Marketing Management

Knowledge and Skills

Marketing Management

Knowledge and Skills

Text Analysis Cases Plans

Third Edition

J. Paul Peter
James R. McManus-Bascom
Professor in Marketing
University of Wisconsin-Madison

James H. Donnelly, Jr.
Turner Professor of Marketing
University of Kentucky

IRWIN
Homewood, IL 60430
Boston, MA 02116

Senior Sponsoring editor:	Stephen Patterson
Developmental editor:	Nancy Barbour
Project editor:	Karen Murphy
Production manager:	Bette K. Ittersagen
Designer:	Larry J. Cope
Compositor:	Graphic World, Inc.
Typeface:	10/12 Century Schoolbook
Printer:	R. R. Donnelley & Sons Company

Library of Congress Cataloging-in-Publication Data

Peter, J. Paul.
  Marketing management : knowledge and skills : text, analysis, cases, plans/J. Paul Peter, James H. Donnelly, Jr.—3rd ed.
      p.   cm.
  Includes bibliographical references and indexes.
  ISBN 0-256-09225-7
  1. Marketing—Management.   2. Marketing—Management—Case studies.
I. Donnelly, James H.   II.   Title.
HF5415.13.P387   1991
658.8—dc20   91–7338

Printed in the United States of America
  2   3   4   5   6   7   8   9   0   DOC   8   7   6   5   4   3   2

Preface

Our goal in the first edition of this text was to develop a complete student resource for marketing management education. This goal has not changed in the present edition. We continue to focus our efforts on enhancing student *knowledge* of marketing management and on developing their *skills* in using this knowledge to develop and maintain successful marketing strategies.

The structure of this edition of our book developed over many years as we experimented successfully and unsuccessfully with various teaching philosophies. Our five-stage learning approach includes (1) learning basic marketing principles; (2) learning approaches and tools for marketing problem analysis; (3) analyzing marketing management cases; (4) analyzing strategic marketing cases; and (5) developing original marketing plans. These five stages are the focus of the seven sections in this book and have as their objective both *knowledge enhancement* and *skill development*. The framework for our book is presented in the following diagram, which will be used throughout the text to integrate the various sections.

STAGE 1: LEARNING OF BASIC MARKETING PRINCIPLES

It is clearly necessary for students to learn and understand basic definitions, concepts and logic before they can apply them in the analysis of marketing problems or attempts to develop marketing plans. Section

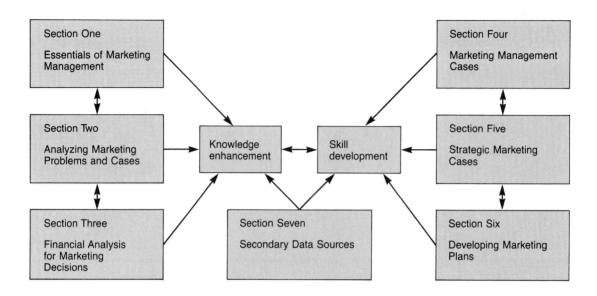

1 of the book contains 14 chapters which we believe present the essentials of marketing management. One problem we continually face in more advanced case-oriented marketing management courses is that most students have long ago discarded or sold their basic texts. Consequently, when they are faced with case problems to analyze they have nothing to rely on but their memories. We believe this seriously detracts from the usefulness of case analysis. Thus, we include this section as a reference source for key marketing concepts. Our objective in this section is to focus on material that is more relevant for analyzing marketing problems. Several of the chapters in this section have been completely revised and updated.

STAGE 2: LEARNING APPROACHES AND TOOLS FOR PROBLEM ANALYSIS

The second stage in our approach involves offering students basic tools and approaches for solving marketing problems. Sections 2 and 3 present these tools in addition to a framework which students can adapt when analyzing marketing problems. Section 7 of the book, an annotated bibliography of important secondary sources of marketing information, will aid students in researching a particular industry or firm and can greatly improve their depth of analysis. Eight classifications of secondary sources are presented: (1) selected periodicals; (2) general marketing information sources; (3) selected marketing information services; (4) selected retail trade publications; (5) financial information sources; (6) basic U.S. statistical sources; (7) general business and industry sources; and (8) indexes and abstracts.

STAGE 3: ANALYZING MARKETING MANAGEMENT CASES

It has been our experience that few students have the confidence and experience necessary to analyze complex strategic marketing cases in their first exposure to this type of learning. We believe it is far better for them to apply their skills at analyzing cases for which traditional marketing principles can be applied somewhat directly before they attempt more challenging problems. Accordingly, Section 4 of the book has been expanded to include 33 marketing management cases, organized into six groups: market opportunity analysis, product strategy, promotion strategy, distribution strategy, pricing strategy, and selected issues in marketing management. Within each group, cases are sequenced so that later cases contain more information and typically require higher levels of marketing management skills than earlier ones.

STAGE 4: ANALYZING STRATEGIC MARKETING CASES

Once students have developed sufficient skills to provide thoughtful analyses of marketing management cases, we believe they are prepared to tackle strategic marketing cases. These cases go beyond traditional marketing principles and focus on the role of marketing in the development of business or organizational strategies. Ten such cases are included in Section 5 of our book. They are sequenced so that the later cases contain more information and require higher levels of management skill to analyze them properly.

STAGE 5: DEVELOPING MARKETING PLANS

The final stage in our approach involves the development of an original marketing plan. We believe that after a two-course sequence in marketing management, students should be able to do one thing very well and should know that they can do it well: Students should be able to construct a quality marketing plan for any product or service. Section 6 provides a framework for developing such a plan. Instructors can consult the *Instructor's Manual* which accompanies this book for alternative ways to incorporate this stage into their course.

We have found that this five-stage process is very flexible and can easily be adapted to the needs of the students and the objectives of the instructor. For example, if the course is the first formal learning experience in marketing, then emphasis could be placed on the first three stages. If students progess well through these stages, then marketing management cases can be assigned on an individual or a group basis.

If the course is for students with one or more previous courses in marketing, or is the capstone marketing management course, then major attention should shift to stages two through five. In this instance, Section 1 becomes a resource for review and reference, and the course can focus on skill development.

Finally, the text can be used for a two-course sequence in marketing management. The first course can emphasize stages one through three and the second concentrate on stages four and five.

PLANNING FOR THIS EDITION

We are indebted to those individuals who contributed cases to our book. Our case search was a long and difficult one. It began with a survey of users. The 57 responses we received were invaluable in planning this edition and in making decisions on replacing cases and selecting new cases. We want to thank those individuals who took the time to complete the survey. We also want to acknowledge the invaluable assistance we received from four detailed reviews of the previous edition. For these we thank John C. Crawford of the University of North Texas, J. Steven Kelly of DePaul University, Edward C. Strong of Tulane University, and Alvin J. Williams of the University of Southern Mississippi. All of the help we received has made this edition a better teaching and learning resource. As a result you will find cases:

• From a variety of time periods
• Set in a variety of industries
• Set in well-recognized organizations
• Focusing on a variety of different types and sizes of both profit and nonprofit organizations
• Dealing with both products and services
• Including problems at all levels of marketing management

The results of our collective efforts yielded what we believe is an outstanding collection, and we want to express our heartfelt thanks to each contributor. This volume would not be possible without them.

Finally, we want to acknowledge Geoff Gordon of the University of Kentucky for his help in many ways throughout this revision.

J. Paul Peter
James H. Donnelly, Jr.

| *CONTENTS*

The Marketing Concept. What is Marketing? What is Strategic
Planning? *Strategic Planning and Marketing Management. The
Strategic Planning Process. The Complete Strategic Plan.* The
Marketing Management Process: *Organizational Mission and
Objectives. Situation Analysis. Marketing Planning. Implementation
and Control of the Marketing Plan. Marketing Information Systems
and Marketing Research.* The Relationship between the Strategic
Plan and the Marketing Plan. Conclusion. Appendix: Portfolio
Models.

Marketing Decision Support Systems: *The Marketing Information
Center. Marketing Decision Making.* Marketing Research: *The
Research Process. Problems in the Research Process.* Conclusion.

The Expenditure Question. The Allocation Question. Sales
Promotion: *Push versus Pull Marketing. Trade Sales Promotions.
Consumer Promotions. What Sales Promotion Can and Can't Do.*
Conclusion. Appendix: Major Federal Agencies Involved in Control
of Advertising.

Chapter 9 Promotion Strategy: Personal Selling 162

Improtance of Personal Selling. The Sales Process: *Selling
Fundamentals.* Managing the Sales Process: *The Sales Management
Task. Controlling the Sales Force.* Conclusion.

Chapter 10 Distribution Strategy 181

The Need for Marketing Intermediaries. Classification of Marketing
Intermediaries and Functions. Channels of Distribution. Selecting
Channels of Distribution: *General Considerations. Specific
Considerations.* Managing a Channel of Distribution: *A Channel
Leader.* Conclusion.

Chapter 11 Pricing Strategy 196

Demand Influences on Pricing Decisions. Supply Influences on
Pricing Decisions: *Pricing Objectives. Cost Considerations in
Pricing. Product Consideration in Pricing.* Environmental Influences
on Pricing Decisions: *Competition. Government Regulations.* A
General Pricing Decision Model. Conclusion.

PART D Marketing in Special Fields 209

Chapter 12 The Marketing of Services 211

Important Characteristics of Services: *Intangibility. Inseparability.
Perishability and Fluctuating Demand. Highly Differentiated
Marketing Systems. Client Relationship. Service Quality. The
Importance of Internal Marketing.* Overcoming the Obstacles in
Service Marketing: *Limited View of Marketing. Limited
Competition. Noncreative Management. No Obsolescence. A Lack of
Innovation in the Distribution of Services.* The Service Challenge:
Implications for Service Marketers. Conclusion.

Chapter 13 International Marketing 231

Organizing for International Marketing: *Problem Conditions:
External. Problem Conditions: Internal. The Multidomestic versus
the Global Approach. Industry Conditions Dictating a Global
Perspective. Internal Factors that Facilitate a Global Strategy.*

Programming for International Marketing: *International Marketing Research. Product Planning for International Markets. International Distribution Systems. Pricing for International Marketing. International Advertising and Sales Promotion.* Strategies for International Marketing. *Strategy One: Same Product, Same Message Worldwide. Strategy Two: Same Product, Different Communications. Strategy Three: Different Product, Same Communications. Strategy Four: Different Product, Different Communications. Strategy Five: Product Invention.* Conclusion.

CASE GROUP B
PRODUCT STRATEGY 365

CASE GROUP C
PROMOTION STRATEGY 472

CASE GROUP F
SELECTED ISSUES IN MARKETING
MANAGEMENT 619

SECTION 5
STRATEGIC MARKETING CASES 689

SECTION 6
DEVELOPING MARKETING PLANS   905

SECTION 7
SECONDARY DATA SOURCES   921

INDEXES

ESSENTIALS OF MARKETING MANAGEMENT

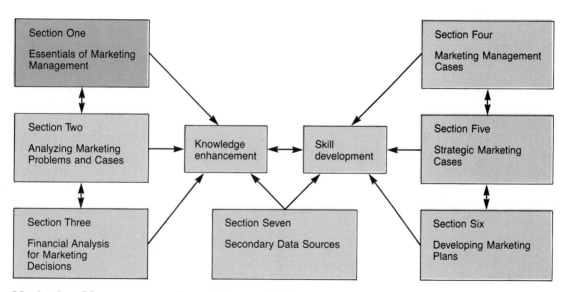

Section One Essentials of Marketing Management	Knowledge enhancement	**Section Four** Marketing Management Cases
Section Two Analyzing Marketing Problems and Cases		**Section Five** Strategic Marketing Cases
Section Three Financial Analysis for Marketing Decisions	Skill development	**Section Six** Developing Marketing Plans
	Section Seven Secondary Data Sources	

Marketing Management: Knowledge and Skills

NOTE TO THE STUDENT

This section contains 14 chapters concerned with basic issues in marketing management. For students who have taken previous courses in marketing, these chapters are designed to provide a useful review. For

1

students who have not taken previous courses in marketing, these chapters should serve as a foundation of basic marketing knowledge. In either case, they provide a resource of marketing logic and information to be used in solving marketing problems and cases and developing marketing plans.

Introduction

CHAPTER 1
Strategic Planning and the Marketing Management Process

Strategic Planning and the Marketing Management Process

The purpose of this introductory chapter is to present the marketing management process and to outline what marketing managers must *manage* if they are to be effective. In doing so, it will also present a framework around which the remaining chapters are organized. Our first task is to review the organizational philosophy known as the marketing concept, since it underlies much of the thinking presented in this book. The remainder of this chapter will focus on the process of strategic planning and its relationship to the process of marketing planning.

THE MARKETING CONCEPT

Simply stated, the marketing concept means that *an organization should seek to make a profit by serving the needs of customer groups.* The concept is very straightforward and has a great deal of common-sense validity. Perhaps this is why it is often misunderstood, forgotten, or overlooked.

The purpose of the marketing concept is to rivet the attention of marketing managers on serving broad classes of customer needs (customer orientation), rather than on the firm's current products (production orientation) or on devising methods to attract customers to current products (selling orientation). Thus, effective marketing starts

---

HIGHLIGHT 1–1
Basic Elements of the Marketing Concept

1. Companywide managerial awareness and appreciation of the consumer's role as it is related to the firm's existence, growth, and stability. As Drucker has noted, business enterprise is an organ of society; thus, its basic purpose lies outside the business itself. And the valid definition of business purpose is the creation of customers.

2. Active, companywide managerial awareness of, and concern with, interdepartmental implications of decisions and actions of an individual department. That is, the firm is viewed as a network of forces focused on meeting defined customer needs, and comprising a system within which actions taken in one department or area frequently result in significant repercussions in other areas of the firm. Also, it is recognized that such actions may affect the company's equilibrium with its external environment, for example, its customers, its competitors.

3. Active, companywide managerial concern with innovation of products and services designed to solve selected consumer problems.

4. General managerial concern with the effect of new products and service introduction on the firm's profit position, both present and future, and recognition of the potential rewards which may accrue from new product planning, including profits and profit stability.

5. General managerial appreciation of the role of marketing intelligence and other fact-finding and reporting units within, and adjacent to the firm, in translating the general statements presented above into detailed statements of profitable market potentials, targets, and action. Implicit in this statement is not only an expansion of the traditional function and scope of formal marketing research, but also assimilation of other sources of marketing data, such as the firm's distribution system and its advertising agency counsel, into a potential marketing intelligence service.

6. Companywide managerial effort, based on participation and interaction of company officers, in establishing corporate and departmental objectives that are understood by and acceptable to these officers, and that are consistent with enhancement of the firm's profit position.

Source: Robert L. King, "The Marketing Concept: Fact or Intelligent Platitude," *The Marketing Concept in Action,* Proceedings of the 47th National Conference (Chicago: American Marketing Association, 1964), p. 657. For an up-to-date discussion of the marketing concept, see Franklin S. Houston, "The Marketing Concept: What It Is and What It Is Not," *Journal of Marketing,* April 1986, pp. 81–87.

---

with the recognition of customer needs and then works backward to devise products and services to satisfy these needs. In this way, marketing managers can satisfy customers more efficiently in the present and anticipate changes in customer needs more accurately in the future. It is hoped that the end result is a more efficient market in which the customer is better satisfied and the firm is more profitable.

The principle task of the marketing function operating under the marketing concept is not to manipulate customers to do what suits the interests of the firm, but rather to find effective and efficient means of making the business do what suits the interests of customers. This is not to say that all firms practice marketing in this way. Clearly, many firms still emphasize only production and sales. However, effective marketing, as defined in this text, requires that consumer needs come first in organizational decision making.

One qualification to this statement deals with the question of a conflict between consumer wants and societal needs and wants. For example, if society deems clean air and water as necessary for survival, this need may well take precedence over a consumer's want for goods and services that pollute the environment.

WHAT IS MARKETING?

One of the most persistent conceptual problems in marketing is its definition.[1] The American Marketing Association has recently defined marketing as "the process of planning and executing conception, pricing, promotion, and distribution of ideas, goods, and services to create exchanges that satisfy individual and organizational objectives."[2] Although this broad definition allows the inclusion of nonbusiness exchange processes (i.e., persons, places, organizations, ideas) as part of marketing, the primary emphasis in this text is on marketing in the business environment. However, this emphasis is not meant to imply that marketing concepts, principles, and techniques cannot be fruitfully employed in other areas of exchange. In fact, some discussions of nonbusiness marketing take place later in the text.

WHAT IS STRATEGIC PLANNING?

Before a production manager, marketing manager, and personnel manager can develop plans for their individual departments, hopefully, some larger plan or blueprint for the *entire* organization has been developed. Otherwise, on what would the individual departmental plans be based?

---

[1] See Reinhard Angelmar and Christian Pinson, "The Meaning of Marketing," *Philosophy of Science,* June 1975, pp. 208–14.

[2] Peter D. Bennett, *Dictionary of Marketing Terms* (Chicago: American Marketing Association, 1988), p. 115.

> **HIGHLIGHT 1–2**
> **Ten Key Principles for Marketing Success**
>
> **Principle 1.** Create Customer Want Satisfaction.
> **Principle 2.** Know Your Buyer Characteristics.
> **Principle 3.** Divide the Market into Segments.
> **Principle 4.** Strive for High Market Share.
> **Principle 5.** Develop Deep and Wide Product Lines.
> **Principle 6.** Price Position Products and Upgrade Markets.
> **Principle 7.** Treat Channels as Intermediate Buyers.
> **Principle 8.** Coordinate Elements of Physical Distribution.
> **Principle 9.** Promote Performance Features.
> **Principle 10.** Use Information to Improve Decisions.
>
> *Source:* Fred C. Allvine, excerpt from *Marketing: Principles and Practices*
> p. viii, copyright © 1987 by Harcourt Brace Jovanovich, Inc. Reprinted by permission of the publisher.

In other words, there is a larger context for planning activities. Let us assume that we are dealing with a large business organization that has several business divisions and several product lines within each division (e.g., General Electric, Philip Morris). Before any marketing planning can be done by individual divisions or departments, a plan has to be developed for the *entire* organization.[3] Then objectives and strategies established at the top level provide the context for planning in each of the divisions and departments by divisional and departmental managers. These lower-level managers develop their plans within the constraints developed at the higher levels.[4]

Strategic Planning and Marketing Management

Many of today's most successful business organizations are here today because many years ago they offered the right product at the right time to a rapidly growing market. The same can also be said for nonprofit and governmental organizations. Many of the critical decisions of the past were made without the benefit of strategic thinking or

---

[3]John H. Grant and William R. King, *The Logic of Strategic Planning* (Boston: Little, Brown, 1982), chap. 1. This section is based on J. H. Donnelly, Jr., J. L. Gibson, and J. M. Ivancevich, *Fundamentals of Management*, 7th ed. (Homewood, Ill: Richard D. Irwin, 1990), chap. 5.

[4]L. Rosenberg and C. D. Schewe, "Strategic Planning: Fulfilling the Promise," *Business Horizons,* July–August 1985, pp. 54–63.

planning. Whether these decisions were based on wisdom or were just luck is not important. They resulted in a momentum which has carried these organizations to where they are today. However, present-day managers are increasingly recognizing that wisdom and intuition alone are no longer sufficient to guide the destinies of their large organizations in today's ever-changing environment. These managers are turning to strategic planning.[5]

Strategic planning includes all of the activities that lead to the development of a clear organizational mission, organizational objectives, and appropriate strategies to achieve the objectives for the entire organization. Figure 1–1 presents the process of strategic planning. It indicates that the organization gathers information about the changing elements of its environment. This information helps the organization to adapt better to these changes through the process of strategic planning.[6] The strategic plan(s) and supporting plan are then implemented in the environment.[7] The results of this implementation are fed back as new information so that continuous adaptation can take place.

The Strategic Planning Process

The output of the strategic planning process is the development of a strategic plan. Figure 1–1 indicates four components of a strategic plan: mission, objectives, strategies, and portfolio plan. Let us carefully examine each one.

Organizational Mission. Every organization's environment supplies the resources that sustain the organization, whether it is a business organization, a college or university, or a governmental agency. In exchange for these resources, the organization must supply the environment with goods and services at an acceptable price and quality.

---

[5]C. Anderson and C. P. Zeithaml, "Stage of the Product Life Cycle, Business Strategy, and Business Performance," *Academy of Management Journal,* March 1984, pp. 5–24.

[6]The process depicted in Figure 1–1 is a generally agreed upon model of the strategic planning process, although some may include or exclude a particular element. For example, see A. A. Thompson and A. J. Strickland III, *Strategic Management: Concepts and Cases,* 6th ed. (Homewood, Ill: Richard D. Irwin, 1990), and Philip Kotler, *Marketing Management: Analysis, Planning, and Control,* 6th ed. (Englewood Cliffs, N.J.: Prentice-Hall, 1988).

[7]The process may differ depending on the type of organization or management approach, or both. For certain types of organizations, one strategic plan will be sufficient. Some manufacturers with similar product lines or limited product lines will develop only one strategic plan. However, organizations with widely diversified product lines and widely diversified markets may develop strategic plans for units or divisions. These plans usually are combined into a master strategic plan.

FIGURE 1–1   The Strategic Planning Process

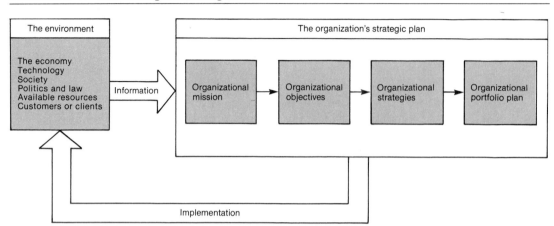

In other words, every organization exists to accomplish something in the larger environment, and that purpose or mission is usually clear at the start. However, as time passes and the organization expands, the environment changes, and managerial personnel change, one or more things are likely to occur. First, the original purpose may become irrelevant as the organization expands into new products, new markets, and even new industries. Second, the original mission remains relevant but some managers begin to lose interest in it. Finally, changes in environment may make the original mission inappropriate. The result of any or all of these three conditions is a "drifting" organization, without a clear mission or purpose to guide critical decisions. When this occurs, management must search for a purpose or restate the original purpose.

The mission statement of an organization should be a long-run vision of what the organization is trying to become: the unique aim that differentiates the organization from similar ones. Note that the need is not a stated purpose, such as "to fulfill the educational needs of college students," that will enable stockholders and managers to feel good or to use for good public relations. The need is for a stated mission that will provide direction and significance to all members of the organization regardless of their level in the organization.

The basic questions that must be answered when an organization decides to examine and restate its mission are: "What is our business?" "What should it be?" While such questions may appear simple, they are in fact such difficult and critical ones that the major responsibility

HIGHLIGHT 1–3
Some Actual Mission Statements

Organization	Mission
1. Office equipment manufacturer	We are in the business of problem solving. Our business is to help solve administrative, scientific, and human problems.
2. Credit union	To produce a selected range of quality services to organizations and individuals to fulfill their continuing financial needs.
3. Large conglomerate	Translating new technologies into commercially salable products.
4. Consumer products paper company	The development and marketing of inedible food store products.
5. State department of health	Administering all provisions of law relating to public health laws and regulations of the State Board of Health, supervising and assisting county and regional boards and departments of health, and doing all other things reasonably necessary to protect and improve the health of the people.
6. Appliance manufacturer	A willingness to invest in any area of suitable profit and growth potential in which the organization has or can acquire the capabilities.

for answering them must lie with top management.[8] In developing a statement of mission, management must take into account three key elements:[9]

1. *The organization's history.* Every organization—large or small, profit or nonprofit—has a history of objectives, accomplishments, mistakes, and policies. In formulating a mission, the critical characteristics and events of the past must be considered.
2. *The organization's distinctive competences.* While there are many things an organization may be able to do, it should seek to do what

---

[8]Lewis W. Walker, "The CEO and Corporate Strategy in the Eighties: Back to Basics," *Interfaces,* January–February 1984, pp. 3–9; Peter Drucker, *Management: Tasks, Responsibilities, Practices* (New York: Harper & Row, 1974), chap. 7.

[9]Kotler, *Marketing Management,* chap. 2.

it can do best. Distinctive competences are things that an organization does well: so well in fact that they give it an advantage over similar organizations. Procter & Gamble could probably enter the synthetic fuel business but such a decision would certainly not take advantage of its major distinctive competence: knowledge of the market for low-priced, repetitively purchased consumer products. No matter how appealing an opportunity may be, the organization must have the competences to capitalize on that opportunity.[10]

3. *The organization's environment.* The organization's environment dictates the opportunities, constraints, and threats that must be identified before a mission statement is developed. Technological developments in the communications field may have a negative impact on travel and should certainly be considered in the mission statement of a large motel chain.[11]

However, it is extremely difficult to write a useful and effective mission statement. It is not uncommon for an organization to spend one or two years developing a useful mission statement. When completed, an effective mission statement will be *focused on markets rather than products, achievable, motivating, and specific.*[12]

Focused on Markets Rather Than Products.   The customers or clients of an organization are critical in determining its mission. Traditionally, many organizations defined their business in terms of what they made—"our business is glass"—and in many cases they named the organization for the product or service (e.g., National Cash Register, Harbor View Savings and Loan Association). Many of these organizations have found that when products and technologies become obsolete, their mission is no longer relevant and the name of the organization may no longer describe what it does. Thus, a more enduring way of defining the mission is needed. In recent years, therefore, a key feature of mission statements has been an *external* rather than *internal* focus. In other words, the mission statement should focus on the broad class of needs that the organization is seeking to satisfy (external focus), *not* on the physical product or service that the organization is

---

[10]For a study of the relationship between corporate distinctive competencies and performance in 185 firms, see M. A. Hitt and R. D. Ireland, "Corporate Distinctive Competence, Strategy and Performance," *Strategic Management Journal,* July–September 1985, pp. 273–93.

[11]See C. Smart and I. Vertinsky, "Strategy and the Environment: A Study of Corporate Responses to Crises," *Strategic Management Journal,* April–June 1984, pp. 199–214. This study of the largest U.S. and Canadian companies examines the relationship between a firm's external environment and its repertoire of strategic responses to cope with crisis.

[12]Drucker, *Management,* pp. 77–89; Kotler, *Marketing Management,* chap. 2.

offering at present (internal focus). This has been clearly stated by Peter Drucker, who argues:

> A business is not defined by the company's name, statutes, or articles of incorporation. It is defined by the want the customer satisfies when he buys a product or service. To satisfy the customer is the mission and purpose of every business. The question "What is our business?" can, therefore, be answered only by looking at the business from the outside, from the point of view of customer and market.[13]

While Drucker was referring to business organizations, the same necessity exists for both nonprofit and governmental organizations.[14] That necessity is to state the mission in terms of serving a particular group of clients or customers and meeting a particular class of need.

Achievable. While the mission statement should "stretch" the organization toward more effective performance, it should, at the same time, be realistic and achievable. In other words, it should open a vision of new opportunities but should not lead the organization into unrealistic ventures far beyond its competences.

Motivational. One of the side (but very important) benefits of a well-defined mission is the guidance it provides employees and managers working in geographically dispersed units and on independent tasks. It provides a shared sense of purpose outside the various activities taking place within the organization. Therefore, such end results as sales, patients cared for, and reduction in violent crimes can then be viewed as the result of careful pursuit and accomplishment of the mission and not as the mission itself.[15]

Specific. As we mentioned earlier, public relations should not be the primary purpose of a statement of mission. It must be specific to provide direction and guidelines to management when they are choosing between alternative courses of action.[16] In other words, "to produce the highest quality products at the lowest possible cost" sounds very good, but it does not provide direction for management.

Organizational Objectives. *Organizational objectives* are the end points of an organization's mission and are what it seeks through the ongoing, long-run operations of the organization. The organizational

---

[13]Drucker, *Management,* p. 79.

[14]Paul C. Nutt, "A Strategic Planning Network for Nonprofit Organizations," *Strategic Management Journal,* January–March 1984, pp. 57–76; Peter Smith Ring and James L. Perry, "Strategic Management in Public and Private Organizations: Implications of Distinctive Contexts and Constraints," *Academy of Management Review,* April 1985, pp. 276–86.

[15]"Who's Excellent Now," *Business Week,* November 5, 1984, pp. 76–88.

[16]Drucker, *Management,* p. 87.

mission is distilled into a finer set of specific and achievable organizational objectives. These objectives must be *specific, measurable, action commitments* by which the mission of the organization is to be achieved.

As with the statement of mission, organizational objectives are more than good intentions. In fact, if formulated properly, they can accomplish the following:

1. They can be converted into specific actions.
2. They will provide direction. That is, they can serve as a starting point for more specific and detailed objectives at lower levels in the organization. Each manager will then know how his or her objectives relate to those at higher levels.
3. They can establish long-run priorities for the organization.
4. They can facilitate management control because they serve as standards against which overall organizational performance can be evaluated.

Organizational objectives are necessary in any and all areas that may influence the performance and long-run survival of the organization. Peter Drucker believes that objectives should be established in at least eight areas of organizational performance. These are market standing, innovations, productivity, physical and financial resources, profitability, manager performance and responsibility, worker performance and attitude, and social responsibility.[17]

The above list of objectives is by no means exhaustive. The important point is that management must translate the organizational mission into specific objectives that will support the realization of the mission. The objectives may flow directly from the mission or be considered subordinate necessities for carrying out the mission of the organization. Table 1–1 presents some examples of organizational objectives. Note that they are broad statements that serve as guides and that they are of a continuing nature. They specify the end points of an organization's mission and the results it seeks in the long run, both externally and internally. Most important, however, the objectives in Table 1–1 are *specific, measurable, action commitments* on the part of the organization.

Organizational Strategies.   Hopefully, when an organization has formulated its mission and developed its objectives, it knows where it wants to go. The next managerial task is to develop a "grand design"

---

[17]Peter Drucker, *The Practice of Management* (New York: Harper & Row, 1954); and reemphasized in Drucker's *Management.*

TABLE 1–1 Sample Organizational Objectives (Manufacturing firm)

Area of Performance	*Possible Objective*
1. Market standing	To make our brands number one in their field in terms of market share.
2. Innovations	To be a leader in introducing new products by spending no less than 7 percent of sales for research and development.
3. Productivity	To manufacture all products efficiently as measured by the productivity of the work force.
4. Physical and financial resources	To protect and maintain all resources— equipment, buildings, inventory, and funds.
5. Profitability	To achieve an annual rate of return on investment of at least 15 percent.
6. Manager performance and responsibility	To identify critical areas of management depth and succession.
7. Worker performance and attitude	To maintain levels of employee satisfaction consistent with our own and similar industries.
8. Social responsibility	To respond appropriately whenever possible to societal expectations and environmental needs.

---

to get there. This grand design constitutes the organizational strategies. The role of strategy in strategic planning is to identify the general approaches that the organization will utilize to achieve its organizational objectives. It involves the choice of major directions the organization will take in pursuing its objectives.

Achieving organizational objectives is accomplished in two ways: by better managing what the organization is presently doing and/or finding new things to do. In choosing either or both of these paths, the organization then must decide whether to concentrate on present customers or to seek new ones, or both. Figure 1–2 presents the available strategic choices. It is known as a product/market matrix and indicates the strategic alternatives available to an organization for achieving its objectives. It indicates that an organization can grow in a variety of ways by concentrating on present or new products and on present or new customers.[18]

---

[18]Originally discussed in the classic H. Igor Ansoff, *Corporate Strategy* (New York: McGraw-Hill, 1965).

FIGURE 1–2 Organizational Growth Strategies

Products / Markets	Present Products	New Products
Present customers	Market penetration	Product development
New customers	Market development	Diversification

Market Penetration Strategies. These organizational strategies focus on improving the position of the organization's present products with its present customers. For example:

- A dairy concentrates on getting its present customers to purchase more of its products.
- A charity seeks to increase contributions from present contributors.
- A bank concentrates on getting present depositors to use additional services.

A market penetration strategy might involve devising a marketing plan to encourage customers to purchase more of a product. Tactics used to carry out the strategy could include price reductions, advertising that stresses the many benefits of the product, packaging the product in different-sized packages, or making the product available at more locations. Likewise, a production plan might be developed to produce more efficiently what is being produced at present. Implementation of such a plan could include increased production runs, the substitution of preassembled components for individual product parts, or the automation of a process that previously was performed manually. In other words, market penetration strategies concentrate on improving the efficiency of various functional areas in the organization.

Market Development Strategies. Following this strategy, an organization would seek to find new customers for its present products. For example:

- A manufacturer of industrial products may decide to develop products for entrance into the consumer market.
- A governmental social service agency may seek individuals and families who have never utilized the agency's services.
- A manufacturer of automobiles decides to sell automobiles in Eastern Europe because of the recent transition to a free market system.

Product Development Strategies. In choosing either of the remaining two strategies, the organization in effect, seeks new things to do. With this particular strategy, the new products developed would be directed to present customers. For example:

- A candy manufacturer may decide to offer a low-calorie candy.
- A social service agency may offer additional services to present client families.
- A college or university may develop programs for senior citizens.

Diversification. An organization diversifies when it seeks new products for customers it is not serving at present. For example:

- A discount store purchases a savings and loan association.
- A cigarette manufacturer diversifies into real estate development.
- A college or university establishes a corporation to find commercial uses for the results of faculty research efforts.

On what basis does an organization choose one (or all) of its strategies? Of extreme importance are the directions set by the mission statement. Management should select those strategies consistent with its mission and capitalize on the organization's distinctive competencies which will lead to a sustainable competitive advantage.[19] A sustainable competitive advantage can be based on either the assets or skills of the organization. Technical superiority, low-cost production, customer service/product support, location, financial resources, continuing product innovation, and overall marketing skills are all examples of distinctive competencies that can lead to a sustainable competitive advantage.[20] For example, Honda is known for providing quality automobiles at a reasonable price. Each succeeding generation of Honda cars has shown marked quality improvement over previous generations. This, in turn, has led to the Honda Accord's becoming the leading selling car in the United States. The key to sustaining a competitive advantage is to continually focus and build on the assets and skills that will lead to long-term performance gains.

Organizational Portfolio Plan. The final phase of the strategic planning process is the formulation of the organizational portfolio plan. In reality, most organizations at a particular time are a portfolio of businesses, that is, product lines, divisions, schools. To illustrate, an appliance

---

[19]N. Venkatramen and J. C. Camillus, "Exploring the Concept of 'Fit' in Strategic Management," *Academy of Management Review,* July 1984, pp. 513–25; H. Mintzberg and J. A. Waters, "Of Strategies, Deliberate and Emergent," *Strategic Management Journal,* July–September 1985, pp. 257–72.

[20]D. Aaker, "Managing Assets and Skills: The Key to a Sustainable Competitive Advantage," *California Management Review,* Winter 1989, pp. 91–106.

EFFECTIVENESS STANDARDS

A. *Sales Criteria*
1. Total sales
2. Sales by product or product line
3. Sales by geographic region
4. Sales by salesperson
5. Sales by customer type
6. Sales by market segment
7. Sales by size of order
8. Sales by sales territory
9. Sales by intermediary
10. Market share
11. Percentage change in sales

B. *Customer Satisfaction*
1. Quantity purchased
2. Degree of brand loyalty
3. Repeat purchase rates
4. Perceived product quality
5. Brand image
6. Number of letters of complaint

EFFICIENCY STANDARDS

C. *Costs*
1. Total costs
2. Costs by product or product line
3. Costs by geographic region
4. Costs by salesperson
5. Costs by customer type
6. Costs by market segment
7. Costs by size of order
8. Costs by sales territory
9. Costs by intermediary
10. Percentage change in costs

EFFECTIVENESS-EFFICIENCY STANDARDS

D. *Profits*
1. Total profits
2. Profits by product or product line
3. Profits by geographic region
4. Profits by salesperson
5. Profits by customer type
6. Profits by market segment
7. Profits by size of order
8. Profits by sales territory
9. Profits by intermediary

Source: Charles D. Schewe, *Marketing: Principles and Strategies* (New York: Random House, 1987), p. 593.

manufacturer may have several product lines (e.g., televisions, washers and dryers, refrigerators, stereos) as well as two divisions, consumer appliances and industrial appliances. A college or university will have numerous schools (e.g., education, business, law, architecture) and several programs within each school. Some widely diversified organizations such as Philip Morris, are in numerous unrelated businesses, such as cigarettes, food products, land development, industrial paper products, and a brewery.

Managing such groups of businesses is made a little easier if resources are plentiful, cash is plentiful, and each is experiencing growth and profits. Unfortunately, providing larger and larger budgets each year to all businesses is seldom feasible. Many are not experiencing growth, and profits and resources (financial and nonfinancial) are becoming more and more scarce. In such a situation, choices must be made, and some method is necessary to help management make the choices. Management must decide which businesses to build, maintain, or eliminate, or which new businesses to add.[21] Indeed, much of the recent activity in corporate restructuring has centered around decisions relating to which groups of businesses management should focus on.

Obviously, the first step in this approach is to identify the various division's product lines and so on that can be considered a "business." When identified, these are referred to as *strategic business units* (SBUs) and have the following characteristics:

- They have a distinct mission.
- They have their own competitors.
- They are a single business or collection of related businesses.
- They can be planned independently of the other businesses of the total organization.

Thus, depending on the type of organization, an SBU could be a single product, product line, division; a department of business administration; or a state mental health agency. Once the organization has identified and classified all of its SBUs, some method must be established to determine how resources should be allocated among the various SBUs. These methods are known as *portfolio models*. For those readers interested, the appendix of this chapter presents two of the most popular portfolio models, the Boston Consulting group model and the General Electric model.

---

[21]There are several portfolio models; each has its detractors and supporters. The interested reader should consult Richard G. Hamermesh and Roderick E. White, "Manage Beyond Portfolio Analysis," *Harvard Business Review*, January–February 1984, pp. 103–9, and J. A. Seeger, "Revising the Images of BCG's Growth/Share Matrix," *Strategic Management Journal*, January–March 1984, pp. 93–97.

The Complete Strategic Plan

Figure 1–1 indicates that at this point the strategic planning process is complete, and the organization has a time-phased blueprint that outlines its mission, objectives, and strategies. Completion of the strategic plan facilitates the development of marketing plans for each product, product line, or division of the organization. The marketing plan serves as a subset of the strategic plan in that it allows for detailed planning at a target market level. Several marketing plans, each one targeted toward a specific market, will evolve from the strategic plan. For example, separate marketing plans would be developed for the various markets that a firm, which produces consumer appliances and industrial electrical products, competes in. Given a completed strategic plan, each area knows exactly where the organization wishes to go and can then develop objectives, strategies, and programs that are consistent with the strategic plan.[22] This important relationship between strategic planning and marketing planning is the subject of the final section of this chapter.

THE MARKETING MANAGEMENT PROCESS

Marketing management can be defined as "the analysis, planning, implementation, and control of programs designed to bring about desired exchanges with target markets for the purpose of achieving organizational objectives. It relies heavily on designing the organization's offering in terms of the target market's needs and desires and on using effective pricing, communication, and distribution to inform, motivate, and service the market."[23] It should be noted that this definition is entirely consistent with the marketing concept, since it emphasizes the serving of target market needs as the key to achieving organizational objectives. The remainder of this section will be devoted to a discussion of the marketing management process in terms of the model in Figure 1–3.

Organizational Mission and Objectives

Marketing activities should start with a clear understanding of the organization's mission and objectives. These factors provide marketing management direction by specifying the industry, the desired role of

---

[22]R. A. Linneman and H. E. Klein, "Using Scenarios in Strategic Decision Making," *Business Horizons,* January–February 1985, pp. 64–74.

[23]Kotler, *Marketing Management,* p. 14.

FIGURE 1–3   Strategic Planning and Marketing Planning

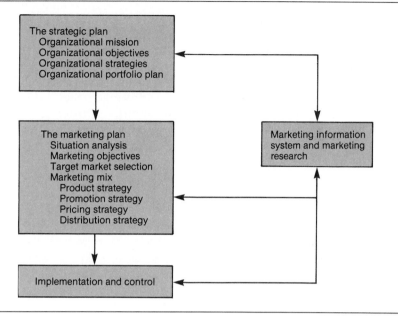

the firm in the industry (such as research-oriented innovator, custom-batch specialist, or mass producer, and hopefully, a precise statement of what the firm is trying to accomplish). However, since written mission statements and objectives are often ambiguous or ill-defined, the marketing manager may have to consult with other members of top management to determine precisely what the firm is trying to accomplish, both overall and during a specific planning period. For example, a commonly stated organizational objective is "growth." Obviously, this objective is so general that it is practically useless. On the other hand, a statement such as "sustained growth of 14 percent in profits before taxes" provides a quantitative goal which the marketing manager can use for determining desired sales levels and the marketing strategies to achieve them. In addition, the marketing manager must monitor any changes in mission or objectives and adapt marketing strategies to meet them.

Situation Analysis

With a clear understanding of organizational objectives and mission, the marketing manager must then analyze and monitor the position of the firm and, specifically, the marketing department, in terms of its past, present, and future situation. Of course, the future situation is of primary concern. However, an analysis of past trends and current situation are most useful for predicting the future situation.

The situation analysis can be divided into six major areas of concern: (1) the cooperative environment; (2) the competitive environment; (3) the economic environment; (4) the social environment; (5) the political environment; and (6) the legal environment. In analyzing each of these environments, the marketing executive must search both for opportunities and for constraints or threats to achieving objectives. Opportunities for profitable marketing often arise from changes in these environments that bring about new sets of needs to be satisfied. Constraints on marketing activities, such as limited supplies of scarce resources, also arise from these environments.

The Cooperative Environment.   The cooperative environment includes all firms and individuals who have a vested interest in the firm's accomplishing its objectives. Parties of primary interest to the marketing executive in this environment are (1) suppliers; (2) resellers; (3) other departments in the firm; and (4) subdepartments and employees of the marketing department. Opportunities in this environment are primarily related to methods of increasing efficiency. For example, a company might decide to switch from a competitive bid process of obtaining materials to a single source that is located near the company's plant. Likewise, members of the marketing, engineering, and manufacturing functions may utilize a teamwork approach to developing new products versus a sequential approach. Constraints consist of such things as unresolved conflicts and shortages of materials. For example, a company manager may believe that a distributor is doing an insufficient job of promoting and selling the product, or a marketing manager may feel that manufacturing is not taking the steps needed to produce a quality product.

The Competitive Environment.   The competitive environment includes primarily other firms in the industry that rival the organization for both resources and sales. Opportunities in this environment include such things as (1) acquiring competing firms; (2) offering demonstrably better value to consumers and attracting them away from competitors; and (3) in some cases, driving competitors out of the industry. For example, one airline purchases another airline, a bank offers depositors a free checking account with no minimum balance requirements, or a grocery chain engages in an everyday low-price strategy that competitors can't meet. The primary constraints in these environments are the demand stimulation activities of competing firms and the number of consumers who cannot be lured away from competition.

The Economic Environment.   The state of the macroeconomy and changes in it also bring about marketing opportunities and constraints.

For example, such factors as high inflation and unemployment levels can limit the size of the market that can afford to purchase a firm's top-of-the-line product. At the same time, these factors may offer a profitable opportunity to develop rental services for such products or to develop less expensive models of the product. In addition, changes in technology can provide significant threats and opportunities.

For example, in the communications industry, technology has developed to a level where it is now possible to provide cable television using phone lines. Obviously such a system poses a severe threat to the existence of the cable industry as it exists today.

The Social Environment.   This environment includes general cultural and social traditions, norms, and attitudes. While these values change slowly, such changes often bring about the need for new products and services. For example, a change in values concerning the desirability of large families brought about an opportunity to market better methods of birth control. On the other hand, cultural and social values also place constraints on marketing activities. As a rule, business practices that are contrary to social values become political issues, which are often resolved by legal constraints. For example, public demand for a cleaner environment has caused the government to require that automobile manufacturers' products meet certain average gas mileage and emission standards.

The Political Environment.   The political environment includes the attitudes and reactions of the general public, social and business critics, and other organizations, such as the Better Business Bureau. Dissatisfaction with such business and marketing practices as unsafe products, products that waste resources, and unethical sale procedures can have adverse effects on corporation image and customer loyalty. However, adapting business and marketing practices to these attitudes can be an opportunity. For example, these attitudes have brought about markets for such products as unbreakable children's toys, high-efficiency air conditioners, and more economical automobiles.

The Legal Environment.   This environment includes a host of federal, state, and local legislation directed at protecting both business competition and consumer rights. In past years legislation reflected social and political attitudes and has been primarily directed at constraining business practices. Such legislation usually acts as a constraint on business behavior, but again can be viewed as providing opportunities for marketing safer and more efficient products. In recent years, there has been less emphasis on creating new laws for constraining business practices. As an example, deregulation has become more common as evidenced by recent events in the airlines, financial services, and telecommunications industries.

HIGHLIGHT 1–5
Some Important Federal Regulatory Agencies

Agencies	Responsibilities
Federal Trade Commission (FTC)	Enforces laws and develops guidelines regarding unfair business practices.
Food and Drug Administration (FDA)	Enforces laws and develops regulations to prevent distribution and sale of adulterated or misbranded foods, drugs, cosmetics, and hazardous consumer products.
Consumer Product Safety Commission (CPSC)	Enforces the Consumer Product Safety Act—which covers any consumer product not assigned to other regulatory agencies.
Interstate Commerce Commission (ICC)	Regulates interstate rail, bus, truck, and water carriers.
Federal Communications Commission (FCC)	Regulates interstate wire, radio, and television.
Environmental Protection Agency (EPA)	Develops and enforces environmental protection standards.
Office of Consumer Affairs (OCA)	Responds to consumers' complaints.

Marketing Planning

In the previous sections it was emphasized that (1) marketing activities must be aligned with organizational objectives; and (2) marketing opportunities are often found by systematically analyzing situational environments. Once an opportunity is recognized, the marketing executive must then plan an appropriate strategy for taking advantage of the opportunity. This process can be viewed in terms of three interrelated tasks: (1) establishing marketing objectives; (2) selecting the target market; and (3) developing the marketing mix.

Establishing Objectives. Marketing objectives usually are derived from organizational objectives; in some cases where the firm is totally marketing-oriented, the two are identical. In either case objectives must be specified and performance in achieving them should be measurable. Marketing objectives are usually stated as standards of performance (e.g., a certain percentage of market share or sales volume) or as tasks to be achieved by given dates. While such objectives are useful, the marketing concept emphasizes that profits rather than sales should be the overriding objective of the firm and marketing

---

HIGHLIGHT 1–6
Key Elements in the Marketing Plan

People	What is the target market for the firm's product(s)? What is its size and growth potential?
Profit	What is the expected profit from implementing the marketing plan? What are the other objectives of the marketing plan, and how will their achievement be evaluated?
Personnel	What personnel will be involved in implementing the marketing plan? Will only intrafirm personnel be involved, or will other firms, such as advertising agencies or marketing research firms, also be employed?
Product	What product(s) will be offered? What variations in the product will be offered in terms of style, features, quality, branding, packaging, and terms of sale and service? How should products be positioned in the market?
Price	What price or prices will products be sold for?
Promotion	How will information about the firm's offerings be communicated to the target market?
Place	How, when, and where will the firm's offerings be delivered for sale to the target market?
Policy	What is the overall marketing policy for dealing with anticipated problems in the marketing plan? How will unanticipated problems be handled?
Period	For how long a time is the marketing plan to be in effect? When should the plan be implemented, and what is the schedule for executing and evaluating marketing activities?

---

department. In any case, these objectives provide the framework for the marketing plan.

Selecting the Target Markets.   The success of any marketing plan hinges on how well it can identify consumer needs and organize its resources to satisfy them profitably. Thus, a crucial element of the marketing plan is selecting the group or segments of potential consumers the firm is going to serve with each of its products. Four important questions must be answered:

1. What do consumers need?
2. What must be done to satisfy these needs?
3. What is the size of the market?
4. What is its growth profile?

Present target markets and potential target markets are then ranked according to (1) profitability; (2) present and future sales volume; and (3) the match between what it takes to appeal successfully to the segment and the organization's capabilities. Those that appear to offer the greatest potential are selected. Chapters 3, 4, and 5 are devoted to discussing consumer behavior, industrial buyers, and market segmentation.

Developing the Marketing Mix.   The marketing mix is the set of controllable variables that must be managed to satisfy the target market and achieve organizational objectives. These controllable variables are usually classified according to four major decision areas: product, price, promotion, and place (or channels of distribution). The importance of these decision areas cannot be overstated and, in fact, the major portion of this text is devoted to analyzing them. Chapters 6 and 7 are devoted to product and new product strategies; Chapters 8 and 9 to promotion strategies in terms of both nonpersonal and personal selling; Chapter 10 to distribution strategies; and Chapter 11 to pricing strategies. In addition, marketing mix variables are the focus of analysis in two chapters on marketing in special fields: the marketing of services (Chapter 12) and international marketing (Chapter 13). Thus, it should be clear to the reader that the marketing mix is the core of the marketing management process.

The output of the foregoing process is the marketing plan. It is a formal statement of decisions that have been made on marketing activities; it is a blueprint of the objectives, strategies, and tasks to be performed.

Implementation and Control of the Marketing Plan

Implementing the market plan involves putting the plan into action and performing marketing tasks according to the predefined schedule. Even the most carefully developed plans often cannot be executed with perfect timing. Thus, the marketing executive must closely monitor and coordinate implementation of the plan. In some cases, adjustments may have to be made in the basic plan because of changes in any of the situational environments. For example, competitors may introduce a new product. In this event, it may be desirable to speed up or delay implementation of the plan. In almost all cases, some minor adjustments or "fine tuning" will be necessary in implementation.

Controlling the marketing plan involves three basic steps. First, the results of the implemented marketing plan are measured. Second, these results are compared with objectives. Third, decisions are made on whether the plan is achieving objectives. If serious deviations exist between actual and planned results, adjustments may have to be made to redirect the plan toward achieving objectives.

Marketing Information Systems and Marketing Research

Throughout the marketing management process, current, reliable, and valid information is needed to make effective marketing decisions. Providing this information is the task of the marketing decision support system (MDSS) and marketing research. These topics are discussed in detail in Chapter 2.

THE RELATIONSHIP BETWEEN THE STRATEGIC PLAN AND THE MARKETING PLAN

Strategic planning is clearly a top-management responsibility. However, marketing managers and mid-level managers in the organization are indirectly involved in the process in two important ways: (1) they often influence the strategic planning process by providing inputs in the form of information and suggestions relating to their particular products, product lines, and areas of responsibility; and (2) they must be aware of what the process of strategic planning involves as well as

FIGURE 1–4   Relating the Marketing Plan to the Strategic Plan

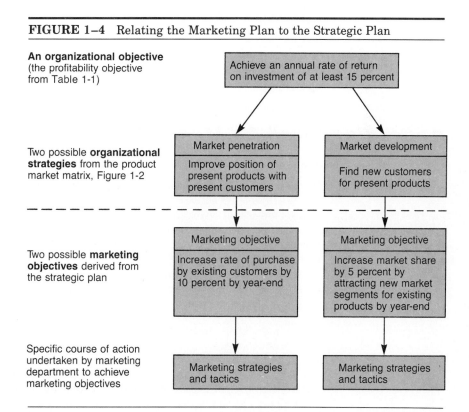

the results because everything they do, the marketing objectives and strategies they develop, must be derived from the strategic plan. There is rarely a strategic planning question or decision that does not have marketing implications.

Thus, if strategic planning is done properly, it will result in a clearly defined blueprint for managerial action at all levels in the organization. Figure 1–4 illustrates the hierarchy of objectives and strategies using one possible objective and two strategies from the strategic plan (above the dotted line), and illustrating how these relate to elements of the marketing plan (below the dotted line). Many others could have been developed, but our purpose is to illustrate how the marketing plan must be derived from and contribute to the achievement of the strategic plan.

CONCLUSION

This chapter has described the marketing management process and provided an outline for many of the remaining chapters in this text. At this point it would be useful for the reader to review Figure 1–3 as well as the Table of Contents. This review will enable you to relate the content and progression of material to the marketing management process.

Appendix   Portfolio Models

Portfolio models have become a valuable aid to marketing managers in their efforts to develop effective marketing plans. The use of these models has become widespread as marketing managers face a situation that can best be described as "more products, less time, and less money." More specifically, (1) as the number of products a firm produces expands, the time available for developing marketing plans for each product decreases; (2) at a strategic level, management must make resource allocation decisions across lines of products and, in diversified organizations, across different lines of business; and (3) when resources are limited (which they usually are), the process of deciding which strategic business units (SBUs) to emphasize becomes very complex. In such situations, portfolio models can be very useful.

Portfolio analysis is not a new idea. Banks manage loan portfolios seeking to balance risks and yields. Individuals who are serious investors usually have a portfolio of various kinds of investments (common stocks, preferred stocks, bank accounts, and the like), each with different characteristics of risk, growth, and rate of return. The investor seeks to manage the portfolio to maximize whatever objectives he or she might have. Applying this same idea, most organizations have a wide range of products, product lines, and businesses, each with different growth rates and returns. Similar to the investor, managers should seek a desirable balance among alternative SBUs. Specifically, management should seek to develop a business portfolio that will assure long-run profits and cash flow.

Portfolio models can be used to classify SBUs to determine the future cash contributions that can be expected from each SBU as well as the future resources that each will require. Remember, depending on the organization, an SBU could be a single product, product line, division, or distinct business. While there are many different types of portfolio models, they generally examine the competitive position of the SBU and the chances for improving the SBU's contribution to profitablility and cash flow.

There are several portfolio analysis techniques. Two of the most widely used are discussed in this appendix. To truly appreciate the concept of portfolio analysis, however, we must briefly review the development of portfolio theory.

A REVIEW OF PORTFOLIO THEORY

The interest in developing aids for managers in the selection of strategy was spurred over 25 years ago by an organization known as the Boston Consulting Group. Its ideas, which will be discussed shortly, and many of those that followed were based on the concept of experience curves.

Experience curves are similar in concept to learning curves. Learning curves were developed to express the idea that the number of labor hours it takes to produce one unit of a particular product declines in a predictable manner as the number of units produced increases. Hence, an accurate estimation of how long it takes to produce the hundredth unit is possible if the production time for the 1st and 10th unit are known.

The concept of experience curves was derived from the concept of learning curves. Experience curves were first widely discussed in the ongoing Profit Impact of Marketing Strategies (PIMS) study conducted by the Strategic Planning Institute. The PIMS project studies 150 firms with more than 1,000 individual business units. Its major focus is on determining which environmental and internal firm variables influence the firm's return on investment (ROI) and cash flow. The researchers have concluded that seven categories of variables appear to influence the return on investment: (1) competitive position; (2) industry/market environment; (3) budget allocation; (4) capital structure; (5) production processes; (6) company characteristics; and (7) "change action" factors.[24]

The experience curve includes all costs associated with a product and implies that the per-unit cost of a product should fall, due to cumulative

---

[24]George S. Day and David B. Montgomery, "Diagnosing the Experience Curve," *Journal of Marketing,* Spring 1983, pp. 44–58.

FIGURE A–1   Experience Curve and Resulting Profit Curve

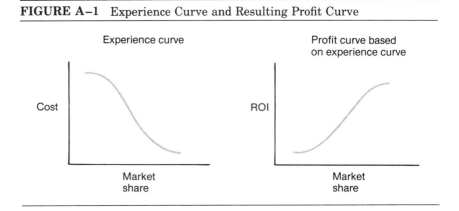

experience, as production volume increases. In a given industry, therefore, the producer with the largest volume and corresponding market share should have the lowest marginal cost. This leader in market share should be able to underprice competitors, discourage entry into the market by potential competitors, and, as a result, achieve an acceptable return on investment. The linkage of experience to cost to price to market share to ROI is exhibited in Figure A–1. The Boston Consulting Group's view of the experience curve led the members to develop what has become known as the BCG Portfolio Model.

THE BCG MODEL

The BCG is based on the assumption that profitability and cash flow will be closely related to sales volume. Thus, in this model, SBUs are classified in terms of their relative market share and the growth rate of the market the SBU is in. Using these dimensions, products are either classified as stars, cash cows, dogs, or question marks. The BCG model is presented in Figure A–2.

- *Stars* are SBUs with a high share of a high-growth market. Because high-growth markets attract competition, such SBUs are usually cash users because they are growing and because the firm needs to protect their market share position.
- *Cash cows* are often market leaders, but the market they are in is not growing rapidly. Because these SBUs have a high share of a low-growth market, they are cash generators for the firm.
- *Dogs* are SBUs that have a low share of a low-growth market. If the SBU has a very loyal group of customers, it may be a source of profits and cash. Usually, dogs are not large sources of cash.
- *Question marks* are SBUs with a low share of a high-growth market. They have great potential but require great resources if the firm is to successfully build market share.

FIGURE A–2   The Boston Consulting Group Portfolio Model

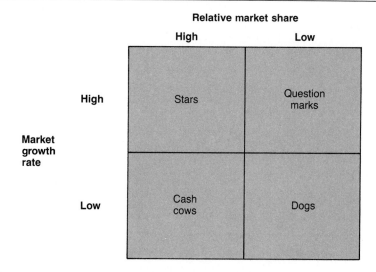

As you can see, a firm with 10 SBUs will usually have a portfolio that includes some of each of the above. Having developed this analysis, management must determine what role each SBU should assume. Four basic objectives are possible:

1. *Build share.* This objective sacrifices immediate earnings to improve market share. It is appropriate for promising question marks whose share has to grow if they are ever to become stars.
2. *Hold share.* This objective seeks to preserve the SBU's market share. It is very appropriate for strong cash cows to ensure that they can continue to yield a large cash flow.
3. *Harvest.* Here, the objective seeks to increase the product's short-term cash flow without concern for the long-run impact. It allows market share to decline in order to maximize earnings and cash flow. It is an appropriate objective for weak cash cows, weak question marks, and dogs.
4. *Divest.* This objective involves selling or divesting the SBU because better investment opportunities exist elsewhere. It is very appropriate for dogs and those question marks the firm cannot afford to finance for growth.

Major criticisms of the BCG Portfolio Model have revolved around its focus on market share and market growth as the primary indicators of profitability. In addition, the BCG model assumes that the major source of SBU financing comes from internal means. While the above criticisms are valid ones, the usefulness of the BCG model in assessing the strategic position of SBUs has enabled it to continue to be utilized extensively by managers across all industries.

FIGURE A–3   The General Electric Portfolio Model

Business strength

		Strong	Average	Weak
	High	A	A	B
Industry attractiveness	Medium	A	B	C
	Low	B	C	C

THE GENERAL ELECTRIC MODEL

Although the BCG model can be useful, it does assume that market share is the sole determinant of an SBU's profitability. Also, in projecting market growth rates, a manager should carefully analyze the factors that influence sales and any opportunities for influencing industry sales.

Some firms have developed alternative portfolio models to incorporate more information about market opportunities and competitive positions. The GE model is one of these. The GE model emphasizes all the potential sources of strength, not just market share, and all of the factors that influence the long-term attractiveness of a market, not just its growth rate. As Figure A–3 indicates, all SBUs are classified in terms of *business strength and industry attractiveness.* Figure A–4 presents a list of items that can be used to position SBUs in the matrix.

Industry attractiveness is a composite index made up of such factors as those listed in Figure A–4. For example: *market size*—the larger the market the more attractive it would be; *market growth*—high-growth markets are more attractive than low-growth markets; *profitability*—high-profit-margin markets are more attractive than low-profit-margin industries.

Business strength is a composite index made up of such factors as those listed in Figure A–4. For example: *market share*—the higher the SBU's share of market, the greater its business strength; *quality leadership*—the higher the SBU's quality compared to competitors, the greater its business strength; *share compared with leading competitor*—the closer the SBU's share to the market leader, the greater its business strength.

FIGURE A–4 Components of Industry Attractiveness and Business Strength at GE

Industry Attractiveness	*Business Strength*
Market size	Market position:
Market growth	Domestic market share
Profitability	World market share
Cyclicality	Share growth
Ability to recover from	Share compared with leading competitor
inflation	Competitive strengths:
World scope	Quality leadership
	Technology
	Marketing
	Relative profitability

Once the SBUs are classified, they are placed on the grid (Figure A–3). Priority "A" SBUs (often called *the green zone*) are those in the three cells at the upper left, indicating that these are SBUs high in both industry attractiveness and business strength, and that the firm should "build share." Priority "B" SBUs (often called *the yellow zone*) are medium in both industry attractiveness and business strength. The firm will usually decide to "hold share" on these SBUs. Priority "C" SBUs are those in the three cells at the lower right (often called *the red zone*). These SBUs are low in both industry attractiveness and business strength. The firm will usually decide to *harvest* or *divest* these SBUs.

Whether the BCG, the GE model, or a variation of these models is used, some analyses must be made of the firm's current portfolio of SBUs as part of any strategic planning effort. Marketing must get its direction from the organization's strategic plan.

Marketing Information, Research, and Understanding the Target Market

Chapter 2

Marketing Decision Support Systems and Marketing Research

It is obvious that the American business system has been capable of producing a vast quantity of goods and services. However, in the past two decades the American business system has also become extremely capable of producing massive amounts of information and data. In fact, the last decade has often been referred to as the "Information Era" and the "Age of Information."

This situation is a complete reversal from what previously existed. In the past, marketing executives did not have to deal with an oversupply of information for decision-making purposes. In most cases they gathered what little data they could and hoped that their decisions would be reasonably good. In fact, it was for this reason that marketing research came to be recognized as an extremely valuable staff function. It provided marketing management with information where previously there had been little or none and, thereby, alleviated to a great extent the paucity of information for marketing decision making. However, marketing management in many companies has failed to store marketing information, and much valuable marketing information is lost when marketing personnel change jobs or companies.

Today, marketing managers often feel buried by the deluge of information and data that comes across their desks. How can it be, then, that so many marketing managers complain that they have insufficient or inappropriate information on which to base their everyday operating decisions? Specifically, most of these complaints fall into the following categories:

1. There is too much marketing information of the wrong kind and not enough of the right kind.
2. Marketing information is so dispersed throughout the company that great effort is usually needed to locate simple facts.
3. Vital information is sometimes suppressed by other executives or subordinates for personal reasons.
4. Vital information often arrives too late to be useful.
5. Information often arrives in a form that provides no idea of its accuracy, and there is no one to turn to for confirmation.

Marketing management requires current, reliable information before it can function efficiently. Because of this need, and the information explosion of the past decade, many large corporations have banked their total marketing knowledge in computers. Well-designed marketing decision support systems (MDSS) can eliminate corporate losses of millions of dollars from lost information and lost opportunities.

This chapter is concerned with marketing decision support systems and marketing research. Since the two concepts are easily confused, it is important initially to distinguish one from the other. In general terms, a marketing decision support system is concerned with the continuous gathering, processing, and utilization of pertinent information for decision-making purposes. The primary objective of the MDSS is to ensure that right information is available to the right decision maker at the right time. Marketing research, on the other hand, usually focuses on a specific marketing problem with the objective of providing information for a particular decision. As such, marketing research is an integral part of the overall marketing decision support system but usually is project oriented rather than a continuous process.

MARKETING DECISION SUPPORT SYSTEMS

A marketing decision support system is a new type of marketing information system. This type of information system is designed to support all phases of marketing decision making—from problem identification to choosing the relevant data to work with, selecting the approach to be used in making the decision, and evaluating alternative courses of action. This type of information system can be defined as

> a coordinated collection of data, system tools, and techniques with supporting software and hardware by which an organization gathers and interprets relevant information from business and the environment and turns it into a basis for making management decisions.[1]

---

[1]Peter D. Bennett, ed., *Dictionary of Marketing Terms* (Chicago: American Marketing Association, 1988), p. 53.

Figure 2–1 illustrates the concept of an MDSS. There are two main changes depicted in this figure: (1) the conversion of data to information; and (2) the conversion of information to action. The first conversion is the task of the marketing information center, while the second is the major purpose of marketing decision making.

The Marketing Information Center

Although the growth of the concept of a marketing decision support system has been fairly recent, most experts agree that a single, separate marketing information center must exist to centralize responsibility for marketing information within the firm. This is necessary because both the users and suppliers of such information are widely scattered throughout the organization, and some unit is needed to oversee the entire operation.

The general purpose of this organizational unit is to maintain, as well as to improve and upgrade, the accuracy, completeness, and timeliness of information for marketing management decisions. Operationally, this means that the information center must gather raw data from various environments and markets and process them so they can be obtained and analyzed by marketing executives. Data must be gathered from both internal and external sources. Internally, such data

FIGURE 2–1   The Marketing Decision Support System

HIGHLIGHT 2–1
Suggestions for Developing an MDSS

The following is a list of suggestions to aid in the effective implementation of an MDSS.

1. Develop small systems first before coordinating them into an overall system.
2. Develop systems relevant to current management practices and organizational structures.
3. Develop decision support system skills internally and do not rely too heavily on outside experts.
4. Involve users of the system in its design and implementation.
5. Build a flexible system to meet the information needs of various levels of management and types of managers.
6. Monitor early usage of the system to ensure success and make sure future users of the system are aware of the success.
7. Build the system in an evolutionary manner, adding complex models only after data storage and retrieval systems are successfully in place.

Source: From Thomas C. Kinnear and Kenneth L. Bernhardt, *Principles of Marketing,* 3rd ed., pp. 218–19. Copyright © 1990, 1986 by Scott, Foresman and Company. Reprinted by permission of Harper Collins, Publishers.

as sales, costs, and profits, as well as other company reports, need to be converted to information and stored in the computer. Externally, data from trade journals, magazines, newspapers, government publications, and other sources of pertinent information used by marketing executives for decision making also must be converted and stored.

A critical point here is that the MDSS converts raw data into information that marketing management can actually use for making intelligent decisions. An MDSS must produce information in a form marketing executives can understand, when it is needed, and have it under the manager's control. In other words, a key distinction that separates an MDSS from other types of marketing information systems is that an MDSS has the direct and primary objective of supporting marketing management decision making.[2] Figure 2–2 provides examples of two firms with conventional MISs and two firms with MDSSs to illustrate this important difference.

---

[2]See Gilbert A. Churchill, Jr., *Marketing Research: Methodological Foundations* (Hinsdale, Ill.: Dryden Press, 1987), chap. 18. Also see George M. Zinkhan, Erich A. Joachimsthaler, and Thomas C. Kinnear, "Individual Differences and Marketing Decision Support System Usage and Satisfaction," *Journal of Marketing Research,* May 1987, pp. 208–14.

FIGURE 2–2   Examples of MISs and MDSSs

A Marketing Information System (MIS) at Savin Corporation

Savin Corporation has installed a computer terminal in each of its warehouses to keep track of every item in its inventory. The system identifies the quantity on hand, the location and movement of stock, and the status of all orders. The system is used to plan shipments, locate single items in inventory, and locate customer records.

A Marketing Information System (MIS) at United Services
Automobile Association

The United Services Automobile Association, the nation's eighth largest insurer of passenger cars, purchased a $4 million system that now contains virtually all of the company's written records. When a customer reports an accident, an adjuster can call up the customer's file, check the coverage, and keep track of all the paperwork through the final settlement of the claim. The company figures that it used to take five people a day-and-a-half to perform tasks that one person now handles in 20 minutes.

A Marketing Decision Support System (MDSS) at Crocker
National Bank

The Crocker National Bank in San Francisco has purchased desk-top terminals for most of its top-level executives. Each terminal is tapped into the huge computers that record all bank transactions. The executives are able to make comparisons, analyze problems, and prepare charts and tables in response to simple commands. For example, they can analyze emerging trends in deposits and loans and monitor the influence of various interest rates and loan maturities.

A Marketing Decision Support System (MDSS) at Gould, Inc.

Gould, Inc., has developed a decision support system to help managers retrieve, manipulate, and display information needed for making decisions. The system combines large visual display and video terminals with a computerized information system. The system is designed solely to assist managers to make comparisons and analyze problems for decision-making purposes. The MDSS instantly prepares tables and color charts in response to simple commands.

Marketing Decision Making

Earlier we stated that the main purpose of marketing executives is to convert information to actions through the process of decision making. Note that, in Figure 2–1, two up-and-down arrows connect marketing decision making with the marketing information center. These arrows represent an important aspect of the MDSS (i.e., it is an *interactive system* in which marketing executives sit at computer terminals and actively analyze information and convert it to actions).

In previous types of marketing information systems, the information center often attempted to prepare reports to meet the individual needs of different marketing executives at different levels in the organization. More often than not, such attempts provided too much information of the wrong kind and not enough information of the right kind. However, in addition to the flexibility, timeliness, and detail provided by an MDSS, such problems do not occur because marketing executives themselves retrieve and manipulate the information.

MARKETING RESEARCH

Marketing research should be an integral part of a marketing decision support system. In essence, marketing research combines insights and intuition with the research process to provide information for making marketing decisions. In general, marketing research can be defined as

> the function that links the consumer, customer, and public to the marketer through information—information used to identify and define marketing opportunities and problems; generate, refine, and evaluate marketing actions; monitor marketing performance; and improve understanding of marketing as a process. Marketing research specifies the information required to address these issues; designs the method for collecting information; manages and implements the data collection process; analyzes the results; and communicates the findings and their implications.[3]

Today's marketing managers should understand the role of research in decision making. It cannot be overstated that *marketing research is an aid to decision making and not a substitute for it*. In other words, marketing research does not make decisions but it can substantially increase the probability that the best decision will be made. Unfortunately, too often marketing managers view marketing research reports as the final answer to their problems. Instead, marketing managers should recognize that (1) even the most carefully controlled research projects can be fraught with pitfalls and (2) decisions should be made in the light of their own knowledge and experience and other factors that are not explicitly considered in the research project. The problems that the Coca-Cola Company faced when it dropped its original formula and introduced New Coke were brought about by both

---

[3]Peter D. Bennett, ed., *Dictionary of Marketing Terms* (Chicago: American Marketing Association, 1988), pp. 117–18.

HIGHLIGHT 2–2
Marketing Research That Influenced Marketing Strategies

Marketing research can be a useful aid in decision making. Below are several examples of marketing research that helped firms develop their marketing strategies.

EASTMAN KODAK COMPANY

The Eastman Kodak Company was faced with flat sales and needed to devise a strategy to improve sales performance. The company knew that amateur photographers goof on more than 2 billion pictures a year and had its technical researchers look at 10,000 photos to see what kinds of things users were doing wrong. The study led to a number of design ideas for the Kodak disc camera that helped eliminate almost one half of the out-of-focus and underexposed shots. The disc camera has been one of the most successful products in Kodak history.

M&M/MARS CANDY COMPANY

In an attempt to determine the proper weight for its candy bars, M&M/Mars Candy Company conducted a 12-month test in 150 stores. For the test it altered the size of its products across the stores but kept the prices constant. It found that, in those stores where the dimensions were increased, sales went up 20 to 30 percent. As a result of this research, the company decided to change almost its entire product line.

AMERICAN EXPRESS

American Express was disappointed with its inability to attract female cardholders. A group of American Express executives listened in on a market research panel of women discussing credit cards. The panel members indicated that they were very familiar with American Express and thought highly of it, but few saw it as a card for them. It seemed that the prestige image promoted for years using various celebrities appealed more to men than to women. Based on this research, the company developed a new ad campaign that did away with celebrities and emphasized that American Express is "part of a lot of interesting lives."

MERCEDES BENZ

When Mercedes Benz made its initial foray into the U.S. market, it conducted consumer surveys. The research showed that people wanted a no-nonsense car with distinct quality, engineering, design, and performance. This research served as the basis for selecting models to be introduced in the United States and also influenced print ads to emphasize facts, rather than gimmickry.

Source: Adapted from Gilbert A. Churchill, Jr., *Marketing Research: Methodological Foundations,* 4th ed. (Hinsdale, Ill.: Dryden Press, 1987), pp. 3–4.

faulty marketing research and a failure of Coke executives to use sound judgment in interpreting the research results.[4]

Although marketing research does not make decisions, it is a direct means of reducing risks associated with managing the marketing mix and long-term marketing planning. In fact, a company's return on investment from marketing research is a function of the extent to which research output reduces the risk inherent in decision making. For example, marketing research can play an important role in reducing new product failure costs by evaluating consumer acceptance of a product prior to full-scale introduction.

In a highly competitive economy a firm's survival depends on the marketing manager's ability to make sound decisions, to outguess competitors, to anticipate consumer needs, to forecast business conditions, and to plan for company growth. Marketing research is one tool to help accomplish these tasks. Research is also vital for managerial control, because without appropriate data, the validity of past decisions on the performance of certain elements in the marketing system (e.g., the performance of the sales force or advertising) cannot be evaluated reliably.

Although many of the technical aspects of marketing research, such as sampling design or statistical analysis, can be delegated to experts, the process of marketing research begins and ends with the marketing manager. In the beginning of a research project it is the marketing manager's responsibility to work with researchers to define the problem carefully. When the research project is completed, the application of the results in terms of decision alternatives rests primarily with the marketing manager.[5] For these reasons, and since the marketing manager must be able to communicate with researchers throughout the course of the project, it is vital for managers to understand the research process from the researcher's point of view.

The Research Process

Marketing research can be viewed as a systematic process for obtaining information to aid in decision making. Although there are many different types of marketing research, the framework illustrated in Figure

---

[4]For a complete discussion of these issues, see Robert F. Hartley, *Marketing Mistakes,* 4th ed. (New York: John Wiley & Sons, 1989), pp. 221–36.

[5]For a discussion of the use of research findings in marketing decision making, see Rohit Deshpande, "The Organizational Context of Market Research Use," *Journal of Marketing,* Fall 1982, pp. 91–101. Also see Rohit Deshpande and Gerald Zaltman, "A Comparison of Factors Affecting Use of Marketing Information in Consumer and Industrial Firms," *Journal of Marketing Research,* February 1987, pp. 114–19.

FIGURE 2–3   The Five Ps of the Research Process

```
        ┌──────────────────────────┐
        │  Purpose of the research │◄──────────┐
        └──────────────────────────┘           │
                     │                          │
                     ▼                          │
        ┌──────────────────────────┐           │
        │   Plan of the research   │◄──────────┤
        └──────────────────────────┘           │
                     │                          │
                     ▼                          │
        ┌──────────────────────────┐           │
        │ Performance of the research │◄───────┤
        └──────────────────────────┘           │
                     │                          │
                     ▼                          │
        ┌──────────────────────────┐           │
        │ Processing of research data │◄───────┤
        └──────────────────────────┘           │
                     │                          │
                     ▼                          │
        ┌──────────────────────────┐           │
        │ Preparation of research report │◄────┘
        └──────────────────────────┘
```

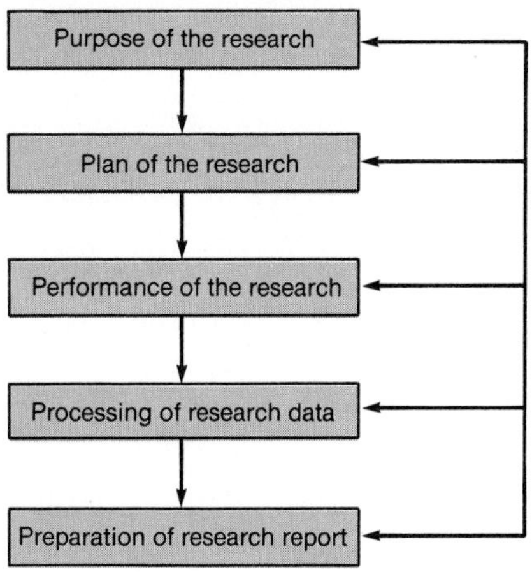

2–3 represents a general approach to defining the research process. Each element of this process will be briefly discussed.

Purpose of the Research.   The first step in the research process is to determine explicitly the purpose of the research. This may well be much more difficult than it sounds. Quite often a situation or problem is recognized as needing research, yet the nature of the problem is not clear or well defined. Thus, an investigation is required to clarify the problem or situation. This investigation includes such things as interviewing corporate executives, reviewing records, and studying existing information related to the problem. At the end of this stage the researcher should know (1) the current situation; (2) the nature of the problem; and (3) the specific question or questions the research is to find answers to—that is, why the research is being conducted.

Plan of the Research.   The first step in the research plan is to formalize the specific purpose of the study. Once this is accomplished, the sequencing of tasks and responsibilities for accomplishing the research are spelled out in detail. This stage is critical since decisions are made that determine the who, what, when, where, and how of the research study.

An initial decision in this stage of the process is the type of data that will be required. The two major types of data are primary and secondary. Primary data is data that must be collected from original sources for the purposes of the study. Secondary data is information that has been previously collected for some other purpose but can be used for the purposes of the study.

If the research project requires primary data, decisions have to be made concerning the following issues:

1. How will the data be collected? Personal interviews? Mail questionnaires? Telephone interviews?
2. How much data is needed?
3. What measures will be used, and how will they be checked for reliability and validity?[6]
4. Who will design the measures and collect the data?
5. Where will the data be collected? Nationally? Regionally? Locally? At home? At work?
6. When and for how long will data be collected?

If secondary data will suffice for the research question(s), similar decisions have to be made. However, since the data are already in existence, the task is much simpler (and cheaper). For example, most of the sources of secondary data listed in Section 5 of this text are available in a public or university library.

In addition to determining data requirements, the research plan also specifies the method of data analysis, procedures for processing and interpreting the data, and the structure of the final report. In other words, the entire research project is sequenced, and responsibility for the various tasks is assigned. Thus, the research plan provides the framework for the coordination and control of the entire project.

When the research plan is fully specified, the time and money costs of the project are estimated. If management views the benefits of the research as worth the costs, the project proceeds to the next phase. A sample research plan is presented in Figure 2–4.

Performance of the Research.   *Performance* is used here in the narrow sense of preparing for data collection and actually collecting the data. It is at this point that the research plan is put into action.

The preparations obviously depend on the type of data desired and method of data collection. For primary research, questions and questionnaire items must be pretested and validated. In addition, preparations for mail surveys include such things as sample selection, questionnaire printing, and envelope and postage considerations. For telephone or personal interviews, such things as interviewer scoring forms, instructions, and scheduling must be taken care of. For secondary data,

---

[6]For sources of information and discussion of reliability and validity issues, see J. Paul Peter and Gilbert A. Churchill, Jr., "The Relationships among Research Design Choices and Psychometric Properties of Rating Scales: A Meta-Analysis," *Journal of Marketing Research,* February 1986, pp. 1–10.

HIGHLIGHT 2–3
A Comparison of Five Methods of Marketing Research

	Definition	Advantages	Disadvantages
Observation	Systematic description of behavior.	Documents the variety of ongoing behavior. Unobtrusive observation captures what happens naturally, when no experimenter is present.	Time consuming. Requires careful training of observers. Observer may interfere with behavior and alter what is happening.
Case study	In-depth description of a single person, family, or organization.	Focuses on the complexity and uniqueness of the individual.	May lack generalizability. Data may reflect the interests and perspective of the investigator.
Survey research	Asking questions to a comparatively large number of people about their opinions, attitudes, or behavior.	Permits data collection from large numbers of subjects.	The way questions are asked can influence the answers. Survey response may not be directly related to behavior.
Experimentation	An analysis of cause-effect relations by manipulating some conditions and holding others constant.	Permits statements about causality. Permits control and isolation of specific variables.	Laboratory findings may not be applicable to other settings.
Correlational research	Assessing the strength of relationship among variables.	Determines whether information on variable A can be used to predict variable B.	Difficult to infer causality. Cannot detect nonlinear relationships.

Source: Adapted from P. R. Newman and B. M. Newman, *Principles of Psychology* (Homewood, Ill.: Dorsey Press, 1983), p. 28.

FIGURE 2–4   Sample Research Plan

 I. *Tentative projective title.*
 II. *Statement of the problem.*
    One or two sentences to outline or to describe the general problem under consideration.
 III. *Define and delimit the problem.*
    Here the writer states the purpose(s) and scope of the problem. *Purpose* refers to goals or objectives. Closely related to this is *justification*. Sometimes this is a separate step, depending on the urgency of the task. *Scope* refers to the actual limitations of the research effort; in other words, what is *not* going to be investigated. Here is the point where the writer spells out the various hypotheses to be investigated or the questions to be answered.
 IV. *Outline.*
    Generally, this is a tentative framework for the entire project by topics. It should be flexible enough to accommodate unforeseen difficulties, show statistical tables in outline form, and also show graphs planned. Tables should reflect the hypotheses.
 V. *Method and data sources.*
    The types of data to be sought (primary, secondary) are briefly identified. A brief explanation of how the necessary information or data will be gathered (e.g., surveys, experiments, library sources) is given. *Sources* refer to the actual depositories for the information, whether from government publications, company records, actual people, and so forth. If measurements are involved, such as consumers' attitudes, the techniques for making such measurements are stated. All of the techniques (statistical and nonstatistical) should be mentioned and discussed about their relevance for the task at hand. The nature of the problem will probably indicate the types of techniques to be employed, such as factor analysis, depth interviews, or focus groups.
 VI. *Sample design.*
    This provides the limits of the universe or population to be studied and how it will be listed (or prepared). The writer specifies the population, states the sample size, whether sample stratification will be employed, and how. If a nonrandom sample is to be used, the justification and the type of sampling strategy to be employed, such as convenience sample, are stated.
 VII. *Data collection forms.*
    The forms to be employed in gathering the data should be discussed and, if possible, included in the plan. For surveys, this will involve either a questionnaire or an interview schedule. For other types of methods, the forms could include IBM cards, inventory forms, psychological tests, and so forth. The plan should state how these instruments have been or will be validated, and the reader should be given some indication of their reliability and validity.

FIGURE 2–4 *(concluded)*

VIII. *Personnel requirements.*

This provides a complete list of all personnel who will be required, indicating exact jobs, time duration, and expected rate of pay. Assignments should be made indicating each person's responsibility and authority.

IX. *Phases of the study with a time schedule.*

This is a detailed outline of the plan to complete the study. The entire study should be broken into workable pieces. Then, considering the person who will be employed in each phase, their qualifications and experience, and so forth, the time in months for the job is estimated. Some jobs may overlap. This plan will help in estimating the work months required. The overall time for the project should allow for time overlaps on some jobs.

Illustration:

1. Preliminary investigation—two months.
2. Final test of questionnaire—one month.
3. Sample selection—one month.
4. Mail questionnaires, field follow-up, and so forth—four months.
5. Additional phases.

X. *Tabulation plans.*

This is a discussion of editing and proof of questionnaires, card punching, and the type of computer analysis. An outline of some of the major tables required is very important.

XI. *Cost estimate for doing the study.*

Personnel requirements are combined with time on different phases to estimate total personnel costs. Estimates on travel, materials, supplies, drafting, computer charges, and printing and mailing costs must also be included. If an overhead charge is required by the administration, it should be calculated and added to the subtotal of the above items.

---

such things as data recording procedures and instructions need attention.

In terms of actual data collection, a cardinal rule is to obtain and record the maximal amount of useful information, subject to the constraints of time, money, and interviewee privacy. Failure to obtain and record data clearly can obviously lead to a poor research study, while failure to consider the rights of subjects or interviewees raises both ethical and practical questions. Thus, both the objectives and constraints of data collection must be closely monitored.

Processing Research Data.   Processing research data includes the preparation of data for analysis and the actual analysis of the data. Preparations include such things as editing and structuring the data,

---

HIGHLIGHT 2–4
Types of Questions that Marketing Research Can Help Answer

I. *Planning*
   A. What kinds of people buy our product? Where do they live? How much do they earn? How many of them are there?
   B. Is the market for our product increasing or decreasing? Are there promising markets that we have not yet reached?
   C. Are there markets for our products in other countries?

II. *Problem Solving*
   A. Product
      1. Which, of various product designs, is likely to be the most successful?
      2. What kind of packaging should we use for our product?
   B. Price
      1. What price should we charge for our new product?
      2. As production costs decline, should we lower our prices or try to develop a higher-quality product?
   C. Place
      1. Where, and by whom, should our product be sold?
      2. What kinds of incentives should we offer to induce dealers to push our product?
   D. Promotion
      1. How effective is our advertising? Are the right people seeing it? How does it compare with the competition's advertising?
      2. What kinds of sales promotional devices—coupons, contests, rebates, and so forth—should we employ?
      3. What combination of media—newspapers, radio, television, magazines—should we use?

III. *Control*
   A. What is our market share overall? In each geographic area? By each customer type?
   B. Are customers satisfied with our product? How is our record for service? Are there many returns?
   C. How does the public perceive our company? What is our reputation with dealers?

Source: Gilbert A. Churchill, Jr., *Basic Marketing Research* (Hinsdale, Ill.: Dryden Press, 1988), p. 8.

---

and perhaps coding and preparing it for computer analysis. Data sets should be clearly labeled to ensure that they are not misinterpreted or misplaced. The data are then analyzed according to the procedure specified in the research plan and are interpreted according to standard norms of the analysis.

HIGHLIGHT 2-5
Techniques of Collecting Survey Data

Personal Interview	*Mail*	*Telephone*
Advantages		
Most flexible means of obtaining data.	Wider and more representative distribution of sample possible.	Representative and wider distribution of sample possible.
Identity of respondent known.	No field staff.	No field staff.
Nonresponse generally very low.	Cost per questionnaire relatively low.	Cost per response relatively low.
Distribution of sample controllable in all respects.	People may be more frank on certain issues (e.g., sex).	Control over interviewer bias easier; supervisor present essentially at interview.
	No interviewer bias; answers in respondent's own words.	Quick way of obtaining information.
	Respondent can answer at his or her leisure, has time to "think things over."	Nonresponse generally very low.
	Certain segments of population more easily approachable.	Callbacks simple and economical.
Disadvantages		
Likely to be most expensive of all.	Bias due to nonresponse often indeterminate.	Interview period not likely to exceed five minutes.
Headaches of interviewer supervision and control.	Control over questionnaire may be lost.	Questions must be short and to the point; probes difficult to handle.
Dangers of interviewer bias and cheating.	Interpretation of omissions difficult.	Certain types of questions cannot be used.
	Cost per return may be high if nonresponse very large.	Nontelephone owners as well as those without listed numbers cannot be reached.
	Certain questions, such as extensive probes, cannot be asked.	
	Only those interested in the subject may reply.	
	Not always clear who replies.	
	Certain segments of population not approachable (e.g., illiterates).	
	Probably slowest of all.	

Preparation of Research Report.   The research report is a complete statement of everything accomplished relative to the research project and includes a writeup of each of the previous stages. Figure 2–5 illustrates the types of questions the researcher should ask prior to submitting the report to the appropriate decision maker.

The importance of clear and unambiguous report writing cannot be overstressed, since the research is meaningless if it cannot be communicated. Often the researcher must trade off the apparent precision of scientific jargon for everyday language that the decision maker can understand. It should always be remembered that research is an aid for decision making and not a substitute for it.

Problems in the Research Process

Although the foregoing discussion presented the research process in a simplified framework, this does not mean that conducting research is a simple task. There are many problems and difficulties that must be overcome if a research study is to be of value. For example, consider the difficulties in one type of marketing research, *test marketing*.

The major goal of most test marketing is to measure new product sales on a limited basis where competitive retaliation and other factors are allowed to operate freely. In this way, future sales potential can be estimated. Test market research is a vital element in new product

---

FIGURE 2–5   Six Criteria for Evaluating Marketing Research Reports

1. Under what conditions was the study made? The report should provide:
   a. Full statement of the problems to be investigated by the study.
   b. Source of financing for the study.
   c. Names of organizations participating in the study, together with their qualifications and vested interests.
   d. Exact time period covered in data collection.
   e. Definitions of terms employed.
   f. Copies of data collection instruments.
   g. Source of collateral data.
   h. Complete statement of method.
2. Has the questionnaire been well designed?
3. Has the interviewing been adequately and reliably done?
4. Has the best sampling plan been followed, or has the best experimental design been used?
5. Was there adequate supervision and control over the editing, coding, and tabulating?
6. Have the conclusions been drawn in a logical and forthright manner?

---

marketing. Listed below are a number of problem areas that can invalidate test market study results.[7]

1. Representative test areas are improperly selected from the standpoint of size, geographical location, population characteristics, and promotional facilities.
2. Sample size and design are incorrectly formulated because of ignorance, budget constraints, or an improper understanding of the test problem.
3. Pretest measurements of competitive brand's sales are not made, which means that the researcher has no realistic base to use for comparison purposes.
4. Attempts are not made to control the cooperation and support of test stores. Consequently, certain package sizes might not be carried, or pricing policies might not be adhered to.
5. Test market products are overadvertised or overpromoted during the test.
6. The full effect of such sales-influencing factors as sales force, season, weather conditions, competitive retaliation, shelf space, and so forth are not fully evaluated.
7. Market test periods are too short to determine whether the product is fully accepted by consumers or only tried on a limited basis.

Similar problems could be listed for almost any type of marketing research. However, the important point to be recognized is that careful planning, coordination, and control are imperative if the research study is to accomplish its objective.

CONCLUSION

This chapter has been concerned with marketing decision support systems and with marketing research. In terms of marketing decision support systems, one of the major reasons for increased interest has been the rapid growth in information-handling technology. However, as we have seen in this chapter, the study of MDSSs is not the study of computers. The study of MDSSs is part of a much larger task: the study of more efficient methods for marketing management decision making.

In terms of marketing research, this chapter has emphasized the importance of research as an aid for marketing decision making. Just

---

[7]For a discussion of some general problems in marketing research, see Alan G. Sawyer and J. Paul Peter, "The Significance of Statistical Significance Testing in Marketing Research," *Journal of Marketing Research,* May 1983, pp. 122–33.

as planning is integral for marketing management, the research plan is critical for marketing research. A research plan not only formalizes the objectives of the study but also details the tasks and responsibilities of the research team as well as cost estimates. Conducting research is a matter of following the research plan and reporting the events of each stage clearly and unambiguously. Finally, emphasis was placed on the extreme care that must be taken to avoid research difficulties and pitfalls.

ADDITIONAL READINGS

Aaker, David A., and George S. Day. *Marketing Research.* 4th ed. New York: John Wiley, 1990.

Boyd, Harper W., Jr.; Ralph Westfall; and Stanley F. Stasch. *Marketing Research: Text and Cases.* 7th ed. Homewood, Ill.: Richard D. Irwin, 1989.

Churchill, Gilbert A., Jr. *Marketing Research: Methodological Foundations.* 4th ed. Hinsdale, Ill.: Dryden Press, 1987.
_____. *Basic Marketing Research.* Hinsdale, Ill.: Dryden Press, 1988.

Dillon, William R.; Thomas J. Madden; and Neil H. Firtle. *Marketing Research in a Marketing Environment.* 2nd ed. Homewood, Ill.: Richard D. Irwin, 1990.

Green, Paul E.; Donald S. Tull; and Gerald Albaum. *Research for Marketing Decisions.* 5th ed. Englewood Cliffs, N.J.: Prentice-Hall, Inc., 1988.

Peterson, Robert A. *Marketing Research.* 2nd ed. Plano, Tex.: Business Publications Inc., 1988.

Tull, Donald S., and Del I. Hawkins. *Marketing Research: Measurement and Method.* 5th ed. New York: Macmillan, 1990.

| *Consumer Behavior*

The marketing concept emphasizes that profitable marketing begins with the discovery and understanding of consumer needs and then develops a marketing mix to satisfy these needs. Thus, an understanding of consumers and their needs and purchasing behavior is integral to successful marketing.

Unfortunately, there is no single theory of consumer behavior that can totally explain why consumers behave as they do. Instead, there are numerous theories, models, and concepts making up the field. In addition, the majority of these notions have been borrowed from a variety of other disciplines, such as sociology, psychology, social psychology, and economics, and must be integrated to understand consumer behavior.

In this chapter some of the many influences on consumer behavior will be examined in terms of the buying process. The reader may wish to examine Figure 3–1 closely, since it provides the basis for this discussion.

The chapter will proceed by first examining the buying process and then discussing the group, product class, and situational influences on this process.

THE BUYING PROCESS

The buying process can be viewed as a series of five stages: need, recognition, alternative search, alternative evaluation, purchase decision, and postpurchase feelings. In this section, each of these stages will be discussed. It should be noted at the outset that this is a general model for depicting a logical sequence of buying behavior. Clearly, individuals will vary from this model because of personal differences

FIGURE 3–1   An Overview of the Buying Process

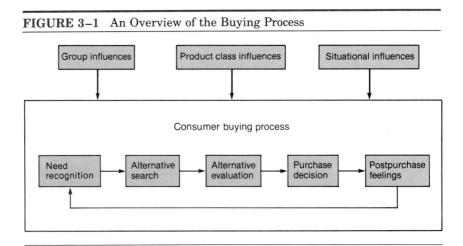

in such things as personality, self-concept, subjective perceptions of information, the product, and the purchasing situation. However, the model provides a useful framework for organizing our discussion of consumer behavior.

Need Recognition

The starting point for this model of the buying process is the recognition of an unsatisfied need by the consumer. Any number of either internal or external stimuli may activate needs or wants and recognition of them. Internal stimuli are such things as feeling hungry and wanting some food, feeling a headache coming on and wanting some Excedrin, or feeling bored and looking for a movie to go to. External stimuli are such things as seeing a McDonald's sign and then feeling hungry or seeing a sale sign for winter parkas and remembering that last year's coat is worn out.

It is the task of marketing managers to find out what needs and wants a particular product can and does satisfy and what unsatisfied needs and wants consumers have for which a new product could be developed. In order to do so, marketing managers should understand what types of needs consumers may have. A well-known classification of needs was developed many years ago by Abraham Maslow and includes five types.[1] Maslow's view is that lower-level needs, starting

---

[1]A. H. Maslow, *Motivation and Personality* (New York: Harper & Row, 1954); also see James F. Engel, Roger D. Blackwell, and Paul W. Miniard, *Consumer Behavior,* 6th ed. (Hinsdale: Dryden Press, 1990), chap. 17 for further discussion of need recognition.

with physiological and safety, must be attended to before higher-level needs can be satisfied. Maslow's hierarchy is described below.

Physiological Needs.   This category consists of the primary needs of the human body, such as food, water, and sex. Physiological needs will dominate when all needs are unsatisfied. In such a case, none of the other needs will serve as a basis for motivation.

Safety Needs.   With the physiological needs met, the next higher level assumes importance. Safety needs consist of such things as protection from physical harm, ill health, economic disaster, and avoidance of the unexpected.

Belongingness and Love Needs.   These needs are related to the social and gregarious nature of humans and the need for companionship. This level in the hierarchy is the point of departure from the physical or quasi-physical needs of the two previous levels. Nonsatisfaction of this level of need may affect the mental health of the individual.

Esteem Needs.   These needs consist of both the need for the self-awareness of importance to others (self-esteem) and actual esteem from others. Satisfaction of these needs leads to feelings of self-confidence and prestige.

Self-Actualization Needs.   This need can be defined as the desire to become more and more what one is, to become everything one is capable of becoming. This means that the individual will fully realize the potentialities of given talents and capabilities. Maslow assumes that satisfaction of these needs is only possible after the satisfaction of all the needs lower in the hierarchy.

While the hierarchy arrangement of Maslow presents a convenient explanation, it is probably more realistic to assume that the various need categories overlap. Thus, in affluent societies, many products may satisfy more than one of these needs. For example, gourmet foods may satisfy both the basic physiological need of hunger as well as esteem and status needs for those who serve gourmet foods to their guests.

Alternative Search

Once a need is recognized, the individual then searches for alternatives for satisfying the need. There are five basic sources from which the individual can collect information for a particular purchase decision.

1. *Internal sources.* In most cases the individual has had some previous experience in dealing with a particular need. Thus, the individual will usually "search" through whatever stored information and experience is in his or her mind for dealing with the need. If a previously acceptable product for satisfying the need is remembered, the individual may purchase with little or no additional information

---

HIGHLIGHT 3–1
How Much Do American Consumers Consume?

It may be difficult for many people to appreciate how much Americans purchase and consume. For example, did you know that *in an average day,* Americans . . .

- Eat 5.8 million pounds of chocolate candy.
- Use 550,000 pounds of toothpaste and gargle 69,000 gallons of mouthwash.
- Buy 190,000 watches, about half of which are for gifts.
- Eat 228,000 bushels of onions.
- Buy 120,000 new radios and 50,000 new television sets.
- Eat 47 million hot dogs.
- Buy over 5.6 million books and 970,000 tapes.
- Buy 99,000 fishing licenses and 78,000 hunting licenses.
- Buy over 30,000 automobiles.
- Spend $200,000 to buy roller skates.
- Spend $40 million on automobile repairs and replacements for damage caused by rust.
- Wear more than 3 million pounds of rubber off their tires, enough to make 250,000 new tires.
- Buy 38,000 Ken and Barbie dolls.
- Buy about 35 million paper clips and 4 million eraser-tipped wooden pencils.
- Buy 12,000 new refrigerators and 10,000 new kitchen ranges.
- And last but not least, snap up 82,000 mousetraps?

Sources: Excerpted from Tom Parker, *In One Day* (Boston: Houghton Mifflin, 1984). Copyright © 1984 by Tom Parker. Reprinted by permission of Houghton Mifflin Co.; and Randolph E. Schmid, "Face It: You're a Statistic," *Wisconsin State Journal,* May 17, 1988, p. 1D.

---

search or evaluation. This is quite common for routine or habitual purchases.

2. *Group sources.* A common source of information for purchase decisions comes from communication with other people, such as family, friends, neighbors, and acquaintances. Generally, some of these (i.e., relevant others) are selected which the individual views as having particular expertise for the purchase decision. Although it may be quite difficult for the marketing manager to determine the exact nature of this source of information, group sources of information often are considered to be the most powerful influence on purchase decisions.

3. *Marketing sources.* Marketing sources of information include such factors as advertising, salespeople, dealers, packaging, and displays.

MARKET ENVIRONMENT
Number of alternatives.
Complexity of alternatives.
Marketing mix of alternatives.
Stability of alternatives on the market (new alternatives).
Information available.

SITUATIONAL VARIABLES
Time pressure.
Social pressure (family, peers, boss).
Financial pressure.
Organizational procedures.
Physical and mental condition.
Ease of access to information sources.

POTENTIAL PAYOFF/PRODUCT IMPORTANCE
Price.
Social visibility.
Perceived risk.
Differences among alternatives.
Number of crucial attributes.
Status of decision-making activity (in family, organization, society).

KNOWLEDGE AND EXPERIENCE
Stored knowledge.
Rate of product use.
Previous information.
Previous choices (number and identity).
Satisfaction.

INDIVIDUAL DIFFERENCES
Training.
Approach to problem solving (compulsiveness, open-mindedness, pre-planning, innovativeness).
Approach to search (enjoyment of shopping, sources of information, etc.).
Involvement.
Demographics (age, income, education, marital status, household size, social class, occupation).
Personality/lifestyle variables (self-confidence, etc.).

CONFLICT AND CONFLICT-RESOLUTION STRATEGIES

Source: Reprinted with permission from "Individual Differences in Search Behavior for a Nondurable," by William L. Moore and Donald R. Lehmann, from the *Journal of Consumer Research,* December 1980, pp. 296–307. For a summary of empirical research on these and other search determinants, see Sharon E. Beatty and Scott M. Smith, "External Search Effort: An Investigation across Several Product Categories," *Journal of Consumer Research,* June 1987, pp. 83–95.

Generally, this is the primary source of information about a particular product. These sources of information will be discussed in detail in the promotion chapters of this text.

4. *Public sources.* Public sources of information include publicity, such as a newspaper article about the product, and independent ratings of the product, such as *Consumer Reports.* Here product quality is a highly important marketing management consideration, since such articles and reports often discuss such features as dependability and service requirements.

5. *Experiential sources.* Experiential sources refer to handling, examining, and perhaps trying the product while shopping. This usually requires an actual shopping trip by the individual and may be the final source consulted before purchase.

Information collected from these sources is then processed by the consumer.[2] However, the exact nature of how individuals process information to form evaluations of products is not fully understood. In general, information processing is viewed as a four-step process in which the individual is (1) exposed to information; (2) becomes attentive to the information; (3) understands the information; and (4) retains the information.[3]

Alternative Evaluation

During the process of collecting information or, in some cases, after information is acquired, the consumer then evaluates alternatives based on what has been learned. One approach to describing the evaluation process can be found in the logic of attitude modeling.[4] The basic logic can be described as follows:

1. The consumer has information about a number of brands in a product class.
2. The consumer perceives that at least some of the brands in a product class are viable alternatives for satisfying a recognized need.

---

[2]For a detailed review of research on external search, see Sharon E. Beatty and Scott M. Smith, "External Search Effort: An Investigation across Several Product Categories," *Journal of Consumer Research,* June 1987, pp. 83–95.

[3]For further discussion of information processing, see J. Paul Peter and Jerry C. Olson, *Consumer Behavior and Marketing Strategy,* 2nd ed. (Homewood, Ill.: Richard D. Irwin, 1990), chap. 3.

[4]For a summary of research on attitude modeling, see Blair H. Sheppard, Jon Hartwick, and Paul R. Warshaw, "The Theory of Reasoned Action: A Meta-Analysis of Past Research with Recommendations for Modification and Future Research," *Journal of Consumer Research,* December 1988, pp. 325–43.

3. Each of these brands has a set of attributes (color, quality, size, and so forth).
4. A set of these attributes are relevant to the consumer, and the consumer perceives that different brands vary in terms of how much of each attribute they possess.
5. The brand that is perceived as offering the greatest number of desired attributes in the desired amounts and desired order will be the brand the consumer will like best.
6. The brand the consumer likes best is the brand the consumer will intend to purchase.

Purchase Decision

If no other factors intervene after the consumer has decided on the brand that is intended for purchase, the actual purchase is a common result of search and evaluation. Actually, a purchase involves many decisions, which include product type, brand, model, dealer selection, and method of payment, among other factors. In addition, rather than purchasing, the consumer may make a decision to modify, postpone, or avoid purchase based on an inhibitor to purchase, or a perceived risk.

Traditional risk theorists believe that consumers tend to make risk-minimizing decisions based on their *perceived* definition of the particular purchase. The perception of risk is based upon the possible consequences and uncertainties involved. Consequences may range from economic loss, to embarrassment if a new food product does not turn out well, to actual physical harm. Perceived risk may be either functional (related to financial and performance considerations) or psychosocial (related to whether the product will further one's self- or reference group image). The amount of risk a consumer perceives in a particular product depends on such things as the price of the product and whether other people will see the individual using the product.

The perceived risk literature emphasizes that consumers generally try to reduce risk in their decision making. This can be done by either reducing the possible negative consequences or by reducing the uncertainty. The possible consequences of a purchase might be minimized by purchasing in small quantities or by lowering the individual's aspiration level to expect less in the way of results from the product. However, this cannot always be done. Thus, reducing risk by attempting to increase the certainty of the purchase outcome may be the more widely used strategy. This can be done by seeking additional information regarding the proposed purchase. In general, the more information the consumer collects prior to purchase, the less likely post-purchase dissonance is to occur.

Postpurchase Feelings

In general, if the individual finds that a certain response achieves a desired goal or satisfies a need, the success of this cue-response pattern will be remembered. The probability of responding in a like manner to the same or similar situation in the future is increased. In other words, the response has a higher probability of being repeated when the need and cue appear together again, and thus it can be said that learning has taken place. Frequent reinforcement increases the habit potential of the particular response. Likewise, if a response does not satisfy the need adequately, the probability that the same response will be repeated is reduced.

For some marketers this means that, if an individual finds that a particular product fulfills the need for which it was purchased, the probability is high that the product will be repurchased the next time the need arises. The firm's promotional efforts often act as the cue. If an individual repeatedly purchases a product with favorable results, loyalty may develop toward the particular product or brand. This loyalty can result in habitual purchases, and such habits are often extremely difficult for competing firms to alter.

Although many studies in the area of buyer behavior center around the buyer's attitudes, motives, and behavior before and during the purchase decision, emphasis has also been given to the study of behavior after the purchase. Specifically, studies have been undertaken to investigate postpurchase dissonance, as well as postpurchase satisfaction.[5]

The occurrence of postdecision dissonance is related to the concept of cognitive dissonance. This theory states that there is often a lack of consistency or harmony among an individual's various cognitions, or attitudes and beliefs, after a decision has been made—that is, the individual has doubts and second thoughts about the choice made. Further, it is more likely that the intensity of the anxiety will be greater when any of the following conditions exist:

1. The decision is an important one psychologically or financially, or both.
2. There are a number of forgone alternatives.
3. The forgone alternatives have many favorable features.

---

[5]For further discussion of consumer satisfaction, see Richard L. Oliver and John E. Swan, "Consumer Perceptions of Interpersonal Equity and Satisfaction in Transactions: A Field Survey Approach," *Journal of Marketing,* April 1989, pp. 21–35; Richard L. Oliver and John E. Swan, "Equity and Disconfirmation Perceptions as Influences on Merchant and Product Satisfaction," *Journal of Consumer Research,* December 1989, pp. 372–83.

These factors can relate to many buying decisions. For example, postpurchase dissonance might be expected to be present among many purchasers of such products as automobiles, major appliances, and homes. In these cases, the decision to purchase is usually an important one both financially and psychologically, and there are usually a number of favorable alternatives available.

When dissonance occurs after a decision has been made, the individual may attempt to reduce it by one or more of the following methods:

1. By seeking information that supports the wisdom of the decision.
2. By perceiving information in a way to support the decision.
3. By changing attitudes to a less favorable view of the forgone alternatives.
4. By avoiding the importance of the negative aspects of the decision and enhancing the positive elements.

Dissonance could, of course, be reduced by admitting that a mistake had been made. However, most individuals are reluctant to admit that a wrong decision has been made. Thus, it is more likely that a person will seek out supportive information to reduce dissonance.

These findings have much relevance for the marketer. In a buying situation, when a purchaser becomes dissonant it is reasonable to predict such a person would be highly receptive to advertising and sales promotion that supports the purchase decision. Such communication presents favorable aspects of the product and can be useful in reinforcing the buyer's wish to believe that a wise purchase decision was made. For example, purchasers of major appliances or automobiles might be given a phone call or sent a letter reassuring them that they have made a wise purchase.[6]

GROUP INFLUENCES ON CONSUMER BEHAVIOR

Behavioral scientists have become increasingly aware of the powerful effects of the social environment and personal interactions on human behavior. In terms of consumer behavior, culture, social class, and reference group influences have been related to purchase and consumption decisions. It should be noted that these influences can have

---

[6]For additional discussion of postpurchase feelings and behavior, see Mary C. Gilly and Betsy D. Gelb, "Post-Purchase Consumer Processes and the Complaining Consumer," *Journal of Consumer Research,* December 1982, pp. 323–28; Jagdip Singh, "Consumer Complaint Intentions and Behavior: Definitional and Taxonomical Issues," *Journal of Marketing,* January 1988, pp. 93–107.

both direct and indirect effects on the buying process. By direct effects we mean direct communication between the individual and other members of society concerning a particular decision. By indirect effects we mean the influence of society on an individual's basic values and attitudes as well as the important role that groups play in structuring an individual's personality.

Cultural and Subcultural Influences

Culture is one of the most basic influences on an individual's needs, wants, and behavior, since all facets of life are carried out against the background of the society in which an individual lives. Cultural antecedents affect everyday behavior, and there is empirical support for the notion that culture is a determinant of certain aspects of consumer behavior.

Cultural values are transmitted through three basic organizations: the family, religious organizations, and educational institutions, and, in today's society, educational institutions are playing an increasingly greater role in this regard. Marketing managers should adapt the marketing mix to cultural values and constantly monitor value changes and differences in both domestic and international markets. To illustrate, one of the changing values in America is the increasing emphasis on achievement and career success. This change in values has been recognized by many business firms that have expanded their emphasis on time-saving, convenience-oriented products.

In a nation as large as the United States, the population is bound to lose a significant amount of its homogeneity, and thus subcultures arise. In other words, there are subcultures in the American culture where people have more frequent interactions than with the population at large and thus tend to think and act alike in some respects. Subcultures are based on such things as geographic areas, religions, nationalities, ethnic groups, and age. Many subcultural barriers are decreasing because of mass communication, mass transit, and a decline in the influence of religious values. However, age groups, such as the teen market, baby boomers, and the mature market, have become increasingly important for marketing strategy. For example, since baby boomers (those born between 1946 and 1962) make up about a third of the U.S. population and soon will account for about half of discretionary spending, many marketers are repositioning products to serve them. Snickers candy bars, for instance, used to be promoted to children as a treat but are now promoted to adults as a wholesome, between-meals snack.

It is important for marketers to understand cultural values and to create and adapt products to the values held by consumers. Below is a description of American cultural values and their relevance to marketing.

Value	General Features	Relevance to Marketing
Achievement and success	Hard work is good; success flows from hard work	Acts as a justification for acquisition of goods ("You deserve it")
Activity	Keeping busy is healthy and natural	Stimulates interest in products that are time-savers and enhance leisure-time activities
Efficiency and practicality	Admiration of things that solve problems (e.g., save time and effort)	Stimulates purchase of products that function well and save time
Progress	People can improve themselves; tomorrow should be better	Stimulates desire for new products that fulfill unsatisfied needs; acceptance of products that claim to be "new" or "improved"
Material comfort	"The good life"	Fosters acceptance of convenience and luxury products that make life more enjoyable
Individualism	Being one's self (e.g., self-reliance, self-interest, and self-esteem)	Stimulates acceptance of customized or unique products that enable a person to "express his or her own personality"
Freedom	Freedom of choice	Fosters interest in wide product lines and differentiated products
External conformity	Uniformity of observable behavior; desire to be accepted	Stimulates interest in products that are used or owned by others in the same social group
Humanitarianism	Caring for others, particularly the underdog	Stimulates patronage of firms that compete with market leaders
Youthfulness	A state of mind that stresses being young at heart or appearing young	Stimulates acceptance of products that provide the illusion of maintaining or fostering youth
Fitness and health	Caring about one's body, including the desire to be physically fit and healthy	Stimulates acceptance of food products, activities, and equipment perceived to maintain or increase physical fitness

Source: Leon G. Schiffman and Leslie Lazar Kanuck, *Consumer Behavior,* 3rd ed. © 1987, p. 506. Reprinted by permission of Prentice Hall, Inc., Englewood Cliffs, N.J.

Social Class

While one likes to think of America as a land of equality, a class structure can be observed. Social classes develop on the basis of such things as wealth, skill, and power. The single best indicator of social class is occupation. However, interest at this point is in the influence of social class on the individual's behavior. What is important here is that different social classes tend to have different attitudinal configurations and values, which influence the behavior of individual members. Figure 3–2 presents a social class hierarchy developed specifically for marketing analysis and describes some of these important differences in attitudes and values.

For the marketing manager, social class offers some insights into consumer behavior and is potentially useful as a market segmentation variable. However, there is considerable controversy as to whether social class is superior to income for the purpose of market segmentation.

Reference Groups

Groups that an individual looks to (uses as a reference) when forming attitudes and opinions are described as reference groups.[7] Primary reference groups include family and close friends, while secondary reference groups include fraternal organizations and professional associations. A buyer may also consult a single individual about decisions, and this individual would be considered a reference individual.

A person normally has several reference groups or reference individuals for various subjects or different decisions. For example, a woman may consult one reference group when she is purchasing a car and a different reference group for lingerie. In other words, the nature of the product and the role the individual is playing during the purchasing process influence which reference group will be consulted. Reference group influence is generally considered to be stronger for products that are "public" or conspicuous—that is, products that other people see the individual using such as clothes or automobiles.

As noted, the family is generally recognized to be an important reference group, and it has been suggested that the household, rather

---

[7]See William O. Bearden and Michael J. Etzel, "Reference Group Influence on Product and Brand Purchase Decisions," *Journal of Consumer Research,* September 1982, pp. 183–94; Peter H. Reingen, Brian L. Foster, Jacqueline Johnson Brown, and Stephen B. Seidman, "Brand Congruence in Interpersonal Relations: A Social Network Analysis," *Journal of Consumer Research,* December 1984, pp. 771–83; Jacqueline Johnson Brown and Peter H. Reingen, "Social Ties and Word-of-Mouth Referral Behavior," *Journal of Consumer Research,* December 1987, pp. 350–62.

FIGURE 3–2 Social Class Groups for Marketing Analysis

Upper Americans (14 percent of population). This group consists of the upper-upper, lower-upper, and upper-middle classes. They have common goals and are differentiated mainly by income. This group has many different lifestyles, which might be labeled postpreppy, conventional, intellectual, and political, among others. The class remains the segment of our society in which quality merchandise is most prized, special attention is paid to prestige brands, and the self-image ideal is "spending with good taste." Self-expression is more prized than in previous generations, and neighborhood remains important. Depending on income and priorities, theater, books, investment in art, European travel, household help, club memberships for tennis, golf, and swimming, and prestige schooling for children remain high consumption priorities.

Middle class (32 percent of population). These consumers definitely want to "do the right thing" and buy "what's popular." They have always been concerned with fashion and following recommendations of "experts" in print media. Increased earnings result in better living, which means a "nicer neighborhood on the better side of town with good schools." It also means spending more on "worthwhile experiences" for children, including winter ski trips, college educations, and shopping for better brands of clothes at more expensive stores. Appearance of home is important, because guests may visit and pass judgment. This group emulates upper Americans, which distinguishes it from the working class. It also enjoys trips to Las Vegas and physical activity. Deferred gratification may still be an ideal, but it is not often practiced.

Working class (38 percent of population). Working-class Americans are "family folk" depending heavily on relatives for economic and emotional support (e.g., tips on job opportunities, advice on purchases, help in times of trouble). The emphasis on family ties is only one sign of how much more limited and different working-class horizons are socially, psychologically, and geographically compared to those of the middle class. In almost every respect, a parochial view characterizes this blue-collar world. This group has changed little in values and behaviors in spite of rising incomes in some cases. For them, "keeping up with the times" focuses on the mechanical and recreational, and thus, ease of labor and leisure is what they continue to pursue.

Lower Americans (16 percent of population). The men and women of lower America are no exception to the rule that diversities and uniformities in values and consumption goals are to be found at each social level. Some members of this world, as has been publicized, are prone to every form of instant gratification known to humankind when the money is available. But others are dedicated to resisting worldly temptations as they struggle toward what some believe will be a "heavenly reward" for their earthly sacrifices.

Source: Excerpted from Richard P. Coleman, "The Continuing Significance of Social Class to Marketing," *Journal of Consumer Research*, December 1983, pp. 265–80.

HIGHLIGHT 3–4
Some Common Verbal Tools Used by Reference Groups

Below are a number of verbal tools used by reference groups to influence consumer behavior. If the statements listed below were made to you by a close friend or someone you admired or respected, do you think that they might change your behavior?

Tools	Definitions	Examples
Reporting	Talking about preferences and behaviors.	"All of us drink Budweiser."
Recommendations	Suggesting appropriate behaviors.	"You should get a Schwinn High Sierra."
Invitations	Asking for participation in events.	"Do you want to go to the Lionel Richie concert with us?"
Requests	Asking for behavior performance.	"Would you run down to the corner and get me a newspaper?"
Prompts	Suggesting desired behaviors.	"It sure would be nice if someone would buy us a pizza!"
Commands	Telling someone what to do.	"Get me some Kleenex, and be quick about it!"
Promises	Offering a reward for performing a behavior.	"If you'll go to Penney's with me, I'll take you to lunch later."
Coercion	Threatening to punish for inappropriate behavior.	"If you don't shut up, I'm going to stuff a sock in your mouth!"
Criticism	Saying something negative about a behavior.	"Quit hassling the salesclerk. You're acting like a jerk."
Compliments	Saying something positive about a behavior.	"You really know how to shop. I bet you got every bargain in the store!"
Teasing	Good-natured bantering about behavior or appearance.	"Man, that shirt makes you look like Bozo the clown!"

Source: J. Paul Peter and Jerry C. Olson, *Consumer Behavior and Marketing Strategy,* 2nd ed. (Homewood, Ill.: Richard D. Irwin, 1990), p. 370.

than the individual, is the relevant unit for studying consumer behavior.[8] This is because within a household the purchaser of goods and services is not always the user of these goods and services. Thus, it is important for marketing managers to determine not only who makes the actual purchase but also who makes the decision to purchase. In addition, it has been recognized that the needs, income, assets, debts, and expenditure patterns change over the course of what is called the *family life cycle*. Basic stages in the family life cycle include:

1. Bachelor stage: young, single people not living at home.
2. Newly married couples: young, no children.
3. Full nest I: young married couples with youngest child under six.
4. Full nest II: young married couples with youngest child six or over.
5. Full nest III: older married couples with dependent children.
6. Empty nest I: older married couples, no children living with them, household head(s) in labor force.
7. Empty nest II: older married couples, no children living at home, household head(s) retired.
8. Solitary survivor in labor force.
9. Solitary survivor, retired.

Because the life cycle combines trends in earning power with demands placed on income, it is a useful way to classify and segment individuals and families.[9]

PRODUCT CLASS INFLUENCES

The nature of the product class selected by the consumer to satisfy an aroused need plays an important role in the decision-making process. Basically, the nature of the product class and the brands within it determine (1) the amount of information the consumer will require before making a decision, and, consequently (2) the time it takes to move through the buying process. In general, product classes in which there are many alternatives that are expensive, complex, or new will require the consumer to collect more information and take longer to make a purchase decision. As illustration, buying an automobile is probably one of the most difficult purchase decisions most consumers make. An automobile is expensive, complex, and there are many new

---

[8]See Rosann L. Spiro, "Persuasion in Family Decision Making," *Journal of Consumer Research,* March 1983, pp. 393–402.

[9]See Janet Wagner and Sherman Hanna, "The Effectiveness of Family Life Cycle Variables in Consumer Expenditure Research," *Journal of Consumer Research,* December 1983, pp. 281–91.

styles and models to choose from. Such a decision will usually require extensive information search and time before a decision is made.

A second possibility is referred to as limited decision making. For these purchases a lesser amount of information is collected and less time is devoted to shopping. For example, in purchasing a new pair of jeans the consumer may already have considerable experience, and price and complexity are somewhat limited. However, since there are many alternative styles and brands, some information processing and decision making is generally needed.

Finally, some product classes require what is called "routinized decision making." For these product classes, such as candy bars or other food products, the consumer has faced the decision many times before and has found an acceptable alternative. Thus, little or no information is collected, and the consumer purchases in a habitual, automatic manner.

SITUATIONAL INFLUENCES

Situational influences can be defined as "all those factors particular to a time and place of observation which do not follow from a knowledge of personal and stimulus attributes and which have a demonstrable and systematic effect on current behavior."[10] In terms of purchasing situations, five groups of situational influences have been identified.[11] These influences may be perceived either consciously or subconsciously and may have considerable effect on product and brand choice.

1. *Physical surroundings* are the most readily apparent features of a situation. These features include geographical and institutional location, decor, sounds, aromas, lighting, weather, and visible configurations of merchandise or other material surrounding the stimulus object.
2. *Social surroundings* provide additional depth to a description of a situation. Other persons present, their characteristics, their apparent roles and personal interactions are potentially relevant examples.

[10]Russell W. Belk, "An Exploratory Assessment of Situational Effects in Buyer Behavior," *Journal of Marketing Research,* May 1974, pp. 156–63. Also see Joseph A. Cote, Jr., "Situational Variables in Consumer Research: A Review," working paper (Washington State University, 1985).

[11]Russell W. Belk, "Situational Variables and Consumer Behavior," *Journal of Consumer Research,* December 1975, pp. 156–64. Also see Jacob Hornik, "Situational Effects on the Consumption of Time," *Journal of Marketing,* Fall 1982, pp. 44–55; C. Whan Park, Easwar S. Iyer, and Daniel C. Smith, "The Effects of Situational Factors on In-Store Grocery Shopping Behavior: The Role of Store Environment and Time Available for Shopping," *Journal of Consumer Research,* March 1989, pp. 422–33.

3. *Temporal perspective* is a dimension of situations that may be specified in units ranging from time of day to season of the year. Time also may be measured relative to some past or future event for the situational participant. This allows such conceptions as time since last purchase, time since or until meals or paydays, and time constraints imposed by prior or standing commitments.

4. *Task definition* features of a situation include an intent or requirement to select, shop for, or obtain information about a general or specific purchase. In addition, task may reflect different buyer and user roles anticipated by the individual. For instance, a person shopping for a small appliance as a wedding gift for a friend is in a different situation than when shopping for a small appliance for personal use.

5. *Antecedent states* make up a final feature that characterizes a situation. These are momentary moods (such as acute anxiety, pleasantness, hostility, and excitation) or momentary conditions (such as cash on hand, fatigue, and illness) rather than chronic individual traits. These conditions are further stipulated to be immediately antecedent to the current situation to distinguish the states the individual brings to the situation from states of the individual resulting from the situation. For instance, people may select a certain motion picture because they feel depressed (an antecedent state and a part of the choice situation), but the fact that the movie causes them to feel happier is a response to the consumption situation. This altered state then may become antecedent for behavior in the next choice situation encountered, such as passing a street vendor on the way out of the theater.

CONCLUSION

The purpose of this chapter was to present an overview of consumer behavior in terms of an analysis of the buying process. The buying process is viewed as a series of five stages: need recognition, alternative search, alternative evaluation, purchase decision, and postpurchase feelings. This process is influenced by group, product class, and situational factors. Clearly, the marketing manager must understand the buying process to formulate effective marketing strategies.

ADDITIONAL READINGS

Assael, Henry. *Consumer Behavior and Marketing Action.* 3rd ed. Boston: PWS-Kent Publishing, 1987.

Engel, James F.; Roger D. Blackwell; and Paul W. Miniard. *Consumer Behavior.* 6th ed. Chicago: Dryden Press, 1990.

Hawkins, Del; Kenneth A. Coney; and Roger Best, Jr. *Consumer Behavior: Implications for Marketing Strategy.* 4th ed. Homewood, Ill: BPI/Irwin, 1989.

Mowen, John C. *Consumer Behavior.* 2nd ed. New York: Macmillan Publishing, 1990.

Peter, J. Paul, and Jerry C. Olson. *Consumer Behavior and Marketing Strategy.* 2nd ed. Homewood, Ill.: Richard D. Irwin, 1990.

Schiffman, Leon G., and Leslie Kanuck. *Consumer Behavior.* 3rd ed. Englewood Cliffs, N.J.: Prentice Hall, 1987.

Wilkie, William L. *Consumer Behavior.* 2nd ed. New York: John Wiley & Sons, 1990.

Appendix *Selected Consumer Behavior Data Sources*

1. Demographic Information:
U.S. Census of Population.
Marketing Information Guide.
A Guide to Consumer Markets.
State and city governments.
Media (newspapers, magazines, television, and radio stations) make demographic data about their readers or audiences available.

2. Consumer Research Findings:

Journal of Consumer Research	*Journal of Advertising Research*
Journal of Marketing	*Journal of Consumer Marketing*
Journal of Marketing Research	*Journal of Applied Psychology*
Journal of Advertising	*Advances in Consumer Research*

3. Marketing Applications:

Advertising Age	*Nation's Business*
Marketing Communications	*Fortune*
Sales Management	*Forbes*
Business Week	Industry and trade magazines

Chapter 4

Organizational Buyer Behavior

Organizational buyers include individuals involved in purchasing products for businesses, government agencies, and other institutions and agencies. Those who purchase for businesses include industrial buyers who purchase goods and services to aid them in producing other goods and services for sale, and resellers who purchase goods and services to resell at a profit. Government agencies purchase products and services to carry out their responsibilities to society; and other institutions and agencies, such as churches and schools, purchase to fulfill their organizational missions.

The purpose of this chapter is to examine the organizational buying process and the factors that influence it. Figure 4–1 provides a model of the organizational buying process that will be used as a framework for discussion in this chapter.

PRODUCT INFLUENCES ON ORGANIZATIONAL BUYING

A major consideration that affects the organizational buying process is the nature of the product itself. Such factors as the price, riskiness, and technical complexity of the product affect the process in three ways. First, they affect how long it will take for the firm to make a purchasing decision. Second, they have an effect on how many individuals will be involved in the purchasing process. Last, these factors may affect whether structural or behavioral influences play the major role in the purchasing process.

FIGURE 4–1 A Model of the Organizational Buying Process

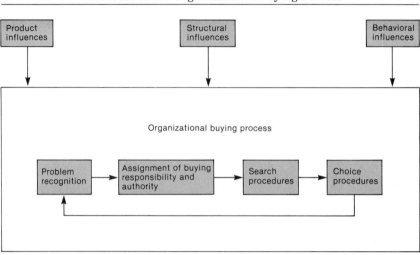

A useful way of examining product class influences is to consider them on the basis of the problems inherent in their adoption.[1] Four basic categories include:

Type I: Routine order products. A Type I product is frequently ordered and used. There is no problem in learning how to use such products, nor is there any question about whether the product will do the job. In short, this type of product is expected to cause no significant problems in use.

Type II: Procedural problem products. For Type II products, the buyer is also confident the product will do the job. However, problems are likely because personnel must be taught how to use the product. A buyer intent on minimizing problems associated with such a product will favor the supplier whose total offering is perceived as likely to reduce to a minimum the time and difficulty required to learn the product's operation.

Type III: Performance problem products. With Type III products, there is doubt whether the product will perform satisfactorily in the application for which it is being considered. Here the problem concerns the technical outcomes of using the product. There is likely to be no firm buying commitment until this problem has been resolved. It is argued that the buyer will favor the supplier who can offer appropriate technical service, providing a free trial period, and who appears flexible enough to adjust to the demands of the buyer's company.

---

[1]Donald R. Lehmann and John O'Shaughnessy, "Difference in Attribute Importance for Different Industrial Products," *Journal of Marketing*, April 1974, pp. 36–42; also see Philip Kotler, *Marketing Management: Analysis, Planning, Implementation, and Control*, 6th ed., Englewood Cliffs, N.J.: Prentice Hall, 1988, chap. 7.

HIGHLIGHT 4–1
Major Differences between Organizational Buyers and Final Consumers

DIFFERENCES IN PURCHASES

1. Organizational buyers acquire for further production, use in operations, or resale to other consumers. Final consumers acquire only for personal, family, or household use.
2. Organizational buyers commonly purchase installations, raw materials, and semifinished materials. Final consumers rarely purchase these goods.
3. Organizational buyers purchase on the basis of specifications and technical data. Final consumers frequently purchase on the basis of description, fashion, and style.
4. Organizational buyers utilize multiple-buying and team-based decisions more often than final consumers.
5. Organizational buyers are more likely to apply value and vendor analysis.
6. Organizational buyers more commonly lease equipment.
7. Organizational buyers more frequently employ competitive bidding and negotiation.

DIFFERENCES IN THE MARKET

1. The demand of organizational buyers is derived from the demand of final consumers.
2. The demand of organizational buyers is more subject to cyclical fluctuations than final-consumer demand.
3. Organizational buyers are fewer in number and more geographically concentrated than final consumers.
4. Organizational buyers often employ buying specialists.
5. The distribution channel for organizational buyers is shorter than for final consumers.
6. Organizational buyers may require special services.
7. Organizational buyers are more likely than final consumers to be able to make goods and services as alternatives to purchasing them.

Source: Reprinted by permission of Macmillan Publishing Company from *Marketing,* 4th ed., p. 186, by Joel R. Evans and Barry Berman. Copyright © 1990 by Macmillan Publishing Company.

Type IV: Political problem products. Type IV products give rise to "political" problems, because there is likely to be difficulty in reaching agreement among those affected if the product is adopted. "Political" problems occur when products necessitate large capital outlays, since there are always allocational rivals for funds. More frequently, political problems arise when the product is an input to several departments whose requirements may not be congruent.

There are two important implications of this classification for marketers. First, in a study of purchasing agents, it was found that different product attributes were rated as relatively more important, depending on the type of product. For example, the most important attributes for Type I products were the reliability of delivery and price; for Type II products, the most important attributes were technical service offered, ease of operation or use, and training offered by supplier; for Type III products, the technical service offered, flexibility of supplier, and product reliability were rated as most important; for Type IV products, the price, reputation of supplier, data on product reliability, reliability of delivery, and flexibility of supplier were rated as most important. Thus, marketing strategy for organizational products should be adapted to variations in buyer perceptions of problems in selection, introduction, and performance.

Second, the type of product may influence whether structural or behavioral factors are relatively more important in the purchasing process. For example, behavioral influences may decrease from Type I to Type IV products while structural influences may increase. A routine order product is most probably the sole responsibility of the purchasing agent. Here organizational influences, such as joint decision making, are minimal, and the purchasing agent may well be more strongly influenced by behavioral influences, such as a personal friendship with the supplier. On the other hand, Type IV product decisions may require considerable joint decision making—such as a purchasing committee—and thus be more influenced by structural factors.

STRUCTURAL INFLUENCES ON ORGANIZATIONAL BUYING

The term *structural influences* refers to the design of the organizational environment and how it effects the purchasing process. Two important structural influences on organizational buying are joint decision making and organization-specific factors.

Joint Decision Making

It is common in organizational buying for more than one department and several persons to be involved in the purchasing process. These people may also play a variety of different roles in arriving at a purchase decision. These roles include:

1. *Users,* or those persons in the organization who actually use the product, for example, a secretary who would use a new word processor.

2. *Influencers,* who affect the buying decision, usually by helping define the specifications for what is bought. For example, an information systems manager would be a key influencer in the purchase of a new mainframe computer.
3. *Buyers,* who have the formal authority and responsibility to select the supplier and negotiate the terms of the contract. For example, in the purchase of a mainframe computer, the purchasing manager would likely perform this role.
4. *Deciders,* who have the formal or informal power to select or approve the supplier that receives the contract. For important technical purchases, deciders may come from R&D, engineering, or quality control.
5. *Gatekeepers,* who control the flow of information in the buying center. Purchasing personnel, technical experts, and secretaries can all keep marketers and their information from reaching people performing the other four roles.[2]

When several persons are involved in the organizational purchase decision, marketers may need to use a variety of means to reach each individual or group. Fortunately, it is often easy to find which individuals in organizations are involved in a purchase because such information is provided to suppliers. Organizations do this because it makes suppliers more knowledgeable about purchasing practices, thus making the purchasing process more efficient.[3]

Organization-Specific Factors

There are three primary organization-specific factors that influence the purchasing process: orientation, size, and degree of centralization. First, in terms of orientation, the dominant function in an organization may control purchasing decisions. For example, if the organization is technology oriented, it is likely to be dominated by engineering personnel, and buying decisions will be made by them. Similarly, if the organization is production oriented, production personnel may dominate buying decisions.

---

[2]This discussion is taken from Eric N. Berkowitz, Roger A. Kerin, and William Rudelius, *Marketing,* 2nd ed., Homewood, Ill.: Richard D. Irwin, 1989, pp. 124–25.

[3]For research on several influences on the industrial buying process, see John R. Ronchetto, Jr., Michael D. Hutt, and Peter Reingen, "Embedded Influence Patterns in Organizational Buying Systems," *Journal of Marketing,* October 1989, pp. 51–62; Ajay Kohli, "Determinants of Influence in Organizational Buying: A Contingency Approach," *Journal of Marketing,* July 1989, pp. 50–65; Daniel H. McQuiston, "Novelty, Complexity, and Importance as Causal Determinants of Industrial Buyer Behavior," *Journal of Marketing,* April 1989, pp. 66–79.

HIGHLIGHT 4–2
Functional Areas and Their Key Concerns in Purchasing

Functional Area	Key Concerns in Purchase Decision Making
Design and development engineering	Name reputation of vendor; ability of vendors to meet design specifications
Production	Delivery and reliability of purchases such that interruption of production schedules is minimized
Sales/marketing	Impact of purchased items on marketability of the company's products
Maintenance	Degree to which purchased items are compatible with existing facilities and equipment; maintenance services offered by vendor; installation arrangements offered by vendor
Finance/accounting	Effects of purchases on cash flow, balance sheet, and income statement positions; variances in costs of materials over estimates; feasibility of make-or-buy and lease options to purchasing
Purchasing	Obtaining lowest possible price at acceptable quality levels; maintaining good relations with vendors
Quality control	Assurance that purchased items meet prescribed specifications and tolerances, governmental regulations, and customer requirements

Source: Michael H. Morris, *Industrial and Organizational Marketing* (Columbus, Ohio: Merrill Publishing, 1988), p. 81.

Second, the size of the organization may influence the purchasing process. If the organization is large, it will likely have a high degree of joint decision making for other than routine order products. Smaller organizations are likely to have more autonomous decision making.

Finally, the degree of centralization of an organization influences whether decisions are made individually or jointly with others. Highly centralized organizations are less likely to have joint decision making. Thus, a privately owned, small company with technology or production orientations will tend toward autonomous decision making while a large-scale, public corporation with considerable decentralization will tend to have greater joint decision making.[4]

---

[4]Jagdish N. Sheth, "A Model of Industrial Buyer Behavior," *Journal of Marketing,* October 1973, pp. 50–56. Also see Paul F. Anderson and Terry M. Chambers, "A Reward/Measurement Model of Organizational Buying Behavior," *Journal of Marketing,* Spring 1985, pp. 7–23.

BEHAVIORAL INFLUENCES ON ORGANIZATIONAL BUYING

Organizational buyers are influenced by a variety of psychological and social factors. We will discuss two of these, personal motivations and role perceptions.

Personal Motivations

Organizational buyers are, or course, subject to the same personal motives or motivational forces as other individuals. Although these buyers may emphasize nonpersonal motives in their buying activities, it has been found that organizational buyers often are influenced by such personal factors as friendship, professional pride, fear and uncertainty (risk), and personal ambitions in their buying activities.

For example, professional pride often expresses itself through efforts to attain status in the firm. One way to achieve this might be to initiate or influence the purchase of goods that will demonstrate a buyer's value to the organization. If new materials, equipment, or components result in cost savings or increased profits, the individuals initiating the changes have demonstrated their value at the same time. Fear and uncertainty are strong motivational forces on organizational buyers, and reduction of risk is often important to them. This can have a strong influence on purchase behavior. Marketers should understand the relative strength of personal gain versus risk-reducing motives, and emphasize the more important motives, when dealing with buyers.[5]

Thus, in examining buyer motivations, it is necessary to consider both personal and nonpersonal motivational forces and to recognize that the relative importance of each is not a fixed quantity. It will vary with the nature of the product, the climate within the organization, and the relative strength of the two forces in the particular buyer.

Role Perception

A final factor that influences organizational buyers is their own perception of their role. The manner in which individuals behave depends on their perception of their role, their commitment to what they believe is expected of their role, the "maturity" of the role type, and the extent to which the institution is committed to the role type.

---

[5]See Christopher P. Puto, Wesley E. Patton III, and Ronald H. King, "Risk Handling Strategies in Industrial Vendor Selection Decisions," *Journal of Marketing,* Winter 1985, pp. 89–98.

HIGHLIGHT 4–3
Twenty Potential Decisions Facing Organizational Buyers

1. Is the need or problem pressing enough that it must be acted upon now? If not, how long can action be deferred?
2. What types of products or services could conceivably be used to solve our need or problem?
3. Should we make the item ourselves?
4. Must a new product be designed, or has a vendor already developed an acceptable product?
5. Should a value analysis be performed?
6. What is the highest price we can afford to pay?
7. What trade-offs are we prepared to make between price and other product/vendor attributes?
8. Which information sources will we rely on?
9. How many vendors should be considered?
10. Which attributes will be stressed in evaluating vendors?
11. Should bids be solicited?
12. Should the item be leased or purchased outright?
13. How far can a given vendor be pushed in negotiations? On what issues will that vendor bend the most?
14. How much inventory should a vendor be willing to keep on hand?
15. Should we split our order among several vendors?
16. Is a long-term contract in our interest?
17. What contractual guarantees will we require?
18. How shall we establish our order routine?
19. After the purchase, how will vendor performance be evaluated?
20. How will we deal with inadequate product or vendor performance?

Source: Michael H. Morris, *Industrial and Organizational Marketing* (Columbus, Ohio: Charles E. Merrill Publishing, 1988), p. 87.

Different buyers will have different degrees of commitment to their buying role which will cause variations in role behavior from one buyer to the next. By commitment we mean willingness to perform their job in the manner expected by the organization. For example, some buyers seek to take charge in their role as buyer and have little commitment to company expectations. The implication for marketers is that such buyers expect, even demand, that they be kept constantly advised of all new developments to enable them to more effectively shape their own role. On the other hand, other buyers may have no interest in prescribing their role activities and accept their role as given to them. Such a buyer is most concerned with merely implementing prescribed company activities and buying policies with sanctioned products. Thus, some buyers will be highly committed to play the role the firm dictates (i.e., the formal organization's perception of their role) while others might be extremely innovative and uncommitted to the expected role performance. Obviously, roles may be heavily influenced by the organizational climate existing in the particular organization.[6]

Organizations can be divided into three groups based on differences in degree of employee commitment. These groups include innovative, adaptive, and lethargic firms. In *innovative* firms, individuals approach their occupational roles with a weak commitment to expected norms of behavior. In an *adaptive* organization, there is a moderate commitment, while in a *lethargic* organization, individuals express a strong commitment to traditionally accepted behavior and behave accordingly. Thus, a buyer in a lethargic firm would probably be less innovative in order to maintain acceptance and status within the organization and would keep conflict within the firm to a minimum.

Buyers' perception of their role may differ from the perception of their role held by others in the organization. This difference can result in variance in perception of the proper and the actual purchase responsibility to be held by the buyer. One study involving purchasing agents revealed that, in every firm included in the study, the purchasing agents believed they had more responsibility and control over certain decisions than the other influential purchase decision makers in the firm perceived them as having. The decisions were (1) design of the product; (2) cost of the product; (3) performance life; (4) naming of the specific supplier; (5) assessing the amount of engineering help available from the supplier; and (6) reduction of rejects. This variance in role perception held true regardless of the size of the firm or the significance of the item purchased to the firm's overall success. It is important, therefore, that the marketer be aware that such perceptual differences may exist and to determine as accurately as possible the amount of control and responsibility over purchasing decisions held by each purchase decision influencer in the firm.

STAGES IN THE BUYING PROCESS

As with consumer buying, most organizational purchases are made in response to a particular need or problem faced by the firm. Recognition of the need, however, is only the first step in the organizational buying process. The following four stages represent one model of the industrial buying process:

---

[6]For research on the role of organizational climate in industrial buying, see William J. Qualls and Christopher P. Puto, "Organizational Climate and Decision Framing: An Integrated Approach to Analyzing Industrial Buying Decisions," *Journal of Marketing Research,* May 1989, pp. 179–92.

HIGHLIGHT 4–4
An Operational View of the Industrial Buying Process

Although there is no single format dictating how industrial companies actually purchase goods and services, a relatively standard process is followed in most cases:

1. A department discovers or anticipates a problem in its operation that it believes can be overcome with the addition of a certain product or service.
2. The department head draws up a requisition form describing the desired specifications he or she believes the product or service must have to solve the problem.
3. The department head sends the requisition form to the firm's purchasing department.
4. Based on the specifications required, the purchasing department conducts a search for qualified sources of supply.
5. Once sources have been located, proposals based on the specifications are solicited, received, and analyzed for price, delivery, service, and so on.
6. Proposals are compared with the cost of producing the product in-house in a make-or-buy decision: if it is decided that the buying firm can produce the product more economically, the buying process for the product in question is terminated; however, if the inverse is true, the process continues.
7. A source or sources of supply is selected from those who have submitted proposals.
8. The order is placed, and copies of the purchase order are sent to the originating department, accounting, credit, and any other interested departments within the company.
9. After the product is shipped, received, and used, a follow-up with the originating department is conducted to determine if the purchased product solved the department's problem.

Although there are many variations of this process in actual operation, this is typical of the process by which industrial goods and services are purchased. It must be understood that in actual practice these steps are combined, not separate.

Source: Robert W. Hass, *Industrial Marketing Management*, 3rd ed. (Boston: Kent Publishing, 1986), p. 96.

---

1. Problem recognition.
2. Organizational assignment of buying responsibility and authority.
3. Search procedures for identifying product offerings and for establishing selection criteria.
4. Choice procedures for evaluating and selecting among alternatives.

Problem Recognition

As mentioned previously, most organizational purchases are made in response to a particular need or problem. The product purchased is hopefully the means to solve the particular problem. Buyers must be concerned with budgets and profits since the firm cannot put forth a great amount of financial resources if it does not have sufficient funds, regardless of the benefits that might be derived from the purchase. However, as was mentioned, there is more subjective buying and persuasion in the organizational buying process than some earlier writers indicated.

Assignment of Buying Authority

The influence of individuals on the buying decision will be determined in part by their responsibility as defined by the formal organization. An individual's responsibility in a given buying situation will be a function of (1) the technical complexity of the product; (2) the product's importance to the firm either in dollar terms or in terms of its relationship with the process or system that will use the product; (3) the individual's product-specific technical knowledge; (4) the individual's centrality in the process or system that will use the product.

In some organizations the responsibility for the purchasing decision is assigned to a centralized purchasing unit. When centralization of the buying function occurs, it is usually based on the assumption that knowledge of the market and not knowledge of the physical product itself is the major consideration in the buying decision. Therefore, the purchasing agent will concentrate on such market variables as price, delivery, and seller performance, rather than on the technical aspects of the product.

Search Procedures

This stage involves the search procedures for identifying product offerings and for establishing selection criteria.[7] Basically, buyers perform two key tasks related to the collection and analysis of information. First, the criteria against which to evaluate potential sellers have to be developed. These are usually based on a judgment about what is

---

[7]See Rowland T. Moriarty and Robert E. Spekman, *Sources of Information Utilized during the Industrial Buying Process: An Empirical Overview.* Report No. 83–101 (Cambridge, Mass.: Marketing Science Institute, 1983).

needed compared to what is available. Second, alternative product candidates must be located in the market. The important point here is that buyers seek sellers just as sellers seek buyers.

Choice Procedures

The final stage in the organizational buying process involves establishing choice procedures for evaluating and selecting among alternatives. Once alternative products and alternative suppliers have been identified, the buyer must choose from among the alternatives. The choice process is guided by the use of decision rules and specific criteria for evaluating the product offering. These decision rules evolve from objectives, policies, and procedures established for buying actions by management. Often some type of rating scheme or value index is used.

The above stages in the organizational buying process have particular significance for marketers in their method of approach to potential buyers. This is not to say that these stages are the only activities organizational buyers go through before making a purchase, or that they are even aware that they are going through them. The stages are presented here only as a convenient way to examine the organizational buying process and the importance of certain activities during particular stages.

CONCLUSION

Organizational buying has long been regarded as the stepchild of marketing in terms of the amount of research effort devoted to its problems. However, considerable recent research has been conducted and in this chapter an overview of the organizational buying process has been presented. Basically, the model viewed organizational buying as a process of problem recognition, assignment of buying authority, search procedures, and choice procedures. Product, structural, and behavioral influences were recognized as playing important roles in terms of the speed and complexity of this process.

ADDITIONAL READINGS

Anderson, Erin; Wujin Chu; and Barton Weitz. "Industrial Purchasing: An Empirical Exploration of the Buyclass Framework." *Journal of Marketing,* July 1987, pp. 71–86.

Frazier, Gary L.; Robert E. Spekman; and Charles R. O'Neal. "Just-in-Time Exchange Relationships in Industrial Markets." *Journal of Marketing,* October 1988, pp. 52–67.

Heide, Jan B., and George John. "Alliances in Industrial Purchasing: The Determinants of Joint Action in Buyer-Seller Relationships." *Journal of Marketing Research,* February 1990, pp. 24–36.

Michaels, Ronald E.; Ralph L. Day; and Erich A. Joachimsthaler. "Role Stress among Industrial Buyers: An Integrative Model." *Journal of Marketing,* April 1987, pp. 28–45.

Morris, Michael H. *Industrial and Organizational Marketing.* Columbus, Ohio: Charles E. Merrill Publishing, 1988.

Reeder, Robert R.; Edward G. Brierty; and Betty H. Reeder. *Industrial Marketing: Analysis, Planning, and Control.* Englewood Cliffs, N.J.: Prentice Hall, 1987.

Robinson, William T. "Sources of Market Pioneer Advantages: The Case of Industrial Goods Industries." *Journal of Marketing Research,* February 1988, pp. 87–94.

| *Market Segmentation*

Market segmentation is one of the most important concepts in the marketing literature. In fact, a primary reason for studying consumer and organizational buyer behavior is to provide bases for effective segmentation, and a large portion of marketing research is concerned with segmentation. From a marketing management point of view, selection of the appropriate target market is paramount to developing successful marketing programs.

The logic of market segmentation is quite simple and is based on the idea that a single product item can seldom meet the needs and wants of *all* consumers. Typically, consumers vary as to their needs, wants, and preferences for products and services, and successful marketers adapt their marketing programs to fulfill these preference patterns. For example, even a simple product like chewing gum has multiple flavors, package sizes, sugar contents, calories, consistencies (e.g., liquid centers), and colors to meet the preferences of various consumers. While a single product item cannot meet the needs of all consumers, it can almost always serve more than one consumer. Thus, there are usually *groups of consumers* who can be served well by a single item. If a particular group can be served *profitably* by a firm, it is a viable market segment. In other words, the firm should develop a marketing mix to serve the group or market segment.

In this chapter we consider the process of market segmentation. We define *market segmentation* as the process of dividing a market into groups of similar consumers and selecting the most appropriate group(s) for the firm to serve. We break down the process of market segmentation into six steps, as shown in Figure 5–1. While we recognize that the order of these steps may vary, depending on the firm and situation, there are few if any times when market segmentation

FIGURE 5–1   A Model of the Market Segmentation Process

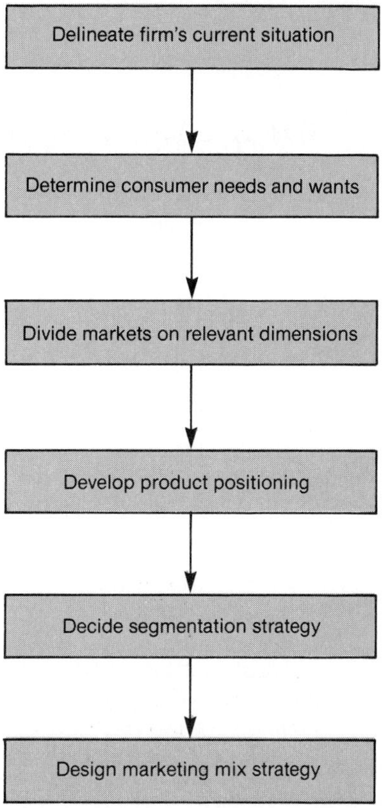

```
┌─────────────────────────────────────┐
│   Delineate firm's current situation │
└─────────────────────────────────────┘
                  │
                  ▼
┌─────────────────────────────────────┐
│  Determine consumer needs and wants  │
└─────────────────────────────────────┘
                  │
                  ▼
┌─────────────────────────────────────┐
│   Divide markets on relevant dimensions │
└─────────────────────────────────────┘
                  │
                  ▼
┌─────────────────────────────────────┐
│      Develop product positioning     │
└─────────────────────────────────────┘
                  │
                  ▼
┌─────────────────────────────────────┐
│      Decide segmentation strategy    │
└─────────────────────────────────────┘
                  │
                  ▼
┌─────────────────────────────────────┐
│      Design marketing mix strategy   │
└─────────────────────────────────────┘
```

analysis can be ignored. In fact, even if the final decision is to "mass market" and not segment at all, this decision should be reached only *after* a market segmentation analysis has been conducted. Thus, market segmentation analysis is a cornerstone of sound marketing planning and decision making.

DELINEATE THE FIRM'S CURRENT SITUATION

As emphasized in Chapter 1, a firm must do a complete situational analysis when embarking on a new or modified marketing program. At the marketing planning level, such an analysis helps determine objectives, opportunities, and constraints to be considered when selecting target markets and developing marketing mixes. In addition,

---

HIGHLIGHT 5–1
Market Segmentation at Campbell Soup Company

Campbell Soup Company recently cooked up its own version of market segmentation, which it calls "regionalization." Basically, the company divided the United States into 22 regions, each with its own marketing and sales force. Each regional staff studies marketing strategies and media buying and has its own ad and trade-promotion budget. Eventually, up to 50 percent of Campbell's ad budget may be the responsibility of the regional groups, rather than corporate headquarters.

Regional staffs have come up with a number of innovative methods to sell Campbell's products, including:

- In Texas and California, where consumers like their food with a bit of a kick, Campbell's nacho cheese soup is spicier than in other parts of the country.
- In New York, when the Giants were bound for the Super Bowl, a local sales manager used part of her ad budget to arrange a football-related radio promotion for Swanson frozen dinners.
- In Nevada, Campbell treats skiers at Ski Incline resort to hot samples of its soup of the day.
- In the South, Campbell has experimented with a creole soup and a red-bean soup for the Hispanic market.

While the company is still ironing out logistical problems, regionalization is a way to deal with the end of the American mass market and perhaps to serve consumers better. Other consumer goods companies are bound to study Campbell's recipe.

---

marketing managers must have a clear idea of the amount of financial and other resources that will be available for developing and executing a marketing plan. Thus, the inclusion of this first step in the market segmentation process is intended to be a reminder of tasks to be performed prior to marketing planning.

DETERMINE CONSUMER NEEDS AND WANTS

As emphasized throughout this text, successful marketing strategies depend on discovering and satisfying consumer needs and wants. In some cases, this idea is quite operational. To illustrate, suppose a firm has a good deal of venture capital and is seeking to diversify its interest into new markets. A firm in this situation may seek to discover a broad variety of unsatisfied needs. However, in most situations, the industry in which the firm operates specifies the boundaries of a firm's need satisfaction activities. For example, a firm in the communication industry may seek more efficient methods for serving consumers' long-distance telephone needs.

As a practical matter, new technology often brings about an investigation of consumer needs and wants for new or modified products and services. In these situations, the firm is seeking the group of consumers whose needs could best be satisfied by the new or modified product. Further, at a strategic level, consumer needs and wants usually are translated into more operational concepts. For instance, consumer attitudes, preferences, and benefits sought, which are determined through marketing research, are commonly used for segmentation purposes.

DIVIDE MARKETS ON RELEVANT DIMENSIONS

In a narrow sense, this step is often considered to be the whole of market segmentation (i.e., consumers are grouped on the basis of one or more similarities and treated as a homogeneous segment of a heterogeneous total market). There are three important questions to be considered here:

1. Should the segmentation be a priori or post hoc?
2. How does one determine the relevant dimensions or bases to use for segmentation?
3. What are some bases for segmenting consumer and industrial buyer markets?

A Priori versus Post Hoc Segmentation

Real-world segmentation has followed one of two general patterns.[1] An *a priori segmentation* approach is one in which the marketing manager has decided on the appropriate basis for segmentation in advance of doing any research on a market. For example, a manager may decide that a market should be divided on the basis of whether people are nonusers, light users, or heavy users of a particular product. Segmentation research is then conducted to determine the size of each of these groups and their demographic or psychographic profiles.

---

[1]Yoram Wind, "Issues and Advances in Segmentation Research," *Journal of Marketing Research,* August 1978, pp. 317–37. Also see T. P. Bean and D. M. Ennis, "Market Segmentation: A Review," *European Journal of Marketing,* no. 5 (1987), pp. 20–42.

Post hoc segmentation is an approach in which people are grouped into segments on the basis of research findings. For example, people interviewed concerning their attitudes or benefits sought in a particular product category are grouped according to their responses. The size of each of these groups and their demographic and psychographic profiles are then determined.

Both of these approaches are valuable, and the question of which to use depends in part on how well the firm knows the market for a particular product class. If through previous research and experience a marketing manager has successfully isolated a number of key market dimensions, then an a priori approach based on them may provide more useful information. In the case of segmentation for entirely new products, a post hoc approach may be useful for determining key market dimensions. However, even when using a post hoc approach, some consideration must be given to the variables to be included in the research design. Thus, consideration must be given to the relevant segmentation dimensions regardless of which approach is used.

Relevance of Segmentation Dimensions

Unfortunately, there is no simple solution for determining the relevant dimensions for segmenting markets. Certainly, managerial expertise and experience are needed to select the appropriate dimensions or bases on which to segment particular markets. In most cases, however, at least some initial dimensions can be determined from previous research, purchase trends, and managerial judgment. For instance, suppose we wish to segment the market for all-terrain vehicles. Clearly, several dimensions come to mind for initial consideration including sex (male), age (18 to 35 years), lifestyle (outdoorsman), and income level (perhaps $15,000 to $25,000). At a minimum, these variables should be included in subsequent segmentation research. Of course, the most market-oriented approach to segmentation is based on the benefits the potential consumer is seeking. Thus, consideration and research of sought benefits is a strongly recommended approach in the marketing literature. This approach will be considered in some detail in the following section.

Bases for Segmentation

A number of useful bases for segmenting consumer and organizational markets are presented in Table 5–1. This is by no means a complete list of possible segmentation variables but represents some useful

TABLE 5–1   Useful Segmentation Bases for Consumer and Industrial Markets

Consumer Markets	
Segmentation Base	*Examples of Base Categories*
Geographic: Region	Pacific, Mountain, West North Central, West South Central, East North Central, East South Central, South Atlantic, Middle Atlantic, New England
City, county, or SMSA size	Under 5,000; 5,000–19,999; 20,000–49,999; 50,000–99,999; 100,000–249,999; 250,000–499,999; 500,000–999,999; 1,000,000–3,999,999; 4,000,000 or over
Population density	Urban, suburban, rural
Climate	Warm, cold
Demographic: Age	Under 6; 6–12; 13–19; 20–29; 30–39; 40–49; 50–59; 60 +
Sex	Male, female
Family size	1–2; 3–4; 5 +
Family life cycle	Young, single; young, married, no children; young, married, youngest child under 6; young, married, youngest child 6 or over; older, married, with children; older, married, no children under 18; older, single; other
Income	Under $5,000; $5,000–$7,999; $8,000–$9,999; $10,000–$14,999; $15,000–$24,999; $25,000–$34,999; $35,000 or over
Occupation	Professional and technical; managers, officials, and proprietors; clerical, sales; craftsmen, foremen; operatives; farmers; retired; students; housewives, unemployed
Education	Grade school or less; some high school; graduated high school; some college; graduated college; some graduate work; graduate degree
Religion	Catholic, Protestant, Jewish, other
Race	White, Black, Oriental, other
Nationality	American, British, German, Italian, Japanese, other
Psychographic: Social class	Lower-lower, upper-lower, lower-middle, upper-middle, lower-upper, upper-upper
Lifestyle	Traditionalist, sophisticate, swinger
Personality	Compliant, aggressive, detached

TABLE 5–1   *(concluded)*

Consumer Markets

Segmentation Base	*Examples of Base Categories*
Cognitive and behavorial:	
Attitudes	Positive, neutral, negative
Benefits sought	Convenience, economy, prestige
Readiness stage	Unaware, aware, informed, interested, desirous, intention to purchase
Perceived risk	High, moderate, low
Innovativeness	Innovator, early adopter, early majority, late majority, laggard
Involvement	Low, high
Loyalty status	None, some, total
Usage rate	None, light, medium, heavy
User status	Nonuser, ex-user, potential user, current user

Organizational Buyer Markets

Segmentation Base	*Examples of Base Categories*
Source loyalty	Purchase from one, two, three, four, or more suppliers
Size of organization	Small, medium, large relative to industry or customer base
Average size of purchase	Small, medium, large
Usage rate	Light, medium, heavy
Product application	Maintenance, production, final product component, administration
Type of organization	Manufacturer, wholesaler, retailer; SIC categories; government agency
Location	North, East, South, West; sales territories
Purchase status	New customer, occasional purchaser, frequent purchaser, non-purchaser
Attribute importance	Reliability of supply, price, service, durability, convenience, reputation of supplier

---

bases and categories. Two commonly used approaches for segmenting markets include benefit segmentation and psychographic segmentation.

Benefit Segmentation.   The belief underlying this segmentation approach is that the benefits people are seeking in consuming a given product are the basic reasons for the existence of true market

HIGHLIGHT 5–2
An Operational Approach to Person-Situation Benefit Segmentation

Peter Dickson argues that market segmentation has focused too narrowly on customer characteristics and needs to include the usage situation in segmentation research. Not only do different types of people purchase different types of products, but they also purchase them for use in different situations. For example, different types of camping gear are needed for cold weather versus hot weather versus mountain-climbing situations. Below is an operational approach for segmenting markets on the basis of both person and situational factors.

Step 1: Use observational studies, focus group discussions, and secondary data to discover whether different usage situations exist and whether they are determinant, in the sense that they appear to affect the importance of various product characteristics.

Step 2: If step 1 produces promising results, undertake a benefit, product perception, and reported market behavior segmentation survey of consumers. Measure benefits and perceptions by usage situation as well as by individual difference characteristics. Assess situation usage frequency by recall estimates or by usage situation diaries.

Step 3: Construct a person-situation segmentation matrix. The rows are the major usage situations; the columns are groups of users identified by a single characteristic or a combination of characteristics.

Step 4: Rank the cells in the matrix in terms of their submarket sales volume. The situation-person combination that results in the greatest consumption of the generic product would be ranked first.

Step 5: State the major benefits sought, the important product dimensions, and the unique market behavior for each nonempty cell of the matrix (some person types will never consume the product in certain usage situations).

Step 6: Position your competitor's offerings within the matrix. The person-situation segments they currently serve can be determined by the product feature they promote and their marketing strategy.

Step 7: Position your offering within the matrix on the same criteria.

Step 8: Assess how well your current offering and marketing strategy meet the needs of the submarkets, compared to the competition.

Step 9: Identify market opportunities based on submarket size, needs, and competitive advantage.

Source: Peter R. Dickson, "Person-Situation: Segmentation's Missing Link," *Journal of Marketing,* Fall 1982, p. 61.

segments.[2] Thus, this approach attempts to measure consumer value systems and consumer perceptions of various brands in a product class. To illustrate, the classic example of a benefit segmentation was provided by Russell Haley and concerned the toothpaste market. Haley identified five basic segments, which are presented in Table 5–2. Haley argued that this segmentation could be very useful for selecting advertising copy, media, commercial length, packaging, and new product design. For example, colorful packages might be appropriate for the Sensory Segment, perhaps aqua (to indicate fluoride) for the Worrier Group, and gleaming white for the Social Segment because of this segment's interest in white teeth.

TABLE 5–2   Toothpaste Market Benefit Segments

	Sensory Segment	*Sociable Segment*	*Worrier Segment*	*Independent Segment*
Principal benefit sought	Flavor and product appearance	Brightness of teeth	Decay prevention	Price
Demographic strengths	Children	Teens, young people	Large families	Men
Special behaviorial characteristics	Users of spearmint flavored toothpaste	Smokers	Heavy users	Heavy users
Brands disproportionately favored	Colgate	Macleans, Ultrabrite	Crest	Cheapest brand
Lifestyle characteristics	Hedonistic	Active	Conservative	Value-oriented

Source: Adapted from Russell I. Haley, "Benefit Segmentation: A Decision-Oriented Research Tool," *Journal of Marketing,* July 1968, pp. 30–35.

---

[2]Russell I. Haley, "Benefit Segmentation: A Decision-Oriented Research Tool," *Journal of Marketing,* July 1968, pp. 30–35; Russell I. Haley, "Benefit Segmentation—20 Years Later," *Journal of Consumer Marketing,* no. 2 (1983), pp. 5–13; Russell I. Haley, "Benefit Segments: Backwards and Forwards," *Journal of Advertising Research,* February–March 1984, pp. 19–25.

Calantone and Sawyer also used a benefit segmentation approach to segment the market for bank services.[3] Their research was concerned with the question of whether benefit segments remain stable across time. While they found some stability in segments, there were some differences in attribute importance, size, and demographics at different times. Thus, they argue for ongoing benefit segmentation research to keep track of any changes that might affect marketing strategy.

Benefit segmentation is clearly a market-oriented approach to segmentation that seeks to identify consumer needs and wants and to satisfy them by providing products and services with the desired benefits. It is clearly very consistent with the approach to marketing suggested by the marketing concept.

Psychographic Segmentation.   Whereas benefit segmentation focuses on the benefits sought by the consumer, psychographic segmentation focuses on the personal attributes of the consumer. The psychographic or lifestyle approach typically follows a post hoc model of segmentation. Generally, a large number of questions are asked concerning consumer's activities, interests, and opinions, and then consumers are grouped together empirically based on their responses. Although questions have been raised about the validity of this segmentation approach, it provides much useful information about markets.[4]

A well-known psychographic segmentation was developed at SRI International in California. The original segmentation divided consumers in the United States into nine groups and was called VALS™, which stands for "values and lifestyles." However, while this segmentation was commercially successful, it tended to place the majority of consumers into only one or two groups, and SRI felt it needed to be updated to reflect changes in society. Thus, SRI developed a new typology called VALS 2.[5]

VALS 2 is based on two national surveys of 2,500 consumers who responded to 43 lifestyle questions. The first survey developed the

[3]Roger J. Calantone and Alan G. Sawyer, "The Stability of Benefit Segments," *Journal of Marketing Research,* August 1978, pp. 395–404; also see James R. Merrill and William A. Weeks, "Predicting and Identifying Benefit Segments in the Elderly Market," in *AMA Educator's Proceedings,* ed. Patrick Murphy et al. (Chicago: American Marketing Association, 1983), pp. 399–403; Wagner A. Kamakura, "A Least Squares Procedure for Benefit Segmentation with Conjoint Experiments," *Journal of Marketing Research,* May 1988, pp. 157–67.

[4]John L. Lastovicka, John P. Murry, Jr., and Eric Joachimsthaler, "Evaluating the Measurement Validity of Lifestyle Typologies with Qualitative Measures and Multiplicative Factoring," *Journal of Marketing Research,* February 1990, pp. 11–23.

[5]This discussion is taken from J. Paul Peter and Jerry C. Olson, *Consumer Behavior and Marketing Strategy,* 2nd ed. (Homewood, Ill.: Richard D. Irwin, 1990), p. 411.

HIGHLIGHT 5–3
Examples of Items Used in Psychographic Segmentation Research

1. I often watch the newspaper advertisements for announcements of department store sales.
2. I like to watch or listen to baseball or football games.
3. I often try new stores before my friends and neighbors do.
4. I like to work on community projects.
5. My children are the most important thing in my life.
6. I will probably have more money to spend next year than I have now.
7. I often seek out the advice of my friends regarding which store to buy from.
8. I think I have more self-confidence than most people.
9. I enjoy going to symphony concerts.
10. It is good to have charge accounts.

(These items are scored on a "agree strongly" to "disagree strongly" scale.)

---

segmentation, and the second validated it and linked it to buying and media behavior. The questionnaire asked consumers to respond to whether they agreed or disagreed with statements such as "My idea of fun at a national park would be to stay at an expensive lodge and dress up for dinner" and "I could stand to skin a dead animal." Consumers were then clustered into the eight groups shown and described in Figure 5–2.

The VALS 2 groups are arranged in a rectangle and are based on two dimensions. The vertical dimension represents resources, which include income, education, self-confidence, health, eagerness to buy, intelligence, and energy level. The horizontal dimension represents self-orientations, and includes three different types. *Principle-oriented consumers* are guided by their views of how the world is or should be; *status-oriented consumers* by the action and opinions of others; and *action-oriented consumers* by a desire for social or physical activity, variety, and risk taking.

Each of the VALS 2 groups represents from 9 to 17 percent of the U.S. adult population. Marketers can buy VALS 2 information for a variety of products and can have it tied to a number of other consumer databases.

FIGURE 5–2   VALS 2™ Eight American Lifestyles

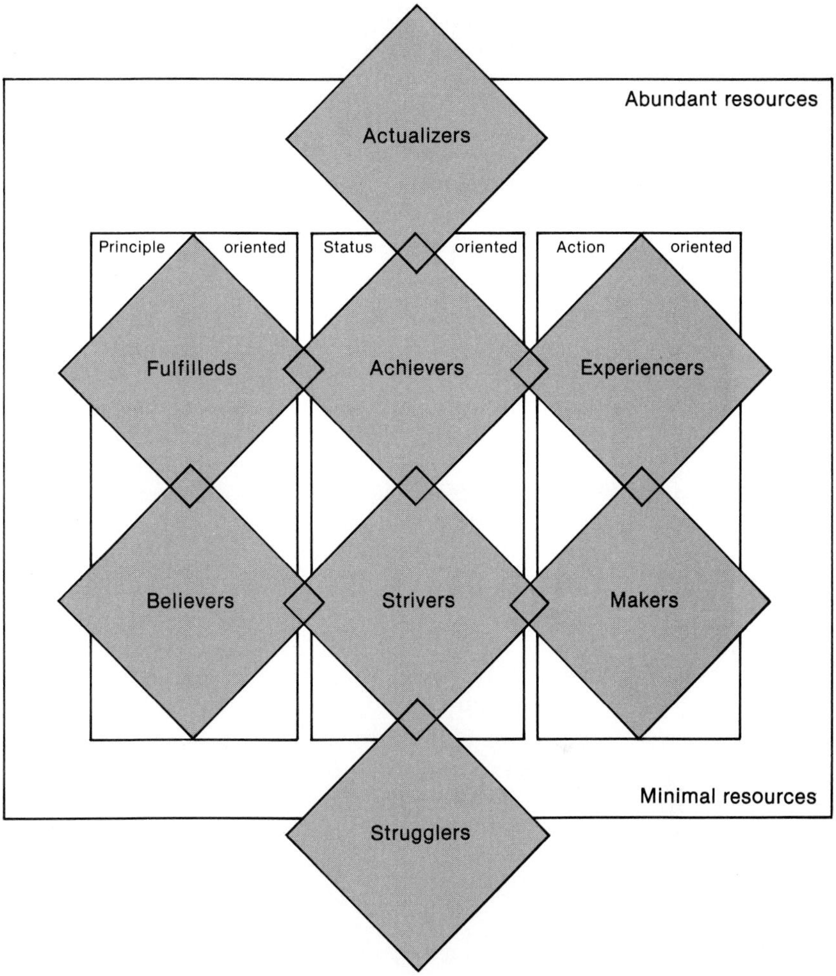

Actualizers. These consumers have the highest incomes and such high self-esteem and abundant resources that they can indulge in any or all self-orientations. They are located above the rectangle. Image is important to them as an expression of their taste, independence, and character. Their consumer choices are directed toward the finer things in life.

Fulfilleds. These consumers are the high-resource group of those who are principle-oriented. They are mature, responsible, well-educated professionals. Their leisure activities center on their homes, but they are well-informed about what goes on in the world, and they are open to new ideas and social change. They have high incomes but are practical consumers.

FIGURE 5–2 *(concluded)*

Believers. These consumers are the low-resource group of those who are principle-oriented. They are conservative and predictable consumers who favor American products and established brands. Their lives are centered on family, church, community, and the nation. They have modest incomes.

Achievers. These consumers are the high-resource group of those who are status-oriented. They are successful, work-oriented people who get their satisfaction from their jobs and families. They are politically conservative and respect authority and the status quo. They favor established products and services that show off their success to their peers.

Strivers. These consumers are the low-resource group of those who are status-oriented. They have values very similar to Achievers but have fewer economic, social, and psychological resources. Style is extremely important to them as they strive to emulate people they admire and wish to be like.

Experiencers. These consumers are the high-resource group of those who are action-oriented. They are the youngest of all the segments with a median age of 25. They have a lot of energy, which they pour into physical exercise and social activities. They are avid consumers, spending heavily on clothing, fast foods, music, and other youthful favorites—with particular emphasis on new products and services.

Makers. These consumers are the low-resource group of those who are action-oriented. They are practical people who value self-sufficiency. They are focused on the familiar—family, work, and physical recreation—and have little interest in the broader world. As consumers, they appreciate practical and functional products.

Strugglers. These consumers have the lowest incomes. They have too few resources to be included in any consumer self-orientation and are thus located below the rectangle. They are the oldest of all the segments with a median age of 61. Within their limited means, they tend to be brand-loyal consumers.

Source: Martha Farnsworth Riche, "Psychographics for the 1990s," *American Demographics,* July 1989, pp. 24–26ff. Adapted with permission. © American Demographics.

DEVELOP PRODUCT POSITIONING

By this time the firm should have a good idea of the basic segments of the market that could potentially be satisfied with its product. The current step is concerned with positioning the product in the minds of consumers relative to competing products. Undoubtedly, the classic example of positioning is the 7UP "Uncola" campaign. Prior to this campaign, 7UP had difficulty convincing consumers that the product could be enjoyed as a soft drink and not just as a mixer. Consumers believed that colas were soft drinks but apparently did not perceive

> **HIGHLIGHT 5–4**
> **Positioning Your Product**
>
> A variety of positioning strategies is available to the advertiser. An object can be positioned by:
>
> 1. Attributes—Crest is a cavity fighter.
> 2. Price/quality—Sears is a "value" store.
> 3. Competitor—Avis positions itself with Hertz.
> 4. Application—Gatorade is for flu attacks.
> 5. Product user—Miller is for the blue-collar, heavy beer drinker.
> 6. Product class—Carnation Instant Breakfast is a breakfast food.
>
> The selection of a positioning strategy involves identifying competitors, relevant attributes, competitor positions, and market segments. Research-based approaches can help in each of these steps by providing conceptualization even if the subjective judgments of managers are used to provide the actual input information to the positioning decision.
>
> *Source:* David A. Aaker and J. Gary Shansby, "Positioning Your Product," *Business Horizons,* May–June 1982, p. 62.

7UP in this way. However, by positioning 7UP as the "Uncola," the company was capable of positioning the product (1) as a soft drink that could be consumed in the same situations as colas and (2) as an alternative to colas. This positioning was very successful.

In determining the appropriate positioning of the product, the firm must consider its offering relative to competition. Some experts argue that different positioning strategies should be used, depending on whether the firm is the market leader or a follower, and that followers usually should not attempt positioning directly against the industry leader.[6] While there are many sophisticated research tools available for investigating positioning, they are beyond the scope of this text. The main point here is that, in segmenting markets, some segments otherwise appearing to be approachable might be forgone, since competitive products may already dominate that segment in sales and in the minds of consumers. Product positioning studies also are useful for giving the marketing manager a clearer idea of consumer perceptions of market offerings.

---

[6]See Al Ries and Jack Trout, *Positioning: The Battle for Your Mind* (New York: Warner Books, 1981); Al Ries and Jack Trout, *Marketing Warfare* (New York: McGraw-Hill, 1986).

HIGHLIGHT 5–5
Segmentation Bases for Particular Marketing
Decision Areas

FOR GENERAL UNDERSTANDING OF THE MARKET:
Benefits sought
Product purchase and usage patterns
Needs
Brand loyalty and switching patterns
A hybrid of the variables above

FOR POSITIONING STUDIES:
Product usage
Product preference
Benefits sought
A hybrid of the variables above

FOR NEW PRODUCT CONCEPTS (AND NEW PRODUCT INTRODUCTION):
Reaction to new concepts (intention to buy, preference over current brand,
    and so on)
Benefits sought

FOR PRICING DECISIONS:
Price sensitivity
Deal proneness
Price sensitivity by purchase/usage patterns

FOR ADVERTISING DECISIONS:
Benefits sought
Media usage
Psychographic/lifestyle
A hybrid (of the variables above or purchase/usage pattern, or both)

FOR DISTRIBUTION DECISIONS:
Store loyalty and patronage
Benefits sought in store selection

Source: Yoram Wind, "Issues and Advances in Segmentation Research," *Journal of Marketing Research,* August 1978, p. 320.

DECIDE SEGMENTATION STRATEGY

The firm is now ready to select its segmentation strategy. There are four basic alternatives. First, the firm may decide not to enter the market. For example, analysis to this stage may reveal no viable market niche for the firm's offering. Second, the firm may decide not to segment but to be a mass marketer. There are at least three situations when this may be the appropriate decision for the firm:

1. The market is so small that marketing to a portion of it is not profitable.
2. Heavy users make up such a large proportion of the sales volume that they are the only relevant target.
3. The brand is the dominant brand in the market, and targeting to a few segments would not benefit sales and profits.[7]

Third, the firm may decide to market to one segment. And fourth, the firm may decide to market to more than one segment and design a separate marketing mix for each. In any case, the firm must have some criteria on which to base its segmentation strategy decisions. Three important criteria on which to base such decisions are that a viable segment must be (1) measurable, (2) meaningful, and (3) marketable.

1. *Measurable.* For a segment to be selected, the firm must be capable of measuring its size and characteristics. For instance, one of the difficulties with segmenting on the basis of social class is that the concept and its divisions are not clearly defined and measured. Alternatively, income is a much easier concept to measure.
2. *Meaningful.* A meaningful segment is one that is large enough to have sufficient sales potential and growth potential to offer long-run profits for the firm.
3. *Marketable.* A marketable segment is one that can be reached and served by the firm in an efficient manner.

Segments that meet these criteria are viable markets for the firm's offering. The firm must now give further attention to completing its marketing mix offering.

DESIGN MARKETING MIX STRATEGY

The firm is now in a position to complete its marketing plan by finalizing the marketing mix or mixes to be used for each segment. Clearly, selection of the target market and designing the marketing mix go hand in hand, and thus many marketing mix decisions should have already been carefully considered. To illustrate, the target market selected may be price sensitive, so some consideration has already been given to price levels, and clearly product positioning has many implications for promotion and channel decisions. Thus, while we place marketing mix design at the end of the model, many of these decisions

---

[7]Shirley Young, Leland Ott, and Barbara Feigin, "Some Practical Considerations in Market Segmentation," *Journal of Marketing Research,* August 1978, p. 405.

HIGHLIGHT 5–6
Differences in Marketing Strategy for Three Segmentation Alternatives

Strategy Elements	Mass Marketing	Single Market Segmentation	Multiple Market Segmentation
Market definition	Broad range of consumers	One well-defined consumer group	Two or more well-defined consumer groups
Product strategy	Limited number of products under one brand for many types of consumers	One brand tailored to one consumer group	Distinct brand for each consumer group
Pricing strategy	One "popular" price range	One price range tailored to the consumer group	Distinct price range for each consumer group
Distribution strategy	All possible outlets	All suitable outlets	All suitable outlets—differs by segment
Promotion strategy	Mass media	All suitable media	All suitable media—differs by segment
Strategy emphasis	Appeal to various types of consumers through a uniform, broad-based marketing program	Appeal to one specific consumer group through a highly specialized, but uniform, marketing program	Appeal to two or more distinct market segments through different marketing plans catering to each segment

Source: Reprinted by permission of Macmillan Publishing Company from *Marketing*, 4th ed., p. 231, by Joel R. Evans and Barry Berman. Copyright © 1990 by Macmillan Publishing Company.

are clearly made in *conjunction* with target market selection. In the next six chapters of this text, marketing mix decisions will be discussed in detail.

CONCLUSION

The purpose of this chapter was to provide an overview of market segmentation. Market segmentation was defined as the process of dividing a market into groups of similar consumers and selecting the most appropriate group(s) for the firm to serve. Market segmentation was analyzed as a six-stage process: (1) to delineate the firm's current situation; (2) to determine consumer needs and wants; (3) to divide the market on relevant dimensions; (4) to develop product positioning; (5) to decide segmentation strategy; (6) to design marketing mix strategy.

ADDITIONAL READINGS

Dickson, Peter R., and James L. Ginter. "Market Segmentation, Product Differentiation, and Marketing Strategy." *Journal of Marketing,* April 1987, pp. 1–10.

Dröge, Cornelia, and René Y. Darmon. "Associative Positioning Strategies through Comparative Advertising: Attribute versus Overall Similarity Approaches." *Journal of Marketing Research,* November 1987, pp. 377–88.

Kahn, Barbara E.; Monohar U. Kalwani; and Donald G. Morrison. "Niching versus Change-of-Pace Brands: Using Purchase Frequencies and Penetration Rates to Infer Brand Positionings." *Journal of Marketing Research,* November 1988, pp. 384–90.

Grover, Rajiv, and V. Srinivasan. "A Simultaneous Approach to Market Segmentation and Market Structuring." *Journal of Marketing Research,* May 1987, pp. 139–53.

Kamakura, Wagner A., and Gary J. Russell. "A Probabilistic Choice Model for Market Segmentation and Elasticity Structure." *Journal of Marketing Research,* November 1989, pp. 379–90.

Shostack, Lynn G. "Service Positioning through Structural Change." *Journal of Marketing,* January 1987, pp. 34–43.

Sujan, Mita, and James R. Bettman. "The Effects of Brand Positioning Strategies on Consumers' Brand and Category Perceptions: Some Insights from Schema Research." *Journal of Marketing Research,* November 1989, pp. 454–67.

Zeithaml, Valarie A. "The New Demographics and Market Fragmentation." *Journal of Marketing,* Summer 1985, pp. 64–75.

The Marketing Mix

| *Product Strategy*

Product strategy is a critical element of marketing and business strategy, since it is through the sale of products and services that companies survive and grow. This chapter discusses four important areas of concern in developing product strategies. First, some basic issues are discussed including product definition, product classification, product mix and product line, and packaging and branding. Second, the product life cycle and its implications for product strategy are explained. Third, the product audit is reviewed, and finally, five ways to organize for product management are overviewed. These include the marketing manager system, product (brand) manager system, product planning committee, new product manager system, and venture team approaches.

BASIC ISSUES IN PRODUCT MANAGEMENT

Successful marketing depends on understanding the nature of products and basic decision areas in product management. In this section, we discuss the definition and classification of products and the nature of a product mix and product lines. Also considered is the role of packaging and branding.

Product Definition

The way in which the product variable is defined can have important implications for the survival, profitability, and long-run growth of the firm. For example, the same product can be viewed at least three

---

HIGHLIGHT 6–1
Elements of Product Strategy

1. *An audit of the firm's actual and potential resources*
   a. Financial strength
   b. Access to raw materials
   c. Plant and equipment
   d. Operating personnel
   e. Management
   f. Engineering and technical skills
   g. Patents and licenses
2. *Approaches to current markets*
   a. More of the same products
   b. Variations of present products in terms of grades, sizes, and packages
   c. New products to replace or supplement current lines
   d. Product deletions
3. *Approaches to new or potential markets*
   a. Geographical expansion of domestic sales
   b. New socioeconomic or ethnic groups
   c. Overseas markets
   d. New uses of present products
   e. Complementary goods
   f. Mergers and acquisitions
4. *State of competition*
   a. New entries into the industry
   b. Product imitation
   c. Competitive mergers or acquisitions

---

different ways. First, it can be viewed in terms of the tangible product—the physical entity or service that is offered to the buyer. Second, it can be viewed in terms of the extended product—the tangible product along with the whole cluster of services that accompany it. For example, a manufacturer of computer software may offer a 24-hour hotline to answer questions users may have, free or reduced-cost software updates, free replacement of damaged software, and a subscription to a newsletter that documents new applications of the software. Third, it can be viewed in terms of the generic product—the essential benefits the buyer expects to receive from the product. For example, many personal care products bring to the purchaser feelings of self-enhancement and security in addition to the tangible benefits they offer.

From the standpoint of the marketing manager, to define the product solely in terms of the tangible product is to fall into the error of "marketing myopia." Executives who are guilty of committing this error define their company's product too narrowly, since overemphasis is placed on the physical object itself. The classic example of this mistake can be found in railroad passenger service. Although no amount of product improvement could have staved off its decline, if the industry had defined itself as being in the transportation business, rather than the railroad business, it might still be profitable today. On the positive side, toothpaste manufacturers have been willing to exercise flexibility in defining their product. For years toothpaste was an oral hygiene product where emphasis was placed solely on fighting tooth decay and bad breath (e.g., Crest with fluoride). More recently, many manufacturers have recognized the need to market toothpaste as a cosmetic item (to clean teeth of stains), as a defense against gum disease (to reduce the buildup of tartar above the gumline), as an aid for denture wearers, and as a breath freshener. As a result, special purpose brands have been designed to serve these particular needs, such as Ultra Brite, Close-Up, Aqua-fresh, Aim, Fresh 'n Brite, and the wide variety of tartar-control formula and gel toothpastes offered under existing brand names.

In line with the marketing concept philosophy, a reasonable definition of product is that it is *the sum of the physical, psychological, and sociological satisfactions the buyer derives from purchase, ownership, and consumption.* From this standpoint, products are consumer-satisfying objects that include such things as accessories, packaging, and service.

Product Classification

A product classification scheme can be useful to the marketing manager as an analytical device to assist in planning marketing strategy and programs. A basic assumption underlying such classifications is that products with common attributes can be marketed in a similar fashion. In general, products are classed according to two basic criteria: (1) end use or market; and (2) degree of processing or physical transformation.

1. *Agricultural products and raw materials.* These are goods grown or extracted from the land or sea, such as iron ore, wheat, sand. In general these products are fairly homogeneous, sold in large volume, and have low value per unit or bulk weight.
2. *Industrial goods.* Such products are purchased by business firms for the purpose of producing other goods or for running the business. This category includes the following:
   a. Raw materials and semifinished goods.
   b. Major and minor equipment, such as basic machinery, tools, and other processing facilities.

    c. Parts or components, which become an integral element of some other finished good.

    d. Supplies or items used to operate the business but that do not become part of the final product.

3. *Consumer goods.* Consumer goods can be divided into three classes:

    a. Convenience goods, such as food, which are purchased frequently with minimum effort. Impulse goods would also fall into this category.

    b. Shopping goods, such as appliances, which are purchased after some time and energy are spent comparing the various offerings.

    c. Specialty goods, which are unique in some way so the consumer will make a special purchase effort to obtain them.

In general, the buying motive, buying habits, and character of the market are different for industrial goods vis-à-vis consumer goods. A primary purchasing motive for industrial goods is, of course, profit. As mentioned in a previous chapter, industrial goods are usually purchased as means to an end, and not as an end in themselves. This is another way of saying that the demand for industrial goods is a derived demand. Industrial goods are often purchased directly from the original source with few middlemen, because many of these goods can be bought in large quantities; they have high unit value; technical advice on installation and use is required; and the product is ordered according to the user's specifications. Many industrial goods are subject to multiple-purchase influence, and a long period of negotiation is often required.

The market for industrial goods has certain attributes that distinguish it from the consumer goods market. Much of the market is concentrated geographically, as in the case of steel, auto, or shoe manufacturing. For certain products there are a limited number of buyers; this is known as a *vertical market,* which means that (1) it is narrow, because customers are restricted to a few industries; and (2) it is deep, in that a large percentage of the producers in the market use the product. Some products, such as office supplies, have a *horizontal market,* which means that the goods are purchased by all types of firms in many different industries. In general, buyers of industrial goods are reasonably well informed. As noted previously, heavy reliance is often placed on price, quality control, and reliability of supply source.

In terms of consumer products, many marketing scholars have found the convenience, shopping, and specialty classification inadequate and have attempted to either refine it or to derive an entirely new typology. None of these attempts appear to have met with complete success.[1]

---

[1]For a review and suggestions for product classification, see Patrick E. Murphy and Ben M. Enis, "Classifying Products Strategically," *Journal of Marketing,* July 1986, pp. 24–42.

HIGHLIGHT 6–2
A. Classes of Consumer Goods—Some Characteristics and Marketing Considerations

Characteristics and Marketing Considerations	Type of Product		
	Convenience	Shopping	Specialty
Characteristics:			
1. Time and effort devoted by consumer to shopping	Very little	Considerable	Cannot generalize; consumer may go to nearby store and buy with minimum effort or may have to go to distant store and spend much time and effort
2. Time spent planning the purchase	Very little	Considerable	Considerable
3. How soon want is satisfied after it arises	Immediately	Relatively long time	Relatively long time
4. Are price and quality compared?	No	Yes	No
5. Price	Low	High	High
6. Frequency of purchase	Usually frequent	Infrequent	Infrequent
7. Importance	Unimportant	Often very important	Cannot generalize
Marketing Considerations:			
1. Length of channel	Long	Short	Short to very short
2. Importance of retailer	Any single store is relatively unimportant	Important	Very important
3. Number of outlets	As many as possible	Few	Few; often only one in a market
4. Stock turnover	High	Lower	Lower
5. Gross margin	Low	High	High
6. Responsibility for advertising	Manufacturer's	Retailer's	Joint responsibility
7. Importance of point-of-purchase display	Very important	Less important	Less important
8. Advertising used	Manufacturer's	Retailer's	Both
9. Brand or store name important	Brand name	Store name	Both
10. Importance of packaging	Very important	Less important	Less important

B. Classes of Industrial Products—Some Characteristics and Marketing Considerations *(concluded)*

Type of Product

Characteristics and Marketing Considerations	Raw Materials	Fabricating Parts and Materials	Installations	Accessory Equipment	Operating Supplies
Example:					
	Iron ore	Engine blocks	Blast furnaces	Storage racks	Paper clips
Characteristics:					
1. Unit Price	Very low	Low	Very high	Medium	Low
2. Length of life	Very short	Depends on final product	Very long	Long	Short
3. Quantities purchased	Large	Large	Very small	Small	Small
4. Frequency of purchase	Frequent delivery; long-term purchase contract	Infrequent purchase, but frequent delivery	Very infrequent	Medium frequency	Frequent
5. Standardization of competitive products	Very much; grading is important	Very much	Very little; custom-made	Little	Much
6. Limits on supply	Limited; supply can be increased slowly or not at all	Usually no problem	No problem	Usually no problem	Usually no problem
Marketing Considerations:					
1. Nature of channel	Short; no middlemen	Short; middlemen for small buyers	Short; no middlemen	Middlemen used	Middlemen used
2. Negotiation period	Hard to generalize	Medium	Long	Medium	Short
3. Price competition	Important	Important	Not important	Not main factor	Important
4. Presale/postsale service	Not important	Important	Very important	Important	Very little
5. Demand stimulation	Very little	Moderate	Salespeople very important	Important	Not too important
6. Brand preference	None	Generally low	High	High	Low
7. Advance buying contract	Important; long-term contracts used	Important; long-term contracts used	Not usually used	Not usually used	Not usually used

Source: William J. Stanton and Charles Futrell, *Fundamentals of Marketing*, 8th ed. (New York: McGraw-Hill, 1987), pp. 195, 198.

Perhaps there is no "best" way to deal with this problem. From the standpoint of the marketing manager, product classification is useful to the extent that it assists in providing guidelines for developing an appropriate marketing mix. For example, convenience goods generally require broadcast promotion and long channels of distribution as opposed to shopping goods, which generally require more targeted promotion and somewhat shorter channels of distribution.

Product Mix and Product Line

The *product mix* is the composite products offered for sale by the firm; *product line* refers to a group of products that are closely related because they satisfy a class of need, are used together, are sold to the same customer groups, are marketed through the same types of outlets, or fall within given price ranges. There are three primary dimensions of a firm's product mix: (1) *width* of the product mix, which refers to the number of product lines the firm handles; (2) *depth* of the product mix, which refers to the average number of products in each line; (3) *consistency* of the product mix, which refers to the similarity of product lines. Thus, McDonald's hamburgers represent a product item in its line of sandwiches, whereas hot cakes or Egg McMuffins represent items in a different line, namely, breakfast foods.

Development of a plan for the existing product line has been called the most critical element of a company's product planning activity.[2] In designing such plans, management needs accurate information on the current and anticipated performance of its products, which should encompass:

1. Consumer evaluation of the company's products, particularly their strengths and weaknesses vis-à-vis competition (i.e., product positioning by market segment information).
2. Objective information on actual and anticipated product performance on relevant criteria, such as sales, profits, and market share.[3]

Packaging and Branding

Distinctive or unique packaging is one method of differentiating a relatively homogeneous product. To illustrate, shelf-stable microwave dinners, pumps rather than tubes of toothpaste or bars of soap, and

---

[2]Yoram Wind and Henry J. Claycamp, "Planning Product Line Strategy: A Matrix Approach," *Journal of Marketing,* January 1976, p. 2.

[3]Ibid.

HIGHLIGHT 6-3
Tips for Developing Effective Packages

1. Ultimate authority and responsibility must lie in the marketing department.
2. A team or systems approach should be utilized including personnel from other areas such as production and engineering.
3. A sequential approach should be followed.
4. Work on new product packages should begin early in the product development process.
5. Needs of both consumers and dealers should be considered.
6. The final package should take into consideration the packages of competitors and any legal or regulatory requirements.
7. The most important objective should be profitability.
8. Packages should not be changed for the sake of change.
9. Consumers and dealers should provide input during the development process.
10. The package should be test-marketed.
11. Package changes should be introduced all at once, not gradually.

Source: Adapted from Richard T. Hise and James U. McNeal, "Effective Package Management," *Business Horizons,* January–February 1988, and reported in Steven J. Skinner, *Marketing* (Boston: Houghton Mifflin Co., 1990), p. 262.

---

different sizes and designs of tissue packages are attempts to differentiate a product through packaging and to satisfy consumer needs at the same time.

In making packaging decisions, the marketing manager must again consider both the consumer and costs. The package must be capable of protecting the product through the channel of distribution to the consumer. In addition, it is desirable for packages to be a convenient size and easy to open. For example, single-serving soups and zip-lock packaging in cereal boxes are attempts by manufacturers to serve consumers better. Hopefully, the package is also attractive and capable of being used as an in-store promotional tool. However, maximizing these objectives may increase the cost of the product to such an extent that consumers are no longer willing to purchase it. Thus, the marketing manager must determine the optimal protection, convenience, and promotional strengths of packages, subject to cost constraints.

As a product strategy, many firms produce and market their own products under a so-called private label. For example, A&P uses the Ann Page label, among others, and Sears uses the Kenmore label, among others. Such a strategy is highly important in industries where the middleman has gained control over distribution to the consumer. The advent of large chain stores, such as K mart, has accelerated the growth of private brands. If a manufacturer refuses to supply certain middlemen with private branded merchandise, the alternative is for these middlemen to go into the manufacturing business, as in the case of Kroger.

As a general rule, private brands are lower priced than national brands because there are some cost savings involved, and this has been the strongest appeal of private brand merchandisers. If a manufacturer is selling its national branded products to middlemen under a private label, then the Robinson-Patman Act requires that any price differential reflect (a) genuine differences in grade and quality; or (b) cost savings in manufacturing or distribution. One of the reasons why manufacturers will supply resellers with private branded merchandise is to utilize their production capacity more fully. Similarly, generic brands use excess capacity and offer manufacturers an alternative for selling their products.

Many companies use branding strategies to increase the strength of the product image. Factors that serve to increase the brand image strength include: (1) product quality, where products do what they do very well (e.g., Windex and Easy-off); (2) consistent advertising and other marketing communications, in which brands tell their story often and well (e.g., McDonald's and Pepsi); and (3) brand personality, where the brand stands for something (e.g., Disney and Marlboro).[4] The brand name is perhaps the single most important element on the package because it serves to identify and differentiate the product from all others. A good brand name can evoke feelings of trust, confidence, security, strength, and many other desirable associations.[5] Consider the case of Bayer aspirin. Bayer can be sold at up to two times the price of generic aspirins due to the strength of its brand image.

In addition, many companies also use branding to carry out market and product development strategies. Line extension is an approach whereby a brand name is used to facilitate entry into a new market segment (e.g., Diet Coke and Liquid Tide). An alternative to line extension is brand extension, whereby a current brand name is used to enter a completely different product class (e.g., Jello pudding pops, Ivory shampoo).[6] A final form of branding commonly used is franchise extension wherein a company attaches the corporate name to a product either to enter a new market segment or different product class (e.g., Honda lawnmower, Toyota Lexus). Each of the above three approaches is an attempt to gain a competitive advantage by making use of an established reputation.

---

[4]James Lowry, "Survey Finds Most Powerful Brands," *Advertising Age,* July 11, 1988, p. 31.

[5]Terance Shimp, *Promotion Management and Marketing Communications,* 2nd ed. (Hinsdale, Ill.: Dryden Press, 1990), p. 67.

[6]David A. Aaker and Kevin Lane Keller, "Consumer Evaluations of Brand Extensions," *Journal of Marketing,* January 1990, pp. 27–41.

HIGHLIGHT 6–4
Marketing Milestones of the Decade

HITS

- **IBM PC.** Big Blue claimed the power to set industry standards.
- **Microwave food.** It's changing our definition of good food.
- **Diet Coke.** Brilliant brand extension.
- **Lean Cuisine.** Pricey diet entrees launched at the height of the recession. Caught the fit-but-fast wave.
- **Macintosh computer.** Apple Computer's new design changed the way people use these machines.
- **Superpremium ice cream.** Häagen-Dazs, Ben & Jerry's, DoveBar, the perfect end to low-calorie meals.
- **Chrysler minivans.** These station wagons of the 80s created a new category of cars.
- **Tartar Control Crest.** P&G's efforts to teach consumers about nasty tooth deposits helped restore its toothpaste market share.
- **Athletic footwear.** After stumbling in 1986, Nike slam-dunked rival Reebok by winning the favor of big-city kids.
- **USA Today.** The colorful national daily is still mired in red ink, but it's changed the way many newspapers look and act.
- **Swatch watches.** A new look at an old product made watches into hot fashion accessories.
- **Nintendo video games.** Games like Super Mario Brothers continue so strong they're zapping the rest of the toy business.
- **SPF sunscreens.** Do you need SPF 5 or SPF 15? High-tech sunscreens sell well to aging baby boomers.

FLASHES

- **Oat bran.** With oat bran snacks and oat bran beer on the market, this one's got to be peaking.
- **Corona beer.** Competition from wine coolers and a decline in beer consumption have hurt this product.

- **Cabbage Patch Kids.** They're still around, although sales have crashed. Maker Coleco wasn't so lucky.
- **Miniskirts.** They're in. They're out. Or are they?
- **Granola bars.** In the mid-1980s, nearly a score of companies battled to be "health" snack king, while consumers snuck back to salty favorites.
- **Dry beer.** Why is it called "dry" again?
- **Wine coolers.** They're sweet as ever, but sales have cooled.

MISSES

- **New Coke.** Fixed what wasn't broken; customers immediately clamored for the original.
- **Premier cigarette.** "Smokeless" cigarette couldn't be lit with matches.
- **IBM PC Jr.** A problematic keyboard contributed to its demise.
- **Yugo.** Yugoslavian minicar was billed as cheapest new car in America, and it showed.
- **LA Beer.** Despite the new sobriety, the market for reduced-alcohol beer has little fizz.
- **Home banking.** Consumers weren't ready for this complicated "service."
- **Pontiac Fiero.** Looked great, but was discontinued after problems with engine fires.
- **Disk camera.** Kodak's Edsel.
- **RCA's SelectaVision.** Bad timing for the videodisc player once lauded as RCA's premier product of the 80s.
- **Generic products.** An 80s flop, if not an 80s innovation; consumers felt queasy about their quality.
- **Fab 1 Shot.** Colgate-Palmolive Co.'s premeasured laundry detergent means consumers can't use just enough for a small load.
- **Holly Farms roasted chickens.** Consumers liked these fully cooked birds, but retailers balked at their short shelf life.

Source: The Wall Street Journal, November 28, 1989, p. B1

PRODUCT LIFE CYCLE

A firm's product strategy must consider the fact that products have a life cycle. Figure 6–1 illustrates this life-cycle concept. Products are introduced, grow, mature, and decline. This cycle varies according to industry, product, technology, and market. Marketing executives need to be aware of the life-cycle concept because it can be a valuable aid in developing marketing strategies.

During the introduction phase of the cycle, there are usually high production and marketing costs, and, since sales are only beginning to materialize, profits are low or nonexistent. Profits increase and are positively correlated with sales during the growth stage as the market begins trying and adopting the product. As the product matures, profits for the initiating firm do not keep pace with sales because of competition. Here the seller may be forced to "remarket" the product, which may involve making price concessions, increasing product quality, or expanding outlays on advertising and sales promotion just to maintain market share. At some time sales decline, and the seller must decide whether to (1) drop the product; (2) alter the product; (3) seek new uses

FIGURE 6–1   The Product Life Cycle

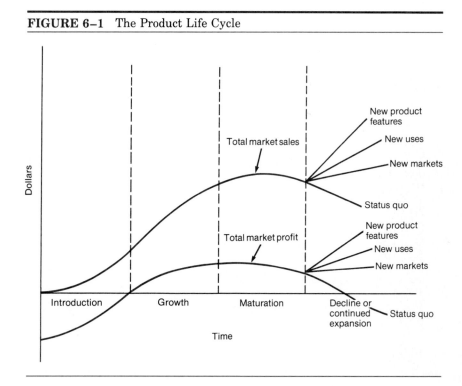

HIGHLIGHT 6-5
Marketing Strategy Implications of the Product Life Cycle

Stages of the Product Life Cycle

Effects/Responses	Introduction	Growth	Maturity	Decline
Competition	None of importance.	Some emulators.	Many rivals competing for a small piece of the pie.	Few in number, with a rapid shakeout of weak members.
Overall strategy	Market establishment; persuade early adopters to try the product.	Market penetration; persuade mass market to prefer the brand.	Defense of brand position; check the inroads of competition.	Preparations for removal; milk the brand dry of all possible benefits.
Profits	Negligible because of high production and marketing costs.	Reach peak levels as a result of high prices and growing demand.	Increasing competition cuts into profit margins and ultimately into total profits.	Declining volume pushes costs up to levels that eliminate profits entirely.
Retail prices	High, to recover some of the excessive costs of launching.	High, to take advantage of heavy consumer demand.	What the traffic will bear; need to avoid price wars.	Low enough to permit quick liquidation of inventory.
Distribution	Selective, as distribution is slowly built up.	Intensive; employ small trade discounts since dealers are eager to store.	Intensive; heavy trade allowances to retain shelf space.	Selective; unprofitable outlets slowly phased out.
Advertising strategy	Aim at the needs of early adopters.	Make the mass market aware of brand benefits.	Use advertising as a vehicle for differentiation among otherwise similar brands.	Emphasize low price to reduce stock.
Advertising emphasis	High, to generate awareness and interest among early adopters and persuade dealers to stock the brand.	Moderate, to let sales rise on the sheer momentum of word-of-mouth recommendations.	Moderate, since most buyers are aware of brand characteristics.	Minimum expenditures required to phase out the product.
Consumer sales and promotion expenditures	Heavy, to entice target groups with samples, coupons, and other inducements to try the brand.	Moderate, to create brand preference (advertising is better suited to do this job).	Heavy, to encourage brand switching, hoping to convert some buyers into loyal users.	Minimal, to let the brand coast by itself.

Source: William Zikmund and Michael D'Amico, *Marketing*, 3rd ed. (New York: John Wiley & Sons, 1989), p. 243.

for the product; (4) seek new markets; or (5) continue with more of the same.[7]

The product life-cycle concept is useful primarily in that it forces management to take a long-range view of marketing planning. In doing so, it should become clear that shifts in phases of the life cycle correspond to changes in the market situation, competition, and demand. Thus, the astute marketing manager should recognize the necessity of altering the marketing mix to meet these changing conditions. It is possible for managers to undertake strategies which, in effect, can lead to a revitalized product life cycle. For example, past advancements in technology led to the replacement of rotary dial telephones by touch-tone, push-button phones. Today, newer technology is allowing the cordless and cellular phone to replace the traditional touch-tone, push-button phone. When applied with sound judgment, the life-cycle concept can aid in forecasting, pricing, advertising, product planning, and other aspects of marketing management.[8] However, the marketing manager must also recognize that the length and slope of the product life cycle varies across products. Thus, while the product life cycle is useful for recognizing the stages a product will go through, it is difficult to forecast the exact time periods for these stages.

THE PRODUCT AUDIT

The product audit is a marketing management technique whereby the company's current product offerings are reviewed to ascertain whether each product should be continued as is, improved, modified, or deleted. The audit should be carried out at regular intervals as a matter of policy. Product audits are the responsibility of the product manager unless specifically delegated to someone else.

Deletions

It can be argued that the major purpose of the product audit is to detect "sick" products and then bury them. Criteria must be developed for deciding whether a product is a candidate for deletion. Some of the more obvious factors to be considered are:

---

[7]Note that the labeling of the new product features, new uses, and new markets curves is arbitrary. In other words, any of the three may result in the highest sales and profits depending on the product and situation.

[8]For an overview of issues concerning the product life cycle, see George Day, "The Product Life Cycle: Analysis and Application Issues," *Journal of Marketing,* Fall 1981, pp. 60–67. This is the introductory article to a special section dealing with the product life cycle.

- *Sales trends.* How have sales moved over time? What has happened to market share? Why have sales declined? What changes in sales have occurred in competitive products both in our line and in those of other manufacturers?
- *Profit contribution.* What has been the profit contribution of this product to the company? If profits have declined, how are these tied to price? Have selling, promotion, and distribution costs risen out of proportion to sales? Does the product require excessive management time and effort?
- *Product life cycle.* Has the product reached a level of maturity and saturation in the market? Has new technology been developed that poses a threat to the product? Are there more effective substitutes on the market? Has the product outgrown its usefulness? Can the resources used on this product be put to better use?

The above factors should be used as guidelines for making the final decision to delete a product. Deletion decisions are very difficult to make because of their potential impact on customers and the firm. For example, eliminating a product may force a company to lay off some employees. There are other factors to consider, such as keeping consumers supplied with replacement parts and repair service and maintaining the good will of distributors who have an inventory of the product. The deletion plan should provide for the clearing out of stock in question.[9]

Product Improvement

One of the other important objectives of the audit is to ascertain whether to alter the product or to leave things as they are. Altering the product means changing one or more of its attributes or marketing dimensions. Attributes refer mainly to product features, design, package, and so forth. Marketing dimensions refer to such things as price, promotion strategy, and channels of distribution.

The product audit can be viewed as a management device for controlling product strategy. Here, control means feedback on product performance and corrective action in the form of product improvement. Product improvement is a top-level management decision, but the information needed to make the improvement decision may come from the consumer or the middlemen. Suggestions are often made by advertising agencies or consultants. Reports by the sales force should be

---

[9]For further discussion of product deletion decisions, see George J. Avlonitis, "Product Elimination Decision Making: Does Formality Matter?" *Journal of Marketing,* Winter 1985, pp. 41–52.

HIGHLIGHT 6–6
A 10-Point Vitality Test for Older Products, or How to Get That Sales Curve to Slope Upward Again

1. Does the product have new or extended uses? Sales of Arm & Hammer baking soda increased considerably after the product was promoted as a refrigerator deodorant.
2. Is the product a generic item that can be branded? Sunkist puts its name on oranges and lemons, thus giving a brand identity to a formerly generic item.
3. Is the product category "underadvertised?" Tampons were in this category until International Playtex and Johnson & Johnson started spending large advertising appropriations, particularly on television ads.
4. Is there a broader target market? Procter & Gamble increased the sales of Ivory soap by promoting it for adults, instead of just for babies.
5. Can you turn disadvantages into advantages? The manufacturer of Smucker's jams and jellies advertised: "With a name like Smucker's, it has to be good."
6. Can you build volume and profit by cutting the price? Sales of Tylenol increased considerably after Johnson & Johnson cut Tylenol's price to meet the lower price set by Bristol-Myers' Datril brand.
7. Can you market unused by-products? Lumber companies market sawdust as a form of kitty litter.
8. Can you sell the product in a more compelling way? Procter & Gamble's Pampers disposable diapers were only a moderate success in the market when they were sold as a convenience item for mothers. Sales increased, however, after the advertising theme was changed to say that Pampers kept babies dry and happy.
9. Is there a social trend to exploit? Dannon increased its sales of yogurt tremendously by linking this product to consumers' interest in health foods.
10. Can you expand distribution channels? Hanes Hosiery Company increased its sales of L'eggs panty hose by distributing this product through supermarkets.

Source: William J. Stanton and Charles Futrell, *Fundamentals of Marketing,* 8th ed. (New York: McGraw-Hill, 1987), p. 224.

structured to provide management with certain types of product information; in fact, these reports can be the firm's most valuable product improvement tool. Implementing a product improvement decision will often require the coordinated efforts of several specialists, plus some research. For example, product design improvement decisions involve engineering, manufacturing, accounting, and marketing. When a firm becomes aware that a product's design can be improved, it is not always clear as to how consumers will react to the various alterations. To illustrate, in blind taste tests, the Coca-Cola Company found that consumers overwhelmingly preferred the taste of a reformulated sweeter new Coke over old Coke. However, when placed on the market in labeled containers, new Coke turned out to be a failure due to consumers' emotional attachments to the classic Coke. Consequently, it is advisable to conduct some market tests in realistic settings.

ORGANIZING FOR PRODUCT MANAGEMENT

A firm can organize for managing its products in a variety of ways.[10] Table 6–1 describes five methods and the types of companies for which they are most useful. Under a *marketing-manager system,* all the functional areas of marketing report to one manager. These include sales, advertising, sales promotion, and product planning. Such companies as PepsiCo, Purex, Eastman Kodak, and Levi Strauss use some form of the marketing-manager system.

With the *product (brand) manager system,* a middle manager in the organization focuses on a single product or a small group of new or existing products. Typically, this manager is responsible for everything from marketing research to package design to advertising. This method of organizing is sometimes criticized because product managers often do not have authority commensurate with their responsibilities. However, such companies as General Mills, Pillsbury, and Procter & Gamble have successfully used this method.

A *product-planning committee* is staffed by executives from functional areas, including marketing, production, engineering, finance, and R&D. The committee handles product approval, evaluation, and development on a part-time basis and typically disbands after a product is introduced. The product then becomes the responsibility of a product manager.

A *new product manager system* uses separate managers for new and existing products. After a new product is introduced, the new product manager turns it over to a product manager. This system can be expensive and can cause discontinuity when the product is introduced. However, such firms as General Foods, NCR, and General Electric have used this system successfully.

A *venture team* is a small, independent department consisting of a broad range of specialists who manage a new product's entire development process. The team disbands when the product is introduced.

---

[10]This section is based on Joel R. Evans and Barry Berman, *Marketing,* 4th ed. (New York: Macmillan, 1990), pp. 273–75.

TABLE 6–1   Five Methods of Organizing for Product Management

| | *Characteristics* | | |
Organization	*Staffing*	*Ideal Use*	*Permanency*
Marketing-manager system	All functional areas of marketing report to one manager.	A company makes one product line or has a dominant line.	The system is ongoing.
Product (brand) manager system	A middle manager focuses on a single product or group of products.	A company makes many distinct products, each requiring expertise.	The system is ongoing.
Product-planning committee	Executives from various functional areas participate.	The committee should supplement another product organization.	The committee meets regularly.
New product manager system	Separate managers direct new products and existing products.	A company makes several existing products, and substantial time, resources, and expertise are needed to develop new products.	The system is ongoing, but new products are shifted to product managers after production.
Venture team	An independent group of specialists guides all phases of a new product's development.	A company wants to create vastly different products than those currently made, and it needs an autonomous structure to aid development.	The team disbands after a new product is introduced, turning responsibility over to a product manager.

Source: Reprinted by permission of Macmillan Publishing Company from *Marketing*, 4th ed., p. 273, by John R. Evans and Barry Berman. Copyright © 1990 by Macmillan Publishing Company.

While it can be an expensive method, Xerox, IBM, and Westinghouse use a venture team approach.

Which method to use depends on the diversity of a firm's offerings, the number of new products introduced, the level of innovation, company resources, and management expertise. A combination of product management methods also can be used, which many firms find desirable.

CONCLUSION

This chapter has been concerned with a central element of marketing management—product strategy. The first part of the chapter discussed some basic issues in product strategy, including product definition and classification, product mix and product lines, and packaging and branding. The product life cycle was discussed as well as the product audit. Finally, five methods of organizing for product management were presented. Although product considerations are extremely important, remember that the product is only one element of the marketing mix. Focusing on product decisions alone, without consideration of the other marketing mix variables, would be an ineffective approach to marketing strategy.

ADDITIONAL READINGS

Dowdy, William L., and Julien Nikolchev. "Can Industries De-Mature?—Applying New Technologies to Mature Industries." *Long Range Planning* 19, no. 2 (1986), pp. 38–49.

Gupta, Ashok K.; S. P. Raj; and David Wilemon. "A Model for Studying R&D—Marketing Interface in the Product Innovation Process." *Journal of Marketing*, April 1986, pp. 7–17.

Park, C. Whan; Bernard J. Jaworski; and Deborah J. Macinnis. "Strategic Brand Concept-Image Management." *Journal of Marketing*, October 1986, pp. 135–45.

Pessemier, Edgar E. *Product Management*. 2nd ed. New York: John Wiley & Sons, 1981.

Quelch, John A. "Why Not Exploit Dual Marketing?" *Harvard Business Review*, January–February 1987, pp. 52–60.

Varadarajan, P. Rajan. "Product Diversity and Firm Performance: An Empirical Investigation." *Journal of Marketing*, July 1986, pp. 43–57.

Wind, Yoram. *Product Policy: Concepts, Methods, and Strategy*. Reading, Mass.: Addison-Wesley Publishing, 1982.

Chapter 7

New Product Planning and Development

New products are a vital part of a firm's competitive growth strategy. Most manufacturers cannot live without new products. It is commonplace for major companies to have 50 percent or more of their current sales in products introduced within the past 10 years. For example, the 3M Corporation insists that 25 percent of each division's annual sales come from products developed within the past five years.

Some additional facts about new products are:

1. Many new products are failures. Estimates of new-product failure range from 33 percent to 90 percent.
2. Companies vary widely in the effectiveness of their new-product programs.
3. Common elements tend to appear in the management practices that generally distinguish the relative degree of efficiency and success between companies.
4. About four out of five hours devoted by scientists and engineers to technical development of new products are spent on projects that do not reach commercial success.[1]

In one recent year, almost 10,000 supermarket items were introduced into the market. Less than 20 percent met sales goals. The cost of introducing a new brand in some consumer markets has been estimated

---

[1] Also see Robert Hisrich and Michael Peters, *Marketing Decisions for New and Mature Products* (Columbus, Ohio: Charles E. Merrill Publishing Co., 1984), chap. 1.

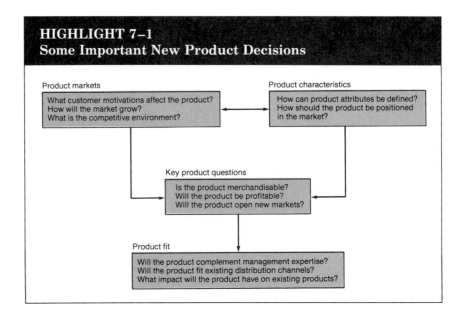

to range from $50 million to the hundreds of millions of dollars.[2] To illustrate, Alpo Petfoods spent over $70 million on advertising and promotion alone in launching their new line of cat food. The Gillette Co. spent over $300 million on R&D and promotion costs in introducing the Sensor razor.[3] In addition to the outlay cost of new product failures, there are also opportunity costs. These opportunity costs refer not only to the alternative uses of funds spent on product failures but also to the time spent in unprofitable product development. Product development can take many years. For example, Hills Brothers spent 22 years developing its instant coffee, while it took General Foods 10 years to develop Maxim, its concentrated instant coffee.

Good management, with heavy emphasis on planning, organization, and interaction among the various functional units (e.g., marketing, manufacturing, engineering, R&D), seems to be the key factor contributing to a firm's success in launching new products. The primary reason for new product failure is the selling company's inability to match up its offerings to the needs of the customer. This inability to satisfy customer needs can be attributed to three main sources:

[2]Paul Brown, "New? Improved?" *Business Week,* October 21, 1985, pp. 108–12; and Edward M. Tauber, "Brand Leverage: Strategy for Growth in a Cost-Controlled World," *Journal of Advertising Research,* August/September 1988, pp. 26–30.
[3]"The $300 Million Shave," *Business Week,* January 29, 1990, pp. 62–64.

(1) inadequacy of upfront intelligence efforts, (2) failure of the company to stick close to what it does best, and (3) the inability to provide better value than competing products and technologies.

NEW PRODUCT POLICY

In developing new product policies, the first question a marketing manager must ask is: "In how many ways can a product be new?" There are at least nine different ways:

1. A product performing an entirely *new function,* such as television, which for the first time permitted the transmission of audiovisual signals.
2. A product that offers *improved performance of an existing function,* such as a wristwatch whose balance wheel has been replaced by a tuning fork.
3. A product that is a *new application of an existing product.* For example, the aerosol bomb, first developed for insecticides, was later applied in paints.
4. A product that offers *additional functions.* The cordless telephone, for instance, does what the earlier telephone did, plus more.
5. An existing product offered to a *new market.* This may be done by repositioning or by taking a regional brand into other regions. For example, Coors Beer used to be sold only in the states surrounding Colorado.
6. A product that through *lower cost* is able to reach more buyers. Hand calculators are an example.
7. An upgraded product defined as an *existing product integrated into another existing product.* The clock-radio is an example.
8. A *downgraded product.* For example, a manufacturer switches from buying a component to producing a cheaper component in-house and marketing it.
9. A *restyled product.* Annual auto and clothing changes are examples.[4]

Another approach to the *new* product question has been developed by H. Igor Ansoff in the form of *growth vectors.*[5] This is the matrix, first introduced in Chapter 1, that indicates the direction in which the organization is moving with respect to its current products and markets. It is shown again in Table 7–1.

---

[4]C. Merle Crawford, *New Product Management,* 2nd ed. (Homewood, Ill.: Richard D. Irwin, 1987), p. 18.

[5]H. Igor Ansoff, *Corporate Strategy* (New York: McGraw-Hill, 1965), pp. 109–10.

TABLE 7–1   Growth Vector Components

Markets	Products	
	Present	*New*
Present	Market penetration	Product development
New	Market development	Diversification

Market penetration denotes a growth direction through the increase in market share for present product-markets. *Market development* refers to finding new customers for present products. *Product development* refers to creating new products to replace existing ones. *Diversification* refers to developing new products and cultivating new markets.

In Table 7–1, market penetration and market development are product line strategies where the focus is upon altering the breadth and depth of the firm's existing product offerings. Product development and diversification can be characterized as product mix strategies. New products, as defined in the growth vector matrix, usually require the firm to make significant investments in research and development and may require major changes in its organizational structure.

It has already been stated that new products are the lifeblood of successful business firms. Thus, the critical product policy question is not whether to develop new products but in what direction to move. One way of dealing with this problem is to formulate standards or norms that new products must meet if they are to be considered candidates for launching. In other words, as part of its new product policy, management must ask itself the basic question: "What is the potential contribution of each anticipated new product to the company?"

Each company must answer this question in accordance with its long-term goals, corporate mission, resources, and so forth. Unfortunately, some of the reasons commonly given to justify the launching of new products are so general that they become meaningless. Phrases such as *additional profits* or *increased growth* or *cyclical stability* must be translated into more specific objectives. For example, one objective may be to reduce manufacturing overhead costs by utilizing plant capacity better. This may be accomplished by using the new product as an offseason filler. Naturally, the new product proposal would also have to include production and accounting data to back up this cost argument.

In every new product proposal some attention must be given to the ultimate economic contribution of each new product candidate. If the

HIGHLIGHT 7–2
Ten Steps in the Development of a New Product Policy

1. Prepare a long-range industry forecast for existing product lines.
2. Prepare a long-range profit plan for the company, using existing product lines.
3. Review the long-range profit plan.
4. Determine what role new products will play in the company's future.
5. Prepare an inventory of company capabilities.
6. Determine market areas for new products.
7. Prepare a statement of new product objectives.
8. Prepare a long-range profit plan, incorporating new products.
9. Assign new product responsibility.
10. Provide for evaluation of new product performance.

argument is that a certain type of product is needed to "keep up with competition" or "to establish leadership in the market," it is fair to ask, "Why?" To put the question another way, top management can ask: "What will be the effect on the firm's long-run profit picture if we do not develop and launch this or that new product?" Policymaking criteria on new products should specify (1) a working definition of the profit concept acceptable to top management; (2) a minimum level or floor of profits; (3) the availability and cost of capital to develop a new product; and (4) a specified time period in which the new product must recoup its operating costs and begin contributing to profits.

NEW PRODUCT PLANNING AND DEVELOPMENT PROCESS

Ideally, products that generate a maximum dollar profit with a minimum amount of risk should be developed and marketed. However, it is very difficult for planners to implement this idea because of the number and nature of the variables involved. What is needed is a systematic, formalized process for new product planning. Although such a process does not provide management with any magic answers, it can increase the probability of new product success. Initially, the firm must establish some new product policy guidelines that include: the product fields of primary interest, organizational responsibilities for managing the various stages in new-product development, and criteria for making go-ahead decisions. After these guidelines are established, a process such as the one shown in Figure 7–1 should be useful in new-product development.

FIGURE 7–1   The New Product Development Process

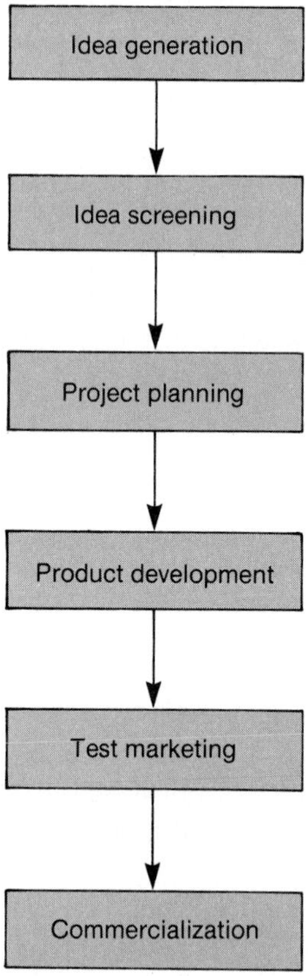

Idea Generation

Every product starts as an idea. But all new product ideas do not have equal merit or potential for economic or commercial success. Some estimates indicate that as many as 60 or 70 ideas are necessary to yield one successful product. This is an average figure, but it serves to illustrate the fact that new product ideas have a high mortality rate. In terms of money, of all the dollars of new product expense, almost three fourths go to unsuccessful products.

The problem at this stage is to ensure that all new product ideas available to the company at least have a chance to be heard and evaluated. This includes recognizing available sources of new product ideas and funneling these ideas to appropriate decision makers for screening.

Top management support is critical to providing an atmosphere that stimulates new product activity. A top management structure that is unwilling to take risks will avoid new product and other innovation activities and instead concentrate on minor areas of product improvement such as simple style changes. To facilitate top management support, it is essential that new product development be focused on meeting market needs.

Both technology push and market pull research activities play an important role in new product ideas and development. By taking a broad view of customer wants and needs, basic research can lead to ideas that will yield profits to the firm. Marketing, on the other hand, is more responsible for gathering and disseminating information gained from customer and competitor contact. This information relates mainly to specific features and functions of the product that can be improved upon or market needs that current products are not satisfying. Both approaches are essential to generating new product ideas.

Idea Screening

The primary function of the screening stage is twofold: first, to eliminate ideas for new products that could not be profitably marketed by the firm and, second, to expand viable ideas into a full product concept. New product ideas may be eliminated either because they are outside the fields of the firm's interest or because the firm does not have the necessary resources or technology to produce the product at a profit. However, organizations should not hastily discount new product ideas due solely to a lack of resources or expertise. Instead, firms should consider forming joint or strategic alliances with other firms. Potential benefits to be gained from alliances include: (1) increased access to technology, funding, and information; (2) market expansion and greater penetration of current markets; and (3) de-escalated competitive rivalries. Motorola has prospered by forming numerous joint ventures with both American and foreign companies.[6]

---

[6]For a more complete discussion on the advantages and disadvantages of strategic alliances see, Godfrey Devlin and Mark Bleackley, "Strategic Alliances—Guidelines for Success," *Long Range Planning* 21, no. 5 (1988), pp. 18–23; Charles W. Joiner, "Harvesting American Technology—Lessons from the Japanese Garden," *Sloan Management Review,* Summer 1989, pp. 61–68; Richard P. Neilson, "Cooperative Strategies in Marketing," *Harvard Business Review,* July–August 1987, pp. 61–68; and Pedro Nueno and Jan Oosterveld, "Managing Technology Alliances," *Long Range Planning* 21, no. 3 (1988), pp. 11–17.

HIGHLIGHT 7–3
Some Sources of New Product Ideas

1. *Sales force*
   a. Knowledge of customers' needs
   b. Inquiries from customers or prospects
   c. Knowledge of the industry and competition
2. *Research and engineering*
   a. Application of basic research
   b. Original or creative thinking
   c. Testing existing products and performance records
   d. Accidental discoveries
3. Other company sources
   a. Suggestions from employees
   b. Utilization of by-products or scrap
   c. Specific market surveys
4. *Outside sources*
   a. Inventors
   b. Stockholders
   c. Suppliers or vendors
   d. Middlemen
   e. Ad agencies
   f. Customer suggestions

Ideas that appear to have adequate profit potential and offer the firm a competitive advantage in the market should be accepted for further study.

Project Planning

This stage of the process involves several steps. It is here that the product proposal is evaluated further and responsibility for the project is assigned to a project team. The proposal is analyzed in terms of production, marketing, financial, and competitive factors. A development budget is established, and some preliminary marketing and technical research is undertaken. The product is actually designed in a rough form. Alternative product features and component specifications are outlined. Finally, a project plan is written up, which includes estimates of future development, production, and marketing costs along with capital requirements and manpower needs. A schedule or timetable is also included. Finally, the project proposal is given to top management for a go or no-go decision.

HIGHLIGHT 7–4
How Much Should You Spend on New Product Development?

Based on a study of 203 new products (123 successes and 80 failures), the researchers concluded that the successful companies:

1. Spend twice as much money and three times as much time for preliminary market assessment.
2. Spend twice as much money for marketing research.
3. Spend twice as much time and twice as much money on preliminary technical assessment.
4. Spend 50 percent more money and 35 percent more time on product development.
5. Spend twice as much money and 50 percent more time on in-house tests.

Source: Based on research conducted by R. G. Cooper and E. J. Kleinschmidt, "Resources Allocation in the New Product Process," *Industrial Marketing Management*, August 1988, pp. 249–62.

Various alternatives exist for creating and managing the project teams. Two of the better-known methods are the establishment of a skunkworks, whereby a project team can work in relative privacy away from the rest of the organization; and a rugby or relay approach, whereby groups in different areas of the company are simultaneously working on the project.[7] The common tie that binds these and other successful approaches is the degree of interaction that develops between the marketing, engineering, production, and other research staff.

Product Development

At this juncture the product idea has been evaluated from the standpoint of engineering, manufacturing, finance, and marketing. If it has met all expectations, it is considered a candidate for further research and testing. In the laboratory, the product is converted into a finished good and tested. A development report to management is prepared that spells out in fine detail: (1) the results of the studies by the engineering

---

[7]James Quinn, "Managing Innovation: Controlled Chaos," *Harvard Business Review*, May–June 1985, pp. 73–84 and Hirotaka Takeuchi and Ikujiro Nonaka, "The New New Product Development Game," *Harvard Business Review*, January–February 1986, pp. 137–46.

HIGHLIGHT 7–5
Six Ss for New Product Success

Below is a list of product attributes that have been found to have a significant effect on new product purchase and acceptance by consumers:

1. *Superiority.* The degree to which the new product has a clear differential or relative advantage over previous products.
2. *Sociability.* The degree to which the new product is compatible or consistent with consumers' existing beliefs, values, and lifestyles.
3. *Satisfaction.* The degree to which the new product satisfies consumers' felt needs.
4. *Simplicity.* The degree to which the new product is easy for consumers to understand and use and for marketers to promote and make available.
5. *Separability.* The degree to which the new product can be tested on a trial basis with limited investment by consumers.
6. *Speed.* The degree to which the benefits of the product are experienced immediately, rather than at a later time.

---

department; (2) required plan design; (3) production facilities design; (4) tooling requirements; (5) marketing test plan; (6) financial program survey; and (7) an estimated release date.

Test Marketing

Up until now the product has been a company secret. Now management goes outside the company and submits the product candidate for customer approval. Test market programs are conducted in lines with the general plans for launching the product. Several of the more commonly utilized forms of test marketing are:[8]

1. *Pseudo sales.* Potential buyers are asked to answer survey questions or pick items off a shelf in a make-believe store. The key factor is that no spending or risk for the consumer takes place.
2. *Cash sales.* Here, the buyer must actually make a purchase. The test may be informal, controlled, or in a full-scale test market. However, it is still research, and no release of the product has been made.

---

[8]The material on test marketing was excerpted from C. Merle Crawford, *New Products Management,* 2nd ed. (Homewood, Ill.: Richard D. Irwin, 1987), pp. 284–98.

3. *Limited marketing.* In this case, the firm decides to market the product gradually. This method allows for continual learning before the product reaches national availability.
4. *National launch.* Here the firm just launches the product on a national scale and makes adjustments as needed.

The main goal of a test market is to evaluate and adjust as necessary the general marketing strategy to be used and the appropriate marketing mix. Test findings are analyzed, forecasts of volume are developed, the product design is frozen into production, and a marketing plan is finalized.

Commercialization

This is the launching step. During this stage, heavy emphasis is placed on the organization structure and management talent needed to implement the marketing strategy. Emphasis is also given to following up such things as bugs in the design, production costs, quality control, and inventory requirements. Procedures and responsibility for evaluating the success of the new product by comparison with projections are also finalized.

The Importance of Time

A company that can bring out new products faster than its competitors enjoys a huge advantage.[9] Today in many industries, Japanese manufacturers are successfully following such a strategy. In projection television, Japanese producers can develop a new television in one third the time required by U.S. manufacturers. Successful time-based innovation can be attributed to the use of short production runs whereby products are improved upon on an incremental basis, the use of cross-functional project teams, decentralized work scheduling and monitoring, and a responsive system for gathering and analyzing customer feedback.

Several U.S. companies, including Procter & Gamble have taken steps to speed up the new product development cycle by giving managers, at the product class and brand family level, more decision-making power. Increasingly, companies are bypassing time-consuming

---

[9]George Stalk, Jr., "Time—The Next Source of Competitive Advantage," *Harvard Business Review,* July–August 1988, pp. 41–51.

regional test markets in favor of national launches. It is becoming, more than ever, crucial that firms do a successful job of developing the new product right the first time.

CAUSES OF NEW PRODUCT FAILURE

Many new products with satisfactory potential have failed to make the grade. Many of the reasons for new product failure relate to execution and control problems. Below is a brief list of some of the more important causes of new product failures after they have been carefully screened, developed, and marketed.

1. Faulty estimates of market potential.
2. Unexpected reactions from competitors.
3. Poor timing in the introduction of the product.
4. Rapid change in the market (economy) after the product was approved.
5. Inadequate quality control.
6. Faulty estimates in production costs.
7. Inadequate expenditures on initial promotion.
8. Faulty market testing.
9. Improper channel of distribution.

Some of the above problems are beyond the control of management; but it is clear that successful new product planning requires large amounts of reliable information in diverse areas. Each department assigned functional responsibility for product development automatically becomes an input to the information system needed by the new product decision maker. For example, when a firm is developing a new product, it is wise for both engineers and marketers to consider both the kind of market to be entered (e.g., consumer, industrial, defense, or export) and specific target segments. These decisions will be of paramount influence on the design and cost of the finished good, which will, of course, directly influence price, sales, and profits.

Need for Research

In many respects it can be argued that the keystone activity of any new product planning system is research—not just marketing research but technical research as well. Regardless of the way in which the new product planning function is organized in the company, new product development decisions by top management require data that provide a base for making more intelligent choices. New product project reports

HIGHLIGHT 7-6
Examples of Misfires in Test Marketing

1. When Campbell Soup first test marketed Prego spaghetti sauce, Campbell marketers say they noticed a flurry of new Ragu ads and cents-off deals that they feel were designed to induce shoppers to load up on Ragu and to skew Prego's test results. They also claim that Ragu copied Prego when it developed Ragu Homestyle spaghetti sauce, which was thick, red, flecked with oregano and basil, and which Ragu moved into national distribution before Prego.
2. P&G claims that competitors stole its patented process for Duncan Hines chocolate chip cookies when they saw how successful the product was in test markets.
3. A health and beauty aids firm developed a deodorant containing baking soda. A competitor spotted the product in a test market, rolled out its own version of the deodorant nationally before the first firm completed its testing, and later successfully sued the product originator for copyright infringement when it launched its deodorant nationally.
4. When P&G introduced its Always brand sanitary napkin in test marketing in Minnesota, Kimberly Clark Corporation and Johnson & Johnson countered with free products, lots of coupons, and big dealer discounts, which caused Always not to do as well as expected.
5. A few years ago, Snell (Booz Allen's design and development division, which does product development work under contract) developed a nonliquid temporary hair coloring that consumers use by inserting a block of solid hair dye into a special comb. "It went to market, and it was a bust," the company's Mr. Schoenholz recalls. On hot days when people perspired, any hair dye excessively applied ran down their necks and foreheads. "It just didn't occur to us to look at this under conditions where people perspire," he says.

Source: G. Churchill, *Basic Marketing Research* (Hinsdale, Ill: Dryden Press, 1988), p. 14.

ought to be more than a collection of "expert" opinions. Top management has a responsibility to ask certain questions, and the new product planning team has an obligation to generate answers to these questions based on research that provides marketing, economic, engineering, and production information. This need will be more clearly understood if some of the specific questions commonly raised in evaluating product ideas are examined:

1. What is the anticipated market demand over time? Are the potential applications for the product restricted?
2. Can the item be patented? Are there any antitrust problems?

3. Can the product be sold through present channels and sales force? How many new salespersons will be needed? What additional sales training will be required?
4. At different volume levels, what will be the unit manufacturing costs?
5. What is the most appropriate package to use in terms of color, material, design, and so forth?
6. What is the estimated return on investment?
7. What is the appropriate pricing strategy?

While this list is not intended to be exhaustive, it illustrates the serious need for reliable information. Note, also, that some of the essential facts required to answer these questions can only be obtained through time-consuming and expensive marketing research studies. Other data can be generated in the engineering laboratories or pulled from accounting records. Certain types of information must be based on assumptions, which may or may not hold true, and on expectations about what will happen in the future, as in the case of "anticipated competitive reaction" or the projected level of sales.

Another complication is that many different types of information must be gathered and formulated into a meaningful program for decision making. To illustrate, in trying to answer questions about return on investment of a particular project, the analyst must know something about (1) the pricing strategy to be used and (2) the investment outlay. Regardless of the formula used to measure the investment worth of a new product, different types of information are required. Using one of the simplest approaches—the payback method (the ratio of investment outlay to annual cash flow)—one needs to estimate the magnitude of the product investment outlay and the annual cash flow. The investment outlay requires estimates of such things as production equipment, R&D costs, and nonrecurring introductory marketing expenditures; the annual cash flow requires a forecast of unit demand and price. These data must be collected or generated from many different departments and processed into a form that will be meaningful to the decision maker.

CONCLUSION

This chapter has focused on the nature of new product planning and development. Attention has been given to the management process required to have an effective program for new product development. It should be obvious to the reader that this is one of the most important and difficult aspects of marketing management. The problem is so complex that, unless management develops a plan for dealing with the problem, it is likely to operate at a severe competitive disadvantage in the marketplace.

ADDITIONAL READINGS

Crawford, C. Merle. *New Products Management*. 2nd ed. Homewood, Ill.: Richard D. Irwin, 1987.

Hauser, John R., and Don Clausing. "The House of Quality." *Harvard Business Review,* May–June 1988, pp. 63–73.

Johne, F. Axel, and Patricia A. Snelson. "Product Development in Established Firms." *Industrial Marketing Management* 18 (1989), pp. 113–24.

Narasimhan, Chakravarthi, and Subrata K. Sen. "New Product Models for Test Market Data." *Journal of Marketing,* Winter 1983, pp. 11–24.

Robertson, Thomas S., and Hubert Gatignon. "Competitive Effects on Technology Diffusion." *Journal of Marketing,* July 1986, pp. 1–12.

von Hippel, Eric. *The Sources of Innovation*. New York: Oxford University Press, 1988.

Chapter 8

Promotion Strategy: Advertising and Sales Promotion

To simplify the discussion of the general subject of promotion, the topic has been divided into two basic categories, personal selling and nonpersonal selling. Personal selling will be discussed in detail in the next chapter, and this chapter will be devoted to nonpersonal selling.

Nonpersonal selling includes all demand creation and demand maintenance activities of the firm, other than personal selling. It is mass selling. In more specific terms, nonpersonal selling includes (1) advertising, (2) sales promotion, and (3) publicity. For purposes of this text, primary emphasis will be placed on advertising and sales promotion. Publicity is a special form of promotion that amounts to "free advertising," such as a writeup about the firm's products in a newspaper article. It will not be dealt with in detail in this text.

THE PROMOTION MIX

The promotion mix concept refers to *the combination and types of promotional effort the firm puts forth during a specified time period.* Most business concerns make use of more than one form of promotion, but some firms rely on a single technique. An example of a company using only one promotional device would be a manufacturer of novelties who markets its products exclusively by means of mail order.

HIGHLIGHT 8–1
Some Advantages and Disadvantages of Major Promotion Methods

Advertising

Advantages	Disadvantages
Can reach many consumers simultaneously. Relatively low cost per exposure. Excellent for creating brand images. High degree of flexibility and variety of media to choose from; can accomplish many different types of promotion objectives.	Many consumers reached are not potential buyers (waste of promotion dollars). High visibility makes advertising a major target of marketing critics. Advertisement exposure time is usually brief. Advertisements are often quickly and easily screened out by consumers.

Personal Selling

Advantages	Disadvantages
Can be the most persuasive promotion tool; salespeople can directly influence purchase behaviors. Allows two-way communication. Often necessary for technically complex products. Allows direct one-on-one targeting of promotional effort.	High cost per contact. Sales training and motivation can be expensive and difficult. Personal selling often has a poor image, making salesforce recruitment difficult. Poorly done sales presentations can hurt sales as well as company, product, and brand images.

Sales Promotion

Advantages	Disadvantages
Excellent approach for short-term price reductions for stimulating demand. A large variety of sales promotion tools to choose from. Can be effective for changing a variety of consumer behaviors. Can be easily tied in with other promotion tools.	May influence primarily brand-loyal customers to stock up at lower price but attract few new customers. May have only short-term impact. Overuse of price-related sales promotion tools may hurt brand image and profits. Effective sales promotions are easily copied by competitors.

Source: J. Paul Peter and Jerry C. Olson, *Consumer Behavior and Marketing Strategy*, 2nd ed. (Homewood, Ill: Richard D. Irwin, 1990), p. 459.

In devising its promotion mix, the firm should take into account three basic factors: (1) the role of promotion in the overall marketing mix; (2) the nature of the product; and (3) the nature of the market. Also, it must be recognized that a firm's promotion mix is likely to change over time to reflect changes in the market, competition, the product's life cycle, and the adoption of new strategies. The following example illustrates how one firm developed its promotion mix along these lines.

When IBM began to market its magnetic character sensing equipment for banks, the company defined the 500 largest banks as its likeliest market, and a research firm was commissioned to study the marketing problems. They selected a representative sample of 185 banks and interviewed the officer designated by each bank as the person who would be most influential in deciding whether or not to purchase the equipment. Researchers sought to establish which of the following stages each banker had reached in the sales process: (1) *awareness* of the new product; (2) *comprehension* of what it offered; (3) *conviction* that it would be a good investment; or (4) the *ordering* stage. They also tried to isolate the promotional factors that had brought the bankers to each stage. IBM's promotional mix consisted of personal selling, advertising, education (IBM schools and in-bank seminars), and publicity (through news releases). Figure 8–1 illustrates the process.

The findings were a revelation to IBM. In marketing such equipment, IBM had consistently taken the position that advertising played a very minor role; that nothing could replace the sales call. IBM found it could cut back on personal selling in the early stages of the selling process, thereby freeing salespeople to concentrate on the vital phase of the process—the actual closing of the sale. While these results may not hold true for all products, they are an excellent example of the concept of the promotion mix and the effectiveness of different combinations of promotion tools for achieving various objectives.

ADVERTISING: PLANNING AND STRATEGY

Advertising seeks to promote the seller's product by means of printed and electronic media. This is justified on the grounds that messages can reach large numbers of people and inform, persuade, and remind them about the firm's offerings. The traditional way of defining advertising is as follows: It is any paid form of nonpersonal presentation of ideas, goods, or services by an identified sponsor.[1]

---

[1]Peter D. Bennett, ed., *Dictionary of Marketing Terms* (Chicago: American Marketing Association, 1988), p. 4.

FIGURE 8–1   An Example of the Role of Various Promotion Tools in the Selling Process

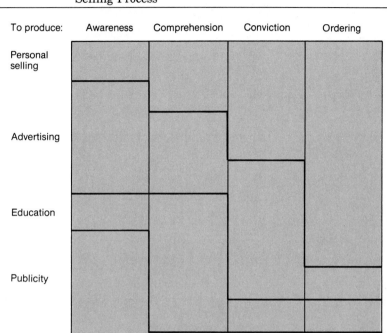

From a management viewpoint, advertising is a strategic device for gaining or maintaining a competitive advantage in the marketplace. For example, in 1988, advertising expenditures went over the $118 billion mark. The top 100 leading national advertisers spent over $27 billion in advertising.[2] Based on past growth patterns, it is expected advertising expenditures will soon reach $175 billion. For manufacturers and resellers alike, advertising budgets represent a large and growing element in the cost of marketing goods and services. As part of the seller's promotion mix, advertising dollars must be appropriated and budgeted according to a marketing plan that takes into account such factors as:

1. Nature of the product, including life cycle.
2. Competition.
3. Government regulations.

---

[2]*Advertising Age,* September 27, 1989, p. 1.

HIGHLIGHT 8–2
Preparing the Advertising Campaign: The Eight-M Formula

Effective advertising should follow a plan. There is no one best way to go about planning an advertising campaign, but, in general, marketers should have good answers to the following eight questions:

1. *The management question:* Who will manage the advertising program?
2. *The money question:* How much should be spent on advertising as opposed to other forms of selling?
3. *The market question:* To whom should the advertising be directed?
4. *The message question:* What should the ads say about the product?
5. *The media question:* What types and combinations of media should be used?
6. *The macroscheduling question:* How long should the advertising campaign be in effect before changing ads or themes?
7. *The microscheduling question:* At what times and dates would it be best for ads to appear during the course of the campaign?
8. *The measurement question:* How will the effectiveness of the advertising campaign be measured and how will the campaign be evaluated and controlled?

---

4. Nature and scope of the market.
5. Channels of distribution.
6. Pricing strategy.
7. Availability of media.
8. Availability of funds.
9. Outlays for other forms of promotion.

Objectives of Advertising

In the long run, and often in the short run, advertising is justified on the basis of the revenues it produces. Revenues in this case may refer either to sales or profits. Economic theory assumes that firms are profit maximizers, and that advertising outlays should be increased in every market and medium up to the point where the additional cost of getting more business just equals the incremental profits. Since most business firms do not have the data required to use the marginal analysis of economic theory, they usually employ a less sophisticated decision-making model. There is also evidence to show that many executives advertise to maximize sales on the assumption that higher sales mean more profits (which may or may not be true).

The point to be made here is that the ultimate goal of the business advertiser is sales and profits. To achieve this goal, an approach to advertising is needed that provides guidelines for intelligent decision making. This approach must recognize the need for measuring the results of advertising, and these measurements must be as valid and reliable as possible. Marketing managers must also be aware of the fact that advertising not only complements other forms of selling but is subject to the law of diminishing returns. This means that for any advertised product it can be assumed a point is eventually reached at which additional advertising produces little or no additional sales.

Specific Tasks of Advertising

There are at least three different viewpoints on the contribution of advertising to the economic health of the firm. The generalist viewpoint is primarily concerned with sales, profits, return on investment, and so forth. At the other extreme, the specialist viewpoint is represented by advertising experts who are mainly concerned with measuring the effects of specific ads or campaigns; here primary attention is given to such matters as the Nielsen Index, Starch Reports, Arbitron Index, Simmons Reports, copy appeal, and so forth. A middle view, one that might be classified as more of a marketing management approach, understands and appreciates the other two viewpoints but, in addition, views advertising as a competitive weapon. Emphasis in this approach is given to the strategic aspects of the advertising problem. Following are some of the marketing tasks generally assigned to the advertising function as part of the overall marketing mix:

1. Maintaining dealer cooperation.
2. Familiarizing the consumer with the use of the product.
3. Emphasizing a trademark or brand.
4. Obtaining a list of prospects.
5. Creating goodwill for the product, brand, or company.
6. Stressing unique features of the product.
7. Introducing new products.
8. Generating store traffic.
9. Informing customers of sales prices.
10. Building customer or brand loyalty.
11. Establishing a relationship between the producer and distributor.

The above list is representative but not exhaustive, and it should be noted that some of the points pertain more to middlemen than to producers. For example, the first point is a "channel task," where advertising and other forms of sales promotion are employed to facilitate the flow of the producer's goods through distributors to the ultimate consumer; "cooperative advertising" programs are specifically designed

---

HIGHLIGHT 8–3
An Advertising Process Model

Consumer Psychosocial State	*Marketing Situation*
1. Ignorance	Consumer has no knowledge of the product.
2. Indifference	Consumer is conscious of product's existence by means of advertising.
3. Awareness	Advertising messages generate an awareness of a need for the product or reinforce a need once generated.
4. Interest	Consumer begins seeking more product-brand information by paying closer attention to various ads.
5. Comprehension	Consumer knows main features of product and various brands after intense ad exposure.
6. Conviction	Consumer is receptive to purchase and ready to act.
7. Action	Consumer shops for the product often as a result of the "act now" advertisements or special sales.

---

to meet this objective. This is where a channel member, such as a retailer, will receive a certain percentage of gross sales as an advertising allowance. Some manufacturers also provide advertising copy, illustrations, and so forth.

ADVERTISING DECISIONS

In line with what has just been said, the marketing manager must make two key decisions. The first decision deals with determining the size of the advertising budget, and the second deals with how the advertising budget should be allocated. Although these decisions are highly interrelated, we deal with them separately to achieve a better understanding of the problems involved.

The Expenditure Question

Most firms determine how much to spend on advertising by one of the following methods:

Percent of Sales. This is one of the most popular rule-of-thumb methods, and its appeal is found in its simplicity. The firm simply takes a percentage figure and applies it to either past or future sales. For example, suppose next year's sales are estimated to be $1 million. Using a 2-percent-of-sales criterion, the ad budget would be $20,000. This approach is usually justified by its advocates in terms of the following argument: (1) advertising is needed to generate sales; (2) a number of cents, that is, the percentage used, out of each dollar of sales should be devoted to advertising in order to generate needed sales; and (3) the percentage is easily adjusted and can be readily understood by other executives. The percent-of-sales approach is popular in retailing.

Per-Unit Expenditure. Closely related to the above technique is one in which a fixed monetary amount is spent on advertising for each unit of the product expected to be sold. This method is popular with higher priced merchandise, such as automobiles or appliances. For instance, if a company is marketing color televisions priced at $500, it may decide that it should spend $30 per set on advertising. Since this $30 is a fixed amount for each unit, this method amounts to the same thing as the percent-of-sales method. The big difference is in the rationale used to justify each of the methods. The per-unit expenditure method attempts to determine the retail price by using production costs as a base. Here the seller realizes that a reasonably competitive price must be established for the product in question and attempts to cost out the gross margin. All this means is that, if the suggested retail price is to be $500 and manufacturing costs are $250, there is a gross margin of $250 available to cover certain expenses, such as transportation, personal selling, advertising, and dealer profit. Some of these expense items are flexible, such as advertising, while others are nearly fixed, as in the case of transportation. The basic problem with this method and the percentage-of-sales method is that they view advertising as a function of sales, rather than sales as a function of advertising.

All You Can Afford. Here the advertising budget is established as a predetermined share of profits or financial resources. The availability of current revenues sets the upper limit of the ad budget. The only advantage to this approach is that it sets reasonable limits on the expenditures for advertising. However, from the standpoint of sound marketing practice, this method is undesirable because there is no necessary connection between liquidity and advertising opportunity. Any firm that limits its advertising outlays to the amount of available funds will probably miss opportunities for increasing sales and profits.

Competitive Parity. This approach is often used in conjunction with other approaches, such as the percent-of-sales method. The basic philosophy underlying this approach is that advertising is defensive. Advertising budgets are based on those of competitors or other members of the industry. From a strategy standpoint, this is a "followership" technique and assumes that the other firms in the industry know what they are doing and have similar goals. Competitive parity is not a preferred method, although some executives feel it is a "safe" approach. This may or may not be true depending in part on the relative market share of competing firms and their growth objectives.

The Research Approach.   Here the advertising budget is argued for and presented on the basis of research findings. Advertising media are studied in terms of their productivity by the use of media reports (such as the Starch Reports) and research studies. Costs are also estimated and compared with study results. A typical experiment is one in which three or more test markets are selected. The first test market is used as a control, either with no advertising or with normal levels of advertising. Advertising with various levels of intensity are used in the other markets, and comparisons are made to see what effect different levels of intensity have. The advertising manager then evaluates the costs and benefits of the different approaches and intensity levels to determine the overall budget. Although the research approach is generally more expensive than some other models, it is a more rational approach to the expenditure decision.

The Task Approach.   Well-planned advertising programs usually make use of the task approach, which initially formulates the advertising goals and defines the tasks to accomplish these goals. Once this is done, management determines how much it will cost to accomplish each task and adds up the total. This approach is often used in conjunction with the research approach. A variation of the task approach is referred to as the *marketing-program approach*. Here all promotional or selling programs are budgeted in relation to each other, and, given a set of objectives, the goal is to find the optimum promotional mix. It should be clear that, in the task or marketing-program approach, the expenditure and allocation decisions are inseparable.

The Allocation Question

This question deals with the problem of deciding on the most effective way to spend advertising dollars. A general answer to the question is that management's choice of strategies and objectives determines the media and appeals to be used. In other words, the firm's or product division's overall marketing plan will function as a general guideline for answering the allocation question.

From a practical standpoint, however, the allocation question can be framed in terms of message and media decisions. A successful ad campaign has two related tasks: (1) say the right things in the ads themselves and (2) use the appropriate media in the right amounts at the right time to reach the target market.

Message Strategy.   The advertising process involves creating messages with words, ideas, sounds, and other forms of audiovisual stimuli that are designed to affect consumer (or distributor) behavior. It follows that much of advertising is a communication process. To be effective, the advertising message should meet two general criteria: (1) it should take into account the basic principles of communication, and (2) it should be predicated upon a sound theory of consumer motivation and behavior.[3]

The basic communication process involves three elements: (1) the sender or source of the communication; (2) the communication or message; and (3) the receiver or audience. Advertising agencies are considered experts in the communications field and are employed by most large firms to create meaningful messages and assist in their dissemination. Translating the product idea or marketing message into an effective ad is termed *encoding*. In advertising, the goal of encoding is to generate ads that are understood by the audience. For this to occur, the audience must be able to decode the message in the ad so that the perceived content of the message is the same as the intended content. From a practical standpoint, all this means is that advertising messages must be sent to consumers in an understandable and meaningful way.

Advertising messages, of course, must be transmitted and carried by particular communication channels commonly known as advertising media. These media or channels vary in efficiency, selectivity, and cost. Some channels are preferred to others because they have less "noise," and thus messages are more easily received and understood. For example, a particular newspaper ad must compete with other ads, pictures, or stories on the same page. In the case of radio or TV, while only one firm's message is usually broadcast at a time, there are other distractions (noise) that can hamper clear communications, such as driving while listening to the radio.

The relationship between advertising and consumer behavior is quite obvious. For many products and services, advertising is an influence that may affect the consumer's decision to purchase a particular

---

[3]For a full discussion of message strategy, see James F. Engel, Martin R. Warshaw, and Thomas C. Kinnear, *Promotional Strategy*, 6th ed. (Homewood, Ill.: Richard D. Irwin, 1987).

Newspapers	*Television*

Advantages

1. Flexible and timely	1. Combination of sight, sound, and motion
2. Intense coverge of local markets	2. Appeals to senses
3. Broad acceptance and use	3. Mass audience coverage
4. High believability of printed word	4. Psychology of attention

Disadvantages

1. Short life	1. Nonselectivity of audience
2. Read hastily	2. Fleeting impressions
3. Small "pass-along" audience	3. Short life
	4. Expensive

Radio	*Magazines*

Advantages

1. Mass use (over 25 million radios sold annually)	1. High geographic and demographic selectivity
2. Audience selectivity via station format	2. Psychology of attention
3. Low cost (per unit of time)	3. Quality of reproduction
4. Geographic flexibility	4. Pass-along readership

Disadvantages

1. Audio presentation only	1. Long closing periods (6 to 8 weeks prior to publication)
2. Less attention than TV	2. Some waste circulation
3. Chaotic buying (nonstandardized rate structures)	3. No guarantee of position (unless premium is paid)
4. Short life	

Outdoor	*Direct Mail*

Advantages

1. Flexible	1. Audience selectivity
2. Relative absence of competing advertisements	2. Flexible
3. Repeat exposure	3. No competition from competing advertisements
4. Relatively inexpensive	4. Personalized

Disadvantages

1. Creative limitations	1. Relatively high cost
2. Many distractions for viewer	2. Consumers often pay little attention and throw it away
3. Public attack (ecological implications)	
4. No selectivity of audience	

product or brand. It is clear that consumers are subjected to many selling influences, and the question arises about how important advertising is or can be. Here is where the advertising expert must operate on some theory of consumer behavior. The reader will recall from the discussion of consumer behavior that the buyer was viewed as progressing through various stages—from an unsatisfied need through and beyond a purchase decision. The relevance of this discussion is illustrated in Table 8–1, which compares the role of advertising in various stages of the buying process.

Planning an advertising campaign and creating persuasive messages requires a mixture of marketing skill and creative know-how. Relative to the dimension of marketing skills, there are some important pieces of marketing information needed before launching an ad campaign. Most of this information must be generated by the firm and kept up to date. Listed below are some of the critical types of information an advertiser should have:

1. *Who* the firms' customers and potential customers are; their demographic, economic, and psychological characteristics; and any other factors affecting their likelihood of buying.
2. *How many* such customers there are.

TABLE 8–1   Advertising and the Buying Process

Stage in the Buying Process	*Possible Advertising Objective*	*Examples*
1. Unsatisfied need	Awareness	"The reciprocating engine is inefficient." "Dishwashing roughens hands."
2. Alternative search and evaluation	Comprehension	"The Wankel engine is efficient." "Palmolive is mild."
3. Purchase decision	Conviction-ordering	"Come in and see for yourself." "Buy some today."
4. Postpurchase feelings	Reassurance	"Thousands of satisfied owners." "Compare with any other brand."

Source: Adapted for the purposes of this text from Ben M. Enis, *Marketing Principles: The Management Process* (Santa Monica, Calif.: Goodyear Publishing, 1980), p. 466.

3. *How much* of the firm's type and brand of product they are currently buying and can reasonably be expected to buy in the short-term and long-term future.
4. *What* individuals, other than customers, and potential customers, *influence* purchasing decisions.
5. *Where* they *buy* the firm's brand of product.
6. *When* they buy, and frequency of purchase.
7. *What* competitive brands they buy and frequency of purchase.
8. *How* they *use* the product.
9. *Why* they buy particular *types* and *brands* of products.

Media Mix.   Media selection is no easy task. To start with, there are numerous types and combinations of media to choose from. Below is a general outline of some of the more common advertising media.

A. Printed media
   1. National
      a. Magazines
      b. Newspapers
      c. Direct mail
   2. Local
      a. Newspapers
      b. Magazines
      c. Direct mail
      d. Handbills or flyers
      e. Yellow Pages
B. Electronic media
   1. National (network)
      a. Radio
      b. Television
   2. Local
      a. Radio (AM–FM)
      b. Television
   3. Individual
      a. Videocassette
      b. Floppy disk
C. Other
   1. Outdoor (example: billboards)
   2. Transit
   3. Specialty (giveaways)
   4. Point-of-purchase
   5. Telemarketing (telephone selling)

Of course, each of the above media categories can be further refined. For example, magazines can be broken down into more detailed classes, such as mass monthlies *(Reader's Digest),* news weeklies *(Time),* men's magazines *(Playboy),* women's fashion magazines *(Vogue),* sports magazines *(Sports Illustrated),* business magazines *(Forbes),* and so forth. Clearly, one dimension of this advertising management problem involves having an overabundance of media to select from. With only four media to choose from, there are 16 possible go or no-go decisions. With 10 media, there would be approximately 1,000 combinations.

Although the number of media and media combinations available for advertising is overwhelming at first glance, four interrelated factors limit the number of practical alternatives. First, *the nature of the product* limits the number of practical and efficient alternatives. For instance, a radically new and highly complex product could not be properly promoted using billboard advertisements. Second, *the nature and size of the target market* also limits appropriate advertising media. For example, it is generally inefficient to advertise industrial goods in mass media publications. Third, *the advertising budget* may restrict the use of expensive media, such as television. And fourth, *the availability* of some media may be limited in particular geographic areas. Although these factors reduce media alternatives to a more manageable number, specific media must still be selected. A primary consideration at this point is media effectiveness or efficiency.

In the advertising industry a common measure of efficiency or productivity of media is "cost per thousand." This figure generally refers to the dollar cost of reaching 1,000 prospects, and its chief advantage is in making media comparisons. Generally, such measures as circulation, audience size, and sets in use per commercial minute are used in the calculation. Of course, different relative rankings of media can occur, depending on the measure used. Another problem deals with what is meant by "reaching" the prospect, and at least five levels of reaching are possible:

1. *Distribution.* This level refers to circulation or physical distribution of the vehicle into households or other decision-making units. In only some of these households or decision-making units are there genuine prospects for the product.
2. *Exposure.* This level refers to actual exposure of prospects to the message. If the TV set is on, distribution is taking place; but only if the program is being watched can exposure occur.
3. *Awareness.* This level refers to the prospect becoming alert to the message in the sense of being conscious of the ad. Actual information processing starts at this point.
4. *Communication.* This level goes one step beyond awareness—to the point where the prospect becomes affected by the message. Here the effect is to generate some sort of change in the prospect's knowledge, attitude, or desire concerning the product.

HIGHLIGHT 8–5
Procedures for Evaluating Advertising Programs and Some Services Using the Procedures

PROCEDURES FOR EVALUATING SPECIFIC ADVERTISEMENTS

1. *Recognition tests:* Estimate the percentage of people claiming to have read a magazine who recognize the ad when it is shown to them (e.g., Starch Message Report Service).
2. *Recall tests:* Estimate the percentage of people claiming to have read a magazine who can (unaided) recall the ad and its contents (e.g., Gallup and Robinson Impact Service, various services for TV ads as well).
3. *Opinion tests:* Potential audience members are asked to rank alternative advertisements as most interesting, most believable, best liked.
4. *Theater tests:* Theater audience is asked for brand preferences before and after an ad is shown in context of a TV show (e.g., Schwerin TV Testing Service).

PROCEDURES FOR EVALUATING SPECIFIC ADVERTISING OBJECTIVES

1. *Awareness:* Potential buyers are asked to indicate brands that come to mind in a product category. A message used in an ad campaign is given and buyers are asked to identify the brand that was advertised using that message.
2. *Attitude:* Potential buyers are asked to rate competing or individual brands on determinant attributes, benefits, characterizations using rating scales.

PROCEDURES FOR EVALUATING MOTIVATIONAL IMPACT

1. *Intention to buy:* Potential buyers are asked to indicate the likelihood they will buy a brand (on a scale from "definitely will not" to "definitely will").
2. *Market test:* Sales changes in different markets are monitored to compare the effects of different messages, budget levels.

Source: Joseph Guiltinan and Gordon Paul, *Marketing Management,* 2nd ed. (New York: McGraw-Hill, 1988), p. 263.

---

5. *Response.* This level represents the overt action that results because of the ad. Response can mean many things, such as a simple telephone or mail inquiry, a shopping trip, or a purchase.

The advertiser has to decide at what level to evaluate the performance of a medium, and this is a particularly difficult problem. Ideally, the advertiser would like to know exactly how many dollars of sales are generated by ads in a particular medium. However, this is very difficult to measure since so many other factors are simultaneously at work that could be producing sales. On the other hand, the distribution of a medium is much easier to measure but distribution figures are much less meaningful. For example, a newspaper may have a distribution (circulation) of 100,000 people, yet none of these people may be prospects for the particular product being advertised. Thus, if this media were evaluated in terms of distribution, it might be viewed as quite effective even though it may be totally ineffective in terms of producing sales. This problem further illustrates the importance of insuring that the media selected are those used by the target market.

From what has been said so far, it should be clear that advertising decisions involve a great deal of complexity and a myriad of variables. Not surprising, therefore, is that application of quantitative techniques have become quite popular in the area. Linear programming, dynamic programming, heuristic programming, and simulation have been applied to the problem of selecting media schedules, and more comprehensive models of advertising decisions have also been developed. Although these models can be extremely useful in advertising decision making, they must be viewed as tools and not as a replacement for sound managerial decisions and judgment.

SALES PROMOTION

In marketing, the word *promotion* is used in many ways. For instance, it is sometimes used to refer to a specific activity, such as advertising or publicity. In the general sense, promotion has been defined as "any identifiable effort on the part of the seller to persuade buyers to accept the seller's information and store it in retrievable form." However, the term *sales promotion* has a more restricted and technical meaning and has been defined by the American Marketing Association as follows:

> Media and nonmedia marketing pressure applied for a predetermined, limited period of time at the level of consumer, retailer, or wholesaler in order to stimulate trial, increase consumer demand, or improve product availability.[4]

The popularity of sales and other promotions has been increasing. In the 10-year period between 1977 and 1987, the promotion-to-advertising expenditure ratio increased from a 58 percent to 42 percent split to a 65 percent to 35 percent level.[5] Current estimates show a similar pattern. Reasons for this growth of sales promotion include a shifting emphasis from pull to push marketing strategies by many

---

[4]Peter D. Bennett, ed., *Dictionary of Marketing Terms* (Chicago: American Marketing Association, 1988), p. 179.

[5]Nathanial Frey, "Ninth Annual Advertising and Sales Promotion Report," *Marketing Communications,* August 1988, p. 11.

HIGHLIGHT 8–6
Some Objectives of Sales Promotion

When directed at consumers:

1. To obtain the trial of a product.
2. To introduce a new or improved product.
3. To encourage repeat or greater usage by current users.
4. To bring more customers into retail stores.
5. To increase the total number of users of an established product.

When directed at salespersons:

1. To motivate the sales force.
2. To educate the sales force about product improvements.
3. To stabilize a fluctuating sales pattern.

When directed at resellers:

1. To increase reseller inventories.
2. To obtain displays and other support for products.
3. To improve product distribution.
4. To obtain more and better shelf space.

Source: Adapted from Steven J. Skinner, *Marketing* (Boston: Houghton Mifflin Co., 1990), p. 542.

firms, a widening of the focus of advertising agencies to include promotional services to firms, an emphasis on the part of management toward short-term results, and the emergence of new technology. For example, supermarket cash registers can now be equipped with a device that will dispense coupons to a customer at the point of purchase. The type, variety, and cash amount of the coupon will vary from customer to customer based on their purchases. In essence, it is now possible for the Coca-Cola Company to dispense coupons to only those customers who purchase Pepsi, thus avoiding wasting promotional dollars on already loyal Coke drinkers.

Push versus Pull Marketing

Push and pull marketing strategies comprise the two options available to firms interested in getting their product into customers' hands. Push strategies include all activities aimed at getting products into the dealer pipeline and accelerating sales by offering inducements to dealers, retailers, and salespeople. Inducements might include introductory price allowances, distribution allowances, and advertising-dollar allowances.[6] A pull strategy, on the other hand, is one whereby a manufacturer relies mainly on product advertising or consumer sales promotions. These activities are aimed at motivating the consumer to pull the product through the channel.

Several forces and developments have contributed to the increasing use of push marketing strategies by many manufacturers.[7]

1. *Changes in the balance of power between manufacturers and retailers.* Due to the decreasing importance of network television and the increasing use of optical scanning equipment, retailers no longer have to depend on manufacturers for facts. This leads to more power on the part of retailers.
2. *Growth and consolidation of retail package goods businesses.* The growth of regional and national grocery chains such as Safeway and Kroger have led to increasing clout for the retailer. For example, many supermarkets now charge manufacturers a slotting allowance on new products. A slotting allowance is a fee manufacturers pay retailers to allocate shelf space to new products.
3. *Reduced product differentiation and brand loyalty.* Due to the similarity of many brands and the growing use of sales promotions, consumers are no longer as brand loyal as they once were. Therefore, more and more sales promotions are needed as an incentive to get the consumer to buy a particular brand. To illustrate, consider the case of domestic car manufacturers. Advertising can no longer be used as a stand-alone promotional strategy to induce consumer automobile purchases. Instead the manufacturer must also offer additional incentives to the consumer through the dealer including rebates, special option packages, and extended warranties.

Trade Sales Promotions

Trade promotions are those promotions aimed at distributors and retailers of products who make up the distribution channel. The major objectives of trade promotions are to: (1) convince retailers to carry the manufacturer's products; (2) reduce the manufacturer's and increase the distributor's or retailer's inventories; (3) support advertising and

---

[6]Definition of push marketing and its activities is from Courtland L. Bovee and William F. Arens, *Contemporary Advertising,* 3rd ed. (Homewood, Ill.: Richard D. Irwin, 1989), p. G–16.

[7]For a fuller explanation of the rise in push marketing strategies, see Terence A. Shimp, *Promotion Management and Marketing Communications,* 2nd ed. (Chicago, Ill.: Dryden Press, 1990), pp. 517–20, and Alvin Achenbaum and F. Kent Mitchel, "Pulling Away from Push Marketing," *Harvard Business Review,* May–June 1987, pp. 38–40.

consumer sales promotions; (4) encourage retailers to either give the product more favorable shelf space or place more emphasis on selling the product; and (5) serve as a reward for past sales efforts.

Types of dealer sales promotions vary. The most common types are:[8]

1. Point-of-purchase displays, including special racks, banners, signs, price cards, and other mechanical product dispensers. For example, an end-of-the-aisle display for Chips Ahoy cookies would be provided to the retailer by Nabisco.
2. Contests in which organizations and individual salespeople are rewarded for sales efforts.
3. Trade shows that are regularly scheduled events where manufacturers display products and provide information.
4. Sales meetings at which information and support materials are presented to dealers.
5. Push money, which is a form of extra payment given to resellers for meeting specified sales goals.
6. Dealer loaders, which are premiums in the form of either merchandise, gifts, or displays given to the reseller for purchasing large quantities of the product.
7. Trade deals, which are price discounts given for meeting certain purchase requirements.
8. Advertising allowances, whereby the manufacturer helps to support retailer advertising efforts in which the manufacturer's product is displayed.

Consumer Promotions

Consumer promotions can fulfill several distinct objectives for the manufacturer. Some of the more commonly sought-after objectives include: (1) inducing the consumer to try the product; (2) rewarding the consumer for brand loyalty; (3) encouraging the consumer to trade up or purchase larger sizes of a product; (4) stimulating the consumer to make repeat purchases of the product; (5) reacting to competitor efforts; and (6) reinforcing and serving as a complement to advertising and personal selling efforts.

Listed below are brief descriptions of some of the most commonly utilized forms of consumer promotion activities.

1. *Sampling.* Consumers are offered regular or trial sizes of the product either free or at a nominal price. For example, Hershey Foods Corp.

---

[8]For a fuller discussion of trade and consumer sales promotion activities, see John Burnett, *Promotion Management,* 2nd ed. (St. Paul, Minn.: West Publishing, 1988), chaps. 13 and 14.

handed out 750,000 candy bars on 170 college campuses as a means of gaining trial.[9]

2. *Price deals.* Consumers are given discounts from the product's regular price. For example, Coke and Pepsi are frequently available at discounted prices.

3. *Bonus packs.* Bonus packs consist of additional amounts of the product that a company gives to buyers of the product. For example, manufacturers of disposable razors frequently add additional razors to their packages at no additional charge.

4. *Rebates and refunds.* Consumers, either on the spot or through the mail, are given cash reimbursements for purchasing products. For example, consumers are offered a $3 mail-in rebate for purchasing a Norelco coffee maker.

5. *Sweepstakes and contests.* Consumers can win cash and/or prizes either through chance selection or games of skill. For example, Marriott Hotels teamed up with Hertz Rent-a-Car in a scratch card sweepstakes that offered over $90 million in prizes.

6. *Premiums.* A premium is a reward or gift that comes from purchasing a product. For example, Coca-Cola gave away an estimated 20 million pairs of 3-D glasses to enable Super Bowl watchers to see their 3-D commercial. AT&T gave away fax and voice-paging machines to purchasers of their small business systems.

7. *Coupons.* Probably the most familiar and widely used of all consumer promotions, coupons are cents-off or added value incentives. Due to the high incidence of coupon fraud, manufacturers including Royal Crown Cola and General Mills are now experimenting with the use of personalized checks as an alternative to coupons. An added advantage of this alternative is a quicker redemption for retailers. As mentioned previously, point-of-purchase coupons are becoming an increasingly efficient way for marketers to target their promotional efforts at specific consumers.

What Sales Promotion Can and Can't Do

Advocates of sales promotion often point to its growing popularity as a justification for the argument that we don't need advertising; sales promotion itself will suffice. Marketers should bear in mind that sales promotion is only one part of a well-constructed overall promotional plan. While proven to be extremely effective in achieving the objectives listed in the previous sections, there are several compelling reasons why sales promotion should not be utilized as the sole promotional tool. These reasons include sales promotion's inability to: (1) generate

---

[9]*Advertising Age,* September 27, 1989, p. 3.

long-term buyer commitment to a brand; (2) change, except on a temporary basis, declining sales of a product; (3) convince buyers to purchase an otherwise unacceptable product; and (4) make up for a lack of advertising or sales support for a product. To illustrate, General Foods cut back the yearly advertising expenditures on Maxwell House coffee by $60 million in the mid 80s and reallocated the funds to sales promotion activities. Within a year, Folger's coffee dislodged Maxwell House as the largest selling brand. It took three years for Maxwell House to finally regain the top spot. In the process, General Foods ended up restoring the advertising budget to an even higher level than it was prior to Maxwell House's fall from grace.

CONCLUSION

This chapter has been concerned with nonpersonal selling. Remember that advertising and sales promotion are only two of the ways by which sellers can affect the demand for their product. Advertising and sales promotion are only part of the firm's promotion mix, and, in turn, the promotion mix is only part of the overall marketing mix. Thus, advertising and sales promotion begin with the marketing plan and not with the advertising and sales promotion plans. Ignoring this point can produce ineffective and expensive promotional programs because of a lack of coordination with other elements of the marketing mix.

ADDITIONAL READINGS

Aaker, David A., and Donald E. Bruzzone. "Causes of Irritation in Advertising." *Journal of Marketing,* Spring 1985, pp. 47–57.

Bovee, Courtland L., and William F. Arens. *Contemporary Advertising.* 3rd ed. Homewood, Ill.: Richard D. Irwin, 1989.

Burnett, John. *Promotion Management.* 2nd ed. St. Paul, Minn.: West Publishing, 1988.

Engel, James F.; Martin R. Warshaw; and Thomas C. Kinnear. *Promotional Strategy: Managing the Marketing Communications Process.* 6th ed. Homewood, Ill.: Richard D. Irwin, 1987.

Healy, John S., and Harold H. Kassarjian. "Advertising Substantiation and Advertiser Response: A Content Analysis of Magazine Advertisements." *Journal of Marketing,* Winter 1983, pp. 107–17.

Heath, Robert L., and Richard A. Nelson, "Image and Issue Advertising: A Corporate and Public Policy Perspective." *Journal of Marketing,* Spring 1985, pp. 58–68.

Pollay, Richard W. "The Subsiding Sizzle: A Descriptive History of Print Advertising, 1900–1980." *Journal of Marketing,* Summer 1985, pp. 24–37.

Pollay, Richard W. "The Distorted Mirror: Reflections on the Unintended Consequences of Advertising." *Journal of Marketing,* April 1986, pp. 18–36.

Rothschild, Michael L. *Advertising.* Lexington, Mass.: D. C. Heath and Co., 1987.

Sandage, C. H.; V. Fryburger; and K. R. Rotzell. *Advertising Theory and Practice,* 11th ed. Homewood Ill.: Richard D. Irwin, 1983.

Sewall, M. A., and D. Sarel. "Characteristics of Radio Commercials and Their Recall Effectiveness." *Journal of Marketing,* January 1986, pp. 52–60.

Shimp, Terence A. *Promotion Management and Marketing Communication.* 2nd ed. Chicago, Ill.: Dryden Press, 1990.

Appendix   Major Federal Agencies Involved in Control of Advertising

Agency	Function
Federal Trade Commission	Regulates commerce between states; controls unfair business practices; takes action on false and deceptive advertising; most important agency in regulation of advertising and promotion.
Food and Drug Administration	Regulatory division of the Department of Health, Education, and Welfare; controls marketing of food, drugs, cosmetics, medical devices, and potentially hazardous consumer products.
Federal Communications Commission	Regulates advertising indirectly, primarily through the power to grant or withdraw broadcasting licenses.
Postal Service	Regulates material that goes through the mails, primarily in areas of obscenity, lottery, and fraud.
Alcohol and Tobacco Tax Division	Part of the Treasury Department; has broad powers to regulate deceptive and misleading advertising of liquor and tobacco.
Grain Division	Unit of the Department of Agriculture responsible for policing seed advertising.
Securities and Exchange Commission	Regulates advertising of securities.

Information Source	Description
Patent Office	Regulates registration of trademarks.
Library of Congress	Controls protection of copyrights.
Department of Justice	Enforces all federal laws through prosecuting cases referred to it by other government agencies.

Chapter 9

Promotion Strategy: Personal Selling

Personal selling, unlike advertising or sales promotion, involves direct face-to-face relationships between the seller and the prospect or customer. The behavioral scientist would probably characterize personal selling as a type of personal influence. Operationally, it is a complex communication process, one not completely understood by marketing scholars.

IMPORTANCE OF PERSONAL SELLING

Most business firms find it impossible to market their products without some form of personal selling. To illustrate, some years ago vending machines became quite popular. The question may be raised about whether or not these machines replaced the salesperson. The answer is both yes and no. In a narrow sense of the word, the vending machine has replaced some retail sales clerks who, for most convenience goods, merely dispensed the product and collected money. On the other hand, vending machines and their contents must be "sold" to the vending machine operators, and personal selling effort must be exerted to secure profitable locations for the machines.

The policies of self-service and self-selection have done much to eliminate the need for personal selling in some types of retail stores. However, the successful deployment of these policies have required manufacturers to do two things: (1) presell the consumer by means of larger advertising and sales promotion outlays; and (2) design packages for their products that would "sell" themselves, so to speak.

HIGHLIGHT 9–1
The Typical American Salesperson

- Age: 33
- Male: 70 percent
- Female: 30 percent
- Some college or degree: 82 percent
- Graduate degree: 9 percent
- Most likely to leave after: 4.3 years
- Average length of service: 6.3 years
- Usual pay: salary, 20 percent; commission, 30 percent; combination, 50 percent
- Earnings per year: trainee, $25,000; experienced salesperson, $40,000
- Cost to train: $18,000
- Length of training: 3 months
- Cost per sales call: $95 to $350
- Sales calls per day: 6.5
- Number of calls to close: 5
- Cost of field expenses: $20,000
- Value of benefits: $14,000
- Average sales volume: $1 million
- Hours per week in selling activities within the territory: 41
- Hours per week in nonselling activities (i.e., paperwork and planning sales calls): 10
- Turnover rate: 20 percent

Source: Charles Futrell, *Fundamentals of Selling*, 3rd ed. (Homewood, Ill.: Richard D. Irwin, 1990), p. 8.

The importance of the personal selling function depends partially on the nature of the product. As a general rule, goods that are new, technically complex, and/or expensive require more personal selling effort. The salesperson plays a key role in providing the consumer with information about such products to reduce the risks involved in purchase and use. Insurance, for example, is a complex and technical product that often needs significant amounts of personal selling. In addition, many industrial goods cannot be presold, and the salesperson (or sales team) has a key role to play in finalizing the sale. However, most national branded convenience goods are purchased by the consumer without any significant assistance from store clerks.

The importance of personal selling also is determined to a large extent by the needs of the consumer. In the case of pure competition (a large number of small buyers with complete market knowledge of a homogeneous product), there is little need for personal selling. A close approximation to this situation is found at auctions for agricultural products, such as tobacco or wheat. At the other extreme, when a product is highly differentiated, such as housing, and marketed to consumers with imperfect knowledge of product offerings, then personal selling becomes a key factor in the promotion mix. In fact, in some cases, the consumer may not even be seeking the product; for instance, life insurance is often categorized as an unsought good. Finally, sellers who differentiate their products at the point of sale will usually make heavy use of personal selling in their promotion mix. For example, automobile buyers are given the opportunity to purchase various extras or options at the time of purchase.

It is important to remember that, for many companies, the salesperson represents the customer's main link to the firm. In fact, to some, the salesperson is the company. Therefore, it is imperative that the company take advantage of this unique link. Through the efforts of the successful salesperson, a company can build relationships with customers that continue long beyond the initial sale. It is the salesperson who serves as the conduit through which information regarding product flaws, improvements, applications, and/or new uses can pass from the customer to the marketing department. To illustrate the importance of using salespeople as an information resource, consider this fact. In some industries, customer information serves as the source for up to 90 percent of new product and process ideas.[1] Along with techniques described in the previous chapter, personal selling provides the push needed to get middlemen to carry new products, increase their amount of purchasing, and devote more effort in merchandising a product or brand.[2]

THE SALES PROCESS

Personal selling is as much an art as it is a science. The word *art* is used to describe that portion of the selling process that is highly creative in nature and difficult to explain. This does not mean there is little control over the personal selling element in the promotion mix. It does imply that, all other things equal, the trained salesperson can outsell the untrained one.

Before management selects and trains salespeople, it should have an understanding of the sales process. Obviously, the sales process will differ according to the size of the company, the nature of the product, the market, and so forth, but there are some elements common to

---

[1]Eric von Hipple, "The Sources of Innovation," *McKinsey Quarterly,* Winter 1988, pp. 72–79.

[2]Terance A. Shimp, *"Promotion Management and Marketing Communication,* 2nd ed. (Chicago: Dryden Press, 1990), p. 602.

almost all selling situations that should be understood. For the purposes of this text, the term *sales process* refers to two basic factors: (1) the sequence of stages or steps the salesperson should follow in trying to sell goods and services; and (2) a set of basic principles that, if adhered to, will increase the likelihood of a sale being made.

The traditional approach to personal selling involves a formula or step-by-step procedure. It is known as the AIDAS formula and has five steps: (1) get the prospect's *attention;* (2) arouse the prospect's *interest;* (3) stimulate the prospect's *desire* for the product; (4) get buying *action;* and (5) build *satisfaction* into the transaction. This approach to selling implies two things. First, the prospect or potential buyer goes through these five steps. Second, the salesperson can influence the behavior of the prospect if this process is managed skillfully. Although this model represents a logical approach to explaining the sales process, it emphasizes a how-to approach to selling, rather than attempting to explain why sales are made, or conversely, why purchases are made.

An explanation of the selling process in terms of why individuals purchase would require a full understanding of consumer behavior. Obviously, as we saw in Chapter 3, this is a difficult task, because so many variables are difficult to measure or control. However, a useful framework for a better understanding of the selling process is illustrated in Figure 9–1.

This approach views the selling process as an input-output system: the inputs are marketing stimuli, such as price, quality, service, and style. Personal selling is viewed as one of the channels by which knowledge about these marketing stimuli are transmitted to the buyer. In this model, the buyer's mind is a processor of the various stimuli, and,

FIGURE 9–1   A Model of the Selling Process

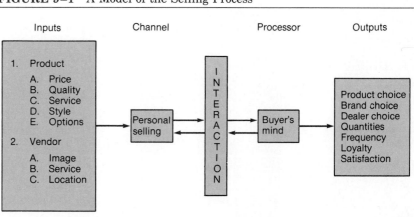

HIGHLIGHT 9–2
Qualities Most Valued, Disliked, and Hated in Salespersons by Purchasing Agents

Most Valued

Reliability/credibility	98.6%
Professionalism/integrity	93.7
Product knowledge	90.7
Innovativeness in problem solving	80.5
Presentation/preparation	69.7

And in the purchasing agents' own words:

Qualities Liked	*Qualities Disliked*	*Qualities Hated*
"Honesty."	"No follow-up."	"Wise-ass attitude."
"Loses a sale graciously."	"Walking in without an appointment."	"Calls me 'dear' or 'sweetheart' (I am female)."
"Admits mistakes."	"Begins call by talking sports."	"Gets personal."
"Problem-solving capabilities."	"Puts down competitor's products."	"Doesn't give purchasing people credit for any brains."
"Friendly but professional."	"Poor listening skills."	"Whiners."
"Dependable."	"Too many phone calls."	"Bullshooters."
"Adaptability."	"Lousy presentation."	"Wines and dines me."
"Knows my business."	"Fails to ask about needs."	"Plays one company against another."
"Well prepared."	"Lacks product knowledge."	"Pushy."
"Patience."	"Wastes my time."	"Smokes in my office."

Source: "PAs Examine the People Who Sell to Them," *Sales and Marketing Management*, November 11, 1985, p. 39.

since the workings of the mind are only partially understood, it can be considered a "black box." The explanation of what goes on in this black box depends on which approach or theory of behavior is employed.[3] The outputs for the model represent purchasing responses, such as brand choice, dealer choice, and the like. Here the sales process is viewed as a social situation involving two persons. The interaction of the two persons depends on the economic, social, physical, and personality characteristics of both the seller and the buyer.[4] A successful sale is situationally determined by these factors and can be considered social behavior as well as individual behavior. The prospect's perception of the salesperson is a key factor in determining the salesperson's effectiveness and role expectations.[5] The salesperson's confidence and ability to "play the role" of a salesperson is crucial in determining behavior and is influenced by personality, knowledge, training, and previous experience.[6]

Selling Fundamentals

From what has been said so far, the only reasonable conclusion that can be drawn is that there is no one clear-cut theory of personal selling nor one single technique that can be applied universally. Most sales training programs attempt to provide the trainee with the fundamentals of selling, placing emphasis on the "how" and "what" and leaving the "why" questions to the theorists.

A primary objective of any sales training program is to impart knowledge and techniques to the participants. An analysis of numerous training manuals reveals subjects or topics common to many programs. Following are brief descriptions of some fundamentals well-trained salespeople should know.

1. They should have thorough knowledge of the company they represent, including its past history. This includes the philosophy of management as well as the firm's basic operating policies.
2. They should have thorough technical and commercial knowledge of their products or product lines. This is particularly true when selling

---

[3]For a review, see J. Paul Peter and Jerry C. Olson, *Consumer Behavior and Marketing Strategy,* 2nd ed. (Homewood, Ill.: Richard D. Irwin, 1990).

[4]Kaylene C. Williams and Rosann L. Spiro, "Communication Style in the Salesperson-Customer Dyad," *Journal of Marketing Research,* November 1985, pp. 434–43.

[5]Barton A. Weitz, Harish Sujen, and Mita Sujen, "Knowledge, Motivation, and Adaptive Behavior: A Framework for Improving Selling Effectiveness," *Journal of Marketing*, October 1986, pp. 174–91.

[6]Alan J. Dubinsky, Roy D. Howell, Thomas N. Ingram, and Danny N. Bellinger, "Salesforce Socialization," *Journal of Marketing,* October 1986, pp. 192–207.

HIGHLIGHT 9–3
A Comparison of Order Takers, Order Generators, and Sales Support Personnel

	Order Takers	Order Generators	Sales Support Personnel
Typical position	Retail sales clerk	IBM mainframe computer salesperson	Pharmaceutical detailer
Purpose	Process routine orders or reorders	Identify new sales opportunities	Promote new products or services
Types of sales transaction	Simple rebuy	New product sales or a modified rebuy situation	Stimulate interest in either a routine rebuy or a new product opportunity
Product line	Well-known, simple products	Complex or customized products	Typically responsible for both simple and complex product lines
Training	Minimum and limited to order processing	Technical skills in addition to extensive skills training	Technical skills and interpersonal communication skills
Compensation	Primarily salary	Either straight commission or combination of salary and a commission	Primarily salary
Source of sales	Existing customers	New customers	Both existing customers and targeted new customers

Source: J. Barry Mason and Hazel F. Ezell, *Marketing: Principles and Strategy* (Homewood, Ill.: Richard D. Irwin Business Publications, Inc., 1987), p. 635.

industrial goods. When selling very technical products, many firms require their salespeople to have training as engineers.

3. They should have good working knowledge of competitor's products. This is a vital requirement because the successful salesperson will have to know the strengths and weaknesses of those products that are in competition for market share.

4. They should have in-depth knowledge of the market for their merchandise. The market here refers not only to a particular sales territory but also to the general market, including the economic factors that affect the demand for their goods.

5. They should have a thorough understanding of the importance of prospecting and the methods used to effectively locate and qualify prospects (the decision-making unit). General issues to be evaluated are the prospective buyer's needs, financial resources, and willingness to be approached.

6. They should have accurate knowledge of the buyer or the prospect to whom they are selling. Under the marketing concept, knowledge of the customer is a vital requirement. Areas of desirable knowledge salespeople should possess include customer applications of the product and customer requirements as they relate to product quality, durability, cost, design, and service. Knowledgeable salespeople should be able to quantify, as well as describe, product benefits to the buyer. Effective selling requires salespeople to understand the unique characteristics of each account.

There are no magic secrets of successful selling. The difference between good salespeople and mediocre ones is often the result of training plus experience. Training is no substitute for experience; the two complement each other. The difficulty with trying to discuss the selling job in terms of basic principles is that experienced, successful salespeople will always be able to find exceptions to these principles. Often successful selling seems to defy logic and, sometimes, common sense. Trying to program salespeople to follow definite rules or principles in every situation can stifle their originality and creativity.[7]

MANAGING THE SALES PROCESS

Every personal sale can be divided into two parts: the part done by the salespeople and the part done for the salespeople by the company. For example, from the standpoint of the product, the company should

---

[7]For a review of research findings regarding factors that are predictive of salespeople's performance, see Gilbert A. Churchill, Jr., Neil M. Ford, Steven W. Hartley, and Orville C. Walker, Jr., "The Determinants of Salesperson Performance: A Meta-Analysis," *Journal of Marketing Research,* May 1985, pp. 87–93.

provide the salesperson with a product skillfully designed, thoroughly tested, attractively packaged, adequately advertised, and priced to compare favorably with competitive products. Salespeople have the responsibility of being thoroughly acquainted with the product, its selling features, points of superiority, and a sincere belief in the value of the product. From a sales management standpoint, the company's part of the sale involves the following:

1. Efficient and effective sales tools, including continuous sales training, promotional literature, samples, trade shows, product information, and adequate advertising.
2. An efficient delivery and reorder system to ensure that customers will receive the merchandise as promised.
3. An equitable compensation plan that rewards performance, motivates the salesperson, and promotes company loyalty. It should also reimburse the salesperson for all reasonable expenses incurred while doing the job.
4. Adequate supervision and evaluation of performance as a means of helping salespeople do a better job, not only for the company but for themselves as well.

The Sales Management Task

Since the advent of the marketing concept, a clear-cut distinction has been made between marketing management and sales management. Marketing management refers to all activities in the firm that have to do with satisfying demand. Sales management is a narrower concept dealing with those functions directly related to personal selling. Generally speaking, sales managers are in middle management and report directly to the vice president of marketing. Their basic responsibilities can be broken down into at least seven major areas: (1) developing an effective sales organization for the company; (2) formulating short-range and long-range sales programs; (3) recruiting, training, and supervising the sales force; (4) formulating sales budgets and controlling selling expenses; (5) coordinating the personal selling effort with other forms of promotional activities; (6) maintaining lines of communication among the sales force, customers, and other relevant parts of the business, such as advertising, production, and logistics; and in some firms, (7) developing sales forecasts and other types of relevant marketing studies to be used in sales planning and control.

Sales managers are line officers whose primary responsibility is establishing and maintaining an active sales organization. In terms of authority, they usually have equivalent rank to that of other marketing executives who manage aspects of the marketing program, such as advertising, product planning, or physical distribution. The sales organization may have separate departments and department heads to perform specialized tasks, such as training, personnel, promotion, and forecasting. Figure 9–2 is an example of such a sales organization.

In other cases, a general marketing manager may have product managers, or directors, reporting to them. This is common in cases where the firm sells numerous products and each product or product line is handled by a separate manager. Another common arrangement is to have sales managers assigned to specific geographic regions or customer groups. This type of specialization enables the sales force to operate more efficiently by avoiding overlaps. Regardless of the method used, the sales force should be structured to meet the unique needs of the consumer, the company, and its management.

Controlling the Sales Force

There are two obvious reasons why it is critical that the sales force be properly controlled. First, personal selling can be the largest marketing expense component in the final price of the product. Second, unless the sales force is somehow directed, motivated, and audited on a continual basis, it is likely to be less efficient than it is capable of being. Controlling the sales force involves four key functions: (1) forecasting sales; (2) establishing sales territories and quotas; (3) analyzing expenses; and (4) motivating and compensating performance.

Forecasting Sales. Sales planning begins with a forecast of sales for some future period or periods. From a practical standpoint, these forecasts are made on a short-term basis of a year or less, although long-range forecasts of one to five years are made for purposes other than

FIGURE 9–2 An Example of a Sales Organization

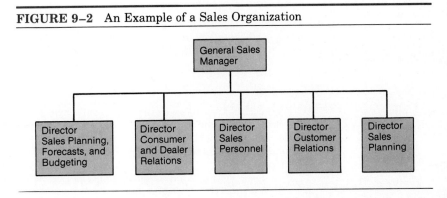

managing the sales force, such as financing, production, and development. Generally speaking, forecasting is the marketing manager's responsibility. In large firms, because of the complexity of the task, it is usually delegated to a specialized unit, such as the marketing research department. Forecast data should be integrated into the firm's marketing decision support system for use by sales managers and other corporate executives. For many companies the sales forecast is the key instrument in the planning and control of operations.[8]

The sales forecast is an estimate of how much of the company's output, either in dollars or in units, can be sold during a specified future period under a proposed marketing plan and under an assumed set of economic conditions. A sales forecast has several important uses: (1) it is used to establish sales quotas; (2) it is used to plan personal selling efforts as well as other types of promotional activities in the marketing mix; (3) it is used to budget selling expenses; and (4) it is used to plan and coordinate production, physical distribution, inventories, personnel, and so forth.

Sales forecasting has become very sophisticated in recent years, especially with the increased availability of computer hardware and software. It should be mentioned, however, that a forecast is never a substitute for sound business judgment. At the present time there is no single method of sales forecasting known that gives uniformly accurate results with infallible precision. Outlined below are some commonly used sales forecasting methods.[9]

1. *Jury of executive opinion method.* This combines and averages the views of top management representing marketing, production, finance, purchasing, and administration.
2. *Sales force composite method.* This is similar to the first method in that it obtains the combined views of the sales force about the future outlook for sales. In some companies all salespeople, or district managers, submit estimates of the future sales in their territory or district.
3. *Customer expectations method.* This approach involves asking customers or product users about the quantity they expect to purchase.
4. *Time series analyses.* This approach involves analyzing past sales data and the impact of factors that influence sales (long-term growth trends, cyclical fluctuations, seasonal variations).

---

[8]For additional discussion on the use of technological systems in sales management, see "Selling Meets the Technological Age," *Sales and Marketing Management* (special section on the "Computer in Marketing"), December 6, 1982, pp. 45–54; and Brad Hamman, "Rebirth of a Salesman: Willy Loman Goes Electronic," *Business Week,* February 27, 1984, p. 103.

[9]Based on a survey by the National Industrial Conference Board: "Forecasting Sales," *Studies in Business Policy,* no. 106.

5. *Correlation analysis.* This involves measuring the relationship between the dependent variable, sales, and one or more independent variables that can explain increases or decreases in sales volumes.
6. *Other quantitative techniques.* Numerous statistical and mathematical techniques can be used to predict or estimate future sales. Two of the more important techniques are (*a*) growth functions, which are mathematical expressions specifying the relationship between demand and time; and (*b*) simulation models, where a statistical model of the industry is developed and programmed to develop values for the key parameters of the model.

Establishing Sales Territories and Quotas.   The establishment of sales territories and sales quotas represents management's need to match personal selling effort with sales potential (or opportunity). Sales territories are usually specified geographic areas assigned to individual salespeople. These areas represent an attempt to make the selling task more efficient.[10] The underlying rationale is that the control of sales operations will be facilitated by breaking down the total market into smaller and more manageable units. Implied here is the notion that there are some distinct economic advantages to dividing the total market into smaller segments. These segments should represent clusters of customers, or prospects, within some degree of physical proximity. Of course, there are criteria other than geography for establishing territories. One important criterion is that of product specialization. In this case, salespeople are specialists relative to particular product or customer situations.

From a marketing management point of view, there are many advantages to establishing sales territories. First, it facilitates the process of sales planning by making it easier to coordinate personal selling, transportation, storage, and other forms of promotion. Second, it promotes better customer relations because salespeople will be more familiar with the accounts they service. Third, it is an effective way of making sure that each market is well covered. Fourth, it aids management in the evaluation and control of selling costs. And fifth, it helps in the evaluation of performance.[11]

The question of managing sales territories cannot be discussed meaningfully without saying something about quotas. *Sales quotas* represent specific sales goals assigned to each territory or sales unit over a

---

[10]For a complete discussion of establishing territories and quotas, see William J. Stanton and Richard H. Buskirk, *Management of the Sales Force,* 7th ed. (Homewood, Ill.: Richard D. Irwin, 1987).

[11]For additional discussion, consult Andris Zoltners and P. Sinha, "Sales Territory Alignment: A Review and Model," *Management Science,* November 1983, pp. 1237–56.

designated time period. Quotas are primarily a planning and control device, because they provide management with measurable, quantitative standards of performance. The most common method of establishing quotas for territories is to relate sales to forecasted sales potential. For example, if the Ajax Drug Company's territory M has an estimated industry sales potential for a particular product of $400,000 for the year, the quota might be set at 25 percent of that potential, or $100,000. The 25 percent figure represents the market share Ajax estimates to be a reasonable target. This $100,000 quota may represent an increase of $20,000 in sales over last year (assuming constant prices) that is expected from new business.

In establishing sales quotas for its individual territories or sales personnel, management needs to take into account three key factors. First, all territories will not have equal potential and, therefore, compensation must be adjusted accordingly. Second, all salespeople will not have equal ability, and assignments may have to be made accordingly. Third, the sales task in each territory may differ from time period to time period. For instance, the nature of some territories may require that salespeople spend more time seeking new accounts, rather than servicing established accounts, especially in the case of so-called new territories. The point to be made here is that quotas can vary, not only by territory but also by assigned tasks. The effective sales manager should assign quotas not only for dollar sales but also for each major selling function. Table 9–1 is an example of how this is done for the

---

TABLE 9–1   Ajax Drug Company Sales Activity Evaluation

Territory: M
Salesperson: Smith

Functions	*(1)* *Quota*	*(2)* *Actual*	*(3)* *Percent* *(2 ÷ 1)*	*(4)* *Weight*	*(5)* *Score* *(3 × 4)*
Sales volume:					
A. Old business	$380,000	$300,000	79%	0.7	55.7
B. New business	$ 20,000	$ 20,000	100	0.5	50.0
Calls on prospects:					
A. Doctors	20	15	75	0.2	15.0
B. Druggists	80	60	75	0.2	15.0
C. Wholesalers	15	15	100	0.2	20.0
D. Hospitals	10	10	100	0.2	20.0
				2.0	175.7

Performance Index = 175.7

Ajax Drug Company, where each activity is assigned a quota and a weight reflecting its relative importance.

Analyzing Expenses.   Sales forecasts should include a sales expense budget. In some companies sales expense budgets are developed from the bottom up. Each territorial or district manager submits estimates of expenses and forecasted sales quotas. These estimates are usually prepared for a period of a year and then broken down into quarters and months. The chief sales executive then reviews the budget requests from the field offices and from staff departments. Expenses may be classified as fixed, semivariable or variable, and direct or indirect. Certain items, such as rent or administrative salaries, are fixed. In field offices, employee compensation is the principal expense, and it may be fixed or semivariable, depending on the plan. Other items, such as travel, samples, or other promotional material, are variable in nature. Some expenses are directly traceable to the sale of specific products, such as samples or displays, while other expenses are indirect, as in the case of administrative salaries and rent. Sales commissions and shipping expenses tend to vary in direct proportion to sales, while travel expense and entertainment may not be tied to sales volume in any direct proportion.

It should be understood that selling costs are budgeted much in the same way as manufacturing costs. Selling costs are usually broken down by product lines, sales region, customers, salespersons, or some other unit. Proper budgeting requires a reasonable cost accounting system. From a budgeting standpoint, the firm should use its accounting system to analyze marketing costs as a means of control.

Motivating and Compensating Performance.   The sales manager's personnel function includes more than motivating and compensating the sales force; but from the vantage point of sales force productivity, these two tasks are of paramount importance. Operationally, it means that the sales manager is responsible for keeping the morale and efforts of the sales force at high levels through supervision and motivation.

These closely related tasks are accomplished through interaction with the sales force, (1) by contacts with supervisors, managers, or sales executives individually or in group meetings; (2) through communication by letters or telephone; and (3) through incentive schemes by which greater opportunity for earnings (as in sales contests) or job promotion may be achieved.

Compensation is a principal method by which firms motivate and retain their sales forces. Devising a compensation plan for a company is a technical matter, but there are some general guidelines in formulating such a plan. First, a firm should be mindful of any modifications necessary to meet its particular needs when adopting another

HIGHLIGHT 9–4
Effort- and Results-Oriented Measures for Evaluating Salespersons

Effort-Oriented Measures	*Results-Oriented Measures*
1. Number of sales calls made	1. Sales volume (total or by product or model)
2. Number of complaints handled	2. Sales volume as a percentage of quota
3. Number of checks on reseller stocks	3. Sales profitability (dollar gross margin or contribution)
4. Uncontrollable lost job time	4. Number of new accounts
5. Number of inquiries followed up	5. Number of stockouts
6. Number of demonstrations completed	6. Number of distributors participating in programs
	7. Number of lost accounts
	8. Percentage volume increase in key accounts
	9. Number of customer complaints
	10. Distributor sales-inventory ratios

Source: Joseph P. Guiltinan and Gordon Paul, *Marketing Management,* 2nd ed. (New York: McGraw-Hill, 1988), p. 341.

company's compensation plan. Second, the plan should make sense (i.e., should have a logical rationale) to both management and the sales force. Third, the plan should not be so overly complex that it cannot be understood by the average salesperson. Fourth, as suggested in the section on quotas, the plan should be fair and equitable to avoid penalizing the sales force because of factors beyond their control; conversely, the plan should ensure rewards for performance in proportion to results. Fifth, the plan should allow the sales force to earn salaries that permit them to maintain an acceptable standard of living. Finally, the plan should attempt to minimize attrition by giving the sales force some incentive, such as a vested retirement plan, for staying with the company.

There are two basic types of compensation: salary and commission. Salary usually refers to a specific amount of monetary compensation at an agreed rate for definite time periods. Commission is usually monetary compensation provided for each unit of sales and expressed as a percentage of sales. The base on which commissions are computed

---

HIGHLIGHT 9–5
Characteristics Related to Sales Performance in Different Types of Sales Jobs

Type of Sales Job	Characteristics That Are Relatively Important	Characteristics That Are Relatively Less Important
Trade selling	Age, maturity, empathy, knowledge of customer needs and business methods	Aggressiveness, technical ability, product knowledge, persuasiveness
Missionary selling	Youth, high energy and stamina, verbal skill, persuasiveness	Empathy, knowledge of customers, maturity, previous sales experience
Technical selling	Education, product and customer knowledge—usually gained through training, intelligence	Empathy, persuasiveness, aggressiveness, age
New business selling	Experience, age and maturity, aggressiveness, persuasiveness, persistence	Customer knowledge, product knowledge, education, empathy

Source: Gilbert A. Churchill, Jr., Neil M. Ford, and Orville C. Walker, *Sales Force Management: Planning Implementation and Control,* 3rd ed. (Homewood, Ill.: Richard D. Irwin, 1990), p. 404.

---

may be: volume of sales in units of product, gross sales in dollars, net sales after returns, sales volume in excess of a quota, and net profits. Very often, several compensation approaches are combined. For example, a salesperson might be paid a base salary, a commission on sales exceeding a volume figure, and a percentage share of the company's profits for that year.

Some other important elements of sales compensation plans are:

1. *Drawing account.* Periodic money advances at an agreed rate. Repayment is deducted from total earnings computed on a commission or other basis, or is repaid from other assets of the salesperson if earnings are insufficient to cover the advance (except in the case of a guaranteed drawing account).
2. *Special payments for sales operations.* Payments in the nature of piece rates on operations, rather than commissions on results. Flat

HIGHLIGHT 9–6
The Most Widely Used Sales-Force Compensation Methods

Method	How Often Used	Most Useful	Advantages	Disadvantages
Straight salary	30.3%	When compensating new salespersons; when firm moves into new sales territories that require developmental work; when salespersons need to perform many non-selling activities.	Provides salesperson with maximum amount of security; gives sales manager large amount of control over salespersons; easy to administer; yields more predictable selling expenses.	Provides no incentive; necessitates closer supervision of salespersons' activities; during sales declines, selling expenses remain at same level.
Straight commission	20.8	When highly aggressive selling is required; when nonselling tasks are minimized; when company cannot closely control sales-force activities.	Provides maximum amount of incentive; by increasing commission rate, sales managers can encourage salespersons to sell certain items; selling expenses relate directly to sales resources.	Salespersons have little financial security; sales manager has minimum control over sales force; may cause salespeople to provide inadequate service to smaller accounts; selling costs less predictable.
Combination	48.9	When sales territories have relatively similar sales potentials; when firm wishes to provide incentive but still control sales-force activities.	Provides certain level of financial security; provides some incentive; selling expenses fluctuate with sales revenue.	Selling expenses less predictable; may be difficult to administer.

Source: Adapted from John P. Steinbrink, "How to Pay Your Sales Force," *Harvard Business Review,* July–August 1978, p. 113.

payments per call or payments per new customer secured can be included in this category. To the extent that these payments are estimated by size of customers' purchases, they resemble commissions and are sometimes so labeled. Other bases for special payments are demonstrations, putting up counter or window displays, and special promotional work.

3. *Bonus payments.* Usually these are lump-sum payments, over and above contractual earnings, for extra effort or merit or for results beyond normal expectation.

4. *Special prizes.* Monetary amounts or valuable merchandise to reward the winners of sales contests and other competitions. Practices vary from firms that never use this device to firm's where there is continuous use and almost every member of the sales force expects to get some compensation from this source during the year, in which case prizes amount to a form of incentive payment.

5. *Profit sharing.* A share of the profits of the business as a whole, figured on the basis of earnings, retail sales, profits in an area, or other factors. Sometimes profit sharing is intended to build up a retirement fund.

6. *Expense allowances.* Provision for travel and other business expenses, which becomes an important part of any compensation plan. No agreement for outside sales work is complete without an understanding about whether the company or the salesperson is to pay travel and other business expenses incurred in connection with work; and, if the company is responsible, just what the arrangements should be. Automobile, hotel, entertainment, and many other items of expense may be included in the agreement.

7. *Maximum earnings or cutoff point.* A limitation on earnings. This figure may be employed for limiting maximum earnings when it is impossible to predict the range of earnings under commission or other types of incentive plans.

8. *Fringe benefits.* Pensions, group insurance, health insurance, and so forth. These are commonly given to sales forces as a matter of policy and become a definite part of the compensation plan.[12]

CONCLUSION

This chapter has attempted to outline and explain the personal selling aspect of the promotion mix. Before ending the discussion, a brief comment might be made concerning the overall value of personal selling.

---

[12]For an excellent review of recruiting, selecting, and motivating sales personnel, see James M. Comer and Alan J. Dubinsky, *Managing the Successful Sales Force* (Lexington, Mass.: D. C. Heath, 1985).

Personal selling in a growing economy must always play an important part in the marketing of goods and services. As long as production continues to expand through the development of new and highly technical products, personal selling will occupy a key role in our marketing system.

ADDITIONAL READINGS

Bellizzi, Joseph A., and Robert E. Hite. "Supervising Unethical Salesforce Behavior." *Journal of Marketing,* April 1989, pp. 36–47.

Brooks, William T. *High Impact Selling: Strategies for Successful Selling.* Engelwood Cliffs, N.J.: Prentice Hall, 1988.

Cron, William L. "Industrial Salesperson Development: A Career Stages Perspective." *Journal of Marketing,* Fall 1984, pp. 41–52.

Dubinsky, Alan J., and Thomas N. Ingram. "Salespeople View Buyer Behavior." *Journal of Personnel Selling and Sales Management,* Fall 1982, pp. 6–11.

Honeycutt, Earl D., and Thomas H. Stevenson. "Evaluating Sales Training Programs." *Industrial Marketing Management* 18 (1989), pp. 215–22.

Ingram, Thomas N., and Danny N. Belenger. "Personal and Organizational Variables: Their Relative Effect on Reward Valences of Industrial Salespeople." *Journal of Marketing Research,* May 1983, pp. 198–205.

Skinner, Steven J.; Alan J. Dubinsky; and James H. Donnelly, Jr. "The Use of Social Bases of Power in Retail Sales." *Journal of Personnel Selling and Sales Management,* November 1984, pp. 48–56.

Chapter 10

Distribution Strategy

Channel of distribution decisions involve numerous interrelated variables that must be integrated into the total marketing mix. Because of the time and money required to set up an efficient channel, and since channels are often hard to change once they are set up, these decisions are critical to the success of the firm.

This chapter is concerned with the development and management of channels of distribution and the process of goods distribution in an extremely complex, highly productive, and specialized economy. It should be noted at the outset that channels of distribution provide the ultimate consumer or industrial user with time, place, and possession utility. Thus, an efficient channel is one that delivers the product when and where it is wanted at a minimum total cost.

THE NEED FOR MARKETING INTERMEDIARIES

A channel of distribution is the combination of institutions through which a seller markets products to the user or ultimate consumer. The need for other institutions or intermediaries in the delivery of goods is sometimes questioned, particularly since the profits they make are viewed as adding to the cost of the product. However, this reasoning is generally falacious, since marketing intermediaries can perform functions *more cheaply and more efficiently* than the producer can. This notion of efficiency is critical when the characteristics of our economy are considered.

For example, our economy is characterized by heterogeneity in terms of both supply and demand. In terms of numbers alone, there are nearly 6 million establishments comprising the supply segment of

> **HIGHLIGHT 10–1**
> **What Intermediaries Add to the Cost of a Compact Disc**
>
> | | |
> |---|---|
> | Production of a disc | .74 |
> | Packaging (tuck box, etc.) | 1.72 |
> | American Federation of Musicians dues | .27 |
> | Songwriters royalties | .39 |
> | Recording artist's royalties | 1.01 |
> | Freight to wholesaler | .36 |
> | Manufacturer's advertising and selling expenses | 1.74 |
> | Manufacturer's administrative expenses | 1.76 |
> | Manufacturer's cost | $7.99 |
> | Manufacturer's profit margin | 1.10 |
> | Manufacturer's price to wholesaler | $9.09 |
> | Freight to retailer | .38 |
> | Wholesaler's advertising, selling, and administrative expense | .47 |
> | Wholesaler's cost | $9.94 |
> | Wholesaler's profit margin | .80 |
> | Wholesaler's price to retailer | $10.74 $6.90 |
> | Retailer's advertising, selling, and administrative expenses | 1.76 |
> | Retailer's profit margin | 3.49 |
> | Retailer's price to consumer | $15.99 |
>
> *Source:* From *Principles of Marketing*, 3rd. ed., p. 339, by Thomas C. Kinnear and Kenneth L. Bernhardt. Copyright © 1990, 1986 by Scott, Foresman and Company. Reprinted by permission of Harper Collins, Publishers.

our economy, and there are close to 90 million households making up the demand side. Clearly, if each of these units had to deal on a one-to-one basis to obtain needed goods and services, and there were no intermediaries to collect and disperse assortments of goods, the system would be totally inefficient. Thus, the primary role of intermediaries is to bring supply and demand together in an efficient and orderly fashion.

CLASSIFICATION OF MARKETING INTERMEDIARIES AND FUNCTIONS

There are many types of marketing intermediaries, many of which are so specialized by function and industry that they need not be discussed here. Figure 10–1 presents the major types of marketing intermediaries common to many industries. Although there is some overlap in this classification, these categories are based on the marketing functions performed. That is, various intermediaries perform different

---

FIGURE 10–1   Major Types of Marketing Intermediaries

Middleman.   An independent business concern that operates as a link between producers and ultimate consumers or industrial buyers.

Merchant middleman.   An intermediary who buys the goods outright and necessarily takes title to them.

Agent.   A business unit that negotiates purchases, sales, or both but does not take title to the goods in which it deals.

Wholesaler.   Merchant establishment operated by a concern that is primarily engaged in buying, taking title to, usually storing, and physically handling goods in large quantities, and reselling the goods (usually in smaller quantities) to retailers or to industrial or business users.

Retailer.   Merchant middleman who is engaged primarily in selling to ultimate consumers.

Broker.   An intermediary who serves as a go-between for the buyer or seller; assumes no title risks, does not usually have physical custody of products, and is not looked upon as a permanent representative of either the buyer or the seller.

Sales agent.   An independent channel member, either an individual or company, who is responsible for the sale of a firm's products or services but does not take title to the goods sold.

Distributor.   A wholesale intermediary, especially in lines where selective or exclusive distribution is common at the wholesale level in which the manufacturer expects strong promotional support; often a synonym for wholesaler.

Jobber.   An intermediary who buys from manufacturers and sells to retailers; a wholesaler.

Facilitating agent.   A business firm that assists in the performance of distribution tasks other than buying, selling, and transferring title (i.e., transportation companies, warehouses, etc.)

Source: Based on Peter D. Bennett, ed., *Dictionary of Marketing Terms* (Chicago: American Marketing Association, 1988).

marketing functions and to different degrees. Figure 10–2 is a listing of the more common marketing functions performed in the channel.

It should be remembered that whether or not a manufacturer utilizes intermediaries to perform these functions, the functions have to be performed by someone. In other words, the managerial question is not whether to perform the functions but who will perform them and to what degree.

CHANNELS OF DISTRIBUTION

As previously noted, a channel of distribution is the combination of institutions through which a seller markets products to the user or ultimate consumer. Some of these links assume the risks of ownership;

FIGURE 10–2   Marketing Functions Performed in Channels of
Distribution

Buying.   Purchasing products from sellers for use or for resale.

Selling.   Promoting the sale of products to ultimate consumers or industrial
buyers.

Sorting.   Function performed by intermediaries in order to bridge the dis-
crepancy between the assortment of goods and services generated by the
producer and the assortment demanded by the consumer. This function includes four distinct processes: sorting out, accumulation, allocation, and
assorting.

Sorting out.   A sorting process that breaks down a heterogeneous supply
into separate stocks that are relatively homogeneous.

Accumulation.   A sorting process that brings similar stocks from a number
of sources together into a larger homogeneous supply.

Allocation.   A sorting process that consists of breaking a homogeneous supply down into smaller and smaller lots.

Assorting.   A sorting process that consists of building an assortment of
products for use in association with each other.

Concentration.   The process of bringing goods from various places together
in one place.

Financing.   Providing credit or funds to facilitate a transaction.

Storage.   Maintaining inventories and protecting products to provide better
customer service.

Grading.   Classifying products into different categories on the basis of quality.

Transportation.   Physically moving products from where they are made to
where they are purchased and used.

Risk-taking.   Taking on business risks involved in transporting and owning
products.

Marketing research.   Collecting information concerning such things as
market conditions, expected sales, consumer trends, and competitive
forces.

Source: Based on Peter D. Bennett, ed., *Dictionary of Marketing Terms* (Chicago: American
Marketing Association, 1988).

others do not. Some perform marketing functions; others perform nonmarketing or facilitating functions, such as transportation. The typical
channel of distribution patterns for consumer goods markets are shown
in Figure 10–3.

Some manufacturers use a direct channel, selling directly to the
ultimate consumer (e.g., Avon Cosmetics). In other cases, one or more
intermediaries may be used. For example, a manufacturer of paper
cartons may sell to retailers, or a manufacturer of small appliances
may sell to retailers under a private brand. The most common channel in the consumer market is the one in which the manufacturer
sells through wholesalers to retailers. For instance, a cold remedy

HIGHLIGHT 10–2
"Are Channels of Distribution What the Textbooks Say?"

The middleman is not a hired link in a chain forged by the manufacturer, but rather an independent market, the focus of a large group of customers for whom he buys. Subsequent to some market analysis of his own, he selects products and suppliers, thereby setting at least one link in the channel.

After some experimentation, he settles upon a method of operation, performing those functions he deems inescapable in the light of his own objectives, forming policies for himself wherever he has freedom to do so. Perhaps these methods and policies conform closely to those of a Census category of middleman, but perhaps they do not.

It is true that his choices are in many instances tentative proposals. He is subject to much influence from competitors, from aggressive suppliers, from inadequate finances and faulty information, as well as from habit. Nonetheless, many of his choices are independent.

As he grows and builds a following, he may find that his prestige in his market is greater than that of the suppliers whose goods he sells. In some instances his local strength is so great that a manufacturer is virtually unable to tap that market, except through him. In such a case the manufacturer can have no channel policy with respect to that market.

Source: Phillip McVey, "Are Channels of Distribution What the Textbooks Say?" *Journal of Marketing*, January 1960, pp. 61–65. This article can be considered a classic in the field of marketing.

FIGURE 10–3   Typical Channels of Distribution for Consumer Goods

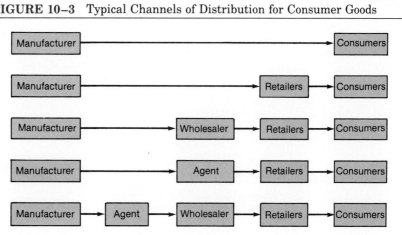

manufacturer may sell to drug wholesalers who, in turn, sell a vast array of drug products to various retail outlets. Small manufacturers may also use agents, since they do not have sufficient capital for their own sales forces. Agents are commonly used intermediaries in the jewelry industry. The final channel in Figure 10–3 is used primarily when small wholesalers and retailers are involved. Channels with one or more intermediaries are referred to as indirect channels.

In contrast to consumer products, the direct channel is often used in the distribution of industrial goods. The reason for this stems from the structure of most industrial markets, which often have relatively few but extremely large customers. Also, many industrial products, such as computers, need a great deal of presale and postsale service. Distributors are used in industrial markets when the number of buyers is large and the size of the buying firm is small. As in the consumer market, agents are used in industrial markets in cases where manufacturers do not wish to have their own sales forces. Such an arrangement may be used by small manufacturers or when the market is geographically dispersed. The final channel arrangement in Figure 10–4 may also be used by a small manufacturer or when the market consists of many small customers. Under such conditions, it may not be economical for sellers to have their own sales organization.

SELECTING CHANNELS OF DISTRIBUTION

General Considerations

Given the numerous types of channel intermediaries and functions that must be performed, the task of selecting and designing a channel of distribution may at first appear to be overwhelming. However, in

FIGURE 10–4   Typical Channels of Distribution for Industrial Goods

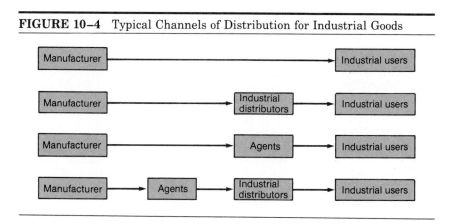

many industries, channels of distribution have developed over many years and have become somewhat traditional. In such cases, the producer may be limited to this type of channel to operate in the industry. This is not to say that a traditional channel is always the most efficient and that there are no opportunities for innovation, but the fact that such a channel is widely accepted in the industry suggests it is highly efficient. A primary constraint in these cases and in cases where no traditional channel exists is that of *availability* of the various types of middlemen. All too often in the early stages of channel design, executives map out elaborate channel networks only to find out later that no such independent intermediaries exist for the firm's product in selected geographic areas. Even if they do exist, they may not be willing to accept the seller's products. In general, there are six basic considerations in the initial development of channel strategy. These are outlined in Table 10–1.

TABLE 10–1 Considerations in Channel Planning

1. *Customer characteristics*
    a. Number
    b. Geographical dispersion
    c. Purchasing patterns
    d. Susceptibilities to different selling methods
2. *Product characteristics*
    a. Perishability
    b. Bulkiness
    c. Degree of standardization
    d. Installation and maintenance services required
    e. Unit value
3. *Intermediary characteristics*
    a. Availability
    b. Willingness to accept product or product line
    c. Strengths
    d. Weaknesses
4. *Competitive characteristics*
    a. Geographic proximity
    b. Proximity in outlet
5. *Company characteristics*
    a. Financial strength
    b. Product mix
    c. Past channel experience
    d. Present company marketing policies
6. *Environmental characteristics*
    a. Economic conditions
    b. Legal regulations and restrictions

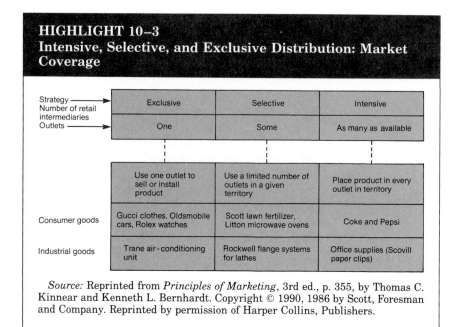

HIGHLIGHT 10–3
Intensive, Selective, and Exclusive Distribution: Market Coverage

Strategy — Number of retail intermediaries	Exclusive	Selective	Intensive
Outlets —	One	Some	As many as available
	Use one outlet to sell or install product	Use a limited number of outlets in a given territory	Place product in every outlet in territory
Consumer goods	Gucci clothes, Oldsmobile cars, Rolex watches	Scott lawn fertilizer, Litton microwave ovens	Coke and Pepsi
Industrial goods	Trane air-conditioning unit	Rockwell flange systems for lathes	Office supplies (Scovill paper clips)

Source: Reprinted from *Principles of Marketing*, 3rd ed., p. 355, by Thomas C. Kinnear and Kenneth L. Bernhardt. Copyright © 1990, 1986 by Scott, Foresman and Company. Reprinted by permission of Harper Collins, Publishers.

It should be noted that for a particular product any one of these characteristics may greatly influence choice of channels. To illustrate, highly perishable products generally require direct channels; or a firm with little financial strength may require middlemen to perform almost all of the marketing functions.

Specific Considerations

The above characteristics play an important part in framing the channel selection decision. Based on them, the choice of channels can be further refined in terms of (1) distribution coverage required; (2) degree of control desired; (3) total distribution cost; and (4) channel flexibility.

Distribution Coverage Required.   Because of the characteristics of the product, the environment needed to sell the product, and the needs and expectations of the potential buyer, products will vary in the intensity of distribution coverage they require. Distribution coverage can be viewed along a continuum ranging from intensive to selective to exclusive distribution.

Intensive Distribution.   Here the manufacturer attempts to gain exposure through as many wholesalers and retailers as possible. Most convenience goods require intensive distribution based on the characteristics of the product (low unit value) and the needs and expectations of the buyer (high frequency of purchase and convenience).

Selective Distribution. Here the manufacturer limits the use of intermediaries to the ones believed to be the best available. This may be based on the service organization available, the sales organization, or the reputation of the intermediary. Thus, appliances, home furnishings, and better clothing are usually distributed selectively. For appliances, the intermediary's service organization could be a key factor, while for better clothing and home furnishings, the intermediary's reputation would be an important consideration.

Exclusive Distribution. Here the manufacturer severely limits distribution, and intermediaries are provided exclusive rights within a particular territory. The characteristics of the product are a determining factor here. Where the product requires certain specialized selling effort and/or investment in unique facilities or large inventories, this arrangement is usually selected. Retail paint stores are an example of such a distribution arrangement.

Degree of Control Desired. In selecting channels of distribution, the seller must make decisions concerning the degree of control desired over the marketing of the firm's products. Some manufacturers prefer to keep as much control as possible over the policies surrounding their product. Ordinarily, the degree of control achieved by the seller is proportionate to the directness of the channel. One Eastern brewery, for instance, owns its own fleet of trucks and operates a wholly owned delivery system direct to grocery and liquor stores. Because its market is very concentrated geographically, with many small buyers, such a system is economically feasible. However, all other brewers in the area sell through wholesalers or distributors.

When more indirect channels are used, the manufacturer must surrender some control over the marketing of the firm's product. However, attempts are commonly made to maintain a degree of control through some other indirect means, such as sharing promotional expenditures, providing sales training, or other operational aids, such as accounting systems, inventory systems, or marketing research data on the dealer's trading area.[1]

Total Distribution Cost. The total distribution cost concept has developed out of the more general topic of systems theory. The concept

---

[1]For further discussion, see John Gaski, "The Theory of Power and Conflict in Channels of Distribution," *Journal of Marketing,* Summer 1984, pp. 9–29; Gul Butaney and Lawrence H. Wortzel, "Distributor Power versus Manufacturer Power: The Customer Role," *Journal of Marketing,* January 1988, pp. 52–63.

A franchise is a means by which a producer of products or services achieves a direct channel of distribution without wholly owning or managing the physical facilities in the market. In effect, the franchiser provides the franchisee with the franchiser's knowledge, manufacturing, and marketing techniques for a financial return.

INGREDIENTS OF A FRANCHISED BUSINESS

Six key ingredients should be included within a well-balanced franchise offered to a franchisee. These are given in order of importance:

- *Technical knowledge* in its practical form is supplied through an intensive course of study.
- *Managerial techniques* based on proven and time-tested programs are imparted to the franchisee on a continuing basis, even after the business has been started or taken over by the franchisee.
- *Commercial knowledge* involving prescribed methods of buying and selling is explained and codified. Most products to be obtained, processed, and sold to the franchisee are supplied by the franchiser.
- *Financial instruction* on managing funds and accounts is given to the franchisee during the indoctrination period.
- *Accounting controls* are set up by the franchiser for the franchisee.
- *Protective safeguards* are included in the intensive training of the franchisee for employees and customers, including the quality of the product, as well as the safeguards for assets through adequate insurance controls.

ELEMENTS OF AN IDEAL FRANCHISE PROGRAM

- *High gross margin.* In order for the franchisee to be able to afford a high franchise fee (which the franchiser needs), it is necessary to operate on a high gross margin percentage. This explains the widespread application of franchising in the food and service industries.
- *In-store value added.* Franchising works best in those product categories where the product is at least partially processed in the store. Such environments require constant on-site supervision—a chronic problem for company-owned stores using a hired manager. Owners simply are willing to work harder over longer hours.
- *Secret processes.* Concepts, formulas, or products that the franchisee can't duplicate without joining the franchise program.
- *Real estate profits.* The franchiser uses income from ownership of property as a significant revenue source.
- *Simplicity.* The most successful franchises have been those that operate on automatic pilot: All the key decisions have been thought through, and the owner merely implements the decisions.

Source: Partially adapted from Philip D. White and Albert D. Bates, "Franchising Will Remain Retailing Fixture, but Its Salad Days Have Long Since Gone," *Marketing News*, February 17, 1984, p. 14.

suggests that a channel of distribution should be viewed as a total system composed of interdependent subsystems, and that the objective of the system (channel) manager should be to optimize total system performance. In terms of distribution costs, it generally is assumed that the total system should be designed to minimize costs, other things being equal. The following is a representative list of the major distribution costs to be minimized.

1. Transportation
2. Order processing
3. Cost of lost business (an "opportunity" cost due to inability to meet customer demand)
4. Inventory carrying costs, including:
   a. Storage-space charges
   b. Cost of capital invested
   c. Taxes
   d. Insurance
   e. Obsolescence and deterioration
5. Packaging
6. Materials handling

The important qualification to the total cost concept is the statement, "other things being equal." The purpose of the total cost concept is to emphasize total system performance to avoid suboptimization. However, other important factors must be considered, not the least of which are level of customer service, sales, profits, and interface with the total marketing mix.

Channel Flexibility.   A final consideration relates to the ability of the manufacturer to adapt to changing conditions. To illustrate, in recent years much of the population has moved from inner cities to suburbs and thus make most of their purchases in shopping centers and malls. If a manufacturer had long-term, exclusive dealership with retailers in the inner city, the ability to adapt to this population shift could have been severely limited. In general, the less certain the future seems to be, the less favorable are channel alternatives involving long commitments.

MANAGING A CHANNEL OF DISTRIBUTION

Once the seller has decided on the type of channel structure to use and selected the individual members, the entire coalition should operate as a total system. From a behavioral perspective, the system can be

---

HIGHLIGHT 10–5
Manufacturers and Intermediaries: A Perfect Working Relationship

THE PERFECT INTERMEDIARY
1. Has access to the market that the manufacturer wants to reach.
2. Carries adequate stocks of the manufacturer's products and a satisfactory assortment of other products.
3. Has an effective promotional program—advertising, personal selling, and product displays. Promotional demands placed on the manufacturer are in line with what the manufacturer intends to do.
4. Provides services to customers—credit, delivery, installation, and product repair—and honors the product warranty conditions.
5. Pays its bills on time and has capable management.

THE PERFECT MANUFACTURER
1. Provides a desirable assortment of products—well designed, properly priced, attractively packaged, and delivered on time and in adequate quantities.
2. Builds product demand for these products by advertising them.
3. Furnishes promotional assistance to its middlemen.
4. Provides managerial assistance for its middlemen.
5. Honors product warranties and provides repair and installation service.

THE PERFECT COMBINATION
1. Probably doesn't exist.

   Source: William J. Stanton and Charles Futrell, *Fundamentals of Marketing*, 8th ed. (New York: McGraw-Hill, 1987), p. 380.

---

viewed as a social system since each member interacts with the others, each member plays a role vis-à-vis the others, and each has certain expectations of the other.[2] Thus, the behavioral perspective views a channel of distribution as more than a series of markets or participants extending from production to consumption.

---

[2]F. Robert Dwyer and M. Ann Welsh, "Environmental Relationships of the Internal Political Economy of Marketing Channels," *Journal of Marketing Research,* November 1985, pp. 397–414; John F. Gaski and John R. Nevin, "The Differential Effects of Exercised and Unexercised Power Sources in a Marketing Channel," *Journal of Marketing Research,* May 1985, pp. 130–42; James C. Anderson and James A. Narus, "A Model of Distributor Firm and Manufacturing Firm Working Partnerships," *Journal of Marketing,* January 1990, pp. 42–58.

HIGHLIGHT 10–6
Pushing or Pulling through the Channel System

A producer has a special challenge with respect to channel systems: How to ensure that the product reaches the end of the channel. Intermediaries—especially retailers—don't have this problem, since they already control that end of the channel.

The two basic methods of recruiting middlemen are *pushing* and *pulling*.

Pushing a product through the channels means using normal promotion effort—personal selling and advertising—to help sell the whole marketing mix to possible channel members. This method is common, since these sales transactions are usually between rational, presumably profit-oriented buyers and sellers. The approach emphasizes the building of a channel—and securing the wholehearted cooperation of channel members. The producer, in effect, tries to develop a team that will work well together to get the product to the user.

By contrast, pulling means getting consumers to ask intermediaries for the product. This usually involves highly aggressive promotion to final consumers or users—perhaps using coupons or samples—and temporary bypassing of intermediaries. If the promotion works, the intermediaries are forced to carry the product to satisfy their customers.

Source: Adapted with permission from E. Jerome McCarthy and William D. Perreault, Jr., *Basic Marketing: A Management Approach,* 10th ed. (Homewood, Ill.: Richard D. Irwin, 1990), p. 288.

A Channel Leader

If a channel of distribution is viewed as a social system comprised of interacting firms with a common set of objectives, then integration among them seems desirable. This is because the channel, as a system, can be conceived as a competitive unit in and of itself; in other words, any success that the product has is determined largely by the effectiveness and efficiency with which human, material, and monetary resources have been mobilized throughout the entire interfirm network.

If the above view is taken, the question arises about who should exert primary leadership in the channel—that is, becomes the "channel captain" or "channel commander." There is little agreement about the answer. Some marketers believe the manufacturer or the owner of the brand name should be the channel captain. The argument here is that the manufacturer or brand name owner (1) has the most to lose if the system malfunctions or fails; (2) has the most technical expertise;

and (3) in many cases has greater resources than other channel members. Others believe the retailer should be the channel captain, since the retailer is the closest link to the consumer and, therefore, can judge better the consumer needs and wants. Still others argue the wholesaler should seek to gain channel control, or that the locus of control should be at the level where competition is greatest.

In some channels of distribution, one member may be large and powerful with respect to other members. It may be a manufacturer, wholesaler, or large retailer. Consider the power Sears, Roebuck has over a small supply manufacturing firm, since 90 percent of Sears products are under its own label. In such cases, the powerful member may assume leadership.

While the issue is certainly not clear, the tendency appears to lean toward channels controlled by the manufacturer, with a few notable exceptions. For example, for their own brands, Sears, Roebuck and K mart likely play the primary leadership role, while the manufacturer plays a subordinate role. In some cases where wholesalers have their own brands, the manufacturer and retailer probably assume a subordinate role. However, in many cases, manufacturers have absorbed functions previously performed by intermediaries and, thereby, obtained even greater channel control.

CONCLUSION

The purpose of this chapter has been to introduce the reader to the process of distribution of goods in an extremely complex, highly productive, and highly specialized economy. It is important that the reader understand the vital need in such an economy for marketing intermediaries to bring about exchanges between buyers and sellers in a reasonably efficient manner. If the reader appreciates this concept, the major objective of this chapter has been achieved. The chapter also examined the typical channels of distribution for both consumer goods and industrial goods, and the various types of marketing intermediaries available to a seller. Finally, two important aspects of channels of distribution were discussed: the selection and management of channels of distribution.

ADDITIONAL READINGS

Achrol, Ravi S., and Louis W. Stern. "Environmental Determinants of Decision-Making Uncertainty in Marketing Channels." *Journal of Marketing Research,* February 1988, pp. 36–50.

Corey, Raymond E.; Frank V. Cespedes; and Kasturi Rangan. *Going to Market.* Boston, Mass.: Harvard Business School Press, 1989.

Dwyer, Robert F., and Sejo Oh. "A Transaction Cost Perspective on Vertical Contractual Structure and Interchannel Competitive Strategies." *Journal of Marketing,* April 1988, pp. 21–34.

Frazier, Gary L.; James D. Gill; and Sudhir H. Kale. "Dealer Dependence Levels and Reciprocal Actions in a Channel of Distribution in a Developing Country." *Journal of Marketing,* January 1989, pp. 50–69.

Hardy, Kenneth G., and Allan J. McGrath. *Marketing Channel Management.* Glenview, Ill.: Scott, Foresman, 1988.

Justis, Robert, and Richard Judd. *Franchising.* Cincinatti, Ohio: South-Western Publishing, 1989.

Rosenbloom, Bert. *Marketing Channels: A Managerial View.* 3rd ed. Chicago: Dryden Press, 1987.

Stern, Louis W.; Adel I. El-Ansary; and James R. Brown. *Management in Marketing Channels.* Englewood Cliffs, N.J.: Prentice-Hall, 1989.

Stern, Louis W., and Adel I. El-Ansary, *Marketing Channels.* 3rd ed. Englewood Cliffs, N.J.: Prentice Hall, 1988.

| *Pricing Strategy*

One of the most important and complex decisions a firm has to make relates to pricing its products or services. If consumers or organizational buyers perceive a price to be too high, they may purchase competitive brands or substitute products, leading to a loss of sales and profits for the firm. If the price is too low, sales might increase, but profitability may suffer. Thus, pricing decisions must be given careful consideration when a firm is introducing a new product or planning a short- or long-term price change.

This chapter discusses demand, supply, and environmental influences that affect pricing decisions, and emphasizes that all three must be considered for effective pricing. However, as will be discussed in the chapter, many firms price their products without explicitly considering all of these influences.

DEMAND INFLUENCES ON PRICING DECISIONS

Demand influences on pricing decisions concern primarily the nature of the target market and expected reactions of consumers to a given price or change in price. The three primary considerations here are demographic factors, psychological factors, and price elasticity.

Demographic Factors. In the initial selection of the target market that a firm intends to serve, a number of demographic factors are usually considered. Demographic factors that are particularly important for pricing decisions include the following:

1. Number of potential buyers.
2. Location of potential buyers.

HIGHLIGHT 11–1
The Meaning of Price

Alternative Terms	What Is Given in Return
Price	Most physical merchandise
Tuition	College courses, education
Rent	A place to live or the use of equipment for a specific time period
Interest	Use of money
Fee	Professional services: for lawyers, doctors, consultants
Fare	Transportation: air, taxi, bus
Toll	Use of road or bridge, or long-distance phone rate
Salary	Work of managers
Wage	Work of hourly workers
Bribe	Illegal actions
Commission	Sales effort

Source: From *Principles of Marketing,* 3rd ed., p. 576, by Thomas C. Kinnear and Kenneth L. Bernhardt. Copyright © 1990, 1986 by Scott Foresman and Company. Reprinted by permission of Harper Collins, Publishers.

3. Position of potential buyers (resellers or final consumers).
4. Expected consumption rates of potential buyers.
5. Economic strength of potential buyers.

These factors help determine market potential and are useful for estimating expected sales at various price levels.

Psychological Factors.   Psychological factors related to pricing concern primarily how consumers will perceive various prices or price changes. For example, marketing managers should be concerned with such questions as:

1. Will potential buyers use price as an indicator of product quality?
2. Will potential buyers be favorably attracted by odd pricing?
3. Will potential buyers perceive the price as too high relative to the service the product gives them?
4. Are potential buyers prestige oriented and therefore willing to pay higher prices to fulfill this need?
5. How much will potential buyers be willing to pay for the product?

While psychological factors have a significant effect on the success of a pricing strategy and ultimately on marketing strategy, answers to the above questions may require considerable marketing research. In fact, a review of buyers' subjective perceptions of price concluded that very little is known about how price affects buyers' perceptions of alternative purchase offers and how these perceptions affect purchase response.[1] However, some tentative generalizations about how buyers perceive price have been formulated. For example, research has found that persons who choose high-priced items usually perceive large quality variations within product categories and see the consequences of a poor choice as being undesirable. They believe that quality is related to price and see themselves as good judges of product quality. In general, the reverse is true for persons who select low-priced items in the same product categories. Thus, although information on psychological factors involved in purchasing may be difficult to obtain, marketing managers must at least consider the effects of such factors on their desired target market and marketing strategy.[2]

Price Elasticity.   Both demographic and psychological factors affect price elasticity. Price elasticity is a measure of consumers' price sensitivity, which is estimated by dividing relative changes in the quantity sold by the relative changes in price:

$$e = \frac{\Delta Q / Q}{\Delta P / P}$$

Although difficult to measure, there are two basic methods commonly used to estimate price elasticity. First, price elasticity can be estimated from historical data or from price/quantity data across different sales districts. Second, price elasticity can be estimated by sampling a group of subjects from the target market and polling them concerning various price/quantity relationships. Although both of these approaches provide estimates of price elasticity, the former approach is limited to the consideration of price changes, while the latter approach is often expensive and there is some question as to the validity of subjects' responses. However, even a crude estimate of price elasticity is a useful input to pricing decisions.[3]

---

[1]Kent B. Monroe, "Buyers' Subjective Perceptions of Price," *Journal of Marketing Research,* February 1973, pp. 70–80; also see Donald R. Lichtenstein and Scot Burton, "The Relationship between Perceived and Objective Price-Quality," *Journal of Marketing Research,* November 1989, pp. 429–43.

[2]For a summary of research concerning the effects of price and several other marketing variables on perceived product quality, see Akshay R. Rao and Kent B. Monroe, "The Effect of Price, Brand Name, and Store Name on Buyers' Perceptions of Product Quality: An Integrative Review," *Journal of Marketing Research,* August 1989, pp. 351–57.

[3]For additional discussion of price elasticity, see Philip Kotler, *Marketing Management: Analysis, Planning and Control,* 6th ed. (Englewood Cliffs, N.J.: Prentice Hall, 1988), pp. 499–501.

HIGHLIGHT 11–2
Some Potential Pricing Objectives

1. Target return on investment
2. Target market share
3. Maximum long-run profits
4. Maximum short-run profits
5. Growth
6. Stabilize market
7. Desensitize customers to price
8. Maintain price-leadership arrangement
9. Discourage entrants
10. Speed exit of marginal firms

SUPPLY INFLUENCES ON PRICING DECISIONS

For the purpose of this text, supply influences on pricing decisions can be discussed in terms of three basic factors. These factors relate to the objectives, costs, and nature of the product.

Pricing Objectives

Pricing objectives should be derived from overall marketing objectives, which in turn should be derived from corporate objectives. Since it is traditionally assumed that business firms operate to maximize profits in the long run, it is often thought that the basic pricing objective is solely concerned with long-run profits. However, the profit maximization norm does not provide the operating marketing manager with a single, unequivocal guideline for selecting prices. In addition, the marketing manager does not have perfect cost, revenue, and market information to be able to evaluate whether or not this objective is being reached. In practice, then, many other objectives are employed as guidelines for pricing decisions. In some cases, these objectives may be considered as operational approaches to achieve long-run profit maximization.

Research has found that the most common pricing objectives are (1) pricing to achieve a target return on investment; (2) stabilization of price and margin; (3) pricing to achieve a target market share; and (4) pricing to meet or prevent competition.

> ## HIGHLIGHT 11–3
> ## Basic Break-Even Formulas
>
> The following formulas are used to calculate break-even points in units
> and in dollars:
>
> $$BEP_{(in\ units)} = \frac{FC}{(SP - VC)}$$
>
> $$BEP_{(in\ dollars)} = \frac{FC}{1 - (VC/SP)}$$
>
> where
>
> FC = Fixed cost
> VC = Variable cost
> SP = Selling price
>
> If, as is generally the case, a firm wants to know how many units or
> sales dollars are necessary to generate a given amount of profit, profit
> (P) is simply added to fixed costs in the above formulas. In addition, if
> the firm has estimates of expected sales and fixed and variable costs, the
> selling price can be solved for. (A more detailed discussion of break-even
> analysis is provided in Section 3 of this book.)

Cost Considerations in Pricing

The price of a product usually must cover costs of production, promotion, and distribution, plus a profit for the offering to be of value to
the firm. In addition, when products are priced on the basis of costs
plus a fair profit, there is an implicit assumption that this sum represents the economic value of the product in the marketplace.

Cost-oriented pricing is the most common approach in practice, and
there are at least three basic variations: *markup pricing, cost-plus
pricing,* and *rate-of-return pricing.* Markup pricing is commonly used
in retailing, where a percentage is added to the retailer's invoice price
to determine the final selling price. Closely related to markup pricing
is cost-plus pricing, where the costs of producing a product or completing a project are totalled and a profit amount or percentage is added
on. Cost-plus pricing is most often used to describe the pricing of jobs
that are nonroutine and difficult to "cost" in advance, such as construction and military weapon development.

Rate-of-return or *target pricing* is commonly used by manufacturers.
In this method, price is determined by adding a desired rate of return
on investment to total costs. Generally, a break-even analysis is performed for expected production and sales levels and a rate of return

is added on. For example, suppose a firm estimated production and sales to be 75,000 units at a total cost of $300,000. If the firm desired a before-tax return of 20 percent, the selling price would be $(300,000 + 0.20 \times 300,000) \div 75,000 = \$4.80$.

Cost-oriented approaches to pricing have the advantage of simplicity, and many practitioners believe that they generally yield a good price decision. However, such approaches have been criticized for two basic reasons. First, cost approaches give little or no consideration to demand factors. For example, the price determined by markup or cost-plus methods has no necessary relationship to what people will be willing to pay for the product. In the case of rate-of-return pricing, little emphasis is placed on estimating sales volume. Even if it were, rate-of-return pricing involves circular reasoning, since unit cost depends on sales volume but sales volume depends on selling price. Second, cost approaches fail to reflect competition adequately. Only in industries where all firms use this approach and have similar costs and markups can this approach yield similar prices and minimize price competition. Thus, in many industries, cost-oriented pricing could lead to severe price competition, which could eliminate smaller firms. Therefore, although costs are a highly important consideration in price decisions, numerous other factors need to be examined.

Product Consideration in Pricing

Although numerous product characteristics can affect pricing, three of the most important are (1) perishability, (2) distinctiveness, and (3) stage in the product life cycle.

Perishability.   Goods that are very perishable in a physical sense must be priced to promote sales without costly delays. Foodstuffs and certain types of raw materials tend to be in this category. Products can be considered perishable in two other senses. High fashion, fad, and seasonal products are perishable not in the sense that the product deteriorates but in the sense that demand for the product is confined to a specific time period. Perishability also relates to consumption rate, which means that some products are consumed very slowly, as in the case of consumer durables. Two important pricing considerations here are that (1) such goods tend to be expensive because large amounts of service are purchased at one time; and (2) the consumer has a certain amount of discretionary time available in making replacement purchase decisions.

Distinctiveness.   Products can be classified in terms of how distinctive they are. Homogeneous goods are perfect substitutes for each other, as in the case of bulk wheat or whole milk, while most manufactured goods can be differentiated on the basis of certain features, such as package, trademark, engineering design, and chemical features. Thus, few consumer goods are perfectly homogeneous, and one of the primary marketing objectives of any firm is to make its product distinctive in the minds of buyers. Large sums of money are often invested to accomplish this task, and one of the payoffs for such investments is the seller's ability to charge higher prices for distinctive products.

Life Cycle.   The stage of the life cycle that a product is in can have important pricing implications. With regard to the life cycle, two approaches to pricing are skimming and penetration price policies. A *skimming* policy is one in which the seller charges a relatively high price on a new product. Generally, this policy is used when the firm has a temporary monopoly and in cases where demand for the product is price inelastic. In later stages of the life cycle, as competition moves in and other market factors change, the price may then be lowered. Digital watches and calculators are examples of this. A *penetration* policy is one in which the seller charges a relatively low price on a new product. Generally, this policy is used when the firm expects competition to move in rapidly and where demand for the product is, at least in the short run, price elastic. This policy is also used to obtain large economies of scale and as a major instrument for rapid creation of a mass market. A low price and profit margin may also discourage competition. In later stages of the life cycle, the price may have to be altered to meet changes in the market.

ENVIRONMENTAL INFLUENCES ON PRICING DECISIONS

Environmental influences on pricing include variables that are uncontrollable by the marketing manager. Two of the most important of these variables are competition and government regulation.

Competition

In setting or changing prices, the firm must consider its competition and how competition will react to the price of the product. Initially, consideration must be given to such factors as:

1. Number of competitors
2. Size of competitors
3. Location of competitors
4. Conditions of entry into the industry

5. Degree of vertical integration of competitors
6. Number of products sold by competitors
7. Cost structure of competitors
8. Historical reaction of competitors to price changes

These factors help determine whether the firm's selling price should be at, below, or above competition. Pricing a product at competition (i.e., the average price charged by the industry) is called "going rate pricing" and is popular for homogeneous products, since this approach represents the collective wisdom of the industry and is not disruptive of industry harmony.[4] An example of pricing below competition can be found in sealed-bid pricing, where the firm is bidding directly against competition for project contracts. Although cost and profits are initially calculated, the firm attempts to bid below competitors to obtain the job contract. A firm may price above competition because it has a superior product or because the firm is the price leader in the industry.

Government Regulations

Prices of certain goods and services are regulated by state and federal governments. Public utilities are examples of state regulation of prices. However, for most marketing managers, federal laws that make certain pricing practices illegal are of primary consideration in pricing decisions. The list below is a summary of some of the more important legal constraints on pricing. Of course, since most marketing managers are not trained as lawyers, they usually seek legal counsel when developing pricing strategies to ensure conformity to state and federal legislation.

1. Price-fixing is illegal per se. Sellers must not make any agreements with (*a*) competitors, or (*b*) distributors concerning the final price of the goods. The Sherman Antitrust Act is the primary device used to outlaw horizontal price fixing. Section 5 of the Federal Trade Commission Act has been used to outlaw price fixing as an "unfair" business practice.
2. Deceptive pricing practices are outlawed under Section 5 of the Federal Trade Commission Act. An example of deceptive pricing would be to mark merchandise with an exceptionally high price and then claim that the lower selling price actually used represents a legitimate price reduction.
3. Price discrimination that lessens competition or is deemed injurious to it is outlawed by the Robinson-Patman Act (which amends Section 2 of the Clayton Act). Price discrimination is not illegal per se, but

---

[4]Kotler, *Marketing Management,* p. 510.

sellers cannot charge competing buyers different prices for essentially the same products if the effect of such sales is injurious to competition. Price differentials can be legally justified on certain grounds, especially if the price differences reflect cost differences. This is particularly true of quantity discounts.

4. Promotional pricing—such as cooperative advertising—and price deals are not illegal per se; but if a seller grants advertising allowances, merchandising service, free goods, or special promotional discounts to customers, it must do so on proportionately equal terms. Sections 2(d) and 2(e) of the Robinson-Patman Act are designed to regulate such practices so that price reductions cannot be granted to some customers under the guise of promotional allowances.[5]

A GENERAL PRICING DECISION MODEL

From what has been discussed thus far, it should be clear that effective pricing decisions involve the consideration of many factors and, depending on the situation, any of these factors can be the primary consideration in setting price. In addition, it is difficult to formulate an exact sequencing of when each factor should be considered. However, several general pricing decision models have been advanced with the clearly stated warning that all pricing decisions will not fit the framework. Below is one such model, which views pricing decisions as a nine-step sequence.

1. *Define market targets.* All marketing decision making should begin with a definition of segmentation strategy and the identification of potential customers.
2. *Estimate market potential.* The maximum size of the available market determines what is possible and helps define competitive opportunities.
3. *Develop product positioning.* The brand image and the desired niche in the competitive marketplace provide important constraints on the pricing decision as the firm attempts to obtain a unique competitive advantage by differentiating its product offering from that of competitors.
4. *Design the marketing mix.* Design of the marketing mix defines the role to be played by pricing in relation to and in support of other marketing variables, especially distribution and promotional policies.

---

[5]For further discussion of legal issues involved in pricing, see Louis W. Stern and Thomas L. Eovaldi, *Legal Aspects of Marketing Strategy* (Englewood Cliffs, N.J.: Prentice Hall, 1984), chap. 5.

HIGHLIGHT 11–4
Some Short-Term Price Reduction Tactics

1. Cents-off deals: "Package price is 20¢ off."
2. Special offers: "Buy one, get one free"; "Buy three tires and get the fourth free."
3. Coupons: Store or manufacturer coupons in newspapers, magazines, flyers, and packages.
4. Rebates: Mail in proof-of-purchase seals for cash or merchandise.
5. Increase quantity for same price: "Two extra ounces of coffee free."
6. Free installation or service for a limited time period.
7. Reduce or eliminate interest charges for a limited time: "90 days same as cash."
8. Special sales: "25 percent off all merchandise marked with a red tag."

Source: J. Paul Peter and Jerry C. Olson, *Consumer Behavior and Marketing Strategy,* 2nd ed. (Homewood, Ill.: Richard D. Irwin, 1990), p. 500.

---

5. *Estimate price elasticity of demand.* The sensitivity of the level of demand to differences in price can be estimated either from past experience or through market tests.
6. *Estimate all relevant costs.* While straight cost-plus pricing is to be avoided because it is insensitive to demand, pricing decisions must take into account necessary plant investment, investment in R&D, and investment in market development, as well as variable costs of production and marketing.
7. *Analyze environmental factors.* Pricing decisions are further constrained by industry practices, likely competitive response to alternative pricing strategies, and legal requirements.
8. *Set pricing objectives.* Pricing decisions must be guided by a clear statement of objectives that recognizes environmental constraints and defines the role of pricing in the marketing strategy while at the same time relating pricing to the firm's financial objectives.
9. *Develop the price structure.* The price structure for a given product can now be determined and will define selling prices for the product (perhaps in a variety of styles and sizes) and the discounts from list price to be offered to various kinds of intermediaries and various types of buyers.[6]

---

[6]Frederick E. Webster, *Marketing for Managers* (New York: Harper & Row, 1974), pp. 178–79; also see Thomas T. Nagle, *The Strategy and Tactics of Pricing* (Englewood Cliffs, N.J.: Prentice Hall, 1987); Kent B. Monroe, *Pricing: Making Profitable Decisions,* 2nd ed. (New York: McGraw-Hill), 1990.

While all pricing decisions cannot be made strictly on the basis of this model, such an approach has three advantages for the marketing manager. First, it breaks the pricing decision into nine manageable steps. Second, it recognizes that pricing decisions must be fully integrated into overall marketing strategy. Third, it aids the decision maker by recognizing the importance of both qualitative and quantitative factors in pricing decisions.

CONCLUSION

Pricing decisions that integrate the firm's costs with marketing strategy, business conditions, competition, consumer demand, product variables, channels of distribution, and general resources can determine the success or failure of a business. This places a very heavy burden on the price maker. Modern-day marketing managers cannot ignore the complexity or the importance of price management. Pricing policies must be continually reviewed and must take into account the fact that the firm is a dynamic entity operating in a very competitive environment. There are many ways for money to flow out of a firm in the form of costs, but often the only way to bring revenues in is by the price-product mechanism.

ADDITIONAL READINGS

Curry, David J., and Peter C. Riesz. "Price and Price/Quality Relationships: A Longitudinal Analysis." *Journal of Marketing,* January 1988, pp. 36–51.

Herr, Paul M. "Priming Price: Prior Knowledge and Context Effects." *Journal of Consumer Research,* June 1989, pp. 67–75.

Lattin, James M., and Randolph E. Bucklin. "Reference Effects of Price and Promotion on Brand Choice Behavior." *Journal of Marketing Research,* August 1989, pp. 299–310.

Lichtenstein, Donald R.; Peter H. Bloch; and William C. Black. "Correlates of Price Acceptability." *Journal of Consumer Research,* September 1988, pp. 243–52.

Mobley, Mary F.; William O. Bearden; and Jesse E. Teel. "An Investigation of Individual Responses to Tensile Price Claims." *Journal of Consumer Research,* September 1988, pp. 273–79.

Monroe, Kent B. *Pricing: Making Profitable Decisions.* 2nd ed. New York: McGraw-Hill, 1990.

Nagle, Thomas T. *The Strategy and Tactics of Pricing.* Englewood Cliffs, N.J.: Prentice Hall, 1987.

Seymour, Daniel T., ed. *Pricing Decisions.* Chicago: Probus Publishing, 1989.

Tellis, Gerard J. "Beyond the Many Faces of Price: An Integration of Pricing Strategies." *Journal of Marketing,* October 1986, pp. 146–60.

Urbany, Joel E.; William O. Bearden; and Dan C. Weilbaker. "The Effect of Plausible and Exaggerated Reference Prices on Consumer Perceptions and Price Search." *Journal of Consumer Research,* June 1988, pp. 95–110.

Zeithaml, Valarie A. "Consumer Perceptions of Price, Quality, and Value: A Means-End Model and Synthesis of Evidence." *Journal of Marketing,* July 1988, pp. 2–22.

Marketing in Special Fields

Chapter 12

The Marketing of Services

For many years, the fastest growing segment of the American economy has not been the production of tangibles but the performance of services. Spending on services has increased to such an extent that today it captures about 50 cents of the consumer's dollar. Meanwhile, the service sector has also grown steadily in its contribution to the U.S. gross national product and now accounts for 71 percent of the country's GNP and 75 percent of its employment.[1] However, for the most part, the entire area of service marketing remains ill-defined.[2]

Unfortunately, many marketing textbooks still devote little, if any, attention to program development for the marketing of services. This omission is usually based on the assumption that the marketing of goods and the marketing of services are the same, and, therefore, the techniques discussed under goods apply as well to the marketing of services. Basically, this assumption is true. Whether selling products or services, the marketer must be concerned with developing a marketing strategy centered around the four controllable decision variables that comprise the marketing mix: the product (or service), the price, the distribution system, and promotion. In addition, the use of marketing research is as valuable to the marketer of services as it is to the marketer of goods.

---

[1] James Brian Quinn, Jordan J. Baruch, and Penny C. Paquette, "Exploiting the Manufacturing-Services Interface," *Sloan Management Review,* Summer 1988, pp. 45–56.

[2] Valerie A. Zeithaml, A. Parasuraman, and L. L. Berry, "Problems and Strategies in Services Marketing," *Journal of Marketing,* Spring 1985, pp. 33–46.

However, because services possess certain distinguishing character-istics, the task of determining the marketing mix ingredients for a service marketing strategy may present different and more difficult problems than may appear at first glance. The purpose of this chapter is threefold. First, the reader will become acquainted with the special characteristics of service marketing. Second, obstacles will be described which, in the past, impeded development of service marketing. Third, current trends and strategies of innovation in service marketing will be explored. Using this approach, the material in the other chapters of the book can be integrated into a better understanding of the mar-keting of services.

Before proceeding, some attention must be given to what the authors refer to when using the term *services*. Probably the most frustrating aspect of the available literature on services is that the definition of what constitutes a service remains unclear. The fact is that no common definition and boundaries have been developed to delimit the field of services. The American Marketing Association has defined services as follows:

> *Service products,* such as a bank loan or home security that are intangible, or at least substantially so. If totally intangible, they are exchanged directly from producer to user, cannot be transported or stored, and are almost instantly perishable. Service products are often difficult to identify, since they come into existence at the same time they are bought and consumed. They are comprised of intangible elements that are inseparable, they usu-ally involve customer participation in some important way, cannot be sold in the sense of ownership transfer, and have no title. Today, however, most products are partly tangible and partly intangible, and the dominant form is used to classify them as either goods or services (all are products). These common, hybrid forms, whatever they are called, may or may not have the attributes just given for totally intangible services.
>
> *Services,* as a term, is also used to describe activities performed by sellers and others which accompany the sale of a product, and aid in its exchange or its utilization (e.g., shoe fitting, financing, an 800 number). Such services are either presale or postsale and supplement the product but do not com-prise it. If performed during sale, they are considered to be intangible parts of the product.[3]

The first definition includes such services as insurance, entertainment, banking, airlines, health care, telecommunications, and hotels; and the second definition includes services such as wrapping and delivery because these services exist in connection with the sale of a product or another service. This suggests that marketers of goods are also

---

[3]Peter D. Bennett, ed. *Dictionary of Marketing Terms* (Chicago: American Market-ing Association, 1988), p. 21.

marketers of services. In fact, more and more manufacturers are exploiting their service capabilities.[4] For example, General Motors, Ford, and Chrysler all offer financing services. Sears has extended financial service offerings to include the Discover Card, which has become a competitor to Visa and Master Card.

IMPORTANT CHARACTERISTICS OF SERVICES

Services possess several unique characteristics that often have a significant impact on marketing program development. These special features of services may cause unique problems and often result in marketing mix decisions that are substantially different from those found in connection with the marketing of goods. Some of the more important of these characteristics are intangibility, inseparability, perishability and fluctuating demand, highly differentiated marketing systems, and a client relationship.

Intangibility

The obvious basic difference between goods and services is the intangibility of services, and many of the problems encountered in the marketing of services are due to the intangibility. To illustrate, how does an airline make tangible a trip from Philadelphia to San Francisco? These problems are unique to service marketing.

The fact that many services cannot appeal to a buyer's sense of touch, taste, smell, sight, or hearing before purchase places a burden on the marketing organization. For example, hotels that promise a good night's sleep to their customers cannot actually show this service in a tangible way. Obviously, this burden is most heavily felt in a firm's promotional program, but, as will be discussed later, it may affect other areas. Depending on the type of service, the intangibility factor may dictate use of distribution channels because of the need for personal contact between the buyer and seller. Since a service firm is actually selling an idea or experience, not a product, it is often difficult to illustrate, demonstrate, or display the service in use. Instead, it must tell the buyer what the service will do. For example, the hotel must somehow describe to the consumer how a stay at the hotel will leave

---

[4]James Brian Quinn, Jordan J. Baruch, and Penny C. Paquette, "Exploiting the Manufacturing-Service Interface," *Sloan Management Review,* Summer 1988, pp. 45–56.

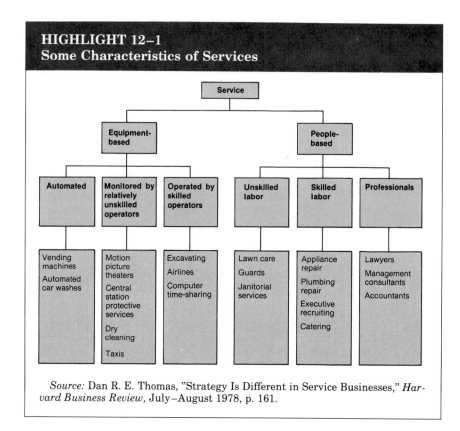

HIGHLIGHT 12–1
Some Characteristics of Services

Service

Equipment-based

People-based

Automated | Monitored by relatively unskilled operators | Operated by skilled operators

Unskilled labor | Skilled labor | Professionals

Vending machines
Automated car washes

Motion picture theaters
Central station protective services
Dry cleaning
Taxis

Excavating
Airlines
Computer time-sharing

Lawn care
Guards
Janitorial services

Appliance repair
Plumbing repair
Executive recruiting
Catering

Lawyers
Management consultants
Accountants

Source: Dan R. E. Thomas, "Strategy Is Different in Service Businesses," *Harvard Business Review,* July–August 1978, p. 161.

the customer feeling well rested and ready to begin a new day. Such a situation not only makes promotion difficult but also leads to problems in offering service quality, as will be shown in a later section.

Inseparability

In many cases, a service cannot be separated from the person of the seller. In other words, the service must often be created and marketed simultaneously. Because of the simultaneous production and marketing of most services, the main concern of the marketer is usually the creation of time and place utility. For example, the barber produces the service of a haircut and markets it at the same time. Many services, therefore, are "tailored" and nonmass-produced.

The implications of inseparability on issues dealing with the selection of channels of distribution and service quality are important. Inseparable services cannot be inventoried, and thus direct sale is the only feasible channel of distribution. Service quality is unable to be completely standardized due to the inability to mechanize the service

HIGHLIGHT 12–2
Intangibility and Marketing Strategy

If marketers of services are to deal effectively with the fact that services are intangible, they must fully understand the concept. The concept of intangibility has two meanings:

1. That which cannot be touched; impalpable.
2. That which cannot be easily defined, formulated, or grasped mentally.

Unfortunately, most services are both of these, or doubly intangible. Overcoming intangibility, therefore, really involves dealing with two problems. Each must be attacked separately, in different ways, and with different elements of the marketing mix. For example:

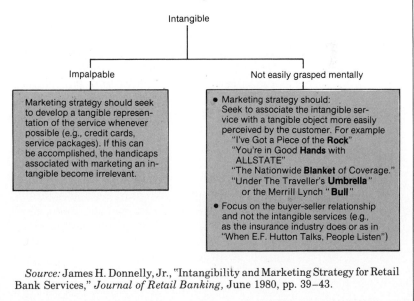

Intangible

Impalpable

Not easily grasped mentally

Marketing strategy should seek to develop a tangible representation of the service whenever possible (e.g., credit cards, service packages). If this can be accomplished, the handicaps associated with marketing an intangible become irrelevant.

- Marketing strategy should:
  Seek to associate the intangible service with a tangible object more easily perceived by the customer. For example
  "I've Got a Piece of the **Rock**"
  "You're in Good **Hands** with ALLSTATE"
  "The Nationwide **Blanket** of Coverage."
  "Under The Traveller's **Umbrella**" or the Merrill Lynch "**Bull**"
- Focus on the buyer-seller relationship and not the intangible services (e.g., as the insurance industry does or as in "When E.F. Hutton Talks, People Listen")

Source: James H. Donnelly, Jr., "Intangibility and Marketing Strategy for Retail Bank Services," *Journal of Retail Banking,* June 1980, pp. 39–43.

encounter. In fact, until recently most service firms did not differentiate between the production and marketing of services and, in many cases, viewed the two as equivalent.

Some industries have been able to modify the inseparability characteristics. In some industries, there may be a tangible representation of the service, such as a contract, by someone other than the producer. In other words, if tangible representations of the service are transferrable, various intermediaries, like agents, can be utilized. The reader is probably familiar with this practice in the marketing of insurance. The service itself remains inseparable from the seller, but the buyer has a tangible representation of the service in the form of a policy. This enables the use of intermediaries in the marketing of insurance. Another example would be in the use of a credit card, whereby the card itself is a tangible representation of a service that is being produced and consumed each time the card is used.

Technology has also aided service companies by allowing for separability between the production and delivery of services. To illustrate, a well-designed voice mail system allows companies and callers to cut down on missed phone calls, eliminate long waits on hold, deliver clear, consistent messages, and answer routine calls automatically.[5] In essence, the service delivery, the passing of the message to the appropriate party, has been separated from the production, creation, and storage of the message. More will be said about the distribution of services later in the chapter.

Perishability and Fluctuating Demand

Services are perishable, and markets for most services fluctuate either by season (tourism), days (airlines), or time of day (movie theaters). Unused telephone capacity and electrical power; vacant seats on planes, trains, busses, and in stadiums; and time spent by bank tellers waiting for customers to use their window represent business that is lost forever.

The combination of perishability and fluctuating demand has created many problems for marketers of services. Specifically, in the area of distribution, channels must be found to have the services available for peak periods, and new channels and strategies must be developed to make use of the service during slack periods. Many firms are attempting to cope with these problems, and several innovations in the distribution of services have occurred in recent years. For example, many electric utilities no longer build to a capacity that will meet peak electrical demand. Instead, they rely on an intricate system of buying unused power from other utilities in other regions of the country. Likewise, to stimulate demand for unused capacity, many downtown hotels offer significant discounts to travelers who stay over on weekends.

Highly Differentiated Marketing Systems

Although the marketer of a tangible product is not compelled to use an established marketing system, such systems often are available and may be the most efficient. If an established system is not available,

---

[5]Andrew Mehlman, "What's Wrong with Voice Mail?" *Services Marketing Newsletter,* Fall 1989, pp. 1–2.

the marketer can at least obtain guidelines from the systems used for similar products. In the case of services, however, there may be little similarity between the marketing systems needed and those used for other services. To illustrate, the marketing of banking and other financial services bears little resemblance to the marketing of computer services, airlines, or telecommunications. The entire area of service marketing, therefore, demands greater creativity and ingenuity on the part of marketing management. For example, Bank One laid out its financial center near Columbus, Ohio, similar to a shopping mall, complete with rock music and neon signs.[6] To reach the tellers, customers walk past minishops selling such offerings as real estate, travel services, and discount stockbrokerage services.

Client Relationship

In the marketing of a great many services, a *client* relationship exists between the buyer and the seller, as opposed to a customer relationship. Examples of a client relationship are the physician-patient and the financial institution-investor relationships. The buyer abides by the suggestions or advice provided by the seller, and these relationships may be of an ongoing nature. Also, since many service firms are client-serving organizations, they may approach the marketing function in a more professional manner, as seen in health care, financial, legal, governmental, and educational services. For example, lawyers and physicians do not utilize comparative advertising where one firm's or physician's services are compared against a named competitor.

A recent study on service marketing by professionals serves to highlight two challenges professionals face.[7] First, in many cases fear or hostility is brought to the purchase. For example, many unpleasant reasons exist for consulting doctors, lawyers, or bankers. These could include fears of surgery, being sued, or having to take out a loan. Second, even high-quality service delivery by the professional can lead to dissatisfied customers. For a physician, the ability to provide quality medical care may be overshadowed by a brusque, unfriendly personality. It is vitally important that professional service providers strive to build long-term, positive relationships with clients.

---

[6]Terence P. Pare, "Banks Discover the Consumer," *Fortune,* February 12, 1990, pp. 96–104.

[7]For a full discussion of problems faced in marketing professional services, see Betsy D. Gelb, Samuel V. Smith, and Gabriel M. Gelb, "Service Marketing Lessons from the Professionals," *Business Horizons,* September–October 1988, pp. 29–34.

Service Quality

The issue of service quality is one of tantamount importance to all service providers. In a recent study, more than 40 percent of all customers surveyed listed poor service as the number one reason for switching to the competition, while only 8 percent listed price as a reason for switching.[8] According to the same study, it is easier and five times cheaper to keep an existing customer than to recruit a new one. Unlike products where quality is often measured against accepted standards, service quality is measured against performance.[9] Since services are frequently produced in the presence of a customer, are labor intensive, and are not able to be stored or objectively examined, the definition and measurement of what constitutes good service quality can be difficult. In general, problems in the determination of good service quality are attributable to differences in the expectations, perceptions, and experiences regarding the service encounter between the service provider and user. These gaps can be classified as:

1. The gap between consumer expectations and management perceptions of the consumer's expectations.
2. The gap between management perceptions of consumer expectations and the firm's service quality specifications.
3. The gap between service quality specifications and actual service quality.
4. The gap between actual service delivery and external communications about the service.

In essence, the customer perceives the level of service quality as being a function of the magnitude and direction of the gap between expected service and perceived service. Management of a company may not even realize that they are delivering poor-quality service due to differences in the way managers and consumers view acceptable quality levels. To overcome this problem and to avoid losing customers,

---

[8]For further details and discussion, see Frank K. Sonnenberg, "Service Quality: Forethought, Not Afterthought," *Journal of Business Strategy,* September/October 1989, pp. 54–57.

[9]The material in this section draws from research performed by Leonard L. Berry, Valerie A. Zeithaml, and A. Parasuraman, "Quality Counts in Services, Too," *Business Horizons,* May–June 1985, pp. 44–52; A. Parasuraman, Valerie A. Zeithaml, and Leonard L. Berry, "A Conceptual Model of Service Quality and Its Implications for Future Research," *Journal of Marketing,* Fall 1985, pp. 41–50; Leonard L. Berry, A. Parasuraman, and Valerie A. Zeithaml, "The Service-Quality Puzzle," *Business Horizons,* September–October 1988, pp. 35–43; and Stephen W. Brown and Teresa A. Swartz, "A Gap Analysis of Professional Service Quality," *Journal of Marketing,* April 1989, pp. 92–98.

firms must be aware of the determinants of service quality. A brief description of these determinants follows.

1. *Reliability* involves dependability and consistency of performance. For example, does a bank always send out accurate customer statements?
2. *Responsiveness* concerns the willingness or readiness of employees to provide service. For example, will a physician see patients on the same day they call in to say they are ill?
3. *Competence* means possession of the necessary skills and knowledge to perform the service. For example, is a bank teller able to give a prospective borrower the name and location of the appropriate loan officer?
4. *Access* involves approachability and ease of contact. For example, banks and other services that have weekend operations are more accessible than those that do not.
5. *Courtesy* involves politeness, respect, consideration, and friendliness of contact personnel.
6. *Communication* means keeping customers informed in language they can understand. It also means listening to customers. For example, a hotel clerk explains in a polite manner why a guest's room is not ready yet.
7. *Credibility* involves trustworthiness, believability, and honesty. For example, a bank's reputation may be built on an ability to always process loans within a promised time period.
8. *Security* is the freedom from danger, risk, or doubt. For example, a telephone company offers 20-minute responses to service calls, or a bank offers bounce-proof checking accounts.
9. *Understanding* the customer involves making the effort to understand the customer's needs. For example, flight attendants on a customer's regular route learn what types of beverages the customer drinks.
10. *Tangibles* include the physical evidence of the service. For example, employees are always visible in a hotel lobby dusting, emptying ashtrays, or otherwise cleaning up.

Each of the above determinants plays an important role in how the customer views the service quality of a firm. What should be obvious is that in order to be successful, a service firm must have dedicated employees and an effective distribution system.

The Importance of Internal Marketing

Service quality goes beyond the relationship between a customer and a company. Rather, it is the personal relationship between a customer *Client* and the particular employee that the customer happens to be dealing

Client

with at the time of the service encounter.[10] The above statement underlies the importance of having customer-oriented, frontline people.[11] If frontline service personnel are unfriendly, unhelpful, uncooperative, or uninterested in the customer, the customer will tend to project that same attitude on the company as a whole. Management must develop programs that will stimulate employee commitment to customer service. In order to be successful, these programs must contain four critical components:

1. A clear, concrete message that conveys a particular service strategy that frontline people can begin to act on.
2. Significant modeling by managers, that is, managers demonstrating the behavior that they intend to reward employees for performing.
3. An energetic follow-through process, in which managers provide the training and support necessary to give employees the capability to provide quality service.
4. An emphasis on teaching employees to have good attitudes. This type of training usually focuses on specific social techniques, such as eye contact, smiling, tone of voice, and standards of dress.

However, organizing and implementing such programs will only lead to temporary results unless managers practice a strategy of internal marketing. The authors define internal marketing as "the continual process by which managers actively encourage, stimulate, and support employee commitment to the company, the company's goods and services, and the company's customers. " Emphasis should be placed on the word *continual*. Managers who consistently pitch in to help when needed, constantly provide encouragement and words of praise to employees, strive to help employees understand the benefits of performing their jobs well, and emphasize the importance of employee actions on both company and employee results are practitioners of internal marketing. In service marketing, successful internal marketing efforts, leading to employee commitment to service quality, are the key to prosperity.

OVERCOMING THE OBSTACLES IN SERVICE MARKETING

The factors of intangibility and inseparability, as well as difficulties in coming up with objective definitions of acceptable service quality, make comprehension of service marketing extremely difficult. However, in view of the size and importance of services in our economy,

---

[10]William A. Sheldon, "Gaining the Service Quality Advantage," *Journal of Business Strategy,* March/April 1988, pp. 45–48.

[11]Much of the material for this section was taken from Karl Albrecht and Ron Zemke, *Service America* (Homewood, Ill.: Dow-Jones Irwin, 1985), chap. 7.

considerable innovation and ingenuity are needed to make high-quality services available at convenient locations for consumers, as well as business people. In fact, the area of service marketing probably offers more opportunities for imagination and creative innovation than does product marketing.

Unfortunately, in the past most service firms have lagged in the area of creative marketing. Even those service firms that have done a relatively good marketing job have been extremely slow in recognizing opportunities in all aspects of their marketing programs. Five reasons can be given for this past lack of innovative marketing on the part of service industries: (1) a limited view of marketing; (2) a lack of competition; (3) a lack of creative management; (4) no obsolescence; and (5) a lack of innovation in the distribution of services.

Limited View of Marketing

Because of the nature of their service, many firms depended to a great degree on population growth to expand sales. A popular example here is the telephone company, which did not establish a marketing department until 1955. It was then that the company realized it had to be concerned not only with population growth, but also with meeting the needs of a growing population. Increases in educational levels and in living standards also bring about the need for new and diversified services. A study conducted by *American Demographics* concluded that college-educated householders are much more likely to buy services—from dry cleaning to financial services—than those with less education.[12] As a well-educated, younger generation replaces the less educated, older one, the demand for services will only increase.

Service firms must meet these changing needs by developing new services and new channels, and altering existing channels, to meet the changing composition and needs of the population. For many service industries, growth has come as a result of finding new channels of distribution. For example, some banks and other financial service companies were able to grow and tap into new markets by establishing limited service kiosks in malls and supermarkets. Airlines have successfully wooed a whole new class of travelers by offering advance-purchase discounted fares. Traditionally, users of these fares either drove or utilized other means of transportation in order to reach their destination.

While many service firms have successfully adopted a marketing perspective, others have been slow to respond. It was not until

---

[12]Judith Waldrop, "Spending by Degree," *American Demographics,* February 1990, pp. 22–26.

deregulation of the telecommunications industry took place in 1984 that the telephone companies began taking a broader view of marketing. Even today, critics of these companies point to the obsession with inventing new technology versus using current technology to meet customer needs. To illustrate, many of these companies began marketing an integrated services digital network (ISDN). Two years after this service came on the market, a majority of potential customers still were not aware of what the service could do and whether and how they could use it.

Limited Competition

A second major cause of the lack of innovative marketing in many service industries was due to the lack of competition. Many service industries, like banking, railroads, and public utilities have, throughout most of their histories faced very little competition; some have even been regulated monopolies. Obviously, in an environment characterized by little competition, there was not likely to be a great deal of innovative marketing. However, two major forces have recently changed this situation. First, in the past two decades the banking, financial services, railroad, cable, airline, and telecommunications industries have all been deregulated in varying degrees. With deregulation has come a need to be able to compete effectively. For example, AT&T was once the sole provider of long-distance telephone service. Now, AT&T has to compete against such companies as MCI and U.S. Sprint, who to a large degree, owe their success to the savvy use of marketing skills. Second, service marketing has taken on an international focus. Today, many foreign companies are competing in domestic service markets. Foreign interests own several banks, many hotels (including Holiday Inn), and shares in major airlines (including Northwest). Likewise, American companies are expanding overseas as markets open up. Each of the seven regional Bell Operating Companies has an equity stake in either cellular, cable television, or telephone network systems in Europe. In the 1990s, the amount of competition facing service companies will continue to increase as the world becomes more and more of a global market.

Noncreative Management

For many years, the managements of service industries have been criticized for not being progressive and creative. Railroad management was criticized for many years for being slow to innovate. More recently, however, railroads have become leaders in the field of freight transportation, introducing such innovations as piggyback service and

containerization, and in passenger service, introducing luxury overnight accommodations on trains with exotic names such as the Zephyr.
Some other service industries, however, have been slow to develop new
services or to innovatively market their existing services.

No Obsolescence

A great advantage for many service industries is the fact that many
services, because of their intangibility, are less subject to obsolescence
than goods. While this is an obvious advantage, it has also led some
service firms to be sluggish in their approach to marketing. Manufacturers of goods may constantly change their marketing plans and seek
new and more efficient ways to produce and distribute their products.
Since service firms are often not faced with obsolescence, they often
failed to recognize the need for change. This failure has led to wholesale
changes in many industries as new operators, who possessed marketing
skills, revolutionized the manner in which the service is performed and
provided. Many a barbershop and hairdresser have gone out of business
due to an inability to compete with the new wave of hairstyling salons.
Many accountants have lost clients to tax preparation services such
as H&R Block, which specialize in doing one task well and have used
technology, including computerized filing services, to their advantage.
Likewise, the old, big, movie house has become a relic of the past as
entrepeneurs realized the advantages to be gained from building and
operating theater complexes that contain several minitheaters in or
near suburban malls.

A Lack of Innovation in the Distribution of Services

As discussed in Chapter 10, the channel of distribution is viewed as
the sequence of firms involved in moving a product from the producer
to the user. The channel may be direct, as when the manufacturer sells
directly to the ultimate consumer, or it may contain one or more institutional intermediaries. Some of the intermediaries assume risks of
ownership, some perform various marketing functions, such as advertising, while others may perform nonmarketing or facilitating functions, such as transporting and warehousing.[13]

---

[13]This section of the chapter draws from James H. Donnelly, Jr., "Marketing Intermediaries in Channels of Distribution for Services," *Journal of Marketing,* January
1976, pp. 55–57; and James H. Donnelly, Jr., and Joseph P. Guiltinan, "Selecting
Channels of Distribution for Services," in *Handbook of Modern Marketing,* ed. Victor
P. Buell (New York: McGraw-Hill, 1986), chap. 24.

Apparently using this concept as a frame of reference, most marketing writers generalize that, because of the intangible and inseparable nature of services, direct sale is the only possible channel for distributing most services. The only traditional indirect channel used involves one agent intermediaries. This channel is used in the distribution of such services as securities, housing, entertainment, insurance, and labor. In some cases, individuals are trained in the production of the service and franchised to sell it, as in the case of dance studios and employment agencies. It is noted that, because they are intangible, services cannot be stored, transported, or inventoried; and since they cannot be separated from the person of the seller, they must be created and distributed simultaneously. Finally, because there is no physical product, traditional wholesalers and other intermediaries can rarely operate in such markets and retailing cannot be an independent activity. For these reasons, it is generally concluded that the geographic area in which most service marketers can operate is restricted.

All of these generalizations are certainly true, using the concept of "channels of distribution" developed for goods. However, the practice of viewing the distribution of services within the framework developed for goods has severely limited innovative thinking. It has focused attention away from understanding the problem and identifying the means to overcome the handicaps of intangibility and inseparability. Most important, however, it has fostered the inability to distinguish conceptually between the production and distribution of services; hence, it supports the idea that services must be created and distributed simultaneously. This had resulted in a lack of attention to channel decisions for producers of services.

THE SERVICE CHALLENGE

Despite the traditional thinking and practices of many marketing managers and writers concerning the similarities between manufacturing and service organizations, the past decade has seen the growth of many innovative ways to meet the service challenge. The service challenge is the quest to: (1) constantly develop new services that will better meet customer needs; (2) improve upon the quality and variety of existing services; and (3) provide and distribute these services in a manner that best serves the customer. This next section illustrates examples of successful innovation in service industries where companies have met the service challenge.

Banking. The days when banking was considered a dead-end career for marketers are over. Perhaps the area of banking best exemplifies the changes that are taking place as service organizations become practitioners of the "marketing concept." In recent years, the banking industry has been very active in the development of new retail banking services, particularly those using the technology or more sophisticated hardware and data processing systems. Direct pay deposit allows employees of businesses and recipients of social security to have their pay deposited directly into their checking accounts. Likewise, direct payment programs allow customers to have payments for such services as Blue Cross and Blue Shield, car loans, and utility bills deducted automatically from their checking accounts.

On another front, Bank of America is developing an expert system that will allow service reps to think like expert problem solvers.[14] Problems that used to take over a month to solve can be taken care of in two weeks. In many banks, computers allow customers to access account information via their telephone on a 24-hour-a-day basis. Using a telephone's push button, customers can get information on account balances, mortgage rates, and other services and can also stop payment on checks. Computers also allow for platform automation, enabling bankers in any branch to bring up on a screen all the information the bank has about the customer. Every face-to-face contact with a customer can now mean an opportunity to make a sale and further the relationship with the customer.

Banks have also learned the value of bundling services. For example, NCNB of Charlotte, North Carolina, offers a Financial Connections account that combines checking, savings, credit card, and auto loan features. Benefits to the customer include free ATM transactions, interest-bearing checking accounts, no-fee credit cards, and the convenience of one-stop banking. In addition, the bank offers preapproved auto loans and cash flow statements. Most banks also offer marketing activities targeted toward senior citizens, which may include discount coupons for entertainment, travel newsletters, and lower monthly minimum required balances.

Citicorp was the first bank to create a national marketing unit for its retail bank operations.[15] The goal of such a unit is to create a "brand approach" to banking whereby a consistent product lineup is available nationwide. By consolidating branch marketing activities, Citicorp is able to enjoy economies of scale, which, until recently, eluded banks with a presence in many regional markets. Banks have also begun extensive promotion campaigns. Numerous banks now offer

---

[14]Much of the material on the marketing activities of banks was taken from Terence P. Pare, "Banks Discover the Consumer," *Fortune,* February 12, 1990, pp. 96–104.

[15]Judith Graham, "Citicorp Bets on McBanking," *Advertising Age,* June 5, 1989, pp. 3, 72.

sweepstakes in conjunction with credit card companies that give customers a chance to win each time they charge a purchase.

Competition in banking will continue to intensify as most states remove barriers to interstate banking. It is estimated that, by the end of the decade, the number of financial institutions will be cut in half as the larger banks expand.[16] The banks that survive will be those that best mastered the skills of service marketing.

Health Care.   The distribution of health care services is of vital concern. In health care delivery, the inseparability characteristic presents more of a handicap than in other service industries because users (patients) literally place themselves in the hands of the seller. Although direct personal contact between producer and user is often necessary, new and more efficient channels of distribution appear to be evolving.

While medical care is traditionally associated with the solo practice, fee-for-service system, several alternative delivery systems have been developed. One method is the health maintenance organization (HMO) concept. This type of delivery system stresses the creation of group health care clinics using teams of salaried health practitioners (physicians, pharmacists, technicians, and so forth) that serve a specific enrolled membership on a prepaid basis.

The HMO performs an intermediary role between practitioner and patient. It increases availability and convenience by providing a central location and "one-stop shopping." For example, a member can visit a general practitioner for a particular ailment and undergo treatment by the appropriate specialist in the same visit. The HMO also assumes responsibility for arranging for or providing hospital care, emergency care, and preventive services. In addition, the prepaid nature of the program encourages more frequent preventive visits, whereas the traditional philosophy of medical care is primarily remedial. HMO programs have inspired similar innovations in other phases of health care, such as dentistry.

The health care industry is becoming highly competitive. Due to a large increase in the number of available beds coupled with government tightening of hospital stay and payment policies, many hospitals are plagued by problems of overcapacity. In order to cope with these problems, some hospitals are developing innovative marketing programs. For example, the Humana Hospital chain offers a Center of Excellence at each of its member hospitals. Each Center of Excellence specializes in treating a specific type of illness. To illustrate, the Center

---

[16]"Consultant Predicts Bank Crisis for This Decade," *Marketing News*, February 5, 1990, p. 8.

of Excellence in Humana's hospital in Lexington, Kentucky, specializes in the treatment of diabetes. In this way, Humana reaps the benefits of economies of scale. Other hospitals have begun targeting specific groups of the population including expectant mothers, senior citizens, and those persons with alcohol or other chemical dependency problems. Current trends show hospitals becoming more and more specialized as they try to differentiate their offerings from those of the competition.

Insurance.   In recent years, the insurance industry has exploded with new product and service offerings. Not too long ago, customers were faced with limited options in choosing life, hospital, or auto insurance. Now, there is a wide array of insurance policies to choose from including universal life policies, which double as retirement savings, nursing care insurance, reversible mortgages, which allow people to take equity from their house while still living in it, and other offerings aimed at serving an aging population. To illustrate, Prudential Insurance Company offers a program whereby terminally ill policyholders are allowed to withdraw funds against the face value of their policy while still alive. In addition to insurance services, most insurance companies now offer a full range of financial services including auto loans, mortgages, mutual funds, and certificates of deposit.

Distribution of insurance services has also been growing. The vending machines found in airports for aircraft insurance have been finding their way into other areas. Travel auto insurance is now available in many motel chains and through the American Automobile Association. Group insurance written through employers and labor unions also has been extremely successful. In each instance, the insurance industry has used intermediaries to distribute its services.

Travel.   The travel industry, most notably the airlines, has been a leader in the use of technology. Computerized reservation systems allow customers to book plane tickets from home or work. Travel agents, who act as intermediaries in the channel of distribution, are conveniently located and easy to access. Technology has also allowed airlines to make strategic pricing decisions through the use of yield management.[17] In yield management, only certain seats on aircraft are discounted. Through the use of computer programs, managers are able to determine who their customer segments are and who is likely to purchase airline tickets when and to where. Package goods manufacturers look with envy at the effective use of these systems by the airlines.

---

[17]"What's Ahead for Travel Industry," *Advertising Age*, January 22, 1990, pp. 20–22.

Recent experiences in the lodging industry point out potential opportunities and pitfalls in service branding strategies.[18] Marriott, one of the most respected names in the lodging industry, is generally regarded as one of the more prestigious hotels. When Marriott decided to enter the lower priced segment of the hotel market, they did so with new brands. By altering the physical appearance and changing the names of their new motels to Courtyard by Marriott and Comfort Inn, Marriott was able to successfully distinguish between their upscale offerings and those that were moderately priced. Holiday Inn, on the other hand, has experienced difficulty in trying to change from its middle-class image. They created Hampton Inns for the budget segment and Crowne Plaza and Embassy Suites for the upscale market. Due to overlapping between segments, Holiday Inn had difficulties in differentiating between the brands, especially in instances when two of the brands were located in the same city. Regardless, the examples point out the necessity of multiple brands for service marketers when practicing market segmentation.

Implications for Service Marketers

The preceding sections emphasized the use of all components of the marketing mix. Many service industries have been criticized for an overdependence on advertising. The overdependence on one or two elements of the marketing mix is one that service marketers cannot afford. The sum total of the marketing mix elements represents the total impact of the firm's marketing strategy. The slack created by severely restricting one element cannot be compensated by heavier emphasis on another, since each element in the marketing mix is designed to address specific problems and achieve specific objectives.

Services must be made available to prospective users, which implies distribution in the marketing sense of the word. The revised concept of the distribution of services points out that service marketers must distinguish conceptually between the production and distribution of services. The problem of making services more efficiently and widely available must not be ignored.

The above sections also pointed out the critical role of new service development. In several of the examples described, indirect distribution of the service was made possible because "products" were developed that included a tangible representation of the service. This

---

[18]Material for the discussion on the lodging industry came from Sak Onkvisit and John J. Shaw, "Service Marketing: Image, Branding, and Competition," *Business Horizons,* January–February 1989, pp. 13–18.

HIGHLIGHT 12–3
Ten Lessons in Good Services Marketing

1. Quality service means never having to say "that's not my job."
2. The delivery of quality service is never the customer's job.
3. Customers should never be inconvenienced because of company policies that are known only to employees and do not become known to customers until they are used against them.
4. Customers should never be required to restate their request or complain to several customers before having it resolved.
5. You will never treat your customers any better than you treat each other.
6. How your employees feel is eventually how your customers will feel.
7. Never allow an employee's work to interfere with their job.
8. If you establish negative expectations for your customers, you will always meet them.
9. A great many customers will not return bad service with bad behavior. They are always polite, never get loud, cause a scene, or scream for the manager. They just never come back.
10. When you lose a customer because of poor service, chances are you will never know it.

Source: Adapted from James H. Donnelly, Jr., and Steven J. Skinner, *The New Banker* (Homewood, Ill.: Dow Jones-Irwin, 1989), chap. 3.

---

development facilitates the use of intermediaries, because the service can now be separated from the producer. In addition, the development of new services paves the way for companies to expand and segment their markets. With the use of varying service bundles, new technology, and alternative means of distributing the service, companies are now able to practice targeted marketing.

Promotional programs, other than advertising, also plays a critical role in service marketing. By running sweepstakes in which contestants were eligible to win prizes each time they used their ATM cards, banks were able to make the public more aware of the ease and convenience of using ATMs. Likewise, no-excuse refunds for poor service have enabled such hotels as Holiday Inn to retain a quality reputation.

CONCLUSION

This chapter has dealt with the complex topic of service marketing. While the marketing of services has much in common with the marketing of products, unique problems in the area require highly creative marketing management skills. Many of the problems in the service area can be traced to the intangible and inseparable nature of services and the difficulties involved in providing service quality. However, considerable progress has been made in understanding and reacting to these difficult problems, particularly in the area of distribution. In view of the major role services play in our economy, it is important that marketing practitioners understand and appreciate the unique problems of service marketing.

ADDITIONAL READINGS

Albrecht, Karl, and Ron Zemke. *Service America! Doing Business in the New Economy*. Homewood, Ill.: Dow Jones-Irwin, 1985.

Berry, Leonard L.; David R. Bennett; and Carter W. Brown. *Service Quality: A Profit Strategy for Financial Institutions*. Homewood, Ill.: Dow Jones-Irwin, 1989.

Brown, Stephens W., and Teresa A. Swartz. "A Gap Analysis of Professional Service Quality." *Journal of Marketing,* April 1989, pp. 92–98.

Donnelly, J. H.; L. L. Berry; and T. W. Thompson. *Marketing Financial Services*. Homewood, Ill.: Dow Jones-Irwin, 1985.

Onkvisit, Sak, and John J. Shaw. "Service Marketing: Image, Branding, and Competition." *Business Horizons,* January–February 1989, pp. 13–18.

Zeithaml, Valerie A.; A. Parasuraman; and Leonard L. Berry. *Delivering Quality Service: Evaluating Customer Perceptions and Expectations*. New York, N.Y.: Free Press, 1990.

Chapter 13

International Marketing

A growing number of U.S. corporations have transversed geographical boundaries and become truly multinational in character. For most other domestic corporations, the question is no longer "should we go international?" Instead, the questions relate to how and where the companies should enter the international marketplace. The past decade has seen the reality of a truly world market unfold. In today's world, the global economy is now over 50 percent integrated versus 25 percent in 1980, and 10 percent in 1950.[1] Primary reasons for individual markets evolving to a network of interdependent economies include:

1. The growing affluence and economic development of lesser developed countries. For example, by the year 2000 it is estimated that Third World nations will account for one fourth of the industrial value-added in the world (versus one eighth today).[2]
2. The integration of world financial markets. For example, interest rate changes occurring in West Germany greatly influence interest rates in the United States and Japan.
3. Increased efficiencies in transportation networks. Consider the case of Western Europe, where airlines are now allowed to schedule flights between two countries other than their home countries.[3]
4. The opening up of new markets. For example, recent political events in Eastern Europe have led to the opening up of a marketplace of over 137 million potential new consumers for U.S. companies.

---

[1]David A. Heenan, "The Case for Convergent Capitalism," *Journal of Business Strategy,* November/December 1988, pp. 54–57.

[2]Ibid.

[3]Eric G. Friberg, "1992: Moves Europeans Are Making," *Harvard Business Review,* May–June 1989, pp. 85–89.

HIGHLIGHT 13–1
Examples of Various Types of Multinational Companies (MNCs)

American-Owned MNCs

General Motors	Ford Motor
IBM	Pan Am
General Electric	American Express
F. W. Woolworth	Bank America
Sears Roebuck	Eastman Kodak
Mobil Oil	Procter & Gamble
ITT	Gulf & Western

Foreign-Owned MNCs

Unilever	Toyota Motors
Royal Dutch/Shell	Sony
Nestlé	Volkswagen
Datsun (Nissan)	Perrier
Honda	Norelco

Nonprofit MNCs

Red Cross (Swiss)
Roman Catholic Church (Italy)
U.S. Army (U.S.)

American Firms Owned by Foreign MNCs

Magnavox	Bantam Books
Gimbel's Department Store	Baskin-Robbins
Libby, McNeill & Libby	Capitol Records
Stouffer Foods	Kiwi Shoe Polish
Saks-Fifth Avenue	Lipton

Multinational firms invest in foreign countries for the same basic reasons they invest in the domestic United States. These reasons vary from firm to firm, but fall under the categories of achieving offensive or defensive goals. Offensive goals are to: (1) increase long-term growth and profit prospects; (2) maximize total sales revenue; (3) take advantage of economies of scale; and (4) improve overall market position. As many American markets reach saturation, American firms look to foreign markets as outlets for surplus productive capacity and potential sources of larger profit margins and returns on investment. For example, in Eastern Europe, less than 15 percent of the population own an automobile. For domestic car manufacturers, this market offers much potential.

Multinational firms also invest overseas to achieve defensive goals. Chief among these goals are the desire to: (1) compete with foreign competitors on their own turf instead of in the United States; (2) have access to technological innovations that are developed in other countries; (3) take advantage of significant differences in operating costs among countries; (4) preempt competitor's global moves; and (5) not be locked out of future markets by arriving too late. To illustrate, in 1988 alone, there were 307 foreign acquisitions of U.S. companies.[4] Such well-known companies as Pillsbury, A&P, Shell Oil, CBS Records, and Firestone Tire & Rubber are now owned by foreign interests. Since 1980, the share of the domestic U.S. high-tech market held by foreign producers has grown from less than 8 percent to over 18 percent.[5] In such diverse industries as power tools, tractors, televisions, and banking, U.S. companies have lost the dominant position they once held. By investing solely in domestic operations, U.S. companies are more susceptible to foreign incursions.

Basically, marketing abroad is the same as marketing at home. Regardless of which part of the world the firm sells in, the marketing program must still be built around a sound product or service that is properly priced, promoted, and distributed to a carefully analyzed target market. In other words, the marketing manager has the same controllable decision variables in both domestic and nondomestic markets.

Although the development of a marketing program may be the same in either domestic or nondomestic markets, special problems may be involved in implementing marketing programs in nondomestic markets. These problems often arise because marketing managers may be unfamiliar with environmental differences that exist among various countries.

This chapter will examine marketing management in an international context. Methods of organizing international versus domestic markets, international market research tasks, methods of entry strategies into international markets, and potential marketing strategies for a multinational firm will be discussed. In examining each of these areas, the reader will find a common thread—knowledge of the local cultural environment—that appears to be a major prerequisite for success in each area.

---

[4]Kenneth M. Davidson, "Fire Sale on America?" *Journal of Business Strategy,* September/October 1989, pp. 9–14.

[5]Gene Koretz, "Has High-Tech America Passed Its High-Water Mark?" *Business Week,* February 5, 1990, p. 18.

With the proper adaptations, U.S. companies do have the capabilities and resources needed to compete successfully in the international marketplace. To illustrate, companies as diverse as Amway, General Electric, Eastman Kodak, Mobil, McDonald's, and Coca-Cola each generate over one-half billion dollars in annual sales in Japan alone.[6] Smaller companies can also be successful. System Software Associates, Inc., of Chicago, a $62 million dollar company, generates more than half its sales outside the United States.[7]

ORGANIZING FOR INTERNATIONAL MARKETING

When compared with the tasks it faces at home, a firm attempting to establish an international marketing organization faces a much higher degree of risk and uncertainty. In a foreign market, management is often less familiar with the cultural, political, and economic situation. Many of these problems arise as a result of conditions specific to the foreign country. Managers are also faced with many decisions relating to internal organization, operation, and control issues. These problems usually come as a result of deciding whether to take a multidomestic or global approach to managing international operations.

Problem Conditions: External

Attention here will focus on those problems U.S. firms most often face when entering foreign markets.

Cultural Misunderstanding. Differences in the cultural environment of foreign countries may be misunderstood or not even recognized because marketing managers tend to use their own cultural values and priorities as a frame of reference. Some of the most common areas of difference lie in the way dissimilar cultures perceive time, thought patterns, personal space, material possessions, family roles and relationships, personal achievement, competitiveness, individuality, social behavior, and other interrelated subjective issues.[8] Another

---

[6]Carla Rapport, "You Can Make Money in Japan," *Fortune,* February 12, 1990, pp. 85–92.

[7]For an explanation of how a small company was able to go international, see Edward R. Koepfler, "Strategic Options for Global Market Players," *Journal of Business Strategy,* July/August, 1989, pp. 46–50.

[8]For a full explanation on cultural differences, see Rose Knotts, "Cross-Cultural Management: Transformations and Adaptations," *Business Horizons,* January-February 1989, pp. 29–33.

important source of misunderstandings is in the perceptions of managers about the people with whom they are dealing. Feelings of superiority can lead to changed communication mannerisms.

The tendency to rely on one's own cultural values has been called the major cause of many international marketing problems. For example, the Japanese often say "yes" when they mean "no."[9] They rarely give a direct negative response—even if they want to deny a request or express a negative intent—especially to a foreigner. They are also wary of the common American practice of bringing lawyers to initial meetings. American managers must make the necessary efforts to learn, understand, and adapt to the cultural norms of the managers and customers they deal with in other parts of the world. Failure to do so will result in missed marketing opportunities.

Political Uncertainty. Because governments are unstable in many countries, social unrest and even armed conflict must sometimes be reckoned with. Other nations are newly emerging and anxious to exert their independence. These and similar problems can greatly hinder a firm seeking to establish its position in a foreign market. For example, in China, many companies had to scale back and adapt their marketing efforts after the government there used military force to quell the student uprisings in 1990.

Import Restrictions. Tariffs, import quotas, and other types of important restrictions hinder international business. These are usually established to promote national self-sufficiency and can be a huge roadblock for the multinational firm. For example, currently a number of countries, including South Korea, Taiwan, Thailand, and Japan, place import restrictions on a variety of goods produced in America, including telecommunications equipment, satellites, rice, and wood products.[10]

Exchange Controls. Often a nation will establish limits on the amount of earned and invested funds that can be withdrawn from that nation. These exchange controls are usually established by nations experiencing balance-of-payment problems. Nevertheless, these and other types of currency regulations are important considerations in the decision to expand into a foreign market. For example, the Soviet ruble is not convertible to hard currency. For foreign companies dealing with the Soviet Union, barter is still the dominant way to buy and sell goods.[11]

---

[9]"In Japan, If Your Prospect Says "Yes," Don't Start Celebrating Yet," *Marketing News,* February 5, 1990, p. 18.

[10]Paul Magnusson and Blanca Riemer, "Carla Hills, Trade Warrior," *Business Week,* January 22, 1990, pp. 50–56.

[11]Karl Seppala and Mark A. Meyer, "Time Ripe for U.S. Firms to Enter Soviet Market," *Marketing News,* February 5, 1990, pp. 6, 9.

Ownership and Personnel Restrictions.   In many nations, governments have a requirement that the majority ownership of a company operating in that nation be held by nationals of the country. Other nations require that the majority of the personnel of a foreign firm be local citizens. Each of these restrictions can act as obstacles to foreign expansion. To illustrate, consider the case of Coca-Cola. In order to comply with foreign ownership requirements, Coca-Cola would have had to share technical knowledge, including the proprietary secret recipe for its soft drink concentrate, with its Indian partners. Coca-Cola refused and instead decided to pull out of India after operating there for over 25 years.[12]

Problem Conditions: Internal

Given the types of external problems just discussed, the reader can see that the external roadblocks to success in a foreign market are substantial. Unfortunately, several major internal problems may also arise.

The Multidomestic versus the Global Approach

There are two distinct kinds of multinational corporations—the multidomestic corporation and the global corporation.[13] The multidomestic company pursues different strategies in each of its foreign markets. Each overseas subsidiary is autonomous. A company's management tries to operate effectively across a series of worldwide positions with diverse product requirements, growth rates, competitive environments, and political risks. Local managers are given the authority and control to make the necessary decisions; however, they are also held responsible for results. In effect, the company competes on a market-by-market basis. Honeywell and General Foods are examples of two American companies that operated well in this manner.

The global company, on the other hand, pits its entire resources against the competition in an integrated fashion. Foreign subsidiaries and divisions are largely interdependent in both operations and strategy. The company operates as though the world were one large market, not a series of individual countries. Since there is no, one, clear-cut

---

[12]Anant R. Negandi and Peter A. Donhowe, "It's Time to Explore New Global Trade Options," *Journal of Business Strategy*, January/February 1989, pp. 27–31.

[13]This section was taken from James F. Bolt, "Global Competitors: Some Criteria for Success," *Business Horizons*, January–February 1988, pp. 34–41.

way to organize a global company, three alternative structures are normally used: (1) worldwide product divisions, each responsible for selling its own products throughout the world; (2) divisions responsible for all products sold within a geographic area; and (3) a matrix system that combines elements of both these arrangements. Many multinational companies already have structured their organization in a global fashion, including IBM, Caterpillar, Timex, General Electric, Siemens, and Mitsubishi. Others are rapidly following.

Most companies are realizing the need to take a global approach to managing their businesses. However, recognizing the need and actually implementing a truly global approach are two distinctly different tasks. For some companies, industry conditions dictate that they take a global perspective. The ability to actually implement a global approach to managing international operations, however, largely depends on factors unique to the company. These industry conditions and internal factors are explored next.

Industry Conditions Dictating a Global Perspective

In determining whether or not to globalize a particular business, managers should look first to the business's industry.[14] Market, economic, environmental, and competitive factors all influence the potential gains to be realized by following a global strategy. Factors constituting the external environment that are conducive to a global strategy are:

1. *Market factors.* Homogenous market needs, global customers, shortening product life cycles, transferable brands and advertising, and the ability to internationalize distribution channels.
2. *Economic factors.* Worldwide economies of scale in manufacturing and distribution, steep learning curves, worldwide sourcing efficiencies, rising product development costs, and significant differences in host-country costs.
3. *Environmental factors.* Falling transportation costs, improving communications, favorable government policies, and the increasing speed of technological change.
4. *Competitive factors.* Competitive interdependencies among countries, global moves of competitors, and opportunities to preempt a competitor's global moves.[15]

---

[14]This section is based on George S. Yip, Pierre M. Loewe, and Michael Y. Yoshino, "How to Take Your Company to the Global Market," *Columbia Journal of World Business,* Winter 1988, pp. 37–48.

[15]Ibid.

Many of the reasons given in the first part of the chapter as to why a domestic company should become a multinational can also be used to support the argument that a firm should take a global perspective. This is because the integration of markets is forcing companies that wish to remain successful not only to become multinationals but also to take a global perspective in doing so. In the past, companies had the option of remaining domestic or going multinational due to the separation of markets. This is no longer the case.

Internal Factors that Facilitate a Global Strategy

Several internal factors can either facilitate or impede a company's efforts to undertake a global approach to marketing strategies. These factors and their underlying dimensions are:

1. *Structure.* The ease of installing a centralized global authority and the absence of rifts between present domestic and international divisions or operating units.
2. *Management processes.* The capabilities and resources available to perform global planning, budgeting, and coordination activities, coupled with the ability to conduct global performance reviews and implement global compensation plans.
3. *Culture.* The ability to project a global versus national identity, a worldwide versus domestic commitment to employees, and a willingness to tolerate interdependence among business units.
4. *People.* The availability of employable foreign nations and the willingness of current employees to commit to multicountry careers, frequent travel, and having foreign superiors.

Overall, whether a company should undertake a multidomestic or global approach to organizing their international operations will largely depend on the nature of the company and its products, how different the foreign culture is from the domestic market, and the company's ability to implement a global perspective.

PROGRAMMING FOR INTERNATIONAL MARKETING

In this section of the chapter, the major areas in developing an international marketing program will be examined. As was mentioned at the outset, marketing managers must organize the same controllable decision variables that exist in domestic markets. However, many firms that have been extremely successful in marketing in the United States have not been able to duplicate their success in foreign markets.

HIGHLIGHT 13–2
Characteristics of Domestic and International Operations

Domestic	*International*
One primary language and nationality.	Multilingual, multinational, and multicultural.
Relatively homogeneous market.	Fragmented and diverse markets.
Data available, usually accurate, and easy to collect.	Data collection formidable task, requiring significantly higher budgets and personnel allocation.
Political factors relatively unimportant.	Political factors frequently vital.
Relative freedom from government interference.	National economic plans, government influences on business decisions common.
Individual corporation has little effect on environment.	"Gravitational" distortion by large companies.
Relatively stable business environment.	Multiple environments, many highly unstable (but potentially very profitable).
Uniform financial climate.	Variety of financial climates, ranging from very conservative to wildly inflationary.
One currency.	Currencies differing in stability and real value.
Business rules mature and understood.	Rules diverse, changeable, and unclear.
Management generally accustomed to sharing responsibilities and using financial controls.	Management frequently autonomous and unfamiliar with budgets and controls.

Source: William C. Cain, "International Planning: Mission Impossible?" *Columbia Journal of World Business,* July–August 1970, p. 58. Although over 20 years old, these ideas still have validity today.

International Marketing Research

Because the risks and uncertainties are so high, marketing research is equally important (and probably more so) in foreign markets than in domestic markets.[16] In attempting to analyze foreign consumers and industrial markets, at least four important dimensions must be considered.

---

[16]S. Tamer Cavusgil, "Guidelines for Export Market Research," *Business Horizons,* November–December 1985, pp. 27–33.

HIGHLIGHT 13–3
Product Categories Most Suited for Global Marketing

1. Computer hardware
2. Airlines
3. Photography equipment
4. Heavy equipment
5. Machine tools
6. Consumer electronics/computer software (tied for 6th)
7. Automobiles
8. Major appliances
9. Hardware/wines and spirits (tied for 10th)
10. Nonalcoholic beverages
11. Tobacco
12. Paper products
13. Cosmetics
14. Beer
15. Household cleaners
16. Toiletries/food (tied for 17th)
17. Confections/clothing (tied for 18th)

Source: "Global Marketing: How Executives Really Feel," *Ad Forum,* April 1985, p. 30.

Population Characteristics. Obviously, population is one of the major components of a market, and significant differences exist between and within foreign countries. The marketing manager should be familiar with the total population and with the regional, urban, rural, and interurban distribution. Other demographic variables, such as the number and size of families, education, occupation, and religion, are also important. In many markets, these variables can have a significant impact on the success of a firm's marketing program. For example, in the United States, a cosmetics firm can be reasonably sure that the desire to use cosmetics is almost universal among women of all income classes. However, in Latin America the same firm may be forced to segment its market by upper-, middle-, and lower-income groups, as well as by urban and rural areas. This is because upper-income women want high-quality cosmetics promoted in prestige media and sold through exclusive outlets. In some rural and less prosperous areas, the cosmetics must be inexpensive, while in other rural areas women do not accept cosmetics. Even in markets that are small in geographical area, consumers may differ in many of the variables mentioned. Any one or set of such differences may have a strong bearing on consumers' ability and willingness to buy.

Ability to Buy. To assess the ability of consumers in a foreign market to buy, four broad measures should be examined: (1) gross national product or per capita national income; (2) distribution of income; (3) rate of growth in buying power; and (4) extent of available financing. Since each of these varies in different areas of the world, the marketing opportunities available must be examined closely.

Willingness to Buy. The cultural framework of consumer motives and behavior is integral to understanding the foreign consumer. Cultural values and attitudes toward the material culture, social organizations, the supernatural, aesthetics, and language should be analyzed for their possible influence on each element in the firm's marketing program. It is easy to see that such factors as the group's values concerning acquisition of material goods, the role of the family, the positions of men and women in society, as well as the various age groups and social classes will all have an effect on marketing, because each influences consumer behavior, values, and the overall pattern of life.

In some areas there appears to be a convergence of tastes and habits, with different cultures becoming more and more integrated into one homogenous culture, although still separated by national boundaries. This appears to be the case in Western Europe, where consumers are developing into a mass market. This obviously will simplify the task for a marketer in this region. However, cultural differences still prevail among most areas of the world and strongly influence consumer behavior.

Differences in Research Tasks and Processes. In addition to the dimensions mentioned above, the processes and tasks associated with carrying out the market research program will also most likely differ from country to country. Many market researchers count on census data for in-depth demographic information. However, in foreign countries the market researcher is likely to encounter a variety of problems in using census data. These include:

1. *Language.* Some nations publish their census reports in English. Other countries offer only their native language.
2. *Data content.* Data contained in a census will vary from country to country and often omit items of interest to researchers. For example, most foreign nations do not include an income question on their census. Others do not include such items as marital status or education levels.
3. *Timeliness.* The United States takes a census every 10 years. Japan and Canada conduct one every five years. However, some northern European nations are abandoning the census as a data collection tool and instead are relying on population registers to account for births, deaths, and changes in marital status or place of residence.

HIGHLIGHT 13–4
The Difficulties of Transcultural Variables

Many firms have found serious problems in international new product marketing:

A firm introduced refrigerators into several Middle Eastern countries and included a photo of a well-stocked refrigerator interior—with a large ham on a central shelf!

Campbell's condensed soups didn't sell well in England because the Campbell's cans appeared small, relative to noncondensed English competitors.

Lever Brothers promised white teeth from its toothpaste, but made the promise to Southeast Asians who held discolored teeth to be a mark of prestige.

Chevrolet introduced its Nova automobile into South America without realizing that "no va" in Spanish means something like "won't go."

Baby food was introduced into several African nations, with baby pictures on the labels. Potential consumers thought the jars contained ground-up babies.

Translators converted:

"Body by Fisher" into "Corpse by Fisher."

"Come Alive with Pepsi" into "Come Alive out of the Grave."

"Car Wash" into "Car Enema."

Source: C. Merle Crawford, *New Products Management,* 2nd ed. (Homewood, Ill.: Richard D. Irwin, 1987), p. 44.

4. *Availability in the United States.* If a researcher requires detailed household demographics on foreign markets, the cost and time required to obtain the data will be significant. For example, to get minimal-quality data on Western Europe and Pacific Rim countries might require trips to over 10 different university libraries, as well as to the U.S. Bureau of the Census and the Library of Congress.[17]

Problems can also be encountered in carrying out research activities.[18] For example, in most nations there are no large-sample theater tests or on-air, day-after recall studies so common in the United States. Other difficulties arise in gathering purchase data. Foreign retailers lag far behind American retailers in the installation and use of checkout scanning devices. Techniques commonly used in the collection of

---

[17]Donald B. Pittenger, "Gathering Foreign Demographics Is No Easy Task," *Marketing News,* January 8, 1990, pp. 23, 25.

[18]Jack J. Honomich, "British, U.S. Researchers Ponder Their Differences," *Advertising Age,* August 28, 1989, pp. 42, 49.

data also differ. For example, while telephone interviewing is the most commonly used survey method in the United States, it's relatively rare in the United Kingdom where most research is conducted door-to-door.

Product Planning for International Markets

Before a firm can market a product, there must be something to sell— a product or service. From this standpoint, product planning is the starting point for the entire marketing program. Once this is accomplished, management can determine whether there is an adequate market for the product and can decide how the product should be marketed. Most firms would not think of entering a domestic market without extensive product planning. Unfortunately, this is often not the case with foreign markets. Often, firms will enter foreign markets with the same product sold in the United States, or at best, one with only minor changes. In many cases, these firms have encountered serious problems. An example of such a problem occurred when American manufacturers began to export refrigerators to Europe. The firms exported essentially the same models sold in the United States. However, the refrigerators were the wrong size, shape, and temperature range for some areas and had weak appeal in others—thus failing miserably. Although adaptation of the product to local conditions may have eliminated this failure, this adaptation is easier said than done. For example, even in the domestic market, overproliferation of product varieties and options can dilute economies of scale. This dilution results in higher production costs, which may make prohibitive the price of serving each market segment with an "adapted" product. The solution to this problem is not easy. In some cases, changes can be made rather inexpensively, while in others the sales potential of the particular market may not warrant extensive product changes. In any case, management must examine these problems carefully to avoid foreign marketing failures.[19]

International Distribution Systems

The role of the distribution network in facilitating the transfer of goods and titles and in the demand stimulation process is as important in foreign markets as it is at home. Figure 13–1 illustrates some of the

---

[19]See Theodore Levitt, "The Globalization of Markets," *Harvard Business Review,* May–June 1983, pp. 92–102, for an excellent discussion of the extent to which a company can market the same product in different countries.

FIGURE 13–1 Common Distribution Channels for International Marketing

---

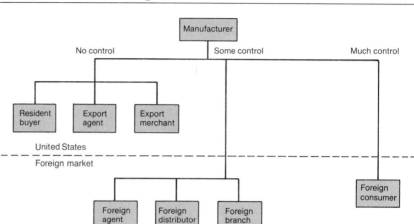

most common channel arrangements in international marketing. The continuum ranges from no control to almost complete control of the distribution system by manufacturers.

The channel arrangement where manufacturers have the least control is shown at the left of Figure 13–1. These are the most indirect channels of distribution. Here manufacturers sell to resident buyers, export agents, or export merchants located in the United States. In reality, these are similar to domestic sales, since all of the marketing functions are assumed by the intermediaries.[20]

Manufacturers become more directly involved and, hence, have greater control over distribution when agents and distributors located in foreign markets are selected. Both perform similar functions, except that agents do not assume title to the manufacturers' products, while distributors do. If manufacturers should assume the functions of foreign agents or distributors and establish their own foreign branch, they greatly increase control over their international distribution system. Manufacturers' effectiveness will then depend on their own administrative organization, rather than on independent intermediaries. If the foreign branch sells to other intermediaries, such as wholesalers and retailers, as is the case with most consumer goods, manufacturers again

---

[20]The manufacturer does have slightly more control over the export agent than the resident buyer or export merchant, since the export agent does not take title to the goods.

relinquish some control. However, since the manufacturers are located in the market area, they have greater potential to influence these intermediaries.

The channel arrangement that enables manufacturers to exercise a great deal of control is shown at the right of Figure 13–1. Here, manufacturers sell directly to industrial users or ultimate consumers. This arrangement is most common in the sale of industrial goods.

Pricing for International Marketing

In domestic markets, pricing is a complex task. The basic approaches used in price determination in foreign markets are the same as those discussed earlier in the chapter on pricing. However, the pricing task is often more complicated in foreign markets, because of additional problems with tariffs, taxes, and currency conversion.

Import duties are probably the major constraint for foreign marketers and are encountered in many markets. Management must decide whether import duties will be paid by the firm, by the foreign consumer, or shared by both. This and similar constraints may force the firm to abandon an otherwise desirable pricing strategy or may force the firm out of a market altogether.

Another pricing problem arises because of the rigidity in price structures found in many foreign markets. Many foreign intermediaries are not aggressive in their pricing policies. They often prefer to maintain high unit margins at the expense of low sales volume, rather than develop large sales volume by means of lower prices and smaller margins per unit. Many times this rigidity is encouraged by legislation that prevents retailers from cutting prices substantially at their own discretion. These are only a few of the pricing problems encountered by foreign marketers.

However, in some cases foreign pricing policies and customs can give the U.S. marketer a competitive advantage. For example, in Japan, American-style shopping malls with stores such as Toys "Я" Us, Talbots, and Virgin Records are able to compete effectively against center-city stores which still adhere to Japanese pricing policies designed to give the retailer huge margins.[21] In fact, imports of consumer goods into Japan hit the $22.6 billion mark in 1988, more than triple the total in 1985. Clearly, the marketer must be aware of both the constraints and opportunities available in foreign market areas.

---

[21]Carla Rapport, "Ready, Set, Sell—Japan Is Buying," *Fortune,* September 11, 1989, pp. 159–64.

International Advertising and Sales Promotion

When expanding their operations into the world marketplace, most firms are aware of the language barriers that exist and realize the importance of translating their messages into the proper idiom. However, numerous other issues must be resolved, such as selecting appropriate media and advertising agencies in foreign markets.

There are many problems in selecting media in foreign markets. Often the media traditionally used in the domestic market are not available in foreign markets. For example, it is estimated that not until 1992 or 1993, at the earliest, will national commercial TV become a reality in the Soviet Union.[22] If media are available, they may be so only on a limited basis or they may not reach the potential buyers. (For example, one firm was forced to use sound trucks or roving movie vans to reach potential buyers in the sub-Sahara area of Africa.) In addition to the problem of availability, other difficulties arise from the lack of accurate media information. There is no rate and data service or media directory that covers all the media available throughout the world. Where data are available, their accuracy is often questionable.

Another important promotion decision that must be made is the type of agency used to prepare and place the firm's advertisements. Along with the growth in multinational product companies, advertising agencies are also taking on a multinational look. Among the top 15 advertising agencies, less than half are U.S. owned.[23] Alliances and takeovers have served to stimulate growth in the formation of global agencies. For the U.S. company, there are two major approaches to choosing an agency. The first is to use a purely local agency in each area where the advertisement is to appear. The rationale for this approach is that a purely local agency employing only local nationals can better adapt the firm's message to the local culture.

The other approach is to use either a U.S.-based multinational agency or a multinational agency with U.S. offices to develop and implement the ad campaign. For example, the Coca-Cola Company uses one agency to create ads for the 80 nations that Diet Coke is marketed in. The use of these so-called super agencies is increasing (annual growth rates averaging over 30 percent in the late 1980s). By using global advertising agencies, companies are able to take advantage of economies of scale and other efficiencies. However, global agencies are not without their critics. Many managers believe that small, local

---

[22]John Iams, "Soviets Plan Private TV Net," *Advertising Age,* August 14, 1989.

[23]Laurel Wentz, "Publicis-FCB Leads Euro-networks," *Advertising Age,* June 12, 1989, p. 36.

agencies in emerging markets take a more entrepreneurial and fresher approach to advertising than do the global agencies.[24] Much discussion has developed over which approach is best, and it appears that both approaches can be used successfully by particular firms.

The use of sales promotion can also lead to opportunities and problems for marketers in foreign markets. Sales promotions often contain certain characteristics that are more attractive than other elements of the promotion mix.[25] In less wealthy countries, consumers tend to be even more interested in saving money through price discounts, sampling, or premiums. Sales promotion can also be used as a strategy for bypassing restrictions on advertising placed by some foreign governments. In addition, sales promotion can be an effective means for reaching people who live in rural locations where media support for advertising is virtually nonexistent.

However, laws in some countries place even more restrictions on sales promotion than those found in the United States. Laws may not permit gifts or premiums to be given, and companies may be required to keep detailed records of promotional transactions. For example, in France a limit is placed on the amount of money companies can spend on sales promotion activities. In addition, retailers and wholesalers in foreign countries may either lack: (1) the appropriate facilities necessary to merchandise the promotional materials; or (2) the capability either to understand how a specific promotion works or to explain it to their customers.

STRATEGIES FOR INTERNATIONAL MARKETING

A major decision facing companies that desire to enter the international marketplace relates to the choice of a market entry strategy. What type of strategy to employ depends on many factors, including the analysis of market opportunities, company capabilities, and the degree of marketing involvement and commitment the company is willing to make.[26] A company can decide to make minimal investments of funds and risks by limiting its efforts to exporting, or it can decide to make large investments of resources and management effort to try

---

[24]Kathleen Barnes, "Nestle Exec Criticizes Sluggish Global Shops," *Advertising Age,* November 13, 1989.

[25]The section on sales promotion is based on John Burnett, *Promotion Management* (St. Paul, Minn.: West Publishing Co.), 1988, chap. 21.

[26]The material for this section comes from Phillip R. Cateora, *International Marketing,* 7th ed. (Homewood Ill.: Richard D. Irwin, 1990), chap. 10.

to establish a permanent share of international markets. Both approaches can be profitable. In general, there are eight ways by which a company can enter the international marketplace:

1. *Exporting.* Exporting occurs when a company produces the product outside the final destination and then ships it there for sale. It is the easiest and most common approach for a company making its first international move.

2. *Licensing.* Companies can grant patent rights, trademark rights, and the rights to use technological processes to foreign companies. It is the favorite strategy for small- and medium-sized companies. Although it may be the least profitable way to enter a market, it also minimizes risks.

3. *Franchising.* Franchising is a form of licensing whereby the franchiser provides a standard package of products, systems, and management services to the franchisee. The foreign franchisee provides market knowledge, capital, and personal involvement in management. Potentially, franchising offers an effective mix of centralized and decentralized decision making.

4. *Joint ventures.* A company may decide to share management with one or more collaborating foreign firms. Advantages of joint ventures include access to a partner's distribution system, access to an otherwise closed market, access to technology, and access to capital or personnel resources. For example, Hercules, Inc., a company that operates in the specialty chemicals, aerospace, and engineered polymers industries, has been involved in joint ventures with companies in Japan, Australia, Italy, and Belgium.[27]

5. *Consortia.* A consortium is similar to a joint venture except for two unique characteristics: consortia typically involve a large number of participants and usually operate in countries or markets in which none of the participants is currently active.

6. *Manufacturing.* Local manufacturing is used when the demand justifies the investment. Low-cost labor/materials or gaining access to otherwise closed markets may provide the impetus for setting up local manufacturing operations. For example, the only way to avoid high tariffs imposed on outsiders by countries in Europe is to establish manufacturing operations.

7. *Management contract.* In this situation, a management company agrees to manage some or all of the functions of another company's operations in exchange for management fees, a share of the profits, or, sometimes, stock options.

---

[27]Walter G. Schmid, "Heinz Covers the Globe," *Journal of Business Strategy,* March/April, 1989, pp. 17–20.

8. *Acquisition.* Some companies prefer to enter markets through the acquisition of other companies. Advantages of acquisition include complete control over operations, the inclusion of local managers in the organization, and the instant credibility and gains realized by owning an already established company. For example, acquisition has been a key element in Heinz's strategy.[28] Seventy percent of the company's products offered worldwide do not bear the Heinz label.

Regardless of the choice of method(s) used to gain entry into a foreign marketplace, companies must somehow integrate these operations. The complexities involved in operating on a worldwide basis dictate that firms decide on a choice of operating strategies.

Although the task of international marketing is similar to that at home, there are significant differences that can have a profound influence on the outcome of a marketing program. These differences must be considered when developing alternative marketing strategies for foreign markets. One critical decision marketing managers must make relates to the extent of adapting the marketing mix elements for the foreign country the company operates in. An approach to this strategy involves five alternative strategies for marketing abroad.[29] Each is based on the idea of adapting either the product, the communication process, or both to the particular market; or operating on a basis where all elements of the marketing mix are standardized.

Strategy One: Same Product, Same Message Worldwide

This approach involves a uniform strategy for each market offering the same product and same advertising appeals. Obviously, this approach has numerous advantages: It is simple, demands on management time are minimal, and it requires no original analysis or data generation. The product is unchanged, so there are opportunities for economies of scale in production as well as marketing. In sum, it is the lowest-cost strategy.

Unfortunately, the uniform strategy does not work for all products, although some firms, such as Pepsi-Cola and Coca-Cola, have been

---

[28]"Building Successful Global Partnerships," *Journal of Business Strategy,* September/October 1988, pp. 12–15.

[29]This section is based on Warren J. Keegan, "Five Strategies for Multinational Marketing," *European Business,* January 1970, pp. 35–40. Also see Warren J. Keegan, "Multinational Product Planning: Strategic Alternatives," *Journal of Marketing,* January 1969, pp. 58–62.

successful using this strategy. Other firms, such as Chrysler and some food product manufacturers, have not been successful with the uniform approach. These firms have been forced to adapt their marketing mix.

Strategy Two: Same Product, Different Communications

This strategy becomes necessary when the product fills a different need or is used differently but under conditions similar to those in the domestic market. Thus, the only adjustment necessary is in marketing communications. Examples of products where this strategy can be used are bicycles and motorcycles. In the United States, they fill a recreation need, while in many parts of the world they serve as basic transportation.

Since the product remains unchanged, this strategy is also a relatively low-cost alternative. Additional costs would be incurred in identifying different product functions and reformulating the advertising and other communications.

Strategy Three: Different Product, Same Communications

This strategy involves a uniform approach to communications with the product being adapted to local conditions. This strategy assumes that the product will serve the same function in the foreign market but under different use conditions. For example, Campbell's Soup initially fared poorly in the English market. The English were not used to condensed soup, so they neglected to add water. Consequently, they thought the soup was too strong and bitter. Realizing this, Campbell's added water to their soups, thus adapting their product to British needs and wants.

Strategy Four: Different Product, Different Communications

This strategy involves adapting both the product and the communications to local conditions. This is necessary because of different market conditions or because the product serves different functions.

Nescafé was forced to use this strategy in England when its instant coffee, which sold well in Europe, did poorly in England. Thus, a special blend was developed for England. When marketing the new blend, it was found that coffee was viewed as a nontraditional drink, since tea was the traditional drink. The firm was forced to develop special advertisements emphasizing that coffee was for the young person looking for something different.

Strategy Five: Product Invention

When customer needs and conditions under which the product is used are in no way similar to the domestic market, this strategy may be necessary. This involves the invention or development of an entirely new product, designed to satisfy specific customer needs at a price within reach of the consumer. While it is often costly to pursue this strategy, it may be a rewarding one for mass markets in less developed nations of the world. Table 13–1 summarizes the five strategies.

The choice of a particular strategy, of course, depends on the specific product-market mix. Depending on the area of the world under consideration and the particular product mix, different degrees of standardization/adaptation to the marketing mix elements may take place.

TABLE 13–1   Multinational Product-Communication Mix: Strategic Alternatives

Product Strategy	Communications Strategy	Product Examples	Product Function or Need Satisfied	Conditions of Product Use
1. Same	Same	Soft drinks, automobiles	Same	Same
2. Same	Different	Bicycles, recreation, transportation	Different	Same
3. Different	Same	Gasoline, detergents	Same	Different
4. Different	Different	Clothing, greeting cards	Different	Different
5. Invention	Develop new communications	Hand-powered washing machine	Same	Different

As a guideline, standardization of one or more parts of the marketing mix is a function of many factors that individually and collectively affect companies in different decision areas.[30] These factors and their resulting influence are:

1. When markets are economically alike, standardization is more practical.
2. When worldwide customers, not countries, are the basis for segmenting markets, a standardization strategy is more effective.
3. The greater the degree of similarity in the markets in terms of customer behavior and lifestyle, the more effective a standardization strategy is.
4. The higher the cultural compatibility of the product across the host countries, the more appropriate is standardization.
5. When a firm's competitive position is similar in different markets, standardization is more practical.
6. When competing against the same adversaries, with similar share positions, in different countries, standardization is more appropriate than when competing against purely local companies.
7. Industrial and high-technology products are more suitable for standardization than consumer products.
8. The greater the differences in physical, political, and legal environments between home and host countries, the greater will be the necessary degree of adaptation.
9. The more similar the marketing infrastructure in the home and host countries, the more likely is the effectiveness of standardization.

Whatever the case, the decision to adapt or standardize marketing should be made only after a thorough analysis of the product-market mix has been undertaken.

CONCLUSION

The world is truly becoming a global market. Many companies that seek to avoid operating in the international arena are destined for failure. For those willing to undertake the challenges and risks necessary to become multinational corporations, the sky is the limit. The purpose of this chapter was to introduce the reader to the opportunities, problems, and challenges involved in international marketing.

---

[30]Material in this section is based on Subhash C. Jain, "Standardization of International Marketing Strategy: Some Research Hypotheses," *Journal of Marketing,* January 1989, pp. 70–79.

ADDITIONAL READINGS

Cateora, Phillip R. *International Marketing.* 7th ed. Homewood, Ill.: Richard D. Irwin, 1990.

Green, Robert, and Arthur Allaway. "Identification of Export Opportunities: A Shift Share Approach." *Journal of Marketing,* Winter 1985, pp. 83–88.

Jain, Subhash C. "Standardization of International Marketing Strategy: Some Research Hypotheses." *Journal of Marketing,* January 1989, pp. 70–79.

Lei, David. "Strategies for Global Competition." *Long-Range Planning* 22, no. 1 (1989), pp. 102–9.

Ohmae, Kenichi. "Planting for a Global Harvest." *Harvard Business Review,* July–August 1989, pp. 136–45.

Onkvisit, Sak, and John J. Shaw. "Marketing Barriers in International Trade." *Business Horizons,* May–June 1988, pp. 64–72.

Raffee, Hans, and Ralf T. Kreutzer. "Organisational Dimensions of Global Marketing." *European Journal of Marketing* 23, no. 5 (1989), pp. 43–57.

Reichel, Jurgen. "How Can Marketing Be Successfully Standardized for the European Market?" *European Journal of Marketing* 23, no. 7 (1989), pp. 60–67.

Root, Franklin R. *Entry Strategies for International Markets.* Lexington, Mass.: Lexington Books, 1987.

West, Phillip R. "Cross-Cultural Literacy and the Pacific Rim." *Business Horizons,* March–April 1989, pp. 3–17.

Marketing Response to a Changing Society

CHAPTER 14
Marketing Management: Social and Ethical Dimensions

Marketing Management: Social and Ethical Dimensions

The primary concern of this chapter is the role of marketing in society. While we believe that marketing and the free enterprise system offer the best and most effective system of exchange that has been developed, we also believe that marketers have a responsibility to society that goes beyond the profit objectives of an organization.[1]

In the remainder of this chapter we first investigate the relative power and rights of marketers and consumers. Then we discuss four influences that act as checks and balances to control the power of business in general and marketing in particular. These include legal, political, competitive, and ethical influences.

THE RIGHTS OF MARKETERS AND CONSUMERS

Both marketers and consumers are granted certain rights by society, and both have a degree of power. Overall, many people believe that marketers have considerably more power than consumers. Several years ago, Professor Philip Kotler provided the following list of rights granted to marketers (sellers):

---

[1]This chapter is based on J. Paul Peter and Jerry C. Olson, *Consumer Behavior and Marketing Strategy*, 2nd ed. (Homewood, Ill.: Richard D. Irwin, 1990), chap. 20.

1. Sellers have the right to introduce any product in any size, style, color, etc., so long as it meets minimum health and safety requirements.
2. Sellers have the right to price the product as they please so long as they avoid discrimination that is harmful to competition.
3. Sellers have the right to promote the product using any resources, media, or message, in any amount, so long as no deception or fraud is involved.
4. Sellers have the right to introduce any buying schemes they wish, so long as they are not discriminatory.
5. Sellers have the right to alter the product offering at any time.
6. Sellers have the right to distribute the product in any reasonable manner.
7. Sellers have the right to limit the product guarantee or postsale services.[2]

While this list is not exhaustive, it does serve to illustrate that marketers have a good deal of power and latitude in their actions.

Since the Consumer Bill of Rights was issued in the early 1960s, consumers have been granted at least four basic rights. First, consumers are granted the *right to safety,* which means the right to be protected against products and services that are hazardous to health and life. Second, consumers are granted the *right to be informed,* which is the right to be protected against fraudulent, deceitful, or misleading advertising or other information that could interfere with making an informed choice. Third, consumers are granted the *right to choose*— the right to have access to a variety of competitive products that are priced fairly and are of satisfactory quality. Finally, consumers are granted the *right to be heard* or the right to be ensured that their interests will be fully and fairly considered in the formulation and administration of government policy. While this list may appear to grant the consumer considerable rights and protection, it has an important weakness: most of these rights depend on the assumption that consumers are both capable of being and willing to be highly involved in purchase and consumption. In fact, however, many consumers are neither. Young children, many elderly people, and the uneducated poor often do not have the cognitive abilities to process information well enough to be protected. Further, even those consumers who do have the capacity often are not willing to invest the time, money, cognitive energy, and effort to ensure their rights.

---

[2]Phillip Kotler, "What Consumerism Means for Marketers," *Harvard Business Review,* May–June 1972, pp. 48–57. Also see Joseph V. Anderson, "Power Marketing: Its Past, Present, and Future," *Journal of Consumer Marketing,* Summer 1987, pp. 5–13.

The right to choose is also predicated on the assumption that consumers are rational, autonomous, knowledgeable information processors and decision makers. While we believe that most consumers are capable of being so, evidence suggests that consumers often do not behave this way. Further, the right to choose ignores the power of marketing to influence attitudes, intentions, and behaviors. Consumers' needs, wants, and satisfaction may be developed by marketers, for instance. Thus, the assumption of consumer autonomy is not easily supported.

Finally, no matter how much effort consumers exert to ensure they are choosing a good product, they cannot process information that is not available. For example, consumers cannot be aware of product safety risks that are hidden from them.

Overall, then, if there were no other forces in society, marketers might well have more rights and power than consumers do. This is not to say that consumers cannot exert countercontrol on marketers or that consumers do not vary in the degree to which they are influenced by marketers. However, as our society and system of government and exchange evolved, a number of constraints or societal influences on marketing activities have also developed. As shown in Figure 14–1, these include legal, political, competitive, and ethical influences.

FIGURE 14–1   Major Sources of Consumer Protection

Before discussing each of these societal influences, three points should be noted. First, as noted earlier, we believe that marketing and the free enterprise system offer the best and most effective system of exchange that has ever been developed. This does not mean that the system could not be improved. For example, there is still a large group of poor, uneducated, hungry people in our society who have little chance of improving their lot.

Second, while marketing usually receives the brunt of society's criticism of business, marketing managers are no more or less guilty of wrong-doing than other business executives. Corporate responsibility to society is a shared responsibility of all business executives, regardless of functional field. In addition, marketing executives are no more or less ethical than most other groups in society. Similarly, while business, particularly big business, is commonly singled out for criticism, there is no question that other fields—including medicine, engineering, and law—also have their share of societal problems. Some consumers could also be criticized for the billions of dollars of merchandise that is shoplifted annually, as well as for other crimes against businesses and society.

Third, while some critics of marketing focus on the field in general, many of the problems are confined to a relatively small percentage of firms and practices. Table 14–1 presents a list of some of the most commonly cited areas of concern, divided into product, promotion,

---

TABLE 14–1 Some Problem Areas in Marketing

Product Issues	*Pricing Issues*
Unsafe products	Deceptive pricing
Poor-quality products	Fraudulent or misleading credit practices
Poor service repair/maintenance after sale	Warranty refund problems
Deceptive packaging and labeling practices	

Promotion Issues	*Distribution Issues*
Deceptive advertising	Sale of counterfeit products and brands
Advertising to children	Pyramid selling
Bait-and-switch advertising	Deceptive in-store selling influences
Anxiety-inducing advertising	
Deceptive personal selling tactics	

pricing, and distribution issues. Many of these practices are subject to legal influences or constraints.

LEGAL INFLUENCES

Legal influences are federal, state, and local legislation and the agencies and processes by which these laws are upheld. Table 14–2 presents examples of recent federal legislation designed to protect consumers. Some federal legislation is designed to control practices in specific industries (such as food); others are aimed at controlling functional areas (such as product safety).

A variety of government agencies are involved in enforcing these laws and investigating business practices. In addition to state and local agencies, this includes a number of federal agencies, such as those listed in Chapter 1.

Legal influences and the power of government agencies to regulate business and marketing practices grew dramatically in the 1970s; but the 1980s witnessed a decrease in many areas of regulation. In fact, deregulation of business was the major thrust in this period, and government agencies considerably reduced their involvement in controlling business practices. Thus, while legal constraints are an important form of consumer protection, it appears that this influence, at least at the federal level, has diminished somewhat.[3]

POLITICAL INFLUENCES

By *political influences* we mean the pressure exerted to control marketing practices by various consumer groups. These groups use a variety of methods to influence marketing practice, such as lobbying with various government agencies to enact legislation, boycotting companies for unfair practices, or working directly with consumers in redress assistance and education. Table 14–3 lists some organizations that are designed to serve consumer interests. These are but a few examples; one tally found over 100 national organizations and over 600 state and local groups that are concerned with consumerism.

---

[3]For complete discussions of legal influences on marketing, see Louis W. Stern and Thomas L. Eovaldi, *Legal Aspects of Marketing Strategy* (Englewood Cliffs, N.J.: Prentice Hall, 1984); Robert J. Posch, Jr., *The Complete Guide to Marketing and the Law* (Englewood Cliffs, N.J.: Prentice-Hall, 1988).

TABLE 14–2   Examples of Recent Consumer-Oriented Legislation

Year	Legislation	Major Provision of Law
1988	Toxic Substances Control Act Amendment	Provides adequate time for planning and implementation of school asbestos management plans.
1988	Federal Food, Drug, and Cosmetic Act Amendment	Bans reimportation of drugs produced in the United States. Places restrictions on distribution of drug samples, bans certain resales of drugs by health care facilities.
1986	Truth in Mileage Act	Amends the Motor Vehicle Information and Cost Savings Act to strengthen, for the protection of consumers, the provisions respecting disclosure of mileage when motor vehicles are transferred.
1986	Petroleum Overcharge Distribution and Restitution Act	Provides for distribution to injured consumers of escrow funds remaining from oil company settlements of alleged price allocation violations under the Emergency Petroleum Allocation Act of 1973.
1986	Superfund Amendments and Reauthorization Act	Extends and amends the Comprehensive Environmental Response Compensation and Liability Act of 1980. Authorizes appropriations for and revises the EPA Hazardous Substance Response Trust Fund program for financing cleanup of uncontrolled hazardous waste sites.
1986	Anti-Drug Abuse Act	Amends the Food, Drug and Cosmetic Act to revise provisions on regulation of infant formula manufacture.
1986	Processed Products Inspection Improvement Act	Amends the Meat Inspection Act to eliminate USDA continuous inspection requirements for meats, poultry, and egg processing plants for a six-year trial period.
1986	Emergency Response Act	Amends the Toxic Substances Control Act to require the EPA to promulgate regulations pertaining to inspections, development of asbestos management plans, and response actions.

TABLE 14–2 *(concluded)*

Year	Legislation	Major Provision of Law
1986	Safe Drinking Water Act Amendments	Amends the Safe Drinking Water Act. Authorizes appropriations for and revises EPA safe drinking water programs, including grants to states for drinking water standards enforcement and groundwater protection programs.
1986	Drug Export Amendments Act	Amends the Food, Drug, and Cosmetic Act to remove restrictions on export of human and veterinary drugs not yet approved by FDA or USDA for use in the U.S., and establishes conditions governing export of such drugs.
1986	Comprehensive Smokeless Tobacco Health Education Act	Provides for public education concerning the health consequences of using smokeless tobacco products. Prohibits radio and television advertising of smokeless tobacco.
1986	Recreational Boating Safety Act Amendment	Enhances boating safety by requiring a report relating to informational displays on gasoline pumps.

Source: John R. Nevin, "Consumer Protection Legislation: Evolution, Structure, and Prognosis," working paper, University of Wisconsin–Madison, August 1989.

TABLE 14–3   Some Political Groups Concerned with Consumerism

Broad-Based National Groups	Special-Interest Groups
Consumer Federation of America National Wildlife Federation Common Cause	Action for Children's Television American Association of Retired Persons Group against Smoking and Pollution

Smaller Multi-Issue Organizations	Local Groups
National Consumer's League Ralph Nader's Public Citizen	Public-interest research groups Local consumer protection offices Local broadcast and newspaper consumer "action lines"

Source: Adapted from Paul N. Bloom and Stephen A. Greyser, "The Maturing of Consumerism," *Harvard Business Review*, November–December 1981, pp. 130–39.

Bloom and Greyser argue that consumerism has reached the mature stage of its life cycle and that its impact has been fragmented.[4] Yet they believe consumerism will continue to have some impact on business, and they offer three strategies for coping with it. First, businesses can try to accelerate the decline of consumerism by *reducing demand* for it. This could be done by improving product quality, expanding services, lowering prices, and toning down advertising claims. Highlight 14–1 describes one industry's attempt to reduce demand for consumerism.

Second, businesses can *compete* with consumer groups by having active consumer affairs departments that offer redress assistance and consumer education. Alternatively, a business could fund and coordinate activities designed to "sell" deregulation and other probusiness causes.

Third, businesses can *cooperate* with consumer groups by providing financial and other support. Overall, most of these strategies would likely further reduce the impact and importance of political influences. However, to the degree that following these strategies leads business firms to increase their social responsibility activities in the long run, the consumer could benefit.

COMPETITIVE INFLUENCES

Competitive influences refer to actions of competing firms intended to affect each other and consumers. These actions can be taken in many ways. For example, one firm might sue another firm or point out its alleged fraudulent activities to consumers. Johnson & Johnson frequently took competitors to court to protect its Tylenol brand of pain reliever from being shown in comparative ads. Burger King publicly accused McDonald's of overstating the weight of its hamburgers.

Perhaps the most important consumer protection generated by competition is that it reduces the impact of information from any single firm. In other words, in a marketing environment where there are many active competitors, no single firm can dominate the information flow to consumers. In this sense, conflicting competitive claims, images, information, and offers may help consumers from being unduly influenced by a single firm or brand. Conversely, it may also lead to information overload.

---

[4]Paul N. Bloom and Stephen A. Greyser, "The Maturing of Consumerism," *Harvard Business Review,* November–December 1981, pp. 130–39; also see Paul N. Bloom and Ruth Belk Smith, *The Future of Consumerism* (Lexington, Mass.: Lexington Books, 1986).

Each of the major television networks has its own set of guidelines for children's advertising, although the basics are very similar. A few rules, such as the requirement of a static "island" shot at the end, are written in stone; others, however, occasionally can be negotiated.

Many of the rules below apply specifically to toys. The networks also have special guidelines for kid's food commercials and for kid's commercials that offer premiums.

	ABC	CBS	NBC
Must not overglamorize product	✔	✔	✔
No exhortative language, such as "Ask Mom to buy . . ."	✔	✔	✔
No realistic war settings	✔		✔
Generally no celebrity endorsements	✔	Case-by-case	✔
Can't use "only" or "just" in regard to price	✔	✔	✔
Show only two toys per child or maximum of six per commercial	✔		✔
Five-second "island" showing product against plain background at end of spot	✔	✔	✔ (4 to 5)
Animation restricted to one third of a commercial	✔		✔
Generally no comparative or superiority claims	Case-by-case	Handle w/care	✔
No costumes or props not available with the toy	✔		✔
No child or toy can appear in animated segments	✔		✔
Three-second establishing shot of toy in relation to child	✔	✔ (2.5 to 3)	
No shots under one second in length		✔	
Must show distance a toy can travel before stopping on its own		✔	

Source: Joanne Lipman, "Double Standard for Kids' TV Ads," *Wall Street Journal,* June 10, 1988, p. 21.

Consumers may also benefit from the development and marketing of better products and services brought about by competitive pressure. Current merger trends and the concentration of various industries may lessen these competitive constraints and societal advantages, however.

ETHICAL INFLUENCES

Perhaps the most important constraints on marketing practices are *ethical influences* and involve *self-regulation* by marketers. Many professions have codes of ethics (see Highlight 14–2), and many firms have their own consumer affairs offices that seek to ensure that the consumer is treated fairly. In addition, some companies have developed a more positive image with consumers by emphasizing consumer-oriented marketing tactics such as offering toll-free hot lines for information and complaints, promoting unit pricing, and supporting social causes.

A difficult problem in discussing ethical constraints is that there is no single standard by which actions can be judged. Laczniak summarizes five ethical standards that have been proposed by various marketing writers:

1. *The Golden Rule:* Act in the way you would expect others to act toward you.
2. *The Utilitarian Principle:* Act in a way that results in the greatest good for the greatest number.
3. *Kant's Categorical Imperative:* Act in such a way that the action taken under the circumstances could be a universal law or rule of behavior.
4. *The Professional Ethic:* Take actions that would be viewed as proper by a disinterested panel of professional colleagues.
5. *The TV Test:* A manager should always ask: "Would I feel comfortable explaining to a national TV audience why I took this action?"[5]

Following these standards could result in many different interpretations of ethical marketing practice. If you doubt this, try applying them to the scenarios in Figure 14–2 and then comparing your answers with those of other readers.

---

[5]Gene R. Laczniak, "Framework for Analyzing Marketing Ethics," *Journal of Macromarketing,* Spring 1983, pp. 7–18; also see Donald P. Robin and R. Eric Reidenbach, "Social Responsibility, Ethics, and Marketing Strategy: Closing the Gap between Concept and Application," *Journal of Marketing,* January 1987, pp. 44–58.

HIGHLIGHT 14–2
Code of Ethics of the American Marketing Association

Members of the American Marketing Association (AMA) are committed to ethical professional conduct. They have joined together in subscribing to this Code of Ethics embracing the following topics:

RESPONSIBILITIES OF THE MARKETER

Marketers must accept responsibility for the consequence of their activities and make every effort to ensure that their decisions, recommendations, and actions function to identify, serve, and satisfy all relevant publics: customers, organizations, and society.

Marketers' professional conduct must be guided by:

1. The basic rule of professional ethics: not knowingly to do harm.
2. The adherence to all applicable laws and regulations.
3. The accurate representation of their education, training, and experience.
4. The active support, practice, and promotion of this Code of Ethics.

HONESTY AND FAIRNESS

Marketers shall uphold and advance the integrity, honor, and dignity of the marketing profession by:

1. Being honest in serving consumers, clients, employees, suppliers, distributors, and the public.
2. Not knowingly participating in conflict of interest without prior notice to all parties involved.
3. Establishing equitable fee schedules including the payment or receipt of usual, customary, and/or legal compensation or marketing exchanges.

RIGHTS AND DUTIES OF PARTIES IN THE MARKETING EXCHANGE PROCESS

Participants in the marketing exchange process should be able to expect that:

1. Products and services offered are safe and fit for their intended uses.
2. Communications about offered products and services are not deceptive.
3. All parties intend to discharge their obligations, financial and otherwise, in good faith.
4. Appropriate internal methods exist for equitable adjustment and/or redress of grievances concerning purchases.

It is understood that the above would include, *but is not limited to*, the following responsibilities of the marketer:

In the area of product development and management,
- Disclosure of all substantial risks associated with product or service usage.
- Identifications of any product component substitution that might materially change the product or impact on the buyer's purchase decision.
- Identification of extra-cost added features.

In the area of promotions,
- Avoidance of false and misleading advertising.
- Rejection of high pressure manipulation, or misleading sales tactics.
- Avoidance of sales promotions that use deception or manipulation.

In the area of distribution,
- Not manipulating the availability of a product for purpose of exploitation.
- Not using coercion in the marketing channel.
- Not exerting undue influence over the reseller's choice to handle the product.

In the area of pricing,
- Not engaging in price fixing.
- Not practicing predatory pricing.
- Disclosing the full price associated with any purchase.

In the area of marketing research,
- Prohibiting selling or fund raising under the guise of conducting research.
- Maintaining research integrity by avoiding misrepresentation and omission of pertinent research data.
- Treating outside clients and suppliers fairly.

ORGANIZATIONAL RELATIONSHIPS

Marketers should be aware of how their behavior may influence or impact on the behavior of others in organizational relationships. They should not demand, encourage, or apply coercion to obtain unethical behavior in their relationships with others, such as employees, suppliers, or customers.

1. Apply confidentiality and anonymity in professional relationships with regard to privileged information.
2. Meet their obligations and responsibilities in contracts and mutual agreements in a timely manner.
3. Avoid taking the work of others, in whole, or in part, and represent this work as their own or directly benefit from it without compensation or consent of the originator or owner.
4. Avoid manipulation to take advantage of situations to maximize personal welfare in a way that unfairly deprives or damages the organization or others.

Any AMA members found to be in violation of any provision of this Code of Ethics may have his or her association membership suspended or revoked.

Source: The American Marketing Association, Chicago.

FIGURE 14-2 Marketing Scenarios That Raise Ethical Questions

Scenario 1

The Thrifty Supermarket Chain has 12 stores in the city of Gotham, U.S.A. The company's policy is to maintain the same prices for all items at all stores. However, the distribution manager knowingly sends the poorest cuts of meat and the lowest-quality produce to the store located in the low-income section of town. He justifies this action based on the fact that this store has the highest overhead due to factors such as employee turnover, pilferage, and vandalism. *Is the distribution manager's economic rationale sufficient justification for his allocation method?*

Scenario 2

The independent Chevy Dealers of Metropolis, U.S.A., have undertaken an advertising campaign headlined by the slogan: "Is your family's life worth 45 mpg?" The ads admit that while Chevy subcompacts are *not* as fuel efficient as foreign imports and cost more to maintain, they are safer according to government-sponsored crash tests. The ads implicitly ask if responsible parents, when purchasing a car, should trade off fuel efficiency for safety. *Is it ethical for the dealers association to use a fear appeal to offset an economic disadvantage?*

Scenario 3

A few recent studies have linked the presence of the artificial sweetener, subsugural to cancer in laboratory rats. While the validity of these findings has been hotly debated by medical experts, the Food and Drug Administration has ordered products containing the ingredient banned from sale in the United States. The Jones Company sends all of its sugar-free J.C. Cola (which contains subsugural) to European supermarkets because the sweetener has not been banned there. *Is it acceptable for the Jones Company to send an arguably unsafe product to another market without waiting for further evidence?*

Scenario 4

The Acme Company sells industrial supplies through its own sales force, which calls on company purchasing agents. Acme has found that providing the purchasing agent with small gifts helps cement a cordial relationship and creates goodwill. Acme follows the policy that the bigger the order, the bigger the gift to the purchasing agent. The gifts range from a pair of tickets to a sports event to outboard motors and snowmobiles. Acme does not give gifts to personnel at companies that they know have an explicit policy prohibiting the acceptance of such gifts. *Assuming no laws are violated, is Acme's policy of providing gifts to purchasing agents morally proper?*

Scenario 5

The Buy American Electronics Company has been selling its highly rated System X Color TV sets (21, 19 and 12 inches) for $700, $500, and $300, respectively. These prices have been relatively uncompetitive in the market. After some study, Buy American substitutes several cheaper components (which engineering says may slightly reduce the quality of performance) and passes on the savings to the consumer in the form of a $100 price reduction on each model. Buy American institutes a price-oriented promotional campaign that neglects to mention that the second-generation System X sets are different from the first. *Is the company's competitive strategy ethical?*

Scenario 6

The Smith & Smith Advertising Agency has been struggling financially. Mr. Smith is approached by the representative of a small South American country that is on good terms with the U.S. Department of State. He wants S & S to create a multi-million dollar advertising and public relations campaign that will bolster the image of the country and increase the likelihood that it will receive U.S. foreign aid assistance and attract investment capital. Smith knows the country is a dictatorship that has been accused of numerous human rights violations. *Is it ethical for the Smith & Smith Agency to undertake the proposed campaign?*

Source: Gene R. Laczinak, "Framework for Analyzing Marketing Ethics," *Journal of Macromarketing,* Spring 1983, p. 8.

Overall, then, what constitutes ethical marketing behavior is a matter of social judgment. Even in the areas such as product safety, what constitutes ethical marketing practices is not always clear. While at first blush it might be argued that all products should either be completely safe or not be allowed on the market, closer inspection reveals questions such as "how safe?" and "for whom?" For example, bicycles often head the list of the most hazardous products, yet few consumers or marketers would argue that bicycles should be banned from the market. Much of the problem in determining product safety concerns the question of whether the harm done results from an inherent lack of product safety or unsafe use by the consumer.

CONCLUSION

This chapter examined some of the important relationships between marketers and consumers that involve questions of social responsibility. Overall, while society offers marketers considerable power and latitude in performing marketing tasks, marketers also have a variety of constraints placed on their behavior. These include legal, political, competitive, and ethical influences.

ADDITIONAL READINGS

Akaah, Ishmael P., and Edward A. Riordan. "Judgments of Marketing Professionals about Ethical Issues in Marketing Research: A Replication and Extension." *Journal of Marketing Research,* February 1989, pp. 112–20.

Bellizzi, Joseph A., and Robert E. Hite. "Supervising Unethical Salesforce Behavior." *Journal of Marketing,* April 1989, pp. 36–47.

Ferrell, O. C., and Steven J. Skinner. "Ethical Behavior and Bureaucratic Structure in Marketing Research Organizations." *Journal of Marketing Research,* February 1988, pp. 103–9.

Garrett, Dennis E. "The Effectiveness of Marketing Policy Boycotts: Environmental Opposition to Marketing." *Journal of Marketing,* April 1987, pp. 46–57.

Hunt, Shelby D.; Van R. Wood; and Lawrence B. Chonko. "Corporate Ethical Values and Organizational Commitment in Marketing." *Journal of Marketing,* July 1989, pp. 79–90.

Laczniak, Gene R., and Patrick E. Murphy, eds. *Marketing Ethics: Guidelines for Managers.* Lexington, Mass.: Lexington Books, 1986.

ANALYZING MARKETING PROBLEMS AND CASES

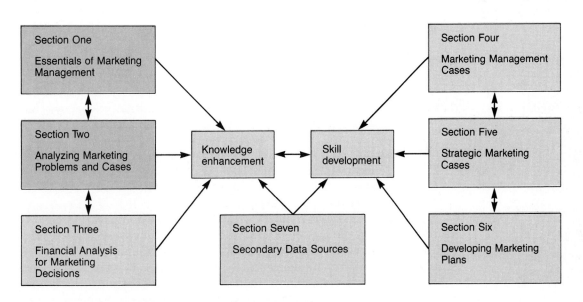

Marketing Management: Knowledge and Skills

NOTE TO THE STUDENT

This section contains a detailed approach to analyzing marketing problems and cases. While the approach is designed primarily for the analysis of comprehensive marketing cases, the logic involved is also applicable to more limited cases. While no approach to marketing problem

271

HIGHLIGHT 1
A Case for Case Analysis

Cases assist in bridging the gap between classroom learning and the so-called real world of marketing management. They provide us with an opportunity to develop, sharpen, and test our analytical skills at:

- Assessing situations.
- Sorting out and organizing key information.
- Asking the right questions.
- Defining opportunities and problems.
- Identifying and evaluating alternative courses of action.
- Interpreting data.
- Evaluating the results of past strategies.
- Developing and defending new strategies.
- Interacting with other managers.
- Making decisions under conditions of uncertainty.
- Critically evaluating the work of others.
- Responding to criticism.

Source: David W. Cravens and Charles W. Lamb, Jr., *Strategic Marketing: Cases and Applications,* 3rd ed. (Homewood, Ill.: Richard D. Irwin, 1990), p. 55.

and case analysis can be expected to fit every situation, we believe that following this approach will direct appropriate analysis and problem recognition for the majority of situations.

The use of business cases was developed by faculty members of the Harvard Graduate School of Business Administration in the 1920s. Case studies have been widely accepted as one effective way of exposing students to the decision-making process.

Basically, cases represent detailed descriptions or reports of business problems. They are usually written by a trained observer who actually had been involved in the firm or organization and had some dealings with the problems under consideration. Cases generally entail both qualitative and quantitative data which the student must analyze to determine appropriate alternatives and solutions.

The primary purpose of the case method is to introduce a measure of realism into management education. Rather than emphasizing the teaching of concepts, the case method focuses on application of concepts and sound logic to real-world business problems. In this way the student learns to bridge the gap between abstraction and application and to appreciate the value of both.

The primary purpose of this section is to offer a logical format for the analysis of case problems. Although there is no one format that can be successfully applied to all cases, the following framework is intended to provide a logical sequence from which to develop sound analyses. This framework is presented for analysis of comprehensive marketing cases; however, the process should also be useful for shorter marketing cases, incidents, and problems.

A CASE ANALYSIS FRAMEWORK

A basic approach to case analysis involves a four-step process. First, the problem is defined. Second, alternative courses of action are formulated to solve the problem. Third, the alternatives are analyzed in terms of their strengths and weaknesses. And fourth, an alternative is accepted, and a course of action is recommended. This basic approach is quite useful for the student well versed in case analysis, particularly for shorter cases or incidents. However, for the newcomer, this framework may well be inadequate and oversimplified. Thus, the following expanded framework and checklists are intended to aid the student in becoming proficient at case and problem analysis.

1. Analyze and Record the Current Situation

Whether the analysis of a firm's problems is done by a manager, student, or paid business consultant, the first step is to analyze the current situation. This does not mean writing up a history of the firm but entails the type of analysis described below. This approach is useful not only for getting a better grip on the situation but also for discovering both real and potential problems—the central concern of any case analysis.

Phase 1: The Environment. The first phase in analyzing a marketing problem or case is to consider the environment in which the firm is operating. The economic environment can have a decided effect on an industry, firm, and marketing program. For example, a depressed economy with high unemployment may not be an ideal situation for implementing a large price increase. The social and cultural environment also can have considerable effect on both multinational and domestic firms. To illustrate, the advent of men's hairstyling could be considered an appropriate reaction to longer hairstyles, whereas a price reduction to stimulate demand for haircuts could well be inappropriate.

Phase 2: The Industry. The second phase involves analysis of the industry in which the firm operates. This phase can be critical, particularly in terms of how the firm's product is defined. A too-narrow definition of the industry and competitive environment can be disastrous not only for the firm but also for the individual analyzing the case. In appraising the industry, it is useful to first categorize it by the

A common criticism of prepared cases goes something like this: "You repeated an awful lot of case material, but you really didn't analyze the case." Yet, at the same time, it is difficult to verbalize exactly what "analysis" means—that is, "I can't explain exactly what it is, but I know it when I see it!"

This is a common problem since the term *analysis* has many definitions and means different things in different contexts. In terms of case analysis, one thing that is clear is that analysis means going beyond simply describing the case information. It includes determining the implications of the case information for developing strategy. This determination may involve careful mathematical analysis of sales and profit data or thoughtful interpretation of the text of the case.

One way of thinking about analysis involves a series of three steps: synthesis, generalizations, and implications. Below is a brief example of this process.

The high growth rate of frozen pizza sales has attracted a number of large food processors, including Pillsbury (Totino's), Quaker Oats (Celeste), American Home Products (Chef Boy-ar-dee), Nestlé (Stouffer's), General Mills (Saluto), and H. J. Heinz (La Pizzeria). The major independents are Jeno's, Tony's, and John's. Jeno's and Totino's are the market leaders, with market shares of about 19 percent each. Celeste and Tony's have about 8 to 9 percent each, and the others have about 5 percent or less.   **Case Material**

The frozen pizza market is a highly competitive and highly fragmented market.   **Synthesis**

In markets such as this, attempts to gain market share through lower consumer prices or heavy advertising are likely to be quickly copied by competitors and thus not be very effective.   **Generalizations**

Lowering consumer prices or spending more on advertising are likely to be poor strategies. Perhaps increasing freezer space in retail outlets could be effective (this might be obtained through trade discounts). A superior product, e.g., better-tasting pizza, microwave pizza, or increasing geographical coverage of the market, may be better strategies for obtaining market share.   **Implications**

Note that none of the three analysis steps includes any repetition of the case material. Rather, they involve abstracting a meaning of the information and, by pairing it with marketing principles, coming up with the strategic implications of the information.

Standard Industrial Classification (SIC) and in terms of the accompanying list.[1]

Class	Possible Implications

1. A few giants (oligopolistic)
Examples:
    Aluminum producers
    Cigarette manufacturers
	Price cutting is fruitless.
	Antitrust action is a hazard.
	Concerned action leads to a monopolistic situation facing the customers.
	Very high capital costs to enter the industry.

2. A few giants and a relatively small number of "independents"
Examples:
    Auto industry
    Oil industry
    Tire industry
    Meat processors
	Price cutting by smaller companies may bring strong retaliation by giants.
	Follow-the-leader pricing.
	Antitrust action against the giants is a hazard.
	Monopolistic prices.
	Squeeze on the independents.
	High capital costs to enter the industry.

3. Many small independent firms
Examples:
    Food brokers
    Sales reps
    Auto supply parts
    Kitchen cabinet manufacturers
    Real estate firms
    Tanneries
	Cost of entry is low.
	Special services.
	Usual local market.
	Threat of regional or national linking into a major competitor.
	Sophisticated business practices often lacking.

4. Professional service firms
Examples:
    CPA firms
    Management consultants
    Marketing research firms
    Advertising agencies
	Confusion of standards.
	Easy entry (and exit).
	Secretive pricing, often based on what the traffic will bear.

5. Government regulated to a degree
Examples:
    Banking
    Stock brokerages
    Rail industry
	Entry is usually difficult.
	Government provides a semimonopoly that may lead to high profits or inability to survive in a changing world.

After initial definition and classification, attention should be paid to such factors as:

1. *Technology*
    a. Level
    b. Rate of change
    c. Technological threats to the industry

---

[1]Robert G. Murdick, Richard H. Eckhouse, R. Carl Moore, Thomas W. Zimmer, *Business Policy: A Framework for Analysis,* 4th ed. (Columbus, Ohio: Grid, 1984), p. 296.

2. *Political-legal-social influences*
   a. Trends in government controls
   b. Specific regulations
   c. Social responsibility pressure
   d. Consumer perceptions of industry
3. *Industrial guidelines and trends*
   a. Pricing policies
   b. Promotion
   c. Product lines
   d. Channels of distribution
   e. Geographic concern
   f. Increases or declines in firms or profitability
4. *Financial indicators*
   a. Financial ratios
   b. Working capital required
   c. Capital structure
   d. Sources and uses of funds
   e. Sales
   f. Profitability[2]

Sources of information and analysis of financial ratios are contained in Section 3 of this book, and sources for the other types of information are contained in Section 4.

Phase 3: The Firm.   The third phase involves analysis of the firm itself, not only in comparison with the industry and industry averages but also internally in terms of both quantitative and qualitative data. Key areas of concern at this stage are such factors as objectives, constraints, management philosophy, strengths, weaknesses, and structure of the firm.

Phase 4: The Marketing Program.   Although there may be internal personnel or structural problems in the marketing department itself that need examination, typically an analysis of the current marketing strategy is the next phase. In this phase the objectives of the marketing department are analyzed in comparison with those of the firm in terms of agreement, soundness, and attainability. Each element of the marketing mix as well as other areas, like marketing research and decision support systems, is analyzed in terms of whether it is internally consistent and synchronized with the goals of the department and firm. Although cases often are labeled in terms of their primary emphasis, such as "Pricing" or "Advertising," it is important to analyze the marketing strategy and entire marketing mix, since a change in one element will usually affect the entire marketing program.

---

[2]This list is based on Murdick et al., *Business Policy,* p. 299.

In performing the analysis of the current situation, the data should be analyzed carefully to extract the relevant from the superfluous. Many cases contain information that is not relevant to the problem; it is the analyst's job to discard this information to get a clearer picture of the current situation. As the analysis proceeds, a watchful eye must be kept on each phase to determine (1) symptoms of problems; (2) current problems; and (3) potential problems. Symptoms of problems are indicators of a problem but are not problems in and of themselves. For example, a symptom of a problem may be a decline in sales in a particular sales territory. However, the problem is the root cause of the decline in sales—perhaps the field representative quit making sales calls and is relying on phone orders only.

The following is a checklist of the types of questions that should be asked when performing the analysis of the current situation:

Checklist for Analyzing the Current Situation

Phase 1: The environment.
1. Are there any trends in the environment that could have an effect on the industry, firm, or marketing program?
2. What is the state of the economy? Inflation? Depression?
3. What is the cultural, social, and political atmosphere?
4. Are there any trends or changes in the environment that could be advantageous or disadvantageous to the industry, firm, or marketing program? Can the marketing program be restructured to take advantage of these trends or changes?

Phase 2: The industry.
1. What industry is the firm in? What class of industry? Are there other industries the firm is competing with?
2. What is the size of the firm relative to the industry?
3. How does the firm compare in terms of market share, sales, and profitability with the rest of the industry?
4. How does the firm compare with other firms in the industry in terms of financial ratio analysis?
5. What is the firm's major competition?
6. Are there any trends in terms of government control, political, or public atmosphere that could affect the industry?

Phase 3: The firm.
1. What are the objectives of the firm? Are they clearly stated? Attainable?
2. What are the strengths of the firm? Managerial expertise? Financial? Copyrights or patents?
3. What are the constraints and weaknesses of the firm?
4. Are there any real or potential sources of dysfunctional conflict in the structure of the firm?
5. How is the marketing department structured in the firm?

Phase 4: The marketing program.
1. What are the objectives of the marketing program? Are they clearly stated? Are they consistent with the objectives of the

firm? Is the entire marketing mix structured to meet these objectives?

2. What marketing concepts are at issue in the program? Is the marketing program well planned and laid out? Is the program consistent with sound marketing principles? If the program takes exception to marketing principles, is there a good reason for it?

3. To what target market is the program directed? Is it well defined? Is the market large enough to be profitably served? Does the market have long-run potential?

4. What competitive advantage does the marketing program offer? If none, what can be done to gain a competitive advantage in the market place?

5. What products are being sold? What is the width, depth, and consistency of the firm's product lines? Does the firm need new products to fill out its product line? Should any product be deleted? What is the profitability of the various products?

6. What promotion mix is being used? Is promotion consistent with the products and product images? What could be done to improve the promotion mix?

7. What channels of distribution are being used? Do they deliver the product at the right time and right place to meet consumer needs? Are the channels typical of those used in the industry? Could channels be made more efficient?

8. What pricing strategies are being used? How do prices compare with similar products of other firms? How are prices determined?

9. Are marketing research and information systematically integrated into the marketing program? Is the overall marketing program internally consistent?

The relevant information from this preliminary analysis is now formalized and recorded. At this point the analyst must be mindful of the difference between facts and opinions. Facts are objective statements, such as financial data, whereas opinions are subjective interpretations of facts or situations. The analyst must make certain not to place too much emphasis on opinions and to carefully consider any variables that may bias such opinions.

Regardless of how much information is contained in the case or how much additional information is collected, the analyst usually finds that it is impossible to specify a complete framework for the current situation. At this point, assumptions must be made. Clearly, since each analyst may make different assumptions, it is critical that assumptions be explicitly stated. When presenting a case, the analyst may wish to distribute copies of the assumption list to all class members. In this way, confusion is avoided in terms of how the analyst perceives the current situation, and others can evaluate the reasonableness and necessity of the assumptions.

2. Analyze and Record Problems and Their Core Elements

After careful analysis, problems and their core elements should be explicitly stated and listed in order of importance. Finding and recording problems and their core elements can be difficult. It is not uncommon on reading a case for the first time for the student to view the case as a description of a situation in which there are no problems. However, careful analysis should reveal symptoms, which lead to problem recognition.

Recognizing and recording problems and their core elements is most critical for a meaningful case analysis. Obviously, if the root problems are not explicitly stated and understood, the remainder of the case analysis has little merit, since the true issues are not being dealt with. The following checklist of questions is designed to assist you in performing this step of the analysis:

Checklist for Analyzing Problems and Their Core Elements

1. What is the primary problem in the case? What are the secondary problems?
2. What proof exists that these are the central issues? How much of this proof is based on facts? On opinions? On assumptions?
3. What symptoms are there that suggest these are the real problems in the case?
4. How are the problems, as defined, related? Are they independent, or are they the result of a deeper problem?
5. What are the ramifications of these problems in the short run? In the long run?

3. Formulate, Evaluate, and Record Alternative Courses of Action

This step is concerned with the question of what can be done to resolve the problem defined in the previous step. Generally, a number of alternative courses of action are available that could potentially help alleviate the problem condition. Three to seven is usually a reasonable number of alternatives to work with. Another approach is to brainstorm as many alternatives as possible initially and then reduce the list to a workable number.

Sound logic and reasoning are very important in this step. It is critical to avoid alternatives that could potentially alleviate the problem, but that at the same time, create a greater new problem or require greater resources than the firm has at its disposal.

After serious analysis and listing of a number of alternatives, the next task is to evaluate them in terms of their costs and benefits. Costs are any output or effort the firm must exert to implement the

HIGHLIGHT 3
Understanding the Current Situation through SWOT Analysis

A useful approach for gaining an understanding of the situation an organization is facing at a particular time is called SWOT analysis. SWOT stands for the organization's *s*trengths and *w*eaknesses and the *o*pportunities and *t*hreats it faces in the environment. Below are some issues an analyst should ask in performing a SWOT analysis.

Internal Analysis

Strengths	*Weaknesses*
• A distinctive competence	• No clear strategic direction
• Adequate financial resources	• A deteriorating competitive position
• Good competitive skills	• Obsolete facilities
• Well thought of by buyers	• Subpar profitability because . . .
• An acknowledged market leader	• Lack of managerial depth and talent
• Well-conceived functional area strategies	• Missing any key skills or competences
• Access to economies of scale	• Poor track record in implementing strategy
• Insulated (at least somewhat) from strong competitive pressures	• Plagued with internal operating problems
• Proprietary technology	• Vulnerable to competitive pressures
• Cost advantages	• Falling behind in R&D
• Competitive advantages	• Too narrow a product line
• Product innovation abilities	• Weak market image
• Proven management	• Competitive disadvantages
• Other?	• Below-average marketing skills
	• Unable to finance needed changes in strategy
	• Other?

External Analysis

Opportunities	*Threats*
• Enter new markets or segments	• Likely entry of new competitors
• Add to product line	• Rising sales of substitute products
• Diversify into related products	• Slower market growth
• Add complementary products	• Adverse government policies
• Vertical integration	• Growing competitive pressures
• Ability to move to better strategic group	• Vulnerability to recession and business cycle
• Complacency among rival firms	• Growing bargaining power of customers or suppliers
• Faster market growth	• Changing buyer needs and tasks
• Other?	• Adverse demographic changes
	• Other?

Source: Adapted from Arthur A. Thompson, Jr., and A. J. Strickland III, *Strategic Management: Concepts and Cases*, 5th ed. (Homewood, Ill.: Richard D. Irwin, 1990), p. 91. Reprinted by permission.

alternative. Benefits are any input or value received by the firm. Costs to be considered are time, money, other resources, and opportunity costs, while benefits are such things as sales, profits, goodwill, and customer satisfaction. The following checklist provides a guideline of questions to be used when performing this phase of the analysis.

Checklist for Formulating and Evaluating Alternative Courses of Action

1. What possible alternatives exist for solving the firm's problems?
2. What limits are there on the possible alternatives? Competence? Resources? Management preference? Social responsibility? Legal restrictions?
3. What major alternatives are now available to the firm? What marketing concepts are involved that affect these alternatives?
4. Are the listed alternatives reasonable given the firm's situation? Are they logical? Are the alternatives consistent with the goals of the marketing program? Are they consistent with the firm's objectives?
5. What are the costs of each alternative? What are the benefits? What are the advantages and disadvantages of each alternative?
6. Which alternative best solves the problem and minimizes the creation of new problems, given the above constraints?

4. Select, Implement, and Record the Chosen Alternative Course of Action

In light of the previous analysis, the alternative is now selected that best solves the problem with a minimum creation of new problems. It is important to record the logic and reasoning that precipitated the selection of a particular alternative. This includes articulating not only why the alternative was selected but also why the other alternatives were not selected.

No analysis is complete without an action-oriented decision and plan for implementing the decision. The accompanying checklist indicates the type of questions that should be answered in this stage of analysis.

Checklist for Selecting and Implementing the Chosen Alternative

1. What must be done to implement the alternative?
2. What personnel will be involved? What are the responsibilities of each?
3. When and where will the alternative be implemented?
4. What will be the probable outcome?
5. How will the success or failure of the alternative be measured?

PITFALLS TO AVOID IN CASE ANALYSIS

Below is a summary of some of the most common errors analysts make when analyzing cases. When evaluating your analysis or those of others, this list provides a useful guide for spotting potential shortcomings.

1. ***Inadequate definition of the problem.*** By far the most common error made in case analysis is attempting to recommend a course of action without first adequately defining or understanding the problem. Whether presented orally or in a written report, a case analysis must begin with a focus on the central issues and problems represented in the case situation. Closely related is the error of analyzing symptoms without determining the root problem.

2. ***The search for "the answer."*** In case analysis, there are no clear-cut solutions. Keep in mind that the objective of case studies is learning through discussion and exploration. There is no one "official" or "correct" answer to a case. Rather, there are usually several reasonable alternative solutions.

3. ***Not enough information.*** Analysts often complain there is not enough information in some cases to make a good decision. However, there is justification for not presenting *all* of the information in a case. As in real life, a marketing manager or consultant seldom has all the information necessary to make an optimal decision. Thus, reasonable assumptions have to be made, and the challenge is to find intelligent solutions in spite of the limited information.

4. ***Use of generalities.*** In analyzing cases, specific recommendations are necessarily not generalities. For example, a suggestion to increase the price is a generality, a suggestion to increase the price by $1.07 is a specific.

5. ***A different situation.*** Considerable time and effort are sometimes exerted by analysts contending that, "If the situation were different, I'd know what course of action to take" or, "If the marketing manager hadn't already fouled things up so badly, the firm wouldn't have a problem." Such reasoning ignores the fact that the events in the case have already happened and cannot be changed. Even though analysis or criticism of past events is necessary in diagnosing the problem, in the end, the present situation must be addressed and decisions must be made based on the given situations.

6. ***Narrow vision analysis.*** Although cases are often labeled as a specific type of case, such as "Pricing," "Product," and so forth, this does not mean that other marketing variables should be ignored. Too often analysts ignore the effects that a change in one marketing element will have on the others.

HIGHLIGHT 4
An Operational Approach to Case and Problem Analysis

1. Read the case quickly to get an overview of the situation.
2. Read the case again thoroughly. Underline relevant information and take notes on potential areas of concern.
3. Review outside sources of information on the environment and the industry. Record relevant information and the source of this information.
4. Perform comparative analysis of the firm with the industry and industry averages.
5. Analyze the firm.
6. Analyze the marketing program.
7. Record the current situation in terms of relevant environmental, industry, firm, and marketing program parameters.
8. Make and record necessary assumptions to complete the situational framework.
9. Determine and record the major issues, problems, and their core elements.
10. Record proof that these are the major issues.
11. Record potential courses of actions.
12. Evaluate each initially to determine constraints that preclude acceptability.
13. Evaluate remaining alternatives in terms of costs and benefits.
14. Record analysis of alternatives.
15. Select an alternative.
16. Record alternative and defense of its selection.
17. Record the who, what, when, where, how, and why of the alternative and its implementation.

7. *Realism.* Too often analysts become so focused on solving a particular problem that their solutions become totally unrealistic. For instance, suggesting a $1 million advertising program for a firm with a capital structure of $50,000 is an unrealistic solution.

8. *The marketing research solution.* A quite common but unsatisfactory solution to case problems is marketing research; for example, "The firm should do this or that type of marketing research to find a solution to its problem." Although marketing research may be helpful as an intermediary step in some cases, marketing research does not solve problems or make decisions. In cases where marketing research is recommended, the cost and potential benefits should be fully specified in the case analysis.

9. ***Rehashing the case material.*** Analysts sometimes spend considerable effort rewriting a two- or three-page history of the firm as presented in the case. This is unnecessary since the instructor and other analysts are already familiar with this information.

10. ***Premature conclusions.*** Analysts sometimes jump to premature conclusions instead of waiting until their analysis is completed. Too many analysts jump to conclusions upon first reading the case and then proceed to interpret everything in the case as justifying their conclusions, even factors logically against it.

COMMUNICATING CASE ANALYSES

The final concern in case analysis deals with communicating the results of the analysis. The most comprehensive analysis has little value if it is not communicated effectively. There are two primary media through which case analyses are communicated—the written report and the oral presentation.

The Written Report

Because the structure of the written report will vary according to the type of case analyzed, this section will not present a "one and only" way of writing up a case, but instead will offer some useful generalizations to aid the student in case writeups.

First, a good written report generally starts with an outline. The purpose of the outline is to:

1. Organize the case material in a sequence that makes it easy for the reader to follow.
2. Highlight the major thoughts of the case and show the relationships among subsidiary ideas and major ideas.
3. Reinforce the analyst's memory of the case ideas and provide the framework for developing these ideas.
4. Serve to refresh the analyst's memory of the case when it has to be referred to weeks later.[3]

The outline format should avoid too fine a breakdown, and there should be at least two subdivisions for any heading. The following is an example of typical outline headings:

---

[3]Murdick et al., *Business Policy*, p. 307.

I. Current Situation
  A. *Environment*
   1. Economic
   2. Cultural and social
   3. Political and legal
  B. *Industry*
   1. Definition
   2. Classification
   3. Technology
   4. Political-legal-social factors
   5. Industrial guidelines and trends
   6. Financial indicators
  C. *Firm*
   1. Objectives
   2. Constraints
   3. Management philosophy
   4. Strengths
   5. Weaknesses
   6. Structure
  D. *Marketing program*
   1. Objectives
   2. Constraints
   3. Strengths
   4. Weaknesses
   5. Target market(s)
   6. Product considerations
   7. Promotion considerations
   8. Pricing considerations
   9. Channel considerations
   10. Information and research considerations
  E. *Assumptions about current situation*

II. Problems
  A. *Primary problem(s)*
   1. Symptoms
   2. Proof
  B. *Secondary problem(s)*
   1. Symptoms
   2. Proof

III. Alternatives
  A. *Alternative 1*
   1. Strengths and benefits
   2. Weaknesses and costs
  B. *Alternative 2*
   1. Strengths and benefits
   2. Weaknesses and costs

   C. *Alternative 3*
      1. Strengths and benefits
      2. Weaknesses and costs
IV. **Decision and Implementation**
   A. *What*
   B. *Who*
   C. *When*
   D. *Where*
   E. *Why*
   F. *How*
 V. **Technical Appendix**

Writing the case report now entails filling out the details of the outline in prose form. Clearly, like any other skill, it takes practice to determine the best method for writing a particular case. However, simplicity, clarity, and precision are prime objectives of the report.

The Oral Presentation

Case analyses are often presented by an individual or team. As with the written report, a good outline is critical, and it is usually preferable to hand out the outline to each class member. Although there is no best way to present a case or to divide responsibility among team members, simply reading the written report is unacceptable since it encourages boredom and interferes with all-important class discussion.

The use of visual aids can be quite helpful in presenting class analyses; however, simply presenting financial statements contained in the case is a poor use of visual media. On the other hand, graphs of sales and profit curves can be more easily interpreted and can be quite useful for making specific points.

Oral presentation of cases is particularly helpful to analysts for learning the skill of speaking to a group. In particular, the ability to handle objections and disagreements without antagonizing others is a skill worth developing.

CONCLUSION

From the discussion it should be obvious that good case analyses require a major commitment of time and effort. Individuals must be highly motivated and willing to get involved in the analysis and discussion if they expect to learn and succeed in a course where cases are utilized. Persons with only passive interest who perform "night before" analyses cheat themselves of valuable learning experiences that can aid them in their careers.

ADDITIONAL READINGS

Bernhardt, Kenneth L., and Thomas C. Kinnear. *Cases in Marketing Management.* 4th ed. Plano, Tex.: Business Publications, 1988.

Cravens, David W., and Charles W. Lamb, Jr. *Strategic Marketing Management: Cases and Applications.* 2nd ed. Homewood, Ill.: Richard D. Irwin, 1990, chap. 3.

O'Dell, William F.; Andrew C. Ruppel; Robert H. Trent; and William J. Kehoe. *Marketing Decision Making: Analytic Framework and Cases.* 4th ed. Cincinnati: South-Western Publishing, 1988, chaps. 1–5.

FINANCIAL ANALYSIS FOR MARKETING DECISION MAKING

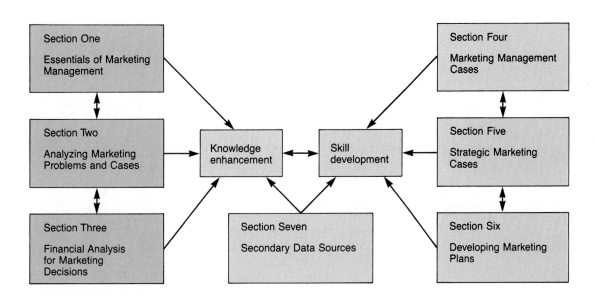

Marketing Management: Knowledge and Skills

NOTE TO THE STUDENT

Financial analysis is an important tool for analyzing marketing problems and cases and is useful for determining problems and defending chosen courses of action. While it is beyond the scope of this text to offer detailed coverage of financial management, we have selected three financial tools which we believe are very useful. These are break-even analysis, net present value analysis, and ratio analysis.

FINANCIAL ANALYSIS

Financial analysis is an important aspect of marketing decision making and planning and should be an integral part of marketing problem and case analysis. In this section we present several financial tools that are useful for analyzing marketing problems and cases. First, we investigate break-even analysis, which is concerned with determining the number of units or dollar sales, or both, necessary to break even on a project or to obtain a given level of profits. Second, we illustrate net present value analysis, which is a somewhat more sophisticated tool for analyzing marketing alternatives. Finally, we investigate ratio analysis, which can be a quite useful tool for determining the financial condition of the firm, including its ability to invest in a new or modified marketing program.

Break-Even Analysis

Break-even analysis is a common tool for investigating the potential profitability of a marketing alternative. The *break-even point* is that level of sales in either units or sales dollars at which a firm covers all of its costs. In other words, it is the level at which total sales revenue just equals the total costs necessary to achieve these sales.

To compute the break-even point, an analyst must have or be able to *obtain* three values. First, the analyst needs to know the *selling price* per unit (SP) of the product. For example, suppose the Ajax Company plans to sell its new electric car through its own dealerships at a retail price of $5,000. Second, the analyst needs to know the level of *fixed costs* (FC). Fixed costs are all costs relevant to the project that do not change, regardless of how many units are produced or sold. For instance, whether Ajax produces and sells 1 or 100,000 cars, Ajax executives will receive their salaries, land must be purchased for a plant, a plant must be constructed, and machinery must be purchased. Other fixed costs include such things as interest, lease payments, and sinking fund payments. Suppose Ajax has totaled all of its fixed costs and the sum is $1.5 million. Third, the analyst must know the *variable costs* per unit (VC) produced. As the name implies, variable costs are those that vary directly with the number of units produced. For example, for each car Ajax produces, there are costs for raw materials and components to build the car, such as batteries, electric motors, steel bodies and tires; there are labor costs for operating employees; and there are machine costs, such as electricity and welding rods. Suppose these are totaled by Ajax, and it is determined that the variable costs for each car produced equal $3,500. With this information, the analyst can now determine the break-even point, which is the number of units that must be sold to just cover the cost of producing the cars. The break-even point is determined by dividing total fixed costs by the *contribution margin*. The contribution margin is simply the difference between the selling price per unit (SP) and variable costs per unit (VC). Algebraically,

$$\text{BEP}_{(\text{in units})} = \frac{\text{Total fixed costs}}{\text{Contribution margin}}$$
$$= \frac{\text{FC}}{\text{SP} - \text{VC}}$$

Substituting the Ajax estimates,

$$\text{BEP}_{(\text{in units})} = \frac{1,500,000}{5,000 - 3,500}$$
$$= \frac{1,500,000}{1,500}$$
$$= 1,000 \text{ units}$$

In other words, the Ajax Company must sell 1,000 cars to just break even (i.e., for total sales revenue to cover total costs).

Alternatively, the analyst may want to know the break-even point in terms of dollar sales volume. Of course, if the preceding analysis has been done, one could simply multiply the BEP (in units) times the selling price to determine the break-even sales volume (i.e., 1,000 units × $5,000/unit = $5 million). However, the BEP (in dollars) can be computed directly, using the formula below:

$$\text{BEP}_{(\text{in dollars})} = \frac{\text{FC}}{1 - \dfrac{\text{VC}}{\text{SP}}}$$
$$= \frac{1,500,000}{1 - \dfrac{3,500}{5,000}}$$
$$= \frac{1,500,000}{1 - .7}$$
$$= \$5,000,000$$

Thus, to break even, Ajax must produce and sell 1,000 cars, which equals $5 million sales. Of course, firms do not want to just break even but want to make a profit. The logic of break-even analysis can easily be extended to include profits (P). Suppose Ajax decided that a 20 percent return on fixed costs would make the project worth the investment. Thus, Ajax would need 20% × $1,500,000 = $300,000 before-tax profit. To calculate how many units Ajax must sell to achieve this level of profits, the profit figure (P) is added to fixed costs in the above formulas. (We will label the break-even point as BEP' to show that we are now computing unit and sales levels to obtain a given profit level.) In the Ajax example:

$$\text{BEP}'_{\text{(in units)}} = \frac{\text{FC} + \text{P}}{\text{SP} - \text{VC}}$$
$$= \frac{1,500,000 + 300,000}{5,000 - 3,500}$$
$$= \frac{1,800,000}{1,500}$$
$$= 1,200 \text{ units}$$

In terms of dollars,

$$\text{BEP}'_{\text{(in dollars)}} = \frac{\text{FC} + \text{P}}{1 - \dfrac{\text{VC}}{\text{SP}}}$$
$$= \frac{1,500,000 + 300,000}{1 - \dfrac{3,500}{5,000}}$$
$$= \frac{1,800,000}{1 - .7}$$
$$= \$6,000,000$$

Thus, Ajax must produce and sell 1,200 cars (sales volume of $6 million) to obtain a 20 percent return on fixed costs. Analysis must now be directed at determining whether a given marketing plan can be expected to produce sales of at least this level. If the answer is yes, the project would appear to be worth investing in. If not, Ajax should seek other opportunities.

Net Present Value Analysis

The profit-oriented marketing manager must understand that the capital invested in new products has a cost. It is a basic principle in business that whoever wishes to use capital must pay for its use. Dollars invested in new products could be diverted to other uses—to pay off debts, pay out to stockholders, or buy U.S. Treasury bonds—which would yield economic benefits to the corporation. If, on the other hand, all of the dollars used to finance a new product have to be borrowed from lenders outside the corporation, interest has to be paid on the loan.

One of the best ways to analyze the financial aspects of a marketing alternative is *net present value* analysis. This method employs a "discounted cash flow," which takes into account the time value of money and its price to the borrower. The following example will illustrate this method.

To compute the net present value of an investment proposal, the cost of capital must be estimated. The cost of capital can be defined as the required rate of return on an investment that would leave the owners of the firm as well off as if the project were not undertaken. Thus, it is the minimum percentage return on investment that a project must make to be worth undertaking. There are many methods of estimating the cost of capital. However, since these methods are not the concern of this text, we will simply assume that the cost of capital for the Ajax Corporation has been determined to be 10 percent.[1] Again, it should be noted that once determined, the cost of capital becomes the minimum rate of return required for an investment—a type of cutoff point. However, in determining their new product investments, some firms select a minimum rate of return that is *above* the cost-of-capital figure to allow for errors in judgment or measurement.

The Ajax Corporation is considering a proposal to market instant developing movie film. After considerable marketing research, sales were projected to be $1 million per year. In addition, the finance department compiled the following information concerning the projects:

New equipment needed	$700,000
Useful life of equipment	10 years
Depreciation	10% per year
Salvage value	$100,000
Cost of goods and expenses	$700,000 per year
Cost of capital	10%
Tax rate	50%

To compute the net present value of this project, the net cash flow for each year of the project must first be determined. This can be done in four steps:

---

[1]For methods of estimating the cost of capital, see Diana R. Harrington and Brent D. Wilson, *Corporate Financial Analysis,* 2nd ed. (Plano, Tex.: Business Publications, 1986), chap. 5.

1. Sales − Cost of goods and expenses = Gross income

$$\$1,000,000 - 700,000 = \$300,000.$$

2. Gross income − Depreciation = Taxable income

$$\$300,000 - (10\% \times 600,000) = \$240,000.$$

3. Taxable income − Tax = Net income

$$\$240,000 - (50\% \times 240,000) = \$120,000.$$

4. Net income + Depreciation = Net cash flow

$$\$120,000 + 60,000 = \$180,000 \text{ per year.}$$

Since the cost of capital is 10 percent, this figure is used to discount the net cash flows for each year. To illustrate, the $180,000 received at the end of the first year would be discounted by the factor $1/(1 + 0.10)$, which would be $180,000 \times 0.9091 = \$163,638$; the $180,000 received at the end of the second year would be discounted by the factor $1/(1 + 0.10)^2$, which would be $180,000 \times 0.8264 = \$148,752$, and so on. (Most finance textbooks have present value tables that can be used to simplify the computations.) Below are the present value computations for the 10-year project. It should be noted that the net cash flow for year 10 is $280,000, since there is an additional $100,000 inflow from salvage value.

Year	Net Cash Flow	0.10 Discount Factor	Present Value
1	$ 180,000	0.9091	$ 163,638
2	180,000	0.8264	148,752
3	180,000	0.7513	135,234
4	180,000	0.6830	122,940
5	180,000	0.6209	111,762
6	180,000	0.5645	101,610
7	180,000	0.5132	92,376
8	180,000	0.4665	83,970
9	180,000	0.4241	76,338
10	280,000	0.3855	107,940
Total	$1,900,000		$1,144,560

Thus, at a discount rate of 10 percent, the present value of the net cash flow from new product investment is greater than the $700,000 outlay required, and so the decision can be considered profitable by this standard. Here the *net present value* is $444,560, which is the

HIGHLIGHT 1
Selected Present Value Discount Factors

Years	8%	10%	12%	14%	16%	18%
1	.9259	.9091	.8929	.8772	.8621	.8475
2	.8573	.8264	.7972	.7695	.7432	.7182
3	.7938	.7513	.7118	.6750	.6407	.6086
4	.7350	.6830	.6355	.5921	.5523	.5158
5	.6806	.6209	.5674	.5194	.4761	.4371
6	.6302	.5645	.5066	.4556	.4104	.3704
7	.5835	.5132	.4523	.3996	.3538	.3139
8	.5403	.4665	.4039	.3506	.3050	.2660
9	.5002	.4241	.3606	.3075	.2630	.2255
10	.4632	.3855	.3220	.2697	.2267	.1911

difference between the $700,000 investment outlay and the $1,144,560 discounted cash flow. The present value ratio is nothing more than the present value of the net cash flow divided by the cash investment. If this ratio is one or larger than one, the project would be profitable for the firm to invest in.

There are many other measures of investment worth, but only one additional method will be discussed. It is the very popular and easily understood "payback method." Payback refers to the amount of time required to pay back the original outlay from the cash flows. Staying with the example, the project is expected to produce a stream of cash proceeds that is constant from year to year, so the payback period can be determined by dividing the investment outlay by this annual cash flow. Dividing $700,000 by $180,000, the payback period is approximately 3.9 years. Firms often set a minimum payback period before a project will be accepted. For example, many firms refuse to take on a project if the pay back period exceeds five years.

This example should illustrate the difficulty in evaluating marketing investments from the standpoint of profitability or economic worth. The most challenging problem is how to develop accurate cash flow estimates, because there are many possible alternatives, such as price of the product and channels of distribution. Also, the consequences of each alternative must be forecast in terms of sales volumes, selling costs, and other expenses. In spite of all the problems, management must evaluate the economic worth of new product decisions, not only to reduce some of the guesswork and ambiguity surrounding marketing decision making, but also to reinforce the objective of trying to make profitable decisions.

Ratio Analysis

Firms' income statements and balance sheets provide a wealth of information that is useful for marketing decision making. Frequently, this information is included in marketing cases, yet analysts often have no convenient way of interpreting the financial position of the firm to make sound marketing decisions. Ratio analysis provides the analyst with an easy and efficient method for investigating a firm's financial position by comparing the firm's ratios across time or with ratios of similar firms in the industry or with industry averages. Ratio analysis involves four basic steps: (1) choose the appropriate ratios; (2) compute the ratios; (3) compare the ratios; (4) check for problems or opportunities.

1. Choose the Appropriate Ratios. The five basic types of financial ratios are: (1) liquidity ratios; (2) asset management ratios; (3) profitability ratios; (4) debt management ratios; and (5) market value ratios.[2] Although calculating ratios of all five types is useful, liquidity, asset management, and profitability ratios provide the information most relevant to marketing decision making. Although many ratios can be calculated in each of these groups, we have selected two of the most commonly used and readily available ratios in each group to illustrate the process.

Liquidity Ratios. One of the first considerations in analyzing a marketing problem is the liquidity of the firm. *Liquidity* refers to the ability of the firm to pay its short-term obligations. If a firm cannot meet its short-term obligations, there is little that can be done until this problem is resolved. Simply stated, recommendations to increase advertising, to do marketing research, or to develop new products are of little value if the firm is about to go bankrupt!

The two most commonly used ratios for investigating liquidity are the *current ratio* and the *quick ratio* (or "acid test"). The current ratio is determined by dividing current assets by current liabilities and is a measure of the overall ability of the firm to meet its current obligations. A common rule of thumb is that the current ratio should be about 2:1.

The quick ratio is determined by subtracting inventory from current assets and dividing the remainder by current liabilities. Since inventory is the least liquid current asset, the quick ratio deals with assets that are most readily available for meeting short-term (one-year)

---

[2]See Eugene F. Brigham, *Fundamentals of Financial Management* (Hinsdale, Ill.: Dryden Press, 1986).

**HIGHLIGHT 2
Financial Ratios: Where to Find Them**

1. *Annual Statement Studies.* Published by Robert Morris Associates, this work includes 11 financial ratios computed annually for over 150 lines of business. Each line of business is divided into four size categories.
2. Dun & Bradstreet provides 14 ratios calculated annually for over 100 lines of business.
3. *Almanac of Business and Industrial Financial Ratios.* The almanac, published by Prentice-Hall, Inc., lists industry averages for 22 financial ratios. Approximately 170 businesses and industries are listed.
4. *Quarterly Financial Report for Manufacturing Corporations.* This work, published jointly by the Federal Trade Commission and the Securities and Exchange Commission, contains balance-sheet and income-statement information by industry groupings and by asset-size categories.
5. Trade associations and individual companies often compute ratios for their industries and make them available to analysts.

Source: James C. Van Horne, *Financial Management and Policy* (Englewood Cliffs, N.J.: Prentice-Hall, 1986), pp. 767–68.

---

obligations. A common rule of thumb is that the quick ratio should be at least 1:1.

Asset Management Ratios.   Asset management ratios investigate how well the firm handles its assets. For marketing problems, two of the most useful asset management ratios are concerned with *inventory turnover* and *total asset utilization.* The inventory turnover ratio is determined by dividing sales by inventories.[3] If the firm is not turning its inventory over as rapidly as other firms, it suggests that too many funds are being tied up in unproductive or obsolete inventory. In addition, if the firm's turnover ratio is decreasing over time, there may be a problem in the marketing plan, since inventory is not being sold as rapidly as it had been in the past. One problem with this ratio is that, since sales usually are recorded at market prices and inventory usually is recorded at cost, the ratio may overstate turnover. Thus, some analysts prefer to use cost of sales rather than sales in computing turnover. We will use cost of sales in our analysis.

---

[3]It is useful to use average inventory rather than a single end-of-year estimate if monthly data are available.

A second useful asset management ratio is total asset utilization. It is calculated by dividing sales by total assets and is a measure of how productively the firm's assets have been used to generate sales. A ratio well below industry figures suggests that marketing efforts may be relatively less effective than other firms' or that some unproductive assets should be disposed of.

Profitability Ratios. Profitability is a major goal of marketing and is an important test of the quality of marketing decision making in the firm. Two key profitability ratios are *profit margin on sales* and *return on total assets*. Profit margin on sales is determined by dividing profit before tax by sales. Serious questions about the firm and marketing plan should be raised if profit margin on sales is declining across time or is well below other firms in the industry. Return on total assets is determined by dividing profit before tax by total assets. This ratio is the return on the investment for the entire firm.

2. Compute the Ratios. The next step in ratio analysis is to compute the ratios. Figure 1 presents the balance sheet and income statement for the Ajax Home Computer Company. The six ratios can be calculated from the Ajax balance sheet and income statement as follows:

Liquidity ratios:

$$\text{Current ratio} = \frac{\text{Current assets}}{\text{Current liabilities}} = \frac{700}{315} = 2.2$$

$$\text{Quick ratio} = \frac{\text{Current assets} - \text{Inventory}}{\text{Current liabilities}} = \frac{270}{315} = .86$$

Asset management ratios:

$$\text{Inventory turnover} = \frac{\text{Cost of sales}}{\text{Inventory}} = \frac{2,780}{430} = 6.5$$

$$\text{Total asset utilization} = \frac{\text{Sales}}{\text{Total assets}} = \frac{3,600}{2,400} = 1.5$$

Profitability ratios:

$$\text{Profit margin on sales} = \frac{\text{Profit before tax}}{\text{Sales}} = \frac{300}{3,600} = 8.3\%$$

$$\text{Return on total assets} = \frac{\text{Profit before tax}}{\text{Total assets}} = \frac{300}{2,400} = 12.5\%$$

3. Compare the Ratios. While rules of thumb are useful for analyzing ratios, it cannot be overstated that comparison of ratios is always the preferred approach. The ratios computed for a firm can be compared in at least three ways. First, they can be compared over time to see if

FIGURE 1   Balance Sheet and Income Statement for Ajax Home Computer Company

AJAX HOME COMPUTER COMPANY
Balance Sheet
March 31, 1980
(in thousands)

Assets		Liabilities and Stockholders' Equity	
Cash	$ 30	Trade accounts payable	$ 150
Marketable securities	40	Accrued	25
Accounts receivable	200	Notes payable	100
Inventory	430	Accrued income tax	40
Total current assets	700	Total current liabilities	315
Plant and equipment	1,000	Bonds	500
Land	500	Debentures	85
Other investments	200	Stockholders' equity	1,500
Total assets	$2,400	Total liabilities and stockholders' equity	$2,400

AJAX HOME COMPUTER COMPANY
Income Statement
For the 12-Month Period Ending March 31, 1980
(in thousands)

Sales		$3,600
Cost of sales:		
Labor and materials	2,000	
Depreciation	200	
Selling expenses	500	
General and administrative expenses	80	
Total cost		2,780
Net operating income		820
Less interest expense:		
Interest on notes	20	
Interest on debentures	200	
Interest on bonds	300	
Total interest		520
Profit before tax:		300
Federal income tax (@40%)		120
Net profit after tax		$ 180

there are any favorable or unfavorable trends in the firm's financial position. Second, they can be compared with the ratios of other firms in the industry of similar size. Third, they can be compared with industry averages to get an overall idea of the firm's relative financial position in the industry.

FIGURE 2 Ratio Comparison for Ajax Home Computer Company

	Ajax	Industry Firms $1–$10 Million in Assets	Industry Median
Liquidity ratios:			
Current ratio	2.2	1.8	1.8
Quick ratio	.86	.9	1.0
Asset management ratios:			
Inventory turnover	6.5	3.2	2.8
Total assets utilization	1.5	1.7	1.6
Profitability ratios:			
Profit margin	8.3%	6.7%	8.2%
Return on total assets	12.5%	15.0%	14.7%

Figure 2 provides a summary of the ratio analysis. The ratios computed for Ajax are presented along with the median ratios for firms of similar size in the industry and the industry median. The median is often reported in financial sources, rather than the mean, to avoid the strong effect of outliers.[4]

4. Check for Problems or Opportunities. The ratio comparison in Figure 2 suggests that Ajax is in reasonably good shape, financially. The current ratio is above the industry figures, although the quick ratio is slightly below them. However, the high inventory turnover ratio suggests that the slightly low quick ratio should not be a problem, since inventory turns over relatively quickly. Total asset utilization is slightly below industry averages and should be monitored closely. This, coupled with the slightly lower return on total assets, suggests that some unproductive assets should be disposed of. While the problem could be ineffective marketing, the high profit margin on sales suggests that marketing effort is probably not the problem.

CONCLUSION

This section has focused on several aspects of financial analysis that are useful for marketing decision making. The first, break-even analysis, is commonly used in marketing problem and case analysis. The

---

[4]For a discussion of ratio analysis for retailing, see Joseph B. Mason and Morris L. Mayer, *Modern Retailing: Theory and Practice,* 5th ed. (Homewood, Ill.: Richard D. Irwin, 1990), chap. 8.

second, net present value analysis, is quite useful for investigating the financial impact of marketing alternatives, such as new product introductions. The third, ratio analysis, is a useful tool sometimes overlooked in marketing problem solving. Performing a ratio analysis, as a regular portion of marketing problem and case analysis, can increase the understanding of the firm and its problems and opportunities.

ADDITIONAL READINGS

Brigham, Eugene F., and Louis C. Gapenski. *Financial Management: Theory and Practice.* 5th ed. Chicago: Dryden Press, 1988.

Brealey, Richard A., and Stewart C. Myers. *Principles of Corporate Finance.* 3rd ed. New York: McGraw-Hill, 1988.

Campsey, B. J., and Eugene F. Brigham. *Introduction to Financial Management.* 2nd ed. Chicago: Dryden Press, 1989.

Day, George, and Liam Fahay. "Valuing Market Strategies." *Journal of Marketing,* July 1988, pp. 45–57.

MARKETING MANAGEMENT CASES

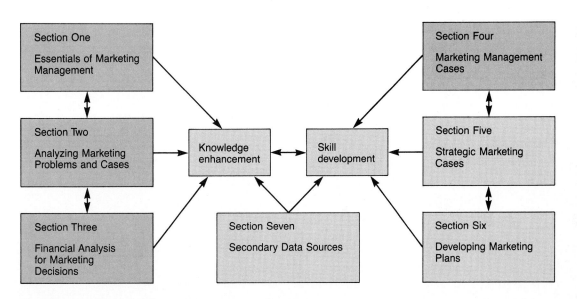

Marketing Management: Knowledge and Skills

NOTE TO THE STUDENT

The primary emphasis of the 33 cases in this section is on marketing as a functional business or organizational area. As such, much of the analysis in these cases involves research and selection of appropriate target markets and the development and management of marketing mix variables.

We have divided these cases into six groups to help focus your analysis. These six groups include cases dealing with market opportunity analysis, product strategy, promotion strategy, distribution strategy, pricing strategy, and selected issues in marketing management. However, keep in mind that regardless of how the case is classified, you should not become too focused on a single issue or marketing mix variable and ignore other elements of marketing strategy.

Marketing Opportunity Analysis

Timex Corp.

J. Paul Peter
University of Wisconsin-Madison

Timex Corp. was one of the first companies to offer low-cost, durable mechanical watches. These watches were mass produced with hard-alloy bearings which were less costly than jeweled bearings. They were also much longer lasting than nonjeweled watches had been before. Timex attempted to sell these watches in jewelry stores offering a 30 percent markup. However, jewelers commonly received 50 percent markup on merchandise and therefore many refused to stock them. The company then began selling direct to drugstores, hardware stores, and even cigar stands. At one point the company had a distribution system of nearly a quarter of a million outlets. This mass-distribution

Sources: "Timex Takes the Torture Test," *Fortune,* June 27, 1983, pp. 112–20; "Can Timex Take a Licking and Keep on Ticking?" *Business Week,* February 20, 1984, p. 102; "The Swiss Put Glitz in Cheap Quartz Watches," *Fortune,* August 20, 1984, p. 102.

strategy was coupled with heavy TV advertising demonstrating the durability of the watches. For example, one of the ads showed a Timex watch being strapped to an outboard motor propellor and continuing to work after the engine had been run for several minutes. Such ads were used to support the contention that Timex watches could "take a licking and keep on ticking." In order to keep dealers and prices firmly in line, Timex limited production to about 85 percent of anticipated demand, making them somewhat scarce.

This strategy was extremely successful. By the late 1960s Timex had 50 percent market share in America and as much as 20 percent of worldwide sales. In 1970, Timex had after-tax profits of $27 million on sales of $200 million.

After a quarter of a century of dominance in the low-price watch market, Timex began to face serious competition by the mid-1970s. One of the major technological advances was the development of electronic watches which Timex executives initially judged to be unimportant. By the time they recognized the importance of this technological change and introduced an electronic watch, competitors had already developed and marketed much-improved models. In fact, the Timex electronic watches were so big and clumsy that employees nicknamed them "quarter pounders" and prices ended up 50 percent above competitive, much more attractive watches.

By 1983 Timex's U.S. market share had plummeted to about 17 percent and operating losses approached $100 million. Distribution outlets had declined to 100,000 outlets. Timex ranked fifth in volume behind Japan's Seiko, Citizen, and Casio, and a Swiss combine, ASUAG-SSIH Ltd. Digital and quartz analog watches dominated the market and even the successful Japanese companies faced increased price competition from manufacturers in Hong Kong. In fact, the export price of the average digital watch dropped from $5 in 1981 to less than $2, and many companies were forced out of business with margins of only a few cents per watch.

At this point Timex decided to attempt to rebuild its watch market. (It also decided to make itself less vulnerable by diversifying into home health care products and home computers.) To rebuild its timekeeping business, the company invested over $100 million to retool and redesign its watch and clock lines. Timex's marketing vice president supported this investment by stating that "we were thick, fat, ugly, overpriced, and behind in technology." The strategy then became to produce watches that were just as attractive as higher-priced brands and keep the major portion of the line priced at under $50. Of course, this forced Timex to compete in a world already overloaded with too many inexpensive watch brands. In addition to watches from Japan and Hong Kong, Swiss manufacturers scored a big hit with a trendy timepiece called Swatch, which was brightly colored plastic and sold for $30. Sales soared to 100,000 units per month and Swatches could not be produced fast enough.

Timex also attempted to compete in the over-$100 price range with its superthin quartz analog Elite collection, which was sold in department and jewelry stores for up to $120. However, as one competitor summed it up in evaluating the market potential of the Timex Elite collection, "It's got one disadvantage; it's got a $12.95 name on it."

DISCUSSION QUESTIONS

1. What opportunities are available to Timex in the low-priced watch market?
2. Assume that Timex Elite watches have variable costs of $30 apiece while overhead and other fixed costs amount to $18 million. What is the break-even point for this product? How many Elite watches would have to be sold to make a profit of $3.6 million?
3. What problems does Timex face in entering the more expensive watch market?

Bally Manufacturing, Corp.: Developing and Marketing Research Strategy

Lawrence F. Cunningham
University of Colorado at Denver

Richard R. Brand
Florida State University

Susan M. Keaveney
University of Colorado at Denver

INTRODUCTION

Dennis Buckley of Project Tourism climbed the steps outside the head-quarters of Bally Manufacturing Corp. As the guard issued him a pass to the executive suite and ushered him to a bank of elevators, he mentally reviewed the circumstances that led to today's appointment.

Two weeks earlier, Dennis, a travel industry consultant, had called on Robert Nero, Bally's director of corporate development. Dennis had pointed out that the travel business was a natural extension of Bally's basic business—entertainment and leisure products and services. Bob Nero listened attentively to Dennis's sales pitch. Eventually he asked Dennis what he thought of the possibility of selling group travel to health club members. He noted that Bally had recently acquired the Health and Tennis Corporation of America (HTCA), the largest health club chain in the country. In particular, Nero wondered whether it

*This case was written as a basis for class discussion rather than to illustrate either effective or ineffective handling of an administrative situation. The names of individuals and some facts and situations presented have been modified in order to aid the development of the case and for teaching purposes.

The authors wish to gratefully acknowledge the contribution of David Pavlich, who served as a Graduate Research Assistant to Drs. Cunningham, Brand, and Keaveney at the University of Colorado and Dennis Buckley of Project Tourism.

would be possible to sell an extensive array of travel packages within the club network.

Dennis left that initial meeting feeling that he might have found a major opportunity to capitalize on his 20 years of travel-industry experience. He had entered the consulting business following a career as director of sales for a large resort in Florida. Buckley had also worked for several wholesale/retail travel agency chains in the Northeast and in Chicago, specializing in group travel. His most recent position had been with First Family of Travel in Chicago.

As Dennis entered Bally's main conference room with Bob Nero, he knew this would not be a casual conversation. The senior vice-president of corporate development, Thomas Ryan, was also seated at the table. Ryan began the conversation:

> "Dennis, I understand that you're interested in helping us determine the potential for group travel packages in our Health and Tennis Corporation subsidiary. We've checked your credentials with several of our contacts in the travel industry and we like what we hear.
>
> However, I want to discuss more than just group travel potential in the health clubs. In fact, Bally has a much more serious problem. As you know, Bally recently acquired the Health and Tennis Corporation of America. When we made this acquisition, we obtained the largest health club chain in America along with a high-quality management team. The management team, however, was more skilled at operations than strategic planning. They were unable to specify a coherent overall strategic plan. While some of the individual clubs had marketing plans in operation, there was little coordination between the clubs, or between the clubs and HTCA management in the area of marketing. Quite frankly, we are questioning their ability to adequately define their markets or even to tell us, in detail, who their customers are or why they buy memberships in the health club chain.
>
> Dennis, you must know some well regarded consultants in the leisure and tourism industries. Can you help with this problem? If you can, we need your suggestions quickly for reasons that I can't discuss right at this moment."

Dennis responded that he felt he knew how to solve some of their problems. After the meeting broke up, Dennis began by conducting a situation analysis of the background surrounding Bally's acquisition of Health and Tennis Corporation of America.

BALLY MANUFACTURING, INC.

Bally Manufacturing Corporation, founded in 1931, was a leader in the leisure and recreation products market. Bally's businesses were broken into three segments: coin-operated amusement and gaming equipment, family amusement parks and amusement centers, and casinos.

Coin-Operated Amusement and Gaming Equipment

Bally's first business segment was coin-operated amusement and gaming equipment. Bally was one of the world's leading manufacturers of coin-operated gaming equipment. According to their 1983 Annual Report, Bally's "fully integrated amusement game operations encompass every aspect of the design, development, engineering, marketing, and distribution of both video and pinball games." It also distributed and sold similar coin-operated equipment that was manufactured by other firms. The company's "Pac-Man" family of games was the most successful in the history of the industry. With such products as slot machines, video gaming machines, electronic slot data computer systems, and German wall-mounted gaming machines (which were manufactured by the Bally-Wulff subsidiary), Bally anticipated leadership in this industry for the foreseeable future.

Bally's Scientific Games, Inc., subsidiary was the leading U.S. designer and supplier for rub-off Instant Lottery games; it sold a record number of such tickets in 1983. Its products were used by 17 of the 18 government-operated lotteries then in existence, as well as by numerous foreign lotteries and various private companies. Working with other Bally subsidiaries, Scientific Games, Inc., had developed a new electronic video Player Activated Lottery Machine (PALM).

Family Amusement Parks and Amusement Centers

A second major business segment included family amusement parks and amusement centers. Bally's Six Flags Corporation subsidiary was acquired in January 1982. Through this subsidiary, Bally operated more theme parks than any other company in the industry; only Disney had larger revenue and attendance figures. Bally's six major theme parks in 1983 were located in Dallas/Fort Worth, Houston, Los Angeles, St. Louis, Atlanta, and Jackson, New Jersey.

During 1983 Bally opened new family-oriented water recreation parks in Houston and Hollywood, Florida. These parks featured wave pools, water slides, diving platforms, and various other water-related attractions. In 1984 Bally planned to open Autoworld in Flint, Michigan. Autoworld was to be an urban entertainment center that was to chronicle America's love affair with the automobile. The company's major theme parks and water recreation parks were located as follows:

Six Flags over Georgia	Atlanta, Ga.
Six Flags over Texas	Dallas/Fort Worth, Tex.
Six Flags over Mid-America	St. Louis, Mo.
Astroworld	Houston, Tex.

Six Flags Great Adventure	Between New York City, N.Y., and Philadelphia, Pa.
Six Flags Magic Mountain	Los Angeles, Ca.
Six Flags Atlantis	Hollywood, Fla.
Water World	Houston, Tex.

Under its Aladdin's Castle, Inc., and related subsidiaries, Bally was the largest operator of family amusement centers in the United States. These amusement centers offered a wide variety of coin-operated amusement games in well-maintained environments ranging in size from 1,500 to 3,000 square feet. Nearly all the approximately 450 centers were located in regional shopping malls.

Casinos

The third major segment of the business was casinos. Bally owned and operated Bally's Park Place Casino Hotel in Atlantic City, New Jersey. This casino-hotel complex contained 512 rooms, a 60,000-square-foot casino, restaurants, shops, and the largest hotel convention facilities in Atlantic City. The next planned improvement for this complex was a 40,000-square-foot health spa.

THE HEALTH AND TENNIS CORPORATION OF AMERICA

On March 31, 1983, Bally Manufacturing, Inc., entered into a series of agreements to acquire HTCA. The terms of purchase called for the payment of up to approximately $77.35 million at closing and an earn-out of up to approximately $66 million, payable over the next five years. The purchase was recorded as $143.35 million added to Bally's assets under the amusement and leisure segment. The acquisition of HTCA widened Bally's chain of family amusement centers to include 280 health and fitness centers across the United States.

The Health and Tennis Corporation of America operated fitness centers across the country, offering such amenities as running tracks, exercise equipment, and instruction. In terms of membership and revenues, HTCA was already the largest operator of fitness centers in the United States. Through wholly owned and partially owned subsidiaries, HTCA operated 280 fitness centers under various names, including Holiday Health Spa, Jack LaLane, Scandinavian, President's First Lady, Chicago Health Clubs, Vic Tanny, The Vertical Clubs, and Holiday Spa. Most of these fitness centers were located in major metropolitan markets, such as New York, Los Angeles, Chicago, Houston, Dallas, Cleveland, Miami, Minneapolis, Baltimore, St. Louis, and

Detroit. Total membership at the time of the acquisition was approximately 1.27 million.

Club membership focused on the use of the fitness centers, which included planned exercise programs and instruction that stressed cardiovascular conditioning, strength development, and improved appearance. In addition, most of the fitness centers offered amenities such as steam rooms, whirlpools and saunas, and a variety of progressive-resistance exercise equipment. The newer centers offered even more services, including indoor swimming pools, jogging tracks and, in many cases, racquetball courts. Several even provided the services of restaurants, bars, and nutrition centers.

Members typically joined these clubs in one of two ways. A "dues" membership permitted members, after paying initial membership fees, to continue membership on a month-to-month basis as long as monthly dues payments were made. With payment of a fixed fee, a "term" membership allowed a member to join for a fixed term, in most cases one or two years. The amount of the membership fee varied by type of facility, services offered, and the degree to which reciprocity among fitness centers was included. For example, the lowest-priced memberships restricted a member's use to a single center. Higher-priced memberships allowed access to most (and for the highest-priced memberships, all) of the health and fitness centers. Only the most expensive memberships were transferrable.

Even though HTCA was the largest operator of fitness centers in the United States in terms of revenues and membership, they were not always the largest operator in each of their markets. The fitness market at this time was extremely competitive. HTCA competed for members and site locations not only with other fitness centers, but with racquet, tennis, and other athletic clubs; country clubs; weight-reducing salons; and physical-fitness and recreational facilities established by local governments, YMCAs, and similar organizations.

Bally had several objectives behind its purchase of Health and Tennis Corporation of America. First, Bally felt that it had ridden the crest of video game popularity, and was looking for ways to diversify away from its dependence upon that segment for its revenues. Second, HTCA was already a profitable enterprise, with a future that appeared positive. Finally, Bally had some plans for making the HTCA purchase an even more profitable undertaking; it was the nature of these plans that had prompted Bally to follow up on Dennis's proposal.

SUBSEQUENT MEETINGS

Dennis called an old friend, Nelson Stevens, a professor of marketing in the graduate school of business at a major university. Nelson and Dennis had worked together on several research projects. Dennis told

Stevens that Bally was interested in conducting a marketing research project, and that if available, he should plan on being in Chicago as soon as possible.

Stevens was in Chicago for the next meeting, which Ryan opened by saying:

> "I wasn't free to totally disclose to Dennis the exact nature of the work that we need completed for Health and Tennis Corporation of America. You have probably been led to believe that our service expansion idea—selling travel-related services through the health clubs—is the reason you're here. Unfortunately, there are other problems. If you'll bear with me I will fill you in on the details.
>
> We bought Health and Tennis with the understanding that we were also getting a super operating management team, able to manage their current service offerings. As Dennis might have indicated, we did in fact inherit a strong management and sales team. However, we have also inherited a few surprises.
>
> The chairman approved the acquisition of Health and Tennis largely on the recommendations of Bob and me. We were convinced, and therefore convinced the chairman, that (1) HTCA was quite profitable (we knew this to be true) and (2) that there were tremendous opportunities to use HTCA to increase the overall ROA of Bally (we believed we could make this happen). In essence, we convinced the chairman that, with only minor additional investment, we could utilize the health clubs as a distribution channel in the sale of a line of highly profitable nonhealth services. One of these suggested services was group travel. However, the list might be expanded to include financial services, magazine subscriptions, or other services. Frankly, we don't care what services they are, so long as they boost ROA of HTCA and, subsequently, Bally."

As a professional consultant, Stevens was understandably concerned that Bally management appeared to have already decided what was needed. Nelson voiced this concern, and asked what purpose a consultant would serve when Bally management already appeared to know what they wanted. Ryan replied:

> "It's rather simple. All we want you to do is develop a strategic marketing plan for us which expands the membership of the club, retains the existing membership, identifies services to introduce that will substantially boost the ROA of HTCA, along with a plan to implement the marketing of those services.
>
> Remember, management of HTCA has been sales-driven and sales-oriented. Prior to and during our acquisition, competition between health clubs was fierce. In order to manage the high fixed costs associated with health and fitness clubs, management typically concentrated on attracting new members. This explains management emphasis on sales and membership drives—they really have little choice. The result is that they have been unable to develop an overall strategic plan for systematically attracting and retaining members. For example, HTCA management had not had the opportunity to even research the characteristics of their membership.

Further, they haven't had the opportunity to do any type of research into the possibilities of expanding their portfolio service offerings to include nonhealth services. That's what we want you to do.

Well, I have to meet with the chairman about another acquisition. Bob will fill you in on any further details. I know you'll come up with some great ideas."

After Ryan left the room, Nero explained that he and Ryan had "sold" their idea of exploiting the health clubs to target customers and to distribute discounted nonhealth services based on the dual effect this strategy would have on ROA. First, the nonhealth services would actually be joint ventures: the prospective partners would pay for access to health club members, believed to be a large, "captive" audience with fairly homogeneous lifestyles. In addition, the partners would share a percentage of revenues (or profits—this was not yet worked out). Because of the possibilities for large-volume sales, Ryan and Nero expected that many of these services could be offered to members at a discount. The effect would be to produce incremental revenues for H&TCA with very small incremental costs and limited, if any, asset commitment. Hence, the ROA would dramatically increase.

Second, it was suggested that offering additional, nonhealth services at a discount could increase retention and attract new members to the clubs. ROA would also be boosted by this effect: variable costs of adding additional members are quite minimal relative to capital investments for the club.

Nero shared many of Ryan's concerns. First, he felt that current club management had sought to develop sales strategies rather than overall marketing strategies for retaining the existing membership. Further, he wondered about their ability to fully exploit the potential markets for the clubs. As Nero put it:

The main difficulty we see with the HTCA managers probably stems from one of their strongest points. Make no mistake about it, they are excellent in their ability to develop and cultivate prospects and close the sale. Without some very good sales strategies, they certainly couldn't have made HTCA the largest health club chain in the country.

Obviously, they must have some instinctive idea of the demographics and psychographics of the membership. They have expressed to me their conviction that their customers are satisfied with the clubs, but they can't specifically answer the question, "Satisfied with what?" What it boils down to is these managers have not had the time, inclination, or training to adopt an overall marketing perspective regarding the clubs. While a sales-oriented approach has served HTCA well in the past, we at Bally feel that due to the changing nature of the market, issues like target markets, segmentation, and customer expectations are critical to the continued success of HTCA, especially when considering the introduction of new products and services.

TABLE 1 Selected Financial Information, Bally Mfg., Inc.

	1983	1982	1981
			(in thousands)
Operating Income (Loss) for the Years Ended Dec. 31:			
Manufacturing and distribution	$ (34,608)	$143,202	$127,749
Amusement and leisure services	63,241*	47,640	21,681
Hotel and casino	60,234	43,135	44,707
Intersegment eliminations	1,987	676	631
TOTAL Income (Loss)	90,856	234,653	194,947
Unallocated corp. expenses, net	(21,457)	(12,381)	(11,140)
Interest expense	(53,489)	(47,766)	(27,802)
Income before income taxes and minority interests	15,910	174,506	156,005
Identifiable Assets at Dec. 31:			
Manufacturing and distribution	372,158	356,788	326,660
Amusement and leisure services	629,167†	342,985	43,551
Hotel and casino	340,373	318,359	330,643
Intersegment eliminations	(67,600)	(14,956)	(12,348)
Total	1,274,098	1,003,176	688,506
Corporate	26,947	11,754	16,754
Consolidated assets	$1,301,045	$1,014,930	$705,260

*Includes income from HTCA from date of purchase through end of year.
†Includes $77.35 million initial payment and $66 million payout for acquisition of the HTCA.

Despite the fact that Bob and Mike Ryan had made the initial recommendation that nonhealth services could be successfully introduced through the health clubs, the fact was that they really hadn't thought through which nonhealth services might work. That is, Bob couldn't say whether travel services would work best or if other types of programs would be a better fit. Further, Bob had no knowledge about how to market these nonhealth services even if Bally ultimately determined that there was, indeed, a market. Thus, what Bally needed at this point was a research design which would allow it to gather and analyze the required data concerning health-club membership and the introduction of nonhealth products.

Dennis who had sat rather passively during most of the conversation interjected:

"Nelson, I know group travel would be a big seller with this crew. If we could present American Express with a well-thought-out plan to sell their group travel packages to a captive market like this at a discount, we could both make a fortune. Bally could take a percentage off the top, or do a joint venture with them and collect a share of the profit. Of course, to entice them we would have to provide American Express with sufficient data regarding numbers of projected travelers, desired destinations, expected service quality levels, and amounts that the membership would be willing to spend. Think of it, Bally/American Express Tours: Another benefit of Bally health clubs. We would be attracting travel dollars and attracting and retaining membership at the same time."

To this Nero added:

"Nelson, Dennis may be right. We could be sitting on a gold mine. Just don't forget that any proposals Mike Ryan and I suggest are subject to financial scrutiny. Specifically, there are people within this organization who would analyze the financial impact of these nonhealth services, including travel programs, not only on the basis of incremental revenues, but on the basis of membership attraction and retention. Don't forget, ROA is the name of the game with the chairman these days. First, we talk ROA and then we talk about market potential."

Nero said that there was approximately $20,000 in the budget for the project, and felt that amount would be sufficient. Stevens responded that there was a diversity of information to be collected and that there really should be several studies conducted, not just one, which would require several different research designs. To this Nero responded:

"I'm sure you'll find a way to get this done, Nelson. Dennis tells me you're one of the best at what you do. I'm afraid that I could stand on my head and the chairman is not going to give us more than $20,000.

Wyler's Unsweetened Soft Drink Mixes*

Don E. Schultz
Mark Traxler
both of Northwestern University

As Mr. Kenneth Otte sat in his office in Northbrook, Illinois, in early August 1977, he felt a bit like Jack in the children's story "Jack and the Beanstalk." He was facing a major challenge against a dominant foe, General Foods' Kool-Aid powdered soft drink mix, the giant of the unsweetened drink mix category.

The question Mr. Otte was considering was whether to recommend a major national introduction of Wyler's Unsweetened Soft Drink Mix against Kool-Aid in 1978 or to continue testing the product. He knew RJR Foods's Hawaiian Punch was considering a national introduction of an unsweetened soft drink mix, and because of Kool-Aid's dominant position in the market—a 92 percent share and virtually unchallenged in its 50-year existence—he questioned whether there was room for two additional brands in the market. If he waited another year, it might be too late. If, however, he introduced a new product in 1978 and Hawaiian Punch did too, then perhaps neither product would be successful.

The question was more complex than whether or not to introduce the product nationally. Wyler's Unsweetened Soft Drink Mix was just completing a test market under Mr. Otte's direction. There was certainly time to make changes and adjustments to the program should he decide to continue testing or launch a national introduction. But the question was: What changes should he investigate or recommend prior to a January meeting with the Wyler sales and broker force?

Management had requested a review of the situation and Mr. Otte's recommendations by October 1, 1977. Since a national introduction in 1978 would require substantial marketing expenditures, Mr. Otte had

---

* This case was prepared by Professor Don E. Schultz and Mark Traxler of Northwestern University as a basis for class discussion and is not designed to illustrate appropriate or inappropriate handling of administrative situations. Revised 1982. Reprinted with permission.

several questions facing him. Should he recommend a national program for 1978? If not, what recommendation should he make? Another test market? A fine tuning of his present program? Major changes? What?

As Mr. Otte prepared to develop his recommendation, he reviewed the entire situation of the category, the product, competition, and test market results. Did he have enough ammunition to challenge Kool-Aid?

WYLER FOODS

Wyler Foods is a Chicago-based company that manufactures consumer products. Their line includes instant soups, bouillion powders and cubes, and powdered soft drink mixes, among other products.

The original company was organized in the late 1920s and in 1930 introduced "Cold Kup" soft drink mix, a presweetened mix in a pouch. It was available in four flavors. About the same time, Peskin Company introduced "Kool-Aid," an unsweetened soft drink mix. Peskin was later acquired by General Foods and Wyler was purchased by Borden. Wyler continued to concentrate on the presweetened soft drink mix market. In 1954 a powdered lemonade mix was introduced very successfully. By 1977 the lemonade flavor accounted for approximately 40 percent of all Wyler soft drink mix sales.

Wyler and Kool-Aid continue to do battle in the soft drink mix market, with Wyler dominant in the presweetened market and Kool-Aid in the unsweetened area. In the early 1960s Kool-Aid entered the presweetened market with an artificially sweetened product using cyclamates. This sweetener was banned by the federal government in 1969 and Wyler, with its sugar sweetening, rapidly gained ground in the mix market. As a result of the ban, Wyler moved up to a 20 percent share of the presweetened market. In 1972 Wyler introduced an industry "first" by packaging presweetened soft drink mixes in cannisters equivalent to 10 to 15 quarts. With this innovation, Wyler's share of the presweetened market increased to over 40 percent. Shares have declined slightly from this level as increased competitive pressures have segmented the market. Wyler did not have an unsweetened entry until initiating the market test described in this case.

SOFT DRINK MIX MARKET

The liquid refreshment market, comprised of hot, cold, and alcoholic beverages, is limited in growth by the "share of belly" concept, which suggests that human beings can consume just so much liquid in a given year. All entries in the soft drink mix market are competing with all other potable refreshments for some space in an unexpandable belly. The level of per-capita liquid consumption, under this concept, is tied to the U.S. population growth rate or changing consumer preferences.

The soft drink mix business, the twelfth-largest dry grocery product category, accounts for about 10 percent of all soft drink sales. It has increased in both quart and dollar sales each year since 1970. This growth is due to a greater demand for more product convenience, a wider assortment of flavors, and a more economical cold beverage alternative to carbonated drinks and single-strength canned drinks. In 1977 soft drink mixes are expected to produce sales of 14.5 million Wyler equivalent cases.[1] Mr. Otte noted industry predictions that with a 5 percent volume growth in 1978, soft drink mixes would generate 15.2 million Wyler equivalent cases.

In comparison with other beverage categories, soft drink mixes are inexpensive, with unsweetened drink mixes the least expensive of all. Mixes cost less than half as much as carbonated beverages and single-strength canned drinks. Unsweetened mixes are least expensive due to the economy of adding one's own sugar. The typical cost per four-ounce serving of unsweetened powdered mix is 3 cents, while the cost of presweetened powdered mix is 4.7 cents. By comparison, the cost per four-ounce serving of carbonated soft drinks and of chilled orange juice is 11.7 cents.

The powdered drink mix market divides as follows. In terms of case volume, the market is divided into 52.4 percent presweetened and 47.6 percent unsweetened. In terms of dollar sales, the split is 74.6 percent presweetened and 25.4 percent unsweetened. The major difference is the cost per quart of the sweetened product versus the unsweetened.

Soft drink mix sales are highly seasonal. Sales peak during the summer months (May–August) and drop off almost entirely during the remainder of the year. Many grocers, particularly those in the northern climates, do not stock soft drink mixes during the winter months after the summer inventory is sold. An attempt to overcome this extreme seasonality was initiated in 1976 by Wyler's. Their "second-season" promotion strategy, which promotes to both the consumer and the trade, was designed to encourage year-round product usage.

SOFT DRINK MIX BUYER

The buyer profile for soft drink mix users shows that about two-thirds of all U.S. households purchase the product. The primary purchaser is the female homemaker between the ages of 18 and 44, with the heaviest

---

[1] One case contains 288 two-quart foil pouches, or the equivalent of 576 quarts of liquid beverage.

concentration in the 25-to-34 age range. She is unemployed and has a high school education. The husband's occupation is blue-collar, clerk, or salesman. Annual household income lies between $10,000 and $20,000. The family has three or more individuals, including children under age 18. Powdered soft drink mix users and heavy users, who consume at least five glasses per day, are concentrated in the north-central and southern states.

More families purchase presweetened soft drink mixes than unsweetened; however, the buyer of unsweetened soft drink mixes appears to be a much heavier consumer (or purchaser at least). The presweetened mix buyer purchases the product an average of every 56.5 days, compared to the more frequent purchase pattern of the unsweetened mix buyer, who purchases every 46.7 days. Consumer panel data show that purchasers of both unsweetened and presweetened mixes pick up an average of six pouches on each shopping occasion.

Unsweetened Soft Drink Mixes

A comparison of the available and most popular flavors shows that the "red" flavors and grape are by far the fastest selling among unsweetened flavors. The available flavors for Wyler's and, in the case of Kool-Aid, the 6 of 16 flavors that constitute 73 percent of their unsweetened mix volume, are shown in Exhibit 1. The flavors listed for Hawaiian Punch are those that have been offered in the presweetened line.

Industry estimates indicate that Kool-Aid accounts for about 92 percent of the unsweetened soft drink mix segment. Private labels such as A&P's Cheri-Aid and Kroger's Flavor-Aid account for the remainder.

The out-of-store or retail price per pouch of unsweetened drink mixes ranges from 10 cents to 13 cents. The suggested retail price is 12 cents, and the typical broker price is 9.4 cents per pouch. The 12 cents price provides a 21.7 percent gross profit margin for grocery retailers, which

EXHIBIT 1   Unsweetened Mix Flavors

Kool-Aid	*Wyler's*	*Hawaiian Punch*
Strawberry	Strawberry	Strawberry
Cherry	Cherry	Cherry
Fruit punch	Fruit punch	Red punch
Grape	Grape	Grape
Orange	Orange	Orange
Lemonade	Lemonade	Lemonade
		Raspberry

is slightly higher than the grocery retailer storewide gross profit margin. The inventory turnover of soft drink mixes is higher than that of most nonperishable grocery store items during the summer peak season.

Unsweetened as well as presweetened soft drink mixes are sold to retailers through food brokers. Brokers, serving as middlemen between the producer and the retailer, receive a 7 percent commission per case for performing the distribution function.

INTRODUCTION OF WYLER'S UNSWEETENED

Target Market Selection

The target market selected for Wyler's introduction differed slightly from the one selected by Kool-Aid. The notable differences were household head's occupation and market size. Exhibit 2 summarizes the market's demographics. The primary users were children aged 2 through 12, who were thought to have little influence on the purchase decision. The female homemaker bought the products she thought best for her family. Hence, most Wyler advertising was directed at mothers.

Advertising and Promotion

Wyler entered the test market with two main copy themes in advertising: (1) "double economy" stressed that Wyler's as an unsweetened drink for the entire family was economical because users added their own sugar and the entire family enjoyed it, and (2) claimed that Wyler's unique flavor boosters (salt and other flavor enhancers) made Wyler's taste better. Both executions emphasized the red flavors and vitamin C content and soft-pedaled lemonade. While the two campaigns were used in the test, they were both considered interim efforts.

EXHIBIT 2 Selected Demographics of Wyler's and Kool-Aid Buyers		
	Wyler's	*Kool-Aid*
Income	$15,000–$19,999	$15,000–$19,999
Household size	3 or more	3 or more
Age of female head	Under 45	Under 45
Age of children	12 and under	Any under 18
Occupation of household head	White-collar	Blue-collar
Market size (population)	500,000–2,500,000	Non-SMSA

The double-economy commercial was tested on two different occasions. One test indicated that the commercial generated high recall among target buyers and particularly among female homemakers between the ages of 25 and 34. However, the other test, while identifying strong awareness of the Wyler brand name, indicated that the specific recall of Wyler's unsweetened mix was low. On the basis of these tests, a different campaign based even more strongly on flavors was being considered. This approach involved the use of Roy Clark, the television personality, who would stress the good taste of Wyler's, as spokesperson.

Kool-Aid's advertising came in three varieties with separate messages for general brand awareness, economy of use, and appeal to children. The general brand-awareness execution, a nostalgia appeal to mothers, said, "You loved it as a kid. You trust it as a mother." The economy-of-use execution showed children's preferences for Kool-Aid's flavor over single-strength beverages and the economy of adding one's own sugar. The execution with child appeal showed the Kool-Aid "smiling pitcher" saving the day by thwarting some dastardly deeds. Most advertising was placed in television: 70 percent network and 30 percent spot evenly divided between day and night.[2] It was anticipated that Hawaiian Punch would take advantage of their character, "Punchy," to introduce the new unsweetened mix, since he had been used extensively before.

For the 1977 test, Wyler had divided the media budget into a peak and second-season push. A total of $10.1 million was invested in spot television in the 33 broker areas that made up the test. From mid-April to mid-August, Wyler had purchased spot TV in prime, day, and early-fringe time. For the second season, the schedule was to be composed of day, early-, and late-fringe time from September until Christmas and from late January into late March. Mr. Otte had already received a suggestion from the agency and his assistant that should the test be continued in 1978, staggered media tests should probably be undertaken since a level spending pattern had been used in the 1977 test markets.

Compared to Wyler's test program, Kool-Aid's program was spending approximately $18 million nationally in measured media in 1977: $6 million was being spent for presweetened, $6 million for unsweetened, and $6 million for the Kool-Aid brand. Two-thirds of the network budget was being used for weekdays and was directed toward women. The remainder was being spent on a Saturday/Sunday rotation directed at children. Spot TV funds were being allocated almost evenly between day (36 percent), night/late night (34 percent), and early

---

[2]Network television provides simultaneous coverage of a nationwide market; spot television involves selecting individual stations to reach specific markets.

fringe (30 percent). During the peak season, Kool-Aid planned on spending $13.405 million divided into $6.58 million in the second quarter and $6.825 million in the third quarter. The second-season expenditure was $4.59 million, divided into $2.57 million in the first quarter and $2.025 million in the fourth quarter. It was expected that Kool-Aid would spend about $20 million in 1978 for consumer advertising in measured media.

Mr. Otte anticipated that Hawaiian Punch, if they introduced nationally, would spend $4.7 million for television in a 1978 introduction. Two-thirds would probably be used in network (33.5 percent each for day and prime) and 33 percent for spot. Advance information indicated that this budget would break down to $3.2 million for network ($1.6 million in prime and daytime) and $1.5 million for spot television.

In addition to the consumer advertising, Wyler's spent $827,670 for consumer promotions during the tests. Expenditures included the cost of samples and coupons. Several print media, such as Sunday supplements and best-food-day newspaper sections, were being used to deliver both coupons and samples. It was still too early to determine the results of these promotions for this year.

Trade promotions during the market tests were budgeted at $292,330. Trade promotions consisted of case allowances to encourage retailers to stock Wyler's unsweetened mix. No matter how much money Wyler's spent on consumer advertising and promotion, it appeared from the tests that grocery retailers would not stock another soft drink mix without sizable case allowances, since most of the soft drink mix inventory traditionally had been sold to retailers using case allowances. Mr. Otte felt that to achieve successful distribution, whether entering additional testing or going national in 1978, a case allowance of $3.60 between the end of February and the end of April would be needed. Given the seasonal nature of the market, approximately 60 percent of annual volume would be shipped during this period. This case allowance would be the highest ever offered in the unsweetened drink mix category, since typical case allowances were $2.88 for Kool-Aid. Industry sources indicated that Hawaiian Punch would offer a case allowance of $1.44.

Preliminary Test Market Results and Options

Wyler's unsweetened mix was introduced into 33 broker areas representing 28 percent of the U.S. population and 40 percent of total unsweetened soft drink mix category sales. Only 25 of the 33 areas had achieved adequate distribution by mid-1977. The 25 successful areas comprised 17.2 percent of the U.S. population and 33.7 percent of total unsweetened mix category volume. Wyler's sold 116,000 cases in the test cities.

As Mr. Otte began to draft his recommendations for the October 1 meeting, he pondered a number of issues. First, if he decided to continue the test market in 1978, Mr. Otte was advised that he would need a minimum expenditure of $4 million for Wyler's unsweetened mix. The plan would involve $2.2 million in media advertising and $1.8 million in consumer promotions, plus the case allowances. If he decided to introduce nationally, he would of course need a substantially larger budget. The expenditure level would be part of his presentation whether or not he recommended a national introduction. Second, the amount of the case allowance was an issue needing attention. He was operating with a $25.20 case price and a 50 percent gross profit margin (excluding case allowances) in the test market at the 9.4 cent price to retailers. If the $3.60 case allowance was adopted, would this trade promotion secure increased distribution coverage and could he afford it? Third, the advertising question loomed. Should another test market or a national introduction include the revised message and claims rather than the "double economy" approach. Also, would the advertising schedule be more potent if it were staggered in a manner similar to Kool-Aid?

What to do? Should he risk another test and perhaps lose the opportunity to go national as Hawaiian Punch was contemplating, or should he develop a plan to invade Kool-Aid's territory in 1978 on a national basis? The risks and the rewards were great either way.

McDonald's Corporation

Henry C. K. Chan

University of West Florida

INTRODUCTION

During the winter of 1990, James Fletcher, who is currently vice president of marketing for McDonald's Corporation, became concerned about the company's recent performance. Careful market expansion, new products, and special promotional strategies have made McDonald's Corporation the leader of the fast-food industry. However, sales per McDonald's store in the United States plummeted to an inflation-adjusted 6 percent during the second quarter of 1989. Fletcher was trying to decide on a set of appropriate marketing strategies for the 1990s in order to stay ahead of competition.

THE FAST-FOOD INDUSTRY

The $60 billion fast-food industry reached a saturation point in the late 1980s. Fletcher expected sales to grow at an inflation-adjusted 2 percent in 1990—down from the double-digit growth rate in the 1970s and early 1980s.

The burger sector accounts for $31 billion of the $60 billion fast-food industry and was growing at 8 percent annually. The pizza sector accounts for $20 billion and has grown 11 percent annually over the past five years. Although fast-food restaurants' sales had slowed, the number of fast-food outlets has increased steadily at a rate of 5 percent annually.

Trends

In recent years, several environmental forces have adversely affected the fast-food industry, especially the burger sector. The traditional frequent users of fast-food restaurants—the 75 million baby boomers, who are now in their 40s and are well established economically—are looking toward the higher-quality and higher-priced entries into the fast-food market. To meet their needs, General Mills, Inc., launched the Olive Garden Italian Restaurant chain in 1982. Red Lobster and other fast-food chains have invested heavily to upgrade their menus.

Over the last decade, consumers' eating habits have changed noticeably. Marketing research findings reveal that American consumers are becoming more health conscious. Nearly 50 percent of U. S. adults are watching their weight. They are seeking fast-foods high in nutritional value and low in saturated fats and cholesterol. Consumers eat less red meat and greasy foods. Per capita consumption of poultry products had increased from 49.8 pounds in 1980 to 62.7 pounds in 1987. Ethnic food preparation at home has also increased rapidly—a 40 percent increase in sales in Italian food, a 21 percent increase in Oriental food, and a 14 percent increase in Mexican food.

Consumers increasingly prefer the convenience of eating quality foods and having a good selection of meals at home. Take-out and home delivery services have therefore emerged as the most rapidly growing business in the fast-food industry. Home delivery has gained widespread acceptance by consumers and has become a formidable competitive strategy in pizza restaurants. Many other fast-food outlets are also experimenting with home delivery. In the Bay Area and in New York City, frazzled two-income families can order their preferred dinners to their tastes and have them delivered to their homes seven days a week. Many small restaurants have experienced great success with this strategy.

In addition, while coping with the consumer's desire for healthier and higher-quality food, fast-food restaurants have been frustrated by rising wholesale food prices and labor costs. Food costs represent approximately 40 to 45 percent of sales in a typical U.S. fast-food restaurant, and labor costs represent about 25 percent of sales. In 1989, beef prices rose 10 percent; and analysts expect beef, wheat, and coffee prices to increase anywhere from 3 to 6 percent in 1990.

The increase in the minimum wage from $3.35 an hour in 1989, to $3.80 in 1990, and to $4.25 in 1991, will further squeeze fast-food restauranteurs' profit margins. Labor costs will go even higher if Congress mandates health insurance coverage for part-time employees.

Fast-food restaurants also face a shortage of workers. The primary labor pool for the industry is declining. The 16- to 24-year-old population, which today stands at 20 percent, is expected to shrink to 15 percent of the total population by the year 2000, and there is no sign of relief in the near future. Many areas of the country have already felt this pinch. Consequently, fast-food outlets have to pay higher wages and develop innovative benefit packages in order to attract workers.

Although the domestic market is reaching a saturation level, one bright spot is the international market, which is growing at a rate almost double that of the United States. The international market was much like that of the United States in the 1960s and 1970s—a period of customer acceptance and rapid economic growth. Major players in the fast-food industry such as McDonald's, Burger King, Wendy's, Pizza Hut, and Kentucky Fried Chicken have aggressively made inroads into these fertile markets.

THE COMPETITIVE ENVIRONMENT

The fierce competition among fast-food chains and from the nonfood outlets in a saturated market forces fast-food chains to frantically woo customers away from each other.

Competition among fast-food restaurants comes from a long list of hamburger and nonhamburger fast-food chains and also from a variety of ethnic food chains and quick-service family restaurants. Major players in the hamburger sector include Burger King, Wendy's, and Hardee's. In the nonhamburger segment, players include Pizza Hut, Kentucky Fried Chicken, Taco Bell, Church's Chicken, and Rax. In recent years, sales of the nonburger segment have outgrown the hamburger segment. Quick-service family dining chains such as Morrison's, Shoney's, Red Lobster, and Roy Rogers have also steadily increased their shares in the industry.

Competition also comes from nonrestaurant stores. Delicatessens and food services are inching their way into supermarkets and traditional nonfood retail outlets. Consumers now can conveniently pick up sandwiches for lunch at supermarkets, convenience stores, and even gas stations. A great variety of microwave oven-ready meals is also available in supermarkets and small grocery stores.

Direct Competition

McDonald's was the leading fast-food restaurant chain in the hamburger segment with a 1988 sales volume exceeding $5.56 billion. Burger King holds the number two position with 1988 sales of approximately $1.4 billion followed by Wendy's, with 1988 sales of about $1.06 billion. In the nonburger sector, Pizza Hut is the world's leading pizza restaurant chain with a 1988 sales volume of $2.8 billion (more than 20 percent of the $13.5 billion U.S. pizza industry). Kentucky Fried Chicken is the world's largest chicken restaurant system. Of the

$6.2 billion U.S. segment, it holds a 46 percent market share with 1988 sales of just under $2.9 billion. Taco Bell is the leading quick-service Mexican food chain with sales of $1.6 billion in 1988.

McDonald's Marketing Strategy

Product.   In the 1960s, the McDonald's menu mainly consisted of hamburgers and french fries. Recognizing changing consumer lifestyles and eating habits, development of new and innovative menu items became McDonald's major focus.

During the 1970s, McDonald's created the breakfast sandwich, which has become a big success. In the early 1980s, McDonald's introduced the Chicken Biscuit Sandwich and McNuggets. McD.L.T. moved nationally in 1985. Salads, introduced in 1987, now bring in about 7 percent of McDonald's total revenue. In 1989, McDonald's introduced McRib in several regional markets and test marketed a 14-inch pizza. The results of the test market are not yet known. Adding menu items is not a panacea for success. McDonald's management is aware that new product introduction is always a gamble; it takes years to develop a new product and millions of dollars to launch it into the market. The failure of the McChicken sandwich is an example of the risk of introducing a new product.

Market Selection.   In addition to developing new products, McDonald's has employed an aggressive market expansion strategy. In 1989, McDonald's had 10,513 outlets and is planning to add 650 new outlets in 1990.

The location of its outlets is one of the pivotal factors that makes McDonald's so successful. McDonald's had typically expanded into suburban areas during the 1960s, and into the crowded downtown markets in the 1970s and 1980s; but now it is opening restaurants in airports and even hospitals. The international market represents an especially lucrative opportunity. In 1988, McDonald's had 2,600 outlets outside the United States. After a 14-year negotiation, McDonald's is completing its first 20 restaurants in the Soviet Union. In the U.S. market, the average annual store sales are about $1.6 million.

Promotion.   McDonald's promotional message focuses on tasty and nutritious food, friendly folks and fun. To accomplish these goals McDonald's has invested heavily in promoting its brand awareness and improving its public image. McDonald's annual Charity Christmas Parade in Chicago and its Ronald McDonald House charity provide the company with beneficial exposure and publicity. A large amount of its market budget is spent on well-planned special promotional programs, including Monopoly II, Scrabble, Kraft salad dressing give-away, Happy Meals, Plush toys, in-store kid videos, and various Big Mac-related promotions.

In 1989, McDonald's spent about $1 billion on marketing and promotion, and the company experimented with music and dim lighting in several test markets.

Pricing. Because price slashing could cheapen the image of fast-food restaurants, discounts have not been widely employed in the industry. However, confronting the intra-industry rivalries and competition from quick-service restaurants and nonfood stores, fast-food chains have no choice but to engage grudgingly in short-term discounts. Discounts of major fast-food chains in late 1989 are shown below:

> *McDonald's:* Offered 99¢ quarter-pound cheeseburgers and Big Macs and 50¢ cheeseburgers, which are regularly $1.90 and 79¢, respectively.
>
> *Wendy's:* Super Value Menu featuring 99¢ junior bacon cheeseburgers and a 99¢ bowl of chili, which is regularly $1.05 and $1.15 respectively.
>
> *Kentucky Fried Chicken:* A $1.99 special on chicken sandwiches and french fries, which is regularly $2.44.
>
> *Hardee's:* A $1.99 special on a regular roast beef sandwich and medium soft drink, which is regularly $2.39.
>
> *Taco Bell:* Tacos and burritos for 59¢ per shell, compared with the regular prices of 79¢ and $1.07 per shell.

Burger King's Strategy

In the late 1980s, Burger King experienced four years of flat sales and a 49 percent decline in profit. In the hope of reversing that trend, Burger King introduced several new menu items, including a salad bar, Chicken Fingers, Chicken Tenders, and Fish Tenders. Burger King was also the first fast-food chain to provide a nutrition guide that includes information on the calories, fats, salt, and protein content of Burger King's foods. To attract new market segments, Haagen-Daz ice cream bars and broiled chicken made their debut at Burger King in 1989. Like McDonald's, Burger King has aggressively expanded its markets in the United States and abroad. In 1986, Burger King began operating 20 mobile food service vehicles to bring its menus to remote locations, such as military bases and national parks. In 1989, Burger King had 5,737 restaurants in the United States; average annual store sales were about $1 million.

Some industry analysts believe that Burger King's poor sales in recent years have been caused by a lack of focus in its advertising campaigns and abrupt changes in promotional strategies. From

1974 to 1989, Burger King changed its advertising themes eight times. Some of its early memorable messages include, "Have It Your Way" (1974–76), "Battle of the Burgers" (1983–86), "We Do It Like You'd Do It" (1988–89), and "Sometimes You've Gotta Break the Rules" (1989–90). Many franchisees were unhappy about the latest campaign theme and criticized the rules-breaking theme as ill-focused and incomprehensible.

In 1989, Burger King's marketing budget was about $250 million, of which $215 million was spent on advertising. Gary Langstaff, vice president of marketing, who left Hardee's in April 1989, indicated that Burger King would place more emphasis on special market segments and brand image and less on product promotion. In order to penetrate the minority markets, Spanish-language songs have been aired in several major Hispanic markets such as Miami, Los Angeles, and San Antonio. However, Burger King once again changed its promotion strategy by pulling its corporate image commercial spots in early 1990.

Hardee's Strategy

To keep abreast of McDonald's and Burger King, Hardee's has diversified and upgraded its limited menu featuring specialty sandwiches— Big Roast Beef sandwich, hamburgers and soft drinks. In 1984, the chain added three entree salads—garden, chef, and shrimp. In 1987, Hardee's rolled out a soft-serve ice cream program in a bid to attract more women, and in 1988, Chicken Stix was introduced. The acquisition of Roy Rogers not only gives Hardee's greater presence in the Northwest but also adds boned chicken to its menu. In June 1990, Hardee's announced the debut of a light hamburger sandwich called "Lean 1" that has about 30 percent less total fat than the chain's other quarter-pound hamburgers.

Founded in 1960, Hardee's has been aggressively expanding into the national market through franchising and acquisitions. Hardee's purchased the 650-unit Burger Chef chain from General Foods Corp. in 1962. Traditionally, Hardee's market strategy focused on small towns, thereby avoiding fierce battles with McDonald's and other major fast-food chains. Now, however, Hardee's is inching into big cities. In 1986, Hardee's signed a contract with Southland, the owner of the largest convenience store chain, to distribute Hardee's sandwiches in Southland's 7,636 Seven-Eleven stores. In April 1990, Hardee's acquired the 638-unit Roy Rogers chain. This move gives the number four fast-food chain a total of 3,968 units and also enables Hardee's to gain vital market in the Northwest United States.

As a small regional fast-food chain in the 1970s, Hardee's had wisely utilized sales promotion and community relations to build its image and sales. Hardee's has sponsored many community events in small towns, such as offering free meals to local high schoolers who make a 3.0 average, and giving special price breaks to bowlers for high scores. In order to transform its small-town appeal into a big-city image, and to differentiate itself from other fast-food chains, Hardee's launched a low-key spot advertising campaign in 1990. The spot commercials make no mention of price cutting and product promotion. They just talk about Hardee's new Grilled Chicken sandwich—in a casual tone directed to consumers as individuals. The only carry-over of the past advertising theme is, "We're out to win you over."

Some industry analysts consider Hardee's to be the most aggressive fast-food chain. Its goal is to pass number two Burger King.

Wendy's Strategy

In the mid-1980s, Wendy's added its very popular Super Bar—a hot and cold buffet. In 1988, Super Bars accounted for about 20 percent of sales in the restaurants carrying it. In 1989, Wendy's tested a new grilled chicken sandwich—the third chicken product, and continued to revamp its breakfast menu. In 1990, the chain publicized using pure vegetable oil for its fried items.

Market segmentation has been Wendy's strategic focus. Its goal is to build sales volume by broadening the base of targeted consumers. For example, in the late 1980s Wendy's experimented with family, weekend, and dinner markets, and added drive-through windows and takeout menus. Although Wendy's has steadily added restaurants in traditional locations, it is now opening restaurants in Sears and even in supermarkets. In 1989, Wendy's had 3,762 outlets in the domestic United States and 241 outlets abroad. The average annual sales volume per U.S. outlet was about $750,000.

Wendy's has consistently promoted an image of quality food, excellent service, and dining ambiance. Its national advertising theme has been, "The Best Burger in the Business and a Whole Lot More." Wendy's has been perceived as a chain at the higher end of the fast-food price spectrum. In order to eliminate the high-price image and expand its customer base, Wendy's launched a new ad campaign in 1990 touting the company's Super Value Menu—an array of 99-cent items. In 1988, service enhancement programs included updating crew and manager training, adding headsets and timers for the drive-through windows, and introducing customer comment cards.

Indirect Competition

The Nonhamburger Fast-Food Chains.   The gradual shift of consumer preference toward hamburger substitutes presents strong competition for hamburger fast-food restaurants. The nonburger fast-food sector grew by about 11 percent in 1989. Pizza and fried chicken had taken the lion's share of this sector.

In the United States, Pizza Hut, Kentucky Fried Chicken, and Taco Bell restaurants hold leading positions in their respective segments with total sales in 1988 amounting to $7.3 billion.

Pizza Hut.   Pizza Hut is the leading pizza restaurant chain in the world with 1988 U.S. sales volume of $2.8 billion. Internationally, there are Pizza Hut restaurants in 50 countries. Two restaurants are currently being constructed in the U.S.S.R.

In the early 1980s the five-minute personal pan pizza was introduced. Hand-tossed traditional pizza was introduced during 1988 and now accounts for about 20 percent of Pizza Hut's total pizza sales.

New Pizza Huts are opening in hospitals, airports, universities, and shopping malls. Pizza Hut Express units, where customers can purchase a personal pan pizza in seconds, have opened in high-traffic areas. Delivery has taken off since mid-1987, and annual sales are growing at double-digit rates. A Pairs Program—offering two pizzas for one low price—is very attractive to both carry-out and delivery customers.

Kentucky Fried Chicken.   Kentucky Fried Chicken is the world's largest quick-service chicken restaurant chain. In 1989, U.S. sales were $2.1 billion, and $2.1 billion in 57 other countries.

New value-oriented products were introduced in the late 1980s, including Chicken Little sandwiches for lunch or snacks, chicken filet burgers, and grilled chicken.

New outlets are opening in shopping malls and other high-traffic areas. Home delivery was tested in several markets in 1989.

Taco Bell.   Taco Bell is the leading U.S. chain in the quick-service Mexican category. Sales in 1988 in the United States and six international markets amounted to $1.6 billion.

In 1987 Taco Bell introduced Steak Fajitas and Chicken Fajitas. In 1988 they introduced Meximelt, a tortilla with melted cheese, a low-cost item that can be eaten either as a main dish or as a side dish.

PepsiCo, the parent company of Kentucky Fried Chicken, Pizza Hut, and Taco Bell, is experimenting with the concept of combining them into one store to provide customers with a greater selection while cutting down on operating expenses.

Sales of major nonburger, fast-food, and quick service family-dining restaurants are given in Exhibit 1.

THE McDONALD'S CORPORATION

McDonald's Corporation was incorporated in Delaware, on March 1, 1965. McDonald's operates in one industry segment. Substantially all revenues result from the sale of menu products, regardless of whether the restaurants are operated by the company, its franchisees, or affiliates. As of January 1990, McDonald's had 11,300 restaurants. Exhibit 2 shows the geographic location of these outlets.

Sales outside of the United States continue to be strong, despite weaker foreign currencies. During the past five years, 41 percent of systemwide restaurants have been added outside of the United States.

EXHIBIT 1   Sales of Major Nonburger and Family Dining Restaurants (in thousands of dollars)

	1987	*1988*
Kentucky Fried Chicken		$6,000,000
Pizza Hut		2,800,000
Taco Bell		1,600,000
Church's Fried Chicken	$400,525	419,600
Morrison's	689,277	829,158
Shoney's	671,124	752,134
Rax	52,825	62,462

Source: Moody's.

EXHIBIT 2   Geographic Locations of McDonald's Restaurants

Location	*Year*					
	1985	*1986*	*1987*	*1988*	*1989*	*1990*[a]
U.S.				7,567		
Outside U.S.A.						
Canada				515		
W. Europe				665		
Pacific				873		
Latin America				85		
Other				462		
Total	8,901	9,410	9,911	10,167	10,513	11,300

[a] Up to February 1990.

Source: InfoTrac.

EXHIBIT 3   McDonald's Sales and Profits by Geographic Segment (in millions of dollars)

	Year			
	1986	*1987*	*1988*	*1989*
Revenue				
U.S.	$3,077	$3,437	$3,716	$3,923
Europe	557	767	1,015	1,168
Canada	435	468	540	621
Other (Pacific and Latin American)	172	221	295	430
Total revenue	$4,240	4,893	5,566	$6,142
Operating Income				
U.S.	809	883	909	995
Europe	70	109	164	204
Canada	84	91	109	118
Other	59	79	102	143
Total operating income	1,021	1,162	1,284	1,459
Interest expense	(173)	(203)	(237)	(302)
Income before provision for income taxes	848	959	1,047	1,157
Assets				
U.S.	4,218	4,509	5,148	5,846
Europe	996	1,460	1,703	2,063
Canada	358	422	511	562
Other	397	591	798	904
Total assets	5,969	6,982	8,160	9,175

Source: InfoTrac.

The major company-operated markets are located in England, Canada, and West Germany. Restaurants operated by affiliates are located primarily in Japan and other Pacific countries due to local business and political conditions.

Sales and profit information by geographic segments are shown in Exhibit 3. Financial statements from 1986 to 1989 are shown in Exhibit 4.

Although Fletcher was satisfied with McDonald's profit margins in recent years, the future prospects for the fast-food industry appear dreadful. Price, product, and locational competition have become so fierce that profit growth may be impossible. How can McDonald's attract health-conscious consumers? What new products should be introduced? Should it go with a McPizza and McRib? Should it expand its menu into new areas? What operational problems may it encounter?

EXHIBIT 4   McDonald's Profit and Loss Statement, 1986–89 (in millions of dollars)

	1986	1987	1988	1989
Net sales	$4,143	$4,894	$5,566	$6,142
Cost of goods	1,808	3,013	2,377	2,581
Gross profit	2,336	1,880	3,189	3,561
Sell gen. & admin. expenses	1,175	525	1,581	1,873
Income before dep. & amort.	1,161	1,355	1,608	1,688
Depreciation and amort.	236	193	324	229
Nonoperating income	97	—	—	—
Interest expenses	173	203	237	302
Net income before taxes	848	959	1,046	1,157
Provision for inc. taxes	368	410	401	430
Net inc. bef. ex. items	480	549	646	727
Ex. items & disc. ops.	—	47	—	—
Net income	480	596	646	727
Outstanding shares	126,985	207,567	207,567	362,000

Source: InfoTrac.

Should it discount? What market expansion and locational strategies should be used in the U.S. market and in the international markets? Which international regions should it focus on? Can it improve profitability in European markets? Fletcher's plan of action would have to convince top management that the new program could be successfully implemented despite a hostile environment.

Prange Meats*

Lawrence M. Lamont
Marc L. Gordon
both of Washington and Lee University

As Toby Prange reviewed the 1988 financial statements for Prange Meats, Inc., he was again reminded that over the past several years, the meat-processing business had shown no sales growth and only a slight improvement in profitability. Sure, the creditors were being paid, but Prange Meats had not met a sales goal in five years. Despite attempts by management to revitalize the company, it seemed to be drifting with no apparent marketing strategy.

Toby and his brother-in-law, Dan Katora, had experimented with several market opportunities in hopes of improving sales and profitability, but generally the results of their efforts had been disappointing. Since 1982, they had developed a new product, experimented with direct-mail marketing of frozen steaks, opened a retail outlet selling a variety of frozen meat products, and had even considered opening a distribution facility in a more desirable location. Recently, Toby Prange had contacted a large Chicago-based mass merchandiser with a proposal to market frozen steaks and hamburger patties through a leased department in their retail stores. Although the new venture seemed attractive, Toby was uncertain about its profitability and he wondered how aggressively it should be pursued. He reflected, "Our efforts at selling directly to consumers have only been modestly successful."

THE HISTORY OF PRANGE MEATS

Anton Prange, the founder of Prange Meats, was discharged from the U.S. Army in 1948. Using his military experience as a cook, he went to work making sausage in a small Polish butcher shop in Chicago on Milwaukee Avenue. In 1963, he rented a building on Chicago's south

*Property of the Washington and Lee University Department of Administration. Case material is prepared as a basis for class discussion, and not designed to present illustrations of either effective or ineffective handling of administrative problems.

The authors gratefully acknowledge the cooperation and assistance of Mr. Toby Prange and Mr. Dan Katora, senior management of Prange Meats, Inc.

side and formed Prange Meats, a sole proprietorship engaged in processing beef into hamburger patties and steaks. Five years later, following hard work and sales growth, Anton borrowed money to purchase a building at 4340 W. Diversey. Equipping the building with used freezers and coolers, Prange began processing beef on a larger scale.

In July 1969, Anton Prange died at the age of 52, leaving three children and his business in the capable hands of his wife Dorothy. She assumed the role of president and incorporated the business. Shortly after his father's death, Michael Prange, the oldest son, joined the company.

The company expanded slowly over the next 11 years, acquiring new processing equipment and an adjoining building to increase production. Shortly after the expansion, Michael Prange died unexpectedly. In 1975, Dan Katora, a son-in-law, joined Prange Meats in a management capacity. He was followed by the Prange's youngest son, Toby, who began to work for the company in 1980.

In October 1986, Mrs. Prange retired from the day-to-day operation of the business, retaining ownership of 100 percent of the common stock and the title of president. She also continued to serve on the company's board of directors. Presently, Toby Prange serves as vice president of administration, and Dan Katora as vice president of production. Figure 1 presents the current organizational structure of

FIGURE 1   Prange Meats, Inc., Organization Chart

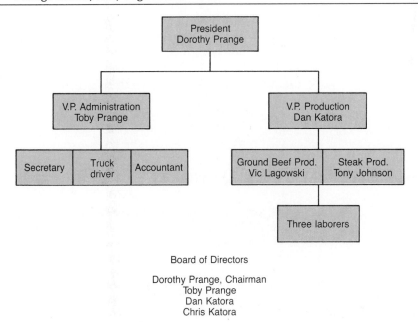

Board of Directors

Dorothy Prange, Chairman
Toby Prange
Dan Katora
Chris Katora

Prange Meats, Inc. The company has 11 employees and has been operating at about 50 percent of capacity for the past several years. Sales were $1.23 million in 1988 and the net income was $6,292.18. The income statement in Table 1 and the balance sheet in Table 2 provide a five-year financial history of operations. It is notable that the company has been conservatively financed and has no long-term debt.

MEAT PROCESSING AND MARKETING

The United States Department of Agriculture (USDA) carefully regulates the processing and marketing of meat. Meat-processing companies, such as Prange, that are involved in interstate commerce are subjected to a daily on-premise federal inspection for sanitation and the accuracy of weights. Additionally, all meat is federally inspected prior to processing and assigned one of five quality ratings:

1. Prime
2. Choice
3. Select/Good
4. Utility
5. Canner and Cutter

Prime is regarded as the superior grade, while Canner and Cutter is an inferior product. Quality is assigned on the basis of gristle, fat content, color, tenderness, and marbleization. A prime piece of beef, for example, comes from a corn-fed steer, has no gristle, little fat (excluding the marbleization), and is extremely tender. Prime products are purchased by commercial establishments such as upscale restaurants and households with discretionary income. While products processed from select and utility grades of beef generally are not regarded as premium, there are advantages to these grades: the steaks provide excellent nutrition and value for volume feeders such as hospitals, restaurants, and institutions; and the lower fat content makes the meat very suitable for the health-conscious consumer.

PRANGE HAMBURGER PATTIES AND STEAKS

Prange Meats, Inc., is primarily involved in processing beef into hamburger patties and steaks. The products are sold frozen and in bulk quantities. The final product is packed in boxes ranging from 2 to 10 pounds and further packaged for delivery in 40- or 50-pound shipping cases. The steaks and patties are separated with a layer of paper and placed in plastic bags within the individual boxes. Cooking instructions appear on the side of the boxes.

The beef used in the Prange hamburger patty line consists of fresh beef chucks, USDA utility grade, 90–92 percent lean, and fresh steer loin trimmings, USDA choice, 50–55 percent lean. Most of the patties processed by Prange contain six percent dry soy protein additive, although pure beef patties are also produced. Hamburger patties range in weight from 2 to 10 per pound and are packed in 5- and 10-pound boxes, sold in 50-pound cases.

Prange steaks are cut from beef graded Utility or better. Large boxes of beef—called "combos"—weighing 2,000 pounds are purchased directly from slaughterhouses or wholesalers and then tenderized prior to being frozen and cut into steaks of various sizes. Prange steaks include T-bone, rib-eye, porterhouse, filet mignon, and New York strip. The steaks are packed in 4- to 10-pound boxes and then sold to customers in 50-pound cases.

ATTEMPTS AT INCREASING SALES AND PROFITS

In 1982, Prange Meats introduced a new product called the Belly-Buster, an oval-shaped, half-pound chopped steak patty with six percent soy protein additive and additional seasonings. The product was favorably accepted. Over the past five years, sales have increased approximately 10 percent annually.

In 1984, Prange attempted to increase sales through direct marketing. A newspaper advertisement was run in Chicago newspapers to promote steaks as a holiday gift for the Christmas season. Two gift assortments were offered, each featuring a selection of Prange steaks at attractive prices. The next year, a second direct marketing effort was attempted. An eight-page, four-color brochure was mailed to 1,400 targeted consumers offering an assortment of steaks and lobster-and-steak combinations. Toby Prange felt that both of these direct marketing programs were unsuccessful because they did not generate an adequate sales volume to defray marketing and administrative costs and provide a satisfactory profit. Competition was a problem. The majority of beef mail-order businesses, such as Omaha Steaks and Phaelser Brothers, operate on a national scale and offer prime and choice steaks with a sophisticated marketing mix targeted to an upscale consumer. Prange, attempting to enter the market offering a lower grade of meat and lower prices, was unable to gain acceptance for its products.

In the summer of 1985, Toby Prange and Dan Katora formed a partnership and opened a retail outlet for Prange Meats. The retail store, called Prange Steaks, was located in a building adjacent to the processing plant and contained about 500 square feet of floor space. The store, equipped with display freezers, sold Prange products as well as

TABLE 1   Income Statement, Prange Meats, Inc.

	1988		1987	
Net Sales		$1,233,708.50		$1,216,873.92
Cost and Expenses:				
1. Cost of sales		$ 870,186.40		$ 886,369.60
2. Selling, admin., & general		233,074.49		217,516.50
expenses:				
Salaries	$176,307.80		$159,576.00	$167,751.50
Rent	6,500.00		4,800.00	4,800.00
Advertising	1,248.16		335.00	1,612.79
Auto and truck exp.	6,496.78		6,639.47	6,341.39
Banking	0.00		0.00	32.27
Business license	288.00		198.00	238.00
Credit card expense	322.86		258.51	1,577.28
Insurance	23,213.07		26,988.00	10,073.90
Legal and accounting	4,255.00		6,100.00	3,605.00
Office expense	1,245.25		1,547.89	1,335.90
Telephone	1,234.39		1,373.85	1,328.07
Uniform and laundry	1,009.33		864.71	882.87
Union dues	2,019.00		2,029.14	1,655.00
Freight	8,934.85		6,805.93	7,004.98
3. Operating supplies:		78,436.56		82,037.14
Repairs and maintenance	4,713.68		6,370.59	6,854.80
Garbage removal	1,444.72		1,210.85	1,042.80
Utilities	19,694.27		22,341.65	19,740.40
Operating supplies	52,583.89		52,114.05	54,632.68
4. Taxes:		18,526.70		17,710.10
State replacement tax	0.00		571.32	471.51
Payroll taxes	14,171.68		12,909.63	13,482.05
Property taxes	4,355.02		3,246.18	1,642.45
State corp. inc. tax	0.00		982.97	739.83
5. Pension plan	0.00	0.00		8,158.85
6. Depreciation	31,633.40	31,633.40		15,048.90
Total costs and expenses		$1,231,857.55		$1,226,841.09
Net operating income (EBIT)		$ 1,850.95		$ (9,967.27)
Interest income		$ 3,051.61		$ 2,687.96
Earnings before taxes		$ 4,902.56		$ (7,279.31)
Income taxes		$ 1,110.38		$ 0.00
Less tax deductions		$ 0.00		$ 0.00
Total taxes		$ 1,110.38		$ 0.00
Extraordinary gain/loss, after tax		$ 2,500.00		$ 5,314.00
Net income available to common stockholders		$ 6,292.18		$ (1,965.31)
Number of common shares outstanding		5,000		5,000
Earnings per share of common stock		$ 1.26		$ (0.39)

1986	1985	1984
$1,136,900.31	$1,169,417.33	$1,291,454.42
$ 788,757.70	$ 841,078.17	$ 958,917.73
208,238.95	193,901.72	180,980.23
$150,452.50		$136,502.00
4,800.00		4,800.00
5,735.50		3,244.74
5,445.18		4,784.72
7.79		125.95
168.00		386.00
133.47		0.00
10,018.00		12,782.00
3,930.00		3,605.00
1,411.82		1,650.18
2,223.89		1,714.93
962.33		817.02
1,614.60		3,018.90
6,998.64		7,548.79
82,270.68	91,286.46	96,949.08
9,227.44		8,051.71
836.00		858.00
19,469.13		18,999.48
61,753.89		69,039.89
16,355.84	16,311.69	14,298.07
364.38		0.00
12,524.66		11,447.14
2,752.34		2,850.93
670.31		0.00
12,618.55	2,699.54	10,383.06
9,286.07	13,125.69	17,634.77
$1,117,507.79	$1,158,403.27	$1,279,162.94
$ 19,392.52	$ 11,014.06	$ 12,291.48
$ 4,909.84	$ 3,794.93	$ 3,663.36
$ 24,302.36	$ 14,808.99	$ 15,954.84
$ 2,957.15	$ 2,576.99	$ 0.00
$ 0.00	$ 1,468.24	$ 510.22
$ 2,957.15	$ 1,108.75	$ 14,444.62
$ 531.96	$ 4,016.53	$ 0.00
$ 21,877.17	$ 17,716.77	$ 14,444.62
5,000	5,000	5,000
$ 4.38	$ 3.54	$ 2.89

TABLE 2 Balance Sheet, Prange Meats, Inc.

	1988	1987	1986	1985	1984
Assets					
Current assets					
1. Cash	$ (4,498.99)	$ 7,706.02	$ 10,323.11	$ 8,110.75	$ (841.10)
2. Accounts receivable	27,009.75	25,249.75	39,569.90	31,652.86	29,959.66
3. Inventory	64,894.81	39,159.49	35,139.60	41,796.81	35,396.54
4. Tax deposits	1,600.00	4,600.00	1,300.00	1,300.00	0.00
Total current assets	$ 89,005.57	$ 76,715.26	$ 86,332.61	$ 82,860.42	$ 64,515.10
Fixed assets (plant)					
1. Land	$ 10,000.00	$ 10,000.00	$ 10,000.00	$ 10,000.00	$ 10,000.00
2. Building	44,561.48	44,561.48	44,561.48	44,561.48	44,561.48
3. Leasehold improvement	62,104.36	61,262.70	5,208.00	6,708.00	19,415.31
4. Machinery and equipment	44,499.50	37,841.60	39,924.67	68,154.96	81,806.42
Total fixed assets	$161,165.34	$153,665.78	$ 99,694.15	$129,424.44	$155,783.21
Allowance for depreciation	77,313.40	60,193.90	47,228.07	78,635.69	91,868.77
Fixed assets less depreciation	$ 83,851.94	$ 93,471.88	$ 52,466.08	$ 50,788.75	$ 63,914.44
Investments					
1. Selected money market funds	$ 60,331.32	$ 55,279.71	$ 85,487.21	$ 55,972.47	$ 35,799.70
2. Stock investments	2,876.11	2,876.11	10,251.11	11,353.46	0.00
3. Other investments	1,000.00	1,000.00	0.00	10,000.00	14,380.57
Total investments	$ 64,207.43	$ 59,155.82	$ 95,738.32	$ 77,325.93	$ 50,180.27
Total assets	$237,064.94	$229,342.96	$234,537.01	$210,975.10	$178,609.81
Liabilities and Stockholders' Equity					
Current liabilities					
1. Accounts payable trade	$ 30,022.28	$ 29,800.36	$ 33,727.57	$ 29,212.60	$ 17,574.72
2. Federal corp. income tax payable	1,110.38	0.00	357.15	2,376.99	130.68
3. Payroll taxes payable	1,153.26	1,055.76	0.14	610.53	46.20
Total current liabilities	$ 32,285.92	$ 30,856.12	$ 34,084.86	$ 32,200.12	$ 17,751.60
Stockholders' equity					
1. Common stock	$ 5,000.00	$ 5,000.00	$ 5,000.00	$ 5,000.00	$ 5,000.00
2. Retained earnings	199,779.02	193,486.84	195,452.15	173,574.98	155,858.21
Total liabilities & stockholders' equity	$237,064.94	$229,342.96	$234,537.01	$210,775.10	$178,609.81

chicken, pork chops and ribs, sausage, hot dogs, seafood, and tamales. Self-service was featured and customers could inspect the products prior to purchase.

As shown in Figure 2, Prange Steaks reached a retail trading area that in 1980 was estimated to have a population of 635,595 people and 153,718 families. A demographic summary of the trading area, shown in Table 3, indicates that it contained ethnic and racial subgroups and that the consumers were low-income wage earners, residing in inexpensive housing. Toby Prange believed that the demographics of the trading area represented the ideal consumer for Prange products, so he was surprised when the retail store's sales were below expectations. Table 4 provides a financial history of Prange Steaks. The retail outlet has remained open in spite of disappointing performance. It is presently staffed by Toby Prange and two part-time female employees. Business hours are 10:00 a.m. to 6:00 p.m., Monday through Friday, and 10:00 a.m. to 3:00 p.m. on Saturday. During the months of January, February, and March, the store is closed on Mondays and Tuesdays because of insufficient customer traffic.

THE CHICAGO MEAT AND PRODUCE MARKETS

Many of Chicago's beef and poultry processors are located in an area referred to as the "market," which is on Randolph Street just west of the city's central business district. Four miles to the south is the South Water Market, which is the major distribution point for fresh produce. The Prange processing plant is located about seven miles northwest of the Randolph Street market, and even farther from the produce market. Figure 2 shows the approximate location of the markets and the Prange processing plant.

Prange's remote location from the market has proven to be a disadvantage because many of the meat and produce buyers from Chicago hotels, restaurants, institutions, and other retail businesses find it convenient to shop both markets for their food provisions. Prange Meats has pursued the option of opening a distribution facility near Randolph Street, but because of the area's inflated real estate and rental prices they have been unable to secure a location. Toby Prange believes that the firm's sales would increase approximately 25 percent with a distribution point more convenient to buyers. He also estimates that the costs to establish and operate a distribution facility would be approximated by those provided in Table 5.

FIGURE 2

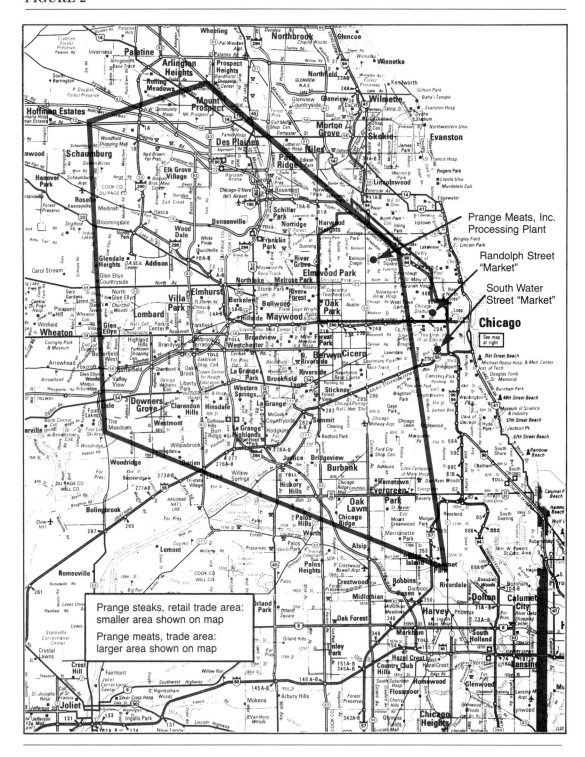

Prange Meats, Inc. Processing Plant

Randolph Street "Market"

South Water Street "Market"

Chicago

Prange steaks, retail trade area: smaller area shown on map

Prange meats, trade area: larger area shown on map

TABLE 3   Demographic Characteristics of Prange Steaks Retail Trade Area

Population	635,595
Families	153,718
Ethnic composition	
Spanish	18.4%
Black	27.9%
Polish	11.8%
Other	41.9%
High school graduates	44.3%
Mean household income	$16,985
Median home value	$37,387

Source: U.S. Bureau of the Census, 1980.

TABLE 4   Prange Steaks—Financial History

	1985	1986	1987	1988
Sales	$52,650[1]	$100,809	$103,353	$83,515
Net profit (loss)	(1,741)	2,742	(701)	(723)
Payments to partners	$ 1,000	$ 2,000	$ 2,000	$ 2,000

[1]Partial year of approximately six months.

Source: Prange Steaks, Inc.

THE MARKETING OF PRANGE MEATS

With the exception of a small quantity of meat sold to consumers by direct mail and through the retail store, most Prange hamburger patties and steaks are sold to middlemen such as wholesalers and jobbers and direct to restaurants and retail stores. Figure 2 shows the trading area in Chicago that would include most of the customers of Prange Meats, Inc. Hamburger patties are the largest-volume product line marketed by Prange. Depending on the customer's needs, patties are marketed in weights ranging from one tenth of a pound to one half pound. With the exception of the belly-buster chopped steak patty, total sales of hamburger patties have declined substantially over the past five years. A summary of annual and quarterly sales volume (in pounds) for 1983–88 is provided in Table 6.

Tenderized steaks are also marketed in different weights and include such cuts as T-bone, rib-eye, New York strip, filet mignon, and porterhouse. As Table 7 shows, annual sales of steaks are down substantially from historical levels.

TABLE 5   Estimated Costs to Establish and Operate a Distribution
Facility

Fixed Costs

Freezers and refrigeration equipment	$ 17,000
Inventory investment	15,000
Business machinery	6,000
Building improvements	1,500
Computer software	1,100
Loading equipment	600

Yearly Operating Costs

Rent	$ 18,000
Salaries	58,200
Utilities	12,000
Insurance	9,600
Vehicles	4,200
Office supplies	4,800
Accounting and legal	600
Advertising	500
Business license	75
Total operating costs	$107,975

Source: Prange Meats, Inc.

TABLE 6   Sales of Ground Beef Patties (lbs.)

	1988	1987	1986	1985	1984	1983
Jan.-Mar.	87,781	73,679	82,413	77,682	102,684	99,186
April-Jun.	93,821	88,083	102,739	95,955	112,878	114,981
July-Sept.	95,996	89,856	97,916	99,301	107,371	129,842
Oct.-Dec.	101,124	72,338	91,963	80,552	87,152	114,558
Total sales	378,722	323,956	375,031	353,490	410,085	458,567

Source: Prange Meats, Inc.

Prange believes that part of the declining sales of its two product lines can be explained by increasing concern over the fat and cholesterol content of red meat. National trends indicate that per capita consumption of beef and pork has declined steadily in recent years, while per capita consumption of chicken and poultry has steadily increased. Figure 3 summarizes these trends. It illustrates that consumer demand for beef dramatically declined in the middle 1980s, and that the decline in per capita consumption is expected to continue into the

TABLE 7   Sales of Steaks (lbs.)

	1988	*1987*	*1986*	*1985*	*1984*	*1983*
Jan.-Mar.	61,897	73,679	82,413	77,682	102,684	53,978
April-Jun.	82,754	88,083	102,739	95,955	112,878	114,981
July-Sept.	72,298	46,402	97,916	99,301	107,371	129,842
Oct.-Dec.	76,284	52,665	91,963	80,552	87,152	114,558
Total sales	293,233	260,829	375,031	353,490	410,085	413,359

Source: Prange Meats, Inc.

FIGURE 3   Per Capita Consumption Trends for Beef, Poultry, Pork, and Chicken

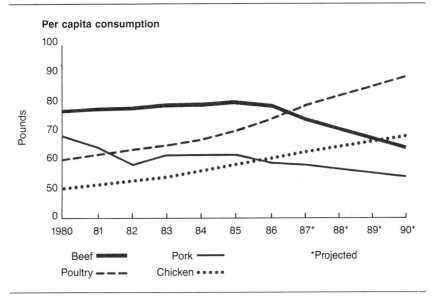

1990s. Toby Prange was aware that the market conditions were generally unfavorable and that his company would have to adjust to new consumer demographics and attitudes toward beef. However, he also knew that the national trends were tempered by the fact that Prange's target consumers generally were heavy consumers of beef and less concerned with nutritional issues.

Approximately 35 percent of Prange's sales (in pounds) were to jobbers who resold the products out of their trucks to restaurants and consumers. Some jobbers purchased exclusively from Prange, but others switched from supplier to supplier depending on the prices of the products they were interested in purchasing. Sales to wholesale distributors, restaurants, and retail stores accounted for 65 percent of Prange's volume. Prange operated a delivery truck that made weekly deliveries to wholesalers, retail grocery stores, and restaurants. The wholesalers resold the Prange products to many of the restaurants and institutions in the Chicago area. Wholesalers usually carried more than one company's product and were not exclusive distributors. The distribution pattern of product sales is shown in Table 8.

Prange Meats currently does not employ a salesperson to service existing customers and solicit new accounts. Toby Prange handles sales, customer service, and customer relations. It is also his responsibility to assure that orders are properly processed and deliveries are promptly made. New customers resulted from the efforts of Toby Prange and Dan Katora. However, since their primary responsibilities were administration and production, the efforts to solicit new customers were quite limited. As Table 9 illustrates, the number of customers of Prange Meats barely changed from 1979 to 1987. At the end of 1987, the company had approximately 78 active accounts which included jobbers, restaurants, wholesalers, and retail grocery stores.

Historically, Prange's promotional efforts have been quite limited. In the late 1970s, the firm employed a salesperson to solicit new customers and service existing accounts. The salesperson was not familiar with the meat-processing industry and was unable to develop new customers. After six months on the job, he was terminated and not replaced. Since the opening of the retail outlet in 1985, advertising expenditures have declined dramatically. In 1988 they were $1,248.16, substantially less than one percent of net sales. In recent years a variety of advertising methods have been used to advertise Prange Steaks, including neighborhood newspapers, direct mail, billboards, and even advertisements on the back of park benches. Over the past three years, Toby Prange has accumulated the names and addresses

TABLE 8 Distribution of Product Sales (lbs.)

Type of Distribution	Percent	Distribution to	Percent
Jobber	35%	Restaurants	15%
		Consumers	20
Wholesale and direct	65	Wholesalers	40
		Retail stores	15
		Restaurants	10
	100%		100%

Source: Prange Meats, Inc.

of 500 retail customers of Prange Steaks. He is considering the use of direct-mail and newspaper advertising during the months of April, May, and June to build sales at the retail store. In general, however, there has been little consistency in the use of advertising, and its economic benefits have never been determined.

Pricing in the meat-processing industry is extremely competitive and prices fluctuate daily in response to supply and demand. Approximately 24 of Prange's competitors are located in the Randolph Street area where they post daily prices on the chalkboards at the market. Because of its remote location from the market, Prange's pricing policy has been to administer prices flexibly and avoid competing strictly on the basis of price. Considering the competitive environment, Prange generally tried to establish prices that would provide a gross margin of 4 to 8 percent on sales of hamburger patties and 20 to 30 percent on steaks.

On July 1, 1988, Prange Meats' prices to jobbers and other customers purchasing directly from the company were as follows:

Steaks		*Hamburger Patties*	
T-bone	$2.29/lb.	Soy-added patties	$1.10/lb
Rib-eye	2.74	All-beef patties	1.33
N.Y. strip (boneless)	2.69	Belly-buster patty	1.33
N.Y. strip (bone-in)	2.19		
Porterhouse	2.29		
Filet mignon	4.65		

All shipments by Prange were F.O.B. delivered. Quantity discounts were also offered. Purchases of 500 pounds or more of a single product resulted in a price reduction of $.05/lb. from posted prices, while orders of a single product in quantities of 1,000 pounds or more earned a quantity discount of $.10/lb. Prices for orders of 1,500 pounds or more were negotiable.

TABLE 9 Changes in Customer Accounts, 1979–1987

Type of Customer	*1979*	*Gained*	*Lost*	*1987*
Wholesalers	40	14	16	38
Jobbers	8	2	1	9
Restaurants and retail stores	28	11	8	31
	76	27	25	78

Source: Prange Meats, Inc.

Prange offered their customers 14 days of revolving credit on purchases, although competitors' standard terms of sale were seven days of credit. Most of the Prange customers were fairly small, with average weekly purchases of about $250, so extra time to settle an account was an important patronage factor. Prange also believed that a liberal credit policy and delivered pricing helped to offset their location disadvantage.

A MARKET OPPORTUNITY FOR PRANGE STEAKS

During 1988, Toby Prange approached a large mass merchandiser having several retail outlets in the Chicago area with an unusual business proposal. Toby proposed that Prange Steaks install, operate, and maintain a frozen boxed beef department in one of its stores. The proposal specified that Prange install display freezers in the store and provide trained employees and management. Prange Steaks would stock the freezers with steaks, hamburger patties, and other frozen products, and provide point-of-purchase and mail-order promotional material. The retailer would provide 250 square feet of floor space near the customer service area on the third floor of the store with the necessary modifications to market the frozen products: utilities, cash registers, video for point-of-purchase promotion, promotional support such as tie-ins with the sale of barbecue grills and patio furniture, and the enclosure of a mail-order brochure in the store's monthly statements. The proposal further stated that all products were to be USDA inspected and supplied by Prange Meats, packed in 4- or 5-pound boxes, and guaranteed for customer satisfaction. The Prange products to be sold consisted of 10 items, with freezer space for two additional products to be offered as specials. A list of the products, the packaging, and proposed retail pricing is shown in Table 10.

The proposal further specified that all sales would be credited to Prange Steaks and deposited weekly into their account. Prange would also be responsible for all state and federal taxes and employee training and management of the leased department. In return for providing merchandising space, utilities, and promotional assistance, the retailer would receive 15 percent of gross sales or a minimum monthly payment of $400.00, whichever was larger.

As he thought about the market opportunity, Toby Prange reflected that even though his proposal seemed to have little risk, it was important that the opportunity be managed carefully to maintain the quality of the merchandising effort as the business developed. He proposed a one-year trial in a single store located at 1900 Lawrence Avenue in Chicago. If the venture proved successful, he felt Prange could be

TABLE 10 Retail Packaging and Pricing for Prange Steaks

Product	Price per Box	Pieces per Box	Price per Piece	Price per Pound
T-bone	$14.75	6	$2.46	$3.69
Rib-eye	16.95	12	1.42	4.23
N.Y. strip (boneless)	16.50	12	1.38	4.12
Porterhouse	14.75	4	3.69	3.69
Filet mignon	24.95	10	2.50	6.24
Pure beef pattie[1]	9.25	16 or 32	.58 or .29	1.85
Seasoned pattie[1]	9.75	10 or 20	.98 or .49	1.95
Pork chop (center cut)	12.50	14	.90	3.13
Pork chop (boneless)	12.95	14	.93	3.24
Back ribs	14.95	5	2.99	2.99
Special				
Special				

[1] Pure beef and seasoned pattie sold in two sizes.

Source: Prange Steaks

prepared to operate a leased department in about 10 stores by the beginning of the third year, with cumulative sales in the $1.5 million range.

Prange hoped to be able to open the department by October 1, 1989. Toby estimated the average retail selling price at $3.36/lb. for 1989–90, and the cost of goods sold at $2.07/lb. He forecasted retail sales for the first several quarters of operation as follows:

Time Period	Retail Sales
Oct.-Dec. 1989	$10,000
Jan.-Mar. 1990	8,000
Apr.-June 1990	16,000
Jul.-Sep. 1990	25,000
Oct.-Dec. 1990	15,000

Table 11 summarizes the fixed costs to establish the leased department in a single store, and the weekly labor expenses to staff and operate it. While Toby believed that most of the costs could be estimated accurately, he knew that the promotion and merchandising expenses to establish the business could vary substantially depending on how the retailing concept was advertised and visually merchandised to the store's customers. After all, it was a bit unusual for frozen hamburger patties and steaks to be sold in this type of a retail environment.

TABLE 11   Costs to Establish and Operate a Retail Boxed Beef
            Department

Item	Estimated Cost
Freezers and display cases	$4,643.00
Fixtures	55.00
Product inventory	2,943.00
Promotional materials	700.00
Business license	68.00
Weekly labor, 37 hrs. @ $5.00/hr.	185.00

Source: Prange Steaks

THE NATIONAL BEEF CAMPAIGN, 1987

To address the problem of declining primary demand for beef, the National Livestock and Meat Board began a $29 million national advertising campaign in 1987 to change the consumer conception that beef is not contemporary, not convenient, and is high in cholesterol. Using the theme, "Beef: Real Food for Real People," the campaign featured Cybil Shepherd and James Garner as spokespersons and used a multimedia approach featuring radio, print, and television. Target audiences of the campaign were persons living a healthy, active lifestyle in the 25- to 54-year age group with $30,000 plus household incomes and above-average educational achievement. A copy of a typical print advertisement from the July 1987 issue of *Gourmet Magazine* is shown in Figure 4. It was expected that the campaign would continue for several years.

LOOKING AHEAD—A MARKETING STRATEGY FOR THE FUTURE

While enthusiasm over the national advertising campaign was high throughout the beef industry, Toby Prange believed it would take time to change consumers' perceptions about beef. In the meantime, he knew that Prange Meats, Inc., had to settle on a marketing strategy for the future. The company's core business of marketing processed meats to jobbers, wholesalers, restaurants, and retail grocery stores had shown little growth in the past several years. The attempts at direct-mail marketing and retailing by Prange Steaks had met with disappointing results. What, if anything, should be done about the pending retailing opportunity wasn't clear to Toby. Time was running out. He had to identify and settle on a marketing strategy that would enable his company to increase sales and profits and strengthen its competitive position.

FIGURE 4 Beef Campaign Advertisement

Good News For People Who Eat.

If your taste buds are not altogether excited about a future of organic fiber flakes, the beef industry would like a few words with you. Even a few from the U.S.D.A. Because the lowdown on beef is probably less than you think—lower in calories, leaner on fat, lighter on cholesterol than you would ever imagine. It's even faster to fix than your mother knows. So read on. And hang on to your forks.

THE LOWDOWN ON CHOLESTEROL.
True fact: beef has only 76 milligrams of cholesterol in a 3-ounce serving. That's only average. Wonderfully average.

GOOD NEWS FOR PEOPLE WHO COOK.
No sauces, no fussing, no frou-frou. Beef doesn't need much help in the kitchen. To cut time, just cut big things in pieces. With stir-fries, sautees, kabobs and marinades, there's never a dull moment. Or a wasted one.

THIS IS YOUR BITE.
3 oz. of lean beef is under 200 calories. But for that fraction of a total day's calories, you get: • 46% of the adult man's RDA for protein • 59% of the adult woman's RDA for protein • 15% of the adult woman's RDA for iron • 40% of the adult RDA for zinc • 76% of the adult RDA for vitamin B-12.

THE UNSATURATION POINT.
Over half the fat in beef is actually mono- or poly-unsaturated. That's why 3 ounces of tenderloin have only 3.1 grams of saturated fat out of 7.9 grams total. May your body and your taste buds make peace.

TERIYAKI BEEF STIR-FRY.
Preparation: 15 min.
Cooking time: 10 min.
Cut 1 lb. top round steak in thin strips. Marinate in 3 Tbs. teriyaki sauce, 1 Tbs. oil and 2 tsp. cornstarch 30 min. Stir-fry 2 bell peppers (3/4" cube) and 6 green onions (2" pieces) in 1 Tbs. oil 3 min.; remove. Stir-fry beef (1/2 at a time) 2-3 min. Return all ingredients. Cook until hot. 4 servings.
Calories: 247 per serving; 162 from beef.

Figures are for 3-ounce servings, cooked and trimmed. •

© 1987 Beef Industry Council and Beef Board

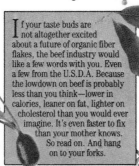

ROUND TIP
6.4 gms total fat*
(2.3 gms sat. fat)
162 calories

TOP LOIN
7.6 gms total fat*
(3.0 gms sat. fat)
172 calories

TOP ROUND
5.3 gms total fat*
(1.8 gms sat. fat)
162 calories

Beef.
Real Food For Real People.
Source: U.S.D.A. Handbook No. 8-13

EYE OF ROUND
5.5 gms total fat*
(2.1 gms sat. fat)
155 calories

TENDERLOIN
7.9 gms total fat*
(3.1 gms sat. fat)
174 calories

SIRLOIN
7.4 gms total fat*
(3.0 gms sat. fat)
177 calories

TenderCare Disposable Diapers*

James E. Nelson

University of Colorado

Tom Cagan watched as his secretary poured six ounces of water onto each of two disposable diapers laying on his desk. The diaper on the left was a new, improved Pampers, introduced in the summer of 1985 by Procter & Gamble. The new, improved design was supposed to be drier than the preceding Pampers. It was the most recent development in a sequence of designs that traced back to the original Pampers, introduced to the market in 1965. The diaper on his right was a TenderCare diaper, manufactured by a potential supplier for testing and approval by Cagan's company, Rocky Mountain Medical Corporation (RMM). The outward appearance of both diapers was identical.

Yet the TenderCare diaper was different. Just under its liner (the surface next to the baby's skin) was a wicking fabric that drew moisture from the surface around a soft, waterproof shield to an absorbent reservoir of filler. Pampers and all other disposable diapers on the market kept moisture nearer to the liner and, consequently, the baby's skin. A patent attorney had examined the TenderCare design, concluding that the wicking fabric and shield arrangement should be granted a patent. However, it would be many months before results of the patent application process could be known.

As soon as the empty beakers were placed back on the desk, Cagan and his secretary touched the liners of both diapers. They agreed that there was no noticeable difference, and Cagan noted the time. They repeated their "touch test" after one minute and again noted no difference. However, after two minutes, both thought the TenderCare diaper to be drier. At three minutes, they were certain. By five minutes, the TenderCare diaper surface seemed almost dry to the touch, even

---

*This case was written by Professor James E. Nelson, University of Colorado. This case is intended for use as a basis for class discussion rather than to illustrate either effective or ineffective administrative decision making. Some data are disguised.
© 1986 by the Business Research Division, College of Business and Administration and the Graduate School of Business Administration, University of Colorado, Boulder, Colorado 80309-0419.

when a finger was pressed deep into the diaper. In contrast, the Pampers diaper showed little improvement in dryness from three to five minutes and tended to produce a puddle when pressed.

These results were not unexpected. Over the past three months, Cagan and other RMM executives had compared TenderCare's performance with 10 brands of disposable diapers available in the Denver market. TenderCare diapers had always felt drier within a two- to four-minute interval after wetting. However, these results were considered tentative because all tests had used TenderCare diapers made by RMM personnel by hand. Today's test was the first made with diapers produced by a supplier under mass manufacturing conditions.

ROCKY MOUNTAIN MEDICAL CORPORATION

RMM was incorporated in Denver, Colorado, in late 1982 by Robert Morrison, M.D. Sales had grown from about $400,000 in 1983 to $2.4 million in 1984 and were expected to reach $3.4 million in 1985. The firm would show a small profit for 1985, as it had each previous year.

Management personnel as of September 1985 included six executives. Cagan served as president and director, positions held since joining RMM in April 1984. Prior to that time he had worked for several high-technology companies in the areas of product design and development, production management, sales management, and general management. His undergraduate studies were in engineering and psychology; he took an M.B.A. in 1981. Dr. Morrison currently served as chairman of the board and vice president for research and development. He had completed his M.D. in 1976 and was board certified to practice pediatrics in the state of Colorado since 1978. John Bosch served as vice president of manufacturing, a position held since joining RMM in late 1983. Lawrence Bennett was vice president of marketing, having primary responsibilities for marketing TenderCare and RMM's two lines of phototherapy products since joining the firm in 1984. Bennett's background included an M.B.A. received in 1981 and three years' experience in groceries product management at General Mills. Two other executives, both also joining RMM in 1984, served as vice president of personnel and as controller.

Phototherapy Products

RMM's two lines of phototherapy products were used to treat infant jaundice, a condition experienced by some 5 to 10 percent of all newborn babies. One line was marketed to hospitals under the trademark Alpha-Lite. Bennett felt that the Alpha-Lite phototherapy unit was superior to competing products because it gave the baby 360-degree exposure to the therapeutic light. Competing products gave less complete exposure, with the result that the Alpha-Lite unit treated more severe cases and produced quicker recoveries. Apart from the Alpha-Lite unit itself, the hospital line of phototherapy products included a light meter, a photo-mask that protected the baby's eyes while undergoing treatment, and a "baby bikini" that diapered the baby and yet facilitated exposure to the light.

The home phototherapy line of products was marketed under the trademark Baby-Lite™. The phototherapy unit was portable, weighing about 40 pounds, and was foldable for easy transport. The unit when assembled was 33 inches long, 20 inches wide, and 24 inches high. The line also included photo-masks, a thermometer, and a short booklet telling parents about home phototherapy. Parents could rent the unit and purchase related products from a local pharmacy or durable medical equipment dealer for about $75 per day. This was considerably less than the cost of hospital treatment. Another company, Acquitron, Inc., had entered the home phototherapy market in early 1985 and was expected to offer stiff competition. A third competitor was rumored to be entering the market in 1986.

Bennett's responsibilities for all phototherapy products included developing marketing plans and making final decisions about product design, promotion, pricing, and distribution. He directly supervised two product managers, one responsible for Alpha-Lite and the other for Baby-Lite. He occasionally made sales calls with the product managers, visiting hospitals, health maintenance organizations, and insurers.

TenderCare Marketing

Right now most of Bennett's time was spent on TenderCare. Bennett recognized that TenderCare would be marketed much differently than the phototherapy products. TenderCare would be sold to wholesalers, who in turn would sell to supermarkets, drugstores, and mass merchandisers. TenderCare would compete either directly or indirectly with two giant consumer goods manufacturers, Procter & Gamble and Kimberly-Clark. TenderCare represented considerable risk to RMM.

Because of the uncertainty surrounding the marketing of TenderCare, Bennett and Cagan had recently sought the advice of several marketing consultants. They reached formal agreement with one, a Los Angeles consultant named Alan Anderson. Anderson had had extensive experience in advertising at J. Walter Thompson. He also had had responsibility for marketing and sales at Mattel and

Teledyne, specifically for the marketing of such products as Intelli-Vision™, the Shower Massage™, and the Water Pik™. Anderson currently worked as an independent marketing consultant to several firms. His contract with RMM specified that he would devote 25 percent of his time to TenderCare the first year and about 12 percent the following two years. During this time, RMM would hire, train, and place their own marketing personnel. One of these people would be a product manager for TenderCare.

Bennett and Cagan also could employ the services of a local marketing consultant who served on RMM's advisory board. The board consisted of 12 business and medical experts who were available to answer questions and provide direction. The consultant had spent over 25 years in marketing consumer products at several large corporations. His specialty was developing and launching new products, particularly health and beauty aids. He had worked closely with RMM in selecting the name TenderCare™, and had done a great deal of work summarizing market characteristics and analyzing competitors.

MARKET CHARACTERISTICS

The market for babies' disposable diapers could be identified as children, primarily below age three, who use the diapers, and their mothers, primarily between ages 18 and 49, who decide on the brand and usually make the purchase. Bennett estimated there were about 11 million such children in 1985, living in about 9 million households. The average number of disposable diapers consumed in these households was thought to range from 0 to 15 and to average about 7.

The consumption of disposable diapers is tied closely to birth rates and populations. However, two prominent trends also influence consumption. One is the disposable diaper's steadily increasing share of total diaper usage by babies. Bennett estimated that disposable diapers would increase their share of total diaper usage from 75 percent currently to 90 percent by 1990. The other trend is toward the purchase of higher-quality disposable diapers. Bennett thought the average retail price of disposable diapers would rise about twice as fast as the price of materials used in their construction. Total dollar sales of disposable diapers at retail in 1985 were expected to be about $3 billion, or about 15 billion units. Growth rates were thought to be about 14 percent per year for dollar sales and about 8 percent for units.

Foreign markets for disposable diapers would add to these figures. Canada, for example, currently consumed about $.25 billion at retail, with an expected growth rate of 20 percent per year until 1990. The U.K. market was about twice this size and growing at the same rate.

The U.S. market for disposable diapers was clearly quite large and growing. However, Bennett felt that domestic growth rates could not be maintained much longer because fewer and fewer consumers were available to switch from cloth to disposable diapers. In fact, by 1995, growth rates for disposable diapers would begin to approach growth rates for births, and unit sales of disposable diapers would become directly proportional to numbers of infants using diapers. A consequence of this pronounced slowing of growth would be increased competition.

COMPETITION

Competition between manufacturers of disposable diapers was already intense. Two well-managed giants—Procter & Gamble and Kimberly-Clark—accounted for about 80 percent of the market in 1984 and 1985. Bennett had estimated market shares at:

	1984	1985
Pampers	32%	28%
Huggies	24	28
Luvs	20	20
Other brands	24	24
	100%	100%

Procter & Gamble was clearly the dominant competitor with its Pampers and Luvs brands. However, Procter & Gamble's market share had been declining, from 70 percent in 1981 to about 50 percent today. The company had introduced its thicker Blue Ribbon™ Pampers recently in an effort to halt the share decline. It had invested over $500 million in new equipment to produce the product. Procter & Gamble spent approximately $40 million to advertise its two brands in 1984. Kimberly-Clark spent about $19 million to advertise Huggies in 1984.

The 24 percent market share held by other brands was up by some 3 percentage points from 1983. Weyerhaeuser and Johnson & Johnson manufactured most of these diapers, supplying private-label brands for Wards, Penneys, Target, K mart, and other retailers. Generic disposable diapers and private brands were also included here, as well as a number of very small, specialized brands that distributed only to local markets. Some of these brands positioned themselves as low-cost alternatives to national brands; others occupied premium ("designer") niches with premium prices. As examples, Universal Converter entered the northern Wisconsin market in 1984 with two brands priced at 78 and 87 percent of Pampers' case price. Riegel Textile Corporation's

Cabbage Patch℠ diapers illustrated the premium end, with higher prices and attractive print designs. Riegel spent $1 million to introduce Cabbage Patch diapers to the market in late 1984.

Additional evidence of intense competition in the disposable diaper industry was the major change of strategy by Johnson & Johnson in 1981. The company took its own brand off the U.S. market, opting instead to produce private-label diapers for major retailers. The company had held about 8 percent of the national market at the time and decided that this simply was not enough to compete effectively. Johnson & Johnson's disposable diaper was the first to be positioned in the industry as a premium product. Sales at one point totaled about 12 percent of the market but began to fall when Luvs and Huggies (with similar premium features) were introduced. Johnson & Johnson's advertising expenditures for disposable diapers in 1980 were about $8 million. The company still competed with its own brand in the international market.

MARKETING STRATEGIES FOR TENDERCARE

Over the past month, Bennett and his consultants had spent considerable time formulating potential marketing strategies for Tender-Care. One strategy that already had been discarded was simply licensing the design to another firm. Under a license arrangement, RMM would receive a negotiated royalty based on the licensee's sales of RMM's diaper. However, this strategy was unattractive on several grounds. RMM would have no control over resources devoted to the marketing of TenderCare: the licensee would decide on levels of sales and advertising support, prices, and distribution. The licensee would control advertising, content, packaging, and even the choice of brand name. Licensing also meant that RMM would develop little marketing expertise, no image or even awareness among consumers, and no experience in dealing with packaged-goods channels of distribution. The net result would be that RMM would be hitching its future with respect to TenderCare (and any related products) to that of the licensee. Three other strategies seemed more appropriate.

The "Diaper Rash" Strategy

The first strategy involved positioning the product as an aid in the treatment of diaper rash. The affliction usually lasts two to three weeks before being cured. Some infants are more disposed to diaper rash than others; however, the ailment probably affects a majority of babies at some point in their diapered lives. The ailment is caused by "a reaction to prolonged contact with urine and feces, retained soaps and topical preparations, and friction maceration" (Nelson's *Text of Pediatrics,* 1979, p. 1884). Recommended treatment includes careful washing of the affected areas with warm water and without irritating soaps. Treatment also includes the application of protective ointments and powders (sold either by prescription or over the counter).

The diaper rash strategy would target physicians and nurses in either family or general practice and physicians and nurses specializing either in pediatrics or dermatology. Bennett's estimates of the numbers of general or family practitioners in 1985 was approximately 65,000. He thought that about 45,000 pediatricians and dermatologists were practicing in 1985. The numbers of nurses attending all these physicians was estimated at about 290,000. All 400,000 individuals would be the eventual focus of TenderCare marketing efforts. However, the diaper rash strategy would begin (like the other two strategies) where approximately 11 percent of the target market was located—California. Bennett and his consultants agreed that RMM lacked resources sufficient to begin in any larger market. California would provide a good test for TenderCare because the state often set consumption trends for the rest of the U.S. market. California also showed fairly typical levels of competitive activity.

Promotion activities would emphasize either direct mail and free samples or in-office demonstrations to the target market. Mailing lists of most physicians and some nurses in the target market could be purchased at a cost of about $60 per 1,000 names. The cost to print and mail a brochure, cover letter, and return postcard was about $250 per 1,000. To include a single TenderCare disposable diaper would add another $400 per thousand. In-office demonstrations would use registered nurses (employed on a part-time basis) to show TenderCare's superior dryness. The nurses could be quickly trained and compensated on a per-demonstration basis. The typical demonstration would be given to groups of two or three physicians and nurses and would cost RMM about $6. The California market could be used to investigate the relative performance of direct mail versus demonstrations.

RMM would also advertise in trade journals such as the *Journal of Family Practice, Journal of Pediatrics, Pediatrics,* and *Pediatrics Digest.* However, a problem with such advertisements was waste coverage because none of the trade journals published regional editions. A half-page advertisement (one insertion) would cost about $1,000 for each journal. This cost would be reduced to about $700 if RMM placed several advertisements in the same journal during a one-year period. RMM would also promote TenderCare at local and state medical conventions in California. Costs per convention were thought to be about $3,000.

The entire promotion budget as well as amounts allocated to direct mail, free samples, advertisements, and medical conventions had yet to be decided.

Prices were planned to produce a retail price per package of 12 TenderCare diapers at around $3.80. This was some 8 to 10 percent higher than the price for a package of 18 Huggies or Luvs. Bennett thought that consumers would pay the premium price because of TenderCare's position: the pennies-per-day differential simply would not matter if a physician prescribed or recommended TenderCare as part of a treatment for diaper rash. "Besides," he noted, "in-store shelf placement of Tender-Care under this strategy would be among diaper rash products, not with standard diapers. This will make price comparisons by consumers even more unlikely." The $3.80 package price for 12 TenderCare diapers would produce a contribution margin for RMM of about 9 cents per diaper. It would give retailers a per-diaper margin some 30 percent higher than that for Huggies or Luvs.

The Special-Occasions Strategy

The second strategy centered around a "special-occasions" position that emphasized TenderCare's use in situations where changing the baby would be difficult. One such situation was whenever diapered infants traveled for any length of time. Another occurred daily at some 10,000 daycare centers that accepted infants wearing diapers. Yet another came every evening in each of the 9 million market households when babies were diapered at bedtime.

The special-occasions strategy would target mothers in these 9 million households. Initially, of course, the target would be only the estimated one million mothers living in California. Promotion would aim particularly at first-time mothers, using such magazines as *American Baby* and *Baby Talk*. Per-issue insertion costs for one full-color, half-page advertisement in such magazines would average about $20,000. However, most baby magazines published regional editions where single insertion costs averaged about half that amount. Black and white advertisements could also be considered; their costs would be about 75 percent of the full-color rates. Inserting several ads per year in the same magazine would allow quantity discounts and reduce the average insertion cost by about one third.

Lately Bennett had begun to wonder if direct-mail promotion could be used instead to reach mothers of recently born babies. Mailing lists of some 1–3 million names could be obtained at a cost of around $50 per 1,000. Other costs to produce and mail promotional materials would be the same as those for physicians and nurses. "I suppose the real issue is, just how much more effective is direct mail over advertising?

We'd spend at least $250,000 in baby magazines to cover California while the cost of direct mail would probably be between $300,000 and $700,000, depending on whether or not we gave away a diaper." Regardless of Bennett's decision on consumer promotion, he knew RMM would also direct some promotion activities toward physicians and nurses as part of the special-occasions strategy. Budget details were yet to be worked out.

Distribution under the special-occasions strategy would have TenderCare stocked on store shelves along with competing diapers. Still at issue was whether the package should contain 12 or 18 diapers (like Huggies and Luvs) and how much of a premium price TenderCare could command. Bennett considered the packaging and pricing decisions interrelated. A package of 12 TenderCare diapers with per-unit retail prices some 40 percent higher than Huggies or Luvs might work just fine. Such a packaging/pricing strategy would produce a contribution margin to RMM of about 6 cents per diaper. However, the same pricing strategy for a package of 18 diapers probably would not work. "Still," he thought, "good things often come in small packages, and most mothers probably associate higher quality with higher price. One thing is for sure—whichever way we go, we'll need a superior package." Physical dimensions for a TenderCare package of either 12 or 18 diapers could be made similar to the size of the Huggies or Luvs package of 18.

The Head-On Strategy

The third strategy under consideration met major competitors in a direct, frontal attack. The strategy would position TenderCare as a noticeably drier diaper that any mother would prefer to use anytime her baby needed changing. Promotion activities would stress mass advertising to mothers using television and magazines. However, at least two magazines would include a dollar-off coupon to stimulate trial of a package of TenderCare diapers during the product's first three months on the market. Some in-store demonstrations to mothers using "touch tests" might also be employed. Although no budget for California had yet been set, Bennett thought the allocation would be roughly 60:30:10 for television, magazines, and other promotion activities, respectively.

Pricing under this strategy would be competitive with Luvs and Huggies, with the per-diaper price for TenderCare expected to be some 9 percent higher at retail. This differential was needed to cover additional manufacturing costs associated with TenderCare's design. TenderCare's package could contain only 16 diapers and show a lower price than either Huggies or Luvs with their 18-count packages.

Alternatively, the package could contain 18 diapers and carry the 9 percent higher price. Bennett wondered if he really wasn't putting too fine a point on the pricing/packaging relationship. "After all," he had said to Anderson, "we've no assurance that retailers or wholesalers would pass along any price advantage TenderCare might have due to a smaller package. Either one or both might instead price TenderCare near the package price for our competitors and simply pocket the increased margin!" The only thing that was reasonably certain was TenderCare's package price to the wholesaler. That price was planned to produce about a 3-cent contribution margin to RMM per diaper, regardless of package count.

Summary of the Three Strategies

When viewed together, the three strategies seemed so complex and so diverse as to defy analysis. Partly the problem was one of developing criteria against which the strategies could be compared. Risk was obviously one such criterion; so were company fit and competitive reaction. However, Bennett felt that some additional thought on his part would produce more criteria against which the strategies could be compared. He hoped this effort would produce no more strategies; three were plenty.

The other part of the problem was simply uncertainty. Strengths, weaknesses, and implications of each strategy had yet to be given much thought. Moreover, each strategy seemed likely to have associated with it some surprises. An example illustrating the problem was the recent realization that the Food and Drug Administration (FDA) must approve any direct claims RMM might make about TenderCare's efficacy in treating diaper rash. The chance of receiving this federal agency's approval was thought to be reasonably high; yet it was unclear just what sort of testing and what results were needed. The worst-case scenario would have the FDA requiring lengthy consumer tests that eventually would produce inconclusive results. The best case could have the FDA giving permission based on TenderCare's superior dryness and on results of a small-scale field test recently completed by Dr. Morrison. It would be probably a month before the FDA's position could be known.

"The delay was unfortunate—and unnecessary," Bennett thought, "especially if we eventually settle on either of the other two strategies." In fact, FDA approval was not even needed for the diaper rash strategy if RMM simply claimed (1) that TenderCare diapers were drier than competing diapers and (2) that dryness helps treat diaper rash. Still, a single-statement, direct-claim position was thought to be more effective with mothers and more difficult to copy by any other manufacturer. And yet Bennett did want to move quickly on TenderCare. Every month of delay meant deferred revenue and other postponed benefits that would derive from a successful introduction. Delay also meant the chance that an existing (or other) competitor might develop its own drier diaper and effectively block RMM from reaping the fruits of its development efforts. Speed was of the essence.

FINANCIAL IMPLICATIONS

Bennett recognized that each marketing strategy held immediate as well as long-term financial implications. He was particularly concerned with finance requirements for start-up costs associated with the California entry. Cagan and the other RMM executives had agreed that a stock issue represented the best option to meet these requirements. Accordingly, RMM had begun preparation for a sale of common stock through a brokerage firm that would underwrite and market the issue. Management at the firm felt that RMM could generate between $1 million and $3 million, depending on the offering price per share and the number of shares issued.

Proceeds from the sale of stock had to be sufficient to fund the California entry and leave a comfortable margin remaining for contingencies. Proceeds would be used for marketing and other operating expenses as well as for investments in cash, inventory, and accounts receivable assets. It was hoped that TenderCare would generate a profit by the end of the first year in the California market and show a strong contribution to the bottom line thereafter. California profits would contribute to expenses associated with entering additional markets and to the success of any additional stock offerings.

Operating profits and proceeds from the sale of equity would fund additional research and development activities that would extend RMM's diaper technology to other markets. Dr. Morrison and Bennett saw almost immediate application of the technology to the adult incontinent diaper market, currently estimated at about $300 million per year at retail. Underpads for beds constituted at least another $50 million annual market. However, both of these uses were greatly dwarfed by another application, the sanitary napkin market. Finally, the technology could almost certainly be applied to numerous industrial products and processes, many of which promised great potential. All these opportunities made the TenderCare situation that much more crucial to the firm: making a major mistake here would affect the firm for years.

Product Strategy

The Seven-Up Company

J. Paul Peter
University of Wisconsin–Madison

7UP was first introduced in 1929 under the name "Bib-Label Lithiated Lemon-Lime Soda." It was soon renamed "7UP" and handily outsold the more than 600 other lemon-lime drinks on the market. It is still the traditional lemon-lime soft drink and the number one seller in that category. It has been promoted over the years with a number of campaigns including, "Nothing does it like 7UP," "Wet and Wild," "The Uncola," "America is turning 7UP," and "Never had it, never will." The last campaign mentioned focused on the fact that 7UP does not have caffeine in it as do most colas. By far, the most successful of these campaigns was "The Uncola" campaign, which positioned 7UP as an alternative to colas rather than just a mixer or a medicinal product.

Sources: "A Slow Rebound for Seven-Up," *Business Week,* October 12, 1981, pp. 107–8; "Seven-Up's Sudden Taste for Cola," *Fortune,* May 17, 1982, pp. 101–3; "Knocked from Third Place, 7UP Is Going Flat," *Fortune,* May 14, 1984, p. 96.

The Seven-Up Company was purchased in 1978 by Philip Morris, a company known for its marketing skills with successful products such as Marlboro cigarettes and Miller Lite beer. However, 7UP has lost money four of the first five years that it has been a Philip Morris company. For example, in 1983, 7UP had an operating loss of $10.8 million on revenues of $650 million.

The soft drink industry is growing about 4 percent per year and is dominated by colas, which account for 62 percent of the $17-billion-a-year U.S. soft drink market. While about 17 percent of adults in the U.S. drink lemon-lime soft drinks, this category accounts for only about 12 percent of total soft drink sales. While 7UP's market share varies, in 1983 it captured 5.6 percent of the soft drink market. While it is traditionally the number three soft drink behind Coke and Pepsi, in 1984 it slid to fourth place behind Diet Coke.

While 7UP faces fierce competition from colas, it also has a variety of competitors in the lemon-lime market. In addition to Bubble-Up and Teem, the Coca-Cola company aggressively promotes Sprite, a 7UP equivalent, with the stated goal of converting 7UP users. In 1981, Sprite was mentioned in twice as many ads as 7UP. In 1984, PepsiCo introduced its own lemon-lime drink, Slice, which contains 10 percent real fruit juice, and aggressively promoted it against both 7UP and Sprite.

As mentioned, 7UP promotion in 1984 focused on the fact that 7UP is caffeine free. Research by the company indicated that 66 percent of American adults and 47 percent of teenagers stated they would be interested in buying a soda without caffeine. The Seven-Up Company used the same caffeine-free positioning in 1982 when it introduced its own cola, Like. While the introduction was supported with a $50-million advertising campaign, Like did not capture a large market share. The anticaffeine position was easily neutralized as both Coke and Pepsi introduced caffeine-free versions of most of their colas.

7UP is distributed by 464 bottlers. Of these, 337 also distribute a competing cola such as Coke, Pepsi, or Royal Crown. It has been reported that there may be more conflict between 7UP and its bottlers than between Coke and Pepsi and their bottlers. For one thing, many of the bottlers viewed 7UP's anticaffeine promotion as a threat to them and the soft drink industry. Also, it has been reported that Coke and Pepsi offer more and better discounts to bottlers than does 7UP. Finally, at the retail level, many restaurants prefer to deal with only one bottler who has a full line of soft drinks. For example, McDonald's has elected to standardize beverages in its 6,250 U.S. restaurants and approves only three drinks: Coke, Sprite, and an orange flavor. However, McDonald's managers can still stock Diet 7UP, as it is on the company-authorized list of optional beverages.

DISCUSSION QUESTIONS

1. What are the major situational factors affecting 7UP?
2. What is 7UP's competitive differential advantage?
3. What is the target market for 7UP?
4. What should 7UP do to regain market share and profitability?

Quality Circuits, Inc.

Herbert E. Brown
Paula M. Saunders
Carolyn Rice
all of Wright State University

INTRODUCTION

One day late in January 1990, Ben Samson, the owner of Quality Circuits, Incorporated, was seated at his desk reading his accountant's latest financial reports. The numbers were good, but not exactly what he had hoped for, and he wondered what he had to do to make Quality Circuits the kind and size of company he had hoped it would be when he founded it.

Quality Circuits is a small electronics business that designs, fabricates, and sells printed circuit boards. The majority of its customers are other small businesses that require these boards for the products they manufacture. The company's primary market is the segment of companies which has a need for small runs of boards or customized boards that the bigger board houses are unwilling to produce. Quality Circuits is located in the mid-Southwest, and most of its customers are from a tri-state area. It has no direct sales staff, and new customers are gained primarily through customer referral.

Over the past eight years, Quality Circuits has experienced steady growth, and even dramatic growth over the past two years (see Exhibits 1 and 2 for Balance Sheet and Income Statements), but it finds itself at a crossroads at this point in time. Although sales have grown substantially, the costs of running a larger operation have also increased dramatically. The company must find ways to increase profits if it is to continue to grow and prosper. Further, although during this time period revenues climbed from about $84,000 to over $414,000, the costs

This case was prepared by Paula M. Saunders, Herbert E. Brown, and Carolyn Rice, Wright State University, and is intended to be used as a basis for class discussion rather than to illustrate either effective or ineffective handling of the situation. The names of the firms, individuals, locations, and/or financial information have been disguised to preserve the firm's desire for anonymity.

EXHIBIT 1   Quality Circuits, Inc. Balance Sheet December 31, 1988

	1988	*1989*
Assets		
Current assets		
Cash in bank	($ 699.27)	$ 1,224.44
Accounts receivable	20,109.10	54,396.08
Inventory	3,654.53	37,000.00
Total current assets	$23,064.36	$ 92,620.52
Fixed assets		
Shop equipment	$ 7,569.29	$ 21,716.63
Office equipment	1,654.26	5,108.64
Vehicle	10,314.70	10,314.70
Leasehold improvements		4,365.11
Less: Accumulated depreciation	9,296.18	13,958.96
Total fixed assets	$10,242.07	$ 27,546.12
Other assets		
PP interest/dfd. comp., etc.	$ 2,498.43	$ 24,908.74
Total assets	$35,804.86	$145,075.38
Liabilities and Shareholders' Equity		
Current liabilities		
Accounts payable—trade		$ 31,216.44
Notes payable	$ 5,111.04	55,437.20
Accrued liabilities	4,160.14	3,750.83
Total current liabilities	$ 9,271.18	$ 90,404.47
Long-term liabilities		
Note payable	$ 8,268.24	$ 8,497.99
Total liabilities	$17,539.42	$ 98,902.46
Shareholders' equity		
Common stock	$ 500.00	$ 500.00
Retained earnings	17,765.44	46,172.92
Total liabilities and shareholders' equity	$35,804.86	$145,075.38

---

of operation have also risen, and there have been times when Quality Circuits has experienced temporary cash flow problems. In fact, recently Quality Circuits found it necessary to establish a line of credit with a local bank to help it meet its cash needs.

One fact is clear to Ben as he sits at his desk pondering his company's situation: Quality Circuits has reached a point at which he must make some carefully considered decisions if he is to propel the company into a state of steady and increasing profitability in the face of technological changes and competition.

EXHIBIT 2   Quality Circuits, Inc. Statement of Income

For Year Ended:	1988	1989
Sales	$84,541.06	$414,065.58
Cost of sales	38,181.49	257,381.21
Gross profit	46,359.57	156,684.37
Less: Operating expenses	25,094.13	118,117.29
Net income before int. & taxes	21,265.44	38,567.08
Interest expense		5,956.89
Net income before corp. income tax		32,610.19
Federal income tax	3,500.00	5,000.00
Net income	$17,765.44	$ 27,610.19

His instincts tell him that his best opportunity would be to increase his firm's surface-mount assembly business and establish Quality Circuits as the market leader in short-run printed circuit board fabrication within the tri-state region. But he is still very unsure as to whether this is the right plan and what the basic course of action should be.

HISTORICAL BACKGROUND

The original idea for Quality Circuits came about in 1982 when Ben Samson was employed as a design engineer for a private telephone company. He was designing circuit boards to be used in the telephone systems that the company installed. The boards were fairly simple, and Ben felt he could assemble them himself for less than what the company was paying. He approached the company with the idea, and they approved his plan.

Ben and his wife, Susan, began assembling boards in their garage at night and on the weekends. The telephone company supplied the parts, and the Samsons supplied the labor. They saw this as a great way to earn some extra spending money.

The Samsons used their entire savings to buy the materials and tools necessary to start the business, but more money was needed to buy the essential equipment needed to run boards more efficiently. Ben's father invested $3,000 in his son's enterprise, which allowed Quality Circuits to buy its first piece of equipment. Ben and his father reached an agreement, and Quality Circuits became a partnership.

For the first year, Quality Circuits continued to assemble boards in Ben's garage. The telephone company was pleased with the arrangement because it was getting boards at a lower cost. It continued to send more and more boards to Ben to assemble. Frequently these boards would have many parts, and it would be a real task to get them delivered on time. The business grew to the point that it was no longer practical to operate out of their garage.

In November 1983 Quality Circuits leased and moved into a 1,000-square-foot space. Office space and work areas were set up to handle the ever-increasing volume of business. Quality Circuits was hearing about board requirements at other companies and was making bids for their business. Customers were pleased with the quality of the work that Quality Circuits produced. Quality Circuits' prices were competitive, and the turnaround time from point-of-order to delivery was excellent. Quality Circuits' business was growing steadily through customer referrals.

Ben Samson continued to work at the telephone company to bring in a steady income, but was finding more and more of his time was needed at Quality Circuits to keep the operation running smoothly. He would go to Quality Circuits before he went to work. He would spend his lunch hour working there, and go straight to Quality Circuits after work—often not getting home until midnight. Even then he would spend a few more hours at his computer designing a board that a particular customer needed.

By the summer of 1988, it was clear to the Samsons that, to be a success, the business would require their full-time energies. So, that summer the Samsons made the decision to devote 100 percent of their resources to making Quality Circuits a success. The company began searching for a suitable location to expand its operations, and in October 1988, new space was leased. The new space was nearly 5,800 square feet—1,600 square feet devoted to office space and the remaining 4,200 square feet to warehousing inventory and assembly. Because much renovation had to be done to get the new location ready and operating, the Samsons divided their time between jobs that needed to be assembled and renovating the new facility. The move was actually made in February 1989, and in April 1989 the new facility was up and running full-time.

THE PRODUCT

Quality Circuits designs and fabricates printed circuit boards to be used by its customers in a wide variety of products. Printed circuit boards are the electronic technology that allows large, bulky cables and wires to be replaced by a single board upon which miniaturized resistors, capacitors, and other electronic components are permanently attached. These circuit boards reduce the size and weight of the electronic devices in which they are used, as well as increase the speed by which the function is performed.

Printed circuit boards are used in all types of electronic equipment. They are used in banking automatic teller machines (ATMs) and are located underneath the pad one touches; these ATMs perform the function one chooses because of the printed circuit board that "tells" that machine what to do. Security systems rely on a circuit board that sends the appropriate alert signal when an alarm is engaged. Plastics manufacturers use circuit boards in the computerized machinery that determines the exact amounts of dye to add to a plastic solution in order to come up with the desired color. Circuit boards are also used in flight simulators, automobiles, computers, telephones, and almost any piece of equipment that uses electronics. Although one may not see these circuit boards unless one removes the cover, these boards enabled machines to be computerized and automated.

A circuit board consists of a board and electronic parts. Quality Circuits does not produce the circuit board upon which the electronic components are placed and then permanently attached. The company can design a circuit board that a customer may need in a certain piece of equipment, but then it orders the actual printed circuit board (PCB) from a PCB manufacturer. Over 90 percent of Quality Circuits' customers supply their own printed circuit boards as well as the electronic components that will be attached to the board at Quality Circuits.

What Quality Circuits does is provide an assembly and/or design service to its customers. Quality Circuits assembles the electronic components such as resistors, transistors, and diodes onto the printed circuit board to meet design specifications. It then solders the parts to the board, cleans the board, and delivers the finished board to a customer to be used as a component of a larger piece of electronic equipment.

CIRCUIT BOARD TECHNOLOGY

There are two major types of printed circuit boards: those that use *through-hole* technology, and those that use *surface-mount* technology. Through-hole technology is the older of the two technologies. Surface-mount technology is gaining acceptance and is rapidly becoming the preferred technology of the future. Quality Circuits currently uses both technologies.

Through-hole technology requires that the component parts be populated or inserted through holes in the single or multilayer circuit board. The component parts, such as resistors, capacitors, transistors, diodes, and semiconductors, are then soldered to the board. This process connects the part to the board both mechanically and electrically.

Surface-mount technology allows the components to be soldered directly to the surface of a printed circuit board. This process also connects the component to the board both mechanically and electrically. Surface-mount technology began to be widely used in 1987 and is gaining in popularity due to its advantages over through-hole technology. It makes it possible to manufacture smaller, higher-density, and faster speed-printed circuit boards. Surface-mount components can be placed closer together and on both sides of the boards. According to *Standard and Poor's Industry Surveys, Volume I* (January 1990), surface-mount boards can be from 40–70 percent smaller than through-hole boards with the same circuitry, depending on whether one or two sides are used. The surface-mount boards can weigh up to 90 percent less than their through-hole counterparts. In addition to the space savings surface-mount boards offer, they are easily automated, which could mean major cost savings for manufacturers. Surface-mount boards may even offer greater reliability because the loose wires associated with through-hole boards have been removed. These advantages point to a promising future for surface-mount technology.

Ben Samson knows that in order to do more surface-mount assembly, Quality Circuits will need to add new equipment. The electronic components that are assembled on a surface-mount board are permanently attached by a heating process that requires a special oven which the company does not presently have. This oven costs $19,000. Surface-mount PCBs can be assembled manually as Quality Circuits currently does, but eventually Quality Circuits will have to acquire automatic placement equipment to keep up with the expected volume. Because of other accompanying production change costs, this equipment could require a total investment of $40,000–$60,000. However, Ben feels that if Quality Circuits is to grow and remain up-to-date with technology trends in the electronics industry, it must expand its current production capacity to accommodate surface-mount assembly.

At the present time, 98 percent of Quality Circuits' current customers use through-hole insertion, and only 2 percent use surface-mount technology. Quality Circuits still does through-hold insertion manually. Although automated through-hole insertion machines can populate boards at the rate of 3,000 parts per hour, Quality Circuits will not switch over to a fully automated operation because automated through-hole insertion requires the use of special types of components. Ninety percent of Quality Circuits' current customers provide their own parts; therefore, Quality Circuits has no control over the types of components their customers choose to use. In addition, these automated insertion machines require a great deal of time to set up. When set-up time is included, small orders, such as Quality Circuits commonly assembles, can be done as quickly by workers as by machine.

PRODUCTION—THE PCB ASSEMBLY PROCESS

Quality Circuits handles orders for boards of all sizes, and each order calls for different layouts of electronic components, depending on the design specifications of the board. An order may be for 10, 100, or even 500 boards. However, Quality Circuits does not usually get orders for more than 1,000 boards at any one time. Regardless of the size or specifications of an order, all boards must follow the same basic steps for assembly. These steps are:

1. Prepping the order
2. Prepping the components
3. Masking the board
4. Populating the board
5. Inspecting pre-soldering
6. Soldering and cleaning
7. Trimming the boards
8. Making final inspection
9. Packaging and shipping.

SUPPLIER RELATIONSHIPS

Quality Circuits does not manufacture any of the electronic components used in the assembly of printed circuit boards. It relies on several different suppliers for these parts. Ben knows that his relationship with suppliers is critical to the company's success. In order to deliver the fully assembled PCBs on time and at a competitive price, Quality Circuits must rely on these suppliers to deliver the ordered parts on schedule. Strong supplier relationships have made it possible for Quality Circuits to build a reputation for quick turnaround times. Ben's insistence that the company maintain a close working relationship with its suppliers has paid off (he is always telling his employees that supplier relationships can make or break a business): a major supplier company that manufacturers the actual printed circuit boards to which the electronic components are attached often recommends Quality Circuits to OEMs (original equipment manufacturers) who inquire about PCB assembly houses. This supplier will even bring the boards directly to Quality Circuits to make it more convenient for the OEM. In return, Quality Circuits recommends this PCB manufacturer to its customers because, not only does it have a good relationship with this supplier, but it knows the boards will be of high quality and fairly priced.

THE MARKET

Quality Circuits' customers can come from any user of printed circuit boards—in other words, from any manufacturer whose product involves computer chip control. This group includes makers of products ranging from automobiles to wristwatches. However, auto companies and other large buyers generally place large orders with "board houses" that are fully automated and able to handle large runs very cost effectively. Also, large-volume users often assemble PCBs in their own in-house assembly facilities. PCB shops like Quality Circuits usually compete most effectively for small orders from customers with one or more of the following characteristics:

1. Their product's volume requires only short runs of PCBs.
2. They are large firms that have occasional short runs that are prohibitively expensive for them or their normal suppliers to set up (with their large-scale capabilities).
3. They make products requiring specialized setups and short runs in support of new product tests, and the like.

INDUSTRY OUTLOOK

According to *U.S. Industrial Outlook 1990: Prospects for Over 350 Industries,* which is produced by the U.S. Commerce Department, the value of all products and services sold by establishments in the printed circuit boards industry will total over $5.1 billion for 1990. This reflects a 5.8 percent inflation-adjusted growth in demand over 1989. The industry experienced an 11.8 percent growth rate from 1987–88, and a 3.6 percent growth rate from 1988–89. The slowdown of growth in 1989 was due to corporate cutbacks on new business-equipment purchases as well as a softening in the automotive market and declining defense department orders.

This report also cited that, in 1980, half of all PCB production occurred as an in-house function. By 1989, due primarily to increasing complexity, expense, and time requirements, this figure had dropped to 35 percent. The development of more and more sophisticated electronic equipment will produce a growing demand for electronic circuitry that is more complex, smaller, and of a higher density. The escalating costs of automated production and test equipment for PCBs as well as OEM vendor cutbacks are expected to force some of the smaller and medium-size board houses to close or be acquired by the larger board houses.

MARKETING

Quality Circuits currently gets all of its new customers through referrals from other satisfied customers. It has no sales representative, does no advertising or any other type of promotions, and has no literature to give to anyone who makes an inquiry about the business.

THE COMPETITION

Ben is very aware of the competition in his industry and area. He frequently talks to his suppliers who keep him informed concerning many of his competitors. Up to now, within its local area, Quality Circuits has served a unique market segment for which no other companies competed as long as the economy stayed strong; however, Ben has some indications that competition may be growing. He has determined that the following six companies comprise Quality Circuits' major competition within its local area:

1. Triton, Inc., is the largest printed circuit board assembly house in the local area. In 1988 Triton's revenues were an estimated $16,000,000. Triton's facilities occupy about 71,500 square feet, of which 56,000 square feet are devoted to production and warehousing and storage. Triton is fully automated and caters to customers with high-volume runs. A typical Triton customer needs more than 1,000 boards per month. In addition, Triton sells its own line of electronic products. Triton is vying for a different market segment than Quality Circuits serves. But Ben admits to himself that if times get tough, even Triton will bid for small orders to help cover its larger costs and overhead.

2. McManus is the second largest printed circuit board assembly house in the local area. McManus handles high-to-medium-volume orders. McManus uses no automation in its assembly—all PCBs are hand-inserted by workers. McManus accepts only those orders in which the customer supplies the parts. McManus has been using surface-mount technology for over ten years; however, because the technology did not become standardized until 1987, much of its equipment for surface mounting is now obsolete.

3. Parton Industries is a much smaller operation than Quality Circuits. Little is known about its business, but it does charge much higher prices and usually provides no direct competition for Quality Circuits.

4. Boardco specializes in cable assemblies but does a limited amount of PCB assembly. Although Quality Circuits rarely finds itself

bidding on the same jobs as Boardco, occasionally they compete for the same job. So far, Quality Circuits has won the bidding with its old customers. Boardco has only been in business since early 1989.

5. Elite Electronics is a new start-up company in the local area. It is very small, and little is known about it yet.
6. Circuitronics provides Quality Circuits with its stiffest competition for orders. Circuitronics is located about 50 miles south and has been making a concerted effort to call on customers in Quality Circuits' immediate area. Circuitronics already does surface-mount assembly. Quality circuits loses an order from time to time because Circuitronics comes in with a lower bid. Quality Circuits believes Circuitronics is aggressively trying to establish a presence in Quality Circuits' local area.

Another source of competition for Quality Circuits is all the OEMs' own in-house printed circuit board assembly facilities. Most of the manufacturers will assemble the boards in-house unless it can be shown it is more cost-effective and efficient to allow an outside contractor such as Quality Circuits to perform this service in which it specializes. There are some, however, who usually contract outside for the work, but when times get rough, they may expand their internal operations and do it in-house.

SUCCESS FACTORS

Ben has spent many hours over the years trying to understand his industry so that a small business like his could be successful. He thinks his success has been due to his understanding of these factors. As he sees it, the salient factors that manufacturers look for when choosing a PCB assembly contractor are quality, turnaround time from order to delivery, and price. Quality is extremely important because if the assembled PCB does not perform as specified or is defective in any way, then the equipment or machine of which it is a component will be defective. Providing a quick turnaround time that is always prompt and on schedule is also of utmost importance to these manufacturers in order to keep their production schedules running smoothly and on time. If two firms are judged to offer the same quality of service with equivalent turnaround time, the order will go to the company that comes in with the lowest bid or price. Quality Circuits has lost bids to competitors before because the competitor's price was $.05 cheaper on a $10.00 board.

Quality Circuits has built a reputation for fine quality workmanship and for providing quick turnaround time on boards. In addition, it is willing to try new techniques or make any adjustments that the manufacturer would like to try. Often an OEM will be working on a prototype for a new piece of equipment. Quality Circuits is willing to try innovations that the engineers are testing, while most of Quality Circuits' competitors would never consider such a request. Quality Circuits has built its business on doing these out-of-the-ordinary type jobs that other board houses consider too time-consuming or unprofitable. For this reason, Quality Circuits dominates the market for small-run and custom board orders in its area.

Electronics technology changes rapidly. A company must keep up to date if it wishes to survive in this industry. Quality Circuits' customers are developing surface-mount prototypes, and it will not be long before they will require surface-mount assembly. However, some electronic components cannot be surface-mounted until more advances in electronics are developed. Until that technology is developed, there will continue to be a demand for through-hole insertion such as Quality Circuits currently does.

THE ORGANIZATION

Quality Circuits is a small business partnership between Ben Samson and his father, Marcus Samson. Marcus would like to be phased out of the business and assume a very limited role with no legal responsibilities. Eight people are on Quality Circuits' payroll. A summary of the organizational structure is as follows:

Ben Samson. Ben is the owner and is ultimately in charge of everything. He makes all management decisions as well as many operations decisions. He continues to design circuit boards as his time allows. He talks with customers about their needs and informally sells Quality Circuits' services. He supervises employees, but has been able to delegate many of these responsibilities to the employee he promoted to be the supervisor. He talks regularly with his suppliers and maintains a strong relationship with them in order to insure prompt delivery of parts when they are scheduled for assembly. Since he is the owner, Ben must meet with the accountant and the banker, and he must make financial decisions. He also meets with salesmen trying to sell him equipment and services, and he is very much involved in the daily operations of the business. These decisions consume almost all of his time, and finding the time to do long-range planning is difficult.

Susan Samson. Susan works full-time at Quality Circuits and is second in command. She does all the bookkeeping and pays all the bills. She performs all secretarial duties as well as serving as the receptionist by answering the telephone and greeting visitors. She is in charge of writing all purchase orders to suppliers, coordinating with the supervisor to keep work in process on schedule, and writing all invoices to customers upon shipment of their orders. It is her responsibility to contact any customers late in paying their bills, and she encourages them to make any overdue payments owed to Quality Circuits. Susan works closely with the accountant to be sure all necessary information is being supplied, and she is responsible for figuring the payroll. She recently began costing out jobs and preparing bids for customers, and she also negotiates with the customers to try to obtain their business. Ben and Susan discuss many of the decisions that must be made and usually arrive at joint decisions. Like her husband, Susan finds herself holding a wide variety of responsibilities at Quality Circuits.

The six other employees of Quality Circuits have more narrowly defined positions. Three of these employees are full-time workers, and the remaining three positions are part-time. Only one full-time employee receives benefits. These employees perform the actual assembly of the printed circuit boards. Their jobs fall into one of the following categories:

1. *Supervisor.* The supervisor of the assembly process checks parts as they arrive, assigns jobs to workers, keeps records of the time and supplies required to perform each job, inspects final products, and coordinates with Susan to be sure all parts and supplies will be on hand when needed. Quality Circuits created this supervisor position this past year. One employee was chosen. This individual, who has a good eye for detail and insists on quality work, also showed an ability to handle extensive responsibility and manage the other employees effectively. With this supervisor, the quality of the boards assembled has remained consistently high. The change has proven beneficial because it has freed up a considerable amount of Ben's time so that he can attend to the demands of running the business.
2. *Full-time assembler.* Two individuals hold this position. These employees assemble parts into boards. They are responsible for following a design layout and populating each board to exactly match the specified design. Only one individual populates any one board. When the assemblers complete boards, they attach their employee identifications to the lower corner of the boards.
3. *Part-time assembler.* Two individuals are employed in this category. One of these employees does all the prepping of components for jobs. The other assembler populates boards. The company allows these individuals to be very flexible in setting their own hours, as long as they put in 20 hours per week.
4. *Bench technician.* One individual is employed part-time as a bench technician. This employee runs the soldering and cleaning equipment and keeps them in good condition. The bench technician also touches up boards, does all hand soldering, puts cable assemblies together, and makes repairs to any board that fails inspection. The bench technician works closely with Ben on the technical aspects of the operation at Quality Circuits.

Quality Circuits is committed to its employees. Lunchtime is often a social time in which someone's birthday or some latest accomplishment is celebrated. The Samsons believe that their employees' satisfaction with both their jobs and responsibilities is a key factor in the company's success. These employees are enthusiastic about Quality Circuits, and they work as a team to help it be successful.

CURRENT SITUATION

As Ben sits at his desk mulling his company's current situation, it occurs to him that he's been here before, and has not done anything about it. In fact, he has frequently said to Susan, "Our problem is that we don't have a business or marketing plan! We have to make some fundamental decisions about what kind of company Quality Circuits will be and how it will get there." Ben believes he must address these needs if the company is to prosper. Assuming you have been retained as a consultant to Quality Circuits, what would you recommend, and why?

QUESTIONS

1. What are Quality Circuits' strengths and weaknesses?
2. What opportunities and threats does Quality Circuits face in its external environment?
3. Explain the role that market segmentation, product positioning, and product differentiation play in developing a marketing strategy for Quality Circuits.
4. What marketing strategy do you recommend? Why?
5. Suggest specific guidelines for implementing this strategy.

Mead Products: The Trapper Keeper®*

Peter S. Carusone

Wright State University

"You know, this just might be the most fantastic product we've ever launched. I think it's really going to shake up the school supplies market!" The man who spoke was Bryant Crutchfield, Mead Products' New Ventures manager.

Mr. Crutchfield had just concluded a meeting in Wichita, Kansas, with Bob Crandall, the regional sales manager, where the two men reviewed results of an August 1978 market test. The purpose of the test was to measure market acceptance of Trapper® Portfolio and the Trapper Keeper® Notebook.

As he prepared to depart Wichita Airport for Dayton, Ohio, Mr. Crutchfield felt good about the success of the test. A new unique product unlike anything else on the market—and a total sell-through in test market.

But Crutchfield also thought about plans for 1979 and the big question yet to be resolved. "How many can we sell nationally?"

MEAD CORPORATION

Mead's traditional base is in forest products. From a strong base in pulp, paper, and paperboard, Mead has developed a family of related businesses. Lumber operations complement those in pulp. Other divisions convert paper and paperboard into packaging, containers, school supplies, and many more industrial and consumer products; some specialize in their distribution.

Still other Mead businesses provide additional growth opportunities and balance—engineered castings, molded rubber parts, distribution of piping and electrical supplies, and advanced digital systems for managing and reproducing vast amounts of information. See Appendix A for a list of the Mead divisions and affiliates.

---

*This case was written by Peter S. Carusone, Professor of Marketing, Wright State University. Copyrighted by Peter S. Carusone. Reprinted with permission.

Innovation at Mead in the 1970s focused on areas beyond but closely related to its traditional businesses. Advanced and sophisticated product developments emerged from expertise and knowledge in printing technology, pollutant management, information handling, and digital technology.

Mead Data Central's LEXIS and NEXIS are the world's most sophisticated services for text research of case law and news materials. Information is channeled into the system from the courts, Congress, news media, and other sources, and flows on demand to thousands of subscriber terminals in the professions, business, government, and education.

Ink-jet printing, which involved the parallel development of hardware and software by Mead Digital Systems, is a new technology that promises to revolutionize the printing industry in many fields. The process results from generating and directing millions of minute drops of ink—precisely and at high speed—to form words, numerals, and images. Ink-jet printing makes it possible to simultaneously compose and imprint personalized materials three times faster than any conventional method.

Mead's CompuChem special chemical analysis service has opened the nation's largest automated laboratory devoted exclusively to the analysis of priority pollutants. Client companies in the petroleum, coal, pulp, paper, rubber, and other industries ship samples to the SuperLab where materials that the Environmental Protection Agency has ruled as potentially hazardous are identified and measured (in parts per trillion).

The Mead Corporation's development philosophy was summarized in the company's 1980 Annual Report:

> Mead's underlying strategic principle is to devote its investment resources to market segments that are growing, that need products and services we are prepared to deliver, and that offer us the opportunity to build or retain a position of cost-effective leadership.

In 1980 Mead sales hit a record $2.7 billion, a 69 percent increase from 1976. The firm employs 25,000 men and women. Its World Headquarters is located in Dayton, Ohio.

MEAD PRODUCTS

A division of Mead Corporation, Mead Products (formerly Westab) is the largest U.S. manufacturer and marketer of school and college supplies, stationery, photo albums, and home/office supplies. Westab was founded in 1927 (as the Western Tablet and Stationery Corp.) and merged with Mead Corporation in 1966.

Since its inception, Mead Products has developed and marketed numerous items which stand as all-time best sellers in the retail school supply and stationery markets. Perhaps it is most famous for its line of Spiral® brand wirebound school supplies that uses a unique method of wire-binding large quantities of tablet paper, and revolutionized the design and production of notebooks, theme books, and memo pads.

The Organizer®, a tri-fold pockets and pad binder, introduced in 1972 was the industry's best-selling school supply item for three consecutive years. Other exclusive Mead Products' introductions include The System® (in 1973), The Spiral Organizer® (in 1974), the Data Center® (in 1975), and The Pinchless One® (in 1976). These also have been best sellers.

Other well-known Mead Products include: The Big Chief® writing tablet, a best seller for over seven generations; The Valet® tablet and envelope stationery line which started a revolution in the 59-cents-per-item market; Academie™ brand artists pads, books, water colors, and crayons; and Montag®, a famous name in quality, boxed stationery. See Appendix B for a list of key Mead Products trademarks.

The company traditionally has been a trendsetter in the industry. In 1966, for example, Mead Products was the first to replace the drab, blue canvas coverings on loose-lead binders with various fabrics in fashionable colors and designs. More recently, through innovative manufacturing techniques, "photo-graphics" have been applied to the covers of numerous school supply items.

Another industry first was Mead Products' decision 12 years ago to advertise on national network television. During the season the commercials are running (late August, early September), Mead Products becomes one of the largest TV advertisers in the country—of any product.

Today, Mead Products, with its own sales force, markets over 3,000 separate items. National distribution is obtained through wholesalers, distributors, and jobbers, as well as direct to chain discount, drug, variety, food and convenience stores, and department and college stores. The company operates seven plants and 12 sales offices/showrooms in 10 states. See Appendix C for facility locations.

HOW THE TRAPPER® AND THE TRAPPER KEEPER® ORIGINATED

The idea for The Trapper® and The Trapper Keeper® was identified by extensive informal exploration of the school supplies market and its total environment. "Management requires us to do a complete situation analysis," Mr. Crutchfield points out. "We have to understand what's happening in the marketplace."

A situation analysis at Mead Products entails extensive study of everything that happens from production of products, through the channels of distribution, to their consumption. It includes analysis of educational trends, consumer trends, sales trends, product usage, competition, the trade, and pertinent external factors.

Consumer Definition

People of all ages involved in the learning process are the consumers of school supplies. The range is from the preschooler just learning how to hold a crayon up to and including the adult taking refresher courses to update professional skills.

Consumer Population

The total student population was projected to continue to increase over the next five years but at a lesser rate than in the past. While the number of grade, junior, and senior high school students was declining slightly, the decline would be more than offset by increases in two other consumer segments: (1) preschool children who in just a few years will become primary customers, and (2) college enrollment and adult basic and occupational education. See Exhibit 1 for consumer population/enrollment trends.

Product Usage

Consumer product usage in the growth market segments (except for preschoolers) was basically the same as that of students in grade and high school: wirebounds, filler, binders, and portfolios. And, increasing in popularity were portfolios, wirebound notebooks, and selected binders. These select binders are those having pads and pockets that provide for versatile storage of a variety of materials. The demand for filler paper and ring notebooks was relatively flat. See Exhibit 1 for product usage by consumer group and consumer expenditures by product category.

Educational Trends

Important educational trends were identified, along with implications for future demand of various kinds of school supplies. It was learned, for example, that students were taking more courses, more advanced

EXHIBIT 1

mead
School Supplies
CONSUMER AND EDUCATIONAL INFORMATION
Consumer Population/Enrollment

	1978	1979	1980	1981	1982	1983
Occupational	10.1	10.9	11.7	12.5	13.3	14.3
Adult Basic	9.7	10.0	10.4	10.8	11.1	11.5
College	12.6	12.9	13.2	13.5	13.6	13.6
9-12 Grade (15-18)	16.8	16.7	16.2	15.8		14.7
4-8 Grade (10-14)	18.6	18.1	17.8	17.8	17.6	17.4
K-3 Grade (5-9)	16.9	16.5	16.1	15.6	15.4	15.5
Pre-School (UNDER 5)	15.3	15.6	16.0	16.6	17.3	17.9
TOTALS	**100.0**	**100.7**	**101.4**	**102.6**	**103.5**	**104.9**

Product Usage by Consumer Group

	HIGH	MEDIUM	BOUGHT BY
Occupational	Wirebound Notebooks Ring Notebooks Notebook Paper Portfolios/Folders		Adult user—some purchased in regular channels others are provided by employers
Adult	Wirebound Notebooks Ring Notebooks Notebook Paper Portfolios/Folders		Adult user
College	Wirebound Notebooks	Ring Notebooks Notebook Paper Portfolios/Folders	Nearly 100% user
9-12 Grade	Wirebound Notebooks Clipboards Ring Notebooks Lt. Wt. Ring Notebooks Portfolios/Folders	Spiral Organizer* Wirebound Data Center* The System* Data Center* Notebook Paper	89% Student 11% Parent (Parents buy primarily parity products)
4-8 Grade	Ring Notebooks Clipboards Notebook Paper The System* The Organizer* Data Center* Portfolios/Folders	Wirebound Notebooks Classifier*	75% Student 25% Parent (Parents buy primarily parity products)
K-3 Grade	Pencil Tablets Folders Drawing Paper	Classifier* The System* The Organizer* Data Center* Ring Notebooks Portfolios/Folders	80-90% Parent 20-10% Student
Pre-School	Drawing Paper Scribble Pads	Pencil Tablets	Parent/child influence

mead
Courthouse Plaza Northeast Dayton Ohio 45463

EXHIBIT 1   *(concluded)*

EDUCATIONAL TRENDS

MORE COURSES
- Today's students are taking more courses. The average student takes in excess of seven...these courses consist of special subjects, like: Black History; Literature; mini-courses in specialized fields; plus, art and hobby and craft courses.
- With this increase in the average number of courses taken, students have increased their usage of lightweight portable supplies (like portfolios and wirebound notebooks). They tend to use one per subject, class or project.

MORE ADVANCED COURSES
- College level courses are being taught more and more in secondary schools—and courses that have traditionally been considered high school courses—languages, mathematics, etc.—are now available at lower levels.
- Students taking these advanced courses have increased their use of college-type products, such as wirebound notebooks with college ruling and, especially, the popular 9½″ x 6″ products.

MORE INDIVIDUALIZED INSTRUCTION
- Individualized instruciton and programmed learning are on the increase and are most frequently coupled with the use of specialized workbooks, multi-media material and computer terminals.
- Loose-leaf filler is on the decline since students tend to use printed workbooks and computer printouts (or readouts), supplemented with bound books (wirebounds, etc.) for notes, and supplies with pockets for filing and organizing handout materials.

INCREASED USE OF TIMELY, SPECIALIZED PORTABLE MATERIALS
- More and more use is being made of Xerography (to produce materials for classrooms, such as handouts), computer retrieval and microfiche.

- Because of the amount of new information, together with the high cost of editing textbooks, pressure on school budgets and the relative decline in copying costs, textbooks are now being updated with Xeroxed handouts. Due to the quantity of handouts, students have shifted to products with pockets (portfolios, wirebounds with pockets, and special ring notebooks) for storing/organizing handout materials.

SHARED CLASSROOMS
- More and more classrooms are shared due to limited specialized teaching materials. Pilferage has increased with this trend.
- Students are forced to carry valuables with them. This creates a need for products capable of housing everything from pencils to calculators.

SMALLER LOCKERS
- New schools are providing smaller lockers for students. This space is often shared. These students are forced to use lightweight portable supplies.
- Portfolios, wirebounds, special notebooks with pockets, and bags are increasing in popularity.

LEFT-HANDED STUDENTS
- 15% to 20% of today's students (estimated) are left-handed.[1] They are becoming vocal about being forced to use products designed for right-handers.
- Top-bound products are increasing in popularity and usage by this group.

ENERGY SHORTAGE
- Energy shortages are changing the traditional school calendars. There is an increase in trimester and year-round schedules with longer breaks during periods when energy use is high.
- These schedule changes mean more promotional opportunities at times other than the normal school opening dates.

CONSUMER EXPENDITURES IN RETAIL DOLLARS[2]
(ESTIMATED)

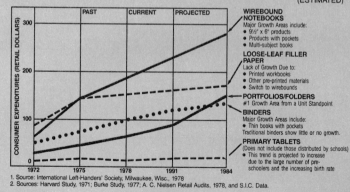

WIREBOUND NOTEBOOKS
Major Growth Areas include:
- 9½″ x 6″ products
- Products with pockets
- Multi-subject books

LOOSE-LEAF FILLER PAPER
Lack of Growth Due to:
- Printed workbooks
- Other pre-printed materials
- Switch to wirebounds

PORTFOLIOS/FOLDERS
#1 Growth Area from a Unit Standpoint

BINDERS
Major Growth Areas include:
- Thin books with pockets
Traditional binders show little or no growth.

PRIMARY TABLETS
(Does not include those distributed by schools)
- This trend is projected to increase due to the large number of pre-schoolers and the increasing birth rate

1. Source: International Left-Handers' Society, Milwaukee, Wisc., 1978
2. Sources: Harvard Study, 1971; Burke Study, 1977; A. C. Nielsen Retail Audits, 1978, and S.I.C. Data.

30-79

©The Mead Corporation—1979

courses, and more individualized instruction. Also uncovered were increased use of timely, specialized portable materials, more use of shared classrooms, and smaller lockers. The impact of the energy shortage and emergence of a market for left-handed students also were assessed. See Exhibit 1 for detailed analysis of educational trends.

Trade Analysis

As changes in education were affecting the need for, and usage of, school supplies, so changes in retail shopping patterns were affecting the opportunities for effective distribution of school supply products. Combination stores (food and drug) were growing. Independent drugstores were declining while the drug chains were merging. Growing rapidly and becoming very popular were the convenience food stores, particularly in certain markets. There were, for example, 864 convenience stores in Houston; 627 in Atlanta. In some cities the number of convenience stores was twice the number of food stores. Another important retail-type store beginning to emerge was the minicombo (convenience and drug combination).

Competition

The school supplies market was very fragmented. Competition was mostly regional due to the high cost of freight. Only one or two companies other than Mead Products were selling nationally. Mead was the leader nationally, but this varied by product line and by region.

Profiling of Consumers.

A NEED UNFULFILLED

The outcome of the situation analysis was that it led Mr. Crutchfield to formulate the following thesis: *There is a need for a notebook to hold and organize the portfolios.*

"We saw that students were taking more courses—some of these a variety of 'mini' courses. We saw an increase in the use of pocket portfolios—growth in excess of 20 percent annually. We knew from research that they were using one portfolio per subject or class. With the increased number of classes and portfolios, a student needs some place to keep them organized. What's more," Mr. Crutchfield points out, "traditional ports with horizontal pockets have a tendency to spill their contents when mistakenly turned upside down. So, the Trapper®

Portfolio and the Trapper Keeper® notebook would provide the student with both better portfolios and a place to keep them organized." Exhibit 2 shows a picture of the two products.

The best-selling portfolio on the West Coast (Pee-Chee®) has a vertical pocket—but it had never been popular east of the Rockies. It is

---

EXHIBIT 2

interesting to note that part of the rationale for the item occurred to Mr. Crutchfield as a result of a conversation at home with his 13-year-old daughter. In retrospect, he describes the experience as one of "creative listening." In asking his daughter about the usage of portfolios in her classes, Mr. Crutchfield thought he heard her relate how the teacher required the students to submit their assignments in portfolios as a time-saving device. The teacher wanted to see the ports for collecting assignments and for redistributing them, along with handouts, so students could pick up their own portfolios and save classtime. When a Mead researcher was dispatched by Mr. Crutchfield to talk with the teacher, he discovered that the teacher never said that. And when the 13-year-old daughter was questioned further, it was found that she never said that either. But, the results of the research were positive. The teacher thought the "nonexistent procedure" was a good one.

Idea generation

TESTING THE TRAPPER KEEPER®

"We saw this to be a fantastic concept," Mr. Crutchfield recalls. "A portfolio with vertical pockets so that everything is trapped inside when they're closed, and a Trapper Keeper® to keep Trapper® ports organized." Other features added to the inside pockets included a metric ruler, an English ruler, multiplication tables, metric conversion charts, and more. The portfolio (the Trapper®) was punched to fit on rings inside a special portfolio notebook (the Trapper Keeper®) designed to hold the Trapper® ports. The Trapper Keeper® was designed, in turn, with nylon, pinchless rings, three Trapper® ports, a pocket for holding loose materials, and a clip that holds a pad for notes and a place for the pencil. After school or class everything can be snapped together for transporting home—nothing falls out.

Teacher Research

Design concept

The next step in development of the Trapper® and Trapper Keeper® was to determine if the basic product concept had merit. Before making any product, illustrations of the concept were drawn and used to conduct a focus group session with teachers. Was there truly a need for this product? Would teachers recommend it?

Basically, teachers said that student organization was their biggest problem, and that they would recommend this or any product that helped students improve their organization.

Market Test

To get some measure of student reaction, a test market was set up in Wichita, Kansas, in August 1978. The primary objectives of the test were to determine:

1. Product salability.
2. Rate of sale compared to The Organizer®, Data Center®, The System®, plus comparable competitive products.

Pricing of the Trapper Keeper® was pegged at the same level as the Data Center® and The Organizer®, ranging from a low of $1.99 (on a weekend sale) to a high of $3.99—the most frequent price being $2.49. The Trapper® ranged from four for 98 cents to 29 cents each—the most frequent price being 29 cents.

The total market (ADI) was monitored from a sell-in and sell-through standpoint. Fifteen representative stores were audited: seven discount, three variety, three drug, and two food. The product was advertised on TV at 180 GRPs, which is equivalent to everyone seeing the commercial 1.8 times. A photoscript of the commerical is presented as Exhibit 3.

The market test results, in audited stores, were as follows:

1. For every 100 Trapper Keeper® notebooks purchased by the consumer, 77 Trapper® portfolios, 90 Data Center®, 65 The Organizer®, and 39 The System® notebooks were sold.
2. Trapper® portfolios totally sold out in over 90 percent of the stores, so the top potential was not known.
3. There was very little cannibalization of The Organizer®, Data Center®, or The System® notebooks. These items sold at approximately the same level this year as last—in some cases, they were totally sold out.
4. Total unit sales of all items increased 38.5 percent in the monitored stores.

Consumer Post-Test Research

Consumer cards were placed in all the test market products offering a free memo book for filling out and returning a questionnaire card. Over 1,500 cards were returned. Some of the results were:

- 62 percent of the purchases were female.
- 35 percent were between the ages of 9 and 12; 44 percent between 13 and 15; 10 percent between 16 and 18.
- 81 percent of the portfolio users preferred the Trapper® pocket design over traditional horizontal pockets.

EXHIBIT 3   Photoscript to Trapper Commercial

Teacher Research

Teachers exposed to the product concept in a focus group session concluded the idea was good—it helps solve one of their greatest problems . . . student's organization. The teachers said they would recommend students use Trapper Keeper® notebooks or any school product that helps them organize their school work.

Market Test

The products were tested for salability and rate of sale compared to The Organizer®, Data Center® and comparable competitive products. Trapper Keeper® outsold them all in monitored stores. For every 100 Trapper Keepers®, 90 Data Centers®, 65 Organizers® and 39 The Systems® were sold. Best of all . . . total unit sales (all items) increased 38.5% in the monitored stores. This means plus business for you as new users were created.

Post Use Research

A sample of Trapper Keeper® notebook purchasers/users were interviewed via phone after 2½ months of product use:
- 95% rated the Trapper Keeper® notebook excellent or good.
- 88% said the Trapper Keeper® notebook was better than previous product used.
- 84% intended to repurchase the Trapper Keeper® notebook.
- Trapper Keeper® notebook users tended to be older.

Introduced to educators in early 1979

Educators will be introduced to Trapper® portfolios and Trapper Keeper® notebooks through contacts at the Board of Education level and through teachers' magazines.

Presold on Network TV in August

The following commercial will be shown on network TV in August. Approximately 250 GRP's, which is equivalent to everyone seeing the following ad 2.5 times.

TWO HIGH SCHOOL BOYS AT THEIR LOCKERS, TAKING OUT THEIR TEXT BOOKS FOR THE NEXT CLASS. ONE BOY HAS ONLY A TRAPPER® PORTFOLIO THE OTHER HAS A THICK NOTEBOOK BRIMMING WITH LOOSE PAPERS. (BELL RINGS)

1ST BOY: That's all you're taking to class?

2ND BOY: Everything I need is in my Trapper Portfolio.

1ST BOY: Trapper?

HE OPENS THE TRAPPER, SLIDES PAPERS IN AND OUT TO DEMONSTRATE.
2ND BOY: It traps in all my papers. The pocket is built this way . . . so . . . .

HE CLOSES THE TRAPPER . . . . THEN SHAKES IT UP AND DOWN . . . DEMONSTRATING HOW THE PAPERS CAN'T FALL OUT.
2ND BOY: . . . close the Trapper . . . and the papers are trapped in. One Trapper for each class.

1ST BOY: Where do you keep um?

CUT TO THE TRAPPER KEEPER.
2ND BOY: In the Trapper Keeper . . .

2ND BOY: . . . which also has a note pad and pencil clip.

HE CLOSES THE TRAPPER KEEPER® NOTEBOOK AND SNAPS IT SHUT.
2ND BOY: After school snap everything in my Trapper Keeper and take it home . . . what could be neater.

GIRL APPROACHES.
1ST BOY: (GESTURING TOWARD THE GIRL) . . . a date with her.

CUT TO PRODUCT SHOT
SUPER: "TRAPPER"
"TRAPPER KEEPER" "MEAD"
VO ANNCR: The Trapper and Trapper Keeper, only from Mead.

2ND BOY INTRODUCES GIRL TO 1ST BOY . . . THE COVER OF 1ST BOY'S BINDER FLOPS OPEN, SPILLING THE PAPERS.
2ND BOY: Hi . . .
MEAD SUPER APPEARS.

- Only 56 percent of the purchasers had used portfolios prior to finding the Trapper®.

Exhibit 4 contains some of the comments of purchasers as to why they purchased Trapper Keeper® rather than other type binders.

Six weeks after the test market, a number of purchasers were interviewed and asked to evaluate the products. The key results of this research were as follows:

- General Reaction:
- 95%—believe Trapper Keeper® to be excellent or good
  88%—rate Trapper Keeper® better than product used previously
- Trapper Keeper® features most liked:
  89%—ports inside, paper won't fall out, and one portfolio for each subject
  84%—intended to repurchase the Trapper Keeper®
- Trapper® features most liked:
  47%—vertical pockets/papers won't fall out
  21%—helpful information (metric conversion, etc.)

NATIONAL PLANS

It was decided to introduce the Trapper Keeper® nationally for school opening 1979. The introduction was to be backed by a national, prime-time, network television campaign of 230 to 250 GRPs—approximately 20 spots.

EXHIBIT 4   Selected Comments from Consumer Cards

- "Because it's new, slender, and the way it's put together."
- "One reason, it had separate folders, but mainly because of the colors."
- "My mother got it by mistake but I'd seen it on TV, so decided to keep it."
- "Because I like neat, and things are easy to find. Thanks."
- "Our teacher made us buy one—but I have been very pleased with it."*
- "I heard it was good. My girlfriend had one."
- "If you trip, all your papers won't go flying all over the place."
- "Because they keep your papers where they belong. They're really great—everybody has got one."
- "I saw an ad on TV."
- "Instead of taking the whole thing you can take only one part home."
- "So when the kids in my class throw it, the papers won't fly all over."
- "It was the only one left in the store."

* Several cards with comments like this were received and traced back to a 9th grade teacher (Mrs. Willard) in Wellington, Kansas. Mrs. Willard agreed to endorse the Trapper Keeper®, and her comments were used in an ad campaign to other teachers. See ad in Exhibit 5.

Products were to be presented to teachers and boards of education during the spring for approval and recommendations at school opening in August/September. Teachers' magazines and personal calls were planned to reach the teachers and administrators. Teachers were offered a sample Trapper Keeper® at a special price to cover handling and postage. A copy of the "Mrs. Willard Testimonial" advertisement to teachers is reproduced in Exhibit 5.

EXHIBIT 5

Why did Mrs. Willard in Wellington, Kansas advise her students to purchase a Mead Trapper Keeper™ Notebook? For the same reasons you will.

"As a 9th grade teacher, I'm always on the lookout for products that will help my students do a better job in school. Last year, I found the Trapper™ portfolio and Trapper Keeper™ notebook from Mead and recommended them to my class.

Mead developed the products because today's students are taking more courses than ever. They average over seven courses per student. They can't carry seven notebooks, so they are switching to portfolios.

Mead has designed a new portfolio called the Trapper. It

traps in all the student's papers so they won't fall out. Mead has also developed a notebook to carry all these portfolios, called the Trapper Keeper.

Most students keep the Trapper Keeper in their locker. Then, they just change Trappers from class to class, taking only one Trapper to each class. With no large notebooks to carry around, they travel light and easy. After school, they take the Trapper Keeper home with all the Trappers inside.

The Trapper and Trapper Keeper have been tested in actual use. Everyone, teachers and students alike, agree that the Trapper and Trapper Keeper make school easier and better."

Special Teacher Offer. Because the Trapper and Trapper Keeper may help you in organizing your classes, Mead wants you to have a sample of the Trapper Keeper (with 3 Trapper portfolios included) for the cost of postage and handling ($2.00). These products will be available to your students the start of school next fall. So, it's a good chance to try it out ahead of your students. You might find you want to recommend it.

---
mead

I'd like to try the Trapper and Trapper Keeper. I'm sending along $2.00 (to cover postage and handling). Would you please send me a set of the 3 Trappers and a Trapper Keeper.

Send to: Mead Products, PO Box 148, 11th & Mitchell Avenue, St. Joseph, Missouri 64502.

Name _____
Address _____
City _____
State _____ Zip _____
Offer expires December 31, 1979

The Trapper® portfolio has a suggested retail price of 29 cents each. Three colors—red, blue, and green—were packaged per assortment. The Trapper Keeper® had a suggested retail of $4.85 each. These were available in three solid colors and three designs: soccer, dog and cat, and Oregon coast.

The distribution plan covered all major types of outlets: mass merchandisers, food, drug, combo stores, variety stores, and others. The strategy would be to concentrate on major regional and national chains.

The sales presentation methods were to include use of a "sell brochure," a slide presentation, a TV commercial, a TV storyboard, and a chain survey sheet.

A sales forecast, by region, would be needed by December 1978. The national account contacts would be made in December and January, with regional sell taking place in February through May. Key account activity would be monitored weekly.

Appendix A   Mead Corporation

Divisions

Mead Paper—Chillicothe (OH)	Mead Merchants
Mead Fine Paper	Gulf Consolidated Services
Mead Publishing Paper	Lynchburg Foundry
Gilbert Paper	Mulga Coal Company
Specialty Paper	Murray Rubber
Mead Paperboard	Mead Data Central
Mead Paperboard Products	Mead Digital Systems
Mead Containers	Mead CompuChem
Mead Packaging	Mead Office Services
Mead Pulp Sales, Inc.	Mead Reinsurance
Mead Products	

Affiliates (50 percent owned)

Georgia Kraft Company
Brunswick Pulp & Paper Company
Northwood Forest Industries Limited
Schoeller Technical Papers, Inc.

Appendix B Key Mead Products Trademarks

The Spiral®
The Organizer®
Data Center®
The System®
The Home Organizers®
The Classifiler®
Twin Wire®
The Pinchless One®
The Valet®

Campus®
Class Mate®
Montag®
Trapper® Portfolio
Trapper Keeper® Notebook
Flex 3™ Notebook
Flex 3™ Expandable
Envelok™ Folio

Appendix C Mead Products Locations

Headquarters
Mead Products
Mead World Headquarters
Courthouse Plaza, Northeast
Dayton, Ohio 45463

Plants
Garden Grove, California
Atlanta, Georgia
Kalamazoo, Michigan
St. Joseph, Missouri
Salem, Oregon
Alexandria, Pennsylvania
Garland, Texas

Sales Offices/Showrooms
Garden Grove, California
San Jose, California
Atlanta, Georgia
Des Plaines (Chicago), Illinois
Braintree, Massachusetts
Kalamazoo, Michigan
Shawnee Mission (Kansas City), Missouri
Union City, New Jersey
Salem, Oregon
Dallas, Texas

MidAmerica BancSystem, Inc.*

James E. Nelson
University of Colorado

Chuck Smith walked briskly across the lobby of the Fairview Heights bank to his office. It was 7:30 A.M., November 2, 1984. He would have at least two hours before the rush of Friday customers would begin. Friday always meant a great deal of "public relations" for Smith in terms of his exchanging greetings and small talk with customers. "Today I could do without it," Smith thought. "I'd much rather work on what the marketing committee discussed yesterday." However, he knew that many customers expected to see his door open and his face break into a smile of recognition whenever they voiced a greeting. Two hours would give him enough time to get some thoughts down on the automated teller machine (ATM) issue. The other topics that he had discussed with the committee would have to wait until the weekend.

MIDAMERICA BANCSYSTEM, INC.

MidAmerica Bank and Trust Company of Fairview Heights was one of six members of MidAmerica BancSystem, Inc., a multibank holding company under the laws of the state of Illinois. Five of the six subsidiaries were located within 25 miles of each other in St. Clair and Madison counties. The sixth, MidAmerica Bank and Trust Company of Carbondale, was almost 80 miles away in Jackson County. St. Clair and Madison counties were due east of St. Louis, Missouri, just across the Mississippi River. Jackson County to the southeast also bordered the Mississippi.

*This case was written by Professor James E. Nelson, University of Colorado. This case is intended for use as a basis for class discussion rather than to illustrate either effective or ineffective administrative decision making. Some data are disguised.
© 1985 by the Business Research Division, College of Business and Administration and the Graduate School of Business Administration, University of Colorado, Boulder, Colorado 80309.

MidAmerica BancSystem, Inc., was formed on August 31, 1982, about one year after enactment of an Illinois law permitting multibank holding companies. Prior to this date, the six subsidiary banks were considered "affiliated" in the sense that they shared a number of officers and directors. MidAmerica BancSystem, Inc., provided auditing, investment, and accounting services for its subsidiaries. It contracted with an independent organization for computer services and managed the ATM service. In short, the holding company had authority and responsibility for major financial and marketing decisions for all subsidiaries. As an example of financial decision making, senior management of the holding company had decided in late 1983 to sell $14.7 million (par value) of long-term securities at a loss of over $1.2 million. The sale made possible the purchase of higher yielding U.S. government securities with much-shortened maturities. Senior management also had charged off about $2.7 million in loans (primarily agricultural) in late 1983, an amount some nine times that for 1982. Together the actions had provided a net loss of $2.9 million for 1983 (see Exhibit 1 for financial data) but promised long-term benefits in terms of liquidity, flexibility, and return.

Senior management had been less decisive in making marketing decisions. However, now that financial matters had been resolved, attention turned to marketing. A marketing committee had been formed at the request of the holding company's new chairman of the board and president, James Watt. Watt had joined the holding company in this capacity in late 1983, replacing David Charles who had served as chairman and president since 1958. Watt's previous experience included positions as senior vice president of Essex County Bank and Trust in Boston, senior vice president of the Bank Marketing Association in Chicago, and vice president of Beverly Bancorporation in Chicago. Watt held an MS in marketing and thus took a keen interest in the marketing issues facing MidAmerica BancSystem, Inc. Chuck Smith chaired the marketing committee.

MARKETING ISSUES

Smith settled into his chair (the office door shut) and reread the four marketing issues he had summarized last night:

1. What should be our response to the Shop and Save proposal to allow installation of MidAmerica ATMs in 20 supermarkets in St. Clair and Madison counties?
2. How can we increase use of our current ATMs?
3. How do we translate corporate financial goals in marketing goals? How do we make marketing goals part of the management process?

EXHIBIT 1   Financial Data

	1981	1982	1983	1984*
Assets	$198,339	$211,067	$202,104	$208,093
Liabilities	183,268	195,415	189,872	194,312
Stockholders' equity	15,071	15,652	12,232	13,781
Interest income	22,687	23,399	20,807	16,871
Interest expense	14,300	15,460	12,871	10,051
Net interest income	8,387	7,939	7,936	6,820
Provision for possible loan losses	285	309	4,140	258
Net interest income after provision for possible loan losses	8,102	7,630	3,796	6,562
Other income	1,676	1,685	711	1,758
Other expenses	7,473	7,924	8,482	6,242
Income (loss) before income taxes and extraordinary item	2,305	1,391	(3,975)	2,078
Income taxes	401	43	(1,080)	803
Income (loss) before extraordinary item	1,904	1,348	(2,895)	1,275
Extraordinary item tax benefit	—	—	—	713
Net income (loss)	1,904	1,348	(2,895)	1,988
Deposit growth (%)	3.9	6.2	−2.0	−1.5
Return on assets (%)	1.0	0.6	−1.4	1.0
Return on equity (%)	12.6	8.6	−23.7	14.4
Capital to assets (%)	7.6	7.4	6.1	6.6

Note: All data are stated in thousands of dollars except data for deposit growth, return on assets, return on equity, and capital to assets.
* As of September 1984.

4. What should be MidAmerica's marketing strategy over the next five years?

Smith knew that senior management of the holding company considered all issues to be high-priority items.

The Shop and Save Proposal

Early in October the president of the Fairview Heights bank had paid a call on the manager of a Shop and Save supermarket located in nearby Belleville, Illinois. The purpose of the call was to see if the store had any interest in installing a MidAmerica ATM. The timing could not have been better—the store was soon to begin a remodeling project and could easily accommodate an ATM. The store's policies did not permit check cashing, nor would they allow a customer to write a check for an amount greater than that purchased. Consequently, the store manager was greatly interested in the installation, provided the system could be used by a large number of the store's customers.

This meant that the ATM had to be available to customers of banks that belonged to Magna Group, Inc., a nine-bank holding company serving many of the same market areas as MidAmerica. Contact with the marketing director for Magna had disclosed that Magna had about 60,000 cards and 36 ATMs in use in the two-county area. These figures greatly exceeded MidAmerica's 10,100 cards and 12 ATMs. The marketing director had shown strong interest in sharing ATM facilities currently in operation, as well as any others either holding company might add. Senior management at both organizations viewed ATMs as a highly desirable service. They also felt that a key to successful implementation of the service was convenient and widespread locations.

A letter from the marketing director summarized Magna's interest and its desire for a $1.50 charge for each interchange transaction. That is, each time a MidAmerica cardholder used a Magna ATM, MidAmerica would be billed $1.50. The same amount would be billed to Magna for each of their cardholders' transactions on a MidAmerica ATM. Smith thought that the charge could be negotiated upward or downward by 25 cents.

Smith was not sure just what sharing meant in terms of interchange usage. He estimated that MidAmerica cardholders might use Magna ATMs for between 10,000 and 30,000 transactions per month. On the other hand, Magna cardholders could use MidAmerica ATMs between 10,000 and 60,000 times per month. The most likely outcome was somewhere in between.

Once MidAmerica had obtained agreement with Magna, negotiations with chain management at Shop and Save could proceed. Chain management had become involved with the Belleville store decision and had quickly proposed that MidAmerica place ATMs in all 20 stores in St. Clair and Madison counties. The chain wanted placement in each store because of its check-cashing policies and what it saw as an opportunity for increased revenues. The proposal called for Shop and Save to receive $600 per ATM per month in rent and 10 cents per each transaction beyond 2,500 per ATM per month. The proposal noted that a similar system in its Springfield, Illinois, stores averaged about 10,000 transactions per ATM per month.

Smith thought that MidAmerica would be lucky to average 4,000 transactions per ATM per month initially in these stores and might reach 10,000 per month in three to five years. He thought the ratio of

MidAmerica cardholder transactions to Magna cardholder transactions would be about 1:3. Shop and Save figures showed the 20 stores to average about 65,000 customers per month, although one store showed only 41,000. Smith thought that Shop and Save might come down somewhat on their rental and transaction charges; he doubted that they would move from their 2,500 figure.

MidAmerica estimates of the installed cost of each ATM were $40,000. The practical life of an ATM was considered to be about six years. Monthly fixed operating costs totalled about $400 per ATM for the computer telephone line, bookkeeping, maintenance, and the service to supply the machines with cash and to collect deposits. The computer service itself charged 40 cents per transaction.

MidAmerica currently billed each of its cardholders $1.00 per transaction. However, many banks in the St. Louis area charged only 50 cents, and some charged nothing. Smith felt that the marketing committee would soon recommend the MidAmerica charge be reduced to 50 cents, although there was some feeling among members that the charge should simply be eliminated.

"Either action should increase usage," Smith thought as he scanned a table of last month's transaction activity. The table showed that usage of cards at MidAmerica's 12 locations actually had fallen 5 percent from September of a year ago. The drop contrasted only slightly with July and August activity, which had shown no growth over usage for the previous year. The 28,400 transactions for September were based on 10,100 cards outstanding, a number that was 4 percent higher than a year ago. Something would have to be done to improve usage to at least 5,000 transactions per ATM per month. This figure was generally considered an industry standard, representing a break-even point between the cost of an ATM and the teller function for which it substituted.

Marketing Goals

The committee also had spent some time discussing marketing goals at MidAmerica. The members' lack of extensive marketing backgrounds made discussion difficult. Nonetheless, Watt and the committee felt it important that MidAmerica personnel at both the holding company and each subsidiary give marketing goals considerable thought. Marketing goals would encourage aggressive marketing actions and give focus to marketing efforts. Marketing goals would also form a standard against which performance could be measured.

This was the first time that the holding company and subsidiaries had ever set marketing goals. Most officers were familiar with financial goal setting and the holding company's financial goals for 1985; an 8 percent growth in deposits, a 1.2 percent return on assets; a 16 percent return on equity; and a 7 percent capital-to-assets ratio. Each subsidiary's financial goals departed somewhat from these figures, dependent on local market conditions and forecasts.

Neither the holding company nor the subsidiaries had translated financial goals into marketing goals. The committee had discussed some criteria for the translation, concluding that marketing goals should be consistent with financial goals and be stated in specific and measurable terms at realistic levels. The committee had even tried to write some marketing goals:

- Obtain 200 Vacation Club accounts by October 1985.
- Increase IRA deposits by 15 percent.
- Book 150 Equity Plus loans by the end of 1985.

Each member had promised to spend more time thinking about marketing goals after yesterday's meeting. Each was also to produce a more complete list of goals by the end of next week, send it to other committee members, and be ready for a discussion at the next meeting. It would be important to get some marketing goals approved at the holding company level before expecting each subsidiary to write its own.

Also at issue was how to integrate marketing goals into the management process. The committee had touched on this matter, noting that marketing goals would be an idle exercise unless officers actually used them. A way to mandate use would be to include marketing goals and marketing performance in each officer's annual performance evaluation. Both the officer and his or her supervisor would then examine each goal and its associated performance and reach formal agreement on progress. However, one committee member strongly opposed such use because of his and MidAmerica's lack of experience with marketing goals. The other members had agreed—something else should be done.

Marketing Strategy

The last major issue discussed by the marketing committee was MidAmerica's marketing strategy over the next five years. Watt had requested that the committee study this topic and propose two options, each with clearly identified strengths and weaknesses. He had also asked for the committee's choice between the options. The committee had until December 31 to complete his request.

The first strategic option was growth via market development. This strategy would emphasize the marketing of existing financial services to new markets defined in terms of either geographic areas or market segments. Growth via new geographic areas could be done three ways.

The first would be to stay in St. Clair and Madison counties and locate in such cities as Cahokia, Collinsville, and Edwardsville, for example. The second would be to expand eastward and southward to other Illinois counties. The third would be to cross the Mississippi and enter the St. Louis market area, perhaps in the St. Charles area about 20 miles west of Alton. MidAmerica could move into Missouri by means of its directors establishing a Missouri corporation in the banking industry. Alternatively, it could enter Missouri by offering a limited-service bank that would provide all MidAmerica's services except commercial loans. A limited-service bank escaped federal and state laws prohibiting interstate banking. However, MidAmerica might be able to expand into Missouri with all of its services as soon as 1986 if an existing bill were enacted by the Illinois and Missouri legislatures. Smith thought that chances of the bill becoming law by 1986 were 50-50.

Watt and the directors wanted any new market area chosen to show a deposit growth potential in excess of 8 percent per year; any new facility should show an operating profit within the first five years. Committee members thought that careful selection of new market areas could meet these criteria. However, the consequences of a mistake in their judgment could be substantial.

Less risky was a market development strategy based not on new geographic areas but on new market segments. These new segments would be in the local community where MidAmerica's reputation was strongest. Examples of new segments were professionals, commercial accounts (mostly retailing and light industry), and the military at nearby Scott Air Force Base. Potential here was probably not as great as with geographic expansion.

The second strategic option was growth via service development. This strategy would emphasize the marketing of new financial services to existing markets. New services could be aimed at either existing consumer or commercial accounts with the goal of increasing deposits, loans, or service fees. There were literally hundreds of new services that MidAmerica could add. Some of the more promising ones had been mentioned in yesterday's meeting. In-home banking would allow customers to link their home computers with the bank's system and pay bills, transfer funds, and check on account balances. Optimistic forecasts here called for about 10 percent of U.S. households to use some form of home banking by the early 1990s. Auto leasing would have MidAmerica as lessor to individual customers. Experts forecast a 10–15 percent annual growth rate for the service, reaching a level of about 40 percent of all new car deliveries in the early 1990s. Personal financial planning would use financial advisers at the bank to investigate middle-aged customers' financial objectives and resources and then recommend a financial program. A "prestige" credit card would provide increased services and higher loan limits to upscale customers. The committee recognized the need for careful research before recommending one new service over another.

The committee also recognized that a recommendation to market any new service would subject MidAmerica to the chance of failure. Costs associated with failure depended on the new service. However, in no case did the committee think that a major new service could be introduced for less than $60,000 in training, marketing, and other start-up costs.

Finally, the committees recognized that growth objectives could be met by either strategy and that MidAmerica almost certainly would not pursue one strategy to the exclusion of the other. A mix between the two would be best; the issue really was which of the two strategies should be emphasized. Further, adoption of either strategy would not mean abandonment of existing customer segments. All MidAmerica subsidiaries would be expected to continue to show growth via penetrating existing segments through the offering of present services.

HOLDING COMPANY STRATEGY

Choosing between a market development and a product development strategy was the final decision in formulating the holding company's strategy. Earlier in the year, Watt and the directors had agreed on other strategic components: profitable growth, liquidity, active asset/ liability management, financial and marketing control over subsidiaries, capable personnel, and market leadership. All components were tied to a community bank orientation: suburban locations, a high profile in local community affairs, personal relationships with customers, and deposits and loans generated in the local community.

"For the next few years, our strategy could also be described as 'conservative,'" Watt had told the committee. He had gone on to explain that a conservative approach was called for because it would:

1. Avoid risk and produce profits (important because of last year's loss).
2. Allow MidAmerica time to train and develop its associates and officers and to improve its management procedures.
3. Minimize the risk of costly mistakes by allowing some important industry trends to emerge.

The net effect of a conservative approach should be intermediate and long-term profitability. However, Watt noted that in the short term, the approach might mean some missed opportunities and some stronger competitors.

Watt and several other officers considered it almost certain that MidAmerica would be sold to a much larger holding company in the next five years. Industry sources predicted hundreds of such sales, beginning shortly after Congress permitted interstate banking. Bank sales and interstate banking were both parts of a broad industry trend called deregulation (see next section). The sale of MidAmerica would take place at a premium if MidAmerica could show capable personnel and strong performance. The present strategy should produce both characteristics by 1987.

DEREGULATION

The term *deregulation* was misleading because governments at federal and state levels would never allow banks to operate without regulation. Instead, deregulation meant reducing regulation, giving banks more freedom to pay and to charge interest rates of their choice, to develop and to market new services, and to locate limited service banks in more than one state. Deregulation had begun in the late 1970s and was expected to continue until at least 1990. Congress, federal regulatory agencies (the Federal Reserve Board, the Federal Deposit Insurance Corporation, the Comptroller of the Currency), and state regulatory agencies all expected that the trend would make banking more competitive and, hence, more efficient.

Increased competition and efficiency would cause some banks to disappear. As of October 1984, there were almost 800 banks on the Federal Reserve Board's problem list. Industry sources expected that about 60 of these would fail in the next 12 months. Already the country had seen 65 failures in 1984, making it a strong candidate for the second highest year for failures since 1937. The same sources predicted that about 2,300 or 15 percent of all U.S. banks would close, merge, or be sold over the next five years. The pace could greatly accelerate if Congress were to permit interstate banking.

Deregulation also meant the threat of other firms competing in the financial service industry. Generally these firms had large retail networks and sophisticated data processing systems. The largest was Sears Roebuck & Co. Sears had purchased Coldwell Banker (the nation's largest real estate broker) and Dean Witter (the nation's fifth-largest investment broker) for over $800 million in 1981. The purchased organizations complemented functions performed by Sears' Allstate Insurance (the nation's second-largest casualty insurer). Sears was expected to place Financial Centers at 300 of its 806 stores by the end of 1984. At each center, a Sears customer could trade securities as well as invest in a money market mutual fund and in certificates of deposit. Increased deregulation might mean that Sears could offer the nation a complete line of what used to be exclusively banking services.

Already banks had seen most of their traditional services extended to savings and loan associations, credit unions, and other institutions inside and outside the financial service industry. Consumers now could keep demand and time deposits, obtain mortgage and installment loans, and, in short, satisfy almost all financial needs at institutions other than banks. Consumers had more choices than ever before.

To some consumers, increased choice meant greater sophistication in managing their finances. Smith thought that these people might be kept by MidAmerica's strategy. They would not move a $20,000 certificate of deposit, for example, just because a competitor's interest rate was 20 basis points higher. The $40 annual difference in interest earned (before taxes) would not be worth the reduction in service. Nor would the higher rate move the deposits of unsophisticated consumers. These people placed greater importance on location and on habit than on return. However, in between these groupings were consumers that Smith worried about. These people would move for $40 per year, not caring about the loss of service or the increased inconvenience.

THE MORNING MAIL

Smith's thoughts were broken by his secretary and the morning mail. A headline on the front page of the St. Louis Business Journal caught his attention: "Citicorp's St. Louis 'Bank' Bid." The accompanying article explained that Citicorp, a New York bank with over $130 billion in assets, had applied to the comptroller of the currency for permission to open a limited-service bank in St. Louis. Citicorp expected to receive permission. However, it would not seek permission from Missouri regulators because Citicorp felt that the planned operation would technically not be a bank and the matter was, therefore, beyond control of the Missouri commissioner of finance. The commissioner was quoted as willing to bring suit to stop Citicorp. Lawyers for Citicorp responded that any suit would be decided in their favor because federal law superseded Missouri law.

The article also summarized fears of the St. Louis banking community that Citicorp's entry would "trigger a bidding war for consumer deposits and hurt local bank earnings." Not only that, the local bankers thought that if Citicorp entered their market, at least three or four other banks would soon follow. The net effect would be much more aggressive marketing of financial services.

A hearty "Hello!" took Smith away from the article. He looked through his now-opened door to see one of the bank's eldest customers. He thought, "It must be 9:30."

| *The Gillette Company**

Charles M. Kummel
Jay E. Klompmaker
both of University of North Carolina

In July 1978, Mike Edwards, brand manager for TRAC II®,[1] is beginning to prepare his marketing plans for the following year. In preparing for the marketing plan approval process, he was to wrestle with some major funding questions. The most recent sales figures show that TRAC II has continued to maintain its share of the blade and razor market. This has occurred even though the Safety Razor Division (SRD) has introduced a new product to its line, Atra. The company believes that Atra will be the shaving system of the future and, therefore, is devoting increasing amounts of marketing support to this brand. Atra was launched in 1977 with a $7 million advertising campaign and over 50 million $2 rebate coupons. In less than a year, the brand achieved a 7 percent share of the blade market and about one third of the dollar-razor market. Thus, the company will be spending heavily on Atra, possibly at the expense of TRAC II, still the number one shaving system in America.

Edwards is faced with a difficult situation, for he believes that TRAC II still can make substantial profits for the division if the company continues to support it. In preparing for 1979, the division is faced with two major issues:

1. What are TRAC II's and Atra's future potentials?
2. Most important, can SRD afford to heavily support two brands? Even if they can, is it sound marketing policy to do so?

COMPANY BACKGROUND

The Gillette Company was founded in 1903 by King C. Gillette, a 40-year-old inventor, utopian writer, and bottle-cap salesman in Boston, Massachusetts. Since marketing its first safety razor and blades,

---

*This case was written by Charles M. Kummel under the direction of Professor Jay E. Klompmaker, Graduate School of Business Administration, University of North Carolina. Copyright © 1982 by Jay E. Klompmaker, reproduced by permission.

[1]TRAC II® is a registered trademark of The Gillette Company.

the Gillette Company, the parent of the Safety Razor Division, has been the leader in the shaving industry. The Gillette safety razor was the first system to provide a disposable blade that could be replaced at low cost and that provided a good inexpensive shave. The early ads focused on a shave-yourself theme: "If the time, money, energy, and brainpower which are wasted (shaving) in the barbershops of America were applied in direct effort, the Panama Canal could be dug in four hours."

The Pre-World War Years

With the benefit of a 17-year patent, Gillette was in a very advantageous position. However, it was not until World War I that the safety razor began to gain wide consumer acceptance. One day in 1917 King Gillette came into the office with a visionary idea: to present a Gillette razor to every soldier, sailor, and marine. Other executives modified this idea so that the government would do the presenting. In this way, millions just entering the shaving age would give the nation the self-shaving habit. In World War I, the government bought 4,180,000 Gillette razors as well as smaller quantities of competitive models.

Daily Shaving Development

Although World War I gave impetus to self-shaving, World War II popularized frequent shaving—12 million American servicemen shaved daily. This produced two results: (1) Gillette was able to gain consumer acceptance of personal shaving, and (2) the company was able to develop an important market to build for the future.

Postwar Years

After 1948, the company began to diversify through the acquisition of three companies which gave Gillette entry into new markets. In 1948, the acquisition of the Toni Company extended the company into the women's grooming aid market. Paper Mate, a leading maker of writing instruments, was bought in 1954, and the Sterilon Corporation, a manufacturer of disposable supplies for hospitals, was acquired in 1962.

Diversification also occurred through internal product development propelled by a detailed marketing survey conducted in the late 1950s. The survey found that the public associated the company as much or more with personal grooming as with cutlery and related products. Gillette's response was to broaden its personal care line. As a result, Gillette now markets such well-known brands as Adorn hair spray, Tame cream rinse, Right Guard anti-perspirant, Dry Look hair spray for men, Foamy shaving cream, Earth Borne and Ultra Max shampoos, Cricket lighter, Pro Max hair dryers as well as Paper Mate, Eraser Mate, and Flair pens.

Gillette Today

Gillette is divided into four principal operating groups (North America, International, Braun AG, Diversified Companies) and five product lines. As Table 1 indicates, the importance of blades and razors to company profits is immense. In nearly all the 200 countries in which its blades and razors are sold, Gillette remains the industry leader. In 1977, Gillette reported increased worldwide sales of $1,587.2 million with income after taxes of $79.7 million (see Table 2). Of total sales, $720.9 million were domestic and $866.3 million were international, with profit contributions of $109 million and $105.6 million, respectively. The company employs 31,700 people worldwide with 8,600 employees in the United States.

Statement of Corporate Objectives and Goals

At a recent stockholders' meeting, the chairman of the board outlined the company's strategy for the future:

TABLE 1   Gillette Sales and Contributions to Profits by Business Segments

	Blades and Razors		Toiletries and Grooming Aids		Writing Instruments		Braun Electric Razors		Other	
	Net Sales	Contributions to Profits	Net Sales	Contributions to Profits	Net Sales	Contributions to Profits	Net Sales	Contributions to Profits	Net Sales	Contributions to Profits
1977	31%	75%	26%	13%	8%	6%	23%	13%	12%	(7)%
1976	29	71	28	15	7	6	21	10	15	(2)
1975	30	73	30	15	7	5	20	8	13	(1)
1974	30	69	31	17	7	6	20	5	12	3
1973	31	64	32	20	7	5	22	10	8	1

Source: Gillette Annual Report for 1977, p. 28.

The goal of The Gillette Company is sustained growth. To achieve this, the company concentrates on two major objectives: to maintain the strength of existing product lines and to develop at least two new significant businesses or product lines that can make important contributions to the growth of the company in the early 1980s.

In existing product lines, the company broadens its opportunities for growth by utilizing corporate technology to create new products. In other areas, growth is accomplished through either internal development or the acquisition of new businesses.

The company uses a number of guidelines to evaluate growth opportunities. Potential products or services must fulfill a useful function and provide value for the price paid; offer distinct advantages easily perceived by consumers; be based on technology available within, or readily accessible outside the company; meet established quality and safety standards; and offer an acceptable level of profitability and attractive growth potential.

THE SAFETY RAZOR DIVISION

The Safety Razor Division has long been regarded as the leader in shaving technology. Building on King Gillette's principle of using razors as a vehicle for blade sales and of associating the name "Gillette" with premium shaving, the division has been able to maintain its number one position in the U.S. market.

TABLE 2   The Gillette Company Annual Income Statements, 1963–1977 (in thousands)

Year	Net Sales	Gross Profit	Profit from Operations	Income before Taxes	Federal and Foreign Income Taxes	Net Income
1977	$1,587,209	$834,786	$202,911	$158,820	$79,100	$79,720
1976	1,491,506	782,510	190,939	149,257	71,700	77,557
1975	1,406,906	737,310	184,368	146,954	67,000	79,954
1974	1,246,422	667,395	171,179	147,295	62,300	84,995
1973	1,064,427	600,805	155,949	154,365	63,300	91,065
1972	870,532	505,297	140,283	134,618	59,600	75,018
1971	729,687	436,756	121,532	110,699	48,300	62,399
1970	672,669	417,575	120,966	117,475	51,400	66,075
1969	609,557	390,858	122,416	119,632	54,100	65,532
1968	553,174	358,322	126,016	124,478	62,200	62,278
1967	428,357	291,916	101,153	103,815	47,200	56,615
1966	396,190	264,674	90,967	91,666	41,800	49,866
1965	339,064	224,995	75,010	75,330	33,000	42,330
1964	298,956	205,884	72,594	75,173	35,500	37,673
1963	295,700	207,552	85,316	85,945	44,400	41,545

Share of Market

Market share is important in the shaving industry. The standard is that each share point is equivalent to approximately $1 million in pretax profits. Over recent history, Gillette has held approximately 60 percent of the total dollar market. However, the division has put more emphasis on increasing its share from its static level.

Product Line

During the course of its existence, Gillette has introduced many new blades and razors. In the past 15 years, the shaving market has evolved from a double-edged emphasis to twin-bladed systems (see Exhibit 1). Besides Atra and TRAC II, Gillette markets Good News! disposables, Daisy for women, double-edge, injector, carbon, and Techmatic band systems (see Table 3). Within their individual markets, Gillette sells 65 percent of all premium double-edged blades, 12 percent of injector sales, and almost all of the carbon and band sales.

EXHIBIT 1   Gillette Percentage of U.S. Blade Sales (estimated market share)

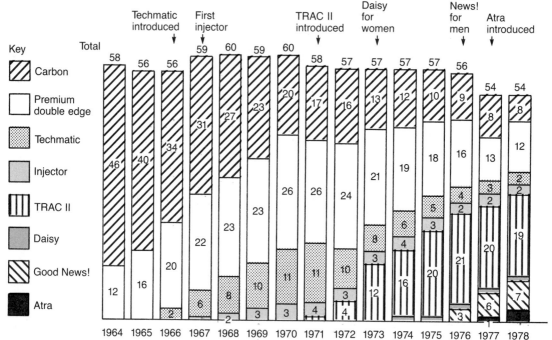

Marketing Approach and Past Traditions

During 1977, the Gillette Company spent $207.9 million to promote all its products throughout the world, of which $133.1 million was spent for advertising, including couponing and sampling, and $74.8 million for sales promotion. In terms of the domestic operation, the Safety Razor Division uses an eight-cycle promotional schedule whereby every six weeks a new program is initiated. During any one cycle, some but

TABLE 3   Safety Razor Division Product Line, June 1978

Product Line	*Package Sizes*	*Manufacturer's Suggested Retail Price*
Blades:		
TRAC II	5, 9, 14, Adjustable 4	$1.60, 2.80, 3.89, 1.50
Atra	5, 10	$1.70, 3.40
Good News!	2	$.60
Daisy	2	$1.00
Techmatic	5, 10, 15	$1.50, 2.80, 3.50
Double-edged:		
Platinum Plus	5, 10, 15	$1.40, 2.69, 3.50
Super-Stainless	5, 10, 15	$1.20, 2.30, 3.10
Carbon:		
Super Blue	10, 15	$1.50, 2.15
Regular Blue	5, 10	$.70, 1.25
Injector:		
Regular	7, 11	$1.95, 2.60
Twin Injector	5, 8	$1.40, 2.20
Razors:		
TRAC II	Regular	$3.50
	Lady	$3.50
	Adjustable	$3.50
	Deluxe	$3.95
Atra		
Double-edged:		
Super Adjustable		$3.50
Lady Gillette		$3.50
Super Speed		$1.95
Twin Injector		$2.95
Techmatic	Regular	$3.50
	Deluxe	$3.95
Three-Piece		$4.50
Knack		$1.95
Cricket Lighters	Regular	$1.49
	Super	$1.98
	Keeper	$4.49

not all the products and their packages are sold on promotion. Usually one of the TRAC II packages is sold on promotion during each of these cycles.

> Gillette advertising is designed to provide information to consumers and motivate them to buy the company's products. Sales promotion ensures that these products are readily available, well located, and attractively displayed in retail stores. Special promotion at the point of purchase offers consumers an extra incentive to buy Gillette products.[2]

In the past the company has concentrated its advertising and promotion on its newest shaving product, reducing support for its other established lines. The theory is that growth must come at the expense of other brands. When TRAC II was introduced, for example, the advertising budget for other brands was cut, with the double-edged portion being decreased from 47 percent in 1971 to 11 percent in 1972 and TRAC II receiving 61 percent of the division budget (see Exhibit 2).

A long-standing tradition has been that razors are used as a means for selling blades. Thus, with razors, the emphasis is on inducing the consumer to try the product by offering coupon discounts, mail samples, and heavy informational advertising. Blade strategy has been to emphasize a variety of sales devices—such as discounts, displays, and sweepstakes at pharmacies, convenience stores, and supermarkets—to encourage point-of-purchase sales. In spite of this tradition, razor sales are a very significant portion of division sales and profits.

At the center of this marketing strategy has been the company's identification with sports. The Gillette "Cavalcade of Sports" began with Gillette's radio sponsorship of the World Series, Super Bowl, professional and NCAA basketball, as well as boxing. During the 1950s and 1960s, Gillette spent 60 percent of its ad dollars on sports programming. Influenced by research showing that prime-time entertainment offered superior audience potential, the company switched to a prime-time emphasis in the early 1970s. However, Gillette has recently returned in the last two years to its sports formula.

Marketing Research

Both product and marketing research have contributed to the success of the company. For example, Gillette was faced in 1917 with the expiration of its basic patents and the eventual flood of competitive models. Six months before the impending expiration, the company came out with new razor models including one for a dollar. As a result, the company made more money than ever before. In fact, throughout the

---

[2]*1977 Gillette Company Annual Report*, p. 14.

EXHIBIT 2   Gillette Advertising Expenditures, 1965–1978 (percentage of total market)

Total market ($ millions):

	1965	1966	1967	1968	1969	1970	1971	1972	1973	1974	1975	1976	1977	1978 (estimate)
Total market ($ millions)	20.5	21.4	21.0	23.6	20.5	21.7	24.8	20.5	23.7	26.5	24.0	24.3	29.8	33.0
Bar top total	43	53	54	46	50	53	38	44	43	39	46	44	38	41

Legend:
- Double-edge
- Bands
- Injector
- TRAC II
- Other
- Daisy
- Atra
- Good News!

Chart segment values:

- 1965: 1, 42
- 1966: 18, 35
- 1967: 25, 29
- 1968: 3, 22, 21
- 1969: 5, 25, 20
- 1970: 4, 16, 33
- 1971: 2, 8, 10, 18
- 1972: 27, 12, 5
- 1973: 21, 6, 8, 8
- 1974: 39, 27, 4, 8
- 1975: 9, 32, 4, 1
- 1976: 25, 7, 12
- 1977: 38, 14, 17, 6, 1
- 1978: 41, 22, 13, 5, 1

history of shaving, Gillette has introduced most of the improvements in shaving technology. The major exceptions are the injector, which was introduced by Schick, and the stainless-steel double-edged blade introduced by Wilkinson.

The company spends $37 million annually on research and development for new products, product improvements, and consumer testing. In addition to Atra, a recent development is a new sharpening process called "Microsmooth" which improves the closeness of the shave and the consistency of the blade. This improvement was to be introduced on all of the company's twin blades by early 1979. Mike Edwards believes that this will help to ensure TRAC II's retention of its market.

At the time of Atra's introduction, Gillette research found that users would come from users of TRAC II and nontwin-blade systems. This projected loss was estimated to be 60 percent of TRAC II users. Recent research indicates that with heavy marketing support in 1978, TRAC II's loss will be held to 40 percent.

THE SHAVING MARKET

The shaving market is divided into two segments, wet and electric shavers. Today, the wet shavers account for 75 percent of the market. In the United States alone, 1.9 billion blades and 23 million razors are sold annually. Gillette participates in the electric market through sales of electric razors by its Braun subsidiary.

Market Factors

There are a number of factors at work within the market: (1) the adult shaving population has increased in the past 15 years to 74.6 million men and 68.2 million women, (2) technological improvements have improved the quality of the shave as well as increased the life of the razor blade, and (3) the volume of blades and razors has begun to level off after a period of declining and then increasing sales (see Exhibit 3). Although the shaving market has increased slightly, there are more competitors. Yet Gillette has been able to maintain its share of the market—approximately two thirds of the dollar-razor market and a little over half of the dollar-blade market.

Market Categories

The market is segmented into seven components: new systems, disposables, injector, premium double-edged, carbon double-edged, continuous bands, and single-edged systems. In the early 1900s the shaving market consisted primarily of straight-edges. During the past 70 years, the market has evolved away from its single- and double-edged emphasis to the present market of 60 percent bonded systems (all systems in which the blade is encased in plastic). Table 4 shows the recent trends within the market categories.

Competitors

Gillette's major competitors are Warner-Lambert's Schick, Colgate-Palmolive's Wilkinson, American Safety Razor's Personna, and BIC. Each has its own strongholds, Schick, which introduced the injector

EXHIBIT 3   Razor and Blade Sales Volume, 1963–1979

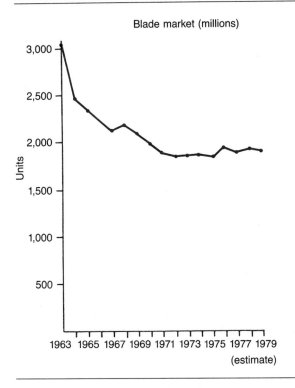

Blade market (millions)

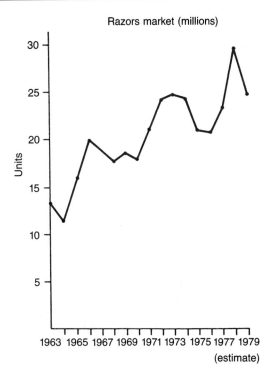

Razors market (millions)

TABLE 4   Recent Share Trends (percent)

Volume	1972	1973	1974	1975	1976	1977	1978, 1st Half
Units:							
New systems	8.8%	20.6%	28.8%	36.2%	39.9%	40.8%	43.8%
Injector	20.2	17.6	17.1	16.3	15.7	14.2	12.8
Double-edged:							
Premium	39.4	34.9	30.8	27.4	24.5	21.1	10.0
Carbon	12.0	10.6	9.4	8.1	7.3	7.6	6.6
Bands	13.1	10.3	8.0	6.4	4.7	3.7	2.7
Disposables	—	—	—	—	2.5	6.9	9.7
Single-edged	6.5	6.0	5.9	5.6	5.4	5.7	5.4
Total market	100.0%	100.0%	100.0%	100.0%	100.0%	100.0%	100.0%
Dollars:							
New systems	11.8%	26.9%	36.9%	46.0%	50.1%	50.1%	52.1%
Injector	21.8	18.6	17.8	16.4	15.0	13.8	12.5
Double-edged:							
Premium	41.5	34.2	28.7	24.0	20.8	18.1	16.1
Carbon	6.1	5.4	4.7	4.2	4.0	4.1	3.5
Bands	15.4	11.8	8.7	6.5	4.8	3.6	2.8
Disposables	—	—	—	—	2.8	7.5	10.5
Single-edged	3.4	3.1	3.2	2.9	2.5	2.8	2.5
Total market	100.0%	100.0%	100.0%	100.0%	100.0%	100.0%	100.0%

TABLE 5   New Product Introductions and Their Effects on the
Market, 1959–1977

Year	Product Segment	Sales Blade/Razor Market ($ millions)	Change (percent)
1959	Carbon	122.4	Base
1960	Super blue	144.1	+ 17.7 over 1959
1963	Stainless	189.3	+ 31.3 over 1960
1965	Super stainless	201.2	+ 6.3 over 1963
1966	Banded system	212.1	+ 5.4 over 1965
1969	Injector	246.8	+ 16.3 over 1966
1972	Twin blades	326.5	+ 32.2 over 1969
1975	Disposable	384.0	+ 17.6 over 1972
1977	Pivoting head	444.9	+ 15.9 over 1975

system, now controls 80 percent of that market. ASR's Personna sells
almost all of the single-edged blades on the market. Wilkinson's
strength is its bonded system which appeals to an older, wealthier
market. BIC has developed a strong product in its inexpensive disposable system.

Competitive pricing structure is comparable to Gillette within the
different system categories. Although all the companies have similar
suggested retail prices, the differences found on the racks in the market
are a function of the companies' off-invoice rates to the trade and their
promotional allowances. It is not much of a factor at this time; private
label covers the range of systems and continues to grow.

Market Segmentation

The success of Gillette's technological innovation can be seen in its
effect on the total shaving market. Although there are other factors
at play in the market, new product introductions have contributed
significantly to market expansion as Table 5 indicates.

TWIN-BLADE MARKET

Research played a key role in the development of twin blades. Gillette
had two variations—the current type in which the blades are in tan-
dem; the other type in which the blades' edges faced each other and

---

TABLE 6   The Twin-Blade Market, 1972–1978 (in millions)

	1972	1973	1974	1975	1976	1977	1978, Estimate	1979, Estimate
Razors	$ 29.5	$ 32.1	$ 31.4	$ 31.3	$ 31.5	$ 39.7	$ 53.8	
Disposables	—	—	—	—	14.5	41.5	64.9	
Blades	31.6	72.0	105.7	147.5	176.3	183.7	$209.2	
Total twin	61.1	104.1	137.1	176.2	222.3	264.9	327.9	
Total market	$326.5	$332.6	$342.5	$384.0	$422.2	$444.9	$491.0	$500.0

required an up-and-down scrubbing motion. From a marketing stand-point, and because the Atra swivel system had problems in testing development, TRAC II was launched first. The research department played a major role in the positioning of the product when it discovered hysteresis, the phenomenon of whiskers being lifted out and after a time receding into the follicle. Thus, the TRAC II effect was that the second blade cut the whisker before it receded.

Since its introduction in 1971, the twin-blade market has grown to account for almost 60 percent of all blade sales. The twin-blade market is defined as all bonded razors and blades (e.g., new systems; Atra and TRAC II; disposables: Good News! and BIC). Table 6 shows the trends in the twin-blade market.

During this period many products have been introduced. These in-clude the Sure Touch in 1971; the Deluxe TRAC II and Schick Super II in 1972; the Lady TRAC II, Personna Double II, and Wilkinson Bonded in 1973; the Personna Flicker, Good News!, and BIC Disposable in 1974; the Personna Lady Double II in 1975; and the Adjustable TRAC II and Schick Super II in 1976.

Advertising

In the race for market share, the role of advertising is extremely im-portant in the shaving industry. Of all the media expenditures, tele-vision is the primary vehicle in the twin-blade market. For Gillette, this means an emphasis on maximum exposure and sponsorship of sports events. The company's policy for the use of television is based on the concept that TV is essentially a family medium and programs should therefore be suitable for family viewing. Gillette tries to avoid programs that unduly emphasize sex or violence.

As the industry leader, TRAC II receives a great deal of competitive pressure in the form of aggressive advertising from competitors and other Gillette twin-blade brands (see Table 7). For example, the theme of recent Schick commercials was the "Schick challenge," and BIC emphasized its lower cost and cleaner shave in relation to those of other twin-blade brands. However, competitive media expenditures are such that their cost per share point is substantially higher than TRAC II's.

Despite competitive pressures, TRAC II is aggressively advertised too. As a premium product, it does not respond directly to competitive challenges or shifts in its own media; rather, the advertising follows a standard principle of emphasizing TRAC II's strengths. As Table 8 and Exhibit 4 indicate, the TRAC II media plan emphasizes diversity with a heavy emphasis on advertising on prime-time television and on sports programs. In addition, TRAC II is continually promoted to retain its market share.

For 1978, the division budgeted $18 million for advertising, with Atra and TRAC II receiving the major portion of the budget (see Table 9). The traditional Gillette approach is for the newest brand to receive the bulk of the advertising dollars (see Exhibit 2). Therefore, it is certain that Atra will receive a substantial increase in advertising for 1979. Whether the division will increase or decrease TRAC II's budget as well as whether it will increase the total ad budget for 1979 is unknown at this time.

TRAC II

The 1971 introduction of TRAC II was the largest in shaving history. Influenced by the discovery of the hysteresis process, by the development of a clogfree dual-blade cartridge, and by consumer-testing data which showed a nine-to-one preference for TRAC II over the panelists' current razors, Gillette raced to get the product to market. Because the introduction involved so many people and was so critical to reversing a leveling of corporate profits (see Table 2), the division president personally assumed the role of product development manager and lived with the project day and night through its development and introduction.[3]

Launched during the 1971 World Series promotion, TRAC II was the most frequently advertised shaving system in America during its introductory period. Supported by $10 million in advertising and promotion, TRAC II results were impressive: 1.7 million razors and 5

---

[3]For an excellent account of the TRAC II introduction, by the president of Gillette North America, see William G. Salatich, "Gillette's TRAC II: The Steps to Success," *Market Communications*, January 1972.

TABLE 7   Estimated Media Expenditures (in thousands)

	1976	1977, 1st Half	1977, 2d Half	Total 1977	1978, 1st Half	Total 1978 Estimate
Companies:						
Gillette	$10,800	$ 4,800	$ 6,400	$11,200	$ 8,100	$13,800
Schick	7,600	3,700	4,300	8,000	4,300	8,900
Wilkinson	2,700	1,400	2,200	3,600	1,400	2,200
ASR	2,600	700	200	900	200	800
BIC	600*	4,300	1,800	6,100	4,000	7,300
Total market	$24,300*	$14,900	$14,900	$29,800	$18,000	$33,000
Brands:						
TRAC II	$ 6,000	$ 3,300	$ 1,700	$ 5,000	$ 2,400	$ 4,000
Atra	—	—	4,000	4,000	4,500	7,500
Good News!	1,900	1,200	600	1,800	700	1,600
Super II	2,600	1,400	2,600	4,000	3,000	4,600

*Product introduction.

TABLE 8   Media Plan, 1976, 1977 (in thousands)

	Quarter				
	1	2	3	4	Total
1976					
Prime	935	575	1,200	500	3,160
Sports	545	305	450	1,040	2,440
Network total	1,480	880	1,650	1,590	5,650
Other	80	85	70	165	400
Total	1,560	965	1,720	1,755	6,000
1977					
Prime	1,300	900	300	—	2,500
Sports	500	400	400	400	1,700
Network total	1,800	1,300	700	400	4,200
Print	—	—	200	200	400
Black	75	75	75	75	300
Military, miscellaneous	25	25	25	15	100
Total	1,900	1,400	1,000	700	5,000

million cartridges were sold in October; and during the first year, the introductory campaign made 2 billion impressions and reached 80 percent of all homes an average of 4.7 times a week. In addition, a multi-million-unit sampling campaign was implemented in 1972 which was the largest of its kind.

EXHIBIT 4 TRAC II Media Plan, 1978 (in thousands)

Media	January	February	March	April	May	June	July	August	September	October	November	December	Totals
Prime TV*	$1,055 — 15 weeks →								$115 — World Series promo				$1,170
Baseball†				$1,278 — 19 weeks + All Star, Playoffs, and World Series →								$1,278
Miscellaneous sports†	$1,062 — 52 weeks →												$1,062
Spot TV											$230 — 4 weeks		$230
Black, military			$260 — 40 weeks →										$260
Sunday newspaper, miscellaneous													$400

* Prime-time TV advertising:

KAZ	Love Boat
ABC Friday Movie	Different Strokes
Tuesday Big Event	Real People
ABC Sunday Movie	Duke
Roots Two	Rockford Files

† Sports TV advertising:

Wide World of Sports
College Basketball
NBA All Star Game
International Team Boxing
Wide World of Sports, Sunday.

NBA Basketball
History of Baseball
Game of the Week Day
This Week Baseball

TABLE 9 Razor Division Marketing Budget, 1978

	Atra Line	TRAC II Line	Good News!	Double-Edged Blades	Double-Edged Razors	Techmatic Line	Daisy	Injector Line	Twin Injector	Total Blade/Razor
Marketing expenses:										
Promotion*	42.3	69.4	65.2	92.2	75.4	52.7	58.4	77.5	48.3	60.7
Advertising†	55.6	28.8	31.2	4.6	—	—	39.0	—	26.3	36.5
Other	2.1	1.8	3.6	3.2	24.6	47.3	2.6	22.5	25.4	2.8
Total marketing	100.0	100.0	100.0	100.0	100.0	100.0	100.0	100.0	100.0	100.0
Percentage Line/total direct marketing	34.1	38.4	14.9	7.6	.4	.3	3.4	.2	.7	100.0
Percentage Line/total full revenue sales	20.5	41.8	13.4	16.8	1.4	2.1	2.2	.6	1.2	100.0

*Defined as off-invoice allowances, wholesale push money, cooperative advertising, excess cost, premiums, contests, and prizes.
†Defined as media, sampling, couponing, production, and costs.

For five years TRAC II was clearly the fastest-growing product on the market, and it helped to shape the switch to twin blades. Its users are predominantly young, college-educated, metropolitan, suburban, and upper-income men. The brand reached its peak in 1976 when it sold 485 million blades and 7 million razors. In comparison, projected TRAC II sales for 1978 are 433 million blades and 4.2 million razors. During this period, TRAC II brand contribution decreased 10 percent (Table 10). Competitors' responsive strategies seem to be effective. The

TABLE 10   TRAC II Line Income Statement, 1972–1978

	*1972**	*1973*	*1974*	*1975*	*Base 1976*	*1977*	*Estimated 1978*
Full revenue sales (FRS):							
Promotional	28	41	71	100	100	110	112
Nonpromotional	38	91	89	83	100	80	65
Total	32	60	78	93	100	99	95
Direct cost of sales:							
Manufacturing	63	77	93	111	100	88	83
Freight	51	80	91	106	100	82	80
Total	62	77	93	111	100	88	83
Standard profit contribution	26	56	75	89	100	101	97
Marketing expenses							
Promotional expenses:							
Lost revenue	26	39	72	100	100	114	126
Wholesale push money	455	631	572	565	100	562	331
Cooperative advertising	27	36	58	71	100	115	133
Excess cost	25	50	59	83	100	63	92
Premiums	3	29	16	28	100	78	217
Contests and prizes	7	21	110	115	100	215	109
Total	26	40	67	90	100	112	129
Advertising:							
Media	90	83	110	119	100	96	75
Production	96	128	130	104	100	196	162
Couponing and sampling	470	344	177	112	100	166	131
Other	19	120	68	78	100	54	54
Total	124	110	108	117	100	96	78
Other marketing expenses	108	120	847	617	100	242	86
Market research	122	65	47	34	100	134	91
Total assignable marketing expenses	67	69	87	102	100	106	108
Net contribution:	14	53	81	85	100	100	94
Percentage of promotional FRS/total FRS	56	43	58	76	63	70	74
Percentage of promotional expense/promo FRS	15	16	16	15	11	17	20
Percentage of promotional expenses/total FRS	9	7	9	10	11	12	15
Percentage of advertising expenses/total FRS	28	13	10	9	7	7	6
Percentage of media expenses/total FRS	17	8	8	8	6	6	5

*Each year's data are shown as a percentage of 1976's line item. For example, 1972 sales were 32 percent of 1976 sales.

growth of Super II during the last two years is attributed to certain advantages it has over TRAC II. Super II has higher trade allowances (20 percent versus 15 percent), improved distribution, an increased media expenditure, and generally lower everyday prices.

In preparing the 1979 marketing plans, the objective for TRAC II was to retain its consumer franchise despite strong competitive challenges through consumer-oriented promotions and to market the brand aggressively year round. Specifically, TRAC II was

1. To obtain a 20 percent share of the cartridge and razor market.
2. To deliver 43 percent of the division's profit.
3. To retain its valuable pegboard space at the checkout counters in convenience, food, and drugstores as well as supermarkets.

In 1978, Mike Edwards launched a new economy-size blade package (14 blades) and a heavy spending campaign to retain TRAC II's market share. He employed strong trade and consumer promotion incentives supported by (1) new improved product claims of a "microsmooth" shave, (2) new graphics, and (3) a revised version of the highly successful "Sold Out" advertising campaign (see Exhibit 5). Midyear results indicated that TRAC II's performance had exceeded division expectations as it retained 21.6 percent of the blade market and its contribution exceeded the budget by $2 million.

ATRA (AUTOMATIC TRACKING RAZOR ACTION)

Origin

Research for the product began in Gillette's United Kingdom Research and Development Laboratory in 1970. The purpose was to improve the high standards of performance of twin-blade shaving and, specifically, to enhance the TRAC II effect. The company's scientists discovered that a better shave could be produced, if, instead of the shaver moving the hand and face to produce the best shaving angle for the blade, the razor head could pivot in such a way as to maintain the most effective twin-blade shaving angle. Once the pivoting head was shown to produce a better shave, test after test, research continued in the Boston headquarters on product design, redesigning, and consumer testing.

The name "Atra" came from two years of intensive consumer testing of the various names which could be identified with this advanced razor. The choice was based on how easy it was to remember the name, how well it communicated the technology, its uniqueness, and the feeling of the future it conveyed. Atra stands for *Automatic Tracking Razor Action.*

Gillette TRAC II

THE GILLETTE COMPANY
SAFETY RAZOR DIVISION

"SOLD OUT"
(MICROSMOOTH-GIRL) SUPER II

BBDO

LENGTH: 30 SECONDS

COMM'L NO.: GSRD 8033

IRVING: Sold out again!???
(SFX: DING!)

CUSTOMER 1: The new improved
Gillette TRAC II, please.

IRVING: Er . . . say . . . who needs
improved when these twin blades'll do.

CUSTOMER 1: TRAC II has micro-
smooth edges . . . makes the blades
smoother than ever.

IRVING: Shave better than these?

CUSTOMER 1: Better, safer, smoother
. . . and comfortable.

IRVING: Comfort . . . schmomfort . . .
you don't have . . . But . . . but . . .b-b . . .

CUSTOMER 2: Do you have the new
improved Gillette TRAC II?

IRVING: Improved TRAC II??
(INNOCENTLY) Improved TRAC II?

A better shave.

ANNCR: The new improved Gillette
TRAC II. Micro-smooth edges make
it a better shave.

Introduction

Atra was first introduced in mid-1977. The introduction stressed the new shaving system supplemented by heavy advertising coupled with $2 razor rebate coupons to induce trial and 50-cent coupons toward Atra blades to induce brand loyalty. An example of Atra advertising is shown in Exhibit 6. During its first year on the national market, Atra was expected to sell 9 million razors, although 85 percent of all sales were sold on a discount basis. Early results showed that Atra sold at a faster level than Gillette's previously most successful product, TRAC II. The Atra razor retails for $4.95. Blades are sold in packages of 5 and 10. Trac II and Atra blades are not interchangeable. Because of Gillette's excellent distribution system, it has not had much problem gaining valuable pegboard space.

CURRENT TRENDS AND COMPETITIVE RESPONSES IN THE TWIN-BLADE MARKET

There was quite a bit of activity in the shaving market during the first half of 1978. Atra has increased the total Gillette share in the razor and blade market. During the June period, Atra razors continued to exceed TRAC II as the leading selling razor, whereas Atra blades share was approximately 8 percent, accounting for most of Gillette's 4 percent share growth since June 1977. Thus, the growth of Atra has put more competitive pressure on TRAC II. In addition, the disposable segment due to BIC and Good News! increased by five share points to a hefty 12 percent dollar share of the blade market. Combined with TRAC II's resiliency in maintaining share, competitive brands lost share: Schick Super II, ASR, and Wilkinson were all down two points since June 1977.

In response to these trends, the TRAC II team expected competition to institute some changes. In an effort to recover its sagging share, Edwards expected the Schick Muscular Dystrophy promotion in October 1977 to help bolster Super II with its special offer. The pressure may have already been appearing with Schick's highly successful introduction of Personal Touch for women in that year, with about 10 percent of the razor market, which had to draw TRAC II female shavers. In addition, it appeared inevitable that Schick would bring out an Atra-type razor. This would remove Atra's competitive advantage, but increase pressure on TRAC II with the addition of a second pivoting head competitor.

Continuing its trends, it appeared that the disposable segment of the market would continue to expand. The first sign of this was the BIC ads offering 12 BIC disposables for $1. Good News! received additional advertising support in the latter half of the year as well as

EXHIBIT 6

Gillette Atra

:30 second commercial   GSRS7013 "Impossible, Yes"   August, 1977

ANNCR (VO): Could Gillette make a razor that does the impossible?

Yes.

Could it shave closer with even more comfort?

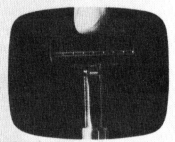

Yes.

Gillette introduces Atra . . .

the first razor with a pivoting head . . .

that safely follows every contour of your face.

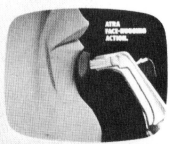

This Atra face-hugging action keeps the twin-blades at the perfect angle.

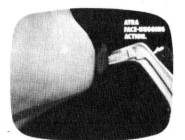

You've never shaved this close with this much comfort.

MAN: Impossible!

*ANNCR: The New Gillette Atra Razor.

Yes, it's the impossible shave.

the introduction of a new package size. One of Edward's major objectives was to emphasize the importance of TRAC II to upper management. Besides the introduction of the microsmooth concept, a price increase on TRAC II products would be implemented soon. It was unclear whether the price change would have an adverse effect on brand sales.

In preparing the 1979 TRAC II marketing plan, Edwards realized that Atra would be given a larger share of the advertising dollars following a strong year, and the disposable market would continue to grow. TRAC II share remained questionable, depending on the level of marketing support it received. Whether TRAC II would be able to continue its heavy spending program and generate large revenues for the division remained to be seen. These factors, as well as the company's support of Atra, made 1979 a potentially tough year for Mike Edwards and TRAC II.

1979 MARKETING PLAN PREPARATION

Edwards received the following memorandum from the vice president of marketing:

Memo to: Brand Group
From: P. Meyers
Date: July 7, 1978
Subject: 1979 Marketing Plans

In preparation for the marketing plan approval process and in developing the division strategy for 1979, I would like a preliminary plan from each brand group by the end of the month. Please submit statements of objective, corresponding strategy, and levels of dollar support requested for the following:

1. Overall brand strategy[4]—target market.
2. Blade and razor volume and share goals.
3. Sales promotion.
4. Advertising.
5. Couponing and sampling.
6. Miscellaneous—new packaging, additional marketing research, marketing cost saving ideas, etc.

See you at the weekly meeting on Wednesday.

---

[4]Brand strategy means positioning the brand in such a way that it appeals to a distinguishable target market.

In developing the TRAC II marketing plan, Edwards had to wrestle with some strategy decisions. To get significant funding, how should he position TRAC II in relation to Atra and the disposables? Also, how does he convince the vice president that dollars spent for TRAC II are more effective than expenditures on Good News! or Gillette's electric razors?

Apple Computers: The First Ten Years*

C. C. Swanger
Stanford University

M. A. Maidique
Florida International University

Apple Computer is a vintage story of American technological entrepreneurship. From the now-famous story of Steve Jobs and Steve Wozniak selling their calculator and van in 1975 to build themselves a microcomputer, to the $1.5 billion in revenues Apple expected to realize during its 1984 fiscal year, Apple's extraordinary success could hardly be questioned. (See Exhibit 1 for selected company financial data.)

The evolution of the company makes a fascinating story. One particularly interesting area was the evolution of the Apple product line and the related waves of renewal that each of Apple's new products had prompted. There had been several successes, but some interwoven failures as well. This posed a complex dilemma, i.e., how should Apple continue to develop as a company and increase the likelihood of product successes?

As Apple matured, so had the personal computer industry. In 1984, the competitive situation was much more complex and the stakes much higher than they had been in 1975. Market growth continued to be strong, but the competitive environment was drastically different.

Numerous firms had entered the personal computer industry during the last decade, including such giants as IBM, Digital Equipment Corporation, and Hewlett-Packard. Most notably, in 1983, IBM had surpassed Apple as the leading personal computer company in terms of sales dollars (though Apple still led in units shipped). Numerous bankruptcies had occurred, particularly among start-up firms (Osborne, Franklin, Victor, and others) and many other firms were in trouble financially.

EXHIBIT 1   Selected Financial Data

	1977	1978	1979	1980	1981	1982	1983	1984
	(Fiscal Year-End September 30)							
Net sales ($000)	774	7,856	47,867	117,126	334,783	583,061	982,769	1,515,876
Net income ($000)	42	793	5,073	11,698	39,420	61,306	76,714	64,055
Earnings per share ($)	.01	.03	.12	.24	.70	1.06	1.28	1.05
Assets ($000)	555	4,341	21,171	65,350	254,838	357,787	556,579	788,786
Research and development ($000)	100	600	3,601	7,282	20,956	37,979	60,040	71,136
Marketing ($000)	200	1,300	4,097	12,619	55,369	119,945	229,961	392,866
Cash and temporary cash investments ($000)	24	775	563	363	72,834	153,056	143,284	114,888
Current liabilities ($000)	N/A	N/A	N/A	37,780	70,280	85,756	128,786	255,184
Noncurrent liabilities ($000)*	N/A	N/A	N/A	1,622	7,171	14,939	49,892	69,037
Ratios:								
Gross margin (%)	N/A	N/A	42.7	42.5	46.1	50.6	48.5	42.0
PAT (%)	5.4	10.1	10.6	10.0	11.8	10.5	7.8	4.2
R&D/Sales (%)	12.9	7.6	7.5	6.2	6.3	6.5	6.1	4.7
Marketing and distribution/Sales (%)	25.8	16.5	8.6	10.8	16.5	20.6	23.4	25.9
Sales/Employee ($000)	77	135	200	176	190	200	212	282

*Noncurrent liabilities consisted of obligations under capital leases plus deferred income taxes. Apple Computer had no long-term debt.

Many questions remained to be resolved regarding Apple's future direction. Developing a new plan required dealing with several complex interconnected issues such as: (1) what to do with the Apple II family; (2) where to go with the Macintosh family; (3) product family integration issues; (4) the role of accessory products; (5) meeting the IBM challenge; (6) managing Apple's growth while maintaining the distinctive culture and working environment; (7) the pursuit of new areas, such as lap-size computers, educational computers, systems, etc.; and (8) evaluating possible diversification alternatives.

COMPUTER INDUSTRY HISTORY

Mainframes

The origins of computers date back to the 1800s when Charles Babbage, George Boole, and Charles Sanders Pierce individually worked on switching circuits and advanced algebraic techniques. As the switching circuits progressed from mechanical to electromechanical during the 1920s and 1930s, to vacuum tubes during the 1940s, the possibility of building commercially useful computers rapidly increased.

Following World War II, the modern computer industry emerged, initially led by the Remington Typewriter Company, which later became Sperry Univac. When International Business Machines (IBM) realized computers were going to take away some of their customers for their large-scale adding machines (such as the U.S. Census Bureau), IBM entered the business. By the late 1950s, Control Data Corporation, an IBM spin-off, was established, and Honeywell, Burroughs, General Electric, RCA, and National Cash Register (NCR) were also producing computers.

IBM quickly came to dominate the industry with a market share that had risen to roughly 70 percent by the early 60s (see Exhibit 2). The computer industry was often referred to as "Snow White" (IBM) and the "Seven Dwarfs" (the other competitors).[1]

In addition to IBM dominance, the computer industry was characterized by continuing and dramatic technological advances, which resulted in increasing computer speed, power, and memory while decreasing costs (see Exhibit 3).

Minicomputers

In the late 1940s and early 1950s, a sequence of technological breakthroughs resulted in the diffused transistor, a microscopic arrangement of crystal layers with electrical properties similar to a vacuum tube amplifier. This development led ultimately to the invention of the integrated circuit around 1960. IBM and most of the other existing computer manufacturers used these advances to increase the speed and power of their computers while reducing the power consumption. Other firms concentrated on using the new technology to design smaller, cheaper computers.

The first firm to commercialize a smaller, cheaper computer was Digital Equipment Corporation (DEC). In 1967, DEC introduced the first "minicomputer," so named after the popular miniskirts of that time. DEC's machine sold in the tens of thousands of dollars and took up much less space than the mainframe computers. Soon thereafter, Hewlett-Packard became the other major minicomputer manufacturer. IBM, however, did not enter the market until much later.[2]

---

[1]Gerald W. Brock, *The U.S. Computer Industry: A Study of Market Power* (Cambridge, Mass.: Ballinger Publishing Company, 1975), pp. 3–24; and Katherine Davis Fishman, *The Computer Establishment* (New York: Harper & Row, 1981), pp. 19–47.
[2]Ibid.

EXHIBIT 2   Mainframe and Minicomputer Manufacturers Market Shares

---

A. Mainframe Computer Manufacturers (percent of market)

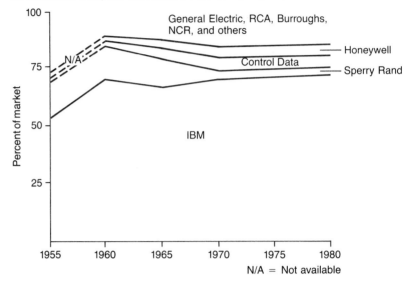

N/A = Not available

Source: 1955–1970: Gerald W. Brock, *The U.S. Computer Industry: A Study of Market Power* (Cambridge, Mass.: Ballinger Publishing Company, 1975), pp. 21–22; 1980: Casewriter's estimate.

B. Minicomputer Manufacturers (percent of market)—General-Purpose Microcomputers

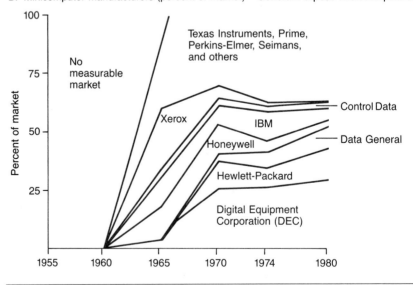

Source: 1960–1974: Montgomery Phister, *Data Processing Technology and Economics*, 1976, p. 291; 1980: Dataquest, Inc., San Jose, California.

EXHIBIT 3   Trends in Microelectronics

Trend in density:
  Maximum number of components per electronic circuit:
    1959 = 1; 1969 = 1.024; 1979 = 1 million; 1985 = over 50 million?
  Maximum number of binary digits (bits) per memory chip:
    1970 = 1,024; 1980 = 65,536; 1985 = over 500,000?

Trend in speed:
  Speed of an electronic logic circuit:
    Mid-1950s (vacuum tube circuit) = one microsecond.
    Early 1960s (transistorized printed circuit) = 100 nanoseconds.
    Late 1970s (integrated circuit chip) = 5 nanoseconds.
    Mid-1980s (integrated circuit chip) = 1 nanosecond?

Trend in cost:
  Cost per integrated circuit chips:
    1964 = $16; 1972 = 75¢; 1977 = 15¢; 1985 = 1¢?
  Cost per bit of integrated circuit memory chip:
    1973 = 0.5¢; 1977 = 0.1¢; 1985 = 0.005¢?

Trend in reliability:
  Reliability of electronic circuits:
    Vacuum tube = One failure every few hours.
    Transistor = 1,000 times more reliable than vacuum tube.
    Integrated circuit = 1,000 times more reliable than transistor.

Source: James A. O'Brien, *Computers and Information Processing* (Homewood, Ill.: Richard D. Irwin, 1983), p. 25.

Personal Computers

In the late 1960s and early 1970s, the trend to continually smaller and less expensive computers was clear. The development of the microprocessor, a fingernail-sized computer central processor, in 1971 provided a key catalyst to the industry.

A number of engineers in the established mainframe and minicomputer firms approached top management with proposals to develop what would have become personal computers. They knew smaller computers could be developed, and their experiences of having to wait to use the larger computers and not be able to work at home provided the real motivation. For a variety of reasons, the major firms chose not to pursue the proposals during the early 1970s. DEC, for example, was one of the most likely candidates to develop personal computers because they already made the smallest computers available, i.e., computers small enough to fit inside the trunk of a car. DEC, however, was interested in industrial markets and had not mastered the art of selling to individual consumers.

Eventually, some engineers and programmers struck off on their own to develop smaller computers. Throughout most of the 1970s, and still to a large extent during the early 1980s, personal computers were developed by entrepreneurs. However, by the mid-1980s, many industry observers believed the industry had entered an era where size and economy of scale were key to survival, thus sharply reducing the possibilities of new Apple-like garage start-ups.

From its modest beginnings as a recognizable industry in the mid-1970s, the personal computer industry reached estimated annual sales of 1.5 million units during 1982, representing revenues in excess of $3 billion. Those sales came from four primary markets: business (975,000 units or 65 percent), science (240,000 units or 16 percent), home (225,000 units or 15 percent), and education (60,000 units or 4 percent).[3] The 1982 factory shipments or wholesale revenues consisted of $.7 billion from units generally priced under $1,500 and used primarily in the home, and $2.6 billion from units generally selling from $1,500 to $5,000 and used in offices. *Business Week* forecasts projected $2 billion and $7 billion revenue, respectively, in 1984 from the two categories.[4] (See Exhibit 4*a*.) Thus, the personal computer industry was forecast to grow at about 65 percent per year from 1982 to 1984.

Three of the initial personal computer developers (MITS, IMSAI, and Process Technology) participated in the business primarily in 1976. From 1978 to 1981, Apple Computer, Inc., Radio Shack (owned by Tandy Corporation), and Commodore Business Machines were the primary manufacturers of personal computers. Radio Shack had the largest market share due primarily to its extensive worldwide network of 8,100 company-owned retail stores. However, Radio Shack's market share declined steadily, and in 1981 Apple surpassed them in number of units shipped. In addition, while Commodore continued to enjoy broad retail distribution internationally, its U.S. share dropped also (see Exhibit 4*b*).

IBM entered the personal computer industry in August 1981, and precipitated dramatic changes in market share and the nature of the industry. As evidence of IBM's commitment and objectives, the company named its computer the IBM Personal Computer, or PC for short. IBM also broke with historic company tradition in several key areas, utilizing outside suppliers and software developers, standard parts, and the so-called "Woz principle" (the principle espoused so strongly by Apple cofounder Steve Wozniak of open computer architecture that allowed independent software developers to write

---

[3]"Personal Computers," *Scientific American,* December 1982, pp. 96, 99.
[4]*Business Week,* June 25, 1984, p. 106; and August 15, 1983, p. 89.

EXHIBIT 4a   U.S. Factory Shipments of Personal Computers

Units generally priced *under $1,500* and used primarily in the home:

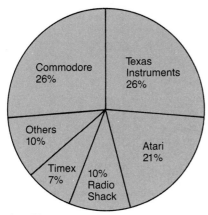

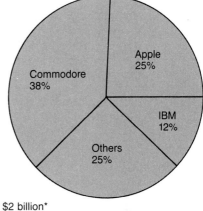

1982 total: $.7 billion   1984 total: $2 billion*

Units generally selling from *$1,500 to $5,000* and used in offices:

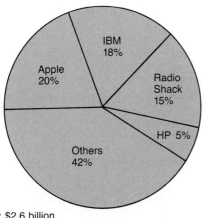

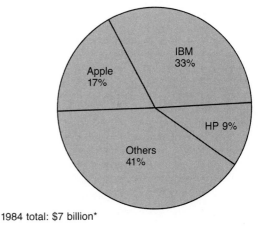

1982 total: $2.6 billion   1984 total: $7 billion*
* Forecasts

Source: *Business Week*, June 25, 1984, p. 106.

programs for the machine).[5] By the end of 1983, IBM had surpassed
Apple in dollar volume, though Apple led slightly in units shipped (see
Exhibit 4c).

---

[5]Paul Freiberger and Michael Swaine, *Fire in the Valley: The Making of the Personal Computer* (Berkeley, Calif.: Osborne/McGraw-Hill, 1984), p. 280.

EXHIBIT 4b U.S. Factory Shipments of Personal Computers
Excluding Peripherals and Software

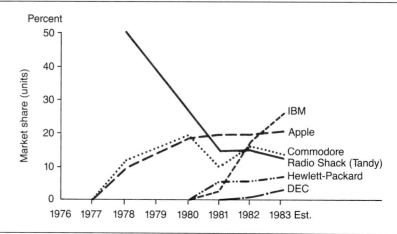

Sources: Scientific American, December 1982, p. 99. *Business Week,* October 3, 1983, p. 77.
Casewriter's estimates.

EXHIBIT 4c

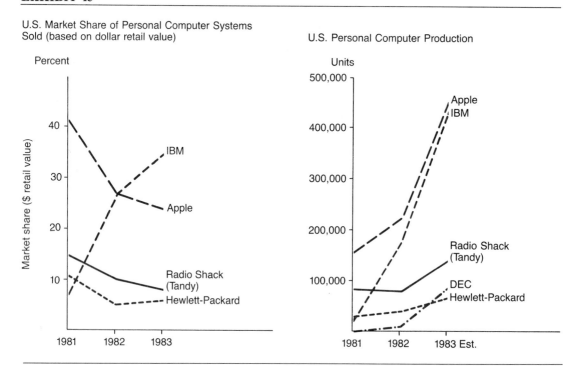

U.S. Market Share of Personal Computer Systems
Sold (based on dollar retail value)

U.S. Personal Computer Production

Source: Business Week, January 16, 1984, p. 79.

Source: Business Week, October 3, 1983, p. 76.

With projected growth rates of 100 percent-plus a year, the personal computer market was a major attraction to a number of firms in the early 80s. In fact, at the beginning of 1983, over 100 companies were each vying for 10 percent to 20 percent of the market. The shakeout that had been predicted for 1985 began in 1983. It was particularly severe in the home computer segment of the personal computer industry.

Apple was the only major competitor whose entire business was built around this single industry. (Even with a quarter of the market in 1983, IBM's personal computer division would account for no more than 5 percent of IBM corporate sales.) Thus, for Apple, its new product activities were not only a response to additional opportunity but a defense of the core of its business.

ORIGINS OF APPLE COMPUTER

Apple Computer Company had been founded in 1975 as a partnership by Steve Wozniak and Steve Jobs. Wozniak, 24, had been working at Hewlett-Packard, designing hand-held calculators, while Jobs, 20, had been designing video games at Atari. Their first product, the Apple I, evolved from their interest in having their own microcomputer. It cost about $10,000 to develop, which they raised from their own savings and by selling a calculator and a van. Once they had built one for each of themselves, they showed it to other members of the Home Brew Computer Club in Palo Alto, and several people wanted one. At first, they built units in their garage but in 1976 decided to farm out the printed circuit board (PCB) operations and to do only the final integration and testing of the finished product.

THE APPLE II

By the fall of 1976, the Apple II had been developed with Wozniak designing the majority of the internal workings and Jobs defining the overall concept and appearance.

Jobs wanted to strip the computer of its mysterious and sometimes threatening reputation. This led to a low profile, a plastic case, and no blinking lights or confusing knobs and dials. In many ways, this design philosophy made the Apple II the first truly successful "personal computer."

While similar to the Apple I, the Apple II included additional circuitry, a built-in, Teletype-style keyboard, BASIC in ROM (Read-Only Memory), high-resolution color graphics, and a 16K memory, all enclosed in a plastic housing (see Exhibit 5 for product specifications).

EXHIBIT 5 Product Specifications

	Base List Price	Microprocessor	RAM	ROM	Operating System
Apple I	N/A		8K		DOS 3.3
Apple II	N/A	8-bit	16K	Including BASIC	DOS 3.3; "Sophisticated Operating System" (SOS)
Apple III and Apple III plus	N/A / $2,995	8-bit / 8-bit	96K / 128K	4K, for self-test diagnostics	DOS 3.3 / Pro DOS
Apple IIe	$1,224	8-bit, 6502 microprocessor	64K	16K bytes including Applesoft BASIC, self-test, and 80-column routines	DOS 3.3 / Pro DOS
Lisa 2	$3,495	32-bit, Motorola 68000	512K	64K bytes	No name given: Apple wants user to think of operating system as "invisible"
Lisa 2/5	$4,495		512K and 5MB hdd*		
Lisa 2/10	$5,495		512K and 10MB hdd*		
Macintosh	$2,195 / $3,195	32-bit, Motorola MC 68000	128K bytes or 512K bytes	64K bytes	No name given; same reasons as for Lisa
Apple IIc	$1,295	65CO2 CMOS version of 6502	128K bytes	16K bytes including Applesoft BASIC and Mousetext	Pro DOS

	Disk Drive	Graphics	Other	Documentation
Apple I			Single printed circuit board; no keyboard; no plastic housing	None
Apple II	One 5¼-inch floppy built in 140K bytes per diskette	Color graphics	Teletype-style keyboard; upper case only; 40-column display	
Apple III and Apple III plus		280 × 192, 16 colors (limited); 140 × 192, 16 colors; 560 × 192 monochromatic; Apple II modes	Aluminum case; 60-key keyboard plus 13-key numeric pad; 80 or 40 character wide columns; upper and lower case letters; Audio-Video output	Instruction manual

Model	Display/Graphics	Disk Drive	Input/Ports	Documentation
Apple IIe	40 × 48, 16 colors; 280 × 192 bit-mapped array (can provide, e.g., 560 × 192 monochromatic limited; 280 × 192 monochromatic; 140 × 192, 4 color)	One 5¼-inch floppy	63-key keyboard; upper and lower case; 7 expansion slots; video interface	Manuals; tutorials
Lisa 2		One 3½-inch floppy w/400K bytes	Mouse; 2 serial ports; video cable	
Lisa 2/5	512 × 342 pixel bit-mapped display; free-hand drawing	Same as Lisa 2, plus 5MB hdd*		Manual; interactive tutorial diskettes
Lisa 2/10		Same as Lisa 2, plus 10MB hdd*		
Macintosh	512 × 342 pixel bit-mapped display; free-hand drawing	One 3½-inch disk drive with 400K bytes	Mouse; 2 serial ports; video cable; numeric pad	Manual; cassette plus tutorial diskettes and tape cassettes
Apple IIc	6-color graphics with 280 × 192 resolution; 16-colors with 560 × 192 resolution	One 5¼-inch low height floppy disk drive	Two keyboard layouts (standard QWERTY, or Dvorak); video cable; 2 serial ports	Manual and six interactive tutorial diskettes

Model	Options	Software
Apple I	—	—
Apple II	Plug-in cards for word processing; 65K maximum memory	
Apple III and Apple III plus	Emulator for All 3 floppy disk drives	Can run majority of Apple IIe software. Included is Information Analyst: word processor, business BASIC, Visicalc
Apple IIe	128K maximum memory; up to 6 140K byte; 5¼" floppy disk drives	Runs most Apple II software; Applewriter IIe word processor; Quickfile IIe data-base system
Lisa 2	1 megabyte memory	Can run most Macintosh software
Lisa 2/15	All Lisas can emulate Macintosh	
Lisa 2/10	Second disk drive; modems	
Macintosh		Included is MacWrite, MacPaint, MacFile
Apple IIc	Mouse; flat-panel LCD display; second disk drive; modems	Can run most Apple IIe software

*hdd = hard disk drive.

On the other hand, the manufacturing process in the Apple II was essentially the same process originally worked out in the garage for the Apple I. Jobs recalled:

> We had learned a lot about product design from the Apple I. We learned that 8K bytes of memory really weren't enough. We were using the new 4K RAMS (Read and Write Memories). At that time, no one else was using RAMS. Going out with a product using only dynamic memories was a risky thing.[6]

With the design and a prototype in hand, Jobs and Wozniak approached Hewlett-Packard and Atari to see if they might be interested in involvement in the project. For a variety of reasons, neither of those firms chose to pursue it, although Commodore did come very close to reaching an agreement with the two partners.

Finally, Jobs decided that a formal corporate organization would need to be developed and that outside financing would be required. In 1977, Mike Markkula, who had previously been employed by Fairchild Semiconductor and Intel but was now "retired," put up $91,000 to supplement the $2,600 each put up by Jobs and Wozniak. Even more important than the money, Markkula agreed to work with Jobs and Wozniak to formalize a strategy and to draw up a business plan. Their concept was to use microprocessor technology to create a personal computer for individuals to use in a wide variety of applications. Another key contribution Markkula made was to identify and bring in Mike Scott as president.

The Apple II was introduced during the summer of 1977 at the West Coast Computer Fair. Its development and introduction had cost approximately $2 million, $1.7 million of which went to development costs.[7]

Apple made available every piece of technical data relating to the machine, a highly unusual move in an industry where secrecy had always been tightly maintained. This open policy allowed sophisticated users to design circuit boards that could plug into the computer and expand its capabilities. In fact, several empty slots were built into the Apple II just for this purpose. Independent vendors soon began marketing hardware and software enhancements.

Because the market was embryonic, the Apple II was a product for which the customer had very low expectations, in part because it had little competition. The early personal computers were purchased by hobbyists. Customers were 98 percent male, typically 25 to 45 years old, earned a salary over $20,000 a year, and had the knowledge to

---

[6]"Apple Computer (A)," Stanford University Graduate School of Business, Case S-BP-229A, revised June 1983, p. 2.

[7]Casewriter's estimate.

program their own routines. (There was little standard software available.) Customers, for instance, commonly programmed games such as Star Trek and Adventure. (See Exhibit 6 for yearly sales.)

The Apple II sold steadily throughout its product life cycle. Demand for the Apple II was enhanced by Visicalc, a financial modeling program developed by two Harvard Business School students. (See the Accessory Products section.) In the summer of 1982, it appeared that sales were slowing, so Apple bundled the II with a monitor and software for $2,000. The results were impressive, with 30,000 units per month being sold during the 1982 Christmas season. The $2,000 price point seemed critical, according to Dave Larson, later the IIe marketing director.[8]

THE APPLE COMPUTER COMPANY

During Apple's first full fiscal year (1978), the company raised $517,000 from outside sources, organized a network of independent distributors, and greatly expanded production of the Apple II. Much of the financing

---

EXHIBIT 6 Yearly Sales of Apple Products (thousands of units)

	1977	1978	1979	1980	1981	1982	1983	1984 est.
Apple I	.2	—	—	—	—	—	—	—
Apple II/ IIe*	.6	7.6	35[1]	78[1]	180[2]	279[3]	420[4]	500+ [5]
Apple III	—	—	—	—	6	20	35[6]	40[6][8]
Lisa	—	—	—	—	—	—	20[7]	100[8]
Macintosh	—	—	—	—	—	—	—	250[9]–500[10]
Apple IIc	—	—	—	—	—	—	—	150[8]–400[12]
Total	.8	7.6	35	78	186	299	475	1,200[11]

*Beginning in 1983, all these units were Apple IIe.

Sources: (1) Paul Freiberger and Michael Swaine, *Fire in the Valley*, 1984, pp. 231, 234.
(2) Apple Computer, Inc., 1981 annual report, p. 6.
(3) Apple Computer, Inc., 1982 annual report, p. 1.
(4) Apple Computer, Inc., 1983 annual report, p. 2.
(5) *InfoWorld*, April 9, 1984, p. 54.
(6) *InfoWorld*, April 9, 1984, p. 55.
(7) *Forbes*, February 20, 1984, p. 88.
(8) Casewriter's estimate.
(9) *Silicon Valley Tech News*, May 21, 1984, p. 4.
(10) *Fortune*, February 20, 1984, p. 100.
(11) *Forbes*, February 13, 1984, p. 40, states that 100,000 Apples are bought each month.
(12) *The Wall Street Journal*, April 24, 1984, p. 23.

---

[8]Interview with Dave Larson, October 1984.

came from Venrock Associates, a New York–based venture capital firm founded by the Rockefeller family to invest in high-technology enterprises. Arthur Rock became a member of Apple's board of directors. (See Exhibit 7 for major company milestones, and Exhibit 8 for organization charts.)

Apple II manufacturing was essentially buy, assemble, and test. Under these manufacturing policies, which later came to be called the "conventional" approach, most components in the Apple II were purchased from outside suppliers who built chips, boards, cases, and other parts to Apple specifications. Only final assembly and test were in-house.

In the testing process, Apple computers with special software performed diagnostic tests to isolate and identify problems. As a part of the final testing procedures, all systems were "burned-in" for two days to provide assurance of electronic and mechanical functions. In addition, the processes used were primarily manual, labor-intensive ones.

With regard to facilities, Apple operated out of one plant in California until June 1980. At that time, Apple instituted the "module" concept. This included the "parent plant" for the Apple II, located near corporate headquarters in California and in close contact with the engineering staff. Satellite production facilities (called "modules") that replicated the assembly and test portion of the parent plant were then developed as additional capacity was required. The satellite facilities for the Apple II were in Dallas, Texas (June 1980), and Cork County, Ireland (November 1980). Apple opened the facility in Ireland because of tax and transportation considerations for selling into the European market, and after coming to believe it would be more effective to sell to the European countries from a nearby location.

The module scheme allowed management and engineers at headquarters to maintain close contact and control over design and manufacturing operations, while spreading some of the risks associated with a single site or an excessively large facility. A module for the Apple II filled 30,000 square feet, required a crew of 70, and produced between 450 and 500 units per day.

By the end of 1980, sales were moving along at a $100 million-plus annual rate through a network of 950 independent retail computer stores in the United States and Canada (serviced by Apple's own sales organization) and 1,300 retail stores elsewhere in the world (serviced by 30 independent distributors). Virtually all of those sales were coming from the Apple II. While the company had introduced some of its own software for that product, it relied on independent developers (often users) to develop the vast majority of the needed software. Apple's policy was to try to price its products so that the retail price equaled approximately four times the manufacturing cost.

EXHIBIT 7 Selected Milestones

Date		Event
Jan. 1975		Development of Apple I.
		Apple Computer Company partnership formed.
Jan. 1976		
	Fall.	Apple II development completed.
Jan. 1977	Jan.	A. C. "Mike" Markkula joined. Mike Scott named president.
	Apr.	Apple II announced and introduction.
Jan. 1978		First full fiscal year.
		Beginning of Apple III development.
Jan. 1979	Mar.	Initial ideas for Lisa.
Jan. 1980	May.	Apple III announced.
	Jul.	Lisa development underway.
	Nov.	Apple III quantity shipments begin.
	Dec.	Initial public offering.
Jan. 1981	Feb.	Apple III production and sales halted.
	Mar.	Macintosh project initiated.
	Mar.	Mike Markkula named president and CEO.
		Steven Jobs, chairman of the board.
	Dec.	Apple III hardware and software reintroduction.
Jan. 1982	May.	Apple IIc work begun.
Jan. 1983	Feb.	Apple IIe introduction.
	Mar.	Lisa introduction.
		John Sculley named president. Markkula became consultant.
	Sept.	Lisa 2 introduction.
Jan. 1984	Jan.	Macintosh introduction.
	Apr.	Apple IIc introduction.
	Jun.	Lisa second-generation software available, and networking and data communications.

EXHIBIT 8 Company Organization, 1978

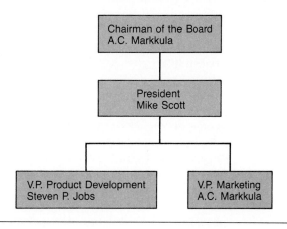

In December of 1980, Apple Computer went public, selling 4.6 million shares at $22 per share, resulting in an overall market value in excess of $1 billion. As a consequence of the offering, over 200 Apple employees became millionaires.

THE APPLE III

In 1981, Apple expanded its product offerings through the development and introduction of the Apple III. This product operated much as the Apple II but included additional features specifically aimed at an office environment.

The project to build the successor to the Apple II began in late 1978. In general, Apple was feeling a need to build a product that would eliminate the Apple II's shortcomings. "We listened very carefully to our customers," remembered Jobs. A great deal of market research had been conducted for the Apple III. Not only did this work help detail technical specifications, it also called for a sense of urgency. "We were told that sales of the Apple II would peak around 10,000 units per month," said Wil Houde, vice president and general manager of the Personal Computer Systems Division (PCSD). In order to sustain the company's growth, the Apple III had to be introduced during the "market window." That window was projected to be in approximately one year, so Apple planned to introduce the III at that time. In fact, the decision to introduce the III by the end of 1980 was announced in the prospectus for Apple's initial public stock offering. As it turned out, however, Apple II sales charged through the 10,000 mark without a pause. Wendell Sander, the Apple III's designer, recalled, "We had no idea back then that the Apple II's popularity would last so long."

The Apple III was envisioned to consolidate Apple's leadership role in personal computers. Although it would be far ahead of any competition, it did not presume to establish radically new standards for the industry. Indeed, some of Apple's best engineers embarked at this time on a separate project named Lisa. Lisa would have a longer time horizon and was expected to be the company's next revolutionary product.

From the beginning, the III was envisioned to have an 80-character wide screen (instead of 40), upper- and lowercase capability, and a built-in disk drive. These made the new machine much closer to a full word processor—an application for which Apple II owners had been buying special plug-in cards. The III was also to have additional memory, since memory limitations appeared to be a second main shortcoming of the II.

Eventually, the Apple III made a transition from an Apple II follow-on product to an entirely new product. The III was to have a numeric keypad in addition to a standard typewriter keyboard, and 96K memory. The hardware was given the Apple look and feel, and enclosed in an aluminum case (see Exhibit 5).

The III was to have an entirely new operating system called the "Sophisticated Operating System," or SOS. SOS made the III more versatile and more user friendly than the II. Indeed, the operating system was considered so advanced that Apple engineers insisted on keeping its specifications secret. However, this technical information was released a few months after the initial product introduction. Apple also decided to incorporate an emulation mode so that the III could simulate a II and run software written for the II. This decision, which was hotly debated, may have added as much as 25 percent to the development costs, which totaled $2.5 million.

Since the Apple III had evolved into a more powerful and expensive machine than the Apple II, the company needed to target a different market segment in order to protect the II's position in the education, small business, and hobbyists segments. It became positioned as a "discretionary purchase by professional people to improve their productivity."

This marketing strategy led to the development of the Information Analyst package of bundled software that included a word processor, business BASIC language, and Visicalc (the popular program for financial planning). User expectations were predicted to be quite different for the III than for the II. While a hobbyist might buy an Apple II and write his or her own programs, an Apple III purchaser would expect a large selection of tools. Unfortunately, software development lagged significantly behind the hardware development and the introduction timetable.

Eight weeks before the National Computer Conference in May 1980, Apple president Mike Scott decided to unveil the Apple III at that conference. At the time, the engineers had numerous design difficulties, most notably with the spacing of components on the printed circuit boards. However, with great effort, the engineers produced several prototypes of the Apple III for the show. Marketing also worked until the last moment to have literature ready for the Information Analyst package. Although everyone at Apple knew that certain bugs still remained to be worked out, the overall attitude at the firm towards the new product was positive.

Amid great publicity and fanfare, the Apple III was introduced as planned at the May 1980 National Computer Conference in Anaheim, California. The product elicited great interest at the conference and Apple rented Disneyland for an evening to celebrate its success, and gave free tickets to anyone who had stopped by the Apple display at the conference. Introduction costs plus later Apple III product launch costs were estimated at $.5 million.

During the fall of 1980, when the transition to volume production was to occur, an endless stream of problems surfaced. Some could be attributed to Apple's rapid growth and the difficulty the company was having managing that growth. Others had to do with supplier problems. Many, however, were related directly to the Apple III design. Apparently, there was unanticipated thermal stress induced by the completely enclosed aluminum case that warped the circuit boards. In addition, the space constraint on the printed circuit board could cause several major failures in the memory board and the copper trace lines that carried the signals between the semiconductor devices.

Nevertheless, the Apple III was shipped and made available to customers in December 1980 as stated in Apple's stock offering prospectus. Of the machines going out the door, 20 percent did not function at all, another 20 percent had major problems, and many more had minor bugs. Some customers brought them back to the dealers four or five times for repairs.

Demand for the Apple III was strong initially, but it declined rapidly as news of the reliability problems spread and as the dealers encouraged potential customers to purchase other machines so they wouldn't have to cope with the extensive repair work the Apple IIIs required.

Because of the severe problems with the Apple III, company executives considered abandoning, replacing, or correcting the machine. In February 1981, the Apple Executive Committee decided to halt production of the III and to redesign it as necessary. The Executive Committee had concluded that the credibility of the entire firm, not just a single product, rested with the future of the Apple III. Mike Markkula announced to the public that Apple would not "abandon" the III. Wil Houde, vice president and general manager of the Personal Computer Systems Division (PCSD), stated: "We felt that we were protecting the reputation of all our future products, not just this one."

Internally, the process of correcting the machine's problems and redesigning the manufacturing process was characterized by one executive as "infinite attention to finite detail." Every major subassembly except the power supply was modified before the computer was ready for reintroduction. Apple IIIs were then subjected to stringent in-house testing, consisting of six phases. Aside from the more rigorous testing, Apple III manufacturing emulated the Apple II processes described earlier in the case. The software bottleneck was overcome by farming out a good deal of the task.

In March, on what came to be called Black Wednesday, Mike Scott fired 40 employees and terminated several hardware development projects he believed were taking too long. The company was stunned by the firings, a substantial number of which many employees believed were unjustified. Shortly thereafter, Mike Scott left Apple, Mike Markkula took over as president, and Steve Jobs became chairman of the board. (See Exhibit 9 for organization chart.)

In December 1981, Apple announced a massive hardware/software reintroduction program for the Apple III. Code-named the THUD project, the company aimed to catch the country's attention with the reintroduction. Apple intended to replace every Apple III that had been sold. The owners would receive completely new machines, including updated software and expanded memory (from 96K to 128K), free of charge. The redesign and reintroduction cost Apple $5 million, bringing the total cost for Apple III development to $8 million. Of the $5 million spent on the redesign and reintroduction, a larger portion went into the reintroduction campaign than had gone to the initial Apple III introduction.[9]

EXHIBIT 9   Company Organization, 1981

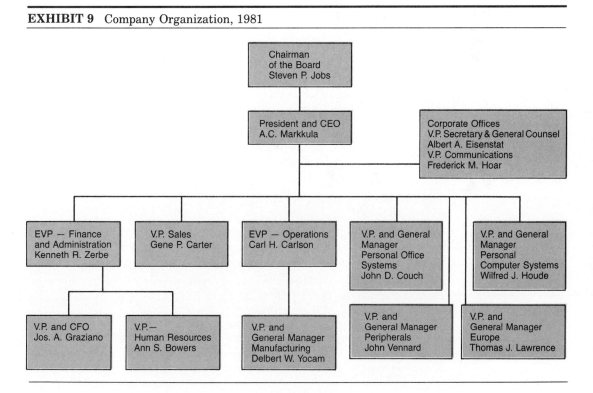

---

[9]Casewriter's estimate.

Following the Apple III reintroduction, numerous Apple managers reflected back:[10]

Design engineers:

Marketing had sold the machine long before it was ready.

If we could have had another six months, none of this would have happened.

Manufacturing engineer:

Design engineering just dumped the design on manufacturing and said, "Build it."

Management:

The Apple II had taken the world by storm. We felt we could do anything. We got cocky.

The Apple III was a machine that an organization had to build, not a small group of individuals.

The people who put the Apple III together weren't here to learn the lessons of the Apple II. They didn't appreciate the details put into the Apple II.

Now we're much more formal. We write things down on paper. But we're still quite unstructured and informal relative to many established firms.

Steve Jobs, chairman of the board, added to these comments:

There is no question that the Apple III was our most maturing experience. Luckily, it happened when we were years ahead of the competition—it was the perfect time to learn.

Despite the reintroduction, sales of the Apple III never accounted for more than a small percentage of Apple II sales. Estimates indicated that approximately 75,000 Apple IIIs had been sold by April 1984,[11] and that at most, 100,000 cumulative would be sold by the end of Apple's fiscal year 1984. (See Exhibit 6.)

APPLE IIe

In February 1983, Apple Computer introduced the IIe, or the so-called "enhanced" Apple II. The IIe had been under development since early 1981 and was initially called the "LCA," for Low Cost Apple. According to Dave Larson, the Apple IIe director of marketing:

The choice was between developing the IIe or what later became the IIc. There were resources available only for one. It was an emotional time at the company. With VLSI (very large scale integrated circuits), it was

---

[10]"Apple Computer (B)," Stanford University Graduate School of Business, Case S-BP-229B, 1983, p. 2.

[11]*InfoWorld,* April 9, 1984, p. 55.

possible to develop a computer with similar capabilities to the II and a 30 percent reduction in the number of chips from the II. Eventually, we decided to develop the IIe—it was a smaller jump . . . a new model for existing markets.

The attitude at the time was that you couldn't make a mistake, like you can now. Anything you could do would be successful. You just had to choose. It was difficult to focus.[12]

The Apple IIe group began with 7 people and eventually grew to 30, and came from a variety of places. These included the Apple II group, the Apple III area, and outside firms. For example, Peter Quinn, who was responsible for designing the integrated circuit, had previously worked for Xilog and Fairchild. Dave Larson, who became the marketing director, came from Measurex via the Apple III group, and other key technical people, including Steve Wozniak, came from the Apple II group.

According to *Byte Publications, Inc.:*

It had been obvious for a while at Apple Computer that a replacement for the Apple II was needed. The Teletype-style keyboard—upper-case-only, 40-column display—and the maximum of 64K bytes of memory were becoming limitations as the marketplace changed and software became more sophisticated. The design was getting old and technology had changed enough to allow a redesign with significantly fewer parts. A new design could also address foreign requirements for special keyboards, displays, and video signals better than the Apple II. Although the Apple II was a tremendous success, it was clearly time to design a successor.[13]

Remarkably, however, less clear was the breadth of support for the project within Apple. Hardware designer Peter Quinn commented:

The IIe was almost a closet project. Of course, we had support from Steve Jobs and Mike Markkula, but everyone pretty much left us alone. Many of the hotshots were working on Macintosh and Lisa at the time, and that left Wozniak free to pursue his interest of customizing the Apple II. Initially, we had 7 people working on the project though that grew to 30. And for most of the year, there was no leader.

We developed the product specs from our gut. We didn't do market research. We had a respected customer base of hobbyists and hackers, and, you know, that's what we were too. So we built the product like we thought it should be built.[14]

The Apple IIe included 64K bytes of memory (expandable to 128K bytes), Applesoft BASIC in ROM, a 63-key keyboard with upper- and lowercase letters, seven expansion slots for I/O (input/output) devices, and a video interface. The keyboard was essentially an improved

---

[12]Interview with Dave Larson, October 1984.

[13]*Byte Publications,* February 1983.

[14]Interview with Peter Quinn, October 1984.

version of the Apple III's keyboard (but without a numeric pad) and was the most visible difference between the II and the IIe.

Internally, though, the IIe was significantly different from the II. The keyboard was completely new, and the main printed circuit board was totally redesigned. The IIe used just 31 integrated circuits compared to approximately 120 in the II to achieve similar capabilities. A substantial part of the reduction resulted from the use of 64K-bit rather than 16K-bit dynamic memories.

Market surveys had indicated that the volume of software available was a key consideration among personal computer purchasers. Therefore, Apple decided the IIe had to be compatible with existing Apple II hardware and software products. This proved to be quite a challenge since the internal workings of the IIe had been designed from scratch. The first two major software products that were designed to use all the II's features (Applewriter IIe and Quickfile IIe) were enhanced versions of the same programs for the Apple III, and were reported to be very user friendly, providing clear prompts, multiple "menus," and numerous "help" screens. Apple also developed a keyboard tutorial and wrote a precise technical manual to aid third-party software development efforts.

Apple spent about $8 million to develop the IIe and $3 million to launch it. According to Dave Larson, the advertising consisted primarily of "corporate umbrella messages," and little advertising in computer magazines. He added that the customer base was not differentiated at this time.[15]

The Apple IIe was manufactured using essentially the same production processes as were used for the II. In fact, at the end of 1982, Apple stopped making IIs completely and started making only IIes. Considering that the II accounted for almost all of the company's revenue stream at the time, this was a bold move.

The printed circuit boards (PCBs) for the IIe were made in Singapore, as they had been with the II since the Singapore facility opened in July 1981. Previously, Apple had been having quality control problems with its eight domestic PCB producers. The first pass yield rate of the PCBs assembled by the eight U.S. firms (i.e., the percentage of PCBs that had zero defects following initial assembly) ranged from 60 to 70 percent. At Apple's Singapore facility, the first pass yield rate ranged from 90 to 98 percent. By 1984, the Singapore facility also handled all the purchasing, board testing, and subcontracting with other Asian countries, in addition to board stuffing. Thirty to 40 percent of the board was stuffed using automated processes, as compared to 0 percent in 1981.

---

[15]Interview with Dave Larson, October 1984.

Regarding the evolution of final assembly and test, Apple began using a series of "linear manufacturing lines" early in 1983. The Dallas facility was responsible for the IIe, III, and upcoming Lisa product, and consequently needed some individual product line flexibility. The design of the lines allowed changeover to another product in the space of a couple of days. The burn-in, or testing time for the IIe, took eight hours, compared to two days when the II was first manufactured.

The manufacturing goal for fiscal years 1984 and 1985 was to develop a "computer integrated flexible manufacturing system." The first step would be to computerize all the work in process inventory tracking and the management information system. The second step would include some degree of workstation automation, automated storage and retrieval, and automated handling. Most of the initiative for automating the IIe derived from the development of the Macintosh factory. (See Macintosh section.)

In the years following the IIe introduction, Apple continued to offer additional enhancements for the product. These included a hard disk, Appleworks integrated software package, a mouse, and MS–DOS add-on capability. Many of these enhancements made the IIe easier to use.

In addition, third-party software developers and users themselves continued to write applications programs for the IIe. Even in 1984, the limits of the machine's capabilities were just beginning to be stretched. With over 10,000 programs written for it, the IIe had had more software developed for it than had any other personal computer.

Marketing at Apple developed through continual refinement and improvement. The retail distribution channel, based on national distribution through manufacturers' representatives, provided the mainstay. The largest retailers, such as Computerland and Businessland, for example, were serviced through a Central Buy organization. A Value-Added Resale channel existed for customers wanting systems integration or customized specific applications. Direct channel representatives sold to both the education—kindergarten through 12th grade—and the adult/university markets. In 1983, the University Consortium was established to sell to selected universities.

The Apple IIe customer mix also changed over the years: from predominantly business and corporate to more small business, school, and some home.

The Apple IIe sold extremely well and captured 55 to 60 percent of the U.S. education market for personal computers. By 1984, roughly 1.5 million Apple IIs and IIes had been sold. (See Exhibit 6.) Thus, the IIe, combined with its direct predecessor, the II, represented one of the most successful products in the history of U.S. business.

However, in late 1983 and early 1984, it appeared that IIe sales were slowing. In response, Apple cut the price from $1,800 to $995 in April 1984.

Peter Quinn reflected on the success of the IIe and the situation in early 1984:

When the IIe came out, it got a corner of the cover of *Popular Computer* magazine, and Lisa got the rest. Yet Apple might not have made it through 1983 if the IIe hadn't existed. Lisa wasn't selling. Mac wasn't available. Sculley arrived in June 1983 and gave a year to Apple. The company was a mess when he arrived. There were shareholders calling all the time.[16]

APPLE IIc

Work on the Apple IIc ("c" for compact) began in mid-1982 when:

Apple chairman Steve Jobs walked into engineer Peter Quinn's office. He slapped an Apple IIe main circuit board on Quinn's desk and plunked a low-profile keyboard at one end of it and a disk drive at the other. Jobs pointed to the assemblage of parts and declared, "*That* is a great product. Do you want to do it?"

Quinn quickly replied, "Sure, Steve, we're half done."

Actually, they weren't even half started. Apple had just introduced the IIe, an enhanced version of the Apple II. But Quinn realized that the work on that computer could be easily applied to the machine Jobs envisioned: a portable Apple II.[17]

By 1982, portable computers had begun to appear in the marketplace. Most notable among these was the Osborne I, which was introduced in April 1981. While the Osborne was not a spectacular machine, it was adequate, it was available, and it proved that one of the next directions for personal computers was toward portability.

Most of the people who developed the IIc came from within Apple, and most notably from the IIe group. Peter Quinn (designer), Dave Larson (marketing), and Dave Patterson (engineering) came from the IIe group, while Wil Houde had been involved with development of the III.

One key issue at the time, according to Dave Larson (marketing manager), was how to get over the hurdle to the next layer of customers. Concurrently, the market for personal computers had become much more complicated. Some Apple managers claimed that more market research went into the development of the IIc than into any other Apple product.

Designed specifically to fit inside any briefcase, the IIc measured 11.5 × 12 × 2.25 inches. The IIc weighed 7.5 pounds, had a single 5.25-inch built-in, low-height disk drive, and 128K bytes of RAM. It had a

---

[16]Interview with Peter Quinn, October 1984.
[17]*Popular Computing,* June 1984.

slightly flatter keyboard than the IIe, utilized the new Motorola 65C02 microprocessor, and needed 21 integrated circuits (compared to the IIe's 31). Importantly, Apple chose to replace many of the IIe expansion slots with fixed functions in the IIc, thus creating a "closed" architecture machine rather than its traditional open architecture approach. This meant that the IIc had limited expansion capabilities and could not run CP/M software. Also, importantly from a technological viewpoint, the IIc had an optional flat-panel LCD (liquid crystal display) display that was reported to be more readable than other flat panel displays available at the time, and to support a full 24 × 80 columns of text and the high-resolution graphics. However, the flat panel was not available at the introduction. The IIc also could be switched from traditional QWERTY keyboard layout (found on virtually all typewriters) to a Dvorak keyboard layout, with the lettered keys arranged differently, which many claimed was easier to learn and use and would become more frequently used than QWERTY. Finally, the IIc included a number of details: a 12-foot video cable, a "splash pad" to protect the circuitry from liquids, auditory-tactile response on the keys. (See Exhibit 5.)

The IIc's software resulted primarily from market research studies Apple conducted to try to understand "popular taste in computers." Some of the managers claimed that the IIc was the first Apple product targeted to a specific customer group. The market research indicated that consumers were spending two to three hours setting up their computers, which was too long. So, Apple built in all the protocols so that the user just needed to plug in the cables in order to begin. The research also showed that consumers became frustrated wading through large manuals. Therefore, Apple decided to bundle an introductory guide and six interactive tutorials with the IIc. Even more significantly, project manager Peter Quinn claimed that 90 to 95 percent of the IIe software was compatible with the IIc. Additional third-party software development was encouraged. Finally, the IIc's ROM included mouse-controlled pictorial icons similar to those used with Lisa and Macintosh. (See Macintosh and Lisa sections.)

Apple targeted the IIc for a broad consumer market, Apple's first product aimed at this market. Specifically, the IIc aimed at "serious home users," i.e., college-educated professionals with school-age children. The company also used consumer-oriented advertising, such as extensive use of TV spots, and more focused, events-oriented promotional activities. Industry observers speculated that the IIc market positioning and strategy represented the influence of Apple's new president, John Sculley. Mr. Sculley, who joined Apple in April 1983, was previously a leading Pepsi-Cola executive and was skilled in mass marketing techniques. He replaced Mike Markkula, who was now worth $100 million and wanted to retire.

Many industry observers claimed that the IIc marked a dramatic change in the Apple II family, both in marketing and product appearance. But also indicated was that Apple had decided to continue the II family. The IIc clearly was positioned against the IBM PCjr, which had been a disappointment for IBM due in large part to its "chiclet" keyboard and its limited memory. In fact, IBM had decided to redesign and reintroduce the machine. Some expected the IIc to cannibalize IIe sales.

The IIc was manufactured according to Apple's conventional manufacturing techniques. The printed circuit boards were assembled in Singapore, most components purchased from subcontractors, and then the final assembly and test performed at Apple's California, Texas, and Ireland facilities.

By the time the Apple IIc was introduced at a computer dealer exposition in San Francisco in April 1984, it had been developed into a fully portable computer with sophisticated software. The IIc development and introduction cost Apple $50 million.[18] Apple spent $15 million on the IIc launch alone. Initial sales reports indicated that the IIc was selling well. One article stated that Apple had forecast 400,000 IIc sales during calendar 1984 and that it would be outselling the IIe by year-end.[19]

ACCESSORY PRODUCTS DIVISION

About 15 percent of Apple's sales were derived from peripheral devices to expand the computer's applications. These hardware devices and software programs did as much as anything to stimulate sales of the Apple II. Apple's most significant innovation, aside from the computers themselves, was the low-cost, 5.25-inch, flexible or "floppy" disk drive for the Apple II, which was introduced in mid-1978. The floppy disk storage replaced the less efficient cassette tape storage. It provided file memory capacity of up to 143K bytes of data, vastly increased data retrieval speed, and provided random access to stored data.

This hardware enhancement increased the power and the speed of the Apple II and also sped up the development of software. Over 100 independent vendors were developing Apple II software and peripheral equipment for text editing, small business accounting, and teaching. Some of these programs were extraordinarily successful. The first bestseller was a financial modeling program called Visicalc that two Harvard Business School students had developed. Over 250,000 copies had been sold by 1982.

---

[18]Interview with Peter Quinn, October 1984.
[19]*The Wall Street Journal*, April 24, 1984, p. 23.

By 1980, Apple had begun to introduce its own software, but they expected to write no more than 1 percent of the software that would eventually be available for their computers. Even 1 percent of the programs would be a large number, since over 10,000 were then available for the Apple II. This "open system" of software development proved crucial to Apple's success.

Apple had also introduced new peripheral devices to expand the computer's applications. In addition to the floppy disk, other peripheral accessories manufactured by Apple included a graphics tablet, a thermal printer, and interface circuit boards. Apple computers incorporated standard interfaces that permitted the use of peripherals designed and manufactured by others as well as those offered by Apple. These included medium-speed letter-quality printers, modems that provided a data communication link over telephone lines, computerized bulletin boards, other computers, music synthesizers, portable power units, and others.

In 1981, Apple introduced the Profile hard disk mass storage unit, initially for the Apple III. It held 5 million bytes and, as such, had 35 times the capacity and 10 times the speed of the standard floppy disk drives available at the time. Apple believed the Profile would be an important building block for future computer products, potentially as important as the Apple II's Disk II was in the 1970s.

In 1982, an Accessory Products Division was formed. The company introduced two brand-name printers, a dot matrix and a letter quality, for the Apple II and III. Nearly 1,000 third-party software suppliers were developing applications for Apples.

Apple established even tighter, stronger links to independent software developers in 1983. The company also reduced efforts in disk drive manufacturing, shifting to outside sources. This decision followed the difficulties and abandonment of development efforts for the "Twiggy" disk drive for the Macintosh.

The Accessory Products Division was located in Garden Grove, California (outside Los Angeles) in 1984. Some keyboards were assembled there, and development of additional add-ons for the IIe continued. As part of the 1984 reorganization, it became part of the Apple II Division.

LISA

During the 1970s, Apple had conducted market research in an effort to understand the Apple II customer base and how the product was being used. The results indicated that by and large, people were using the Apple IIs for basic spreadsheet and word processing activities (text editing and filing). They also needed graphics and communications capabilities. More importantly, however, the research indicated that the average consumer spent 30 to 40 hours learning how to use their new personal computer. The top managers and engineers at Apple, represented most vocally by Steve Jobs, concluded in 1981 that the key to expanding the personal computer market was in making a machine that was significantly more user-friendly. Only by doing so, the argument went, would large numbers of new users be attracted to personal computers. In fact, Jobs had held this view since at least 1976 when he designed the Apple II to be less threatening than traditional mainframe computers.

The ideas for the Lisa originated in 1979 with Steve Wozniak and Steve Jobs. Wozniak wanted to design a computer using a bit slice central processor, i.e., a computer that would include a purchased central part of the processor and an Apple-designed control for the processor. Jobs, then chairman of the board and vice president of product marketing, had an initial concept to produce an advanced, easy-to-use office computer. Jobs envisioned a computer with five integrated software applications, i.e., a computer with which data could be moved between the software applications packages relatively easily. The original target market was to be the "productivity marketplace," primarily executives.

Later in 1979, Jobs and some of the engineers visited Xerox's Palo Alto Research Center (PARC). The visit proved particularly stimulating. Some of the Xerox people, including noted developer Alan Kay, were also focusing on increasing personal computers' user-friendliness. They had developed a language called Smalltalk, which used a "mouse" or hand-held pointing device that greatly reduced the number of complex commands a user needed to type into the computer. Also, advances had been made with bit map displays where every pixel or point on the computer screen could be controlled, thus greatly expanding graphics capabilities.

Work on the Lisa project began in earnest in mid-1979 and accelerated during 1980. Some engineers from within Apple joined the group, notably Bill Atkinson, who rejoined Apple at this time and who played a critical role in the software development. Atkinson had previously developed the Pascal programming language for use on the Apple II, and more recently had studied neurology at the University of California at San Diego and the University of Seattle. Others from outside Apple joined the project also, including about 15 engineers from Xerox's PARC facility and several people from DEC.[20]

Mike Scott, Apple's president, named John Couch as head of the Lisa project, insisting that Steve Jobs was too inexperienced to manage such a large project. Jobs remained as vice president of product marketing. The Lisa project staff began with a core of approximately 20 Apple

---

[20]*Newsweek,* January 31, 1984, p. 74.

people. In addition, 40 outsiders were subsequently hired, including some from Hewlett-Packard and a handful from Xerox. Ultimately, about 100 people worked on Lisa. The total development cost approached $40 million.

During 1980, hardware development breakthroughs occurred after three quarters of a year of false starts. The Motorola 68000 microprocessor replaced the Intel 8086 because it was more powerful for supporting graphics than the 8086.

Also during 1980, the software engineers began to solve the problems of integrating the software. A key to Lisa was the "windows" software, which allowed a user to view on one screen parts of several different "screens" of information at once. The Lisa also used a mouse, or hand-held pointing device, which facilitated movement around the screen. Instead of hitting cursor keys, the mouse would be moved over the desktop surface, and its movement translated into cursor movements on the screen.

By September 1980, three or four simple electronics prototypes were running, and demonstration software was available. Essentially, the hardware never changed after the end of 1980. The plan was to ship beginning in May 1981.

Wayne Rosing, general manager, recalled his perspectives from this time:

> With only six months until the projected product release date, we were in a "Lisa late" mode. No one had a total vision of the product, and the vision people did have was out of sync with the marketplace. The engineering group had no clear leader at the top, no single technical visionary, no intellectual. Instead, there were four or five warring camps. The product concept decision led to a political atmosphere resembling guerrilla camps. In addition, no one in the marketing group (which was more loyal to Jobs than Couch) had ever done a major new product.[21]

As development on Lisa continued, it became clear that a hard disk would be required to handle the massive software programs that would be run on the machine. But this was hard to swallow: it made Lisa expensive. In early 1981, Steve Jobs stated that Lisa had lost it—that it was just too big, that what he wanted was a "personal productivity appliance." Shortly thereafter, Jobs initiated work on what became the Macintosh.[22]

During 1982, an outside consultant brought a PERT program to Apple for the Lisa, and work began on a terminal emulator. Apple began introducing potential corporate customers to Lisa in June 1982 through the Lisa Sneak Program. The vast majority of

---

[21]Interview with Wayne Rosing, July 1984.
[22]Ibid.

the potential customers thought the product was great, except that it didn't have data communications, programmability, or networking capabilities.

The Wall Street Journal reported in January 1983 that:

> One reason the Lisa has taken so long getting to market is that Apple was undertaking an enormous development job for such a young company. It is understood to have written all the basic programs itself, even though most personal computer manufacturers use independent authors, even for the most fundamental software. Apple is also said to have devised its own video tube, disk drive, and mouse, which required considerable time and capital.
>
> Apple also had little incentive to move faster until recently, when competition increased so dramatically. The Apple II was selling well, and other companies were coming out with products that could be added to the Apple II to increase its capacity and keep it competitive.
>
> In addition, three years ago, when Apple introduced its last entry, the Apple III, it stumbled badly. A lot of the bugs hadn't been worked out, and the machine had to be redesigned.[23]

Apple targeted the Lisa at large corporate customers, a market traditionally dominated by IBM and new to Apple. Apple initially supplied only 150 dealers with Lisa, out of 1,800 total dealers, and expanded the national sales force to 100.

Beginning in the latter part of 1982, Lisa received worldwide news coverage, allegedly more than any other product except the IBM 370, according to Apple executives. The advanced technology captured people's imaginations. Apple spent approximately $10 million introducing and launching the Lisa.

Apple introduced the Lisa in March 1983, at a price of $9,995. The product was manufactured in California using conventional Apple manufacturing techniques, including overseas parts suppliers and assembly and only final assembly and test performed in-house. The Lisa hardware that had been developed in 1980 remained virtually unchanged.

Though Lisa had sparked tremendous interest within the computer industry, the fanfare did not materialize into high sales volume. As President John Sculley said in October 1984, "Lisa captured people's imaginations with its technology, but it did not capture the desktops of America."[24]

The 16,000-machine backlog that existed in September 1983 evaporated 1,200 machines later,[25] and only 20,000 were sold during all of calendar 1983.[26] Apple had difficulty closing sales to large corporations

---

[23]*The Wall Street Journal,* January 1983.
[24]Speech by John Sculley, Stanford Graduate School of Business, October 1984.
[25]Personal communication, Apple manager.
[26]*Forbes,* February 20, 1984, p. 88.

and was unaccustomed to operating in the corporate environment where purchase decisions often took a year. In addition, Apple sold the Lisa from stock in distribution (rather than through classic bookings), so didn't know the demand at any particular point in time. The competitive environment had toughened, also, due in large part to IBM's introduction of its Personal Computer and Vision's "Windows" programs in August 1983. Some Apple executives claimed in retrospect that Lisa sales would have been lower if it hadn't been for several popular software programs.

Apple's 1983 annual report said:

> Sales of the Lisa system, while on track with our early, modest expectations, were generally disappointing in fiscal 1983. Partly because of lengthy evaluation and purchasing cycles, we did not receive the volume orders we would have liked from the *Fortune* 1000 market, upon which we focused to the exclusion of other segments.
>
> Lisa should be viewed as much as a beginning—the threshold of new technology that will give rise to a family of new products from Apple—as it is an end in itself. Lisa technology is what Apple Computer is all about—in terms of the elegance of the product, ease of learning how to use it, and what its development says about Apple's commitment to innovation.[27]

In the fall of 1983, with less than 20,000 Lisas sold in total, Apple announced that Lisa manufacturing would be consolidated in the Texas and Ireland high-volume plants earlier than expected. Apple also increased the number of authorized Lisa dealers, unbundled the software, and introduced three modified versions of the Lisa. Each had different memory configurations and lower prices than the original version:

	Memory	*Price*
Lisa 2	512K	$3,495
Lisa 5	512K, 5MB hard disk drive	$4,495
Lisa 10	512K, 10MB hard disk drive	$5,495

By mid-1984, second-generation software was available, and networking and data communications capabilities had been added. Company executives claimed demand was brisk because of the improved price/performance characteristics and the fact that some potential Macintosh customers (see following section) were deciding they preferred a machine with larger memory (such as the Lisa). Discussion about the future of the Lisa continued within Apple.

Business Week reported that Lisa had missed its goal because of several marketing mistakes, notably lack of ability to communicate with other computers (which was later remedied), and too-slow dealer and sales-force training. Tom Peters added:

---

[27]Apple Computer, Inc., 1983 annual report, p. 6.

Apple suffered from technological hubris. It took the native Silicon Valley view that Lisa would walk into the boardrooms of corporate America and sell itself.[28]

MACINTOSH[29]

When Steve Jobs chose to pursue a different product from the Lisa, he was adamant about certain features for the new computer: price around $2,000, user-friendliness, and short initial learning time. He also wanted to automate manufacturing.

In order to focus on these objectives, a separate team of people was assembled to work on the project. Some key Macintosh technical people came from other parts of Apple, including the Apple II group and Lisa (Bill Atkinson and the Lisa graphics code). Many others were hired from outside Apple from firms including Xerox PARC, Texas Instruments, Hewlett-Packard, and Four-Phase (see Exhibit 10).

In the words of Joseph Graziano, vice president of finance and chief financial officer, "The Macintosh was intended to be like a car. We don't think much anymore of driving our car—we just get in and do it. We want to make this product equally as comfortable and natural." An important aspect of making the Macintosh "natural" or, in computer terms, "user-friendly," was the development of software that would make the human interaction with the Macintosh much easier than with traditional computers. This had been accomplished in the product design through the development of pictorial or visually oriented commands and a mouse that permitted the user to move a pointer (cursor) on the video screen. In developing the software, the Macintosh people benefited greatly from Lisa's graphics systems and development systems (i.e., the systems that programs are developed on). Also, the Lisa programs provided the Macintosh team with a base of experience and a standard against which to measure themselves and their improvement.

A second feature of the Macintosh, intended to increase user-friendliness, was a substantial decrease in the initial learning time required for the new user. This was achieved through the development of a more conversational language and ancillary support materials that did not require a computer background for understanding. When combined with a price under $2,500, top management expected the "every person's computer" to reach a large and primarily untapped number of

---

[28]*Business Week*, January 16, 1984, p. 78.

[29]The majority of this section comes from "Apple Computer, Inc.—Macintosh (A)," Stanford University Graduate School of Business Case S-BP-234, pp. 5–8, 11.

EXHIBIT 10 Company and Macintosh Organization (February 1983)

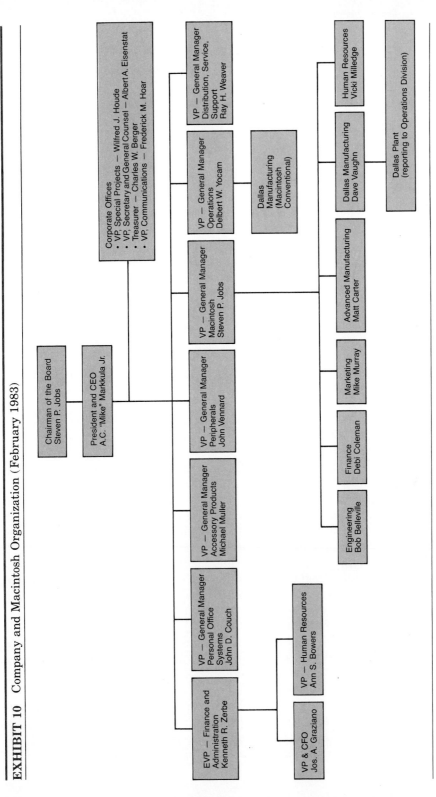

Source: "Apple Computer, Inc.—Macintosh (A)," Stanford University, Graduate School of Business Case #S-BP-234, p. 25, revised 3/12/84.

customers, eventually realizing volumes of up to 1 million units of Macintosh per year. (Final Macintosh specifications are summarized in Exhibit 5.)

In terms of product positioning and target market segments, Mike Murray, director of marketing for the Macintosh, described the product as "a desktop appliance for the knowledge worker." The idea was to provide knowledge workers, that is, people whose major resource was information and ideas (and who in their jobs would take information and ideas and turn them into memos, reports, policies, and plans), with an "appliance" that would enhance their productivity and creativity. (The type of audience at whom the Macintosh was aimed could be described graphically as shown in Exhibit 11.) When initially introduced, it would focus primarily on the office segment and have only small penetration in the fields of education, home, and small business. However, by 1985, the Macintosh was envisioned as the heart of Apple's product offerings in sales volume. As suggested in Exhibit 11, a replacement for the IIe would complement the Macintosh and Lisa products.

From the point of view of all of those working closely with the Macintosh project, the product design represented only half the challenge and half the opportunity associated with Macintosh. The other half involved the transformation of the manufacturing function itself. Here Macintosh not only differed from the Apple II, IIe, and III, but also differed significantly from the Lisa. All of these products were manufactured using the company's "conventional" manufacturing approach (described earlier in the case).

The ideas regarding manufacturing for the Macintosh originated with Steve Jobs and Rod Holt. Rod Holt was an Apple Fellow, one of about half a dozen leaders in the field who were employed by Apple to pursue whatever they wanted. Holt came to Apple in 1977 following work at both National Semiconductor and Kodak. Steve Jobs had read about Japanese manufacturing techniques and became convinced Apple needed to learn and adopt those techniques in order to compete versus IBM and Japan in the long run. Rod Holt had been introduced to automated manufacturing at Kodak and was just as much in favor of it as was Steve.

The manufacturing approach proposed for the Macintosh involved several basic changes from Apple's conventional one. Two of these were particularly significant—the involvement of manufacturing in the product design stage and the incorporation of new technology in the final production process.

In the conventional design process, the product development team essentially completed its design of the product before getting involved with manufacturing as to how the product would be produced. Since Apple (and most other electronics equipment firms, for that matter)

EXHIBIT 11   Product Positioning and Target Segments for Apple Products

A. 1981

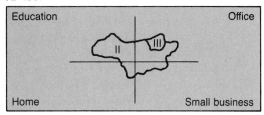

B. 1983–1984 Macintosh introduction

Target markets for Apple IIe		Target markets for Macintosh	
Business	42%		
Family	30%	Business	70%
Education	20%	College	20%
Science/Industry	8%	Home	10%

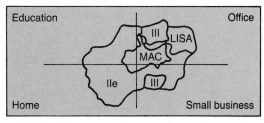

C. 1985–1986

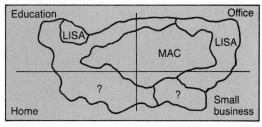

Source: "Apple Computer, Inc.—Macintosh (A)," Stanford University, Graduate School of Business Case #S-BP-234, revised 3/12/84, p. 21.

tended to use simple, readily available, worker dependent manufacturing process technologies, products often could be designed without much consideration of tight tolerances or new capabilities that would require uniqueness in the product's manufacturing process. In fact, in some companies this product design-manufacturing handoff sequence was referred to as "throwing it (the design) over the wall."

The Macintosh was to be designed for manufacturability using a parallel, interactive process between product development and manufacturing process development. In the short term, it was hoped that this parallel, interactive approach would lead to a smoother start-up of production. In the intermediate term, it was intended to result in a more manufacturable product design, providing more stable design, thereby giving lower costs and higher quality. In the long term, an additional potential benefit was that more (and) better features could be built into next-generation products because better processes would have been developed to provide such features. (That is, the product designers would be able to take better advantage of enhanced process capabilities.) In addition, further automation could take place in manufacturing because the initial design would have incorporated the tighter tolerances needed for that automation.

Unfortunately, in the near term, this approach had at least two significant drawbacks: product designers could feel a loss of freedom and, they would argue, a resulting decline in creativity because they were constrained by manufacturing; and, the development process initially might take longer because the systems for the interaction would need to be developed and installed.

A second particularly important aspect of the proposed Macintosh manufacturing approach was that of automation. Simply stated, the concept was to provide better—more efficient, higher quality, and more reliable—production processes. The Macintosh team referred to this as "an enhanced manufacturing capability." One aspect of this enhanced capability was that it required broadening the scope of activities performed on site: that is, with the automated process, more of the manufacturing tasks would be done by Apple rather than being subcontracted or done at Apple's Singapore site. Another was that it implied putting in place a form of technology with the expectation that it would be continually upgraded and enhanced (rather than being put in place once and for all and left unchanged until completely replaced). Two other aspects of this enhanced capability were the development of a focused facility that used a single process technology to produce a single product, and development of a set of control systems uniquely designed to operate that facility.

A third part of the plan called for closer ties to parts vendors and subcontractors. Apple wanted to establish stronger relationships in order to work with the vendors to decrease the percentage of defective parts.

Finally, the Macintosh team planned to automate in two stages. Phase I, to be part of the initial plant construction, would include automated testing, parts documentation, storage and loading, automatic insertion of components into printed circuit boards, and automated final test. Phase I would not impact future product design flexibility and provided somewhat of a hedge against the automation since all of the individual parts of the process had been done somewhere else before. What was different was that no one had put them all together as yet. Phase II would encompass additional automation but would not be developed until 1985, when the Mac team would have more hands-on automated manufacturing experience.

Debi Coleman, controller for the Macintosh, had summarized some of the team's views with regard to the automated production option:

> The automation issue is really one of out-Japanesing the Japanese. Can we? Should we? If we were to do Mac the old way, would we be giving the business away to the Japanese? . . . The type of equipment we'll be using to manufacture Mac has been used in Japan for three to five years. What's new is to put it all together in one factory.[30]

Great debate occurred within Apple regarding the Macintosh manufacturing process. Many people believed the Macintosh team was wildly optimistic about the time frame required to build and ramp up an automated manufacturing facility. There was considerable risk associated with an automated plant: the schedule couldn't slip too much without significant competitive implications regarding the appropriate time to introduce the Macintosh, yet everyone remembered the Apple III problems and so wanted to be absolutely sure the product was debugged, inventory in place, and production ramp-up well under way before the Macintosh was announced. Also, questions arose about the reporting relationships. Traditionally, the product and engineering groups turned the plant over to the Manufacturing Division once it was operational. But the Manufacturing Division had little experience with automated production, and the Macintosh team did not want to turn it over to manufacturing.

For quite some time, the plan was to set up a conventional manufacturing line that would be phased out within about six months, after the automated facility was up and running. However, in the spring of 1984, Steve Jobs decided to cancel the conventional line. At about the same time, the plant location was moved from Dallas, Texas, to Fremont, California, in order for it to be near corporate engineering and headquarters. Apple also decided to do Phase I of the automation at start-up, and Phase II a year later in 1985. Steve Jobs summarized some of his views about the Macintosh and its significance to the entire corporation this way:

> Mac is the Apple II of the 80s. Apple needs to become a manufacturing company and the Macintosh strategy is an offensive manufacturing strategy. With regard to some of the manufacturing options being discussed, I don't believe in alternatives. I believe in putting all my eggs in one basket

---

[30]"Apple Computer, Inc.—Macintosh (A)," Stanford University Graduate School of Business, Case S-BP-234, revised March 1984, p. 11.

and then watching the basket carefully. Then I either succeed or fail co-
lossally. We have three to four years before the Japanese figure out about
computers. We made the decision to do Mac essentially because we wanted
to do it; it's a long-term decision.[31]

The development of the Macintosh cost Apple approximately $35
million. Apple introduced Macintosh on January 24, 1984, with a $15
million launch campaign. On May 21, the company reported it had
shipped more than 70,000 Macintosh computers and that it expected
to sell 250,000 by the end of 1984. In order to meet the demand, Apple
announced that Macintosh manufacturing capacity would be doubled
by the end of 1984.[32]

Sales was a key criterion by which Apple had chosen to measure the
success of the Macintosh during the first 100 days. Other criteria included response from independent software developers and dealers.
Apple reported it received over 5,000 inquiries from independent software developers during the first 100 days, sold 1,000 machines to these
firms, and anticipated 150 software programs by the end of 1984 (50
by the end of the summer). Steve Jobs, chairman, commented:

> Apple set very aggressive goals and we believe that we have exceeded those
> goals. Based on the response we've had so far, we feel that the Macintosh
> is on its way towards becoming the third industry standard product in the
> personal computer business.[33]

THE SITUATION IN LATE 1983 AND EARLY 1984

The second half of calendar 1983 saw IIe sales weaken, Lisa and
III sales continue low, depressed earnings, and the stock price
fall from a high of $63 to $17 per share. Apple management presented a plan to securities analysts which stated that Apple would
be a marketing innovator and an equal leader with IBM in the
personal computer industry—and that they would do it in a year
through new product introductions, a $100 million advertising budget,
and depressed fiscal year 1984 earnings. As President John Sculley
later said, "There's nothing like a life-and-death situation to focus your
priorities."[34]

In January 1984, Apple announced a major company reorganization
into two divisions: the Apple II Division and the Apple 32 Division

---

[31]Ibid., p. 1.
[32]*Silicon Valley Tech News,* May 21, 1984.
[33]Ibid.
[34]Speech by John Sculley, Stanford Graduate School of Business, October 1984.

(referring to the 32-bit microprocessor used in the Lisa and Macintosh products). The divisions were essentially parallel in structure and included all the major functional areas.

The Apple II family would include the IIe, III, and IIc products. It would focus on the home, education, kindergarten-through-12th-grade, and small business markets. It represented older technologies, a consumer goods orientation, and computer ease of use that was more likely to be added on than built in. Del Yocam, who had been vice president of manufacturing, was named executive vice president of the Apple II Division.

The Apple 32 Division would house Lisa and Macintosh and focus more on the college education and corporate environment markets. It had newer technology, and the ease-of-use characteristics tended to be built into the computers rather than added on through enhancements. About a month later, the new division was renamed the Macintosh Division. Steve Jobs, 29, became general manager and retained the role of chairman of the board. As Steve explained, "He (Sculley) is my boss, but in a sense I'm his boss."[35] The majority of the other key management positions in the new division went to Macintosh people. (See Exhibit 12 for mid-1984 company organization chart.)

The marketing function also underwent change. In the summer of 1984, Apple announced that it would terminate its manufacturing representatives and replace them with Apple-trained and -employed reps. Bill Campbell took over as head of the sales area.

Future products allegedly under development included a "Fat Mac" with expanded memory, a terminal emulator, a lap-sized Mac coordinated by Alan Kay, and possibly an educational product.

THE COMPETITIVE ENVIRONMENT, 1984

By 1984, the competitive situation in the personal computer industry was ferocious. IBM continued to gain market share but had been hampered by poor sales of its PCjr. Bill Gates, chairman of the board of Microsoft and the developer of the IBM PC operating system MS–DOS, stated, "IBM is committed to the PCjr. It just has to get the formula right."[36] IBM announced it would modify the PCjr, and in August 1984 announced a much improved machine that included a keyboard similar to the PC, 256K memory (which meant virtually all the PC programs could now be run on the PCjr, including the best-selling integrated spreadsheet program 1-2-3® from Lotus®), and memory expandable to

---

[35]"Apple Bites Back," *Fortune,* February 20, 1984, p. 100.
[36]Freiberger and Swaine, *Fire in the Valley.*

EXHIBIT 12 Company Organization, September 1984

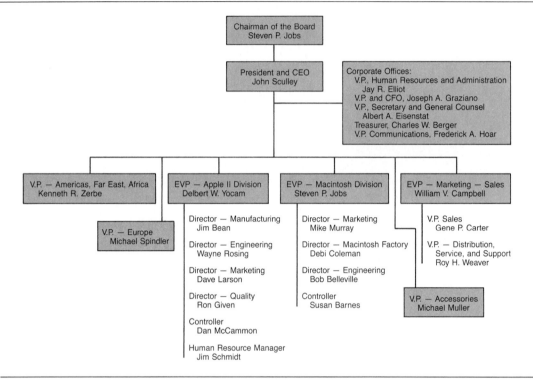

512K. A few weeks later, IBM announced two PC networking products. (See Exhibit 13 for Apple and IBM product and price comparisons.) In many ways, IBM had broken with their corporate tradition to do things the way other personal computer firms did (e.g., open hardware architecture, use of outside suppliers and software developers, distribution through retail channels). However, the question remained whether the personal computer market would ever resemble the mainframe market of the 1960s when a popular saying was that "IBM was not the Competition, it was the Environment."[37]

Hewlett-Packard was also clearly committed to the personal computer market, although H-P got a slow start, having begun development of a personal computer in 1976 but not having introduced one until 1981. H-P's 150 was reputed to be selling well to corporate accounts (their historic strengths), though not nearly as well through retail distribution channels.

---

[37]Ibid., p. 276.

EXHIBIT 13   Selected Apple and IBM Product Offerings* (Retail Prices, October 1984)

Price	Apple	IBM
$0		
		■ Notebook (anticipated) ($800–900) – 16-bit, 128K – No monitor
$1,000		
	■ IIe ($1,224) – 8-bit, 64K, 1dd† ■ IIc portable ($1,295) – 8-bit, 128K ■ IIe ($1,795) – 8-bit, 128K, 2dd	
$2,000		
	■ Macintosh ($2,195) – 32-bit, 128K, 1dd, mouse ■ III + ($2,995) – 8-bit, 256K, 1dd	■ PCjr expanded ($2,035) – 16-bit, 128K, 1dd ■ PC ($2,920) – 16-bit 256K, 2dd – Color monitor
$3,000		
	■ Macintosh ($3,195) – 32-bit, 512K, 1dd, mouse ■ Lisa 2 ($3,495) – 32-bit, 512K, 1dd, mouse	■ PC ($3,920) – 16-bit, 512K, 2dd – Color monitor
$4,000		
	■ Lisa 2/5 ($4,495) – Same as Lisa 2, plus 5MB‡ hdd	■ PC XT ($4,800) – 16-bit, 256K, 1dd, 10MB hdd
$5,000		
	■ Lisa 2/10 ($5,495) – Same as Lisa 2, plus 10MB hdd	■ PC AT ($5,220) – 16-bit, 256K, 1.2MB dd
$6,000		
		■ PC AT enhanced ($6,320) – 16-bit, 512K, 1.2MB dd, 20MB hdd
$7,000		

* All product prices include a monochrome monitor and adapter (if needed), unless otherwise stated.
† 8-bit microprocessor. 64 kilobytes memory. 1 floppy disk drive.
‡ MB = megabyte. hdd = hard disk drive.

Sources: Businessland sales representative, Los Altos, California; Computerland sales representative, Los Altos, California; *The Wall Street Journal*, August 15, 1984, p. 3; *Fortune*, February 20, 1984, p. 88.

The demise of four other personal computer manufacturers had occurred in the previous 12 months: Victor, Franklin, Atari, and Osborne. Gavilan Corporation, which had planned to introduce a lap-sized computer in mid-1983, still couldn't ship product due to manufacturing difficulties. As a result, Gavilan had missed its window of opportunity in the marketplace, and many industry observers believed the company would not survive. Grid Systems, one of the first firms to develop a portable computer, was now focusing primarily on military applications and customers since its high quality and high price were out of most business and consumer price/performance ranges.

There also continued to be concern about the Japanese. One key concern was potential aggressive entry into the U.S. personal computer market by Japanese firms. Another was the projection that by the end of 1984, the Japanese would have overtaken the United States in *every* major consumer electronics industry.

THE SITUATION IN 1984, AND A LOOK TOWARD THE FUTURE

As computer industry experts observed the personal computer industry in mid-1984 and speculated on Apple Computer, Inc.'s, future, the key question regarding Apple was "Where to go from here?"

There was a whole range of strategic questions for Apple to confront:

1. What will their long-term position be vis-à-vis IBM in 1987 or 1990, when the personal computer market reaches $25 billion in size? Will Apple be able to maintain a large market share?
2. What should be done with the Apple II family? Especially given the fact that the IIe was back selling well above company expectations, and that initially, at least, it appeared that Macintosh sales were not cannibalizing IIe sales to the degree that had been anticipated.
3. Where to go with the Macintosh?
4. What to do about the Accessory Products Division?
5. How to handle issues related to systems integration and integrating communications capabilities (many other firms were entering partnerships in these areas)?
6. How to continue managing growth, at approximately 25 percent per year, while maintaining the Apple culture?
7. How to improve the product development process and related questions of organization, learning, etc.?

John Sculley, president and CEO of Apple since June 1983, summarized his views on Apple's past, present, and future:

> In the past, people at Apple were free to work on any neat idea. There was no strategic plan, no strategic discipline, little thought of where products fit in the marketplace.
>
> From day 1 of my arrival through month 10, I spent lots of time delineating a product line strategy. Now, all products fit into our two families of products: the Apple II family for education, small business, and serious home users and the Macintosh Division for users in an office environment.

I want to cautiously avoid market research. The industry is too new, market research doesn't have a good track record; intuition and insight are still required. I'm against market research designing products. If research did it, there'd be other great products on the market. I think research designed the IBM PCjr. However, I firmly believe you still have to do lots of basic homework before you design a product: such things as technology, competition, distribution. Then I prefer a small team of people.

Apple is a great product company. It has a group of people who love great products, who have driving passion. But I want it to be a great product marketing company also.[38]

---

[38]Interview with John Sculley, September 18, 1984.

Research Policy, December 1985. © 1985, Elsevier Science Publishers B.V. (North-Holland). Reprinted with permission.

Promotion Strategy

General Foods*

Jerry C. Olson

Penn State University

In 1984, General Foods' Post cereal division suffered a drubbing at the hands of Kellogg, the market leader. Kellogg had begun to turn up the competitive heat in the early 1980s by increasing advertising expenditures and introducing a stream of new cereal products. During 1984, Kellogg increased its market share by 2 percent (up to 40 percent), while number-three-ranked GF dropped 2 percent (down to a 14 percent market share). The number two company, General Mills, held on to about a 20 percent market share, which had not changed significantly since 1980. These were not small changes. The ready-to-eat cereal market is a $4 billion market, so each share point was worth about $40 million in sales.

*This case was written by Jerry C. Olson, George and Lillian Binder Professor of Marketing, Penn State University. It is adapted from J. Paul Peter and Jerry C. Olson, *Consumer Behavior: Marketing Strategy Perspectives* (Homewood Ill.: Richard D. Irwin, 1987), pp. 657–58. Original source: Excerpted from Pamela Sherrid, "Fighting Back at Breakfast," *Forbes,* October 7, 1985, pp. 126–30.

Post did have one hugely successful product in 1984, Fruit & Fiber, which cleverly satisfied two potentially contradictory desires of adult cereal consumers—a healthful cereal that tastes good. On the negative side was the costly failure of Smurfberry Crunch that fizzled early despite very heavy advertising promotion. The heavy ad expenditures on these two brands had left little for promoting the other Post brands. So, while Kellogg was gearing up for its ad blitz, Post actually reduced ad spending by 24 percent to $44 million. Instead, GF spent additional promotional dollars on cents-off coupons and discounts to grocers. This strategy encouraged one-time sales, but didn't build long-term loyalty the way advertising does. In 1984, the disparity got worse, Kellogg increased its advertising spending by 49 percent to $160 million, while GF's rose only 16 percent to $52 million. At the same time Post's share sank from 15.5 to 14.6 percent.

But a different strategy was being planned at GF. Management decided to increase ad spending to match Kellogg's—but not over all its 14 brands. Instead, it would concentrate its dollars on five core brands—Raisin Bran, Grape Nuts, Fruit & Fiber, Super Golden Crisp, and Pebbles—which together account for 75 percent of Post's cereal sales. They increased ad expenditures by 40 percent in 1984 and again in 1985. But dollars alone don't do the trick in the cereal business. According to David Hurwitt, who runs GF's $500-million Post cereal business, "It costs just as much to run a lousy commercial as a good one." In fact, one of the reasons Post ad spending had decreased in 1983 was because GF (and their ad agencies) couldn't come up with the right advertising strategies and campaigns. Why spend money to show ineffective advertising?

More than most products, cereal is what marketers call "marketing sensitive." Dollars spent on mediocre marketing simply fall into the void—they have no noticeable effect. The same amount of money, however, spent on a well-designed communication strategy can dramatically increase sales. For instance, Post's Grape Nuts campaign—with its tag line "Are you right for Grape Nuts?"—offended many people. However, sales increased about 10 percent, compared to industry growth of only 3 percent.

Post's strategy was illustrated by the new campaign for Raisin Bran, launched in late 1985 at a cost of about $15 million. Hurwitt had changed the product to fit people's tendencies to eat what they think are "natural" foods. He removed the preservatives, increased the fiber, and took the sugar off the raisins. Then he hired singer John Denver—to some people the essence of all that is wholesome—for about $1 million to pitch the new product in a series of TV ads. Late in 1985, GF introduced another new cereal called Horizon, aimed at the active adult segment. The cereal is based on a "trail mix" concept, which means peanuts and grains clumped together, not in flakes.

Will Post's strategies work? The odds aren't good. Of dozens of new product entries, only a few cereals such as General Mill's Honey Nut Cheerios and Post's Fruit & Fiber have earned a sustainable 1 percent share in recent years. It's a big risk, but the potential payoffs are big, too.

Discussion Questions

1. Assume you are the brand manager for Raisin Bran. Present your arguments explaining why it is reasonable to spend $15 million in advertising on your brand even though only small (perhaps only 1 percent) shifts in market share are likely to be created. Make assumptions about the other costs that may be involved.
2. What are the relative advantages and disadvantages of using advertising and sales promotion strategies such as cents-off coupons, price reductions, and prizes and premiums to promote breakfast cereals?

Outdoor Sporting Products, Inc.*

Zarrel V. Lambert

Auburn University

Fred W. Kniffen

University of Connecticut

The annual sales volume of Outdoor Sporting Products, Inc., for the past six years had ranged between $6.2 million and $6.8 million. Although profits continued to be satisfactory, Mr. Hudson McDonald, president and chief operating officer, was concerned because sales had not increased appreciably from year to year. Consequently, he asked a consultant in New York City and the officers of the company to submit proposals for improving the salesmen's compensation plan, which he believed was the basic weakness in the firm's marketing operations.

Outdoor's factory and warehouse were located in Albany, New York, where the company manufactured and distributed sporting equipment, clothing, and accessories. Mr. Hudson McDonald, who managed the company, organized it in 1956 when he envisioned a growing market for sporting goods resulting from the predicted increase in leisure time and the rising levels of income in the United States.

Products of the company, numbering approximately 700 items, were grouped into three lines: (1) fishing supplies, (2) hunting supplies, and (3) accessories. The fishing supplies line, which accounted for approximately 40 percent of the company's annual sales, included nearly every item a fisherman would need such as fishing jackets, vests, caps, rods and reels of all types, lines, flies, lures, landing nets, and creels. Thirty percent of annual sales were in the hunting supplies line, which consisted of hunting clothing of all types including insulated and thermal underwear, safety garments, shell holders, whistles, calls, and gun cases. The accessories line, which made up the balance of the company's annual sales volume, included items such as compasses, cooking kits, lanterns, hunting and fishing knives, hand warmers, and novelty gifts.

---

*Adapted from a case written by Zarrel V. Lambert, Auburn University, and Fred W. Kniffen, University of Connecticut, Stamford. Used with permission.

While the sales of the hunting and fishing lines were very seasonal, they tended to complement one another. The January-April period accounted for the bulk of the company's annual volume in fishing items, and most sales of hunting supplies were made during the months of May through August. Typically, the company's sales of all products reached their lows for the year during the month of December.

Outdoor's sales volume was $6.57 million in the current year with self-manufactured products accounting for 35 percent of this total. Fifty percent of the company's volume consisted of imported products, which came principally from Japan. Items manufactured by other domestic producers and distributed by Outdoor accounted for the remaining 15 percent of total sales.

Mr. McDonald reported that wholesale prices to retailers were established by adding a markup of 50 to 100 percent to Outdoor's cost for the item. This rule was followed on self-manufactured products as well as for items purchased from other manufacturers. The resulting average markup across all products was 70 percent on cost.

Outdoor's market area consisted of the New England states, New York, Pennsylvania, Ohio, Michigan, Wisconsin, Indiana, Illinois, Kentucky, Tennessee, West Virginia, Virginia, Maryland, Delaware, and New Jersey. The area over which Outdoor could effectively compete was limited to some extent by shipping costs, since all orders were shipped from the factory and warehouse in Albany.

Outdoor's salesmen sold to approximately 6,000 retail stores in small- and medium-sized cities in its market area. Analysis of sales records showed that the firm's customer coverage was very poor in the large metropolitan areas. Typically, each account was a one- or two-store operation. Mr. McDonald stated that he knew for a fact that Outdoor's share of the market was very low, perhaps 2 to 3 percent; and for all practical purposes, he felt the company's sales potential was unlimited.

Mr. McDonald believed that with few exceptions, Outdoor's customers had little or no brand preference and in the vast majority of cases they bought hunting and fishing supplies from several suppliers.

It was McDonald's opinion that the pattern of retail distribution for hunting and fishing products had been changing during the past 10 years as a result of the growth of discount stores. He thought that the proportion of retail sales for hunting and fishing supplies made by small- and medium-sized sporting goods outlets had been declining compared to the percent sold by discounters and chain stores. An analysis of company records revealed Outdoor had not developed business among the discounters with the exception of a few small discount stores. Some of Outdoor's executives felt that the lack of business with discounters might have been due in part to the company's pricing policy and in part to the pressures which current customers had exerted on company salesmen to keep them from calling on the discounters.

Outdoor's Sales Force

The company's sales force played the major role in its marketing efforts since Outdoor did not use magazine, newspaper, or radio advertising to reach either the retail trade or consumers. One advertising piece that supplemented the work of the salesmen was Outdoor's merchandise catalog. It contained a complete listing of all the company's products and was mailed to all retailers who were either current accounts or prospective accounts. Typically, store buyers used the catalog for purposes of reordering.

Most accounts were contacted by a salesman two or three times a year. The salesmen planned their activities so that each store would be called upon at the beginning of the fishing season and again prior to the hunting season. Certain key accounts of some salesmen were contacted more often than two or three times a year.

Management believed that product knowledge was the major ingredient of a successful sales call. Consequently, Mr. McDonald had developed a "selling formula," which each salesman was required to learn before he took over a territory. The "formula" contained five parts: (1) the name and catalog number of each item sold by the company; (2) the sizes and colors in which each item was available; (3) the wholesale price of each item; (4) the suggested retail price of each item; and (5) the primary selling features of each item. After a new salesman had mastered the product knowledge specified by this "formula," he began working in his assigned territory and was usually accompanied by Mr. McDonald for several weeks.

Managing the sales force consumed approximately one third of Mr. McDonald's efforts. The remaining two thirds of his time was spent purchasing products for resale and in general administrative duties as the company's chief operating officer.

Mr. McDonald held semiannual sales meetings, had weekly telephone conversations with each salesman, and had mimeographed bulletins containing information on products, prices, and special promotional deals mailed to all salesmen each week. Daily call reports and attendance at the semiannual sales meetings were required of all salesmen. One meeting was held the first week of January to introduce the spring line of fishing supplies. The hunting line was presented at the second meeting, which was scheduled in May. Each of these sales meetings spanned four to five days so the salesmen were able to study the new products being introduced and any changes in sales and company policies. The production manager and comptroller attended these sales meetings to answer questions and to discuss problems the salesmen might have concerning deliveries and credit.

On a predetermined schedule each salesman telephoned Mr. McDonald every Monday morning to learn of changes in prices, special promotional offers, and delivery schedules of unshipped orders. At this time the salesman's activities for the week were discussed, and sometimes the salesman was asked by Mr. McDonald to collect past-due accounts in his territory. In addition, the salesmen submitted daily call reports, which listed the name of each account contacted and the results of the call. Generally, the salesmen planned their own itineraries in terms of the accounts and prospects that were to be contacted and the amount of time to be spent on each call.

Outdoor's sales force during the current year totaled 11 full-time employees. Their ages ranged from 23 to 67 years, and their tenure with the company ranged from 1 to 10 years. Salesmen, territories, and sales volumes for the previous year and the current year are shown in Exhibit 1.

EXHIBIT 1   Salesmen: Age, Years of Service, Territory, and Sales

| | | | | Sales | |
| | | | | *Previous* | *Current* |
Salesmen	*Age*	Years of *Service*	*Territory*	*Year*	*Year*
Allen	45	2	Illinois and Indiana	$ 330,264	$ 329,216
Campbell	62	10	Pennsylvania	1,192,192	1,380,240
Duvall	23	1	New England	—	414,656
Edwards	39	1	Michigan	—	419,416
Gatewood	63	5	West Virginia	358,528	358,552
Hammond	54	2	Virginia	414,936	414,728
Logan	37	1	Kentucky and Tennessee	—	447,720
Mason	57	2	Delaware and Maryland	645,032	825,088
O'Bryan	59	4	Ohio	343,928	372,392
Samuels	42	3	New York and New Jersey	737,024	824,472
Wates	67	5	Wisconsin	370,712	342,200
Salesmen terminated in previous year				1,828,816	—
House account				257,384	244,480
Total				$6,478,816	$6,374,816

Compensation of Salesmen

The salesmen were paid straight commissions on their dollar sales volume for the calendar year. The commission rate was 5 percent on the first $300,000, 6 percent on the next $200,000 in volume, and 7 percent on all sales over $500,000 for the year. Each week a salesman could draw all or a portion of his accumulated commissions. Mr. McDonald encouraged the salesmen to draw commissions as they accumulated since he felt the men were motivated to work harder when they had a very small or zero balance in their commission accounts. These accounts were closed at the end of the year so each salesman began the new year with nothing in his account.

The salesmen provided their own automobiles and paid their traveling expenses, of which all or a portion were reimbursed per diem. Under the per diem plan, each salesman received $70 per day for Monday through Thursday and $42 for Friday, or a total of $322 for the normal workweek. No per diem was paid for Saturday, but a salesman received an additional $70 if he spent Saturday and Sunday nights in the territory.

In addition to the commission and per diem, a salesman could earn cash awards under two sales incentive plans that were installed two years ago. Under the Annual Sales Increase Awards Plan, a total of $10,400 was paid to the five salesmen having the largest percentage increase in dollar sales volume over the previous year. To be eligible for these awards, a salesman had to show a sales increase over the previous year. These awards were made at the January sales meeting, and the winners were determined by dividing the dollar amount of each salesman's increase by his volume for the previous year with the percentage increases ranked in descending order. The salesmen's earnings under this plan for the current year are shown in Exhibit 2.

Under the second incentive plan, each salesman could win a Weekly Sales Increase Award for each week in which his dollar volume in the current year exceeded his sales for the corresponding week in the previous year. Beginning with an award of $4 for the first week, the amount of the award increased by $4 for each week in which the salesman surpassed his sales for the comparable week in the previous year. If a salesman produced higher sales during each of the 50 weeks in the current year, he received $4 for the 1st week, $8 for the 2nd week, and $200 for the 50th week, or a total of $4,100 for the year. The salesman had to be employed by the company during the previous year to be eligible for these awards. A check for the total amount of the awards accrued during the year was presented to the salesmen at the sales meeting held in January. Earnings of the salesmen under this plan for the current year are shown in Exhibit 2.

EXHIBIT 2   Salesmen's Earnings and Incentive Awards in the Current Year

Salesmen	Sales Previous Year	Sales Current Year	Annual Sales Increase Awards Increase in Sales (percent)	Annual Sales Increase Awards Award	Weekly Sales Increase Awards (total accrued)	Earnings*
Allen	$ 330,264	$ 329,216	(0.3%)	—	$1,012	$30,000†
Campbell	1,192,192	1,380,240	15.8	$3,000 (2d)	2,244	88,167
Duvall	—	414,656	—	—	—	30,000†
Edwards	—	419,416	—	—	—	30,000†
Gatewood	358,528	358,552	(0.1)	400 (5th)	1,104	18,513
Hammond	414,936	414,728	—	—	420	30,000†
Logan	—	447,720	—	—	—	30,000†
Mason	645,032	825,088	27.9	4,000 (1st)	3,444	49,756
O'Bryan	343,928	372,392	8.3	1,000 (4th)	1,512	19,344
Samuels	737,024	824,472	11.9	2,000 (3d)	1,300	49,713
Wates	370,712	342,200	(7.7)	—	612	17,532

*Exclusive of incentive awards and per diem.
†Guarantee of $600 per week or $30,000 per year.

The company frequently used "spiffs" to promote the sales of special items. The salesman was paid a spiff, which usually was $4, for each order he obtained for the designated items in the promotion.

For the past three years in recruiting salesmen, Mr. McDonald had guaranteed the more qualified applicants a weekly income while they learned the business and developed their respective territories. During the current year five salesmen—Allen, Duvall, Edwards, Hammond, and Logan—had a guarantee of $600 a week, which they drew against their commissions. If the year's cumulative commissions for any of these salesmen were less than their cumulative weekly drawing accounts, they received no commissions. The commission and drawing accounts were closed on December 31 so each salesman began the new year with a zero balance in each account.

The company did not have a stated or written policy specifying the maximum length of time a salesman could receive a guarantee if his commissions continued to be less than his draw. Mr. McDonald held the opinion that the five salesmen who currently had guarantees would quit if these guarantees were withdrawn before their commissions reached $30,000 per year.

Mr. McDonald stated that he was convinced the annual earnings of Outdoor's salesmen had fallen behind earnings for comparable selling positions, particularly in the past six years. As a result, he felt that the company's ability to attract and hold high-caliber professional salesmen was being adversely affected. He strongly expressed the opinion that each salesman should be earning $50,000 annually.

Compensation Plan Proposals

In December of the current year, Mr. McDonald met with the comptroller and production manager, who were the only other executives of the company, and solicited their ideas concerning changes in the company's compensation plan for salesmen.

The comptroller pointed out that the salesmen having guarantees were not producing the sales that had been expected from their territories. He was concerned that the annual commissions earned by four of the five salesmen on guarantees were approximately half or less than their drawing accounts.

Furthermore, according to the comptroller, several of the salesmen who did not have guarantees were producing a relatively low volume of sales year after year. For example, annual sales remained at relatively low levels for Gatewood, O'Bryan, and Wates, who had been working four to five years in their respective territories.

The comptroller proposed that guarantees be reduced to $250 per week plus commissions at the regular rate on all sales. The $250 would not be drawn against commissions as was the case under the existing plan but would be in addition to any commissions earned. In the comptroller's opinion, this plan would motivate the salesmen to increase sales rapidly since their incomes would rise directly with their sales. The comptroller presented Exhibit 3, which showed the incomes of the five salesmen having guarantees in the current year as compared with the incomes they would have received under his plan.

From a sample check of recent shipments, the production manager had concluded that the salesmen tended to overwork accounts located within a 50-mile radius of their homes. Sales coverage was extremely light in a 60- to 100-mile radius of the salesmen's homes, with somewhat better coverage beyond 100 miles. He argued that this pattern of sales coverage seemed to result from a desire by the salesmen to spend most evenings during the week at home with their families.

He proposed that the per diem be increased from $70 to $90 per day for Monday through Thursday, $42 for Friday, and $90 for Sunday if the salesman spent Sunday evening away from his home. He reasoned that the per diem of $90 for Sunday would act as a strong incentive for the salesmen to drive to the perimeters of their territories on Sunday evenings rather than use Monday morning for traveling. Further, he believed that the increase in per diem would encourage the salesmen

EXHIBIT 3   Comparison of Earnings in Current Year under Existing Guarantee Plan with Earnings under the Comptroller's Plan*

| | | *Existing Plan* | | | *Comptroller's Plan* | | |
| | | Com- | Guar- | | Com- | Guar- | |
Salesmen	Sales	missions	antee	Earnings	missions	antee	Earnings
Allen	$329,216	$16,753	$30,000	$30,000	$16,753	$12,500	$29,253
Duvall	414,656	21,879	30,000	30,000	21,879	12,500	34,379
Edwards	419,416	22,165	30,000	30,000	22,165	12,500	34,665
Hammond	358,552	18,513	30,000	30,000	18,513	12,500	31,013
Logan	447,720	23,863	30,000	30,000	23,863	12,500	36,363

*Exclusive of incentive awards and per diem.

to spend more evenings away from their homes, which would result in a more uniform coverage of the sales territories and an overall increase in sales volume.

The consultant from New York City recommended that the guarantees and per diem be retained on the present basis and proposed that Outdoor adopt what he called a "Ten Percent Self-Improvement Plan." Under the consultant's plan each salesman would be paid, in addition to the regular commission, a monthly bonus commission of 10 percent on all dollar volume over his sales in the comparable month of the previous year. For example, if a salesman sold $40,000 worth of merchandise in January of the current year and $36,000 in January of the previous year, he would receive a $400 bonus check in February. For salesmen on guarantees, bonuses would be in addition to earnings. The consultant reasoned that the bonus commission would motivate the salesmen, both those with and without guarantees, to increase their sales.

He further recommended the discontinuation of the two sales incentive plans currently in effect. He felt the savings from these plans would nearly cover the costs of his proposal.

Following a discussion of these proposals with the management group, Mr. McDonald was undecided on which proposal to adopt, if any. Further, he wondered if any change in the compensation of salesmen would alleviate all of the present problems.

Hanover-Bates Chemical Corporation*

Robert E. Witt

University of Texas–Austin

James Sprague, newly appointed northeast district sales manager for the Hanover-Bates Chemical Corporation, leaned back in his chair as the door to his office slammed shut. "Great beginning," he thought. "Three days in my new job and the district's most experienced sales representative is threatening to quit."

On the previous night, James Sprague, Hank Carver (the district's most experienced sales representative), and John Follet, another senior member of the district sales staff, had met for dinner at Jim's suggestion. During dinner Jim had mentioned that one of his top priorities would be to conduct a sales and profit analysis of the district's business in order to identify opportunities to improve the district's profit performance. Jim had stated that he was confident that the analysis would indicate opportunities to reallocate district sales efforts in a manner that would increase profits. As Jim had indicated during the conversation, "My experience in analyzing district sales performance data for the national sales manager has convinced me that any district's allocation of sales effort to products and customer categories can be improved." Both Carver and Follet had nodded as Jim discussed his plans.

Hank Carver was waiting when Jim arrived at the district sales office the next morning. It soon became apparent that Carver was very upset by what he perceived as Jim's criticism of how he and the other district sales representatives were doing their jobs—and, more particularly, how they were allocating their time in terms of customers and products. As he concluded his heated comments, Carver said:

> This company has made it darned clear that 34 years of experience don't count for anything . . . and now someone with not much more than two years of selling experience and two years of pushing paper for the national sales

---

*This case was prepared by Professor Robert E. Witt, University of Texas, Austin, and is intended to serve as a basis for class discussion rather than to illustrate effective or ineffective management.

manager at corporate headquarters tells me I'm not doing my job. . . . Maybe it's time for me to look for a new job . . . and since Trumbull Chemical [Hanover-Bates's major competitor] is hiring, maybe that's where I should start looking . . . and I'm not the only one who feels this way.

As Jim reflected on the scene that had just occurred, he wondered what he should do. It had been made clear to him when he had been promoted to manager of the northeast sales district that one of his top priorities should be improvement of the district's profit performance. As the national sales manager had said, "The northeast sales district may rank third in dollar sales, but it's our worst district in terms of profit performance."

Prior to assuming his new position, Jim had assembled the data presented in Exhibits 1 through 6 to assist him in analyzing district sales and profits. The data had been compiled from records maintained in the national sales manager's office. Although he believed the data would provide a sound basis for a preliminary analysis of district sales and profit performance, Jim had recognized that additional data would probably have to be collected when he arrived in the northeast district (District 3).

In response to the national sales manager's comment about the northeast district's poor profit performance, Jim had been particularly interested in how the district had performed on its gross profit quota. He knew that district gross profit quotas were assigned in a manner that took into account variation in price competition. Thus he felt that poor performance in the gross profit quota area reflected misallocated sales efforts either in terms of customers or in the mix of product line items sold. To provide himself with a frame of reference, Jim had also requested data on the north-central sales district (District 7). This district was generally considered to be one of the best, if not the best,

---

EXHIBIT 1   Hanover-Bates Chemical Corporation: Summary Income Statements, 1981–1985

	1981	*1982*	*1983*	*1984*	*1985*
Sales	$19,890,000	$21,710,000	$19,060,000	$21,980,000	$23,890,000
Production expenses	11,934,000	13,497,000	12,198,000	13,612,000	14,563,000
Gross profit	7,956,000	8,213,000	6,862,000	8,368,000	9,327,000
Administrative expenses	2,606,000	2,887,000	2,792,000	2,925,000	3,106,000
Selling expenses	2,024,000	2,241,000	2,134,000	2,274,000	2,399,000
Pretax profit	3,326,000	3,085,000	1,936,000	3,169,000	3,822,000
Taxes	1,512,000	1,388,000	790,000	1,426,000	1,718,000
Net profit	$ 1,814,000	$ 1,697,000	$ 1,146,000	$ 1,743,000	$ 2,104,000

in the company. Furthermore, the north-central district sales manager, who was only three years older than Jim, was highly regarded by the national sales manager.

THE COMPANY AND INDUSTRY

The Hanover-Bates Chemical Corporation was a leading producer of processing chemicals for the chemical plating industry. The company's products were produced in four plants located in Los Angeles, Houston,

EXHIBIT 2   District Sales Quota and Gross Profit Quota Performance, 1985

District	Number of Sales Reps	Sales		Gross Profit	
		Quota	Actual	Quota*	Actual
1	7	$ 3,880,000	$ 3,906,000	$1,552,000	$1,589,000
2	6	3,750,000	3,740,000	1,500,000	1,529,000
3	6	3,650,000	3,406,000	1,460,000	1,239,000
4	6	3,370,000	3,318,000	1,348,000	1,295,000
5	5	3,300,000	3,210,000	1,320,000	1,186,000
6	5	3,130,000	3,205,000	1,252,000	1,179,000
7	5	2,720,000	3,105,000	1,088,000	1,310,000
		$23,800,000	$23,890,000	$9,520,000	$9,327,000

*District gross profit quotas were developed by the national sales manager in consultation with the district managers and took into account price competition in the respective districts.

EXHIBIT 3   District Selling Expenses, 1985

District	Sales Rep Salaries*	Sales Commission	Sales Rep Expenses	District Office	District Manager Salary	District Manager Expenses	Sales Support	Total Selling Expenses
1	$177,100	$19,426	$56,280	$21,150	$33,500	$11,460	$69,500	$ 388,416
2	143,220	18,700	50,760	21,312	34,000	12,034	71,320	351,346
3	157,380	17,030	54,436	22,123	35,000†	12,382	70,010	368,529
4	150,480	16,590	49,104	22,004	32,500	11,005	66,470	348,153
5	125,950	16,050	42,720	21,115	33,000	11,123	76,600	326,558
6	124,850	16,265	41,520	20,992	33,500	11,428	67,100	315,655
7	114,850	17,530	44,700	22,485	31,500	11,643	58,750	$ 300,258
								$2,398,915

*Includes cost of fringe-benefit program, which was 10 percent of base salary.
†Salary of Jim Sprague's predecessor.

EXHIBIT 4   District Contribution to Corporate Administrative Expense and Profit, 1985

District	Sales	Gross Profit	Selling Expenses	Contribution to Administrative Expense and Profit
1	$ 3,906,000	$1,589,000	$ 388,416	$1,200,544
2	3,740,000	1,529,000	351,346	1,177,654
3	3,406,000	1,239,000	368,529	870,471
4	3,318,000	1,295,000	348,153	946,847
5	3,210,000	1,186,000	326,558	859,442
6	3,205,000	1,179,000	315,376	863,624
7	3,105,000	1,310,000	300,258	1,009,742
	$23,890,000	$9,327,000	$2,398,636	$6,928,324

EXHIBIT 5   Northeast (#3) and North-Central (#7) District Sales and Gross Profit Performance by Account Category, 1985

District	(A)	(B)	(C)	Total
Sales by Account Category				
Northeast	$915,000	$1,681,000	$810,000	$3,406,000
North-central	751,000	1,702,000	652,000	3,105,000
Gross Profit by Account Category				
Northeast	$356,000	$ 623,000	$260,000	$1,239,000
North-central	330,000	725,000	255,000	1,310,000

Chicago, and Newark, New Jersey. The company's production process was, in essence, a mixing operation. Chemicals purchased from a broad range of suppliers were mixed according to a variety of user-based formulas. Company sales in 1985 had reached a new high of $23.89 million, up from $21.98 million in 1984. Net pretax profit in 1985 had been $3.822 million, up from $3.169 million in 1984. Hanover-Bates had a strong balance sheet, and the company enjoyed a favorable price-earnings ratio on its stock, which traded on the OTC market.

Although Hanover-Bates did not produce commodity-type chemicals (e.g., sulfuric acid and others), industry customers tended to perceive minimal quality differences among the products produced by Hanover-Bates and its competitors. Given the lack of variation in product quality and the industrywide practice of limited advertising expenditures, field sales efforts were of major importance in the marketing programs of all firms in the industry.

EXHIBIT 6   Potential Accounts, Active Accounts, and Account Call Coverage: Northeast and North-Central Districts, 1985

District	Potential Accounts			Active Accounts			Account Coverage (total calls)		
	(A)	*(B)*	*(C)*	*(A)*	*(B)*	*(C)*	*(A)*	*(B)*	*(C)*
Northeast	90	381	635	53	210	313	1,297	3,051	2,118
North-central	60	286	499	42	182	218	1,030	2,618	1,299

Hanover-Bates's market consisted of several thousand job-shop and captive (in-house) plating operations. Chemical platers process a wide variety of materials including industrial fasteners (e.g., screws, rivets, bolts, washers, and others), industrial components (e.g., clamps, casing, coupling, and others), and miscellaneous items (e.g., umbrella frames, eyelets, decorative items, and others). The chemical plating process involves the electrolytic application of metallic coatings such as zinc, cadmium, nickel, brass, and so forth. The degree of required plating precision varies substantially, with some work being primarily decorative, some involving relatively loose standards (e.g., 0.0002 zinc, which means that anything over two ten-thousandths of an inch of plate is acceptable) and some involving relatively precise standards (e.g., 0.0003–0.0004 zinc).

Regardless of the degree of plating precision involved, quality control is of critical concern to all chemical platers. Extensive variation in the condition of materials received for plating requires a high level of service from the firms supplying chemicals to platers. This service is normally provided by the sales representatives of the firm(s) supplying the plater with processing chemicals.

Hanover-Bates and the majority of the firms in its industry produced the same line of basic processing chemicals for the chemical plating industry. The line consisted of a trisodium phosphate cleaner (SBX), anesic aldahyde brightening agents for zinc plating (ZBX), cadmium plating (CBX) and nickel plating (NBX), a protective post-plating chromate dip (CHX), and a protective burnishing compound (BUX). The company's product line is detailed as follows:

Product	Container Size	List Price	Gross Margin
SPX	400-lb. drum	$ 80	$28
ZBX	50-lb. drum	76	34
CBX	50-lb. drum	76	34
NBX	50-lb. drum	80	35
CHX	100-lb. drum	220	90
BUX	400-lb. drum	120	44

COMPANY SALES ORGANIZATION

Hanover-Bates's sales organization consisted of 40 sales representatives operating in seven sales districts. Sales representatives' salaries ranged from $14,000 to $24,000, with fringe-benefit costs amounting to an additional 10 percent of salary. In addition to their salaries, Hanover-Bates's sales representatives received commissions of 0.5 percent of their dollar sales volume on all sales up to their sales quotas. The commission on sales in excess of quota was 1 percent.

In 1983 the national sales manager of Hanover-Bates had developed a sales program based on selling the full line of Hanover-Bates products. He believed that if the sales representatives could successfully carry out his program, benefits would accrue to both Hanover-Bates and its customers:

1. Sales volume per account would be greater and selling costs as a percentage of sales would decrease.
2. A Hanover-Bates's sales representative could justify spending more time with such an account, thus becoming more knowledgeable about the account's business and becoming better able to provide technical assistance and identify selling opportunities.
3. Full-line sales would strengthen Hanover-Bates's competitive position by reducing the likelihood of account loss to other plating chemical suppliers (a problem that existed in multiple-supplier situations).

The national sales manager's 1983 sales program had also included the following account call-frequency guidelines:

- A accounts (major accounts generating $12,000 or more in yearly sales)—two calls per month.
- B accounts (medium-sized accounts generating $6,000–$11,999 in yearly sales)—one call per month.
- C accounts (small accounts generating less than $6,000 yearly in sales)—one call every two months.

The account call-frequency guidelines were developed by the national sales manager after discussions with the district managers. The national sales manager had been concerned about the optimum allocation of sales effort to accounts and felt that the guidelines would increase the efficiency of the company's sales force, although not all of the district sales managers agreed with this conclusion.

It was common knowledge in Hanover-Bates's corporate sales office that Jim Sprague's predecessor as northeast district sales manager had not been one of the company's better district sales managers. His attitude toward the sales plans and programs of the national sales manager had been one of reluctant compliance rather than acceptance and support. When the national sales manager succeeded in persuading Jim Sprague's predecessor to take early retirement, he had been faced with the lack of an available qualified replacement.

Hank Carver, who most of the sales representatives had assumed would get the district manager job, had been passed over in part because he would be 65 in three years. The national sales manager had not wanted to face the same replacement problem again in three years and also had wanted someone in the position who would be more likely to be responsive to the company's sales plans and policies. The appointment of Jim Sprague as district manager had caused considerable talk, not only in the district but also at corporate headquarters. In fact, the national sales manager had warned Jim that "a lot of people are expecting you to fall on your face ... they don't think you have the experience to handle the job, in particular, and to manage and motivate a group of sales representatives, most of whom are considerably older and more experienced than you." The national sales manager had concluded by saying, "I think you can handle the job, Jim. ... I think you can manage those sales reps and improve the district's profit performance ... and I'm depending on you to do both.

Wind Technology*

Ken Manning
University of South Carolina

Jakki Mohr
University of Colorado

WIND TECHNOLOGY

Kevin Cage, general manager of Wind Technology, sat in his office on a Friday afternoon watching the snow fall outside his window. It was January 1991 and he knew that during the month ahead he would have to make some difficult decisions regarding the future of his firm, Wind Technology. The market for the wind profiling radar systems that his company designed had been developing at a much slower rate than he had anticipated.

Wind Technology

During Wind Technology's 10-year history, the company had produced a variety of weather-related radar and instrumentation. In 1986, the company condensed its product mix to include only wind-profiling radar systems. Commonly referred to as wind profilers, these products measure wind and atmospheric turbulence for weather forecasting, detection of wind direction at NASA launch sites, and other meteorological applications (i.e., at universities and other scientific monitoring stations). Kevin had felt that this consolidation would position the company as a leader in what he anticipated to be a high-growth market with little competition.

Wind Technology's advantages over Unisys, the only other key player in the wind-profiling market, included the following: (1) The company adhered stringently to specifications and quality production; (2) Wind Technology had the technical expertise to provide full system integration. This allowed customers to order either basic components or a full

---

system including software support; (3) Wind Technology's staff of meteorologists and atmospheric scientists provided the customer with sophisticated support, including operation and maintenance training and field assistance; (4) Finally, Wind Technology had devoted all of its resources to its wind-profiling business. Kevin believed that the market would perceive this as an advantage over a large conglomerate like Unisys.

Wind Technology customized each product for individual customers as the need arose; the total system could cost a customer from $400,000 to $5 million. Various governmental entities, such as the Department of Defense, NASA, and state universities had consistently accounted for about 90 percent of Wind Technology's sales. In lieu of a field sales force, Wind Technology relied on top management and a team of engineers to call on prospective and current customers. Approximately $105,000 of their annual salaries was charged to a direct selling expense.

The Problem

The consolidation strategy that the company had undertaken in 1986 was partly due to the company being purchased by Vaitra, a high-technology European firm. Wind Technology's ability to focus on the wind-profiling business had been made possible by Vaitra's financial support. However, since 1986 Wind Technology had shown little commercial success, and due to low sales levels, the company was experiencing severe cash-flow problems. Kevin knew that Wind Technology could not continue to meet payroll much longer. Also, he had been informed that Vaitra was not willing to pour more money into Wind Technology. Kevin estimated that he had from 9 to 12 months (until the end of 1991) in which to implement a new strategy with the potential to improve the company's cash flow. The new strategy was necessary to enable Wind Technology to survive until the wind-profiler market matured. Kevin and other industry experts anticipated that it would be two years until the wind-profiling market achieved the high growth levels that the company had initially anticipated.

One survival strategy that Kevin had in mind was to spin-off and market component parts used in making wind profilers. Initial research indicated that, of all the wind-profiling system's component parts, the high-voltage power supply (HVPS) had the greatest potential for commercial success. Furthermore, Kevin's staff on the HVPS product had demonstrated knowledge of the market. Kevin felt that by marketing the HVPS, Wind Technology could reap incremental revenues, with very little addition to fixed costs. (Variable costs would include the costs of making and marketing the HVPS. The accounting department had estimated that production costs would run approximately 70 percent of the selling price, and that 10 percent of other expenses—such as top management direct-selling expenses—should be charged to the HVPS.)

High-Voltage Power Supplies

For a vast number of consumer and industrial products that require electricity, the available voltage level must be transformed to different levels and types of output. The three primary types of power supplies include linears, switchers, and converters. Each type manipulates electrical current in terms of the type of current (AC or DC) and/or the level of output (voltage). Some HVPS manufacturers focus on producing a standardized line of power supplies, while others specialize in customizing power supplies to the user's specifications.

High-voltage power supplies vary significantly in size and level of output. Small power supplies with relatively low levels of output (under 3 kV[1]) are used in communications equipment. Medium-sized power supplies that produce an output between 3 and 10 kV are used in a wide range of products including radars and lasers. Power supplies that produce output greater than 10 kV are used in a variety of applications, such as high-powered X rays and plasma-etching systems.

Background on Wind Technology's HVPS

One of Wind Technology's corporate strategies was to control the critical technology (major component parts) of its wind-profiling products. Management felt that this control was important since the company was part of a high-technology industry in which confidentiality and innovation were critical to each competitor's success. This strategy also gave Wind Technology a differential advantage over its major competitors, all of whom depended on a variety of manufacturers for component parts. Wind Technology had successfully developed almost all of the major component parts and the software for the wind profiler, yet the development of the power supply had been problematic.

To adhere to the policy of controlling critical technology in product design (rather than purchasing an HVPS from an outside supplier), Wind Technology management had hired Anne Ladwig and her staff

---

[1]kV (Kilovolt): 1,000 volts.

of HVPS technicians to develop a power supply for the company's wind-profiling systems. Within six months of joining Wind Technology, Anne and her staff had completed development of a versatile power supply which could be adapted for use with a wide variety of equipment. Some of the company's wind-profiling systems required up to ten power supplies, each modified slightly to carry out its role in the system.

Kevin Cage had delegated the responsibility of investigating the sales potential of the company's HVPS to Anne Ladwig since she was very familiar with the technical aspects of the product and had received formal business training while pursuing an MBA. Anne had determined that Wind Technology's HVPS could be modified to produce levels of output between 3 and 10 kV. Thus, it seemed natural that if the product was brought to market, Wind Technology should focus on applications in this range of output. Wind Technology also did not have the production capabilities to compete in the high-volume, low-voltage segment of the market, nor did the company have the resources and technical expertise to compete in the high-output (10 kV +) segment.

The Potential Customer

Power supplies in the 3–10 kV range could be used to conduct research, to produce other products, or to place as a component into other products such as lasers. Thus, potential customers could include research labs, large end-users, OEM's, or distributors. Research labs each used an average of three power supplies; other types of customers ordered a widely varying quantity.

HVPS users were demanding increasing levels of reliability, quality, customization, and system integration. *System integration* refers to the degree to which other parts of a system are dependent upon the HVPS for proper functioning, and the extent to which these parts are combined into a single unit or piece of machinery.

Anne had considered entering several HVPS market segments in which Wind Technology could reasonably compete. She had estimated the domestic market potential of these segments at $237 million. To evaluate these segments, Anne had compiled growth forecasts for the year ahead and had evaluated each segment in terms of the anticipated level of customization and system integration demanded by the market. Anne felt that the level of synergy between Wind Technology and the various segments was also an important consideration in selecting a target market. Exhibit 1 summarizes this information. Anne believed that if the product was produced, Wind Technology's interests would be best served by selecting only one target market on which to concentrate initially.

EXHIBIT 1 HVPS Market Segments in the 3–10 kV Range

Application	Forecasted Annual Growth (%)	Level of Customization/ Level of System Integration*	Synergy Rating**	Percent of $237 Million Power Supply Market***
General/Univ. laboratory	5.40	medium/medium	3	8
Lasers	11.00	low/medium	4	10
Medical equipment	10.00	medium/medium	3	5
Microwave	12.00	medium/high	4	7
Power modulators	3.00	low/low	4	25
Radar systems	11.70	low/medium	5	12
Semiconductor	10.10	low/low	3	23
X-ray systems	8.60	medium/high	3	10

*The level of customization and system integration generally in demand within each of the applications is defined as low, medium, or high.

**Synergy ratings are based on a scale of 1 to 5; 1 is equivalent to a very low level of synergy and 5 is equivalent to a very high level of synergy. These subjective ratings are based on the amount of similarities between the wind-profiling industry and each application.

***Percentages total 100 percent of the $237 million market in which Wind Technology anticipated it could compete.

Note: This list of applications is not all-inclusive.

Competition

To gather competitive information, Anne contacted five HVPS manufacturers. She found that the manufacturers varied significantly in terms of size and marketing strategy (see Exhibit 2). Each listed a price in the $5,500–$6,500 range on power supplies with the same features and output levels as the HVPS that had been developed for Wind Technology. After she spoke with these firms, Anne had the feeling that Wind Technology could offer the HVPS market superior levels of quality, reliability, technical expertise, and customer support. She optimistically believed that a one-half percent market share objective could be achieved the first year.

Promotion

If Wind Technology entered the HVPS market, they would require a hard-hitting, thorough promotional campaign to reach the selected target market. Three factors made the selection of elements in the promotion mix especially important to Wind Technology: (1) Wind Technology's poor cash flow, (2) the lack of a well-developed marketing department, and (3) the need to generate incremental revenue from

---

EXHIBIT 2   Competitor Profile (3–10 kV range)

Company	Gamma	Glassman	Kaiser	Maxwell*	Spellman
Approximate annual sales	$2 million	$7.5 million	$3 million		$7 million
Market share	1.00%	3.00%	1.50%		2.90%
Price**	$5,830	$5,590	$6,210	$5000–$6000	$6,360
Delivery	12 weeks	10 weeks	10 weeks	8 weeks	12 weeks
Product customization	No	Medium	Low	Medium	Low
System integration experience	Low	Low	Low	Medium	Low
Customer targets	Gen. lab.	Laser	Laser	Radar	Capacitors
	Space	Medical	Medical	Power mod.	Gen. lab.
	Univ. lab.	X ray	Microwave	X ray	Micro-
			Semiconductor	Medical	wave
				equip.	X ray

*Maxwell was in the final stages of product development and stated that the product would be available in the spring. Maxwell anticipated that the product would sell in the $5,000–$6,000 range.
**Price quoted for an HVPS with the same specifications as the "standard" model developed by Wind Technology.

---

sales of the HVPS at a minimum cost. In fact, a rule of thumb used by Wind Technology was that all marketing expenditures should be about 9 to 10 percent of sales. Kevin and Anne were contemplating the use of the following elements:

1. Collateral Material.   Sales literature, brochures, and data sheets are necessary to communicate the product benefits and features to potential customers. These materials are designed to be (1) mailed to customers as part of direct-mail campaigns or in response to customer requests, (2) given away at trade shows, and (3) left behind after sales presentations.

Because no one in Wind Technology was an experienced copywriter, Anne and Kevin considered hiring a marketing communications agency to write the copy and to design the layout of the brochures. This agency would also complete the graphics (photographs and artwork) for the collateral material. The cost for 5,000 pieces (including the 10 percent mark-up for the agency) was estimated to be $5.50 each.

2. Public Relations.   Kevin and Anne realized that one very cost-efficient tool of promotion is publicity. They contemplated sending out new product announcements to a variety of trade journals whose readers were part of Wind Technology's new target market. By using this tool, interested readers could call or write to Wind Technology, and the company could then send the prospective customers collateral material. The drawback of relying too heavily on this element was very obvious to Kevin and Anne—the editors of the trade journals could choose not to print Wind Technology's product announcements if their new product was not deemed "newsworthy."

The cost of using this tool would include the time necessary to write the press release and the expense of mailing the release to the editors. Direct costs were estimated by Wind Technology to be $500.

3. Direct Mail.   Kevin and Anne were also contemplating a direct-mail campaign. The major expenditure for this option would be buying a list of prospects to whom the collateral material would be mailed. Such lists usually cost around $5,000, depending upon the number of names and the list quality. Other costs would include postage and the materials mailed. These costs were estimated to be $7,500 for a mailing of 1,500.

4. Trade Shows.   The electronics industry had several annual trade shows. If they chose to exhibit at one of these trade shows, Wind Technology would incur the cost of a booth, the space at the show, and the travel and incidental costs of the people attending the show to staff the booth. Kevin and Anne estimated these costs at approximately $50,000 for the exhibit, space, and materials, and $50,000 for a staff of five people to attend.

5. Trade Journal Advertising.   Kevin and Anne also contemplated running a series of ads in trade journals. Several journals they considered are listed in Exhibit 3, along with circulation, readership, and cost information.

6. Personal Selling.

(a.) Telemarketing (Inbound/Inside Sales).[2] Kevin and Anne also considered hiring a technical salesperson to respond to HVPS product inquiries generated by product announcements, direct mail, and advertising. This person's responsibilities would include answering phone calls, prospecting, sending out collateral material, and following up with potential customers. The salary and benefits for one individual would be about $50,000.

(b.) Field Sales. The closing of sales for the HVPS might require some personal selling at the customer's location, especially if Wind Technology pursued the customized option. Kevin and Anne realized

---

[2]"Inbound" refers to calls that potential customers make to Wind Technology, rather than "outbound," in which Wind Technology calls potential customers (i.e., solicits sales).

EXHIBIT 3   Trade Publications

Trade Publication	Editorial	Cost per Color Insertion (1 page)	Circulation
Electrical manufacturing	For purchasers and users of power supplies, transformers, and other electrical products.	$4,077	35,168 nonpaid
Electronic component news	For electronics OEM's. Products addressed include work stations, power sources, chips, etc.	$6,395	110,151 nonpaid
Electronic manufacturing news	For OEM's in the industry of providing manufacturing and contracting of components, circuits, and systems.	$5,075	25,000 nonpaid
Design news	For design OEM's covering components, systems, and materials.	$8,120	170,033 nonpaid
Weatherwise	For meteorologists covering imaging, radar, etc.	$1,040	10,186 paid

Note: This is a partial list of applicable trade publications. Standard Rate and Data Service lists other possible publications.

that potentially this would provide them with the most incremental revenue, but it also had the potential to be the most costly tool. Issues such as how many salespeople to hire, where to position them in the field (geographically), and so on, were major concerns. Salary plus expenses and benefits for an outside salesperson were estimated to be about $80,000.

Decisions

As Kevin sat in his office and perused the various facts and figures, he knew that he would have to make some quick decisions. He sensed that the decision about whether or not to proceed with the HVPS spin-off was risky, but he felt that to not do something to improve the firm's cash flow was equally risky. Kevin also knew that if he decided to proceed with the HVPS, there were a number of segments in that market in which Wind Technology could position its HVPS. He mulled over which segment appeared to be a good fit for Wind Technology's abilities (given Anne's recommendation that a choice of one segment would be best). Finally, Kevin was concerned that if they entered the HVPS market, that promotion for their product would be costly, further exacerbating the cash flow situation. He knew that promotion would be necessary, but the exact mix of elements would have to be designed with financial constraints in mind.

Chili's Restaurant

Sexton Adams
North Texas State University

Adelaide Griffin
Texas Women's University

THE STORY

It was 5:20 P.M. Norman Brinker sat in his car and put his seat belt on. "That's right, seat belts are mandatory now," he thought. He left his office building, 6820 LBJ Freeway, Dallas, still worrying about the earlier meeting.

Although Chili's had maintained its average store volumes at 1985 levels during 1986, market conditions were rather bad. With 66 percent of the restaurants located in the economically impacted energy-belt states, Chili's would have to concentrate its efforts on the future expansion of the company.

Traffic was heavy on LBJ Freeway. Norman turned on the radio to relax and keep his mind away from the difficult two and a half hours he had just spent with his colleagues. Bruce Springsteen was singing again, the same song, over and over. "That's enough for the day," Norman thought. "I have already heard this song three times today." He turned the radio off and decided to take advantage of the traffic jam to direct his thoughts to his business. He tried to recall the conversation he had had with his partners during the meeting.

THE COMPANY

In 1975 Larry and Jack Lavine, two brothers, opened the first Chili's restaurant on Greenville Avenue in Dallas, Texas. The Lavines were banking on a new niche in the restaurant industry between fast food

Source: This case was prepared by L. Miklichansky and B. Logan under the supervision of Professor Sexton Adams, North Texas State University, and Professor Adelaide Griffin, Texas Women's University.

and midscale restaurants. They were bent on a commitment to the quality burger. Their first restaurant offered the customer two new appealing qualities for this time period: fast, full service specializing in quality hamburgers.

Through 1982 the Lavines opened up 17 more Chili's restaurants, primarily in the Southwest. Over this period of 1975 to 1982 investors and restaurant analysts started following the growth of Chili's with interest. As of June 30, 1986, Chili's had expanded to 80 units in 12 states (see Exhibit 1). Chili's initial expansion strategies were that of establishing themselves in Sunbelt cities with somewhat of a "youthful" atmosphere, for example, Dallas, Houston, Atlanta, Tampa, Orlando, Los Angeles, and San Franciso.

In 1983 Norman Brinker, a well-respected restaurant industry pioneer, paid $12 million for 35 percent of Chili's stock. The company up to this time was privately held by the Lavine brothers. In January

EXHIBIT 1   Chili's Restaurant Units Open as of June 30, 1986

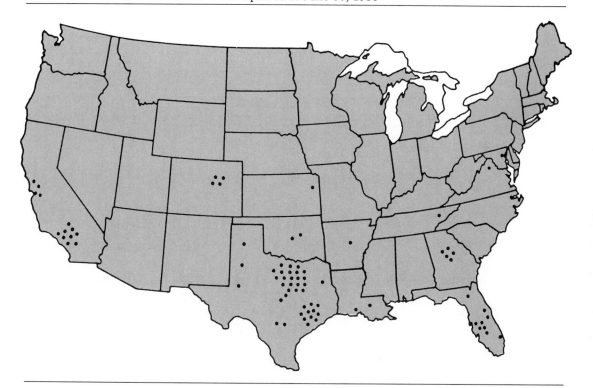

Source: Chili's 1986 Annual Report.

1984 Chili's had its first public stock offering on the over-the-counter exchange.

Since the initial public stock offering, the company opened more than 50 restaurants. In 1986 Chili's had 65 company-owned units, 14 joint-venture-owned units, and one franchised unit.[1] Chili's had signed two primary joint-venture agreements, one with Sunstate Restaurant Corporation in the Southeast and one with Dunkin' Ventures Corporation in the Northeast. The Sunstate agreement allowed Chili's to penetrate the Florida market. The agreement with Dunkin' was signed in October 1985, giving Chili's 50 percent ownership in more than 50 restaurants expected to be developed in New England, eastern Canada, and upstate New York.[2,3]

In 1986 Chili's was a restaurant concept that appealed to winners. Fiscal year 1985 had been a landmark year for Chili's in terms of operating and financial results (see Exhibit 2). Management felt that it had been able to leverage its talents toward the expansion processes it was undergoing. The year 1986 brought menu introductions, new marketing efforts, and a 25 percent increase in total employment, to 4,500 employees from 3,600 employees. Chili's at this point in time was considering the following nonexclusive alternatives:

EXHIBIT 2

Chili's Inc. Selected Financial Data (in thousands)	Year Ended June 30		
	1986	*1985*	*1984*
Revenues	$106,990	$69,301	$43,157
Net income	$4,799	4,131	$1,990
Weighted average shares out- standing	5,230	4,714	3,982
Working capital	$2,375	$1,453	($230)
Total assets	63,110	41,147	22,209
Long-term debt	10,739	8,483	3,528
Stockholders' equity	38,500	23,307	12,535
Number of restaurants open at year end	65	45	28

Source: Chili's 1986 Annual Report.

---

[1]Donald Smith, "Romancing the Burger," *Nation's Restaurant News*, February 10, 1986, p. F9.

[2]Ibid.

[3]Don Jeffrey, "Smaller Dinner Houses Rely on Local Marketing," *Nation's Restaurant News*, March 10, 1986, p. F8.

- National expansion
- Further existing market penetration
- New product introductions

As Chili's Chairman of the Board and Chief Executive Officer Norman Brinker said, "We have an unusually dedicated, talented group. That's the difference. A company is simply the sum total of individual efforts toward a common goal."[4]

THE ECONOMY

Industry observers saw 1986 as a year of considerable change within the restaurant industry. Oil prices had plunged, inflation was falling, and the stock market was soaring. Cheaper oil prices were hitting the Southwest harder and faster than expected. Energy companies were slashing capital spending budgets and laying off workers. Other industries both directly and indirectly related to energy were also suffering. Restaurant companies located in the economically impacted energy-belt states had reported sluggish market conditions.

Another element which presented a direct threat to the restaurant industry was the 1986 Tax Reform Act. This act eliminated 20 percent of the expense-account write-off for business-related dining and also eliminated the investment tax credit. Industry analysts felt that less businessmen would eat out due to this reform. And, in the case of rapidly expanding companies, the investment tax credit meant beneficial tax savings. Chili's recognized investment tax credits of over $1.5 million in 1985 and 1986.[5]

As opposed to tightened economic conditions in the U.S. market, volatility of world politics and increased terrorism abroad persuaded many Americans to consider the advantages of traveling in the United States rather than in foreign countries. Industry experts considered this trend an opportunity for the U.S. hotel and restaurant businesses.

Demographers had pointed out the aging of the population. The baby-boom generation had reached maturity. The tastes and values of upwardly mobile young professionals, less concerned with price than with variety and style, would benefit full-service sit-down restaurants and cafeterias, industry experts believed. These restaurant categories offered a wide selection of items and an atmosphere favored by a broad section of the population. The trend was toward the "gourmet" eating experience, coupled with nutrition and weight consciousness.

---

[4]"The Restaurant Chain Industry," *Nation's Restaurant News,* August 11, 1986, pp. F3–F70.
[5]Chili's Annual Report, 1986.

Also influencing the restaurant industry was consumer retrenchment. Spending on restaurant meals was one of the first areas to be affected by changes in the financial condition of consumers. Growth in real disposable income and employment, the two key supports for restaurant sales, had moderated in 1986. When combined with relatively high debt loads and a low savings rate, the customers' propensity to eat away from home had declined.[6]

Sales of hard goods had been relatively strong in early 1986. While purchases of autos, furniture, appliances, and other consumer durables obviously were substitutes for restaurant sales, they channeled an amount of buying power away from meals eaten outside the home. However, their impact on restaurant sales was expected to be short-lived since much of the strength in hard goods sales had been promotionally induced and was probably not sustainable.[7]

The differential had widened between the cost of food prepared at home and the prices in restaurants. According to *The Nation's Restaurant News,* an industry journal, the average monthly increase in 1985 in the cost of food eaten away from home was 3.9 percent while the average monthly increase in the cost of food eaten at home was 1.5 percent. In 1984 these figures were 4.2 percent and 3.7 percent, respectively.[8]

The restaurant industry had become more competitive. Competition was coming from nonrestaurant food retailers as well as from other restaurants. By providing new alternatives for the consumer, convenience stores, deli counters and salad bars at supermarkets, and restaurants within department stores were among the nontraditional food outlets that were capturing more of the market for food consumed outside the home.[9]

In addition to general economic trends and consumer demand influences, direct operation factors had an impact on restaurant companies. The industry was facing rising insurance costs. Third-party liability awards and workers' compensation claims were climbing, leading to substantially higher insurance premiums. Those operators whose restaurants had a high alcohol mix had been hit especially hard. Encouraging alcoholic beverage sales was no longer commonplace in the wake of consumer awareness, such as Mothers Against Drunk Driving.[10]

---

[6]Don Jeffrey, p. F8.
[7]Ibid.
[8]"The Restaurant Chain Industry," pp. F3–F70.
[9]Don Jeffrey, p. F8.
[10]Ibid.

According to a report published by the National Restaurant Association, the nation's food-service industry will face a shortage of 1.1 million workers by 1994.[11] This industry, which employed 150,000 restaurant cashiers in 1984, will need 216,000 cashiers in 1995, a 36.7 percent jump. The need for cooks and chefs will expand to 435,000 in 1995 from 331,000 in 1984, a 31.4 percent increase, the NRA said.

The need for bartenders will rise 29.8 percent, to 353,000 in 1995 from 272,000 in 1984. The industry labor shortages were exacerbated by high turnover rates in food service, according to the report, which was prepared in conjunction with the consulting firm of Arthur D. Little, Inc. Food counter and fountain workers and waiter and waitress assistants all demonstrated a 43 percent turnover rate, followed by kitchen workers' and waiters' and waitresses' 32 percent rates in 1984. Even supervisors had a 24 percent turnover rate. In addition, the industry was facing a labor crisis because its employment rate would swell 21.7 percent over the next ten years, to 8.9 million persons, while overall employment would increase only 14.9 percent. Consequently, for most operators, wage rates were being bid up and recruiting and training had intensified.

THE INDUSTRY

As of January 1986, the restaurant chain industry consisted of approximately 100,000 outlets, an increase of 9 percent over the previous year.[12]

The restaurant chain industry included 10 different segments (see Exhibit 3), the largest of which was the burger segment, accounting for 40 percent of sales dollars in the industry.[13] However, the fastest-growing segment was pizza chains, registering an annual sales growth rate of 23 percent for 1985. Industry observers attributed this result to increased consumer demand for speed and convenience, home delivery, and variety of product. Contract feeders, snack chains, and fast-food chains were all growing and reaping market share gains. Dinner houses, chicken chains, family restaurants, family steak houses, and cafeterias were showing slower sales growth than the industry as a whole (see Exhibit 4).

---

[11]"Food Service Facing Shortage of 1.1 Million Workers by 1995," *Nation's Restaurant News,* July 28, 1986, p. 61.
[12]"The Restaurant Chain Industry," pp. F3–F70.
[13]Ibid.

EXHIBIT 3   Restaurant Chain Industry Segments

Segment	*Major Chains*
Burger	McDonald's, Burger King
Contract	Marriott Food Service, ARA Services
Family restaurant	Denny's, International House of Pancakes
Pizza	Pizza Hut, Domino's
Chicken	Kentucky Fried Chicken, Church's
Dinner house	Bennigan's, Red Lobster
Snack	Dairy Queen, Dunkin' Donuts
Family steak house	Ponderosa, Western Sizzlin
Cafeteria	Luby's, Wyatt's
Fish	Long John Silver's, Captain D's

Source: Nation's Restaurant News, August 11, 1986.

EXHIBIT 4   Burgers Do the Biggest Business but Pizza is Growing the Fastest

Top 100 Systemwide Sale by Segment, in Billions

Burger[1]	$27.5
Contract	6.8
Family restaurant	5.5
Pizza	5.4
Chicken	4.9
Dinner house	3.7
Snack	9.7
Family steak house	2.7
Cafeteria	1.2
Fish	1.1

Top 100 1986 Growth Rate by Segment

Burger[1]	13.6%
Contract	15.3
Family restaurant	5.8
Pizza	22.7
Chicken	6.5
Dinner house	8.8
Snack	6.9
Family steak house	8.0
Cafeteria	9.1
Fish	14.1

[1]Includes roast beef.

Source: Nation's Restaurant News, August 11, 1986.

DINNER HOUSE SEGMENT

Restaurant analysts considered Chili's within the dinner house segment, defined as the niche between the fast-food and midscale restaurants. "It is one of the most effectively positioned restaurant concepts," said Donald Smith, professor of Hotel Restaurant and Institutional Management at Michigan State University.[14] The late 1960s saw the development of the concept, representing the birth of the American tavern. These restaurants were neighborhood eating, drinking, and meeting places, right on target for the hungry, lonely young adult audience. They emphasized casual dining atmosphere, good quality, and variety accompanied by alcoholic beverages at reasonable prices.

In 1985, the top ten dinner house chains had an average of 182 units with annual sales of $2.1 million. The average guest check was $10 per person, up 0.8 percent from the previous years (see Exhibit 5).

As a result of consumer awareness programs and governmental regulations concerning alcohol sales and consumption, the new strategy in the dinner house segment was one of menu expansion to offset decreased sales of alcoholic beverages. Alcoholic beverage sales in this segment ranged from 15 percent of total sales to 40 percent, but with increased awareness the norm seemed to fall off to about 20 percent of total sales.

EXHIBIT 5   1985 Dinner House Segment Data

	Average Guest Check	Systemwide Sales (millions)	Number of Units	Sales $ Market Share
Red Lobster	$10.75	$ 925	400	25.09%
Bennigan's	8.04	455	223	12.34
Chi-Chi's	7.82	435	217	11.80
El Torito	n/a	383	196	10.39
T.G.I. Friday's	10.00	366	123	9.93
Steak & Ale	13.00	295	190	8.00
Stuart Anderson's	n/a	275	120	7.46
Ground Round	n/a	220	201	5.97
Chili's	6.81	185	97	5.02
Brown Derby	n/a	148	56	4.01
		$3,687	1,823	100.00%

Source: Nation's Restaurant News, August 11, 1986.

[14]Donald Smith, p. F9.

HUMAN RESOURCES

Restaurant analysts saw Chili's as a very well-managed company headed by experienced and creative restaurant veterans. This dynamic outlook filtered down to the restaurant level where there was an energy and attitude present about the employees. Chili's offered a comprehensive training program and an attractive compensation and benefits package in order to develop and keep talented restaurant management. As a result, Chili's boasted a 15 percent management turnover rate, one of the industry's lowest.[15] In 1986 Chili's had approximately 4,500 employees, up from 3,600 in 1985.[16] Chili's organization was very structured in terms of operating autonomy. This can be seen in the Organization Chart (see Exhibit 6).

THE KEY PLAYERS

A major turning point for Chili's came in 1983 when, as previously mentioned, Norman Brinker and several other top executives were brought in to replace the Lavine brothers. The new team was known in the restaurant industry for holding aggressive marketing philosophies and growth-oriented attitudes. The key executives averaged more than 13 years of experience in the restaurant industry.

Norman Brinker, 54, joined Chili's in 1983 as chairman of the board and chief executive officer. He had 27 years of experience in the food-service industry. In 1966, he started the Steak & Ale restaurant chain. The Bennigan's chain followed in 1976. He sold both of the chains to Pillsbury in 1976 and went to work for that company as the chairman of Steak & Ale. He also served as chairman and chief executive officer of Burger King Corporation, a subsidiary of Pillsbury.

Ron McDougall was named president and chief operating officer of Chili's in 1983, after serving as senior vice president for Steak & Ale Restaurant Corporation, where he helped create the Bennigan's concept. His experience also included senior management positions with Burger King Corporation, the Pillsbury Company, Sara Lee, and Procter & Gamble. Under his direction, Chili's corporate expansion strategy took on a more quantitative approach to market penetration, restaurant design/construction, site selection procedures, and advertising

---

[15]Charles Glousky and Steven Rockwell, "Here Comes the Shakeout," *Nation's Restaurant News,* March 10, 1986, p. F37.

[16]Chili's Annual Report, 1986.

EXHIBIT 6   Chili's Organization Chart

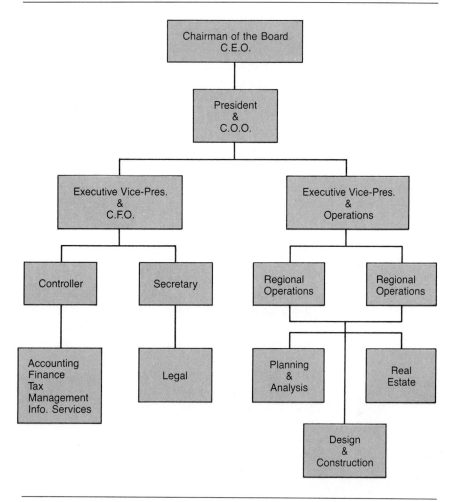

Source: Company data.

in the form of demographic studies, competitive studies, and site selection models.

Jim Parrish, executive vice president and chief financial officer, joined Chili's in 1983. His prior experience included serving as chief financial officer for companies in the restaurant, agricultural processing, and oil and gas industries.

Creed Ford III, who had been with Chili's since 1976, was named director of operations in 1978 and promoted to executive vice president of operations in 1986.

John Titus, a real estate and construction officer from Steak & Ale, was elected vice president of real estate in 1983.

Ed Palms, previously Steak & Ale director of design, also joined Chili's in 1983 as vice president of design after serving Steak & Ale for nine years.[17]

All of the aforementioned executives were aggressive and risk taking in their management styles, restaurant analysts felt. Chili's had installed the right mixture of leadership and know-how to position themselves for the future.

CHILI'S MENU CONCEPT AND SERVICE

Chili's restaurants' distinctive buildings became well-established and familiar landmarks in the markets in which the company operated. Market analyses, conducted in 1984 on management's behalf, indicated that by making some design modifications to the Chili's standardized buildings, the company could increase the appeal of the existing restaurants while significantly reducing maintenance costs. Management decided to undertake a remodeling program includng the installation of effective signage, improved lighting, and custom-designed awnings. These changes made significant contributions to the exterior appearance and visibility of each Chili's location. Other key improvements involved a new kitchen layout to increase operational efficiency, a reconfiguration of the customer areas to raise table turnover, and a low-maintenance brick exterior.[18]

In 1986 the decor of a Chili's restaurant consisted of booth seating, tile-top tables, hanging plants, and wood and brick walls covered with interesting memorabilia. Each restaurant had a casual atmosphere and was open seven days a week, for lunch, dinner, and late-night meals. Chili's restaurants featured quick, efficient, and friendly service. Most were free-standing units of approximately 6,000 square feet, with 156–178 dining seats.[19] Table turnover was 45 minutes.[20]

Management placed emphasis on serving customers substantial portions of high-quality food and beverages at moderate prices. Full bar service was available, with frozen margaritas offered as a specialty drink. Draft and bottled domestic and imported beers were served in frosted mugs. In 1986, Chili's introduced a premium "Top Shelf"

---

[17]Ibid.
[18]Chili's Annual Report, 1984.
[19]Ibid.
[20]Chili's Annual Report, 1986.

margarita and premium wines which were available by the glass or bottle.[21] Thanks to these new drinks liquor sales had held steady at about 20 percent of total revenues. Although Chili's did not downplay liquor, its focus was on food, and a substantial portion of alcohol sales was made to customers waiting for tables. As Ron McDougall said, "We are not a watering hole."[22]

Chili's menu was designed to be varied enough to accommodate a diverse customer group yet limited enough so that all offerings could still be "prepared from substantially fresh products each day" on the premises, said Normal Brinker.[23] Thirteen varieties of half-pound hamburgers were available with a wide range of toppings. Other selections included the ever-popular "bowl of red" ; Mexican-style specialties such as nachos, soft tacos, and quesadillas; and meal-sized salads.

In 1985, Chili's scored big gains with the introduction of chicken and beef fajitas, a chicken sandwich, and two new appetizers—Buffalo chicken wings and cheese fries. Seeking to broaden its market base, Chili's extended its menu early in 1986 by adding other nonburger items—the Chicken Frisco Salad, the Monterey Chicken Platter, the Country Fried Steak, and the BBQ Baby Back Ribs.

These products were targeted toward a growing consumer demand for variety, according to Chili's chairman, Norman Brinker. "Burgers are still king, but people just want more different things more often," he said.[24] Burgers, which once accounted for more than 50 percent of sales, according to the company, made up less than 35 percent by 1986.[25] Also in response to customer requests, a children's menu and desserts, which included hot fudge sundaes and a cinnamon apple sundae delight, were introduced.[26] New product introductions were very well received, and boosted Chili's per person check average from $6.50 to $6.81.[27]

At Chili's, a new item strategy was pursued, as long as the dishes would meet the goals of high quality, simple preparation, fast service, and outstanding price/value. Further, through a diversified menu, Chili's intended to maintain and enlarge its customer loyalty. Internal research had shown that more than half of the customers visited Chili's restaurants an average of three times per month.[28]

---

[21]Ibid.
[22]Don Jeffrey, p. F8.
[23]Charles Glousky and Steven Rockwell, p. F37.
[24]Ibid.
[25]Ibid.
[26]Chili's Annual Report, 1986.
[27]Ibid.
[28]Ibid.

ADVERTISING CAMPAIGN

Prior to the change in management at Chili's, almost no money was spent on advertising and promotion. Success, such as it was, was due almost exclusively to word of mouth. In October 1983, Chili's engaged New York-based McCann-Erickson to handle its advertising. However, soon thereafter, in February 1984, the $1 million account was awarded to Dallas-based Levenson, Levenson, and Hill. McDougall attributed the change primarily to management's dissatisfaction with the advertising strategies taken by McCann-Erickson. Additionally, the change enabled Chili's executives to work with the top agency people as opposed to a branch office of a large agency.[29]

In mid-1984, the "No Place Else Is Chili's" campaign debuted. Phase one lasted about a year and focused on both television and radio spots. March 1985 began the second phase of the campaign with two national television commercials and four new radio spots. Chili's commercials took viewers inside Chili's restaurants to eavesdrop on conversations at various tables. Scenarios included a couple reminiscing over old times and mutual friends, and a group of neighbors relaxing after a garage sale. According to the president of the ad agency, Bill Hill, "You can't do it by showing pretty food alone. You have to create a personality for them [the restaurants]." Levenson, Levenson, and Hill conducted market research to answer the question "What is Chili's?" The agency concluded that Chili's was an original, rather than an imitator or a fad—thus the reason for the slogan "No Place Else."[30]

In February 1986, to make up for its concentration in the oil-depressed Southwest, Chili's launched a two-pronged plan of new product introductions and television advertising in a stepped-up effort to stimulate sales. The advertising campaign was targeted at key oil-sensitive markets in Dallas, Houston, Austin, Denver, and Oklahoma City.[31]

FINANCE AND ADMINISTRATION

Chili's became a publicly held company on January 6, 1984. Since Chili's went public, the company has posted sales gains exceeding 50 percent in each of the two years. Same-store sales in 1986 were

---

[29]D. S. Hansard, "Chili's Picks Dallas Ad Agency," *Dallas Morning News,* February 22, 1984, p. 2D.

[30]D. S. Hansard, "Chili's Expands Ad Campaign," *Dallas Morning News,* March 15, 1985, p. 1D.

[31]David Zuckerman, "Chili's Introduces New Products, Ads," *Nation's Restaurant News,* April 28, 1986, pp. 2, 59.

relatively unchanged from 1985, although expansion of new restaurants boosted revenues. New menu items introduced in 1986 raised cost of sales by 0.4 percent from 27.2 percent in 1985. In 1984 cost of sales was 26.0 percent. Operating expenses, including marketing, had risen from 49.4 percent in 1984 to 52.5 percent in 1986. This cost increase was made up of first-year and start-up expenses associated with opening new restaurants and with rising insurance costs. In 1986 management believed it had positioned itself for future growth with adequate personnel and support functions in place. The growth throughout 1985 and 1986 resulted in lower general and administrative expenses as a percent of sales. The largest operating expense realized by the company in 1986 outside of salaries was rent expense, totaling $8.5 million. This, coupled with depreciation expense of $6.7 million, represented 14.2 percent of total sales. In 1984 the same expenses were 4.7 percent of sales. This 300 percent increase reflected 50 additional restaurant locations, a 267 percent increase in unit growth. Chili's profit margin in 1986 dropped to 4.5 percent from 6.0 percent in 1985. Company officials believed that they could see lower profit margins during periods of heavy growth in return for higher margins in later years.[32]

Management believed that financially Chili's was in relatively good shape in 1986. Total assets had experienced a 285 percent growth rate since 1984 and working capital was strong. Company officials believed that funds generated from operations, from built-to-suit agreements with landlords, and available under a revolving loan agreement and lines of credit with various Dallas banks were adequate to finance capital expenditures.[33] (See Exhibits 8 and 9.)

EXPANSION

Chili's expansion plan was twofold: first, it clustered restaurants in preexisting markets to obtain complete market penetration; and, second, it entered new geographic territories with one unit at a time or through joint-venture agreements with outside investors. Chili's had 20 units in Dallas/Fort Worth, 10 units in Houston, 9 units in Los Angeles and 4 to 6 units each in San Francisco, Denver, Atlanta, and Tampa/St. Petersburg in 1986. The biggest event in the story of Chili's expansion was an agreement signed in October 1985 with Dunkin' Ventures, operator of the world's largest donut shop chain. The 20-year agreement would allow the 50 percent joint venture to build and

---

[32]Chili's Annual Report, 1986.
[33]Ibid.

EXHIBIT 8   Chili's, Inc., Consolidated Balance Sheet (in thousands)

	June 30	
	1986	*1985*
Assets		
Current assets:		
Cash & equivalent	$2,581	$308
Inventories	1,046	594
Other current assets	8,543	7,193
Total current assets	12,170	8,095
Property & equipment	54,933	34,117
Less: accumulated depreciation	(10,209)	(5,732)
Net property & equipment	44,724	28,385
Other assets	6,216	4,667
	$63,110	$41,147
Liabilities		
Current liabilities		
Current portion of		
long-term debt	$362	$586
Accounts payable	5,842	3,558
Accrued liabilities	3,591	2,498
Total current liabilities	9,795	6,642
Long-term debt	10,739	8,483
Deferred income taxes	3,840	2,453
Deferred gain on sale & leaseback	236	262
Stockholders' equity:		
Common stock—authorized 20		
million shares of $.10 par		
value: 5,222,818 and 4,661,038		
shares issued and outstanding		
in 1986 and 1985, respectively	522	466
Additional paid in capital	25,847	15,509
Retained earnings	12,131	7,332
Total stockholders' equity	38,500	23,307
	$63,110	$41,147

Source: Chili's 1986 Annual Report.

EXHIBIT 9   Chili's, Inc., Consolidated Statement of Income (in thousands, except per share data)

| | Year Ended June 30 | | |
	1986	1985	1984
Revenues	*$106,990*	*$69,301*	*$43,157*
Costs & expenses:			
Costs of sales	29,504	18,882	11,200
Operating expenses	56,165	34,891	21,320
General & administrative	7,483	5,887	4,880
Depreciation & amortization	6,730	3,378	2,040
Interest	470	301	774
	100,352	62,339	40,214
Income before taxes	6,638	5,962	2,943
Income taxes	1,839	1,831	953
Net income	$4,799	$4,131	$1,990
Net income per share	$0.92	$0.88	$0.50
Weighted average shares outstanding	5,230	4,714	3,982

Source: Chili's 1986 Annual Report.

operate more than 50 Chili's in New England and Canada. Norman Brinker said that Chili's management was impressed with Dunkin's food service operations and expansion plans. The first unit should open in the Boston area in fiscal 1987.[34,35]

In 1986 Chili's also had joint-venture agreements with Chesapeake Seafood Co. in the Washington, D.C., area and with Tampa-based Sunstate Restaurant Corporation. Chesapeake operated 9 units and Sunstate operated 10 units in 1986. The strategy behind the joint-venture agreements allowed Chili's to approach unfamiliar territories with limited-financial risk.

At the start of fiscal 1986 Chili's plan was to grow to 80 restaurants by June 30, 1986. This goal was accomplished through a systematic, disciplined approach to expansion. Chili's vice presidents of design and

[34]Ibid.
[35]J. Fine, "Chili's Franchise Agreement Fits in With Its Long-Range Expansion Plan," *Dallas Business Courier,* October 14, 1985, p. 3.

EXHIBIT 10 Chili's, Inc., Sales Growth

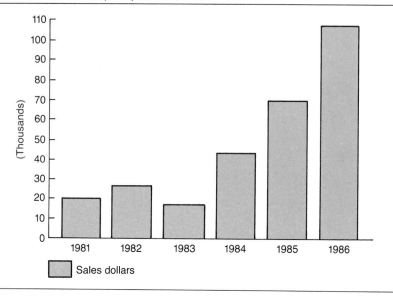

Source: Chili's 1986 Annual Report.

EXHIBIT 11 Chili's, Inc., Unit Growth

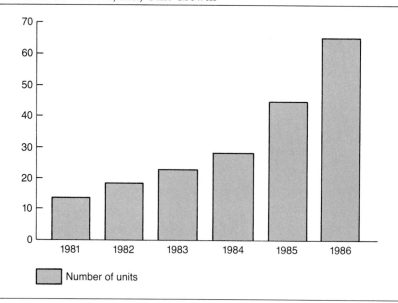

Source: Chili's 1986 Annual Report.

construction and real estate employed sophisticated site models in the selection of Chili's restaurant locations. In addition, rigorous financial analyses and experienced managerial instincts were used.

FUTURE DIRECTIONS

The future of the restaurant industry was not very glamorous by the fall of 1986. According to *Standard & Poor,* profits of restaurants and lodging companies had dropped 22 percent during 1986, third quarter, in comparison with 1985, same period. This result was mainly due to increased competition among restaurant chains and to an increase in the popularity of cheaper ready-made packaged foods that people could eat at home.[36] Some chains had been forced to close units; others had reckoned on introduction of new menu items; and others were seeking geographical expansion.

Chili's plans for fiscal 1987 were the continuation of national expansion, clustering units in markets where the company already had restaurants, and entering new markets to develop broader national exposure. Chili's specific objectives were:[37]

- Add approximately 35 new restaurants.
- Expand from 12 to 22 states.
- Maintain unit management turnover below 17 percent.
- Improve the ratio of sales to investment.
- Introduce an exciting new prototype for future Chili's restaurants.

[36]Laurie Baum, "Profits Look Muscular—But Not for Long," *Business Week,* November 17, 1986, p. 175.

[37]Chili's Annual Report, 1986.

S. C. Johnson— The Agree Line*

Stephen B. Ash
Sandra Safran
both of the University of Western Ontario

As Mel Liston reviewed the latest material received from the firm's advertising agency, he felt very pleased that his recommendations on product positioning had been approved by senior management. These recommendations centered around a new targeting strategy for Agree Shampoo and Agree Creme Rinse and Conditioner that would shift marketing effort away from the "all women, aged 18 to 45" segment toward the "teenage female" segment of the market. As product manager of the Agree line at S. C. Johnson & Son, Ltd., in Brantford, Ontario, his current task was to develop a comprehensive marketing communications program aimed at the new target audience for the fiscal year (FY) 1980–81. It was May 1980, and he would have to make strategic decisions on advertising, consumer sales promotion, and trade promotion within the next few weeks in order to finalize a plan that could be implemented by July 1, the start of the new fiscal year.

COMPANY BACKGROUND

S. C. Johnson & Son, Ltd., better known as Johnson Wax, was founded in 1886 in Racine, Wisconsin, as a manufacturer of parquet flooring. When customers became concerned with the care and protection of their flooring, Johnson began making and selling a prepared paste wax. The popularity of parquet flooring began to fade, and by 1917 the company was concentrating solely on floor wax and other wood finishing products. The Canadian operation was created in 1920, by which time there were also plants in England and Australia.

---

*This case was prepared by Stephen B. Ash and Sandra Safran, University of Western Ontario, as a basis for class discussion and is not intended to illustrate effective or ineffective handling of administrative situations. Used with permission.

By 1980, the company had grown into a $2 billion corporation with operations in 41 countries and 110 distribution centers around the world. At that time, 78 percent of the company's sales were derived from the Consumer Products Group which comprised the U.S. Division and the International Division. The Canadian company was part of the latter group, although it had a separate management structure and research facilities. This arrangement ensured a high degree of autonomy in decisions related to marketing, finance, and research and development. Some products were developed in Canada—for example, Glade Flo-Thru Air Freshener and Super Soap—and these were frequently adopted by other subsidiaries. Other products were developed abroad and were later marketed in Canada.

Until the late 1970s, Johnson's primary emphasis was on floor- and furniture-care products. These were relatively mature markets that, in recent years, had suffered a slow but steady decline. Two reasons accounted for this slowdown: no-wax floors were becoming increasingly popular, and consumers' attitudes toward floor and furniture care were softening with the growth of low-maintenance chrome, glass, and wood-veneer products. At this time, Johnson controlled over two thirds of the shrinking floor market. The company responded to these trends by improving and repositioning existing products as well as by adding new products to the line. Although the company believed that these tactics helped it to maintain a market leadership position, management recognized that it would have to look farther afield in order to sustain existing sales and profitability.

NEW MARKET OPPORTUNITY

Personal-care products were designated by Johnson as a key growth area at this time, and the firm began to explore the possibility of entering these markets. Market research indicated that after-shampoo products had grown recently by more than 20 percent per year despite the fact that users were apparently dissatisfied with the feel of their hair after using these oily conditioning products. Research findings suggested that consumers wanted control and softness in hair that both looked and felt clean. Owing to its wide-ranging R&D program, Johnson had developed the technology to formulate a unique creme rinse product that was 99 percent oil-free but still conditioned hair.[1] The company had recently hired personnel who were experienced in the production and marketing of hair care products.

---

[1]The 1 percent oil component was included to provide a fragrance base. At that time, a major competing brand, Tame, contained approximately 40 percent oil.

Agree Creme Rinse and Conditioner (CRC), was first launched in the United States in 1976. During the fall of that year, marketing research was undertaken in Canada to develop profiles of typical shampoo and/or CRC consumers. Findings from the "Usage and Attitude Study" indicated that 95 percent of all Canadians used a shampoo product, with women accounting for the heaviest usage. The rate of usage varied, however, from once a day to once a week or less. In addition, the study found that 40 percent of all women used CRCs "some of the time."

Agree CRC was then introduced in Canada in June 1977 and became the Canadian CRC market leader by 1979 (see Exhibit 1). Some of its success was due to Johnson's Canadian advertising budget, set at $700,000 in the launch year compared to $868,000 for all other firms in the CRC industry, including $200,000 spent by Gillette on its CRC product, Tame, the market leader prior to Agree's introduction.[2] The Johnson product was also successful because of its superior formulation, which was emphasized in its advertising (see Exhibit 2). Finally, a large-scale sampling promotion contributed to the early success of Agree CRC.[3]

The extraordinary success of Agree CRC prompted Johnson to introduce a second Agree product. Johnson entered the large, highly competitive and fragmented shampoo market early in 1978, almost a

---

EXHIBIT 1   S. C. Johnson—Agree, Creme Rinse and Conditioner, Market Shares for the 12 Months Ending September/ October 1975–1979 (percentages)

Brand	*1975*	*1976*	*1977*	*1978*	*1979*
Tame	23.3	23.5	18.1	13.7	11.2
Clairol (total)*	18.3	16.2	13.2	9.1	10.8
Alberto Culver	9.4	8.0	—	—	—
Breck Clean Rinse	4.0	3.9	—	—	—
Revlon Flex	—	5.2	11.7	11.4	13.3
Wella Balsam	—	—	5.2	6.0	7.8
Agree	—	—	—	13.5	13.8
All others	45.0	41.6	47.0	41.0	40.0

*Includes Herbal Essence, Balsam, and Clairol Conditioner.

Source: Company records.

---

[2]Many of Johnson's figures have been disguised, but basic relationships have not been altered significantly.

[3]During the sampling campaign, ¾-ounce sachets were distributed in a full national mailing to approximately 3.2 million Canadian households.

EXHIBIT 2   S. C. Johnson—Agree, 1977 Advertisement for Agree Creme Rinse and Conditioner

"I used to get the greasies."

"With Agree I can forget the greasies!"

New Agree
Creme Rinse & Conditioner
Helps Stop the "Greasies"

The "greasies." That's oily, greasy hair too soon after using some creme rinse and conditioners. But now there's new Agree. New Agree Creme Rinse and Conditioner *actually helps stop the greasies.*

New Agree is 99% Oil Free
Agree's formula is very different. Some

creme rinse and conditioners contain oil up to 40% oil. And oil causes the greasies. *Agree's formula is actu-* ally 99% oil free. So there's no oil to give you the greasies. Yet, be assured, Agree still gives you beautiful wet combing, great conditioning.

Does Agree Really Work?
Yes. Agree was tested. And re-tested. People like yourself were asked to use Agree and compare it with the leading creme rinse and conditioner. Agree was pre-ferred. *It actually helped solve the problem of the greasies.*

Agree's Wet Combing is Proved Effective in Detangling Hair.
More tests were conducted at the Hair Care Laboratories of

S. C. Johnson & Son. A laboratory instrument (com-monly called an In-stron) measured the force required to remove tangles. *Agree removed the tangles significantly easier than the leading creme rinse and conditioner.*

Agree Actually Conditions Hair
Shown below are actual exam-ples of damaged and healthy-looking hair. The conditioners in Agree, used reg-ularly, will

reduce fly-away, make wet comb-ing easy and add body and shine, all signs of healthy looking hair.

Agree is pH Balanced
Most hair care experts agree that normal healthy-looking hair is mildly acidic with a pH range from 4.0 to 5.0. Agree has a compatible pH level of 4.0 to 5.0.

The people of the Hair Care Labora-tories, Personal Care Division of Johnson believe that Agree is the finest creme rinse and conditioner available in either salons or retail stores. Try Agree for yourself.

© S. C. Johnson and Son, Inc. Racine, Wisconsin 53401

EXHIBIT 3	S. C. Johnson—Agree, Market Shares of Shampoos, Early 1978	

Leading Brands	*Share*
Head & Shoulders	16
Johnson & Johnson Baby Shampoo	12
Clairol Herbal Essence	5
Breck Golden	6
Revlon Flex	4
Short & Sassy	3
Earth Born	3

Sales by Formula Type (percentage)

Dandruff medicated segment	20
Cosmetic segment (including baby shampoos)	80

Note: The total shampoo category consisted of over 150 brands and more than 700 sizes and types.

Source: Company records.

year after its Agree CRC introduction (see Exhibit 3). Agree shampoo was formulated to clean hair more thoroughly than most of the shampoos then on the market. The slogan, "Helps stop the greasies between shampoos," combined with the Agree name helped to make the new shampoo number three in the market within six months, close behind Head & Shoulders and Johnson & Johnson (J&J) Baby Shampoo.

By 1979, most other CRCs on the market were reformulated to be oil-free, thus converting Agree's main benefit into a generic one. Management recognized the potential threat posed by this move and began to consider alternative steps that could be taken to prevent any erosion of Agree's market share.

PRODUCT MANAGEMENT

S. C. Johnson employed a product management system to guide the strategic plans and activities of the firm's marketing department. Under this system, the director of marketing delegated responsibility for specific groups of products to group product managers (e.g., personal-care products, furniture and floor care), who, in turn, reassigned responsibility for one or more brands within the group to product managers and assistant product managers.

Product managers at Johnson adhered to a well-defined policy governing new product development. Under this policy, a new product was permitted to lose money during its introductory year(s) but was expected to achieve annual corporate profitability goals thereafter. Because the CRC and the shampoo had been introduced at different times, the goal for the full Agree line had been set at 11 percent in FY 1979–80. A target of 12.5 percent had been set for FY 1980–81.

From the inception of Agree shampoo in 1978 until late 1979, Agree CRC and shampoo were handled by two separate product managers within Johnson. The rationale for this division of responsibility reflected management's belief that the competitive environments for CRCs and shampoos were quite distinct during that period. This policy resulted in the development of separate advertising and pricing strategies for Agree CRC and shampoo.

During the latter part of 1979, market analysis was undertaken by S. C. Johnson to identify and describe Agree CRC and shampoo users (see Exhibit 4). Management was quite surprised to discover that the user base for Agree was not women aged 18 to 45, but primarily girls in the 12-to-24 age group. This study also showed that there was as high as 65 percent cross-usage between the Agree CRC and shampoo brands, one of the highest nationally, although they were not advertised as being essential to one another. Interestingly, earlier advertising tracking studies had indicated that approximately 24 percent of viewers of any Agree shampoo commercial recalled it as one for Agree CRC and vice versa.

In view of these research results, the product management group for Agree became increasingly convinced that consumers seemed to think about Agree products as a unit. As a result, the separate product manager positions for Agree CRC and shampoo were combined in order to achieve economies of scale and to foster better communications. As part of this integration, management decided that Agree products eventually would share a common pricing strategy together with joint trade and consumer promotions. Since Agree products would now be viewed as a family, advertising would be scheduled to alternate between shampoo and CRC. The combined FY 1979–80 sales for these products were estimated to total $12 million at retail.

Mel Liston had recently been appointed product manager for both Agree CRC and shampoo products. As a result of the 1979 market research study, he believed that repositioning Agree would strengthen its chances for continued success. In particular, the information pertaining to the current user base for Agree products led Mel Liston to define the primary target market as girls in the 12-to-18 age bracket and the secondary target market as women aged 19 to 24. New advertising copy and media schedules aimed at implementing the revised strategy for Agree were requested from Johnson's advertising agency.

Mel Liston said, "If we're going to be the 'bubble gum' shampoo, we have to gear most of our plans to this new market. We must change our thinking in order to fully exploit our knowledge of the consumer base for Agree."

EXHIBIT 4 S. C. Johnson—Agree, Shampoo/CRC Markets, Importance by Sex and Age Group

Group	Population (millions)	Percentage Who Use	Frequency of Use per Year	Number of Uses (millions)	Adjusting Factors	Equivalent Volume Used	Percentage of Volume Represented	Percentage of Volume of Agree Used
A. Hair Conditioner Market: Importance by Sex and Age Group								
Females:								
12–18	1.35	80	200	216	1.25	270	23	32
19–24	1.37	93	157	200	1.1	220	19	10
25–34	1.96	84	134	220	1.0	220	19	13
35–54	2.60	87	98	221	0.75	166	15	15
55+	2.33	85	70	138	0.60	83	7	4
Males:								
13–34	5.2	57	53	157	1.0	157	14	24
35+	4.8	42	11	22	0.8	18	3	2
B. Shampoo Market: Importance by Sex and Age Group								
Females:								
12–18	1.35	100	260	351	1.25	439	15	23
19–24	1.37	100	239	327	1.1	360	12	8
25–34	1.96	100	208	407	1.0	407	14	11
35–54	2.60	100	175	455	0.75	341	11	12
55+	2.33	100	95	221	0.6	132	4	3
Males:								
13–34	5.2	99	175	900	1.0	900	30	37
35+	4.8	97	102	474	0.8	380	14	6

Source: Company records.

THE AGREE MARKET

By May 1980, both Agree CRC and Agree shampoo were being offered on a continuous basis in three regular sizes and three formulas (see Exhibit 5). A fourth size, 50 ml, was offered each year, although mainly as a back-to-school trial size. This trial size was typically offered in promotional packages containing other personal care products sold by a variety of companies.

At that time, there were at least 150 kinds of shampoos and 80 CRCs on the market. Less than half of them were branded, and of these, only about 10 were supported by an advertising or consumer promotion. The rest were "price brands"—reasonably priced, acceptable products that were low-priced to consumers and were promoted heavily to the trade. Two of the more familiar of the price brands were Unicare and Suave.

Market share estimates for the different shampoo and CRC sizes are summarized in Exhibit 6. By May 1980 the total CRC market in Canada had reached almost $37.5 million and was growing at an annual

EXHIBIT 5   S. C. Johnson—Agree, Types, Sizes, and Colors of Agree Products, 1980

CRCs

Formula Name	*Bottle Color*	*Sales Volume (percentage)*
Extra Body with Balsam	Orange	27%
Regular Formula	Green	41
For Extra Oily Hair	Yellow	32

Shampoos

Formula Name	*Shampoo Color (bottle is clear plastic)*	*Sales Volume (percentage)*
Extra Gentle	Orange	29%
Regular	Green	40
Oily Hair	Yellow	31

Size	*Type*
50 ml	Trial (promotional only)
225 ml	Regular
350 ml	Family
450 ml	Economy (introduced in Feb. 1980)

Source: Company records.

EXHIBIT 6 S. C. Johnson—Agree, Market Shares for Agree
Shampoo/CRC

	Share of Dollar Sales		Share of Volume Sales	
	*1979–80 to Date**	*Percentage Change from 1978–79*	*1979–80 to Date*	*Percentage Change from 1978–79*
A. Shampoo				
Total market volume	107,742,000	11	6,725†	1
Total Agree	6.3	32	5.5	37
50 ml	0.1		0.1	
225 ml	1.5		1.1	
350 ml	4.1		3.7	
450 ml	0.7		0.6	
Head & Shoulders	16.5	22	10.8	16
J&J	7.6	2	7.9	(7)
Body on Tap	3.5	66	3.6	64
Revlon Flex	5.8	22	5.6	15
All others	60.3	6	67.4	(5)
B. CRC				
Total market volume	37,455,600	21	2,034.4	12
Total Agree	13.8	19	14.5	15
50 ml	0.3		0.5	
225 ml	2.8		2.4	
350 ml	6.1		6.5	
450 ml	4.6		5.2	
Tame	8.0	(2)	10.9	(11)
Silkience	2.9	N‡	1.2	N‡
Revlon Flex	10.5	43	12.0	29
Condition II	4.0	N	6.1	N
All others	60.8	10	55.3	1

*Based on approximately 10 months of sales. FY 1979–1980 ends on June 30.
†Represents the liquid measure of millions of cases of 12 350-ml bottles.
‡New; no data for year ago.

Source: Company records.

rate of approximately 20 percent. At that time, Agree CRC was the
leading brand in the category, with sales of $5.2 million at retail representing almost 13.8 percent of the total CRC market in dollar terms.
The total shampoo market had risen to almost $108 million, with a

growth rate of about 12 percent per year. Agree was second in terms of market share, with sales amounting to $6.8 million or close to 6.3 percent of the total shampoo market. The 350-ml bottle accounted for the bulk of total Agree sales, both in the CRC and shampoo categories (see Exhibit 6).

THE CONSUMER

Company sales records indicated that by May 1980 consumers were purchasing 75 percent as much Agree CRC as shampoo. Buying habits for these two items were quite different from those associated with Johnson's other products. For example, a 1979 market research study indicated that purchase frequency was relatively high—every few weeks as opposed to every few months. If the product that the consumer wanted was not on the shelf, she would rarely postpone her purchase until the following week. Instead, she normally would switch to another brand.

According to the 1979 study, the consumer typically owned about three brands at a time. Many of the purchasers, principally women, apparently believed that they became sensitized to one particular brand after a while.[4] Consequently, they would try another brand in their "evoked brand set"—those four or five brands that they were prepared to buy at any one time. Since people tended to rotate between brands within their own set, a key objective of management was to encourage users to come back to Agree more often, thereby ensuring its position as the brand with the highest frequency of use in the category. Purchases tended to be made largely on impulse, particularly for conditioners, which generally were considered to be less essential in the household than shampoos.

SALES AND DISTRIBUTION

When Agree CRC was first introduced in 1977, Johnson's distribution system was oriented primarily toward the food trade. However, the launch of Agree, a personal-care item, underscored the need for greater dependency on the drug trade in order to obtain widespread distribution for this type of product. Management decided to partially realign

---

[4]As a rule, people consider their hair-care requirements to be highly unique. After repeated uses of any single brand, many people gradually become concerned that the brand no longer works as effectively as it once did. It is this concern that prompts brand-switching behavior.

EXHIBIT 7   S. C. Johnson—Agree, Sales Percentage by Outlet Type

	Food	*Drug*	*Mass Merchandise*
Industry shampoo sales, 1978	43*	42	15
Industry CRC sales, 1978	36	42	22
Agree shampoo sales, 1979–80	47.4	38.5	17.0
Agree CRC sales, 1979–80	35	46.3	18.5

*To be read: "43% of all units sold were purchased in food stores."

Source: Company records.

its field sales effort in order to place increased emphasis on the drug trade. By 1980 more than 97 percent of the drug stores in Canada were included as part of the Johnson distribution system. Food stores constituted the primary outlets for Agree products, followed by drug and mass merchandising outlets, such as Woolco, K mart, and Zellers (see Exhibit 7).

Johnson had clear objectives for shelf management. In particular, it sought to have the 18 different bottles arranged at the retail outlet in a "billboard" or "ribbon" effect for maximum eye-catching appeal. Inserts and shelf talkers were frequently included to increase the likelihood of eye contact (see Exhibit 8).[5] Most retail outlets did not, in fact, carry every size and formula of the Agree line, despite aggressive sales force efforts to achieve this stocking pattern.

Johnson maintained its own sales force of approximately 80 people, who were required to sell all of its products, including Agree. By May 1980 additional penetration of distribution channels was no longer a primary objective. However, it was recognized that continued trade support would depend, in part, on the frequency and quality of both consumer and trade promotions. Sales representatives were well trained and were compensated by a salary-plus-incentives scheme, where the incentives included things like free trips and prizes. Management attempted to provide strong support for the sales force through regular meetings and discussions and by furnishing selling aids. Some of the Johnson products which the sales group sold—for example, "Raid" and "Off"—were seasonal. In the case of Agree, however, the variation per season was slight, averaging 3 or 4 percent higher in midsummer and 1 or 2 percent lower in winter.

---

[5]*Case inserts* are written instructions indicating where to stock the brand on the shelf. *Shelf talkers* are small signs attached to the front of a shelf on which the product is stocked.

EXHIBIT 8   S. C. Johnson—Agree, Case Insert (top) and Shelf
Talker (bottom)

Stock Agree next to Tame as shown for maximum shelf movement

Yellow Bottle for Extra Oily Hair   Green Bottle Regular Formula   Orange Bottle Extra Body with Balsam

"I used to get the greasies."   "With Agree I can forget the greasies."   New **Agree** ™   *Creme Rinse & Conditioner*   **helps stop the greasies**

PRICING

When Agree CRC was first introduced, the retail price was pegged to that of the leading brand, Tame. The regular cost to the retailer initially was $12.86 per case for one dozen 225-ml bottles and $16.94 per case for 350-ml bottles. At that time, retail selling prices ranged from $1.39 to $1.79 for the 225-ml size and from $1.79 to $2.39 for the 350-ml size. By May 1980 trade costs and suggested retail selling prices for Agree CRC were as follows:

Bottle Size	Trade Cost (per case)	Suggested Retail Selling Prices
225 ml	$14.65	$1.59–$1.79
350 ml	$19.20	$2.09–$2.29
450 ml	$23.50	$2.59–$2.79

The suggested retail selling prices for Agree CRC provided trade margins in the 23–31 percent range.

By May 1980, trade costs and suggested retail selling prices for Agree shampoo were as follows:

Bottle Size	Trade Cost (per case)	Suggested Retail Selling Prices
225 ml	$16.55	$1.79–$1.99
350 ml	$24.25	$2.59–$2.79
450 ml	$28.00	$2.99–$3.19

Suggested retail selling prices for Agree shampoo typically provided trade margins in 23-27 percent range.

The initial pricing strategy for Agree CRC was to introduce the product at a consumer price equal to that of Tame, or to Gillette Earth Born if Tame was not stocked in a particular outlet. A similar pricing strategy was pursued for Agree shampoo in that the pricing objective was parity with Johnson & Johnson Baby Shampoo, or with Clairol Herbal Essence if the former was not available. Over the next few years, Agree CRC and shampoo moved to a slight premium price relative to the top selling brands.

ADVERTISING

Mel Liston was about to set a marketing communications budget that would include expenditures for advertising, consumer promotion, and trade promotion. As a starting point, he examined the budgets for the fiscal years 1978–79 and 1979–80 (see Exhibit 9). In doing so, however, he recognized that some important factors had changed in the interim. For example, deal and promotional costs had been higher in FY 1978–79 than in the following year because of the introductory expenses incurred for the launch of Agree shampoo. Although the current year was estimated to be slightly below target, his projected budget for FY 1980–81 would still have to provide for a pretax profit level of at least 12.5 percent.

Foote, Cone & Belding, Johnson's advertising agency, was requested to prepare scripts that would direct advertising toward the new target audience. The agency created material that it felt would be effective and then made suggestions about how to use the advertising package— for example, the level of frequency required to achieve maximum impact with a particular audience. The agency commission would be included in Mr. Liston's budget as a fixed percent of his expected net revenue (see Exhibit 9).

The primary marketing objective was to maintain or increase current sales levels for Agree. To meet this goal, Mel Liston believed that it would be necessary to achieve a 90 percent awareness level for Agree within the new primary target audience of women aged 12 to 18. A secondary target audience was defined as women aged 19 to 24 and he hoped to achieve at least a 60 percent awareness level for this group.

EXHIBIT 9 S. C. Johnson—Agree, Mel Liston's P&L Worksheet for His 1980–81 Budget (CRC and Shampoo Combined)

	1978–79 ($000)	Percentage of Net Sales	1979–80* ($000)	Percentage of Net Sales	1980–81 ($000)	Percentage of Net Sales
Net sales	8,158	100	9,300	100		100
Cost of goods sold†	2,941	36	3,160	34		33
Gross profit	5,217	64	6,140	66		
Advertising	1,875	23	1,578	17		
Consumer promotion	816	10	553	6		
Deals	1,225	15	1,197	13		
Other‡	890	11	920	10		
Total promotion	4,806	59	4,248	46		
Functional expenses§	900	11	927	10		
Operating profit	489	(6)	965	10		≥12.5

*Projected from mid-May to June 30 year end.
†Includes labor, materials, standard overhead.
‡Includes external marketing services, sales meetings, agency fees.
§Overhead allocations and fixed costs.

Source: Company records.

Research undertaken by the advertising agency on Canadian teens' and young women's television viewing habits indicated a national weekly reach of 99 percent for the 12-to-18 age bracket and 98 percent for the 19-to-24-year-old group, with average weekly viewing times of 21.3 and 21.5 hours, respectively. One of the tasks facing Mel Liston was to select specific programs and parts of the day (e.g., 4:00–9:00 P.M.) that achieved optimal viewing levels within the budget that he set. He felt that consumer magazine advertising was important as a support vehicle to television, since magazines provided increased reach against the light television viewer (see Exhibit 10).

The agency proposed a television commercial for each Agree product, scripts for radio advertising, and layouts for print media. Total media costs to run the television commercials on a complete network daily basis were estimated at $1.05 million for 52 weeks if late afternoon time slots were scheduled versus $1.6 million for a prime time insertion schedule. These figures incorporated a discount, which could range from 10 to 15 percent on a full 52-week purchase. In keeping with Agree's younger image, the agency recommended a fast-paced, exciting commercial featuring a strong musical beat, which appeared to be favored by teens.

The product management group also considered radio advertising, which had been directed mainly at the "teen" segment of the Agree market during the previous two years. In FY 1979–80, Johnson ran a

---

EXHIBIT 10 S. C. Johnson—Agree, Media Plan Excerpts

A. Quintile Analysis

The quintiles of the 1980–81 media plan were compared with the quintiles of a television-only campaign, which would run for 52 weeks with a 45 percent weekly reach. The target group was women aged 12–18.

TV Watcher Quintile	*TV Only— % Total Impressions*	*Index*	*TV/Consumer Magazines— % Total Impressions*	*Index*
1 + 2 (light)	15.9	100	25.9	163
3 (medium)	21.5	100	33.6	156
4 + 5 (heavy)	62.6	100	40.6	70

B. Publication Costs (for full-page ads)

Publication	*Cost/Insertion(s)*	*Total Readers Women 12–18 (000)*	*CPM*($)*
Chatelaine (E)	15,078.15	350	43.08
Flare	5,174.80	224	23.10
Homemaker's	14,614.00	176	83.03
Chatelaine (F)	4,996.85	42	118.97
Madame au Foyer	4,199.13	27	155.52
Clin d'Oeil	1,921.50	60	32.01

Note: The above analysis reflects the fact that the inclusion of consumer magazines provides increased reach against the light TV viewer. In addition, the multimedia schedule provides a more even distribution of impressions against the light, medium, and heavy quintiles.
*Cost per thousand impressions.

Source: Foote, Cone and Belding.

seven-week radio campaign (see Exhibit 11). For FY 1980–81, it was estimated by the agency that the media cost for 27-station national radio would amount to approximately $35,000 per week.

Since its introduction, Agree had been promoted regularly in magazines and newspapers. During the launch periods, seven American and three Canadian magazines had carried full-page color advertisements for Agree. In Canada, Johnson had paid for the Canadian material and had received the American magazine spillover, estimated at approximately $200,000 per year, at no cost, although it was recognized that U.S. advertising would still be directed at the historical U.S. target audience, women aged 18 to 45.

EXHIBIT 11   S. C. Johnson—Agree, Agree Radio Plan

Target group: Primary   Teens   12–18
Target group: Secondary   Women   19–24
Reach objective: 55% weekly
Announcements: 30 seconds
Duration: 7 weeks

Market	Number of Stations	Number of Weekly Announcements for Each Product
Vancouver	2 CKLG/CFUN	40
Victoria	1 CKDA	20
Calgary	1 CKXL	25
Edmonton	1 CHED	25
Regina	1 CJME	25
Saskatoon	1 CKOM	25
Winnipeg	2 CKRC/CFRW	35
Toronto	3 CHUM-FM/CFTR/CHUM	50
Hamilton	1 CKOC	25
Ottawa	2 CFRA/CFGO	45
Kitchener	1 CHYM-AM	30
London	1 CJBK	25
Montreal		
English	2 CKGM/CHOM-FM	40
French	2 CKLM/CKAC	30
Quebec City	2 CHOI-FM/CFLS	50
Halifax	1 CJCH	20
St. John/Moncton	2 CFBC/CKCW	20
St. John's	1 VOCM	20

Source: Company records.

As Mel Liston began to work on developing a marketing communications program for FY 1980–81, he tried to imagine a profile of a typical teen girl and the type of advertising she would be most likely to notice. Studies on women 18 years old and over had shown that heavy users of hair products were not necessarily heavy watchers of television. However, he wondered how applicable this result was, given the age disparity with the Agree primary target group. There was even less statistical information on magazine readership in the target age group. Thus, Mel Liston wondered whether or not the reading habits of the typical young female consumer would justify spending a significant part of his budget on print advertising, in either magazines

or newspapers. If a decision was reached to run a print campaign, he
believed that any print advertising that did appear would have to be
young and vibrant like the ads that the agency was proposing for the
coming year (see Exhibit 12).

EXHIBIT 12   S. C. Johnson—Agree, 1980–81 Proposed Print Ad

CONSUMER PROMOTION

Johnson had introduced its Agree products with heavy consumer promotion. The CRC was introduced with a six-month sampling campaign, which consisted of a direct mailing to approximately three million potential users of a 3/4-ounce plastic sachet good for about two uses. This was followed by a second six-month campaign, which included 400,000 3/4-ounce plastic sachets and 15-cent coupons using a cross-promotion with Close-Up toothpaste.[6] Agree shampoo was introduced by using similar sachets to 3.2 million homes, and this campaign included a fact book and another 15-cent coupon. The net effective coverage of these promotional events was approximately 50 percent of Canadian homes.

Another launch promotion for Agree consisted of ¾-ounce pouches of free shampoo, which were attached to CRC bottles. One million of these pouches were distributed free to stores, in addition to 1.5 million 50-ml samples, which were prepriced at 39 cents each. The unit cost to Johnson was 5 cents per sachet of CRC and 7 cents per sachet of shampoo. Bulk distribution costs were estimated at $30 per thousand. Although sales for each product increased significantly during the trial period, the cost to Johnson of distributing such high quantities of free or virtually free merchandise was very high.

After Agree CRC and shampoo had been launched, other consumer promotion opportunities were considered. Refund campaigns were run twice during FY 1979–80. Coupons that offered 50 cents off the next purchase were distributed in bulk mailings and in magazines directed toward homemakers. Cash refunds of one dollar were later offered in exchange for two Agree labels. The redemption rates were 3 percent and 2 percent, respectively. This coupon program proved rather disappointing, since there was little, if any, change in sales volume during the promotion period.

In 1979, Agree in the United States had been packaged with a free Warner-Lambert razor, normally sold at $3.69. Although the perceived value of this "gift" was high, the impact on sales during the promotion period was disappointing. After calculating the total cost of the distributed premiums, this campaign was responsible for a substantial loss incurred by American Agree. A similar promotion was tried in the United States six months later. Free pantyhose were attached to Agree products. During the promotion period, sales remained relatively stable. However, the result of this promotion was less damaging to profits than the free razor campaign, since the cost to Johnson was only 40 cents per pair of pantyhose. Despite these results, Mel Liston

---

[6]Cross-promotions are samples, coupons, and the like placed on or inside the package of a noncompeting product usually sharing the same market as the promoted brand.

was unwilling to describe either of the premium campaigns as a failure, since other long-term objectives such as increases in usage frequency and brand loyalty appeared to have been met. Furthermore, in judging any sales promotion campaign, he realized, as a general rule, that most promotion events did lose money during the deal period.

One promotion being considered by Mel Liston was an "instant win" tag, whereby the purchaser would be notified if she had won a free pair of Jordache jeans. Jordache would be asked to supply the jeans free in exchange for being featured in advertising and in-store promotion. Other costs for this contest would include plastic prize tickets, special labels, backer cards, and labor. Some of these expenses would overlap into the trade promotion category. Total promotional costs for the Jordache Sweepstakes were estimated at $120,000, at least $20,000 of which would include store items such as end-aisle displays.

Mel Liston believed that consumer promotions were important merchandising devices, since all customers who learned about such offers could take advantage of them. In contrast, trade promotions, particularly off-invoice allowances, were important to retailers, but the benefits from these deals were not necessarily passed along to consumers in the form of lower prices. The primary objective of a consumer promotion was to induce the consumer to buy Agree more often, perhaps every other time, rather than every fourth or fifth time.

Since the product was in the non–price-sensitive 50 percent of the market where consumers tended to buy on impulse, Mel Liston felt that nonprice promotions might be very effective. Deals such as bonus packs were nondiscretionary in that anyone who bought the product received the bonus. However, Mr. Liston wondered whether bonuses were merely a way to subsidize or reward the already loyal purchaser. In his mind, it was unclear whether or not larger amounts of an untried product would, in fact, induce trial.

As Mel Liston began to think about consumer promotion plans for the coming year, he recognized the importance of establishing a clearly defined personality for Agree CRC and shampoo. One possible promotion event consisted of a contest that would offer as the grand prize a rock group concert at the winner's school or community center. Although somewhat unusual, this type of promotion might reinforce the image he was trying to project for Agree. He said, "We want a commercial image with an underlying message which tells the kids that the music and the special Agree products are mainly for them; they're not something meant to appeal to the whole family." Other consumer promotion possibilities included couponing and redemption ideas. For example, one opportunity under consideration was cross-ruff couponing, perhaps on Pledge or Flo-Thru Air Freshener or one of the company's other home-care products.

TRADE PROMOTION

Trade spending was something that companies such as Johnson felt they *had* to do; it was not truly discretionary. As part of each year's budget, a percentage of sales dollars was set aside in order to meet shelf space objectives. The FY 1979–80 discretionary pool of funds was set at 7.9 percent of projected sales. Without special deals, there might be insufficient reason for stores to try to sell Agree instead of competing brands.

Johnson allocated funds to trade promotion for two main reasons. First, trade deals were viewed as essential simply to get and keep products listed. A variety of trade deals were possible such as off-invoice allowances (e.g., $1.20 off each case ordered during the deal period). During FY 1979–80, trade spending varied widely both in the CRC and shampoo markets (see Exhibit 13).

The other reason for trade spending was related to cooperative advertising. Contributions to these programs normally were calculated according to a formula that included some percentage of a retailer's previous sales, typically around 2 percent. Advertising "slicks" (see Exhibit 14) were provided to retailers to encourage their active participation in coop advertising campaigns.[7]

To encourage retailers to sell stock at "feature prices" from time to time, S. C. Johnson provided off-invoice allowances (also called *deal money*) to the trade. Deal money was occasionally passed on to consumers as reduced prices but frequently was viewed by the retailer as a means to increase the trade margin. For example, Mel Liston estimated that only 40–50 percent of all stock sold on deal to the trade was actually retailed at the feature price. The balance was sold at the regular price, thereby increasing the retailer's trade margin. It seemed to Mel Liston that a large number of retailers were more concerned about obtaining deal money than about an extensive advertising campaign that the manufacturer might undertake to build a longer-term brand franchise.

Although advertising was sometimes cut if fourth-quarter sales were disappointing, trade deals hardly ever were cut. The risk of suffering a loss in shelf positioning was considered too great to justify a reduction in trade promotion activity. Retailers typically tried to buy and stock up at the end of a deal period to keep annual inventory costs down as much as possible. Retailer expectations regarding trade deals were not expected to change in FY 1980–81.

---

[7]Advertising "slicks" are reproducible copy and pictures supplied by manufacturers to participating retailers during a cooperative advertising campaign.

EXHIBIT 13 S. C. Johnson—Agree, Selected Promotional Influences for Major Brands, July–August 1979 to March–April 1980 (three periods)

A. Shampoo

	Agree			Head & Shoulders			Johnson & Johnson			Body on Tap			All Others		
	1979 July Aug.	1979 Nov. Dec.	1980 Mar. Apr.	1979 July Aug	1979 Nov. Dec.	1980 Mar. Apr.	1979 July Aug.	1979 Nov. Dec.	1980 Mar. Apr.	1979 July Aug.	1979 Nov. Dec.	1980 Mar. Apr.	1979 July Aug.	1979 Nov. Dec.	1980 Mar. Apr.
Sales share	6.4	5.4	5.7	9.5	10.8	10.1	7.3	7.3	8.6	4.0	3.3	3.9	72.7	73.1	71.7
Deal percentage of market*	2.8	1.2	0.4	0.1	0	0	0.5	0.8	0.4	1.5	0.5	1.0	7.5	7.0	6.4
	(43.8)	(22.2)	(7.0)	(1.0)	(0.0)	(0.0)	(6.8)	(10.9)	(4.7)	(37.5)	(15.2)	(25.6)	(10.3)	(9.6)	(8.9)
TV advertising ($000)	12.9	40.8	181.2	157.5	152.8	151.1	186.2	0	169.8	24.6	28.3	115.3	456	283	856
Radio advertising ($000)	139	3.7	0	31.3	7.0	36.2	0	0	10.9	0	0	0	5	2	15
Press advertising ($000)	0	0	17.2	13.7	16.2	7.4	0	0	0	7.1	0	11.0	105	46	220
Total advertising volume ($000)	152	45	198	203	176	195	186	2	181	31.8	28.3	126.3	566	331	1091
Advertising share:†	13.4	4.6	11.1	17.8	31.3	10.9	16.4	0.2	10.1	2.8	5.0	7.1	49.7	58.8	60.9
Co-op share:‡															
Food	32	20	31	35	30	34	53	61	59	29	1	10			
Drug	48	44	72	64	64	86	56	57	76	41	20	31			
Mass merchandiser	83	10	59	113	46	95	64	87	102	64	29	55			
Displays share:‡															
Food	9	6	8	16	7	8	6	14	13	3	2	4			
Drug	13	16	21	21	20	19	19	17	19	7	7	15			
Mass merchandiser	34	3	50	25	22	28	28	45	50	9	10	43			

B. CRC

	Agree			Revlon Flex			Silkience			Tame			Condition II			All Others		
	1979 July Aug.	1979 Nov. Dec.	1980 Mar. Apr.	1979 July Aug.	1979 Nov. Dec.	1980 Mar. Apr.	1979 July Aug.	1979 Nov. Dec.	1980 Mar. Apr.	1979 July Aug.	1979 Nov. Dec.	1980 Mar. Apr.	1979 July Aug.	1979 Nov. Dec.	1980 Mar. Apr.	1979 July Aug.	1979 Nov. Dec.	1980 Mar. Apr.
Sales share	15.6	15.1	13.7	14.5	11.1	12.8	2.7	4.5	6.1	9.2	10.3	9.2	7.1	8.1	9.2	50.9	51.8	51.2
Deal percentage of market*	4.6	5.3	2.1	6.0	2.1	1.4	0	0	0	1.3	2.5	1.1	1.5	2.6	0.9	10.5	11.2	9.9
	(29.5)	(35.1)	(15.3)	(41.4)	(18.9)	(10.9)	(0.0)	(0.0)	(0.0)	(14.1)	(24.3)	(11.9)	(21.1)	(32.1)	(14.5)	(20.6)	(21.6)	(19.3)

TV advertising ($000)	33.7	243.8	0	58.9	7.3	0	133.0	100.8	75.7	0	0	85.1	11.8	5.8	8.9	124.6	81.5	41.3
Radio advertising ($000)	47.5	0	0	0	0	0	0	0	0	0	0	0	0	0	0	0	0	0
Press advertising ($000)	0	0	0	0	0	0	0	19.0	30.4	35.1	0	5.2	0	10.4	28.0	71.8	7.6	99.8
Total advertising volume ($000)	81.1	243.8	0	58.9	7.3	0	133.0	119.8	106.1	35.1	0	90.3	11.8	16.2	37	198.2	89.1	141.1
Advertising share†	16.8	47.7	0	12.2	1.4	0	27.5	23.4	25.6	6.9	0	21.8	2.4	3.2	8.9	41.0	17.4	43.7
Co-op share:‡																		
Food	19	15	15	19	5	14	7	14	15	13	17	17	1	7	6			
Drug	36	31	43	15	21	29	45	40	46	29	28	26	27	42	32			
Mass merchandiser	53	16	32	40	10	33	29	26	29	44	26	50	31	45	36			
Displays shares:§																		
Food	9	4	2	5	5	7	3	8	8	13	7	6	1	4	1			
Drug	20	15	18	17	12	19	13	24	12	22	23	5	10	14	8			
Mass merchandiser	37	22	50	6	16	21	19	13	7	34	6	18	15	35	21			

$$\frac{12.9 + 139.0}{(12.9 + 139.0) + (157.5 + 31.3 + 13.7) \ldots + (456.0 + 5.0 + 105.0)} = 13.4\% \text{ (rounded)}$$

*The Neilsen Market Survey defines a deal as any package/price configuration that is different from the company's regular market configuration. The figures in the row are the proportion of brand sales that were sold on deal. For example, during July–August 1979 in the shampoo market, approximately 43.8 percent (6.4 ÷ 2.8) of Agree shampoo sales were "on deal," compared to 22.2 percent (5.4 ÷ 1.2) of sales for Agree during November–December 1979.

† Advertising share denotes Agree share of total advertising expenditures on the product category during each period. For example, the calculation for July–August 1979:

‡Co-op share is supplied by A. C. Neilsen. It is a period result defined as the number of stores that did co-op advertising (i.e., newspapers, flyers) weighted by their sales importance to the shampoo category. For example, in July–August 1979, food stores doing 32 percent of shampoo sales in the food trade had co-op advertising on Agree.

§Display share is the unweighted percentage of stores that had display activity when the store was audited by A. C. Neilsen at the end of the bimonthly period. For example, at the end of August 1979, 9 percent of food stores had Agree on display. Display is defined by Neilsen as the product being somewhere in the store other than its normal shelf position.

EXHIBIT 14 S. C. Johnson—Agree, Example of an Advertising Slick

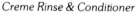

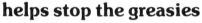

THE TASK

As Mel Liston began to think about developing a comprehensive marketing communications program for the Agree line in FY 1980–81, he remembered that the first step in the process was to establish a set of clear and specific objectives against which campaign results could be measured. In addition, he understood that decisions about advertising, consumer promotions, and trade deals were highly interrelated. Thus, overall success in implementing the revised positioning strategy for Agree CRC and shampoo would depend on his ability to design a well-integrated communications program. In this type of program, decisions across advertising, consumer, and trade promotion activities would have to be well coordinated with in-store merchandising to achieve a strong reinforcing effect.

Mr. Liston was frequently overheard explaining this philosophy to new people in his department. He told them that exposure was worth more than price—that is, an end-aisle display with 10 cents off was more valuable to the company than a one-dollar sale sitting on a shelf—but that both types of promotion might be necessary. In addition, he believed that an end-aisle display with no cents off or no contest was merely a nice arrangement of stock instead of a sales booster.

The complete marketing communications plan was required by July 1, 1980. The document itself would outline decisions reached in the following areas: total communications budget for FY 1980–81 and allocation of those funds across advertising, consumer, and trade promotion activities; message strategy; and selection and scheduling of advertising media, consumer promotions, and trade deals. In addition, the plan would outline any steps needed to coordinate the marketing communications activities proposed for FY 1980–81. Given the importance of these decisions to the future position of Agree CRC and shampoo in the market, Mel Liston planned to consult other members of the Agree product management group before finalizing the plan.

Distribution Strategy

Tupperware

J. Paul Peter

University of Wisconsin–Madison

In 1958 Justin Dart purchased Tupperware from former Du Pont chemist Earl Tupper for $10 million. From that time until 1983 Tupperware earned an estimated $1.5 billion pretax and had a phenomenal 25-year record of doubling sales and earnings every 5 years. In 1983, Tupperware sales slipped 7 percent to $827 million and operating profits sank 15 percent to $192 million.

Tupperware is sold by 90,000 part-time salespeople and 10,000 full-time managers in the United States. The plastic products are sold at in-house Tupperware parties which consist of a part-time salesperson inviting friends over and displaying the many varieties of plastic products. The party typically includes refreshments, a free sample of Tupperware, casual conversation, and formal offering of Tupperware products. Customers order at the party and pay for the products on delivery by the salesperson.

Sources: "Tupperware's Party Times Are Over," *Fortune,* February 20, 1984, pp. 113–20; "Dart & Kraft Turns Back to Its Basic Business—Food," *Business Week,* June 11, 1984, pp. 100–105.

Four explanations have been offered for the decline in Tupperware sales in 1983. First, since the economy was recovering, many of the part-time salespeople quit to take full-time jobs with other companies. This resulted in 7 percent fewer salespeople and 5 percent fewer parties in the first 11 months of the year.

Second, Tupperware commissions to salespeople are somewhat less than other in-home sellers such as Avon and Mary Kay cosmetics. Avon pays commissions of 35 percent to 50 percent depending on sales volume and Mary Kay pays from 40 percent to 50 percent. Tupperware pays a flat 35 percent commission to dealers. Tupperware does offer merchandise bonuses but their value has been decreasing. As one executive put it, "Salespeople aren't stupid. They can see they're being asked to sell more to win goods that have less value. People aren't as motivated to sell as hard, because the thrill of earning those big-ticket gifts isn't what it used to be."

Third, one study found that the average family of four owned 28 pieces of Tupperware. While this might not be a concern given the broad product line, some questions could be raised concerning market saturation.

Fourth, competition increased greatly in the inexpensive plastic bowl market. For example, Eagle Affiliates ran a series of national TV ads pointing out that it was more convenient and less expensive to buy these products in supermarkets rather than purchase them at an in-home party. Rubbermaid also increased its marketing effort to sell an expanded line of plastic bowls in supermarkets.

One approach taken by Tupperware to overcome its dealer recruiting problems and to position the firm for the long run was the development of new products. For example, the company introduced a new line called Modular Mates. These compact, stackable containers were targeted at smaller families with less storage space available. In addition, a line of cookware for microwave ovens was developed. Most analysts agreed that Tupperware would revive but would never again grow at 17 percent compounded annually as it did in the 1970s.

Discussion Questions

1. What accounts for the overall success of Tupperware?
2. Evaluate each of the reasons given for the decrease in sales and operating profits in 1983.
3. In addition to offering new products, what else should Tupperware do to avoid losses in sales and profits?

Cub Foods*

J. Paul Peter

University of Wisconsin–Madison

Leslie Wells's recent expedition to the new Cub Foods store in Melrose Park, Illinois, was no ordinary trip to the grocery store. "You go crazy," says Wells, sounding a little shell-shocked. Overwhelmed by Cub's vast selection, tables of samples, and discounts as high as 30 percent, Wells spent $76 on groceries—$36 more than she planned. Wells fell prey to what a Cub executive calls "the wow factor"—a shopping frenzy brought on by low prices and clever marketing. That's the reaction Cub's super warehouse stores strive for—and often get.

Cub Foods has been a leader in shaking up the food industry and forcing many conventional supermarkets to lower prices, to increase services, or—in some cases—to go out of business. With Cub and other super warehouse stores springing up across the country, shopping habits are changing, too. Some shoppers drive 50 miles or more to a Cub store instead of going to the nearest neighborhood supermarket. Their payoff is that they find almost everything they need under one roof, and most of it is cheaper than at competing supermarkets. Cub's low prices, smart marketing, and sheer size encourage shoppers to spend far more than they do in the average supermarket.

The difference between Cub and most supermarkets is obvious the minute a shopper walks through Cub's doors. The entry aisle, called by some the "power alley," is lined two stories high with specials, such as bean coffee at $2 a pound and half-price apple juice. Above, the ceiling joists and girders are exposed, giving "the subliminal feeling of all the spaciousness up there. It suggests there's massive buying going on that translates in a shopper's mind that there's tremendous savings going on as well," says Paul Suneson, director of marketing research for Cub's parent, Super Valu Stores Inc., the nation's largest food wholesaler.

---

*This case is taken from J. Paul Peter and Jerry C. Olson, *Consumer Behavior: Marketing Strategy Perspectives* (Homewood, Ill.: Richard D. Irwin, 1987), pp. 655–56. Based on Steve Weiner and Betsy Morris, "Bigger, Shrewder and Cheaper Cub Leads Food Stores into the Future," *The Wall Street Journal,* August 26, 1985, p. 17.

Cub's wider-than-usual shopping carts, which are supposed to suggest expansive buying, fit easily through Cub's wide aisles, which channel shoppers toward high-profit impulse foods. The whole store exudes a seductive, horn-of-plenty feeling. Cub customers typically buy in volume and spend $40 to $50 a trip, four times the supermarket average. The average Cub store has sales of $800,000 to $1 million a week, quadruple the volume of conventional stores.

Cub Foods has a simple approach to grocery retailing: low prices, made possible by rigidly controlled costs and high-volume sales; exceptionally high quality for produce and meats—the items people build shopping trips around; and immense variety. It's all packaged in clean stores that are twice as big as most warehouse outlets and four times bigger than most supermarkets. A Cub store stocks as many as 25,000 items, double the selection of conventional stores, mixing staples with luxury, ethnic, and hard-to-find foods. This leads to overwhelming displays—88 kinds of hot dogs and dinner sausages, 12 brands of Mexican food, and fresh meats and produce by the ton.

The store distributes maps to guide shoppers. But without a map or a specific destination, a shopper is subliminally led around by the arrangement of the aisles. The power alley spills into the produce department. From there the aisles lead to highly profitable perimeter departments—meat, fish, bakery, and frozen food. The deli comes before fresh meat, because Cub wants shoppers to do their impulse buying before their budgets are depleted on essentials.

Overall, Cub's gross margin—the difference between what it pays for its goods and what it sells them for—is 14 percent, six to eight points less than most conventional stores. However, because Cub relies mostly on word-of-mouth advertising, its ad budgets are 25 percent less than those of other chains.

Discussion Questions

1. List at least five marketing tactics Cub Foods employs in its stores to increase the probability of purchases.
2. What accounts for Cub's success in generating such large sales per customer and per store?
3. Given Cub's lower prices, quality merchandise, excellent location, and superior assortment, what reasons can you offer for why many consumers in its trading areas refuse to shop there?

Thompson Respiration Products, Inc.*

James E. Nelson
William R. Woolridge
both of the University of Colorado

Victor Higgins, executive vice president for Thompson Respiration Products, Inc. (TRP), sat thinking at his desk late one Friday in April 1986. "We're making progress," he said to himself. "Getting Metro to sign finally gets us into the Chicago Market . . . and with a good dealer at that." *Metro,* of course, was Metropolitan Medical Products, a large Chicago retailer of medical equipment and supplies for home use. "Now, if we could just do the same in Minneapolis and Atlanta," he continued.

However, getting at least one dealer in each of these cities to sign a TRP Dealer Agreement seemed remote right now. One reason was the sizeable groundwork required—Higgins simply lacked the time to review operations at the well over 100 dealers currently operating in the two cities. Another was TRP's lack of dealer-oriented sales information that went beyond the technical specification sheet for each product and the company's price list. Still another concerned two conditions in the Dealer Agreement itself—prospective dealers sometimes balked at agreeing to sell no products manufactured by TRP's competitors and differed with TRP in interpretations of the "best efforts" clause. (The clause required the dealer to maintain adequate inventories of TRP products, contact four prospective new customers or physicians or respiration therapists per month, respond promptly to sales inquiries, and represent TRP at appropriate conventions where it exhibited.)

"Still," Higgins concluded, "we signed Metro in spite of these reasons, and 21 others across the country. That's about all anyone could expect—after all, we've only been trying to develop a dealer network for a year or so."

---

*This case was written by Professor James E. Nelson and DBA Candidate William R. Woolridge, the University of Colorado. This case illustrates neither effective nor ineffective administrative decision making. Some data are disguised. © 1986 by the Business Research Division, College of Business and Administration and the Graduate School of Business Administration, University of Colorado, Boulder, Colorado 80309.

THE PORTABLE RESPIRATOR INDUSTRY

The portable respirator industry began in the early 1950s when polio-stricken patients who lacked control of muscles necessary for breathing began to leave treatment centers. They returned home with hospital-style iron lungs or fiber-glass chest shells, both being large chambers that regularly introduced a vacuum about the patient's chest. The vacuum caused the chest to expand and, thus, the lungs to fill with air. However, both devices confined patients to a prone or semiprone position in a bed.

By the late 1950s, TRP had developed a portable turbine blower powered by an electric motor and battery. When connected to a mouthpiece via plastic tubing, the blower would inflate a patient's lungs on demand. Patients could now leave their beds for several hours at a time and realize limited mobility in a wheelchair. By the early 1970s, TRP had developed a line of more sophisticated turbine respirators in terms of monitoring and capability for adjustment to individual patient needs.

At about the same time, applications began to shift from polio patients to victims of other diseases or of spinal cord injuries, the latter group existing primarily as a result of automobile accidents. Better emergency medical service, quicker evacuation to spinal cord injury centers, and more proficient treatment meant that people who formerly would have died now lived and went on to lead meaningful lives. Because of patient's frequently younger ages, they strongly desired wheelchair mobility. Respiration therapists obliged by recommending a Thompson respirator for home use or, if unaware of Thompson, recommending a Puritan-Bennett or other machine.

Instead of a turbine, Puritan-Bennett machines used a bellows design to force air into the patient's lungs. The machines were widely used in hospitals but seemed poorly suited for home use. For one thing, Puritan-Bennett machines used a compressor pump or pressurized air to drive the bellows, much more cumbersome than Thompson's electric motor. Puritan-Bennett machines also cost approximately 50 percent more than a comparable Thompson unit and were relatively large and immobile. On the other hand, Puritan-Bennett machines were viewed by physicians and respiration therapists as industry standards.

By the late 1970s, TRP had developed a piston and cylinder design (similar in principle to the bellows) and placed it on the market. The product lacked the sophistication of the Puritan-Bennett machines but was reliable, portable, and much simpler to adjust and operate. It also maintained TRP's traditional cost advantage. Another firm, Life Products, began its operations in 1981 by producing a similar design. A third competitor, Lifecare Services, had begun operations somewhat earlier.

Puritan-Bennett

Puritan-Bennett was a large, growing, and financially sound manufacturer of respiration equipment for medical and aviation applications. Its headquarters were located in Kansas City, Missouri. However, the firm staffed over 40 sales, service, and warehouse operations in the United States, Canada, the United Kingdom, and France. Sales for 1985 exceeded $100 million, while employment was just over 2,000 people. Sales for its Medical Equipment Group (respirators, related equipment, and accessories, service, and parts) likely exceeded $40 million for 1985; however, Higgins could obtain data only for the period 1981–84 (see Exhibit 1). Puritan-Bennett usually sold its respirators through a system of independent, durable medical equipment dealers. However, its sales offices did sell directly to identified "house accounts" and often competed with dealers by selling slower-moving products to all accounts. According to industry sources, Puritan-Bennett sales were slightly more than three fourths of all respirator sales to hospitals in 1985.

However, these same sources expected Puritan-Bennett's share to diminish during the late 1980s because of the aggressive marketing efforts of three other manufacturers of hospital-style respirators: Bear Medical Systems, Inc.; J. H. Emerson; and Siemens-Elema. The latter

---

EXHIBIT 1   Puritan-Bennett Medical Equipment Group Sales

	1981	1982	1983	1984
Domestic sales:				
Model MA-1:				
Units	1,460	875	600	500
Amount ($ millions)	8.5	8.9	3.5	3.1
Model MA-2:				
Units	—	935	900	1,100
Amount ($ millions)	—	6.0	6.1	7.8
Foreign sales:				
Units	250	300	500	565
Amount ($ millions)	1.5	1.8	3.1	3.6
IPPB equipment ($ millions)	6.0	6.5	6.7	7.0
Parts, service, accessories ($ millions)	10.0	11.7	13.1	13.5
Overhaul ($ millions)	2.0	3.0	2.5	2.5
Total ($ millions)	28.0	34.0	35.0	37.5

Source: The Wall Street Transcript.

firm was expected to grow the most rapidly, despite its quite recent entry into the U.S. market (its headquarters were in Sweden) and a list price of over $16,000 for its basic model.

Life Products

Life Products directly competed with TRP for the portable respirator market. Life Products had begun operations in 1981 when David Smith, a TRP employee, left to start his own business. Smith had located his plant in Boulder, Colorado, less than a mile from TRP headquarters.

He began almost immediately to set up a dealer network and by early 1986 had secured over 40 independent dealers located in large metropolitan areas. Smith had made a strong effort to sign only large, well-managed durable medical equipment dealers. Dealer representatives were required to complete Life Product's service training school, held each month in Boulder. Life Products sold its products to dealers (in contrast to TRP, which both sold and rented products to consumers and to dealers). Dealers received a 20 to 25 percent discount off suggested retail price on most products.

As of April 1986, Life Products offered two respirator models (the LP3 and LP4) and a limited number of accessories (such as mouthpieces and plastic tubing) to its dealers. Suggested retail prices for the two respirator models were approximately $3,900 and $4,800. Suggested rental rates were approximately $400 and $500 per month. Life Products also allowed Lifecare Services to manufacture a respirator similar to the LP3 under license.

At the end of 1985, Smith was quite pleased with his firm's performance. During Life Products' brief history, it had passed TRP in sales and now ceased to see the firm as a serious threat, at least according to one company executive:

> We really aren't in competition with Thompson. They're after the stagnant market and we're after a growing market. We see new applications and ultimately the hospital market as our niche. I doubt if Thompson will even be around in a few years. As for Lifecare, their prices are much lower than ours but you don't get the service. With them you get the basic product, but nothing else. With us, you get a complete medical care service. That's the big difference.

Lifecare Services, Inc.

In contrast to the preceding firms, Lifecare Services, Inc., earned much less of its revenues from medical equipment manufacturing and much more from medical equipment distributing. The firm primarily resold products purchased from other manufacturers, operating out of its headquarters in Boulder as well as from its 16 field offices (Exhibit 2). All offices were stocked with backup parts and an inventory of respirators. All were staffed with trained service technicians under Lifecare's employ.

Lifecare did manufacture a few accessories not readily available from other manufacturers. These items complemented the purchased products and, in the company's words, served to "give the customer a complete respiratory service." Under a licensing agreement between Lifecare and Life Products, the firm manufactured a respirator similar to the LP3 and marketed it under the Lifecare name. The unit rented for approximately $175 per month. While Lifecare continued to service the few remaining Thompson units it still had in the field, it no longer carried the Thompson line.

Lifecare rented rather than sold its equipment. The firm maintained that this gave patients more flexibility in the event of recovery or death and lowered patients' monthy costs.

THOMPSON RESPIRATION PRODUCTS, INC.

TRP currently employed 13 people, 9 in production and 4 in management. It conducted operations in a modern, attractive building (leased) in an industrial park. The building contained about 6,000 square feet of space, split 75/25 for production/management purposes. Production operations were essentially job shop in nature: skilled technicians assembled each unit by hand on work benches, making frequent quality control tests and subsequent adjustments. Production lots usually ranged from 10 to 75 units per model and probably averaged around 40. Normal production capacity was about 600 units per year.

EXHIBIT 2   Lifecare Services, Inc., Field Offices

Augusta, Ga.	Houston, Tex.
Baltimore, Md.	Los Angeles, Calif.
Boston, Mass.	New York, N.Y.
Chicago, Ill.	Oakland, Calif.
Cleveland, Ohio	Omaha, Nebr.
Denver, Colo.	Phoenix, Ariz.
Detroit, Mich.	Seattle, Wash.
Grand Rapids, Mich.*	St. Paul, Minn.

*Suboffice.

Source: Trade literature.

Product Line

TRP currently sold seven respirator models plus a large number of accessories. All respirator models were portable but differed considerably in terms of style, design, performance specifications, and attendant features (see Exhibit 3). Four models were styled as metal boxes

---

EXHIBIT 3   TRP Respirators

Model*	Style	Design	Volume (cc)	Pressure (cm. H_2O)
M3000	Metal box	Volume	300–3,000	+10 to +65
MV Multivent	Metal box	Pressure (positive or negative)	n.a.	−70 to +80
Minilung M15	Suitcase	Volume	200–1,500	+5 to +65
Minilung M25 Assist (also available without the assist feature)	Suitcase	Volume	600–2,500	+5 to +65
Bantam GS	Suitcase	Pressure (positive)	n.a.	+15 to +45
Compact CS	Metal box	Pressure (positive)	n.a.	+15 to +45
Compact C	Metal box	Pressure (positive)	n.a.	+15 to +45

Model	Breaths per minute	Weight (lbs.)	Size (cubic ft.)	Features
M3000	6 to 30	39	0.85	Sigh, four alarms, automatic switchover from AC to battery
MV Multivent	8 to 24	41	1.05	Positive or negative pressure, four alarms, AC only
Minilung M15	8 to 22	24	0.70	Three alarms, automatic switchover from AC to battery
Minilung M25 Assist (also available without the assist feature)	5 to 20	24	0.70	Assist, sigh, three alarms, automatic switchover from AC to battery
Bantam GS	6 to 24	19	0.75	Sigh, six alarms, automatic switchover from AC to battery
Compact CS	8 to 24	25	0.72	Sigh, six alarms, automatic switchover from AC to battery
Compact C	6 to 24	19	0.50	Sigh, four alarms, automatic switchover from AC to battery

Note: n.a. = not applicable.
*Five other models considered obsolete by TRP could be supplied if necessary.

Source: Company sales specification sheets.

with an impressive array of knobs, dials, indicator lights, and switches. Three were styled as less imposing "overnighter" suitcases with less prominently displayed controls and indicators. (Exhibit 4 reproduces part of the specification sheet for the M3000, as illustrative of the metal box design.)

Four of the models were designed as *pressure machines,* using a turbine pump that provided a constant, usually positive, pressure. Patients were provided intermittent access to this pressure as breaths per minute. However, one model, the MV Multivent, could provide either a constant positive or a constant negative pressure (i.e., a vacuum, necessary to operate chest shells, iron lungs, and body wraps). No other portable respirator on the market could produce a negative pressure. Three of the models were designed as *volume machines,* using a piston pump that produced intermittent, constant volumes of pressurized air as breaths per minute. Actual volumes were prescribed by each patient's physician based on lung capacity. Pressures depended on the breathing method used (mouthpiece, trach, chest shell, and others) and on the patient's activity level. Breaths per minute also depended on the patient's activity level.

Models came with several features. The newest was an assist feature (currently available on the Minilung M25 but soon to be offered also on the M3000) that allowed the patient alone to "command" additional breaths without having someone change the dialed breath rate. The sigh feature gave patients a sigh, either automatically or on demand. Depending on the model, up to six alarms were available to indicate a patients' call, unacceptable low pressure, unacceptable high pressure, low battery voltage/power failure, failure to cycle, and the need to replace motor brushes. All models but the MV Multivent also offered automatic switchover from alternating current to either an internal or an external battery (or both) in the event of a power failure. Batteries provided for 18 to 40 hours of operation, depending on usage.

Higgins felt that TRP's respirators were superior to those of Life Products. Most TRP models allowed pressure monitoring in the airway itself rather than in the machine, providing more accurate measurement. TRP's suitcase-style models often were strongly preferred by patients, especially the polio patients who had known no others. TRP's volume models offered easier volume adjustments and all TRP models offered more alarms. On the other hand, he knew that TRP had recently experienced some product reliability problems of an irritating—not life threatening—nature. Further, he knew that Life Products had beaten TRP to the market with the assist feature (the idea for which had come from a Puritan-Bennett machine).

TRP's line of accessories was more extensive than that of Life Products. TRP offered the following for separate sale: alarms, call switches, battery cables, chest shells, mouthpieces, plastic tubing, pneumobelts

EXHIBIT 4   The M3000 Minilung

M3000 MINILUNG
PORTABLE VOLUME VENTILATOR

What it can mean to the User . . .

• The M3000 is a planned performance product designed to meet breathing needs. It is a significant step in the ongoing effort of a company which pioneered the advancement of portable respiratory equipment.

• This portable volume ventilator sets high standards for flexibility of operation and versatility in use. The M3000 has gained its successful reputation as a result of satisfactory usage in hospitals, for transport, in rehabilitation efforts and in home care. This model grew out of expressed needs of users for characteristics which offer performance PLUS. It is engineered to enable the user to have something more than just mechanical breathing.

• Now breathing patterns can be comfortably varied with the use of a SIGH, which can be obtained either automatically or manually.

• Besides being sturdy and reliable, the M3000 can be adjusted readily.

• Remote pressure sensing in the proximal airway provides for more accurate set up of the ventilator pressure alarms.

• This model has the option of a patient-operated call switch.

• AC-DC operation of the M3000 is accomplished with ease because automatic switch-over is provided on AC power failure, first to external battery, then to internal battery.

THOMPSON takes pride in planning ahead.

See reverse for specifications.

Innovators in Respiratory Equipment for Over 25 Years
Thompson Respiration Products, Inc.   1680 Range Street   Boulder Colorado 80301   303/443-3350

M3000 MINILUNG
Portable Volume Ventilator

SPECIFICATIONS:

300 to 3000 ml adjustable volume

10 to 65 cm. water pressure

6 to 30 breaths per minute

Automatic or Manual Sigh

Alarms:
Patient operated call alarm
Low Pressure alarm and light
High Pressure alarm and light
Low Voltage light with delayed alarm
Automatic switchover provided on AC power failure,
   first to external battery, then to internal battery
Alarm delay switch

Pilot lamps color-coded and labeled

Remote pressure connector

Self-contained battery for 2 hour operation — recharges automatically

Power sources:
120 volt, 60 hz; 12 volt external battery; and internal battery

Size: 12⅝ W x 11¼ D x 10¼ inches H

Weight: 39 pounds (Shipping weight: 48 pounds)

and bladders (equipment for still another breathing method that utilized intermittent pressure on a patient's diaphragm), and other items. Lifecare Services offered many similar items.

Distribution

Shortly after joining TRP, Higgins had decided to switch from selling and renting products directly to patients to selling and renting products to dealers. While it meant lower margins, less control, and more infrequent communication with patients, the change had several advantages. It allowed TRP to shift inventory from the factory to the dealer, generating cash more quickly. It provided for local representation in market areas, allowing patients greater feelings of security and TRP more aggressive sales efforts. It shifted burdensome paperwork (required by insurance companies and state and federal agencies to effect payment) from TRP to the dealer. It also reduced other TRP administrative activities in accounting, customer relations, and sales.

TRP derived about half of its 1985 revenue of $3 million directly from patients and about half from the dealer network. By April 1986, the firm had 22 dealers (see Exhibit 5) with 3 accounting for over 60 percent of TRP dealer revenues. Two of the three serviced TRP products as did two of the smaller dealers; the rest preferred to let the factory take care of repairs. TRP conducted occasional training sessions for dealer repair personnel but distances were great and turnover in the position high, making such sessions costly. Most dealers requested air shipment of respirators, in quantities of one or two units.

EXHIBIT 5   TRP Dealer Locations

Bakersfield, Calif.	Salt Lake City, Utah
Baltimore, Md.	San Diego, Calif.
Birmingham, Ala.	San Francisco, Calif.
Chicago, Ill.	Seattle, Wash.
Cleveland, Ohio	Springfield, Ohio
Fort Wayne, Ind.	Tampa, Fla.
Greenville, N.C.	Tucson, Ariz.
Indianapolis, Ind.	Washington, D.C.
Newark, N.J.	Montreal, Canada
Oklahoma City, Okla.	Toronto, Canada
Pittsburgh, Pa.	

Source: Company records.

Price

TRP maintained a comprehensive price list for its entire product line. (Exhibit 6 reproduces part of the current list.) Each respirator model carried both a suggested retail selling price and a suggested retail rental rate. (TRP also applied these rates when it dealt directly with patients.) The list also presented two net purchase prices for each model along with an alternative rental rate that TRP charged to dealers. About 40 percent of the 300 respirator units TRP shipped to dealers in 1985 went out on a rental basis. The comparable figure for the 165 units sent directly to consumers was 90 percent. Net purchase prices allowed an approximate 7 percent discount for orders of three or more units of each model. Higgins had initiated this policy early last year with the aim of encouraging dealers to order in larger quantities. To date one dealer had taken advantage of this discount.

Current policy called for TRP to earn a gross margin of approximately 35 percent on the dealer price for one or two units. All prices included shipping charges by United Parcel Service (UPS); purchasers requesting more expensive transportation service paid the difference between actual costs incurred and the UPS charge. Terms were net 30 days with a 1.5 percent service charge added to past due accounts. Prices were last changed in late 1985.

CONSUMERS

Two types of patients used respirators, depending on whether the need followed from disease or from injury. Diseases such as polio, sleep apnea, chronic obstructive pulmonary disease, and muscular dystrophy annually left about 1,900 victims unable to breathe without a

EXHIBIT 6 Current TRP Respirator Price List

	Suggested Retail		Dealer Rent/month	Dealer Price	
Model	Rent/month	Price		1–2	3 or More
M3000	$380	$6,000	$290	$4,500	$4,185
MV Multivent	270	4,300	210	3,225	3,000
Minilung M15	250	3,950	190	2,960	2,750
Minilung M25	250	3,950	190	2,960	2,750
Bantam GS	230	3,600	175	2,700	2,510
Compact CS	230	3,600	175	2,700	2,510
Compact C	200	3,150	155	2,360	2,195

Source: Company sales specification sheets.

respirator. Injury to the spinal cord above the fifth vertebra caused a similar result for about 300 people per year. Except for polio, incidences of the diseases and injury were growing at about 3 percent per year. Most patients kept one respirator at bedside and another mounted on a wheechair. However, Higgins did know of one individual who kept eight Bantam B models (provided by a local polio foundation, now defunct) in his closet. Except for polio patients, life expectancies were about five years. Higgins estimated the total number of patients using a home respirator in 1981 as follows:

Polio	3,000
Other diseases	6,500
Spinal cord injury	1,000

Almost all patients were under a physician's care as well as that of a more immediate nurse or attendant (frequently a relative). About 95 percent paid for their equipment through insurance benefits or foundation monies. About 90 percent rented their equipment. Almost all patients and their nurses or attendants had received instruction in equipment operation from respiration therapists employed by medical centers or by dealers of durable medical equipment.

The majority of patients were poor. Virtually none was gainfully employed and all had seen their savings and other assets diminished to varying degrees by treatment costs. Some had experienced a divorce. Slightly more patients were male than female. About 75 percent lived in their homes, with the rest split between hospitals, nursing homes, and other institutions.

Apart from patients, Higgins thought that hospitals might be considered a logical new market for TRP to enter. Many of the larger and some of the smaller general hospitals might be convinced to purchase one portable respirator (like the M3000) for emergency and other use with injury patients. Such a machine would be much cheaper to purchase than a large Puritan-Bennett and would allow easier patient trips to testing areas, X-ray, surgery, and the like. Even easier to convince should be the 14 regional spinal cord injury centers located across the country (Exhibit 7). Other medical centers that specialized in treatment of pulmonary diseases should also be prime targets. Somewhat less promising but more numerous would be public and private schools that trained physicians and respiration therapists. Higgins estimated the number of these institutions at:

General hospitals (100 beds or more)	3,800
General hospitals (fewer than 100 beds)	3,200
Spinal cord injury centers	14
Pulmonary disease treatment centers	100
Medical schools	180
Respiration therapy schools	250

EXHIBIT 7 Regional Spinal Cord Injury Centers

Birmingham, Ala.	Houston, Tex.
Boston, Mass.	Miami, Fla.
Chicago, Ill.	New York, N.Y.
Columbia, Mo.	Philadelphia, Pa.
Downey, Calif.	Phoenix, Ariz.
Englewood, Colo.	San Jose, Calif.
Fishersville, Va.	Seattle, Wash.

DEALERS

Dealers supplying homecare medical products (as distinct from dealers supplying hospitals and medical centers) showed a great deal of diversity. Some were little more than small areas in local drugstores that rented canes, walkers, and wheelchairs in addition to selling supplies like surgical stockings and colostomy bags. Others carried nearly everything needed for home nursing care—renting everything from canes to hospital beds and selling supplies from bed pads to bottled oxygen. Still others specialized in products and supplies for only certain types of patients.

In this latter category, Higgins had identified dealers of oxygen and oxygen-related equipment as the best fit among existing dealers. These dealers serviced victims of emphysema, bronchitis, asthma, and other respiratory ailments, a growing market that Higgins estimated was about 10 times greater than that for respirators. A typical dealer had begun perhaps 10 years ago selling bottled oxygen (obtained from a welding supply wholesaler) and renting rather crude metering equipment to patients at home under the care of a registered nurse. The same dealer today now rented and serviced oxygen concentrators (a recently developed device that extracts oxygen from the air), liquid oxygen equipment and liquid oxygen, and much more sophisticated oxygen equipment and oxygen to patients cared for by themselves or by relatives.

Most dealers maintained a fleet of radio-dispatched trucks to deliver products to their customers. Better dealers promised 24-hour service and kept delivery personnel and a respiration therapist on call 24 hours a day. Dealers usually employed several respiration therapists who would set up equipment, instruct patients and attendants on equipment operation, and provide routine and emergency service. Dealers often expected the therapists to function as a sales force. The therapists would call on physicians and other respiration therapists at hospitals and medical centers, on discharge planners at hospitals, and on organizations such as muscular dystrophy associations, spinal cord injury associations, and visiting nurse associations.

Dealers usually bought their inventories of durable equipment and supplies directly from manufacturers. They usually received a 20 to 25 percent discount off suggested list prices to consumers and hospitals. Only in rare instances might dealers instead lease equipment from a manufacturer. Dealers aimed for a payback of one year or less, meaning that most products began to contribute to profit and overhead after 12 months of rental. Most products lasted physically for upwards of 10 years but technologically for only 5 to 6: every dealer's warehouse contained idle but perfectly suitable equipment that had been superseded by models demanded by patients, their physicians, or their attendants.

Most dealers were independently owned and operated, with annual sales ranging between $5 million and $10 million. However, a number had recently been acquired by one of several parent organizations that were regional or national in scope. Such chains usually consisted of from 10 to 30 retail operations located in separated market areas. However, the largest, Abbey Medical, had begun operations in 1924 and now consisted of over 70 local dealers. Higgins estimated 1985 sales for the chain (which was itself acquired by American Hospital Supply Corporation in April 1981) at over $60 million. In general, chains maintained a low corporate visibility and provided their dealers with working capital, employee benefit programs, operating advice, and some centralized purchasing. Higgins thought that chain organizations might grow more rapidly over the next 10 years.

THE ISSUES

Higgins looked at his watch. It was 5:30 and really time to leave. "Still," he thought, "I should jot down what I see to be the immediate issues before I go—that way I won't be tempted to think about them over the weekend." He took a pen and wrote the following:

1. Should TRP continue to rent respirators to dealers?
2. Should TRP protect each dealer's territory (and how big should a territory be)?
3. Should TRP require dealers to stock no competing equipment?
4. How many dealers should TRP eventually have? Where?
5. What sales information should be assembled in order to attract high-quality dealers?
6. What should be done about the "best efforts" clause?

As he reread the list, Higgins considered that there probably were still other short-term-oriented questions he might have missed. Monday would be soon enough to consider them all.

Until then, he was free to think about broader, more strategic issues. Some reflections on the nature of the target market, a statement of marketing objectives, and TRP's possible entry into the hospital market would occupy the weekend. Decisions on these topics would form a substantial part of TRP's strategic marketing plan, a document Higgins hoped to have for the beginning of the next fiscal year in July. "At least I can rule out one option," Higgins thought as he put on his coat. That was an idea to use independent sales representatives to sell TRP products on commission: recently completed two-month search for such an organization had come up empty. "Like my stomach," he thought, as he went out the door.

| *Lands' End**

Peter G. Goulet
Lynda L. Goulet
both of the University of Northern Iowa

Lands' End, Inc. (LEI) was founded in 1963 by Gary C. Comer, an avid sailor and an award-winning copywriter with the advertising agency of Young & Rubican. LEI was founded to sell equipment to racing sailors by direct mail. Its unique name was the result of a mistake in its first printed mailing piece. Lands' End was meant to be Land's End, the name of a famous English seaport. The error was left uncorrected and the firm was off and running. Mr. Comer has said, "For me Lands' End is a dream that came true. I always wanted to create a company of my own and here it is."

From its founding until 1976, LEI emphasized the sales of sailing gear while gradually adding related traditional recreational clothing and soft luggage to its product line. The clothing and luggage became so popular among the firm's upscale clientele that by 1976, LEI shifted its focus entirely to these more popular items. In 1979, having outgrown its Chicago location, LEI moved to its current headquarters in Dodgeville, Wisconsin. The Chicago facility which once housed the whole firm was retained as the location of its marketing creative staff of 35 people.

In its first 25 years Lands' End has grown to sales of over $335 million, making it one of the nation's largest merchants selling entirely through the medium of the direct-mail catalog. In the five years between 1982 and 1987, LEI's sales more than tripled and the firm set a goal of doubling fiscal 1986 sales by 1991. LEI went public in October 1986, achieving listing on the New York Stock Exchange in late 1987. LEI's 20,040,000 shares had a market value of $560 million in September 1988. For the fiscal year ending in January 1989, Lands' End

*This case was prepared by Peter G. Goulet and Lynda L. Goulet of the University of Northern Iowa and is intended to be used as a basis for class discussion rather than to illustrate either effective or ineffective handling of an administrative situation. The authors thank Julie Coppock, a UNI graduate student, and Stephen Ashley of Blunt, Ellis, and Loewi for their help in the preparation of this case.

Presented to and accepted by the refereed Midwest Society for Case Research. All rights reserved to the authors and to the MSCR. © 1988 by Peter G. Goulet and Lynda L. Goulet.

TABLE 1 Income Statements for the Fiscal Years Ended January 31 (thousands of dollars), Lands' End

	1988	%	1987	%	1986	%	1985	%
Net sales	$336,291	100.0%	$265,058	100.0%	$227,160	100.0%	$172,241	100.0%
Cost of sales	190,348	56.6%	152,959	57.7%	135,678	59.7%	101,800	59.1%
Gross profit	145,943	43.4%	112,099	42.3%	91,482	40.3%	70,441	40.9%
Operating expense	104,514	31.0%	80,878	30.5%	67,781	29.9%	55,431	32.2%
Depreciation	3,185	1.0%	2,576	1.0%	1,867	.8%	1,435	.8%
Operating income	38,244	11.4%	28,645	10.8%	21,834	9.6%	13,575	7.9%
Interest expense	1,357	−0.4%	(1,488)	−0.6%	(1,579)	−0.7%	(1,697)	−1.0%
Other income	1,441	0.4%	1,329	0.5%	1,329	0.6%	938	0.5%
Income before tax	38,328	11.4%	28,486	10.7%	21,584	9.5%	12,816	7.4%
Income tax (1)	15,523	4.6%	13,881	5.2%	10,314	4.5%	6,076	3.5%
Net income	22,805	6.8%	14,605	5.5%	11,270	5.0%	6,740	3.9%
Per share (2)	$1.14		$0.73		$0.56			
Catalogs mailed	63.5 mil.		50.0 mil.		44.0 mil.		29.0 mil.	
Quarterly percents	Sales	Gr. Pr.	Sales	Gr. Pr.	Sales	Gr. Pr.		
Feb–Apr	18.0%	17.6%	17.8%	16.7%	19.1%	19.5%		
May–July	19.0	18.8	19.9	18.7	19.4	18.1		
Aug–Oct	23.8	24.1	24.5	25.3	23.7	24.4		
Nov–Jan	39.1	39.4	37.8	39.3	37.8	38.0		

Lands' End was a Subchapter S corporation through part of 1987. Therefore: (1) Income taxes from 1985–87 are estimated to reflect a normal corporate structure. (2) Earnings per share are estimated based on shares outstanding in 1988.

TABLE 2   Statement of Changes in Working Capital for Fiscal Years Ended (thousands of dollars), Lands' End

	1988	%	1987	%	1986	%	1985	%
Sources:								
Operations (1)	$25,668		$21,804		$23,451		$14,251	
Long-term debt			264		316			
Sale of stock			22,584				520	
Fixed assets, net	776		38		243		205	
Total sources	$26,444		$44,690		$24,010		$14,976	
Uses:								
Dividends (2)	$ 4,008		$28,000		$13,775		$11,755	
Fixed assets	5,862		9,595		6,631		2,658	
Reduce L.T. debt	1,918						478	
Other			40		24			
Total uses	$11,788		$37,635		$20,430		$14,891	
Net incr. w. cap.	$14,656		$ 7,055		$ 3,580		$ 85	

(1) Cash flow from operations consists of net income, depreciation, and additions to deferred taxes. (2) Lands' End was a subchapter S corporation through part of 1987. Therefore, dividends from 1985–87 are subchapter S distributions.

is expected to circulate 72 million catalogs, achieve sales of $388 million, and earn profits of $26 million, or $1.30 per share.[1] Further financial information is presented in Tables 1–3.

BUSINESS AND CUSTOMERS

Lands' End is a clothing retailer serving the market by direct mail through its extensive catalog of traditional clothing and related items. The main types of products sold include men's dress shirts, slacks, ties, and accessories, as well as sport clothes such as sweaters, shoes, jogging suits, and "sweats," and a myriad of styles of knit shirts. The women's line includes similar sport clothing, as well as traditional natural fiber shirts, skirts, slacks, shoes, and accessories. The firm also offers a limited, but growing, line of children's clothing in styles similar to the adult lines. Finally, the firm manufactures and sells a line of soft luggage products and has recently introduced a line of linen and bedding.

---

[1]All financial data in this case comes from Lands' End annual reports and analytical reports prepared by Stephen Ashley of Blunt, Ellis, and Loewi, Inc. (August 4, 1987 and November 23, 1987).

TABLE 3   Balance Sheets for the Fiscal Years Ended January 31
(thousands of dollars), Lands' End

	1988	1987	1986
Current assets			
Cash & m. secur.	$ 28,175	$16,032	$ 3,578
Receivables	274	238	319
Inventories	46,444	40,091	31,057
Other	3,363	1,299	733
Total current	$ 78,256	$57,660	$35,687
Plant & equipment			
Land & buildings	15,114	13,809	9,499
Equipment	21,974	19,667	13,266
Leashold improv.	908	661	584
Other	674		1,250
Total	38,670	34,137	24,599
Depreciation	9,947	7,315	4,758
Net fixed as-sets	28,723	26,822	19,841
Total assets	$106,979	$84,482	$55,528
Current liabilities			
Curr. portion long-term debt	$ 1,918	$ 321	$ 193
Accounts payable	21,223	16,791	13,927
Order advances	453	449	193
Accruals	7,226	4,394	2,589
Profit sharing	2,646	1,707	830
Taxes payable	5,394	9,258	
Total current	38,860	32,920	18,002
Long-term debt	8,667	10,585	10,321
Deferred inc. tax	2,778	3,100	
	50,305	46,605	28,323
Stockholders' equity			
Common stock	200	100	95
Paid-in-capital	22,308	22,408	73
Retained earnings	34,166	15,369	27,037
Total equity	56,674	37,877	27,205
Total debt and own-ers' equity	$106,979	$84,482	$55,528

The Lands' End customer is reasonably affluent. Sixty percent have incomes in excess of $35,000. Most have been to college and are employed in professional or managerial jobs. Table 4 compares the typical Lands' End customer to its counterpart in the population as a whole. In 1986, LEI estimated that there were 23 million households in the United States that met its typical customer characteristics. Moreover,

TABLE 4 Lands' End Customer Analysis

	Median Household Income	Women, Percent Employed	Percent, Ages 25–49	Growth 25–49 >$30K*	Percent Employed Professionals
LEI	$46,000	75%	69%	3.2%	70%
U.S.	24,500	<50%	50%	<1.0%	<25%

*Annual growth expected from 1985 to 1995 for the population group with incomes over $30,000, and from 25 to 49 years of age.

this group was growing more than three times as fast as the population as a whole. Further, it typically spends a larger proportion of its income on apparel than the average for the population.

The Direct Marketing Association (DMA) estimated that 10.1 percent of the total female population and 5.4 percent of the male population ordered at least one item of clothing from a catalog or other direct-mail merchant in 1986. On average, between 9 percent and 10 percent of all the people with incomes over $30,000 made a direct-mail clothing purchase. In addition, DMA has estimated that 10.7 percent of college graduates and 10.5 percent of professional/managerial households made such a purchase. Overall, it would appear that about 10 percent of the group Lands' End considers to be its prime customers can be expected to make a direct-mail clothing purchase from some firm in a given year. Out of the base of 23 million customers, this would imply an average of 2.3 million active customers per year. In fact, LEI estimates that in the 36 months preceding February 1988, it had made at least one sale to 3.4 million different persons.

INDUSTRY ENVIRONMENT

Lands' End is part of the catalog apparel industry, which accounts for approximately 10 percent of all apparel sales. Recent data for these markets is shown in Table 5. In 1988 the firm held about a 4 percent share of the catalog apparel market, making it the seventh largest direct-market or catalog-apparel retailer (see Table 6 for a list of selected competitors). This market has enjoyed recent growth of 8.6 percent per year and is expected to continue to grow at 10 percent per year through 1991. Lands' End has grown roughly two to three times as fast as the market since calendar 1985.

Though catalog retailing is expected to grow faster than retailing in general in the next three to five years, there are some clouds on the horizon. The prospects for growth have caused a sharp increase in the

TABLE 5   Retail Sales Data ($ billions)

	1985	1986	1987E	1988E	Growth Rate†
Retail sales	1374.0	1454.0	1541.0	1633.0	5.9%
Retail apparel	74.0	81.0	86.7	92.8	7.8
Catalog sales*	26.0	27.5	29.7	32.1	7.3
Catalog apparel*	7.5	8.2	8.9	9.6	8.6
Lands' End	.23	.26	.34	.39	19.2
share cat. app'l.	3.1%	3.1%	3.8%	4.1%	

*Estimated.
†Average annual growth, 1985–88.

Source: U.S. Commerce Department.

number of catalogs directed to the buying public. In 1985, a total of 10 billion catalogs were mailed, rising to 11.8 billion in 1987.[2] In addition, poor service on the part of some catalog merchants may help create a negative image for the segment in general. *Consumer Reports* has recently published ratings of catalog retailers to help consumers determine the relative service quality of many of the larger firms, including Lands' End. Lands' End was beaten only by L. L. Bean in these initial consumer ratings.

Another threat to catalog retailers is the rising cost of shipping goods and mailing catalogs. Early in 1988, the postal service raised postage rates for catalogs 25 percent and U.P.S. raised surface shipping costs as well. In addition, catalog production costs are also rising, as are catalog sizes. The typical cost for a catalog the size and quality of that published by Lands' End can run a high as $750–$800 per thousand, exclusive of mailing and handling costs. A typical 64-page catalog in two or four colors costs around $350–$400 per thousand. To partially offset these rising costs, some catalog retailers—such as Bloomingdale's—have begun to sell their catalogs in major chain bookstores and to sell advertising space in the catalogs.

Finally, most states do not require catalog retailers to charge sales tax on catalog sales outside of the states in which the firm operates. Recently, however, states are beginning to view this practice as a significant source of lost revenue. In 1988, Iowa was added to a small but growing list of states which will require catalog firms to remit sales tax on all purchases made from catalogs by residents of the state,

---

[2]A. Hagedorn, "'Tis the Season for Catalog Firms," *The Wall Street Journal*, November 24, 1987, p. 6.

regardless of where the catalog firm is located. If all states move to this type of policy it will reduce one of the key advantages to catalog retailers and could create significant overhead expenses for keeping the records required to satisfy each state.

A segment of the direct-market retailing industry outside of the catalog segment may also pose a threat to catalog retailers. Home shopping directed through cable television was expected to generate an estimated $1.75 billion in sales in 1987. The companies in this segment, of which the largest is the Home Shopping Network, Inc., were estimated to have reached over 40 million households in that year. Further, though some view the cable shopping phenomenon as a fad, DMA estimates that by 1992 this industry segment could be generating $5.6 billion in sales and be reaching nearly 80 million households. If this is true it represents a 26 percent average annual growth rate for the period. Given the growth of retail sales in general and forecasts for direct-market retailing, this would seem to be growth that could easily come at the expense of other direct marketers.

Though entry into direct marketing does not demand the same level of investment required to generate similar sales in the normal retail market, the costs may still be significant. To provide sufficient service requires expertise and may involve a large equipment investment. To develop a mailing list is also important and expensive. Name rental may run anywhere from $60–$100 per thousand names annually, or upwards of $100,000 for a million quality, proven names. As established firms such as Lands' End and L. L. Bean become large, economies of scale and learning curve effects may make it difficult for new firms to enter the business in all but small niche markets.

Pure catalog retailers have a number of significant advantages over conventional retailers. The most obvious of these is that they have no stores to operate and have, therefore, lower costs. Passing on some of these cost savings can create a competitive advantage. Yet in spite of this inherent advantage, several major catalog competitors have chosen to operate store locations in addition to their catalog operation. What these firms have attempted to do is improve their performance as traditional retailers by using higher-profit catalog sales as an adjunct to normal store-based selling. The Limited, Eddie Bauer, Talbots, J. C. Penney, and Sears, for example, operate anywhere from several dozen to several hundred stores each.

In addition to lower costs and prices, catalog retailers offer the customer the advantage of convenience. Being able to shop through a catalog and call in an order even in the middle of the night may be of great benefit to households where, for example, both spouses work outside the home. Using a catalog also allows the consumer to think about the purchase and compare alternate sources without costly transportation and sales pressure. Finally, catalog shopping is a convenience for people who live in smaller communities where a variety of upscale goods, in particular, is not typically available; obtaining such goods from a conventional store would be even more inconvenient than purchasing through a catalog.

The biggest weaknesses of catalog shopping involve the inability to see an item before buying it and the cost and inconvenience of having to return an unsatisfactory purchase. In spite of these issues, however, a Gallup poll reported by the DMA in 1987, shows that two thirds of the population would consider making a direct/catalog purchase even if the item were available in conventional stores.

LANDS' END'S STRATEGY

Catalog retailers must adhere to most of the principles that govern traditional store-based retailers. Merchandise must be fresh, varied, and of satisfactory quality. By maintaining itself as a retailer of traditional clothing, Lands' End does not have the concerns with fad and fashion faced by such combination in-store and direct-mail retailers as the Limited and Bloomingdales, for example. However, the firm does have to offer new merchandise regularly. Its most recent introductions have been its line of linens and children's clothing. Other featured items include its knit shirts and rugby shirts, the latter having been chosen by the U.S. National Rugby Team as their official jersey.

All Lands' End merchandise carries the firm's private label. All catalog items except luggage are produced by outside vendors. The luggage is manufactured by the firm at its plant in West Union, Iowa. Product quality is assured by frequent inspections of goods, both at the manufacturer's facility and at the company. The firm even maintains a Lear jet to fly its staff of quality assurance personnel to the factories of domestic manufacturers to direct production according to Lands' End specifications. Further, ten percent of every shipment received at Dodgeville is inspected to assure continuing quality. Critical products are purchased from more than one vendor and consistency between them is maintained by strict specifications. To further assure quality and service from vendors, officers of these companies are regularly brought to Dodgeville to see the Lands' End operation.

Lands' End understands that catalog retailing is a difficult business in which to create a competitive advantage. Its catalogs, therefore, are produced with what the firm calls an "editorial" approach. Goods are not merely described in short, dry prose. Rather, key product lines are given half- or full-page descriptions designed to be interesting, appealing, and original. The catalog also contains several pages devoted to editorials, essays, and witty commentary dealing with a variety of subjects of interest to the firm's clientele. Two pages in the April 1988, issue described glass blowing. This kind of content is not unique to Lands' End. The catalog issued by the trendy Banana Republic employs a similar approach. However, because different writers and subjects are involved in each catalog, Lands' End's catalogs are unique and difficult to copy.

The quality and presentation of the Lands' End catalog is tightly controlled and merchandise is presented in "life-style" settings designed to appeal to the firm's clientele. Merchandise is grouped in "programs" to promote multiple-item sales. This magazine-style approach is further supported by the use of product teams: new items are studied by a team consisting of a writer, an artist, and a buyer to make certain that each item is presented properly in the catalog.

To interest prospective customers, Lands' End utilizes print advertising. The cost of this national campaign in selected upscale publications such as *The Wall Street Journal* and the *New Yorker* is approximately 1 percent of sales. The campaign is designed to be compatible with the firm's editorial catalog structure and contains copy in a similar style.

Lands' End considers itself a "direct merchant" and summarizes its marketing and operations strategy as:

1. Establishing a strong, unique consumer brand image.
2. Placing an emphasis on product quality and value.
3. Identifying and expanding an active customer base.
4. Creating a continuous relationship with active customers.
5. Building customer confidence and convenience through service.

SERVICE

At least part of the success of Lands' End has been attributed to its customer-oriented marketing philosophy. This customer orientation is reflected in a number of ways. Prompt service is supported by rapid response and personal attention. The firm claims its 24-hour-a-day 800 number—which is the source of 73 percent of all incoming orders—rarely requires more than two rings before it is answered. In addition, 99 percent of its orders are shipped within 24 hours of receipt. This level of service is facilitated by a dedicated staff, a sophisticated computerized operating system, and a distribution center recently doubled in size to 275,000 square feet. The DMA reports in its 1987 survey of customer attitudes that 83 percent of all direct-mail customers have some sort of complaint about direct-mail purchasing. Though the most common complaints center on the inability to tell what one is likely to receive, or that one will have been deceived by the merchandise, a significant percentage either object to poor service (20 percent) or inconvenience of some kind (16 percent). In addition, over half of consumers surveyed by DMA say they would buy more from direct marketers who provide prompt delivery.

Lands' End deals with customer complaints with the same commitment they have to customers placing orders. This is essential if the firm is to retain its strong group of dedicated customers. The DMA reports that though a high proportion of customers may have some complaint with mail order, 73 percent will become repeat customers if the complaint is satisfactorily handled, compared to 17 percent if it is not.

Lands' End sums up its marketing and service philosophy through its "Principles of Doing Business." These principles have been published in the catalog, annual reports, and advertising copy produced by the company:

Principle 1. We do everything we can to make our products better. We improve material, and add back features and construction details that others have taken out over the years. We never reduce the quality of a product to make it cheaper.

Principle 2. We price our products fairly and honestly. We do not, have not, and will not participate in the common retail practice of inflating markups to set up a future phony "sale."

Principle 3. We accept any return, for any reason, at any time. Our products are guaranteed. No fine print. No arguments. We mean exactly what we say: GUARANTEED. PERIOD.

Principle 4. We ship faster than anyone we know of. We ship items in stock the day we receive the order. At the height of the last Christmas season the longest time an order was in the house was 36 hours, excepting monograms which took another 12 hours.

Principle 5. We believe that what is best for our customer is best for all of us. Everyone here understands that concept. Our sales and service people are trained to know our products, and to be friendly and helpful. They are urged to take all the time necessary to take care of you. We even pay for your call, for whatever reason you call.

Principle 6. We are able to sell at lower prices because we have eliminated middlemen; because we don't buy branded merchandise with high protected markups; and because we have placed our contracts with manufacturers who have proved they are cost conscious and efficient.

Principle 7. We are able to sell at lower prices because we operate efficiently. Our people are hard working, intelligent, and share in the success of the company.

Principle 8. We are able to sell at lower prices because we support no fancy emporiums with their high overhead. Our main location is in the middle of a 40-acre cornfield in rural Wisconsin. We still operate our first location in Chicago's Near North tannery district.

OPERATIONS

The heart of any catalog retailing operation is, of course, the catalog itself. Lands' End currently mails thirteen 140-page (average) catalogs a year to its proven customers. In all, the firm circulated a total of 50 million catalogs in fiscal 1987. That number is expected to rise to 63.5 million in 1988 and is expected to reach 72 million in 1989, up from 18 million in 1984, the firm's most productive year in terms of sales per catalog mailed.

Another key to effective catalog retailing is the mailing list. Firms the size of Lands' End commonly maintain lists of 5 million or more names. The firm itself maintains a proprietary list of 7.8 million names. Although many catalog retailers obtain names from mailing-list brokers and even competitors, Lands' End has attempted to build its list internally, as much as possible, as a source of competitive advantage. It has also reduced its participation in the mailing-list rental market.

Catalog retailing also depends on order fulfillment and service. Merchandise is stored in and distributed from the firm's 275,000-square-foot distribution center. In spite of the size of this facility, however, it is only expected to be able to satisfy the firm's needs through 1989, when another 250,000-square-foot addition is expected to be completed. Through this center, Lands' End processed approximately 31,000 orders per day in 1987, with a high of 75,000 orders on its peak day. The center has the capacity to process 35,000 orders per nine-hour shift.

To facilitate the function of the distribution center, manage inventories, and minimize shipping costs, the firm utilizes an optical-scanning sorting system. Orders are processed through the firm's mainframe computer system, based on three very large Series 3090 IBM computers. Through this computer system, management can obtain real-time information on any part of its current operation status. In addition, during 1987, the firm installed a new computer-controlled garment-moving system and an inseaming system as part of $6 million in capital expenditures. Finally, an automated receiving system installed during 1987, has increased the firm's receiving capacity from 4,000 to 10,000 boxes per day.

Phone service is maintained through company phone centers. This service was recently enlarged by the addition of an auxillary center designed to handle seasonal overload traffic. The phone system now operates on a fiber-optic cable system to increase communication quality. Through the computer system, each operator has access to customer records and past sales history, as well as a fact file on each catalog item. In normal times, it is not unusual for this system to handle 75 calls at a time, around the clock, with a much higher load during the Christmas season.

Though 95 percent of all sales are through the catalog, and Lands' End operates no retail stores, it does maintain nine "outlet stores" at various locations in Chicago and Wisconsin. The firm also utilizes a "Lands' End Outlet" section in its catalog to help dispose of overstocks.

As the firm has grown, so has the number of employees. The firm now employs more than 2,200 people, with as many as 1,200 added to handle the extra load during the busy fourth quarter. Both the founder and the current president have extensive advertising experience as well as considerable experience with the company. New additions to the list of top managers include experts in catalog merchandising, quality assurance, and other related specialties.

Lands' End realizes the importance of a quality work force. It has worked with the University of Wisconsin, Platteville, to set up an extension in Dodgeville to help workers increase their skills at company expense. Part-time workers earn full-time benefits after they work 1,040 hours in a year. All workers receive the right to an employee discount on the firm's products and they share in the LEI's profits. The firm also plans to provide a $5 million employee fitness center in 1988. Overall, wage levels in this industry average approximately $5.75 per hour.

COMPETITORS

Dozens of catalog retailers sell apparel, even in the market dominated by Lands' End. However, in its specific target market, LEI has apparently become the market leader. LEI's competitors can be classified into several basic categories. Firms such as the J. Crew unit of Popular Services, Inc. (men's clothing), Talbots (women's clothing, formerly owned by General Mills), and The Company Store (linens), compete directly with a product segment served by Lands' End. Other firms, such as Hanover House, produce multiple catalogs serving a wide variety of customer product and demographic segments. Some of these segments may overlap with those served by LEI. Major retailers such as Sears, J. C. Penney, and Spiegel produce large, seasonal, full-line catalogs selling a wide variety of merchandise, of which apparel is only a part. These large firms, as well as other smaller catalog retailers who also operate retail stores, tend to compete more closely with traditional retailers. Table 6 identifies a number of major catalog retailers and competitors for LEI. Table 7 describes and contrasts several operating characteristics of LEI's closest competitors.

TABLE 6   Direct/Catalog Sales, 1985 Largest Direct-Mail/Catalog-
Apparel Firms

Firm	Direct/Catalog Total 1985 Sales
Fingerhut Corp/Cos.	$1,485 million
Spiegel	847 million
Sears	695 million
The Limited/Brylane	612 million
J. C. Penney	510 million
New Process	330 million
Combined International	227 million
Lands' End	227 million
L. L. Bean	220 million
Hanover House	212 million
Avon Direct Response	205 million
Bear Creek	130 million
General Mills	104 million
CML Group	55 million
Popular Services	40 million

Source: Maxwell Sroge *(Inside the Leading Mail Order Houses,* 1985).

TABLE 7   Competitor Characteristics, 1985 Lands' End

Company	Catalog Sales ($ mil.)	Catalogs Mailed (mil.)	Sales per Catalog	Active Buyers (mil.)	Stores and/or Notes
Lands' End	$227	44	$5.16	3.43	9 outlets
Hanover House	212	250	0.85	4.00	20 catalogs
L. L. Bean	221	68	3.25	2.15	1 store
Popular Services:					
J. Crew	30	7	4.29	.45	
Cliff & Wills	10	2	5.00	.20	
CML Group	55	25	2.20	.49	5 catalogs 100 stores
General Mills (1985)					
Talbots	47	38	1.25	.47	59 stores
Eddie Bauer	57	25	2.28	.72	39 stores
General Mills (1987)					
Talbots	84	60+	<1.40	.65+	109 stores
Eddie Bauer	76	N/A	N/A	1.00	39 stores

PERFORMANCE

Since 1984, when Lands' End achieved sales of $123.4 million and net profits of $7.3 million, the firm's sales and profits have grown annually at 22.2 percent and 25.6 percent, respectively. Sales and profit growth in the first half of fiscal 1989 were 33.7 percent and 64.6 percent higher than the same period in 1988, respectively. Gross margins have improved steadily and may be compared to a level of approximately 42.5 percent typical for apparel retailers in general. Net profit margins have also improved and may be compared to a recent level of about 3.5 percent for large retailers. The percentage of debt to equity has declined steadily throughout the period. The net profit to total assets measure of return on investment has averaged 21 percent over the last five years, compared to 4.4 percent for the nation's 33 largest value retail firms (including LEI) in 1988, and approximately 7.5 percent for all retail establishments. LEI's return on stockholder's equity has averaged 40.4 percent since 1984, having earned 40.2 percent in 1988, compared to 15.4 percent for the 33 largest firms. Financial results for Lands' End are presented in Tables 1–3.

Although Lands' End's recent performance is spectacular and far exceeds industry standards, it remains to be seen how long their growth and margins can be maintained. As the catalog market becomes increasingly competitive, new products and marketing methods will have to be developed. In spite of the prospect of future pressures, the sale of General Mills's catalog operations in 1988 brought the firm $585 million, or about 19 times the pretax operating earnings of this unit.

REFERENCES

1987 Supplement to the Fact Book. Direct Marketing Association. New York: DMA, 1987.

Inside the Leading Mail Order Houses. 3rd edition. Colorado Springs: Maxwell Sroge Publishing, 1987.

Lands' End Annual Reports, 1987 and 1988.

1988 Industrial Outlook. U.S. Department of Commerce.

Pricing Strategy

Delta Airlines*

Margaret L. Friedman

University of Wisconsin–Whitewater

Nowhere has the flexibility and importance of the price variable been more boldly illustrated than in the airline industry since its deregulation in late 1978. In this free-market environment, when one carrier initiates a fare change (typically a fare decrease), other airlines follow suit, usually in a matter of a few hours using sophisticated computer technology. A typical day in the tariff department at Delta Airlines requires comparison of Delta's more than 70,000 fares against the industry's 5,000 price changes of the past 24-hour period. Since deregulation, Delta's tariff department has grown from 27 employees to approximately 150.

Prior to deregulation, U.S. government dictated all aspects of airline route and fare structures. Under regulation, competitors filed comparable fare increase requests with the Civil Aeronautics Board on a

*This case was prepared by Margaret L. Friedman, Assistant Professor, School of Business, University of Wisconsin–Whitewater. Based on "Fare Bargains on Planes Spur Odd Routing," *The Wall Street Journal*, December 8, 1982; "Fare Wars: Have the Big Airlines Learned to Win?", *Fortune*, October 29, 1984, pp. 24–28; "Learning How to Fly," *Barron's*, November 19, 1984, pp. 8–9 and 30–38.

regular basis in order to recover the rising costs of labor, fuel, and debt. All requests were restricted to increases no higher than 5 percent above the "standard industry fare level" or 5 percent below that level, and all such requests were granted. In addition, the federal government put a 12.5 percent ceiling on allowable rate of return in the industry. In this controlled macroenvironment, price was not an important factor in competitive success. Individual members of the industry acted in concert with one another in the spirit of a fraternity. The major carriers attempted to differentiate themselves on the basis of product attributes such as the thickness of the steak served on their flights, the friendliness of their flight attendants, and overall image.

When the industry was deregulated, price suddenly became the single most important factor in competitive strategy. On almost a moment's notice carriers could raise fares by 30 percent or decrease them by 100 percent from standard levels. In other words, the airlines were allowed to give their service away and some did just that. For example, Midway Airlines offered round-trip tickets at the one-way price plus a penny. Jet America offered 405 passengers a one-way fare between Long Beach, California, and Chicago for $4.05. Texas International Airlines promoted free service to four cities for the first 100 passengers who came to them wearing Santa Claus costumes.

On the other hand, it should be noted that while the discount fares attracted a lot of attention, the average price of a ticket rose 71 percent between 1978 and 1982 to $106.34 (the consumer price index rose 43 percent during the same period), because fares increased on less-traveled routes. For example, it cost $.29 a seat per mile to travel between Peoria, Illinois, and Wichita, Kansas, versus $0.6 a seat per mile between Chicago and San Francisco.

The post-deregulation era in the airlines industry has been marked by other serious problems. These include a massive strike among air traffic controllers, a recessionary glut of airplane seats, and a tripling of fuel prices from 1979 to 1981. Most established carriers enthusiastically turned to price to: (1) stimulate demand for their service which was in oversupply, (2) smooth demand in an environment where supply and demand change drastically from day to day, from city to city, and from flight to flight, and (3) compete against the lower prices offered by new, "no frills" carriers which sprang up almost overnight, especially on high-volume routes. The results for the industry were large operating losses ($680 million in 1982) and several bankruptcies.

The new discount carriers had a pricing advantage over established airlines because of their lower labor costs. For example, PEOPLExpress avoided labor unions and persuaded employees to accept lower wages in return for a mandatory but generous stock-ownership plan. Management also instituted a unique method to increase labor productivity called *cross-utilization,* whereby a pilot, when not flying, might do accounting or personnel work or a flight attendant might help out at the ticket counter. Also, customer services, such as food ($.50 for a cup of coffee) and baggage handling ($3.00 for each bag checked), are charged separately so that the price of the ticket is "honest," that is, reflective only of the cost of travel. This approach resulted in some dramatic differences in costs. For example, six years after deregulation Delta Airlines' expenses were approximately $.08 a seat per mile while PEOPLExpress' expenses were $.053 a seat per mile.

Delta Airlines had historically been considered the industry's best-managed company. However, in 1982 a market survey revealed that few travelers called Delta as their first choice when making travel plans because Delta had acquired a reputation for being high-priced in the new deregulated environment. Based on this survey, Delta introduced a promotion offering to match any competitor's fare on any of its more than 5,000 routes. While Delta was successful in attracting passengers, the number paying full fare dropped to 8 percent of all seats sold, creating Delta's first annual deficit in 47 years of business. Delta's pricing decisions, like those of other carriers in the industry, became increasingly complex. Prices varied on the same route according to time of day, day of the week, season of the year, advance purchase requirements, length of stay, class of service, connections, and stopovers. In one informal survey it was reported that eight different Delta agents quoted seven different fares for the exact same travel itinerary.

Delta's computer technology was critical in helping to make pricing decisions, particularly with respect to determining how many discount seats to make available. Sophisticated programs analyzed historical travel patterns on flights and compared them to present bookings on future flights. On the basis of such seat analyses, the number of discount seats available on a flight was in a constant state of flux. Consequently, a passenger who was told on one occasion that no low fare seats were available would suddenly find them available if he/she called back in a day or two. At one point it was reported that 50 Delta reservation agents worked full time at computer terminals monitoring minute-by-minute booking patterns. Their primary task was to divide up the number of discount and full-fare seats on future flights in order to maximize revenue per flight.

Discussion Questions

1. What are some of the distinguishing characteristics of a service such as air transportation that are particularly relevant to pricing strategy?

2. How did pricing methods change over time from the period during regulation, to immediately after deregulation, to six years after deregulation?
3. What should Delta Airlines do to compete successfully against the low-cost entrants in the market?
4. What do you think the long-run effect of deregulation will be on ticket prices? Consider this question from the perspective of the established carriers and from the perspective of the newer low-cost carriers.

Young Attitudes—Pricing a New Product Line*

Jon M. Hawes

University of Akron

Young Attitudes is a large, well-known clothing store chain with more than 400 retail outlets located throughout the United States and Canada. Appealing to the teenage and young adult consumer, the success enjoyed by Young Attitudes is based largely on the firm's ability to market fashionable merchandise at reasonable and competitive prices. While Young Attitudes stocks a limited selection of national manufacturer's brands (e.g., Levi's and Haggar) to enhance its store image and to generate consumer traffic, the vast majority of each outlet's merchandise consists of the firm's own private retailer brands. To ensure a reliable source of supply for their private labels, Young Attitudes purchased the Fashion-Plus Clothing Company (FPCC) in 1982. At the time of the takeover, FPCC was a well-established national manufacturer of high-quality, fashionable apparel. FPCC's product mix consisted of a wide line of both men's and women's wearing apparel.

The recent increase in the popularity and acceptance of fleece wearing apparel by many diverse consumer groups throughout all market areas of the country prompted Ralph West, the general merchandise manager for Young Attitudes, to investigate the possibility of adding a new line of men's shirts. Preliminary results of that investigation led Ralph to conclude that such a line would appeal to the consumer group the firm identified as "the comfort-seekers"—a consumer market segment wanting stylish, leisure clothing of good quality. While quality is a concern for these people, cost is also an important consideration in the selection of clothing apparel. As far as Ralph is concerned, the addition of a new line of men's fleece shirts makes good merchandising sense. However, it will be up to the production people at Fashion-Plus

---

*This case was prepared by Jon M. Hawes, Professor of Marketing, Department of Marketing, University of Akron. Copyright © 1988 by Jon M. Hawes.

to determine whether the new line is feasible given the price, cost, and profit constraints under which they must produce the product.

While Fashion-Plus is a wholly owned subsidiary of Young Attitudes, FPCC's management is responsible for making all production decisions. Presently under consideration is Ralph's request for the new line of fleece shirts. To determine the feasibility of new product lines, Bill Morris (manager for new product development) must collect the necessary information to make a cost and break-even analysis, to project expected profits, and to recommend a suggested retail price as well as a manufacturer's price (the price that Fashion-Plus should charge Young Attitudes). Having spent the last two weeks collecting data, Bill feels he now has the necessary information to make the required evaluations of the new fleece shirt project. Before proceeding with his analysis, Bill reviews the following information he has collected:

1. Several competitors have recently introduced similar lines of men's fleece shirts. Market research indicates that these lines are selling at a brisk pace at competitive retail stores for the following prices:

Retail Selling Prices	*Number of Times Observed*
$14.00	2
15.00	7
16.00	5
17.00	3

2. Young Attitudes will apply a 40-percent initial markup on the retail selling price of shirts.
3. Production costs for the new shirt are estimated to be:

Cloth	$2.20 per shirt
Buttons	.05 per shirt
Thread	.05 per shirt
Direct labor	20 minutes per shirt
Shipping weight	2 pounds per packaged shirt

4. Basic marketing costs for introducing the new line of shirts are estimated to be $300,000 the first year if a penetration pricing policy is used or $340,000 if a skimming pricing policy is employed.
5. Being a large company, FPCC has 15 production facilities strategically located throughout the United States. Last year, the average round-trip distance from FPCC production facilities to Young Attitudes outlets was 225 miles. Current plans are to produce the new line of shirts at each of FPCC's production facilities.

6. An examination of FPCC's annual report reveals the following information:

Managerial salaries	$1,500,000
Rent and utilities expense	1,200,000
Transportation costs (1,250,000 miles)	750,000
Depreciation on plant and equipment	1,300,000
Other overhead	2,000,000
Direct labor costs (2,000,000 hours)	8,000,000
Total company sales	45,000,000
Average order size	1,000 pounds

7. The Midwest Market Research Corporation was hired to develop a sales forecast for the new line of western shirts. Their research findings estimate that if a skimming pricing policy were used, Young Attitudes could expect to sell approximately 110,000 to 130,000 shirts. Under a penetration-type pricing policy, Midwest estimates a unit sales volume of approximately 130,000 to 150,000 shirts.

The Problem

Assume that Bill Morris was unexpectedly called out of town and he has asked you to prepare the analysis and written report on the project's feasibility and then to recommend the pricing strategy he should use. At a minimum, your analysis should include a cost analysis (variable cost per shirt, fixed cost allocation for the line, and total cost per shirt), a break-even analysis in units and dollars, a determination of the manufacturer's price and suggested retail price, and a statement as to expected profit the company can derive from the new line.

| *SnowGo**

Nabil Hassan
Herbert E. Brown
Paula M. Saunders
all of Wright State University

BACKGROUND INFORMATION

Stanlan, Inc., is a privately owned, diversified company with eight separate divisions selling distinctly different products to very different markets. Carl Brauer is the president and CEO of Stanlan, Inc. He recently attended a national workshop on "responsibility centers." Material presented there led him to decide that each of his company's eight divisions should be a separate and distinct investment and profit center as prescribed by the responsibility center concept. This concept requires each division manager to see himself or herself as the president of his/her own company. Corporate management, and Carl Brauer in particular, would have to take a hands-off approach and exercise control through a minimum rate-of-return-on-invested-capital objective for each company division. In effect, each division manager would have completely decentralized authority over costs and investments, as well as the responsibility for them and for revenues.

After much discussion with experts, Brauer decided to set a uniform 14 percent minimum rate of return for all divisions. He notified all of his division managers of this decision, and also informed them that each would get a $20,000 bonus for each percentage point return greater than 14 percent. He based this idea on what is known as the "residual income concept." Residual income is the difference between net income after tax for each division and the minimum rate of return on invested capital. Tom Van Lier, general manager of the Snow Mobile

*This case was prepared by Nabil Hassan, Herbert E. Brown, and Paula M. Saunders, all of Wright State University, and is intended to be used as a basis for class discussion rather than to illustrate either effective or ineffective handling of the situation.

Presented and accepted by the Midwest Society for Case Research. All rights reserved to the authors and by the MSCR. Copyright © 1990 by Nabil Hassan, Herbert E. Brown, and Paula M. Saunders.

Division, was very enthusiastic after receiving notice of the new approach, along with a commitment from Stanlan, Inc., for $20 million in new investment money for the next fiscal year.

THE SNOW MOBILE DIVISION

The Snow Mobile Division is a typical Stanlan, Inc., division. It is producing a variety of winter sports products, including snowmobiles. Its current invested capital is an estimated $120 million. The division was purchased by Stanlan, Inc., in 1983. Since then, profits have increased approximately six percent every year. It is widely believed that these results are primarily due to the division's exceptional distribution capabilities. These center around an exclusive relationship with a large winter sports retailing chain that has many excellent locations around the nation and a reputation for hard-hitting promotion campaigns at the beginning of the snow and snow-skiing seasons. Tom Van Lier's strong leadership and management is also thought to be a factor.

When Brauer asked all division managers to submit a condensed income statement for the year ended December 31, 1989, the income statement for Tom Van Lier's Snow Mobile Division included the following information:

Sales	$ 100,000,000	100%
Less cost of goods sold	40,000,000	40
= Gross Profit	$ 60,000,000	60
Less administrative expenses	12,000,000	12
Less selling expenses	10,000,000	10
Less financial expenses	2,000,000	2
Less research & development expenses	6,000,000	6
= Net income before taxes	$ 30,000,000	30
Less income taxes (30%)	9,000,000	9
= Net income after taxes	$ 21,000,000	21

OTHER BACKGROUND INFORMATION ON STANLAN INC.'S SNOW MOBILE DIVISION

The major profitmaker for the Snow Mobile Division is its snowmobile line. Van Lier has known for some time that he must come up with something new, possibly even a new product line. He and his marketing staff have promoted the sport of snowmobiling and sold it aggressively as an alternative to skiing. This approach has built sales. Unfortunately, the growth potential and overall attractiveness of the snowmobile market appears to be limited. Several reasons were cited for this. One is that high-quality snowmobiles last an average of seven years, and although most buyers plan to purchase a second one when that becomes necessary, only one out of every four buyers actually does so. There is also bad publicity generated by occasional accidents; these usually result in major sales fluctuations and in temporary but serious unplanned revenue shortfalls.

In early 1988, potential problems in the snowmobile market coupled with increased concern about the division's dependency on the snowmobile, led Van Lier to direct his research and development people to search for a major new product addition. He also initiated an aggressive program to find products already on the market which could be sold through the division's current distribution network. These efforts proved timely. In early 1989 the Snow Mobile Division introduced a prototype of a new product called "SnowGo."

THE SNOWGO

As a first step in the product-development process, an independent marketing research firm was commissioned to conduct a scientific survey of 500 households. These households were selected from the direct-mail lists of Stanlan's primary distributor/retailer in three major "snow product" markets, namely, New York, Michigan, and Colorado. The study focused on family members' current and past recreational activities and was designed to obtain demographic, personality, and lifestyle data on snow sport participants.

One especially interesting finding was that in many households, individuals who had become skiing or snowmobile enthusiasts could not convince other family members to try the sport. Those members who refused to join them cited fear of injury, as in the case of skiing, as well as the amount of time needed for older individuals to become proficient. As a result, many families' members were forced to take separate vacations or to participate in separate sports activities.

Thus, the "big idea" that guided development of the "SnowGo" was a product concept that would satisfy the winter outdoor recreational needs of a wider range of the population while reducing the learning curve for participation below that of skiing. It would also offer lower risk factors than either skiing or snowmobiling. And, it would provide buyers with greater recreational versatility. Such a product would give the Snow Mobile Division a significantly larger winter sport customer base than its current snowmobile market.

DESIGNING AND DEVELOPING A PROTOTYPE

The product that emerged from this development effort resembles a narrow one-person golf cart. The rider sits snugly on a benchlike seat inside a durable foam-type substance. The product has large, soft-cushion tires and can travel at 15–20 miles per hour. The driver steers the SnowGo with his hands and regulates its speed with a foot pedal. The driver is in much more control than if on skis and is much more protected in case of an accident. The SnowGo stops when pressure is not applied to the pedal, and it is not easily turned over. The SnowGo itself is composed of fiberglass, foam rubber, and rubber tires, and is propelled by a battery-operated motor. The battery is rechargeable in a 110-amp outlet and will last approximately four hours without re-charging. The entire SnowGo can be folded into a rectangular shape the size of a 3-foot-by-2-foot box with a depth of 2 feet. Its tires act as rollers when the SnowGo is in its "fold-away" or travel position.

DISTRIBUTION

The plan was to sell SnowGo through sports stores and to and through golf course pro shops, which in turn, would either sell or rent the product, or both. After the SnowGo was designed, the marketing de-partment confidentially approached 12 golf course managers around the country about the likelihood that such a product would be allowed on courses in winter. Initially, many of the managers were not en-couraging. However, after some discussion, several actually became excited about the additional revenue that the SnowGo could generate during the dead season. Clearly, though, their enthusiasm was tem-pered by their concern about damage to their courses and liability suits in case of injuries.

After the prototype was produced, a few course owners were brought in to see the SnowGo demonstrated. They went away very enthusiastic about the opportunity for more people to participate in a cold-weather activity at their location. One owner said that whereas he did not think his board of directors would open its course to the public, he did think it would consider opening the course to "SnowGoing" by its private members.

Van Lier and his staff are not sure whether the SnowGo would be a substitute for skiing, an additional activity for skiers, or a recreational activity for those who don't presently ski or snowmobile. However, all these markets appear to have excellent potential, especially since it could be used by anyone, age eight and up. And there would be the additional advantage of accessibility in being able to use it on golf courses, cross-country skiing areas, and snowmobile facilities, all of which can be found in residential communities. It is even possible that some people, particularly the elderly, could use it as a vehicle in re-tirement villages where large amounts of snow fall.

ESTIMATES OF COSTS AND SALES

The SnowGo's tires, battery, and motor would have to be replaced periodically. The battery would need replacement annually if used frequently. Since the tires, battery, and motor (which would represent approximately a third of the retail price) would be specially designed, this would create a nice aftermarket for the company. A patent would provide time to gain a foothold on the market, particularly in the distribution and rental ends.

Tom Van Lier asked Nancy Castle, the division's controller, to present to him a report indicating projected sales, cost of goods sold, and expected net income of the new product SnowGo. He emphasized that Nancy would have to work with marketing, production, and research and development, and make projections regarding sales and profitability. Her final report—which reflects the best thinking of accounting, marketing, and other people in the company concerning sales and costs—contains the following information, based on a $2,000 unit price when producing 10,000 units of the SnowGo product:

Expected sales	$ 20,000,000	100%
Less expected cost of goods sold	11,000,000	55
= Expected gross profit	$ 9,000,000	45
Less expected administrative, financial, selling expenses	$ 5,000,000	25
= Expected net income before tax	$ 4,000,000	20
Less expected tax expenses (30%)	1,200,000	6
= Expected net income after tax	$ 2,800,000	14

For the proposed product line, SnowGo, the manufacturing costs and nonmanufacturing expenses were forecast to be as follows:

Cost of Goods Manufactured:	
Direct materials costs	$ 5,000,000
Direct labor costs	3,000,000
Variable manufacturing overhead costs	1,000,000
Fixed overhead costs	2,000,000
Total manufacturing costs	$11,000,000
Nonmanufacturing Expenses:	
Variable administrative, financial, & selling expenses	$ 3,000,000
Fixed administrative, financial, or selling expenses	2,000,000
Total nonmanufacturing expenses	$ 5,000,000

Further Cost Breakdown:
Variable Costs:

Direct materials costs	$ 5,000,000
Direct labor costs	$ 3,000,000
Variable manufacturing overhead costs	1,000,000
Variable administrative, financial, & selling costs	3,000,000
Total variable costs	$12,000,000

Fixed Costs and Expenses:

Fixed manufacturing overhead costs	$ 2,000,000
Fixed administrative, financial, & selling expenses	2,000,000
Total fixed costs & expenses	$ 4,000,000

President Brauer is excited about the SnowGo. He believes that his company's Snow Mobile Division can capture a bigger share of the winter recreation market and increase overall company profits. Furthermore, he has confidence in Tom Van Lier and his management team. What he doesn't know yet is whether and to what extent the benefits of the responsibility center concept will outweigh its negatives, given the nature of his particular business and the forces it brings to bear on general managers. But he's willing to take the risk.

S. C. Johnson and Son, Limited (R)*

Carolyn Vose
University of Western Ontario

Four months ago, in November, George Styan had been appointed division manager of Innochem, at S. C. Johnson and Son, Limited[1] (SCJ), a Canadian subsidiary of S. C. Johnson & Son, Inc. Innochem's sole product line consisted of industrial cleaning chemicals for use by business, institutions, and government. George was concerned by the division's poor market share, particularly in Montreal and Toronto. Together, these two cities represented approximately 35 percent of Canadian demand for industrial cleaning chemicals, but less than 10 percent of Innochem sales. It appeared that SCJ distributors could not match the aggressive discounting practiced by direct-selling manufacturers in metropolitan markets.

Recently, George had received a rebate proposal from his staff designed to increase the distributor's ability to cut end-user prices by "sharing" part of the total margin with SCJ when competitive conditions demanded discounts of 30 percent or more off the list price to end users. George had to decide if the rebate plan was the best way to penetrate price-sensitive markets. Moreover, he wondered about the plan's ultimate impact on divisional profit performance. George either had to develop an implementation plan for the rebate plan or draft an alternative proposal to unveil at the Distributors' Annual Spring Convention, three weeks away.

---

*This case was written by Carolyn Vose under the supervision of Associate Professor Roger More for the sole purpose of providing material for class discussion at the School of Business Administration. Any use or duplication of the material in this case is prohibited except with the written consent of the School. Copyright © 1987, University of Western Ontario. Used with permission.

[1]Popularly known as Canadian Johnson Wax.

THE CANADIAN MARKET FOR INDUSTRIAL CLEANING CHEMICALS

Last year, the Canadian market for industrial cleaning chemicals was approximately $100 million at end-user prices. Growth was stable at an overall rate of approximately 3 percent per year.

"Industrial cleaning chemicals" included all chemical products designed to clean, disinfect, sanitize, or protect industrial, commercial, and institutional buildings and equipment. The label was broadly applied to general purpose cleaners, floor maintenance products (strippers, sealers, finishes, and detergents), carpet cleaners and deodorizers, disinfectants, air fresheners, and a host of specialty chemicals such as insecticides, pesticides, drain cleaners, oven cleansers, and sweeping compounds.

Industrial cleaning chemicals were distinct from equivalent consumer products typically sold through grocery stores. Heavy-duty industrial products were packaged in larger containers and bulk and marketed directly by the cleaning chemical manufacturers or sold through distributors to a variety of end users. Exhibit 1 includes market segmentation by primary end-user categories, including janitorial service contractors and the in-house maintenance departments of government, institutions, and companies.

BUILDING MAINTENANCE CONTRACTORS

In Canada, maintenance contractors purchased 17 percent of the industrial cleaning chemicals sold during 1980 (end-user price). The segment was growing at approximately 10–15 percent a year, chiefly at the expense of other end-user categories. *Canadian Business* reported, "Contract cleaners have made sweeping inroads into the traditional preserve of in-house janitorial staffs, selling themselves on the strength of cost efficiency."[2] Maintenance contract billings reached an estimated $1 billion last year.

Frequently, demand for building maintenance services was highly price sensitive, and since barriers to entry were low (small capitalization, simple technology), competition squeezed contractor gross margins below 6 percent (before tax). Variable cost control was a matter of survival, and only products bringing compensatory labour savings could command a premium price in this segment of the cleaning chemical market.

A handful of contract cleaners did specialize in higher-margin services to prestige office complexes, luxury apartments, art museums,

---

[2]"Contract Cleaners Want to Whisk Away Ring-around-the-Office," *Canadian Business,* 1981, p. 22.

EXHIBIT 1   Segmentation of the Canadian Market for Industrial Cleaning Chemicals

By End-User Category

End User	Percent Total
Retail outlets	25%
Contractors	17
Hospitals	15
Industrial and office	13
Schools, colleges	8
Hotels, motels	6
Nursing homes	5
Recreation	3
Government	3
Fast food	2
Full-service restaurants	2
All others	1
Total	100% = $95 million

By Product Category

Product	Percent Total
Floor care products	40%
General purpose cleaners	16
Disinfectants	12
Carpet care products	8
Odor control products	5
Glass cleaners	4
All others	15
Total	100% = $95 million

and other "quality-conscious" customers. However, even contractors serving this select clientele did not necessarily buy premium cleaning supplies.

IN-HOUSE MAINTENANCE DEPARTMENTS

Government

Last year, cleaning chemical sales to various government offices (federal, provincial, and local) approached $2 million. Typically, a government body solicited bids from appropriate sources by formally advertising for quotations for given quantities of particular cleaning chemicals. Although bid requests often names specific brands, suppliers were permitted to offer "equivalent substitutes." Separate competitions were held for each item and normally covered 12 months' supply with provision for delivery "as required." Contracts were frequently awarded solely on the basis of price.

Institutions

Like government bodies, most institutions were price sensitive owing to restrictive budgets and limited ability to "pass on" expenses to users. Educational institutions and hospitals were the largest consumers of cleaning chemicals in this segment. School boards used an open-bid system patterned on the government model. Heavy sales time requirements and demands for frequent delivery of small shipments to as many as 100 locations were characteristic.

Colleges and universities tended to be operated somewhat differently. Dan Stalport, one of the purchasing agents responsible for maintenance supplies at the University of Western Ontario, offered the following comments:

> Sales reps come to UWO year 'round. If one of us (in the buying group) talks to a salesman who seems to have something—say, a labour-saving feature—we get a sample and test it. Testing can take up to a year. Floor covering, for example, has to be exposed to seasonal changes in weather and traffic.
>
> If we're having problems with a particular item, we'll compare the performance and price of three or four competitors. There are usually plenty of products that do the job. Basically, we want value—acceptable performance at the lowest available price.

Hospitals accounted for 15 percent of cleaning chemical sales. Procurement policies at University Hospital (UH), a medium-sized (450-bed) facility in London, Ontario, were typical. UH distinguished between "critical" and "noncritical" products. Critical cleaning chemicals (i.e., those significantly affecting patient health, such as phenolic germicide) could be bought only on approval of the staff microbiologist, who tested the "kill factor." This measure of effectiveness was regularly retested, and any downgrading of product performance could void a supplier's contract. In contrast, noncritical supplies, such as general purpose cleaners, floor finishes, and the like, were the exclusive province of Bob Chandler, purchasing agent attached to the housekeeping department. Bob explained that performance of noncritical cleaning chemicals was informally judged and monitored by the housekeeping staff:

Just last year, for example, the cleaners found the floor polish was streaking badly. We (the housekeeping department) tested and compared five or six brands—all in the ballpark pricewise—and chose the best.

Business

The corporate segment was highly diverse, embracing both service and manufacturing industries. Large-volume users tended to be price sensitive—particularly when profits were low. Often, however, cleaning products represented such a small percentage of the total operating budget that the cost of searching for the lowest-cost supplier would be expected to exceed any realizable saving. Under such conditions, the typical industrial customer sought efficiencies in the purchasing process itself, for example, by dealing with the supplier offering the broadest mix of janitorial products (chemicals, paper supplies, equipment, etc.). Guy Breton, purchasing agent for Securitech, a Montreal-based security systems manufacturer, commented on the time economies of "one-stop shopping":

> With cleaning chemicals, it simply isn't worth the trouble to shop around and stage elaborate product performance tests. I buy all our chemicals, brushes, dusters, toweling—the works—from one or two suppliers . . . buying reputable brands from familiar suppliers saves hassles—back orders are rare, and Maintenance seldom complains.

DISTRIBUTION CHANNELS FOR INDUSTRIAL CLEANING CHEMICALS

The Canadian market for industrial cleaning chemicals was supplied through three main channels, each characterized by a distinctive set of strengths and weaknesses:

1. Distributor sales of national brands.
2. Distributor sales of private label products.
3. Direct sale by manufacturers.

Direct sellers held a 61 percent share of the Canadian market for industrial cleaning chemicals, while the distributors of national brands and private label products held shares of 25 percent and 14 percent, respectively. Relative market shares varied geographically, however. In Montreal and Toronto, for example, the direct marketers' share rose to 70 percent and private labelers' to 18 percent, reducing the national brand share to 12 percent. The pattern, shown in Exhibit 2, reflected an interplay of two areas of channel differentiation, namely, discount capability at the end-user level and the cost of serving distant, geographically dispersed customers.

EXHIBIT 2   Effect of Geography on Market Share of Different
Distribution Channels

Supplier Type		Share Nationwide	Share in Montreal and Toronto
Direct marketers		61%*	70%
Private label distributors		14	18
National brands distributors		25†	12

*Dustbane	17%	†SCJ	8%
G. H. Wood	31	N/L	4
All others	13	Airkem	3
Total	61%	All others	10
		Total	25%

Distributor Sales of National Brand Cleaning Chemicals

National brand manufacturers, such as S. C. Johnson and Son, Airkem, and National Labs, produce a relatively limited range of "high-quality" janitorial products, including many special purpose formulations of narrow market interest. Incomplete product range, combined with shortage of manpower and limited warehousing, made direct distribution unfeasible in most cases. Normally, a national brand company would negotiate with middlemen who handled a broad array of complementary products (equipment, tools, and supplies) by different manufacturers. "Bundling" of goods brought the distributors cost efficiencies in selling, warehousing, and delivery by spreading fixed costs over a large sales volume. Distributors were, therefore, better able to absorb the costs of after-hour emergency service, frequent routine sales and service calls to many potential buyers, and shipments of small quantities of cleaning chemicals to multiple destinations. As a rule, the greater the geographic dispersion of customers, and the smaller the average order, the greater the relative economies of distributor marketing.

Comparatively high gross margins (approximately 50 percent of wholesale price) enabled national brand manufacturers to offer distributors strong marketing support and sales training along with liberal terms of payment and freight plus low minimum order requirements. Distributors readily agreed to handle national brand chemicals, and in metropolitan markets, each brand was sold through several distributors. By the same token, most distributors carried several directly competitive product lines. George suspected that some distributor salesmen only used national brands to "lead" with and tended to offer private label whenever a customer proved price sensitive, or a competitor handled the same national brand(s). Using an industry rule of thumb, George estimated that most distributors needed at least 20 percent gross margin on retail sales to cover sales commission of 10 percent, plus delivery and inventory expenses.

Distributor Sales of Private Label Cleaning Chemicals

Direct-selling manufacturers were dominating urban markets by aggressively discounting end-user prices—sometimes below the wholesale price national brand manufacturers charged their distributors. To compete against the direct seller, increasing numbers of distributors were adding low-cost private label cleaning chemicals to their product lines. Private labeling also helped differentiate a particular distributor from others carrying the same national brand(s).

Sizable minimum order requirements restricted the private label strategy to only the largest distributors. Private label manufacturers produced to order, formulating to meet low prices specified by distributors. The relatively narrow margins (30–35 percent wholesale price) associated with private label manufacturers characteristically provided to distributors. Private label producers pared their expenses further still by requiring distributors to bear the cost of inventory and accept rigid terms of payment as well as delivery (net 30 days, FOB plant).

In addition to absorbing these selling expenses normally assumed by the manufacturer, distributors paid salesmen higher commissions on private label sales (15 percent of resale) than on national brands (10 percent of resale). However, the incremental administration and selling expenses associated with private label business were more than offset by the differential savings on private label wholesale goods. By pricing private label chemicals at competitive parity with national brands, the distributor could enjoy approximately a 50-percent gross margin at resale list, while preserving considerable resale discount capability.

Private label products were seldom sold outside the metropolitan areas where most were manufactured. First, the high costs of moving bulky, low-value freight diminished the relative cost advantage of private label chemicals. Second, generally speaking, it was only in metro areas where distributors dealt in volumes great enough to satisfy the private labeler's minimum order requirement. Finally, outside the city, distributors were less likely to be in direct local competition with others handling the same national brand, reducing value of the private label as a source of supplier differentiation.

For some very large distributors, backward integration into chemical production was a logical extension of the private labeling strategy. Recently, several distributors had become direct marketers through acquisition of captive manufacturers.

Direct Sale by Manufacturers of Industrial Cleaning Chemicals

Manufacturers dealing directly with the end user increased their gross margins to 60–70 percent of retail list price. Greater margins increased their ability to discount end-user price—a distinct advantage in the price-competitive urban marketplace. Overall, direct marketers averaged a gross margin of 50 percent.

Many manufacturers of industrial cleaning chemicals attempted some direct selling, but relatively few relied on this channel exclusively. Satisfactory adoption of a full-time direct-selling strategy required the manufacturer to match distributor's sales and delivery capabilities without sacrificing overall profitability. These conflicting demands had been resolved successfully by two types of company: large-scale powder chemical manufacturers and full-line janitorial products manufacturers.

Large-Scale Powder Chemical Manufacturers.   Economies of large-scale production plus experience in the capital-intensive manufacture of powder chemicals enabled a few established firms, such as Diversey-Wyandotte, to dominate the market for powder warewash and vehicle cleansers. Selling through distributors offered these producers few advantages. Direct-selling expense was almost entirely commission (i.e., variable). Moreover, powder concentrates were characterized by comparatively high value-to-bulk ratios, and so could absorb delivery costs even where demand was geographically dispersed. Thus, any marginal benefits from using middlemen were more than offset by the higher margins (and associated discount capability) possible through direct distribution. Among these chemical firms, competition was not limited to price. The provision of dispensing and metering equipment was important, as was 24-hour servicing.

Full-Line Janitorial Products Manufacturers.   These manufacturers offered a complete range of maintenance products, including paper supplies, janitorial chemicals, tools, and mechanical equipment. Although high margins greatly enhanced retail price flexibility, overall profitability depended on securing a balance of high- and low-margin business, as well as controlling selling and distribution expenses. This was accomplished in several ways, including:

- Centering on market areas of concentrated demand to minimize costs of warehousing, sales travel, and the like.
- Increasing average order size, either by adding product lines which could be sold to existing customers, or by seeking new large-volume customers.
- Tying sales commission to profitability to motivate sales personnel to sell volume, without unnecessary discounting of end-user price.

Direct marketers of maintenance products varied in scale from established nationwide companies to hundreds of regional operators. The two largest direct marketers, G. H. Wood and Dustbane, together supplied almost a third of Canadian demand for industrial cleaning chemicals.

S. C. JOHNSON AND SON, LIMITED

S. C. Johnson and Son, Limited (SCJ), was one of 42 foreign subsidiaries owned by the U.S.-based multinational, S. C. Johnson & Son, Inc. It was ranked globally as one of the largest privately held companies. SCJ contributed substantially to worldwide sales and profits and was based in Brantford, Ontario, close to the Canadian urban markets of Hamilton, Kitchener, Toronto, London, and Niagara Falls. About 300 people worked at the head office and plant, while another 100 were employed in field sales.

Innochem Division

Innochem (Innovative Chemicals for Professional Use) was a special division established to serve corporate, institutional, and government customers of SCJ. The division manufactured an extensive line of industrial cleaning chemicals, including general purpose cleansers, waxes, polishes, and disinfectants, plus a number of specialty products of limited application, as shown in Exhibit 3. Last year, Innochem sold $4.5 million of industrial cleaning chemicals through distributors and $0.2 million direct to end users. Financial statements for Innochem are shown in Exhibit 4.

INNOCHEM MARKETING STRATEGY

Divisional strategy hinged on reliable product performance, product innovation, active promotion, and mixed channel distribution. Steve Remen, market development manager, maintained that "customers know our products are of excellent quality. They know that the products will always perform as expected."

At SCJ, performance requirements were detailed and tolerances precisely defined. The Department of Quality Control routinely inspected and tested raw materials, work in process, packaging, and finished goods. At any phase during the manufacturing cycle, Quality Control was empowered to halt the process and quarantine suspect product or materials. SCJ maintained that nothing left the plant "without approval from Quality Control."

EXHIBIT 3 Innochem Product Line

Johnson Wax is a systems innovator. Frequently, a new product leads to a whole new system of doing things—a Johnson system of "matched" products formulated to work together. This makes the most of your time, your effort, and your expense. Call today and see how these Johnson systems can give you maximum results at a minimum cost.

For all floors except unsealed wood and unsealed cork.
Stripper:
  Step-Off—powerful, fast action
Finish:
  Pronto—fast-drying, good gloss, minimum maintenance
Spray-buff solution:
  The Shiner Liquid Spray Cleaner or **The Shiner Aerosol Spray Finish**
Maintainer:
  Forward—cleans, disinfects, deodorizes, sanitizes

For all floors except unsealed wood and unsealed cork.
Stripper:
  Step-Off—powerful, fast stripper
Finish:
  Carefree—tough, beauty, durable, minimum maintenance
Maintainer:
  Forward—cleans, disinfects, deodorizes, sanitizes

For all floors except unsealed wood and unsealed cork.
Stripper:
  Step-Off—for selective stripping
Sealer:
  Over & Under-Plus—undercoater-sealer
Finish:
  Scrubbable Step-Ahead—brilliant, scrubbable
Maintainer:
  Forward—cleans, disinfects, sanitizes, deodorizes

For all floors except unsealed wood and cork.
Stripper:
  Step-Off—powerful, fast stripper

Finish:
  Easy Street—high solids, high gloss, spray buffs to a "wet look" appearance
Maintainer:
  Forward—cleans, disinfects, deodorizes
  Expose—phenolic cleaner disinfectant

For all floors except unsealed wood and unsealed cork.
Stripper:
  Step-Off—for selective stripping
Sealer:
  Over & Under-Plus—undercoater-sealer
Finishes:
  Traffic Grade—heavy-duty floor wax
  Waxtral—extra tough, high solids
Maintainer:
  Forward—cleans, disinfects, sanitizes, deodorizes

For all floors except asphalt, mastic, and rubber tile.
Use sealer and wax finishes on wood, cork, and cured concrete; sealer-finish on terrazzo, marble, clay, and ceramic tile; wax finish only on vinyl, linoleum, and magnesite.
Sealer:
  Johnson Gym Finish—sealer and topcoater, cleans as it waxes
Wax finishes:
  Traffic Wax Paste—heavy-duty buffing wax
  Beautiflor Traffic Wax—liquid buffing wax
Maintainers:
  Forward—cleans, disinfects, sanitizes, deodorizes
  Conq-r Dust—mop treatment
Stripper:
  Step-Off—stripper for sealer and finish

EXHIBIT 3   Innochem Product Line *(concluded)*

Sealer:
  Secure—fast-bonding, smooth, long-lasting
Finish:
  Traffic Grade—heavy-duty floor wax
Maintainer:
  Forward or **Big Bare**
Sealer-finish:
  Johnson Gym Finish—seal and top-coater
Maintainer:
  Conq-r-Dust—mop treatment

General cleaning:
  Break-Up—cleans soap and body scum fast
  Forward—cleans, disinfects, sanitizes, deodorizes
  Bon Ami—instant cleaner, pressurized or pump, disinfects
Toilet-urinals:
  Go-Getter—"Working Foam" cleaner
Glass:
  Bon Ami—spray-on foam or liquid cleaner
Disinfectant spray:
  End-Bac II—controls bacteria, odors
Air freshener:
  Glade—dewy-fresh fragrances
Spot cleaning:
  Johnson's Pledge—cleans, waxes, polishes
  Johnson's Lemon Pledge—refreshing scent
  Bon Ami Stainless Steel Cleaner—cleans, polishes, protects
All-purpose cleaners:
  Forward—cleans, disinfects, sanitizes, deodorizes
  Break-Up—degreaser for animal and vegetable fats
  Big Bare—heavy-duty industrial cleaner
Carpets:
  Rugbee Powder & Liquid Extraction Cleaner
  Rugbee Soil Release Concentrate—for prespraying and bonnet buffing

Rugbee Shampoo—for power shampoo machines
Rugbee Spotter—spot remover
Furniture:
  Johnson's Pledge—cleans, waxes, polishes
  Johnson's Lemon Pledge—refreshing scent
  Shine-Up Liquid—general purpose cleaning
Disinfectant spray air freshener:
  End-Bac II—controls bacteria, odors
  Glade—dewy-fresh fragrances
Glass:
  Bon Ami—spray-on foam or liquid cleaner
Cleaning:
  Break-Up—special degreaser designed to remove animal and vegetable fats
Equipment:
  Break-Up Foamer—special generator designed to dispense Break-Up cleaner
General cleaning:
  Forward—fast-working germicidal cleaner for floors, walls, all washable surfaces
  Expose—phenolic disinfectant cleaner
Sanitizing:
  J80 Sanitizer—liquid for total environmental control of bacteria; no rinse necessary if used as directed
Disinfectant spray:
  End-Brac II Spray—controls bacteria, odors
Flying insects:
  Bolt Liquid Airborne or **Pressurized Airborne,** P3610 through E10 dispenser
Crawling insects:
  Bolt Liquid Residual or **Pressurized Residual,** P3610 through E10 dispenser
  Bolt Roach Bait
Rodents:
  Bolt Rodenticide—for effective control of rats and mice, use with Bolt Bait Box

---

EXHIBIT 4

S. C. JOHNSON AND SON, LIMITED
Profit Statement of the Division
(in $ thousands)

Gross sales:	$4,682
Returns	46
Allowances	1
Cash discounts	18
Net sales	4,617
Cost of sales	2,314
Gross profit:	2,303
Advertising	75
Promotions	144
Deals	—
External marketing services	2
Sales freight	292
Other distribution expenses	176
Service fees	184
Total direct expenses	873
Sales force	592
Marketing administration	147
Provision for bad debts	—
Research and development	30
Financial	68
Information resource management	47
Administration management	56
Total functional expenses	940
Total operating expenses	1,813
Operating profit	490

"Keeping the new product shelf well stocked" was central to divisional strategy, as the name Innochem implies. Products launched over the past three years represented 33 percent of divisional gross sales, 40 percent of gross profits, and 100 percent of growth.

Mixed Distribution Strategy

Innochem used a mixed distribution system in an attempt to broaden market coverage. Eighty-seven percent of divisional sales were handled by a force of 200 distributor salesmen and were serviced from 50 distributor warehouses representing 35 distributors. The indirect channel was particularly effective outside Ontario and Quebec. In part, the tendency for SCJ market penetration to increase with distances from Montreal and Toronto reflected Canadian demographics and the general economics of distribution. Outside the two production centres, demand was dispersed and delivery distances long.

Distributor salesmen were virtually all paid a straight commission on sales, and were responsible for selling a wide variety of products in addition to S. C. Johnson's. Several of the distributors had sales levels much higher than Innochem.

For Innochem, the impact of geography was compounded by a significant freight cost advantage: piggybacking industrial cleaning chemicals with SCJ consumer goods. In Ontario, for example, the cost of SCJ to a distributor was 30 percent above private label, while the differential in British Columbia was only 8 percent. On lower value products, the "freight effect" was even more pronounced.

SCJ had neither the salesmen nor the delivery capabilities to reach large-volume end users who demanded heavy selling effort or frequent shipments of small quantities. Furthermore, it was unlikely that SCJ could develop the necessary selling and distribution strength economically, given the narrowness of the division's range of janitorial products (i.e., industrial cleaning chemicals only).

THE REBATE PLAN

The key strategic problem facing Innochem was how best to challenge the direct marketer (and private label distributor) for large-volume, price-sensitive customers with heavy service requirements, particularly in markets where SCJ had no freight advantage. In this connection George had observed:

> Our gravest weakness is our inability to manage the total margin between the manufactured cost and consumer price in a way that is equitable and sufficiently profitable to support the investment and expenses of both the distributors and ourselves.
>
> Our prime competition across Canada is from direct-selling national and regional manufacturers. These companies control both the manufacturing and distribution gross margins. Under our pricing system, the distributor's margin at end-user list on sales is 43 percent. Our margin (the manufacturing margin) is 50 percent on sales. When these margins are combined, as in the case of direct-selling manufacturers, the margin becomes 70 percent at list. This long margin provides significant price flexibility in a price-competitive marketplace. We must find a way to profitably attack the direct marketer's 61 percent market share.

The rebate plan George was now evaluating had been devised to meet the competition head-on. "Profitable partnership" between Innochem and the distributors was the underlying philosophy of the plan.

EXHIBIT 5 Distributors' Rebate Pricing Schedule: An Example Using Pronto Floor Wax

Code: 04055
Product description: Pronto Fast-Dry Finish
Size: 209-Litre
Pack: 1

EFF. DATE: 03-31-81
Resale Price List 71   613.750
Distributor Price List 74   349.837
Percent Markup on Cost with Carload and Rebate

Discount Percent[1]	Quote (federal sales tax included)[2]	Rebate Percent[3]	Rebate Dealers[4]	2% Net[5]	2% Markup Percent[6]	3% Net	3% Markup Percent	4% Net	4% Markup Percent	5% Net	5% Markup Percent
30.0	429.63	8.0	27.99	314.85	36	311.35	38	307.86	40	304.36	41
35.0	398.94	12.0	41.98	300.86	33	297.36	34	293.86	36	290.36	27
40.0	368.25	17.0	59.47	283.37	30	279.87	32	276.37	33	272.87	35
41.0	362.11	17.5	61.22	281.62	29	278.12	30	274.62	32	271.12	34
42.0	355.98	18.0	62.97	279.87	27	276.37	29	272.87	30	269.37	32
43.0	349.84	18.5	64.72	278.12	26	274.62	27	271.12	29	267.63	31
44.0	343.70	19.0	66.47	276.37	24	272.87	26	269.37	29	265.88	29
45.0	337.56	20.0	69.97	272.87	24	269.37	25	265.88	28	262.38	29
46.0	331.43	20.5	71.72	271.12	22	267.63	24	264.13	27	260.63	27
47.0	325.29	21.0	73.47	269.37	21	265.88	22	262.38	25	258.88	26
48.0	319.15	21.5	75.21	267.63	19	264.13	21	260.63	24	257.13	24
49.0	313.01	22.0	76.96	265.88	18	262.38	19	258.88	22	255.38	23
50.0	306.88	23.0	80.46	262.38	17	258.88	19	255.38	21	251.88	22
51.0	300.74	24.0	83.96	258.88	16	255.38	18	251.88	20	248.38	21
52.0	294.60	25.0	87.46	255.38	15	251.88	17	248.38	19	244.89	20
53.0	288.46	26.0	90.96	251.88	15	248.38	16	244.89	19	241.39	19
54.0	282.33	28.0	97.95	244.89	15	241.39	17	237.89	18	234.39	20
55.0	276.19	30.0	104.95	237.89	16	234.39	18	230.89	20	227.39	21

[1]Discount extended to end user on resale list price.
[2]Resale price at given discount level (includes federal sales tax).
[3]Percentage of distributor's price ($613.75) rebated by SCJ.
[4]Actual dollar amount of rebate by SCJ.
[5]Actual net cost to distributor after deduction of rebate and "carload" (quantity) discount.
[6]Effective rate of distributor markup.

Rebates offered a means to "share fairly the margins available between factory cost and consumer price." Whenever competitive conditions required a distributor to discount the resale list price by 30 percent or more, SCJ would give a certain percentage of the wholesale price back to the distributor. In other words, SCJ would sacrifice part of its margin to help offset a heavy end-user discount. Rebate percentages would vary with the rate of discount, following a set schedule. Different schedules were to be established for each product type and size. Exhibits 5, 6, and 7 outline the effect of rebates on both the unit gross margins of SCJ and individual distributors for a specific product example.

The rebate plan was designed to be applicable to new, "incremental" business only, not to existing accounts of the distributor. Distributors would be required to seek SCJ approval for end-user discounts of over 30 percent or more of resale list. The maximum allowable end-user discount would rarely exceed 50 percent. To request rebate payments, distributors would send SCJ a copy of the resale invoice along with a written claim. The rebate would then be paid within 60 days. Currently, Innochem sales were sold by distributors at an average discount of 10 percent off list.

EXHIBIT 6   Effect of Rebate Plan on Manufacturer and Distributor Margins: The Example of One 209-Litre Pack of Pronto Floor Finish Retailed at 40 Percent below Resale List Price

I. Under present arrangements

Base price to distributor	$349.84
Price to distributor, assuming 2 percent carload discount*	342.84
SCJ cost	174.92
∴ SCJ margin	$167.92
Resale list price	613.75
Resale list price minus 40 percent discount	368.25
Distributor price, assuming 2 percent carload discount	342.84
∴ Distributor's margin	$ 25.41

II. Under rebate plan

Rebate to distributor giving 40 percent discount off resale price amounted to 17 percent distributor's base price	$ 59.47
SCJ margin (minus rebate)	108.45
Distributor margin (plus rebate)	84.88

III. Competitive prices

For this example, George estimated that a distributor could buy a private brand "comparable" product for approximately $244.

*A form of quantity discount, which, in this case, drops the price the distributor pays to SCJ from $349.84 to $342.84.

EXHIBIT 7 Effect of End-User Discount Level on Manufacturer and Distributor Margins under Proposed Rebate Plan: The Example of One 209-Litre Pack of Pronto Fast-Dry Finish*

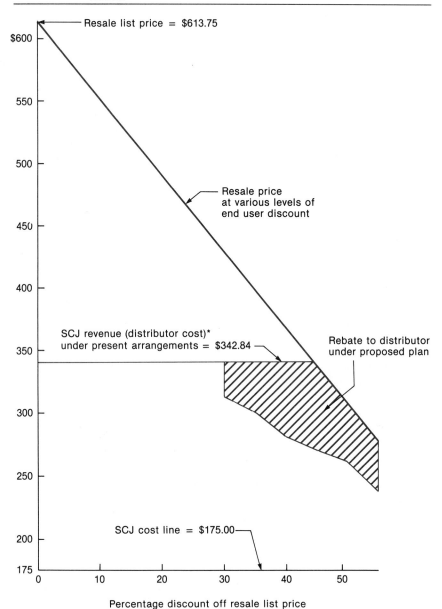

*Assuming 2 percent quantity ("carload") discount off price to distributor.

Proponents of the plan maintained that the resulting resale price flexibility would not only enhance Innochem competitiveness among end users but would also diminish distributor attraction to private label.

As he studied the plan, George questioned whether all the implications were fully understood and wondered what other strategies, if any, might increase urban market penetration. Any plan he devised would have to be sold to distributors as well as to corporate management. George had only three weeks to develop an appropriate action plan.

Island Shores*

Cynthia J. Frey

Boston College

In February 1982, Tom Smith, vice president and project manager of Enterprise Developers, Inc., was contemplating marketing alternatives available to the firm and the associated risks inherent in real estate development during such turbulent economic times. As Mr. Smith sat in his St. Petersburg, Florida, office trying to organize his thoughts and the market information at his disposal in some meaningful fashion, he was well aware that should the firm act on his recommendation, tens of millions of dollars would be at stake. Within the firm Smith was known for his good insights and solid judgment. While his previous decisions had successful outcomes, there was no guarantee that he was immune to mistakes, and in this business mistakes were costly. Corporate expectations to meet a target return on investment of 18 percent added to the pressure that the selected project be more than marginally successful. The final plan to be submitted to the board of directors would have to include consideration of the designated target market, site selection, and architectural design requirements as well as price and promotional strategy.

COMPANY BACKGROUND

The history of Enterprise Developers was characterized by risk taking and an unusually high rate of success. The firm was founded by three businessmen from New York who had grown up in one of the worst boroughs in the city. They had banded together in the late 1950s to renovate and refurbish a neighborhood tenement building. After buying the burned-out shell from the city for $1,000, they rebuilt it themselves with sweat equity into a model example of low-income housing worth several hundred thousand dollars. The group invested the profits from the sale of this building into other pieces of real estate. Middle-income housing, apartment buildings, and townhouses followed. With

---

*This case was written by Cynthia J. Frey, Assistant Professor of Marketing, Boston College, and Maria Sannella as a basis for class discussion rather than to illustrate either effective or ineffective handling of an administrative situation.

each renovation success the profits were reinvested in more property. The group was always alert to a new opportunity.

Encouraged by a friend and the possibility of more lucrative ventures, the trio moved to Miami in 1969. The next five years were spent developing rental units in the central city area. Close to the major business district, these midrise-style buildings provided convenient access to the city for office workers. The skills that Enterprise acquired in New York City developing high-density, urban-living units were equally successful in Miami.

During this time period, extensive condominium development was occurring along Florida's east coast, particularly in the Fort Lauderdale area. Two of the primary groups of buyers were retirees desiring low-maintenance home ownership in a warm climate, and investment buyers who might spend three or four weeks a year in their unit and rent the remaining weeks to Florida vacationers looking for an alternative to high-price, crowded hotel accommodations. While this was a time of extraordinary growth for east coast condominium building, with units being sold before construction was even started, little of this development was occurring on the west side of the state.

In an attempt to take advantage of the condominium boom in the early 1970s, Enterprise investigated possible sites throughout the Florida peninsula but found most of the areas best suited to resort or retirement communities vastly overpriced or unavailable. One alternative which caught the trio's interest was a so-called spoil spot in Boca Ciega Bay, 350 miles from Miami between St. Petersburg and Clearwater. From dredging operations by the Army Corps of Engineers, a 320-acre island had been formed. Two bridges connected the island with the northernmost portions of the city of St. Petersburg 25 minutes away by car. The island was comprised of coarse bottom sand from the Bay. Vegetation was sparse and uncultivated giving the area a decidedly remote and desolate atmosphere.

The 320-acre island was offered for sale by a prominent insurance company. Although friends and business associates advised against the acquisition of the parcel for the planned high-amenity community, Enterprise purchased the site for $18 million. While clarification of zoning ordinances was the first concern for the developers, taming the wilderness to support human creature comforts would be a time-consuming task.

ST. PETERSBURG AREA

St. Petersburg is known for its mild temperatures and beautiful year-round weather. According to the local paper, the *St. Petersburg Independent,* 361 days of sunshine per year are guaranteed. On days when the sun does not appear by 3 P.M., the newspaper distributes the afternoon edition free of charge. Since 1910, only 30 editions have been given away. The record for consecutive days with sunshine is 546.

St. Petersburg, the fourth largest city in Florida, is located on the southern tip of the Pinellas Peninsula. This point of land takes its name from the Spanish Punta Pinales or Point of the Pine Trees. Tampa Bay is on the east and to the south; the Gulf of Mexico on the west. St. Petersburg Beach, on Long Key, is one of the Holiday Isles, a ribbon of keys separated from the mainland and St. Petersburg by Boca Ciega Bay (see Exhibit 1).

Although the Spanish explorer Narvaez landed on the peninsula in 1528 and marched to Tampa Bay, John C. Williams of Detroit is credited as the city's founder. Williams acquired 1,700 acres of wilderness land in 1876, which later became the nucleus of downtown St. Petersburg. Williams's intention was to establish a resort community to take advantage of the fine weather. However, his remote location had no transportation connection with other Florida population centers. As a result, he agreed to a partnership with Russian exile Piotr Alexeitch Dementieff (a.k.a. Peter Demens), contingent on Demens's completion of a railroad trunk line into the area.

The Orange Belt Line from Lake Monroe near Sanford, Florida, was completed in 1888 when Williams's little community had a population of 30. As the story goes, Williams and Demens flipped a coin to decide who would name the new town. Demens won and elected to name the town St. Petersburg after his birthplace. Williams's resort hotel, completed around 1890, was fittingly named The Detroit.

As early as 1885 the American Medical Association praised the climate and healthful surroundings as ideal. With its accessibility improved by the Orange Belt Line, the population had climbed to 300 by 1892 when the town was incorporated. Many of the early settlers were British who had emigrated to the Bahamas and Key West. In an effort to expand the resort reputation of St. Petersburg, the Chamber of Commerce established its first promotional budget of $150 in 1902. In 1907 a special tax was levied on year-round residents to support tourist promotion.

Today, thousands of people arrive daily at the Tampa International Airport which also serves St. Petersburg and Clearwater. Considered one of the most modern and efficient airports in the world, Tampa International has shuttle trains from the main terminal to the gates, an assortment of restaurants and boutiques, and a hotel with a revolving penthouse. Fifteen major air carriers fly into the airport, many with international routes to Central and South America and Europe.

St. Petersburg is also known as the Boating Capital of the United States. With boating activity supported by the Municipal Marina downtown and the St. Petersburg Yacht Club, St. Petersburg is home base

EXHIBIT 1

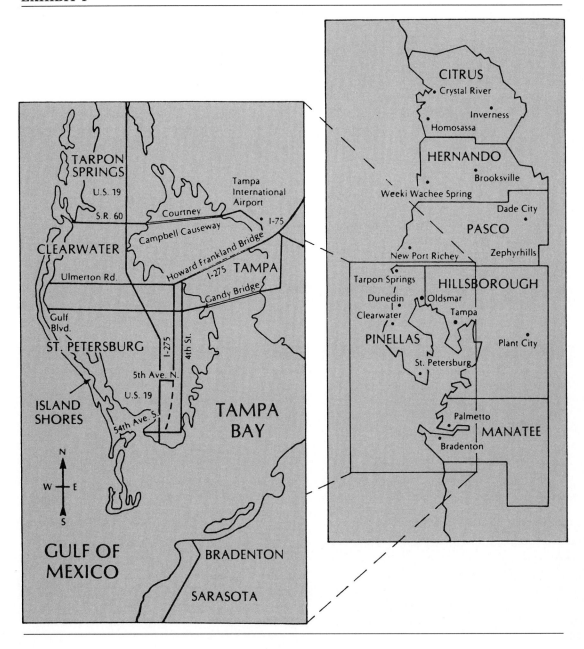

EXHIBIT 2 Population and Population Characteristics Change, 1970 to 1979

	Metro Area			Pinellas			Hillsborough			Pasco		
	April 1, 1979 Population	Percent of Total	Percent Change Since 1970	April 1, 1979 Population	Percent of Total	Percent Change Since 1970	April 1, 1979 Population	Percent of Total	Percent Change Since 1970	April 1, 1979 Population	Percent of Total	Percent Change Since 1970
Total population	1,521,799	100.0%	+39.8%	725,457	100.0%	+38.9%	634,469	100.0%	+29.4%	161,873	100.0%	+113.1%
0–14 years	285,296	18.8	+14.7	112,546	15.5	+14.8	147,088	23.2	+7.0	25,662	15.9	+93.7
15–24 years	217,866	14.3	+43.3	82,771	11.4	+40.1	117,580	18.5	+38.8	17,515	10.8	+111.6
25–44 years	323,700	21.3	+51.2	129,227	17.8	+49.0	170,511	26.9	+46.3	23,962	14.8	+122.1
45–64 years	338,423	22.2	+38.4	171,011	23.6	+37.3	127,884	20.2	+27.4	39,528	24.4	+101.5
65 and over	356,514	23.4	+55.6									
18 and over	1,165,496	76.6	+47.9									
Median age	40.9 years	—	+2.5 years									
White	1,385,288	91.0%	+42.5%									
Nonwhite	136,511	9.0	+17.2									
Male	716,075	47.1	+39.1									
Female	805,724	52.9	+40.4									

Continued (age/race/sex detail — county headers not shown on this page):

	Population	Percent of Total	Percent Change Since 1970	Population	Percent of Total	Percent Change Since 1970	Population	Percent of Total	Percent Change Since 1970
65 and over	229,902	31.7	+ 49.4	55,206	34.1	+129.8	71,406	11.2	+ 39.5
18 and over	584,955	80.6	+ 45.5	130,413	80.6	+117.6	450,128	70.9	+ 38.1
Median age	49.5 years	—	+1.4 years	52.0 years	—	−1.4 years	31.2 years	—	+2.7 years
White	671,331	92.5%	+40.4%	157,783	97.5%	+119.4%	556,174	87.7%	+31.8%
Nonwhite	54,126	7.5	+22.2	4,090	2.5	+ 1.5	78,295	12.3	+ 14.9
Male	334,017	46.0	+38.9	77,599	47.9	+110.7	304,459	48.0	+ 28.1
Female	391,440	54.0	+38.8	84,274	52.1	+115.4	330,010	52.0	+ 30.6

	Manatee			Citrus			Hernando		
	April 1, 1979 Population	Percent of Total	Percent Change Since 1970	April 1, 1979 Population	Percent of Total	Percent Change Since 1970	April 1, 1979 Population	Percent of Total	Percent Change Since 1970
Total population	141,188	100.0%	+45.4%	42,397	100.0%	+120.9%	38,182	100.0%	+124.5%
0–14 years	23,837	16.9	+27.2	7,155	16.9	+ 85.1	7,399	19.4	+ 73.8
15–24 years	15,049	10.6	+37.1	3,717	8.8	+ 81.7	4,166	10.9	+ 93.8
25–44 years	24,504	17.4	+58.1	6,215	14.6	+113.4	7,104	18.6	+120.7
45–64 years	33,874	24.0	+50.1	11,909	28.1	+121.4	10,268	26.9	+161.9
65 and over	43,924	31.1	+49.8	13,401	31.6	+168.4	9,245	24.2	+167.4
18 and over	112,346	80.0	+51.3	33,869	79.9	+134.5	29,253	76.6	+144.9
Median age	49.2 years	—	+.5 years	51.9 years	—	+2.8 years	45.8 years	—	+7.6 years
White	128,068	90.7%	+50.1%	40,622	95.8%	+134.3%	35,833	93.8%	+146.1%
Nonwhite	13,120	9.3	+11.5	1,775	4.2	− 4.4	2,349	6.2	− 3.9
Male	66,700	47.2	+46.7	20,397	48.1	+119.9	18,833	49.3	+125.7
Female	74,488	52.8	+44.2	22,000	51.9	+121.8	19,349	50.7	+123.5

Source: University of Florida, Bureau of Economic and Business Research, "Age, Race, and Sex Components of Florida Population—1979," and 1970 Census. Prepared by Research Department, *St. Petersburg Times* and *Evening Independent*, May 1980.

to some of the most important sailboat and powerboat races in the Gulf. The Swift Hurricane Classic, Isla de Mujeres Race, and the Southern Ocean Racing Conference championships represent the highlights of the season.

Fishing is also a favorite pastime in St. Petersburg where people can be seen lining the bridges fishing late into the night. Golf courses are widely available as are tennis courts.

While St. Petersburg has become a preferred retirement community for many, the city has tried to promote business development in the area to balance the population demographics. Since 1970, construction of new plants and plant expansions has totaled 1,196, and 19,005 new jobs have been created. Changes in population demographics in St. Petersburg and the surrounding counties between 1970 and 1979 are presented in Exhibit 2.

A survey of newcomers to the St. Petersburg area conducted by Suncoast Opinion Surveys in 1980 reveals some further information. This group of newcomers is considered to represent approximately 19 percent of the adult population in Pinellas County. Survey results are presented in Exhibit 3.

BACKGROUND ON ISLAND SHORES

Given their previous experience, management at Enterprise was convinced that careful planning and gradual development would be critical to the success of the Island Shores project. In order to appeal to both retiree and second-home vacationers, Island Shores had to represent a distinct combination of benefits. While many of the Florida condominium complexes were just places to hang one's hat and residents were dependent on the Ft. Lauderdale or Miami communities for things to do and places to go, the location of Island Shores required that many entertainment and recreation options be available on the island. Enterprise's plan called for development of the following amenities: angling, beaches, golf, jogging and bicycle paths, open areas, clubhouse and restaurant, sailing, shopping, sunbathing, swimming pools, tennis and racquetball courts, and water skiing. In order to attract buyers in the early stages of development at least some of these planned benefits had to be apparent, so the golf course and clubhouse went into construction immediately.

The plan for the island called for high-density residential units to be built on the water's edge and a golf course in the center. Since the golf course was considered a major drawing feature, the problems associated with growing grass where none had grown before had to be faced immediately. In 1974 work on the golf course began at the same time as condominium construction. After several false starts and

EXHIBIT 3   Demographic Profile of Pinellas Residents

	Total Pinellas Adults	*By Length of Residency*		
		Newcomers (2 years or less)	*Midterm Residents (3–10 years)*	*Long-Term Residents (over 10 years)*
Total population	100%	19%	35%	46%
Sex				
Male	45%	46%	51%	40%
Female	55	54	49	60
Age				
18–24 years	10%	25%	7%	6%
25–34 years	17	20	22	13
35–49 years	21	24	18	22
50–64 years	22	19	23	22
65–74 years	18	10	22	18
75 years and over	12	2	8	19
Median adult age (years)	51.4	38.1	52.0	56.1
Where born:*				
Pinellas County	8%	1%	1%	16%
Other Florida	5	7	4	5
Northeast	32	31	37	29
Midwest	31	35	31	29
South	15	17	14	14
West	3	3	4	2
Outside United States	6	6	9	5
Education				
Grammar school	4%	1%	4%	6%
Some high school	11	6	12	12
High school graduate	34	28	32	37
Technical, business school graduate	7	8	8	7
Some college	21	24	21	20
College graduate	23	33	23	18
Employment status				
Employed full time	43%	56%	46%	35%
Employed part time	7	5	7	7
Temporarily out of work	3	6	1	3
Retired	32	19	35	34
Housewife	11	11	7	15
Disabled	2	1	3	3
Other	2	2	1	3
Women				
Employed outside home	40%	49%	41%	36%
Not employed outside home	60	51	59	64

EXHIBIT 3   Demographic Profile of Pinellas Residents *(continued)*

	Total Pinellas Adults	By Length of Residency		
		Newcomers (2 years or less)	Midterm Residents (3–10 years)	Long-Term Residents (over 10 years)
Household income				
Under $10,000	23%	21%	18%	28%
$10,000–$15,000	18	24	16	17
$15,000–$20,000	19	12	23	19
Over $20,000	40	43	43	36
Median	$17,400	$17,100	$18,500	$16,300
Own/rent residence				
Own, with mortgage	47%	37%	52%	47%
Own, no mortgage	33	19	32	40
Rent	19	42	15	13
Other	1	2	1	†
Type of residence				
Single family	69%	53%	68%	77%
Apartment	11	19	10	7
Condominium	9	11	10	7
Mobile home	9	11	10	7
Other	2	6	2	2
Household size				
1 person	21%	14%	16%	26%
2 persons	41	45	48	35
3 persons	13	15	9	14
4 persons	15	15	15	16
5 or more persons	10	11	12	9
Average	2.5	2.6	2.6	2.5
Children present in household				
No children present	69%	68%	69%	69%
Child(ren) present	31	32	31	31
Race				
White	96%	97%	98%	94%
Nonwhite	4	3	2	6
Household income sources				
Wages/salaries only	40%	53%	39%	36%
Wage/salary and other regular sources‡	25	21	26	26
Other regular sources only	34	26	34	37
No income sources	1	—	1	1

EXHIBIT 3   Demographic Profile of Pinellas Residents *(continued)*

	Total Pinellas Adults	By Length of Residency		
		Newcomers (2 years or less)	Midterm Residents (3–10 years)	Long-Term Residents (over 10 years)
Number of wage earners in household				
None	35%	26%	35%	39%
One wage earner	31	30	33	30
Two wage earners	26	36	19	27
Three wage earners	6	6	11	2
Four or more	2	2	2	2
Average	1.1	1.3	1.1	1.0
Residence				
North of Ulmerton Road	43%	55%	44%	37%
South of Ulmerton Road	57	45	56	63
Daily newspapers read regularly				
St. Petersburg Times	83%	83%	82%	84%
Evening Independent	22	15	18	27
Clearwater Sun	23	23	28	20
Tampa Tribune	3	6	4	2
Other	3	4	2	3
None	4	3	3	5
Daily newspapers read yesterday				
St. Petersburg Times	67%	59%	68%	69%
Evening Independent	16	11	8	23
Clearwater Sun	18	18	21	15
Tampa Tribune	2	3	2	2
Other	1	1	—	2
None	15	21	13	14
Sunday newspaper read last Sunday				
St. Petersburg Times	74%	72%	70%	78%
Clearwater Sun	17	16	19	15
Tampa Tribune	1	2	2	—
Broadcast media				
Watched television yesterday:				
6:00–8:59 A.M.	8%	7%	6%	8%
9:00–10:59 A.M.	10	7	10	11
Noon–5:59 P.M.	34	37	27	35
6:00–8:59 P.M.	67	66	70	65
9:00–10:59 P.M.	61	63	63	59
11:00 P.M. or later	30	26	30	31
Don't know when watched	1	—	2	1

EXHIBIT 3 Demographic Profile of Pinellas Residents *(concluded)*

	Total Pinellas Adults	By Length of Residency		
		Newcomers (2 years or less)	Midterm Residents (3–10 years)	Long-Term Residents (over 10 years)
Broadcast media (continued)				
Did not watch TV yesterday	11%	13%	8%	13%
Subscriber to cable TV	11	11	14	9
Not cable TV subscriber	89	89	86	91
Listened to radio yesterday:				
6:00–8:59 A.M.	34%	39%	38%	30%
9:00–11:59 A.M.	28	28	29	26
Noon–5:59 P.M.	32	27	37	31
6:00–8:59 P.M.	15	13	14	16
9:00–10:59 P.M.	9	2	11	10
11:00 P.M. or later	7	2	10	8
Don't know when listened	2	2	1	3
Did not listen to radio yesterday	37	38	34	40
Checking account	90%	92%	91%	88%
Savings account	89%	82%	92%	90%
At bank	74	76	77	71
At savings and loan	43	34	38	51
At credit union	26	21	30	24
MasterCard or Visa	55%	56%	59%	52%
MasterCard	36	39	41	31
Visa	46	48	46	45
Other credit cards:				
American Express	10%	18%	13%	6%
Diners Club	3	4	4	2
Carte Blanche	2	2	3	2
Passport	18	11	22	18
Base	(501)	(93)	(175)	(233)

Northeast includes Connecticut, Maine, Massachusetts, New Hampshire, New Jersey, New York, Pennsylvania, Rhode Island, and Vermont.
Midwest includes Illinois, Indiana, Iowa, Kansas, Michigan, Minnesota, Missouri, Nebraska, North Dakota, Ohio, South Dakota, and Wisconsin.
South includes Alabama, Arkansas, Delaware, Washington, D.C., Georgia, Kentucky, Louisiana, Maryland, Mississippi, North Carolina, Oklahoma, South Carolina, Tennessee, Texas, Virginia, and West Virginia.
West includes Alaska, Arizona, California, Colorado, Hawaii, Idaho, Montana, Nevada, New Mexico, Oregon, Utah, Washington, and Wyoming.
†Less than one half of 1 percent.
‡Other regular sources = Other than wages and salaries; includes social security, dividends, interest, alimony, child support, disability, pension, welfare, or other benefits.

experimentation with many varieties of grass, ground-covers, and shrubs, reasonably well-manicured greens appeared three years later. It became painfully clear that landscaping a "spoil spot" would take perseverance, patience, and a great deal of money. Costs associated with construction of the golf course alone totaled a million dollars.

Michele Perez, an award-winning architect from California, was responsible for designing the residential structures in harmony with the island environment. Due to the priority given the 18-hole golf course in the 320-acre parcel and the desire to maximize picturesque views from each condo unit, the residential development plan called for high-density construction along the water's edge. The land utilization goal of 14 condominiums per acre was met by Perez's plan for positioning units diagonally to the water rather than lining them up parallel to the beach frontage in traditional fashion. These clusters form miniature neighborhoods while maximizing ocean views. For each cluster a swimming pool and sunbathing deck was constructed to act as a social gathering spot and provide a recreational area with a relatively large amount of privacy. The large "community pool" concept was considered by Enterprise to be unappealing to many potential residents who were expected to value easy access to the pool's ambience more than its Olympic proportions. Resident parking was designed underneath the buildings to minimize the asphalt perspective so typical of high-density living environments.

Four-story and 12-story high-rise units, 2-story townhouses, and free-standing condominium villas were constructed. The units in greatest demand between 1975 and 1980 were villas. Many of them sold before construction was even begun. Two-bedroom units in the mid- and high-rise buildings were also very popular. One-bedroom high-rise units and townhouses were still available, although on a limited basis. The primary construction materials were stucco and wood which blended with the Spanish architectural influence throughout the St. Petersburg area. As each building was completed, landscaping was carefully undertaken. The landscape architects working for Enterprise were sent to Disney World in Orlando to study plantings. Using similar shrubs which could adapt to conditions at Island Shores, sculptured shrubs and ever-blooming varieties of plants created a garden atmosphere. In 1981 alone, the cost of landscaping approached $1.5 million, not counting individual building phases.

In 1975 the condominiums on Island Shores ranged in price from $42,000 to $50,000. The average market value of these units for resale in 1982 was $108,034. Smith's records showed that in December 1981, 70 units had been sold for a total of $7,562,389. Overall, new sales in 1980 were $32 million and sales in 1981 were $34 million. Prices for units still under construction in the Colony Beach portion of the project as of 1982 are shown in Exhibit 4.

EXHIBIT 4

Colony Beach (6 story)

Model	Size	Price
Madrid	1 bedroom—1½ bath	$70,000–$ 92,900
Sevilla	2 bedroom—2 bath	$90,900–$125,000
Villa	2 bedroom—2 bath	$86,900–$107,000

Colony Beach (12 story)

Model	Size	Price
Barcelona	2 bedroom—2 bath	$133,000–$162,000
Sevilla	2 bedroom—2 bath	$135,000–$166,000
Villa	2 bedroom—2 bath	$110,000–$117,000

Prices vary for the models depending on what floor they are on in the building and their relative exposure. Each unit has its own balcony, carpeting, a full set of appliances, and assigned parking. Two-bedroom, two-bath models had been the most in demand with different square footage and floor plans distinguishing Sevilla, Villa, and Barcelona models. Recent prices at Island Shores for villas had been in the range of $79,000 to $112,000, mid-rise units from $70,000 to $150,000, and high-rise units $95,000 to $166,000. Smith was concerned that as costs escalated the project was being priced out of the reach of most people in the market for vacation homes. While the number of one-bedroom units could be increased, in the future they did not appear to be the most desirable. He wondered if square footage in the two-bedroom, two-bath models could be reduced further or if the target market should be narrowed to primary home buyers rather than including vacation home buyers. This would have implications for the physical design of the units and the required storage space. The Colony Beach area with a planned 1,200 units was not scheduled for completion until 1988. Based on previous experience, it was currently estimated that the 340 units, as yet unsold, would be fully occupied by the end of 1984.

COMPETITION

Smith knew from friends in the business and his own observations that competitors' sales had declined in recent months. While he felt Island Shores was more desirable than similar high-rise condominium units located on the Intracoastal Waterway or the Mandalay Channel, he had collected pricing information hoping it would help him develop his

---

EXHIBIT 5   Competitive Prices

Marina Walk

Model	Description	Price Range	Units/Building
J	2 bedroom, 2 bath	$125,000–$150,000	20
K	2 bedroom, den, 2 bath	$140,000–$165,000	20
L	2 bedroom, 2 bath	$112,500–$142,000	20
M	1 bedroom, 1½ bath	$ 90,000–$110,000	20
NE	2 bedroom, 2 bath	$155,000–$185,000	20
NW	2 bedroom, 2 bath	$167,500–$202,500	20

Sailfish Key

Model	Description	Price Range	Units/Building
Sunfish	1 bedroom, 1 bath	$ 97,900–$ 99,900	6
Yacht	1 bedroom, 1½ bath	$110,000–$126,400	10
Corsair	2 bedroom, 2 bath	$136,500–$149,500	12
Brigantine	2 bedroom, 2 bath	$167,000–$175,000	6
Galleon	2 bedroom, 2 bath*	$171,000–$179,500	10
Frigate	2 bedroom, 2 bath—den	$215,000	2
Clipper	3 bedroom, 2½ bath	$270,000	2

*Corner.

---

marketing plan. In general, unit square-footage ranges from 950 to 1,450 and the selling price from $77 to $115 per square foot. Exhibit 5 presents data for projects comparable to the units in Colony Beach.

It was clear that the development firms behind the competition were aggressive and unlikely to give market share to Island Shores without a battle. Smith didn't know for sure how they would respond to the recent market downturn, but he suspected it would be through strengthened promotional efforts. It was likely that the promotion budget for the Colony Beach community would have to be increased just to keep pace with the competition and maintain the build-out schedule for 1984–85.

BUYER PROFILES

In 1975 the average age of Island Shores condominium buyers was 58. More recently, the average age had decreased to approximately 52, with many buyers in their late 40s. Smith was unsure how to interpret this trend. During the early stages of development, many retirees and investment buyers came from Illinois, Ohio, and Michigan. As economic conditions in these areas worsened, fewer and fewer newcomers seemed to come from the Midwest. To Smith's surprise, an increasing number of European and South Americans were coming to Island Shores over any number of other condominium areas. It seemed that there were growing numbers of buyers from West Germany, France, Venezuela, Argentina, and Mexico. Each nationality tended to cluster together at Island Shores and to maintain close social ties. Whether this pattern would present problems in the long run for the total community was unclear.

A growing concern voiced by condominium residents was the issue of security. The small groupings of units actually facilitated security, since neighbors knew each other's comings and goings and watched out for one another. The problem seemed to be caused by transients. When investment buyers rented their condominiums long distance they could exercise very little control over their tenants. Similarly, management at Island Shores had scant information about renters and no power to intervene unless explicit rules and regulations were being violated. Compared to other condominium developments in the St. Petersburg area the relative crime rate at Island Shores was very low. St. Petersburg itself had little crime compared to other major cities like Miami. Smith began to wonder whether the residents' perceptions of security were more at issue than the occasional burglary. Since one of the objectives of the management was to create an atmosphere of stability in a relaxing environment, any tensions caused by real or imagined security problems would have to be resolved.

Smith wondered if there was some way to encourage more permanent residents and fewer speculative investors to minimize the transient issue. If security personnel were increased it was not clear whether the result would be to alarm or calm the residents and potential buyers. As it had turned out so far, some of the individuals sampling life at Island Shores by renting from absentee owners eventually purchased units on the island, although the number of such individuals was small.

MARKETING DECISIONS

Before Smith could recommend a marketing program, he needed to establish the basic target market and whether or not to continue building at Island Shores. Secondary data showed that more people leave New York than any other state for the South every year. If this market was to be reached, however, there would be a lengthy process of registering Enterprise with New York state authorities in order to promote land sales to New York residents. Smith estimated this process would take about a year. Enterprise was already registered in Michigan, Illinois, Indiana, Ohio, and Pennsylvania.

Another possible market was comprised of people already in the St. Petersburg area. Considering the escalation of land values in recent years, many individuals could sell their existing property for twice its purchase price. In this event the extensive amenity package at Island Shores, offering both quality golf and boating, might prove very attractive. Promotional efforts would certainly be reduced in reaching this market segment, Smith thought.

The international market seemed to be one of growing importance. If this market was actively pursued, the cost and methods of reaching buyers were difficult to determine. The long-run potential of this market was unclear. Smith became even more unsure as he thought about international currency fluctuations and the recent devaluation of the peso.

Expanding on the plan for development at Island Shores was by far the easiest plan of action to adopt in the short run, but Smith wondered if perhaps a lower amenity package with a golf course but no ocean access might not recapture the Midwest market. He knew of projects such as The Westside near Tampa Airport which concentrated on patio homes, both attached and detached, with prices from $45,000 to $70,000. The patio home concept was relatively new. There was no yard to speak of, just the fenced patio. In some parts of the country they were known as zero-lot homes. They offered single-family housing with very low maintenance which might prove appealing to retirees and young families. Patio homes had gained acceptance as starter homes for young couples and there seemed to be encouragement to expand the target market.

A parcel of 200 acres just east of Bradenton in Manatee County was available for purchase which might prove suitable. With the lower yield per acre of about 6 units compared to 14 units per acre at Island Shores, Smith felt there would be a potential 350–380 units with the remaining land used for a golf course. While the price of the parcel was open to negotiation, the asking figure was $6 million. Smith had 10 days to pick up a 90-day option on this property. This would mean a commitment of $5,000.

If building was continued immediately at Island Shores, the mix of high-rise, mid-rise, and villas needed to be considered as did the two-bedroom and one-bedroom proportion. If prices were to be reduced, something would have to change. Existing plans called for development of the Ocean Watch portion of the project which was a mid-rise building series with 50 two- and three-bedroom condominum units from $175,000 to $260,000. This was a 1982 estimate, but completion was not scheduled until 1985, when prices would certainly be higher. The current plan called for surface preparation of the area beginning in 1983. If the market became highly price-sensitive, a potential option was to sell the units under a time-sharing arrangement. Smith knew that existing owners in Colony Beach had voiced objection to such a proposal earlier, but then again, Ocean Watch was a different situation. The target market for this type of vacation home would be a totally new one for Enterprise.

Smith realized that forecasting the demand for seasonal vacation homes versus year-round retirement homes was a critical issue that would strongly influence project location and physical design decisions. Until the best target market was identified, little in the way of price or promotional decisions could be resolved. The person interested in a $200,000 condominium would not likely be the same individual considering a $60,000 patio home.

Since the attributes and amenities of the projects would be very different, the promotional messages would also be very different. Smith was responsible for developing the overall marketing strategy for his projects and would make decisions on promotional strategy as well. A local advertising agency would handle the details of implementation such as art, collateral materials, production, and media buying.

Smith felt strongly that when the real estate market picked up, the Tampa–St. Petersburg area would be among the first to lead the upturn. It was difficult to determine, however, which segments of the market represented the best opportunities for Enterprise. As Smith tried to evaluate the different opportunities facing him, he knew that it was going to be a long weekend. Next Wednesday's board meeting would come all too soon.

Selected Issues in Marketing Management

Tylenol*

Margaret L. Friedman

University of Wisconsin–Whitewater

Pain relievers are a lucrative, $1.2-billion-a-year industry. Until recently, there were no chemical or medicinal differences among brands of nonaspirin pain relievers, and so aggressive marketing was the key to gain market share. For example, in a recent year $130 million was spent on advertising for pain relievers. Johnson & Johnson, producer of Tylenol analgesic, developed very successful marketing strategies and obtained the largest share of the pain reliever market, 37 percent, in a matter of a few years. Then a tragedy threatened their strong position.

---

*This case was prepared by Margaret L. Friedman, Assistant Professor, School of Business, University of Wisconsin–Whitewater. Used by permission. Based on "Tylenol, the Painkiller, Gives Rivals Headache in Stores and in Court," The Wall Street Journal, September 2, 1982; "A Death Blow for Tylenol?", Business Week, October 18, 1982, p. 151; "The Fight to Save Tylenol," Fortune, November 29, 1982, pp. 44–49; "Rivals Go After Tylenol's Market, But Gains May Be Only Temporary," The Wall Street Journal, December 2, 1982, pp. 25ff.

In 1959 Johnson & Johnson acquired McNeil Laboratories which had introduced the Tylenol brand in 1955 in the form of an elixir for children as an alternative to aspirin and its irritating side effects. Traditionally, Tylenol was sold "ethically," through physicians and pharmacists and not directly to end-use consumers. Specifically, it was sold only as a prescription drug until 1960, and then as a nonprescription drug advertised only to doctors and pharmacists, who, in turn, recommended it to patients.

In 1975 Bristol-Meyers introduced Datril, a nonaspirin pain reliever, and successfully marketed it directly to end users. Datril's success forced Johnson & Johnson to expand its marketing effort to end users. The company cut prices, formed a sales force, and spent $8 million on advertising in which Tylenol was represented as an alternative to aspirin. Tylenol's solid reputation among pharmacists and physicians gave it a definite competitive advantage with end-use consumers as it was perceived to be a safe product endorsed by health professionals. In fact, two of every three Tylenol customers started using the product because it was recommended by their doctors.

In 1976 Extra-Strength Tylenol was introduced and was the first product to contain 500 milligrams of painkiller per tablet. Market research had indicated that many consumers believed that Tylenol was too gentle to be effective. Extra-Strength Tylenol was advertised as the most "potent pain reliever available without a prescription." Tylenol's market share rose from 4 percent to 25 percent in 1979, due largely to the extra-strength version of the brand. In 1982 Tylenol had 37 percent market share as shown in Exhibit 1.

Competitors frantically tried to defend their brands against Tylenol. Excedrin, Anacin, and Bayer each introduced extra-strength versions of their brands, with little success. Datril turned out to be a noncontender in the fight for market share because of failure to build a favorable reputation among physicians and pharmacists. Tylenol seemed unbeatable. The product became the largest-selling health and beauty aid, breaking the 18-year dominance of Procter & Gamble's Crest toothpaste.

Tylenol employed very aggressive competitive tactics in order to dominate the industry. For example, court litigation was a very important competitive strategy, since Johnson & Johnson took several competitors to court with claims of infringement on Tylenol's trademark and name. Tylenol found that through the use of litigation, competitors could be barred from active competition for up to two years. After that time the competition was in a weakened market position and seldom recovered. This strategy was especially effective against Anacin. Tylenol sued Anacin four times, once for trademark infringement and three times for false advertising, and won each suit. One marketing expert went so far as to credit Johnson & Johnson with inventing the fifth "P" of marketing—plaintiff.

EXHIBIT 1 Market Shares: Pain Reliever Industry

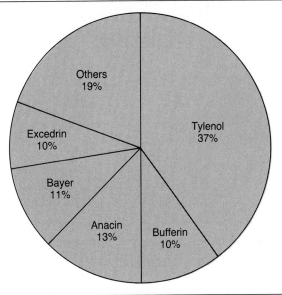

In the early fall of 1982 eight Chicago-area consumers of Extra-Strength Tylenol died tragically. These consumers had taken Tylenol capsules that had been tampered with and laced with cyanide. The coupling of the Tylenol name with the eight deaths caused Tylenol's market share to drop from 37 percent to 7 percent overnight.

Research indicated that many consumers had misconceptions about the poisoning incidents. For example, many consumers were not aware that (1) the company was absolved of all responsibility by the investigating authorities, (2) Tylenol's production process conformed to all safety standards, (3) only Tylenol capsules were involved, not tablets, and (4) the tragic deaths were confined to the Chicago area.

Tylenol's competitors benefited greatly from the tragedy. Anacin won about 25 percent of Tylenol's lost business, mainly by aggressively advertising Anacin-3, and Bufferin and Bayer each took 20 percent of Tylenol's business. Most experts predicted that the Tylenol brand would never recover. The situation was described as a consumer goods marketer's darkest nightmare.

Very soon after the crisis, Johnson & Johnson made a strategic decision to attempt to save the brand that had been so successful and profitable. The company had built up a reservoir of consumer trust and loyalty which management felt would play a key role in the Tylenol brand's recovery. The company had always tried to live up to the credo set for it in 1940s by its leader, General Robert Wood Johnson: "We believe our first responsibility is to the doctors, nurses, and patients, to mothers and all others who use our products and services. In meeting their needs, everything we do must be of high quality."[1] Company management interpreted the crisis as a monumental challenge to live up to this credo against overwhelming odds.

Discussion Questions

1. What tactics should Johnson & Johnson use to rebuild consumer trust in Tylenol?
2. What lessons are there for marketers of drug products in Tylenol's response to the crisis which resulted in the recovery of 90 percent of the lost market share in less than one year?
3. Should Johnson & Johnson have abandoned Tylenol and marketed a new brand?

---

[1] *The Wall Street Journal,* October 8, 1982.

DENVER ART MUSEUM*

Patricia Stocker

University of Maryland

The Denver Art Museum, the major visual arts institution for the Rocky Mountain region, was founded as an artists' club in 1893. It had no collection and no permanent building. By 1932 it became the official art institution for Denver, but until 1971 the collection was divided among various locations, including an old mansion and a remodeled automobile showroom.

In 1971 the Denver Art Museum's spectacular six-story building was opened. The striking silver-gray structure, designed by Gio Ponti of Milan and James Sudler of Denver, was located near downtown in the city's Civic Center. The opening of that new building marked a significant boost to the visual arts of the area. According to Thomas N. Maytham, who became museum director in 1974, "In the new building, we had a doubled budget, a new board of trustees, quadrupled attendance, and a challenging question: How can we best use this building?"

The answer continued to change, but by most measures the museum had been very successful. The permanent collection numbered 35,000 objects valued at more than $70 million. The major areas in the collection were European Art, American Art, New World (including Pre-Columbian Art), Oriental Art, Native Arts (including American Indian Art), and Contemporary Art. The largest single area in the museum's collection was American Indian Art, which numbered more than 13,000 objects and was among the finest assemblages of its type in the world. It had been described as the finest collection of American Indian works in any art museum.

About 20 special circulating exhibitions were also shown at the museum each year. These were usually borrowed from other museums or from private collections. The exhibitions ranged in scope from the

---

*This case was prepared by Dr. Patricia Stocker, Associate Dean and Director of the Executive Program for the College of Business and Management at the University of Maryland at College Park. Used by permission.

EXHIBIT 1 Attendance at Selected Temporary Exhibitions (six-week showings)

Armand Hammer Collection	152,106
Masterpieces of French Art	56,836
Art of the Muppets	115,531
Heritage of American Art	22,583
Frederick Remington: The Late Years	35,000
Silver in American Life	30,000

---

well-known Armand Hammer collection of European and American masterpieces and "Masterpieces of French Art," to "Art of the Muppets" and "Secret Splendors of the Chinese Court," a costume collection (see Exhibit 1). The museum had not been on the tour for such "block-buster" exhibitions as King Tut or Picasso.

The museum also had a number of educational programs including lectures, tours, films, seminars, dance, mime, music, and other performing arts. These programs were generally planned around the circulating exhibitions or the museum's permanent collection and were designed to increase the visitors' appreciation of the visual arts they were seeing.

BACKGROUND INFORMATION

Although the Denver Art Museum was not strictly a government agency, its assets were held by a Colorado nonprofit educational corporation for the benefit of the public. It served as the official arts agency for the city and county of Denver. (The city and the county were one entity.) The museum was managed by an elected, unpaid board of trustees including civic leaders in the community and those who had special skills needed by the museum, such as lawyers, advertising agency executives, professional artists, business managers, and others.

Attendance averaged between 500,000 and 600,000 a year (see Exhibit 2), which put it ahead of the Boston, Houston, and Philadelphia art museums. Perhaps more significantly, the museum boasted the highest attendance on a per capita basis of any major art museum in the country. Of the visitors to the Denver Art Museum, about 28 percent came from out of state, another 40 percent came from Colorado but outside of Denver, and the remaining 32 percent from the city and county of Denver. Included in these attendance figures were visits from students as part of gallery tours led by museum guides. The largest community in the Rocky Mountain region, Denver had a population of 500,000, but the population of the metropolitan area was 1,650,000.

EXHIBIT 2   Total Yearly Denver Art Museum Attendance

1972	674,299
1973	527,311
1974	555,058
1975	524,193
1976	527,859
1977	530,000
1978	608,178*
1979	466,361
1980	598,648
1981	500,000†

*The popular Armand Hammer Collection was included this year.
†Preliminary figure.

The museum was open 40 hours per week, including one evening. It was closed on Mondays. There were 105 employees, about half on the security force and the other half in curatorial and administrative positions.

The Denver Art Museum had traditionally been free to the public. However, admission fees had been charged for major circulating exhibitions. Over the past three years, the museum had collected an average of $160,000 per year in fees for these special exhibitions.

There were about 15,000 museum members, the majority of these family memberships at $30 per family per year. The greatest impetus to membership had been the major exhibitions for which admission fees were charged, because members had been admitted free. Among other membership benefits were 10 percent discounts at the museum on purchases of $5 or more, a monthly newsletter about museum activities, and previews of the 9 or 10 major traveling exhibitions per year. At each preview showing, light refreshments were served free of charge and there was a cash bar. At a few previews an arts celebrity, patron, or collector appeared, a recent example being Baron Thyssen von Bornemiza, when a portion of his collection was exhibited.

The museum had been more marketing-oriented than most other art museums, with marketing considerations in terms of exhibitions, educational programs, fund raising, and acquisitions of art objects for the permanent collection. The museum had traditionally been supported financially by local, state, and federal allocations, gifts from private foundations, and museum memberships. The trend had been toward a greater percentage of the budget each year being raised from private sources. To succeed in this change, the museum had instituted a number of innovative funding ideas, such as the successful museum associates program, for which membership was limited to those individuals who contributed at least $1,250 each year in unrestricted funds for museum support. This was in contrast to restricted funds contributed by individuals and others for specific purposes, such as the support of special exhibitions or the purchase of a specific piece of art for the museum's permanent collection. In its solicitation of funds from private foundations, companies, and individuals for those restricted uses, the museum had been successful by demonstrating its relationship to the quality of life in Denver and by including recognition to the donors, such as associating a special exhibition with the sponsoring organization in the publicity about that exhibition.

The museum also had received substantial support from the federal government. In 1981, the museum received about $200,000 from federal sources, including the national Endowment for the Arts, the National Endowment for the Humanities, and the Institute for Museum Services. Much of this support had come as matching grants. Matching grants required the museum to raise $3 for each $1 of the grant. Walter Rosenberry, chairman of the museum's board of trustees, explained that these challenge grants had had a "tremendously stimulating effect" on private contributions.

The museum budget for 1981 was $3.8 million. The city provided about 24 percent of that amount, with state appropriations making up another 10 percent of the total. However, that situation began to change dramatically in 1982.

THE FUNDING CRUNCH

A combination of government cuts, inflation, and changes in tax deductions for private contributions were forcing changes in the museum's funding picture. The total allocation from the state of Colorado and the city and county of Denver was reduced by $320,000, about 25 percent, in 1982. At the same time, federal funds were slated for a 50 percent cut. This meant that the $200,000 received by the museum in 1981 would be reduced to $100,000 for 1982. Museum director Maytham noted that the halving of funds from the National Endowments for the Arts and Humanities could cut back funds for purchase of art works and for traveling exhibitions.

The museum generated about $2.4 million of its operating budget of $3.8 million in 1981 from gifts, grants, memberships, and admission fees at special exhibitions. Changes in federal tax laws for charitable contributions were also expected to reduce revenues for the museum. With the announced budget cuts for 1982, Maytham expected the Denver Art Museum to receive $420,000 less than in 1981. With 10 percent added to the budget for inflation, 1982 expenses were expected to be $380,000 higher than in 1981. This left an $800,000 gap between revenue and expenses.

BRIDGING THE GAP

Museum employees and trustees responded to the cuts by increasing their solicitation of individual, corporate, and foundation gifts. Also planned were cutbacks in the number of traveling exhibitions, with more emphasis on the museum's own permanent collection. Fewer exhibits were to be sent around the state from Denver and fewer exhibitions of international collections would be brought to Denver.

Management planned to expand the museum's retail shop to increase sales and to close a small gallery called the Discovery Gallery used for specialized shows. Maytham estimated that $30,000 a year would be saved on packing, shipping, insurance, staff time, fees to lending institutions, and other costs associated with exhibitions in that small gallery. The space would be given to the shop for expansion.

On a long-range basis, the museum would attempt to establish a substantial endowment through foundation and individual gifts, which would allow the museum more flexibility in meeting inflation and other unpredictable contingencies.

However, the most noticeable action taken by the museum was the institution of an admission fee. For about a decade, the museum had vigorously opposed such a fee, although the city administration and others had proposed the charge as a way to avoid increasing city and state aid to the museum.

Museum officials had debated not only the imposition of a fee but also what form of admission charge would be most effective in terms of generating the greatest revenue with the smallest drop in attendance. Maytham suggested as an alternative to mandatory entrance fees, a "recommended contribution" along with a sign, "Pay what you wish, but you must pay something." This flexible type of admission fee was pioneered by New York's Metropolitan Museum of Art, where it had been used with success since 1971. The Metropolitan had signs suggesting certain donations. Several months after the flexible fee was introduced by the Metropolitan Museum, the Art Institute of Chicago adopted the system, which it continues to use today.

The Denver Art Museum trustees decided to adopt this "recommended" admission fee. Maytham explained that the museum expected to net approximately $340,000 with the new fee. "While we regret that we must institute the fee," he said, "we hope the flexible system will encourage people to come to the museum regardless of their financial means."

"Our two major goals connected with inauguration of the fee are an increase in critically needed revenue and retention of our healthy attendance goals," he continued. Recommended contributions at the Denver Art Museum were $2 for adults and $1 for senior citizens and students. Museum members and children under 12 would be admitted free. There would not be separate charges for special traveling exhibitions, which had previously brought in about $160,000 each year.

Costs of implementing the fee collection were $60,000, which included such items as cash registers and turnstiles, according to Steven Schmidt, the museum's public relations director. He noted that the museum expected to generate a 26 percent increase in memberships in 1982, from about 15,000 to 19,000, in view of the free admission given to museum members.

Schmidt noted that the Denver Art Museum decision relied heavily on the experience at the Metropolitan Museum and Chicago's Art Institute and that the differences in the Denver museum and its audience might make the flexible fee more or less successful. For this reason, he suggested that the imposition of the fee be closely evaluated, and if the flexible fee was not successful, a fixed fee would be considered.

A fixed fee had been avoided by museum officials because of other museums' experiences in instituting such fees. "With a fixed fee, we'd expect a drop in attendance of 20 to 30 percent at first," Schmidt explained, "with rebuilding after that." He noted that education and advance notification might offset some of the drop in attendance.

The drop associated with a fixed fee was of particular concern in terms of the museum's efforts to attract lower-income visitors. It saw its mission as education, and museum officials worried that attendance might become restricted to middle and upper economic classes.

E. & J. GALLO WINERY*

A. J. Strickland III
Daniel C. Thurman
both of The University of Alabama

In the mid-1980s, alcohol consumption in the United States had been declining in virtually every category except low-priced wines. A number of producers in the wine industry did not believe they should be producing what they called skid-row wines (wines fortified with additional alcohol and sweetener and sold in screw-top, half-pint bottles). Richard Maher, president of Christian Brothers Winery in St. Helena, California, who once was with E. & J. Gallo Winery, said he didn't think Christian Brothers should market a product to people, including many alcoholics, who were down on their luck. "Fortified wines lack any socially redeeming values," he said.

Major producers of the low-end category of wines, called "dessert" or "fortified" (sweet wines with at least 14 percent alcohol), saw their customers otherwise. Robert Hunington, vice president of strategic planning at Canandaigue (a national wine producer whose product, Wild Irish Rose, was the number one low-end wine), said 60 percent to 75 percent of its "pure grape" Wild Irish Rose was sold in primarily black, inner-city markets. Hunington described Wild Irish Rose's customer in this $500 million market as "not super-sophisticated," lower middle-class, and low-income blue-collar workers and mostly men. However, Canandaigua also estimated the annual national market for dessert category wine to be 55 million gallons; low-end brands accounted for 43 million gallons, with as much as 50 percent sold in pints (typically the purchase choice of winos—alcoholics with a dependency on wine). Daniel Solomon, a Gallo spokesman, said Gallo's Thunderbird

---

*Prepared by Daniel C. Thurman, doctoral student, under the supervision of A. J. Strickland III, both of The University of Alabama.

had lost its former popularity in the black and skid-row areas and was consumed mainly by retired and older people who didn't like the taste of hard distilled products or beer.[1]

Tony Mayes, area sales representative for Montgomery Beverage Company, Montgomery, Alabama, said one-third of the total revenue from wine sales in the state of Alabama was from the sale of one wine product—Gallo's Thunderbird. Sales crossed all demographic lines. According to Mayes, a consumer developed a taste for wine through an education process that usually began with the purchase of sweet wines from the dessert category. He attributed the high sales of Thunderbird to the fact that the typical wine drinker in Alabama was generally not the sophisticated wine drinker found in California or New York.

COMPANY HISTORY AND BACKGROUND

The E. & J. Gallo Winery, America's biggest winery, was founded by Ernest and Julio Gallo in 1933. More than 55 years later, the Gallo Winery was still a privately owned and family-operated corporation actively managed by the two brothers. The Gallo family had been dedicated to both building their brands and the California wine industry.

The Gallos started in the wine business working during their spare time in the vineyard for their father, Joseph Gallo. Joseph Gallo, an immigrant from the Piedmont region in northwest Italy, was a small-time grape grower and shipper. He survived Prohibition because the government permitted wine for medicinal and religious purposes, but his company almost went under during the Depression. During the spring of 1933, Joseph Gallo killed his wife and chased Ernest and Julio with a shotgun. He killed himself following their escape. Prohibition ended that same year, and the Gallos, both in their early 20s and neither knowing how to make wine, decided to switch from growing grapes to making wine. With $5,900 to their names, Ernest and Julio found two thin pamphlets on wine-making in the Modesto Public Library and began making wine.[2]

The Gallos had always been interested in quality and began researching varietal grapes in 1946. They planted more than 400 varieties in experimental vineyards during the 1950s and 1960s, testing

[1]Alix M. Freedman, "Misery Market—Winos & Thunderbird Are a Subject Gallo Doesn't Like to Discuss," *The Wall Street Journal,* February 25, 1988, pp. 1, 18.

[2]Jaclyn Fierman, "How Gallo Crushes the Competition," *Fortune,* September 1, 1986, pp. 24–31.

each variety in the different growing regions of California for its ability to produce fine table wines. Their greatest difficulty was to persuade growers to convert from common grape varieties to the delicate, thin-skinned varietals because it took at least four years for a vine to begin bearing and perhaps two more years to develop typical, varietal characteristics. As an incentive, in 1967, Gallo offered long-term contracts to growers, guaranteeing the prices for their grapes every year, provided they met Gallo quality standards. With a guaranteed long-term "home" for their crops, growers could borrow the needed capital to finance the costly replanting, and the winery was assured a long-term supply of fine wine grapes. In 1965, Julio established a grower relations staff of skilled viticulturists to aid contract growers. This staff still counsels growers on the latest viticultural techniques.[3]

Private ownership and mass production were the major competitive advantages contributing to Gallo's success. Gallo could get market share from paper-thin margins and absorb occasional losses that stockholders of publicly held companies would not tolerate. Gallo was vertically integrated, and wine was its only business. While Gallo bought about 95 percent of its grapes, it virtually controlled its 1,500 growers through long-term contracts. Gallo's 200 trucks and 500 trailers constantly hauled wine out of Modesto and raw materials in. Gallo was the only winery to make its own bottles (2 million a day) and screw-top caps. Also, while most of the competition concentrated on production, Gallo participated in every aspect of selling its product. Julio was president and oversaw production, while Ernest was chairman and ruled over marketing, sales, and distribution. Gallo owned its distributors in about a dozen markets and probably would have bought many of the more than 300 independents handling its wines if laws in most states had not prohibited it.

Gallo's major competitive weakness over the years had been an image associated with screw tops and bottles in paper bags that developed because of its low-end dessert wine, Thunderbird.[4] There were stories, which Gallo denied, that Gallo got the idea for citrus-flavored Thunderbird from reports that liquor stores in Oakland, California, were catering to the tastes of certain customers by attaching packages of lemon Kool-Aid to bottles of white wine to be mixed at home.[5]

Thunderbird became Gallo's first phenomenal success. It was a high-alcohol, lemon-flavored beverage introduced in the late 1950s. A radio jingle sent Thunderbird sales to the top of the charts on skid rows across the country: "What's the word? Thunderbird. How's it sold? Good

---

[3]"The Wine Cellars of Ernest & Julio Gallo, a Brief History," a pamphlet produced by Ernest & Julio Gallo, Modesto, Calif.

[4]Fierman, "How Gallo Crushes the Competition."

[5]Freedman, "Misery Market."

and cold. What's the jive? Bird's alive. What's the price? Thirty twice." Thunderbird has remained a brand leader in its category ever since. In 1986, Ernest Gallo poured $40 million into advertising aimed at changing Gallo's image to one associated with quality wines.

Information on Gallo's finances were not publicly available, and the brothers maintained a tight lid on financial details. In a 1986 article, *Fortune* estimated that Gallo earned at least $50 million a year on sales of $1 billion. By comparison, the second leading winery, Sea-gram's (also the nation's largest distillery), had approximately $350 million in 1985 wine revenues and lost money on its best-selling table wines. *Fortune* stated that several of the other major Gallo competitors made money, but not much.[6]

Gallo produced the top-selling red and white table wines in the country. Its Blush Chablis became the best-selling blush-style wine within the first year of its national introduction. Gallo's award-winning varietal wines were among the top sellers in their classification. The company's Carlo Rossi brand outsold all other popular-priced wines. Gallo's André Champagne was by far the country's best-selling champagne, and E & J Brandy has outsold the number two and three brands combined. Gallo's Bartles & Jaymes brand was one of the leaders in the new wine cooler market.[7]

THE U.S. WINE INDUSTRY

Wine sales in the United States grew from about 72 million gallons in 1940 to over 600 million gallons, accounting for retail sales in excess of $9 billion (see Exhibit 1). This retail sales volume had exceeded such major established grocery categories as detergents, pet foods, paper products, and canned vegetables. While wine consumption had grown at an astonishing rate, trends toward moderation and alcohol-free lifestyles made this growth rate impossible to maintain. Nevertheless, annual growth was projected to be 3.2 percent through 1995.

Per capita consumption of wine was low in the late 1950s and early 1960s because wine drinking was perceived as either the domain of the very wealthy or the extreme opposite. "Fortified" dessert wines were the top-selling wines of the period. The first surge in consumption in the late 1960s was the result of the introduction of "pop" wines, such as Boones Farm, Cold Duck, and Sangrias. These wines were bought by baby boomers, who were now young adults. Their palates were

---

[6]Fierman, "How Gallo Crushes the Competition."
[7]"Gallo Sales Development Program," a pamphlet produced by Ernest & Julio Gallo, Modesto, Calif.

EXHIBIT 1   The National Wine Market (1977–86)

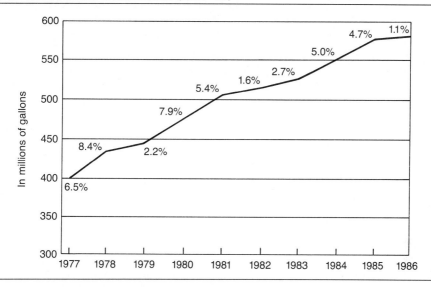

Source: National Beverage Marketing Directory, 10th ed., 1988.

unaccustomed to wine drinking and these wines were suited to them. By the mid-1970s, the pop wine drinkers were ready to move up to Lambruscos and white wine "cocktails," and per capita consumption increased (see Exhibit 2). The wine spritzer became the trend, still the alternative to more serious wines for immature palates. Just as this surge began to wane, wine coolers were introduced in 1982 and exploded on the market in 1983. Wine coolers were responsible for a 5 percent market surge in 1984 and experienced four consecutive years of very high growth rates, rising 6 percent in 1987 to 72.6 million nine-liter cases.

The imported wines category enjoyed an upward growth rate from 6.6 percent of the market in 1960 to a high of 27.6 percent in 1985 (see Exhibits 3 and 4). The category lost market share to 23.1 percent in 1986 primarily because of the shift from Lambruscos to wine coolers. Additional factors were the weakening dollar and an overall improved reputation for domestic wines.

There were about 1,300 wineries in the United States. *Fortune* identified the major market-share holders in the U.S. market in a September 1986 article. It showed Gallo as the clear leader, nearly outdistancing the next five competitors combined (see Exhibit 5).

EXHIBIT 2   Per Capita Consumption of Wine in the U.S.

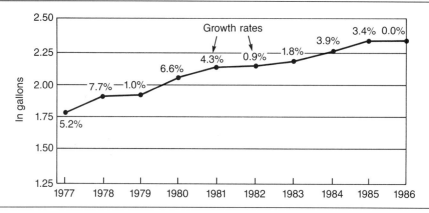

Source: National Beverage Marketing Directory, 10th ed., 1988.

EXHIBIT 3   Wine Production by Place of Origin (millions of nine-liter cases)

| Origin | 1970 | 1975 | 1980 | 1985 | 1986 | Average Annual Compound Growth Rate | | | Percent change |
						1970–75	1975–80	1980–85	1985–86
California	82	115	139.5	133.2	133.3	7.0%	3.9%	−0.9%	0.1%
Other states*	18	19	18.7	16.9	17.3	1.4	−0.3	−2.0	2.4
United States	100	134	158.2	150.1	150.6	6.1	3.3	−1.0	0.3
Imports	13	21	43.1	57.2	45.3	10.5	15.8	5.8	−20.8
Total†	113	115	201.3	207.3	195.9	6.6%	5.4%	0.6%	−5.5%

*Includes bulk table wine shipped from California and blended with other state wines.
†Addition of columns may not agree because of rounding.

Source: Impact 17, no. 11 (June 1, 1987), p. 4.

A number of threats had faced the wine industry, not the least of which had been the national obsession with fitness and the crackdown on drunken driving. Americans drank 6.5 percent less table wine in 1985 than in 1984 (see Exhibits 6 and 7), and consumption was projected to be down another 5 percent in 1986. The industry answer to this problem had been introduction of wine coolers. Gallo's Bartles and Jaymes Coolers were number one until they lost the lead by only a slight margin to a Seagram's brand in 1987.

EXHIBIT 4   Market Share Trends in Wine Production

Place Produced	1970	1975	1980	1985	1986	Share Point Change		
						*1970–80**	*1980–85*	*1985–86*
California	73%	74%	69.3%	64.3%	68.0%	4	−5.0	3.8
Other states	16	12	9.3	8.2	8.8	−7	1.1	0.7
United States	88	86	78.6	72.4	76.9	−10	−6.2	4.5
Imports	12	14	21.4	27.6	23.1	9	6.2	−4.5
Total†	100%	100%	100.0%	100.0%	100.0%	—	—	—

*1980 based on unrounded data.
†Addition of columns may not agree because of rounding.

Source: Impact 17, no. 11 (June 1, 1987), p. 4.

EXHIBIT 5   1985 Share of U.S. Wine Market

Company	Percent
E. & J. Gallo Winery	26.1%
Seagram & Sons	8.3
Canandiagua Wine	5.4
Brown-Forman	5.1
National Distillers	4.0
Heublein	3.7
Imports	23.4
All others	24.0
Total	100.0%

Source: Jaclyn Fierman, "How Gallo Crushes the Competition," *Fortune,* September 1, 1986, p. 27.

Another trend had been a shift toward a demand for quality premium wines made from the finest grapes. Premium wines increased market share from 8 percent in 1980 to 20 percent in 1986. Again, Gallo had sold more premium wine than any other producer, but Gallo's growth had been limited by its lack of snob appeal.[8]

Although more than 80 percent of the U.S. adult population enjoyed wine occasionally, Gallo's research indicated most Americans were still infrequent wine drinkers by global standards. Only about one in four

[8]Fierman, "How Gallo Crushes the Competition."

EXHIBIT 6 Shipments of Wine Entering U.S. Trade Channels by Type (millions of nine-liter cases)

Type	1970	1975	1980	1984	1985	1986	Average Annual Compound Growth Rate 1970–75	1975–80	1980–85	Percent Change* 1985–86
Table	55.9	88.9	150.8	170.9	159.2	147.1	9.9%	11.2%	1.1%	−7.4%
Dessert	31.1	28.2	19.1	15.5	14.3	14.7	−2.0	−7.5	−5.7	3.2
Vermouth	4.2	4.2	3.7	3.0	2.9	2.7	—	−2.5	−4.8	−6.9
Sparkling	9.3	8.4	12.7	19.7	19.4	18.7	−1.9	8.6	8.6	−4.5
Special natural	11.8	24.0	13.6	10.9	10.7	10.9	15.3	−10.7	−4.7	1.9
Imported specialty†	0.3	1.0	1.5	1.0	0.9	1.8	25.4	8.1	−9.7	104.7
Total‡	112.6	154.7	201.3	220.1	207.3	195.9	6.6%	5.4%	0.6%	−5.5%

*Based on unrounded data.
†Imported fruit wines and wine specialties (includes sangria and fruit-flavored wines).
‡Addition of columns may not agree because of rounding.

Source: Impact 17, no. 11 (June 1, 1987), p. 3.

EXHIBIT 7 Share of Market Trends in Shipments of Wine Entering U.S. Trade Channels, by Type

Type	1970	1975	1980	1984	1985	1986	Share Point Change 1970–80*	1980–85	1985–86
Table	50%	57%	74.9%	77.2%	76.8%	75.1%	25	1.9	−1.7
Dessert	28	18	9.5	7.0	6.9	7.5	−18	−2.6	0.6
Vermouth	4	3	1.8	1.4	1.4	1.4	−2	−0.4	†
Sparkling	8	5	6.3	9.0	9.4	9.5	−2	3.0	0.2
Special natural	10	16	6.8	5.0	5.2	5.6	−3	−1.6	0.4
Imported specialty	‡	1	0.7	0.5	0.4	0.9	+	−0.3	0.5
Total	100%	100%	100.0%	100.0%	100.0%	100.0%	—	—	—

*1980 based on unrounded data.
†Addition of columns may not agree because of rounding.
‡Less than 0.05%.

Source: Impact 17, no. 11 (June 1, 1987), p. 3.

Americans drank wine as often as once a week. Per capita consumption in the United States was less than 2.5 gallons per year, compared to about 20 gallons in some Western European countries.[9]

Though the health-consciousness and alcohol-awareness of the 1980s had a moderating influence on wine growth patterns as consumers traded up in quality and drank less, long-term growth was expected to be steady but slower than that of the 1970s and early 1980s. Exhibit 8 provides drinking patterns for 1986. Personal disposable income was expected to grow in the United States through 1995; busy life-styles contributed to more dining out; and sale of wine in restaurants was expected to increase. As the aging baby boomers grew in number and importance, their wine purchases were expected to increase. All these factors contributed to the projected average yearly increase in growth rate of 3.2 percent through 1995.[10]

THE DESSERT WINE INDUSTRY

Dessert wine represented a 55 million-gallon, $500 million industry. The dessert wine category, also called fortified wines, included wines that contained more than 14 percent alcohol, usually 18 percent to 21 percent. They were called fortified because they usually contained added alcohol and additional sugar or sweetener. This category included a group of low-end priced brands that had been the brunt of significant controversy. Canandaigua's Wild Irish Rose had been the leading seller in this category, with Gallo's Thunderbird claiming second place, followed by Mogen David Wine's MD 20/20.[11]

Dessert wines had shown a decreasing trend both in amount of wine consumed and in market share from 1970 through 1985. However, the trend changed in 1986 when dessert wine's market share rose six-tenths of a share point to 7.5 percent of the total wine market (see Exhibit 7). The rise was attributed in large measure to the 19 percent federal excise tax increase on distilled spirits. An additional factor in the increase in the dessert wine category was the shift to fruit-flavored drinks, which also affected the soft drink industry and wine coolers.[12]

A number of factors indicated that the growth trend would continue for the $500 million dessert-wine category. The desire to consume beverages that contained less alcohol than distilled spirits and were less expensive than distilled spirits, the desire for fruit flavor, and the

---

[9]"Gallo Sales Development Program."

[10]"Coolers Providing Stable Growth," *Beverage Industry Annual Manual,* 1987.

[11]Freedman, "Misery Market."

[12]"U.S. News and Research for the Wine, Spirits and Beer, Executive," *IMPACT* 17, no. 11 (June 1, 1987); and *IMPACT* 17, no. 18 (September 15, 1987).

EXHIBIT 8   Beverage Consumption Patterns

1986 National Beverage Consumption by Gender (% of volume):

Gender	Malt Beverages	Wine	Distilled Spirits	Coolers	Total Nonalcoholic Beverages	Total Beverages
Male	80.8%	51.6%	62.6%	44.9%	51.1%	52.7%
Female	19.2	48.4	37.4	55.1	48.9	47.3
Total	100.0%	100.0%	100.0%	100.0%	100.0%	100.0%

1986 National Alcoholic Beverage Consumption by Household Income (% of volume):

Household Income	Malt Beverages	Wine	Distilled Spirits	Coolers	Total Alcoholic Beverages
Under $15,000	26.1%	11.7%	19.7%	22.3%	26.5%
$15,000–$24,999	19.1	13.9	18.1	19.5	21.3
$25,000–$29,999	10.8	14.2	6.6	10.9	12.1
$30,000–$34,999	11.7	9.9	14.7	7.9	10.3
$35,000 & over	32.3	50.3	40.9	39.4	29.8
Total	100.0%	100.0%	100.0%	100.0%	100.0%

1986 National Beverage Consumption by Time of Day (% of volume):

Time of Day	Malt Beverages	Wine	Distilled Spirits	Coolers	Total Nonalcoholic Beverages	Total Beverages
Breakfast/morning	2.7%	2.1%	4.6%	1.5%	32.7%	30.6%
Lunch	6.8	5.8	4.2	4.4	20.8	19.8
Snack	27.5	19.0	31.9	27.0	10.9	12.0
Dinner	14.2	45.8	15.5	13.7	22.9	22.6
Evening	48.8	27.3	43.8	53.4	12.7	15.0
Total	100.0%	100.0%	100.0%	100.0%	100.0%	100.0%

1986 National Beverage Consumption by Location of Consumption (% of volume):

Location	Malt Beverages	Wine	Distilled Spirits	Coolers	Total Nonalcoholic Beverages	Total Beverages
Total home	64.6%	75.8%	61.4%	76.9%	76.1%	75.5%
Total away from home	35.4%	24.2%	38.6%	23.1%	23.9%	24.5%

Source: Impact 17, no. 18 (September 15, 1987), pp. 3–4.

American trend toward eating out at restaurants more often contributed to the trend toward increased consumption of dessert wines. Additionally, the dessert wine category had survived relatively well with virtually no promotion or advertising. This had been possible because, of the category's 55 million gallons, low-end brands accounted for 43 million gallons, approximately 50 percent of which was sold in half pints; and this market had not been accessible by traditional advertising or promotion.

The dessert wine category had been a profitable venture because many of the wines in this category were made with less expensive ingredients, packaged in less expensive containers, and had usually been sold without promotion. Canandaigua estimated that profit margins in this category were as much as 10 percent higher than those of ordinary table wines. Gallo said this was not true for its products, but it would not reveal the figures.

The low-end dessert wines were a solid business. *The Wall Street Journal* reported that, of all the wine brands sold in America, Wild Irish Rose was the number 6 best seller, Thunderbird was 10th, and MD 20/20 was 16th. In contrast to the growth expectations of other brands and categories, sales of these low-end brands were expected to be up almost 10 percent. Yet the producers of these top-selling wines distanced themselves from their products by leaving their corporate names off the labels, obscuring any link to their products. Paul Gillette, publisher of the *Wine Investor,* was quoted in a discussion of this unsavory market as saying: "Makers of skid-row wines are the dope pushers of the wine industry."[13]

---

[13]Freedman, "Misery Market."

LEVI'S—WORLDWIDE STRATEGY OR LOCALIZED CAMPAIGN?

Philip R. Cateora
University of Colorado

The Levi Strauss Company, manufacturer of the famous Levi's jeans and other wearing apparel, markets its products in 70 countries. The company owns and operates plants in 25 countries and has licensees, distributors, and joint ventures in others.

The company is now in the process of evaluating its advertising policy to determine whether to apply a worldwide strategy to all advertising or settle on localized campaigns for each country in which it sells its products.

You have been asked to evaluate its present programs and to make recommendations that will assist management in deciding whether it is better to (1) create advertising campaigns locally or regionally but with a good deal of input and influence from headquarters as they presently do; (2) allow campaigns to be created independently by local advertising companies; or (3) centralize at national headquarters all advertising and develop a consistent worldwide advertising campaign.

You are asked to do the following:

1. Prepare a report listing the pros and cons of each of these three approaches.
2. Make a recommendation about the direction the company should take.
3. Support your recommendation and outline major objectives for whichever approach you recommend.

The information in Exhibit 1 should be of assistance in completing this assignment:

EXHIBIT 1   Sales/Profits ($ millions)

	Total	United States	Europe	Other International
Sales	$2,840	$1,888	$526	$426
Profits	468	314	92	62
Assets	1,375	882	240	253

Company Objectives

In a recent annual report, the following statement of objectives of Levi Strauss International was made:

> In addition to posting record sales [see Exhibit 1], Levi Strauss International continued to advance toward two long-term objectives.
>
> The first is to develop a solid and continuing base of regular jeans business in markets throughout the world, thus providing a foundation for product diversification into women's-fit jeans, youthwear, menswear, and related tops.
>
> The second objective is to attain the greatest possible self-sufficiency in each of the major geographic areas where Levi Strauss International markets: Europe, Canada, Latin America, and Asia/Pacific. This requires the development of raw material resources and manufacturing in areas where the products are marketed, thus reducing exposure to long supply lines and shipping products across national borders.
>
> Unlike some competitors, Levi Strauss International does not, in its normal markets, seek targets of opportunity, that is, large one-time shipments to customers it may never serve again. Rather, the goal is to develop sustainable and growing shipment levels to long-term customers.

Organization

Western European Group.   The company's European operations began in 1959 with a small export business, and, in 1965, an office was opened in Brussels. The company now has 15 European manufacturing plants and marketing organizations in 12 countries. This group includes all Western Europe served by the Continental and Northern European divisions.

The Continental European Division is headquartered in Brussels and is responsible for operations in Germany, France, Switzerland, the Benelux countries, Spain, and Italy. The Northern European Division is headquartered in London and is responsible for all marketing and production in the United Kingdom and the Scandinavian nations.

Other International Group.   The divisions in this group report directly to the president of Levi Strauss International. They are Canada, Latin America, and Asia/Pacific.

The Canadian Division consists of two separate operating units: Levi Strauss of Canada and GWG. Levi Strauss Company is sole owner of GWG which manufactures and markets casual and work garments under the GWG brand.

The Latin American Division traces its origins to 1966 when operations began in Mexico. In the early 1970s, the business was expanded to Argentina, Brazil, and Puerto Rico. In addition to these countries, the division now serves Chile, Venezuela, Uruguay, Paraguay, Peru, Colombia, and Central America. Plans call for the division to explore new markets in Central America and the Andean Region.

The Asia/Pacific Division had its beginning in the 1940s when jeans reached this market through U.S. military exchanges. In 1965 a sales facility was established in Hong Kong. Markets now served include Australia and Japan, the two largest, as well as Hong Kong, the Philippines, Singapore/Malaysia, and New Zealand. Business in Indonesia and Thailand is handled through licenses. The markets served by this division present opportunity for growth in jeanswear. However, diversification potential in Asia/Pacific is centered in Japan and Australia.

Other Operating Units.   One other unit, EXIMCO, not aligned with either Levi Strauss USA or Levi Strauss International, reports directly to the president.

EXIMCO has two major responsibilities; market development and joint ventures in Eastern Europe, the USSR, and the People's Republic of China, and directing offshore contract production for the company's division.

Comments

The director of advertising and communications for International shares with you the following thoughts about advertising:

- The success of Levi Strauss International's advertising derived principally from their judging it consistently against three criteria: (1) Is the proposition meaningful to the consumer? (2) Is the message believable? and (3) Is it exclusive to the brand?
- A set of core values underlies advertising wherever it is produced and regardless of strategy: honesty/integrity, consistency/reliability, relevance, social responsibility, credibility, excellence, and style. The question remains whether a centralized advertising campaign can be based on this core of values.

- Levi Strauss' marketing plans must include 70 countries and recognize the cultural and political differences affecting advertising appeals.
- Uniform advertising (i.e., standardized) could ignore local customs and unique product uses, while locally prepared advertising risks uneven creative work, is likely to waste time and money on preparation, and might blur the corporate image.
- Consistency in product image is a priority.
- International advertising now appears in 25 countries. Levi currently uses seven different agencies outside the United States, although one agency handles 80 percent of the business worldwide. In Latin America, it uses four different agencies, and still a different agency in Hong Kong.
- Levi is not satisfied with some of the creative work in parts of Latin America. The company wants consistency in Latin American strategy rather than appearing to be a different company in different countries. They are not satisfied with production costs and casting of commercials, and the fact that local agencies are often resistent to outside suggestions to change. They feel there is a knee-jerk reaction in Latin America that results in the attitude that everything must be developed locally.
- The risks of too closely controlling a campaign result in uninteresting ads compared with decentralizing all marketing which produces uneven creative quality.

Competition

At the same time that Levi is looking at more centralized control of its advertising, another jeans maker is going in the opposite direction. Blue Bell International's Wrangler jeans company has just ended a six-month review of its international advertising and decided against coordinating its advertising more closely in Europe.

The concept of one idea that will work effectively in all markets is attractive to Wrangler. Yet the disadvantages are just as clear: the individual needs of each market cannot be met, resistance from local managers could be an obstacle, and the management of a centralized advertising campaign would require an organizational structure different from the present one.

To add to the confusion, a leading European jeans manufacturer, the Spanish textile company Y Confecciones Europeas, makers of Louis jeans, recently centralized its marketing through one single advertising agency. Louis—fourth-largest jeans maker after Levi, Lee Cooper, and Wrangler—is intent on developing a worldwide international image for its Louis brand.

Review of Current Ads

A review of a selection of Levi advertisements from around the world provided the following notes:

- European television commercials for Levi's were supersexy in appeal, projecting, in the minds of some at headquarters, an objectionable personality for the brand. These commercials were the result of allowing complete autonomy to a sales region.
- Levi's commercials prepared in Latin America projected a far different image than those in Europe. Latin American ads addressed a family-oriented, Catholic market. However, the quality of the creative work was far below the standards set by the company.
- Ads for the United Kingdom, emphasizing that Levi's are an American brand, star an all-American hero, the cowboy, in fantasy wild West settings. In Northern Europe, both Scandinavia and the United Kingdom consumers are buying a slice of America when they buy Levi's.
- In Japan, where an attitude similar to that in the United Kingdom prevails, a problem confronted Levi's. Local jeans companies had already established themselves as very American. To overcome this, Levi's positioned itself against these brands as legendary Americans jeans with commercials themed "Heroes Wear Levi's," featuring clips of cult figures such as James Dean. These commercials were very effective and carried Levi's from a 35 percent to a 95 percent awareness level in Japan.
- In Brazil, unlike the United Kingdom, consumers are more strongly influenced by fashion trends emanating from the European Continent rather than from America. Thus, the Brazilian-made commercial filmed in Paris featured young people, cool amidst a wild traffic scene—very French. This commercial was intended to project the impression that Levi's are the favored brand among young, trend-setting Europeans.
- Australian commercials showed that creating brand awareness is important in that market. The lines, "fit looks tight, doesn't feel tight, can feel comfortable all night," and "a legend doesn't come apart at the seams" highlighted Levi's quality image, and "since 1850 Levi jeans have handled everything from bucking broncos . . ." amplified Levi's unique positioning. This campaign resulted in a 99-percent brand awareness among Australians.*

---

*Information for this case was taken in part from the following sources: Levi Strauss and Company, Annual Report, 1980, "Exporting a Legend," *International Advertising,* November–December 1981, pp. 2–3, and "Levi Zipping up World Image," *Advertising Age,* September 14, 1981, pp. 35–36.

Lime Kiln Arts, Inc.

Lawrence M. Lamont
Ashley F. Hayes
Lizabeth Ashley Hoopes
Brian S. Tanis
all of Washington and Lee University

INTRODUCTION

> Where master stonemasons once plied their trade and kilns burned red-hot with the making of lime, actors and musicians now entertain audiences on pleasant summer evenings. With a star-studded sky as a roof, and earthen floor and stone walls as a stage, Lime Kiln was called the most unusual theater setting in the United States. *Lime Kiln Arts Brochure, 1988.*

In early 1990, Caro Hall, director of operations, and Don Baker, the artistic director at Lime Kiln Arts in Lexington, Virginia, were discussing the upcoming summer season. Lime Kiln had experienced rapid growth since its first season in 1985, but attendance at the outdoor theater was beginning to level off and had actually declined in 1989. Management wondered if changes in marketing strategy would help the theater regain its momentum and restore the previous rate of growth.

An analysis of attendance data for the 1989 season indicated that only about 30 percent of the audience came from Rockbridge County and the cities of Lexington and Buena Vista, the immediate area around the theater. Caro Hall suspected that Lime Kiln had not sufficiently penetrated the local market and if some changes in marketing strategy were made, attendance could be increased. She was also troubled by the fact that the marketing position in the Lime Kiln organization had remained unfilled for several months. It seemed to her that without the appropriate personnel, whatever changes were needed would never be made.

Property of the Washington and Lee University Department of Administration. Case material is prepared as a basis for class discussion, and not designed to present illustrations of either effective or ineffective handling of administrative problems.

The authors gratefully acknowledge the cooperation and assistance of Ms. Caroline Hall and Mr. Donald Baker, management of Lime Kiln Arts, Lexington, Virginia.

In the fall of 1989, Caro had authorized a market research study to learn more about the local residents and their entertainment interests. The research, conducted in February and March of 1990, used the survey method with 100 personal interviews: 62 with residents who had never attended a Lime Kiln event and 38 with residents who had attended at least once in the past two years. Caro hoped the research would provide some information about the community awareness of Lime Kiln and an evaluation of its theater and concert program. She also hoped to use the research to formulate a marketing strategy that would focus on the residents who had not attended Lime Kiln. As Caro contemplated the research findings, she thought of some of the issues that needed to be addressed:

1. How could Lime Kiln increase the attendance of local residents?
2. What marketing strategy should be used to stimulate the demand for Lime Kiln events among local residents?
3. Should the vacant marketing position be filled? If so, by whom?

Historical Development of Lime Kiln Arts

In the late 1960s, Don Baker was a fine-arts student at Washington and Lee University in Lexington, Virginia. While spending summer vacation in Lexington, he stumbled upon the site used by A. T. Barclay in 1896 to harvest limestone for the Rockbridge Stone and Lime Company. Baker, involved in the theater arts at the university, was struck by the natural beauty of the quarry and its surroundings and thought they would be a perfect setting for Shakespeare's play, *A Midsummer Night's Dream.* Baker obtained permission from the landowner to direct and stage the play at the old kiln ruins. The success of the production intrigued Baker and played an important part in his return to the site several years later.

Following graduation, Baker studied acting and performed and directed for theater organizations in Washington, D.C., and Kentucky. In 1981, on a trip through Lexington, Baker met with Thomas Spencer, a local attorney and former classmate who had worked on *A Midsummer Night's Dream,* to discuss developing the lime company ruins into an outdoor theater. They met again with the landowner, who agreed to let them use the quarry site as a theater for the arts.

Lime Kiln Arts was incorporated in 1982 by Baker and Spencer as a nonprofit organization to offer artistic and cultural events to a broad audience. The founders believed that the enjoyment of professional theater should not be reserved for the wealthy few. The theatrical works developed by Lime Kiln capture the life, heritage, and culture of the Southern Appalachian people. The philosophy of the founders is reflected in the mission statement: "The more personally we speak, the more universally we are understood." Figure 1 contains the mission statement of Lime Kiln Arts as conceived by the founders.

The outdoor theater had a preview season in 1984 and a full season in the summer of 1985. The preview season received such an enthusiastic response from the community that Baker and Spencer enlisted local volunteer support to create the all-natural 299-seat outdoor theater that exists today. Spencer, Lime Kiln Arts' first chairman of the board, was responsible for much of the fund raising needed to get the theatrical organization started. His persistence and popularity in the community enabled him to raise the funds necessary to support the first seasons.

Six concerts featuring regional music such as bluegrass, folk, and country were added to the 1985 summer season. Since then, the product mix has expanded to include artistic performances with a foundation in other regions and cultures. The number of concerts has also increased to over 20 during a season. The concert site is a grassy, natural amphitheater located approximately 100 yards from the quarry. This area has an audience capacity of approximately 420.

Each year, in addition to theater and concerts, Lime Kiln sponsors a special presentation such as an international theater group or similar one-time event. Since 1985, Lime Kiln has sponsored the Palestinian Theater Company, the Leningrad Clown Mime Theater, the Txsuma Noh theater from Japan, as well as a production of *Red Fox/Second Hangin'*, a Baker original. In 1990, the season will feature an American Movement Festival during the first three weeks of June.

FIGURE 1 Lime Kiln Arts, Inc., Mission Statement

Lime Kiln Arts is an organization and the Kiln is a place dedicated to presenting artistic and cultural events and performances of professional quality. The mission of Lime Kiln Arts is to encourage, produce, and create experiences which will endow the broadest possible audience with the full enjoyment and understanding of the arts. The founders of Lime Kiln Arts believe that the enjoyment of works of art of high quality and intrinsic value need not be an experience reserved for few. The founders also believe that the most accessible creative works of art reflect a strong sense of place and personal involvement—that the more personally we speak, the more universally we are understood. The organization, therefore, intends to focus on those works which reflect the life, history, and heritage of the people rooted in this place.

Source: Lime Kiln Arts.

In recent years, a touring company sponsored by Lime Kiln has performed at theaters and schools throughout the Southeast, including performances at the Baltimore Theater Project and the ROOTS festival. Unfortunately, scheduled touring for 1989 was canceled due to a lack of funding. However, a short tour is planned for March 1990 at schools and local theaters in Virginia. Lime Kiln hopes to establish a resident theatrical troupe which will form the core of the summer theater and touring companies. This troupe will spend two or three months each year developing and rehearsing new theatrical works.

Management and Organization Structure

Lime Kiln Arts is governed by a 27-member board of directors which has the responsibility for fund raising and organization development. Board members represent a diverse range of occupations and backgrounds. Of the 24 voting members, 18 live in Lexington or nearby communities. The remaining five members live in other Virginia cities and one resides in New York. Historically, board members have been chosen for their ability to support Lime Kiln financially and to solicit contributions from acquaintances and friends. However, some have played only a minor role in Lime Kiln's development and do not regularly attend board meetings.

Members of the board serve on five standing committees: executive, nominating, finance, audience development, and fund raising. The executive committee is concerned with operations. Caro Hall and Don Baker are members, and as shown in Figure 2, they manage the administrative and artistic activities of the organization.

Caro Hall is director of operations and manages Lime Kiln's marketing and general office activities. Over the past year, Hall has had to assume responsibility for marketing because the position has remained unfilled. She is also responsible for the activities of the Lime Kiln volunteers, a group of 137 persons called FOLKS (Friends of Lime Kiln) who help prepare the costumes and stage props, sell tickets and concessions, and usher patrons during the summer season.

Don Baker, the artistic director, is responsible for all artistic aspects of Lime Kiln and is the creator and writer for most of the theatrical productions. In addition, Baker directs the stage manager, production manager, and the artistic company which is hired to perform his work.

In February 1990, Lime Kiln hired Steven Carr, former president of the Virginia School of Arts in Lynchburg, Virginia, to become the managing director. While it is not clear where he will fit in the organization chart, his primary responsibility will be fund raising. He will also guide the board of directors in selecting new members and will teach the board how to solicit funds. His previous experience in

FIGURE 2 Lime Kiln Arts, Inc., Organization Chart

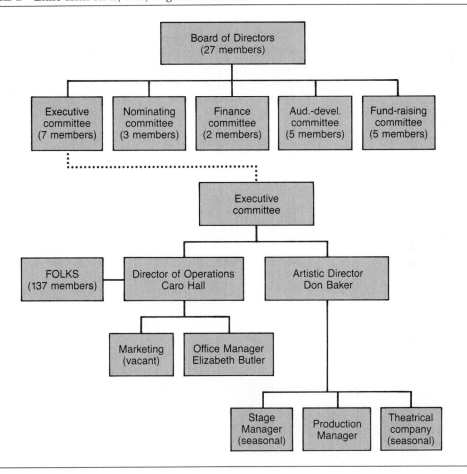

Source: Lime Kiln Arts.

directing an organization with a combination of artistic and administrative operations is expected to improve Lime Kiln's public relations, as well as the working relationships between the board of directors and the Lime Kiln staff.

Financial Performance

The financial goal of Lime Kiln Arts is to generate sufficient revenue and funding to support annual operations. Revenues from ticket and concession sales historically have accounted for less than 50 percent of the funds needed to cover annual operating expenses. The balance has come from donated gifts, annual giving, grants, and miscellaneous gifts.

The income statement, showing sources of revenue and support and operating expenses for the three most recent fiscal years, is in Table 1. In fiscal year 1990, Lime Kiln experienced a decline in revenue, explained in part by the wet weather conditions that prevailed throughout the 1989 summer season. The productions were interrupted on several occasions by rain, resulting in a decline in attendance and concession sales.

Lime Kiln's balance sheet for the fiscal years 1988–90 is presented in Table 2. The organization is mainly concerned with meeting short-term obligations, which are usually adequately covered by current assets. The $104,000 note is payable in annual installments of $6,000 plus accrued interest, with a balloon payment due on March 1, 1999, for the outstanding balance.

Because revenues from ticket and concession sales are insufficient to cover operating expenses, fund raising is an important part of the Lime Kiln operation. Table 3 illustrates the fund-raising efforts over the past four years and the dependency on gifts, grants, and other sources for Lime Kiln's continued existence.

Table 4 presents a schedule of functional expenses allocated across the major program and support categories for the 1990 fiscal year. Program services which total the direct costs for the product lines account for about 66 percent of expenses, while overhead support services, including marketing and promotion, account for the balance.

LIME KILN GEOGRAPHIC MARKETS

Lime Kiln attracts its audience from three geographic markets: tourists visiting Lexington, Virginia, residents living within a 50- to 75-mile radius of Rockbridge County, and local residents living in Lexington, Buena Vista, and Rockbridge County. Approximately 40 percent of Lime Kiln's attendance comes from the tourist market, 30 percent from residents outside Rockbridge County, and 30 percent from local residents.

Virginia is known for its rich history and scenic beauty. Tourists, traveling in tour groups and as families, are attracted to Rockbridge County because it is the home of Civil War heroes Thomas "Stonewall" Jackson and Robert E. Lee; famous inventor Cyrus McCormick; and pioneer Sam Houston. Lexington, the county seat of Rockbridge County, is itself an historic landmark.

During the summer, tourists visit Lexington to tour the many historic sites. Among the most popular are the Jackson House, the

TABLE 1 Lime Kiln Arts, Inc., Income Statement

	FY Ended Feb. 28, 1990		FY Ended Feb. 28, 1989		FY Ended Feb. 29, 1988	
Revenue and support:						
Revenue and support from operations:		$175,007		$198,080		$149,901
Admissions	132,806		126,029		95,985	
Concessions	42,201		72,051		53,916	
Nonoperating support:		318,258		259,744		174,122
Donated services	15,000		20,163		3,600	
Annual giving	196,533		170,046		107,471	
Grants	90,544		68,286		62,479	
Miscellaneous	1,181		1,249		572	
Total revenue and support		$493,265		$457,824		$324,023
Operating expenses:						
Plays	190,461		$156,020		$129,985	
Touring	43,140		22,657		20,760	
Special presentations	27,765		24,019		22,400	
Concerts	66,116		45,106		23,448	
General and administrative expenses	105,322		107,965		85,199	
Marketing and promotion expenses	59,751		40,712		46,134	
Fund raising	5,476		37,275		24,791	
Total operating expenses		$498,031		$433,754		$352,717
Net income (EBI)		($4,766)		$24,070		($28,694)
Interest income		$1,041		$1,752		$278
Excess (deficiency) from current endeavors		($3,725)		$25,822		($28,416)

Source: Lime Kiln Arts financial statements.

TABLE 2   Lime Kiln Arts, Inc., Balance Sheet

	FY Ended Feb. 28, 1990	FY Ended Feb. 28, 1989	FY Ended Feb. 28, 1988
Assets			
Current assets:			
Cash	21,494	$19,669	$16,206
Accounts receivable	3,451	53	2,069
Grants receivable	13,031	54,914	2,710
Pledges receivable	1,750	1,550	4,200
Inventories	2,139	3,128	402
Prepaid expenses	780	726	850
Total current assets	42,645	80,040	26,437
Noncurrent assets:			
Investment securities	80,000	80,065	40,051
Property and equipment	141,843	145,813	163,385
Scripts and copyrights	26,126	26,813	27,500
Total noncurrent assets	247,969	252,691	230,936
Total assets	290,614	$332,731	$257,373
Liabilities and Entity Capital			
Current liabilities:			
Accounts payable	5,635	$1,610	$7,959
Accrued salaries payable	6,374	2,812	3,290
Payroll taxes payable	5,494	5,494	5,831
Accrued interest payable	170	170	1,622
Deferred revenue	6,381	48,290	6,738
Current notes payable	6,000	6,000	40,000
Total current liabilities	30,054	64,376	65,440
Long-term liabilities:			
Long-term notes payable	104,000	104,000	163,400
Deferred revenue	80,000	80,000	40,000
Total long-term liabilities	184,000	184,000	203,400
Contingencies			
Entity capital:			
Plant fund	141,843	145,813	138,385
Unrestricted funds	(65,283)	(61,458)	(149,852)
Total entity capital	76,560	84,355	(11,467)
Total liabilities and entity capital	290,614	$332,731	$257,373

Source: Lime Kiln Arts financial statements.

TABLE 3   Lime Kiln Arts, Inc., Fund Raising

Fiscal Year	Individual Gifts	Grants State/Fed.	Other	Total Fund Raising
1987	$130,801	$34,421	$ 6,884	$172,106
1988	111,071	24,082	38,969	174,122
1989	190,209	40,045	29,090	259,744
1990	190,093	73,316	24,869	288,278

Source: Lime Kiln Arts.

residence of Stonewall Jackson; Lee Chapel, the burial site of Robert E. Lee; the Marshall Museum, a memorial to World War II hero George C. Marshall; the Virginia Military Institute and Washington and Lee University; and the Virginia Horse Center, a nonhistoric facility for equine shows and competition. As Table 5 indicates, over the past six summers the number of registered guests to visit the area has steadily increased.

The market outside the local area consists of the cities and counties that are within a 50- to 75-mile radius of Lexington. Some of the cities, such as Charlottesville, Harrisonburg, and Roanoke offer summer theater, symphony orchestra programs, and concerts. They compete with Lime Kiln, but none offers an assort of entertainment products that is directly comparable.

Most of the cities and counties, shown in Table 6, are expected to experience slow growth over the next decade. Approximately 30 percent of Lime Kiln's audience comes from this geographic market.

Rockbridge County, including the cities of Lexington and Buena Vista, has a population of 31,500. Centrally located in the scenic Shenandoah Valley in west-central Virginia, the county encompasses 607 square miles of rolling terrain and parts of the Blue Ridge and Allegheny mountain ranges. Figure 3 is a map of Rockbridge County showing the locations of Lexington and Buena Vista.

Lexington, located at the intersection of interstate highways I-81 and I-64, is the retail, commercial, and administrative center of the county. It has a high concentration of well-educated residents, many of whom are employed in government service and education. Buena Vista is the center of industry and manufacturing in Rockbridge County and is located six miles east of Lexington. Manufacturing firms employ almost half of the persons working in Buena Vista. The population and income characteristics of Buena Vista, Lexington, and Rockbridge County are shown in Table 7, which presents an area profile. Approximately 2,400 college students are included in the population of Lexington, but only about 300 reside in the area during the summer.

TABLE 4 Lime Kiln Arts, Inc., Supplementary Schedule of Functional Expenses

Description of Expenses:	Plays	Touring	Special Pres.	Concerts	Total Program Services	General and Admin.	Marketing and Promotion	Fund Raising	Total Support Services	Tot FY Ended 1990
Salaries and fees	$129,730	$31,456	$18,529	$48,955	$228,669	$42,433	$10,286	$0	$52,719	$281,388
Payroll taxes	8,773	2,517	439	1,096	12,825	3,541	888	0	4,429	17,254
Benefits	2,154	3,721	78	194	6,147	3,474	615	0	4,089	10,236
Travel, meals, and entertainment	2,504	4,790	782	402	8,478	1,552	301	78	1,931	10,409
Printing	1,185	0	169	423	1,778	0	26,323	1,860	28,183	29,961
Repairs and maintenance	136	0	10	34	180	119	0	0	119	299
Miscellaneous	635	0	95	238	968	1,900	1,918	1,979	5,797	6,765
Technical, lighting, and sound	10,164	0	3,994	4,125	18,283	0	0	0	0	18,283
Props, pyro, costumes, and make-up	6,247	656	0	0	6,903	0	0	0	0	6,903
Stage, house, and box office	4,243	0	606	1,515	6,365	0	0	0	0	6,365
Concessions	7,493	0	1,070	2,676	11,239	0	0	0	0	11,239
Utilities	1,755	0	251	627	2,632	1,197	0	0	1,197	3,829

Supplies	0	0	0	0	0	4,036	0	0	4,036	4,036
Postage and shipping	0	0	0	0	0	4,129	3,000	956	8,085	8,085
Insurance	0	0	0	0	0	4,240	0	0	4,240	4,240
Telephone	0	0	0	0	0	7,735	0	0	7,735	7,735
Rent	8,000	0	1,143	2,857	12,000	3,600	0	0	3,600	15,600
Dues and conferences	0	0	0	0	0	1,723	1,129	0	2,852	2,852
Advertising	0	0	0	0	0	25	6,678	0	6,703	6,703
Taxes	0	0	0	0	0	1,981	0	0	1,981	1,981
Professional services	0	0	0	0	0	4,663	1,950	0	6,613	6,613
Interest expense	0	0	0	0	0	2,976	0	0	2,976	2,976
Media	0	0	0	0	0	0	1,944	0	1,944	1,944
Depreciation	6,755	0	600	2,173	9,528	471	0	471	942	10,470
Events and recognition	0	0	0	0	0	7,201	0	132	7,333	7,333
Service fees	0	0	0	0	0	1,500	0	0	1,500	1,500
Company housing	0	0	0	0	0	6,826	0	0	6,826	6,826
Design	0	0	0	0	0	0	1,229	0	1,229	1,229
Campaign	0	0	0	0	0	0	3,490	0	3,490	3,490
Accommodations	0	0	0	800	800	0	0	0	0	800
Support services	0	0	0	0	0	0	0	0	0	0
Amortization	687	0	0	0	687	0	0	0	0	687
	$190,461	$43,140	$27,765	$66,116	$327,482	$105,322	$59,751	$5,476	$170,549	$498,031

Source: Lime Kiln Arts financial statements.

TABLE 5 Lexington, Virginia Visitor Information

	1984		1985		1986		1987		1988		1989	
	Summer	Year Total	Summer	Year Total	Summer	Year Total	Summer	Year Total	Summer	Year Total	Summer	Year Total
Visitor Center	26,439	49,038	27,016	51,252	32,389	61,274	40,803	73,069	42,408	81,539	43,803	84,484
Jackson House	11,234	22,170	13,584	26,030	15,049	29,863	14,413	28,332	11,110	23,167	16,553	31,744
Lee Chapel	18,677	41,546	19,315	39,952	23,014	43,883	21,884	42,332	25,861	48,949	22,628	46,481
Marshall Museum	6,211	15,771	6,801	14,823	7,823	19,126	8,877	22,302	10,594	24,402	11,054	27,193
VMI Museum	16,680	35,359	17,639	38,290	19,987	42,981	22,629	43,795	22,368	46,954	23,475	51,844
Virginia Horse Center									1,183	2,573	1,398	2,943

Note: Summer totals include June, July, August, and September.

Source: City of Lexington, Visitor Center, Lexington, VA.

TABLE 6 Virginia Counties and Cities, Population Projections

	1990	2000	Percent Change
Virginia Counties			
Albemarle	66,500	75,700	13.8%
Alleghany	13,400	13,000	(3.0)
Amherst	29,200	29,900	2.4
Augusta	53,000	54,800	3.4
Bath	5,000	5,200	4.0
Bedford	43,400	50,900	17.3
Botetourt	25,900	28,000	8.1
Nelson	12,900	13,400	3.9
Roanoke	77,000	80,000	3.9
Rockbridge	18,200	18,500	1.6
Rockingham	57,800	61,800	6.9
Virginia Cities			
Bedford	6,300	6,600	4.8
Buena Vista	6,300	6,100	(3.2)
Charlottesville	42,800	44,200	3.3
Clifton Forge	5,000	4,900	(2.0)
Covington	7,100	6,900	(2.8)
Harrisonburg	28,600	32,100	12.2
Lexington	7,000	7,200	2.9
Lynchburg	70,000	73,000	4.4
Roanoke	99,000	99,000	0.0
Salem	24,500	25,000	2.0
Staunton	24,200	25,000	3.3
Waynesboro	18,500	19,000	2.7

Source: Virginia Department of Planning and Budget, *Virginia Population Projections,* January 1990.

Residents have a high awareness of Lime Kiln, but the decision to attend a performance is influenced by the availability of a variety of competing activities. Market research respondents reported summer participation in outdoor sports, camping, leisure reading, movies, concerts, and simply relaxing at home and watching television. Attendance has varied by geographic location and demographic characteristic. Lexington residents have been more inclined to attend Lime Kiln than residents of Buena Vista and Rockbridge County. As illustrated by Tables 8, 9, and 10, market research indicates that residents who have attended a Lime Kiln performance in the past two years generally are older with higher household incomes and more education than

FIGURE 3

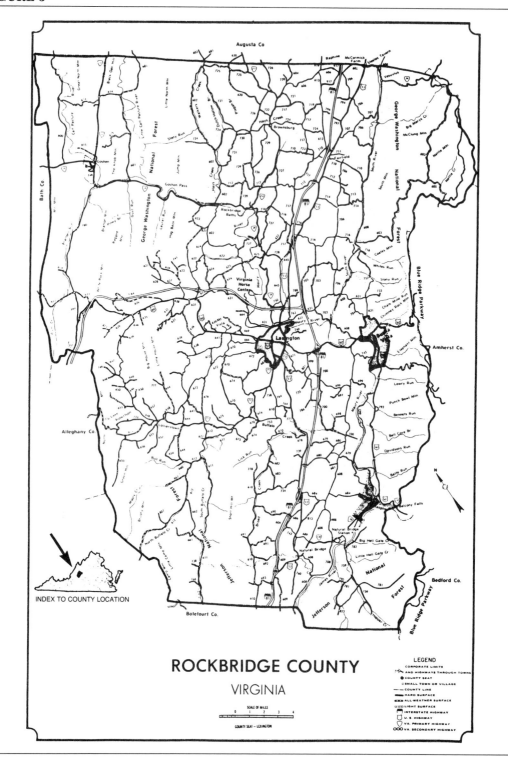

INDEX TO COUNTY LOCATION

ROCKBRIDGE COUNTY
VIRGINIA

SCALE OF MILES

0   1   2   3   4

COUNTY SEAT – LEXINGTON

LEGEND
CORPORATE LIMITS
AND HIGHWAYS THROUGH TOWNS
COUNTY SEAT
SMALL TOWN OR VILLAGE
COUNTY LINE
HARD SURFACE
ALL WEATHER SURFACE
LIGHT SURFACE
INTERSTATE HIGHWAY
U.S. HIGHWAY
VA. PRIMARY HIGHWAY
VA. SECONDARY HIGHWAY

TABLE 7   Population Characteristics, 1988, Area Profile

	Buena Vista	Lexington	Rockbridge County
Population			
Median age	33.9	24.7	33.1
Age distribution (%)			
18–24 years	10.0	38.2	14.5
25–34 years	16.2	10.4	15.4
35–49 years	21.9	13.3	21.0
50 and over	26.3	24.6	26.1
Income			
Median household	$22,072	$22,429	$20,370
Income distribution (%)			
$10,000–19,999	26.9	24.2	27.1
20,000–34,999	35.9	22.7	29.6
35,000–49,999	15.6	13.1	13.5
50,000 and over	5.3	19.6	7.8

Source: Sales and Marketing Management, *1989 Survey of Buying Power,* August 7, 1989.

those who have not attended. Caro Hall believes that a substantial market opportunity exists if Lime Kiln can further penetrate the local market.

MARKETING AT LIME KILN ARTS

The Lime Kiln season features theater, concerts, and special presentations. The common thread in the three product lines is the presentation of artistic and cultural experiences that have relevance in a rural setting and offer entertainment which reflects a unique cultural heritage.

The theatrical productions have been developed by Don Baker and performed by professional actors under contract with Lime Kiln for the summer season. Concerts and special presentations have generally featured bands and independent theatrical organizations hired to complete the summer season and generate additional ticket and concession revenue. They usually perform once or a few times and then move on to another engagement. The mix of entertainment has been enthusiastically received and as indicated in Table 11, Lime Kiln attendance and revenue expanded rapidly from 1985 to 1988. The 1990 summer

TABLE 8   Lime Kiln Arts, Inc., Age and Attendance Data

Age	Attended		Have Not Attended	
	No.	*Percent*	*No.*	*Percent*
18–24 years	4	10.5%	11	17.7%
25–34 years	9	23.7	16	25.8
35–49 years	11	28.9	13	21.0
50 and over	14	36.8	22	35.5
Totals	38	100.0%	62	100.0%

Source: Independent Market Research.

TABLE 9   Lime Kiln Arts, Inc., Income and Attendance Data

Yearly Income	Attended		Have Not Attended	
	No.	*Percent*	*No.*	*Percent*
$10,000–$19,999	11	28.9%	29	46.8%
$20,000–$34,999	6	15.8	17	27.4
$35,000–$49,999	7	18.4	6	9.7
$50,000 and over	5	13.2	1	1.6
No response	9	23.7	9	14.5
Totals	38	100.0%	62	100.0%

Source: Independent Market Research.

TABLE 10   Lime Kiln Arts, Inc., Education and Attendance Data

Education	Attended		Have Not Attended	
	No.	*Percent*	*No.*	*Percent*
High school or less	9	23.7%	41	66.2%
Some college	6	15.8	14	22.6
College degree or higher	22	57.9	7	11.3
No response	1	2.6	0	0.0
Total	38	100.0%	62	100.0%

Source: Independent Market Research.

TABLE 11   Lime Kiln Arts, Inc., Aggregate Attendance

Year	No. of Performances	Total Audience	Total Revenue
1985	38	5,185	$ 28,998
1986	45	9,473	52,595
1987	64	13,677	88,874
1988	78	16,929	117,995
1989	84	16,663	133,558
1990	80		

Source: Lime Kiln Arts.

season is being planned to include multiple performances of three original theatrical works, a concert series with 27 different groups, and a special presentation called the American Movement Festival which features three theatrical groups. The season is scheduled to run from May 31 until September 2.

Theater and Artistic Development

Lime Kiln has functioned successfully as an originating, producing, and performing theater. Theater attendance and revenue, shown in Table 12, have increased significantly since the first full summer season in 1985.

Don Baker is responsible for most of the original theatrical works and adaptations performed at Lime Kiln. His first production was an adaptation of Shakespeare's *Cymbeline,* which he set in 1984 just outside of Lexington. Baker used about an hour and a half of Shakespeare's words and 45 minutes of his own. He claims, "It's a lesser-known play, so we can fiddle around with it without upsetting too many people. Mainly, we're going to tell the tale, and try to do it the way Shakespeare would have done it if he were living today in Rockbridge County." Baker also wrote and produced Lime Kiln's best-known production, *Stonewall Country.* This play explores through music, drama, and dance the infinite contradictions of the confederate legend, Stonewall Jackson. Historians and scholars were asked to read and criticize drafts of the play, and Baker revised it from their ideas and comments. *Stonewall Country,* widely acclaimed and extremely popular with tourists, finished its fourth season in 1989. *Munci Meg,* an original adaptation of an Appalachian mountain folk tale that has special appeal to children, was produced in 1989, and *Virgil Powers,* a musical that draws on the true life story of an Appalachian man and his family who are

---

TABLE 12   Lime Kiln Arts, Inc., Theater Attendance

Year	No. of Performances	Total Audience	Total Revenue
1985	22	3,371	$20,268
1986	31	6,452	35,173
1987	39	8,616	57,005
1988	55	10,321	72,494
1989	56	9,474	84,664
1990	44		

Source: Lime Kiln Arts.

---

deeply affected by the man's visions, will premiere during the 1990 season. The artistic themes and plays developed by Don Baker reflect the cultural dialect and heritage of the Appalachian people. Baker chooses local stories and legends that contain controversial and emotional themes such as slavery, racism, truth, loyalty, and war. He seeks to challenge audiences with difficult questions and encourages them to reach their own conclusions. Baker sees it as the "artists job to reflect and clarify the issues and help the audience become a part of the thinking process." Lime Kiln's theatrical productions address these issues but intentionally take no position.

Figure 4 illustrates the artistic development process that Baker has implemented at Lime Kiln. When he finds a story that seems appealing for a theatrical production, he consults with his staff, artistic confidants, and others in the community for their general impression of the subject matter. Once a story is selected for production, Baker researches it and begins to conceptualize the play. Depending on the complexity of the story and the availability of historical information, the research process may require as much as two years. Following the research, Baker either hires a company to write the play, or he writes it himself. Generally, it takes from one to three months to complete the writing. The average production time for a play, from the first rehearsal to opening night, is about six to eight weeks. Usually, several changes are made during the production process. Depending upon the time and funding available, a theatrical play will be market-tested by performing it on tour prior to performing it during the regular summer season. Once a new play becomes part of the summer theater offering, it is evaluated and allowed to run as long as it keeps Baker and the organization artistically interested and satisfactory attendance levels are maintained. Music for the productions is typically original work written and performed by two nationally acclaimed songwriters.

FIGURE 4   Lime Kiln Arts, Inc., Artistic Development

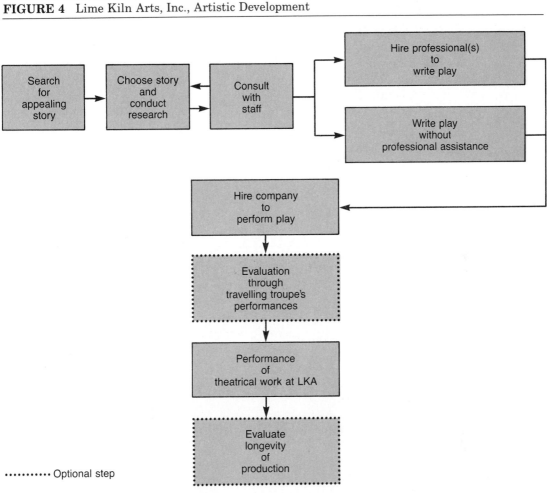

Concerts and Special Presentations

Lime Kiln presents a variety of concerts and special presentations. The three-month summer season will include 27 concerts featuring such groups as The Seldom Scene, Bela Fleck and the Flecktones, and individual performers such as Livingston Taylor, John McCutcheon, and Robin and Linda Williams. Concerts are offered on Sunday and Wednesday evenings throughout the summer with music ranging from mountain music, bluegrass, folk, and country to string bands, an African rhythm band, and a Cajun-based musical gumbo. Special presentations have featured the Leningrad Clowns and the Palestinian Theater of Jerusalem. The special presentation for the 1990 season will be an American Movement Festival to be held during the first three weeks of the summer season. It will feature the Ukelele Vaudeville Review, the American Dance Theater, and the Seattle Mime Theater.

Concerts and special presentations have not been as popular as the theater, but they have enabled Lime Kiln to broaden its audience because of their appeal to families and younger adults. Table 13 summarizes the attendance for concerts and Table 14 presents similar information for the special presentations sponsored by Lime Kiln.

TABLE 13   Lime Kiln Arts, Inc., Concerts Attendance

Year	No. of Performances	Total Audience	Total Revenue
1985	5	1,049	$ 5,456
1986	11	2,282	13,342
1987	14	3,747	24,748
1988	16	4,423	31,965
1989	20	4,708	38,520
1990	27		

Source: Lime Kiln Arts.

TABLE 14   Lime Kiln Arts, Inc., Special Presentations Attendance

Year	No. of Performances	Total Audience	Total Revenue
1985	9	765	$ 3,274
1986	3	609	4,081
1987	9	1,314	7,121
1988	5	1,918	13,536
1989	8	1,212	10,373
1990	9		

Source: Lime Kiln Arts.

Touring

Lime Kiln performs theatrical works on tour when resources are available. In the past, a touring company has been hired to perform in theaters and schools throughout the Southeast, but touring was dropped in 1989 because of insufficient funding. Touring dates have again been scheduled in 1990 for performances of *Munci Meg* in Virginia schools and theaters. Management views touring as an excellent way to market test new theatrical work and stimulate the demand for summer season theater.

Market research indicates that the quality of Lime Kiln events is favorably evaluated by local residents. As shown in Table 15, of the local residents who have attended a Lime Kiln performance during the past two years, about 95 percent rated its overall quality as excellent or very good. Management was pleased with the ratings, but they knew that responding to the areas entertainment interests and offering events consistent with the mission of Lime Kiln would always be a challenge.

The Outdoor Theater and Concert Site

The theater and concert site, located in a remote area outside the city of Lexington, are reached by a one-way, unpaved, access road. Lime Kiln volunteers (FOLKS) direct visitors to one of two infield parking areas located within 200 yards of the theater and concert areas. However, parking space is limited and late arrivals often have to park outside of the designated parking areas and walk as much as a half

TABLE 15 Lime Kiln Arts, Inc., Customer Evaluation of Lime Kiln Events

Quality Rating	No.	Percent
Excellent	21	55.3%
Very good	15	39.5
Good	2	5.3
Fair	0	0.0
Poor	0	0.0
Total	38	100.0%

Source: Independent Market Research.

mile to reach the site. Following an evening performance, patrons exit the theater and concert site in the dark and use a different one-way road to return to Lexington.

Location may be a problem according to the independent market research conducted for Lime Kiln. When survey respondents who had never attended a performance were asked if they knew where the out-door theater was located, 42 percent responded that they did not. The City of Lexington has cooperated with Lime Kiln to make the theater easier to locate by allowing the placement of small signs along the route to the theater. The signs are helpful to local residents, but visitors unfamiliar with the community and its roads still experience difficulty locating the site.

Tickets are purchased at the theater box office, or customers can phone the business office in Lexington to reserve tickets for pick-up prior to the performance. A brochure which includes a map is available to help ticket holders locate Lime Kiln. Upon arrival, a unique rustic quarry welcomes patrons to the outdoor theater. After almost a century, the kiln remains essentially intact. The theater stage, located on a harvested lime hill, is directly next to the original giant metal kiln. Don Baker keeps the rare personality of the theater in mind when he creates new works, making sure the props are simple in order to em-phasize the natural beauty of the site. Figure 5 shows the theater site and provides additional descriptive information about Lime Kiln.

Concerts are held in a spacious natural amphitheater about 100 yards from the quarry. The amphitheater is an open, informal setting with room for people to sit or dance on the grass. The concert area accommodates up to 420 people. Lime Kiln has a relaxed, casual, come-as-you-are atmosphere and visitors are invited to picnic on the grounds before a performance. In case of rain, the scheduled performance is held in a tent located next to the kiln.

Promotion

Lime Kiln uses publicity and advertising for most of its promotion. Regular press releases featuring news about Lime Kiln and its schedule of performances are sent to over 90 local and regional newspapers, radio and television stations, and regional magazines. Lime Kiln is featured quite often in local weekly newspapers such as the *Lexington News Gazette* and the *Rockbridge Weekly*. In 1989, *Southern Living* magazine wrote a feature article praising Lime Kiln for its unique portrayal of Southern culture. The publicity has contributed to very high awareness in the local area. According to the market research, about 88 percent of local residents have heard of Lime Kiln and 76 percent are able to describe what the organization does. Repeat

FIGURE 5 Lime Kiln Arts, Inc., Theater Site and Descriptive Information

attendance by local residents is a concern, however. Of survey respondents who reported attending Lime Kiln in the past two years, 69 percent had attended three times or less.

In spite of the favorable publicity, Lime Kiln does not have the resources to determine exactly how many of its press releases are printed and the extent to which they lead to ticket sales. Further, most regional newspapers will only run a feature on Lime Kiln every two to three years. Lime Kiln emphasizes in its press releases that it is nonprofit, in order to increase the likelihood of receiving print space in magazines and newspapers.

Local newspaper advertising is used twice during the summer season to supplement publicity. While advertising is used sparingly, market research indicates that about 69 percent of survey respondents rely on newspapers for information about entertainment. Of those respondents who were aware of Lime Kiln, 34 percent mentioned newspapers as a source of information where they learned about the organization.

Publicity and advertising are supplemented with posters distributed for placement in retail store windows. An attractive four-color brochure, which included a calendar of performances, ticket pricing, and a map, was distributed to area motels and tourist attractions by FOLKS to target the tourist market. Lime Kiln also retained the services of an advertising agency to distribute its brochures to travel agents in Washington, D.C., Richmond, and other areas in an effort to reach tourists and family vacationers planning to visit the Shenandoah Valley.

Pricing

During 1988, Lime Kiln priced theater tickets at $8.00 and $12.00 (depending on the proximity of the seat to the stage), and increased prices to $10.00 and $12.00 in 1989. However, some of the more expensive seats did not offer a better view than the less expensive seats at the back of the theater. Customers could not understand why they paid more for what was essentially the same theatrical experience. In planning for the 1990 season, Lime Kiln is considering a flat price of $12.00 on all tickets for theatrical performances and special presentations. Concert tickets are expected to sell at a single price between $10.00 and $14.00 depending on the individual or group performing. Table 16 summarizes the ticket pricing for theater, concerts, and special presentations.

Pricing is controversial among Lime Kiln management, so a part of the market research study was designed to gather information on prices of Lime Kiln presentations. As shown in Table 17, most of respondents who had attended Lime Kiln during the 1988 and 1989 summer seasons thought that ticket prices in the $8.00 to $12.00 range were "just about right." Caro Hall wondered what impact the proposed prices for the 1990 season would have on ticket sales. After all, it was quite a change and consumer behavior had always been difficult to predict.

In 1989, Lime Kiln offered discounts on ticket prices for theater, concerts, and special presentations. Senior citizens received a $2.00 discount and children under 10 years of age were admitted at half-price. Tickets for theater previews and matinee performances were also discounted and special prices were available for groups and families. These policies were to remain about the same for 1990.

Theater and concert packages featuring reduced ticket prices were also offered in an attempt to encourage customers to attend multiple performances. Four packages were offered in 1989 including special prices for: all theatrical performances, all concerts, all opening night shows with a champagne reception following the performance, and four theatrical performances. Most of the packages featured a 10 to 25

TABLE 16 Lime Kiln Arts, Inc., Ticket Prices for Lime Kiln Events

	1990[1]	*1989*	*1988*
Theater	$12.00	$10.00 & $12.00	$8.00 & $10.00
Special presentations	$12.00	$10.00 & $12.00	$8.00 & $10.00
Concerts[2]	$10.00–$14.00	$4.00–$14.00	$3.00–$12.00

[1] Proposed for 1990.
[2] Ticket price depends on concert.

Source: Lime Kiln Arts.

TABLE 17 Lime Kiln Arts, Inc., Customer Evaluation of Lime Kiln Ticket Prices

Ticket Price	*No.*	*Percent*
Too high	0	0.0%
High	1	2.6
Just about right	33	86.8
Low	3	7.9
Too low	0	0.0
Free ticket	1	2.6
Total	38	100.0%

Source: Independent Market Research.

percent discount with prices ranging from $24.00 to $153.00. Similar packages are proposed for the 1990 summer season, with prices between $40.00 and $250.00. The discounted ticket packages have not been very popular.

Promotional packages were also sponsored with local motels in an attempt to attract tourists visiting Lexington as part of a tour group. For example, Lime Kiln sponsors the "Performance Tour," in conjunction with the local Best Western motel. The package includes a discount on the room and a ticket for members of the tour group. The tour groups are seen by Lime Kiln as excellent prospects because they are already visiting in the area.

Marketing the 1990 Summer Season

Caro Hall knew that Lime Kiln had to find the formula for a successful marketing strategy. Lime Kiln attendance was below capacity for the 1989 summer season, and after considering the effects of bad weather and the number of performances offered, it appeared that growth was beginning to stall. The market research had stimulated her thinking about how promotion might be used more effectively to expand the demand for Lime Kiln performances. Was it time to place more emphasis on advertising and sales promotion, and if so, what media and methods would be most effective? Ticket prices for the 1990 summer season were also a concern. After all, if higher prices reduced the demand for tickets, Lime Kiln might actually experience a decline in ticket and concession revenue. Given the difficulty of raising funds from grants and donations to cover operating expenses, this would be a problem. How to further penetrate the local market was of concern to Caro. She wondered what should be done to encourage more residents from Buena Vista and Rockbridge County to attend Lime Kiln events. Perhaps additional ticket locations would be helpful. "Its all meaningless unless we can find some enthusiastic person to fill our marketing position," she remarked.

Rogers, Nagel, Langhart (RNL PC), Architects and Planners*

H. Michael Hayes

University of Colorado–Denver

It was August 1984. John B. Rogers, one of the founders and a principal stockholder in RNL, had just completed the University of Colorado's Executive MBA program. Throughout the program John had tried to relate the concepts and principles covered in his courses to the problems of managing a large architectural practice. In particular, he was concerned about the marketing efforts of his firm. As he put it, "Marketing is still a new, and sometimes distasteful, word to most architects. Nevertheless, the firms that survive and prosper in the future are going to be those which learn how to market as effectively as they design. At RNL we are still struggling with what it means to be a marketing organization, but we feel it's a critical question that must be answered if we're going to meet our projections of roughly doubling by 1989, and we're giving it lots of attention."

RNL

In 1984, with sales (design fees) of approximately $3,300,000, RNL was one of the largest local architectural firms in Denver and the Rocky Mountain region. The firm evolved from the individual practices of John B. Rogers, Jerome K. Nagel, and Victor D. Langhart. All started their architectural careers in Denver in the 1950s. The partnership of

---

* This case was prepared by H. Michael Hayes, Professor of Marketing and Strategic Management, University of Colorado at Denver, as the basis for class discussion rather than to illustrate either effective or ineffective handling of an administrative situation. Copyright © 1985 by H. Michael Hayes.

Rogers, Nagel, Langhart was formed from the three individual proprietorships in 1966, and became a professional corporation in 1970.

In 1984 the firm provided professional design services to commercial, corporate, and governmental clients, not only in Denver but throughout Colorado and, increasingly, throughout the western United States. In addition to basic architectural design services, three subsidiaries had recently been formed:

- Interplan, which provides pre-architectural services, programming, planning, budgeting, scheduling, and cost projections, utilized in corporate budgeting and governmental bond issues.
- Denver Enterprises, formed to hold equity interests in selected projects designed by RNL and to take risk by furnishing design services early in a project and by participating in the capital requirements of a project.
- Space Management Systems, Inc. (SMS), which provides larger corporations with the necessary services (heavily computer system supported) to facilitate control of their facilities with respect to space, furnishings, equipment, and the cost of change.

In 1984, the firm had 72 employees. John Rogers served as chairman, and Vic Langhart served as president. Nagel had retired in 1976. (See Exhibit 1 for an organization chart.) Development of broad-based management had been a priority since 1975. The firm had seven vice presidents. Two of these vice presidents, Phil Goedert and Rich von Luhrte, served on the board of directors, together with Rogers and Langhart.

Growth was financed through retained earnings. In addition, a plan to provide for more employee ownership, principally through profit sharing (ESOP in 1984), was initiated in 1973. Rogers and Langhart held 56 percent of RNL stock, and 66 percent was held by the four board members. The Colorado National Bank Profit Sharing Trust held 12 percent in its name. The remaining 22 percent was controlled by 23 other employees, either personally or through their individual profit-sharing accounts. It was a goal of the firm to eventually vest stock ownership throughout the firm, in the interest of longevity and continuity.

The firm's principal assets were its human resources. Rogers and Langhart, however, had significant ownership in a limited partnership, which owned a 20,000-square-foot building in a prestigious location in downtown Denver. In 1984, RNL occupied 15,000 square feet. Use of the remaining 5,000 square feet could accommodate up to 30 percent growth in personnel. Through utilization of automation and computers, RNL felt it could double its 1984 volume of work without acquiring additional space.

EXHIBIT 1   Corporate Organization

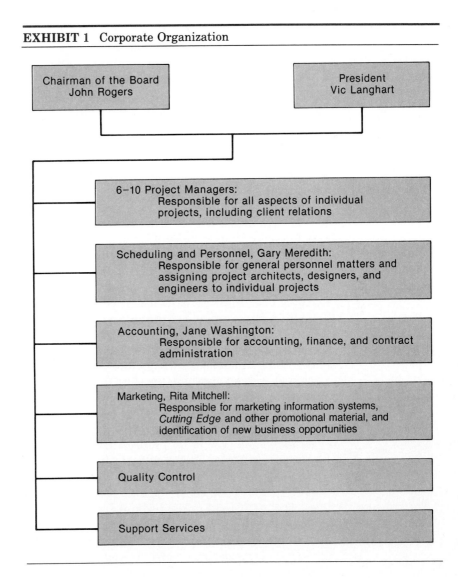

Chairman of the Board
John Rogers

President
Vic Langhart

6–10 Project Managers:
Responsible for all aspects of individual projects, including client relations

Scheduling and Personnel, Gary Meredith:
Responsible for general personnel matters and assigning project architects, designers, and engineers to individual projects

Accounting, Jane Washington:
Responsible for accounting, finance, and contract administration

Marketing, Rita Mitchell:
Responsible for marketing information systems, *Cutting Edge* and other promotional material, and identification of new business opportunities

Quality Control

Support Services

ARCHITECTURAL SERVICES

Architecture: the profession of designing buildings, open areas, communities, and other artificial constructions and environments, usually with some regard to aesthetic effect. The professional services of an architect often include design or selection of furnishings and decorations, supervision of construction work, and the examination, restoration, or remodeling of existing buildings. *(Random House Dictionary)*

Demand for architectural services is closely tied to population growth and to the level of construction activity. The population in the Denver metropolitan area grew from 929,000 in 1960 to 1,620,000 in 1980, and it is estimated to grow to 1,958,000 by 1990. Denver's annual population change of 3.4 percent in the decade 1970–80 ranked 10th for major American cities (Dallas and Phoenix ranked 1 and 2). The projected population growth for the Denver metropolitan area from 1978 to 1983 ranked third in the nation, and Colorado was predicted to be one of the 10 fastest-growing states during the 1980s.

Commercial construction permits grew from 340 in 1970 with an estimated value of $70,818,000, to 1,235 in 1980 with an estimated value of $400,294,000. This growth was not steady, however. Year-to-year changes in dollar value of commercial construction varied from 0.2 percent to 91.6 percent, and the number of permits dropped from a high of 2,245 in 1978 to 1,235 in 1980. Similar patterns of growth and variation characterized industrial construction.

Translating construction growth into estimates of demand for architectural services is difficult. One rule of thumb holds that each additional person added to the population base requires 1,000 square feet of homes, schools, churches, offices, hospitals, manufacturing facilities, retail and shopping facilities, and transportation facilities. In the Denver metro area alone, this could mean 338 million square feet. At $50 average per square foot, total construction expenditure over the decade could reach $16.9 billion, involving as much as $845 million in design fees during the 1980s.

The past and projected growth in demand for architectural services was accompanied by a significant growth in the number of architects in Colorado. From 1979 to 1982, the number of state registrations of individual architects grew from 1,400 to 3,381, an increase of 141.5 percent. Over 100 architectural firms competed actively in the Denver market. (Over 500 architects are listed in the Yellow Pages of the Denver metro area phone directory.) In recent years, a number of national firms (e.g., Skidmore, Owens and Merrill) opened offices in Denver. Other major firms came to Colorado to do one job and then returned to their home offices (e.g., Yamasaki for the Colorado National Bank Office Tower, TAC for Mansville World Headquarters). Of the 26 major firms working on 38 selected jobs in Denver in 1983, 16, or 61.5 percent, were Denver-based. Of the other 10, which have headquarters offices elsewhere, all but 2 had offices in Denver.

Major categories of customers for architectural services include:

- Industrial
- Commercial
    Owner
    Developer

- Government
  - Federal
  - State
  - Municipal
- Residential (Note: RNL did not compete in this market.)

Within these categories, however, not all architectural work is available to independent firms, and not all architectural work on a project is awarded to one architect. A recent Denver survey, for example, indicated that of 49 commercial jobs under construction with a known architect, 11 were handled by an "inside" architect. Of the remaining 38 jobs, 20 included shell and space design whereas 18 involved space design only. In the 18 space designs, only 50 percent were actually done by architects.

The rapid growth in the construction market in Denver came to an abrupt halt in February 1982. Triggered by the broad realization that the oil boom was over, or had at least slowed significantly, project after project was put on hold. Construction of office space literally came to a halt. Of particular concern to RNL, which had just completed negotiations for a $1 million contract with Exxon, was the Exxon announcement of the closure of its Colorado Oil Shale activities at Parachute, Colorado.

It was against the backdrop of these changes that RNL felt the pressing need to review its marketing activities.

MARKETING OF ARCHITECTURAL SERVICES

The basis of competing for architectural work has changed dramatically over the past several decades. As John Rogers recalled:

> At the beginning of my practice in 1956, you could establish an office, put a sign on your door, print calling cards, and have a "news" announcement with your picture in the *Daily Journal* that you had established a new practice of architecture. Beyond that, it was appropriate to suggest to friends and acquaintances that I was in business now and I hoped that they might recommend me to someone they knew. The Code of Ethics of the American Institute of Architects, like many other professions at the time, prohibited any kind of aggressive marketing or sales effort as practiced in recent times.
>
> In fact, after convincing one school board member (an artist) in Jefferson County that design was important, and then being awarded a commission to design an elementary school, which led to another and another, it was not surprising to read in the *Daily Journal* that the school board had met the previous evening and had elected me to design a new junior high school, one that I hadn't even known about. I called and said, "Thank you." Marketing expense was zero with the exception of an occasional lunch or courtesy call here and there.

Today, the situation is vastly different. We have to compete for most jobs, against both local firms and, increasingly, large national firms. Clients are becoming more sophisticated regarding the purchase of architectural services [see Exhibit 2 for a brief description of buyer behavior]. Promotion, of some kind, and concepts such as segmentation have become a way of life.

During the 1960s, development of an architectural practice was a slow process, characterized by heavy reliance on word of mouth regarding professional experience and expertise. Overt communication about an architect's qualifications was limited to brochures. Personal acquaintances played a significant role in the development of new clients. Personal relations between principals and clients were an important part of continuing and new relations. This method of practice development tended to favor local firms, whose reputation could be checked out on a personal basis, and small firms, whose principals could provide personal management and design of client projects.

As Denver grew, the market changed. The advantage of being a successful, local architect and knowing the local business community diminished. Newcomers to Denver tended to rely on relationships with architects in other cities. For local architects there wasn't time to rely on traditional communication networks to establish relationships with these newcomers. The size of projects grew, requiring growth in the size of architectural staffs. Personal attention to every client by principals was no longer possible.

Concomitantly, there was a growing change in the attitude toward the marketing of professional services. New entrants in the fields of medicine and law, as well as architecture, were becoming impatient with the slowness of traditional methods of practice development. A Supreme Court decision significantly reduced the restrictions that state bar associations could impose on lawyers with respect to their pricing and advertising practices. In a similar vein, the American Institute of Architects signed a consent decree with the Justice Department, which prohibited the organization from publishing fee schedules for architectural services.

Perhaps of most significance for architects, however, was the start of the so-called proposal age. Investigations in Maryland and Kansas, among other states, had revealed improper involvement of architects and engineers with state officials. Financial kickbacks were proven on many state projects. Formal proposals, it was felt, would eliminate or reduce the likelihood of contract awards made on the basis of cronyism or kickbacks. Starting in the government sector, the requirement for proposals spread rapidly to all major clients. In 1984, for example, even a small church could receive as many as 20 detailed proposals on a modestly sized assignment.

EXHIBIT 2 Buyer Behavior

Purchase of architectural services is both complex and varied. Subject to many qualifications, however, there seems to be a number of steps that most buying situations have in common:

1. Development of a list of potential architects.
2. Identification of those architects from whom proposals will be solicited for a specific job (usually called the short list).
3. Invitations to submit proposals.
4. Evaluation of proposals and screening of final candidates.
5. Selection of a finalist, based on proposal evaluation, or invitations to finalists to make oral presentations to an evaluation group.

From a marketing standpoint, the focus of interest is the process of getting on the short list and the process by which the final selection is made.

The Short List

Prospective clients find out about architects in a variety of ways. Those who are frequent users of architectural services will generally keep a file of architects, sometimes classified as to type or practice. Additions to the file can come from mailed brochures, personal calls, advertisements, press releases, or, in fact, almost any form of communication. When a specific requirement develops, the file is reviewed for apparent fit. With many variations, a short list is developed and proposals are solicited.

Those who use architects infrequently tend to rely on various businesses of social networks to develop what is in essence their short list. In either case, a previously used architect is almost always on the short list, provided the past experience was satisfactory.

As the largest single customer for architectural services, agencies of the federal government follow a well-defined series of steps, including advertisements in the *Commerce Business Daily* and mail solicitation of local firms.

The Selection Process

The selection process is significantly influenced by the nature and scope of the work and its importance to the firm. Architect selection on major buildings is usually made at the highest level in the organization: by a principal or the president in a private organization or by various forms of boards in not-for-profit organizations such as churches. In some instances, the principal, president, or board are actively involved in all phases of the process. In others, the management of the process is delegated to others who develop recommendations to the decision makers. On smaller jobs, and those of an ongoing nature (e.g., space management), the decision is usually at lower levels and may involve a plant engineer or facilities manager of some kind.

Regardless of the level at which the selection process is made, there seem to be two well-defined patterns to the process. The first, and predominant one, evaluates the firms on the short list, taking into prime consideration nonprice factors such as reputation, performance on previous jobs, and current workload. Based on this evaluation, one firm is selected and a final agreement is then negotiated as to the scope of the work, the nature of the working relationship, the project team, and specific details as to price. The second, and of limited but growing use, pattern attempts to specify the requirements so completely that a firm price can accompany the proposal. In some instances, the price and the proposal are submitted separately. Evaluation of the proposals includes a dollar differential, and these dollar differentials are applied to the price quotation to determine the low evaluated bidder.

EXHIBIT 2   *(concluded)*

Regardless of the process, there appear to be three main criteria on which firms are evaluated:

1. *The ability of the firm to perform the particular assignment.* For standard work this assessment is relatively easy and relies on the nature of past work, size of the organization, current backlogs, and so forth. For more creative work the assessment becomes more difficult. Much importance is put on past work, but the proposal starts to take on additional importance. Sketches, drawings, and, sometimes, extensive models may be requested with the proposal. In some instances, there may actually be a design competition. Much of this evaluation is, perforce, of a subjective nature.
2. *The comfort level with the project team that will be assigned to do the work.* For any but the most standard work there is recognition that there will be constant interaction between representatives of the client's organization and members of the architectural firm. Almost without exception, therefore, some kind of evaluation is made of the project team, or at least its leaders, in terms of the client's comfort level with the personalities involved.
3. *Finally, the matter of cost.* While direct price competition is not a factor in most transactions, the cost of architectural services is always a concern. This has two components. First, there is concern with the total cost of the project, over which the architect has great control. Second, there is growing concern with the size of the architect's fee, per se.

At least some assessment of the reputation of the architect with respect to controlling project costs is made in determining the short list. Once final selection is made, there is likely to be much discussion and negotiation as to the method of calculating the fee. The traditional method of simply charging a percentage of the construction price seems to be on the wane. Increasingly, clients for architectural services are attempting to establish a fixed fee for a well-defined project. The nature of architectural work, however, is such that changes are a fact of life and that many projects cannot be sufficiently defined in the initial stages to allow precise estimation of the design costs. Some basis for modifying a basic fee must, therefore, be established. Typically this is on some kind of direct cost basis plus an overhead adder. Direct costs for various classes of staff and overhead rates obviously become matters for negotiation. In the case of the federal government, the right is reserved to audit an architect's books to determine the appropriateness of charges for changes.

MARKETING AT RNL

In 1984, RNL was engaged in a number of marketing activities. In addition to proposal preparation, major activities included:

- Professional involvement in the business community by principals, which provides contacts with potential clients. This included memberships in a wide variety of organizations such as the Downtown Denver Board, Chamber of Commerce, and Denver Art Museum.
- Participation in, and appearances at, conferences, both professional and business oriented.

- Daily review of *Commerce Business Daily* (a federal publication of all construction projects) along with other news services that indicate developing projects.
- Maintenance of past client contacts. (RNL found this difficult but assigned the activity to its project managers.)
- Development of relationships with potential clients, usually by giving a tour through the office plus lunch.
- VIP gourmet catered lunches for six invited guests, held once a month in the office. These involved a tour of the office and lively conversation, with some attempt at subsequent follow-up.
- Participation in appropriate local, regional, or national exhibits of architectural projects.
- Occasional publicity for a project or for a client.
- The *Cutting Edge*.[1]
- An assortment of brochures and information on finished projects.
- Special arrangements with architectural firms in other locations to provide the basis for a variety of desirable joint ventures.

RNL participated in a number of market segments, which it identified in Exhibit 4, together with its view of the required approach.

Net fee income and allocation of marketing expenses by major segments is given in Exhibit 5. The general feeling at RNL was that there is a lapse of 6 to 18 months between the marketing effort itself and tangible results such as fee income.

Salient aspects of budgeted marketing expense for 1985, by segment, were:

1. *Government.* Heavy emphasis on increased trips to Omaha (a key Corps of Engineers location), Washington, and other out-of-state (as well as in-state) locations plus considerable emphasis on participation in municipal conferences.
2. *Private.* Personal contact at local, state, and regional levels with corporations, banks, developers, and contractors plus local promotion through Chamber of Commerce, clubs, VIP lunches, *Cutting Edge,* promotion materials, and initiation of an advertising and public relations effort.
3. *Semiprivate.* Increased level of personal contact and promotional effort.
4. *Interiors.* Major allocation of salary and expenses of a new full-time marketing person to improve direct sales locally plus other promotional support.

---

[1]The *Cutting Edge* is an RNL publication designed to inform clients and prospects about new developments in architecture and planning and about significant RNL accomplishments (see Exhibit 3 for an example of an article on a typical issue).

EXHIBIT 3

The Cutting Edge

Planning for Parking

The recent boom in downtown Denver office building has resulted in tremendous increases in population density in Denver's core, bringing corresponding increases in the number of vehicles and their related problems as well.

Auto storage, or parking, is one of the major resulting problems. Most building zoning requires parking sufficient to serve the building's needs. Even building sites not requiring parking are now providing parking space to remain competitive in the marketplace.

RNL's design for this above-grade parking structure at 1700 Grant aided in facilitating lease of the office building.

Parking solutions can range from a simple asphalt lot to a large multi-floor parking structure; the decision is based on many factors including site access, required number of spaces, land costs, budget and user convenience.

For many suburban sites, where land costs are sufficiently low to allow on-grade parking, design entails mainly the problems of circulation and landscaping. Circulation includes issues of easy site access and optimal efficient use of the site. Landscaping, including landforming, can visually screen automobiles and break up ugly seas of asphalt common to poorly designed developments.

At the opposite end of the parking spectrum are downtown sites where high land costs necessitate careful integration of parking into the building concept. This is often accomplished by building parking underground, below the main structure. Parking design, in this case, becomes a problem of integrating the circulation and the structure of the building above. While building underground eliminates the need for

acceptable outer appearance, the costs of excavation, mechanical ventilation, fire sprinklering and waterproofing make this one of the most expensive parking solutions.

Between on-grade parking and the underground structure is the above-grade detached or semi-detached parking structure. This solution is very common in areas of moderate land cost where convenience is the overriding factor.

Site conditions do much to generate the design of an above-grade parking structure, but where possible the following features should ideally be included:

1. Parking is in double loaded corridors, i.e. cars park on both sides of the circulation corridor to provide the most efficient ratio of parking to circulation area;

2. Parking at 90 degrees to circulation corridors rather than at angles, once again the most efficient use of space;

3. Access to different garage levels provided by ramping the parking floors, efficiently combining vertical circulation and parking;

4. A precast prestressed concrete structure (this structure economically provides long spans needed to eliminate columns which would interfere with parking circulation and the fireproof concrete members have a low maintenance surface that can be left exposed).

5. Classification as an "open parking garage" under the building code, meaning that the structure has openings in the walls of the building providing natural ventilation and eliminating the need for expensive mechanical ventilation of exhaust fumes;

6. A building exterior in a precast concrete finish, allowing the designer to combine structure and exterior skin into one low cost element.

RNL recently completed work on the $20,000,000 1700 Grant Office Building for Wickliff & Company. The inclusion of a 415 car parking garage in the 1700 Grant project provided one of the amenities necessary for successful leasing in a very depressed leasing market.

A Publication of **RNL**/Inerplan ● by Richard T. Anderson ● Vol. II No. I ● 1576 Sherman Street Denver, Co. 80203 (303) 832-5599

EXHIBIT 4

Segment	*Approach*
Government	
City and county governments	Personal selling, political involvement.
School districts	Personal selling (professional educational knowledge required).
State government	Political involvement, written responses to RFPs (request for proposals, from clients), personal selling.
Federal government	Personal selling, very detailed RFP response, no price competition in the proposal stage.
Private sector	Personal selling, social acquaintances, referrals, *Cutting Edge,* preliminary studies, price competition.
Semiprivate sector (includes utilities)	Personal selling, *Cutting Edge,* referrals, continuing relationships, some price competition.

EXHIBIT 5

	1982		*1983*		*1984 (estimated)*		*1985 (estimated)*	
	Net Fee	*Marketing Expense*	*Net Fee*	*Marketing Expense*	*Net Fee*	*Marketing Expense*	*Net Fee*	*Marketing Expense*
Government	$ 800	$104	$1,220	$101	$1,012	$150	$1,200	$140
Private	1,376	162	1,261	140	1,200	195	1,616	220
Semiprivate	88	11	118	24	100	25	140	30
Interiors	828	40	670	30	918	100	1,235	110
Urban design	95	20	31	10	170	30	220	40
Total	$3,187	$337	$3,300	$305	$3,400	$500	$4,411	$540

Note: All amounts are in $000s.

---

5. *Urban design.* Some early success indicates that land developers and urban renewal authorities are the most likely clients. Planned marketing expense is primarily for personal contact.

Additional marketing efforts being given serious consideration included:

- A more structured marketing organization with more specific assignments.
- Increased visibility for the firm through general media and trade journals, paid or other (e.g., public relations).
- Appearances on special programs and offering special seminars.
- Use of more sophisticated selling tools such as video tapes and automated slide presentations.
- Increased training in client relations/selling for project managers and other staff.
- Hiring a professionally trained marketing manager.
- Determining how the national firms market (i.e., copy the competition).
- Expansion of debriefing conferences with successful and unsuccessful clients.
- Use of a focus group to develop effective sales points for RNL.
- Training a marketing MBA in architecture versus training an architect in marketing.

RNL CLIENTS

RNL described its clients as:

1. Having a long history of growing expectations with respect to detail, completeness, counseling, and cost control.
2. Mandating the minimization of construction problems, including changes, overruns, and delays.
3. Having an increased concern for peer approval at the completion of a project.
4. Having an increased desire to understand and be a part of the design process.

Extensive interviews of clients by independent market researchers showed very favorable impressions about RNL. Terms used to describe the firm included:

- Best and largest architectural service in Denver.
- Innovative yet practical.
- Designs large projects for "who's who in Denver."
- Long-term resident of the business community.
- Lots of expertise.
- Designs artistic yet functional buildings.

RNL's use of computer-aided design systems was seen as a definite competitive edge. Others mentioned RNL's extra services, such as interior systems, as a plus, although only 35 percent of those interviewed were aware that RNL offered this service. In general, most clients felt that RNL had a competitive edge with regard to timeliness, productivity, and cost consciousness.

Two major ways that new clients heard about RNL were identified. One was the contact RNL made on its own initiative when it heard of a possible project. The other was through personal references. All those interviewed felt advertising played a minor role, and, in fact, several indicated they had questions about an architectural firm that advertises.

Clients who selected RNL identified the following as playing a role in their decision:

- Tours of RNL's facilities.
- Monthly receipt of *Cutting Edge*.
- Low-key selling style.
- RNL's ability to focus on their needs.
- Thoroughness in researching customer needs and overall proposal preparation and presentation.
- RNL's overall reputation in the community.
- Belief that RNL would produce good, solid (not flashy) results.

Clients who did not select RNL identified the following reasons for their decision:

- RNL had less experience and specialization in their particular industry.
- Decided to stay with the architectural firm used previously.
- Decided to go with a firm that has more national status.
- Other presentations had more "pizazz."

Overall, clients' perceptions of RNL were very positive. There was less than complete understanding of the scope of RNL services, but its current approach to clients received good marks.

MARKETING ISSUES AT RNL: SOME VIEWS OF MIDDLE MANAGEMENT

Richard von Luhrte joined RNL in 1979, following extensive experience with other firms in Chicago and Denver. In 1984, he led the firm's urban design effort on major projects, served as a project manager, and participated actively in marketing. He came to RNL because the firm "fits my image." He preferred larger firms that have extensive and complementary skills. He commented on marketing as follows:

> RNL has a lot going for it. We have a higher overhead rate, but with most clients you can sell our competence and turn this into an advantage. I think RNL is perceived as a quality firm, but customers are also concerned that

we will gold-plate a job. I'd like to be able to go gold-plate or inexpensive as the circumstances dictate. But it's hard to convince a customer that we can do this.

For many of our clients continuity is important and we need to convey that there will be continuity beyond the founders. RNL has done well as a provider of "all things for all people," and our diversification helps us ride through periods of economic downturn. On the other hand, we lose some jobs because we're not specialized. For instance, we haven't done well in the downtown developer market. We're starting to do more, but if we had targeted the shopping center business we could have had seven or eight jobs by now. One way to operate would be to jump on a trend and ride it until the downturn and then move into something else.

There's always the conflict between specialization and fun. We try to stay diversified, but we ought to be anticipating the next boom. At the same time, there's always the problem of overhead. In this business you can't carry very much, particularly in slow times.

I like the marketing part of the work, but there's a limit on how much of it I can, or should, do. Plus, I think it's important to try to match our people with our clients in terms of age and interests, which means we need to have lots of people involved in the marketing effort.

Oral presentations are an important part of marketing, and we make a lot of them. You have to make them interesting, and there has to be a sense of trying for the "close." On the other hand, I think that the presentation is not what wins the job, although a poor presentation can lose it for you. It's important that the presentation conveys a sense of enthusiasm and that we really want the job.

As comptroller, Jane Washington was involved extensively in the firm's discussions about its marketing efforts. As she described the situation:

There is little question in my mind that the people at the top are committed to developing a marketing orientation at RNL. But our objectives still aren't clear. For instance, we still haven't decided what would be a good mix of architecture, interiors, and planning. Interiors is a stepchild to some. On the other hand, it is a very profitable part of our business. But it's not easy to develop a nice neat set of objectives for a firm like this. Two years ago we had a seminar to develop a mission statement, but we still don't have one. This isn't a criticism. Rather, it's an indication of the difficulty of getting agreement on objectives in a firm of creative professionals.

One problem is that our approach to marketing has been reactive rather than proactive. Our biggest marketing expenditure is proposal preparation, and we have tended to respond to RFPs as they come in, without screening them for fit with targeted segments. From a budget standpoint we have not really allocated marketing dollars to particular people or segments, except in a pro forma kind of way. As a result, no one person is responsible for what is a very large total expenditure.

Another problem is that we don't have precise information about our marketing expenditures or the profitability of individual jobs. It would be impractical to track expenditures on the 500–1,000 proposals we make a year, but we could set up a system that tracks marketing expenditures in, say, 10 segments. This would at least let individuals see what kind of money we're spending for marketing, and where. We also could change from the present system, which basically measures performance in terms of variation from dollar budget, to one that reports on the profitability of individual jobs. I've done some studies on the profitability of our major product lines, but those don't tie to any one individual's performance.

Rita Mitchell, who has an MS in library science and information systems, joined RNL in 1981. Originally her assignment focused on organizing marketing records and various marketing information resources. In her new role as new business development coordinator she had a broader set of responsibilities. According to Rita;

> We definitely need some policies about marketing, and these ought to spell out a marketing process. In my present job, I think I can help the board synthesize market information and so help to develop a marketing plan.
>
> I do a lot of market research based on secondary data. For instance, we have access to Dialog and a number of other online databases, using our PC. Based on this research, and our own in-house competence, I think I can do some good market anticipation. The problem is what to do with this kind of information. If we move too fast, based on signals about a new market, there is obviously the risk of being wrong. On the other hand, if we wait until the signals are unmistakably clear, they will be clear to everyone else, and we will lose the opportunity to establish a preeminent position.
>
> With respect to individual RFPs, our decision on which job to quote is still highly subjective. We try to estimate our chances of getting the job, and we talk about its fit with our other work, but we don't have much hard data or policy to guide us. We don't, for instance, have a good sense of other RFPs that are in the pipeline and how the mix of the jobs we're quoting and the resulting work fits with our present work in progress. The Marketing Committee [consisting of John Rogers, Vic Langhart, Phil Goedert, Rich Von Luhrte, Dick Shiffer, Rita Mitchell, and, occasionally, Bob Johnson] brings lots of experience and personal knowledge to bear on this, but it's not a precise process.
>
> We have a number of sources of information about new construction projects: the *Commerce Business Daily* [a federal government publication], the *Daily Journal* [which reports on local government construction], the Western Press Clipping Bureau, Colorado trade journals, and so forth. Monitoring these is a major activity, and then we have the problem of deciding which projects fit RNL.

Bob Johnson, a project manager and member of the Marketing Committee, commented:

> The way the system works now we have four board members and 12 project managers, most of whom can pursue new business. They bring these opportunities before the Marketing Committee, but it doesn't really have the

clout to say no. As a result, people can really go off on their own. I'd like to see the committee flex its muscles a little more on what jobs we go after. But there's a problem with committing to just a few market segments. Right now we're involved in something like 30 segments. If we're wrong on one it's not a big deal. But if we were committed to just a few then a mistake could have really serious consequences.

For many of us, however, the major problem is managing the transfer of ownership and control to a broader set of individuals. Currently the prospective owners don't really have a forum for what they'd like the company to be. My personal preference would be to go after corporate headquarters, high-tech firms, speculative office buildings, and high-quality interiors. But there probably isn't agreement on this.

MARKETING ISSUES: THE VIEWS OF THE FOUNDERS

Vic Langhart started his practice of architecture in 1954 and has taught design in the Architecture Department of the University of Colorado. He was instrumental in developing new services at RNL, including Interplan and SMS, Inc., and was heavily involved in training of the next level of management. In 1984, he supervised day-to-day operations and also served as president of Interplan and SMS, Inc. Looking to the future, Vic observed:

Our toughest issue is dealing with the rate of change in the profession today. It's probably fair to say there are too many architects today. But this is a profession of highly idealistic people, many of whom feel their contribution to a better world is more important than dollars of income and so will stay in the field at "starvation wages." We wrestle with the question of "profession or business?" but competition is now a fact of life for us. The oil boom of the 1970s in Denver triggered an inrush of national firms. Many have stayed on, and we now have a situation where one of the largest national firms is competing for a small job in Durango. We're also starting to see more direct price competition. Digital Equipment recently prequalified eight firms, selected five to submit proposals that demonstrated understanding of the assignment, and asked for a separate envelope containing the price.

Our tradition at RNL has been one of quality. I think we're the "Mercedes" of the business, and in the long haul an RNL customer will be better off economically. A lot of things contribute to this—our Interplan concept, for instance—but the key differentiation factor is our on-site-planning approach.

In 1966–68, we were almost 100 percent in education. Then I heard that they were closing some maternity wards, and we decided to diversify. Today we have a good list of products, ranging from commercial buildings to labs and vehicle maintenance facilities. In most areas, the only people who can beat us are the superspecialists, and even then there's a question. Our diversification has kept our minds free to come up with creative approaches. At Beaver Creek, for example, I think we came up with a better approach to condominium design than the specialists. Plus, we can call in special expertise, if it's necessary.

Over the past several years we've had a number of offers to merge into national, or other, firms. We decided, however, to become employee owned. Our basic notion was that RNL should be an organization that provides its employees a long-time career opportunity. This is not easy in an industry that is characterized by high turnover. Less than 10 percent of architectural firms have figured out how to do it. But we're now at 35 percent employee ownership.

I'm personally enthusiastic about Interplan. It has tremendous potential to impact our customers. In Seattle, for instance, a bank came to us for a simple expansion. Our Interplan approach, however, led to a totally different set of concepts.

We've had some discussion about expansion. Colorado Springs is a possibility, for instance. But there would be problems of keeping RNL concepts and our culture. We work hard to develop and disseminate an RNL culture. For example, we have lots of meetings, although John and I sometimes disagree about how much time should be spent in meetings. A third of our business comes from interiors, and there is as much difference between interior designers and architects as there is between architects and mechanical engineers.

In somewhat similar vein, John Rogers commented:

In the 1960s, RNL was primarily in the business of designing schools. We were really experts in that market. But then the boom in school construction came to an end, and we moved into other areas. First into banks and commercial buildings. We got started with Mountain Bell, an important relationship for us that continues today. We did assignments for mining companies and laboratories. In the late 1960s, no one knew how to use computers to manage office space problems, and we moved in that direction, which led to the formation of Interplan. We moved into local and state design work. One of our showcase assignments is the Colorado State Judicial/ Heritage Center.

In the 1980s, we started to move into federal and military work, and this now represents a significant portion of our business.

We have done some developer work, but this is a tough market. It has a strong "bottom line orientation," and developers want sharp focus and expertise.

As we grow larger we find it difficult to maintain a close client relationship. The client wants to know who will work on the assignment, but some of our staff members are not good at the people side of the business.

Currently we're still doing lots of "one of a kind" work. Our assignment for the expansion of the *Rocky Mountain News* building, our design of a condominium lodge at Beaver Creek, and our design of a developer building at the Denver Tech Center are all in this category. A common theme, however, is our "on-site" design process. This is a process by which we make sure that the client is involved in the design from the start and that we are really tuned in to his requirements. I see this as one of our real competitive advantages. But I'm still concerned that we may be trying to spread ourselves too thin. Plus, there's no question that there is an increased tendency to specialization: "shopping center architects," for example.

We need to become better marketers, but we have to make sure that we don't lose sight of what has made us the leading architectural firm in Denver: service and client orientation.

STRATEGIC MARKETING CASES

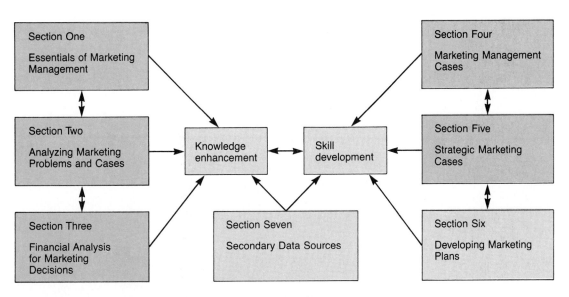

Marketing Management: Knowledge and Skills

NOTE TO THE STUDENT

The 10 cases in this section emphasize the role of marketing in developing successful business or organizational strategies. While marketing is critical in these cases, successful analysis and strategy formulation will often involve other areas in the organization as well.

The knowledge and skills you've developed in the analysis of the cases in the previous section provide a useful foundation for analyzing the cases in this section. However, these cases are intended to broaden your knowledge of marketing and your skills at analyzing various strategic problems.

Maytag Company*
Lester Neidell

University of Tulsa

The Maytag Company of Newton, Iowa, has maintained an enviable position in the home-laundry market. Despite increased competition, and a price premium charged to consumers of roughly $100 per unit, it has continued to capture a "traditional" 15 percent share of the washing machine market, and has enjoyed profit margins roughly twice that of competitors. Operating results for the period 1974–81 are given in Exhibit 1. The largest competitive share growth in laundry equipment has gone to Whirlpool, who, buoyed by the surge of its private-label sales to Sears and by Frigidaire's abandonment of the market, now sells approximately 45 percent of all home-laundry equipment in the United States.

Maytag Company backs its premium policy with a product consistently evaluated as superior in quality. The famous lonely Maytag repairman hammers home the theme that the purchase price premium buys lower service costs. But the quality gap appears to be lessening. Arnold Consdorf, editor of the trade journal *Appliance Manufacturer,* noted, "The quality gap that existed 5 or 10 years ago doesn't exist anymore. Model for model, I really don't see much difference as far as premium quality goes." A retailer notes, "The critical thing is that the rationale to run out and buy a Maytag has declined."

Maytag values highly its retail dealer relationships. A feature of the company's 1979 Annual Report was this assessment:

> Among Maytag's more than 10,000 independent retailers are most of the leading merchandisers in North America. While the wide geographic dispersion of so many dealers provides Maytag with outstanding service coverage, it is the mass merchandisers who generate much of the volume that keeps us growing. . . .

*Copyright © 1982 by Lester A. Neidell. Sources: "The Problems of Being Premium," *Forbes* (May 29, 1978), pp. 56–57; "A Duel of Giants in the Dishwasher Market," *Business Week* (October 9, 1978), pp. 137–38; Lawrence Ingrassia, "Staid Maytag Puts in Money on Stoves But May Need to Invest Expertise, Too," *The Wall Street Journal* (July 23, 1980), p. 27; "The New Maytag Recipe for Going into Kitchens," *Business Week* (May 24, 1982), pp. 48–49; and Maytag Company Annual Reports.

EXHIBIT 1   Financial Summary for Maytag Company, 1974–81 (in $ millions)

	1974	*1975*	*1976*	*1977*	*1978*	*1979*	*1980*	*1981*
Net sales	229	238	275	299	325	369	349	409
Net income	21.1	25.9	33.1	34.5	36.7	45.3	35.6	37.4

Historically, Maytag . . . sought dealer coverage in each community and thus had product availability, along with service, throughout the United States and Canada. [C]hanging . . . competition [required] developing quality volume accounts in major markets.

Because selling quality appliances requires well-trained salespersons and outstanding parts and service availability . . . Maytag has stopped short of attempting to market its products through self-service "shopping cart" outlets. Nor do we have dealer arrangements with any chains across the board nationally, requiring instead that dealer selection be made in each market by those responsible for generating our market share in that locality.

A natural expansion of Maytag's home-laundry emphasis has been the commercial laundromat business. This business was pioneered in the 1930s when coin meters were attached to Maytag wringer-type washers. Rapid growth of coin-operated laundries occurred in the United States during the late 1950s and early 1960s. Increased competition and soaring energy costs of the 1970s cut deeply into laundromat profits. In 1975 Maytag introduced new energy-efficient machines and a "Home Style" store concept that has rejuvenated this business. More than 1,000 Home Style stores are currently in operation in the United States.

Until recently, Maytag's other major product effort has been dishwashers. Here the leading competitor is Design & Manufacturing, Inc., (D & M), whose "bread and butter" are private-label dishwashers for Sears, other retailers, and other appliance manufacturers. D & M's market share is approximately 45 percent. Other major dishwasher competitors include General Electric and Hobart Corporation's KitchenAid brand, each with approximately 19 percent shares. Maytag, who has been making dishwashers since 1966, has generally obtained annual shares in the 4–6 percent range. The "premium" price-quality segment is dominated by KitchenAid, and despite Maytag's efforts, little recognition of the Maytag name is apparent in the dishwasher business. Maytag's president, Daniel Krumm, admitted in 1978, "We might as well be selling the Jones dishwasher." A revamped 1979 product line provided an increase in sales but it is too soon to tell if the share increase is permanent.

Other product lines include food waste disposers and cooking appliances. Maytag's entry into cooking has been achieved by acquisition. In 1981 the Hardwick Stove Company was purchased for $28 million. Early 1982 saw the introduction of Maytag microwave ovens, produced by the Hardwick subsidiary. In April 1982, Maytag reached agreement with United Technologies to acquire its Jenn-Air subsidiary for an estimated $75 million. Jenn-Air is a producer of indoor barbeque grills and other innovative cooking and kitchen ventilation equipment.

President Krumm, explaining the Maytag thrust into kitchen appliances, noted, "Cooking equipment is a mature market, but it is an exciting one because product innovation is changing the traditional way people cook and broadening sales opportunities."

Maytag expects a profitable future:

> High inflation has not been especially detrimental to our sales, as consumers seem to buy better-quality goods during inflationary periods. Rising energy costs will play an especially important part in future sales for both home and commercial appliances. The energy-saving Maytag washers and dryers will have potentially large markets as both households and self-service laundries replace the millions of appliances purchased in the 1960s. Home kitchens and laundries will be upgraded, compensating for the slump in new housing construction. The changing composition of the American family, with more women working and subsequent increase in family incomes, will produce a growing demand for labor- and time-saving appliances.

TSR Hobbies, Inc.— "Dungeons and Dragons"*

Margaret L. Friedman

University of Wisconsin–Whitewater

TSR (Tactical Studies Rules) Hobbies, Inc., had grown rapidly since its start in 1973 to sales of $27 million in fiscal 1983. TSR's star product responsible for this rapid growth was "Dungeons and Dragons," a unique fantasy/adventure game. The game was unique because it happened largely in the minds of its players. Its emphasis on cooperation among players and dependence upon their imaginative powers set it apart from traditional board games.

OVERVIEW

Company History

TSR Hobbies, Inc., was founded by E. Gary Gygax in a small Wisconsin resort town. Gygax never graduated from high school, but pursued his passion for fantasy in the forms of war games and science fiction books. When Gygax lost his job as an insurance underwriter in 1970, he started developing fantasy games almost full-time, while supporting his family with a shoe repair business in his basement. In 1973 Gygax persuaded a boyhood friend and fellow war game enthusiast, Donald Kaye, to borrow $1,000 against his life insurance and TSR Hobbies, Inc., was founded.

The two gamers published a popular set of war games rules for lead miniatures called "Cavaliers and Roundheads." In January 1974 another inveterate gamer friend, Brian Blume, invested $2,000 in the company, and the three partners printed the first set of rules for

*This case was prepared by Margaret L. Friedman, Assistant Professor, School of Business, University of Wisconsin–Whitewater.

"Dungeons and Dragons." The game was assembled in the Gygax home and was sold through an established network of professional gamers. In 1974, 1,000 sets of the "Dungeons and Dragons" game were sold. Eight years later it was selling at the rate of 750,000 per year. The sales history for the product is shown in Exhibit 1.

The rapid growth of TSR was not necessarily a reflection of keen and experienced management skill. The three top officers in the company all lacked formal management training, but felt they could remedy this deficiency by taking management courses and seminars. Although TSR wanted to attract older, experienced toy and game managers to their ranks, most of their recruits came from outside the toy/game/hobby industry.

Between 1977 and 1982 the TSR workforce grew from 12 to more than 250 employees. Gygax's original partner, Donald Kaye, died of a

EXHIBIT 1   TSR Hobbies Sales

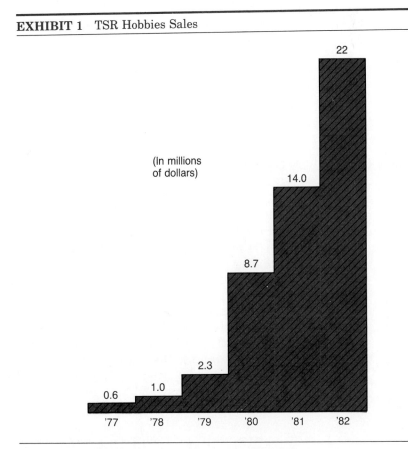

Source: Adapted from *The Wall Street Journal*, January 7, 1983.

heart attack in 1975, and so the partnership was assumed by Gygax and brothers Brian and Kevin Blume. Gygax was president of TSR, Kevin was chief executive, and Brian was executive vice president. All company decisions were directed through Kevin Blume, from major decisions down to authorization for a $12 desk calendar for a secretary. There was some personnel turnover and evidence of employee dissatisfaction due to nepotism in the company's hiring policies. It was reported that between 10 and 20 of Brian Blume's relatives were on the company's payroll.

The "Dungeons and Dragons" Game

"Dungeons and Dragons" represented a significant innovation in the game and hobby industry. A basic set for a "Dungeons and Dragons" game consisted of a lengthy instruction book, dice, and a wax pencil, all of which sold for $12.

The game begins when each player generates a mythical character with a role of the dice. The personality profile for each character is determined according to rigorous guidelines given in the instruction booklet. For example, there is a Dungeon Master role in each game. It is the Dungeon Master who develops a map of the dungeon layout as there is no game board. Each character has particular spells and powers which are critical in negotiating the game's adventure. The goal is to navigate through a treacherous dungeon, arrive at a particular destination, and depart alive with the treasure. The combination of mythical characters and adventure is why "Dungeons and Dragons" is called a role-playing/fantasy/adventure game. No two "Dungeons and Dragons" games are alike since the way the game unfolds depends upon the players' imaginations.

To survive, players must work together, rather than against one another, winding their way through a dangerous path to the treasure. Players are confronted with conquest after conquest involving ghouls, monsters, dragons, and other obstacles to finding the treasure and escaping with it. The instruction booklet describes the various powers and spells available to the different characters and general rules for behaving in the dungeon. The crayon is used to keep track of pathways taken and used-up spells. The game can last from two hours to weeks on end—it is all up to the imaginative powers of the players.

MARKETING STRATEGY

TSR's goal was to double sales every year. The strategy used to achieve this goal was based heavily on target market expansion, product line expansion, expansion of promotional activities, and more intensive distribution.

Expansion of Target Market

When "Dungeons and Dragons" was first introduced, it was targeted solely to experienced gamers. The first edition of the game came in a plain brown bag and the rules were so complex that only experienced gamers could decipher them. Word of the game spread to college campuses with the help of publicity involving a Michigan State University student who was rumored to be lost in the steam tunnels under the campus while playing a "live" "Dungeons and Dragons" game. This potentially negative publicity for "Dungeons and Dragons" turned into an advantage for the company since it created word-of-mouth advertising and interest among college students.

As the product matured, the median age of new buyers dropped from college age to the 10-to-14-year-old bracket. Typically, these consumers were boys described as introverted, intelligent, nonathletic, and very imaginative. The game provided an outlet for such boys to join in a group activity and helped bring them out of their shells. In fact, educators noted that "Dungeons and Dragons" welds a group of players into an ongoing joint project that teaches participation, assertiveness, and cooperation.

To further increase sales of the product, TSR targeted the product to new consumer groups. For example, at one point, women made up only 12 percent of the total number of purchasers. TSR conducted consumer research and found that women felt the game was created as a release for "macho" fantasies. Many women also stated that the lengthy instruction manual (63 pages) would take too long to read and be a waste of their time. In response to such perceptions, TSR (1) publicized the fact that the game is not cutthroat and competitive, (2) reduced the length of the instruction manual, and (3) created a game that can be played in a limited amount of time. TSR also targeted downward to the younger children's market with a product that transferred the "Dungeons and Dragons" theme to a more conventional board game called "Dungeons!"

Expansion of Product Lines

Initially, the basic "Dungeons and Dragons" set was marketed as a hobby, rather than as a game. A hobby involves a starter toy which is enhanced with a myriad of add-ons. For example, a miniature train is considered a hobby since the engine and track form the basis for building an entire railroad system, including special cars, track, scenery, stations, and so on over time. Similarly, for each $12 basic "Dungeons and Dragons" set sold, retailers could expect an additional $150 in satellite or captive product purchases in the form of modules that provide supplemental adventures of varying complexity. There were at least 50 such satellite products on the market.

Since TSR management recognized that their short product line was vulnerable to competition from such toy and game giants as Mattel, Parker Brothers, Milton Bradley, and Ideal, several other new products were introduced to extend the line. Most of these new introductions followed the role-playing, fantasy theme. For example, since each fantasy world in a "Dungeons and Dragons" game has its own set of characters and monsters, a line of miniature lead figurines of these creatures was introduced. These included miniature dragons, wizards, and dwarfs. Although these figures are not necessary to play the game, it was hoped that a market of figurine collectors would develop.

TSR also marketed a number of other role-playing games, including "Top Secret," a spy adventure game, "Boot Hill," a western adventure game, "Gamma World," a futuristic game, and "Star Frontiers," a science fiction game—all of which were quite successful. Somewhat less successful have been TSR's other board game entrants, "Snit's Revenge," "The Awful Green Things from Outer Space," "Escape from New York," and "Dungeons!" These more conventional board games were intended to change the company's image from that of a producer of complex, esoteric games to a producer of a broader range of game products.

TSR also added new lines to their product mix. For example, they produced a feature-length film using a "Dungeons and Dragons" theme, as well as a successful Saturday morning cartoon program for children and an hour-long pilot for a radio-theater program.

TSR's other ventures included purchase of *Amazing* magazine, the oldest science fiction magazine on the market (since 1926), and publishing *Dragon* magazine, which began in 1976 and obtained a circulation of over 70,000 copies per issue. The Dragon Publishing division of TSR also produced calendars and anthologies of fiction, nonfiction, and humor. TSR's most popular publications included *Endless Quest* books. Young readers determine the plot of these stories by making choices for the main character. Depending on the choices made, the reader is directed to different pages in the book. Therefore, each book contains a number of different adventure stories. TSR also developed a line of books called *Heart Quest,* which are romance novels for teenagers in this same create-your-own-plot format. TSR had performed consulting services for a failing needlework company owned by a friend of Gygax. To further its diversification efforts TSR acquired this company briefly, realizing soon, however, that it was a poor investment.

TSR found licensing to be a profitable form of product line expansion. Arrangements were made to permit 14 companies to market products that displayed the TSR and "Dungeons and Dragons" name. For example, Mattel, Inc., was sold a license for an electronic version of "Dungeons and Dragons," and St. Regis Paper Company was sold a license for a line of notebooks and school supplies.

Expansion of Promotional Activities

In the beginning, TSR relied on word-of-mouth advertising among gamers to sell the "Dungeons and Dragons" game. As their markets expanded, TSR employed other promotional methods, including television commercials and four-color magazine ads. TSR's ad budget in 1981 was $1,194,879 which was divided as follows: 13 percent on trade magazines, 28 percent on consumer magazines, and 59 percent on spot television. During the Christmas season of 1982, $1 million was spent on a television campaign for the "Dungeons!" board game.

The company's logo and accompanying slogan were updated in 1982. Formerly, the logo showed a wizard next to the letters TSR and the slogan "The Game Wizards." The updated logo included a stylized version of the letters "TSR" and the slogan, "Products of the Imagination." This updated logo and slogan were designed to convey an image with broader market appeal.

TSR sponsored an annual gamers convention which attracted dozens of manufacturers and thousands of attendees to Kenosha, Wisconsin. This became the largest role-playing convention in the world which included four days of movies, demonstrations, tournaments, seminars, and manufacturers' exhibits. The company also sponsored the Role-Playing Game Association. This association offered newsletters and informational services and was responsible for calculating international scoring points to rate players in official tournaments. It also provided a gift catalog of premiums available only to RPGA members.

In the beginning, the printing and artwork needed for the "Dungeons and Dragons" instruction booklet were contracted with suppliers outside of TSR. The company has since engaged in backward vertical integration into the manufacturing process by hiring a staff of artists and purchasing its own printing facility.

Expansion of Distribution Channels

Retail distribution was originally concentrated in hobby stores, but expanded rapidly into department stores and bookstores, although some mass market retailers such as Sears, Penneys, and K mart were reluctant to stock all of the satellite products generated by the basic "Dungeons and Dragons" set. This evolution from exclusive distribution through hobby stores to intensive distribution followed naturally from the concomitant expansion of target markets and product lines.

Over time TSR employed as many as 15 manufacturers' representatives who marketed the product through independent wholesalers in nine territories. One problem with this distribution system was that the company did not have close contact with its wholesalers, and hence, were not able to offer much merchandising assistance.

TSR opened its own retail hobby shop for a brief period. However, this outlet attracted a lot of mail-order business, creating channel conflict among other retail hobby outlets, and the shop was closed in 1984.

EXPANSION PROBLEMS

TSR obviously grew quickly and expanded in many different directions which caused several problems. For example, TSR announced it would hire over 100 new employees, and 50 new hires were actually made in June of 1983. However, by April 1984, over 230 employees were laid off. The rapid loss of personnel resulted in coordination problems. For example, two different products were packaged in boxes with identical graphics on the covers. The layoffs also created morale problems.

In an effort to "tighten the reigns," Kevin Blume eliminated half of the company's 12 divisions to streamline accounting, reporting, and general decision making. TSR was then divided into four separate companies: TSR, Inc., for publishing games and books, TSR Ventures, Inc., for supervising trademark licensing, TSR Worldwide Ltd. for managing international sales, and Dungeons and Dragons Entertainment Corporation for producing cartoons. Each company functioned independently of the others, with its own stock and board of directors. Still, the three partners sat on all four boards in order to maintain tight control over the company.

TSR's full-fledged entry into the mass market also drained their cash reserves, creating cash flow problems. Business practices in the mass market were different than what TSR was accustomed to in the specialized hobby market. For example, it is common to cater to mass retailers by allowing six months' payment, whereas 30 days or less is more usual for small hobby shops. Also, demand is relatively smooth in the hobby market unlike the mass market which experiences a Christmas buying rush. Thus, TSR was not prepared for the retail Christmas buying rush and many items ordered were out-of-stock.

TSR also faced an image problem in the mass market, illustrated in the positioning map shown in Exhibit 2. The early success of "Dungeons and Dragons" depended largely upon its image as a mysterious hobby

EXHIBIT 2 Positioning Map

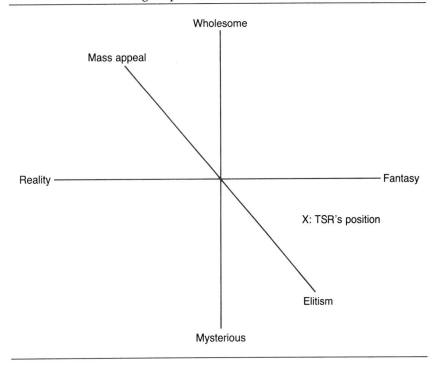

that was not for just anyone, but only for an elite few. Because of this image, many consumers in the mass market were convinced that the "Dungeons and Dragons" game was "bad for the mind" because it involved hours and hours of make-believe. Dr. Joyce Brothers was engaged to endorse the product and to legitimize its role-playing format. In supporting the product she pointed to research results illustrating that children who played "Dungeons and Dragons" developed better reading skills, math skills, and basic logic and problem-solving skills.

TSR faced formidable competition in the mass market. Large companies such as Milton Bradley, Mattel, and Parker Brothers spent more on advertising each year than TSR earned in profits. However, TSR's fantasy/role-playing concept was unique. Only Mattel's "He Man" and "Masters of the Universe" could be remotely compared to TSR's product concept. While the other traditional toy and game giants had no comparable fantasy/role-playing games, they dominated the northwest quadrant of the map in Exhibit 2, the market TSR wanted to enter. Though TSR was a market leader in fantasy/role-playing games in the hobby market, it remained to be seen whether this type of product could gain a respectable share of the mass market.

Caterpillar Tractor Company*

Donald W. Eckrich
Ithaca College

INTRODUCTION

In January 1984, Caterpillar Tractor Company Chairman Lee L. Morgan was actively involved in corporate-wide planning efforts. These efforts were directed at reestablishing Caterpillar's tradition of profitability and world leadership in the heavy equipment and machinery industry. Looking to the coming year, he reported:

> 1984 should be a markedly better year. The 1983 loss of $345 million reflected the deep recession in most of the world's economies. Current indicators suggest . . . strong sales increases for our kinds of products. Sales should be significantly higher in 1984, and we expect to be profitable.

By year end, it was anticipated, specific plans detailing actions on new business opportunities would be completed and long-term sales and profit strategies would be identified, effective through 1995.

HISTORY

Headquartered in Peoria, Illinois, and currently the largest multinational company which designs, manufactures, and markets construction equipment, machinery, engines, and parts, Caterpillar's roots date back to the late 19th century and the evolution of mechanized agricultural equipment. In February 1889, Daniel Best introduced the first steam-powered harvester, replacing the 40-horse-drawn combine with an eight-man, 11-ton, self-propelled tractor using eight-foot wheels.

*This case was prepared by Donald W. Eckrich, Associate Professor and Chairman, Department of Marketing, Ithaca College, as the basis for class discussion rather than to illustrate either effective or ineffective handling of administrative situations and problems. A special thanks for their invaluable assistance throughout the preparation of this case is due Charles F. Maier and Barbara A. Wright.

Shortly thereafter, Benjamin Holt began field testing the first crawler-type equipment, built simply by replacing the wheels on existing equipment with new "track" structures—pairs of treads comprised of wooden slats linked loosely together.

Driven by increasing demand in agriculture, road building, military equipment, and industrial construction, the two companies prospered. The introduction of the internal combustion engine provided yet another boost for the evolving heavy equipment industry.

In 1925, the Holt and Best Companies merged to form Caterpillar Tractor Co., thereby setting the stage for several decades of dramatic and systematic growth through technological leadership and new applications in the emerging equipment and machinery industry. Agricultural applications quickly gave way to forestry opportunities, which in turn gave way to oil field and highway operations.

In 1931, the first Caterpillar Diesel Tractor was introduced. This product initiated an incredible six-year sales growth spurt from $13 million to $63 million and launched the track-type tractor into prominence as the single largest user of diesel power.

Caterpillar's growing reputation for industry leadership and technological superiority was further strengthened during World War II by U.S. government defense contracts. These contracts included demand for both existing equipment (e.g., bulldozers and graders) and special government requests for revolutionary and sophisticated equipment such as air-cooled diesel engines for advanced military operations.

Throughout the postwar years, the Korean conflict, and into the 1970s, Caterpillar generally concentrated on the development of large, industrial-sized machines and engines. In 1944, Caterpillar announced its plans to build a line of matched earthmoving equipment, and quickly found a receptive and profitable market. Later, in 1951, the Trackson Company of Milwaukee was purchased to produce hoists, pipe layers, and hydraulically operated tractor shovels for Caterpillar crawlers. In 1965, Towmotor Corporation was acquired, continuing the expansion into heavy equipment with forklift trucks and straddle carriers for a wide range of materials handling in industrial, shipping, warehousing, and other markets. Thus, by the early 1970s, Caterpillar had achieved at least foothold positions in a variety of heavy equipment product lines, with the objective of achieving industry leadership in each of the new areas.

In 1977, Caterpillar unveiled the single-largest, most technologically advanced tractor in the world—the D-10. Foremost among its advantages were (1) an elevated drive sprocket and (2) modular-designed major components. The elevation of the drive sprocket removed it from high-wear and shock-load areas, reduced overall stress on the undercarriage, and produced a smoother ride. The modular design of major components not only permitted faster and more efficient servicing, but also provided the opportunity to pretest components before final assembly. Modular designs thereby reduced repair and overall downtime in some cases by as much as 80 percent. Perhaps most significant regarding the D–10 and its modular-designed components was the extent to which they reflected the intense product quality and service orientations adhered to throughout Cat's history. It had long been assumed by management that industrial users' needs would best be served through the progress of technology, largely irrespective of the effects on pricing.

Only four years later, in 1981, several more years of research and development were capped off with the introduction of a 16-cylinder, 1,600 horsepower, 1200 kilowatt engine—also stressing modular design and repair convenience. In early 1982, a new D8L crawler tractor was introduced, the third in a series of crawler tractors to employ the elevated sprocket. Finally, several other technological advances previously introduced on smaller, track-type loaders were extended to larger models, thereby permitting the relocation of the engine to the rear and correspondingly, improving balance, operator visibility, and serviceability.

Thus, over several decades, Caterpillar Tractor Co. managed to establish a pace-setting position in the heavy equipment industry by focusing directly on state-of-the-art technology and continuous product redesign. Specifically, concern for increased *user productivity* through greater equipment capacities, enhanced reliability, and quicker serviceability contributed most heavily to Cat's success and superior image. Maintenance of this leadership position across numerous product lines has also translated into the industry's highest prices.

MANUFACTURING AND WAREHOUSING

Caterpillar manufactures products in two principal categories: (1) machines and parts (M&Ps), which includes track-type machinery like bulldozers, tractors, rippers, and track-loaders, as well as several wheel-type machines such as motor graders, loaders, off-highway trucks, and tractor-scrapers; and (2) engines, used to power a variety of equipment for highway, marine, petroleum, agricultural, industrial, and electric power generation applications, ranging from diesel to natural gas and turbines. The category of M&Ps, it should be noted, includes all related parts and equipment for all of the machines. Exhibits 1, 2, 3, and 4 present sales, profit, and other financial data for the years 1979 to 1983.

Manufacturing and warehousing activities take place worldwide through 22 plants in the United States and several wholly or partly owned subsidiaries located in Australia, Belgium, Brazil, Canada,

EXHIBIT 1   Consolidated Sales and Profit Data

	1983	*1982*	*1981*	*1980*	*1979*
Sales	$5,424	$6,469	$9,154	$8,598	$7,613
Profit (loss) for year-consolidated	(345)	(180)	579	565	492
Profit (loss) per share of common stock	(3.74)	(2.04)	6.64	6.53	5.69
Return on average common stock equity	(10.1)%	(4.9)%	15.9%	17.4%	16.9%
Dividends paid per share of common stock	$ 1.50	$ 2.40	$ 2.40	$2,325	$ 2.10
Current ratio at year-end	2.15 to 1	2.87 to 1	1.50 to 1	1.71 to 1	1.88 to 1
Total assets at year-end	$6,968	$7,201	$7,285	$6,098	$5,403
Long-term debt due after one year at year-end	1,894	2,389	961	932	952
Capital expenditures for land, buildings, machinery, and equipment	324	534	836	749	676
Depreciation and amortization	506	505	448	370	312

Source: Caterpillar Tractor Company Annual Report, 1983.

EXHIBIT 2   Total Sales by Category (billions)

	1983	*1982*	*1981*	*1980*	*1979*
Inside the United States					
Machines and parts	$2.08	$1.84	$2.62	$2.84	N/A
Engines and parts	.85	.96	1.35	.85	N/A
Total inside	$2.93	$2.80	$3.97	$3.69	$3.51
Outside the United States					
Machines and parts	$2.08	$2.92	$4.48	$4.36	N/A
Engines and parts	.41	.75	.70	.55	N/A
Total outside	$2.49	$3.67	$5.28	$4.91	$4.10
By country (millions)					
Africa/Mid East	$ 680	$1,062	$1,886	$1,282	$ 960
Europe	771	927	993	1,267	1,153
Asia/Pacific	515	800	927	922	764
Latin America	266	637	903	879	716
Canada	262	239	472	563	505
Combined totals	$5.42	$6.47	$9.15	$8.60	$7.60

EXHIBIT 3   Research and Engineering Costs (in millions)

	1983	*1982*	*1981*	*1980*	*1979*	*1978*
New product development and major project improvements	n.a.*	$230	$227	$200	$191	$160
Other—general	n.a.*	146	136	126	92	96
Total	$340	376	363	326	283	256
Percent of sales	6.3%	5.8%	3.9%	3.8%	3.7%	3.6%

*n.a. = not available.

EXHIBIT 4   Heavy Equipment and Machinery Manufacturer Earnings (in millions)

	1983	*1982*	*1981*	*1980*	*1979*
Caterpillar Tractor Co.	($ 345)	($ 180)	$ 579	$ 565	$ 492
International Harvester*	(539)	(1,738)	(393)	(397)	369
Deere*	(.052)	(.039)	.250	.228	.310
Allis-Chalmers	(133)	(207)	(28)	47	81
Clark Equipment	(.012)	(.155)	.029	.051	.106

*Fiscal year ends October 31; latest year's figures are estimates. Losses indicated in ( ).

Source (in part): Harlan S. Byrne, "For Heavy Equipment Makers, Recovery to Be Delayed Another Year," *The Wall Street Journal,* November 3, 1982.

France, Japan, India, Indonesia, Mexico, and the United Kingdom. Each international location has been carefully selected to provide significant cost advantages by reducing global transportation costs, eliminating duty applicable to U.S.-built machinery, and by capitalizing on the manufacturing cost advantage derived from lower foreign wage levels. Such trends, it should be noted, have not been without some repercussions. The United Automobile Workers, for instance, representing over 80 percent of Cat's stateside hourly employees, ever alert to this threat to their jobs, became vitally concerned and quite vocal regarding possible extensions of foreign plants.

In addition, major warehouses and emergency parts' depots are strategically located throughout the world. As a result, these combined facilities form a worldwide organizational network which attempts to maximize Caterpillar's flexibility and customer responsiveness. All parts manufactured by any one plant are completely interchangeable with the same parts manufactured by any other plant. Thus, replacement parts are generally available on extremely short notice wherever

Caterpillar machines are deployed throughout the world. In short, all dealers and customers recognize Cat's parts and distribution as one of the two or three major advantages of owning Cat equipment. Heavy equipment purchasers widely acknowledge that no other firm in the industry can touch Cat in this category.

DEALERS

Recognized as the strongest in the industry, Caterpillar's dealer network handles all sales and service worldwide, with the exception of direct sales to the U.S. government, the Soviet Union, and the People's Republic of China, which are handled by a subsidiary division of Cat known as CIPI (Caterpillar Industrial Products, Inc.). Comprised of 213 independent dealers (84 in the United States), Caterpillar dealers represent an enterprise almost as large as the company. They operate 1,050 sales, parts, and service outlets in more than 140 countries, employ about 75,000 people, and have a combined net worth of approximately $3.1 billion. A typical dealership sells and services Caterpillar equipment exclusively, represents an average net worth of approximately $12 million, and is likely in a second or third generation of affiliation. Industry estimates place the capitalization of Caterpillar's dealer network at 10 times that of any competitor.

With Caterpillar's sales and service activities outside the direct control of Caterpillar executives, increasing efforts have been directed at improving service to dealers and informing users of the advantages of Caterpillar products. In 1978, a computerized dealer terminal system was completed which linked dealers and Caterpillar facilities to the European parts distribution department in Belgium. Essentially it provided direct computer access for ordering and locating parts for dealers in Europe, Africa, and the Middle East. In 1979, more than 3,000 consumers and dealer personnel attended Caterpillar-sponsored seminars, 47,000 visitors viewed Caterpillar products and manufacturing operations, and representatives from 26 countries attended a weeklong International Agricultural Seminar.

Comparable levels of seminar and visitation activity can be noted throughout the past few years, further promoting selective demand to both engine and equipment users. In one instance, 400 representatives of energy-related mining operations attended a seminar held at a West Virginia coal mine which not only highlighted the use of Cat machines, but perhaps more important, the dealers' capabilities to support special needs of mine operators. In another instance, in order to demonstrate dealer commitment to servicing the on-highway truck industry, Cat co-sponsored the National Fuel Economy Challenge, a competition open to owners of new trucks equipped with Caterpillar 3406 and 3408

Economy Engines. Results confirmed impressive fuel economy statistics for Caterpillar engines and provided hands-on exposure to dealer support facilities.

In what was called "target marketing" by Cat executives, the predominant dealer support theme during the past few years has begun to focus dealer efforts on special end-user groups. U.S. dealers brought over 1,000 owners of competitive equipment to Peoria to learn about Cat equipment, its advantages and capabilities, as well as to actually operate Cat equipment. In another program, "Build Your Future," small machine owners, unfamiliar with the differential advantages of Caterpillar equipment and dealer support capabilities, were instructed on various general business topics and specific Caterpillar operations capabilities including equipment maintenance. Factory tours and machine demonstrations were also provided.

In 1983, the continuing efforts to improve service to users and dealers achieved a milestone with a major restructuring of the company's marketing organizations in the United States and Far East. The changes generally consisted of moving from a centralized, functional organization to a geographically dispersed, marketing-oriented team structure. As a result, the new structure recognizes the growing diversity of competition and product applications and the need for more individually tailored programs. It is more responsive to dealer needs and opportunities, shortens the lines of communication, and speeds up vital decision-making processes. As a result, Caterpillar's dealer organization has become widely regarded and consistently mentioned by customers as a prime reason for purchasing Cat equipment and represents Cat's single largest advantage over all competitors, both in the United States and internationally.

RESEARCH AND ENGINEERING

Improving quality and technological leadership have long been key ingredients of Caterpillar's long-term growth strategy. In a 1983 statement to stockholders, Chairman Morgan asserted, "We will not allow our product leadership to be diminished." Expenditures for research and engineering (R&E) have consistently ranked number one in the industry, and have permitted Caterpillar to develop state-of-the-art products, manufacturing processors, and apparatus. In 1982, for example, expenditures for R&E reached a record $376 million (data on other recent research and engineering expenditures appear in Exhibit 3). As a result, Caterpillar's product leadership is not only widely recognized, but manufacturing facilities, as well, are considered the most modern and best equipped in the industry.

A carryover of this commitment to product leadership is the general practice of passing along specific product advances as soon as reliably feasible rather than accumulating several modifications and incorporating them all simultaneously in periodic model changes. Not only would the latter fail to permit the entire line to be completely up-to-date at all times, but it would also fail to insure maximum sales opportunities for existing, but aging, products. As an example of the success of this market penetration strategy, a simple addition of rubber grousers on tractors used primarily for log skidding created 200 immediate new machine sales for other agricultural users.

COMPETITION

As a result of decades of domination of the heavy equipment and construction industry, Caterpillar has an estimated 45–50 percent share for earthmoving machinery in the U.S. market and roughly 30–35 percent of the market worldwide. Mr. Morgan readily admits the toughest competition facing Caterpillar is from Komatsu Ltd., of Tokyo, which has rapidly grown to second place in worldwide sales. In addition, considerable domestic competitive pressures come from J.I. Case, Inc., and Deere & Company, considered No. 2 and No. 3, respectively.

In 1981, the president of Komatsu Ltd. stated a goal of achieving 20 percent of the U.S. market within five years; the company has succeeded in boosting market share from approximately 2 percent in 1974 to 15 percent in 1983. Komatsu is gaining sales basically in selected markets such as specialty bulldozers (i.e., including amphibians and remote-controlled units especially for underground use), and in equipment larger than Caterpillar's largest. Number one in terms of the latter is Komatsu's 1,000 Hp. tractor bulldozer, which far surpasses Cat's biggest, the D–10 with only 700 Hp. In these specialty areas, Komatsu does particularly well. Projections are that Komatsu Ltd., as a result of aggressiveness, adaptability, and a number of complex economic factors, will continue to encroach into the U.S. market largely at the expense (or demise) of many smaller competitors. As one industry analyst put it, "When elephants fight, the grass dies."

Nevertheless, despite claims of durability and efficiency which rival Caterpillar's, Komatsu probably will not match the current Cat sales in the United States. With approximately 60 part-time dealerships in America (i.e., those who sell Komatsu and other manufacturer's equipment simultaneously), and several competitive handicaps in the United States, such as ocean freight costs and narrow product lines, Komatsu cannot compete head-to-head with Cat. Thus the company initially adopted a strategy of allying itself, through joint-venture subsidiaries, with International Harvester (IH) and Bucyrus-Erie (B-E) to manufacture wheeled vehicles and excavators. In 1980, Komatsu bought out B-E with financial assistance provided directly by Japan's Fair Trade Commission and, in 1982, IH's share of the joint venture was also purchased. Thus, domestic entrance for Komatsu has been achieved through limited and well-conceived flanking attacks providing American-based manufacturing facilities and distribution links.

The U.S. presence of Komatsu, however, is considered by industry analysts more a matter of competitive visibility than an operational threat to Caterpillar's leadership position. The most direct threats to Caterpillar's domestic markets are J.I. Case and John Deere & Co. J.I. Case has an estimated 35 percent share of the earthmoving equipment market and John Deere has an estimated 30 percent share of the farm-machinery market.

However, each of these organizations, as well as several others (Allis-Chalmers, Clark Equipment, Harnischfeger Corp., IH, and Massey-Ferguson), has been undergoing considerable upheaval as a result of the early 1980s worldwide recession (see Exhibit 4 for performance data from selected competitors). As one analyst put it:

> Producers of construction, farm, and other heavy equipment have been in varying degrees of recession . . . and had expected recovery to start by now. Instead, widespread weakness is showing up, and companies are awash in red ink.
>
> Executives and analysts have been surprised by the depths and breadth of the slump. In past recessions, declines in some markets have been at least partly offset by strengths in others. Not so today. Practically all major markets are weak. For instance, the collapse of the oil and gas drilling boom and the financial problems of many countries weren't anticipated. And the farm depression has been deeper and more prolonged than machinery makers expected.[1]

Thus, although Caterpillar has probably fared better than the other firms, the most significant domestic problem for Caterpillar is the delay in the recovery of the market.

Internationally, and despite the worldwide slump, Komatsu Ltd. is Caterpillar's single-largest and growing competitor with 15 percent share of the *world market* (second only to Caterpillar) and 60 percent of the Japanese market. Cat accounts for roughly 50 percent of the world market but only 30 percent of the Japanese market (Caterpillar Mitsubishi).

Typical of many Japanese manufacturing firms, Komatsu's competitive thrust focuses directly on a long-term strategy to equal or exceed

---

[1]Harlan S. Byrne, "For Heavy Equipment Makers, Recovery To Be Delayed Another Year," *The Wall Street Journal,* November 3, 1982.

Caterpillar's position. Considering Cat vulnerable to superior managerial efficiency and operating flexibility, Komatsu's broad marketing strategy has emphasized expanding market share, largely on the basis of lower prices and efforts to match Caterpillar's follow-up service and parts capabilities. The slogan "Maru-C" is widely acknowledged as one of Komatsu's greatest challenges—to "engulf Caterpillar." Komatsu offers customers prices up to 15 percent below Caterpillar and endeavors to accommodate every conceivable special heavy equipment need through continual *adaptation* of existing products. In one instance, special equipment was developed exclusively for the particular needs of Australian coal miners. In another instance, an electric-powered bulldozer was developed for a small number of contractors whose special needs required them to operate equipment within legal noise limits.

Determined to produce the world's best earthmoving equipment, Komatsu executives lay claim to offering superior equipment in terms of power, durability, and lower fuel consumption.[2] Indeed, considerable evidence is available to support such claims, and industrial customers have responded to Komatsu's discount pricing and manufacturing flexibility. In terms of follow-up support, Komatsu maintains a crew of salespeople (engineers), ready to fly anywhere in the world to solve Komatsu equipment problems. Within the United States, Komatsu maintains five regional centers to directly support dealer efforts.

OTHER PROBLEMS

The suddenness of Caterpillar's 1982 $180 million loss, the first in 50 years, found President Robert E. Gilmore and Chairman Lee Morgan stunned and hopeful of a quick return to profitability. In a 1983 joint address to stockholders they reported:

> We hope that the worldwide economic malaise is coming to an end, and that people will soon be able to return to more normal lives.
>
> The economy will recover, and the world will need capital goods of the kinds made by Caterpillar. Roads will be built . . . ore and coal will be mined . . . fields will be cleared and dams constructed . . . oil and gas will be produced. These and other applications for our products are essential to a growing world population.
>
> Our concern isn't whether demand will revive and grow. It will.

However, by early 1984 Caterpillar's troubles were beginning to prove far more pervasive and devastating than first thought.

---

[2]Bernard Krisher, "Komatsu on the Track of Cat," *Fortune,* April 20, 1981, pp. 164–74.

In retrospect, several contributing factors began emerging as much as five years earlier, and not without Caterpillar's awareness. For instance, as the only manufacturer of pipelayers in the United States, Caterpillar was particularly hard hit by President Carter's 1979 "high tech" export control measures against the Soviet Union. Caterpillar was on the verge of a multimillion (perhaps billion) dollar contract with the Soviet Union for 2,000 heavy tractors at approximately $500,000 each and hundreds of pipelayers at $250,000 each. However, the export control measures ended this opportunity and the sale went to Komatsu.

Later in 1979, additional clouds surfaced. As a result of ever-increasing oil prices, worldwide economic growth abruptly halted. Adding to the U.S. problems, the growing and unprecedented international trade deficits of the 1970s prompted ever-higher interest rates and greater uncertainty regarding the future of the international trading system, and contributed significantly to inflation. The Consumer Price Index in 1979 was up 13 percent and Chairman Morgan noted that "inflation has become deeply embedded," and "solutions will neither be simple nor quick."

By 1981, effects of the world's economic recession began to appear at Caterpillar as physical sales volume declined "moderately"—as the company called it. Slowdowns in world markets, considered the most significant long-term growth opportunities for heavy construction equipment manufacturers, were particularly difficult to manage insofar as the U.S. competitive posture was slumping in general. Unlike the embargo against the Soviet Union, some developing world markets were being diminished by a variety of anti-U.S. export/import restrictions issued by developing countries themselves. Loss of accessibility to such markets, restricted information flows, and the growing trend in foreign government subsidies were leaving Caterpillar in a hopeful, but retrospective, position, as noted in a joint letter to stockholders by Chairman Morgan and President Gilmore:

> We have a competitive edge. . . . Outside authorities frequently confirm that ours is the preferred product. Our very substantial capital investment and research and engineering programs . . . should help us maintain a technological lead. . . . Toward that end, we seek the renewed commitment of Caterpillar people everywhere.

Unfortunately, throughout 1982, conditions continued to deteriorate. After the first quarter of operations, management began imposing numerous temporary plant shutdowns and indefinite layoffs. Domestic interest rates were sufficiently high to cause most U.S. capital spending to be abandoned. Worldwide, the previous decade of accelerated oil explorations and refinement had resulted in over-production such that oil prices also began to slump, which further resulted in reduced energy development and construction. Facing the unprecedented reduction in practically all markets simultaneously, Caterpillar experienced a 29 percent sales decline, and reported the first loss in common stock prices in 50 years. Common stock prices plunged from $55–$60 per share in 1981 to $35 per share in 1982.

On October 1, 1982, the United Auto Workers Union struck (20,400 members or roughly 80 percent of Cat's active, U.S. hourly employees), seeking an extension of the existing contract. For almost 30 years, the UAW labor contract had established a pattern that provided workers with automatic, annual, 3 percent wage increases. Management now resisted these increases because the increase in labor costs would make it even more difficult to compete. Recent data, for instance, placed Cat's per capita U.S. labor costs at roughly twice those of Japanese firms.

Throughout 1983, even well after the labor settlement, ripple effects of the dispute continued to emerge. Inventory shortages of both parts and equipment resulted in lost sales, lost good will, and a considerable strain on efforts to return to profitability. These efforts included reductions in expenditures for perhaps Cat's most sacred budget item— research and engineering—as well as the second annual cut in the capital expenditures budget—from $836 million in 1981, down to $324 million in 1983. These cost-cutting efforts resulted in layoffs and plant closings, leaving employment figures at the end of 1983 markedly reduced from previous years. Hourly employees, reduced in 1982 by 21,501, dropped another 624 in 1983, while the number of salaried employees was cut 3,077 and 2,585 in these two years.

The combination of a deteriorating worldwide economic climate and postsettlement reconstruction efforts required management to assume an adaptive posture while long-term solutions were worked out. Perhaps most noteworthy in this regard is the Cost Reduction Program (CRP), aimed at positioning Cat's 1986 cost levels more than 20 percent below those of 1981 (in constant dollars adjusted for volume). These cost reductions were intended to be *permanent* and included plant closings, new applications of computer and scientific technology, inventory reduction programs, and faster deliveries from suppliers. At the end of 1983 considerable efforts were being directed at achieving a scaled-down, more efficient organization.

The achievement of a long-term, strategic growth perspective has captured management's attention. Beginning in late 1982, management initiated efforts to focus planning specifically on future opportunities in diesel, natural gas, and turbine engines, and to review the basic role of the lift truck in Cat's product mix. In 1983, Caterpillar management held a Business Strategy Conference which developed specific objectives along with a timetable for activities through 1995. The plan involves what are designed to be the most productive means of "establishing, confirming, or modifying current strategies for . . . existing business; developing, evaluating, recommending, and selecting for implementation 'new' strategic growth opportunities; and developing corporate goals consistent with the findings and decisions produced by the conference."

Based on this planning, U.S. dealers recently launched a marketing program targeted at non-Caterpillar owners. Recognizing the strategic growth opportunities associated with market development, this program, called PLUS 3, provided a means for end users of competitors' equipment to gauge the superiority of Cat *dealers* in after-sales parts support and service. Specifically, the program guaranteed a 48-hour repair turnaround or the customer would be given a machine to use from the dealer's rental fleet, and a 48-hour parts delivery or the customer would receive the part free. It also included one of the most extensive power train warranties in the industry—36 months or 5,000 hours, whichever came first. Results of PLUS 3 were quite favorable, most notably among small- and medium-sized machine owners.

As a result of additional analyses regarding the role of the lift truck to Caterpillar, at least one U.S. plant was closed and management began labor negotiations with two non-U.S. production facilities. Indications were quite strong that more and more production throughout the product mix will be moved overseas in the future (e.g., lift trucks to Korea). Identifying future growth opportunities and detailing appropriate marketing strategies for the next decade were seen as becoming more critical as no significant upturn had been experienced through mid-1984, and the future seemed to be even more unstable and uncertain.

| *Hershey Foods**

Richard T. Hise

Texas A & M University

Milton S. Hershey, the founder of the giant chocolate-manufacturing firm bearing his name, did not find the road to success an easy one. He tried a number of business ventures before eventually succeeding in the chocolate business. In his early teens, he found that he was not cut out to be an apprentice typesetter, but did enjoy his four-year stint as an apprentice candy maker for Joseph H. Royer, a Lancaster, Pennsylvania, confectioner.

At the age of 19, Hershey decided to go into the candy business for himself. His venture in Philadelphia failed, as did efforts with his father in Denver and Chicago. Another solo attempt in New York also failed.

Back in his native Lancaster, Hershey began to manufacture caramels, an operation with which he was experienced, and the caramel business expanded rapidly. In 1900, he sold his company for $1 million, an unheard-of price in those days, and used the proceeds to begin construction of a chocolate processing plant in Derry Township, about 15 miles east of Harrisburg.

Within 10 years, the company prospered so much that Hershey and his wife were accumulating more money than they could possibly spend. In 1909, Mrs. Hershey suggested they build a home for unfortunate boys. Hershey eagerly agreed, feeling that, although his own childhood had not been all he had wished it to be, he could try to provide security and love for others. Thus, 486 acres of the initial 1,000-acre construction tract were set aside for the Hershey Industrial School.

In subsequent years, other community projects were built by the Hershey Company. The Community Building, containing two theaters, a dining room and cafeteria, a gymnasium, swimming pool, bowling

---

*This case was written as a basis for class discussion rather than to illustrate either effective or ineffective marketing management. Reprinted with permission from Richard T. Hise and Stephen W. McDaniel, *Cases in Marketing Strategy*, Columbus, Ohio: Charles E. Merrill Publishing Co., 1984.

alley, fencing and boxing room, and photographic room was finished in 1933. The Hershey Hotel was also completed in 1933. The 7,200-seat Hershey Sports Arena was constructed in 1936, and the Hershey Stadium was finished in 1939. Later, Hershey constructed Hershey's Chocolate World, which contains a free ride through a simulated chocolate manufacturing operation; Hershey Park, a theme park; the Hershey Museum of American Life; and the Hershey Gardens.

In the 1920s, Milton Hershey decided to reorganize the company. The Hershey Chocolate Company was dissolved, and three separate companies were organized: the Hershey Chocolate Corporation controlled all of the chocolate properties; the Hershey Corporation was responsible for the Cuban sugar interests; and the Hershey Estates was established to conduct the various businesses and municipal services in the town of Hershey.

The Hershey Trust Company administers the funds of the Milton Hershey School. As trustee for this school, it owns or controls the other three companies because Milton Hershey provided the trust with a sizable block of shares of common stock. In 1981, the Hershey Trust Company owned about 51 percent of the company's common stock.

The Hershey Chocolate Corporation continued to prosper. During World War II, the army commissioned Hershey to develop a chocolate bar for troops in the field; the result was the "Field Ration D," and the company was soon producing 500,000 bars a day.

Milton S. Hershey died on October 13, 1945. For 15 years after his death, the Hershey Chocolate Corporation continued to emphasize its chocolate products. Since 1960, however, the company has pursued a strategy of becoming a multiproduct corporation. The name of the Hershey Chocolate Corporation was changed to the Hershey Foods Corporation, its current name. In 1961, the company's sales were $185 million, compared to over $1.4 billion in 1981.

MAJOR PRODUCT GROUPS

In 1982, Hershey had three major product groups: the chocolate and confectionery group; restaurant operations (Friendly Ice Cream Corporation); and the other food products and services group—San Giorgia-Skinner (pasta) and Cory Food Services, Inc. The chocolate and confectionery group has grown through both internal means and acquisitions, while the other two groups have grown primarily through acquisitions. Exhibits 1 and 2 show overall company performance between 1971 and 1981. Exhibit 3 shows performance figures for the various product groups between 1979 and 1981.

Chocolate and Confectionery Group

The company produces a broad line of chocolate and confectionery products. The major product lines in the chocolate and confectionery group are bar goods, bagged items, baking ingredients, chocolate drink mixes, and dessert toppings. Hershey uses a variety of packages, such as boxes, trays, and bags for bar products. Sizes include standard, large, and giant bars, and about 30 brand names are used. The most important of these are Hershey's Almond Bars, Hershey's Chips, Hershey's Cocoa, Hershey's Kisses, Hershey's Milk Chocolate Bar, Hershey's Miniatures, Hershey's Syrup, Kit Kat, Mr. Goodbar, Reese's Peanut Butter Cup, Reese's Pieces, Rolo, and Whatchamacallit.

While most of the company's chocolate and confectionery items have been developed internally, some were acquired or made available through licensing agreements. The Reese's products were added to Hershey's product lines through acquisition of the H. B. Reese Candy Company of Hershey, Pennsylvania, in 1963. H. B. Reese, a former Hershey employee, began operations in 1923. Since one of the major ingredients in the Reese's line is peanut butter, Hershey executives believe that these items reduce to some extent the firm's dependency on the cacao bean, the chief raw ingredient in chocolate. Y&S Candies, Inc., a licorice manufacturer with facilities in Lancaster, Pennsylvania, Moline, Illinois, Farmington, New Mexico, and Montreal, Canada, was acquired in 1977 to serve the same purpose.

A licensing agreement with Rountree Mackintosh Limited of England gives Hershey the right to manufacture and market the Kit Kat and Rolo brands. The agreement with the English firm also allows Hershey to import, manufacture, and market After Eight, a thin dinner mint. This product was being test marketed in 1981.

Hershey has three other licensing arrangements. One is with AB Marabou of Sundbyberg, Sweden, the leading Scandinavian chocolate and confectionery company. Several AB Marabou products have been imported and marketed since 1978. Hershey owns 50 percent of Nacional de Dulces, S.A. de C.V., a manufacturer and marketer of chocolate and confectionery products in Mexico. The other licensing arrangement gives Hershey the right to import and sell various high-quality licorice products of the Geo. Bassett & Co. of England. In 1981, Hershey executives did not consider any of these agreements to be large moneymarkets.

Exhibit 4 delineates the company's most important chocolate and confectionery products, and when they were developed. While Hershey has had a number of successful new products, there have also been several disappointments. Chocolate-covered raisins were introduced in

EXHIBIT 1 Five-Year Financial Summary, 1971–1975 (all figures in thousands—except market price and per share statistics)

	1975	1974	1973	1972	1971
Summary of earnings:					
Continuing operations					
Net sales	$ 556,328	$ 491,995	$ 415,944	$ 392,004	$ 379,229
Cost of goods sold	368,992	357,830	294,174	255,162	247,784
Operating expenses	105,102	81,792	88,318	91,595	86,439
Interest expense (net)	1,259	2,190	4,848	3,246	2,610
Income taxes	41,682	25,812	13,929	20,679	21,947
Income from continuing operations	39,293	24,371	14,675	21,322	20,449
Losses from discontinued operations	(1,433)	(2,277)	(369)	(680)	44
Loss related to disposal of discontinued operations	(4,898)	—	—	—	—
Net income	32,962	22,094	14,306	20,642	20,493
Net income per share of common stock					
Continuing operations	3.02	1.87	1.13	1.63	1.55
Discontinued operations					
Losses from operations	(.11)	(.17)	(.03)	(.05)	—
Loss related to disposal	(.38)	—	—	—	—
Net income	2.53	1.70	1.10	1.58	1.55
Dividends per common share	.85	.80	1.10	1.10	1.10
Dividends per preferred share	.60	.60	.60	.60	.60

718

Average number of common shares and equivalents outstanding during the year	13,024	13,024	13,024	13,064	13,212
Percent of net income to sales*	7.1%	5.0%	3.5%	5.4%	5.4%
Financial statistics:					
Capital expenditures	$ 10,203	$ 10,887	$ 17,564	$ 25,137	$ 22,602
Depreciation*	7,541	7,912	7,010	5,622	5,597
Advertising*	9,325	1,744	9,565	13,954	10,506
Current assets	151,217	124,172	97,106	108,667	102,965
Current liabilities	52,494	57,579	23,456	29,789	44,486
Working capital	98,723	66,593	73,650	78,878	58,479
Current ratio	2.9:1	2.2:1	4.1:1	3.6:1	2.3:1
Long-term debt	$ 29,856	$ 31,730	$ 51,470	$ 51,364	$ 26,533
Debt-to-equity percent	15%	18%	32%	32%	17%
Stockholders' equity	$ 195,847	$173,173	$ 160,777	$ 159,714	$ 156,280
Stockholders' data:					
Outstanding common shares at year-end	13,024	11,824	11,824	11,824	11,977
Market price of common stock—					
At year-end	$ 18⅝	$ 9¾	$ 12⅝	$ 23⅞	$ 28
Range during year	$10⅛–20⅞	$ 8½–15	$12½–24¾	$21⅛–28¾	$26–31⅜
Number of common stockholders	19,279	19,362	19,095	17,980	18,346
Employees' data:					
Payrolls	$ 74,329	$ 72,936	$ 74,464	$ 67,700	$ 62,189
Number of employees—year-end	7,150	7,200	8,500	8,530	9,140

*Restated to reflect continuing operations only.

EXHIBIT 2 Six-Year Financial Summary, 1976–1981 (all figures in thousands except market price and per share statistics)

	1981	1980	1979	1978	1977	1976
Summary of earnings:						
Continuing operations						
Net sales	$1,451,151	$1,335,289	$1,161,295	$ 767,880	$ 671,227	$ 601,960
Cost of sales	1,015,767	971,714	855,252	560,137	489,802	417,673
Operating expenses	267,930	224,615	184,186	128,520	110,554	94,683
Interest expense	15,291	16,197	19,424	2,620	2,422	2,240
Interest (income)	(2,779)	(2,097)	(1,660)	(5,303)	(2,931)	(1,883)
Income taxes	74,580	62,805	50,589	40,450	35,349	45,562
Income from continuing operations	80,362	62,055	53,504	41,456	36,031	43,685
Income from discontinued operations	—	—	—	—	—	1,112
Gain related to disposal of discontinued operations	—	—	—	—	5,300	—
Net income	$ 80,362	$ 62,055	$ 53,504	$ 41,456	$ 41,331	$ 44,797
Income per common share						
Continuing operations	$ 5.61	4.38	3.78	3.02	2.62	3.18
Discontinued operations	—	—	—	—	—	.08
Gain related to disposal	—	—	—	—	.39	—
Net income	5.61	4.38	3.78	3.02	3.01	3.26
Cash dividends per common share	$ 1.75	$ 1.50	$ 1.35	$ 1.225	$ 1.14	$ 1.03
Average number of common shares and equivalents outstanding during the year	14,322	14,160	14,153	13,742	13,722	13,720
Percent of income from continuing operations to sales	5.5%	4.6%	4.6%	5.4%	5.4%	7.3%

Financial statistics:						
Capital additions	$ 91,673	$ 59,029	$ 56,437	$ 37,425	$ 27,535	$ 20,722
Depreciation	27,565	24,896	20,515	8,850	7,995	7,539
Advertising	56,516	42,684	32,063	21,847	17,637	13,330
Current assets	287,030	221,367	170,250	216,659	221,202	169,872
Current liabilities	117,255	111,660	103,826	74,415	83,149	47,309
Working capital	169,775	109,707	66,424	142,244	138,053	122,563
Current ratio	2.4:1	2.0:1	1.6:1	2.9:1	2.7:1	3.6:1
Long-term debt and lease obligations	$ 158,182	$ 158,758	$ 143,700	$ 35,540	$ 29,440	29,440
Debt-to-equity percent	34%	44%	45%	13%	11%	13%
Stockholders' equity	$ 469,664	$ 361,550	$ 320,730	$ 284,389	$ 259,668	$ 233,529
Total assets	$ 806,800	$ 684,472	$ 607,199	$ 422,004	$ 396,153	$ 331,870
Return on average stockholders' equity	19.3%	18.2%	17.7%	15.2%	16.8%	20.5%
Aftertax return on average invested capital	13.9%	12.8%	14.3%	13.0%	14.2%	17.1%
Stockholders' data:						
Outstanding common shares at year-end	15,669	14,160	14,159	13,745	13,730	13,720
Market price of common stock						
At year-end	$ 36	$ 23½	$ 24⅝	$ 20⅝	$ 19⅞	$ 22⅜
Range during year	$ 41–23⅛	$ 26–20	$26½–17⅜	$23½–18½	$22⅜–16⅝	$27½–18½
Number of common stockholders at year-end	16,817	17,774	18,417	18,735	19,694	20,421
Employees' data:						
Payrolls	$ 273,097	$ 253,297	$ 227,987	$ 112,135	$ 99,322	$ 88,848
Number of full-time employees at year-end	12,450	12,430	11,700	8,100	7,660	7,670

EXHIBIT 3   Product Group Information for the Years Ended December 31 (in thousands)

	1981	1980	1979
Net sales:			
Chocolate and confectionery	$1,015,106	$ 929,885	$ 822,813
Restaurant operations	302,908	274,297	224,072
Other food products			
and services	133,137	131,107	114,410
Total net sales	$1,451,151	$1,335,289	$1,161,295
Operating income:			
Chocolate and confectionery	$ 142,658	$ 118,435	$ 99,880
Restaurant operations	29,309	25,567	23,322
Other food products			
and services	7,250	5,148*	6,397
Total operating income	179,217	149,150	129,599
General corporate			
expenses	(11,763)	(10,190)	(7,742)
Interest expense (net)	(12,512)	(14,100)	(17,764)
Income before taxes	154,942	124,860	104,093
Less: income taxes	74,580	62,805	50,589
Net income	$ 80,362	$ 62,055	$ 53,504
Identifiable assets:			
Chocolate and confectionery	$ 445,815	$ 333,232	$ 297,296
Restaurant operations	223,265	219,196	207,125
Other food products			
and services	63,446	62,553	63,886
Corporate	74,274	69,491	38,892
Total identifiable assets	$ 806,800	$ 684,472	$ 607,199
Depreciation:			
Chocolate and confectionery	$ 9,554	$ 8,469	$ 7,389
Restaurant operations	14,379	13,015	10,283
Other food products			
and services	2,675	2,671	2,185
Corporate	957	741	658
Total depreciation	$ 27,565	$ 24,896	$ 20,515
Capital additions:			
Chocolate and confectionery	$ 57,504†	$ 27,061†	$ 29,472
Restaurant operations	22,098	24,468	20,965
Other food products			
and services	5,525	6,141	2,233
Corporate	6,546	1,359	3,767
Total capital additions	$ 91,673	$ 59,029	$ 56,437

*After a writeoff of deferred location costs of Cory Food Services in the amount of $1.4 million.
†Includes $37.8 million in 1981 and $6.5 million in 1980 for a new manufacturing facility currently being constructed.

EXHIBIT 4 Development of Hershey Products

1894	Hershey Bar and Almond Bar
	Hershey's Cocoa, Hershey's Baking Chocolate
1907	Hershey's Kisses
1923	Reese's Peanut Butter Cups
	Y&S Nibs
1925	Mr. Goodbar
1926	Hershey's Syrup
1928	Y&S Twizzlers
1938	Krackel
1939	Hershey's Miniatures
1940	Hershey's Hot Chocolate (now Hot Cocoa Mix)
1941	Dainties (now Semi-Sweet Chocolate Chips)
1952	Chocolate Fudge Topping
1956	Instant Cocoa Mix (Hershey's Instant)
1970	Kit Kat
1971	Special Dark
1976	Reese's Crunchy
1977	Reese's Peanut Butter Flavored Chips
	Golden Almond
1978	Reese's Pieces, Giant Kiss
1979	Whatchamacallit

Source: Company document.

1975 and withdrawn the same year. The Rally Bar, a chocolate, caramel, and peanut candy bar, was removed from the market; one of its problems was that, in the initial formula, the peanuts became soggy on the retailers' shelves. The original formula was modified, but the product did not measure up to sales expectations. Exhibit 5 shows the importance of new and current products for the Chocolate and Confectionery Division from 1963 to 1977.

Restaurant Operations

This division was acquired in January 1979. The Friendly Ice Cream Corporation consists of about 626 restaurants (1982) in 16 states, primarily in the Northeast and Midwest. Exhibit 6 shows the number of restaurants in each state. The division's headquarters and major plant are in Wilbraham, Massachusetts; another plant is in Troy, Ohio. Both plants manufacture the ice cream, syrups, and toppings used by the restaurants, and their capacities are considered sufficient for the current number of restaurants, as well as for some future expansion. The

EXHIBIT 5   Sales of New and Present Chocolate and Confectionery Products, 1963–1977

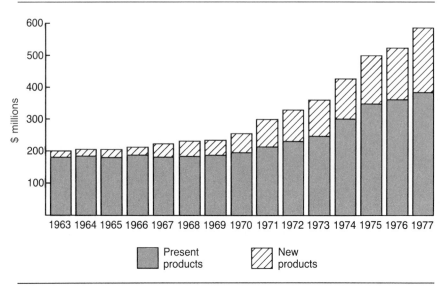

Source: The Wall Street Transcript, November 13, 1978, by permission.

Wilbraham plant processes the meat required by the restaurants; it is shipped frozen to the individual restaurant units. Some items (milk, cream, baked goods, eggs, and produce) are purchased by the restaurants from local sources which are designated by Friendly's central purchasing department.

Friendly Restaurants serve high-quality food at moderate prices, specializing in sandwiches, platters, and ice cream products. All units are owned outright by Friendly; there are no franchise agreements.

There are three major types of Friendly Restaurants. The *traditional* Friendly ice cream and sandwich shop offers a limited menu, featuring ice cream, hamburgers, breakfast items, platters, salad, french fries, beverages, and soup and sandwiches. Customers are served in booths or counters, or by take-out service. (The average seating capacity is 60.) There were 213 traditional operations in 1981. The 351 *modified* shop units offer most of the items available in the traditional shop, but serve a wider variety of full meals and platters. Unlike in the traditional shop, food is prepared out of the customer's sight. The modified units offer take-out service, but have a greater proportion of booth seats than the traditional restaurants. (Seating capacity averages 70 seats.) They also have more personalized service and a more pleasant dining atmosphere. The 50 *family* restaurants have the broadest menu, serving seafood, chicken, and other dinners, along with more varied

---

EXHIBIT 6   Location of Friendly Restaurants

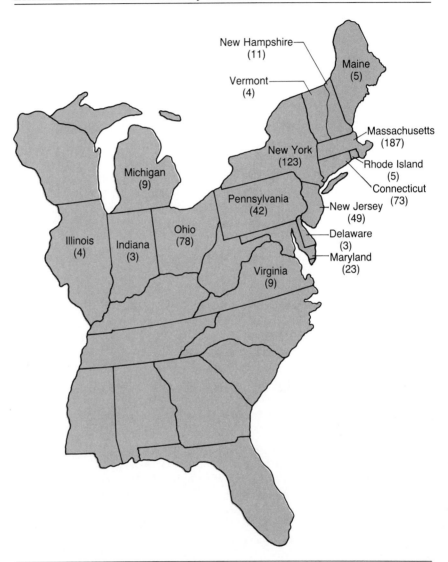

---

breakfasts and platter meals. Desserts other than ice cream are available, and some units serve beer and wine. Seating is primarily booths
and tables, and the floors are usually carpeted. (Seating capacity is
from 90 to 120.)

Menus and portions in each type of restaurant are standardized, but
prices may vary, generally according to geographical location. Most of

the units sell prepackaged ice cream for home consumption. Friendly restaurants feature a colonial decor, and free parking is available.

The Friendly Corporation has followed a policy of refurbishing its restaurants and opening newer ones. The remodeling policy involves converting traditional units into modified units; as of January 1, 1981, 351 units had been modified. Other units have been modernized. In 1980, 20 additional units, 14 of which are family restaurants, were opened; 11 units were closed in 1980. All units use modern construction methods. Almost 400 Friendly units have opened since 1970.

As of January 1, 1981, 419 of the Friendly units were free-standing, while the rest were located in shopping centers. Seventy percent of the free-standing sites are owned by Friendly; the other 30 percent are leased, as are all the shopping center sites. Friendly's executives believe that the great majority of its customers are residents of the immediate area surrounding the restaurant. Virtually all units are in suburban areas.

Other Food Products and Services

Pasta.   Four acquisitions comprise Hershey's pasta group. San Giorgio Macaroni, Inc., was acquired in 1966, with major markets in Philadelphia, Washington, D.C., Pittsburgh, and New York. Its primary plant is in Lebanon, Pennsylvania, about 20 miles from Hershey. San Giorgio produces 65 varieties of pasta and noodle products. Delmonico Foods, Inc., of Louisville, Kentucky, was also acquired in 1966, and was merged with San Giorgio in 1975. Its manufacturing facility is in Louisville, and the company's products are distributed chiefly in Kentucky, Ohio, and parts of West Virginia. The Procino-Rossi Corporation was acquired in 1978. Its brands (P & R brands) are distributed chiefly in upstate New York. The largest pasta acquisition is the Skinner Macaroni Co. of Omaha, Nebraska. Purchased in 1979, it distributes its products to 20 states in the West, Southwest, and South. In 1980, Hershey merged all four pasta companies into one organization, called San Giorgio-Skinner Company.

San Giorgio-Skinner Company produces and sells a great variety of pasta items, including small shells, jumbo shells, large shells, manicotti, lasagna, rippled-edge lasagna, macaroni, large elbow macaroni, shell macaroni, spaghetti, long spaghetti, thin spaghetti, curly spaghetti, mostaccioli, egg noodles, extra-wide egg noodles, rigatoni, alphabets, linguine, perciatelli, fettucini, soupettes, cut ziti, and spaghetti sauce.

Cory Food Services.   Cory Food Services, Inc., founded by Harvey Cory in 1933, was acquired in 1967. Cory developed a vacuum glass brewer with a glass filter that brewed a delicious coffee. In 1964, Cory introduced its coffee service to the business community in the United States and Canada. Cory's corporate headquarters is in Chicago, and the company has 51 branch offices in the United States. These branch offices are grouped into five regional offices: Arlington Heights, Illinois; Long Island, New York; Rockville, Maryland; Glendale, California; and Dallas, Texas. Six branch offices in Canada are serviced by the regional office in Toronto.

As a complement to its coffee business, Cory introduced leased water treatment units, compact refrigerator units, and microwave ovens suitable for offices. The latter two were expanded into more areas in 1981. Growth in these new ventures was good in 1981 and further expansion was anticipated in 1982.

STRATEGIC PLANNING

Hershey began to emphasize strategic planning in the late 1970s. William E. C. Dearden, Hershey's chief executive officer, stated that strategic planning was his number one priority. In 1978, Mr. Dearden established the position of vice president of corporate development, which reports directly to him.

Hershey's strategic plan for accomplishing its basic corporate objectives has centered on its efforts to diversify. In the company's 1980 annual report, Chairman of the Board Harold S. Mohler, Chief Executive Officer William E. C. Dearden, and the company's President and Chief Operating Officer, Richard A. Zimmerman, stated, "In keeping with our strategic plan, we shall continue our drive to become a major, diversified, international food and food-related company." This strategic plan is also reflected in the Statement of Corporate Philosophy developed by the same executives (see Exhibit 7). The statement also includes the company's basic objectives: "We are in business to make a reasonable profit, and to enhance the value of our shareholders' investment."

The company, however, faces strong competition. In the early 1970s, Hershey lost its lead in market share for candy bars to Mars, the privately owned, Hackettstown, New Jersey, company which markets such well-known brands as Milky Way, Snickers, Three Musketeers, and m&m's. At one time, Mars had a 40 percent share of the candy bar market, compared to Hershey's 23 percent. By 1979, Mars had slipped to 36 percent of candy bar sales, while Hershey increased to 27 percent. Hershey executives maintained that in 1979 it was ahead of Mars in total candy sales.[1]

---

[1]"Hershey Steps Out," *Forbes,* March 17, 1980, p. 64.

EXHIBIT 7

✖ Hershey Foods Corporation
Hershey, Pennsylvania 17033

STATEMENT OF CORPORATE PHILOSOPHY

We are in business to make a reasonable profit and to enhance the value of our shareholders' investment. We recognize that, to achieve this objective, we must use our resources efficiently, and we must provide for the proper balance between the fundamental obligations that we have to our shareholders, employees, customers, consumers, suppliers and society in general.

We will continue to pursue a policy of profitable growth by maintaining the excellence of our current businesses while concurrently utilizing our financial resources and the expertise and ingenuity of our people to further diversify into other food and food-related businesses, and/or such other businesses which offer significant opportunity for growth.

In seeking to balance our desire for profitable growth with the obligations which we have to the other various interests, we recognize that:

— All employees should be treated fairly and with dignity. They should be provided with good working conditions and competitive wages, and should be rewarded according to performance. To the fullest extent possible, in line with good business practices, promotions should be made from within the Corporation.

— Our Affirmative Action Program is a sincere commitment. Each of us has an obligation to follow it both in the spirit and letter of the law.

— We should be results oriented, and all employees should be given the opportunity to express individual initiative and judgment. Responsibility and authority, however, must be appropriately delegated.

— To successfully conduct the business of the Corporation, it is necessary that each employee strive to improve the communications relating to his or her area of responsibility.

— Our individual and company relationships should be conducted on the basis of the highest standards of conduct and ethics, and it is important that we recognize that the success of our business depends upon the character and integrity of people working in a spirit of constructive cooperation.

— We need to provide to our customers and consumers products of consistent excellent quality at competitive prices that will insure an adequate return on investment.

— We have an inherent responsibility to be a good neighbor and to support community projects, and all employees are encouraged to take an active part in improving the quality of community life.

— We have a responsibility to conduct our operations within the regulatory guidelines and in a manner that does not adversely affect our environment.

It is imperative that we create a climate throughout our entire organization which causes these philosophies to become a way of life.

Adopted: July 26, 1976
Affirmed: April 11, 1980

Chairman of the Board   Vice Chairman and   President and
                             Chief Executive Officer   Chief Operating Officer

Source: Company document.

Another impediment is the slide in candy consumption. In 1978, Americans consumed an annual per capita average of about 15 pounds of candy. A decade earlier, the figure was about 20 pounds. The highest per capita annual candy consumption was in the 1940s, and the 1978 figure was the lowest since 1935.[2] Competition is also stiff in the pasta division. In 1979, its San Giorgio, Delmonico, Procino-Rossi, and Skinner brands had a 10.2 percent market share. This was well under the 18 percent shares of the industry leader, C. F. Mueller Co., a subsidiary of Foremost-McKesson, Inc.[3] To implement its strategic plan, Hershey has developed the corporate organization presented in Exhibit 8. Gary W. McQuaid is the vice president of marketing for the chocolate and confectionery group; John D. Burke is Friendly's vice president of marketing; and Clifford K. Larsen serves in this capacity for San Giorgio-Skinner.[4]

RESEARCH AND DEVELOPMENT

In 1979, Hershey's 114,000-square-foot technical center was completed at a cost of $7.4 million. Management believes this facility and its staff will give it one of the best research and development capabilities in the industry. Included in the facility are offices, laboratories, a library, test kitchen, auditorium, animal testing facilities, and a pilot plant. A year before completion of the technical center, a major reorganization of the company's R&D effort was announced, and a new vice president of science and technology was named. This office, consisting of four groups, is responsible for heading up the company's entire R&D effort.

The *research group's* efforts have focused on three areas: vegetable fat chemistry, chocolate flavor research, and raw materials, such as peanuts and almonds. There are three subgroups in the research group: (1) The analytical research group emphasizes chocolate analysis, and has received international acclaim for its efforts; it has compiled one of the world's largest data banks on the nutritional content of chocolate and cocoa. (2) Microbiological research focuses on cocoa bean microbiology. This group's importance has increased as the company has purchased more chocolate liquor and less raw cocoa. (3) The nutrition group engages in basic nutrition research projects, on subjects like

[2]"Indulge, Indulge! Enjoy, Enjoy!" *Forbes,* October 15, 1979, p. 45.
[3]"Hershey Steps Out."
[4]*Advertising Age,* September 9, 1982, p. 106.

EXHIBIT 8 Hershey's Corporate Organization*

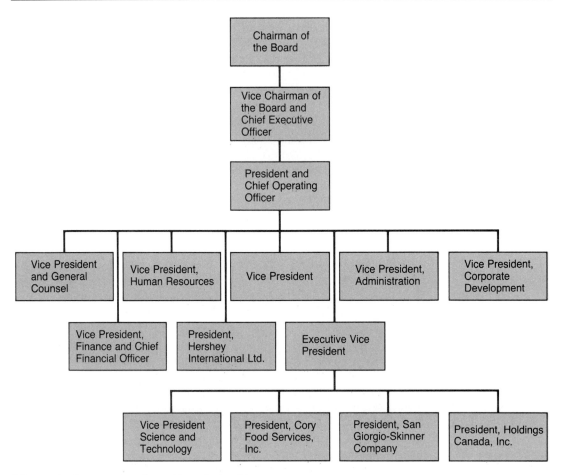

*Case writer's perception of reporting relationships.

tooth decay, acne, chocolate allergies, and nutrition, and it works closely with the technical committee of the Chocolate Manufacturers Association.

The *product and process development group* continually monitors consumer trends and behavioral patterns to define product opportunities. San Giorgio's Light 'n Fluffy Noodles and the Whatchamacallit candy bar were developed in response to consumers' demand for "lightness."

The *engineering group* is mainly responsible for assisting capital programs, and it also provides some engineering skills for moving new products into production.

The *equipment design and developing group* provides support for producing new products and improving existing manufacturing systems. This group designs special equipment not generally available and integrates purchased equipment into the production line. In addition, it is responsible for designing special methods and devices unique to Hershey's products and conditions.

One of the major reasons for Hershey's purchase of Marabou in Sweden was to exchange technological information, with special emphasis on new confectionery products. An interest in Chadler Industrial de Bahia of Brazil was purchased for the same reason. Hershey was interested in Chadler's conversion processes which make chocolate liquor, cocoa butter, and cocoa powder from cacao beans. Hershey has also acquired interests in several cocoa-growing ventures in Costa Rica, the Dominican Republic, and Belize, to try to increase yields from cacao bean production. Hershey is committed to continued support of the American Cocoa Research Institute, which works to improve the volume and quality of cacao bean production in the western hemisphere.

The company's R&D efforts have paid important dividends. Whatchamacallit and Reese's Pieces are two successful products which were developed by the company, and their success has encouraged further research. A significant technological breakthrough was the development of a peanut-butter-flavored ingredient which reduces dependence on high-priced cacao beans.

Future corporate research and development is expected to continue to work toward creating new ingredients that are readily available domestically and will reduce the dependency on imported commodities. Two major emphases have been testing alternate fat products for cocoa butter and experimenting with new high-fructose corn syrup, which could be used as a sucrose alternate in certain kinds of products.

INTERNATIONAL OPERATIONS

In recent years, Hershey has increased its overseas marketing efforts. As of 1981, the company believes that "overall sales and earnings from international operations remain modest in comparison with the corporation's total performance." However, the company is pleased with its expansion in international sales.

Hershey's major foreign market is Canada. Although some sales growth occurred in Canada in 1980, company executives considered these results well below expectations. As in the United States, higher operating costs forced the company to raise prices to 35 cents for the standard-size candy bar.

During 1979 and 1980, several new products were successfully introduced in Canada. Brown Cow proved to be an immediate success, and became one of the company's leading brands in Canada. Brown Cow is a chocolate syrup milk modifier in a plastic dispenser bottle. Top Scotch, a butterscotch sundae topping, was introduced in 1979. Three other products entered the Canadian market in 1970: Special Crisp, the Canadian version of Whatchamacallit; Reese's Crunchy Peanut Butter Cups; and a boxed version of Y&S All Sorts (licorice). 1980 saw the introduction of Reese's Pieces and two clear plastic-bag packages of Y&S All Sorts.

Hershey has a number of supply points for cacao beans. The major ones are La Guaria, Venezuela; Guayaquil, Ecuador; Ilheus, Brazil; Abidjan, Ivory Coast; Accra, Ghana; Lagos, Nigeria; and Douala, Cameroon.

Hershey has a policy of joint ventures in entering foreign markets. This strategy allows the company to work with well-established partners with considerable knowledge of local market conditions. Hershey entered a joint venture in 1979 with the Fujiya Confectioning Company, Ltd. of Tokyo. This Japanese firm has been in existence since 1910, and is a leader in chocolate and confectionery products, snack foods, beverages, ice cream, and bakery products in that country; it also has important restaurant operations. The joint venture agreement enables Hershey's products to be imported, manufactured, and sold in Japan, and company executives believe that this arrangement has already resulted in increased Japanese sales. Another joint venture arrangement in Mexico with Nacional de Dulces, S.A. has resulted in increased sales and earnings in that country. The company expects demand for its products to increase, and a new Mexican manufacturing facility is under construction. Two joint ventures exist in Brazil: one with Chadler Industrial de Bahia S.A. involves sales of chocolate and confectionery products. A new joint venture with S.A. Industrias Reunidas F. Matarazzo is concerned with pasta sales. Early indications were that the pasta joint venture was successful. However, the continued devaluation of the cruzeiro has adversely affected the firm's Brazilian operations.

In Sweden, AB Marabou acquired Göteborgs Kex, that country's leading cookie and cracker manufacturer. These additional sales contributed to Hershey's revenues; Hershey has a 20 percent interest in AB Marabou. In the Philippines, Hershey began in 1980 to furnish technical manufacturing assistance and cocoa-growing advice to the Philippine Coca Corporation.

In 1981, Hershey formed a new subsidiary company, Hershey International Ltd. This company is responsible for Hershey's international operations outside Canada, especially those in Mexico, Brazil, the Philippines, Sweden, and Japan. Company executives believed this "consolidation will further strengthen the overall monitoring, control, and reporting of international operations." Richard M. Marcks, vice president, international, was named president of the new subsidiary company and his old position was abolished.

DISTRIBUTION

The company believes that its distribution system is critical in maintaining sales growth and providing service to its distributors. Hershey attempts to anticipate distributors' optimum stock levels and provide them with reasonable delivery times. To achieve these objectives, Hershey uses 35 field warehouses throughout the United States, Puerto Rico, and Canada. Hershey uses public carriers, contract carriers, and some private trucks to move its products from manufacturing plants to field warehouses, and then to customers. For example, a fleet of company-owned refrigerated trucks transports food and supplies from the two Friendly production sites to the individual restaurants. Some shipments go directly from manufacturing plants to customers. Hershey's executives believe that the distribution system has been very helpful in successfully introducing new products nationally.

Hershey has five major manufacturing plants in the United States and Canada for chocolate and confectionery products, with an additional manufacturing site under construction. Four of the present plants (two in Hershey, one in Oakdale, California, and one in Smith Falls, Ontario) produce primarily chocolate products. The Lancaster, Pennsylvania, plant produces licorice products. A future manufacturing plant in Stuart's Draft, Virginia, will produce chocolate items.

Hershey's chocolate and confectionery products are sold mainly to wholesale, chain, and independent grocers, candy and tobacco stores, syndicated and department stores, vending and concessions, drug stores, and convenience stores. Exhibit 9 shows the percentage of sales of each of these distribution outlets. Exhibit 10 shows the geographical sales pattern for chocolate and confectionery products. Over 375 sales representatives throughout the United States and Canada service over 20,000 direct-sales customers. Company executives estimate that over 1 million retail outlets are served in 20,000 cities and towns, and that no single customer accounts for more than 4 percent of the total sales of chocolate and confectionery items. The company's sales representatives are specialized according to the product sold. One type is responsible for candy bars, packaged items, and grocery products. The other handles specialty products, food service, and industrial products.

Hershey's pasta products are sold to supermarket chains, cooperatives, independent wholesalers, and wholesaler-sponsored volunteers. Four brand names are marketed (San Giorgio, Skinner, Delmonico, and P&R), but some private label merchandise is also marketed.

EXHIBIT 9   Percentage of Chocolate and Confectionery Sales by Type of Distribution
Outlet

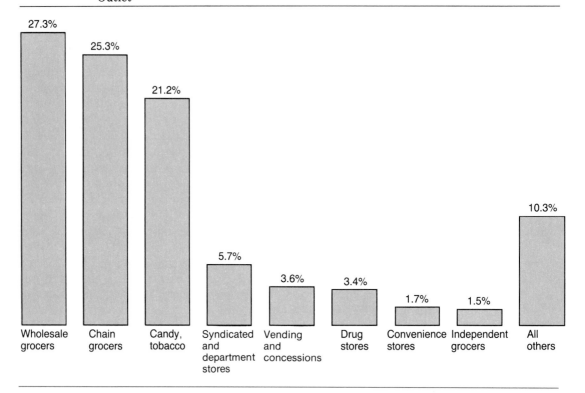

Source: The Wall Street Transcript, November 13, 1978, by permission.

EXHIBIT 10   Geographical Sales

Region	Percentage of Sales	Percentage of U.S. Population
North	31.9%	27.6%
South	24.2	27.4
Midwest	25.9	27.9
West	18.0	17.1
Total U.S.	100.0%	100.0%

Source: The Wall Street Transcript, November 13, 1978, by permission.

ADVERTISING

For its first 66 years, Hershey did not advertise. The company relied on the quality of its products and its extensive channels of distribution system to gain acceptance in the marketplace. Milton Hershey said, "Give them quality. That's the best kind of advertising in the world." However, Hershey did use various forms of sales promotion, such as the plant tour, to promote sales. The plant tour, seen by almost 10 million people, was replaced by Hershey's Chocolate World in 1973.

In 1968, over 20 years after the death of its founder, Hershey announced plans to initiate a consumer advertising program for its confectionery and grocery products. On July 19, 1970, the program was launched with a full-page ad for Hershey's Syrup, which appeared in 114 newspaper supplements. National radio and television advertising appeared in September.

Hershey decided to advertise for several reasons. There was increased competition in the confectionery industry—increased competition which often involved heavy advertising. There was the need to better acquaint people under 25 with Hershey products. In 1970, these people accounted for half of the U.S. population. And as Hershey developed new products, executives believed that advertising would promote mass distribution, which would, in turn, spur mass production.

Exhibit 11 shows advertising expenditures from 1971 through 1981. Hershey's $43 million of advertising in 1980 moved it into the top 100 of U.S. advertisers, and its 1981 expenditures ranked it 86th. Mars, Inc., spent $78.4 million on advertising in 1981, good for the 69th spot. Exhibit 12 shows 1981 advertising expenditures for Hershey's major

---

EXHIBIT 11   Annual Advertising

Year	Amount
1971	$10,506,000
1972	13,954,000
1973	9,565,000
1974	1,744,000
1975	9,499,000
1976	13,330,000
1977	17,637,000
1978	21,847,000
1979	32,063,000
1980	42,684,000
1981	56,516,000

Source: Company Annual Reports.

EXHIBIT 12   Most Heavily Advertised Products in 1981

Product	*Advertising Expenditure*
Hershey's Candy Bars	$7.0 million
Reese's Candies	4.6 million
Hershey's Chocolate Kisses	3.7 million
Whatchamacallit	3.7 million
Hershey's Chocolate Syrup	3.1 million
Reese's Pieces	2.9 million
Chocolate Chips	2.3 million
Rolo Candy	1.6 million
Hershey's Candies	1.4 million

Source: Reprinted with permission from the September 9, 1982, issue of *Advertising Age.* Copyright 1982 by Crain Communications, Inc.

brands. Sales promotion efforts are directed to consumers by such point-of-purchase materials as shelf-takers and case cards, and by coupon and premium offers.

The company has had to defend its advertising from attacks on two fronts: some of the advertising is directed toward children, and some of its products may promote tooth decay. Hershey estimates that about 30 percent of its advertising is directed at children. The Federal Trade Commission on May 28, 1980, began considering a trade regulation which would adversely affect the advertising of many of the company's products. At that time, however, Congress narrowed the FTC's authority to adopt such a trade rule. As of January 1, 1981, company executives were not sure whether the FTC would continue its efforts to regulate advertising to children. In most cases, it would take several years to adopt such a trade rule. Hershey executives announced they were opposed to "any attempt to limit its rights to advertise truthfully its products to any audience." Hershey has developed material about the controversy surrounding tooth decay and nutrition. An example of these materials is presented in Exhibit 13. Exhibit 14 shows the nutritional value per serving of various foods.

PRICING

Pricing is a particularly important element of the marketing mix for Hershey, and it is difficult for a number of reasons. Hershey's chocolate and confectionery products depend on raw materials. The suppliers of these raw materials are usually in foreign countries and their supplies are frequently curtailed because of bad weather or other factors.

EXHIBIT 13   Example of a Hershey's Advertisement

Good Nutrition Makes Good Sense

Everyone agrees that good nutrition makes good sense. But what is good nutrition? Nowadays many people are readily willing to answer this question, but many of their answers are contradictory.

While we do not advertise our chocolate products as especially nutritious foods, they do have nutritional value and do contribute to the overall diet since they are composed of such food ingredients as milk, various nuts, chocolate, and sugar.

Nearly all Hershey's Chocolate and Confectionery Division products have nutrition information printed on their labels. This practice was begun voluntarily in 1973, and to date we are the only manufacturer in the chocolate and confectionery industry to provide this consumer service. Our effort to convey this information is one clear indication of Hershey's concern for good nutrition and our respect for the consumer's right to know.

Good nutrition comes from a balanced diet, one that provides the right amounts and the right kinds of proteins, vitamins, minerals, fats, and carbohydrates. The chart on page 739 provides an interesting basis of comparison between Hershey Food's products and other snack items commonly cited as "more nutritious."

Chocolate and confectionery products and other sugar-containing snacks have been coming under attack recently. They are accused of being "empty calorie" or so-called junk foods.

We all have substantial caloric needs. At Hershey Foods we believe obtaining the right amount of calories is especially important for active, growing children. Calories come from nutrients, namely carbohydrates, fats, and proteins. Our products supply these nutrients and do contribute to good nutrition.

Throughout the world, carbohydrates are the largest single component of the diet. In the United States, about half of all calories (i.e., energy) are provided by carbohydrates

commonly referred to as sugars and starches. As far as the body is concerned, all carbohydrates must be reduced to simple sugars before they can be used. Once sugars and starches reach the stomach, their dietary origin is lost. It makes no difference whether they come from fruits, vegetables, milk, honey, or Hershey Bars—before entering the blood stream, they are all alike.

Sugar is currently bearing the brunt of the attack from a variety of sources. Since sugar is a significant component of many Hershey Foods' chocolate and confectionery products, we are naturally concerned about these attacks and the types of evidence used to support them.

At present sugar is not linked in substantive research to the variety of health problems usually mentioned in this context. As for dental caries, a complex issue, there is evidence that sugar, both naturally occurring and added, plays a role. On the other hand, a number of studies in dental literature show that chocolate, especially milk chocolate, does not cause an increase in dental caries.

Researchers report that milk chocolate has a high content of protein, calcium, phosphate and other minerals, all of which have exhibited positive effects on tooth enamel. In addition due to its natural fat (cocoa butter) content, milk chocolate clears the mouth quickly in comparison to some other foods. These factors are thought to be responsible for making milk chocolate less likely to cause dental caries than certain other foods.

The American public is being inundated with numerous attacks on sugar and the role it plays in the diet. Many assertions are made on a partial understanding of the facts or without substantiating research.

Unfortunately the crusade against sugar-containing products is well underway despite a lack of adequate, factual support. Federal, state, and local governmental bodies have

---

EXHIBIT 13 *(concluded)*

---

entered the fray, and considerable media interest has been generated. We fear that great misunderstanding will be created before the issue is resolved, although as a company and an industry, we are trying to raise the information level on all fronts.

One aspect of this very complex situation is the role the Federal Trade Commission has been asked to play regarding the advertisement of products containing sugar. At the present time, the FTC is considering various means of limiting our industry's ability to advertise its products.

Hershey Foods has and will continue to oppose any attempt to limit its right to advertise. We believe we have the right to advertise to all of our audiences and we do not think our advertising has been out of balance. In 1978, less than one third of all our advertising impressions will be received by children.

Hershey Foods has always been concerned about the content of its advertising as well as the type of programs it supports. We have helped in the development of voluntary codes through the Children's Review Unit of the National Advertising Board, and our ads are constantly reviewed by child psychologists and public affairs specialists to make sure they are not misleading and cannot be misunderstood.

Our standard bar line, which accounts for the majority of advertising expenditures, represents an inexpensive group of products. We feel that children can be appropriately informed about them, especially in light of their nutritional value and the parental approval they have received for generations in the United States. We believe we have the right to remind consumers of our products and to inform new consumers about products their parents have used, enjoyed, and approved.

Perhaps the most paradoxical aspect of this issue is the fact that chocolate and confectionery consumption in the United States is not excessive, representing only about one percent of total food intake. What's more, consumption of these foods has not increased in the last 40 years. Since mass media advertising did not really come into being until the 1950s, it is evident that television advertising has not contributed to increased consumption of chocolate and confectionery products. As far as our industry is concerned, however, advertising has simply fostered competition.

The so-called junk food issue in all its complexity will continue to be an important challenge to Hershey Foods Corporation. We shall stand firmly in our position that Hershey's products are mixtures of ingredients that inherently have nutritional value. Hershey has manufactured chocolate and confectionery products of the highest quality for over 80 years. We are very proud of these products and the role they play in the lives of people throughout the world.

Cacao beans are the major raw materials for the Chocolate and Confectionery Division; two thirds of the world's supply is grown in West Africa, chiefly in Ghana. Prices fluctuated widely in the 1970s because of weather conditions, consuming countries' demands, sales policies of the producing countries, speculative influences, worldwide inflation, and currency movements. Hershey attempts to minimize the effects of bean price fluctuations through forward purchasing of large quantities of cacao beans, cocoa butter, and chocolate liquor. Cocoa future contracts are purchased and sold, and the company holds memberships in the London Cocoa Terminal Market Association and the Coffee, Sugar, and Cocoa Exchange, Inc., in New York. Crop forecasts, chiefly in West Africa and Brazil, are also made.

EXHIBIT 14 Nutritional Value per Serving of Various Foods‡

	A Milk Chocolate	B Mr. Goodbar	C Reese Cup	D Ice Cream	E Saltine Crackers	F Graham Crackers	G Cheese/Peanut Butter Crackers	H Apple	I Dried Dates
Serving size	1.05 oz	1.3 oz	1.2 oz	8 fl oz (1 cup)	1 oz	1 oz	1.5 oz	3¼ in. diam.	1.4 oz
Calories	160	210	190	260	120	110	210	120	120
Protein (grams)	2	5	4	6	2	2	6	0	1
Carbohydrate (grams)	17	18	18	28	20	20	24	30	29
Fat (grams)	10	13	11	14	3	2	10	1	0
Vitamin A*	*	*	*	*	*	*	*	2	*
Vitamin C†	*	*	*	*	*	*	*	10	*
Thiamine†	4	2	2	2	*	*	*	2	2
Riboflavin†	*	4	2	15	*	4	2	2	2
Niacin†	*	8	8	*	*	2	8	*	4
Calcium†	6	4	2	20	*	*	2	*	2
Iron†	2	2	2	*	2	2	2	2	6

*Contained less than 2 percent of the U.S. RDA of these nutrients.
†Vitamin and mineral levels are expressed as a percentage of the U.S. RDA.
‡Information for foods other than Hershey products derived from U.S.D.A. Handbook No. 456, *Nutritive Value of American Foods*.
Items A, B, & C, according to at least one state's legislators' list, would be included in a "low-nutritious" category.
Items D through I are identified on that list as nutritious food.

Source: Company document.

Despite these efforts, the prices of cacao beans skyrocketed in the 1970s. The following is the average price of cacao beans for October 1 through September 30, the normal crop year:

Year	Cents per Pound
1969–70	32.5
1970–71	26.3
1971–72	26.3
1972–73	44.5
1973–74	62.7
1974–75	57.3
1975–76	72.1
1976–77	150.1
1977–78	141.1
1978–79	156.4
1979–80	138.8

Source: Company document.

The other major ingredient is sugar. Like cacao beans, many factors affect the price of sugar, including quantities available, demand by consumers, speculation, currency movements, and the International Sugar Agreement. Another price determinant is the price support provided domestic sugar by the Agriculture Adjustment Act of 1978. The average price per pound of refined sugar, as reported by the U.S. Department of Agriculture, FOB Northeast, has been steadily increasing:

1977	17.3 cents
1978	20.8 cents
1979	23.2 cents
1980	41.0 cents
1981	36.1 cents

Three other raw materials are important. The company is the largest domestic user of almonds, using only almonds grown in California. The price of almonds doubled in 1979 due to a poor California crop in 1978, and have remained high despite a good 1979 California crop. Marginal crops in the rest of the world kept prices high. In 1980, the peanut crop in the United States was poor, causing significant price increases. The supply of peanuts is expected to be low in 1981, but Hershey did not expect any problem obtaining enough for production. The price of milk has also increased greatly in recent years; both milk and peanut prices are affected by various Federal Marketing Orders and by U.S. Department of Agriculture subsidy programs.

More expensive cacao beans, sugar, almonds, peanuts, and milk have forced Hershey to raise prices. The sizes of various products have also been modified. Below are the price/size adjustments for Hershey's Standard Milk Chocolate Bar since 1949:

Common Retail Price: 5 Cents

1949	1 oz.
March 1954	$^7/_8$ oz.
June 1955	1 oz.
January 1958	$^7/_8$ oz.
August 1960	1 oz.
September 1963	$^7/_8$ oz.
September 1965	1 oz.
September 1966	$^7/_8$ oz.
May 1968	$^3/_4$ oz.
Discontinued	11-24-69

Common Retail Price: 10 Cents

November 1969	$1^1/_2$ ozs.
March 1970	$1^3/_8$ ozs.
January 1973	1.26 ozs.
Discontinued	1-1-74

Common Retail Price: 15 Cents

January 1974	1.4 ozs.
May 1974	1.2 ozs.
September 1974	1.05 ozs.
January 1976	1.2 ozs.
Discontinued	12-31-76

Common Retail Price: 20 Cents

December 1976	1.35 ozs.
April 1977	1.2 ozs.
July 1977	1.05 ozs.
Discontinued	12-1-78

Common Retail Price: 25 Cents

December 1978	1.2 ozs.
March 1980	1.05 ozs.

Source: Company documents.

Friendly Restaurants use many raw materials. Rising prices of items such as beef, cream, condensed milk, whole milk, and sugar and corn syrup in the late 70s forced Friendly to raise menu prices. Pasta is made from durum wheat flour grown almost exclusively in North

Dakota. Poor weather conditions in 1980 sharply reduced the quality of the durum wheat crop, resulting in a 60 percent increase in price. Hershey was forced to raise prices twice in 1980. Coffee prices declined in 1980 from 1979 levels, down from historic highs earlier in the decade, and the Cory Division was able to reduce its prices during 1980.

Hershey uses price concessions to induce its distributors to carry its products. The company hopes that the distributor will feature the item because the price reductions provide them with a higher-than-normal profit.

TOWARD THE FUTURE

As Hershey Foods Corporation moved into 1982, company executives decided to thoroughly review past performance and strategy, and use these assessments to chart the future direction of the firm. Several aspects of the company's operations were chosen for appraisal:

1. Have the company's diversification efforts been effective in accomplishing its objectives? What should Hershey's future diversification strategy be?
2. How effective has Hershey's advertising been? How much emphasis should the company place on advertising in the future?
3. How effective has the company's distribution strategy been? What changes would be appropriate in the future?
4. Has Hershey been able to reduce the risks which appear to be inherent in the kinds of products it sells? What can be done to reduce these risks?
5. How viable is the company's corporate organization? What are its strengths and weaknesses? What modifications are needed?

| *Nike, Inc.*

Robert C. Wirthlin
Anthony P. Schlichte
both of Butler University

In June 1984, the senior management met to review the events of the past fiscal year that ended May 31. Although the company reported a net income of $40.6 million, this represented a 20 percent decrease from the previous year despite a 6 percent increase in revenues. All were aware of the problems facing the company. The athletic-footwear industry had become keenly competitive, forcing price reductions. In addition, the domestic market for athletic shoes was decreasing. Consumers were changing their preference from the athletic look to a more fashionable and traditional style. Furthermore, the demand for running shoes, the company's leading revenue producer, was declining very rapidly. This was partly due to demographics. The industry's primary market was the baby boomers born between 1946 and 1964. With that market saturated and its leading-edge age approaching 40, the industry was hard-pressed to maintain the substantial early growth it enjoyed.

At the beginning of fiscal 1984, Nike was caught in this changing market with an all-time-high inventory of 22 million pairs of shoes. Although by year end the inventory level had been reduced to 17 million pairs, this buildup was costly. The effects of price cutting, slow-moving merchandise, and inventory write-downs to market value decreased the gross margin by 3.5 percent. This translated into $32 million of additional costs.

No one was happy. Fiscal 1984 was the first year since the company was founded that had failed to produce an increase in net income.

COMPANY HISTORY

In 1958, Phil Knight was an aspiring miler at the University of Oregon. His coach, Bill Bowerman, was considered by many to be the premier track coach in the United States. In 1960, Knight went on to Stanford's Graduate School of Business. While fellow students were doing their market research papers on computers and electronics, Knight was only interested in running. His research paper asserted that there was an enormous potential in the United States for athletic shoes. Furthermore, he concluded the Japanese could become a dominant market force in athletic shoes. Following his graduation in 1962, Knight celebrated with a trip around the world. He stopped in Japan and placed his first shoe order with Onitsuka, which manufactured Tiger running shoes. When his shipment of 300 pairs of shoes finally arrived in December 1963, nearly 14 months after the order, Knight took the shoes to his former coach for his opinion. Bowerman was enthusiastic and joined Knight in a partnership called Blue Ribbon Shoes (BRS). They each put up $500 to order more shoes. In the first year, BRS sold 1300 pairs of shoes for a total revenue of $8000. Within two years, BRS had opened its first office and warehouse in Tigard, a Portland suburb. Then in 1969, Knight resigned his accounting position with Coopers and Lybrand to devote his full time to the company. Now employing 20, and having three retail outlets, BRS attained $100,000 in revenues.

In 1972, a dispute over their distribution agreement led to litigation between BRS and Onitsuka. BRS launched a new shoe line under its own label. The name Nike, after the Greek goddess of victory, was chosen. Bowerman was selected as head track and field coach for the U.S. Olympic team. Several members of his team wore Nike shoes in competition. Sales for the first year were $1.90 million.

In 1973, John Anderson won the Boston Marathon wearing Nike shoes. Ilie Nastase, playing in Nike, was ranked number one tennis player in the world. One year later, the company opened its first manufacturing facility in Exeter, New Hampshire. Nike also expanded its sales overseas to Australia. Worldwide revenues reached $4.8 million.

In 1975, taking a clue from his traditional Sunday breakfast, Bill Bowerman created the first "waffle" sole using raw rubber and a kitchen waffle iron. The resulting studded design revolutionized running by providing a high-traction, lightweight, durable outsole. This invention was patented and the design was quickly grasped by the emerging jogging boom. Sales for the year shot to $8.3 million.

In 1977, Nike made a commitment to the amateur sports by organizing Athletics West (AW). This club was the first track and field training club for Olympic contenders. AW members included Mary Decker, Alberto Salazar, Willie Banks, and Carl Davis. In the same year, Nike established factory sources in Taiwan and Korea. Nike shoes were sold for the first time in Asia. Sales more than doubled over 1976 to $28.7 million.

By 1979, Nike had signed agreements with distributors in all European countries. In that same year, Nike shoes became the most popular athletic shoes in the United States and Canada. In 1980, the company went public and offered 2 million shares of common stock. In 1980, the company also signed new manufacturing contracts in Thailand, Malaysia, and the Philippines.

In October 1981, the company formed a 51 percent owned subsidiary in Japan with Nissho Iwai Corporation to market Nike products in Japan. The company continued its explosive growth in sales, and by May 1984, revenues had grown to $919 million. In just 12 years, the company's revenues went from $1.96 million to $919 million and the company was in a strong financial position to continue this growth. (See financial statements, Exhibits 1–3.)

PRODUCTS

The company produces a broad line of athletic shoes for men, women, and children for competitive and recreational wear. The majority of the footwear products are designed for a specific athletic use. However, more and more shoes are being purchased and worn for casual or leisure purposes.

The company also manufactures a line of active-sports apparel including running shoes and shirts, tennis clothing, warmup suits, socks, jackets, athletic bags, and accessories. Apparel and accessories are designed to complement the company's footwear products featuring the "swoosh" design and the Nike trademark.

EXHIBIT 1   Nike, Inc., Consolidated Statement of Income (in thousands except per share data)

	Year Ended May 31		
	1983	*1982*	*1981*
Revenues	$867,212	$693,582	$457,742
Costs and expenses			
Cost of sales	589,986	473,885	328,133
Selling and administrative	132,400	94,919	60,953
Interest	25,646	24,538	17,859
Other expenses	1,057	435	92
	749,089	593,777	407,037
Income before provision for income taxes and minority interest	118,123	99,805	50,705
Provision for income taxes	60,922	50,589	24,750
Income before minority interest	57,201	49,216	25,955
Minority interest	197	180	—
Net income	$ 57,004	$ 49,036	$ 25,955
Net income per common share	$ 1.53	$ 1.37	$ .76
Average number of common and common equivalent shares	37,158	35,708	34,031

EXHIBIT 2 Nike, Inc., Consolidated Balance Sheet (in thousands)

	May 31	
	1983	1982
Assets:		
Current assets	$ 13,038	$ 4,913
Cash		
Accounts receivable, less allowance for doubtful accounts of $3,751		
and $3,877, respectively	151,581	130,438
Inventories	283,788	202,817
Deferred income taxes and purchased tax benefits	10,503	2,145
Prepaid expenses	6,625	5,198
Total current assets	465,535	345,511
Property, plant, and equipment	61,359	41,407
Less accumulated depreciation	21,628	12,485
	39,731	28,922
Other assets	2,762	1,040
	$508,028	$375,473
Liabilities and Shareholders' Equity:		
Current liabilities		
Current portion of long-term debt	$ 2,347	$ 3,936
Notes payable to banks	132,092	112,673
Accounts payable	91,102	74,064
Accrued liabilities	19,021	22,894
Income taxes payable	11,102	19,774
Total current liabilities	255,664	233,341
Long-term debt	10,503	9,086
Commitments and contingencies	—	—
Minority interest in consolidated subsidiary	948	− 86
Redeemable preferred stock	300	300
Shareholders' equity		
Common stock at stated value Class A convertible—18,837 and		
11,976 shares outstanding	225	166
Class B—18,434 and 5,555 outstanding	2,646	1,414
Capital in excess of stated value	77,457	27,020
Unrealized translation gain (loss)	70	(67)
Retained earnings	160,215	103,427
	240,613	131,960
	$508,028	$375,473

Shown in Exhibit 4 is a breakdown of revenues in the United States by product category, and revenues from foreign markets.

The company's products are designed for the high-quality market. At the end of 1984, the company's product line included 235 basic footwear models. Running, basketball, racquet, and children's shoes

EXHIBIT 3 Nike, Inc., Consolidated Statement of Changes in Financial Position (in thousands)

	Year Ended May 31		
	1983	1982	1981
Financial resources were provided by:			
Net income	$ 57,004	$ 49,036	$25,955
Income charges (credits) not affecting working capital			
Depreciation	9,421	5,135	3,774
Minority interest	197	180	—
Other	(188)	194	131
Working capital provided by operations	66,434	54,545	29,860
Net proceeds from sale of class B common stock in October 1982 and December 1980	51,442	—	27,890
Purchased tax benefits becoming current	14,270	—	—
Additions to long-term debt	4,135	4,477	4,392
Disposal of property, plant, and equipment	584	343	134
Proceeds from exercise of stock options	100	—	450
Minority shareholder contribution	—	648	—
	136,965	60,013	62,726
Financial resources were used for:			
Additions to property, plant, and equipment	21,031	18,228	9,914
Purchase of tax benefits	15,277	—	—
Long-term debt becoming current	2,368	4,002	7,049
Additions to other assets	527	161	670
Unrealized loss from translation of statements of foreign operations, including minority interest	31	109	—
Dividends on redeemable preferred stock	30	30	30
	39,264	22,530	17,663
Increase in working capital	$ 97,701	$ 37,483	$45,063

Analysis of Changes in Working Capital

	1983	1982	1981
Increase (decrease) in current assets			
Cash	$ 8,125	$ 3,121	$ (35)
Accounts receivable	21,143	43,202	23,375
Inventories	80,971	82,588	64,288
Deferred income taxes and purchased tax benefits	8,358	845	1,165
Prepaid expenses	1,427	2,711	336
	120,024	132,467	89,129
Increase (decrease) in current liabilities			
Current portion of long-term debt	(1,589)	(2,684)	2,753
Notes payable to banks	19,419	51,483	24,690
Accounts payable	17,038	31,572	5,560
Accrued liabilities	(3,873)	7,493	5,102
Income taxes payable	(8,672)	7,120	5,961
	22,323	94,984	44,066
Increase in working capital	$ 97,701	$ 37,483	$45,063

EXHIBIT 4 Breakdown of Nike's Revenues in the United States and Abroad

	Year Ended May 31[1]							
	1981		1982		1983		1984	
U.S. Revenues								
Footwear								
Running	$149,300	33%	$236,300	34%	$267,600	31%	$240,200	26%
Court								
Basketball	104,500	23	144,400	21	122,400	14	125,100	14
Racquet	60,700	13	58,600	9	62,100	7	81,400	9
Field sports	8,700	2	13,600	2	41,300	5	42,200	5
Other								
Children's	64,300	14	106,100	15	120,800	14	97,100	10
Leisure/other	11,400	2	21,300	3	52,300	6	53,600	6
	398,900	87	580,300	84	666,500	77	639,600	70
Apparel	33,100	7	70,300	10	107,400	12	121,800	13
Total United States	432,000	94	650,600	94	773,900	89	761,400	83
Foreign revenues	25,700	6	43,000	6	93,300	11	158,400	17
Total revenues	$457,700	100%	$693,600	100%	$867,200	100%	$919,800	100%

[1] Dollars in thousands.

were expected to continue to account for the majority of the company's shoe sales in the near future. However, the company planned to continue to place significant emphasis on the development and production of a broader line of leisure shoes.

DOMESTIC SALES AND MARKETING

Nearly 83 percent of the company's sales in fiscal 1984 were made in the United States to approximately 12,000 retail accounts consisting of department stores, shoe stores, sporting good stores, specialty stores, tennis shops, and other retail outlets. During fiscal 1984, no single customer accounted for more than 9.0 percent of the company's sales, and the three largest customers accounted for only 17 percent of sales.

Sales are solicited in the United States by 24 independent regional sales representative firms which are compensated on a commission basis. These firms do not take title to the inventory. Additionally, the company supports it reps with in-house sales personnel. Company sales and credit personnel review all orders and new accounts and are responsible for collecting receivables. Bad-debt losses have been minimal.

The company operates seven Nike retail stores which carry a full line of products. One store carries primarily close-out merchandise.

The company feels these stores are valuable for promotional purposes as well as a training ground for employees.

During 1984, nearly 60 percent of the company shipments were made under the "futures" program. This program, started in 1982, allows dealers to order six months in advance of delivery and be guaranteed that 90 percent of their order will be shipped within 15 days of the requested delivery date at a specified price. Retailers benefit from this program because prices are fixed, promotional activities are planned in advance, and sufficient inventories are assured to meet seasonal peak demands. These orders can be cancelled with penalties.

The company distributes its footwear products in the United States through three large warehouse facilities. The western United States is served from Portland; the East is served from Greenland, New Hampshire; and, the Midwest and south by Memphis, Tennessee. Apparel products are distributed from Beaverton, Oregon, and Memphis, Tennessee.

FOREIGN SALES

Nike products are sold in 50 countries in addition to the United States. In most countries, Nike is represented by independent distributors, several of whom are licensed to manufacture and sell Nike brand products. Licensing arrangements provide for the company's approval of product lines and on-site quality-control inspection.

In larger foreign markets, Nike has become directly responsible for the marketing of its products by opening its own branches and acquiring subsidiaries (Nissho Iwai Corporation to market Nike products in Japan and the acquisition of the Canadian distributorship).

PROMOTION AND ADVERTISING

Since 1972, the company has spent the majority of its annual promotion and advertising budget on having athletes wear and endorse Nike products. Shoes and equipment are provided to outstanding athletes and teams, athletes are hired as consultants, and product endorsements are obtained from leading professional athletes. The company uses this form of promotion to establish product credibility with customers.

The company founded Athletics West in 1972 to provide coaching, training, and financial support for postgraduate athletes. Presently there are 80 athletes in this club. During 1984, the company sponsored or assisted nearly 1,000 road races, marathons, and other sporting events across the United States.

Although the company spends the majority of its advertising budget on promotional activites, it does limited advertising on television and in athletic and trade magazines, and it assists retailers with local advertising. The company supplies dealers with brochures, posters, and other point-of-purchase promotional material.

MANUFACTURING

Nearly 95 percent of the footwear produced for the company is manufactured by 35 foreign suppliers, primarily in South Korea and Taiwan. The remaining portion is manufactured by three contract suppliers in the United States and its own plants in Massachusetts, Ireland, and England. The U.S. facilities produce approximately 100,000 pairs of shoes per month, or roughly 2 percent of the current requirements. U.S. production is concentrated on the most expensive models. In fiscal 1984, South Korea and Taiwanese suppliers accounted for 63 percent and 15 percent respectively of total footwear production for the company. The company also obtains production from contract suppliers in the People's Republic of China, Spain, Yugoslavia, Malaysia, the Philippines, Brazil, and Italy. No single supplier accounted for more than 12 percent of that 1984 production.

All foreign and domestic contract manufacturing is performed to detailed specifications furnished by the company. The company closely monitors such production to ensure compliance with such specifications. Foreign operations are subject to the usual risks such as revaluation of currency, export duties, quotas, restrictions on the transfer of funds, and political instability. To date, Nike has not been materially affected by any such risk. However, the company has developed alternative sources of supply for such products.

Since 1972, Nissho Iwai American Corporation (NIAC), a subsidiary of Nissho Iwai Corporation, a large Japanese trading company, has performed significant financing and export-import services for the company. The company purchases through NIAC substantially all of the athletic shoes and apparel it acquires from overseas suppliers for sale in the United States. The company's agreements with NIAC expired on September 30, 1985.

COMPETITION

There are approximately 50 companies worldwide that produce athletic footwear and apparel. The industry has experienced substantial growth the past ten years and is becoming increasingly competitive. Adidas is the leader in worldwide sales. Nike is the largest producer in the

EXHIBIT 5   Income Statements for Two of Nike's Competitors

	Year Ended December 31		10-Month Period Ended December 31,
	1984	*1983*	*1982*
Converse Inc.			
Net revenues	$265,598,000	$209,470,000	$150,844,000
Cost of sales	179,730,000	137,580,000	97,824,000
Gross profit on sales	85,868,000	71,890,000	53,020,000
Other expenses			
Marketing, general and administrative	52,910,000	44,043,000	27,548,000
Research and development	2,107,000	1,588,000	1,031,000
Income from operations	30,851,000	26,259,000	24,441,000
Other income, net	842,000	236,000	141,000
Interest expense	(7,581,000)	(7,601,000)	(10,207,000)
Income before income taxes	24,112,000	18,894,000	14,375,000
Income taxes	9,645,000	7,784,000	6,564,000
Net income	14,467,000	11,110,000	7,811,000
Less cumulative preferred dividends and amortization	—	(309,000)	(707,000)
Net income available to common stockholders	$ 14,467,000	$ 10,801,000	$ 7,104,000
Net income per common share	$ 2.54	$ 2.07	$ 1.63
	1984	*1983*	*1982*
Hyde Athletic Industries			
Net sales	$ 47,313,237	$ 44,556,716	$ 36,877,503
Costs and expenses			
Cost of sales	28,176,286	27,381,355	23,663,233
Depreciation and amortization	487,516	316,948	279,813
Selling and administrative expenses	13,160,584	10,557,907	6,939,945
Total costs and expenses	41,824,386	38,256,210	30,882,991
Operating income	5,488,851	6,300,506	5,994,512
Interest expense	890,104	492,656	1,065,482
Income before income taxes	4,598,747	5,807,850	4,929,030
Income taxes	1,917,721	2,944,111	2,440,000
Net income	$ 2,681,026	$ 2,863,739	$ 2,489,030
Net income per share of common stock based on the average number of shares outstanding	$ .92	$ 1.06	$ 1.01

United States and second largest in the world and estimates it has 30 percent of the worldwide market. Although there are no comprehensive independent trade statistics, Nike believes its running, basketball, and tennis shoes have the highest sales volume in the United States (see Exhibit 5).

RESEARCH AND DEVELOPMENT

Nike has always relied heavily on its technical competence and innovation and feels its success will depend on continued emphasis on research and development for the elimination of injury and for performance maximization of its products. Many of the 150 people employed in R&D hold degrees in biochemics, exercise physiology, engineering,

EXHIBIT 6

Name	Age	Title	Years with Nike	Background
Philip Knight	46	Chairman and president	14	Accountant
William J. Bowerman	73	Vice chairman and vice president	14	Track coach
Robert L. Woodell	40	Executive vice president	14	Salesman
Delbert J. Hayes	49	Executive vice president	9	Accountant
Henry C. Carsh	45	Vice president and manager—international operations	7	Accountant
David P. C. Chang	54	Vice president—foreign production	3	Architect
Neil Goldschmidt	43	Vice president—international marketing	3	Former secretary of treasury under President Carter and Portland mayor
John E. Jaqua	63	Secretary	14	Attorney
Gary D. Kurtz	38	Treasurer	3	Banker
James L. Manns	46	Vice president—finance	5	Accountant
Ronald E. Nelson	41	Vice president—apparel division	8	Accountant
George E. Porter	53	Vice president—footwear division	2	Accountant
Robert J. Strasser	36	Vice president—marketing and planning	8	Attorney
Richard H. Werschkul	38	Vice president and counsel	1	Attorney

industrial design, and chemistry. The company also utilizes advisory boards, which include coaches, athletes, trainers, equipment managers, podiatrists, and orthopedists to review designs and concepts aimed at improving shoes.

TRADEMARKS AND PATENTS

The Nike trademark and "swoosh" design are two of the company's most valuable assets. Both are registered in over 70 countries.

The company has an exclusive worldwide license to manufacture and sell footwear using the patented Nike-Air midsole unit. This unit utilizes pressurized gas encapsulated in a polyurethane midsole. The company also has a number of patents covering component features used in various athletic shoes.

MANAGEMENT AND EMPLOYEES

Nike management in 1984 is shown in Exhibit 6. Nike employs 4,100 people. Approximately 1,300 are engaged in footwear production, 600 in apparel operations, 375 in sales and marketing, 100 in retail stores, 500 in footwear warehousing, 150 in product research and development, 600 in foreign operations, and 475 in general management and administration. Except for 120 employees in Ireland, none of the company's employees is represented by a union.

The American Express Company

James R. Lang

Virginia Polytechnic Institute and State University

By the middle of 1981, the finance-related and insurance industries were in periods of rapid change and turmoil. Each industry was facing problems resulting from general economic conditions and intensified competition. The basis for competition was changing as companies departed traditional and historic roles, new and powerful entrants threatened, and technological innovation was obvious everywhere. As an active participant in these industries, American Express was also experiencing a year of transition and challenge. James D. Robinson III, chief executive officer, offered his view of the future:

> By 1990, you'll have a stockbroker in California, a banker in New York, an insurance agency in Maryland, and a realtor jetting between Chicago and Boston. All your purchases will be on the American Express Card, of course. And within the decade you'll have the option of banking by mail or by cable television.[1]

The challenge for American Express is to chart a course to this vision.

CREDIT CARD INDUSTRY

The first credit cards in the United States were issued in the 1920s by oil companies as a means of promoting brand loyalty and providing a billing convenience for traveling customers. Use of cards was expanded slightly during the 1930s when department stores issued cards to their charge account customers and major oil companies developed reciprocal billing arrangements. This relatively limited use of cards was abruptly changed in the early 1950s when the credit card industry was born with the formation of Diners Club. Diners Club began in February 1950 with 22 restaurants and 200 cardholders. After a first year loss of $158,730, Diners Club earned a $61,222 profit in its second year and

---

[1]Thomas O'Donnell, "The Tube, the Card, the Ticker, and Jim Robinson," *Forbes*, May 25, 1981.

then continually expanded the scope of its operations during the 1950s. American Express entered the industry in 1958 and took over industry leadership in 1959 by acquiring two smaller competitors. Carte Blanche became industry competitive in 1959 when Hilton Hotels added establishments outside of the Hilton chain to its credit card system.

Banks entered the industry in the late 1950s when the first bank credit card was issued by Franklin National Bank. Through the 1960s the bank cards grew by offering cards to a wider segment of the population and by allowing use for goods and services beyond travel and entertainment.

By 1980 there were over 600 million credit cards in circulation in the United States and it was estimated that there would be 1 billion cards worldwide by 1985. Americans are by far the greatest users of credit cards, holding about 82 percent of all cards. As of 1978 American consumers held an average of 5.2 cards and business persons an average of 11.3 cards each. Of the 1979 total installment borrowing of $300 billion in the United States, about $100 billion was through credit cards.

In spite of their early entry in the industry, travel and entertainment (T&E) cards have not maintained a significant share in terms of number of cards in circulation. In 1980 T&E accounted for one half of the cards in existence, with Sears Roebuck & Co. the single largest issuer. In 1978 Sears alone had 47 million cards in circulation. The proportion of retailers' cards has been on the decline, however, as smaller retailers are being absorbed by conglomerates which tend to favor the use of bank credit cards. In 1979 there were about 115 million bank cards in circulation and that number is expected to increase to 255 million by 1985. Oil companies maintained about 22 percent of the cards outstanding in 1980 and all other types (airlines, etc.) had about 3 percent.

Bank Cards

In 1980 banks held about 22 percent of the number of cards outstanding, but were by far the most aggressive segment of the industry. Traditionally, the bank cards have been differentiated by the fact that they extend a line of credit to the cardholder, whereas the T&E cards demand payment on request each month. Young families, families with children, and families headed by those without a college degree are most likely to use the credit features of cards, while others use the cards primarily to facilitate transactions. In the mid- to late 1970s the use of the credit feature grew rapidly. In 1978 for instance, there was $23 billion of credit outstanding on bank cards, which was a 33 percent increase over the previous year. By the late 1970s, interest charges provided 70 percent of the bank's credit card earnings, which was far greater than the percentages received from merchant discounts (about 2 percent of the amount purchased) and fees. Recently, however, the costs of financing receivables have increased markedly and many banks have begun to charge annual fees of $10 to $15 or transactions fees to offset these costs. Transaction fees are typically 12 cents per transaction. In 1980 about one half of all bank card holders paid either annual or transaction fees. In 1979 there were practically none. In other moves to combat higher financing costs, some banks have been moving their operations to states that allow higher than the standard 18 percent interest rate.

In spite of these changes to improve position, most banks lost money on their credit card operations in late 1979 and 1980. More and more customers were paying off their accounts within the interest-free grace period. In 1980 the banks seemed to suffer no significant drop-off of business because of the institution of fees, but the proportion of billings incurring no interest approached 50 percent. This pay-off phenomenon has led many banks to conclude that they are not selling credit so much as convenience or "transfer of value." This conclusion has led the banks to consider offering other transfer of value instruments such as debit cards[2] and travelers' checks as potential services. For instance, bank cards have teamed up with Western Union's emergency money order service to allow callers to wire up to $300 to any of 8,100 offices in the United States and to have the amount charged to their credit cards. It is generally felt that if consumers should continue to decrease their amounts of credit card debt, the competition will intensify and bank cards will move more aggressively into travelers' checks and other segments of the travel and entertainment segment. In fact, surveys already show that more consumers are using bank cards than are using T&E cards for restaurant checks and hotel bills. As of 1978, Visa and MasterCard claimed 2.5 million outlets accepting cards; Diners Club, 400,000; American Express, 350,000; and Carte Blanche, 250,000.

The two strongest competitors among bank cards are Visa and MasterCard. While Visa has recently overtaken MasterCard as the leader in worldwide volume and number of holders, MasterCard still retains an edge in the United States. Both provide debit cards and are venturing into the travelers' check business.

Visa changed its name from BankAmericard in 1977 in order to shed its national identity with its political connotations and to project more of a worldwide image. The number of Visa cardholders increased

---

[2]Debit cards operate similarly to credit cards except than when the bank is notified of a sale, it immediately deducts the amount from an account balance that the consumer maintains with the bank, much in the same manner as with a checking account.

dramatically during the late 1970s with over 70 million by 1979. The volume of Visa transactions also has increased rapidly (91 percent in 1977–79 period), primarily from retail stores and restaurants.

Visa presents increasingly formidable competition in the credit card industry, displaying corporate agility that fostered innovations such as the debit card (800,000 accounts in 1980), the single, trendy name, and strong initiatives in foreign markets. Although Visa's management sees travelers' checks as a regression into paper processing (which runs counter to their electronic processing strength), they have aggressively entered the travelers' check market. Depending upon cooperation with Barclay's (presently fourth-largest issuer of travelers' checks), Visa's business has been growing at a 15 percent annual rate. In 1980 Visa had 8 percent of the U.S. market and was expecting a 40 percent share by 1985. As of 1980 about 90 percent of the checks processed were, in fact, Barclay's. The largest bank to build Visa travelers' checks sales from scratch was First National Bank of Chicago. As of 1980 that bank had sold $50 million in checks. Visa's plan for the travelers' check business is to allow participating banks to place their own names on the checks. Visa hopes this approach will lure banks who have been selling American Express checks.

MasterCard, with its 65 million worldwide cardholders in 1979, has been fighting the Visa challenge with larger advertising outlays (40 percent increase in 1979), a name change from Master Charge to MasterCard, debit cards, and a delayed venture into travelers' checks. The travelers' check delay was caused by a legal roadblock set up by Citibank, a member of the MasterCard system, who already held 12 percent of the world travelers' check market. Along with Visa, the MasterCard system is large enough and integrated enough to provide economies of scale advantages in authorization and interchange procedures.

Travel and Entertainment Cards

In 1978 it was estimated that $385 billion was spent on domestic and international travel and that by 1988 the amount spent will be $755 billion. American Express is by far the largest T&E card company, with 11.9 million cardholders in 1980. The American Express card is held by more than half of the country's families who earn more than $25,000 annually. They engage in heavy advertising campaigns and frequently cosponsor ads with hotels and restaurants that accept their card.

Diners Club intensified their marketing efforts in the late 1970s with large increases in marketing budgets. In 1979 Diners Club claimed 2.5 million cardholders, with about 60 percent of the holders residing outside of the United States. Carte Blanche, with 800,000 holders in 1979, serves the affluent, has snob appeal, and turned down 75 percent of its 40,000 monthly applicants in 1978. Acquired from AVCO by Citicorp in 1979, Carte Blanche was generally thought to be in need of new marketing emphasis in order to survive.

In contrast to bank cards, which credit merchants' accounts on the same day an invoice is received, T&E cards generally cause the merchants to wait several days for payments. T&E cards also charge a higher discount to the merchants, typically 3.5 to 4 percent of the price of purchase. American Express, for example, offers retailers the option of being paid in from 1 to 30 days after receipt, with the discount rate correspondingly lower as the period is extended.

Travelers' Checks

Closely related to the T&E credit card segment is the travelers' check industry. Started in 1891 by American Express, which maintains 60 percent of the market, the major competitors are Bank of America, Citibank, Barclays, and Thomas Cook. In 1978, 735 million travelers' checks were sold at a value of $25 billion. The five major U.S. and British issuers earned an estimated total of $239 million. In the five-year period 1974–79, the industry sales grew 120 percent, and by 1979 worldwide sales had reached $30 billion.

Most income on travelers' checks is made not on the nominal fee charged (usually 1 percent of face value), but on the "float"—that is, on checks which are purchased and paid for, but not yet cashed. The average float period for travelers' checks is about two months. The companies can then invest this cash for two months until the checks are cashed. American Express, for instance, had about $2.3 billion in travelers' check float in 1979. Thus, industry experts indicate that it is unlikely that a company can be profitable in travelers' checks with an annual volume of less than $2 billion.

PROPERTY/CASUALTY INSURANCE INDUSTRY

In contrast to the concentration of the credit card industry, the property/casualty (P-C) insurance industry has a large number of competitors, with 200 companies that have written over $40 million in premiums in 1980. Many, but not all, of the leading P-C companies are also leaders in life insurance (see Exhibit 1). Even within the P-C segment, not all companies offer full lines of P-C insurance services. The importance of the various insurance lines in the P-C segment is shown in Exhibit 2.

EXHIBIT 1 Leading Property/Casualty Companies and Groups (1980 net premiums in thousands)

	Rank	Total P-C Company Premiums	Life Insurance Premiums	Total Premium Volume	Rank	Percent Increase 1 Year	Percent Increase 5-Year Compound
State Farm	1	8,011,787	551,365	8,563,152	3	10.83	19.10
Allstate	2	5,270,426	240,300	5,515,454	6	9.89	12.27
Aetna Life & Casualty	3	4,558,426	3,939,761	10,284,080	1	3.72	16.05
Travelers	4	2,888,253	2,526,244	7,128,640	4	9.05	5.64
Liberty Mutual	5	2,867,423	39,677	2,911,727	10	4.29	18.47
Continental Insurance	6	2,822,595	44,886	2,883,049	11	6.25	7.61
Hartford Fire	7	2,661,964	301,050	3,217,105	9	4.73	9.83
Farmers Insurance	8	2,552,756	133,413	2,719,557	13	7.32	20.69
INA	9	2,550,211	458,050	3,349,209	8	6.08	9.20
Fireman's Fund	10	2,350,283	75,354	2,525,217	17	2.43	12.94
U.S. Fidelity & Guaranty	11	2,043,653	48,008	2,093,985	20	2.63	16.40
Nationwide	12	1,951,339	574,703	2,590,320	15	10.95	18.21
Kemper	13	1,689,683	363,964	2,053,740	21	5.48	12.55
Home Insurance	14	1,689,386	45,964	1,814,049	22	4.04	14.26
Crum and Forester	15	1,620,970	—	1,620,970	25	2.38	13.07
St. Paul	16	1,520,073	96,832	1,682,636	23	9.00	14.18
CNA	17	1,418,916	413,262	2,469,170	18	8.61	16.20
American International	18	1,374,564	203,950	1,632,035	24	10.34	24.82
Chubb	19	1,142,373	88,380	1,281,117	27	6.21	9.31
Commercial Union	20	1,115,897	20,939	1,137,437	28	15.19	8.58
Prudential of America	21	1,023,892	5,847,490	9,681,087	2	11.82	28.79
Connecticut General	22	1,011,796	629,059	2,872,063	12	-1.76	10.88
Royal Insurance	23	957,059	8,890	956,949	35	3.27	7.55
American Financial	24	898,823	177,897	1,079,999	29	9.64	4.82
Reliance	25	875,799	107,299	1,036,609	30	-3.67	10.48

Source: Adapted from *Best's Review: Property/Casualty Insurance Edition,* June 1981.

EXHIBIT 2 Property/Casualty Insurance Industry (premium distribution by line)

	Total Premiums*	Percent of Total	Gain in Premiums*	Loss Ratio† 1980	1979	1978	1977
Fire	2,887,770	3.0	−19,425	51.6	51.6	47.5	51.0
Allied lines	1,673,619	1.7	44,043	69.1	67.9	57.1	46.6
Farmowners multi-peril	594,335	0.6	60,316	76.5	61.4	60.3	61.0
Homeowners multi-peril	10,012,854	10.4	982,901	67.1	61.5	53.5	53.1
Commercial multi-peril	7,663,589	7.9	320,269	55.4	52.9	44.4	42.9
Earthquake	53,558	0.1	11,934	5.0	1.8	1.9	.9
Ocean marine	1,015,670	1.1	74,631	87.9	82.5	66.1	60.8
Inland marine	2,744,061	2.8	383,791	68.9	58.1	51.6	49.1
Group A&H	1,853,362	1.9	143,767	80.8	76.4	77.5	78.2
All other A&H	655,389	0.7	1,704	64.2	62.5	62.4	60.2
Worker's compensation	15,743,510	16.3	1,411,445	70.4	75.3	77.9	74.1
Total miscellaneous liability:	9,408,956	9.7	−148,140	60.9	55.4	50.6	40.4
Medical malpractice	1,491,403	1.5	85,412	82.6	75.3	60.6	41.8
Other liability	7,917,553	8.2	−233,552	57.1	51.6	48.7	40.1
Private passenger auto liability:	18,564,090	19.2	1,188,824	67.6	66.4	64.7	63.4
No fault	2,170,962	2.2	116,823	78.3	74.0	76.7	78.3
Other liability	16,393,128	17.0	1,072,001	66.2	65.4	63.1	61.5
Commercial auto liability:	4,936,684	5.1	136,871	69.0	66.4	61.7	57.9
No fault	154,251	0.2	−9,769	71.1	62.7	60.3	64.9
Other liability	4,782,433	4.9	146,640	68.9	66.5	61.7	57.7
Private passenger auto physical damage	13,188,141	13.6	1,161,405	64.9	68.7	65.2	61.6
Commercial auto physical damage	2,726,160	2.8	112,358	59.4	59.6	55.4	53.2
Aircraft	389,376	0.4	71,892	82.3	78.6	101.0	63.3
Fidelity	399,686	0.4	18,517	48.1	44.8	55.2	56.0
Surety	1,000,732	1.0	98,180	46.1	33.2	43.5	36.3
Glass	31,666	0.0	−972	54.1	50.6	47.8	46.6
Burglary & theft	125,653	0.1	−1,831	37.3	36.6	25.8	26.4
Boiler & machinery	377,519	0.4	8,908	49.4	40.4	31.9	31.7
Credit	79,229	0.1	8,840	56.7	35.1	37.9	38.7
Miscellaneous	584,253	0.6	−54,299	54.3	85.2	46.7	46.2
Totals	96,709,863	100.0	6,015,930	65.5	64.3	60.8	57.7

*Dollars in thousands.

†Loss ratio = $\dfrac{\text{Losses incurred}}{\text{Premiums earned} - \text{Dividends}}$

Source: Adapted from *Best's Review: Property/Casualty Insurance Edition,* July 1981.

A historical characteristic of the insurance business is the underwriting cycle. The cycle affects profitability of insurance companies through the relationship between premium pricing and claims costs. At the peak of the cycle, competition is intense and prices are forced to a low level. When claims begin to come in at a level higher than provided for in the reserves, losses occur. At this point there is a shakedown of sorts, with some companies dropping from the competition in their less profitable segments and the remaining companies raising their premiums.

The overall industry growth rate has slowed from 10.7 percent in 1980. This slowing of premium growth rate is indicative of another trough in the underwriting cycle and stiff price competition. In 1980 the top 100 companies averaged an underwriting loss of 3.53 percent of earned premiums (after dividends to policy holders). This loss totaled $2.8 billion for the industry. The forecasts for 1981 indicate that it could be even more competitive, with worse results than 1980. Most insurance companies have been able to offset underwriting losses with investment income. *Best's* reported, however, that 5 of the top 100 firms were not, in fact, able to offset underwriting losses in 1980. Some industry experts predicted that this pressure, following the 1973–75 trough by only five years, may force weaker firms into insolvency.

The use of investment income to offset underwriting losses has kept the industry profitable, exhibiting a strong capital surplus in spite of the downturn in the cycle (see Exhibit 3). The increasing dependence of companies on investment income is shown dramatically in Exhibit 4 and may have permanently changed the nature of the insurance business. Some analysts feel that the ability to depend on investment

---

EXHIBIT 3   Summary of Five-Year Industry Results ($ billions)

Year	Premiums Written	Rate of Increase (percent)	Pretax Underwriting Profits*	Capital Gains	Surplus
1976	$ 60.4	21.9%	$ −2.2	$ 2.0	$24.6
1977	72.4	19.8	1.1	−0.8	29.3
1978	81.6	12.8	1.3	0.5	35.2
1979	90.1	10.3	−1.3	2.3	42.8
1980	96.3	6.9	−3.4	4.8	52.3
Total	400.8	14.3	−4.5		

*After dividends.

Source: Best's Review: Property/Casualty Insurance Edition, September 1981.

EXHIBIT 4   Underwriting and Investment Income Growth Trends

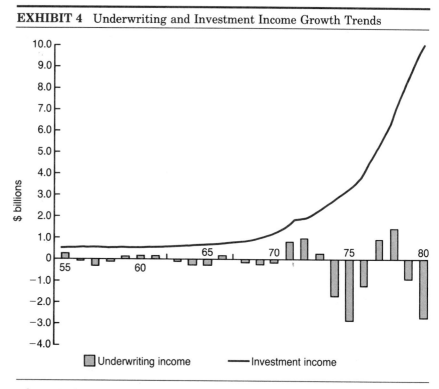

Source: *Best's Review: Property/Casualty Insurance Edition*, September 1981.

income will delay the normal shakeout of unprofitable lines and companies and will prolong the present trough much longer than usual.

Given the prospect of extended competitive pricing, attention to cost reduction may be one of the keys to survival. The current trends in the industry are summarized in *Best's* as follows:

1. As product and service distinctiveness becomes more difficult to maintain, insurance is taking on the aspects of a commodity game where low-cost producers are winners.
2. Competitive pricing is assuming growth importance.
   a. Competition from major new entrants is forcing insurers to offer a competitive price.
   b. Independent agencies are undergoing structural changes that are increasing price competition.
   c. Customers are becoming more price conscious as insurance costs rise.
3. As competition increases among all types of insurers, companies are seeking new revenue avenues such as a fee-based administration, loss control, and claim services.

4. Since price increases and premium growth are not keeping up with inflation, primarily because of competition, companies with uncompetitive expense ratios[3] may pay a substantial penalty for their inefficiency.[4]

Among the suggestions provided for increasing expense ratios are the following:

1. Programs to increase productivity.
2. Investment in automated systems.
3. Delegation of expense management responsibilities to branches.
4. Building expense accountability into the reward systems.

AMERICAN EXPRESS COMPANY

American Express was founded in 1850 and boasts of 114 years of uninterrupted profitability. The chairman of the board and chief executive officer is James D. Robinson III, who succeeded Harold L. Clark in 1977. In the 17 years of Clark's tenure, American Express revenues grew from $77 million to $3.4 billion in 1977. Clark ran the company with a very personal style of management that minimized bureaucratic controls and allowed a great deal of latitude to the division heads. He also recognized the importance of good relationships with banks to the success of American Express's business and used these contacts to build the business. When he left the company, four of the six largest banks were represented on the American Express Board of Directors.

Robinson, who has been at American Express since 1970, has indicated that "our prime objective is to provide, directly with banks, the widest variety of consumer financial services available from any single source." The transition from Clark to Robinson was orderly and gradual, with Clark maintaining active company involvement for some time after the official transfer of duties in 1977. Although Clark and Robinson are both conservative in financial matters, differences in their management styles have become apparent. American Express has evolved into a more highly structured organization. Along with Roger Morely (who succeeded him as president), Robinson implemented a rigorous system of planning and control, which included not only annual plans, but also divisional level monthly forecasts. Morely was

---

[3]Expense ratio $= \dfrac{\text{Operating costs}}{\text{Premiums earned}}$

[4]William F. Kinder, "A Look at the Leaders: Has the Game Changed?" *Best's Review: Property/Casualty Insurance Edition 82* (September 1981), p. 132.

replaced as president in 1979 by Alva Way, formerly the chief financial officer at General Electric. Among the qualities in Way that were found attractive by Robinson were his abilities in strategic planning, data processing, and communications. Observers feel that all of this organizational emphasis has paid off in the form of significant improvements in the coordination among the divisions within the last few years.

A major part of American Express's growth has been through acquisition. In 1968 American Express acquired Fireman's Fund Insurance, the nation's ninth largest property-liability insurer. In 1972 the company bought 25 percent interest in Donaldson, Lufkin and Jenrett, but sold the interest in 1975 at a $23 million loss. Within Robinson's first three years, American Express attempted to make four acquisitions: Walt Disney Productions, Book-of-the-Month Club, Philadelphia Life Insurance, and McGraw-Hill. The company's recent acquisitions are listed in Exhibit 5, the most significant and most recent being the merger with Shearson Loeb Rhoades.

As of early 1981, American Express was organized into four major business areas: Travel Services Group, Warner Amex Cable Services, International Banking Services, and Insurance Services. The company had assets of $19.7 billion, 44,000 employees, 1,000 travel offices, and 77 international banking and investment offices. Total revenues for 1980 were $5.5 billion with a net income of $376 million. In 1980, dividends were increased from 45 to 50 cents per share, the sixth increase in five years. The consolidated financial statements are shown in Exhibit 6 and contributions of the various segments are summarized in Exhibit 7. The scope of the company's international operations is shown in Exhibit 8.

EXHIBIT 5

Acquisition	*Date*
American Express Direct Response	April 1979
Warner Amex Cable Communications (joint venture)	December 1979
First Data Resources	January 1980
Southern Guaranty Insurance Company	September 1980
Food and Wine magazine	September 1980
Mitchell Beazley Ltd.	November 1980
WATS Marketing of America	December 1980
Interstate Group of Insurance Companies	December 1980
New England Bank Card Association	March 1981
Shearson Loeb Rhoades	Awaiting approval

Source: Moody's Bank and Finance Manual.

Travel Services Group

The Travel Services Group includes the card division, travelers' cheque division, travel division, communications division, and the financial institutions services division. Revenues for the group increased 34 percent from 1979 to $1.7 billion in 1980 and net income rose 17 percent to $177 million, which is 47 percent of the company's total earnings.

EXHIBIT 6

AMERICAN EXPRESS COMPANY
Consolidated Income Statement
(in $ million)

	1980	*1979*	*1978*	*1977*	*1976*
Revenues:					
Commissions and fees....................	$ 1,522	$ 1,130	$ 912	$ 738	$ 643
Interest and dividends...................	1,264	1,007	759	580	496
Property-liability and life insurance premiums	2,589	2,450	2,341	2,080	1,771
Other.....................................	129	80	64	48	48
Total revenues	5,504	4,667	4,076	3,446	2,948
Expenses:					
Provisions for losses:					
Insurance.............................	1,545	1,482	1,393	1,255	1,142
Banking, credit, financial paper, other	214	161	127	108	100
Salaries and employee benefits...........	833	685	578	472	421
Interest..................................	870	572	368	249	208
Commissions and brokerage..............	403	371	355	311	275
Occupancy and equipment	247	187	141	125	105
Advertising and promotion..............	187	140	127	84	66
Taxes other than income taxes...........	145	133	120	101	85
Telephone, telegraph, postage............	117	93	83	74	63
Financial paper, forms, and other printed matter	82	65	51	45	35
Claims adjustment service	78	102	116	130	90
Other.....................................	362	285	234	188	162
Total expenses	5,083	4,276	3,693	3,142	2,752
Pretax income	421	391	383	304	196
Income tax provision	45	46	69	52	17
Net operating income.....................	376	345	314	252	179
Gains on sale of investment securities	—	—	—	10	15
Net income	376	345	314	262	194
Net income per share.....................	$ 5.27	$ 4.83	$ 4.39	$ 3.65	$ 2.70

EXHIBIT 6   *(continued)*

AMERICAN EXPRESS COMPANY
Consolidated Income Statement
(in $ million)

	1980	1979	1978	1977	1976
Assets					
Cash	$ 1,069	$ 1,051	$ 844	$ 674	$ 542
Time deposits..............................	1,084	976	891	858	821
Investment securities (cost):					
U.S. government	750	519	435	459	429
State and municipal......................	4,070	4,104	3,808	3,167	2,458
Other bonds and obligations	1,200	1,044	735	720	710
Preferred stocks	$ 57	$ 52	$ 48	$ 48	$ 43
Total*	6,077	5,719	5,026	4,388	3,640
Investment securities (lower of cost or market):					
Preferred stocks	67	83	99	111	95
Common stocks..........................	99	83	72	66	56
Total†	166	166	171	177	151
Investment securities (market):					
Preferred stocks	63	57	50	49	45
Common stocks..........................	$ 783	$ 652	$ 563	$ 507	$ 506
Total‡	846	709	613	556	551
Accounts receivable and accrued interest, less reserves: 1980, $287; 1979, $213; 1978, $171; 1977, $146; 1976, $125.................	4,887	3,597	2,705	2,164	1,754
Loans and discounts, less reserves: 1980, $89; 1979, $82; 1978, $75; 1977, $60; 1976, $52.........................	3,690	3,369	3,320	2,571	2,073
Land, buildings and equipment (cost), less depreciation	448	347	285	263	239
Prepaid policy acquisition expenses	271	244	206	153	130
Other assets	1,171	930	637	542	467
Total assets...............................	$19,709	$17,108	$14,698	$12,346	$10,368

The card division provides corporate and personal credit card services to 11.9 million card holders. The familiar "green card" is marketed not as a credit card implying a line of credit, but as a convenience device. As such, payment-in-full is required on demand, with the exception of certain tour plans and airplane tickets that can be financed over an extended period. There are approximately 6.5 million personal green cardholders who pay an annual fee of $35. About 1.5 million customers

EXHIBIT 6 *(concluded)*

AMERICAN EXPRESS COMPANY
Consolidated Income Statement
(in $ million)

	1980	*1979*	*1978*	*1977*	*1976*
Liabilities					
Customers deposits and credits held by subsidiaries	$ 5,087	$ 4,749	$ 4,192	$ 3,755	$ 3,024
Travelers cheques outstanding	2,542	2,343	2,105	1,859	1,716
Money orders and drafts outstanding	212	289	324	175	140
Accounts payable	1,020	889	785	593	471
Reserves for:					
Property-liability losses and expenses....	2,589	2,364	2,057	1,723	1,363
Unearned premiums	1,008	974	875	792	673
Life and disability policies	259	227	184	147	130
Short-term debt............................	2,302	1,595	1,117	776	555
Long-term debt	1,099	689	479	330	304
Deferred income taxes.....................	161	135	108	117	117
Other..................................	$ 1,244	$ 996	$ 852	$ 711	$ 621
Total liabilities......................	17,523	15,250	13,078	10,978	9,114
Preferred stock	24	25	27	28	30
Common stock (100,000,000 shares authorized, 60 cents par values; 71,274,306 outstanding in 1980)	43	43	43	43	43
Capital surplus	208	204	202	200	201
Net unrealized security gains	208	115	87	78	116
Retained earnings	1,703	1,471	1,261	1,019	864
Total common shareholders' equity........	2,162	1,833	1,593	1,340	1,224
	$19,709	$17,108	$14,698	$12,346	$10,368

*Market: 1980, $4,612; 1979, $5,070; 1978, $4,686; 1977, $4,396; 1976, $3,612.
†Cost: 1980, $191; 1979, $192; 1978, $188; 1977, $188; 1976, $167.
‡Cost: 1980, $531; 1979, $523; 1978, $471; 1977, $433; 1976, $370.

Source: Annual Reports.

hold the "gold cards" at an annual fee of $50. In addition to the charge features, the gold card allows members to finance purchases and to obtain cash through a line of credit that American Express has established with 1,800 participating banks.

The American Express cards are issued in 23 currencies and are honored by 438,000 establishments worldwide. The company has been attempting to build the number of establishments and added about 50,000 new establishments during 1980. Expanding beyond the

EXHIBIT 7 American Express Company, Industry Segments 1980 (in $ millions)

	Travel Related Services	International Banking Services	Insurance Services	Other and Corporate	Adjustments and Eliminations	Consolidated
Revenues	$1,661	$ 930	$2,914	$ 35	$ (36)	$ 5,504
Pretax income before general corporate	236	67	215	16	—	534
General corporate expenses	—	—	—	(113)	—	(113)
Pretax income	236	67	215	(97)	—	421
Net income	177	41	210	(52)	—	376
Assets	$6,877	$6,926	$5,846	$469	$(409)	$19,709

Insurance services comprised of:

	Commercial Lines	Personal Lines	Investment Income	Other	Total	Total Insurance Services
Revenues	$1,788	$626	$282	$218	$2,696	$2,914
Pretax income	$ (37)	$(39)	$277	$ 14	$ 201	$ 215

Source: Annual Report.

EXHIBIT 8   American Express Company, Geographic Operations (in $ millions)

	United States	Europe	Asia/ Pacific	All Other	Adjustments and Eliminations	Consolidated
Revenues	$ 3,953	$ 700	$ 281	$ 604	$ (34)	$ 5,504
Pretax before general corporate expenses	435	21	15	63	—	534
General corporate expenses	(113)	—	—	—	—	(113)
Pretax income	322	21	15	63	—	421
Assets	11,718	3,704	1,774	2,603	(528)	19,271
Corporate assets						438
Total assets						$19,709

Source: Annual Report.

traditional emphasis on food, lodging, and travel is a new emphasis on recruiting prestigious retail and department stores that are likely to provide a high average purchase value.

A major cost of the card business is the financing of card receivables. American Express sells its receivables to Credco, a wholly owned subsidiary. Credco then finances them through commercial paper, equity capital, lines of credit, and long-term debt. In 1980 Credco purchased $19.2 billion of receivables, up from $14.6 billion in 1979. The weighted average interest cost of all Credco financing rose from 8.48 percent in 1978 to 15.7 percent during the first two months of 1980. These increased financing costs have led American Express to tighten its collection policies by reducing the grace period and increasing the finance charge.

American Express cards have achieved a high degree of market penetration in the United States. It is estimated that about 50 percent of the families with incomes greater than $25,000 have the card, as do 64 percent of those with incomes greater than $50,000, and 71 percent with incomes over $75,000. Growth rates in membership have averaged 11 percent over the last three years. A major contribution to the growth rate has come from countries outside of the United States, where the growth rates have been on the order of 25 percent. The number of cardholders outside of the United States was 2.7 million in 1980.

The charge card volume has increased at annual rates of 26 percent (1978), 29 percent (1979), and 32 percent (1980). This positive trend in the face of government controls on credit spending during the period has reinforced management's view that the card is used by consumers as a convenience rather than a credit device. Customers also seem to be attracted to the country-club style of itemizing the bills (a feature not provided by bank cards), the absence of charge limits, check cashing privileges, and the snob appeal of the card.

American Express travelers' checks are sold through 105,000 outlets worldwide, including banks, travel agents, credit unions, etc. Although check buyers are charged a fee of 1 percent of the check's face value, the issuing banks retain about two thirds of that fee. The primary source of travelers' check revenues for American Express is from the "float," or cash, the company controls from checks that have not yet been cashed. This float is invested by American Express in tax-free securities and has provided a significant amount of the company's total revenues in 1980. The average period that the checks are outstanding is two months. An advertising campaign begun in 1979, featuring actor Karl Malden, appealed to consumers to hold unused checks for emergencies—an attempt to extend the float period. The dollar value of the travelers' checks outstanding at year end increased from $1.72 billion to 1976 to $2.5 billion in 1980.

Increasing competitive pressure is being felt in the travelers' check industry, and the growth rate of American Express checks has been slowing over the last three years. Many banks, which sell the majority of the checks, are now selling their own checks under Visa or MasterCard trademarks. American Express also now owns 34 percent of Sociéte Francais du Chèque de Voyage, which began issuing French franc travelers' checks in 1980. American Express has converted all of its French franc business to the new checks.

The travel division offers retail and wholesale (tours) travel services worldwide through 1,000 offices in 126 countries. Services include trip planning, reservations, ticketing, and other incidental services. Revenues for the division are earned through commissions from carriers, hotels, and through fees from customers for incidental services.

American Express reported major changes in the travel division in 1980 including a restructuring of the organization to decentralize along geographic lines. It is anticipated that this move will provide greater flexibility to respond to localized customer needs and opportunities. The company has also been redesigning its tour packages to achieve greater consumer affordability and to eliminate low-revenue programs. A major automation step was taken in 1980 with the implementation of a computerized Travel Information Processing System (TRIPS). TRIPS eventually will become an integrated worldwide information and reservation system.

The financial performance of the travel division has varied over the years, with weak years during the period 1973–76. A stronger revenues showing was reported for 1977, although it is not clear whether the division was profitable. In 1979 and 1980 the division reported losses, this in spite of increased revenues during 1980. The company explained that part of the problem in 1980 was due to slackened demand for tours, lower margins on discount ticket purchasing, and the costs of restructuring the division.

The communications division was formed in January 1980 and has responsibility for American Express Publishing Corporation, Merchandise Sales, American Express Direct Response (ADR), and Mitchell Beazley Limited, a London-based international publishing house.

The division has recently taken over publication of *Food and Wine* magazine and has published *Travel and Leisure* magazine (circulation 925,000) since 1970. A growing emphasis in the division is in direct-mail marketing through Merchandise Sales (revenues increased by 70 percent in 1980), supported by the computer services of ADR. ADR also supplies direct-mail marketing services to outside businesses and to other American Express divisions.

The financial institutions services division was formed in 1980 to consolidate operations relating to the financial community. Within the division is First Data Resources, Inc., a recently acquired provider of data and telephone marketing services to financial institutions and merchandisers. Also included are the Money Order Division and Payment Systems, Inc., which provides information and research in payment systems and electronic funds transfer.

Warner Amex Cable Services

In 1979 American Express paid $175 million for one half interest in Warner Cable Company, which was owned by Warner Communications. The joint venture includes the subsidiaries, Warner Amex Cable Communications, Inc., and Warner Amex Satellite Entertainment Company. American Express sees the cable systems as the technical hardware link for the financial supermarket of the future, which they expect to build around the television screen.

Warner Cable Company owns and operates 141 cable television systems with 736,000 subscribers in 27 states. Among the most recent awards are major franchises in Pittsburgh, Dallas, Cincinnati, and in areas surrounding St. Louis, Boston, Chicago, and Akron. These awards provide the potential for entering 1.1 million households.

Most Warner Amex systems have 12 to 30 channels; however, new systems will provide many more channels. The company has a head start on its competition in two-way cable systems with a system called Qube. Warner Amex spent $20 million to develop the Qube system and it is presently operating in Columbus and in Cincinnati. Although the talkback feature of Qube is used primarily for entertainment purposes such as voting on boxing matches, answering viewer polls, and calling plays for football games, the two-way link is critical for potential home selling, burglar alarm, and financial transaction uses. The Qube system is now offering a retrieval service for business analysis and money management information. A 24-hour security system has recently been added to the Columbus system and is now servicing 2,500 households and businesses.

Warner Amex Satellite Entertainment Company (WASEC) operates five satellite transponders which receive television signals and transmit them over the entire country. The entertainment company offers two major services: "The Movie Channel" and "Nickelodeon." "The Movie Channel" offers 24-hour feature films, while "Nickelodeon" provides varied programming for children and young adults. The company is planning a joint venture with ABC Video Enterprises, Inc., called the Alpha Repertory Television Service which will provide programming devoted to the performing and visual arts. Firm plans also have been made to offer "The Music Channel," which will provide continuous popular music with complementary visual material.

Although a significant amount of risk exists in the cable video industry in that franchises must be awarded by local governments, Warner Amex has proven to be an effective competitor. In 1980 Warner Amex won 1.1 million of the 1.6 million households up for bids in the United States. The company anticipates a need for significant financing to support future expansion efforts. In 1980 they received a $250 million line of credit from a group of banks, but additional capital will be needed in 1981 from external sources, and from the parent companies, where appropriate.

Insurance Services

Fireman's Fund Insurance was founded in 1863 and was acquired by American Express in 1968. Fireman's Fund provides a broad range of insurance services including commercial and personal property liability insurance and life insurance and annuities. Policies are sold in the United States through 11,000 independent agents and brokers. The company also operates overseas through AFIA World Wide insurance, a consortium of United States insurance companies. The Fireman's Fund commercial insurance lines include property, general liability, multiple peril, and worker's compensation, while the personal lines include homeowners' and automobile insurance. Life insurance is offered through Fireman's Fund American Life Insurance Company (FFAL), which sells a full portfolio of life insurance products including ordinary and term life insurance, annuities, group term life insurance, and group accident and health insurance. FFAL also underwrites the supplemental life insurance offered to American Express cardholders.

Fireman's Fund was caught in the insurance underwriting cycle in 1974 when earnings dropped by 17 percent. Even at this amount, the drop was softened since the company called upon $9 million from a "catastrophe reserve" built up during more profitable years. This practice of banking earnings has since been ordered abolished for the entire industry by the Financial Accounting Standards Board, since it was considered to be misleading to investors.

Following the 1974 experience, American Express decided to institute policies to avoid the cycle. They vowed to price more aggressively when premium rates are rising and not to write unprofitable policies by cutting prices when competition stiffens.

Feeling the competitive pressures of the most recent trough in the underwriting cycle, the growth rate in premiums written has been declining as the company has attempted to concentrate on more profitable business in underwriting and investment. In 1980 $2.4 billion in premiums were written, which is a 2.5 percent increase. The increase in 1979 was 4.5 percent and in 1978 the increase was 9.1 percent.

Fireman's Fund gross revenues for 1980 were $2.9 billion, which is a 7.2 percent increase over 1979. A significant contribution to the increase in revenues has been from specialized products in rural markets, commercial group packages, and reinsurance. The company has suffered underwriting losses for the past three years due to higher claims costs which were not offset by premiums revenues. The underwriting losses were $76 million (1980), $53 million (1979), and $13 million (1978). According to *Best*, Fireman's Fund ranked 53rd in the industry in underwriting performance with a loss ratio of 58:1. These losses were offset by investment income, which increased by 21 percent in 1980. Fireman's Fund is attempting to remedy the losses through rate increases, increased deductibles, and obtaining shorter terms so that premiums can be adjusted more frequently.

The underwriting expense ratio has been increasing over the last three years, from 30.8 percent in 1978 to 33.3 percent in 1980. This increase has been attributed to slower premium growth and long-term development spending. The company has been increasing the number of branch offices, automating its network of offices, and has been developing a program of standardization of field office procedures.

International Banking Services

American Express International Banking Company (AEIBC) accounts for 17 percent of American Express's total revenues, 35 percent of the company's total assets, and 11 percent of the net income. AEIBC operates 83 offices in 34 countries, providing commerical banking services, investment banking, wholesale banking, equipment finance, and financial advisory services. It also offers consumer banking service in certain locations, including contracted services on overseas U.S. military bases. The bank does not provide services in the United States except as incidental to its foreign operations. AEIBC is also an active dealer in foreign exchange markets; these activites contributed $35 million in revenues in 1980.

Income from interest increased 21 percent to $197 million in 1980, while commissions fees revenues increased 14 percent to $100 million in 1980. The latter increase reflects an emphasis on the expansion of nonasset-related sources of revenues. In 1980 operating costs rose 19 percent, primarily as a result of inflation and automation of the banking network.

THE SHEARSON MERGER

In April 1981, American Express and Shearson Loeb Rhoades, Inc., announced that they had reached agreement on a merger. The terms were 1.3 American Express shares for each Shearson share. At the time of the merger Shearson brought into American Express 11,000 employees and $8 billion in assets, mostly in money market funds. The company reported $653 million in revenues in 1980 and had an estimated 500,000 customers.

The level of revenues in 1980 put Shearson in the number two position in the brokerage industry and is largely the product of eight acquisitions in the 10 years since Shearson went public. Shearson's acquisitions were usually of "old line" brokerage houses that were having financial difficulty. To make the acquisitions work, Shearson cut out levels of management, consolidated and automated the "back office" operations into a strong network, and added new services. The consolidated financial statements for the company are shown in Exhibit 9.

Under the terms of the merger Sanford I. (Sandy) Weill remained in charge of Shearson and headed American Express' executive committee, while Robinson became chairman of the merged entity. After the transaction Weill personally owned an estimated 0.6 percent of American Express's stock. Weill built a reputation of competence along with his building of Shearson and demonstrated a willingness and an ability for making fast decisions.

The merger was seen by many as giving strong impetus to a trend in the financial industry where many of the leading brokerage companies are looking for capital inputs to remain competitive on a national scale. The competitive surge appears to be aimed at providing consolidated "one-stop" financial services. Several securities dealers

EXHIBIT 9

SHEARSON LOEB RHOADES, INC.
Consolidated Income Statement
(in thousands)

	1980*	1979*	1978*
Revenues:			
Commissions.....................................	$ 327,497	$ 188,744	$ 136,732
Principal transactions	82,038	17,427	16,299
Interest	128,961	56,293	36,674
Investment banking	57,203	23,900	23,339
Mortgage banking	28,455	6,008	—
Other..	28,312	11,658	8,181
Total revenues...............................	652,466	304,030	221,225
Expenses:			
Employee compensation	310,065	152,802	113,078
Floor broker commissions.......................	26,703	16,785	12,658
Interest	57,407	21,178	18,037
Other operating expenses.......................	142,653	73,180	57,591
Total expenses...............................	536,828	263,945	201,364
Income before distribution	115,638	40,085	19,861
Distribution to profits participation.................	10,669	—	—
Pretax income...................................	104,969	40,085	19,861
Income taxes	49,162	20,010	9,857
Net income......................................	55,805	20,075	10,004
Net income per share	$6.99	$3.78	$2.11
Dividends per share..............................	$ .40	$ .34	$ .27

Assets

Cash..	$ 52,768	$ 15,372	$ 7,110
Segregated cash and treasury bills	316,739	167,085	123,226
Securities and deposit............................	52,514	9,853	13,963
Receivables from customers......................	966,759	547,677	485,588
Receivables from brokers	461,126	135,360	88,676
Mortgages and construction loans	69,481	92,146	—
Other receivables	17,651	7,164	7,176
Spot commodities owned	—	—	254
Securities owned (market)	248,769	127,586	122,960
Secured demand notes	716	7,394	7,394
Exchange membership............................	5,175	2,883	2,874
Investments in affiliates	3,203	—	—
Securities purchased	1,849	9,630	184,927
Purchased mortgage contracts	6,778	7,197	—
Deferred income taxes	5,610	—	—
Office equipment, etc.............................	22,011	12,197	8,286
Excess acquisition cost...........................	14,559	4,647	4,245
Differed expenses and other assets.................	21,983	8,358	3,433
Total assets	$2,267,691	$1,154,549	$1,060,114

EXHIBIT 9 *(concluded)*

SHEARSON LOEB RHOADES, INC.
Consolidated Income Statement
(in thousands)

	1980*	1979*	1978*
Liabilities			
Bank loans	$ 212,668	$ 154,377	$ 149,393
Payables to brokers	557,752	154,743	109,556
Payables to customers............................	607,497	292,992	196,189
Accrued liabilities, etc............................	341,465	255,874	168,355
Securities sold†.....................................	166,260	127,683	115,583
Repurchased securities sold.......................	43,517	1,966	211,565
Deferred income tax...............................	—	662	749
Term notes	26,503	17,826	7,513
Subordinate debt..................................	137,671	61,233	32,994
Secured demand obligation	—	7,394	7,394
Contributions of profit participation agreement	30,113	—	—
Preferred stock....................................	175	1,482	2,026
Common stock.....................................	661	527	487
Paid in capital	50,665	29,639	26,259
Retained earnings.................................	96,295	51,713	33,546
Reacquired stock	(3,561)	(3,562)	(1,496)
Total liabilities	$2,267,691	$1,154,549	$1,060,114

*Year ended June 30th.
†Securities sold, but not yet purchased.

Source: Annual Reports, Moody's Bank and Finance Manual.

---

who have survived a tight decade and are showing profitable years now appear attractive to the larger insurance and other financial firms.

The trend in these acquisitions may have been triggered by Merrill Lynch, Pierce, Fenner & Smith, Inc., which is the industry's number one brokerage house and has considerable capital ($1 billion) strength of its own. In 1977 Merrill Lynch broke with tradition and created a cash management account that allows customers to access cash in the account and money funds as well as providing a line of credit. All of this can be accomplished through special VISA cards or through Merrill Lynch checks. This move proved attractive to customers and was difficult for the smaller companies to match.

In March 1981 Prudential Insurance merged with Bache Group, Inc. Through the merger it is expected that Prudential can provide not only the financial stability to remain competitive and to ride out the fiscal variability that is a problem in the brokerage business, but also to provide marketing and promotional support as well as new services to the Bache customers.

The American Express-Shearson merger announcement has caused considerable concern for banks, who see a new kind of financial institution that can offer a broad range of services that banks are not allowed to sell. Banks are presently prohibited from selling securities by the Glass-Steagall Act of 1933. Their reaction has been in several directions. Larger banks have been lobbying to have the government restrictions on themselves lifted so that they can enter the competitive field, but others have been attempting to block formation of such strong competition. The Independent Bankers Association has written to the Justice Department asking that the American Express-Shearson merger be delayed pending investigation of the deal's "potential anticompetitive effects." The strength of the overall opposition to the merger is difficult to assess without the support of the larger banks. But given the present political trends toward less government involvement, it is unlikely that the merger will be disapproved.

Coke Tries to Counter the Pepsi Challenge*

Dhruv Grewal

Virginia Polytechnic Institute and State University

INTRODUCTION

The Coca-Cola Company was ranked as the 46th largest industrial corporation on the basis of sales in 1984. With 36.4 percent of the domestic soft drink sales volume, Coca-Cola was still ahead of its nearest rival, Pepsi Company, Inc., which had 25.6 percent of the domestic sales volume. Still, Coca-Cola needed to address several issues to ensure its leadership and growth in the soft drink industry. One issue was how best to deal with increased competition in a maturing soft drink industry. Another more specific issue was what to do about Pepsi which was gaining on Coke in recent years. These and other factors meant more intense competition within the soft drink industry.

HISTORY

Coca-Cola, perhaps the world's most renowned trademarked product, was created by Dr. Pemberton in 1886 by stirring various ingredients into a brass pot. His partner and bookkeeper, Frank Robinson, named the product Coca-Cola, something he felt would be easily remembered by customers. The product was first sold at drugstore fountains for 5 cents a glass and sales averaged 13 glasses per day during 1886. During the first year, Dr. Pemberton earned $50.00; however, he spent $73.96 on advertising alone.

---

*This case was written by Dhruv Grewal (Ph.D. student in Marketing at Virginia Polytechnic Institute and State University) under the direction of Larry D. Alexander (Associate Professor of Strategic Management), Department of Management, R. B. Pamplin College of Business, Virginia Polytechnic Institute and State University, Blacksburg, Virginia 24061. Copyright © by Dhruv Grewal.

Later, in 1889, Joseph Whitehead and Benjamin Thomas secured the exclusive rights from the company to bottle and sell Coca-Cola throughout the United States, except for six New England states, Texas, and Mississippi. This contract started the unique relationship that the Coca-Cola Company enjoyed with its largely independent bottlers. By 1894, Joseph Biedenharn started bottling the Coca-Cola product at his own facilities.

The Coca-Cola Company (which replaced the 1892 firm which was incorporated in Georgia) was incorporated in Delaware in 1919. Still, the company's headquarters remained in Atlanta, Georgia. Clearly, several of the most vital assets of the Coca-Cola Company were its trademarks. "Coca-Cola" was registered in the U.S. Patent and Trademark Office in 1893, and the shortened "Coke" was similarly registered much later in 1945. In addition, its unique contoured bottle was registered as a trademark in 1960.

The Coca-Cola Company was best known for manufacturing and distributing soft drink syrups and flavoring concentrates. While the company also operated a separate food division which produced and marketed citrus and other fruit juices, coffee, and plastic products, the focus of this case is on its soft drink division. Some of its products in this category included Hi-C fruit drinks, various Minute Maid juices, and Five-Alive beverages. The Coca-Cola Company significantly diversified its operations when it acquired Columbia Pictures in 1982. That acquired firm was engaged in the production and distribution of motion pictures and television shows. Other entertainment-related activities that Columbia participated in included the publication and distribution of sheet music and song books.

THE PEPSI CHALLENGE

In 1975, Pepsi started its "Pepsi Challenge," aimed directly at Coca-Cola through its various comparative ads. By 1983, Pepsi was targeting the teenage population, claiming it to be the "Choice of a New Generation." Popular music and television personalities endorsed Pepsi products in the advertisements. Pepsi even agreed to partially finance the Jackson Brothers' Victory Tour of 30 cities if they would appear in two Pepsi commercials. Pepsi's name would also be on all the tickets and promotions of the tour and several radio and print advertisements that featured the Jacksons. Other celebrities who signed contracts to endorse Pepsi products in recent years include singer Lionel Richie, television actor Don Johnson, rock musician Glen Frey, actor Michael J. Fox, and comedian Billy Crystal. Clearly, the Pepsi challenge had strengthened the number two soft drink manufacturer, which captured 33 percent of the food-store market by 1985.

Pepsi made other changes in its strategy to more effectively compete against Coca-Cola. Pepsi began to acquire some of its largest bottlers. By acquiring its third largest bottler, MEI Bottling Corporation in Minnesota, Pepsi was able to cover 33 franchise markets. Pepsi-Cola also acquired the Allegheny Bottling Company, another major bottler, which served an area stretching from south-central Pennsylvania to the coastal area of Virginia. The financial statements of PepsiCo, Inc. are presented in Exhibit 1.

Pepsi's challenge to Coke's supremacy has been felt the most in recent years. During 1983 alone, Coca-Cola lost both its Burger King and Wendy's accounts to Pepsi. A major aspect of the Pepsi challenge was its comparative advertising in which Pepsi claimed its products were superior to Coke. Later in 1985, Pepsi reaped benefits when arch rival Coke first discontinued old Coke and later reintroduced it. So happy was Pepsi management that it gave its employees the day off when old Coke was discontinued, since they felt it confirmed that Pepsi was superior. Exhibit 2 shows that PepsiCo had the dominant share of the caffeine-free market. It also shows that coke had increased its position in the diet soft drink market with its newly introduced diet Coke, the most popular diet drink.

Clearly, Coke and Pepsi were locked into a competitive battle for the number one position in the industry. For years, Coke's profit margins had declined while Pepsi's market share increased. To improve its profit margin, Coke replaced weak bottlers, bought Columbia Pictures, and introduced diet Coke, caffeine-free Coke and Cherry Coke. These moves increased Coke's profit margin by 20 percent and doubled Coke's stock price. Still, Pepsi was outperforming Coke in the grocery stores with ads targeted at the teenage market. Meanwhile, Coke had been concentrating on the Baby-Boomer market, people born after World War II (between 1946 and 1962). By the 1980s, the Baby Boomers were aging, which caused the teenage population to increase.

PepsiCo's attempt to acquire Seven-Up from Philip Morris in 1985 might make the Pepsi challenge an every greater threat. Philip Morris had already agreed to sell Seven-Up to PepsiCo for $380 million. All that remained for PepsiCo was to obtain approval from the Antitrust Division of the Department of Justice. If the Seven-Up acquisition is approved, PepsiCo's share of the lemon-lime soft drink would rise to 60 percent. With Seven-Up's addition, PepsiCo would have two additional soft drinks which accounted for 13 percent of the total industry sales. While Seven-Up suffered losses in past years, PepsiCo believed that its pending acquisition complemented PepsiCo's operations and would help increase its share of the soft drink market to 35 percent, only a few percentage points behind Coke.

EXHIBIT 1

PEPSI-CO, INC., AND SUBSIDIARIES
Consolidated Statement of Income and Retained Earnings
Years ended December 29, 1984, December 31, 1983,
and December 25, 1982
(in thousands except per share amounts)

		1984 (52 weeks)	1983 (53 weeks)	1982 (52 weeks)
Revenues	Net Sales	**$7,698,678**	$7,165,586	$6,810,929
Costs and expenses	Cost of sales	**3,149,940**	3,007,398	2,949,160
	Marketing, administrative, and other expenses	**3,853,540**	3,629,509	3,233,050
	Interest expense	**206,956**	176,759	165,270
	Interest income	**(86,131)**	(53,650)	(49,325)
		7,124,305	6,760,016	6,298,155
Income from continuing operations before unusual charges and income taxes	....	**574,373**	405,570	512,774
Unusual charges	Provision for restructuring	**220,000**	—	—
	Reduction in net assets of foreign bottling operations (without tax benefit)	**—**	—	79,400
Income from continuing operations before income taxes	....	**354,373**	405,570	433,374
	Provision for United States and foreign income taxes	**147,701**	134,233	220,947
Income from continuing operations	....	**206,672**	271,337	212,427
Discontinued operations	Income from discontinued operations (net of income taxes of $14,915, $6,728 and $5,846 in 1984, 1983, and 1982, respectively)	**20,875**	12,774	11,861
	Loss on disposal (net of $500 tax benefit)	**(15,000)**	—	—
		5,875	12,774	11,861
Net income	....	**212,547**	284,111	224,288
	Retained earnings at beginning of year ...	**1,622,550**	1,489,797	1,412,636
	Cash dividends (per share 1984–$1.665; 1983–$1.62; 1982–$1.58)	**(156,185)**	(151,358)	(147,127)
	Retained earnings at end of year	**$1,678,912**	$1,622,550	$1,489,797
Net income per share	Continuing operations	**$ 2.19**	$ 2.88	$ 2.27
	Discontinued operations	**.06**	.13	.13
	Net income	**$ 2.25**	$ 3.01	$ 2.40

EXHIBIT 1 *(concluded)*

PEPSI-CO, INC., AND SUBSIDIARIES
Consolidated Balance Sheet
(in thousands)

	Year Ended December 29 1984	Year Ended December 31 1983
Assets		
Current assets		
Cash	$ 28,139	$ 24,434
Marketable securities	784,684	529,326
Notes and accounts receivable, less allowance 1984–$31,966; 1983–$33,738	640,081	647,329
Inventories	451,781	375,606
Prepaid expenses, taxes and other current assets	242,181	159,247
Net assets of the transportation segment held for disposal	143,210	149,504
	2,290,076	1,885,446
Long-term receivables and investments		
Long-term receivables and other investments	178,647	161,283
Investment in tax leases	73,236	77,941
	251,883	239,224
Property, plant, and equipment		
Land	$ 218,231	$ 190,942
Buildings	819,990	732,999
Machinery and equipment	1,988,112	1,891,046
Capital leases	191,924	190,842
Bottles and cases, net of customers' deposits, 1984–$11,678; 1983–$32,777	23,785	56,550
	3,242,042	3,062,379
Less accumulated depreciation and amortization	1,079,029	1,019,000
	2,163,013	2,043,379
Goodwill	163,904	235,768
Other assets	81,358	88,919
Total assets	$4,950,234	$4,492,736
Liabilities and Shareholders' Equity		
Current liabilities		
Notes payable (including current installments on long-term debt and capital lease obligations)	$ 284,280	$ 276,062
Accounts payable	505,843	406,339
United States and foreign income taxes	114,372	80,329
Other accrued taxes	64,338	66,144
Other current liabilities	656,499	521,704
	1,625,332	1,350,578
Long-term debt	541,076	668,294
Deferred income taxes	621,300	387,000
Capital lease obligations	145,218	147,519
Other liabilities and deferred credits	163,932	145,187
Shareholders' equity		
Capital stock par value 5¢ per share authorized 135,000,000 shares issued 1984–95,164,331 shares; 1983–94,986,557 shares	$ 4,758	$ 4,749
Capital in excess of par value	251,915	245,030
Retained earnings	1,678,912	1,622,550
Cumulative translation adjustment	(49,426)	(40,976)
Less cost of repurchased shares 1984–1,256,768; 1983–1,425,915	(32,783)	(37,195)
	1,853,376	1,794,158
Total liabilities and shareholders' equity	$4,950,234	$4,492,736

Source: Pepsico, Inc., 1984 Annual Report, pp. 41–43.

EXHIBIT 2

A. Diet Soft Drink Consumption—Market Share (percent)

	1980	1981	1982	1983	1984
Coca-Cola	28.5%	28.8%	30.2%	40.9%	43.5%
PepsiCo	23.7	24.3	23.2	22.0	21.4
Seven-Up	8.5	8.4	8.7	8.0	7.6
Dr Pepper	9.2	11.7	10.8	7.2	6.0
Royal Crown Cola	5.4	4.4	3.9	2.6	2.8
R. J. Reynolds	3.1	3.6	3.2	3.2	2.3
Sugar Free A&W	2.4	2.4	2.4	2.0	1.5
Dad's	0.9	0.8	0.8	0.6	0.5
Others	18.2	17.6	17.5	15.0	14.3
Percentage of total market	12.8	13.8	14.6	17.3	19.2

B. Caffeine-Free Consumption—Market Share (percent)

	1983	1984
PepsiCo	43.8%	40.5%
Coca-Cola	20.5	28.6
Dr Pepper	5.5	4.9
Seven-Up	7.7	6.2
Royal Crown Cola	19.8	14.8
Others	2.7	5.0
Percentage of total market	5.6	5.9

Source: Adapted from *Beverage Industry*, March 1985, p. 68.

COCA-COLA'S FUNCTIONAL AREA STRATEGIES

Marketing/Sales

The major markets for Coke products are vending machines, restaurant sales, and grocery and convenience stores. In 1985, The Coca-Cola Company produced many soft drinks. They included the following:

Classic Coke, New Coke, caffeine-free Coke, diet Coke, caffeine-free diet Coke, Cherry Coke, TAB, caffeine-free TAB, Sprite, diet-Sprite, Fresca, Mr. PiBB, sugar-free Mr. PiBB, Mello-Yello, Fanta, diet-Fanta, Hi-C soft drinks, Ramblin' Root Beer, sugar-free Ramblin' Root Beer, and Santiba.

The firm's product pricing structure worked in the following manner. Coca-Cola USA, which was a division of The Coca-Cola Company, manufactured the beverage syrups and concentrates. They were sold by

Coca-Cola USA to bottlers at an established price. The bottlers, in turn, charged a wholesale price to the retailers in their territories, who then sold at a retail price to the ultimate consumers. In recent years, Coke has increased its price discounting in order to increase its market share in the food store segment.

Coca-Cola had always emphasized a strong role for advertising to sell its soft drinks. In its various advertising campaigns in recent years, Coca-Cola utilized such major themes as "Things go better with Coke," "Coke is it," "The one you grow up with," and others to sell its products. Its ad campaigns seemed to be in line with the tempo of life for the period. Before an advertising campaign was approved, months of work were spent on thorough market research. The campaign was then pretested in one or several target markets and, if the results proved favorable, a final approval was given for it to be undertaken with a full-scale effort.

To increase consumer awareness, Coke refined its popular "Coke is it" general advertising campaign in 1984. In its place, it introduced a number of commercials targeted at specific consumer groups. Different commercials were aimed at the young and old and showed Coke was "the one you grow up with." Music video commercials were aimed at the young, and comedian/actor Bill Cosby was used to emphasize the fact that Coke was not as sweet as its competitors' products. This campaign was successful since it increased unit sales and market shares in food stores, vending machines, and all other segments. One 1986 advertisement featured William Perry, the huge football star of the Superbowl Champion Chicago Bears, drinking a whole case of the New Coke.

In April 1985, the company announced the reformulation of the world's best-selling soft drink, Coke. It was a sweeter cola drink, hopefully more appealing to the teen market. Coke had spent four years doing market research before introducing the newly formulated Coke. Taste tests all pointed to New Coke as being more desirable. Once the new Coke was introduced, however, the company soon discovered just how loyal the old Coke customers were. The New Coke was losing ground to old Coke and, more important, to Pepsi. After the new Coke had been on the market for only two months, Coca-Cola president Donald Keough announced that old Coke would be reintroduced as Coca-Cola Classic, but the new Coke would remain Coca-Cola.

The blunder of reformulating Coke had caused several problems. Bottlers had to deal with double inventory and increased production scheduling problems. Coke also faced the problem of limited shelf space from retailers. Many of the retailers did not have space for all of Coke's different products. Fast food restaurants, which provided a large percentage of Coke's income, likewise lacked enough room for all of Coke's products. As a result, restaurant owners and retailers let consumer preferences decide what to carry. Still, the market share for Coke products increased, since the new Coke and Coca-Cola Classic provided consumers with more choices.

The company's fountain sales continued to grow strongly in the 1980s. Overall, fountain sales represented 33 percent of total U.S. volume. The firm's aggressive marketing of Sprite resulted in McDonald's authorizing its use in all of its 6,500 restaurants. In 1985, Coca-Cola USA managed to obtain the Baskin-Robbins contract to supply Ramblin' Root Beer for its root beer floats. Baskin-Robbins, with over 3,000 stores in the U.S. and 17 foreign countries, represented over 1 million gallons of soft drink sales annually. Under this agreement, Coke, diet Coke, Sprite, and Ramblin' Root Beer would all be available to Baskin-Robbins' customers.

Manufacturing Operations

Coca-Cola USA manufactured the beverage syrups and concentrates that were sold to more than 1,500 bottlers in over 155 countries. These bottlers were generally independent businesses who invested their own capital to purchase the necessary land, buildings, machinery and equipment, trucks, bottles, and cases. These bottlers packaged, distributed, and marketed the products throughout their respective territories. In addition to syrups and concentrates, Coca-Cola USA provided management guidance in such areas as quality control, marketing, advertising, engineering, financing, and personnel to help bottlers maintain product quality and be profitable.

Soft drink syrups and concentrates were manufactured by the company and sold to bottlers and fountain wholesalers. The syrups were a mixture of sweeteners, water, and flavoring concentrate. Bottlers or canning operators combined the syrups with carbonated water, packaged the soft drinks in cans, bottles, and plastic containers, and then sold them to retailers. Fountain retailers purchased the syrups from fountain wholesalers and sold the product in cups and glasses. Major sweeteners that Coca-Cola used included sugar, high fructose corn syrup (HFCS-55), saccharin, and aspartame.

The company's operations were broken down into geographical subdivisions, which were each headed up by an area manager. To ensure smooth operations, the company had developed a strong and committed bottling network. In 1984, Coca-Cola sold 68 percent of its soft drink syrup and concentrate to approximately 500 U.S. bottlers. The remaining 32 percent was sold to approximately 4,000 fountain wholesalers, who sold the product to restaurants. The company continued to use multiple sweeteners in its products. It had an agreement from G. D. Searle & Co. to supply aspartame for its diet/low-calorie drinks.

In 1979, Coca-Cola initiated a program to strengthen its bottling network which had high turnover. Company projections estimated that about 50 percent of its franchise ownerships would change hands during a five-year period. The company devoted a great deal of time and money to facilitate transfers or financial restructures of its bottlers. The company invested over $100 million in 1983 alone to strengthen its bottling operations to support the company's ambitious future growth goals.

Finance/Accounting

The consolidated statement of income for the Coca-Cola Company is shown in Exhibit 3 for 1982 through 1984. Its net operating revenues for 1984 were $7,363,993,000 and its net income after taxes was $628,818,000. Historically, its net operating revenues had increased from $2,425 billion in 1974 to over $7 billion in 1984. Furthermore, its net income increased from $204 million to over $600 million during that same period.

The Coca-Cola Company had recently deemphasized stock financing in favor of long-term debt. For example, in 1984 alone, the company bought back over $6 million shares of common stock, which resulted in higher earnings per share. In turn, the company started utilizing more low-cost debt to finance its investment programs. In total, the company more than doubled its total debt in 1984 alone. The firm's consolidated balance sheets (including its majority-owned subsidiaries) are shown in Exhibit 4.

In the last five years, sales have exhibited a 10.7 percent growth rate, while net income has reflected a 12.4 percent growth rate. In 1984, selling, general, and administrative expenses totaled over $2 billion. Of this amount, approximately $5 million in salaries were paid to officers. The highest salaries were paid to Roberto C. Goizueta, the chief executive officer and chairman of the board, and Donald R. Keough, president and chief operating officer. These two officers earned approximately $1.7 million and $1.2 million in salaries, respectively.

Innovation Research and Development

To maintain its number one position, Coke constantly introduced new products. In recent years this included New Coke, Cherry Coke, diet Coke, caffeine-free diet Coke, caffeine-free TAB, and others. As Brian Dyson, Coca-Cola's USA president, said to assembled bottlers, "If there's a better product we'll make it . . . if there's a better way we'll

EXHIBIT 3

THE COCA-COLA COMPANY
Consolidated Statement of Income
(in thousands except per share data)

	Year Ended December 31		
	1984	*1983*	*1982*
Net operating revenues	$7,363,993	$6,828,992	$6,021,135
Costs and services	3,992,923	3,772,741	3,310,847
Gross profit	3,371,070	3,056,251	2,710,288
Selling, administrative, and general expenses	2,313,562	2,063,626	1,830,527
Operating income	1,057,508	992,625	879,761
Interest income	128,837	82,912	106,172
Interest expense	123,750	72,667	74,560
Other income (deductions)—net	5,438	(2,528)	6,679
Income from continuing operations before income taxes	1,068,033	1,000,332	918,052
Income taxes	439,215	442,072	415,076
Income from continuing operations	628,818	558,260	502,976
Income from discontinued operations (net of applicable income taxes of $414 in 1983 and $4,683 in 1982)	—	527	9,256
Net income	$ 628,818	$ 558,787	$ 512,232
Per share:			
Continuing operations	$4.76	$4.10	$3.88
Discontinued operations	—	—	.07
Net income	$4.76	$4.10	$3.95
Average shares outstanding	132,210	136,222	129,793

Source: The Coca-Cola Company, Annual Report, 1984.

find it."[1] In addition to new product development, the company also tried to improve the taste of existing products, like TAB, by using a blend of Saccharin and Aspartame to sweeten them.

Coke had recently introduced many new drinks. It had come out with new diet Fanta flavors such as orange, ginger ale, strawberry, grape, root beer, and cherry. All its Fanta products were caffeine free. Its new introduction, Cherry Coke, might result in the emergence of a new soft drink segment. Coke emphasized that its Cherry Coke was not aimed at the Dr Pepper market and that the product had its own light, smooth,

---

[1]Anonymous. "Coke Foresees New Products, Innovation," *Beverage Industry*, July 1984, p. 1.

EXHIBIT 4

THE COCA-COLA COMPANY
Consolidated Balance Sheet
(in thousands except per share data)

	Year Ended December 31	
	1984	**1983**
Assets		
Current assets		
Cash	$ 307,564	$ 319,385
Marketable securities, at cost (approximate market)	474,575	292,084
Trade accounts receivable, less allowance of $20,670 in 1984 and		
$20,169 in 1983	872,332	779,729
Inventories and unamortized costs	740,063	744,107
Prepaid expenses and other assets	241,326	195,009
Total current assets	2,635,860	2,330,314
Investments, film costs, and other assets		
Investments (principally investments in affiliates)	334,220	241,780
Unamortized film costs	341,662	252,612
Long-term receivables and other assets	408,324	240,880
	1,084,206	735,272
Property, plant, and equipment		
Land	130,883	128,642
Buildings and improvements	645,150	618,586
Machinery and equipment	1,518,264	1,412,697
Containers	337,993	341,597
	2,632,290	2,501,522
Less allowance for depreciation	1,009,715	940,716
	1,622,575	1,560,806
Goodwill and other intangible assets	615,428	601,430
Total assets	$5,958,069	$5,227,822

and satisfying taste with a slight taste of cherry. Rather, this product was targeted at consumers in the 12-to-29 age group. Other introductions included new Minute Maid Orange soda, which contained 10 percent fruit juice, and a reformulation of Fresca by adding 1 percent grapefruit juice. These drinks were targeted at the growing health-conscious and juice-drinking segments. Fresca was being targeted at the over-25 age group, and was being positioned as an alternative to other soft drinks and wine coolers.

Coca-Cola had developed a number of new distributing, vending, and packaging systems over the years. For example, in 1983, the company developed a compact, integrated, and self-contained beverage dispenser

EXHIBIT 4   *(concluded)*

	Year Ended December 31	
	1984	*1983*
Liabilities and Shareholders' Equity		
Current		
Loans and notes payable	$ 502,216	$ 85,913
Current maturities of long-term debt	120,300	20,783
Accounts payable and accrued expenses	1,020,807	910,951
Participations and other entertainment obligations	192,537	154,213
Accrued taxes—including income taxes	186,942	219,240
Total current liabilities	2,022,802	1,391,100
Participation and other entertainment obligations	175,234	226,129
Long-term debt	740,001	513,202
Deferred income taxes	241,966	176,635
Shareholders' equity		
Common stock, no par value—		
Authorized: 180,000,000 shares in 1984 and 1983;		
Issued: 137,263,936 shares in 1984 and 136,653,676		
shares in 1983	69,009	68,704
Capital surplus	532,186	500,031
Reinvested earnings	2,758,895	2,494,215
Foreign currency translation adjustment	(234,811)	(130,640)
Total shareholders' equity	3,125,279	2,932,310
Less treasury stock, at cost (6,438,873 shares in		
1984; 300,588 shares in 1983)	347,213	11,554
....	2,778,066	2,920,756
Total liabilities and shareholders' equity	$5,958,069	$5,227,822

Source: The Coca-Cola Company, Annual Report, 1984.

(BTS 150) which utilized patented syrup packages. This dispenser was designed for the large untapped office market. During 1985, it was working on the final stages of a futuristic computerized vending machine, which featured a video display screen, voice simulator, and coupon dispenser. When completed, this machine would offer a wide range of Coca-Cola soft drinks for varying container sizes and prices.

Coke always had stressed consumer convenience and had continuously introduced new ways of packaging its product. Examples would include the two-liter bottles and six-packs in plastic bottles, among others. In 1985, Coke test marketed a 12-ounce plastic can, which was made up of uncoated plastic (PET) and had an aluminum end.

Human Resources Personnel

Overall, The Coca-Cola Company and its subsidiaries employed more than 40,500 people. Of this, 18,200 persons worked within the United States. The company contributed to various pension plans covering the majority of its employees in the United States, and certain foreign employees. Pension expenses incurred in 1984 for its present and retired employees were estimated to be about $36 million. The company also provided health care plans and life insurance benefits to most of its U.S. employees. It even provided health care benefits to most domestic employees who had retired after five or more years of service.

The company introduced a new and more attractive thrift plan for its employees in 1984. SODA, which stood for "Savings on Deferred Accounts," allowed employees to contribute up to 10 percent of their salaries while the company matched the first 3 percent of their salaries. Internal Revenue Service ruling permitted employees to contribute pre-tax dollars and this money could accumulate tax-free until the employee reached 59.5 years of age. Furthermore, employees could withdraw money from the plan at any time without penalty. They just had to declare the withdrawn money in the present year as additional income.

Management

The Coca-Cola Company was headed by Roberto Goizueta, who was both chairman of the board and chief executive officer. Directly under him was Donald Keough, president and chief operating officer. These two top management officials had established (1) growth in annual earnings per share and (2) increased return on equity as the company's two main goals. The firm's various aggressive financial policies helped to support these goals by letting it exploit high return opportunities.

Under Goizueta's leadership, Coca-Cola's management had followed an aggressive pricing policy combined with new product development to win back market share. It found that this new approach was necessary to respond to changing market conditions and increased competition. The company had changed from being a sleeping giant to an aggressive risk taker.

Goizueta established a guideline that each business segment must satisfy the 20 percent corporate rate of return on investment. In accord with this guideline, the company sold its Wine Spectrum division which could not achieve this ROI level. According to Sergio Zyman, senior vice president of marketing, Coke had experienced a cultural revolution since Goizueta took over as chairman. As Zyman noted, "Before, if you were aggressive, you were out" while today "if you're not aggressive, you're out."[2]

Coca-Cola management began taking a much tougher stance and had started to face competition in a head-on manner. Coca-Cola, which had never put its famous trademark on any other product, used it for the first time on its new product, diet Coke. Goizueta said this was done because "we didn't have the Coca-Cola trademark on the fastest-growing segment [diet-drink market] of the soft drink business."[3] Diet Coke benefited from this brand identification, which made it not only the largest-selling diet soft drink, but also the third largest-selling soft drink product.

International Operations

In its international operations, Coca-Cola Company's key objective was growth. To attract customers to drink more of its products, Coke was making its products more readily available and increasing the product variety. The particular types of drinks that the company was targeting for international sales were low calorie (in some developed countries such as Japan), lemon lime, and others.

To increase consumption internationally, Coca-Cola was trying to increase use of its products through vending machines and fountain outlets. The company had also increased the popularity of its products by offering larger package sizes, emphasizing their convenience and economy. The large amount of capital required by bottlers had prevented vending machines from becoming a major factor in penetrating international markets. Japan was one exception where vending machine sales were a large percentage, some 44 percent, of total company sales. Equipment investment was also a major factor in developing more fountain sales. Recent investments in equipment combined with effective merchandising and advertising had led to substantial gains in this area.

One key factor that contributed to international growth was a strong bottler network. In 1984, the company spent $100 million reconstructing its bottler system. Bottling facilities in Japan and Australia were sold to local operators while bottling facilities in South England, which

---

[2]Thomas E. Ricks, "Coca-Cola's Tough New Ads Take Aim at the Competition," *The Wall Street Journal*, July 26, 1984, p. 29.

[3]Eric Morgenthaler, "Diet Coke Is a Big Success in Early Going, Spurring a Gush of Optimism at Coca-Cola," *The Wall Street Journal*, December 22, 1982, p. 17.

included London, were purchased. The company changed the management at these facilities and participated in ownership changes at other facilities. These changes were made to ensure commitment to its goals for international growth.

In the low-calorie segment, diet Coke had the most growth potential. Diet Coke's sales averaged 8 percent of Coca-Cola sales in international markets. Particular markets where diet Coke has been popular included Ireland, Australia, South Africa, and Japan. In these markets, diet Coke sales were greater in volume than those of the primary brand of the company's largest competitor. In Japan, diet Coke captured 68 percent of the low-calorie carbonated soft drink segment.

Sprite was Coca-Cola's entry in the lemon-lime segment. The company had started marketing this product aggressively, focusing on Argentina, the Philippines, and Mexico. Mexico was the company's second largest market by volume and through this aggressive marketing the company was able to increase Sprite sales volumes there by 71 percent.

Coca-Cola sales were approximately 69 percent of the company's international volume. Coca-Cola was first made available in the Soviet Union in 1985, reaching a potential market of 275 million people. Sudan, Congo, and the German Democratic Republic were other possibilities for new markets.

THE SOFT DRINK INDUSTRY

The commercial sale of soda water first began in the United States in about 1806 by Benjamin Silliman. Initially, carbonated drinks were considered to have medicinal values. The industry made great progress with the introduction of the cork bottle cap which enabled carbonated soda to remain inside the bottle. Later, the painter's foot-operated machine allowed syruping, filling, and capping to be done simultaneously.

More recently, the soft drink industry had become a highly competitive one. Major competitors included The Coca-Cola Company, Pepsi Cola Company, 7-Up, Dr Pepper Company, and Royal Crown Cola Competitors in the industry included a wide variety of international, national, regional, and private-label producers.

The soft drink industry was influenced by the general economic outlook. Domestic sales increased as the U.S. economy experienced a growing economy in 1984 and 1985. Similarly, sales remained flat during the 1981–83 recession. Soft drink sales were clearly related to per capita income. Still, the per capita consumption of soft drinks of 19.1 gallons in 1964 increased to 41.5 gallons in 1983, as shown in Exhibit 5. Soft drink industry sales were also subjected to seasonal fluctuations due to weather conditions, with higher sales coming in the warmer, summer months and lower sales during colder, winter months.

EXHIBIT 5 U.S. Liquid Consumption Trends (gallons per capita)

	1964	1965	1966	1967	1968	1969	1970	1971	1972	1973	1974	1975	1976	1977	1978	1979	1980	1981	1982	1983	1984E
Soft drinks	19.1	20.3	22.3	23.5	24.8	25.9	27.0	28.6	30.1	31.5	31.4	31.0	33.7	35.9	37.1	38.1	38.8	39.5	40.1	41.5	43.2
Coffee*	38.8	37.8	37.4	37.0	37.0	36.2	35.7	35.3	35.2	35.1	33.8	33.0	29.4	28.0	27.0	29.2	28.7	28.5	27.8	27.0	27.3
Beer	15.9	15.9	16.5	16.8	17.3	17.8	18.5	19.2	19.7	20.5	21.3	21.6	21.8	22.5	23.1	23.8	24.5	24.7	24.4	24.3	24.0
Milk†	25.9	26.0	25.9	25.3	25.6	25.3	23.1	23.0	23.1	22.7	22.0	22.1	21.9	21.5	21.3	21.0	20.7	20.4	20.0	20.9	21.1
Juices	3.5	3.8	4.0	4.8	4.7	4.8	5.2	5.7	6.0	5.2	6.1	6.8	6.8	6.8	6.5	6.7	6.9	6.7	6.8	7.7	6.1
Tea*	6.3	6.3	6.3	6.4	6.6	6.6	6.5	6.7	6.8	7.2	7.3	7.3	7.4	7.7	7.6	7.6	7.3	7.5	7.5	7.2	7.3
Powdered drinks	—	—	—	—	—	—	—	—	—	—	—	4.8	5.5	5.9	6.1	6.0	6.0	6.0	6.0	6.5	6.3
Wine	1.0	1.0	1.0	1.0	1.1	1.2	1.3	1.5	1.6	1.7	1.7	1.7	1.7	1.8	2.1	2.2	2.3	2.3	2.3	2.4	2.5
Bottled water	—	—	—	—	—	—	—	1.1	—	—	—	1.2	1.2	1.3	1.4	1.5	1.6	1.9	2.2	2.7	3.0
Distilled spirits	1.4	1.5	1.6	1.6	1.7	1.8	1.8	1.9	1.9	1.9	2.0	2.0	2.0	2.0	2.0	2.0	2.0	2.0	1.9	1.8	1.8
Subtotal	111.9	112.6	115.0	116.4	118.8	119.6	119.1	123.0	124.4	125.8	125.6	131.5	131.4	133.4	134.3	138.1	138.8	139.5	139.0	142.0	144.6
Inputed water consumptions‡	70.6	69.9	67.5	66.1	63.7	62.9	63.4	59.5	58.1	56.7	56.9	51.0	51.1	49.1	48.2	44.4	43.7	43.0	43.5	40.5	37.9
Total	182.5	182.5	182.5	182.5	182.5	182.5	182.5	182.5	182.5	182.5	182.5	182.5	182.5	182.5	182.5	182.5	182.5	182.5	182.5	182.5	182.5

*Coffee and tea data are based on a three-year moving average to counterbalance swings, thereby portraying consumption more realistically. Tea numbers have been restated to reflect this.
†Certain milk figures have been changed based on revisions to USDA data.
‡Includes all others.

Sources: USDA, DSI, MABO, ABWA, Laidlaw Ansbacher Research Estimates 1985; and "Soft Drinks, Juices, Bottled Water Pace Gains," Beverage Industry, February 1985, p. 38. Copyright John C. Maxwell, Beverage Industry, February 1985.

The U.S. population had started to become very health conscious. As this trend continued, combined with the aging of the American population, the consumption of beer, wine, and spirits decreased, while the consumption of soft drinks increased. This trend had been further accelerated by the raising of legal drinking ages in several states and the growing public sentiment against drunken driving.

Advertising played a major role in the soft drink industry. Soft drink manufacturers spent $367,300,000 collectively on advertising in 1984. Top media expenditures for regular soft drinks of major brands are shown in Exhibit 6. The selection of which media to use depended on a number of factors, including the product, its popularity, the age group it was being targeted at, and whether it was a new or old product, among others. The amount spent on television promotions had increased in 1984 over the prior year. In 1984, spot advertisements increased 9 percent for regular drinks and 5 percent for diet drinks, whereas network advertisements increased 18.7 percent for regular drinks and 125.5 percent for diet drinks. Radio spot commercials were highly effective at targeting certain audiences such as teenagers and younger people who were devoted radio music listeners. The use of billboard advertising, on the other hand, had been decreasing in recent years.

Segmentation

The soft drink industry was segmented into six categories on the basis of drink types. The six categories included cola drinks, lemon-lime drinks, pepper drinks, orange drinks, root beer drinks, and all other

EXHIBIT 6   Top Media Expenditures of Regular Soft Drink Brands (in thousands)

Product	4-Media Total	Magazines	Network Television	Spot Television	Outdoor
Coca-Cola	$48,298.3	$252.9	$24,764.9	$20,647.4	$2,633.1
Pepsi-Cola	33,013.5	—	9,028.6	22,845.1	1,139.8
Sprite	23,161.7	72.4	15,399.6	7,669.5	20.0
7UP	22,759.8	95.0	13,317.0	8,926.1	431.8
Canada Dry	9,004.9	—	4,534.9	4,510.0	—
Dr Pepper	8,321.7	—	2,433.5	5,685.8	202.4
Mountain Dew	7,772.9	—	558.3	7,191.7	22.9
Sunkist	4,438.1	—	138.9	4,292.9	6.3
A&W	4,348.7	—	2,273.3	2,075.4	—
Royal Crown	4,103.0	—	—	4,099.9	3.1

Source: Leading National Advertisers Broadcast Advertiser's Report. Copyright *Beverage Industry,* July 1985.

soft drinks. Among these groups, the cola category had always been the dominant segment. Its staggering 62.6 percent market share in 1981 increased to 63.2 percent in 1984. The market shares for cola and lemon lime had remained fairly steady, whereas the pepper-type drinks had increased. The orange and root beer categories, however, had decreased from 1971 to 1984.

There were certain newly emerging segments. Squirt Company introduced Diet Squirt Plus in 1985, which became the first company to use 100 percent NutraSweet in its diet drinks. This use was considered to be partially responsible for the tremendous increase in consumption of diet drinks. Diet Squirt Plus contained 50 percent of the recommended daily dosage of Vitamin C and 10 percent of the daily dosage of five important B complex vitamins. In coming years, this new drink could possibly establish a new vitamin-fortified soft drink segment. Other emerging segments may be the diet chocolate soda segment, the cherry coke segment, and the carbonated juice segment.

A more basic way of segmenting the soft drink industry was into full-calorie regular drinks and diet drinks. Back in 1980, diet drinks constituted only 12.8 percent of the market. Their sales rose, however, to 17.3 percent in 1983 and to 19.2 percent of the market by 1984. Their sales were further stimulated in 1984 by the introduction of NutraSweet and the increase in sales of diet Coke. Thus, diet drinks were the newest and fastest-growing segment in the soft drink industry.

Threats

One potential problem facing the soft drink industry was the Federal Trade Commission's complaint that the industry's exclusive territorial franchise agreements with their bottlers unnecessarily restricted competition. This complaint was still under review in mid-1985.

On another issue, there had been constant concern about whether the artificial sweeteners used in soft drinks caused cancer. This concern had been directed especially toward saccharin. The other widely used noncaloric sweetener, aspartame, had an alleged inability to remain stable at high temperatures. This problem was causing some health concerns even though it received Food and Drug Administration Approval in 1981.

The entrance of the Procter & Gamble Co. (P&G) as a small, yet potentially powerful competitor in the soft drink industry was still another threat to Coke. P&G, with 1984 sales of approximately $13 billion, acquired Orange Crush for $55 million. P&G was also trying to buy the Lexington-based Coca-Cola Bottling Mideast, Inc., to learn more about how to bottle and distribute soft drinks. Coca-Cola had filed a restraining order to try to prevent this acquisition by its leading competitor. According to Brian Dyson, president of Coca-Cola USA, "The record indicates that they [P&G] have not entered the soft drink industry in a casual way."[4] Senior Vice President Allen McCusker was even more vocal about the subject and said, "They [P&G] could be our biggest competitor."[5] There were speculations that since P&G did not possess a cola product, it might try to acquire Royal Crown Cola. This would provide them with a strong, well-established bottler network. Another possibility was that P&G might sell its product directly to the supermarkets without even going through bottlers. If successful, this change could have a major impact on the soft drink industry.

The growing sense of awareness against littering posed another potential threat to Coke and the industry. Several states had passed antilitter laws. Various studies had found that disposable packages constituted a major portion of the litter. As a result, some states had passed, or were considering, laws against nonreturnable containers.

A final threat was the aging of the American population. The American population was growing older largely due to the fact that the population birth rate was slowing down and medical facilities were improving for Americans of all ages. These trends had resulted in a reduction of the number of youths, who were the major consumers of regular soft drink products.

Substitutes

Soft drinks compete for the consumer dollar spent on all beverages. Major drinks and beverages consumed by the American population were soft drinks, water, coffee, beer, milk, fruit juice, tea, wine, distilled spirits, and others. Soft drinks had experienced tremendous growth from a paltry 9.4 percent in 1960 to 25.5 percent of the beverage consumption in 1984. The overall consumption of beverages had increased from 35 billion gallons in 1960 to 45 billion gallons in 1984. The beverage industry expected sales of beverages such as light beer, wine coolers, specialty coffees and teas, decaffeinated and flavored teas, rum, diet and caffeine-free soft drinks, and fruit juices to increase tremendously. The products that were increasing in popularity were the ones that catered to the largely health-conscious public. Out of the 483 million gallons of increased consumption of soft drinks, 465 million gallons were for diet drinks. Alcoholic beverage sales had declined largely due to increased public opinion against alcohol abuse, drunk driving, and increased drinking age laws.

---

[4]"Is P&G Thirsty for Some of Coke's Know-How?" *Business Week*, May 30, 1983, p. 62.
[5]Ibid.

Suppliers

A major material cost incurred by the soft drink industry was the sweetener. The major types of sweeteners used were sugar, high fructose corn syrup (HFCS-55), saccharin, and aspartame. The increased consciousness among many consumers to be slim had resulted in the growing popularity of diet drinks utilizing noncaloric sweeteners. The two major noncaloric sweeteners being used were saccharin and aspartame. Aspartame was a low-calorie sweetening agent produced in the United States and many foreign countries. Sales of NutraSweet, the trade name for aspartame, had risen from $12 million in 1981 to $110 million in the first half of 1983 alone. Even though aspartame has received FDA approval, there were certain unanswered questions regarding its safety.

FDA proposed a ban against saccharin in 1977, but a congressional moratorium was applied to give further time for testing and researching whether the product was carcinogenic or not. The moratorium was again extended in April 1985. Thus far, this proposed ban had not seemed to have had an effect on the sales of saccharin.

Sugar was another raw material utilized in manufacturing soft drinks. It was purchased from numerous domestic and international sources and was subject to vast price fluctuations. A large number of major soft drink manufacturers, like The Coca-Cola Company, had been authorized to utilize 100 percent high fructose corn syrup (HFCS-55) in their products.

Sugar was the major sweetener used by the soft drink industry to sweeten their products. Quotas on sugar imports resulted in artificially high prices for domestic sugar. This quota had caused soft drink manufacturers to switch from sugar to high fructose corn syrup (HFCS-55). With the increase in the consumption of diet drinks, it had resulted in the increased use of noncaloric sweeteners. By 1985, there were some other noncaloric sweeteners, such Acesulfame K and left-handed sugars, which were awaiting FDA approval.

Another major material cost of the soft drink industry was packaging. The major types of materials used in packaging soft drinks were plastic containers, aluminum cans, glass bottles, and aseptic paper packages. Greatest growth had been experienced by plastic containers, aluminum cans, and aseptic paper packages, whereas glass containers application had steadily decreased.

Buyers

In the soft drink industry, the buyers of the syrups and concentrates were bottlers and fountain wholesalers. Bottlers were the ones who subsequently manufactured the finished product, packaged it, and then sold it to retailers. Still, retailers were the primary customers of the bottlers and wholesalers, not the consumers. To ensure successful sales, the bottlers and wholesalers had to cultivate a positive relationship with their retailers.

Bottlers had broadened the use of various retail outlets to sell their soft drinks in recent years. In 1974, 53 percent of their soft drinks were sold through food stores, whereas in 1984 they sold 46.2 percent. This shift was a result of the increased competition in the soft drink industry, especially between Coke and Pepsi, which resulted in numerous products being introduced in the markets. This had further resulted in reduced shelf space being available in the supermarkets and food stores to any one soft drink manufacturer. All the bottlers were fighting to increase their sales by various methods, such as increased price discounting, promotions, and maintaining full shelves of their product to consumers in stores. To incresae product availability, bottlers had resorted to increased distribution through other retail outlets besides food stores. Other retail outlets included convenience stores and general merchandising stores, as well as vending machines.

Expressing market share as a percentage of soft drink sales through retail establishments, convenience stores increased their market share from 17.4 percent in 1974 to 19.6 percent in 1984, whereas food stores decreased their market share from 53 percent in 1974 to 42.6 percent in 1984. An increasingly important success factor was to get the product to the consumers, wherever they wanted it. As the number of two-wage-earner families increased, it resulted in more frequent shopping for just a few items. This trend had resulted in increased soft drink sales through convenience stores and vending machines, where a customer could make a purchase very quickly.

Vending sales clearly were on the increase. Furthermore, this was a very profitable segment since it did not include any promotional price discounting. In part, due to the new attractive machines that changed dollar bills and had video displays and voice simulators, the sales through vending machines increased 20–25 percent. The soft drink manufacturers had even developed mini vending machines that dispensed three products for the largely untapped office market.

NEW PRODUCTS/MARKET OPPORTUNITIES

Coca-Cola had introduced new products such as diet drinks, caffeine-free drinks, and juice soda drinks aimed at the health- and diet-conscious market. In anticipation of this new market, Coke had introduced diet Coke, diet Sprite, diet Fanta, caffeine-free Coca-Cola, caffeine-free diet Coke, caffeine-free TAB, sugar-free Mr. PiBB, sugar-free Ramblin' Root Beer, Minute Maid Orange Soda, and new improved Fresca.

Other product opportunities that Coca-Cola could take advantage of were the multivitamin juices and multivitamin soda segments. This might follow the lead of the successful introduction of Diet Squirt Plus. Coke had already started to take advantage of the growing carbonated juice drink market by introducing Minute Maid Orange Soda and new improved Fresca. The juice market in schools and health care institutions might prove to be a good opportunity for market development. This market could be served through mini juice-vending machines which had recently been developed. In addition, these mini vending machines could be used to serve the growing office market.

Another product opportunity might be apple-flavored sodas, which were gaining tremendous popularity in Australia, Ireland, and most of Europe.

Another fast growing segment is the diet-chocolate fudge soda. If this segment captured a portion of the soft drink market, it may be an area in which Coke could introduce a product.

The international markets might provide tremendous opportunities for increasing soft drink sales. Coca-Cola products had been doing extremely well internationally. Their international soft drink sales volume increased by 4 percent alone in 1984. To further increase international sales, the company was focusing on product availability and product variety. In 1985, Coca-Cola Company products will be available for the first time in Russia, Sudan, Congo, and the German Democratic Republic.

Other important domestic segments might be the Black and Hispanic markets. The Black population in the United States represented $140 billion in purchasing power and the U.S. Hispanics represented $50–$70 billion in purchasing power. Some marketing efforts in the 1980s were not spending all of their advertising dollars on campaigns designed to reach certain segments of the population in the most cost-effective manner. Television advertising utilizing certain sitcoms, sport events, and other shows to reach certain targeted audiences had increased. Outdoor advertising was being utilized to reach a particular segment of the population without other segments even being aware of it. This outdoor advertising was being increasingly used by beverage marketers to reach the Black and Hispanic markets.

In considering any product/market opportunity, The Coca-Cola Company should examine the existing soft drink firms, their product offerings, and market shares. Exhibit 7 does just this by providing market shares for each soft drink offered by the various manufacturers from 1980 through 1984. By studing these statistics and trends, hopefully it will provide support for whatever new products Coke might introduce.

EXHIBIT 7 Consumption of Soft Drinks by Company

	Market Share				
	1980	*1981*	*1982*	*1983*	*1984*
Coca-Cola Co.					
Coca-Cola	24.3%	24.2%	23.9%	22.5%	21.8%
Diet Coke	—	—	0.3	3.2	5.1
Sprite	2.9	2.9	2.8	2.8	3.3
Tab	3.2	3.6	3.8	2.7	1.6
Fanta	1.7	1.5	1.3	1.1	1.6
Caffeine-Free Diet Coke	—	—	—	0.5	1.0
Mello Yello	0.8	0.9	0.8	0.6	0.9
Caffeine-Free Coke	—	—	—	0.5	0.6
Diet Sprite	—	—	0.4	0.3	0.5
Mr. PiBB	0.7	0.6	0.5	0.4	0.3
Caffeine-Free Tab	—	—	—	0.2	0.2
Fresca	0.4	0.4	0.3	0.2	0.1
Others	0.4	0.4	0.4	0.4	0.4
Total	34.4	34.5	34.5	35.3	36.4
Pepsico, Inc.					
Pepsi-Cola	17.9%	18.3%	18.1%	16.9%	17.0%
Mountain Dew	2.9	3.0	2.8	2.7	2.7
Diet Pepsi	2.6	2.9	2.9	2.4	2.9
Pepsi Free	—	—	—	1.5	1.4
Sugar-Free Pepsi Free	—	—	0.3	1.0	1.0
Pepsi Light	0.4	0.5	0.5	0.4	0.2
Teem	0.3	0.2	0.2	0.2	0.1
Others	0.3	0.2	0.2	0.2	0.3
Total	24.4	25.1	25.0	25.3	25.6
Seven-Up Co.					
7Up	5.4	5.0	5.2	5.4	5.2
Diet 7Up	1.1	1.2	1.3	1.3	1.4
Like	—	—	0.3	0.4	0.3
Sugar-Free Like	—	—	—	0.1	0.1
Dixie Cola	0.2	0.1	0.1	0.1	—
Howdy Flavors	—	—	—	—	—
Total	6.7	6.3	6.9	7.3	7.0
Dr Pepper					
Dr Pepper	5.5	5.4	5.1	4.9	5.1
Sugar-Free Dr Pepper	1.2	1.3	1.3	1.1	1.0
Sugar-Free Pepper Free	—	—	—	0.2	0.1
Pepper Free	—	—	—	0.2	0.1
Welch's	0.5	0.5	0.5	0.5	0.4
Total	7.2	7.2	6.9	6.9	6.8
R. J. Reynolds' Canada Dry Corp.					
Ginger Ale	1.0	1.1	1.1	1.2	1.2
Club Soda/Seltzer	0.5	0.5	0.6	0.6	0.6
Tonic, Bitter Lemon	0.4	0.5	0.5	0.5	0.4
Barrelhead	0.3	0.2	0.2	0.2	0.1
Wink	0.2	0.1	0.1	—	—
Others	0.5	0.4	0.3	0.3	0.3
Total	2.9	2.8	2.8	2.8	2.6
Sunkist					
Sunkist	1.3	1.5	1.6	1.5	1.5
Diet Sunkist	—	0.1	0.3	0.3	0.2
Total	1.3	1.6	1.9	1.8	1.7

Source: Adapted from *Beverage Industry*, March 1985, pp. 17–18.

COCA-COLA'S FUTURE

The Coca-Cola Company, the original inventor of cola drinks, obviously looked forward to a bright future. It had been facing more vigorous competition with the soft drink industry as a whole in recent years. Still, it was the number one soft drink manufacturer in the world. On the other hand, the gains achieved by Pepsi-Cola in recent years were substantial. Just what Coca-Cola would do to counter this growing competitive challenge in coming years remained to be seen.

Campbell Soup Company*

Arthur A. Thompson
Sharon Henson
both of the University of Alabama

In mid-1985, five years after he had been appointed president and chief executive officer of Campbell Soup Company, Gordon McGovern decided it was time to review the key strategic theme he had initiated— new product development. Shortly after he became Campbell's CEO, McGovern reorganized the company into autonomous business units to foster entrepreneurial attitudes; his ultimate objective was to transform Campbell from a conservative manufacturing company into a consumer-driven, new product-oriented company. As a result of McGovern's push, Campbell had introduced 334 new products in the past five years—more than any other company in the food processing industry.

During the 1970s Campbell's earnings had increased at an annual rate just under 9 percent—a dull performance compared to the 12 percent average growth for the food industry as a whole. With prior management's eyes fixed mainly on production aspects, gradual shifts in consumer buying habits caused Campbell's unit volume growth to flatten. McGovern's five-year campaign for renewed growth via new product introduction had produced good results so far. By year-end 1984 sales were up 31 percent—to $3.7 billion—and earnings had risen by 47 percent—to $191 million. But now it appeared that Campbell's brand managers may have become so involved in new product development that they had neglected the old stand-by products, as well as not meeting cost control and profit margin targets. Campbell's growth in operating earnings for fiscal year 1985 fell far short of McGovern's 15 percent target rate. Failure to control costs and meet

*Prepared by graduate researcher, Sharon Henson, under the supervision of Professor Arthur A. Thompson, University of Alabama. Copyright © 1986 by Sharon Henson and Arthur A. Thompson.

EXHIBIT 1 Financial Summary, Campbell Soup Company, 1979–85 (in thousands of dollars)

	1979	1980	1981	1982	1983	1984	1985
Total sales (includes interdivisional)	n.a.	$2,566,100	$2,865,600	$2,995,800	$3,359,300	$3,744,600	$4,060,800
Net sales (excludes interdivisional)	$2,248,692	2,560,569	2,797,663	2,955,649	3,292,433	3,657,440	3,988,705
Cost of products sold	1,719,134	1,976,754	2,172,806	2,214,214	2,444,213	2,700,751	2,950,204
Marketing and sales expenses	181,229	213,703	256,726	305,700	367,053	428,062	478,341
Administrative and research expenses	94,716	102,445	93,462	136,933	135,855	169,614	194,319
Operating earnings	253,613	276,869	280,355	309,283	349,116	378,316	389,488
Interest—net	1,169	10,135	30,302	21,939	39,307	26,611	32,117
Earnings before taxes	252,444	257,532	244,367	276,863	306,005	332,402	333,724
Taxes on earnings	119,700	122,950	114,650	127,250	141,000	141,200	135,800
Net earnings, after taxes	119,817	134,582	129,717	149,613	165,005	191,202	197,824
Percent of sales	5.3%	5.3%	4.6%	5.1%	5.0%	5.2%	5.0%
Percent of stockholders' equity	13.8%	14.6%	13.2%	14.6%	15.0%	15.9%	15.0%
Per share of common stock	1.80	2.04	2.00	2.32	2.56	2.96	3.06
Dividends declared per share	.86	.93	1.02	1.05	1.09	1.14	1.22
Average shares outstanding	66,720	65,946	64,824	64,495	64,467	64,514	64,572
Salaries, wages, pensions, etc	$ 543,984	$ 609,979	$ 680,946	$ 700,940	$ 755,073	$ 889,450	$ 950,143
Current assets	680,955	861,845	845,343	921,501	932,099	1,063,330	1,152,761
Working capital	362,187	405,628	368,246	434,627	478,899	541,515	579,490
Plant assets—gross	1,134,571	1,248,735	1,368,663	1,472,693	1,607,634	1,744,866	1,856,122
Accumulated depreciation	520,603	560,730	613,643	657,315	718,478	774,004	828,662
Plant assets purchased and acquired	159,603	155,796	155,275	175,928	178,773	201,864	222,321
Total assets	1,325,823	1,627,565	1,722,876	1,865,519	1,991,526	2,210,115	2,437,525
Long-term debt	36,298	137,879	150,587	236,160	267,465	283,034	297,146
Stockholders' equity	900,017	958,443	1,000,510	1,055,762	1,149,404	1,259,908	1,382,487
Depreciation	60,360	67,958	75,118	83,813	93,189	101,417	119,044

Source: Annual reports of Campbell Soup Company.

earnings targets threatened to leave Campbell without the internal cash flows to fund its new-product strategy. Exhibit 1 offers a summary of Campbell Soup's recent financial performance.

THE FOOD PROCESSING INDUSTRY

In the early 19th century small incomes and low urban population greatly limited the demand for packaged food. In 1859 one industry — grain mills — accounted for over three fifths of the total U.S. food processing. Several industries were in their infancy: evaporated milk, canning, candy, natural extracts, and coffee roasting. From 1860 to 1900 the industry entered a period of development and growth that made food processing the leading manufacturing industry in the United States. The driving forces behind this growth were increased urbanization, cheaper rail transport, and the advent of refrigeration and tin can manufacturing.

At the beginning of the 20th century the food processing industry was highly fragmented; the thousands of local and regional firms were too small to capture scale economies in mass production and distribution as was occurring in other industries. During the 1920s, industry consolidation via acquisition and merger began; the process was evolutionary not revolutionary and continued on into the 1960s and 1970s. Companies such as Del Monte and Kraft, whose names have since become household words, were established, as were the first two multiline food companies — General Foods and Standard Brands (later part of Nabisco Brands). With consolidation came greater production cost efficiency and national market coverages. Following World War II the bigger food companies made moves toward more product differentiation and increased emphasis on advertising. Some became multinational in scope, establishing subsidiaries in many other countries. Starting in the 1960s and continuing into the 1980s the industry went through more consolidation; this time the emphasis was on brand diversification and product line expansion. Acquisition-minded companies shopped for smaller companies with products having strong brand recognition and brand loyalty.

Then in the 1980s giants began acquiring other giants. In 1984 Nestlé acquired Carnation for $3 billion. In 1985 R. J. Reynolds purchased Nabisco Brands for $4.9 billion (and then changed its corporate name to RJR Nabisco), and Philip Morris acquired General Foods Corporation for $5.7 billion — the biggest nonoil deal in U.S. industry. In 1985 the U.S. food processing industry had sales over $100 billion and combined net profits of over $4 billion. Exhibit 2 shows data for leading companies in the industry in 1985.

EXHIBIT 2   The Top 15 Companies in the Food Processing Industry, 1985
(millions of dollars)

Company		Sales	Profits	Assets	Return on Common Equity	Example Brands
1. RJR Nabisco	1985	$ 16,595	$2,163	$16,930	20.3%	Nabisco, Del Monte
	1984	12,974	1,619	9,272	22.1	
2. Dart & Kraft	1985	9,942	466	5,502	17.0	Velveeta, Parkay,
	1984	9,759	456	5,285	16.5	Miracle Whip
3. Beatrice	1985	12,595	479	10,379	21.8	Swiss Miss, Wesson,
	1984	9,327	433	4,464	20.4	Tropicana
4. Kellogg	1985	2,930.1	281.1	1,726.1	48.0	Mrs. Smith's, Eggo,
	1984	2,602.4	250.5	1,667.1	27.0	Rice Krispies
5. H. J. Heinz	1985	4,047.9	266	2,473.8	22.6	Star-Kist Tuna,
	1984	3,953.8	237.5	2,343	21.0	Heinz Ketchup
6. Ralston Purina	1985	5,863.9	256.4	2,637.3	26.7	Hostess Twinkies,
	1984	4,980.1	242.7	2,004.2	23.1	Meow Mix
7. Campbell Soup	1985	3,988.7	197.8	2,437.5	15.0	Prego, Le Menu,
	1984	3,657.4	191.2	2,210.1	15.9	Vlasic pickles
8. General Mills	1985	4,285.2	(72.9)	2,662.6	(6.5)	Cheerios, Betty
	1984	5,600.8	233.4	2,858.1	19.0	Crocker
9. Sara Lee	1985	8,117	206	3,216	20.5	Popsicle, Bryan,
	1984	7,000	188	2,822	19.4	Rudy's Farm
10. CPC International	1985	4,209.9	142.0	3,016.6	10.5	Mazola, Skippy,
	1984	4,373.3	193.4	2,683.4	14.7	Hellmann's
11. Borden	1985	4,716.2	193.8	2,932.2	14.3	Wyler's, Bama,
	1984	4,568	182.1	2,767.1	13.7	Cracker Jack
12. Pillsbury	1985	4,670.6	191.8	2,778.5	17.3	Green Giant,
	1984	4,172.3	169.8	2,608.3	17.0	Häagen-Dazs
13. Archer Daniels	1985	4,738.8	163.9	2,967.1	10.8	LaRosa, Fleisch-
	1984	4,907	117.7	2,592.7	NA	mann's
14. Quaker Oats	1985	3,520.1	156.6	2,662.6	20.3	Gatorade, VanCamp's
	1984	3,334.1	138.7	1,806.8	19.8	
15. Hershey Foods	1985	1,996.2	112.2	1,197.4	16.6	Delmonico, Hershey's
	1984	1,848.5	108.7	1,122.6	17.3	Chocolate
Industry composite	1985	$101,669	$4,004	$58,294	16.5%	

NA = Not available.

Source: Ranking by market value of common stock according to *Business Week,* April 18, 1986. Financial data from annual reports.

COMPANY BACKGROUND

Campbell Soup Company was one of the world's leading manufacturers and marketers of branded consumer food products. In 1985 the company had approximately 44,000 employees and 80 manufacturing plants in 12 nations, with over 1,000 products on the market. Its major products were Prego spaghetti sauces, Le Menu frozen dinners, Pepperidge Farm baked goods, Mrs. Paul's frozen foods, Franco-American canned spaghettis, Vlasic pickles, and its flagship red-and-white-label canned soups.

Founded in 1869 by Joseph Campbell, a fruit merchant, and Abram Anderson, an ice-box maker, the company was originally know for its jams and jellies. In 1891 it was incorporated as the Joseph Campbell Co. in Camden, New Jersey. In 1899 John T. Dorrance, a brilliant 24-year-old with a Ph.D. from MIT, developed a process for canning soup in condensed form. He was also a master salesman who came up with the idea of attaching snappy placards to the sides of New York City streetcars as a way of promoting the company's products.

From 1900 to 1954 the company was owned entirely by the Dorrance family. It was incorporated as the Campbell Soup Company in 1922. When Dorrance died in 1930 after running the company for 16 years, he left an estate of over $115 million, the third-largest up to that time. He also left a company devoted to engineering, committed to supplying value (in recessions it would rather shave margins than lower quality or raise prices), and obsessed with secrecy. John T. Dorrance, Jr., ran the company for the next 24 years (1930–54) and few, if any, important decisions were made at Campbell without his approval. In 1954 the company went public, with the Dorrance family retaining majority control. In 1985 the Dorrance family still held about 60 percent of Campbell's stock and picked the top executives of the company. In 1984 John Dorrance III became a member of the board. The more than eight decades of family dominance contributed to what some insiders described as a conservative and paternalistic company culture at Campbell.

Over the years Campbell had diversified into a number of food and food-related businesses—Swanson frozen dinners, Pepperidge Farm bakery products, Franco-American spaghetti products, Recipe pet food, fast-food restaurant chains, Godiva chocolates, and even retail garden centers. Still, about half of the company's revenues came from the sale of its original stock-in-trade: canned soup. Throughout most of its history, the company picked its top executives from among those with a production background in the soup division—most had engineering training and good track records in furthering better manufacturing efficiency. One such person, Harold A. Shaub, a 30-year veteran of the company, was named president in 1972. An industrial engineer, Shaub placed a premium on controlling production cost while maintaining acceptable product quality. There were occasions when Shaub, during unannounced inspection tours, had shut down a complete plant that didn't measure up to the strict standards he demanded.

During his tenure Shaub began to set the stage for change at Campbell, acknowledging that "the company needed changes for the changing times."[2]* He restructured the company into divisions built around major product lines. Then in 1978, realizing that Campbell's marketing skills were too weak, he hired aggressive outsiders to revitalize the company's marketing efforts. That same year Campbell purchased Vlasic Foods, Inc., the largest producer of pickles in the United States.

Also in 1978 Campbell launched Prego spaghetti sauce products, the first major new food items introduced by Campbell in 10 years. The former Campbell policy required a new product had to show a profit within a year and the pay-out on Prego was expected to be three years. But because the policy held back new product development, Shaub changed it and set a goal of introducing two additional products each year.

In 1980 Campbell broke a 111-year-old debt-free tradition, issuing $100 million in 10-year notes. Until then the company had relied primarily on internally generated funds to meet long-term capital requirements.

Because of company tradition, everyone expected Shaub's successor to come from production. Thus it came as a surprise to Gordon McGovern, president of Connecticut-based Pepperidge Farm and a marketing man, when Shaub called him into his office and said, "I'd like you to come down here and take my place."[1] When McGovern became Campbell's president and CEO on December 1, 1980, Shaub remained on the board of directors.

McGovern was at Pepperidge Farm when the company was bought by Campbell in 1961. He was in business school when Margaret Rudkin, founder of Pepperidge Farm, spoke to his class. She told how she had built her bread company from scratch in an industry dominated by giants. McGovern was impressed. He wrote to Rudkin for a job, received it in 1956, and began his climb through the ranks. When Campbell acquired Pepperidge Farm in 1961 it had sales of $40 million. When McGovern became its president in 1968 sales had reached $60 million. When he left to become president of Campbell in 1980, Pepperidge Farms' sales had climbed to $300 million. McGovern brought some of what he considered Pepperidge's success strategy with him to Campbell: experimentation, new product development, marketing savvy, and creativity.

---

*Numbers in brackets refer to references listed at the end of this case.

MANAGEMENT UNDER McGOVERN

Every Saturday morning McGovern did his family's grocery shopping, stopping to straighten Campbell's displays and inspect those of competitors, studying packaging and reading labels, and trying to learn all he could about how and what people were eating. He encouraged his managers to do the same. Several board meetings were held in the backrooms of supermarkets so that afterward directors could roam the store aisles interviewing customers about Campbell products.

McGovern's style of management was innovative to a company known as much for its stodginess as for its red-and-white soup can. For decades Campbell Soup operated under strict rules for decorum. Eating, smoking, or drinking coffee was not permitted in the office. Managers had to share their offices with their secretaries, and an unwritten rule required executives to keep their suitcoats on in the office. When McGovern joined Campbell he drove to work in a yellow Volkswagen that stuck out in his parking space so much that the garagemen quietly arranged to have it painted. Finding the atmosphere at headquarters stifling, he promised a change.

He began wandering through the corridors every day, mingling easily among the employees. McGovern's voluble personality and memory for names made him popular with many employees. But not everyone was impressed by McGovern's style. Some production people were suspicious of his marketing background. Others believed that his grocery trips and hobnobbing with employees were ploys calculated to win him support and a reputation. But McGovern pressed forward with several internal changes: (1) a day-care center for the children of employees (complete with Campbell Kids posters on the wall), (2) a health program including workouts in a gymnasium, and (3) an unusual new benefit program which covered adoption expenses up to $1,000 and gave time off to employees who adopted children—in the same way that women were given maternity leave. He appointed the first two women vice presidents in the company's history; one of these, a former director of the Good Housekeeping Institute, was hired to identify consumers' food preferences and needs.

McGovern decentralized Campbell management to facilitate entrepreneurial risk-taking and new product development, devising a new compensation program to reward these traits. He restructured the company into some 50 autonomous units and divided the U.S. division into eight strategic profit centers: soups, beverages, pet foods, frozen foods, fresh produce, main meals, grocery, and food service. Units were encouraged to develop new products even if another unit would actually produce the products. Thus, the Prego spaghetti sauce unit—not the frozen food group—initiated frozen Mexican dinners. And although it wasn't his job, the director of market research created "Today's Taste," a line of refrigerated entrees and side dishes. "It's like things are in constant motion," the director said. "We are overloaded, but it's fun."[3]

The new structure encouraged managers, who had to compete for corporate funding, to be more aggressive in developing promising products. According to McGovern:

> These integral units allow the company to really get its arms around chunks of the business. The managers are answerable to the bottom line—to their investments, their hiring, their products—and it's a great motivation for performance.[4]

As part of this motivation, Campbell began annually allotting around $30 million to $40 million to support new ventures, each requiring a minimum of $10 million. This strategy was intended to encourage star performers while enabling management to weed out laggards. McGovern felt that this was much easier to determine when everyone knew where the responsibilities lay—but that it was no disgrace to fail if the effort was a good one. An employee noted that McGovern was endorsing "the right to fail," adding that "it makes the atmosphere so much more positive."[4]

Every Friday McGovern held meetings to discuss new products. The fact-finding sessions were attended by financial, marketing, engineering, and sales personnel. Typical McGovern questions included: "Would you eat something like that?" "Why not?" "Have you tried the competition's product?" "Is there a consumer niche?" The marketing research director noted that in Shaub's meetings the question was, "Can we make such a product cost-effectively?"[3]

Under Shaub the chain of command was inviolable, but McGovern was not hesitant about circumventing the chain when he felt it was warranted. He criticized one manager's product to another manager, expecting word to get back to the one with the problem. Although this often motivated some to prove McGovern wrong, others were unnerved by such tactics. When he became aware of this, McGovern eased up a bit.

In the past under prior CEOs, cost-cutters got promoted; now in McGovern's more creative atmosphere, the rules weren't so well defined. As one insider put it, "There's a great deal of uncertainty. No one really knows what it takes to get ahead. But that makes us all work harder."[3]

When hiring managers, McGovern, himself a college baseball player, tended to favor people with a competitive sports background. "There's teamwork and determination, but also the idea that you know how to lose and get back up again. 'Try, try, try' is what I say. I can't stress how important that is."[4]

STRATEGY

The strategic focus was on the consumer—considered to be the key to Campbell's growth and success in the 1980s. The consumer's "hot buttons" were identified as nutrition, convenience, low sodium, price, quality, and uniqueness—and managers were urged to "press those buttons." General managers were advised to take into account the consumer's perceptions, needs, and demands regarding nutrition, safety, flavor, and convenience. Key strategies were: (1) improving operating efficiency, (2) developing new products for the modern consumer, (3) updating advertising for new and established products, and (4) high quality.

When he took over, McGovern developed a five-year plan that included four financial performance objectives: a 15 percent annual increase in earnings, a 5 percent increase in volume, a 5 percent increase in sales (plus inflation), and an 18 percent return on equity by 1986. His long-range strategy included making acquisitions every two years that would bring in $200 million in annual sales. Campbell's acquisition strategy was to look for small, fast-growing food companies strong in product areas where Campbell was not and companies on the fast track that were in rapidly growing parts of their industries. Under McGovern, Campbell made a number of acquisitions:

1982
- Mrs. Paul's Kitchens, Inc., a processor and marketer of frozen prepared seafood and vegetable products, with annual sales of approximately $125 million (acquired at a cost of $55 million).
- Snow King Frozen Foods, Inc., engaged in the production and marketing of a line of uncooked frozen specialty meat products, with annual sales of $32 million.
- Juice Bowl Products, Inc., a Florida producer of fruit juices.
- Win Schuler Foods, Inc., a Michigan-based producer and distributor of specialty cheese spreads, flavored melba rounds, food service salad dressings, party dips, and sauces, with annual sales of $6.5 million.
- Costa Apple Products, Inc., a producer of apple juice retailed primarily in the Eastern United States, with annual sales of $6 million.

1983
Acquired several small domestic operations at a cost of $26 million, including:
- Annabelle's restaurant chain of 12 units in the southeastern United States.
- Triangle Manufacturing Corp., a manufacturer of physical fitness and sports medicine products.

1984
- Mendelson-Zeller Co., Inc., a California distributor of fresh produce.

1985

- Continental Foods Company S.A. and affiliated companies which produced sauces, confectioneries, and other food products in Belgium and France; the cost of the acquisition was $17 million.

Campbell was by no means alone in adding companies to its portfolio; many major mergers in the food industry were taking place (see Exhibit 3). Several factors were at work:

- Many food companies had been stung by ill-fated diversification forays outside food. In the 1960s when industry growth had slowed, it was fashionable to diversify into nonfoods. Many of the acquired companies turned out to be duds, draining earnings and soaking up too much top management attention. Now food companies were refocusing their efforts on food—the business they knew best.
- Even though the food industry was regarded as a slow-growth/low-margin business, the fact remained that stable demand, moderate capital costs, and high cash flows had boosted returns on equity to almost 20 percent for some companies. Food processors discovered that they were earning better returns on their food products than they were earning in the nonfood businesses they had earlier diversified into.

While companies such as Beatrice, the nation's largest food company, and Nestlé, the world's largest, paid substantial sums to buy out large established companies with extensive brand stables, others—such as Campbell—followed the route of concentrating on internal product development and smaller, selective acquisitions to complement their existing product lines. In fact Campbell was considered the leader among the food processors who were striving to limit acquisitions in favor of heavy, in-house product development. Campbell's emphasis on new product development was not without risk. It took $10 to $15 million in advertising and couponing to launch a brand. Because of the hit-or-miss nature of new products, only about one out of eight products reaching the test market state were successful. Moreover, industry analysts predicted that the continuing introduction of new products would lead to increased competition for shelf space and for the consumer's food dollar.

MARKETING

The outsiders Shaub had hired to revitalize Campbell's marketing included a vice president for marketing who was an eight-year veteran of a New York advertising firm and a soup general manager who was

EXHIBIT 3   Examples of Major Acquisitions in the Food Processing Industry, 1982–85

Buyer	Acquired Company	Year	Price (millions of dollars)	Products/Brands Acquired
Beatrice	Esmark	1984	$2,800	Swift, Hunt-Wesson Brands
CPC	C. F. Mueller	1983	122	Makes CPC biggest U.S. pasta maker
ConAgra	Peavey	1982	NA	Jams & syrups
	ACLI Seafood	1983	NA	
	Armour Food	1983	166	
	Imperial Foods' Country Poultry	1984	18	Processed meats
Dart & Kraft	Celestial Seasonings	1984	25	Herbal teas
Esmark	Norton Simon	1983	1,100	Hunt-Wesson
General Foods	Entenmann's	1982	315	Baked goods
	Otto Roth	1983	NA	Specialty cheeses
	Monterey	1983	NA	
	Peacock Foods	1983	NA	
	Ronzoni	1984	NA	Pasta
	Oroweat	1984	60	Bread
McCormick	Patterson Jenks	1984	53	Major British spice and food distributor
Nestlé	Carnation	1984	3,000	Evaporated milk, Friskies pet food
Philip Morris	General Foods	1985	5,750	Jell-O, Maxwell House
Pillsbury	Häagen-Dazs	1983	75	Ice cream
	Sedutto	1984	5	
Quaker Oats	Stokely-Van Camp	1983	238	Baked beans, canned goods
Ralston Purina	Continental Baking	1984	475	Hostess Twinkies, Wonder Bread
R. J. Reynolds	Nabisco Foods	1984	4,900	Oreo cookies, Ritz crackers, ginger ale, soda, tonic
	Canada Dry	1984	175	

NA = Not available.

Source: Data compiled from various sources.

a former Wharton business school professor. In addition to those hired by Shaub, the rest of McGovern's marketing-oriented executive team included: a frozen foods manager (a former marketing manager with General Foods), the head of the Pepperidge Farm Division, and the head of the Vlasic Foods division (both marketing men from Borden). This team boosted Campbell's marketing budget to $428 million by 1984 (up 57 percent from 1982). Advertising spending grew from $67 million in 1980 to $179 million in 1985. Prior to McGovern, Campbell used to cut ad spending at the end of a quarter to boost earnings. Besides hurting the brands, it gave the company an unfavorable reputation among the media. In 1985 the marketing expenditures (including advertising and promotion) of some of the leading food companies were: Campbell—approximately $488 million, Quaker—$619 million, Heinz—$303 million, Pillsbury—$365 million, and Sara Lee—$594 million.

In 1982 McGovern was named *Advertising Age's* Adman of the Year for his efforts in transforming Campbell into "one of the most aggressive market-driven companies in the food industry today."[4] *Advertising Age* noted that McGovern had almost doubled the advertising budget and had replaced the company's longtime ad agency for its soups, leading to a new ad campaign that helped reverse eight years of flat or lower sales. The new campaign emphasized nutrition and fitness, as opposed to the former "mmm, mmm, good" emphasis on taste. Print ads included long copy that referred to major government research studies citing soup's nutritional values. The new slogan was: "Soup is good food." New products and advertising were aimed at shoppers who were dieting, health conscious, and usually in a hurry. In keeping with the new fitness image, the 80-year-old Campbell Kids, although still cherubic, acquired a leaner look. Campbell's marketing strategy under McGovern was based on several important market research findings and projections:

- Women now comprised 43 percent of the workforce, and a level of 50 percent was projected by 1990.
- Two-income marriages represented 60 percent of all U.S. families. These would take in three out of every five dollars earned.
- Upper-income households would grow 3.5 times faster than total household formations.
- More than half of all households consisted of only one or two members.
- There were 18 million singles, and 23 percent of all households contained only one person.
- The average age of the population was advancing with the number of senior citizens totaling 25 million-plus and increasing.

- The percentage of meals eaten at home was declining.
- Nearly half of the adult meal-planners in the United States were watching their weight.
- Poultry consumption had increased 26 percent since 1973.
- Ethnic food preparation at home was increasing, with 40 percent, 21 percent, and 14 percent of household preparing Italian, Mexican, and Oriental foods, respectively, at home from scratch.
- There was growing consumer concern with food avoidance: sugar, salt, calories, chemicals, cholesterol, and additives.
- The "I am what I eat" philosophy had tied food in to lifestyles along with Nautilus machines, hot tubs, jogging, racquetball, backpacking, cross-country skiing, and aerobic dancing.

In response to growing ethnic food demand, Campbell began marketing ethnic selections in regions where interests were highest for particular food types. For instance, it marketed spicy Ranchero Beans only in the South and Southwest and planned to market newly acquired Puerto Rican foods in New York City.

The product development priorities were aimed at the themes of convenience, taste, flavor, and texture. The guidelines were:

- Prepare and market products that represent superior value to consumers and constantly strive to improve those values.
- Develop products that help build markets.
- Develop products that return a fair profit to Campbell and to customers.

In support of these guidelines, Campbell adopted several tactics:

- Use ongoing consumer research to determine eating habits by checking home menus, recipe preparation, and foods that are served together. Study meal and snack-eating occasions to determine which household members participate so that volume potential can be determined for possible new products and product improvement ideas.
- Develop new products and produce them in small quantities that simulate actual plant production capabilities.
- Test new or improved products in a large enough number of households which are so distributed throughout the United States that results can be projected nationally. Once the product meets pretest standards, recommend it for market testing.
- Once packaging and labels have been considered, design and pretest introductory promotion and advertising.
- Introduce a new product into selected test markets to determine actual store sales which can be projected nationally.
- If test marketing proves successful, roll out the new product on a regional or national plan using test market data as a rationale for expansion.

A key part of the strategy was the "Campbell in the Kitchen" project, consisting of some 75 homemakers across the country. Three to five times a year Campbell asked this "focus group" to try different products and give opinions. McGovern regularly dispatched company executives to the kitchens of these homemakers to observe eating patterns and see how meals were prepared. He sent Campbell's home economists into some of the households to work with the cooks on a one-to-one basis.

All this was in sharp contrast to the pre-McGovern era. Campbell averaged about 18 new product entries a year through the late 1970s. Many of these were really line extensions rather than new products. Substantial numbers flopped, partly because they had often been subjected to only the most rudimentary and inexpensive tests. Sometimes the testing had consisted only of a panel of the company's advertising and business executives sipping from teaspoons.

In 1983 Campbell was the biggest new-products generator in the combined food and health and beauty aids categories with a total of 42 new products. Second was Esmark, 36; followed by Lever/Lipton, 33; Nabisco Brands, 25; Beatrice and General Foods, 24 each; American Home Products, 23; Quaker Oats, 21; Borden, 19; and General Mills and Noxell, 17 each. Exhibit 4 shows Campbell's leading new products from 1982 to 1985.

PRODUCTION

McGovern summarized Campbell's philosophy on quality: "I want zero defects. If we can't produce quality, we'll get out of the business."[5] In 1984 Campbell held its first Worldwide Corporate Conference dedicated to quality. Hundreds of Campbell managers from all levels and most company locations spent three days at this conference. Campbell

---

EXHIBIT 4   Campbell's Leading New Products Total $600 Million in Sales for Fiscal 1985

1985 Ranking	Year Introduced
Le Menu Frozen Dinner	1982
Prego Spaghetti Sauce	1982
Chunky New England Clam Chowder	1984
Great Starts Breakfasts	1984
Prego Plus	1985

Source: The Wall Street Journal, August 14, 1985.

believed that the ultimate test of quality was consumer satisfaction, and its goal was to maintain a quality-conscious organization at every employee level in every single operation.

Before McGovern took over, Campbell used to emphasize new products compatible with existing production facilities. For example, a square omelet was designed for Swanson's frozen breakfasts because it was what the machine would make. After McGovern's appointment, although low-cost production was still a strategic factor, consumer trends—and not existing machinery—were the deciding factors for new product development. Other important factors considered in the production process included:

- The growing move toward consumption of refrigerated and fresh product in contrast to canned or frozen products.
- The emerging perception that private label and/or generic label merchandise would drive out weak national and secondary brands unless there was a clear product superiority and excellent price/value on the part of the brands supported by consumer advertising.
- The polarization of food preparation time with long preparation on weekends and special occasions, but fast preparation in between via microwaves, quick foods, and instant breakfasts.
- The cost of the package—especially metal packaging—which was outrunning the cost of the product it contained.
- Energy and distribution costs—these were big targets for efficiency with regional production, aseptic packaging, and packages designed for automatic warehouse handling and lightweight containers becoming standard.

The bulk of $154 million in capital expenditures in 1983 went into improvement of production equipment, expenditures for additional production capacity, the completion of the $100 million canned foods plant in North Carolina, and the start of a mushroom-producing facility at Dublin, Georgia. In 1984 construction began on a $9 million Le Menu production line in Sumter, South Carolina. Capital expenditures in 1985 totaled $213 million. Most of this went into improvements of production equipment, packaging technology, and expenditures for additional production capacity.

Campbell was considered a model of manufacturing efficiency. Production was fully integrated from the tomato patch to the can-making factory. Campbell was the nation's third largest can manufacturer behind American Can Company and Continental Group. Yet Campbell, which made the red-and-white soup can with the gold medallion an American institution, had recently concluded that food packaging was headed in the direction of snazzier and more convenient containers. McGovern compared sticking with the can to the refusal of U.S. automobile makers to change their ways in the face of the Japanese challenge:

There's a tremendous feeling of urgency because an overseas company could come in here with innovative packaging and technology and just take us to the cleaners on basic lines we've taken for granted for years.[6]

Other soup companies—including Libby, McNeill & Libby, a Nestlé Enterprises, Inc., unit that made Crosse & Blackwell gourmet soup— had already started experimenting with can alternatives. Campbell's testing was considered the most advanced, but a mistake could mean revamping production facilities at a cost of $100 million or more.

Researchers at the Campbell Soup Company's DNA Plant Technology Corporation were working toward the development of the "perfect tomato." They were seeking ways to grow tasty, high solids tomatoes under high-temperature conditions that would cause normal plants to droop and wither. They also hoped to crossbreed high-quality domestic tomatoes with tough, hardy, wild tomatoes that could withstand cold weather. A breakthrough in this area could result in two harvests a year. Conceding that they were latecomers (Heinz began similar research several years after Campbell), Campbell researchers estimated that they were four to five years ahead of Heinz.

Campbell believed its key strengths were: (1) a worldwide system for obtaining ingredients, (2) a broad range of food products that could be used as a launching pad for further innovation, and (3) an emphasis on low-cost production.

CAMPBELL'S OPERATING DIVISIONS

Campbell Soup Company was divided into six operating units—Campbell U.S., Pepperidge Farm, Vlasic Foods, Mrs. Paul's Kitchens, Other United States, and International. Sales and profit performance by division are shown in Exhibit 5.

Campbell U.S.

In 1985 the Campbell U.S. Division was Campbell's largest operating unit, accounting for almost 62 percent of the company's total consolidated sales. Operating earnings increased 5 percent over 1984. Unit volume rose 7 percent in 1983, 9 percent in 1984, and 4 percent in 1985. The Campbell U.S. division was divided into eight profit centers: soup, frozen foods, grocery business, beverage business, food service business, poultry business, fresh produce business, and pet foods business. Exhibit 6 shows the brands Campbell had in this division and the major competitors each brand faced.

The soup business group alone accounted for more than 25 percent of the company's consolidated sales (as compared to around 50 percent

EXHIBIT 5   Sales and Earnings of Campbell Soup, by Division, 1980–85 (millions of dollars)

	1980	1981	1982	1983	1984	1985
Campbell U.S.:						
Sales	$1,608	$1,678	$1,773	$1,987	$2,282	$2,500
Operating earnings	205	190	211	250	278	292
Pepperidge Farm:						
Sales	283	329	392	433	435	426
Operating earnings	29	35	41	43	35	39
Vlasic Foods:						
Sales	130	137	149	168	193	199
Operating earnings	8	10	12	13	14	16
Mrs. Paul's Kitchens:						
Sales				108	126	138
Operating earnings				10	14	11
Other United States:						
Sales	35	27	56	64	84	81
Operating earnings	1	(1)	(1)	(1)	(2)	(3)
International:						
Sales	512	694	643	599	624	716
Operating earnings	33	46	46	33	34	35

Source: Campbell's annual reports.

in the 1970s). Campbell's flagship brands of soups accounted for 80 percent of the $1 billion-plus annual canned soup market; in 1985 Campbell offered grocery shoppers over 50 varieties of canned soups. Heinz was second with 10 percent of the market. Heinz had earlier withdrawn from producing Heinz-label soup and shifted its production over to making soups for sale under the private labels of grocery chains; Heinz was the leading private-label segment. See Exhibit 6 for information on competitors and their brands.

Although the soup business was relatively mature (McGovern preferred to call it underworked), Campbell's most ambitious consumer research took place in this unit. McGovern planned to speed up soup sales by turning out a steady flow of new varieties in convenient packages: "Ethnic, dried, refrigerated, frozen, microwave—you name it, we're going to try it."[7]

In 1985 Campbell began an assault on the $290 million dry-soup mix market dominated by Thomas J. Lipton, Inc., a unit of the Anglo-Dutch Unilever Group. This move was made because dry-soup sales in the United States were growing faster than sales of canned soup. Lipton's aggressive response to test marketing of an early Campbell dry-soup product resulted in Campbell's rushing a six-flavor line into national distribution ahead of schedule.

EXHIBIT 6   The Campbell U.S. Division; Products, Rival Brands, Competitors

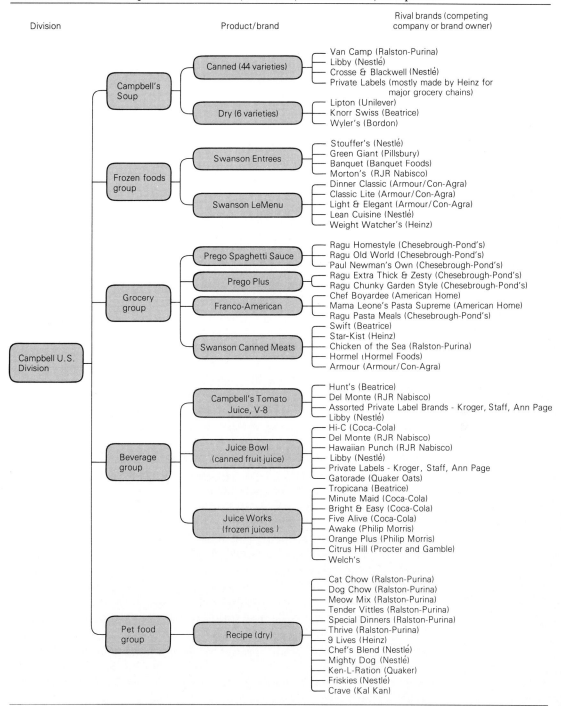

Division	Product/brand	Rival brands (competing company or brand owner)
Campbell's Soup	Canned (44 varieties)	Van Camp (Ralston-Purina) Libby (Nestlé) Crosse & Blackwell (Nestlé) Private Labels (mostly made by Heinz for major grocery chains)
	Dry (6 varieties)	Lipton (Unilever) Knorr Swiss (Beatrice) Wyler's (Bordon)
Frozen foods group	Swanson Entrees	Stouffer's (Nestlé) Green Giant (Pillsbury) Banquet (Banquet Foods) Morton's (RJR Nabisco)
	Swanson LeMenu	Dinner Classic (Armour/Con-Agra) Classic Lite (Armour/Con-Agra) Light & Elegant (Armour/Con-Agra) Lean Cuisine (Nestlé) Weight Watcher's (Heinz)
Grocery group	Prego Spaghetti Sauce	Ragu Homestyle (Chesebrough-Pond's) Ragu Old World (Chesebrough-Pond's) Paul Newman's Own (Chesebrough-Pond's)
	Prego Plus	Ragu Extra Thick & Zesty (Chesebrough-Pond's) Ragu Chunky Garden Style (Chesebrough-Pond's)
	Franco-American	Chef Boyardee (American Home) Mama Leone's Pasta Supreme (American Home) Ragu Pasta Meals (Chesebrough-Pond's)
	Swanson Canned Meats	Swift (Beatrice) Star-Kist (Heinz) Chicken of the Sea (Ralston-Purina) Hormel (Hormel Foods) Armour (Armour/Con-Agra)
Beverage group	Campbell's Tomato Juice, V-8	Hunt's (Beatrice) Del Monte (RJR Nabisco) Assorted Private Label Brands - Kroger, Staff, Ann Page Libby (Nestlé)
	Juice Bowl (canned fruit juice)	Hi-C (Coca-Cola) Del Monte (RJR Nabisco) Hawaiian Punch (RJR Nabisco) Libby (Nestlé) Private Labels - Kroger, Staff, Ann Page Gatorade (Quaker Oats)
	Juice Works (frozen juices)	Tropicana (Beatrice) Minute Maid (Coca-Cola) Bright & Easy (Coca-Cola) Five Alive (Coca-Cola) Awake (Philip Morris) Orange Plus (Philip Morris) Citrus Hill (Procter and Gamble) Welch's
Pet food group	Recipe (dry)	Cat Chow (Ralston-Purina) Dog Chow (Ralston-Purina) Meow Mix (Ralston-Purina) Tender Vittles (Ralston-Purina) Special Dinners (Ralston-Purina) Thrive (Ralston-Purina) 9 Lives (Heinz) Chef's Blend (Nestlé) Mighty Dog (Nestlé) Ken-L-Ration (Quaker) Friskies (Nestlé) Crave (Kal Kan)

Campbell U.S. Division

In 1982 McGovern caused a stir when he announced publicly that Campbell's Swanson TV-dinner line was "junk food": "It was great in 1950, but in today's world it didn't go into the microwave; it didn't represent variety or a good eating experience to my palate."[7] He maintained that consumers had discovered high-quality options to the TV-dinner concept. The market niche for more exotic, better quality entrees was being exploited by Nestlé's Stouffer subsidiary and Pillsbury's Green Giant division (Exhibit 6).

Campbell's frozen foods group answered the challenge by producing its own frozen gourmet line, Le Menu. Campbell committed about $50 million in manufacturing, marketing, and trade promotion costs on the basis of encouraging marketing tests. In the five years prior to Le Menu, Swanson's sales volume had slipped 16 percent. Its biggest volume decline (23 percent) was in the area that had been its stronghold: sales of dinners and entrees. Overall industry sales in dinners and entrees grew to $2 billion during 1982. The single-dish entree market had increased 58 percent since 1978, with sales being dominated by Stouffer's Lean Cuisine selections.

Le Menu—served on round heatable plates and consisting of such delicacies as chicken cordon bleu, al dente vegetables, and sophisticated wine sauces—produced 20 percent growth in the frozen meal unit with sales of $150 million during its first year of national distribution (1984). This was double Campbell's earlier projection of sales.

Under Project Fix, Swanson dinners were overhauled, putting in less salt and more meat stock in gravies and adding new desserts and sauces. The revamped line had new packaging and a redesigned logo. The frozen foods business unit reported an overall volume increase of 3 percent in 1983, 27 percent in 1984, and 2 percent in 1985. In 1985 the unit had a 52 percent increase in operating earnings as sales rose 10 percent.

Meanwhile, Pillsbury had targeted the $4 billion-a-year frozen main meal market and the rapidly expanding market in light meals and snacks as vital to its future. In 1984 Pillsbury purchased Van de Kamp's, a market leader in frozen seafood and ethnic entrees for $102 million. During 1985 Van de Kamp's became the number one seller of frozen Mexican meals. Pillsbury also sold more than one third of the 550 million frozen pizzas consumed in the United States in 1985 and made substantial investments in quality improvements and marketing support to maintain the number one position in frozen pizza.

The grocery business unit's star was Prego Spaghetti Sauce that in 1984 had obtained 25 percent of the still-growing spaghetti sauce market and was the number two sauce, behind Chesebrough-Pond's Ragu. (Exhibit 6 lists competing brands.) Chesebrough had recently introduced Ragu Chunky Gardenstyle sauce to try to convert cooks who still made their own sauce (about 45 percent of all spaghetti sauce users still cooked their own from scratch). The new Ragu product came in three varieties: mushrooms and onions, green peppers and mushrooms, and extra tomatoes with garlic and onions. Campbell had no plans for a similar entry because copying Ragu wouldn't be innovative. However, a Prego Plus Spaghetti Sauce line completed its first year of national distribution in 1985. To show "old-fashioned concern," all three sizes of Prego sauce came in jars with tamper-evident caps; Campbell would buy back from grocery shelves all jars that had been opened.

The Beverage group's 1985 operating earnings were affected by a slower-than-anticipated introduction of Juice Works—a line of 100 percent natural, no-sugar-added, pure, blended fruit juices for children. This was attributed to intense competitive pressure and major technological problems. Campbell's Tomato Juice and V-8 Cocktail Vegetable Juice also reported disappointing earnings. Juice Bowl, however, showed improved earnings in 1985. Campbell's competition in this area came from Hunt's, Del Monte, and private label brands (Exhibit 6).

The Poultry business unit sales were up 13 percent in 1985. Operating earnings for the year were positive, compared to a loss in 1984. These results stemmed from the national rollout of frozen "finger foods"—Plump & Juicy Dipsters, Drumlets, and Cutlets—and sales of Premium Chunk White Chicken. Some of the competitors were Banquet's Chicken Drum-Snackers and Tyson's Chick'n Dippers.

Pepperidge Farm

Pepperidge Farm, Campbell's second-largest division with 12 percent of the company's consolidated sales, reported a decline in operating income and a sales gain of less than 1 percent between 1983 and 1984. In 1980 it was one of the fastest-growing units; sales had risen 14 percent annually, compounded.

1984's disappointing results were largely blamed on losses incurred in the apple juice (Costa Apple Products, Inc., purchased in 1982) and "Star Wars" cookies businesses. When Pepperidge Farm introduced Star Wars cookies, McGovern called them a "travesty" because they were faddish and did not fit the brand's high-quality, upscale adult image. Plus, at $1.39 a bag, he maintained that it was a "lousy value." But he didn't veto them because, "I could be wrong."[6] As the popularity of the movie series waned, so did sales.

The frozen biscuit and bakery business unit volume was also down. New products such as Vegetables in Pastry and Deli's reportedly did not receive enough marketing support.

To remedy the division's growth decline, a number of steps were taken:

- Apple juice operations were transferred to the Campbell U.S. division beverage unit.
- During the year Pepperidge divested itself of operations that no longer fit into its strategic plan, including Lexington Gardens, Inc., a garden center chain.
- Deli's went back into research and development to improve quality.
- By the start of the 1985 fiscal year a new management team was in place and a comprehensive review of each product was being conducted in an effort to return emphasis to traditional product lines and quality standards which accounted for its success and growth in the past.

At the end of 1985, Pepperidge Farm showed an 11 percent increase in operating earnings over the previous year in spite of a 2 percent drop in sales. This was considered a result of the transfer of Pepperidge Farm beverage operations to the Campbell U.S. beverage group and the sale of the Lexington Gardens nursery chain. During 1985 sales in the convectionery business unit increased 22 percent and seven Godiva boutiques were added. Goldfish Crackers and Puff Pastry contributed to a volume increase in the food service business unit, while some varieties of Deli's and the Snack Bar products were discontinued.

One of Pepperidge Farm's major competitors in frozen bakery products was Sara Lee, which had 40 percent of the frozen sweet goods market and an ever-increasing 33 percent share of the specialty breads category. Pepperidge Farm's fresh breads and specialty items competed against a host of local, regional, and national brands. Exhibit 7 presents more details.

Vlasic Foods

Campbell's third largest domestic division enjoyed an 11 percent increase in operating earnings in 1985. Vlasic maintained its number one position with a 31 percent share of the pickles market. Seventeen percent of Vlasic's sales were in the food service category.

In 1985 Vlasic implemented new labels which used color bands and a flavor rating scale to help consumers find their favorite tastes quickly on the supermarket shelf. Taking advantage of their marketing research, which indicated consumer desires for new and interesting flavors, Vlasic introduced "Zesty Dills" and "Bread & Butter Whole Pickle" lines in 1985. Heinz was Campbell's leading national competitor in this area (Exhibit 8), but there were a number of important regional and private label brands which competed with Heinz and Vlasic for shelf space.

EXHIBIT 7   The Pepperidge Farm Division: Products, Rival Brands, Competitors

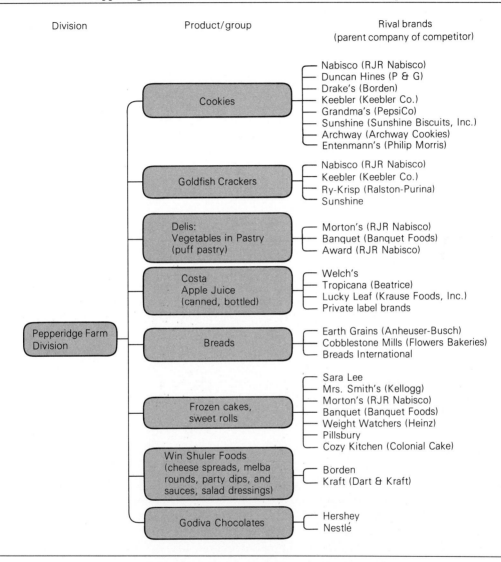

Division	Product/group	Rival brands (parent company of competitor)

Pepperidge Farm Division

Cookies
- Nabisco (RJR Nabisco)
- Duncan Hines (P & G)
- Drake's (Borden)
- Keebler (Keebler Co.)
- Grandma's (PepsiCo)
- Sunshine (Sunshine Biscuits, Inc.)
- Archway (Archway Cookies)
- Entenmann's (Philip Morris)

Goldfish Crackers
- Nabisco (RJR Nabisco)
- Keebler (Keebler Co.)
- Ry-Krisp (Ralston-Purina)
- Sunshine

Delis: Vegetables in Pastry (puff pastry)
- Morton's (RJR Nabisco)
- Banquet (Banquet Foods)
- Award (RJR Nabisco)

Costa Apple Juice (canned, bottled)
- Welch's
- Tropicana (Beatrice)
- Lucky Leaf (Krause Foods, Inc.)
- Private label brands

Breads
- Earth Grains (Anheuser-Busch)
- Cobblestone Mills (Flowers Bakeries)
- Breads International

Frozen cakes, sweet rolls
- Sara Lee
- Mrs. Smith's (Kellogg)
- Morton's (RJR Nabisco)
- Banquet (Banquet Foods)
- Weight Watchers (Heinz)
- Pillsbury
- Cozy Kitchen (Colonial Cake)

Win Shuler Foods (cheese spreads, melba rounds, party dips, and sauces, salad dressings)
- Borden
- Kraft (Dart & Kraft)

Godiva Chocolates
- Hershey
- Nestlé

Win Schuler, the Vlasic subsidiary purchased in 1982, reported flat sales in 1984 due to a general economic decline in the Michigan and upper Midwest markets where its products were sold. In 1985 it was moved to Campbell's refrigerated foods business unit where there were plans to begin producing a wider range of food products under the Win Schuler brand name.

EXHIBIT 8 Vlasic Division: Products, Rival Brands, and Competitors

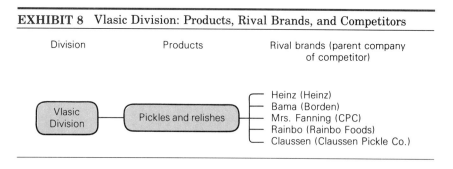

EXHIBIT 9 The Mrs. Paul's Kitchen Division: Products, Rival
Brands, National Competitors

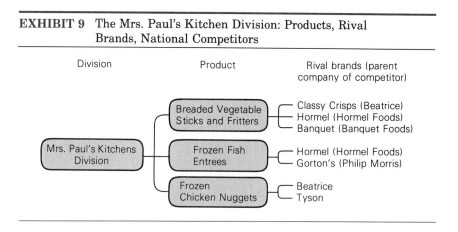

Mrs. Paul's Kitchens

Sales of this division for 1984 were up 16 percent over the previous
year, operating earnings increased 36 percent, and unit volume increased 9 percent. Mrs. Paul's sales represented just over 3 percent of
Campbell's total business; all results exceeded goals set for the year.
However, strong competitive pressure on its traditional lines was
blamed for the unit's drop in operating earnings for 1985. Competing
brands included Hormel and Gorton's (Exhibit 9).

When Campbell acquired Mrs. Paul's in 1982, it was rumored that
Heinz and Pillsbury, among others, were considering the same acquisition. Shortly after the acquisition, Campbell responded to consumer
preferences for convenience seafood products that were nutritious, low
in calories, microwavable, and coated more lightly, by introducing

Light & Natural Fish Fillets in 1983. Quality improvements were made to existing products, and a promising new product, Light Seafood entrees, was introduced in 1984. Market share increased about 25 percent over 1983, and Light Seafood Entrees went national in 1985. This line, which featured seven varieties of low-calorie, microwavable, seafood dishes, accounted for 11 percent of 1985's volume. However, sales of the company's established product lines of breaded frozen seafood items dipped below the 1984 level.

Campbell's Other U.S. Businesses

Beyond the base of Campbell's main operating groups there were several additional small businesses: Triangle Manufacturing Corp., a health- and fitness-products manufacturer; Campbell Hospitality, the restaurant division; and Snow King Frozen Foods, Inc., a manufacturer of frozen meat specialty products.

In 1984, the Hospitality Division, encompassing 59 Pietro's restaurants, 15 Annabelle's, and 6 H. T. McDoogal's, reported an operating loss slightly less than 1983. During the year the division added one H. T. McDoogal's, two Annabelle's, and nine Pietro's units.

In 1985 Annabelle's experienced a 14 percent increase in sales and a 43 percent rise in operating earnings. During the year Campbell announced its intention to sell four H. T. McDoogal's restaurants. Snow King reported a sales decline of 19 percent and an operating loss of almost $1 million.

Competing food companies in the restaurant business included General Mills and Pillsbury. General Mills' Red Lobster unit was the nation's largest full-service dinner-house chain. Red Lobster had 1985 sales of $827 million—an all-time high—and its operating profits also set a record. Pillsbury's Restaurants Group was comprised of Burger King and Steak & Ale Restaurants; both achieved record sales and earnings in 1985. Pillsbury opened 477 new restaurants in 1985—the most ever in a single year—bringing the total to 4,601.

Triangle, Campbell's physical fitness subsidiary, in its second full year of operation in 1985, reported that sales had more than tripled, but that increased marketing costs aimed at securing brand recognition resulted in an operating loss. Sales growth was a result of doubling the size of Triangle's distribution system. Its best-known product line, "The Band" wrist and ankle weights, maintained the number two position in its category with a 14 percent market share. Triangle planned to build on its strengths by entering the exercise equipment category and by marketing its products internationally.

Campbell's International Division

Campbell's international division provided 18 percent of the company's consolidated sales in 1984. Campbell had subsidiaries in 11 foreign countries and was planning to expand further. Total restructuring of the international division was in progress with goals of increasing sales and earnings and building a solid base for growth.

In 1985 steps were taken toward the division's goal of contributing 25 percent of Campbell's corporate sales and earnings. A number of operations were consolidated, and new businesses were added. Other international objectives were to improve Campbell's presence in all international markets and to make Campbell into a premier international company.

RECENT EVENTS

During 1985 the market price of Campbell's stock reached a new high of $80.50 a share. In July the stock was split two for one. At year-end 1985 the market price was $51.50 and the stock price was up $4 during one December week. Analysts were puzzled by this sudden rise in market price, and there were rumors of a takeover.

Analysts observed that the company had been hurt by fierce competition in 1985, an increasing softness in many of its markets, and mistakes on new product introduction. In its *1985 Annual Report* Campbell acknowledged increased competition in the marketplace:

> The supermarket has become an arena of intense competitive activity as food companies introduce a steady stream of new consumer-oriented products and support them with massive marketing dollars in an attempt to carve out a first or second place position in the respective categories. That competitive activity is keeping the pressure on Campbell's operating results.

REFERENCES

1. *Forbes,* December 7, 1981, p. 44.
2. *The Wall Street Journal,* September 17, 1984, p. 1.
3. *The Wall Street Journal,* September 17, 1984, p. 10.
4. *Advertising Age,* January 3, 1983, p. 38.
5. *Savvy,* June 1984, p. 39.
6. *Business Week,* November 21, 1983, p. 102.
7. *Business Week,* December 24, 1984, p. 67.

The Kellogg Company and the Ready-to-Eat Cereal Industry*

Joseph A. Schenk
Dan S. Prickett
Stanley J. Stough
all of The University of Dayton

You take care of the outside.
We'll help take care of the inside—1985 Ad for Kellogg's All Bran.

Advertising campaigns for Kellogg products in the 1980s stress the healthy, nutritious quality of cereal flakes—corn, bran, wheat, oats— a Kellogg theme that began almost a century ago. Dr. John H. Kellogg and W. K. Kellogg sought to develop a cereal that could replace meat in the diets of the patients at the Battle Creek sanitarium that the Kelloggs managed. The product of their efforts, Corn Flakes, became popular enough with the patients that the Kelloggs formed two companies that became the Kellogg Company in 1899.

Eighty-six years later Kellogg is one of the largest food companies in the world, with annual sales exceeding $2.5 billion and earnings greater than $250 million. Kellogg has established a position in the ready-to-eat (RTE) cereal market almost twice as large as either of the two nearest competitors, General Mills and General Foods. "Kellogg knows the cereal business better than anyone else," said William Wason of Brown Brothers Harriman & Co., "and the management has had the wisdom to stick with what they know." In December 1985, Kellogg was named one of the five best-managed companies in the United States by *Dun's Business Month*. Kellogg won this acclaim

*Address reprint requests to: Joseph A. Schenk, Management Department, University of Dayton, 300 College Park, Dayton, OH 45469–0001. Copyright © 1986 by Joseph A. Schenk.

because of its performance throughout the 1970s and early 1980s, the darkest time in the industry's history, and the progress Kellogg made in recovering during 1984 and 1985.

THE READY-TO-EAT CEREAL INDUSTRY

The RTE cereal industry is composed of firms that are engaged in the manufacture and sale of prepackaged, processed foodstuffs made primarily of grain products. The user does not have to prepare the product prior to use, and it can be eaten in dry form or with the addition of other substances, such as milk and sugar. Advantages of the products from a consumer perspective include convenience of use and easy satisfaction of nutritional requirements. Consumption of the product takes place primarily at breakfast, but they are also used as between-meal snacks. The first products in the market were introduced by W. K. Kellogg, Wheat Flakes in 1894, and Corn Flakes in 1898.

The $4 billion RTE cereal industry is composed of several large companies that dominate the market. Led by Kellogg, the industry includes General Mills, General Foods, Quaker Oats, Ralston Purina, and Nabisco. Exhibit 1 lists the market share performance of the major competitors as of 1984.

The significance of cereals within the product lines of the competitors changes as a result of competition and developments within the companies themselves. Although cereals represent more than 75 percent of Kellogg sales, cereals are estimated to constitute no more than 13 percent of General Foods sales and 7 percent of General Mills sales. Kellogg sales and estimated operating profits by division are listed in Exhibit 2.

Vigorous competition in the RTE cereal industry requires intensive and decisive actions to expand investments in research, in the development of new products, and in marketing. Marketing plans generally center on facing the competition squarely and forcefully. Budgets for advertising and promotions have increased substantially in recent years, both to give additional support to established products and to successfully support new product introductions. Market shares for the top ten products in the industry are listed in Exhibit 3. Selected information regarding each major competitor is presented below.

General Mills

General Mills managed to increase its market share significantly during the 1976–81 period. Since then, market share has stabilized and General Mills has been able to maintain a share position in the industry

EXHIBIT 1

Company	1976	1977	1978	1979	1980	1981	1982	1983	1984
Kellogg	42.6%	42.5%	42.0%	41.5%	40.9%	39.3%	38.5%	38.5%	40.3%
General Mills	20.8	20.5	20.4	22.2	22.4	23.0	23.1	23.2	23.1
General Foods	15.7	16.8	16.0	15.4	15.0	15.0	16.0	16.1	13.3
Quaker Oats	8.9	8.9	8.7	8.6	8.6	8.6	8.9	8.9	8.6
Ralston Purina	4.9	3.4	5.7	5.6	6.2	6.1	5.6	6.1	6.3
Nabisco	4.0	4.2	4.2	4.1	3.8	3.9	3.8	3.8	4.2
All others	3.1	3.7	3.0	2.6	3.1	4.1	4.1	3.4	4.2

Source: *Advertising Age,* Aug. 5, 1985, p. 42; Jun. 14, 1982, p. 62; May 25, 1981, p. 62; Aug. 28, 1978, p. 217.

EXHIBIT 2 Kellogg Company: Operating Profit at Year End December, Estimated by Division ($ millions)

	1982	1983	1984	1985	1986 (est.)
Net sales	$2,367	$2,381	$2,602	$2,930	$3,250
Operating profits					
Domestic RTE Cereals	238.0	255.0	311.0	395.0	450.0
Mrs. Smith's	29.0	28.5	31.5	36.9	43.0
Salada	9.0	10.0	11.0	12.5	14.0
Fearn	13.8	15.5	17.0	19.0	21.0
International	107.9	105.4	96.7	95.0	110.0
Total operating income	397.7	414.4	467.2	558.4	638.0
Net income	$ 227.8	$ 242.7	$ 250.5	$ 281.3	$ 320.5

Source: Prudential-Bache Securities, Inc., Apr. 2, 1986.

EXHIBIT 3 Cold Cereal's Top Ten in Market Share (in percent)

Brand (company)	1983		1984	
	Pounds	Dollars	Pounds	Dollars
Corn Flakes (K)	6.8%	4.7%	6.8%	4.7%
Frosted Flakes (K)	5.2	4.8	5.6	5.2
Cheerios (GM)	5.5	5.8	5.2	5.5
Raisin Bran (K)	4.6	4.1	4.5	4.0
Chex (RP)	4.3	4.4	4.3	4.6
Shredded Wheat (N)	4.0	3.1	4.0	3.3
Rice Krispies (K)	3.6	3.9	3.5	3.8
Raisin Bran (GF)	3.0	2.5	2.7	2.1
Cap'n Crunch (Q)	2.9	3.5	2.7	3.2
Honey-Nut Cheerios (GM)	2.3	2.6	2.6	2.9
Total	42.2%	39.4%	41.9%	39.3%

Abbreviations: K = Kellogg; GM = General Mills; GF = General Foods; Q = Quaker Oats; N = Nabisco; RP = Ralston Purina.

Source: *Advertising Age,* Aug. 5, 1985, p. 42.

at about 23 percent. Recent new product activity included the national roll-out of E.T.s, which failed to produce significant sales, reflecting a decline of consumer interest in licensed properties. Cinnamon Toast Crunch, Fiber One, Bran Muffin Crunch, and S'More's Crunch are all expected to perform well after national roll-out in early 1986. General Mills's brands and the market share performance of each brand for the period 1982–84 are shown in Exhibit 4.

General Mills has concentrated its efforts on its snack food, yogurt, and restaurant businesses. It has divested some toy operations and repurchased 7 million shares of its own stock (44 million shares outstanding). General Mills's net sales and operating profit by segment are listed in Exhibit 5.

General Foods

Throughout the 1970s, General Foods relied on coffee—Maxwell House, Sanka, Yuban, and Brim—for approximately 40 percent of its total revenue (*New York Times,* Sept. 15, 1985). Since then, it has made major acquisitions. Currently, the company gets 40 percent of its revenues from packaged groceries, 28 percent from coffee products, and 18 percent from processed meats (*Economist,* 1985). Coffee is still General Foods's largest single product, and it holds a 38 percent share of the coffee market (Philip Morris, 1986). In fiscal year 1985, General Foods achieved total revenues of $9 billion and the RTE cereal sales accounted for $512 million of total sales (Drexel, Burnham, & Lambert, May 20, 1985).

Sales of Post Toasties and Grape Nuts are eroding. Raisin Bran and Honey Nut Crunch Raisin Bran are reported to be performing well in the health-conscious market segment (*New York Times,* Sept. 15, 1985). Exhibit 6 lists General Foods's RTE cereal products and market share performance for the 1982–84 period.

Most of General Foods's development in the 1980s consisted of creating or acquiring product lines to enter new markets, particularly convenience, low-calorie foods. Acquisitions include Oscar Meyer, Entenmann's bakery, Ronzoni, and Orowheat. New products developments include Crystal Light, Pudding Pops, Sun Apple, Lean Strips, and Crispy Cookin' French Fries, of which only Crystal Light and Pudding Pops had met with success as of the end of 1985.

Simultaneously, General Foods has divested its pet foods division and the Burger Chef restaurant chain and repurchased 11 percent of its stock. In 1985, Philip Morris acquired General Foods to integrate its food operations into the tobacco products company. General Foods's sales and operating profits by segment are listed in Exhibit 7.

EXHIBIT 4   General Mills's Ready-to-Eat Cereals: Market Share Data (in percent)

Brand	1982		1983		1984	
	Pounds	*Dollars*	*Pounds*	*Dollars*	*Pounds*	*Dollars*
Cheerios	5.6%	5.9%	5.5%	5.8%	5.2%	5.5%
Honey Nut Cheerios	2.1	2.4	2.3	2.6	2.6	2.9
Total	1.7	2.4	1.9	2.6	2.1	2.8
Lucky Charms	1.7	2.2	1.6	2.1	1.7	2.1
Trix	1.5	1.9	1.5	1.9	1.5	1.9
Wheaties	2.5	1.9	2.3	1.7	2.0	1.4
Golden Grahams	1.3	1.3	1.3	1.3	1.3	1.3
Crispy Wheats 'n Raisins	1.1	1.3	1.1	1.3	1.0	1.1
Licensed Products	0.4	0.5	1.1	1.3	0.7	1.0
Monsters, etc.	0.7	1.0	0.6	0.9	0.5	0.8
Cinnamon Toast Crunch	—	—	—	—	0.6	0.7
Cocoa Puffs	0.7	1.8	0.7	0.8	0.6	0.7
Buc Wheats	0.5	0.6	0.4	0.5	0.3	0.4
Others	0.3	0.2	0.5	0.4	0.6	0.5
Total	20.7%	23.1%	20.8%	23.2%	20.7%	23.1%

Source: Advertising Age, Aug. 5, 1985, p. 42.

EXHIBIT 5   General Mills: Operating Profit at Year End May, by Segment

	1983	1984	1985	1986 (est.)
Net sales	$4,082	$4,118	$4,285	$4,550
Operating profits				
Consumer foods	269.4	275.3	265.6	300.0
Restaurants	80.0	70.0	91.5	97.0
Specialty retailing and other (loss)	10.4	19.8	(1.7)	23.0
Total operating profit	359.8	365.1	355.4	420.0
Net income (loss)	$ 245.1	$ 233.4	$ (72.9)	$ 182.9

Source: Prudential-Bache Securities, Inc., Apr. 2, 1986.

Quaker Oats

In the 1960s, Quaker Oats acquired many diverse businesses. By the 1980s, Quaker Oats had divested its restaurants and chemical products units and was concentrating on acquiring packaged foods and specialty companies including Brookstone (tools), Jos. A. Bank (clothiers),

EXHIBIT 6 General Foods' Ready-to-Eat Cereals: Market Share Data (in percent)

Brand	1982		1983		1984	
	Pounds	*Dollars*	*Pounds*	*Dollars*	*Pounds*	*Dollars*
Post Raisin Bran	3.1%	2.8%	3.0%	2.5%	2.7%	2.1%
Grape-Nuts	2.9	2.4	2.5	1.9	2.2	1.5
Super Sugar Crisp	1.4	1.6	1.5	1.6	1.4	1.4
Honeycombs	1.1	1.5	1.2	1.5	1.1	1.3
Post Fruit & Fibre	1.5	1.7	1.3	1.4	1.3	1.4
Pebbles	1.2	1.4	1.2	1.4	1.1	1.3
Smurf Berry Crunch	—	—	1.0	1.1	0.5	0.6
Post Toasties	1.3	0.9	1.2	0.9	1.0	0.8
Alpha-Bits	0.8	0.9	0.8	0.9	0.7	0.8
Bran Flakes	0.8	0.8	0.8	0.8	0.8	0.8
Honey-Nut Crunch Raisin Bran	0.3	0.3	0.7	0.7	0.2	0.2
Raisin Grape-Nuts	0.8	0.8	0.6	0.6	0.4	0.4
Fortified Oat Flakes	0.6	0.5	0.6	0.5	0.5	0.4
C. W. Post Hearty Granola	0.2	0.2	—	0.1	0.1	0.1
Others	0.4	0.2	0.1	0.2	0.3	0.2
Total	16.4%	16.0%	16.6%	16.1%	14.3%	13.3%

Source: Advertising Age, Aug. 5, 1985, p. 42.

EXHIBIT 7 General Foods: Operating Profit at Year End March, by Segment ($ millions)

	1983	*1984*	*1985*	*1986 (est.)*
Net sales	$8,256	$8,599	$9,022	$9,500
Operating profits				
Packaged groceries	427.8	470.5	419.3	451.0
Coffee	131.1	107.9	127.2	135.0
Processed meats	90.1	96.9	104.2	115.1
Food services and other	38.4	39.9	51.2	55.0
Total operating income	686.6	715.2	701.9	756.1
Net income	$ 288.5	$ 317.1	$ 302.8	$ 316.4

Source: Prudential-Bache Securities, Inc., Oct. 1, 1985.

Eyelab (eyeware retailing), and Stokely Van Camp (pork and beans, Gatorade). In addition, Quaker Oats repurchased 5 percent of its own shares in March 1985. The 1980s witnessed an aggressive Quaker Oats expanding its operations throughout its product lines.

EXHIBIT 8   Quaker Oats' Ready-to-Eat Cereals: Market Share Data (in percent)

| | 1982 | | 1983 | | 1984 | |
Brand	Pounds	Dollars	Pounds	Dollars	Pounds	Dollars
Cap'n Crunch	3.2%	3.8%	2.9%	3.5%	2.7%	3.2%
Life	2.5	2.3	2.4	2.2	2.4	2.2
100% Natural	1.6	1.5	1.6	1.5	1.5	1.4
Halfsies	—	—	0.7	0.7	0.2	0.3
Corn Bran	0.7	0.6	0.7	0.6	0.6	0.6
Others	0.9	0.7	0.6	0.4	0.9	0.9
Total	8.9%	8.9%	8.9%	8.9%	8.3%	8.6%

Source: Advertising Age, Aug. 5, 1985, p. 42.

EXHIBIT 9   Quaker Oats: Operating Profit at Year End June, by Segment ($ millions)

	1983	1984	1985	1986 (est.)
Net sales	$2,611	$3,344	$3,520	$3,650
Operating profits				
U.S. and Canadian grocery	193.8	219.5	250.0	272.0
International grocery	49.1	32.9	49.7	60.0
Fisher-Price	29.6	43.6	47.1	50.0
Specialty retailing	15.8	12.7	15.2	18.0
Total	288.3	308.7	362.0	400.0
Net income	$ 119.3	$ 138.7	$ 156.6	$ 174.2

Source: Prudential-Bache Securities, Inc., Apr. 2, 1986.

Quaker Oats has bundled its product development (20 new products and line extensions since 1983) under the Quaker umbrella and has pushed those lines in which it has a leadership position: hot cereals, granola bars, and Gatorade. Spending $200 million in 1985 for advertising, Quaker Oats showed a 16 percent growth in advertising expenditures and a 31 percent growth in merchandising expenditures since 1984.

As a result of this stategy and increasing new product development at Kellogg, General Mills, and Ralston Purina, Quaker Oats has allowed its share of the RTE cereal market to erode from 8.9 percent in 1983 to 8.6 percent in 1984. Halfsies and Cap'n Crunch have lost market share, whereas Life and 100% Natural have maintained their sales levels. Quaker Oats's RTE cereal brands and market share performance are listed in Exhibit 8, and Quaker Oats's net sales and operating profits by segment are shown in Exhibit 9.

Ralston Purina

Ralston Purina led the RTE cereal industry in restructuring through the use of share repurchase. Ralston Purina has acquired almost 40 million shares of its own stock, and, through divestiture of its Food-maker division, can acquire more. Ralston Purina acquired Continental Baking in 1984, which added the Hostess brands to the Ralston Purina product lines.

Ralston Purina is expected to focus on its pet food operations and the Hostess lines for the foreseeable future. New product activity in 1985, greatest in company history, brought extension of the Chuck Wagon line with three new dog food products, expansion of the dog treats line with Waggles and T-Bonz, and new cat foods. New products in cereals include Sun Flakes, Rainbow Brite, and Cabbage Patch. Ralston Purina's RTE cereal products and market share performance for the 1982–84 period are presented in Exhibit 10. Ralston Purina's net sales and operating profits by segment are listed in Exhibit 11.

Nabisco

Since 1983, Nabisco has introduced 140 new products and line extensions globally. This aggressive posture indicated a recognition by Nabisco of the importance of the international market, which accounts for 40 percent of its normalized operating income.

In 1985, Nabisco was acquired by R. J. Reynolds, a tobacco products company. The combined R. J. Reynolds and Nabisco advertising budget weighs in at $1 billion. This financial strength is to be applied, among other things, to joint product marketing. For example, Del Monte coupons may come with Shredded Wheat. It is hoped that this mixed marketing approach will boost sales of product lines throughout the combined companies.

Nabisco's major product in the RTE cereals market is Shredded Wheat. Shredded Wheat held a 3.3 percent dollar market share in 1984 (4.0 percent in pounds). All Nabisco RTE cereal products held a total market share of 4.2 percent on a dollar basis (4.9 percent on a poundage basis) (*Advertising Age,* Aug. 5, 1985).

INDUSTRY CHALLENGES

The RTE cereal industry emerged from the 1970s facing continuing challenges from the Federal Trade Commission (FTC). Founded in 1914 to combat monopolies, the FTC is charged with preventing unfair methods of competition and unfair or deceptive acts or practices that affect

EXHIBIT 10   Ralston Purina's Ready-to-Eat Cereals: Market Share Data (in percent)

	1982		1983		1984	
Brand	*Pounds*	*Dollars*	*Pounds*	*Dollars*	*Pounds*	*Dollars*
Chex	4.2%	4.0%	4.3%	4.4%	4.3%	4.6%
Donkey Kong	—	—	0.7	0.7	0.6	0.6
Cookie Crisp	0.6	0.6	0.5	0.7	0.4	0.7
Others	0.3	0.2	0.3	0.2	0.6	0.4
Total	5.9%	5.6%	5.9%	6.1%	5.9%	6.3%

Source: Advertising Age, Aug. 5, 1985, p. 42.

EXHIBIT 11   Ralston Purina: Operating Profit at Year End September, by Segment
($ millions)

	1982	1983	1984	1985	1986 (est.)
Net sales	$4,803	$4,872	$4,980	$5,864	$5,350
Operating profits					
Pet food	227.0	263.5	303.0	350.0	399.0
Seafood (loss)	(11.0)	14.5	9.5	10.0	11.5
Cereals	38.5	43.5	41.5	45.5	50.0
Continental baking	—	—	—	84.0	94.0
Other consumer goods	3.7	5.5	1.6	6.6	8.0
Agriculture	96.6	105.6	92.5	74.9	82.0
Restaurant	46.7	58.5	61.4	47.2	0.0
Diversified operations	27.1	33.6	35.9	24.2	30.0
Total operating income	428.6	524.7	545.4	642.4	674.5
Net income	$ 69.1	$ 256.0	$ 242.7	$ 256.4	$ 371.0

Source: Prudential-Bache Securities, Inc., Apr. 2, 1986.

commerce. For almost a decade, the FTC had pursued the RTE industry leaders on two issues: children's television programming and advertising, and the operation of an oligopolistic "shared monopoly."

Children's Television and Advertising

As early as 1970, consumer groups pressed for greater regulation of children's television and advertising (*Federal Register,* vol. 49). A group called Action for Children's Television (ACT) prodded the FTC to establish minimum requirements for age-specific programming for

children. In 1971, ACT petitioned the FTC to ban all vitamin advertising on programs intended for children. (One third of advertising on
TV programs for children had been for vitamin products.) To avoid
further pressure, the manufacturers voluntarily complied with the pe-
tition (Ward, 1978).

From 1971 through 1974, the Children's Television Task Force studied the state of children's television and recommended that licensees
increase the amount of television programming created for children,
particularly programs of educational and informational content. The
task force recommended that selling, promotion, or endorsement of a
product by the host of the program be prohibited, and that program
content be clearly distinguished from commercial messages.

The ACT and other watchdog groups increased their efforts to influence the FTC in the late 1970s, with the result that the FTC introduced
proposals for regulations to limit advertising on programs whose primary audience was children. Despite efforts toward self-regulation by
industry groups such as the Children's Advertising Review unit of the
National Council of Broadcasters and the Codes of the National Association of Broadcasters (Ward, 1978), the FTC banned all commercials on shows aimed at children of a very young age and commercials
for highly sugared foods on programs directed at older children. The
regulation also required advertisers to devote money to public service
announcements to promote good dental and nutritional habits.

In 1980, Congress limited the scope of the FTC's attempts to regulate
children's advertising to matters of deception and "unfair" or misleading advertising (Dewar, 1980). By October 1981, the FTC dropped its
pursuit of the broadcasters and advertisers with respect to "Kid Vid"
issues (*Federal Register,* vol. 46). The ACT continues to monitor television and file complaints to the FTC on those companies that ACT
believes exploit the innocence of youth. The ACT has filed against
Quaker Oats (1982), General Mills (1983), and General Foods (1983),
charging unfair or deceptive advertising by each company (*Associated
Press,* Jul. 18, 1983).

In 1983, Kellogg was brought to court in Canada to force the company
to cease advertising to children. Kellogg claimed that such a ban would
limit the company's ability to release new products and thus freeze
competitors' present market shares. The availability of U.S. television
in Canada obscures any verification of Kellogg's claim. However, Kellogg and other companies marketing products aimed at children, including games, toys, and foods, were restricted from advertising to
children on Canadian television. The Canadian court stated that ads
are presumed to be intended for children if they include "themes related
to fantasy, magic, mystery, suspense or adventure," if they depict authority figures, role models, heroes, animals, or "imaginary or fanciful

creatures," or if they rely on cartoons, children's music, or attention-getting technical devices (Lippman, 1983). Products of interest to children can be presented on Canadian television only if addressed to adults in a mature fashion.

Shared Monopoly

In the ten years that followed the FTC's initial complaint against Kellogg, General Mills, General Foods, and Quaker Oats, 243 days of testimony produced more than 36,000 pages of transcript and 60,000 pages of documents. The FTC charged the industry leaders with operating a "shared monopoly" that resulted not from conspiracy or collusion but from the collective power of the few firms (Kiechel, 1978).

The concept of shared monopoly arose from a study by a Massachusetts Institute of Technology economist, Richard L. Schmalensee. He argued that the cereal companies crowded the supermarket shelves with a large number of brands that left little space for new entrants. The flood of products into the market invited competition among those brands with similar characteristics—crunchiness, flavor, sweetness—but not competition among all brands on the market. The profusion of brands ensured that only existing firms could afford to compete; a new entrant would be required to invest $150 million in development with little assurance that it could gain the 3–5 percent share necessary to gain scale economy in production (Sebastian, 1979).

Specifically, the FTC charged the companies with the following practices (*FTC* vs *Lonning & Kellogg*).

- *Brand proliferation.* "The four companies introduce a profusion of ready-to-eat cereal brands into the market," that fill the "perceptual space" of the consumer with over 200 brands on the supermarket shelves.
- *Aggressive marketing.* "The brands are promoted by intensive advertising aimed primarily at children, which . . . conceals the true nature of these cereals." For example, Honey and Nut Corn Flakes implies significant sweetening by honey; in fact the flakes contain more brown sugar, white refined sugar, vegetable oil, salt, and malt flavoring than honey (Sebastian, 1979).
- *Product differentiation.* The four companies produce "basically similar" ready-to-eat cereals that are artificially differentiated through trivial differences.

In addition to creating barriers to entry into the RTE cereal market, the companies were also accused of other unfair methods of competition in advertising and product promotion. The charges included:

1. Cereal advertising is false and misleading. This issue, also raised by ACT, pits the claims of nutrition and health against the high sugar content of many cereals. The sugar content has been blamed for health and dental problems.

2. Kellogg's program of shelf-space allocation, a program emulated by other cereal manufacturers, controls the exposure of breakfast food products. Kellogg records the sales of cereals in the supermarket and recommends brand selection and shelf-space allocation to the supermarket manager.

3. The companies made numerous acquisitions to eliminate competition in the RTE cereal market. These acquisitions have enhanced the shared monopoly structure of the industry.

4. The companies have exercised monopoly power by refusing to engage in price competition or other consumer-directed promotions.

The FTC claimed that the results of these acts were artificially inflated prices, excessive profits, and an absence of price competition. Government economists used the concept of shared monopoly to explain the reluctance of large consumer-products companies, such as Procter and Gamble, to enter the lucrative, albeit competitive, cereal market.

The FTC hoped to apply shared monopoly or oligopolistic behavior restrictions to other industries after establishing the validity of the concept in a landmark decision with references to the RTE cereals industry case. Any industry in which relatively few companies hold 90 percent market share (examples include telecommunications, oil, automobiles, and computers) would then be vulnerable to FTC action (Cowan, 1981; *Time,* Oct. 5, 1981).

Demographic Changes

Another basic challenge facing the industry has been a slowdown in the rate of growth of cereal consumption, brought about, in part, by the aging of the U.S. population. The U.S. median age is now 30 and is forecasted to reach 35 by the year 2000. The total population is expected to grow by less than 1 percent per year during the 1980s, primarily because of a slowdown in the U.S. birthrate.

Age-group populations do show different growth rates. Several changes expected in the 1980–90 decade are listed below.

- The 15–24 year age group will decrease by 17 percent or 7.1 million.
- The 25–34 year age group will undergo a strong 14 percent increase.
- The 35–54 year age group will undergo the largest increase of all age groups, 25 percent.
- The 55–64 year age group will shrink by 2 percent.
- The over-65 age group will show the second largest increase, up by 20 percent (*Newsweek,* Jan. 17, 1983).

These demographic trends pose a threat to companies that sell a significant portion of their production to the youth market. The greatest consumers of RTE cereals are children under the age of 13. In the 1970s, the industry had experienced a decline in the population of this group. Exhibits 12–15 provide additional data on demographic changes facing the industry and on consumption of RTE cereal products.

Despite the challenges faced by the industry, the 1980s held some promise for the RTE cereal makers. Grain prices were weakening, with strong gains in production continuing through mid-decade. Moreover, cereal companies were able to levy 5 percent and 6 percent price increases while maintaining cereal at the lowest cost-per-serving of any breakfast food.

EXHIBIT 12   Age Distribution Changes and Composite Percentage Change

Age (yr.)	1970–80	1980–85	1985–90 (est.)
<5	− 8.7%	32.1%	7.6%
5–13	− 16.3	1.2	25.6
14–17	2.3	− 11.6	− 11.3
18–21	16.6	− 9.9	− 6.1
22–24	21.6	2.3	− 14.3
25–34	38.5	13.8	3.1
35–44	8.6	24.8	16.6
45–54	− 1.5	− 2.2	12.7
55–64	12.3	3.7	− 4.4
65 +	22.8	10.7	9.2
Total	8.1%	7.4%	6.6%

Source: U.S. Bureau of Census.

EXHIBIT 13   Ready-to-Eat Cereal Consumption: Percent of Total Consumption by Age Group

Age (yr.)	1984	1983	1982	1981	1980	1979	1976	1972
<13	31.0%	31.5%	31.5%	31.6%	31.8%	31.9%	32.2%	36.1%
13–18	13.9	13.9	13.8	13.8	13.8	13.9	14.0	12.9
19–49	28.9	28.1	28.0	28.2	28.1	28.0	27.9	25.7
50 +	26.2	26.5	26.7	26.4	26.3	26.2	25.9	25.3
Total	100%	100%	100%	100%	100%	100%	100%	100%

Source: Drexel, Burnham, & Lambert Brokerage House Report, "Kellogg Co.," Apr. 8, 1985.

EXHIBIT 14   Pounds Per Capita Ready-to-Eat Cereal Consumption by Age Group

Age (yr.)	Pounds
<6	11.5
6–11	14.3
12–17	13.4
18–24	7.0
25–34	5.6
35–49	5.8
50–64	7.7
65 +	11.3

Source: Kellogg Company publication.

EXHIBIT 15   Ready-to-Eat Cereals: Consumption and Tonnage Shipped

Year	Pounds Consumed per Capita	Percent Change in Year-to-Year Tonnage
1971	6.76	3.00%
1972	7.75	9.30
1973	8.30	15.20
1974	8.62	7.20
1975	9.03	5.40
1976	9.06	5.80
1977	8.89	1.00
1978	9.07	0.20
1979	9.07	1.30
1980	9.13	2.80
1981	9.26	2.40
1982	9.30	2.10
1983	9.41	2.30
1984	9.74	4.20

Source: Drexel, Burnham, & Lambert Brokerage House Report "Kellogg Co.," Apr. 8, 1985.

KELLOGG'S BUSINESS SITUATION

For Kellogg, the end of the 1970s and the beginning of the 1980s was an era of severe problems. The company retained its market leadership position, but their erosion of market share in the United States was a growing concern.

EXHIBIT 16   Kellogg's Principal Products' Sales Trends ($ millions)

Product	1983	1984	Change (%)
Corn Flakes	$141.3	$162.5	15.0%
Rice Krispies	144.1	141	−2.2
Raisin Bran	134.3	151.9	13.1
Special K	70.3	82.9	17.8
Fruit Loops	88.9	103.6	16.5
Frosted Flakes	188.8	217.9	15.4
Total	$767.5	$859.7	12.0%

Source: Drexel, Burnham, & Lambert, Inc.

Domestic Sales

The introduction of generic and private-label brands contributed to a loss of Kellogg market share. Kellogg's position in the industry weakened as its market share dropped from a high of 43 percent in 1972 to a low of 38.5 percent in 1983. Consumers appeared to switch to the less-expensive generic brands as the rate of inflation grew to double digits in the 1970s. The cost of this share erosion was substantial: each percent of the RTE cereal market is valued at approximately $40 million.

Kellogg executive Arnold Langbo stated that Kellogg was particularly vulnerable to the generic and private-label inroads in the RTE cereal market. He observed, "The whole philosophy or principle of the private label is to copy the leading products in the market" (Johnson, 1983).

Kellogg fought the invasion of generic and private-label cereals with aggressive price decreases, recovering 1.8 percent of market share in 1984 as generic goods dropped 10 percent in tonnage shipped. Kellogg's two primary competitors held 36.4 percent of the market, considerably less than Kellogg's 40.3 percent share. In 1984, General Foods market share dropped 2.8 percent to 13.3 percent; General Mills held constant at a 23 percent share. Sales trends for several of Kellogg's products are presented in Exhibit 16. Market share performance of the Kellogg brands for the years 1982–1984 is presented in Exhibit 17.

Research and Development

In addition to price decreases, Kellogg increased its efforts in research and development (R & D) advertising and new product introduction. With an R & D budget of $6.5 million in 1978, Kellogg began to develop cereals to appeal to different segments of the cereal market. By 1981, Kellogg was investing $20 million a year in research. Kellogg built two advanced research centers and acquired Agrigentics, a research company exploring improvements in grain development. Kellogg's efforts in research produced the first flaked cereal with no sugar or preservatives, Nutri Grain in 1981; the first cereal to combine two grains with identity separation, Crispix in 1983; and the first cereals to fully enrobe fruit, Raisin Squares and OJ's in 1984 (patent numbers: 4,178,392, 4,103,035, and 3,952,112).

EXHIBIT 17   Kellogg's Ready-to-Eat Cereals: Market Share Data (in percent)

	1982		1983		1984	
Brand	*Pounds*	*Dollars*	*Pounds*	*Dollars*	*Pounds*	*Dollars*
Frosted Flakes	5.2%	4.8%	5.2%	4.8%	5.6%	5.2%
Corn Flakes	6.8	4.7	6.8	4.7	6.8	4.7
Raisin Bran	4.7	4.2	4.6	4.1	4.5	4.0
Rice Krispies	3.9	4.2	3.6	3.9	3.5	3.8
Fruit Loops	2.2	2.8	2.2	2.8	2.3	2.9
Special K	1.5	2.1	1.7	2.3	1.9	2.5
Bran Products	2.7	2.0	2.8	2.1	3.1	2.3
Frosted Mini-Wheats	1.8	1.8	1.8	1.8	1.9	1.9
Apple Jacks	1.0	1.5	1.0	1.5	1.0	1.5
Sugar Smacks	1.3	1.3	1.3	1.3	1.2	1.3
Sugar Pops	1.1	1.3	1.0	1.2	1.1	1.2
Product 19	0.8	1.1	0.8	1.1	0.9	1.1
Nutri-Grain	1.0	1.0	1.0	1.0	1.2	1.1
Crispix	—	—	0.7	0.7	0.5	0.5
Honey & Nut Corn Flakes	0.6	0.7	0.6	0.7	0.5	0.6
Marshmallow Krispies	0.5	0.7	0.5	0.7	0.4	0.6
Cocoa Krispies	0.5	0.7	0.5	0.7	0.6	0.8
Frosted Rice	0.6	0.8	0.5	0.6	0.4	0.4
Fruitful Bran	—	—	—	—	0.7	0.6
C-3PO	—	—	—	—	0.5	0.6
Apple Raisin Crisp	—	—	—	—	0.5	0.6
Raisin Squares	—	—	—	—	0.3	0.3
Most	0.3	0.4	0.3	0.4	0.2	0.3
Raisins Rice & Rye	0.5	0.6	0.3	0.4	0.1	0.1
Others	1.2	1.4	1.0	1.3	0.8	1.4
Total	38.5%	38.5%	38.5%	38.5%	40.5%	40.3%

Source: Advertising Age, Aug. 5, 1985, p. 42.

Advertising

In 1984, Kellogg increased its advertising budget by 49 percent to $160 million, an aggressive move when compared to the 16 percent increase (to $52 million) of General Foods, and the 1 percent decrease in advertising by Post. As General Foods limited its primary advertising on its top five (of 14) leading brands, Kellogg was able to devote considerable push to its new products (*Forbes,* Oct. 7, 1985). Kellogg advertising themes for selected products are presented in Exhibit 18.

EXHIBIT 18   Kellogg's Cereal: Products and Advertising Themes

Product	*Themes*
Special K	Thanks to the K, Staying in Shape Never Tasted So Good—Can't Pinch an Inch
Product 19	Flaky, Bumpy, Crispy, Crunchy *Vitamins*—100% of Your Daily Allowance of 10 Vitamins
Fruitful Bran	Bushels of Taste!—Fiber Rich
Nutri-Grain	Whole Grain Goodness . . . No Sugar Added—Dedicated to the Ones We Love
Apple Raisin Crisp	New Great Taste—New, Big, Juicy Chunks of Real Apple
Frosted Flakes	Gr-r-reat Taste—Tony the Tiger—The Taste Adults Have Grown to Love
Raisin Bran	Two Scoops of Raisins—Fiber Rich—Here is the Goodness of Fiber
All Bran	High Fiber—The Highest Fiber Cereal Ever
Rice Krispies	More Vitamin Nutrition than Old Fashioned Oatmeal—Snap! Crackle! and Pop!—The Talking Cereal Talks about Nutrition
Corn Flakes	The Original and Best—Provides 8 Essential Vitamins and Iron—How 'bout these Kellogg's Corn Flakes Now?—The Surprise is the People Who Eat Them
Just Right	High Nutrition . . . Uncompromising Taste—Kellogg's Just Right Cereal
Bran Flakes	Fiber-rich *Bran Flakes*—We'll Help Take Care of the Inside, You Take Care of the Outside
Fruit Loops	Natural Fruit Flavors with 100% U.S. RDA of Vitamin C—All Natural Flavors: Orange, Lemon, Cherry—Delicious Natural Fruit Flavors with a Full Day's Supply of Vitamin C

Source: Kellogg advertisements.

Kellogg was able to take advantage of reports connecting a high-fiber diet with a reduced risk of colon cancer and they positioned their new All Bran cereal as a cancer-preventive tool. Kellogg advertised, "At last, some news about cancer you can live with." By the end of 1984, $250 million of Kellogg's sales came from bran cereals: All Bran, Bran Buds, Cracklin' Oat Bran, Fruitful Bran, Kellogg's Bran Flakes, Kellogg's Raisin Bran, and, in 1985, All Bran with Extra Fiber (Tracy, 1985).

The advertising campaign sparked controversy among industry, medical, and government groups. Officials at the FTC hailed the campaign as "the type of advertisement that we believe should be encouraged" (Kronhelm, 1985; Wollenberg, 1985). The Food and Drug Administration, however, protested that Kellogg was making medical claims for its product and considered seizing all boxes of All Bran from the shelves (Marwick, 1985). The National Food Processors Association petitioned the FDA to allow its member manufacturers to tout the health benefits of their products as long as the labeling was truthful and could be substantiated.

"Everyone has his opinions of advertising, but we didn't think anyone would misinterpret our commercials," explained Kellogg Vice President of Public Affairs, Peggy Wollerman. "Our goal is to communicate recommendations of the National Cancer Institute's findings that maintaining a high-fiber diet is a direct means of reducing the risk of cancer" (Rotenberk, 1984). The Kellogg advertisement had been cleared by Kellogg and National Cancer Institute scientists and lawyers for accuracy, and it had been passed by lawyers for the three television networks.

Until 1970, the FDA prohibited manufacturers from making any health claims on behalf of food products. In the following years, the FDA relaxed its standard for claims of "low calorie" and "low cholesterol." If a product is claimed to be useful in the treatment of a disease, it is considered a drug and the manufacturer must prove the efficacy of its claims (Cowart, 1985).

New Marketing Developments

Kellogg's move into the adult market in the late 1970s and early 1980s signaled a new direction for the cereal industry. Kellogg's strategy included promoting vitamin-enriched, whole grain, and sugarless cereals to the 25–49 year age group, high fiber to the 65+ age group, and C-3POs and OJs to the under-17 market (*Business Week,* Jan. 8, 1977).

Recognizing sociological changes in the United States, Kellogg introduced all-family cereals to enhance the convenience of shopping. Kellogg also introduced Smart Start, a cereal aimed at the working woman (*Business Week,* Nov. 26, 1979). Key to Kellogg's development and marketing were the themes of health, diet, convenience, and taste (Brody, 1985). Numerous surveys and surveying organizations, including the Bureau of Labor Statistics, have recorded significant social demographic changes in the last 15 years. A few of the changes that Kellogg and the other cereal companies had to address are listed below.

- In 1985, the numbers of families with school-age or preschool-age children increased by 460,000; the number of employed mothers increased by 765,000 to 18.2 million.
- In 1985, the median family wage and salary earnings increased 4.6 percent. Since 1982, the median family earnings increased 16 percent, compared to a consumer price increase of 11 percent over the same period (*New York Times,* Feb. 19, 1986).

In the 1980s, breakfast has become a more significant part of the American diet, with 89 percent of the populace eating breakfast each day. Frozen breakfast foods were also becoming an important part of the breakfast food industry. In 1985, sales of all frozen foods totalled $849.3 million, 15 percent more than in 1984. In part, this increase was caused by the fact that more than 44 percent of American homes now had a microwave oven, making cooking at home easier. Sales of frozen breakfast entrees tripled from 1979 to 1985: sales of frozen pancakes increased 390 percent; frozen toaster items increased 1,000 percent. Moreover, between 1978 and 1984, the number of Americans eating breakfast at a restaurant increased 45.7 percent compared to the overall restaurant increase of only 6.3 percent (Callahan, 1986).

Despite the decline in the population of children under 13 years of age, competition in the breakfast food market segment continued without any slackening of intensity. As consumers of the greatest per capita amounts of cereal, children have long been the focus of cereal company advertising. Although Tony the Tiger has represented Kellogg's Sugar Frosted Flakes for many years, General Mills broke new ground in products for children with the first licensed character, Strawberry Shortcake. This was a move to link the cereal with other commercial media. Other RTE cereal companies followed quickly. The RTE cereal companies' licensed character products now include General Mills's ET, General Foods's Smurf Berry Crunch, Ralston Purina's Donkey Kong, Rainbow Brite, and Gremlins, and Kellogg's C-3POs.

The benefit of tying a cereal to an established figure from television, movies, comics, or toys (character licensing) is a quick gain in market share through exposure in a good trial period. Although traditional cereal products have existed for more than 30 years, the licensed-character cereal may have a life cycle of only 6–18 months. "The first licensed characters did well for about a year. Now their life span is about six months," said Nomi Ghez of Goldman Sachs & Co. (Spillman,

1985). The editor of *New Products News,* Martin Friedman, stated, "The characters that have been created by cereal companies go on forever, and the others don't" (Hollie, 1985). To seek a license for a character, Kellogg depended on assurances that the character would continue, that the character had personality and integrity, and that the character would not alienate adults.

By 1986, the cereal companies had less interest in developing licensed-character products because of a general decrease in the popularity of the characters with consumers (Friedman, 1986).

International Operations

By 1980, Kellogg measured sales in 130 countries from 19 manufacturing locations (Kellogg Annual Report, 1982). Kellogg International was divided into four divisions: Canada; United Kingdom and Europe; Latin America; and Africa, Australia, and Asia. International sales accounted for 30 percent of Kellogg's total sales. In France, Kellogg planned to target all segments of the population in hopes of replacing the croissant with cereal. In Japan, Kellogg has targeted children to establish the habit of eating cereal (*Dun's Business Month,* Dec., 1985). Financial results for several geographic operating segments are detailed in Exhibit 19.

Federal Trade Commission Case Revisited

In addition to the problems created by the introduction of generic and private-label brands, Kellogg management also attributed the previously mentioned loss of market share to the inability of top management to concentrate on operating the business. The Chairman of the Board, William E. Lamothe, estimated in 1982 that 40 percent of top management time had been spent on the FTC litigation (*Business Week,* Dec. 6, 1982).

For Kellogg, losing the FTC case would have significant effect. If the FTC had won the case, it would have divided Kellogg into five separate operating companies organized around its major product lines. Additionally, the FTC would have required Kellogg to license its brands to smaller, regional manufacturers. Kellogg argued that such actions would place Kellogg at a competitive disadvantage in the RTE market and would produce inconsistent quality within Kellogg's brands.

As the trial entered the 1980s, Kellogg changed its passive strategy of litigation, becoming an aggressive champion of the industry's positions. Kellogg sponsored intense letter-writing campaigns to

EXHIBIT 19   Kellogg Company: Geographic Operating Segments ($ millions)

	1985	1984	1983	1982	1981
Sales					
United States	$2,074.9	$1,789.6	$1,560.0	$1,514.3	$1,454.0
Canada	177.6	178.9	176.0	169.0	170.2
Europe	474.9	425.9	437.8	453.0	435.9
Other	202.7	208.0	207.3	230.8	261.2
Total	$2,930.1	$2,602.4	$2,381.1	$2,367.1	$2,321.3
Net Earnings					
United States	$ 222.7	$ 194.7	$ 170.5	$ 163.0	$ 150.7
Canada	11.7	11.6	27.6	15.2	13.1
Europe	38.8	35.0	38.6	36.9	34.0
Other	7.9	9.2	6.0	12.7	7.6
Total	$ 281.1	$ 250.5	$ 242.7	$ 227.8	$ 205.4
Assets					
United States	$ 833.6	$ 731.6	$ 677.1	$ 639.0	$ 606.9
Canada	262.7	247.5	192.3	143.4	130.2
Europe	337.9	223.3	195.4	199.0	197.5
Other	158.9	148.6	139.8	153.7	178.0
Corporate	133.0	316.1	262.6	162.3	166.5
Total	$1,726.1	$1,667.1	$1,467.2	$1,297.4	$1,279.11

Source: Kellogg Annual Reports.

congressional representatives from districts in which Kellogg maintained facilities. As a result, the FTC received numerous inquiries from congressional representatives regarding the efficacy of continuing the case further (*Business Week,* Nov. 26, 1979).

In 1981, Kellogg created Project Nutrition, a teaching unit for secondary grade school children, as well as nutrition inserts for children's television. Kellogg also provided cereals in 33,000 school breakfast programs. In 1982, Kellogg introduced Fitness Focus, a physical education program for high schools. Kellogg believed that the program would enhance its image as a producer of health-related foods, an image that could benefit Kellogg in its case against the FTC as well as in its position in the market.

Procedural errors in the handling of the case by the administrative judge and the FTC raised challenges from Kellogg and the other cereal companies. Judge Harry R. Hinkes decided in 1978 to retire from the judiciary in order to gain full pension benefits, some of which he would lose if he postponed his retirement. The FTC, fearing a considerable delay and possible dismissal of the case, offered the judge a salary to stay on the case. The impropriety of such an arrangement, alleging a possible conflict of interest, was raised by Kellogg as grounds for dismissal. A new judge was appointed to continue the suit in 1981. Later, in 1982, the FTC dropped its suit (*Federal Register,* vol. 47).

Following the collapse of the FTC lawsuit against its four largest companies, the RTE industry witnessed increased competitive rivalry. This increased rivalry manifested itself in new product releases and advertising, and in corporate-development activities including acquisitions, divestitures, and share repurchases.

Diversification

The slowing growth rate in the cereal industry compelled Kellogg to look toward diversification for continued growth and comparable rates of returns for reinvestment of its retained earnings. In 1970, Kellogg entered the frozen food industry with the acquisition of Fearn International. In 1976, Kellogg acquired Mrs. Smith's Pie Co. and in 1977, it acquired Pure Packed Foods. Products such as Eggo waffles, salad dressings, LeGout soups, Salada Tea, Whitney Yogurt, Mrs. Smith's Pies, and pickles entered Kellogg's lines. Kellogg consolidated its frozen food operations under the Mrs. Smith's label in 1980 to gain greater efficiencies in manufacturing, warehousing, transportation, and marketing as well as a stronger product identity in the marketplace (Prokesch, 1985). By 1984, 25 percent of Kellogg's sales were noncereal (Blyskal, 1984). Exhibit 20 presents net income contributions of several elements of Kellogg, and Exhibit 21 presents sales and operating income for several segments of the company.

Despite LaMothe's declaration that Kellogg was "gung ho" on diversification, Kellogg lost in three attempts to acquire Tropicana and in attempts to acquire Binney and Smith (manufacturers of Crayola crayons) and Seven-Up. Kellogg believed in each case that the price was too high for the company. "Today we are kind of glad we did [lose]," said LaMothe, "There is no embarrassment in losing. The big embarrassment is to win by paying too much and then never being able to make a return to your shareholders" (*Dun's Business Month,* Dec., 1985).

Capital Projects

Productivity improvements were made at many Kellogg manufacturing facilities in the late 1970s and 1980s, culminating in a $100 million expansion and improvement in the Battle Creek plant in 1985, the largest single capital expenditure in the company's history. Kellogg's ability to improve productivity is demonstrated by the 50 percent increase in revenues per employee that the company enjoyed between

EXHIBIT 20   Kellogg Company: Net Income Contributions

Product Division	1981	1982	1983	1984	1985 (est.)	1986 (est.)
Domestic cerals	$121.0	$135.7	$138.0	$169.9	$206.0	$231.0
Canadian operation	11.0	13.0	13.8	9.4	10.0	12.0
Salada	12.1	13.0	14.0	15.0	16.0	18.0
Fearn International	9.0	9.5	10.5	11.6	12.0	14.0
Mrs. Smith's Pie Co.	8.7	7.0	8.0	8.9	10.0	11.0
Kellogg International	41.6	49.6	44.6	39.2	42.0	50.0
Total	$203.4	$227.8	$228.9	$254.0	$296.0	$336.0

Source: Drexel, Burnham, & Lambert, Inc., Oct. 7, 1985.

EXHIBIT 21   Kellogg Company: Estimated Sales and Operating Income ($ millions)

	1979	1980	1981	1982	1983	1984	1985
Sales							
RTE Cereals	$1,426	$1,687	$1,802	$1,792	$1,755	$2,000	$2,260
Salada	128	140	154	165	182	180	190
Fearn International	118	132	145	165	177	165	180
Mrs. Smith's Pie Co.	157	172	200	218	239	222	235
Other	18	19	20	27	50	35	35
Total	1,847	2,150	2,321	2,367	2,381	2,602	2,900
Operating income							
RTE Cereals	240	297	331	343.7	370	408.2	510
Salada	12	12	13	14	16	14	15
Fearn International	8	9	10	11	12.5	11.5	13
Mrs. Smith's Pie Co.	19	20	22	24	27.5	25	28
Other	2	2	2	3	4	4.5	5
Total	$ 281	$ 340	$ 378	$ 395.7	$ 430	$ 463.2	$ 571

Source: Merrill, Lynch, Pearce, Fenner, & Smith brokerage house report: "Kellogg Co.," Oct. 31, 1985.

1979 and 1985 (Drexel, Burnham, & Lambert, Oct. 7, 1985). Early in 1986, Kellogg ended a long practice of public tours of the Battle Creek facility because of a desire to protect proprietary information. Several Kellogg capital projects for the years 1980–83 are listed in Exhibit 22.

Preventing Takeover

Matching Kellogg's rates of return in an acquisition candidate is difficult. Moreover, the consumer-products companies such as Kellogg are attractive takeover targets themselves because of their high returns.

EXHIBIT 22   Kellogg Company: Capital Projects

Year	Location	Project
1980	Rexdale, Ontario	Frozen food manufacturing facility
	Wrexham, England	Expanded capacity for Super Noodles
	Valls, Spain	New cereal plant
	Rooty Hill, Australia	Expansion of frozen food plant
	Queretro, Mexico	New corn milling operation
	Sao Paolo, Brazil	Expansion of cereal plant
	Maracay, Venezuela	New office building, processing, and packing
	Guatemala	Expansion of grain storage
	Arlington, TN	Pure Packed dry materials warehouse
	McMinnville, OR	Expansion of Mrs. Smith's plants
	San Jose, CA	Expansion of plant
	Blue Anchor, NJ	Mrs. Smith's facility
	Milpitas, CA	Eggo salad dressing plant
1981	Battle Creek, MI	Expanded for Nutri-Grain cereal
	Lancaster, PA	Increased capacity for cereal
	Battle Creek, MI	Advanced technology facility for research and development
	South Korea	New processing plants
	London, Ontario	Advanced technology center
	Manchester, England	Expansion of packing facility
	Bremen, West Germany	Purchased land
1982	London, Ontario	Expansion of plant
	Seoul, South Korea	Plant completed
	Manchester, England	Conversion of packing line
	Sao Paolo, Brazil	Expansion of facilities
1983	Pottstown, PA	Expansion of office space, storage Warehouse

Source: Kellogg Annual Reports.

To reduce the risk of a takeover, Kellogg purchased 20 percent of its own stock in 1984, an "investment in our own business," said LaMothe. The effect of the stock repurchase added $500 million of debt to the Kellogg balance sheet. Before the transaction, Kellogg enjoyed only $19 million of debt against $1 billion in equity. The 20 percent block of stock had been held by the Kellogg Foundation. Any potential sale of the stock, said LaMothe, was a "cloud we didn't think was good to leave hanging out there in today's time" (Willoughby, 1985).

Kellogg's competitors employed a range of strategies in response to the same takeover challenge. Ralston Purina also acquired blocks of its own stock, continuing this strategy through mid-decade. In

---

EXHIBIT 23   Recent Acquisitions of Established Brands

Buyer	*Acquisition*	*Brands*
Procter and Gamble	Richardson-Vicks	NyQuil, Vidal Sassoon, Clearasil
Philip Morris	General Foods	Jell-O, Maxwell House
Monsanto	G. D. Searle	Nutrasweet, Metamusil
Brown-Forman	California Cooler	California Cooler
Greyhound	Purex Cleaning	Purex Bleach, Brillo
Sara Lee	Nicholas Kiwi	Kiwi shoe polish
Nestlé	Carnation	Carnation Milk, Friskies pet food
Ralston Purina	Continental Baking	Hostess Twinkies, Wonder Bread
	Nabisco Foods	Oreo cookies, Life Savers, Ritz Crackers, Shredded Wheat
Beatrice Foods	Esmark	Wesson Oil, Playtex
R. J. Reynolds	Canada Dry	Canada Dry soft drinks
Quaker Oats	Stokely-Van Camp	Gatorade, canned goods

Source: Brown (1985).

1985, R. J. Reynolds acquired Nabisco Brands, itself a result of a merger between Nabisco and Standard Brands. Philip Morris acquired General Foods. Exhibit 23 lists several recent acquisitions of established brands.

Some of the largest companies in the food industry have been built through a series of acquisitions. Beatrice and Sara Lee Corporation are both the products of acquisitions. Traditionally, regional brands were acquired to take advantage of a larger, national sales force, as well as the financial strength of the parent company. When product lines of the two companies overlapped, the strength of the broader product line commanded greater influence in attracting shelf space in the supermarket, and greater discounts in advertising rates (Brown, 1985).

For Reynolds and Philip Morris, acquisition of food products carried other benefits. Slower sales of cigarettes and pending lawsuits and legislation about smoking are expected to eventually erode profitability in the cigarette industry. The higher-than-average returns of the cereal and food companies, with a strong brand image of health and nutrition, is an attractive inducement for investment.

According to Marc C. Patricelli of Booz Allen & Hamilton Inc., 19 of 24 RTE cereal brands retained their leadership position from 1923 to 1983, "So if a company buys a leader, and if they run it correctly, they are buying an annuity, because brand leadership is sustainable" (Brown, 1985). Kellogg's financial performance and dominance in the cereal industry makes it an appealing target for merger or acquisition. Exhibits 24–26 give financial information on Kellogg.

EXHIBIT 24   Kellogg Company: Consolidated Balance Sheet ($ millions)

	1985	1984	1983	1982	1981
Current Assets:					
Cash and temporary investments	$ 127.8	$ 308.9	$ 248.8	$ 159.8	$ 163.7
Accounts receivable	203.9	182.5	157.1	140.7	158.9
Inventory					
Raw materials	135.6	119.7	115.7	128.8	129.4
Finished goods and work in progress	110.3	101.4	101.1	98.9	101.8
Prepaid expenses	40.5	39.0	40.4	35.9	28.4
Total current assets	618.1	751.5	663.1	564.1	582.2
Property:					
Land	25.6	25.6	26.3	25.1	24.0
Buildings	321.2	277.7	274.1	263.4	263.8
Machinery and equipment	903.2	762.4	692.7	677.6	620.6
Construction in progress	280.4	215.7	143.7	83.5	90.0
Total property	1,503.4	1,281.4	1,136.8	1,049.6	998.4
Less accumulated depreciation	494.5	425.4	393.6	367.4	340.0
Net property	1,035.9	856.0	743.2	682.2	658.4
Intangible assets	28.3	30.5	29.0	33.6	32.2
Other assets	43.8	29.1	31.9	17.5	6.3
Total assets	1,726.1	1,667.1	1,467.2	1,297.4	1,279.1
Current Liabilities:					
Current maturities of debt	34.8	340.6	20.0	6.5	16.5
Accounts payable	189.7	127.4	116.8	99.1	104.5
Accrued liabilities					
Income tax	29.4	51.4	85.0	81.9	77.4
Salaries and wages	41.8	38.7	36.2	31.4	29.9
Promotion	71.3	60.2	66.4	45.0	30.9
Other	46.4	45.8	36.3	43.7	41.7
Total current liabilities	444.3	664.1	360.7	307.6	300.9
Long-term debt	392.6	364.1	18.6	11.8	88.2
Other liabilities	12.3	9.5	9.2	11.0	9.8
Deferred income tax	193.9	142.2	100.8	82.3	69.9
Shareholders' Equity:					
Common stock	38.4	38.4	38.2	38.2	38.2
Capital in excess of par value	44.5	40.8	34.4	32.9	32.5
Retained earnings	1,288.5	1,118.4	991.5	872.8	761.6
Treasury stock	−576.8	−577.8			
Currency translation adjustment	−111.6	−132.6	−86.2	−59.2	−22.0
Total equity	683.0	487.2	977.9	884.7	810.3
Total liabilities and equity	$1,726.1	$1,667.1	$1,467.2	$1,297.4	$1,279.1

Source: Kellogg Annual Reports.

EXHIBIT 25   Kellogg Company: Consolidated Earnings and Retained Earnings ($ millions)

	1985	*1984*	*1983*	*1982*	*1981*	*1980*
Net sales	$2,930.1	$2,602.4	$2,381.1	$2,367.1	$2,331.3	$2,150.9
Interest revenue	7.2	27.7	18.6	21.3	18.2	18.7
Other, net	−2.8	3.9	18.1	2.1	0.0	0.0
Total revenue	2,934.5	2,634.0	2,417.8	2,390.5	2,339.5	2,169.6
C.O.G.S.	1,605.0	1,488.4	1,412.3	1,442.2	1,447.8	1,385.2
S.G. & A exp.	766.7	650.8	554.4	529.2	501.1	435.7
Interest exp.	35.4	18.7	7.1	8.2	12.0	10.4
Total	2,407.1	2,157.9	1,973.8	1,979.6	1,960.9	1,831.3
EBT	527.4	476.1	444.0	410.0	378.6	338.3
Income taxes	246.3	225.6	201.3	183.1	173.2	154.3
Net earnings	281.1	250.5	242.7	227.8	205.4	184.0
Retained earnings, Jan. 1	1,118.4	991.5	872.8	761.6	665.1	583.5
Dividends	−111.0	−123.6	−124.0	−116.6	−108.9	−102.4
Retained earnings, Dec. 31	$1,288.5	$1,184.4	$ 991.5	$ 872.5	$ 761.6	$ 665.1

Source: Kellogg Annual Reports.

CONCLUSION

"The question is not whether this is a mature market," said LaMothe, "it's whether we can be inventive enough. . . . [Americans now have] the highest level of per capita [cereal] consumption in U.S. history. A lot of areas are close to 13 pounds. Why not make the whole country average 13?" (Willoughby, 1985). Kellogg's challenge is to increase the market for cereals, both domestic and foreign, by increasing consumption. In the United States, middle-aged and older Americans are the target segments. According to LaMothe (*Dun's Business Month,* Dec. 1985):

> Dr. Kellogg and Mr. Kellogg were going on either intuition or their basic beliefs coming out of a Seventh Day Adventist background, where they believed that meats were not healthful for the diet. . . . We think that it (cereal) has a tremendous future. . . . The whole grains . . . healthy life-style . . . avoidance of major disease in the Western world . . . more grains, fruit, and vegetables. Where else can you get such nutrition for 20 cents a serving? There will be 6 billion people on the face of the earth by the year 2000 and grains will continue to be the most efficient way for most people to get their calories and nutrition. We are going to help feed them. That's what Kellogg is all about.

EXHIBIT 26   Kellogg Company: Changes in Consolidated Financial Position ($ millions)

	1985	1984	1983	1982	1981	1980
Source of funds:						
Net earnings	$ 281.1	250.5	242.7	227.7	205.4	184.0
Depreciation	75.4	63.9	62.8	55.9	49.1	44.7
Deferred tax/other	54.9	62.6	12.0	27.1	10.4	12.0
Total funds provided by operations	411.4	377.0	317.5	310.7	264.9	240.7
Changes in working capital components:						
Accounts receivable	− 21.4	− 25.4	− 16.4	18.2	− 9.2	− 17.0
Inventory	− 24.8	− 4.3	10.9	3.5	26.1	− 19.2
Prepaid expenses	− 1.5	1.4	− 4.5	− 7.5	− 3.7	− 7.1
Current debt maturity	− 305.8	320.6	13.5	− 10.0	− 10.0	5.7
Accounts payable	62.3	10.6	17.7	− 5.4	− 1.5	− 9.8
Accrued liability	23.7	− 27.9	21.9	22.1	25.2	46.2
Net change	− 267.5	275.1	43.1	20.9	26.9	− 1.2
Funds provided by operations and changes in working capital	143.9	652.1	360.6	331.6	291.8	239.5
Long-term debt	31.5	348.1	1.5	0.0	7.9	0.4
Common stock	3.7	6.7	1.1	0.4	0.0	0.0
Property disposal	4.3	12.0	38.0	5.3	2.9	5.0
Tax-lease benefits	1.2	3.1	6.2	12.0	0.0	0.0
Other	7.9	0.9	0.5	3.1	0.5	1.4
Total source of funds	192.1	1,022.9	407.9	352.4	303.1	246.3
Use of funds:						
Property	245.6	228.9	156.7	121.1	146.4	122.9
Cash dividends	111.0	123.6	124.0	116.6	108.9	102.4
Treasury stock purchases	0.0	577.9	0.0	0.0	0.0	
Investment in tax leases	0.0	0.0	11.6	14.2	0.0	0.0
Long-term debt reduction	2.8	2.7	3.6	75.7	0.4	2.8
Other	23.8	14.7	10.5	13.9	6.4	1.1
Total use of funds	383.2	947.7	306.4	341.5	262.1	229.2
Exchange rate effect on working capital	10.0	− 15.1	− 12.5	− 14.9	− 9.1	0.0
Increase in cash and temporary investments	$ − 181.1	$ 60.1	$ 89.0	$ − 4.0	$ 31.9	$ 17.1

Source: Kellogg Annual Reports.

REFERENCES

Advertising Age, Aug. 5, 1985, p. 42.

Associated Press, "FTC Accused of Sanctioning Bad Advertising Practice," Jul. 18, 1983.

Blyskal, Jeff, "Branded Foods," *Forbes,* Jan. 2, 1984, p. 208.

Brody, Jane E., "America Leans to a Healthier Diet," *New York Times,* Oct. 13, 1985, p. 32, sect. 6.

Brown, Paul B., et al. (1985). "NEW? IMPROVED? The Brand Name Mergers," *Business Week,* Oct. 21, p. 108.

Business Week, Industrial Edition, Jan. 8, 1977, p. 46.

Business Week, Industrial Edition, Nov. 26, 1977, p. 80.

Business Week, "Too Many Cereals for the FTC," Mar. 20, 1978, p. 166+.

Business Week, "Still the Cereal People," Nov. 26, 1979, p. 80+.

Business Week, "Kellogg Looks Beyond Breakfast," Dec. 6, 1982, p. 66+.

Callahan, Tom, "What's New with Breakfast; Morning Meals, Fresh from the Freezer," *New York Times,* Feb. 16, 1986, p. 17, sect. 3.

Cowan, Edward, "FTC. Staff Is Rebuffed on Cereals," *New York Times,* Sep. 11, 1981, p. D1.

Cowart, V., "Keeping Foods Safe and Labels Honest; Food Safety and Applied Nutrition," *Journal of the American Medical Association* 254 (1985) 2228–29.

Dewar, Helen, "FTC Curbs Are Adopted by Senate," *Washington Post,* Feb. 8, 1980, p. A1.

Drexel, Burnham, & Lambert, Brokerage House Report, "Kellogg Co.," Apr. 8, 1985.

Drexel, Burnham, & Lambert, Brokerage House Report, "General Foods," May 20, 1985.

Drexel, Burnham, & Lambert, Kellogg Company, Research Abstracts; Food Processors, Oct. 7, 1985.

Dun's Business Month, "Kellogg: Snap, Crackle, Profits," Dec. 1985, p. 32+.

The Economist, "Philip Morris/General Foods: Chow Time for the Marlboro Cowboy," Oct. 5, 1985.

Federal Register, Federal Trade Commission, "Children's Advertising," 46 FR 48710.

Federal Register, "Children's Television Programming and Advertising Practices," 49 FR 1704.

Federal Register, Federal Trade Commission, "Kellogg Company et al: Prohibitive Trade Practices, and Affirmative Correction Actions," 47 FR 6817.

Federal Trade Commission v. *J. E. Lonning, President, and Kellogg Company, a Corporation,* Appellants, 539 F2nd 202.

Forbes, Oct. 7, 1985, p. 126.

Friedman, Martin, "Cereal Bowls Spill over with Nuttiness," *Adweek*, Feb. 10, 1986.

Hollie, Pamela G., "New Cereal Pitch at Children," *New York Times*, Mar. 27, 1985, p. D1.

Johnson, Greg, "Who's Afraid of Generic Cereals?" *Industry Week*, May 16, 1983, p. 33.

Kellogg Company Annual Reports, 1981, 1982, 1983, 1984, 1985.

Kiechel, Walter III, "The Soggy Case against the Cereal Industry," *Fortune*, Apr. 10, 1978, p. 49.

Kornhelm, William, "Should Food Labels Carry Health Claims? FDA's Policy Challenged," *Associated Press*, May 15, 1985.

Lippman, Thomas W., "Quebec's Ad Ban No Child's Game; Advertisers, TV Try to Adjust," *Washington Post*, Apr. 17, 1983, p. G1.

Marwick, C., "FDA Prepares To Meet Regulatory Challenges of 21st Century," *Journal of the American Medical Association* 254 (1985), 2189–2201.

Meadows, Edward, "Bold Departures in Antitrust," *Fortune*, Oct. 5, 1981, p. 180.

Newsweek, "A Portrait of America," Jan. 17, 1983, pp. 20–33.

New York Times, Sep. 15, 1985, sect. 3, p. 1.

New York Times, "More Mothers Are Working," Feb. 19, 1986, p. C4+.

Patent Number 3,952,112, "Method for Treating Dried Fruits to Improve Softness Retention Characteristics," Fulger et al., April 20, 1976.

Patent Number 4,103,035, "Method for Retaining Softness in Raisins," Fulger et al., July 25, 1978.

Patent Number 4,178,392, "Method of Making a Ready-to-Eat Breakfast Cereal," Gobble et al., December 11, 1979.

Philip Morris Co., press release, Apr. 24, 1986.

Prokesch, Steven, "Food Industry's Big Mergers," *New York Times*, Oct. 14, 1985, p. D1.

Prudential-Bache Securities, Inc., Oct. 1, 1985.

Prudential-Bache Securities, Inc., Apr. 1, 1986.

Rotenberk, Lori, "Ad Exec Blasts JWT's All-Bran Ad," *Adweek* (Eastern edition), Oct. 29, 1984.

Sebastian, John V., "A Slight Taste of Honey," *Business Week*, Reader's Report, Dec. 17, 1979, p. 10.

Spillman, Susan, "It's a Kid's Market," *USA Today*, Oct. 7, 1985.

Tracy, Eleanor Johnson, "Madison Avenue's Cancer Sell Spreads," *Fortune*, Aug. 19, 1985, p. 77.

Ward, S., "Compromise in Commercials for Children," *Harvard Business Review*, Nov. 1978, p. 128+.

Willoughby, Jack, "The Snap, Crackle, Pop Defense," *Forbes*, Mar. 25, 1985, p. 82.

Wollenberg, Skip, "Reagan's Cancer Diagnosis Sparks Prevention Ads," *Associated Press*, Jul. 29, 1985.

Mary Kay Cosmetics, Inc.*

Arthur A. Thompson, Jr.
Robin Romblad
both of the University of Alabama

In spring 1983 Mary Kay Cosmetics, Inc. (MKC), the second largest direct sales distributor of skin care products in the United States, encountered its first big slowdown in recruiting women to function as Mary Kay beauty consultants and market the Mary Kay cosmetic lines. As of April, MKC's sales force of about 195,000 beauty consultants was increasing at only a 13 percent annual rate, down from a 65 percent rate of increase in 1980. The dropoff in the percentage of new recruits jeopardized MKC's ability to sustain its reputation as a fast-growing company. MKC's strategy was predicated on getting ever larger numbers of beauty consultants to arrange "skin care classes" at the home of a hostess and her three to five guests; at the classes consultants demonstrated the Mary Kay approach to skin care, gave makeup instruction with samples from the Mary Kay Cosmetics line, and usually sold anywhere from $50 to $200 worth of Mary Kay products. MKC's historically successful efforts to build up the size of its force of beauty consultants had given the company reliable access to a growing number of "showings" annually.

Even though MKC's annual turnover rate for salespeople was lower than that of several major competitors (including Avon Products), some 120,000 Mary Kay beauty consultants had quit or been terminated in 1982, making the task of recruiting a growing sales force of consultants a major, ongoing effort at MKC. Recruiting success was seen by management as strategically important. New recruits were encouraged to spend between $500 and $3,000 for sales kits and startup

*Prepared by graduate researcher Robin Romblad and Professor Arthur A. Thompson, Jr., the University of Alabama. The assistance and cooperation provided by many people in the Mary Kay organization is gratefully acknowledged. Copyright © 1986 by Arthur A. Thompson, Jr.

inventories; the initial orders of new recruits accounted for over one third of MKC's annual sales. The newest recruits were also instrumental in helping identify and attract others to become Mary Kay beauty consultants.

Richard Rogers, MKC's cofounder and president, promptly reacted to the recruiting slowdown by announcing five changes in the company's sales force program:

- The financial incentives offered to active beauty consultants for bringing new recruits into the Mary Kay fold were increased by as much as 50 percent.
- A new program was instituted whereby beauty consultants who (1) placed $600 a month in wholesale orders with the company for three consecutive months and (2) recruited five new consultants who together placed $3,000 in wholesale orders a month for three straight months would win the free use of a cream-colored Oldsmobile Firenza for a year (this program supplemented the existing programs whereby top-performing beauty consultants could win the use of a pink Cadillac or pink Buick Regal).
- The minimum order size required of beauty consultants was increased from $400 to $600.
- The prices at which MKC wholesaled its products to consultants were raised by 4 percent.
- The requirements for attaining sales director status and heading up a sales unit were raised 25 percent; a sales director had to recruit 15 new consultants (instead of 12), and her sales unit was expected to maintain a monthly minimum of $4,000 in wholesale orders (up from $3,200).

In addition, MKC's 1984 corporate budget for recruiting was more than quadrupled and, as a special recruiting effort, the company staged a National Guest Night in September 1984, that consisted of a live closed-circuit telecast to 78 cities aired from Dallas, Texas, where MKC's corporate headquarters was located. Mary Kay salespeople all over the United States were urged to invite prospective recruits and go to one of the 78 simulcast sites.

NATIONAL GUEST NIGHT IN BIRMINGHAM

Jan Currier, senior sales director for MKC in the Tuscaloosa, Alabama, area, invited two other ladies and the casewriter to drive to Birmingham in her pink Buick Regal to attend what was billed as "The Salute to the Stars." On the way, Jan explained that as well as being entertaining, the evening's event would give everyone a chance to see firsthand just how exciting and rewarding the career opportunities were with MKC; she noted with pride that Mary Kay Cosmetics was one of the companies featured in the recent book, *The 100 Best Companies to Work for in America.* As the Tuscaloosa entourage neared the auditorium in Birmingham, the casewriter observed numerous pink Cadillacs and pink Buick Regals in the flow of traffic and in the parking lot. Mary Kay sales directors were stationed at each door to the lobby enthusiastically greeting each person and presenting a gift of Mary Kay cosmetics. Guests were directed to a table to register for prizes to be awarded later in the evening.

Inside the auditorium over 1,500 people awaited at the beginning of the evening's program. A large theater screen was located at center stage. The lights dimmed promptly at 7 P.M. and the show began. The casewriter used her tape recorder and took extensive notes to capture what went on:

Mark Dixon *[national sales administrator for the south-central division, appears on stage in Birmingham]:*

> Welcome, ladies and gentlemen, to National Guest Night, Mary Kay's Salute to the Stars. Tonight, you're going to be a part of the largest teleconference ever held by a U.S. corporation. Now please help me welcome someone all of us at Mary Kay love very dearly, National Sales Director from Houston, Texas, Lovie Quinn. *[The crowd stands and greets Lovie with cheers and applause.]*

Lovie Quinn *[comes out on stage in Birmingham to join Mark Dixon. Lovie is wearing this year's Mary Kay national sales director suit of red suede with black mink trim]:*

> Good evening ladies and gentlemen and welcome to one of the most exciting events in the history of Mary Kay. An evening with Mary Kay as she Salutes the Stars. . . . During the evening you'll learn about career opportunities. There will be recognition of our stars. We'll see the salute to them with gifts and prizes you hear about at Mary Kay. You'll hear about . . . pink Cadillacs, . . . pink Buick Regals, and Firenza Oldsmobiles. You're going to hear about and see diamond rings and beautiful full-length mink coats. And of course we'll talk about MONEY.
>
> If you've never attended a Mary Kay function you might very easily get the impression that we brag a lot. We like to think of it as recognition. . . . But we would not be able to give this recognition of success if you, the hostesses, our special guests, did not open up your homes so we may share with you and some of your selected friends the Mary Kay skin care program. For that reason we would like to show our appreciation at this time. Will all the special guests please stand up. *[About 40 percent of the audience stands and the remainder applaud the guests.]*

Lovie Quinn:

> Now I need to have all our directors line up on stage. *[Each one is dressed in a navy blue suit with either a red, green, or white blouse—the color of the blouse signifies director, senior director, or future director status.]* Enthusiasm and excitement are at the root of the Mary Kay philosophy. This is why we always start a meeting like this with a song. We invite all of you to join with the directors and sing the theme song, "That Mary

Kay Enthusiasm." *[Lovie motions for the audience to stand; the choir of directors begins to clap and leads out in singing. The audience joins in quickly.]*

> I've got that Mary Kay enthusiasm up in my
>   head, up in my head, up in my head.
> I've got that Mary Kay enthusiasm up in my
>   head, up in my head to stay.
> I've got that Mary Kay enthusiasm down in my
>   heart, down in my heart, down in my heart.
> I've got that Mary Kay enthusiasm down in my
>   heart, down in my heart to stay.
> I've got that Mary Kay enthusiasm down in my
>   feet, down in my feet, down in my feet.
> I've got that Mary Kay enthusiasm down in my
>   feet, down in my feet to stay.
>   all over me, all over me.
>   all over me to stay.
> I've got that Mary Kay enthusiasm up in my
>   head, down in my heart, down in my feet.
> I've got that Mary Kay enthusiasm all over me,
>   all over me to stay.

[The song concludes to a round of applause. The crowd is spirited.]

Lovie Quinn

Now we'd like to recognize a group of very special consultants. These ladies have accepted a challenge from Mary Kay and have held 10 beauty shows in one week. This is something really terrific. It demonstrates the successful achievement of a goal. We have found when you want to do something for our Chairman of the Board, Mary Kay Ash . . . you don't have to give furs. The most special gift you can give to Mary Kay is your own success. *[All of those recognized are seated in the first 10 rows with their guests; seating in the front rows is a special reward for meeting the challenge. The crowd applauds.]*

Lovie Quinn

It is almost time for the countdown to begin, but before it does, one more special group must be recognized. These ladies are Mary Kay's Gold Medal winners. In one month they recruited *five* new consultants. *[A number of ladies stand; they beam with pride and each has been awarded a medal resembling an Olympic Gold. The audience gives them a nice round of applause. Lovie continues to fill the crowd with excitement and anticipation.]:* The countdown is going to be in just a few moments. It will be a treat for those of you that have not met Mary Kay before. Please help me count down the final 10 seconds before the broadcast.

[But the crowd is so excited it starts the countdown when one minute appears on the screen. As the seconds wind down, the crowd gets louder with anticipation and then gets in sync chanting: 10, 9, 8, 7, 6, 5, 4, 3, 2, 1. More screams and applause.

On the screen a Gold Mary Kay medallion appears, then the production lines at the plant are shown, and then trucks shipping the products. The audience claps as they see these on the screen. Headquarters is shown. Now a number of the Mary Kay sales directors are shown framed in stars on the screen. People clap when they recognize someone from their district. Loud applause fills the auditorium when Mary Kay Ash, MKC's chairman of the board and company cofounder, is shown in a star.

The Dallas-based part of the simulcast opens with female dancers dressed in pink and male dancers dressed in gray tuxedos. They perform the "Mary Kay Star Song," which includes a salute to various regions in the United States. The Birmingham crowd cheers when the South is highlighted.

A woman is chased out of the audience in Dallas. Her name is Susan; the audience is told that at various intervals in the broadcast we will see her evolution into a successful Mary Kay Beauty consultant. Initially we see her get a feeling that maybe she can be a Mary Kay star. The message is that personal dreams of success can come true. Will she be successful? The answer comes back, "Yes, She Can Do It."

Mary Kay Ash is escorted on stage by her son Richard Rogers. She is elegantly dressed with accents of diamonds and feathers. The applause, the loudest so far, is genuinely enthusiastic and many in both the Dallas and Birmingham audiences are cheering loudly.]

Mary Kay Ash:

Welcome everyone to our very first Salute to the Stars, National Guest Night. How exciting it is to think that right now over 100,000 people are watching this broadcast all over the United States. . . . Even though I can't see all of you, I can feel your warmth all the way to Dallas.

During the program this evening, one expression you're going to hear over and over again is YOU CAN DO IT. . . . This is something we really believe in. What we have discovered is the seeds of greatness are planted in every human being. . . . Tonight we hope to inspire you, to get you to reach within yourself, to bring out some of those star qualities that I know you have. And no matter who you are and no matter where you live, I believe you can take those talents and go farther than you ever thought possible and we have a special place waiting just for you.

Now I would like to introduce someone who has a special place in my heart. Someone who has been beside me from the very beginning. Without him Mary Kay Cosmetics would not be what it is today. Please welcome your president and cofounder of our company, my son, Richard Rogers.

Richard Rogers *[steps to the microphone, accompanied by respectful applause]:*

When we started this company over 20 years ago my mother and I never dreamed we would be standing here talking live to over 100,000 of you all across the country. . . . Tonight we've planned a memorable evening just for you. A program that conveys the spirit of Mary Kay. Going back 21 years ago, Mary Kay saw a void in the cosmetics industry. The observation she made was that others were just selling products. No one was teaching women about their skin and how to care for it. . . . This is the concept on which she based her company. So on September 13, 1963, Mary Kay Cosmetics opened its doors in Dallas, Texas.

Throughout the decade Mary Kay's concept continued to flourish. . . . By the end of the 60s Mary Kay Cosmetics had become a fully integrated manufacturer and distributor of skin care products. In 1970 the sales force had grown to 7,000 consultants in Texas and four surrounding states.

California was the first state MKC designated for expansion. When we first went there no one had ever heard of Mary Kay Cosmetics. Within three years California had more consultants selling Mary Kay Cosmetics than the state of Texas. . . . With this success, expansion continued throughout the United States. . . . By 1975 MKC had grown to 700 sales directors, 34,000 consultants, and $35 million in sales.

International expansion was initiated in 1978 by selling skin care products in Canada. In just 36 months MKC became the fourth largest Canadian cosmetic company. . . . Since that time Mary Kay has expanded to South America, Australia, and in September we opened for business in the United Kingdom.

At the end of 1983 MKC had over 195,000 consultants. Sales had reached over $600 million around the world. . . . With total commitment to excellence setting the pace, MKC is still working toward achieving the goal of being the finest teaching-oriented skin care organization in the world. . . . Mary Kay is proud to have the human resources necessary to meet this goal. At Mary Kay, P&L means more than profit and loss. It also stands for People and Love. People have helped MKC reach where it is today, and they will play a big part in where it will be tomorrow.

Tonight we're proud to announce the arrival of a book that expresses the Mary Kay philosophy of Golden Rule management, a book that outlines the management style that has contributed to the success of Mary Kay Cosmetics. The new book is *Mary Kay on People Management. [The crowd applauds at this announcement.]*

Mary Kay Ash *[reappears on stage]:*

We're so excited about the new book. I am pleased to have the opportunity to talk with you about it tonight. Actually, I started to write that book over 20 years ago. I had just retired from 25 years of direct sales. I wanted to share my experiences, so I wrote down my thoughts about the companies I had worked for. What had worked and what had not. . . . After expressing my ideas I thought how wonderful it would be to put these ideas of a company designed to meet women's needs into action. That is when Mary Kay Cosmetics was born. . . . The company helps women meet the goals they set for themselves. . . . I feel this is what has contributed to the success of the organization. Everyone at MKC starts at the same place, as a consultant, and everyone has the same opportunities for success.

[The broadcast returns to the scenario of Susan as she becomes a new Mary Kay consultant. Susan sings about the doubts people have about her joining Mary Kay. She disregards this and decides to climb to success. At the end of the scene, she projects a positive, successful image that her friends and family recognize. The audience responds favorably.]

Dale Alexander *[national sales administrator for Mary Kay Cosmetics appears on stage in Dallas]:*

It is a great honor to be with you tonight and I want to add my most sincere welcome. . . . Recognition is one of the original principles on which our company is based. It's an essential ingredient in the Mary Kay formula for success. . . . I want to start out by recognizing the largest group, the group of independent businesswomen who are out there every day holding beauty shows, teaching skin care, selling our products, and sharing the Mary Kay opportunity. At this time will all of the Mary Kay beauty consultants across the nation stand to be recognized? *[In Birmingham the lights go up and the crowd applauds the consultants in the audience.]* Next we want to recognize the Star Consultants. . . . Will these ladies stand?

Many of our people are wearing small golden ladders. This is our Ladder of Success. Each ladder has a number of different jewels awarded for specific accomplishments during a calendar quarter. Star consultants earn rubies, sapphires, and diamonds to go on their ladders. The higher they climb the more dazzling their ladders become. A consultant with all diamonds is known at Mary Kay as a top Star Performer. It is like wearing a straight A report card on your lapel.

In addition to ladders, consultants have an opportunity to earn great prizes each quarter. . . . This quarter's theme is Salute to the Stars . . . and these prizes are out of this world.

[The scene shifts to a description of the fall 1984 sales program; it utilizes a "Star Trek" theme, and across the screen is emblazoned "Starship Mary Kay in Search of the Prize Zone." Captain Kay appears with members of her crew on Starship Mary Kay. She remarks their mission is to seek out prizes to honor those that reach for the sky. They are approaching the prize zone. The awards and prizes are flashed onto the screen.

The Prize Zone
Bonus Prizes Available
Based on Fourth-Quarter Sales

$1,800 wholesale sales	*Cubic zirconia necklace and earrings or travel set with hair dryer*
$2,400 wholesale sales	*Leather briefcase with matching umbrella*
$3,000 wholesale sales	*Diamond earrings with 14K gold teardrops*
$3,600 wholesale sales	*Telephone answering machine*
$4,200 wholesale sales	*Sapphire ring*
$4,800 wholesale sales	*Electronic printer by Brother—fits in a briefcase*
$6,000 wholesale sales	*Diamond pendant—nine diamonds—.5 karat on an 18K gold chain*

Even though this "space" presentation of prizes is humorous, the ladies know that the rewards are real; they respond as the scene ends with a round of applause and a buzz of excitement. The scene concludes with the message, "When you reach for the sky, you bring home a star."]

Mary Kay *[returns to the stage]:*

You can climb that ladder of success at Mary Kay. It is up to you to take that very first step. . . . There are so many rewards for being a Mary Kay consultant. There are top earnings, prizes, and lots of recognition. But there is even more to a Mary Kay career and that is the fulfilment of bringing beauty into the lives of others. . . .

When a woman joins our company she knows she can do it. But not alone. She'll receive support from many people. A big-sister relationship will form between a new consultant and her recruiter. . . . Whoever invited you tonight thought you were a special person. She wanted to share this evening and introduce you to our company and let you see for yourself the excitement and enthusiasm Mary Kay people have when they are together. . . . The enthusiasm of our consultants and directors is responsible for our success.

[The vignette about Susan returns to the screen. This time she is thinking about concentrating her effort on recruiting. After five recruits she will become a team leader—a good goal to strive for, she thinks. A woman that had doubted Susan's career earlier is the first one recruited. Then four more ladies are recruited: a waitress, a teacher, a stewardess, and a nurse. All kinds of people can be Mary Kay consultants. Susan has reached her goal—she is a team leader. The crowd applauds her success.]

Dale Alexander *[returns to the microphone in Dallas]:*

There is the perfect goal of a Mary Kay career. And now it is time to recognize a very special group of individuals who are proof of this point. Will all the team leaders please stand and remain standing for a few moments? *[The lights go up and team leaders stand. All are wearing red jackets.]*

To qualify for a team leader each consultant must recruit five new consultants. . . . And now will you please recognize these ladies' achievements with a round of applause? *[The audience applauds.]* Now it is time to draw for the prizes. In each of the 75 locations two names will be drawn. These lucky people will both win this exquisite 14K diamond earring and pendant set. *[The crowd oohs and aahs when the jewelry is shown on the screen.]* These two winners will also be eligible for the prize to be given by Mary Kay when the broadcast resumes.

[The lights go up in the Birmingham auditorium. Lovie draws two tickets from a big box. When she calls out the names, the winners scream and run on stage to accept their gifts. The crowd applauds the winners.]

Lovie Quinn *[on the stage in Birmingham]:*

Please join me in counting down the final seconds left before we rejoin the broadcast. *[Everyone stands and enthusiastically counts off "11, 10, 9, 8, 7, 6, 5, 4, 3, 2, 1." The crowd applauds and cheers.]*

Mary Kay *[appears on the screen as the broadcast from Dallas is rejoined]:*

I wish I could be there to congratulate each winner. . . . The two lucky winners in each of the 75 cities are eligible to win the grand prize. . . . It used to be you just drew a number out of a hat. Now that is considered old-fashioned. Tonight, we'll use a computer. All I have to do is push a button and a city will be randomly selected. The local winners in that city will also win this .75 karat diamond ring. *[The crowd buzzes as a close-up of the ring is shown on the giant screen.]* Are you ready? OK. Here goes. *[Mary Kay presses a button.]* The lucky city is Philadelphia. *[The crowd applauds.]* Congratulations Philadelphia, and we will be sending each of you a ring real soon.

By the way, while we are talking about prizes, would you happen to have a spare finger for a diamond ring? *[The crowd cheers.]* Or could you squeeze into your closet room for a full-length mink coat? *[The crowd is really excited.]* Or is there by any chance, a space in your driveway for a car? *[The crowd cheers and applauds. One member of the audience remarks how she would be glad to get rid of that old blue thing she is driving.]* Well, all you have to do is set your Mary Kay career goals high enough to achieve the recognition and rewards available just for you. . . .

I remember the first sales competition I set my goals to win. I worked so hard and all I won was a flounder light. *[The audience laughs.]* Does anyone know what you do with it? It is something you use when you put on waders and jig for fish. *[The audience laughs again.]* I thought the prize was awful. . . . but my manager was a fisherman and he thought it was great.

Winning that flounder light taught me a lesson. I decided if I was ever in a position to give awards they would be things women appreciate, *not* flounder lights. . . . Prizes would be things women would love to have. Absolutely no washing machines and certainly no ironing boards. *[The audience shows their approval by cheers and applause.]* At MKC you are rewarded for consistent sales and recruiting performance. . . . This past spring a new program was added. . . . We call it our VIP program. It stands for Very Important Performer. . . . This program allows a person to win a cream-colored Oldsmobile Firenza with rich brown interior. . . . A consultant is eligible for this prize only three months after joining MKC. . . .

Mary Kay Cosmetics can offer several unique career opportunities:

- A 50 percent commission on everything you sell.
- Earnings of a 12 percent commission on your recruit's sales.
- You work your own hours.
- After three months you can be eligible for a car. The car is free. MKC pays the insurance.
- When you do well you get a lot of recognition. Not dumb old things like turkeys and hams. We're talking diamonds and furs.
- You work up to management because of your own efforts and merit.

Other companies would think these things are part of a dream world. At Mary Kay we do live in a dream world and our dreams do come true.

[The audience applauds loudly. The broadcast then returns to the scenario about Susan. She sets a goal to be a VIP. Through song and dance her group illustrates setting goals and receiving recognition. Step by step they climb the ladder of recognition. The audience applauds this short scene on success.]

Dale Alexander *[comes back to the Dallas stage]:*

We have some VIPs among us tonight. . . . Mary Kay's Very Important Performers. Will all the VIPs now stand? *[The lights go up in Birmingham; the VIPs stand and the audience applauds.]* Through her enthusiasm and hard work each VIP has worked hard to achieve this status. And to recognize her accomplishments she was awarded an Oldsmobile Firenza to show off her achievement of success. Now let's give all our VIPs a round of applause. *[The Birmingham and Dallas audiences respond with more applause.]*

Mary Kay Ash *[comes onto the stage in Dallas and the crowd in Birmingham turns its attention to the screen]:*

With Mary Kay you can achieve success. . . . All you have to do is break down your goals into small manageable steps. . . . You are able to move on to bigger accomplishments as you gain confidence in yourself.

Let's look at some of the provisions of the Mary Kay career plan and see how it works:

* Your products are purchased directly from the company.
* Generous discounts are offered on large orders.
* There are no territories. You can sell and recruit wherever you want.
* We provide our customers the best possible way to buy cosmetics. They can try the products in their own home before they buy.
* All Mary Kay products are backed by a full 100 percent money-back guarantee.

Mary Kay is a good opportunity to go into business for yourself. . . . There are many benefits of running your own business. . . . You meet new sisterhood. . . . Plus you earn financial rewards as well as prizes. . . .

Now we need to talk about the position of Mary Kay sales director. Directors receive income not only from shows, facials, and reorders but also from recruit commissions. . . . In addition they earn unit and recruiting bonuses from Mary Kay. . . .Some earn over $30,000 a year. And today in our company we have more women earning over $50,000 a year than any other company in America. *[The audience applauds.]* At the very top are our national sales directors. . . . Their average is about $150,000 a year in commissions. How about that? *[The audience applauds.]* Everyone at Mary Kay starts at the same place with the same beauty showcase. I've always said you can have anything in this world if you want it badly enough and are willing to pay the price. With that kind of attitude anyone can succeed at Mary Kay.

[The vignette about Susan comes back onto the screen. Susan sets a goal to become sales director. She sings about how invigorating her new career is and how she now wants to be a coach, a teacher, a counselor, and a friend to others. Everyone around her recognizes how her success has positively affected her whole life. The scene ends and the audience applauds.]

Dale Alexander *[comes onto the screen from Dallas]:*

Those individuals that advance on to directorship lead our organization. They set the pace for their units. Will all our sales directors please stand? *[The sales directors stand as the lights go up in Birmingham and the audience applauds.]* Among all our directors there are some that have reached a very special level. They have earned the privilege of driving one of Mary Kay's famous pink cars. . . . One thing is guaranteed. Whenever you see one of those pink cars on the road you know there is a top achiever behind the wheel. At this time we want to honor all these ladies. *[First the Regal drivers stand and then the Cadillac drivers. The audience recognizes each group with applause.]* Finally, there is one last group we want to recognize. A group whose members have already committed to a future with Mary Kay. . . . They are our DIQs or directors in qualification. They are working toward meeting the goals to qualify for directorship. . . . Will all the DIQs stand for a round of applause? *[The lights go up and the DIQs stand. They are recognized with applause from the audience. The lights fade and the scene shifts back to Dallas.]*

Mary Kay:

I want to congratulate these ladies. Next week I'll have the pleasure of hostessing our traditional tea for the DIQs at my home. *[The audience applauds.]* Our DIQs are a perfect example of one of the points we have tried to make this evening. . . . You can set your goals and achieve them if you want them badly enough.

I've always felt our most valuable asset is not our product but our people. . . . I wish I could tell you all the success stories of consultants at MKC. . . . We have chosen a few stories we think best represent Mary Kay consultants. The first person you'll meet is Rena.

[The audience applauds; Rena is recognized by the Mary Kay people present. The narrator of the film clip tells us that Rena has been with MKC for 17 years. She has been Queen of Unit Sales four consecutive years, an honor which was earned when the sales unit she managed exceeded $1 million in sales in one year. Her reward was four $5,000 shopping sprees at Neiman-Marcus Co. in Dallas. When she started she was living on $300 a month in government housing with her husband and three small children. One day a friend offered to buy her dinner and pay for a babysitter if she would attend a meeting. She couldn't pass up this offer so she went to the Mary Kay meeting. The meeting inspired her and she joined MKC. At the end we learn that Rena has had cancer for the last eight years, a fact that is not well known; the point is made that it has never affected her ability to succeed with Mary Kay Cosmetics. The crowd applauds her success story.

Next comes a film clip about Ruel; the audience is told that Ruel was raised in Arkansas, a daughter of a sharecropper. She joined Mary Kay in 1971. By 1976 she was a national sales director. A career with Mary Kay has given her confidence. She has two children in medical school and one of her sons just won a national honor, the Medal of Valor. All of this she attributes to Mary Kay. Her children saw her achieve and they knew they could too. Her career with Mary Kay has allowed her to climb up the scale from a poor sharecropper's daughter to become financially independent. Along the way she has the opportunity to meet many wonderful people. As her success story ends, the audience applauds.

The third story is about Arlene. Arlene has been a national sales director since 1976. She achieved this just five short years after joining MKC. She had been at home for 13 years and wanted to have her own business, set her own hours, and write her own checks. She found she could achieve these goals in a career with Mary Kay. Arlene, we are told, has been able to reach inside herself and achieve great success. Arlene testifies that one of her biggest rewards at Mary Kay has been helping other women achieve the goals they set. The audience loudly applauds the last of the success stories.]

Mary Kay:

I am so proud of all these ladies. . . . It makes me feel good to be able to offer all these wonderful opportunities to so many women. Every journey begins with just a single step. All you have to do is make up your mind that YOU can do it! Isn't it exciting. YOU can do it.

All you need to start a Mary Kay career is a beauty case. It carries everything: vanity trays, mirrors, products, and product literature. To-night it becomes easier. . . . If you join us as a beauty consultant tonight, we will give you your beauty showcase. *[The audience interrupts with a round of applause.]* When you submit your beauty consultant agreement along with your first wholesale order, you will receive the beauty case free, an $85 value.

At Mary Kay you'll make lasting friends and you'll achieve a feeling of growth. . . . Tonight we wanted to give you a feel for Mary Kay Cosmetics. We have a place for you to shine. . . . Believe in yourself and you can do anything. *[The broadcast from Dallas concludes; the audience stands and applauds the program.]*

Lovie Quinn *[comes onto stage in Birmingham]:*

I started at Mary Kay just to earn money for Christmas. I told Mary Kay I could only work four hours a week. Believe it or not Mary Kay welcomed me into the organization.

Things were different then. There were no manuals or guides. I was given my first cosmetics in a shoe box. Mary Kay Cosmetics has come a long way. Each consultant has her own beauty case and is trained in skin care.

Last year I earned over $112,000. This does not include my personal sales. . . . I am now driving my 13th pink Cadillac. . . . For three years I have been in the half million dollar club. The prizes for this honor include either a black mink, a white mink, or a diamond ring, all worth $10,000 each. I have all three.

Mary Kay Cosmetics offers many opportunities to women. . . . Tonight, if you join MKC, I would be honored to sign your agreement. This will let Mary Kay know you made your commitment tonight. *[Lovie invites the new consultants to meet her up front. The audience applauds her. Many of the women eagerly go up to meet Lovie and have their agreements signed.]*

THE DIRECT SALES INDUSTRY

In 1984 Avon was the acknowledged leader among the handful of companies that chose to market cosmetics to U.S. consumers using direct sales techniques. Avon, with its door-to-door sales force of 400,000 representatives, had worldwide sales of about $2 billion. Mary Kay

Cosmetics was the second leading firm (see Exhibit 1). Other well-known companies whose salespeople went either door-to-door with their products or else held "parties" in the homes of prospective customers included Amway Corp. (home cleaning products), Shaklee Corp. (vitamins and health foods), Encyclopaedia Britannica, Tupperware (plastic dishes and food containers), Consolidated Foods' Electrolux division (vacuum cleaners), and StanHome (parent of Fuller Brush). The direct sales industry also included scores of lesser known firms selling about every product imaginable—clothing, houseplants, toys, and financial services. Although Stanley Home Products invented the idea, Mary Kay and Tupperware were the best-known national companies using the "party plan" approach to direct selling.

The success enjoyed by Avon and Mary Kay was heavily dependent upon constantly replenishing and expanding their sales forces. New salespeople not only placed large initial orders for products but they also recruited people into the organization. Revenues and revenue

EXHIBIT 1   Estimated Sales of Leading Direct Selling Cosmetic Companies, 1983

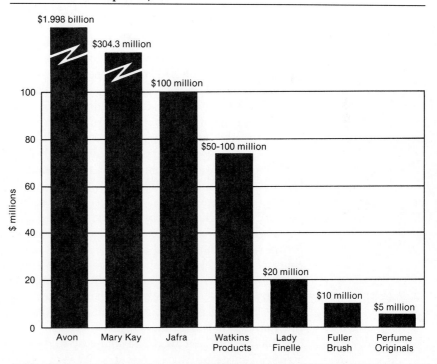

Source: "Reopening the Door to Door-to-Door Selling," *Chemical Business,* February 1984.

growth thus were a function of the number of representatives as well as the sales productivity of each salesperson. Market size was not seen as a limiting factor for growth because direct sales companies typically reached fewer than half the potential customer base.

Direct selling was grounded in capitalizing in networking relationships. Salespeople usually got their starts by selling first to relatives, friends, and neighbors, all the while looking for leads to new prospects. Direct sales specialists often believed that party-plan selling was most successful among working class, ethnic, and small-town population groups where relationships were closer knit and where the social lives of women had a high carryover effect with work and high school. However, industry analysts saw several trends working against the networking approach and party-plan type of direct selling: rising divorce rates; the scattering of relatives and families across wider geographic areas; weakening ties to ethnic neighborhoods; declines in the number and strength of "the old girls" networks in many towns and neighborhoods; increased social mobility; the growing popularity of apartment and condominium living, where acquaintances and relationships were most transient; and the springing up of bedroom communities and subdivisions populated by commuters and/or by families that stayed only a few years.

In the 1980s direct selling companies began to have problems recruiting and retaining salespeople, partly because of these trends but even more because of shifting employment patterns and preferences. During the two most recent recessionary periods in the United States, it was thought that the pool of potential saleswomen available for recruitment into direct sales careers would expand owing to above-normal unemployment rates. It didn't happen. As it turned out, many women became the sole family support and even greater numbers sought steady, better paying jobs in other fields. Part-time job opportunities mushroomed outside the direct sales field; many service and retailing firms started hiring part-time permanent workers rather than full-time permanent staffs because part-time workers did not have to be paid the same extensive fringe benefits that full-time employees normally got. When the economy experienced upturns, the pool of direct sales recruits shrank even more as people sought security in jobs offering regular hours and a salary; in 1983 all direct sales companies reported increased difficulty in getting people to accept their part-time, sales-oriented, commission-only offers of employment.

Avon and Mary Kay were both caught offguard by these unpredicted events. Staffing plans at Avon had originally called for expansion in the number of sales force representatives from 400,000 in 1983 to 650,000 by 1987; in 1984 the company revised the 1987 goal down to 500,000 representatives. Four straight years of declining earnings convinced Avon that the traditional approach of depending on increasing the number of representatives for growth was no longer feasible.

Sarah Coventry, a home-party jewelry firm, decided in 1984 that relying solely upon direct selling approaches would not only be a continuing problem but a growing problem. The company began to look for ways to supplement its direct sales methods and shortly announced a plan to begin to sell Sarah Coventry products in retail stores. Fuller Brush, a long-standing door-to-door seller, began to distribute mail-order catalogs displaying a wider line of "househelper" products.

As of 1984 virtually every company in the direct sales industry was critically evaluating the extent to which changes in the economy and in employment demographics would affect the success of direct selling. Many firms, including Avon and Mary Kay, were reviewing their incentive programs and sales organization methods. A number of industry observers as well as company officials believed some major changes would have to be made in the way the direct sales industry did business.

MARY KAY ASH

Before she reached the age of 10, Mary Kay was responsible for cleaning, cooking, and caring for her invalid father while her mother worked to support the family. During these years, Mary Kay's mother encouraged her daughter to excel. Whether at school or home, Mary Kay was urged to put forth her best efforts. By the time she was a teenager, Mary Kay had become a classic overachiever, intent on getting good grades and winning school contests. Over and over again she heard her mother say "you can do it." Years later Mary Kay noted on many occasions, "The confidence my mother instilled in me has been a tremendous help."[1]

Deserted by her husband of 11 years during the Great Depression, Mary Kay found herself with the responsibility of raising and supporting three children under the age of eight. Needing a job with flexible hours she opted to try a career in direct sales with Stanley Home Products, a home-party housewares firm. One of the first goals Mary Kay set at Stanley was to win Stanley's Miss Dallas Award, a ribbon honoring the employee who recruited the most new people in one week; she won the award during her first year with Stanley. After 13 years with Stanley, Mary Kay joined World Gift, a direct sales company involved in decorative accessories; a few years later she was promoted to national training director. Her career and life were threatened in 1962 by a rare paralysis of one side of the face.

After recovery from surgery she decided to retire from World Gift; by then she had remarried and lived in a comfortable Dallas neighborhood. She got so bored with retirement she decided to write a book

---

[1]Mary Kay Ash, *Mary Kay* (New York: Harper & Row, 1981), p. 3.

on her direct sales experiences. The more she wrote, the more she came to realize just how many problems women faced in the business world. Writing on a yellow legal pad at her kitchen table, Mary Kay listed everything she thought was wrong with male-run companies; on a second sheet she detailed how these wrongs could be righted, how a company could operate in ways that were responsive to the problems of working women and especially working mothers, and how women could reach their top potential in the business world. Being restless with retirement, she decided to do something about what she had written on the yellow pad and began immediately to plan how she might form a direct sales company that had no sales quotas, few rules, flexible work hours, and plenty of autonomy for salespeople.

Finding a product to market was not a problem. In 1953 when she was conducting a Stanley home party at a house "on the wrong side of Dallas," she had noticed that all the ladies present had terrific-looking skin. It turned out that the hostess was a cosmetologist who was experimenting with a skin care product and all the guests were her guinea pigs. After the party everyone gathered in the hostess's kitchen to get samples of her latest batch. The product was based on a formula that the woman's father, a hide tanner, developed when he accidentally discovered that some tanning lotions he made and used regularly had caused his hands to look much younger than his face. The tanner decided to apply these solutions to his face regularly, and after a short time his facial skin began looking more youthful too. The woman had since worked with her father's discovery for 17 years, making up batches which had the chemical smell of tanning solutions, putting portions in empty jars and bottles, and selling them as a sideline; she gave out instructions for use written in long-hand on notebook paper. Mary Kay offered to try some of the hostess's latest batch and, despite the fact that it was smelly and messy, soon concluded that it was so good she wouldn't use anything else. Later, she became convinced that the only reason the woman hadn't made the product a commercial success was because she lacked marketing skills.

In 1963, using $5,000 in savings as working capital, she bought the formulas and proceeded to organize a beauty products company that integrated skin care instruction into its direct sales approach. The company was named Beauty by Mary Kay; the plan was for Mary Kay to take responsibility for the sales part of the company and for her second husband to serve as chief administrator. One month before operations were to start, he dropped dead of a heart attack. Her children persuaded her to go ahead with her plans, and Mary Kay's 20-year-old son, Richard Rogers, agreed to take on the job of administration of the new company. In September 1963 they opened a small store in Dallas with one shelf of inventory and nine of Mary Kay's friends as saleswomen. Mary Kay herself had limited expectations for the company and never dreamed that its sphere of operations would extend beyond Dallas.

All of Mary Kay's life-long philosophies and experiences were incorporated into how the company operated. The importance of encouragement became deeply ingrained in what was said and done. "You Can Do It" was expanded from a technique used by her mother to a daily theme at MKC. Mary Kay's style was to "praise people to success." She put into practice again the motivating role that positive encouragement had played in her own career; recognition and awards were made a highlight of the sales incentive programs that emerged. By 1984, recognition at MKC ranged from a simple ribbon awarded for a consultant's first $100 show to a $5,000 shopping spree given to million-dollar producers.

The second important philosophy Mary Kay stressed concerned personal priorities: "Over the years I have found that if you have your life in the proper perspective, with God first, your family second, and your career third, everything seems to work out."[2] She reiterated this belief again and again, regularly urging employees to take stock of their personal priorities and citing her own experience and belief as a positive example. She insisted on an all-out, firmwide effort to accommodate the plight of working mothers. Mary Kay particularly stressed giving beauty consultants enough control over how their selling efforts were scheduled so that problems with family matters and sick children were not incompatible with a Mary Kay career. A structure based on no sales quotas, few rules, and flexible hours was essential, Mary Kay believed, because working mothers from time to time needed the freedom to let work demands take a backseat to pressing problems at home.

Fairness and personal ethics were put in the forefront, too. The Golden Rule (treating others as you would have them treat you) was high on Mary Kay's list of management guidelines:

> I believe in the Golden Rule and try to run the company on those principles. I believe that all you send into the lives of others will come back into your own. I like to see women reaching into themselves and coming out of their shells as the beautiful person that God intended them to be. In my company women do not have to claw their way to the top. They can get ahead based on the virtue of their own ethics because there's enough for everyone.[3]

To discourage interpersonal rivalry and jealousy, all rewards and incentives were pegged to reaching plateaus of achievement; everybody

---

[2]Ibid., p. 56.

[3]As quoted in "The Beauty of Being Mary Kay," *Marketing and Media Decisions*, December 1982, pp. 150, 152.

who reached the target level of performance became a winner. Sales contests based on declaring first place, second place, and third place winners were avoided.

MKC INC.

The company succeeded from the start. First-year wholesale sales were $198,000; in the second year sales reached $800,000 At year end 1983, wholesale revenues exceeded $320 million and MKC's staff of consultants numbered over 195,000. Major geographical expansion was initiated during the 1970s. Distribution centers were opened in California, Georgia, New Jersey, and Illinois, and the company expanded its selling efforts internationally to Canada, Argentina, Australia, and the United Kingdom.

Early on, Mary Kay and Richard decided to consult a psychologist to learn more about their personalities. Testing revealed that Mary Kay was the type who, when encountering a person bleeding all over a fine carpet, would think of the person's plight first while Richard would think first of the carpet. This solidified their decision for Mary Kay to be the company's inspirational leader and for Richard to concentrate on overseeing all the business details.

In 1968 the company name was changed to Mary Kay Cosmetics, Inc. During that year the company went public and its stock was traded in the over-the-counter market. In 1976 MKC's stock was listed on the New York Stock Exchange. Income per common share jumped from $0.16 in 1976 to $1.22 in 1983. A 10-year financial summary is presented in Exhibit 2; Exhibits 3 and 4 provide additional company data.

Richard Rogers, president, gave two basic reasons for the success of MKC:

> We were filling a void in the industry when we began to teach skin care and makeup artistry and we're still doing that today. And second, our marketing system, through which proficient consultants achieve success by recruiting and building their own sales organization, was a stroke of genius because the by-product has been management. In other words, we didn't buy a full management team; they've been trained one by one.[4]

One of the biggest challenges MKC had to tackle during the 1970s was how to adapt its strategy and operating style in response to the influx of women into the labor force. Full- and part-time jobs interfered with attending beauty shows during normal working hours, and many working women with children at home had a hard time fitting beauty

---

[4]Mary Kay Cosmetics, Inc., "A Company and a Way of Life," company literature.

EXHIBIT 2 Selected Financial Data, Mary Kay Cosmetics, Inc., 1973–83 (in thousands except per share data)

	1973	*1974*	*1975*	*1976*	*1977*	*1978*	*1979*	*1980*	*1981*	*1982*	*1983*
Net sales	$22,199	$30,215	$34,947	$44,871	$47,856	$53,746	$91,400	$166,938	$235,296	$304,275	$323,758
Cost of sales	6,414	9,054	10,509	14,139	14,562	17,517	27,584	52,484	71,100	87,807	88,960
Selling, general, and administrative expenses	9,674	13,128	15,050	19,192	21,394	27,402	45,522	86,998	120,880	154,104	168,757
Operating income	6,111	8,033	9,388	11,540	11,900	8,827	18,304	27,456	43,316	62,364	66,041
Interest and other income, net	377	443	202	501	175	660	493	712	1,485	2,763	3,734
Interest expense	58	54	60	43	212	504	958	635	1,014	1,284	2,886
Income before income taxes	6,430	8,422	9,530	11,998	11,863	8,983	17,839	27,533	43,787	63,843	66,889
Provision for income taxes	3,035	3,973	4,480	5,854	5,711	4,110	8,207	12,398	19,632	28,471	30,235
Net income	$ 3,395	$ 4,449	$ 5,050	$ 6,144	$ 6,152	$ 4,873	$ 9,632	$ 15,135	$ 24,155	$ 35,372	$ 36,654
Net income per common share	$ .09	$ .11	$ .13	$ .16	$ .17	$ .15	$ .33	$ .52	$ .82	$ 1.18	$ 1.22
Cash dividends per share	$ .01	$ .03	$ .03	$ .05	$ .05	$ .06	$ .06	$ .09	$ .10	$ .11	$ .12
Average common shares	38,800	38,864	38,928	39,120	35,480	33,408	29,440	28,884	29,324	29,894	30,138
Total assets	$19,600	$24,743	$27,996	$34,331	$35,144	$36,305	$50,916	$ 74,431	$100,976	$152,457	$180,683
Long-term debt	$ 756	$ 87	$ 42	—	$ 5,592	$ 3,558	$ 4,000	$ $3,000	$ 2,366	$ 4,669	$ 3,915
Return on average stockholders' equity			21%	23%	24%	20%	38%	48%	48%	45%	32%
Stock prices											
Year high			2¾	2⅞	2⅝	1⅞	3⅞	8¾	18¾	28½	47⅞
Year low			1⅞	1¾	1½	1¼	1¼	3	6⅛	8⅜	13⅛

Source: Mary Kay Cosmetics, Inc., *1983 Annual Report*.

EXHIBIT 3   Growth in the Number of MKC Sales Directors and Beauty Consultants, 1973–83

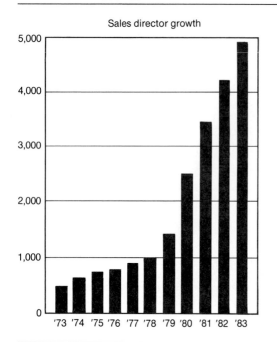

Sales director growth

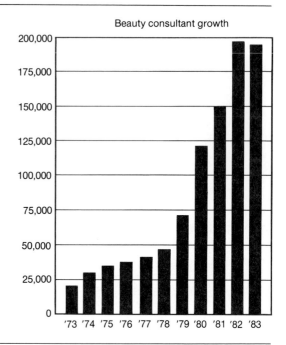

Beauty consultant growth

Source: 1983 Annual Report.

EXHIBIT 4   Percentage Breakdown of Product Sales at Mary Kay Cosmetics, 1979–83

	1979	*1980*	*1981*	*1982*	*1983*
Skin care products for women	49%	52%	49%	46%	44%
Skin care products for men	1	2	1	1	1
Makeup items	26	22	26	26	30
Toiletry items for women	10	10	10	12	11
Toiletry items for men	2	2	2	2	2
Hair care	2	2	2	2	2
Accessories	10	10	10	11	10
Total	100%	100%	100%	100%	100%

Source: 1983 Annual Report.

shows on weeknights and weekends into their schedules. To make the beauty show sales approach more appealing to working women, the company began to supplement its standard "try before you buy" and "on-the-spot-delivery" sales pitch themes. Consultants were trained to tout the ease with which MKC's scientifically formulated skin care system could be followed, the value of investing in good makeup and attractive appearance, the up-to-date glamor and wide selection associated with MKC's product line, the flexibility of deciding what and when to buy, and the time-saving convenience of having refills and "specials" delivered to their door instead of having to go out shopping. Mary Kay consultants quickly picked up on the growing popularity of having beauty shows on Tuesday, Wednesday, and Thursday nights; a lesser proportion of weekday hours were used for morning and afternoon showings, and a greater proportion came to be used for seeking and delivering reorders from ongoing users.

MKC's corporate sales goal for the 80s was to reach $500 million in revenues by 1990. As of 1984 about 65 percent of total sales were made to customers at beauty shows. However, it was expected that as the size of the company's customer base grew, the percentage of orders from repeat buyers would rise well above the present 35 percent level. MKC estimated that the average client spent over $200 a year on cosmetics. The company saw its target clientele as middle-class women in the 18–34 age group primarily and in the 35–44 age group secondarily, and believed that a big percentage of its customers consisted of suburban housewives and white-collar clerical workers. The company's literature always pictured upscale women, dressed in a classy and elegant yet understated way, in either the role of a Mary Kay beauty consultant or the role of a user of Mary Kay cosmetics. As company figurehead, Mary Kay Ash personally made a point of being fashionably and expensively dressed, with perfect makeup and hairdo—a walking showcase for the company's products and a symbol of the professionally successful businesswoman (Exhibit 5).

MANUFACTURING

When Mary Kay Cosmetics commenced operations in 1963, the task of making the products was contracted out to a private Dallas-based manufacturing company. Mary Kay explained why:

> In 1963 I had no previous experience in the cosmetics industry; my forte was recruiting and training salespeople. After I acquired the formulas for the skin-care products, the first thing I did was seek out the most reputable cosmetics manufacturer I could find. Specifically I wanted a firm that not only made quality products, but observed the Food and Drug Administration's regulatory requirements to the letter. I knew it would be a fatal

---

EXHIBIT 5 Mary Kay Ash in 1983

Source: 1983 Annual Report (picture on front cover).

mistake to attempt to cut corners. With the right people in charge, we would never have to concern ourselves with that aspect of the business.[5]

In 1969 MKC built a 300,000-square-foot manufacturing and packaging facility adjacent to corporate headquarters. Packaging, warehousing, purchasing, and research labs were all housed in this location. Also included was a printing set-up which created Mary Kay labels in English, Spanish, and French. Many of the operations were automated.

The company's scientific approach to skin care was supported by a staff of laboratory technicians skilled in cosmetic chemistry, dermatology, physiology, microbiology, and package engineering. On-going tests were conducted to refine existing items and to develop new

---

[5]Mary Kay Ash, *Mary Kay on People Management* (New York: Warner Books, 1984), p. 13.

products. Laboratory staffs were provided with the comments and reactions about the products that came in from beauty consultants and
their customers; consultants were strongly encouraged to report on
their experiences with items and to relay any problems that consultants had directly to the laboratory staff. About 80 percent of the R&D
budget was earmarked for improving existing products.

MKC believed that it was an industry leader in researching (1) the
biophysical properties of the skin (as concerning skin elasticity and
moisture) and (2) skin structure and anatomical quality. Much of the
research at MKC was performed in cooperation with academic institutions, particularly the University of Pennsylvania and the University of Texas Health Science Center.

PRODUCT LINE AND DISTRIBUTION POLICIES

As of 1984 the Mary Kay product line consisted of the basic skin care
program for various skin types, the glamour collection, the body care
products line, and a line of men's products called Mr. K. Most of the
women's products were packaged in pink boxes and jars. When the
company first began operations, Mary Kay personally put a lot of
thought into packaging and appearance:

> Since people do leave their toiletries out, I wanted to package our cosmetics
> so beautifully that women would *want* to leave them out. So I was looking
> for a color that would make a beautiful display in all those white bathrooms.
> There were some shades of blue that were attractive, but the prettiest
> complementary color seemed to be a delicate pink. It also occurred to me
> that pink is considered a more feminine color. But my main reason for
> choosing it was that delicate pink seemed to look prettier than anything
> else in those white tile bathrooms. And from that I gained a *pink* reputation![6]

Mr. K, the men's line, was introduced in the 1960s in response to a
number of confessions from men who used their wives' Mary Kay products. A rich chocolate brown package accented with silver was chosen
for Mr. K. The men's line included a basic skin care program as well
as lotions and colognes. The majority of Mr. K purchases were made
by women for their husbands and boyfriends.

Consultants bought their supplies of products directly from MKC at
wholesale prices and sold them at a 100 percent markup over wholesale.
To make it more feasible for consultants to keep an adequate inventory
on hand, the product line at MKC was kept streamlined, about 50
products. Mary Kay consultants were encouraged to carry enough
products in their personal inventories that orders could be filled on
the spot at beauty shows. As an incentive to support this practice,

---

[6]Ash, *Mary Kay*, pp. 150–51.

MKC offered special awards and prizes when consultants placed orders of $1,500 or more.

A consultant could order as many or as few of the company's products as she chose to inventory. Most consultants stockpiled those items that sold especially well with their own individual clientele, and consultants also had the freedom to offer special promotions or discounts to customers. Nearly 50 percent of sales were for the skin care products which had evolved from the hide tanner's discovery. Consultants were required to pay for all orders with cashier's checks or money orders prior to delivery. MKC dealt only on a cash basis to minimize accounts receivables problems. According to Mary Kay, "Bad debts are a major reason for failure in other direct sales companies." In 1984 the average initial order of new consultants for inventory was about $1,000 ($2,000 in retail value). Consultants who decided to get out of the business could resell their inventories to MKC at 90 percent of cost.

During the company's early years, consultants were supplied only with an inventory of items to sell; shipments arrived in plain boxes. There were no sales kits and no instruction manuals to assist in sales presentations. However, by the 1970s each new recruit received training in skin care techniques and was furnished with a number of sales aids. Later new consultants were required to buy a beauty showcase containing everything needed to conduct a beauty show (samples, pink mirrors, pink trays used to distribute the samples, and a step-by-step sales manual that included suggested dialogue). In 1984 the showcase was sold to new consultants for $85. Along with the showcase came a supply of beauty profile forms to use at showings; guests filled out the form at the beginning of the show, and from the information supplied a consultant could readily prescribe which of several product formulas was best suited for the individual's skin type.

In addition to the income earned from product sales, consultants earned bonuses or commissions on the sales made by all of the recruits they brought in. MKC paid consultants with one to four recruits a bonus commission equal to 4 percent of the recruits' wholesale orders. A consultant with five or more recruits earned an 8 percent commission on the orders placed by recruits, or 12 percent if she also placed $600 a month in wholesale orders herself. MKC consultants who were entitled to a 12 percent commission and who had as many as 24 recruits were averaging about $950 monthly in bonuses and recruitment commissions as of 1984.

MKC'S SALES ORGANIZATION

The basic field organization unit for MKC's 195,000-person force of beauty consultants was the sales unit. Each sales unit was headed by a sales director who provided leadership and training for her group of beauty consultants. The top-performing sales directors were designated as national sales directors, a title that signified the ultimate achievement in the Mary Kay career sales ladder. A corporate staff of seven national sales administrators oversaw the activities of the sales directors in the field and their units of beauty consultants.

The sales units were not organized along strict geographical lines, and sales directors were free to recruit consultants anywhere:

> One of the first things I wanted my dream company to eliminate was assigned territories. I had worked for several direct-sales organizations in the past, and I knew how unfairly I had been treated when I had to move from Houston to St. Louis because of my husband's new job. I had been making $1,000 a month in commissions from the Houston sales unit that I had built over a period of eight years and I lost it all when I moved. I felt that it wasn't fair for someone else to inherit those Houston salespeople whom I had worked so hard to recruit and train.
>
> Because we don't have territories at Mary Kay Cosmetics, a director who lives in Chicago can be vacationing in Florida or visiting a friend in Pittsburgh and recruit someone while there. It doesn't matter where she lives in the United States; she will always draw a commission from the company on the wholesale purchases made by that recruit as long as they both remain with the company. The director in Pittsburgh will take the visiting director's new recruit under her wing and train her; the recruit will attend the Pittsburgh sales meetings and participate in the local sales contests. Although the Pittsburgh director will devote a lot of time and effort to the new recruit, the Chicago director will be paid the commissions. We call this our "adoptee" program.
>
> The Pittsburgh recruit may go on to recruit new people on her own. No matter where she lives, she becomes the nucleus for bringing in additional people for the director who brought her into the business. As long as they're both active in the company, she will receive commissions from the company on her recruit's sales activity.
>
> Today we have more than 5,000 sales directors, and most of them train and motivate people in their units who live outside their home states. Some have beauty consultants in a dozen or more states. Outsiders look at our company and say, "Your adoptee progam can't possibly work!" But it does work. Each director reaps the benefits from her recruits in other cities and helps other recruits in return.[7]

THE BEAUTY CONSULTANT

Nearly all of MKC's beauty consultants had their first contact with the company as a guest at a beauty show. A discussion of career opportunities with Mary Kay was a standard part of the presentation at

---

[7]Ash, *People Management,* pp. 2–3.

each beauty show. As many as 10 percent of the attendees at beauty shows were serious prospects as new recruits.

All beauty consultants were self-employed and worked on a commission basis. Everyone in the entire MKC sales organization started at the consultant level. The progression of each consultant up the "ladder of success" within the MKC sales organization was tightly linked to (1) the amount of wholesale orders the consultant placed with MKC, (2) her abilities to bring in new sales recruits, and (3) the size of the wholesale orders placed by these recruits. There were five rungs on the ladder of success for consultants, with qualifications and rewards as follows:

1. *New beauty consultant* (member of "Perfect Start Club").
   Qualifications:
   - Study and complete Perfect Start workbook.
   - Observe three beauty shows.
   - Book a minimum of eight shows within two weeks of receiving beauty showcase.
   Awards and recognition:
   - Receives "Perfect Start" pin.
   - Earns 50 percent commission on retail sales (less any discounts given to customers on "special promotions").
   - Becomes eligible for a 4 percent recruiting commission on wholesale orders placed by active personal recruits (to be considered "active," a consultant had to place at least a $600 minimum wholesale order during the current quarter).
   - Is eligible for special prizes and bonuses given for current quarter's sales and recruiting contest.

2. *Star consultant.*
   Qualifications
   - Must have three active recruits.
   - Be an active beauty consultant (place a minimum wholesale order of $600 within the current calendar quarter).
   Awards and recognition:
   - Earns a red blazer.
   - Earns a star pin.
   - Earns "Ladder of Success" status by placing $1,800 in wholesale orders in a three-month period.
   - Earns 50 percent commission on personal sales at beauty shows.
   - Earns 4 percent personal recruiting commission on wholesale orders placed by active personal recruits.
   - Is eligible for special prizes and awards offered during quarterly contest.
   - Receives a Star of Excellence ladder pin by qualifying as a star consultant for 8 quarters (or a Double Star of Excellence pin for 16 quarters).

3. *Team leader.*

Qualifications:
- Must have five or more active recruits.
- Be an active beauty consultant.

Awards and recognitions:
- Earns 50 percent commission on sales at own beauty shows.
- Earns a "Tender Loving Care" emblem for red blazer.
- Earns an 8 percent personal recruiting commission on wholesale orders of active personal recruits.
- Earns a 12 percent personal recruiting commission if *(a)* five or more active personal recruits place minimum $600 wholesale orders during the current month and *(b)* the team leader herself places a $600 wholesale order during the current month.
- Receives Team Leader pin in ladder of success program.
- Is eligible for quarterly contest prizes and bonuses.

4. *VIP (Very Important Performer).*

Qualifications:
- Must have obtained Team Leader status.
- Must place wholesale orders of at least $600 for three consecutive months.
- Team must place wholesale orders of at least $3,000 each month for three consecutive months.

Awards and recognition:
- Earns the use of an Oldsmobile Firenza.
- Earns 50 percent commission on sales at own beauty shows.
- Earns a 12 percent personal recruiting commission.
- Receives VIP pin in ladder of success program.
- Is eligible for quarterly contest prizes and bonuses.

5. *Future director.*

Qualifications:
- Must have qualified for Team Leader status.
- Must have 12 active recruits at time of application.
- Must make a commitment to Mary Kay to become a sales director by actually giving her letter of intent date.

Awards and recognition:
- Earns a Future Director crest for red jacket.
- Plus all the benefits accorded Team Leaders and VIPs, as appropriate, for monthly and quarterly sales and recruiting performance.

New recruits were required to submit a signed Beauty Consultant Agreement, observe three beauty shows conducted by an experienced consultant, book a minimum of eight beauty shows, and hold at least five beauty shows within their first two weeks. Each consultant was asked to appear in attractive dress and makeup when in public and to project an image of knowledge and confidence about herself and the

MKC product line. Mary Kay felt the stress on personal appearance was justified: "What we are selling is beauty. A woman is not going to buy from someone who is wearing jeans and has her hair up in curlers. We want our consultants to be the type of woman others will want to emulate."[8]

Consultants spent most of their work hours scheduling and giving beauty shows. A showing took about two hours (plus about an hour for travel time), and many times the hostess and one or more of the guests turned out to be prospective recruits. New consultants were coached to start off by booking showings with friends, neighbors, and relatives and then network these into showings for friends of friends and relatives of relatives.

Consultants were instructed to follow up each beauty show by scheduling a second facial for each guest at the showing. Many times a customer would invite friends to her second facial and the result would be another beauty show. After the follow-up facial, consultants would call customers periodically to check on whether the customer was satisfied, to see if refills were needed, and to let the customer know about new products and special promotions. Under MKC's "dovetailing" plan, a consultant with an unexpected emergency at home could sell her prearranged beauty show to another consultant and the two would split the commissions generated by the show.

THE SALES DIRECTOR

Consultants who had climbed to the fifth rung of the consultants' ladder of success were eligible to become sales directors and head up a sales unit. In addition to conducting her own beauty shows, a sales director's responsibilities included training new recruits, leading weekly sales meetings, and providing assistance and advice to the members of her unit. Sales directors, besides receiving the commissions on sales made at their own showings, were paid a commission on the total sales of the unit they headed and a commission on the number of new salespeople they recruited. In June 1984 the top 100 recruiting commissions paid to sales directors ranged from approximately $660 to $1,900. It was not uncommon for sales directors to have a total annual earnings in the $50,000–$100,000 range; in 1983 the average income of the 4,500 sales directors was between $25,000 and $30,000.

---

[8]Rebecca Fannin, "The Beauty of Being Mary Kay," *Marketing & Media Decisions* 17 (December 1982), pp. 59–61.

There were six achievement categories for sales directors, with qualifications and awards as shown below:

1. *Director in Qualification (DIQ).*
   Qualifications:
   - Must have 15 active personal recruits.
   - Submits a letter of intent to obtain directorship.
   - Gets the director of her sales unit to submit a letter of recommendation.
   - Within three consecutive months:
     a. Must recruit an additional 15 consultants for a total of 30 personal active recruits.
     b. The unit of 30 personal active recruits must place combined wholesale orders of $4,000, $4,500, and $5,000 for months one, two, and three respectively.
   Awards and recognition:
   - Earns personal sales and personal recruiting commissions (as per schedules for at least Team Leader status).
   - Eligible for prizes and bonuses in quarterly contests.
2. *Sales director.*
   Qualifications:
   - Sales unit must maintain a minimum of $4,000 in wholesale orders each month for the sales director to remain as head of her unit.
   Awards and recognition:
   - Receives commissions of 9 percent to 13 percent on unit's wholesale orders.
   - Receives monthly sales production bonuses:
     a. $300 monthly bonus if unit places monthly wholesale orders of $3,000–$4,999.
     b. $500 monthly bonus if unit places monthly wholesale orders of $5,000 and up.
   - Receives a monthly recruiting bonus (for personal recruits or for recruits of other consultants in the sales unit):
     a. $100 bonus if 3–4 new recruits come into unit.
     b. $200 bonus if 5–7 new recruits come into unit.
     c. $300 bonus if 8–11 new recruits come into unit.
     d. $400 bonus for 12 or more recruits..
   - Is given a designer director suit.
   - Is entitled to all commission schedules and incentives of future sales directors.
3. *Regal director.*
   Qualifications:
   - Members of sales unit must place wholesale orders of at least $24,000 for two consecutive quarters.

- Must qualify every two years.

Awards and recognition:

- Earns the use of a pink Buick Regal.
- Is entitled to all the commission percentages, bonuses, and other incentives of a sales director.

4. *Cadillac director.*

Qualifications:

- Sales unit members must place at least $36,000 in wholesale orders for two consecutive quarters.
- Must qualify every two years.

Awards and recognition:

- Earns the use of a pink Cadillac.
- Is entitled to all the commission percentages, bonuses, and other incentives of a sales director.

5. *Senior sales director.*

Qualifications:

- From 1 to 4 sales directors emerge from her unit.

Awards and recognition:

- Earns a 4 percent commission on offspring director's consultants.
- Is entitled to all the commission percentages, bonuses, and other incentives of at least a sales director.

6. *Future national director.*

Qualifications:

- Five or more active directors emerge from her unit.

Awards and recognition:

- Is entitled to all commission percentages, bonuses, and other incentives of a senior sales director.

As of late 1983 the company had about 700 Regal directors and about 700 Cadillac directors; in one recent quarter 81 sales directors had met the qualifications for driving a new pink Cadillac.

THE NATIONAL SALES DIRECTOR

Top-performing sales directors became eligible for designation as a national sales director, the highest recognition bestowed on field sales personnel. NSDs were inspirational leaders and managers of a group of sales directors and received commissions on the total dollar sales of the group of sales units they headed. In 1984 MKC's 50 national sales directors had total sales incomes averaging over $150,000 per year. A 1985 *Fortune* article features Helen McVoy, a MKC national sales director since 1971, as one of the most successful salespeople in the United States; in 1984 she earned $375,000. McVoy began her career with Mary Kay in 1965 at the age of 45. Her family was on a tight budget, having lost all of their savings in a bad mining investment. To support her plant-collecting hobby, Helen started selling Mary Kay products on a part-time basis—two hours a week. Her original investment was for a beauty case; by the end of her first year she had made $17,000. From 1970 through 1984 she was the company's top volume producer.

TRAINING

Before holding a beauty show a new consultant had to observe three beauty shows, attend orientation classes conducted by a sales director, and complete a self-study set of MKC training materials. This training covered the fundamentals of conducting skin care shows, booking future beauty shows, recruiting new Mary Kay consultants, personal appearance, and managing a small business. Active consultants were strongly encouraged to continue to improve their sales skills and product knowledge. In addition to weekly sales meetings and frequent one-on-one contact with other consultants and sales directors, each salesperson had access to a variety of company-prepared support materials—videotapes, films, slide shows, and brochures.

In 1983 a new educational curriculum was introduced to support each phase of a Mary Kay career. A back-to-basics orientation package provided a foundation for the first stage of career development. A recruitment notebook provided dialogue of mock recruiting conversations, and sales directors were provided with an organizational kit to help them make a smooth transition from being purely a consultant to being a sales manager as well as a consultant.

Additional learning opportunities were provided in the form of special product knowledge classes, regional workshops, and annual corporate-sponsored seminars.

MOTIVATION AND INCENTIVES

New sales contests were introduced every three months. Prizes and recognition awards were always tied to achievement plateaus rather than declaring first, second, and third place winners. Top performers were spotlighted in the company's full-color monthly magazine, *Applause* (which had a circulation of several hundred thousand).

Mary Kay Ash described why MKC paid so much attention to recognition and praise:

I believe praise is the best way for a manager to motivate people. At Mary Kay Cosmetics we think praise is so important that our entire marketing plan is based upon it.

Praise is an incredibly effective motivator; unfortunately, many managers are reluctant to employ it. Yet I can't help feeling that they know how much praise means, not only to others, but to themselves. . . . I believe that you should praise people whenever you can; it causes them to respond as a thirsty plant responds to water.

The power of positive motivation in a goal-oriented structure such as ours cannot be overstated. This is what inspires our consultants to maximize their true potentials.

As a manager you must recognize that everyone needs praise. But it must be given sincerely. You'll find numerous occasions for genuine praise if you'll only look for them.

Because we recognize the need for people to be praised, we make a concentrated effort to give as much recognition as possible. Of course with an organization as large as ours not everyone can make a speech at our seminars, but we do attempt to have many people appear on stage, if only for a few moments. During the Directors' March, for example, hundreds of directors parade on stage before thousands of their peers. In order to appear in the Directors' March a director must purchase a special designer suit. Likewise we have a Red Jacket March, in which only star recruiters, team leaders, and future directors participate. Again, a special uniform is required for participation.

How important are these brief stage appearances? Frankly I think it means more for a woman to be recognized by her peers on stage than to receive an expensive present in the mail that nobody knows about! And once she gets a taste of this recognition, she wants to come back next year for more![9]

SEMINAR

MKC staged an annual "Seminar" as a salute to the company and to the salespeople who contributed to its success. The first Seminar was held on September 13, 1964 (the company's first anniversary); the banquet menu consisted of chicken, jello salad, and an anniversary cake while a three-piece band provided entertainment. By 1984, Seminar had grown into a three-day spectacular repeated four consecutive times with a budget of $4 million and attended by 24,000 beauty consultants and sales directors who paid their own way to attend the event. The setting, the Convention Center in Dallas (see Exhibit 6), was decorated

---

[9]Ash, *People Management,* pp. 21, 23, 26–28.

EXHIBIT 6   "Share the Spirit," 1984 Annual Seminar, Mary Kay Cosmetics

Source: Mary Kay Cosmetics, Inc., Interim Report, 1984.

in red, white, and blue in order to emphasize the theme, "Share the Spirit." The climactic highlight of Seminar was Awards Night, when the biggest prizes were awarded to the people with the biggest sales. The company went to elaborate efforts to ensure the Awards Night was charged with excitement and emotion; as one observer of the 1984 Awards Night in Dallas described it, "The atmosphere there is electric, a cross between a Las Vegas revue and a revival meeting. Hands reach up to touch Mary Kay; a pink Cadillac revolves on a mist-shrouded pedestal; a 50-piece band plays; and women sob."

Mary Kay Ash customarily made personal appearances throughout the Seminar period. In addition to Awards Night, Seminar featured sessions consisting of informational and training workshops, motivational presentations by leading sales directors, and star entertainment (Paul Anka performed in 1984, and in previous years there had been performances by Tennessee Ernie Ford, John Davidson, and Johnny

Mathis). Over the three days, Cadillacs, diamonds, mink coats, a $5,000 shopping spree at Neiman-Marcus for any director whose team sold $1 million worth of Mary Kay products, and lesser assorted prizes were awarded to the outstanding achievers of the past year. Gold-and-diamond bumblebee pins, each containing 21 diamonds and retailing for over $3,600, were presented to the Queens of Sales on Pageant Night; these pins were not only the company's ultimate badge of success, but Mary Kay felt they also had special symbolism:

> It's a beautiful pin, but that isn't the whole story. We think the bumblebee is a marvelous symbol of woman. Because, as aerodynamic engineers found a long time ago, the bumblebee cannot fly! Its wings are too weak and its body is too heavy to fly, but fortunately, the bumblebee doesn't know that, and it goes right on flying. The bee has become a symbol of women who didn't know they could fly but they DID! I think the women who own these diamond bumblebees think of them in their own personal ways. For most of us, it's true that we refused to believe we couldn't do it. Maybe somebody said, "It's really impossible to get this thing off the ground." But somebody else told us, "You can do it!" So we did.[10]

On the final day of Seminar the Sue Z. Vickers Memorial Award—Miss Go Give—was presented. This honor was given to the individual who best demonstrated the Mary Kay spirit—a spirit described as loving, giving, and inspirational.

CORPORATE ENVIRONMENT

The company's eight-story, gold-glass corporate headquarters building in Dallas was occupied solely by Mary Kay executives. An open-door philosophy was present at MKC. Everyone from the mailroom clerk to the chairman of the board was treated with respect. The door to Mary Kay Ash's office was rarely closed. Often people touring the building peeked in her office to get a glimpse of the pink and white decor. Mary Kay and all other corporate managers took the time to talk with any employee.

First names were always used at MKC. Mary Kay herself insisted on being addressed as Mary Kay; she felt people who called her Mrs. Ash were either angry at her or didn't know her. In keeping with this informal atmosphere, offices didn't have titles on the doors, executive restrooms didn't exist, and the company cafeteria was used by the executives (there was no executive dining room).

---

[10]Ash, *Mary Kay,* p. 9.

To further enhance the informal atmosphere and enthusiasm at MKC, all sales functions were started with a group sing-along. Mary Kay offered several reasons for this policy:

> Nothing great is ever achieved without enthusiasm. . . . We have many of our own songs, and they're sung at all Mary Kay get-togethers, ranging from small weekly meetings to our annual Seminars. Our salespeople enjoy this activity, and I believe the singing creates a wonderful esprit de corps. Yet outsiders, especially men, often criticize our singing as being "strictly for women." I disagree. Singing unites people. It's like those "rah-rah-rah for our team" cheers. If someone is depressed, singing will often bring her out of it.[11]

The company sent Christmas cards, birthday cards, and anniversary cards to every single employee each year. Mary Kay personally designed the birthday cards for consultants. In addition, all the sales directors received Christmas and birthday presents from the company.

THE PEOPLE MANAGEMENT PHILOSOPHY AT MKC

Mary Kay Ash had some very definite ideas about how people ought to be managed, and she willingly shared them with employees and, through her books, with the public at large. Some excerpts from her book on *People Management* reveal the approach taken at Mary Kay Cosmetics.

> People come first at Mary Kay Cosmetics—our beauty consultants, sales directors, and employees, our customers, and our suppliers. We pride ourselves as a "company known for the people it keeps." Our belief in caring for people, however, does not conflict with our need as a corporation to generate a profit. Yes, we keep our eye on the bottom line, but it's not an overriding obsession. . . .
>
> Ours is an organization with few middle management positions. In order to grow and progress, you don't move upward; you expand outward. This gives our independent sales organization a deep sense of personal worth. They know that they are not competing with one another for a spot in the company's managerial "pecking order." Therefore the contributions of each individual are of equal value. No one is fearful that his or her idea will be "stolen" by someone with more ability on the corporate ladder. And when someone—anyone—proposes a new thought, we all analyze it, improve upon it, and ultimately support it with the enthusiasm of a team. . . .
>
> Every person is special! I sincerely believe this. Each of us wants to feel good about himself or herself, but to me it is just as important to make

---

[11]Ash, *People Management,* p. 59.

others feel the same way. Whenever I meet someone, I try to imagine him wearing an invisible sign that says: MAKE ME FEEL IMPORTANT! I respond to this sign immediately and it works wonders. . . .

At Mary Kay Cosmetics we believe in putting our beauty consultants and sales directors on a pedestal. Of all people I most identify with them because I spent many years as a salesperson. My attitude of appreciation for them permeates the company. When our salespeople visit the home office, for example, we go out of our way to give them the red-carpet treatment. Every person in the company treats them royally. . . .

We go first class across the board, and although it's expensive, it's worth it because our people are made to feel important. For example, each year we take our top sales directors and their spouses on deluxe trips to Hong Kong, Bangkok, London, Paris, Geneva, and Athens, to mention a few. We spare no expense, and although it costs a lot extra per person to fly the Concorde, cruise on the Love Boat, or book suites at the elegant George V in Paris, it is our way of telling them how important they are to our company. . . .

My experience with people is that they generally do what you expect them to do! If you expect them to perform well, they will; conversely, if you expect them to perform poorly, they'll probably oblige. I believe that average employees who try their hardest to live up to your high expectations of them will do better than above-average people with low self-esteem. Motivate your people to draw on that untapped 90 percent of their ability and their level of performance will soar! . . .

A good people manager will never put someone down; not only is it nonproductive—it's counterproductive. You must remember that your job is to play the role of problem solver and that by taking this approach instead of criticizing people you'll accomplish considerably more.

While some managers try to forget problems they encountered early in their careers, I make a conscious effort to remember the difficulties I've had along the way. I think it's vital for a manager to empathize with the other person's problem, and the best way to have a clear understanding is to have been there yourself.[12]

Interviews with Mary Kay consultants gave credibility to the company's approach and methods. One consultant described her experience thusly:

I had a lot of ragged edges when I started. The first time I went to a Mary Kay seminar, I signed up for classes in diction and deportment, believe me, I needed them. I didn't even have the right clothes. You can only wear dresses and skirts to beauty shows, so I sank everything I had into one nice dress. I washed it out every night in Woolite and let it drip dry in the shower.

But I was determined to follow all the rules, even the ones I didn't understand—*especially* the ones I didn't understand. At times, it all seemed foolish, especially when you consider that all my clients were mill workers

---

[12]Ibid, pp. xix, 6, 11–12, 15, 17, 19, 20.

and didn't exactly appreciate my new grammar. But I kept telling myself to hang in there, that Mary Kay knew what was good for me.

When I first started, I won a pearl and ruby ring. A man or a man's company may say I'd have been better off with the cash, but I'm not so convinced. Mary Kay is on to something there. From the moment I won that ring, I began thinking of myself as a person who deserved a better standard of living. I built a new life to go with the ring.[13]

Another consultant observed:

The essential thing about Mary Kay is the quality of the company. When you go to Dallas, the food, the hotel, and the entertainment are all top notch. Nothing gaudy is allowed in Mary Kay.[14]

When asked if she didn't think pink Cadillacs were a tad gaudy, she responded in a low, level tone: "When people say that, I just ask them what color car their company gave them last year."

On the morning following Awards Night 1984, a group of Florida consultants were in the hotel lobby getting ready to go to the airport for the flight home.[15] One member had by chance met Mary Kay Ash in the ladies room a bit earlier and had managed to get a maid to snap a Polaroid photograph of them together. She proudly was showing her friends the snapshot and was the only one of the group who had actually met Mary Kay. The consultant said to her friends, "She told me she was sure I'd be up there on stage with her next year. She said she'd see me there." Her sales director, in noting the scene, observed, "She's got the vision now. She really did meet her. And you've got to understand that in Mary Kaydom that's a very big deal."

THE BEAUTY SHOW

It was a few minutes past 7 P.M. on a weeknight in Tuscaloosa, Alabama. Debbie Sessoms and three of her friends (including the casewriter) were seated around the dining room table in Debbie's house. In front of each lady was a pink tray, a mirror, a pencil, and a blank personal Beauty Profile form. Jan Currier stood at the head of the table. She welcomed each of the ladies and asked them to fill out the personal Beauty Profile form in front of them.

When they were finished, Jan started her formal presentation, leading off with how MKC's products were developed by a tanner. She used a large display board to illustrate the topics she discussed. Next Jan told the group about the company and the founder, Mary Kay Ash.

---

[13]As quoted in Kim Wright Wiley, "Cold Cream and Hard Cash," *Savvy,* June 1985, p. 39.

[14]Ibid., p. 41.

[15]Ibid.

She showed a picture of Mary Kay and explained she was believed to be in her 70s—though no one knew for sure because Mary Kay maintained that "a woman who will tell her age will tell anything." Jerri, one of the guests, remarked that she couldn't believe how good Mary Kay looked for her age. Jan told her that Mary Kay had been using her basic skin care formulas since the 1950s.

Jan went on to talk about the growth of the sales force from nine consultants to over 195,000 in 1984. She explained how the career oppportunities at MKC could be adapted to each consultant's ambitions. A consultant, she said, determined her own work hours and could choose either a full-time or part-time career. Advancement was based on sales and recruiting abilities. The possible rewards included diamonds, minks, and pink Cadillacs.

Before explaining the basic skin care program, Jan told the ladies that with the Mary Kay money-back guarantee, products could be returned for any reason for a full refund. Jan distributed samples to each of the guests based on the information provided in the personal Beauty Profiles. Under Jan's guidance the ladies proceeded through the complete facial process, learning each of the five basic skin care steps advocated by Mary Kay. There was a lot of discussion about the products and how they felt on everyone's skin.

When the presentation reached the glamour segment, each guest was asked her preference of makeup colors. Jan encouraged everyone to try as many of the products and colors as they wanted. Jan helped the guests experiment with different combinations and worked with each one personally, trying to make sure that everyone would end up satisfied with her own finished appearance.

After admiring each other's new looks, three of the ladies placed orders. Jan collected their payments and filled the orders on the spot. No one had to wait for delivery.

When she finished with the orders, Jan talked with Debbie's three guests about hostessing their own shows and receiving hostess gifts. Chris agreed to book a show the next week. Debbie was then given her choice of gifts based on the evening's sales and bookings. To close the show, Jan again highlighted the benefits of a Mary Kay career—being your own boss, setting your own hours—and invited anyone interested to talk with her about these opportunities. Debbie then served some refreshments. Shortly after 9 P.M., Jan and Debbie's three guests departed.

Walking to Jan's car, the casewriter asked Jan if the evening was a success. Jan replied that it had been "a pretty good night. Sales totaled $150, I got a booking for next Wednesday. I made $75 in commissions in a little over two hours, the guests learned about skin care and have some products they are going to like, and Debbie got a nice hostess gift."

THE WEEKLY SALES MEETING

Jan Currier, senior sales director, welcomed the consultants to the weekly Monday night meeting of the members of her sales unit.[16] After calling everyone's attention to the mimeographed handout on everybody's chair (Exhibit 7), she introduced the casewriter to the group and then invited everyone to stand and join in singing the Mary Kay enthusiasm song. As soon as the song was over Jan started "the Crow

---

EXHIBIT 7   Excerpt from Sales Director's Mimeographed Weekly Newsletter Distributed to Members of Sales Unit

---

You Are Special

Once upon a time a very competent woman went into a beautiful designer furniture store and said to the owner, "Sir, I would like to work for you. I will work hard. I will do a *Great* job for you, but I ask for the following:

1. For everything I sell I want to make a 50 percent profit.
2. I know others that I will get to sell for you too, and I want to be paid a commission on all they do, say 4 percent to 12 percent.
3. I want to work my own hours. No Sundays—just a few nights . . . . God and my family will *always* come first.
4. I will also need a car after I bring in five successful people to work for you, at no cost to me—not even insurance.
5. When I do really well, I want to receive bonuses, not little meaningless things, but things like *mink coats* and *diamonds!*

"Can you give these things to me?"

The store owner was in shock with her requests. He roared with condescending laughter. Then came his reply, "No, not one! No one could."

Only your own beautiful *Mary Kay!* You have it all right at your fingertips! Go after it! You and your family deserve it! This is your year, 1984!

Consider this story and think seriously about what you have in this wonderful opportunity!!!

You are indeed *special!* You are appreciated and loved. I'm so very proud of you. Share what you have. . . .

Jan

---

[16]Most sales directors had their sales meetings on Monday night, a practice urged upon them by Mary Kay Ash. Mary Kay saw the Monday night meeting as a good way to start the week: "If you had a bad week—you need the sales meeting. If you had a good week, the sales meeting needs you! When a consultant leaves a Monday meeting excited, she has an entire week to let excitement work for her." Ash, *Mary Kay,* p. 40.

Period" by asking Barbara, team leader, to stand and tell about her achievement of VIP (Very Important Performer) status. Barbara told of setting and achieving the goals necessary to win the use of an Oldsmobile Firenza. Her new goal was to assist and motivate everyone on her team to do the same. Jan recognized Barbara again for being both the Queen of Sales and the Queen of Recruiting for the previous month.

Jan began the educational segment by instructing the consultants on color analysis and how it related to glamour. She continued the instruction by explaining the proper techniques of a man's facial.

Next everyone who had at least a $100-week in sales was asked to stand. Jan began the countdown "110, 120, 130 . . . 190." Barbara sat down to a round of applause for her $190 week in sales. "200, 220 . . . 270." Melissa sat down. The ladies applauded her efforts. Mary was the only one left standing. There was anticipation of how high her sales reached as the countdown resumed. "280, 290, 300 . . . 335." Mary sat down. Everyone applauded this accomplishment of a consultant who had only been with MKC for four months and who held a 40-hour-week full-time job in addition to her Mary Kay sales efforts.

At this time Jan asked Linda and Susan to join her up front. She pinned each lady and congratulated them on joining her team. The Mary Kay pin was placed upside down on the new consultant's lapels. Jan explained this was so people would notice and ask about it. When they did, a consultant was to respond by saying; "My pin is upside down to remind me to ask if you've had a Mary Kay facial." The pin would be turned right side up when the consultant got her first recruit. Each of the new consultants also received a pink ribbon. This marked their membership in the Jan's Beautiful People sales unit. Both Linda and Susan were given some material Jan had prepared (Exhibits 8, 9, and 10); Jan said she would go over it with them after the meeting.

Next a new competition was announced. This contest focused on recruiting. For each new recruit a consultant would receive one stem of Romanian crystal. So everyone could see how beautiful the rewards were, Jan showed a sample of the crystal.

A final reminder was made for attendance at the upcoming workshop on motivation. Jan sweetened the pot by providing a prize to the first one in her unit to register and pay for the seminar. Next week she would announce the winner.

The meeting was adjourned until next Monday evening.

AN INTERVIEW WITH JAN CURRIER

One night shortly after attending the meeting of Jan's Beautiful People sales unit, the casewriter met with Jan to ask some questions:

EXHIBIT 8   Example of a Sales Director's Mimeographed Handout
to New Mary Kay Recruits

GETTING STARTED

Jan Currier,
Senior Sales Director

HELLO . . . AND WELCOME TO . . .
THE BEAUTIFUL PEOPLE UNIT!!

1. You will need:
   A. Cotton balls.
   B. Swabs.
   C. Large and small zip-lock bags.
   D. Five subject spiral notebooks for note-taking.
2. This is the time to decide which merchandise order you will need. Just fill in your name and address on one of the sample orders. It's ready to go. Or change one to suit you, using the blank order. Beginning with at least $1,500 section one only. . . . makes you a ladder or success winner.
3. Be a professional consultant by ordering the "consultant's kit" (1,000 gold labels, rubber stamp, name badge, 500 facial cards—style B—"Rip-off type"—for $21.95). Send check or money order to Labeling Inc., P.O. Box 476, Lakewood, CA 90714.
4. "Buff brushes" may be ordered from Silverset Brush Co., P.O. Box 53, Greenvale, New York 11548 . . . 20 cents each ($2.00 shipping charge) style 2900 *pink* handle . . . minimum order $25. Suggest sharing an order with other Beauty Consultants where possible.
5. Write your mileage in your datebook today . . . for income tax purposes.
6. Memorize:
   A. Hide tanners story (it *is* a true story).
   B. Correct booking approach.
   C. Four-point recruiting plan.
7. Read and read again your beauty consultant's guide. *Everything* you really need to know is in the book!! Listen to your training tape over and over again. If yours hasn't arrived yet, ask to borrow your recruiter's.
8. Obtain list of beauty consultants and their telephone numbers in your area from your recruiter or local director. Call and ask to observe shows. *If you are out of town* . . . call the local director, ask to attend her training classes and meetings, be helpful, and let her know that you support her. Always keep a positive attitude . . . especially at the sales meetings.
9. Begin booking your shows for two weeks from now. You will want to get off to a *"Perfect Start"* by *holding* at least five shows during your beginning two weeks. Realizing that some of these may *postpone* (never "cancel"), you will want to book *twice as many*. These are only practice shows. (You will have products with you should they decide to buy, of course!)

Submit names, dates, times, and telephone numbers to your recruiter. She will call or write them, thanking them for helping you get started.

EXHIBIT 8   Example of a Sales Director's Mimeographed Handout
to New Mary Kay Recruits *(concluded)*

Again, these are just "practice" shows. Simply ask your friends to "help
you" get started by letting you "practice" on them. (Part of your training is to get their *honest opinions*.)

Re-book each and every basic customer for a *second* facial. . . . preferably
within a week to 10 days. Then . . . "Oh, by the way, you are *entitled* to
invite a few friends over to *share* your second facial, it's so much more fun
and *you* win some *free!* In other words, you receive a *discount* on what-
ever *they* buy. In other words, THE MORE THEY BUY . . . THE *MORE
YOU* RECEIVE *FREE!!* BUT WE CAN'T DO MORE THAN SIX. . . . IT'S
NOT A PARTY. . . . IT'S A CLASS, SO WE ARE LIMITED. YOU CAN
DECIDE WHAT YOU PREFER TO DO. . . . I'LL JUST GIVE YOU THIS
SUGGESTIONS FOR THE HOSTESS (comes with your Beauty Case)
AND I WILL BE CALLING YOU IN A DAY OR SO." Give her: *Beauty
Book, Suggestions for the Hostess,* and *Saturday Evening Post* reprint if
she looks like she would be a good recruit. *BE SURE YOUR NAME IS
ON EVERYTHING!!* Send a reminder card within two days.

Vow never to miss a sales meeting. This is your continuous training . . . and
it is for you. And . . . always try to bring prospective recruits as your
guests. And a very, very positive attitude.

AND . . . YOU ARE OFF TO A BEAUTIFUL START!!!!

Casewriter:

How many are in your unit?

Jan:

We're down right now. I had a small unit to start with. I only had 56. . . . A
decent unit has got a hundred, 75 to 100 at least.

Casewriter:

Is it the size of the town that hampers you?

Jan:

No, no, it's me who hampers me. The speed of the leader is the speed of
the unit. If I'm not out there doing it, then they're not going to be doing
it. If I'm recruiting, they're recruiting.

Casewriter:

What about your leader, is your leader not fast?

Jan:

No, it's me; see when you point a finger, three come back.

Casewriter:

How do you handle a situation where a consultant would like to do well
but she doesn't put in the time necessary to do well?

EXHIBIT 9   Example of Material Provided to New Beauty
Consultants at Weekly Sales Meeting

Goal Setting is the most powerful force for human motivation.
   Goal + Plans + Action = Success!!!
My Goal is: _____

Circle Number of Classes You Will Put On Each Week	Class Time Plus Travel Time	Sales Based on each $150 Class (minutes)	Approximate Gross Profit per Week (before expenses)
1	3 hours	$ 150	$ 75
2	6	300	150
3	9	450	225
4	12	600	300
5	15	750	375
6	18	900	450
7	21	1,059	525
8	24	1,200	600
9	27	1,350	675
10	30	1,500	750
11	33	1,650	825
12	36	1,800	900
13	39	1,950	975
14	42	2,100	1,050
15	45	2,250	1,125
16	48	2,400	1,200
17	51	2,550	1,275
18	54	2,700	1,350
19	57	2,850	1,425
20	60	3,000	1,500

Note: Hostess credit and hostess gift will be deducted from your gross profit.
However, everything you give away is tax deductible.
   Your *Attitude* and Your *Consistency* Will Determine . . .
          Your Goals . . . *Your* Success!

                                              Jan Currier
                                              Senior Sales Director

---

Jan:

   You have to go back to that premise, that whole philosophy that you're in
   business for yourself but not by yourself. So if a girl comes in and says I
   want to make X number of dollars, then I will work with her and we will
   do it. I try to get them to set goals and really look at them every week
   and work for it. One gal comes in and wants to make $25 a week and
   another says, "I have to support my family." There's a big difference.

EXHIBIT 10   Example of Material Provided to new Beauty
Consultants at Weekly Sales Meeting

The Mary Kay Opportunity

	Yearly Total
3 Shows per week with $150.00 sales per show	
Less 15 percent hostess credit = $191.25 profit (per week)	
Three persons buying per show, three shows per week	$ 9,945
468 prospective customers per year	
Average selling to 7 out of 10	
327 new customers per year	
Call customers at least six times per week	
Average $15.00 in sales per call	
Yearly reorder profits will be	14,715
1 Facial per week—52 prospective customers per year	
Average selling to 7 of 10, 36 new customers	
If each buys a basic, your facial profits will be	702
36 New customers from facials	
Call each customer six times per year	
Average $15.00 in sales per call	
Your yearly *reorder* profit will be	1,620
Recruit one person per month	
Each with at least a $1,500 initial order (wholesale)	
Ordering only $500.00 every month thereafter	
Your 4 percent—8 percent commission checks from these 12 recruits	3,490
Your yearly profits will be approximately	$30,472

This is a simple guideline designed to show you, in figures, approximately how much you can benefit from your Mary Kay career. These figures may vary a little, due to price changes. These totals are based on orders placed at our maximum discount level and do not include referrals, dovetail fees, and prizes.

Working hours per week for the above should not exceed 20 hours, if your work is well planned. Attitude and consistency are the keys to your success.

Jan Currier
Senior Sales Director

Casewriter:

How do you handle those that only want to make $25 a week?

Jan:

If you get rid of the piddlers you wouldn't have a company. It's the piddlers that make up the company. There are only going to be one or two superstars.

Casewriter:

How do you motivate the girls in your unit?

Jan:

The only way you can really motivate is to call, encourage, write notes, and encourage recognition at the sales meetings and recognition in the newsletter. If they're not doing anything they usually won't come to the sales meeting, but once in a while maybe, they'll find excuses.

Casewriter:

What do you do when a girl hits that stage?

Jan:

Everybody has to go through that phase . . . If you're smart, you'll go to your director, read your book and go back to start where you were before— with what was working to begin with and you'll pull out of it. There are a lot of them who never pull out of it. They came in to have fun.

Casewriter:

And the fun wears out.

Jan:

Let's face it. This is a job. It's work, it's the best-paying hard work around, but it's work. I just finished with one gal last week who ended up saying, "Well, I just thought it would be fun. I thought it was just supposed to be fun." And I said, "Yes, but it's a job."

Casewriter:

Can you tell before a girl starts if she'll be successful?

Jan:

There's no way to predict who's going to make it, the one you think is going to be absolutely a superstar isn't. You give everybody a chance. I measure my time with their interest and I tell them that. I'll encourage them, but they are going to pretty much do what they want to do. I learned that the hard way. There is no point to laying guilt trips, no point pestering them to death, and pressure doesn't work.

Casewriter:

Do you feel recognition is the best motivator?

Jan:

Absolutely, recognition and appreciation. I think appreciation more than anything else. Little notes, I'm finally learning that too. Some of us are slow learners. . . . So I'll write little notes telling someone, I really appreciate your doing this, or I'm really proud of you for being a star consultant this quarter, or I'm so glad you went with us to Birmingham to the workshop.

Casewriter:

Does it upset you when people don't come to the sales meetings?

Jan:

I use to grieve when they wouldn't come to sales meetings. I'd ask what am I doing wrong. . . . Finally I realized that no matter how many people aren't there, the people who are there care and they are worth doing anything for. It's strange we seem to get a different batch every meeting.

Casewriter:

I get the impression that you are always looking for new recruits.

Jan:

Yes, I've gotten more picky. I'm looking more for directors. I'm looking for people who really want to work. I look for someone who is older, not just the 18-year-olds because they don't want to work. They want to make money but they don't want to work. . . . I'd like to build more offspring directors.

Casewriter:

What kind of people do you look for?

Jan:

Not everybody's right for Mary Kay. It takes somebody who genuinely cares about other people.

Casewriter:

Is there a common scenario that fits most new recruits?

Jan:

Mary Kay attracts a lot of insecure women who are often married to insecure men. And that woman is told over and over by Mary Kay how wonderful she is and how terrific she is and how she can do anything with God's help. She can achieve anything. And like me she is dumb enough to believe it and go along with it.

Casewriter:

What do you feel is the reason for the slowdown in recruiting at Mary Kay?

Jan:

The key to this drop has been partly the economy but partly a lot of people are weeding out. That's OK because the cream is going to rise to the top. I really believe that. We're going to have a stronger, much better company. I could see it at leadership (conference). The quality of people was much higher. It gets higher every year.

MKC'S FUTURE

MKC's sales in 1984 fell 14 percent to $278 million (down from $324 million in fiscal year 1983). The company's stock price, after a two-for-one split at about $44, tumbled from $22 in late 1983 to the $9–$12 range in 1984. Profits were down 8 percent to $33.8 million. The declines were blamed on a dropoff in recruiting and retention (owing to reduced attractiveness of part-time employment) and to the expense of starting up the European division. As of December 31, 1984, the company had about 152,000 beauty consultants and 4,500 sales directors as compared to 195,000 beauty consultants and 5,000 sales directors at year end 1983. Average sales per consultant in 1984 were $1,603, versus $1,655 in 1983 and a 1980–82 average of $1,753; only 60,000 of the 152,000 consultants were thought to be significantly productive. A cosmetics analyst for one Wall Street securities firm, in talking about the company's propsects, said, "Brokers loved this stock because it had such a great story. But the glory days, for the time being, are certainly over.[17]

The company's mystique was upbeat, however. Mary Kay Ash was on the UPI list of the most interviewed women in America. And when the Republicans chose Dallas for its 1984 convention, the Chamber of Commerce had to persuade Mary Kay to change the date of the 1984 Seminar, which was slated for the same week in the same convention center. Positive anecdotes about Mary Kay Ash and how MKC was operated were cited in numerous books and articles.

Mary Kay Ash indicated that the company had no plans for changing the main thrust of company's sales and recruiting strategies:

> This is an excellent primary career for women, not just a way to get pin money. We see no need to alter one basic approach. It's taken us this far.[18]
>
> We have only 4 percent of the total retail cosmetics market. The way I see it 96 percent of the people in the United States are using the wrong product. There's no reason why we can't become the number one cosmetics company in the United States.[19]

---

[17]As quoted in Wiley, "Cold Cream and Hard Cash," p. 40.

[18]Ibid.

[19]As quoted in *Business Week,* March 28, 1983, p. 130.

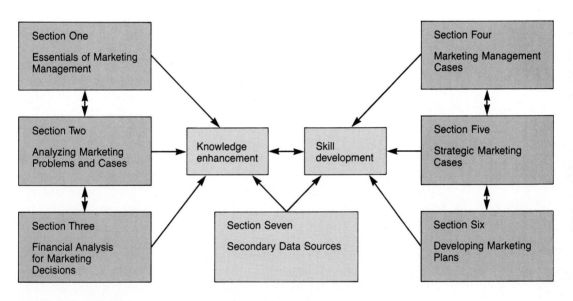

DEVELOPING
MARKETING PLANS

Section One Essentials of Marketing Management	**Section Four** Marketing Management Cases
Section Two Analyzing Marketing Problems and Cases	Knowledge enhancement / Skill development	**Section Five** Strategic Marketing Cases
Section Three Financial Analysis for Marketing Decisions	**Section Seven** Secondary Data Sources	**Section Six** Developing Marketing Plans

Marketing Management: Knowledge and Skills

NOTE TO THE STUDENT

This section contains an approach to developing marketing plans. It is intended to help you develop practical skills by providing a general format for structuring actual marketing plans. It also offers sources from which important marketing information can be found and explains what types of information to include in various parts of the plan.

Imagine this scenario: After receiving your bachelor's or master's degree in marketing, you are hired by a major consumer goods company. Because you've done well in school, you are confident that you have a lot of marketing knowledge and a lot to offer to the firm. You're highly motivated and are looking forward to a successful career.

After just a few days of work you are called in for a conference with the vice president of marketing. The vice president welcomes you and tells you how glad the firm is that you have joined them. The vice president also says that, since you have done so well in your marketing courses and have had such recent training, he wants you to work on a special project.

He tells you that the company has a new product, which is to be introduced in a few months. He also says, confidentially, the recent new product introductions by the company haven't been too successful. Suggesting that the recent problems are probably because the company has not been doing a very good job of developing marketing plans, the vice president tells you not to look for marketing plans for the company's other products.

Your assignment, then, is to develop a marketing plan for the proposed product in the next six weeks. The vice president explains that a good job here will lead to rapid advancement in the company. You thank the vice president for the assignment and promise that you'll do your best.

How would you feel when you returned to your desk? Surely, you'd be flattered that you had been given this opportunity and be eager to do a good job. However, how confident are you that you could develop a quality marketing plan? Would you even know where to begin?

We suspect that many of you, even those who have an excellent knowledge of marketing principles and are adept at solving marketing cases, may not yet have the skills necessary to develop a marketing plan from scratch. Thus, the purpose of this section is to offer a framework for developing marketing plans. In one sense, this section is no more than a summary of the whole text. In other words, it is an organizational framework based on the text material that can be used to direct the development of marketing plans.

Students should note that we are not presenting this framework and discussion as the only way to develop a marketing plan. While we believe this is a useful framework for logically analyzing the problems involved in developing a marketing plan, other approaches can be used just as successfully.

Often, successful firms prepare much less detailed plans, since much of the background material and current conditions are well known to everyone involved. However, our review of plans used in various firms suggests that something like this framework is not uncommon.

We would like to mention one other qualification before beginning our discussion. Students should remember that one important part of the marketing plan involves the development of a sales forecast. While we have discussed several approaches to sales forecasting in the text, we will detail only one specific approach here.

A MARKETING PLAN FRAMEWORK

Marketing plans have three basic purposes., First, they are used as a tangible record of analysis to investigate the logic involved. This is done to ensure the feasibility and internal consistency of the project and to evaluate the likely consequences of implementing the plan. Second, they are used as roadmaps or guidelines for directing appropriate actions. A marketing plan is designed to be the best available scenario and rationale for directing the firm's efforts for a particular product or brand. Third, they are used as tools to obtain funding for implementation. This funding may come from internal or external sources. For example, a brand manager may have to present a marketing plan to senior executives in a firm to get a budget request filled. This would be an internal source. Similarly, proposals for funding from investors or business loans from banks often require a marketing plan. These would be external sources.

Table 1 presents a format for preparing marketing plans. Each of the 10 elements will be briefly discussed. We will refer to previous chapters and sections in this text and to other sources where additional information can be obtained when a marketing plan is being prepared. We also will offer additional information for focusing particular sections of the plan as well as for developing financial analysis.

TABLE 1   A Marketing Plan Format

- Title page
- Executive summary
- Table of contents
- Introduction
- Situational analysis
- Marketing planning
- Implementation and control of the marketing plan
- Summary
- Appendix: Financial analysis
- References

Title Page

The *title page* should contain the following information: (1) the name of the product or brand for which the marketing plan has been prepared—for example, Marketing Plan for Little Friskies Dog Food; (2) the time period for which the plan is designed—for example, 1990–91; (3) the person(s) and position(s) of those submitting the plan—for example, submitted by Amy Lewis, brand manager; (4) the persons, group, or agency to whom the plan is being submitted—for example, submitted to Lauren Ellis, product group manager, and (5) the date of submission of the plan—for example, June 30, 1990.

While preparing the *title page* is a simple task, remember that it is the first thing readers see. Thus, a title page that is poorly laid out, is smudged, or contains misspelled words can lead to the inference that the project was developed hurriedly and with little attention to detail. As with the rest of the project, appearances are important and affect what people think about the plan.

Executive Summary

The *executive summary* is a two- to three-page summary of the contents of the report. Its purpose is to provide a quick summary of the marketing plan for executives who need to be informed about the plan but are typically not directly involved in plan approval. For instance, senior executives for firms with a broad product line may not have time to read the entire plan but need an overview to keep informed about operations.

The executive summary should include a brief introduction, the major aspects of the marketing plan, and a budget statement. This is not the place to go into detail about each and every aspect of the marketing plan. Rather, it should focus on the major market opportunity and the key elements of the marketing plan that are designed to capitalize on this opportunity.

It is also useful to state specifically how much money is required to implement the plan. In an ongoing firm, many costs can be estimated from historical data or from discussions with other executives in charge of specific functional areas. However, in many situations (such as a class project), sufficient information is not always available to give exact costs for every aspect of production, promotion, and distribution. In these cases, include a rough estimate of total marketing costs of the plan. In many ongoing firms, marketing cost elements are concentrated in the areas of promotion and marketing research, and these figures are integrated with those from other functional areas as parts of the overall business plan.

Table of Contents

The table of contents is a listing of everything contained in the plan and where it is located in the report. Reports that contain a variety of charts and figures may also have a table of exhibits listing their titles and page numbers within the report.

In addition to using the table of contents as a place to find specific information, readers may also review it to see if each section of the report is logically sequenced. For example, situational analysis logically precedes marketing planning as an activity, and this ordering makes sense in presenting the plan.

Introduction

The types of information and amount of detail reported in the *introduction* depend in part on whether the plan is being designed for a new or existing product or brand. If the product is new, the introduction should explain the product concept and the reasons why it is expected to be successful. Basically, this part of your report should make the new idea sound attractive to management or investors. In addition, it is useful to offer estimates of expected sales, costs, and return on investment.

If the marketing plan is for an existing brand in an outgoing firm, it is common to begin the report with a brief history of the brand. The major focus here is on the brand's performance in the last three to five years. It is useful to prepare graphs of the brand's performance that shows its sales, profits, and market share for previous years and to explain the reasons for any major changes. These exhibits can also be extended to include predicted changes in these variables given the new marketing plan. A brief discussion of the overall strategy followed in previous years also provides understanding of how much change is being proposed in the new marketing plan.

Also useful is to offer a precise statement of the purpose of the report as well as a "roadmap" of the report in the introduction. In other words, tell readers what this report is, how it is organized, and what will be covered in the following sections.

Situational Analysis

The *situational analysis* is not unlike the analysis discussed in Chapter 1 and Section 2 of this text. The focus remains on the most critical and relevant environmental conditions (or changes in them) that affect the success or failure of the proposed plan. While any aspect of the

> ## HIGHLIGHT 1
> ## Some Questions to Consider in Competitive Analysis
>
> Understanding an industry and the actions of competitors is critical to developing successful marketing plans. Below is a list of some questions to consider when performing competitive analysis. Thinking about these questions can aid the marketing planner in developing better marketing strategies.
>
> 1. Which firms compete in this industry, and what is their financial position and marketing capability?
> 2. What are the relative market shares of various brands?
> 3. How many brands and models does each firm offer?
> 4. What marketing strategies have the market leaders employed?
> 5. Which brands have gained and which have lost market share in recent years, and what factors have led to these changes?
> 6. Are new competitors likely to enter the market?
> 7. How quickly do competitive firms react to changes in the market?
> 8. From which firms or brands might we be able to take market share?
> 9. What are the particular strengths and weaknesses of competitors in the industry?
> 10. How do we compare with other firms in the industry in terms of financial strength and marketing skills?

economic, social, political, legal, or cooperative environments might deserve considerable attention, there is seldom if ever a marketing plan in which the competitive environment does not require considerable discussion. In fact, the competitive environment may be set off as a separate section called *industry analysis*. The strengths and weaknesses of major competitors, their relative market shares, and the success of various competitive strategies are critical elements of the situation analysis.

Section 5 of the text offers some sources of information for analyzing the competitive environment, such as the *Audits and Surveys National Total-Market Index* and the *Nielson Retail Index*. In addition, trade association publications, *Fortune, Business Week*, and *The Wall Street Journal*, frequently have useful articles on competitive strategies. Firms' annual reports often provide considerable useful information.

Marketing Planning

Marketing planning is, of course, a critical section of the report. As previously noted, it includes three major elements: marketing objectives, target market(s), and the marketing mix.

Marketing Objectives. Marketing objectives are often stated in plans in terms of the percentage of particular outcomes to be achieved; for example, 80 percent awareness of the brand in particular markets, increase in trial rate by 30 percent, distribution coverage of 60 percent, increase in total market share by 3 percent over the life of the plan. Similarly, there may also be objective statements in terms of sales units or dollars or increases in these. Of course, the reasons for selecting the particular objectives and rationale are important points to explain.

Target Markets. The *target market(s)* discussion explains the customer base and rationale or justification for it. An approach to developing appropriate target markets is contained in Chapter 5 of this text, and a useful source of secondary data for segmenting markets is the *National Purchase Diary Panel.*

This section also includes relevant discussion of changes or important issues in consumer or industrial buyer behavior; for example, what benefits consumers are seeking in this products class, what benefits does the particular brand offer, or what purchasing trends are shaping the market for this product. Discussions of consumer and industrial buyer behavior are contained in Chapters 3 and 4 of this text.

Marketing Mix. The marketing mix discussion explains in detail the selected strategy consisting of product, promotion, distribution, and price, and the rationale for it. Also, if marketing research has been done on these elements or is planned, it can be discussed in this section.

Product. The product section details a description of the product or brand, its packaging and attributes. Product life-cycle considerations should be mentioned if they affect the proposed plan.

Of critical importance in this discussion is the competitive differential advantage of the product or brand. Here it must be carefully considered whether the brand really does anything better than the competition or is purchased primarily on the basis of image. For example, many brands of toothpaste have fluoride, yet Crest has the largest market share primarily through promoting this attribute of its brand. Thus, does Crest do anything more than other toothpastes, or is it Crest's image that accounts for sales?

Discussion of product-related issues is contained in Chapters 6 and 7, and services are discussed in Chapter 12 of this text. For discussion of marketing plans for products at the international level, see Chapter 13.

Promotion. The promotion discussion consists of a description and justification of the planned promotion mix. It is useful to explain the theme of the promotion and to include some examples of potential ads

HIGHLIGHT 2
Stating Objectives: How to Tell a "Good" One from a "Bad" One

For the direction-setting purpose of objectives to be fulfilled, objectives need to meet five specifications:

1. An objective should relate to a single, specific topic. (It should not be stated in the form of a vague abstraction or a pious platitude: "We want to be a leader in our industry" or, "Our objective is to be more aggressive marketers.")
2. An objective should relate to a result, not to an activity to be performed. (The objective is the result of the activity, not the performing of the activity.)
3. An objective should be measurable (stated in quantitative terms whenever feasible).
4. An objective should contain a time deadline for its achievement.
5. An objective should be challenging but achievable.

Consider the following examples:

Poor: Our objective is to maximize profits.

Remarks: How much is "maximum"? The statement is not subject to measurement. What criterion or yardstick will management use to determine if and when actual profits are equal to maximum profits? No deadline is specified.

Better: Our total profit target in 1989 is $1 million.

Poor: Our objective is to increase sales revenue and unit volume.

Remarks: How much? Also, because the statement relates to two topics, it may be inconsistent. Increasing unit volume may require a price cut, and if demand is price inelastic, sales revenue would fall as unit volume rises. No time frame for achievement is indicated.

Better: Our objective this calendar year is to increase sales revenues from $30 million to $35 million. We expect this to be accomplished by selling 1 million units at an average price of $35.

Poor: Our objective in 1989 is to boost advertising expenditures by 15 percent.

Remarks: Advertising is an activity, not a result. The advertising objective should be stated in terms of what result the extra advertising is intended to produce.

Better: Our objective is to boost our market share from 8 percent to 10 percent in 1989 with the help of a 15 percent increase in advertising expenditures.

Poor: Our objective is to be a pioneer in research and development and to be the technological leader in the industry.

Remarks: Very sweeping and perhaps overly ambitious; implies trying to march in too many directions at once if the industry is one with a

HIGHLIGHT 2 *(concluded)*

wide range of technological frontiers. More a platitude than an action commitment to a specific result.

Better: During the 1980s our objective is to continue as a leader in introducing new technologies and new devices that will allow buyers of electrically powered equipment to conserve on electric energy usage.

Poor: Our objective is to be the most profitable company in our industry. *Remarks:* Not specific enough by what measures of profit—total dollars or earning per share or unit profit margin or return on equity investment or all of these? Also, because the objective concerns how well other companies will perform, the objective—while challenging—may not be achievable.

Better: We will strive to remain atop the industry in terms of rate of return on equity investment by earning a 25 percent after-tax return on equity investment in 1989.

   Source: Arthur A. Thompson, Jr., and A. J. Strickland, *Strategic Management: Concepts and Cases.* 5th ed. (Homewood, Ill.: Richard D. Irwin, 1990), pp. 23–34.

as well as the nature of the sales force, if one is to be used. For mass-marketed consumer goods, promotion costs are clearly significant and need to be considered explicitly in the marketing plan.

Discussion of promotion-related issues is contained in Chapters 8 and 9 of this text. Secondary sources, such as *Standard Rate and Data*, *Simmons Media/Market Service*, *Starch Advertising Readership Service*, and the *Nielson Television Index*, provide useful information for selecting, budgeting, and justifying media and other promotional decisions.

Distribution.   The distribution discussion describes and justifies the appropriate channel or channels for the product. This includes types of intermediaries and specifically who they will be. Other important issues concern the level of market coverage desired, cost, and control considerations. In many cases, the channels of distribution used by the firm, as well as competitive firms, are well established. For example, General Motors and Ford distribute their automobiles through independent dealer networks. Thus, unless there is a compelling reason to change channels, the traditional channel will often be the appropriate alternative. However, serious consideration may have to be given to methods of obtaining channel support—for example, trade deals to obtain sufficient shelf space.

Discussion of distribution-related issues is contained in Chapter 10 of this text. Useful retail distribution information can be found in the *Nielson Retail Index* and the *Audits and Surveys National Total-Market Index.*

HIGHLIGHT 3
Some Questions to Consider in Consumer Analysis

Knowledge of consumers is paramount to developing successful market-ing plans. Below is a list of questions that are useful to consider when analyzing consumers. For some of the questions, secondary sources of information or primary marketing research can be employed to aid in decision making. However, a number of them require the analyst to do some serious thinking about the relationship between brands of the prod-uct and various consumer groups to better understand the market.

1. How many people purchase and use this product?
2. How many people purchase and use each brand of the product?
3. Is there an opportunity to reach nonusers of the product with a unique marketing strategy?
4. What does the product do for consumers functionally, and how does this vary by brand?
5. What does the product do for consumers in a social or psychological sense, and how does this vary by brand?
6. Where do consumers currently purchase various brands of the product?
7. How much are consumers willing to pay for specific brands, and is price a determining factor for purchase?
8. What is the market profile of the heavy user of this product, and what percentage of the total market are heavy users?
9. What media reach these consumers?
10. On average, how often is this product purchased?
11. How important is brand image for consumers of this product?
12. Why do consumers purchase particular brands?
13. How brand loyal are consumers of this product?

Price.   The pricing discussion starts with a specific statement of the price of the product. Depending on what type of channel is used, manufacturer price, wholesale price, and suggested retail price need to be listed and justified. In addition, special deals or trade discounts that are to be employed must be considered in terms of their effect on the firm's selling price.

Discussion of price-related issues is contained in Chapter 11. In ad-dition to a variety of other useful information, the *Nielson Retail Index* provides information on wholesale and retail prices.

Marketing Research.   For any aspect of marketing planning, there may be a need for marketing research. If such research is to be per-formed, it is important to justify it and explain its costs and benefits. Such costs should also be included in the financial analysis.

HIGHLIGHT 4
Some Questions to Consider in Marketing Planning

Below is a brief list of questions to ask yourself about the marketing planning section of the report. Answering them honestly and recognizing both the strengths and weaknesses of your marketing plan should help you improve it.

1. What are the key assumptions that were made in developing the marketing plan?
2. How badly will the product's market position be hurt if these assumptions turn out to be incorrect?
3. How good is the marketing research?
4. Is the marketing plan consistent? For example, if the plan is to seek a prestige position in the market, is the product priced, promoted, and distributed to create this image?
5. Is the marketing plan feasible? For example, are the financial and other resources (such as a distribution network) available to implement it?
6. How will the marketing plan affect profits and market share, and is it consistent with corporate objectives?
7. Will implementing the marketing plan result in competitive retaliation that will end up hurting the firm?
8. Is the marketing mix designed to reach and attract new consumers or increase usage among existing users or both?
9. Will the marketing mix help to develop brand loyal consumers?
10. Will the marketing plan be successful not just in the short run but also contribute to a profitable, long-run position?

If marketing research has already been conducted as part of the marketing plan, it can be reported as needed to justify various decisions that were reached. To illustrate, if research found that two out of three consumers liked the taste of a new formula Coke, this information would likely be included in the product portion of the report. However, the details of the research could be placed here in the marketing research section. Discussion of marketing research is contained in Chapter 2.

Implementation and Control of the Marketing Plan

This section contains a discussion and justification of how the marketing plan will be implemented and controlled. It also explains who will be in charge of monitoring and changing the plan should

Implementation and control of a marketing plan require careful scheduling and attention to detail. While some firms have standard procedures for dealing with many of the questions raised below, thinking through each of the questions should help improve the efficiency of even these firms in this stage of the process.

1. Who is responsible for implementing and controlling the marketing plan?
2. What tasks must be performed to implement the marketing plan?
3. What are the deadlines for implementing the various tasks, and how critical are specific deadlines?
4. Has sufficient time been scheduled to implement the various tasks?
5. How long will it take to get the planned market coverage?
6. How will the success or failure of the plan be determined?
7. How long will it take to get the desired results from the plan?
8. How long will the plan be in effect before changes will be made to improve it based on more current information?
9. If an ad agency or other firms are involved in implementing the plan, how much responsibility and authority will they have?
10. How frequently will the progress of the plan be monitored?

unanticipated events occur, and how the success or failure of the plan will be measured. Success or failure of the plan is typically measured by comparing the results of implementing the plan with the stated objectives.

For a marketing plan developed within an ongoing firm, this section can be quite explicit, since procedures for implementing plans may be well established. However, for a classroom project, the key issues to be considered are the persons responsible for implementing the plan, a timetable for sequencing the tasks, and a method to measure and evaluate the plan's success or failure.

Summary

This *summary* need not be much different than the executive summary stated at the beginning of the document. However, it is usually a bit longer, more detailed, and states more fully the case for financing the plan.

Appendix—Financial Analysis

Financial analysis is a very important part of any marketing plan. While a complete business plan often includes extensive financial analysis, such as a complete cost breakdown and estimated return on investment, marketing planners frequently do not have complete accounting data for computing these figures. For example, decisions concerning how much overhead is to be apportioned to the product are not usually made solely by marketing personnel. However, the marketing plan should contain at least a sales forecast and estimates of relevant marketing costs.

Sales Forecast.   As noted, there are a variety of ways to develop sales forecasts. Regardless of the method, however, they all involve trying to predict the future as accurately as possible. It is, of course, necessary to justify the logic for the forecasted figures, rather than offer them with no support.

One basic approach to developing a sales forecast is outlined in Table 2. This approach begins by estimating the total number of persons in the selected target market. This estimate comes from the market segmentation analysis and may include information from test marketing and from secondary sources, such as *Statistical Abstracts of the United States*. For example, suppose a company is marketing a solar-powered watch designed not only to tell time but to take the wearer's pulse. The product is targeted at joggers and others interested in aerobic exercise. By reviewing the literature on these activities, the marketing planner, John Murphy, finds that the average estimate of this market on a national level is 60 million persons and is growing by 4 million persons per year. Thus, John might conclude that the total number of people in the target market for next year is 64 million. If he has not further limited the product's target market and has no other information, John might use this number as a basis for starting the forecast analysis.

The second estimate John needs is the annual number of purchases per person in the product's target market. This estimate could be quite large for such products as breakfast cereal, or less than one (annual purchase per person) for such products as automobiles. For watches, the estimate is likely to be much less than one, since people are likely to buy a new watch only every few years. Thus John might estimate the annual number of purchases per person in the target market to be .25. Of course, as a careful marketing planner, John would probably carefully research this market to refine this estimate. In any event, multiplying these two rough numbers gives John an estimate of the *total potential market*, in this case, 64 million times .25 equals 16

TABLE 2   A Basic Approach to Sales Forecasting

Total number of people in target markets *(a)*	a
Annual number of purchases per person *(b)*	$\times\ b$
Total potential market *(c)*	$=\ c$
Total potential market *(c)*	c
Percent of total market coverage *(d)*	$\times\ d$
Total available market *(e)*	$=\ e$
Total available market *(e)*	e
Expected market share *(f)*	$\times\ f$
Sales forecast (in units) *(g)*	$=\ g$
Sales forecast (in units) *(g)*	g
Price *(h)*	$\times\ h$
Sales forecast (in dollars) *(i)*	$=\ i$

---

million. In other words, if next year alone John's company could sell the watch to every jogger or aerobic exerciser who is buying a watch, the company could expect sales to be 16 million units.

Of course, the firm cannot expect to sell every jogger a watch for several reasons. First, it is unlikely to obtain 100 percent market coverage in the first year, if ever. Even major consumer goods companies selling convenience goods seldom reach the entire market in the first year and many never achieve even 90 percent distribution. Given the nature of the product and depending on the distribution alternative, John's company might be doing quite well to average 50 percent market coverage in the first year. If John's plans call for this kind of coverage, his estimate of the total available market would be 16 million times .5, which equals 8 million.

A second reason why John's plans would not call for dominating the market is that his company does not have the only product available or wanted by this target market. Many of the people who will purchase such a watch will purchase a competitive brand. He must, therefore, estimate the product's likely market share. Of all the estimates made in developing a sales forecast, this one is critical, since it is a reflection of the entire marketing plan. Important factors to consider in developing this estimate include: (1) competitive market shares and likely marketing plans; (2) competitive retaliation, should the product do well; (3) differential advantage of the product, such as lower price; (4) promotion mix and budget relative to competitors; and (5) market shares obtained by similar products in the introductory year.

Overall, suppose John estimates the product's market share to be 5 percent, since other competitive products have beat his company to the market and because the company's differential advantage is only a slightly more stylish watch. In this case, the sales forecast for one year would be 8 million times .05, which equals 400,000 units. If the manufacturer's selling price was $50, then the sales forecast in dollars would be 400,000 times $50, which equals $20 million.

This approach can also be used to extend the sales forecast for any number of years. Typically, estimates of most of the figures change from year to year, depending on changes in market size, changes in distribution coverage, and changes in expected market shares. The value of this approach is that it forces an analyst to carefully consider and justify each of the estimates offered, rather than simply pulling numbers out of the air. In developing and justifying these estimates, many of the sources listed in Section 5 provide a good place to start searching for information—for example, *Selling Areas Marketing, Inc.*, or SAMI data.

Estimates of Marketing Costs. A complete delineation of all costs, apportionment of overhead, and other accounting tasks usually are performed by other departments within a firm. All of this information, including expected return on investment from implementing the marketing plan, is part of the overall business plan.

However, the marketing plan should at least contain estimates of major marketing costs. These include such things as advertising, sales-force training and compensation, channel development, and marketing research. Estimates may also be included for product development and package design.

For some marketing costs, reasonable estimates are available from sources such as *Standard Rate and Data.* However, some cost figures, such as marketing research, might be obtained from asking various marketing experts for the estimated price of proposed research. Other types of marketing costs might be estimated from financial statements of firms in the industry. For example, Morris's *Annual Statement Studies* offers percentage breakdowns of various income statement information by industry. These might be used to estimate the percentage of the sales-forecast figure likely to be spent in a particular cost category.

References

This section contains the sources of any secondary information that was used in developing the marketing plan. This information might include company reports and memos, statements of company objectives, and articles or books used for information or support of the marketing plan.

References should be listed alphabetically using a consistent format. One way of preparing references is to use the same approach used in marketing journals. For example, the format used for references in *Journal of Marketing* articles is usually acceptable.

CONCLUSION

Suppose you're now sitting at your desk faced with the task of developing a marketing plan for a new product. Do you believe that you might have the skills to develop a marketing plan? Of course, your ability to develop a quality plan will depend on your learning experiences during your course work and the amount of practice you've had. For example, if you developed a promotion plan in your advertising course, it is likely that you could do a better job on the promotion phase of the marketing plan. Similarly, your experiences in analyzing cases should have sharpened your skills at recognizing problems and developing solutions to them. But inexperience (or experience) aside, hopefully you now feel that you understand the process of developing a marketing plan. You at least know where to start, where to seek information, how to structure the plan, and what are some of the critical issues that require analysis.

ADDITIONAL READINGS

Ames, Charles B. "How to Devise a Winning Business Plan." *Journal of Business Strategy*, May/June 1989, pp. 26–30.

Cohen, William A. *Developing a Winning Marketing Plan*. New York: John Wiley & Sons, 1987.

Lehmann, Donald R., and Russell S. Winer. *Analysis for Marketing Planning*. Plano, Tex: Business Publications, 1988.

SECONDARY DATA SOURCES

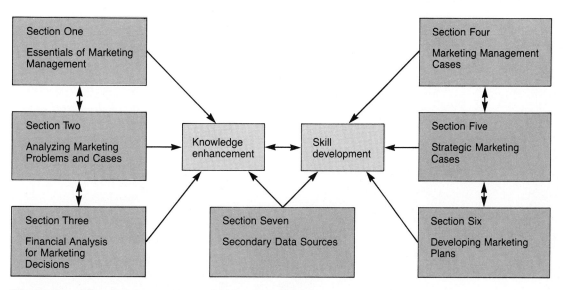

Marketing Management: Knowledge and Skills

NOTE TO THE STUDENT

This section contains a variety of information sources for enhancing your knowledge of marketing and developing your marketing and planning skills. The information is divided into the following categories:

Selected periodicals
General marketing information
   sources
Selected marketing information
   services
Selected retail trade publications

Financial information sources
Basic U.S. statistical sources
General business and industry sources
Indexes and abstracts

In analyzing and presenting cases and developing marketing plans, it is often very useful for analysts to be able to find outside data sources to support their recommendations or conclusions. The data referred to here are from secondary sources and can be located in most business libraries. The purpose of this section is to list and briefly describe some of the key data sources available to analysts. The references are listed under eight specific headings: selected periodicals, general marketing information sources, selected marketing information services, selected retail trade publications, financial information sources, basic U.S. statistical sources, general business and industry sources, and indexes and abstracts.

SELECTED PERIODICALS

Advertising Age

American Demographics

Business Horizons

Business Week

California Management Review

Columbia Journal of World Business

Conference Board Record

Forbes

Fortune

Harvard Business Review

Industrial Marketing Management

Journal of the Academy of Marketing Science

Journal of Advertising

Journal of Advertising Research

Journal of Consumer Research

Journal of Experimental Psychology

Journal of Macro Marketing

Journal of Marketing

Journal of Marketing and Public Policy

Journal of Marketing Research

Journal of Personal Selling and Sales Management

Journal of Psychology

Journal of Retailing

Marketing Communications

Marketing News

Marketing Science

Michigan Business Review

Michigan State University Business Topics

Nations Business

Sales Management

GENERAL MARKETING INFORMATION SOURCES

Commercial Atlas and Marketing Guide. Skokie, Ill.: Rand-McNally & Co. Statistics on population, principal cities, business centers, trading areas, sales and manufacturing units, transportation data, and so forth.

Editor and Publisher "Market Guide." Market information for 1,500 American and Canadian cities. Data include population, household, gas meters, climate, retailing, and newspaper information.

Guide to Consumer Markets. New York: The Conference Board. This useful annual compilation of U.S. statistics on the consumer marketplace covers population, employment, income, expenditures, production, and prices.

Marketing Information Guide. Washington, D.C.: Department of Commerce. Annotations of selected current publications and reports, with basic information and statistics on marketing and distribution.

Milutinovich, J. S. "Business Facts for Decision Makers: Where to Find Them." *Business Horizons,* March–April 1985, pp. 63–80.

Population and Its Distribution: The United States Markets. J. Walter Thompson Co. New York: McGraw-Hill Book Co. A handbook of marketing facts selected from the *U.S. Census of Population* and the most recent census data on retail trade.

Sales and Marketing Management. (Formerly *Sales Management,* to October 1975.) This valuable semimonthly journal includes four useful annual statistical issues: *Survey of Buying Power* (July), *Survey of Buying Power, Part II* (October); *Survey of Industrial Purchasing Power* (April); *Survey of Selling Costs* (January). These are excellent references for buying income, buying power index, cash income, merchandise line, manufacturing line, and retail sales.

SELECTED MARKETING INFORMATION SERVICES[1]

Audits and Surveys National Total-Market Index. Contains information on various product types, including total market size, brand market shares, retail inventory, distribution coverage, and out of stock.

Dun & Bradstreet Market Identifiers. Relevant marketing information on over 4.3 million establishments for constructing sales prospect files, sales territories, sales territory potentials, and isolating potential new customers with particular characteristics.

National Purchase Diary Panel (NPD). Monthly purchase information based on the largest panel diary in the United States with detailed brand, frequency of purchase, characteristics of heavy buyers, and other market data.

Nielson Retail Index. Contains basic product turnover data, retail prices, store displays, promotional activity, and local advertising based on a national sample of supermarkets, drugstores, and mass merchandisers.

Nielson Television Index. Well-known index which provides estimates of the size and nature of the audience for individual television programs.

---

[1]Excerpted from Gilbert A. Churchill, Jr., *Marketing Research,* 4th ed. (Hinsdale, Ill.: Dryden Press, 1987), pp. 188–202.

Selling Areas Marketing, Inc. Reports on warehouse withdrawals of various food products in each of 42 major markets covering 80 percent of national food sales.

Simmons Media/Marketing Service. Provides cross-referencing of product usage and media exposure for magazine, television, newspaper, and radio based on a strict national probability sample.

Standard Rate and Data. Nine volumes on major media which include a variety of information in addition to prices for media in selected markets.

Starch Advertising Readership Service. Measures the reading of advertisements in magazines and newspapers and provides information on overall readership percentages, readers per dollar, and rank when grouped by product category.

SELECTED RETAIL TRADE PUBLICATIONS[2]

American Druggist (monthly), Hearst Corporation, 959 Eighth Avenue, New York, N.Y. 10019.

Auto Chain Store Magazine (ACS) (monthly), Babcox Publications, Inc., 11 South Forge Street, Akron, OH 44304.

Body Fashions & Intimate Apparel (monthly), Harcourt Brace Jovanovich Publications, 757 Third Avenue, New York, N.Y. 10017.

C. Store Business (10 times/year), Maclean Hunter Media 1351 Washington Boulevard, Stamford, Conn. 06902.

Catalog Showroom Business (monthly), Gralla Publications, 1515 Broadway, New York, N.Y. 10036.

Catalog Showroom Merchandiser (monthly), CSM Marketing, Inc., 1020 West Jericho Turnpike, Smithtown, N.Y. 11787.

Chain Drug Review (biweekly), Racher Press, Inc., 1 Park Avenue, New York, N.Y. 10016.

Chain Store Age—Executive Edition (monthly), Lebhar-Friedman, Inc., 425 Park Avenue, New York, N.Y. 10022.

Chain Store Age—General Merchandise Edition (monthly), Lebhar-Friedman, Inc., 425 Park Avenue, New York, N.Y. 10022.

Chain Store Age—Supermarkets Edition (monthly), Lebhar-Friedman, Inc., 425 Park Avenue, New York, N.Y. 10022.

CompetitivEdge (monthly), National Home Furnishings Association, 405 Merchandise Mart, Chicago, Ill. 60654.

Consumer Electronics Monthly (monthly), CES Publishing Corporation, 135 West 50th Street, New York, N.Y. 10020.

---

[2]This list is from William R. Davidson, Daniel J. Sweeney, and Ronald W. Stampfl, *Retailing Management,* 5th ed. (New York: John Wiley & Sons, 1984), pp. 764–66.

Convenience Store Merchandiser (monthly), Associated Business Publications, Inc., 41 East 42nd Street, New York, N.Y. 10017.

Convenience Store News (monthly, with additional issues in March, April, August, and October), BMT Publications, Inc., 254 West 31st Street, New York, N.Y. 10001.

Daily News Record (daily), Fairchild Publications, 7 East 12th Street, New York, N.Y. 10003.

Decorating Retailer (monthly), National Decorating Products Association, 1050 North Lindbergh Boulevard, St. Louis, Mo. 63132.

Decorative Products World (monthly, except January), 2911 Washington Avenue, St. Louis, Mo. 63103.

Direct Marketing (monthly), Hoke Communications, Inc., 224 Seventh Street, Garden City, N.Y. 11530.

Discount Merchandiser (monthly), Schwartz Publications, 2 Park Avenue, New York, N.Y. 10016.

Discount Store News (biweekly except May and December), Lebhar-Friedman, Inc., 425 Park Avenue, New York, N.Y. 10022.

Drug Store News (biweekly), Lebhar-Friedman, Inc., 425 Park Avenue, New York, N.Y. 10022.

Drug Topics (biweekly), Medical Economics Company, Inc., 680 Kinderkamack Road, Oradell, N.J. 07649.

Earnshaw's Infants Girls Boys Wear Review (monthly), Earnshaw Publications, Inc., 393 Seventh Avenue, New York, N.Y. 10001.

Electronics Retailer (monthly, except combined issues in January–February, and June–July), Fairchild Publications, 7 East 12th Street, New York, N.Y. 10003.

Floor Covering Weekly (weekly), Hearst Business Communications, Inc., 645 Steward Avenue, Garden City, N.Y. 11530.

Food Merchandising for Nonfood Retailers (quarterly), Lebhar-Friedman, Inc., 425 Park Avenue, New York, N.Y. 10022.

Furniture/Today (biweekly), Communications/Today Ltd., 200 S. Mai Street, High Point, N.C. 27261.

Garden Supply Retailer (monthly), The Miller Publishing Company, 2501 Wayzata Blvd., Minneapolis, Minn. 55440.

Giftware Business (monthly), Gralla Publications, 1515 Broadway, New York, N.Y. 10036.

Hardware Age (monthly), Chilton Company, Chilton Way, Radnor, Pa. 19089.

Hardware Merchandiser (monthly), Irving-Cloud Publishing Company, 7300 North Cicero Avenue, Lincolnwood, Ill. 60646.

Home & Auto (semimonthly except November and December), Harcourt Brace Jovanovich Publications, 757 Third Avenue, New York, N.Y. 10017.

Home Center (monthly), Vance Publishing Corporation, 300 West Adams, Chicago, Ill. 60606.

Housewares (semimonthly plus January, July, and December issues), Harcourt Brace Jovanovich Publications, 757 Third Avenue, New York, N.Y. 10017.

Lawn & Garden Marketing (10 times annually), Intertec Publishing Corporation, 9221 Quivira Road, Overland Park, Kan. 66212.

Mart (monthly), Morgan-Grampian Publishing Co., 2 Park Avenue, New York, N.Y. 10016.

Men's Wear (semimonthly), Fairchild Publications, 7 East 12th Street, New York, N.Y. 10003.

Merchandising (monthly), Gralla Publications, 1515 Broadway, New York, N.Y. 10036.

NARDA News (monthly), NARDA, Inc., 2 North Riverside Plaza, Chicago, Ill. 60606.

Nation's Restaurants News (biweekly), Lebhar-Friedman, Inc., 425 Park Avenue, New York, N.Y. 10022.

National Jeweler (bimonthly), Gralla Publications, 1515 Broadway, New York, N.Y. 10036.

National Mall Monitor (bimonthly), National Mall Monitor, 2280 U.S. 19 North, Suite 264, Clearwater, Fla. 33575.

National Petroleum News (NPN) (monthly), Hunter Publishing Company, 950 Lee Street, Des Plaines, Ill. 60016.

Non-Foods Merchandising (monthly), Charleson Publishing Co., 124 East 40th Street, New York, N.Y. 10016.

Non-Store Marketing Report (biweekly), Maxwell Sroge Publishing Inc., Sroge Building, 731 North Cascade Avenue, Colorado Springs, Colo. 80903.

Outdoor Retailer (bimonthly), Pacifica Publishing Corporation, 31652 Second Avenue, South Laguna, Calif. 92677.

Private Label (monthly), E. W. Williams Publishing Co., 80–88th Avenue, New York, N.Y. 10011.

Professional Furniture Merchant (monthly), Vista Publications, Inc., 9600 W. Sample Road, Coral Springs, Fla. 33065.

Progressive Grocer (monthly), Maclean Hunter Media, 1351 Washington Boulevard, Stamford, Conn. 06901.

Restaurants & Institutions (semimonthly), Cahners Publishing Co., 221 Columbus Avenue, Boston, Mass. 02116.

Retail Control (monthly except April–May and June–July, when bimonthly), NRMA—Financial Executives Division, 100 West 31st Street, New York, N.Y. 10001.

Retailing Home Furnishings (weekly), Fairchild Publications, 7 East 12th Street, New York, N.Y. 10003.

Shopping Center World (monthly), Communications Channels, Inc., 6255 Barfield Road, Atlanta, Ga. 30328.

Sporting Goods Business (monthly), Gralla Publications, 1515 Broadway, New York, N.Y. 10036.

Sporting Goods Dealer (monthly), Sporting News Publishing Company, 1212 North Lindbergh Boulevard, St. Louis, Mo. 63132.

Sports Retailer (monthly), National Sporting Goods Association, 1699 Wall Street, Mt. Prospect, Ill. 60056.

Stores (monthly), National Retail Merchants Association, 100 W. 31st Street, New York, N.Y. 10001.

Supermarket Business (monthly), Fieldmark Media, Inc., 25 West 43rd Street, New York, N.Y. 10036.

Supermarket News (weekly), 71 West 35th Street, Suite 1600, New York, N.Y. 10001.

Teens and Boys Magazine (monthly), 71 West 35th Street, Suite 1600, New York, N.Y. 10001.

Tire Review (monthly), Babcox Publications, 11 South Forge Street, Akron, Ohio 44304.

Toys Hobbies & Crafts (monthly except June), Harcourt Brace Jovanovich Publications, 1 East First Street, Duluth, Minn. 55802.

Video Store (monthly), Hester Communications, Inc., 1700 East Dyer Road, Suite 250, Santa Ana, Calif. 92705.

Visual Merchandising & Store Design (monthly), Signs of the Times Publishing Company, 407 Gilbert Avenue, Cincinnati, Ohio 45202.

Women's Wear Daily (daily), Fairchild Publications, 7 East 12th Street, New York, N.Y. 10003.

FINANCIAL INFORMATION SOURCES

Blue Line Investment Survey. Quarterly ratings and reports on 1,000 stocks; analysis of 60 industries and special situations analysis (monthly); supplements on new developments and editorials on conditions affecting price trends.

Commercial and Financial Chronicle. Variety of articles and news reports on business, government, and finance. Monday's issue lists new securities, dividends, and called bonds. Thursday's issue is devoted to business articles.

Dun's Review. Dun & Bradstreet. This monthly includes very useful annual financial ratios for about 125 lines of business.

Fairchild's Financial Manual of Retail Stores. Information about officers and directors, products, subsidiaries, sales, and earnings for apparel stores, mail order firms, variety chains, and supermarkets.

Federal Reserve Bulletin. Board of Governors of the Federal Reserve System. The "Financial and Business Statistics" section of each issue of this monthly bulletin is the best single source for current U.S. banking and monetary statistics.

Financial World. Articles on business activities of interest to investors, including investment opportunities and pertinent data on firms, such as earnings and dividend records.

Moody's Bank and Finance Manual; Moody's Industrial Manual; Moody's Municipal & Government Manual; Moody's Public Utility Manual; Moody's Transportation Manual; Moody's Directors Service. Brief histories of companies and their operations, subsidiaries, officers and directors, products, and balance sheet and income statements over several years.

Moody's Bond Survey. Moody's Investors Service. Weekly data on stocks and bonds, including recommendations for purchases or sale and discussions of industry trends and developments.

Moody's Handbook of Widely Held Common Stocks. Moody's Investors Service. Weekly data on stocks and bonds, including recommendations for purchases or sale and discussions of industry trends and developments.

Security Owner's Stock Guide. Standard & Poor's Corp. Standard & Poor's rating, stock price range, and other helpful information for about 4,200 common and preferred stocks.

Security Price Index. Standard & Poor's Corp. Price indexes, bond prices, sales, yields, Dow Jones averages, etc.

Standard Corporation Records. Standard & Poor's Corp. Published in loose-leaf form, offers information similar to Moody's manuals. Use of this extensive service facilitates buying securities for both the individual and the institutional investor.

BASIC U.S. STATISTICAL SOURCES

Business Service Checklist. Department of Commerce. Weekly guide to Department of Commerce publications, plus key business indicators.

Business Statistics. Department of Commerce. (Supplement to *Survey of Current Business.*) History of the statistical series appearing in the *Survey.* Also included are source references and useful explanation notes.

Census of Agriculture. Department of Commerce. Data by states and counties on livestock, farm characteristics, values.

Census of Manufacturers. Department of Commerce. Industry statistics, area statistics, subjects reports, location of plants, industry descriptions arranged in Standard Industrial Classification, and a variety of ratios.

Census of Mineral Industries. Department of Commerce. Similar to *Census of Manufacturers.* Also includes capital expenditures and employment and payrolls.

Census of Retail Trade. Department of Commerce. Compiles data for states, SMSAs, counties, and cities with populations of 2,500 or more by kind of business. Data include number of establishments, sales, payroll, and personnel.

Census of Selected Services. Department of Commerce. Includes data on hotels, motels, beauty parlors, barber shops, and other retail service organizations.

Census of Transportation. Passenger Transportation Survey, Commodity Transportation Survey, Travel Inventory and Use Survey, Bus and Truck Carrier Survey.

Census Tract Reports. Department of Commerce, Bureau of Census. Detailed information on both population and housing subjects.

Census of Wholesale Trade. Department of Commerce. Similar to *Census of Retail Trade*—information is for wholesale establishment.

County and City Data Book. Department of Commerce. Summary statistics for small geographical areas.

Current Business Reports. Department of Commerce. Reports monthly department store sales of selected items.

Economic Report of the President. Transmitted to the Congress, January (each year), together with the *Annual Report* of the Council of Economic Advisers. Statistical tables relating to income, employment, and production.

Handbook of Basic Economic Statistics. Economic Statistics Bureau of Washington, D.C. Current and historical statistics on industry, commerce, labor, and agriculture.

Statistical Abstract of the United States. Department of Commerce. Summary statistics in industrial, social, political, and economic fields in the United States. It is augmented by the *Cities Supplement, The County Data Book,* and *Historical Statistics of the United States.*

Statistics of Income: Corporation Income Tax Returns. Internal Revenue Service. Balance sheet and income statement statistics derived from corporate tax returns.

Statistics of Income: U.S. Business Tax Returns. Internal Revenue Service. Summarizes financial and economic data for proprietorships, partnerships, and small business corporations.

Survey of Current Business. Department of Commerce. Facts on industrial and business activity in the United States and statistical summary of national income and product accounts. A weekly supplement provides an up-to-date summary of business.

GENERAL BUSINESS AND INDUSTRY SOURCES

Aerospace Facts and Figures. Aerospace Industries Association of America.

Annual Statistical Report. American Iron and Steel Institute.

Chemical Marketing Reporter. Schnell Publishing. Includes lengthy, continuing list of "Current Prices of Chemicals and Related Materials."

Computerworld. Computerworld, Inc. Last December issue includes "Review and Forecast," an analysis of computer industry's past year and the outlook for the next year.

Construction Review. Department of Commerce. Current statistics on construction put in place, costs, and employment.

Distribution Worldwide. Chilton Co. Special annual issue, *Distribution Guide,* compiles information on transportation methods and wage.

Drug and Cosmetic Industry. Drug Markets, Inc. Separate publication in July, *Drug and Cosmetic Catalog,* provides list of manufacturers of drugs and cosmetics and their respective products.

Electrical World. January and February issues include two-part statistical report on expenditures, construction, and other categories by region; capacity; sales, and financial statistics for the electrical industry.

Encyclopedia of Business Information Sources. Paul Wasserman et al., eds., Gale Research Company. A detailed listing of primary subjects of interest to managerial personnel, with a record of sourcebooks, periodicals, organizations, directories, handbooks, bibliographies, and other sources of information on each topic. Two vols., nearly 17,000 entries in over 1,600 subject areas.

Forest Industries. Miller Freeman Publications, Inc. The March issue includes "Forest Industries Wood-Based Panel," a review of production and sales figures for selected wood products; extra issue in May includes a statistical review of the lumber industry.

Implement and Tractor. Intertec Publishing Corporation. January issue includes equipment specifications and operating data for farm and industrial equipment. November issue includes statistics and information on the farm industry.

Industry Surveys. Standard & Poor's Corp. Continuously revised analysis of leading industries (40 industries made up of 1,300 companies). Current analysis contains interim operating data of investment comment. Basic analysis features company ratio comparisons and balance sheet statistics.

Middle Market Directory. Dun & Bradstreet. Inventories approximately 18,000 U.S. companies with an indicated worth of $500,000 to $999,999, giving officers, products, standard industrial classification, approximate sales, and number of employees.

Million Dollar Directory. Dun & Bradstreet. Lists U.S. companies with an indicated worth of $1 million or more, giving officers and directors, products, standard industrial classification, sales, and number of employees.

Modern Brewery Age. Business Journals, Inc. February issue includes a review of sales and production figures for the brewery industry. A separate publication, *The Blue Book,* issued in May, compiles sales and consumption figures by state for the brewery industry.

National Petroleum News. McGraw-Hill, Inc. May issue includes statistics on sales and consumption of fuel oils, gasoline, and related products. Some figures are for 10 years, along with 10-year projections.

Operating Results of Department and Specialty Stores. National Retail Merchants Association.

Petroleum Facts and Figures. American Petroleum Institute.

Poor's Register of Corporations, Directors, and Executives of the United States and Canada. Standard & Poor's Corp. Divided into two sections. The first gives officers, products, sales range, and number of employees for about

30,000 corporations. The second gives brief information on executives and directors.

Quick-Frozen Foods. Harcourt Brace Jovanovich Publications. October issue includes "Frozen Food Almanac," providing statistics on the frozen food industry by product.

Statistical Sources. Paul Wasserman et al., eds. Gale Research Corp., 4th ed., 1974. A subject guide to industrial, business, social, educational, financial data, and other related topics.

The Super Market Industry Speaks. Super Market Institute.

Vending Times. February issue includes "The Buyers Guide," a special issue providing information on the vending industry; June issue includes "The Census of the Industry," a special issue containing statistics on the vending industry.

INDEXES AND ABSTRACTS

Accountants Digest. L. L. Briggs. A digest of articles appearing currently in accounting periodicals.

Accountants Index. American Institute of Certified Public Accountants. An index to books, pamphlets, and articles on accounting and finance.

Accounting Articles. Commerce Clearing House. Loose-leaf index to articles in accounting and business periodicals.

Advertising Age Editorial Index. Crain Communications, Inc. Index to articles in *Advertising Age*.

American Statistical Index. Congressional Information Service. A comprehensive two-part annual index to the statistical publications of the U.S. government.

Applied Science & Technology Index (formerly *Industrial Arts Index* to 1958). H. W. Wilson Co. Reviews over 200 periodicals relevant to the applied sciences, many of which pertain to business.

Battelle Library Review (formerly *Battelle Technical Review* to 1962). Battelle Memorial Institute. Annotated bibliography of books, reports, and articles on automation and automatic processes.

Bulletin of Public Affairs Information Service. Public Affairs Information Service, Inc. (Since 1915—annual index.) A selective list of the latest books, pamphlets, government publications, reports of public and private agencies, and periodicals relating to economic conditions, public administration, and international relations.

Business Education Index. McGraw-Hill Book Co. (Since 1940—annual index.) Annual author and subject index of books, articles, and theses on business education.

Business Periodicals Index. H. W. Wilson Co. A subject index to the disciplines of accounting, advertising, banking, general business, insurance, labor, management, and marketing.

Catalog of United States Census Publication. Washington, D.C.: Dept of Commerce, Bureau of Census. Indexes all available at Census Bureau Data. Main divisions are: agriculture, business, construction, foreign trade, government, guide to locating U.S. census information.

Computer and Information Systems. (Formerly *Information Processing Journal* to 1969.) Cambridge Communications Corporation.

Cumulative Index of NICB Publications. The National Industrial Conferences Board. Annual index of NICB books, pamphlets, and articles in the area of management of personnel.

Funk and Scott Index International. Investment Index Company. Indexes articles on foregin companies and industries from over 1,000 foreign and domestic periodicals and documents.

Guide to U.S. Government Publications. McLean, Va., Documents Index. Annotated guide to publications of various U.S. government agencies.

International Abstracts in Operations Research. Operations Research Society of America.

International Journal of Abstracts of Statistical Methods in Industry. The Hague, Netherlands: International Statistical Institute.

Management Information Guides. Gale Research Company. Bibliographical references to information sources for various business subjects.

Management Review. American Management Association.

Monthly Catalog of U.S. Government Publications. U.S. Government Printing Office. Continuing list of federal government publications.

Monthly Checklist of State Publications. U.S. Library of Congress, Exchange and Gift Division. Record of state documents received by Library of Congress.

New York Times Index. New York. Very detailed index of all articles in the *Times,* arranged alphabetically with many cross-references.

Psychological Abstracts. American Psychological Association.

Public Affairs Information Service. Public Affairs Information Service, Inc. A selective subject list of books, pamphlets, and government publications covering business, banking, and economics as well as subjects in the area of public affairs.

Reader's Guide to Periodical Literature. H. W. Wilson Co. Index by author and subject to selected U.S. general and nontechnical periodicals.

Sociological Abstracts. American Sociological Association.

The Wall Street Journal Index. Dow Jones & Company, Inc. An index of all articles in *The WSJ* grouped in two sections: corporate news and general news.

Case Index

| *Name Index*

Section 1 lists names found in the text. Section 2 lists names found in notes and bibliographies. Some names appear in both sections.

(1)

(2)

│ *Subject Index*